Arkansas, Kansas, Missouri & Oklahoma

Are we meeting your travel needs?
Send written comments to:

AAA Member Comments
1000 AAA Drive, Box 61
Heathrow, FL 32746-5063

Published by AAA Publishing
1000 AAA Drive
Heathrow, FL 32746-5063
Copyright AAA 2006

**Advertising Rate and Circulation
Information: (407) 444-8280**

**Printed in the USA by
Quebecor World, Buffalo, NY**

Photo Credit: (Cover & Title Page)
Flint Hills, Riley County, KS
© James Nedresky

Printed on recyclable paper.
Please recycle whenever possible.

Mixed Sources
Product group from well-managed
forests and other controlled sources
www.fsc.org Cert no. SW-COC-1610
© 1996 Forest Stewardship Council
FSC

Stock #4603

Arkansas, Kansas, Missouri & Oklahoma

Featured Information

■ *Oklahoma*

4

Find Hotels As Easy As 1-2-3-4-5!

For reliable hotel stays matched to your needs, every time, use AAA's valuable two-part rating system:

- First, rest assured that *every* hotel designated **AAA Approved** upholds qualities important to members – cleanliness, service, and value.

- Focus your selection using the descriptive one-to-five **AAA Diamond Ratings** assigned exclusively to Approved properties to help you match your expectations.

Find AAA Approved and Diamond rated properties in the TourBook®, in print and on aaa.com. Look for the AAA logo on signage and billboards.

Read about **AAA Diamond Ratings** on page 20-21or visit aaa.com/Diamonds.

Make it a point
to plan your next
trip on aaa.com
Get the BEST price on aaa.com
aaa.com

For hotel reservations and vacation planning, get right to the point on *aaa.com*. Reserve AAA approved and Diamond rated hotels at the lowest online prices. Plus, enjoy these additional tools and benefits:

AAA.com TourBook® – Find thousands of AAA Approved and Diamond rated hotels and restaurants, plus destinations, attractions, & events.

AAA.com TripTik® – Get complete trip routings with hotel reservations, sightseeing stops, member discount locations, and more.

AAA Drive Trips – Enjoy nearly 100 flexible, preplanned driving itineraries for popular destinations.

Vacation Getaways – Get exclusive benefits on flights, tours, cruises, and Disney vacation packages from AAA's Preferred Travel Partners.

Hertz – Save up to 20% on car rental.

Show Your Card & Save® – Search for exclusive member savings at 150,000 locations worldwide at AAA.com/save.

AAA Travel Money – Get no-fee travelers cheques, foreign currency, and prepaid cards.

Books – Save 5% on AAA travel publications at aaa.com/barnesandnoble.

AAA Credit Card – Get up to 5% gas rebate.

AAA Approved Auto Repair – Find reliable service facilities at home and away.

Plan your next trip on *aaa.com* — the only travel Web site backed by thousands of highly trained travel professionals at more than 1,000 AAA/CAA offices!

aaa.com
Plan to go.

Attractions, lodgings and restaurants are listed on the basis of merit alone after careful evaluation and approval by one of AAA/CAA's full-time, professionally trained Tourism Editors. Evaluations are unannounced to ensure that we see an establishment just as you would see it.

An establishment's decision to advertise in the TourBook guide has no bearing on its evaluation or rating. Advertising for services or products does not imply AAA endorsement.

All information in this guide was reviewed for accuracy before publication. However, since changes inevitably occur between annual editions, we suggest you work with your AAA travel professional or check on AAA.com to confirm prices and schedules.

How the TourBook Guide is Organized

The TourBook guide is organized into three distinct sections.

The **Points of Interest** section helps you plan daily activities and sightseeing excursions and provides details about the city or attraction you are visiting.

The **Lodgings and Restaurants** section helps you select AAA Approved accommodations and dining facilities meeting your specific needs and expectations.

The **Reference** section provides indexes for locating information within this guide and items to aid the trip planning process.

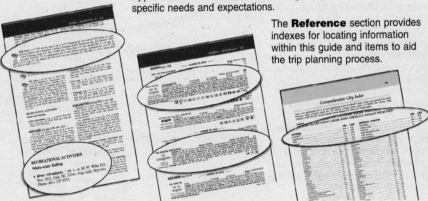

Locating the Attractions, Lodgings and Restaurants

Attractions, lodgings and restaurants are listed under the city in which they physically are located - or in some cases under the nearest recognized city. Most listings are alphabetically organized by state, province, region or island, then by city and establishment name.

A color is assigned to each state or province so that you can match the color bars at the top of the page to switch from the **Points of Interest** section to the **Lodgings and Restaurants** section.

Spotting maps help you physically locate points of interest, lodgings and restaurants in the major destinations.

The Comprehensive City Index located in the **Reference** section contains an A-to-Z list of cities.

Destination Cities and Destination Areas

Destination cities, established based on government models and local expertise, include metropolitan areas plus nearby vicinity cities. **Destination areas** are regions with broad tourist appeal; several cities will comprise the area.

If a city falls within a destination's vicinity, the city name will appear at its alphabetical location in the book, and a cross reference will give you the exact page on which listings for that city begin.

An orientation map appears at the beginning of each destination section to orient you to that destination.

Understanding the Points of Interest Listing

GEM Designation

A ▽GEM indicates the attraction has been rated a AAA GEM, a "must see" point of interest that offers a *Great Experience for Members®*. These attractions have been judged to be of exceptional interest and quality by AAA Tourism Editors.

A GEM listing page with a brief description of individual GEM attractions follows the Orientation map near the beginning of each state or province Points of Interest section. Cross-references guide the reader to the attraction's listing page.

Discount Savings

The SAVE icon denotes those attractions offering AAA/CAA, AAA MasterCard, AAA VISA or international Show Your Card & Save discount cardholders a discount off the attraction's standard admission. Present your card at the attraction's admission desk.

A list of participating points of interest appears in the Reference section of this guide.

Shopping establishments preceded by a SAVE icon also provide to AAA/CAA members a discount and/or gift with purchase; present your card at the mall's customer service center to receive your benefit.

Exceptions

- Members should inquire in advance concerning the validity of the discount for special rates.
- The SAVE discount may not be used in conjunction with other discounts.
- Attractions that already provide a reduced senior or child rate may not honor the SAVE discount for those age groups.
- All offers are subject to change and may not apply during special events, particular days or seasons or for the entire validity period of the TourBook guide.

Shopping areas: Mast General Store, 630 W. King St., operates out of a 1913 building, stocked with a variety of goods

Swa
Box

RED OAK, is off I-95 exit 4A, just n. to Dogw restored 1812 house has eight 60-foot columns ar Allow 1 hour minimum. Daily 9-5, Apr. 1-Labor Labor Day-Nov. 30; by appointment rest of year. 6-12, $5; ages 2-5, $4; family rate (two adults and two ch 5555 or (800) 555-5555.

RED OAK, is off I-95 exit 4A, just n. to Dogwood Dr., then 2 mi. e. to 610 Magnolia St. The restored 1812 house has eight 60-foot columns and is furnished in period. Costumed guides demonstrate the 1812 lifestyle. Allow 1 hour minimum. Daily 9-5, Apr. 1-Labor Day; Thurs.-Sun. 9-5, Feb.-Mar. 31 and day after Labor Day-Nov. 30; by appointment rest of year. Closed holidays. Admission $8; over 65 and ages 6-12, $5; ages 2-5, $4; family rate (two adults and two children) $12. DS, MC, VI. ($10). Phone (828) 555-5555 or (800) 555-5555.

RECREATIONAL ACTIVITIES
White-water Rafting

- **River Adventures,** 1 mi. s. on SR 50. Write P.O Box 1012, Gale, NC 35244. Trips daily May-Oct Phone (828) 555-5555.

BREVARD (F-3) pop. 6,789, elev. 2,229'

The town is a popular summer resort at the e trance to Pisgah National Forest (*see place listi p. 165*). Brevard is in an area known as the "La of Waterfalls," sporting more than 250 named v terfalls such as Laughing Falls and Courtho Falls. Brevard Music Center offers concerts nigh last weekend in June to mid-August

Brevard i porti

RECREATIONAL ACTIVI
White-water Rafting

- **River Adventures,** 1 mi. s Box 1012, Gale, NC 3524 Phone (828) 555-5555.

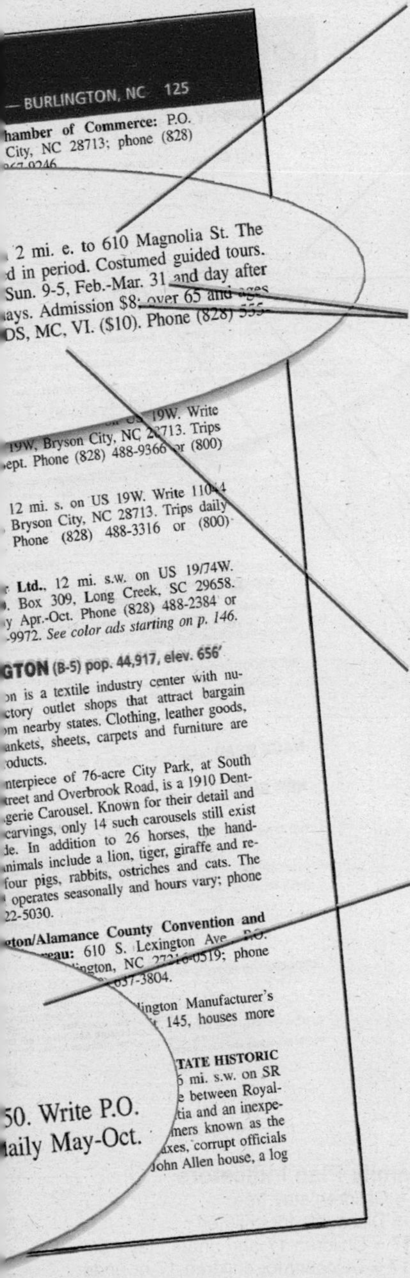

Directions

Unless otherwise specified, directions are given from the center of town, using the following highway designations:

I=interstate highway
SR=state route
FM=farm to market
Mex.=Mexican highway

US=federal highway
CR=county road
FR=forest road
Hwy.=Canadian or Caribbean highway

Prices and Dates of Operations

Admission prices are quoted without sales tax. Children under the lowest age specified are admitted free when accompanied by an adult. Days, months and age groups written with a hyphen are inclusive.

Prices pertaining to points of interest in the United States are quoted in U.S. dollars; points of interest in Canada are quoted in Canadian dollars; prices for points of interest in Mexico and the Caribbean are quoted as an approximate U.S. dollar equivalent.

Credit Cards Accepted

AX=American Express
CB=Carte Blanche
DC=Diners Club
DS=Discover

JC=Japan Credit Bureau
MC=MasterCard
VI=VISA

Bulleted Listings

Casino gambling establishments are visited by AAA personnel to ensure safety; casinos within hotels are presented for member information regardless of whether the lodging is AAA Approved.

Recreational activities of a participatory nature (requiring physical exertion or special skills) are not inspected.

Wineries are inspected by AAA Tourism Editors to ensure they meet listing requirements and offer tours.

All are presented in an abbreviated bulleted format for informational purposes.

BURLINGTON, NC 125

hamber of Commerce: P.O.
City, NC 28713; phone (828)
...0246

2 mi. e. to 610 Magnolia St. The
...d in period. Costumed guided tours.
Sun. 9-5, Feb.-Mar. 31 and day after
...ays. Admission $8; over 65 and ages
DS, MC, VI. ($10). Phone (828) 555-

...19W. Write
19W, Bryson City, NC 28713. Trips
...ept. Phone (828) 488-9366 or (800)

12 mi. s. on US 19W. Write 110-4
, Bryson City, NC 28713. Trips daily
Phone (828) 488-3316 or (800)

...Ltd., 12 mi. s.w. on US 19/74W.
, Box 309, Long Creek, SC 29658.
y Apr.-Oct. Phone (828) 488-2384 or
...9972. See color ads starting on p. 146.

...GTON (B-5) pop. 44,917, elev. 656'
...n is a textile industry center with nu-
...ctory outlet shops that attract bargain
...m nearby states. Clothing, leather goods,
...ankets, sheets, carpets and furniture are
...oducts.

...nterpiece of 76-acre City Park, at South
...treet and Overbrook Road, is a 1910 Dent-
...gerie Carousel. Known for their detail and
...carvings, only 14 such carousels still exist
...de. In addition to 26 horses, the hand-
...nimals include a lion, tiger, giraffe and re-
...four pigs, rabbits, ostriches and cats. The
...operates seasonally and hours vary; phone
...22-5030.

...gton/Alamance County Convention and
...eau: 610 S. Lexington Ave., P.O.
...lington, NC 2721...0519; phone
...657-3804.

...ington Manufacturer's
...t 145, houses more

...TATE HISTORIC
...50. Write P.O.   6 mi. s.w. on SR
...aily May-Oct.   e between Royal-
                        ...tia and an inexpe-
                        ...ners known as the
                        ...xes, corrupt officials
                        ...John Allen house, a log

Official Appointment

🔺🔺🔺 or 🔺🔺🔺 indicates our Official Appointment (OA) lodgings. These properties guarantee members the lowest public rate available at the time of booking for the dates of stay or a minimum 10% discount off the standard room rates published in TourBook guides. We highlight these properties with red and a ⟨SAVE⟩ icon to help you quickly identify them.

Diamond Rating

The number of diamonds informs you of the overall complexity of a lodging's amenities and service. Red indicates an Official Appointment lodging. An fyi in place of diamonds indicates the property has not been rated but is included as an "information only" service. A detailed description of each rating level appears on page 20.

Classification

All diamond rated lodgings are classified using three key elements: style of operation, overall concept and service level. See pages 22-23 for details on our classifications.

Online Reservations

This notation indicates AAA/CAA members can conveniently check room availability, validate room rates and make reservations for this property in a secure online environment at AAA.com.

Rates

Shown from left to right: dates the rates are effective; any meal plan included in the rates (see below); standard room rates for 1 person (1P) or 2 persons (2P); extra person charge (XP); and any applicable family plan indicator (see below).

Rates are provided to AAA by each lodging and represent the regular (rack) rate ranges for a standard room. Rates are rounded to the nearest dollar and do not include taxes. U.S., Mexican and Caribbean rates are in U.S. dollars; rates for Canadian lodgings are in Canadian dollars.

Meal Plan Indicators

AP = American Plan of three meals daily
BP = Breakfast Plan of full hot breakfast
CP = Continental Plan of pastry, juice and another beverage
ECP = Expanded Continental Plan, which offers a wider variety of breakfast items
MAP = Modified American Plan of two meals daily

See individual listing "Terms" for additional meal plans not included in the room rate.

Family Plan Indicators

F = Children stay free
D = Discounts for children
F17 = Children 17 and under stay free
D17 = Discount for children 17 or under

The number displayed will reflect the property's age policy.

Credit Cards Accepted

AX=American Express   **JC**=Japan Credit Bureau
CB=Carte Blanche   **MC**=MasterCard
DC=Diners Club   **VI**=VISA
DS=Discover

Spotting Symbol

Black ovals with white numbers are used to locate, or "spot," lodgings on maps we provide for larger cities.

Service Availability

Unit types, amenities and room features preceded by the word "Some" indicate the item is available on a limited basis, potentially within only one unit.

Free Special Amenities

Some OA properties offer special amenities such as Continental breakfast; expanded Continental breakfast or full breakfast; early check-in and late check-out; room upgrade or preferred room; local phone calls; or daily newspaper. This does not imply that only these properties offer these amenities.

Icons

Lodging icons represent some of the member values, services and facilities offered.

Discounts

ASK May offer discount

S10 Offers minimum 10% senior discount to members over 59

Member Services

Airport transportation

Pets allowed

Restaurant on premises

Restaurant off premises (walking distance)

24 24-hour room service

Cocktail lounge

Child care

Accessibility Features

&M Accessible features

Hearing-impaired equipment available

Roll-in showers

In-Room Amenities

Designated non-smoking rooms

VCR VCR

Movies

Refrigerator

Microwave

Coffee maker

No air conditioning

No TV

No cable TV

No telephones

Leisure Activities

Full-service casino

Pool

Health club on premises

Health club off premises

Recreational activities

Safety Features (see page 24)
(Mexico and Caribbean only)

S Sprinklers

D Smoke detectors

SOME UNITS printed above the icons indicates the amenity is available on a limited basis, potentially in only one unit. **FEE** appearing below an icon indicates that an extra charge applies.

Understanding the Restaurant Listing

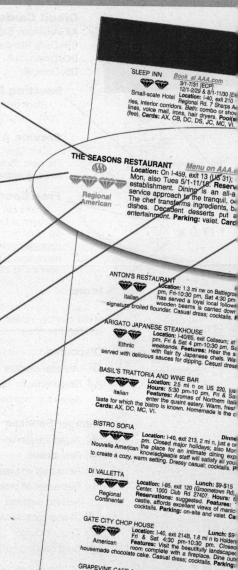

Official Appointment

AAA or CAA indicates our Official Appointment (OA) restaurants. The OA program permits properties to display and advertise the AAA or CAA emblem. We highlight these properties in red to help you quickly identify them. The AAA or CAA Approved sign helps traveling members find restaurants that want member business.

Diamond Rating

The number of diamonds informs you of the overall complexity of food, presentation, service and ambience. Red indicates an Official Appointment restaurant. A detailed description of each diamond level appears on page 21.

Cuisine Type

The cuisine type helps you select a dining facility that caters to your individual taste. AAA currently recognizes more than 90 different cuisine types.

Menus

This notation indicates AAA/CAA members can conveniently view the restaurant's menu in a secure online environment at AAA.com.

Credit Cards Accepted

AX=American Express
CB=Carte Blanche
DC=Diners Club
DS=Discover
JC=Japan Credit Bureau
MC=MasterCard
VI=VISA

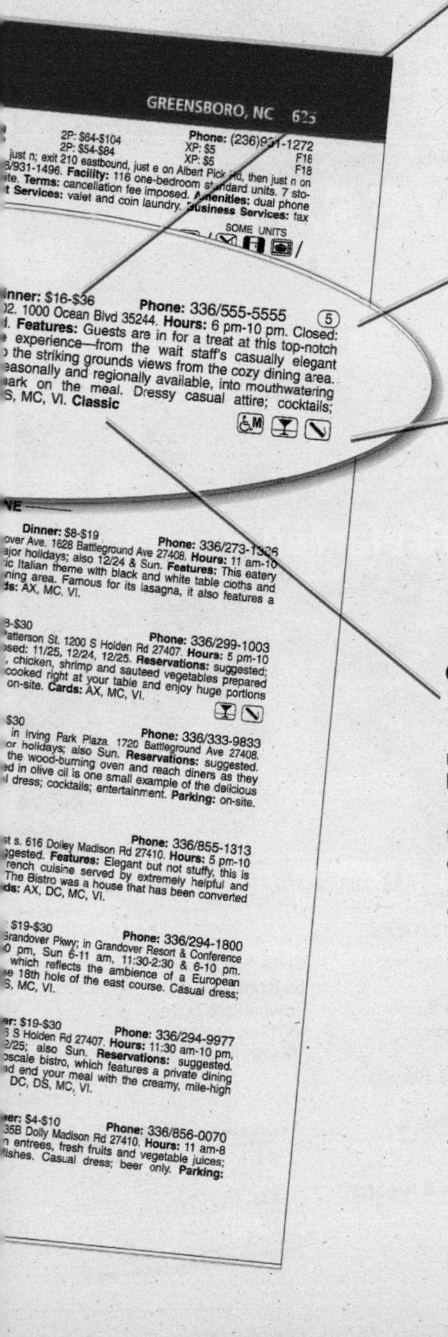

Prices

Rates shown represent the minimum and maximum entree cost per person. Exceptions may include one-of-a-kind or special market priced items. Rates are rounded to the nearest dollar and do not include taxes. U.S., Mexican and Caribbean rates are in U.S. dollars; rates for Canadian restaurants are in Canadian dollars.

Spotting Symbol

White ovals with black numbers serve as restaurant locators and are used to locate, or "spot," restaurants on maps we provide for larger cities.

Icons

Icons provide additional information about services and facilities.

🧊 No air-conditioning

&M Accessible features

🍸 Cocktail lounge

🚬 Designated smoking section available

Classifications

If applicable, a restaurant may be defined as:

Classic - renowned and/or landmark restaurant in business longer than 25 years, known for unique style and ambience.

Historic - properties must meet one of the following criteria:

- Listed on the U.S. National Register of Historic Places
- Designated a U.S. National Historic Landmark
- Located in a U.S. National Register Historic District

Separate criteria designate historic properties in Canada, Mexico and the Caribbean.

GREENSBORO, NC 625

2P: $64-$104   Phone: (236)951-1272
2P: $54-$84   XP: $5
just n; exit 210 eastbound, just e on Albert Pick Rd,   XP: $5   F18
3/931-1496. **Facility:** 116 one-bedroom standard units. 7 sto-   F18
te. **Terms:** cancellation fee imposed. **Amenities:** dual phone
t **Services:** valet and coin laundry. **Business Services:** fax

SOME UNITS

inner: $16-$36   Phone: 336/555-5555   (5)
2. 1000 Ocean Blvd 35244. **Hours:** 6 pm-10 pm. Closed:
. **Features:** Guests are in for a treat at this top-notch
experience—from the wait staff's casually elegant
the striking grounds views from the cozy dining area.
easonally and regionally available, into mouthwatering
ark on the meal. Dressy casual attire; cocktails;
S, MC, VI. **Classic**

&M 🍸 🚬

NE

Dinner: $8-$19   Phone: 336/273-1526
over Ave. 1628 Battleground Ave 27408. **Hours:** 11 am-10
ajor holidays; also 12/24 & Sun. **Features:** This eatery
ic Italian theme with black and white table cloths and
ning area. Famous for its lasagna, it also features a
s: AX, MC, VI.

3-$30   Phone: 336/299-1003
atterson St. 1200 S Holden Rd 27407. **Hours:** 5 pm-10
osed: 11/25, 12/24, 12/25. **Reservations:** suggested.
chicken, shrimp and sauteed vegetables prepared
cooked right at your table and enjoy huge portions
on-site. **Cards:** AX, MC, VI.

🍸 🚬

$30   Phone: 336/333-9833
in Irving Park Plaza. 1720 Battleground Ave 27408.
or holidays; also Sun. **Reservations:** suggested.
the wood-burning oven and reach diners as they
ed in olive oil is one small example of the delicious
al dress; cocktails; entertainment. **Parking:** on-site.

t s. 616 Dolley Madison Rd 27410. **Phone:** 336/855-1313
ggested. **Features:** Elegant but not stuffy, this is
rench cuisine served by extremely helpful and
The Bistro was a house that has been converted
ds: AX, DC, MC, VI.

$19-$30   Phone: 336/294-1800
Grandover Pkwy; in Grandover Resort & Conference
0 pm, Sun 6-11 am, 11:30-2:30 & 6-10 pm.
which reflects the ambience of a European
e 18th hole of the east course. Casual dress;
S, MC, VI.

er: $19-$30   Phone: 336/294-9977
S Holden Rd 27407. **Hours:** 11:30 am-10 pm,
2/25; also Sun. **Reservations:** suggested.
oscale bistro, which features a private dining
end your meal with the creamy, mile-high
DC, DS, MC, VI.

er: $4-$10   Phone: 336/856-0070
35B Dolly Madison Rd 27410. **Hours:** 11 am-8
n entrees, fresh fruits and vegetable juices;
ishes. Casual dress; beer only. **Parking:**

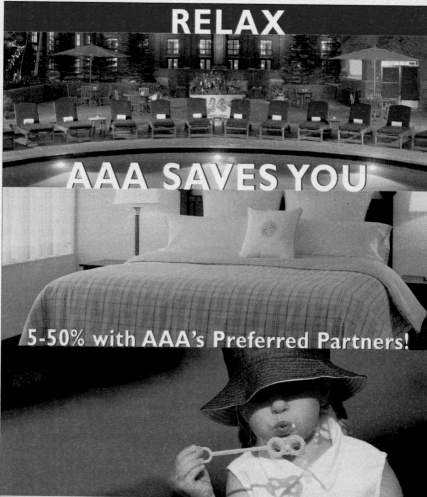

RELAX

AAA SAVES YOU

5-50% with AAA's Preferred Partners!

Visit Over 1,000 AAA Offices **Click** AAA.com/save **Call** 866-AAA-SAVE

AAA Preferred Lodging Partners

Best Western	Hyatt Hotels & Resorts	SpringHIll Suites
Clarion	La Quinta Inn	St. Regis
Comfort Inn	La Quinta Inn & Suites	TownePlace Suites
Comfort Suites	Luxury Collection	W Hotels
Courtyard by Marriott	MainStay Suites	Westin Hotels & Resorts
Doubletree Hotel & Suites	Marriott Hotels & Resorts	
Fairfield Inn	Quality	
FourPoints by Sheraton	Renaissance Hotels &	
Hampton Inn	Resorts	
Hampton Inn & Suites	Residence Inn	
Hilton Inn & Suites	Sheraton Hotels & Resorts	
Hilton Garden Inn	Sleep Inn	

– see page 19 for full details.

Visit Click, Call for member savings.

Lodging Rates Guaranteed

AAA/CAA members are guaranteed they will not be charged more than the maximum regular rate printed in the TourBook guide in each rate range for a standard room. Rates may vary within the range, depending on season and room type. Listed rates are based on last standard room availability. Obtain current AAA/CAA member rates and make reservations at AAA.com.

Discounts

Member discounts will apply to rates quoted within the rate range and are applicable at the time of booking. Special rates used in advertising, as well as special short-term promotional rates lower than the lowest listed rate in the range, are not subject to additional member discounts.

Exceptions

Rates for properties operating as concessionaires for the U.S. National Park Service are not guaranteed due to governing regulations. Rates in the Mexico TourBook are not guaranteed and may fluctuate based on the exchange rate of the peso.

Lodgings may temporarily increase room rates, not recognize discounts or modify pricing policies during special events. Examples of special events range from Mardi Gras and the Kentucky Derby (including pre-Derby events) to college football games, holidays, holiday periods and state fairs. Although some special events are listed in AAA/CAA TourBook guides and on AAA.com, it is always wise to check in advance with AAA travel professionals for specific dates.

Get the Room You Reserved

When making your reservation, identify yourself as a AAA or CAA member and request written confirmation to guarantee: type of room, rate, dates of stay, and cancellation and refund policies. At registration, show your membership card.

When you find your room is not as specified, and you have written confirmation of reservations for a certain type of accommodation, you should be given the option of choosing a different room or finding one elsewhere. Should you choose to go elsewhere and a refund is refused or resisted, submit the matter to AAA/CAA within 30 days, along with complete documentation, including your reasons for refusing the room and copies of your written confirmation and any receipts or canceled checks associated with this problem.

If you are charged more than the maximum rate listed in the TourBook guide for a standard

room, question the additional charge. If management refuses to adhere to the published rate, pay for the room and submit your receipt and membership number to AAA/CAA within 30 days. Include all pertinent information: dates of stay, rate paid, itemized paid receipts, number of persons in your party and the room number you occupied, and list any extra room equipment used. A refund of the amount paid in excess of the stated maximum will be made if our investigation indicates that unjustified charging occurred.

Deposit, Refund and Cancellation Policies

Most establishments give full deposit refunds if they have been notified at least 48 hours before the normal check-in time. Listing prose will note if more than 48 hours' notice is required for cancellation. Some properties may charge a cancellation or handling fee. When this applies, "cancellation fee imposed" will appear in the listing. If you cancel too late, you have little recourse if a refund is denied.

When an establishment requires full or partial payment in advance and your trip is cut short, a refund may not be given.

When canceling a reservation, phone the lodging immediately. Make a note of the date and time you called, the cancellation number if there is one, and the name of the person who handled the cancellation. If your AAA/CAA club made your reservation, allow them to make the cancellation for you as well, so you will have proof of cancellation.

Check-in and Check-out Times

Check-in and check-out times are shown in the lodging listings, under Terms, only if they are before 10 a.m. or after 3 p.m. respectively.

Members Save With Our Partners

These National Show Your Card & Save® partners provide the listed member benefits. Admission tickets that offer greater discounts may be available for purchase at the local AAA/CAA club. A maximum of six tickets is available at the discount price at the gate. Visit AAA.com to discover all the great Show Your Card & Save® discounts in your area.

SeaWorld/Busch Gardens AAA.com/SeaWorld

- Save $5 on 1-day gate admission at SeaWorld, Busch Gardens, and Sesame Place

- Save $3 on 1-day admission at Water Country USA and Adventure Island

- Save 10% on select up-close dining. Reservations are required; visit Guest Relations for details

AAA.com/BuschGardens

Six Flags Theme Parks

- 10% OFF Brunch with Bugs

- 10% OFF merchandise purchases of $15 or more at all Six Flags operated locations.

Universal Orlando AAA.com/Universal

- Save $4 on a 2-day/2-park pass at Universal Orlando's theme parks (savings apply to tickets purchased at the gate)

- Save 10% on select dining and souvenirs at both Universal Orlando theme parks and at select Universal CityWalk Orlando restaurants (excludes Emeril's)

Universal Studios Hollywood

- Save $3 on a 1-day Universal Studios Hollywood pass (savings applies to tickets purchased at the gate) AAA.com/Universal

- Save 10% on select dining and souvenirs at Universal Studios Hollywood and Universal CityWalk

Gray Line
AAA.com/GrayLine

- Save 10% on sightseeing tours of 1 day or less

Landry's Seafood House, The Crab House, Chart House, Muer Seafood Restaurants, Joe's Crab Shack and Aquarium and Downtown Aquarium Restaurants

- 10% discount on food and non-alcoholic beverages at all of the above restaurants.

- 10% discount on novelty merchandise at Joe's Crab Shacks and Aquarium and Downtown Aquarium Restaurants.

Hard Rock Cafe

- Save 10% on food, beverage and merchandise at all U.S. and select Canadian and international locations

Restaurant Partner Savings applies to AAA/CAA members and up to five guests.

Tanger Outlet Centers www.tangeroutlet.com

- Save up to 20% on total purchase at select merchants with AAA/CAA coupon booklet

- Member BONUS: FREE $5 gift card for each additional Tanger Outlet Center visited after first within same calendar year

Tanger Outlets

- Show membership card and register at the AAA customer service desk when you visit

Lodging Partners

SAVINGS. SELECTION. SATISFACTION.—When contacting one of these lodging partners, you will be given AAA/CAA's best rates for your dates of stay. Your valid membership card must be presented at check-in. Select the chain you want and have your membership card available when making a reservation and checking in. Let the property know if you are dissatisfied with any part of your stay. If the matter cannot be resolved, you are entitled to recompense (see page 17).

Offer good at time of publication; chains and offers may change without notice. Lodging partners offering discounts to AAA/CAA members may vary in Mexico and the Caribbean.

Visit	Over 1,000 AAA/CAA Offices	Click	AAA.com	Call	866-AAA-SAVE

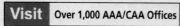

CHOICE HOTELS INTERNATIONAL ™

  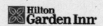

Understanding the Diamond Ratings

AAA/CAA Tourism Editors have evaluated and rated each of the 60,000 lodging and restaurant establishments in the TourBook series to ensure quality travel information for our members. All properties must meet AAA's 27 minimum requirements (for lodgings) concerning cleanliness, comfort and security - or - AAA's 12 minimum requirements (for restaurants) pertaining to cleanliness, food preparation and service.

Eligible applicants receive an unannounced evaluation by a AAA/CAA Tourism Editor that includes two distinct components:

- AAA Approval: The Tourism Editor first must determine whether the property meets the criteria required to be AAA Approved. Every establishment that meets these strict guidelines offers AAA members the assurance that, regardless of the diamond rating, it provides acceptable quality, cleanliness, service and value.
- AAA Diamond Rating: Once an establishment becomes AAA Approved, it is then assigned a rating of one to five diamonds, indicating the extensiveness of its facilities, amenities and services, from basic to moderate to luxury. These diamond ratings guide members in selecting establishments appropriately matched to their needs and expectations.

LODGINGS

1 Diamond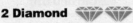

One diamond lodgings typically appeal to the budget-minded traveler. They provide essential, no-frills accommodations and basic comfort and hospitality.

2 Diamond

Two diamond lodgings appeal to family travelers seeking affordable yet more than the basic accommodations. Facilities, decor and amenities are modestly enhanced.

3 Diamond

Three diamond lodgings offer a distinguished style. Properties are multi-faceted, with marked upgrades in physical attributes, amenities and guest comforts.

4 Diamond

Four diamond lodgings are refined and stylish. Physical attributes are upscale. The fundamental hallmarks at this level include an extensive array of amenities combined with a high degree of hospitality, service and attention to detail.

5 Diamond

Five diamond lodgings provide the ultimate in luxury and sophistication. Physical attributes are extraordinary in every manner. Service is meticulous, exceeding guest expectations and maintaining impeccable standards of excellence. Extensive personalized services and amenities provide first-class comfort.

fyi The lodging listings with **fyi** in place of diamonds are included as an *information only* service for members. The icon indicates that a property has not been rated for one or more of the following reasons: too new to rate, under construction, under major renovation, not evaluated, may not meet all AAA requirements.

A property not meeting all AAA requirements is included for either its member value or because it may be the only accommodation available in the area. Listing prose will give insight as to why the **fyi** designation was assigned.

RESTAURANTS

1 Diamond

One diamond restaurants provide simple, familiar specialty food (such as burgers, chicken, pizza or tacos) at an economical price. Often self-service, basic surroundings complement a no-nonsense approach.

2 Diamond

Two diamond restaurants offer a familiar, family-oriented experience. Menu selection includes home-style foods and family favorites, often cooked to order, modestly enhanced and reasonably priced. Service is accommodating yet relaxed, a perfect complement to casual surroundings.

3 Diamond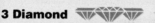

Three diamond restaurants convey an entry into fine dining and are often positioned as adult-oriented experiences. The atypical menu may feature the latest cooking trends and/or traditional cuisine. Expanded beverage offerings complement the menu. The ambience is well coordinated, comfortable and enhanced by a professional service staff.

4 Diamond

Four diamond restaurants provide a distinctive fine-dining experience that is typically expensive. Surroundings are highly refined with upscale enhancements throughout. Highly creative chefs use imaginative presentations to augment fresh, top-quality ingredients. A proficient service staff meets or exceeds guest expectations. A wine steward may offer menu-specific knowledge to guide selection.

5 Diamond

Five diamond restaurants are luxurious and renowned for consistently providing a world-class experience. Highly acclaimed chefs offer artistic menu selections that are imaginative and unique, using only the finest ingredients available. A maitre d' leads an expert service staff in exceeding guest expectations, attending to every detail in an effortless and unobtrusive manner.

fyi The restaurants with **fyi** in place of diamonds are included as an *information only* service for members. These listings provide additional dining choices but have not yet been evaluated.

Understanding the Lodging Classifications

To ensure that your lodging needs and preferences are met, we recommend that you consider an establishment's classification when making your travel choices. While the quality and comfort at properties with the same diamond rating should be consistent (regardless of the classification), there are differences in typical decor/theme elements, range of facilities and service levels.

Large-scale Hotel

A multistory establishment with interior room entrances. A variety of guest unit styles is offered. Public areas are spacious and include a variety of facilities such as a restaurant, fitness center, spa, business center, shops or meeting rooms.

Hotel Royal Plaza, Lake Buena Vista, FL

Small-scale Hotel

A multistory establishment typically with interior room entrances. A variety of guest unit styles is offered. Public areas are limited in size and/or the variety of facilities available.

Baymont Inn, Dallas Ft. Worth-Airport N, TX

Motel

A 1- to 3-story establishment typically with exterior room entrances facilitating convenient access to parking. The standard guest units have one bedroom with a bathroom and are typically similar in decor and design throughout. Public areas are limited in size and/or the variety of facilities available.

Best Western Deltona Inn, Deltona, FL

Country Inn

Similar in definition to a bed and breakfast but usually larger in scale, with spacious public areas offering a dining facility that serves at least breakfast and dinner.

Greenville Inn, Greenville, ME

Bed & Breakfast

Small-scale properties emphasizing a high degree of personal touches that provide guests an "at home" feeling. Guest units tend to be individually decorated. Rooms may not include some modern amenities such as televisions and telephones, and may have a shared bathroom. Usually owner-operated with a common room or parlor separate from the innkeeper's living quarters, where guests and operators can interact during evening and breakfast hours. Evening office closures are normal. A Continental or full, hot breakfast is served and is included in the room rate.

1884 Paxton House Inn, Thomasville, GA

Condominium

Vacation-oriented or extended-stay, apartment-style accommodations that are routinely available for rent through a management company. Units vary in design and decor and often contain one or more bedrooms, a living room, full kitchen and an eating area. Studio-type models combine the sleeping and living areas into one room. Typically, basic cleaning supplies, kitchen utensils and complete bed and bath linens are supplied. The guest registration area may be located off-site.

Sands of Kahana, Kahana, Maui, HI

Cabin/Cottage

Vacation-oriented, small-scale, freestanding houses or cabins. Units vary in design and decor and often contain one or more bedrooms, a living room, kitchen, dining area and bathroom. Studio-type models combine the sleeping and living areas into one room. Typically, basic cleaning supplies, kitchen utensils, and complete bed and bath linens are supplied. The guest registration area may be located off-site.

Desert Rose Inn, Bluff, UT

Ranch

Typically a working ranch with an obvious rustic, Western theme. In general, equestrian-related activities are featured, but ranches may include other animals and activities as well. A variety of guest unit styles is offered in a family-oriented atmosphere.

C Lazy U Ranch, Granby, CO

Vacation Home

Vacation-oriented or extended-stay, large-scale, freestanding houses that are routinely available for rent through a management company. Houses vary in design and decor and often contain two or more bedrooms, a living room, full kitchen, dining room and multiple bathrooms. Typically, basic cleaning supplies, kitchen utensils, and complete bed and bath linens are supplied. The guest registration area may be located off-site.

ResortQuest, Hilton Head Island, SC

Lodging Subclassifications

The following are subclassifications that may appear along with the classifications listed previously to provide a more specific description of the lodging.

Casino

Extensive gaming facilities are available such as blackjack, craps, keno and slot machines. Note: This subclassification will not appear beneath its diamond rating in the listing. It will be indicated by a ⊛ icon and will be included in the row of icons immediately below the lodging listing.

Classic

Renowned and landmark properties, older than 50 years, well-known for their unique style and ambience.

Historic

These properties are typically over 75 years of age and exhibit many features of a historic nature with respect to architecture, design, furnishings, public record or acclaim. Properties must meet one of the following criteria:

- Maintained the integrity of the historical aspect
- Listed on the U.S. National Register of Historic Places
- Designated a U.S. National Historic Landmark
- Located in a U.S. National Register Historic District

Separate criteria designate historic properties in Canada, Mexico and the Caribbean.

Vacation Rental

Typically houses, condos, cottages or cabins; these properties are a "home away from home" offering more room and greater value for the money and generally provide the conveniences of home, such as full kitchens and washers/dryers. They are located in resort or popular destination areas within close proximity to major points of interest, attractions, or recreation areas. These properties may require a pre-arranged reservation and check-in at an off-site location. Housekeeping services may be limited or not included.

Resort

Recreation-oriented, geared to vacation travelers seeking a specific destination experience. Travel packages, meal plans, themed entertainment, and social and recreational programs are typically available. Recreational facilities are extensive and may include spa treatments, golf, tennis, skiing, fishing, water sports, etc. Larger resorts may offer a variety of guest accommodations.

Guest Safety

Room Security

In order to be approved for listing in AAA/CAA TourBook guides for the United States and Canada, accommodations must have dead-bolt locks on all guest room entry doors and connecting room doors.

If the area outside the guest room door is not visible from inside the room through a window or door panel, viewports must be installed on all guest room entry doors. Bed and breakfast properties and country inns are not required to have viewports. Ground floor and easily accessible sliding doors must be equipped with some type of secondary security locks.

Even with those approval requirements, AAA cannot guarantee guest safety. Tourism Editors view a percentage of rooms at each property since it is not feasible to evaluate every room in every lodging establishment. Therefore, AAA cannot guarantee that there are working locks on all doors and windows in all guest rooms.

Fire Safety

Because of the highly specialized skills needed to conduct professional fire safety inspections, AAA/CAA Tourism Editors cannot assess fire safety.

Properties must meet all federal, state and local fire codes. Each guest unit in all U.S. and Canadian lodging properties must be equipped with an operational, single-station smoke detector. A AAA/CAA Tourism Editor has evaluated a sampling of the rooms to verify this equipment is in place.

Mexico and the Caribbean

Requirements for some features, such as door locks and smoke detectors/sprinkler systems, differ in Mexico and the Caribbean. If a property met AAA's security requirements at the time of the evaluation, the phrase "Meets AAA guest room security requirements" appears in the listing.

Service Animals

The Americans with Disabilities Act (ADA) prohibits U.S. businesses that serve the public from discriminating against persons with disabilities. Some businesses have mistakenly denied access to persons who use service animals. Businesses must permit entry to guests and their service animals, as well as allow service animals to accompany guests to all public areas of a property.

A property is permitted to ask whether the animal is a service animal or a pet, and whether the guest has a disability. The property may not, however, ask questions about the nature of the disability, the service provided by the animal or require proof of a disability or certification that the animal is a service animal. These regulations may not apply in Canada, Mexico or the Caribbean.

No fees or deposits, even those normally charged for pets, may be charged for service animals. Service animals fulfill a critical need for their owners—they are not pets.

Savings for all Seasons

Hertz rents Fords and other fine cars. ® REG. U.S. PAT. OFF. © HERTZ SYSTEM INC., 1999/2006-99.

No matter the season, Hertz offers AAA members exclusive discounts and benefits.

Operating in 150 countries at over 8,100 locations, Hertz makes traveling more convenient and efficient wherever and whenever you go. Hertz offers AAA members discounts up to 20% on car rentals worldwide.

To receive your exclusive AAA member discounts and benefits, mention your AAA membership card at time of reservation and present it at time of rental. **In addition**, to receive a free one car class upgrade on daily, weekly or weekend rental in the United States and Canada, mention PC# 969194, and in Puerto Rico mention PC# 969183 at the time of reservation. Offer available through 12/15/07.

For reservations and program details, visit aaa.com/hertz, call your AAA Travel office or the Hertz/AAA Desk at **1-800-654-3080.**

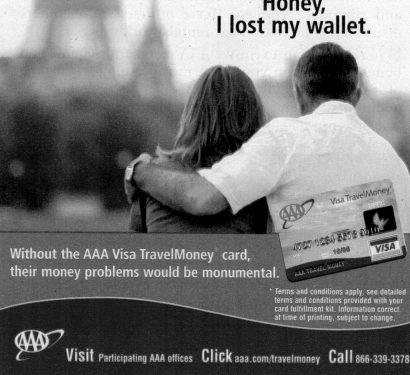

With the AAA Visa TravelMoney® card, worry-free travel is here. Like travelers cheques, this card has replacement and refund options, emergency assistance service, zero liability, purchase security, and even luggage protection.

You don't have to worry about unauthorized spending because the funds are not linked to a bank account.

By keeping a pre-paid amount on your card, you can track what you spend and not go over your budget.

The next time you travel, don't forget to pack the AAA Visa TravelMoney card.

**Honey,
I lost my wallet.**

Without the AAA Visa TravelMoney® card,
their money problems would be monumental.

* Terms and conditions apply, see detailed terms and conditions provided with your card fulfillment kit. Information correct at time of printing, subject to change.

AAA

Visit Participating AAA offices **Click** aaa.com/travelmoney **Call** 866-339-3378

Arkansas

Where the West Begins
Frontier spirit of the West blended with Southern hospitality

"Diamonds Are a Girl's Best Friend"
Search for new friends at Crater of Diamonds State Park—and it's finders keepers

Arkansas Architecture
Frontier log cabins, Victorian homes and Thorncrown Chapel

Yellowstone's Big Brother
Hot Springs National Park preserves access to "therapeutic" springs

19th-century Spa
Eureka Springs now is a resort area and center of holistic healing

Cossatot River, east of Vandervoort / Arkansas Dept of Parks & Tourism
Chuck Haralson

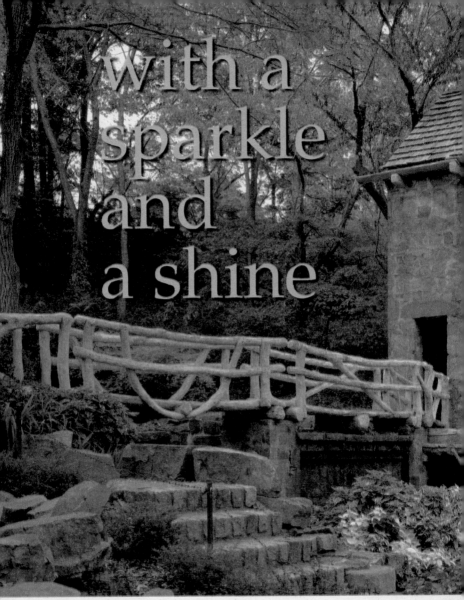

with a sparkle and a shine

The Old Mill, North Little Rock / © Gene Ahrens / SuperStock

When evaluating a diamond, it's essential to keep the four "C's" in mind: Cut, color, clarity and carat highlight the qualities of the stone and define its natural beauty.

Like the gem, Arkansas also boasts four "C's." Clear lakes and streams, caves and colorful countryside accentuate the beauty of the Diamond State. And let's not forget Bill Clinton.

Waves calmly lap the shores of Bull Shoals Lake and lakes Norfork and Ouachita. The Arkansas and White rivers meander across the state, joining with the great Mississippi.

Underground caves offer a different view of Arkansas—from the bottom up. And if you're feeling lucky, you may unearth a jewel of your own at Crater of

Diamonds State Park; a 16-carat diamond was found here in 1975.

Arkansas' countryside adds a splash of color. Sunsets on the rivers are known to mix shades of pinks, reds and yellows; trees among some 17 million acres of national forests don a rust-colored coat in the fall.

Fans of our 42nd president will find monuments to William Jefferson Clinton in Hope, Hot Springs and Little Rock. Walking tours in these cities point out numerous stops on his path to the presidency.

Come appraise the Diamond State. You're sure to find it full of wealth.

French explorers first started the Arkansas name game. Scouting the area now designated as the Diamond State, they met the Ugukhpah Indians, also known by the sobriquets Quapaw, Arkansas and Arkansa. One of these was adopted to identify the territory. Simple enough, right?

Well, not really. When Jacques Marquette and Louis Joliet explored the Mississippi and Arkansas rivers in 1673, the name appeared as *Akansea* in their journal. René-Robert Cavelier, sieur de La Salle, recorded his 1680 trip on a map showing *Acansa*. Another map drawn 1718-22 by Bénard de la Harpe referred to the territory as *Arkansas* and the inhabitants as *Les Arkansas*. Still later, Zebulon Pike spelled it *Arkansaw*.

You get the general idea. But how to pronounce it? Early senators were at odds; one was reputed to have introduced himself as the senator from Ar-*kansas;* the other called his home state Arkan-*saw.* To squelch any future confusion, the General Assembly passed a resolve in 1881 that the state name be spelled Arkansas, but pronounced Arkan*saw.*

Clearly, the evolving name game was much like finding a diamond in the rough—a jewel of an idea that just needed a little polishing to reveal its brilliance. The final decision conveys a melding of its cultural origins—the pronunciation respects the heritage of the land's earliest inhabitants, while the French spelling adds a bit of panache.

What's in a Name?

Little Rock, ironically the largest city in the state, also had French origins. The same man who dubbed the state *Arkansas* also is credited with naming its capital. After hearing from American Indians that a large "emerald stone" sat along the Arkansas River, de la Harpe and his party sought the treasure but found only a small rock, greenish in hue. He called it *"la petite roche,"* and the name stuck.

Nowadays, the capital is anything but a small green rock. The swiftly moving waters of the Arkansas reflect both the glitter of Little Rock's contemporary skyline and its success as a primary river port. Reminders of early days float right by you in the form of barges, still traversing the river.

Petit Jean Mountain, the centerpiece of Petit Jean State Park, is named for a French girl who dressed as a boy to be with her beau. But the park has more than a nifty name—lush foliage surrounds Cedar Falls, which

Exploration of the region begins under Hernando de Soto's leadership.
1541

Library of Congress

Henry de Tonty establishes the Mississippi Valley's first permanent European settlement.
1686

Spain gains control of the area but 37 years later returns it to France.
1763

The United States acquires the region as part of the Louisiana Purchase, which includes most of the land between the Mississippi River and the Rockies.
1803

Arkansas Historical Timeline

©Bettmann/Corbis

1836
Arkansas enters the Union as a slave-holding state.

drops almost 100 feet into a rocky pool. And from the top of the peak, you can see both the Ozark and Ouachita mountain ranges.

Rising steam from more than 40 boiling springs coined the name of Hot Springs, once known as the Valley of the Vapors. Literally a hot spot for centuries, Indians were drawn to the area for what they believed were healing potions bestowed by the Great Spirit. Rumors of "magic waters" spread, and after Hernando de Soto stumbled across the area in 1541, those suffering from rheumatism frequented bathhouses in hope of a cure.

The terrain, now a national park and health resort, still attracts visitors for its therapeutic aura, but it also has a more recent claim to fame—as the boyhood home of our 42nd president. A walking tour through downtown Hot Springs identifies noteworthy places in Bill Clinton's pre-presidential existence.

There are a few reasons why Arkansas is called the Diamond State: The 40-carat Uncle Sam, the 16-carat Amarillo Starlight, the 34-carat Star of Murfreesboro and the 15-carat Star of Arkansas rank high on the list of sensational finds at Crater of Diamonds State Park near Murfreesboro. The only public diamond mine in the country, visitors keep what they find.

And the hamlet of Mount Ida in the Ouachita Mountains offers more than outstanding scenery; clear quartz crystals hide in red clay, waiting to be unearthed by rockhounds. Once shaped and used by Indians as arrowheads, the crystals are believed by some to have healing powers.

Going Down Under

Exploring Arkansas' caverns is a way to discover some objects with interesting names. Once secret hideaways for Indians, dark and chilly caves throughout the state sport funky formations, subterranean lakes, mazes and tunnels.

Most cave deposits are named after things they resemble: You can see a pipe organ, a witch's fireplace, soda straws, popcorn, frozen waterfalls and a friendly dragon—all hidden beneath the earth in grottoes that date back almost 350 million years.

In Arkansas, it's easy to play the name game. Visit and you may coin some terms of your own—rich, serene, sparkling. . .

You name it.

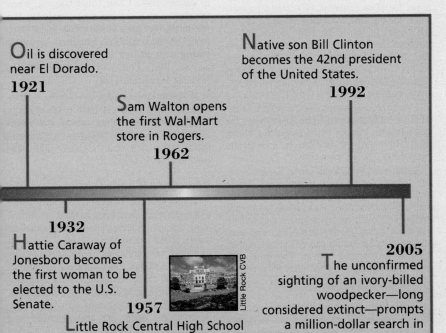

Oil is discovered near El Dorado.
1921

Native son Bill Clinton becomes the 42nd president of the United States.
1992

Sam Walton opens the first Wal-Mart store in Rogers.
1962

1932
Hattie Caraway of Jonesboro becomes the first woman to be elected to the U.S. Senate.

1957
Little Rock Central High School resists federally mandated public school desegregation.

Little Rock CVB

2005
The unconfirmed sighting of an ivory-billed woodpecker—long considered extinct—prompts a million-dollar search in Arkansas' Big Woods.

Recreation

The harnessing of rivers in Arkansas for water power and flood control has created a haven for anyone who enjoys being in, on or near the water. Be sure to include fishing poles, flippers, water wings, paddles and bathing suits on your packing list.

Gone Fishin'

Fishing holes throughout the state lure anglers to reservoirs, natural lakes and streams for a variety of good catches. Lake Norfork is best known for its lunker and striped bass. Nearby Bull Shoals Lake, which stretches across five counties in northern Arkansas, is fantastic for catfish, crappie, lunker bass, trout and walleye.

An annual stocking program helps ensure plentiful bites in both lakes, where bass swim alongside trout. **Night fishing** in summer increases your chance for hooking white bass and crappie. Daytime fishing is best in deeper waters. **Spearfishing** is permitted in both Bull Shoals and Lake Norfork; interested parties should contact the Arkansas Game and Fish Commission.

Looking for trout? Head north. The White River, a world-class cold trout stream, is famous for huge cutthroat, brown and rainbow trout; for big fins, your best bet is to cast in the waters of the North Fork section, where honeysuckle perfumes the air. You can witness the rhythmic maneuvers of **fly-fishing** just south of Norfork Dam. People clad in waders carefully cast in hopes of reeling in record-breaking trout.

Don't forget to check out the waters of the Missouri, Arkansas and Little Red rivers—the last holds the current world record for brown trout. Tailwaters below Beaver and Greers Ferry lakes also are trout runs.

Surrounded by a pecan grove, Lake Chicot, the largest natural lake in the state, offers crappie. Some navigation is required on the lake at Millwood State Park, where boat lanes meander through timber marshes and oxbow cutoffs. Catches in this tree-filled area vary with the season; spring and fall bring crappie, summer bream and catfish. The park also gives **birdwatchers** a good view of wintering bald eagles, migrating pelicans and ducks in autumn.

The Buffalo River yields smallmouth bass. It also features a great spot on its upper reaches where brave souls go **canoeing** on the challenging white water. Experienced canoeists and **kayakers** take on the rough waters in the rocky canyon where the Cossatot River plummets to form Cossatot Falls. Limestone bluffs provide a dramatic backdrop for a float down the Buffalo National River in the central Ozarks. Canoes also dot the White River from Fayetteville to Brashears.

The waters of Lake Norfork are wonderful for **boating, swimming** and **water skiing.** For **scuba diving,** head to limpid Lake Ouachita. Gigantic Bull Shoals Lake is called the "Caribbean of the Midwest" for a good reason: The blue, crystal-clear depths provide amazing visibility and an open invitation for diving and scavenging.

Take A Hike

Pinnacle Mountain State Park, within the Ouachita National Forest, offers many **hiking** trails that will afford visitors countless hours of pleasure. Nature enthusiasts will appreciate the varied wildlife and array of plant life while exploring the trails, which range from easy to strenuous in terms of difficulty. It is said that the view from atop Pinnacle Mountain is breathtaking.

At Petit Jean State Park, trails lead you past forests, canyons, streams, meadows and mountainsides to Cedar Creek Canyon, where the creek drops and becomes a waterfall that just might take your breath away. Want to explore on two wheels? Excellent **mountain biking** trails include Womble, Wolf Pen Gap and the Black Fork portion of the Ouachita National Recreation Trail.

If **spelunking** is your style, bring a flashlight and head to one of eight caves in northern Arkansas. Wandering among stalagmites and stalactites, you'll discover subterranean lakes, mazes and weird creatures like blind trout and albino crawfish.

Recreational Activities

Throughout the TourBook, you may notice a Recreational Activities heading with bulleted listings of recreation-oriented establishments listed underneath. Similar operations also may be mentioned in Destination City recreation sections. Since normal AAA inspection criteria cannot be applied, these establishments are presented only for information. Age, height and weight restrictions may apply. Reservations often are recommended and sometimes are required. Addresses and/or phone numbers are provided so visitors can contact the attraction for additional information.

Fast Facts

POPULATION: 2,673,400.

AREA: 51,945 square miles; ranks 29th.

CAPITAL: Little Rock.

HIGHEST POINT: 2,753 ft., Mount Magazine.

LOWEST POINT: 55 ft., Ouachita River.

TIME ZONE(S): Central. DST.

MINIMUM AGE FOR UNRESTRICTED DRIVER'S LICENSE: 16.

SEAT BELT/CHILD RESTRAINT LAWS: Seat belts are required for driver and front-seat passengers over age 15. Children ages 6-15 who weigh at least 60 pounds must wear a seat belt; child restraints are required for under age 6 and under 60 pounds.

HELMETS FOR MOTORCYCLISTS: Required for riders under 21.

RADAR DETECTORS: Permitted.

FIREARMS LAWS: Vary by state and/or county. Contact the Arkansas State Police, 1 State Police Plaza, Little Rock, AR 72209; phone (501) 618-8600.

HOLIDAYS: Jan. 1; Martin Luther King Jr. Day/Robert E. Lee's Birthday, Jan. 19; Washington's Birthday, Feb. (3rd Mon.); Memorial Day, May (last Mon.); July 4; Labor Day; Veterans Day, Oct. (4th Mon.); Election Day; Thanksgiving; Christmas, Dec. 25.

TAXES: Arkansas' statewide sales tax is 6 percent with local options to impose additional increments. A 2 percent Tourism Gross Receipts Tax is levied on lodgings statewide; some cities may levy an additional 1 percent.

INFORMATION CENTERS: State welcome centers are 3 mi. n. of Bentonville on US 71; n. of Harrison on US 65; in Mammoth Spring on US 63N; 5 mi. s. of the Missouri state line on I-55S at Blytheville; 6 mi. n. of Corning on US 67N; 2 mi. e. of the Oklahoma state line on I-40W at Fort Smith/Van Buren; 5 mi. n. of the Louisiana state line on US 167S/SR 7 at junction with US 82 at El Dorado; on US 49 Bypass at Helena; 10 mi. w. of the Mississippi state line off US 82 at Lake Village; on I-30 in Texarkana; on US 71 on the Red River n. of Texarkana; on US 412W at Siloam Springs; 3 mi. w. of West Memphis on I-40; and at One Capitol Mall in Little Rock.

The centers are open daily 8-6, Memorial Day weekend-Labor Day; 8-5, rest of year. Helena and Red River are open daily 8-5, Memorial Day weekend-Labor Day; 8-4, rest of year. Centers are closed Jan. 1, Easter, Thanksgiving and Dec. 25.

FURTHER INFORMATION FOR VISITORS:

Arkansas Department of Parks & Tourism
One Capitol Mall
Little Rock, AR 72201
(800) 628-8725
See color ad p. 38

FISHING AND HUNTING REGULATIONS:

Game and Fish Commission
2 Natural Resource Dr.
Little Rock, AR 72205
(501) 223-6300

NATIONAL FOREST INFORMATION:

Southern Region
1720 Peachtree Rd., Suite 760
Atlanta, GA 30309
(404) 347-4177
(877) 444-6777 (reservations)

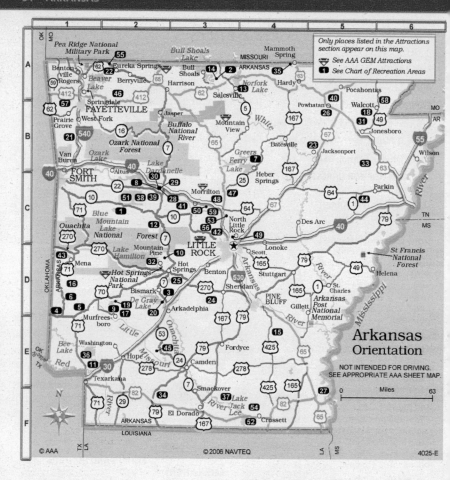

Arkansas Orientation

NOT INTENDED FOR DRIVING.
SEE APPROPRIATE AAA SHEET MAP.

Only places listed in the Attractions section appear on this map.
⬧ See AAA GEM Attractions
1 See Chart of Recreation Areas

Miles 0 — 63

© AAA   ©2006 NAVTEQ   4025-E

Arkansas Temperature Averages
Maximum/Minimum
From the records of The Weather Channel Interactive, Inc.

	JAN	FEB	MAR	APR	MAY	JUN	JUL	AUG	SEP	OCT	NOV	DEC
Fort Smith	50 / 29	55 / 33	63 / 40	74 / 50	81 / 59	90 / 67	95 / 71	94 / 70	87 / 62	77 / 51	62 / 38	53 / 32
Little Rock	51 / 31	55 / 34	63 / 41	74 / 51	82 / 60	90 / 68	93 / 71	92 / 70	86 / 62	76 / 50	61 / 38	52 / 32
Texarkana	53 / 35	59 / 38	66 / 44	75 / 53	82 / 61	90 / 69	93 / 72	93 / 72	88 / 65	79 / 54	65 / 42	57 / 37

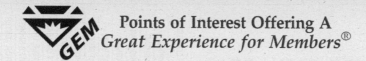

Points of Interest Offering A
Great Experience for Members®

Eureka Springs (A-2)

"THE GREAT PASSION PLAY"—A cast of 250, meticulous costuming, special lighting and sound effects combine in this amphitheater to retell the story of Jesus of Nazareth. See p. 42.

Hot Springs National Park (D-2)

HOT SPRINGS NATIONAL PARK—The water from these springs is so free of bacteria and contaminants that it was used to store moon rocks. See p. 48.

Little Rock (D-3)

WILLIAM J. CLINTON PRESIDENTIAL LIBRARY AND MUSEUM—Explore the Clinton White House era through the exhibits in this 21st-century structure. See p. 52.

Morrilton (C-3)

PETIT JEAN STATE PARK—Leave your campsite or lodge room for a day of fishing, swimming, wading in streams, splashing in springs, viewing a waterfall, exploring caves or traipsing through the woods in one of the state's finest parks. See p. 54.

Mountain View (B-3)

BLANCHARD SPRINGS CAVERNS—Spectacular mineral deposits creating the columns, stalactites, stalagmites and flowstone in these "living" caverns are still forming. See p. 54.

OZARK FOLK CENTER—The period 1820-1920 in the Ozark Mountains is captured in crafts demonstrations, music and food of the people in this isolated valley surrounded by misty blue mountains. See p. 54.

RECREATION AREAS	MAP LOCATION	CAMPING	PICNICKING	HIKING TRAILS	BOATING	BOAT RAMP	BOAT RENTAL	FISHING	SWIMMING	PETS ON LEASH	BICYCLE TRAILS	WINTER SPORTS	VISITOR CENTER	LODGE/CABINS	FOOD SERVICE
NATIONAL PARKS *(See place listings)*															
Hot Springs (D-2) 5,839 acres.		●	●	●						●			●		
NATIONAL FORESTS *(See place listings)*															
Ouachita 1,613,120 acres. West-central Arkansas and southeastern Oklahoma. Horse trails.		●	●	●	●	●	●	●	●	●	●		●	●	●
Ozark 1,123,079 acres. Northwestern Arkansas. Horse trails.		●	●	●	●	●	●	●	●	●	●		●	●	●
St. Francis 20,977 acres. East-central Arkansas.		●	●	●	●	●		●	●	●					
NATIONAL RIVERS *(See place listings)*															
Buffalo River (B-3) 95,730 acres. Northwestern Arkansas.		●	●	●	●	●	●	●	●	●			●		●
ARMY CORPS OF ENGINEERS															
Blue Mountain Lake (C-2) 17,000 acres 1.5 mi. s.w. of Waveland on SR 10. Scuba diving, water skiing.	❶	●	●		●	●		●	●						
Bull Shoals Lake (A-3) 101,196 acres 8 mi. w. of Mountain Home on SR 178. Sailing, scuba diving, water skiing.	❷	●	●		●	●	●	●	●						●
DeGray Lake (D-2) 31,800 acres. Sailing, scuba diving, water skiing. *(See Bismarck p. 39)*	❸	●	●		●	●	●	●	●				●	●	●
DeQueen Lake (D-1) 7,150 acres 4 mi. n.w. of DeQueen on SR 71. Scuba diving, water skiing.	❹	●	●		●	●		●	●						
Dierks Lake (D-1) 8,100 acres 5 mi. n.w. of Dierks on SR 70. Scuba diving, water skiing.	❺	●	●		●	●		●	●						
Gillham Lake (D-1) 9,000 acres 6 mi. n.e. of Gillham on SR 71. Scuba diving, water skiing.	❻	●	●		●	●		●	●	●					

RECREATION AREAS

	MAP LOCATION	CAMPING	PICNICKING	HIKING TRAILS	BOATING	BOAT RAMP	BOAT RENTAL	FISHING	SWIMMING	PETS ON LEASH	BICYCLE TRAILS	WINTER SPORTS	VISITOR CENTER	LODGE/CABINS	FOOD SERVICE
Greers Ferry Lake (B-4) 40,914 acres. Sailing, scuba diving, water skiing. *(See Heber Springs p. 45)*	7	•	•	•	•	•	•	•	•	•			•	•	•
Lake Dardanelle (C-2) 52,570 acres 4 mi. w. of Russellville on SR 7.	8	•	•		•	•	•	•	•	•			•	•	•
Lake Greeson (D-2) 15,842 acres 7 mi. n. of Murfreesboro on SR 19. Sailing, scuba diving, water skiing; motorcycle trails.	9	•	•	•	•	•	•	•	•	•			•	•	•
Lake Ouachita (D-3) 82,373 acres 12 mi. n. of Mountain Pine on SR 227. Sailing, scuba diving, water skiing.	10	•	•	•	•	•	•	•	•	•			•	•	•
Millwood Lake (E-1) 101,790 acres 9 mi. e. of Ashdown on SR 32.	11	•	•		•	•	•	•		•			•		
Nimrod Lake (C-2) 24,840 acres on SR 60 w. of SR 7 at Fourche Junction. Scuba diving, water skiing.	12	•	•	•	•	•	•	•	•	•	•				
Norfork Lake (A-4) 54,000 acres. Sailing, scuba diving, water skiing. *(See Salesville p. 59)*	13	•	•	•	•	•	•	•	•	•			•	•	•
STATE															
Bull Shoals-White River (A-3) 663 acres 6 mi. n. of Mountain Home on SR 5, then 8 mi. w. on SR 178. Scuba diving, trout fishing, water skiing.	14	•	•	•	•	•	•	•		•			•	•	•
Cane Creek (E-4) 2,053 acres 4 mi. e. of Star City on SR 293.	15	•	•	•	•	•		•		•	•		•		
Cossatot River (D-1) 5,484 acres 9 mi. e. of Vandervoort on SR 246. Natural area. Canoeing, kayaking.	16			•				•	•	•			•		
Crater of Diamonds (D-2) 887 acres. Diamond hunting. *(See Murfreesboro p. 55)*	17	•	•	•					•	•			•		•
Crowley's Ridge (B-5) 270 acres. *(See Walcott p. 61)*	18	•	•	•	•	•		•	•	•			•	•	•
Daisy (D-2) 272 acres .2 mi. s. of Daisy off US 70.	19	•	•	•	•	•		•		•	•		•		
DeGray Lake Resort (D-2) 938 acres. Golf (18 holes), sailing, scuba diving, tennis, water skiing. *(See Bismarck p. 39)*	20	•	•	•	•	•	•	•	•	•	•		•	•	•
Devil's Den (B-1) 2,000 acres 17 mi. s.w. on SR 170. Canoe, pedal boats, tandem kayaks and water bicycle rentals; swimming pool. Scenic. *(See West Fork p. 62)*	21	•	•	•			•	•		•	•		•	•	•
Hobbs State Park-Conservation Area (A-2) 38,045 acres 10 mi. e. of Rogers on SR 12. Bridle/multi-use trails, firing range, interpretive programs, primitive campsites; hunting. *(See Rogers p. 58)*	22	•	•	•	•	•		•		•	•		•		
Jacksonport (B-5) 157 acres. *(See Jacksonport p. 49)*	23	•	•	•	•	•		•	•	•			•	•	
Jenkins' Ferry (D-3) 40 acres 13 mi. s. of Sheridan on SR 46.	24		•					•	•	•					
Lake Catherine (D-3) 2,180 acres 15 mi. n.w. of Malvern on SR 171.	25	•	•	•	•	•	•	•	•	•			•	•	•
Lake Charles (B-5) 140 acres 8 mi. n.w. of Hoxie on US 63, then 6 mi. s.w. on SR 25.	26	•	•	•	•	•	•	•	•	•			•		
Lake Chicot (F-5) 132 acres 8 mi. n.e. of Lake Village on SR 144.	27	•	•	•	•	•	•	•	•	•			•	•	
Lake Dardanelle															
Dardanelle (C-3) 90 acres 4 mi. w. of Dardanelle. Scuba diving, water skiing.	28	•	•	•	•	•	•	•		•					
Ouita (C-3) 20 acres .7 mi. e. of Russellville on SR 326. Scuba diving, water skiing.	29	•	•		•	•		•		•					
Russellville (C-2) 184 acres 4 mi. s. of Russellville on SR 326. Miniature golf, scuba diving, water skiing.	30	•	•		•	•	•	•	•	•			•		
Lake Frierson (B-5) 114 acres 10 mi. n. of Jonesboro on SR 141.	31	•	•	•	•	•		•		•			•		
Lake Ouachita (D-2) 370 acres. Scuba diving, water skiing. *(See Mountain Pine p. 54)*	32	•											•	•	•
Lake Poinsett (B-5) 111 acres 1 mi. e. of Harrisburg on SR 14, then 3 mi. s. on SR 163.	33	•	•	•	•	•		•		•			•	•	
Logoly (F-2) 345 acres .7 mi. e. of McNeil on CR 47. Playground.	34	•	•	•				•							
Mammoth Spring (A-4) 62 acres. Scenic. Historic. *(See Mammoth Spring p. 53)*	35		•	•				•		•			•		

RECREATION AREAS

	MAP LOCATION	CAMPING	PICNICKING	HIKING TRAILS	BOATING	BOAT RAMP	BOAT RENTAL	FISHING	SWIMMING	PETS ON LEASH	BICYCLE TRAILS	WINTER SPORTS	VISITOR CENTER	LODGE/CABINS	FOOD SERVICE
Millwood (E-1) 823 acres 9 mi. e. of Ashdown on SR 32.	36	•	•	•	•	•	•	•	•	•			•		
Moro Bay (F-3) 117 acres 20 mi. n.e. of El Dorado on SR 15.	37	•	•	•	•	•	•	•	•	•					
Mount Magazine (C-2) 2,200 acres 17 mi. s. of Paris on SR 309.	38	•	•	•								•	•	•	
Mount Nebo (C-2) 2,812 acres 7 mi. w. of Dardanelle on SR 155. Tennis.	39	•	•	•					•	•		•	•	•	
Old Davidsonville (A-5) 173 acres. Historic. *(See Pocahontas p. 57)*	40	•	•	•	•	•	•	•		•			•		
Petit Jean (C-3) 2,896 acres. Scenic. Tennis. *(See Morrilton p. 54)*	41	•	•	•	•	•	•	•	•	•			•	•	•
Pinnacle Mountain (C-3) 2,000 acres 13 mi. w. of Little Rock on SR 10, then 2 mi. n. on SR 300. Arboretum. Interpretive programs. Scenic.	42		•	•	•	•		•		•			•		
Queen Wilhelmina (D-1) 460 acres. *(See Mena p. 53)*	43	•	•	•						•			•	•	•
Village Creek (C-5) 6,909 acres 13 mi. n. of Forrest City on SR 284. Tennis.	44	•	•	•	•	•	•	•	•	•	•		•	•	
White Oak Lake (E-2) 666 acres 2 mi. s.e. of Bluff City on SR 387.	45	•	•	•	•	•		•		•					
Withrow Springs (A-2) 786 acres 5 mi. n. of Huntsville on SR 23. Tennis. Canoe shuttle service and rental, playground, pool.	46	•	•	•	•	•	•	•	•	•			•		•
Woolly Hollow (C-3) 399 acres 12 mi. n. of Conway on US 65, then 6 mi. e. on SR 285.	47	•	•	•	•	•	•	•	•	•			•		•
OTHER															
Beaverfork Lake (C-3) 900 acres 3 mi. n. of Conway off US 65 or SR 25.	48		•		•			•	•	•					
Burns Park (C-4) 1,575 acres. *(See North Little Rock p. 55)*	49	•	•	•	•	•		•		•			•		
Cadron Settlement (C-3) 80 acres 5 mi. w. of Conway on US 64, then 1.5 mi. s. on SR 319.	50		•	•	•	•		•		•			•		
Cove Lake (C-2) 160 acres s.e. of Paris on SR 309 near Mount Magazine.	51	•	•		•	•		•	•	•					
Crossett Harbor (F-4) 300 acres 8 mi. w. of Crossett.	52	•	•		•	•		•		•			•		•
Lake Conway (C-3) 6,700 acres 3 mi. s. of Conway on SR 365.	53	•	•		•	•	•	•							
Lake Georgia-Pacific (F-4) 1,700 acres 10 mi. n.w. of Crossett.	54	•	•		•	•		•							
Lake Leatherwood (A-2) 1,600 acres 2 mi. w. of Eureka Springs off US 62. Canoe and paddleboat rental.	55	•	•	•	•	•	•	•	•	•	•			•	
Lake Maumelle (C-3) 8,900 acres 12 mi. w. of Little Rock on SR 10.	56		•	•	•	•		•		•					
Lake Wedington (B-1) 139 acres 13 mi. w. of Fayetteville on SR 16. Canoeing.	57	•	•	•	•	•		•	•	•				•	
Reynolds Park (A-6) 80 acres on n. edge of Paragould.	58	•	•			•		•	•						
Toad Suck Park (C-3) 78 acres 5 mi. w. of Conway on SR 60 on the Arkansas River.	59	•	•		•	•		•		•			•		

Points of Interest

ALTUS (C-2) pop. 817, elev. 538'

ST. MARY'S CATHOLIC CHURCH is atop Mount Bethel, 5 mi. s. of I-40 exit 41 on SR 186. This basilica-type church was dedicated in 1879 and is known for its original paintings by German artist Fridolin Fuchs. Four bells, weighing a total of nearly 6,400 pounds, hang in a 120-foot tower, and 29 stained-glass windows grace the interior. The altar and frescoes are covered in gold leaf. Open daily 7-7. Free. Phone (479) 468-2585.

WINERIES

• **Post Familie Vineyards & Winery** is 1 blk. n. of US 64 on SR 186. Tasting room open Mon.-Sat. 9:30-6, Sun. noon-5. Guided 20-minute winery tours Mon.-Sat. 11-3:40. Phone (479) 468-2741.

• **Wiederkehr Wine Cellars** is 4 mi. s. on SR 186, off I-40 exit 41. Guided 25-minute tours and tastings daily every 45 minutes 9-4:30. Last tour begins at closing. Phone (479) 468-9463.

ARKADELPHIA (D-3) pop. 10,912, elev. 189'

Founded in 1839 and built along the bluffs of the Ouachita Valley, Arkadelphia was a river port during the steamboat days. The town is an agricultural and light industrial center producing aluminum, boats, clothing and wood products. It also has two colleges: Henderson State University has 5,000 students; Ouachita Baptist College's enrollment is 3,000.

Arkadelphia Area Chamber of Commerce: 6th and Caddo sts., P.O. Box 38, Arkadelphia, AR 71923; phone (870) 246-5542.

Self-guiding tours: The Arkadelphia Historic Homes Tour is a driving tour featuring several homes dating from the 1840s. A brochure with a map of the path and descriptions of the homes is available from the chamber of commerce.

DeGRAY DAM VISITOR CENTER is 7 mi. n. on SR 7, then 2 mi. w. on entrance road. Displays and 3-D models illustrate the dam's construction and operational features. The center also features a wildlife exhibit and Caddo Indian artifacts. Daily 8-4:15; closed Jan. 1 and Dec. 25. Free. Phone (870) 246-5501. *See Recreation Chart and the AAA South Central CampBook.*

DEGRAY LAKE RESORT STATE PARK— *see Bismarck p. 39*

ARKANSAS POST NATIONAL MEMORIAL (D-5)

On SR 169, 7 miles south of Gillett along the lower Arkansas River, the Arkansas Post National Memorial occupies 389 acres. Erected as a fort by the French in 1686, Arkansas Post was the first permanent European settlement in the lower Mississippi Valley. Ownership passed to Spain 1765-1800, then briefly reverted to France. With the Louisiana Purchase the post became a frontier village.

Arkansas Post was the home of Arkansas' first newspaper, the *Gazette*, and the first capital of the Arkansas Territory. In 1821 both the newspaper and the capital moved to Little Rock. The site continued as a river port until the Civil War, when it became the scene of one of the state's major battles.

A visitor center and museum contain historical exhibits. Visitors can tour the town site, hike nature trails and fish, as well as enjoy bird-watching opportunities available due to the memorial's location along the Mississippi Flyway. Memorial open daily 8-dusk. Visitor center daily 8-5; closed Jan. 1, Thanksgiving and Dec. 25. Free. Phone (870) 548-2207.

BATESVILLE (B-4) pop. 9,445, elev. 338'

MARK MARTIN MUSEUM is at 1601 Batesville Blvd. This museum at Martin's Ford Mercury dealership features racing memorabilia, trophies and vehicles from his NASCAR career. Video displays tell the racing history of the cars he drove to win a record-setting 47 Busch Series victories and five IROC titles in one year. Mon.-Fri. 8-6, Sat. 9-5. Free. Phone (870) 793-4461 or (800) 566-4461.

BENTON (D-3) pop. 21,906, elev. 416'

GANN MUSEUM OF SALINE COUNTY is at 218 S. Market St. Built in 1893, this structure is said to be the only known building in the world constructed of bauxite, or aluminum ore. Once the medical office of Dr. Dewell Gann Sr., the building was erected by his patients who could not afford to pay their bills. Exhibits also include a collection of Niloak pottery. Allow 30 minutes minimum. Tues.-Thurs. 10-4; closed July 4, Thanksgiving and Dec. 24-25. Donations. Phone (501) 778-5513.

BENTONVILLE (A-1)
pop. 19,730, elev. 1,280'

THE PEEL MANSION & HERITAGE GARDENS is at 400 S. Walton Blvd. Col. Samuel West Peel, a pioneer businessman, Indian agent, Confederate soldier, and congressman, built this Italianate mansion in 1875. He and his wife, Mary Emaline Berry Peel, raised nine children here. The house is furnished in period. A garden comprising historic roses, perennials and native plants also is on site. The mansion is available for viewing by guided tour only.

Allow 30 minutes minimum. Tues.-Sat. 10-4; closed Christmas week. Admission $3; ages 6-12, $1. MC, VI. Phone (479) 273-9664.

BERRYVILLE (A-2) pop. 4,433, elev. 1,246'

The "Turkey Capital of Arkansas," Berryville raises more than 500,000 turkeys each year. North on US 62 is a scenic drive through the Ozarks.

Berryville Chamber of Commerce: P.O. Box 402, Berryville, AR 72616; phone (870) 423-3704.

CARROLL COUNTY HERITAGE CENTER MUSEUM is at 403 Public Sq. Three floors of displays in the 1889 Carroll County Courthouse include a pioneer-era schoolroom and funeral parlor, moonshine still, miniature train room, clock collection and genealogy department. Allow 1 hour minimum. Mon.-Fri. 9-4, Apr.-Oct.; Tues.-Fri. 9-4, rest of year. Admission $2; under 13, $1. Phone (870) 423-6312.

SAVE **COSMIC CAVERN** is just n.e. off SR 21. Guided 75-minute tours into this former onyx mine cover one-third mile and travel to such features as two underground lakes and a 9-foot-long soda straw stalactite. The cave maintains a constant temperature of 62 F.

Picnicking is permitted. Allow 1 hour, 30 minutes minimum. Tours depart daily every 25 minutes 9-6, June-Aug.; every 45 minutes daily 9-5, Mar.-May and Sept.-Oct.; Fri.-Tues. 9-5, Nov.-Dec.; Sat.-Sun. 9-5, rest of year (weather permitting). Last tour begins 10 minutes before closing. Closed Dec. 24-25. Phone to verify winter schedule. Fee $12.89; ages 5-12, $7.50. AX, DS, MC, VI. Phone (870) 749-2298.

SAUNDERS MEMORIAL MUSEUM is 1 blk. e. of Main St. at 113-115 Madison Ave. Col. C.B. Saunders' collection of pistols and revolvers includes a Chinese pistol more than 500 years old and side arms that belonged to Jesse James, Wild Bill Hickok, Pancho Villa and Annie Oakley. The museum also contains antique furniture, Persian rugs, European and American silverware and an Arabian sheik's tent.

Allow 1 hour minimum. Mon.-Sat. 10:30-5, Apr. 15-early Nov. Admission $3; ages 6-12, $1.50. Phone (870) 423-2563.

BISMARCK (D-2) elev. 531'

In the foothills of the Ouachita Mountains, 13,800-acre DeGray Lake is one of the state's most popular recreation destinations *(see Recreation Chart)*. The Army Corps of Engineers created this clear body of water in 1972 with completion of the DeGray Dam and Power Plant; the visitor center is on the southern end of the lake near Arkadelphia *(see attraction listing p. 38)*.

DeGRAY LAKE RESORT STATE PARK is off I-30 exit 78, then 6 mi. n. on SR 7. Interpretive programs at this 938-acre park include guided lake cruises, snorkeling and kayaking trips, trail hikes and wildlife demonstrations. Eagles Et Cetera in January spotlights the park's American bald eagles and other birds of prey. Facilities include an 18-hole championship golf course, a lodge and campsites, a swimming beach, picnic facilities and a marina that rents fishing tackle, boats, canoes and personal watercraft.

Park open daily dawn-10 p.m. Visitor facilities Sun.-Thurs. 8-5, Sat.-Sun. 8-8. Free. Boat tours $6; ages 6-12, $3. Phone (501) 865-2801 for the park, or (501) 865-2811 for the marina. *See Recreation Chart and the AAA South Central CampBook.*

BUFFALO NATIONAL RIVER (B-3)

Reached via US 65 or SRs 7, 14 or 21 in northwestern Arkansas, Buffalo National River stretches through the rugged Ozark Mountains. While the Buffalo River courses 150 miles through the Ozarks, only its lower 135 miles and adjacent land are designated a national river. To protect the natural beauty of this area, Congress declared it a national river in 1972, thereby preserving it from development and population encroachment.

A variety of wildlife, including bears, whitetail deer, bobcats, raccoons opossums, beavers and minks, as well as geological features as distinct as caves, sinkholes, waterfalls, springs and bluffs, combine to provide a tranquil setting for hiking, fishing, camping and canoeing. More than 100 miles of hiking trails are available, and some allow horseback riding.

Interpretive programs are offered throughout the spring, summer and fall and include such activities as campfire programs, guided walks and hikes, canoe and float trips, and craft and folk music demonstrations. Backpacking is popular in the three wilderness areas. Hunting is permitted in season. Tyler Bend, the main visitor center, is 9 miles north of Marshall on US 65.

The national river is accessible daily 24 hours; Tyler Bend Visitor Center is open daily 8:15-4:45. The visitor center is 11 miles north of Marshall off US 65. There is no admission charge but camping fees are imposed at Buffalo Point campground. For information contact the Superintendent, Buffalo National River, P.O. Box 1173, Harrison, AR 72602-1173; phone (870) 741-5443. *See Recreation Chart and the AAA South Central CampBook.*

BULL SHOALS (A-3) pop. 2,000, elev. 800′

Bull Shoals is a rural resort area on the shores of Bull Shoals Lake. This 101,196-acre reservoir offers fishing, camping, boating, picnicking and other recreational opportunities. *See Recreation Chart and the AAA South Central CampBook.*

Bull Shoals Lake-White River Chamber of Commerce: SR 178, P.O. Box 354, Bull Shoals, AR 72619; phone (870) 445-4443 or (800) 447-1290.

[SAVE] **MOUNTAIN VILLAGE 1890** is at 1011 C.S. Woods Blvd., just off SR 178 following signs. This historic re-creation of an Ozark town is a living tribute to the pioneers who settled in this remote part of the country. Many of the buildings contain original furnishings.

Allow 1 hour, 30 minutes minimum. Daily 9-6, mid-May through Labor Day; Wed.-Sun. 10-5, mid-Mar. to mid-May; Thurs.-Mon. 10-5, day after Labor Day-Oct. 31; Fri.-Sun. 10-4, in Nov. Admission $10; ages 6-11, $6. Combination admission for village and caverns $18; ages 6-11, $10.80. AX, DS, MC, VI. Phone (870) 445-7177 or (800) 445-7177.

[SAVE] **Bull Shoals Caverns** is in Mountain Village 1890 at 1011 C.S. Woods Blvd., just off SR 178 following signs. Guided 45-minute tours take visitors through caverns formed 350 million years ago. Allow 1 hour minimum. Daily every half-hour 9-6, mid-May through Labor Day; Wed.-Sun. 10-5, mid-Mar. to mid-May; Thurs.-Mon. 10-5, day after Labor Day-Oct. 31; Fri.-Sun. 10-4, in Nov. Last tour departs 45 minutes before closing. Tour $10; ages 6-11, $6. Combination admission for village and caverns $18; ages 6-11, $10.80. AX, DS, MC, VI. Phone (870) 445-7177 or (800) 445-7177.

TOP O' THE OZARKS TOWER is atop Bull Mountain, 1 mi. w. on SR 178 at Tower Rd. This 20-story-high tower offers a view of Bull Shoals Lake and Dam and the White River as well as the surrounding Ozark hill country, lakes, rivers and streams. Allow 30 minutes minimum. Daily 9-5, Mar. 15-Oct. 31; Fri.-Sun. in Nov. Admission $5; ages 7-12, $2.50. Phone (870) 445-4302.

CAMDEN (E-3) pop. 13,154, elev. 149′

Camden, overlooking the Ouachita River, was an ancient American Indian trail crossing. Early French settlers named the town Fabre's Hill. American pioneers arrived during the 1820s, and soon a thriving cotton-growing industry was established. The proximity of the river made easy the transport of up to 40,000 bales a season. Wiped out by the Civil War, the cotton industry was replaced by timber production.

River Drive and Sandy Beach Park offer good views of the river; the latter also provides a boat ramp. Nearby White Oak Lake State Park provides camping, swimming, canoes, rental boats and fishing *(see Recreation Chart and the AAA South Central CampBook).*

Camden Area Chamber of Commerce: 141 Jackson S.W., P.O. Box 99, Camden, AR 71701; phone (870) 836-6426.

McCOLLUM-CHIDESTER HOUSE is .5 mi. w. on SR 4 at 926 Washington St. This 1847 house was an early stage stop and was occupied by a Union commander during the Civil War. Original furnishings are displayed, and bullet holes are visible in the upstairs walls. Allow 1 hour minimum. Wed.-Sat. 9-4, Mar.-Jan; closed Jan. 1, Thanksgiving and Dec. 24-25. Admission $5; ages 6-17, $2. Phone (870) 836-9243.

CROSSETT (F-4) pop. 6,097, elev. 159′

The Crossett division of Georgia-Pacific Corp. has gained national recognition for its tree-farming methods. Its large, scientifically managed prime forest supports plywood, paper and chemical plants. The company's Levi Wilcoxon Demonstration Forest, 15 miles east of Crossett, contains a series of marked trails with trees and plants identified by signs.

Felsenthal National Wildlife Refuge, 7 miles west on US 82, offers camping, picnicking, hiking trails, boating and fishing.

Crossett Area Chamber of Commerce: 101 W. First Ave., Crossett, AR 71635; phone (870) 364-6591 or (870) 364-8648.

DES ARC (C-4) pop. 1,933, elev. 202'

Settled in the early 1800s by fur traders, Des Arc sits on a bend of the White River. Its name in French refers to that curve. Farming is one of the area's chief industries, with rice the major crop.

LOWER WHITE RIVER MUSEUM STATE PARK is at the w. end of Main St. Arkansas rivers and associated lifestyles are the focus of this museum, with displays depicting life and the river-based economy, mainly from 1831 to 1931. Various mussels, which were used for trade as well as to make buttons and jewelry and for food, are exhibited. Tues.-Sat. and Mon. holidays 8-5, Sun. 1-5; closed Jan. 1, Thanksgiving and Dec. 24-25. Admission $3; ages 6-12, $1.75; family rate $9. Phone (870) 256-3711.

EL DORADO (F-3) pop. 21,530, elev. 250'

Until 1921 the town of El Dorado was quiet and peaceful. In that year, however, oil was discovered, and the once tranquil city was transformed into a boomtown whose population increased 10-fold in a 4-year span. Gamblers and moonshiners soon arrived, as did H.L. Hunt, who began his oil empire in El Dorado after winning an interest in an oil well in a poker game.

The oil business is still important, but it has been joined by timber, poultry production and chemical manufacturing to form a more diverse economic base.

El Dorado Chamber of Commerce: 201 N. Jackson, El Dorado, AR 71730; phone (870) 863-6113.

Self-guiding tours: A brochure outlining a walking tour of El Dorado's historic downtown area is available at the chamber of commerce.

SOUTH ARKANSAS ARBORETUM is 1 mi. n. off SR 82B at 501 Timberlane. This 13-acre site features plants native to the state's Gulf Coastal Plain region as well as other species such as azaleas and camellias. Botanist-led guided tours may be arranged in advance. Allow 1 hour minimum. Daily 8-5; closed state holidays. Free. Phone (870) 862-8131, ext. 188.

EUREKA SPRINGS (A-2)
pop. 2,278, elev. 1,130'

The waters around Eureka Springs had been touted for alleged medicinal powers by American Indians and settlers alike long before Dr. Alvah Jackson established a clinic in the area in 1850. By the late 1870s a busy resort had developed; the arrival of the railroad in 1883 made the spa more accessible, and the sick and weary came great distances to be healed.

Modern medicine caused a drastic decline in the use of the springs, but recreational and artistic businesses have kept the city alive. Eureka Springs offers a variety of activities that cater to both body and mind. Country music shows abound throughout the year. The annual Eagle Watch, the last weekend in January, draws thousands of visitors from a four-state region.

A European-style farmer's market is held Sunday 9-4 early May through mid-October in a parking lot at One North Main St. Offerings range from produce to arts and crafts works to antiques and flea-market finds. Capping the day is the Lucky 13 Starlight Outdoor Cinema showing of films on a 17-by-25-foot screen painted on an outside wall of a building in the parking lot. Live entertainment before the screening is appropriate to the theme of the film, and audience members are encouraged to dress in garb in keeping with the film being shown.

Eureka Springs Visitor Information Center: 516 Village Circle Dr., Eureka Springs, AR 72632; phone (479) 253-8737 or (800) 638-7352.

Self-guiding tours: Elegant Victorian houses built at the turn of the 20th century can be seen in the city's historic district. Brochures outlining walking tours of Eureka Springs are available from the chamber of commerce.

Shopping areas: Pine Mountain Jamboree Village, 1 mile north on US 62E, is a Victorian-style shopping and entertainment complex with stores that specialize in local crafts. About 125 gift shops and restaurants are concentrated in the historic downtown district near the intersection of SRs 62 and 62B.

ABUNDANT MEMORIES HERITAGE VILLAGE is 2.5 mi. n. to 2434 SR 23. This re-creation of an early 19th-century town includes 26 furnished shops, offices, houses and forts. Antiques and memorabilia add to the atmosphere. Performances at the Historama Theatre bring historical events to life. Allow 2 hours minimum. Daily 9:30-3:30, May 15-Oct. 31. Historama performances daily at 10:30. Admission $9; ages 12-18, $4.50; ages 5-11, $3.50. Phone (479) 253-6764.

BELLE OF THE OZARKS can be reached off SR 187 at 354 CR 146; take Mundell Rd. 4 mi. into Starkey Park, after the gatehouse turn right to lower-level parking, following signs. This 12-mile, 75-minute excursion of Beaver Lake *(see attraction listing*) features sightseeing of Beaver Dam, White House Bluffs, the Ozark Bluff Dweller's burial ground, the Lost Bridge area and a 200-acre game preserve island.

Allow 1 hour, 30 minutes minimum. Cruises depart Thurs.-Tues. at 11, 1 and 3, May-Oct. An evening cruise is available Thurs.-Tues. at 6, Memorial Day weekend-Labor Day. Fare $18; ages 2-11, $7.50. Phone (479) 253-6200 or (800) 552-3803.

SAVE **BLUE SPRINGS HERITAGE CENTER** is 5.5 mi. w. off US 62, following signs. The 33-acre complex, which features informal meadow, rock and wildflower gardens, also includes one of the largest natural springs in the Ozark Mountains. Several million gallons of water flow here each day. A 20-minute, three-screen presentation offers information about the area's history. Allow 1 hour minimum. Daily 9-6, Apr.-Oct.; 9-5, in Mar. and Nov. Admission $7.25; ages 10-17, $4. DS, MC, VI. Phone (479) 253-9244.

EUREKA SPRINGS AND NORTH ARKANSAS RAILWAY departs from the town's original depot at 299 N. Main St. Narrated 45-minute rides are offered aboard a restored steam train. Lunch and dinner trips also are available. Departures Tues.-Sat. 10-4, early Apr.-late Oct. Fare $10; ages 4-9, $5. Reservations are suggested for meal trips. AX, DS, MC, VI. Phone (479) 253-9623 or (479) 253-9677.

EUREKA SPRINGS HISTORICAL MUSEUM is at 95 S. Main St. Exhibits chronicling Eureka Springs' history occupy three floors of an 1889 stone house. Allow 1 hour minimum. Mon.-Sat. 9:30-4, Sun. 11-4; closed Jan. 1, Thanksgiving and Dec. 25. Admission $5, children $2.50, under 6 free. Phone (479) 253-9417.

GEM **"THE GREAT PASSION PLAY"** is 3 mi. e. off US 62, following signs. This production depicts the days leading to Christ's death, followed by the resurrection and the ascension. The staging area represents the streets of Jerusalem at the time of Christ. A special interactive Christmas nativity, "Beyond Dickens," is presented before the show in November and December.

Food is available from 4:30 until 30 minutes before show time. Curtain time Mon.-Tues. and Thurs.-Sat. at 8:30 p.m. (7:30 p.m. after Labor Day), last Fri. in Apr.-last Sat. in Oct. Two special performances are presented at 8:30 on the Sundays before Memorial Day and Labor Day. Tickets $23.25; ages 6-11, $10; under 6 free when held on the lap. Price includes admission to the Bible Museum and the Sacred Arts Center. DS, MC, VI. Phone (479) 253-9200 for information, or (800) 882-7529 for reservations. *See color ad.*

Bible Museum is on the lower level of Smith Memorial Chapel, 3 mi. e. on US 62, then 1.2 mi. n. on Statue Rd. The museum contains more than 6,000 Bibles in 625 languages and dialects as well as a large collection of parchments and artifacts.

Mon.-Tues. and Thurs.-Sat. 10-8, Apr. 30-Labor Day; Mon.-Tues. and Thurs.-Sat. 10-7, day after Labor Day-last Sat. in Oct. Admission $6. Combination admission with New Holy Land Tour and Sacred Arts Center $15; ages 6-11, $5.50. DS, MC, VI. Phone (479) 253-8559.

The Christ of the Ozarks is 3 mi. e. on US 62, then 1.5 mi. n. on Passion Play Rd. Towering seven stories above Magnetic Mountain and weighing more than 500 tons, the statue has outspread arms which measure 65 feet across, giving it the appearance of an immense cross when viewed from a distance. Daily 24 hours. Free.

New Holy Land Tour is 3 mi. e. off US 62, following signs; tours depart the ticket office across from the Eastern Gate. The guided 2-hour bus tour covers a 50-acre tract that re-creates the features of the region where Christ lived. Re-creations of biblical scenes include Moses' Wilderness Tabernacle, the inn at Bethlehem and a "Visit with Peter Simon beside the Sea of Galilee." Visitors disembark at several stops along the route and continue on another bus.

Allow 2 hours, 30 minutes minimum. Tours depart every 15 minutes Mon.-Tues. and Thurs.-Sat. 10-3:30, late Apr.-last Sat. in Oct. Fare (includes Bible Museum and Sacred Arts Center) $15; ages 6-11, $5.50. DS, MC, VI. Phone (479) 253-9200.

Sacred Arts Center is 3 mi. e. on US 62, then 1.2 mi. n. on Statue Rd. The center displays more than 1,000 pieces of biblical art in 64 media, including sculptured marble, mosaics and needlepoint. Mon.-Tues. and Thurs.-Sat. 10-8, late Apr.-Labor Day; Mon.-Tues. and Thurs.-Fri. 10-7, Sat. 10-7:30, day after Labor Day-last Sat. in Oct. Admission $6. Combination admission with Bible Museum and New Holy Land Tour $15; ages 6-11, $5.50. DS, MC, VI.

HOBBS STATE PARK-CONSERVATION AREA—
see Rogers p. 58.

SAVE   **ONYX CAVE PARK** is 3 mi. e. on US 62, then 3.5 mi. n. on Onyx Cave Rd. Self-guiding 30-minute tours feature taped narration. The site includes the free Gay '90s Button and Doll Museum. Picnicking is permitted. Daily 8:30-5, May-Sept.; 8:30-4 in Apr. and Oct.-Nov. (weather permitting). Admission $5; ages 3-13, $2.50. AX, MC, VI. Phone (479) 253-9321.

THE QUEEN ANNE MANSION is on US 62 at jct. SR 23 and US 62B. This three-story Victorian house contains original beveled and stained-glass windows, period furnishings and original oak and cherry woodwork, including seven fireplaces. **Note:** the mansion was closed for renovations at press time; phone to confirm schedule. Guided tours are available. Allow 30 minutes minimum. Self-guiding tours daily 11-5, Mar.-Oct.; 1-5, rest of year.. Admission $8; ages 6-12, $4. MC, VI. Phone (479) 253-8825 or (800) 626-7466.

ST. ELIZABETH CHURCH is just off US 62B on Crescent Dr. The church is unusual in that it is entered through the bell tower. Along the walkway are the Stations of the Cross. A prayer garden at the side of the church provides a good view of the "Christ of the Ozarks" statue nearby. Daily 8:30-6. Free. Phone (479) 253-9853.

THORNCROWN CHAPEL is just w. off US 62. This modern glass and wood chapel is noted for its innovative architecture. Woods and trails surround the chapel, which is open for Sunday services. Daily 9-4, Apr.-Oct.; 11-4, Nov.-Dec. and in Mar. Donations. Phone (479) 253-7401.

FAYETTEVILLE (B-1)
pop. 58,047, elev. 1,416'

Lots first were sold in Fayetteville in 1828, and the town soon became known for an interest in education. Several small colleges were founded in the 1840s and '50s. Arkansas Industrial University, established in 1871, became the University of Arkansas with an enrollment in excess of 14,000.

Walton Arts Center is home to the North Arkansas Symphony, which presents several concerts throughout the year; phone (479) 443-5600.

Guided walking tours of the Washington-Willow Historic District, a neighborhood with Victorian houses and large shade trees, can be arranged through the Washington County Historical Society.

The society also offers living history tours of the 1853 Headquarters House Museum by appointment; phone (479) 521-2970. Nearby Lake Wedington offers camping, cabins, a boat ramp, boat rental and fishing *(see Recreation Chart and the AAA South Central CampBook).*

The Battle of Fayetteville Re-enactment is held on a weekend close to the anniversary of the April 18, 1863, engagement; living-history demonstrations include battle camp cooking, weaving, quilting and other crafts of the Civil War period. The 4-day Bikes, Blues & BBQ Motorcycle Rally brings some 250,000 visitors into town in late September or early October; phone (479) 527-9993. The War Eagle Arts and Crafts Fair is in nearby Hindsville in October.

Fayetteville Convention & Visitors Bureau: 123 W. Mountain St., P.O. Box 1166, Fayetteville, AR 72702; phone (479) 521-5776 or (800) 766-4626.

SAVE   **ARKANSAS AIR MUSEUM** is 5 mi. s. on US 71 next to the Fayetteville Municipal Airport. The museum houses racing planes of the 1920s and '30s, open cockpit biplanes and early aircraft engines. Most of the planes are maintained in flying condition. Various exhibits trace the history of manned flight. Antique airplanes are restored in the museum's shop. Allow 30 minutes minimum. Sun.-Fri. 11-4:30, Sat. 10-4:30; closed major holidays. Admission $4; senior citizens $3.60; ages 6-12, $2. Phone (479) 521-4947.

FINE ARTS CENTER is on the University of Arkansas campus at 1125 Maple St. Theatrical and musical performances are presented in its theater and concert hall. An art gallery also is part of the center. Most events are held during the school year. Art gallery open Mon.-Fri. 10-4. Many events are free. Gallery free. Phone (479) 575-4701 for concert information, or (479) 575-4752 for theater schedule.

FORDYCE (E-3) pop. 4,799, elev. 285'

From the age of 10, legendary football coach Paul "Bear" Bryant grew up in Fordyce. In 1927, when Bryant was 13 or 14, a promoter at the Fordyce Theatre offered a dollar to anyone who would wrestle a bear—Bryant took him up on the offer, thereby earning his nickname. The mainstays of the local economy are logging and wood products.

There are 18 Craftsman-style houses in the Charlotte Street Historic District of Fordyce, some designed by Charles Thompson in the early 1900s. The First Presbyterian Church on West 4th Street has 36 stained-glass windows.

Fordyce Chamber of Commerce: 101 S. Main St., Fordyce, AR 71742; phone (870) 352-2198.

DALLAS COUNTY HISTORICAL MUSEUM is at 221 S. Main St. The museum traces the history of the county. Exhibits include tools and housewares from the early 1900s and photographs of legendary football coach Paul "Bear" Bryant, who attended high school in Fordyce. Allow 30 minutes minimum. Tues.-Fri. 11-4, Sat. 11-3; closed major holidays. Free. Phone (870) 352-7202.

FORT SMITH (C-1) pop. 80,268, elev. 439′

In 1817 Maj. Stephen H. Long selected a site at the confluence of the Arkansas and Poteau rivers as the location for the region's first military fort. Named for Gen. Thomas Smith, the fort prompted settlement and the resultant town shared the fort's name. With the discovery of natural gas in nearby Mansfield, a large and diverse manufacturing industry developed; Fort Smith remains one of Arkansas' leading manufacturing cities.

A navigation channel on the Arkansas River connects Fort Smith with other ports. Fort Smith is a convenient starting point for picturesque drives through the Ozark, Ouachita and Kiamichi mountains and the Cookson Hills via two of the state's scenic highways, US 71 and I-40.

A 35-minute interpretive tour by trolley of the Belle Grove Historic District is available from Miss Laura's Visitors Center (see attraction listing). Tours begin and end at the center.

Fort Smith Chamber of Commerce: 612 Garrison Ave., P.O. Box 1668, Fort Smith, AR 72902; phone (479) 783-6118.

ARKANSAS AND MISSOURI RAILROAD—
see Van Buren p. 60.

THE CLAYTON HOUSE is at 514 N. 6th St. William Henry Harrison Clayton, district attorney under Judge Isaac C. Parker, purchased this antebellum house in the 1880s and added onto it. Clayton lived there until 1897. Restored and furnished in period, this example of Classic Revival Victorian architecture contains Clayton belongings, artifacts and other memorabilia.

Allow 30 minutes minimum. Wed.-Fri. noon-4, Sat.-Sun. 1-4; closed Jan. 1, Thanksgiving and Dec.

DID YOU KNOW

Arkansas borders six states: Louisiana, Texas, Oklahoma, Missouri, Tennessee, and Mississippi.

25. Hours may vary; phone for schedule. Admission $2; ages 12-18, $1. Phone (479) 783-3000.

THE DARBY HOUSE is at 311 General Darby St. This was the boyhood home of Brig. Gen. William O. Darby, the organizer and commander of the U.S. Army's 1st Ranger Battalion. Two rooms are open to the public: the living room, restored to its appearance when Darby's parents were informed of his death on May 1, 1945, and another room containing memorabilia and tributes. Allow 30 minutes minimum. Mon.-Fri. 8-1, Sat.-Sun. by appointment; closed holidays. Free. Phone (479) 782-3388.

FORT SMITH ART CENTER is at 423 N. 6th St. The center, which occupies a restored Victorian house built about 1870, contains permanent displays of works by local artists and a variety of traveling exhibits. Allow 1 hour minimum. Tues.-Sat. 9:30-4:30; closed July 4, Thanksgiving and Dec. 25-Jan. 1. Free. Phone (479) 784-2787.

[SAVE] **FORT SMITH MUSEUM OF HISTORY** is at 320 Rogers Ave. Chronicling the development of Fort Smith, museum collections include an early 20th-century pharmacy and soda fountain, the area's first steam-powered fire pump and memorabilia of World War II hero Brig. Gen. William O. Darby. Weaving demonstrations are given on weekends. A restored trolley offers trips through the historic district; tokens may be purchased at the museum.

Allow 2 hours minimum. Museum open Tues.-Sat. 10-5 (also Sun. 10-5, June-Aug.); closed Jan. 1, Thanksgiving and Dec. 24-25. Museum admission $5; ages 6-11, $2. Trolley fare $2; under 13, $1. VI. Phone (479) 783-7841 or (479) 783-1237.

FORT SMITH NATIONAL CEMETERY is at 522 Garland St. at S. 6th St. Established in 1867, the cemetery contains the graves of many who were important to the area, including Brig. Gen. William O. Darby, organizer of Darby's Rangers; Maj. William C. Bradford, who established the first fort; and Judge Isaac C. Parker, who held court in Fort Smith during the years of the Indian Territory days. Gates open daily 24 hours. Office open Mon.-Fri. 8-4:30; closed holidays. Free. Phone (479) 783-5345.

FORT SMITH NATIONAL HISTORIC SITE is at 3rd and Garland sts. Incorporating the remains of two successive frontier forts, the site chronicles the frontier years 1817-96. Themes include military history, westward expansion, Indian Removal along the Trail of Tears, the Indian Territory, law and order in the late 19th century and the diverse people who lived in the region.

Seventy-nine felons were hanged at the fort during Judge Isaac C. Parker's 21 years on the bench of the U.S. District Court for Western Arkansas—outlaws dubbed him the "hanging judge." The fort's visitor center in his restored courtroom features original furnishings and exhibits, a 15-minute DVD program about the fort's history and a reproduction of the gallows.

Daily 9-5; closed Jan. 1 and Dec. 25. Site admission free. Visitor center $4, under 16 free, family rate $8. Phone (479) 783-3961.

MISS LAURA'S VISITORS CENTER is at 2 N. B St. This turn-of-the-20th-century brothel eventually became one of the most celebrated bordellos in the Southwest. Laura Ziegler owned the establishment that now is furnished in period. Transoms show the names of women who worked there. Allow 30 minutes minimum. Guided 30-minute tours of the house are offered as necessary Mon.-Sat. 9-4, Sun. 1-4:30; closed major holidays. Last tour begins 30 minutes before closing. Donations. Phone (479) 783-8888 or (800) 637-1477.

GILLETT (D-4) pop. 819, elev. 188

ARKANSAS POST STATE MUSEUM is at jct. US 165 and SRs 1 and 169. Five buildings house artifacts illustrating local history. Mon.-Sat. 8-5, Sun. 1-5; closed Jan. 1, Thanksgiving and Dec. 24-25. Admission $2.75; ages 6-12, $1.75. Phone (870) 548-2634.

HARDY (A-4) pop. 578, elev. 358

Hardy is set in the Ozark Mountain foothills along the banks of Spring River. The river provides white-water canoeing and fishing, while the town serves up its own brand of entertainment—music. Country sounds abound in musical productions, music theaters and weekly outdoor jam sessions. The downtown district has remained virtually unchanged since the 1920s and features 43 historic buildings.

Spring River Area Chamber of Commerce: P.O. Box 300, Hardy, AR 72542; phone (870) 856-3210.

[SAVE] **GOOD OLD DAYS VINTAGE MOTORCAR MUSEUM** is at 301 W. Main St. More than 50 rare and vintage cars, trucks, motorcycles and bicycles are displayed. A large collection of cars from the 1915-29 era also is featured. Some vehicles still have all their original parts. The museum's collection is constantly changing. Allow 30 minutes minimum. Mon.-Fri. 9-5, Sat. 10-5, Sun. noon-5. Admission $7.50; ages 1-12, $3.50. MC, VI. Phone (870) 856-4884.

HARRISON (A-3) pop. 12,152, elev. 1,061

The "Crossroads of the Ozarks," Harrison is the center of a rustic resort community in the valley of Crooked Creek, one of the most scenic sections of the Arkansas Ozarks. The town is home to the two-year North Arkansas College.

Running from the state's northern border through Hot Springs National Park (see place listing p. 48) and ending in Arkadelphia, SR 7 encompasses lofty mountains and numerous lakes and rivers. The road is popular for leisurely drives and photographic opportunities. En route to Hot Springs, SR 7 crosses two national forests, the Ozark (see place listing p. 56) and the Ouachita (see place listing p. 56), and the Buffalo National River (see place listing p. 40).

See Recreation Chart and the AAA South Central CampBook.

Harrison Convention & Visitors Bureau: 623 S. Pine St., P.O. Box 940, Harrison, AR 72602; phone (870) 741-1789 or (888) 283-2163.

BOONE COUNTY HERITAGE MUSEUM is at 110 S. Cherry St. This three-story museum features large collections of railroad memorabilia and antique clocks, a room devoted to medical instruments of the past, American Indian artifacts and World Wars I and II memorabilia. A genealogy library also is available. Allow 1 hour minimum. Mon.-Fri. 10-4, Mar.-Nov.; Thurs. 10-4, rest of year. Closed holidays. Admission $2, under 12 free with adult. Phone (870) 741-3312.

MARINE CORPS LEGACY MUSEUM is on the n.w. corner of the town square at 125 W. Rush Ave. Using displays of uniforms, weapons and equipment, this museum traces the history of marine forces from 400 BC through the founding of the United States Marine Corps in 1775, to the present. Allow 1 hour minimum. Tues.-Sat. 10-5; closed major holidays. Admission $5; under 12, $3. Phone (870) 743-1680.

[SAVE] **MYSTIC CAVERNS** is 8 mi. s. on SR 7. Guided 70-minute tours feature two Ozark caverns with well-lighted walkways and wide steps. The temperature in the caves is a constant 58 F. A jacket is advised. Food is available. Allow 30 minutes minimum. Tours Mon.-Sat. every 40 minutes 9-6, June-Aug.; Mon.-Sat. 9-5, Mar.-May and Sept.-Oct.; Mon.-Sat. 9-4, Nov.-Dec.; Wed.-Sat. 10-4, in Feb. (weather permitting). Closed Thanksgiving and Dec. 25. Last tour begins at closing. Tour $11.95; ages 5-12, $5.95. MC, VI. Phone (870) 743-1739 or (888) 743-1739.

HEBER SPRINGS (E-4) pop. 6,432, elev. 348

The hallmark of Heber Springs, at the foot of Round Mountain, is water. The springs for which the town is named are downtown. Other waters also are important to the community; the Little Red River offers excellent fishing for rainbow trout, thanks to stocking by the federal trout hatchery just north of Greers Ferry Dam.

Heber Springs Area Chamber of Commerce: 1001 W. Main St., Heber Springs, AR 72543; phone (501) 362-2444.

GREERS FERRY DAM AND LAKE is 3.5 mi. n.e. on SR 25. Completed in 1962, the dam is part of the White River Basin power and flood control project. Sugar Loaf Mountain in the middle of Greers Ferry Lake has hiking and nature trails. Opportunities for fishing and other aquatic activities are available. The visitor center at the west end of the dam presents historical exhibits and a 20-minute slide show. A trout hatchery and an aquarium are 1.5 miles north of the dam off SR 25N.

Visitor center open daily 10-6, May-Sept.; Thurs.-Tues. 10-6, in Apr. and Oct.; Sat.-Sun. 10-4, in Mar. and Nov. Trout hatchery and aquarium open daily 7-3. Free. Phone (501) 362-9067, or (501) 362-3615 for the hatchery and aquarium. *See Recreation Chart and the AAA South Central CampBook.*

HELENA (D-6) pop. 6,323

Founded in 1820, Helena enacted early laws that set the speed limit at a trot or pace and required that guns be fired within town limits only with just cause. Such cause was found on July 4, 1863, during the bloody Battle of Helena, when Confederate troops tried in vain to recapture the town from occupying Union forces.

Helena now is a river port; it also was the hometown of lyric soprano Frances Greer; country singer Harold Jenkins, better known as Conway Twitty; and blues singer Sonny Boy Williamson II. A mural depicting musicians stretches for a block beginning at 95 Missouri St., on the levee walk.

The Wild Hog Music Festival & Motorcycle Rally zooms into town in April. The Delta Cultural Center retells the story of the Delta region and its people and hosts the late May The Arkansas Delta Family Gospel Festival; phone (870) 338-4350 or (800) 358-0972. The town celebrates its musical talent again in October with the 4-day, well-known Arkansas Blues and Heritage Festival, formerly the King Biscuit Blues Festival; phone (870) 338-8798.

Guided tours of some of Helena's historic houses are available year-round by appointment. For further information contact the chamber of commerce.

Phillips County Chamber of Commerce: 111 Hickory Hill Dr., P.O. Box 447, Helena, AR 72342; phone (870) 338-8327.

CONFEDERATE MILITARY CEMETERY is n. off US 49 Bus. Rte. to Columbia St., 2 blks. e. on McDonough St. to Holly St., then 4 blks. n. to Maple Hill Cemetery, following signs. This cemetery contains approximately 100 marked and unmarked graves of Confederate soldiers. The site offers views of the Mississippi River. Daily 9-5. Free. Phone (870) 338-8221.

PHILLIPS COUNTY LIBRARY AND MUSEUM is 2 blks. e. of US 49 Bus. Rte. at Porter and Pecan sts. The museum displays memorabilia from the Spanish-American and Civil wars as well as artworks and period costumes. The library is among the oldest in the state. Free guided 1-hour tours of the library depart on demand Mon.-Fri. 7-5. Museum open Tues.-Sat. 10-4; closed holidays. Last tour begins 1 hour before closing. Free. Phone (870) 338-7790.

HOPE (E-2) pop. 10,616, elev. 355'

Known as the birthplace of Bill Clinton, Hope was settled in 1852 and named after the daughter of a railroad commissioner. Local growers began cultivating watermelons for rail shipment in the early 1900s and soon began breaking world records for giant-sized melons. Today's entries regularly tip the scales at 250 pounds.

Hope-Hempstead County Chamber of Commerce: 108 W. 3rd St., P.O. Box 250, Hope, AR 78101; phone (870) 777-3640.

Self-guiding tours: Information about self-guiding walking tours of the area is available at the chamber of commerce.

THE CLINTON CENTER is at 117 S. Hervey St. This 2-story house was the birthplace of William Jefferson Clinton, 42nd president of the United States, and is furnished to reflect his boyhood years in the 1950s. A visitors' center features Clinton exhibits and memorabilia. Mon.-Sat. 10-5. Last tour departs 1 hour before closing. Visitor center free. House tour $5; over 54, $4; ages 7-18, $3; family rate $12. Phone (870) 777-4455.

HOT SPRINGS (D-3) pop. 35,750, elev. 632'

The city of Hot Springs is a year-round health and pleasure resort. Hot Springs sponsors a variety of events, including the Oaklawn Horse Race Meet held during February, March and April, and Arkansas Derby Day in early April. Both of these events take place at Oaklawn Park race course; phone (501) 623-4411. The Arkansas Oktoberfest is a fixture in mid-October. Beginning the fourth Friday in October and running for 10 days, is the Hot Springs Documentary Film Festival.

Note: Policies concerning admittance of children to pari-mutuel betting facilities vary. Phone for information.

The Hot Springs region is rich in quartz crystals of superior hardness and brilliance; the finest are in the veins of Crystal Mountain. Locally mined novaculite is used worldwide as a commercial whetstone.

Hot Springs Convention and Visitors Bureau: 134 Convention Blvd., Hot Springs, AR 71901; phone (501) 321-2277 or (800) 772-2489.

Shopping areas: Temperance Hill Square, SR 7 at Central Avenue, features specialty stores including Bon Worth and Van Heusen. Cornerstone Mall, off the US 270/70 Bypass, includes Chico's, Old Navy and Pier 1.

[SAVE] **ARKANSAS ALLIGATOR FARM AND PETTING ZOO** is at 847 Whittington Ave. Four ponds are stocked with alligators of different sizes. A petting zoo also is featured. Daily 9:30-5. Feeding time is Thurs. and Sat.-Sun. at noon. Admission $6; ages 3-12, $5. MC, VI. Phone (501) 623-6172.

ART CENTRAL is at 405 Park Ave. The center presents changing exhibitions and special events. Center open Mon.-Fri. 10-2. Free. Phone (501) 625-3992.

BELLE OF HOT SPRINGS departs from 5200 Central Ave. The 220-passenger riverboat offers narrated 75-minute daytime and 2-hour evening sightseeing cruises on Lake Hamilton. Lunch and dinner cruises also are available.

Departures daily at 1, 3, and 7 (also Sat. at 6 and 8:30, July-Aug.), Memorial Day-Labor Day; at 1 and 6, day after Labor Day-Oct. 31; at 1 and 5, in Nov.; at 1 and 7, Feb. 1-day before Memorial Day; schedule varies rest of year. Times are subject to change. Evening fare $13.99; over 54, $12.99; ages 2-12, $7.49. Daytime fare $12.99; over 54, $11.99; ages 2-12, $6.99. AX, DS, MC, VI. Phone (501) 525-4438.

GARVAN WOODLAND GARDENS is at 550 Arkridge Rd. This 210-acre botanical garden features almost 2 miles of walking trails that provide visitors access to a variety of plant collections, flower borders, rock and antique rose gardens, waterfalls, pools and a bird sanctuary. A welcome center also is on-site.

Pets on leash and picnicking are permitted. Free kennels are available. Food is available. Allow 1 hour, 30 minutes minimum. Daily 9-6, Apr.-Oct.; noon-9, Thanksgiving week-Dec. 31; 10-5, rest of year. Closed Jan. 1, Thanksgiving and Dec. 25. Admission $7; over 55, $6; ages 6-12, $4. Pets on leash $4. DS, MC, VI. Phone (501) 262-9300 or (800) 366-4664.

JOSEPHINE TUSSAUD WAX MUSEUM is at 250 Central Ave. Representations of historical figures range from 16th-century explorer Hernando de Soto to former president Bill Clinton. Daily 9-8, Memorial Day weekend-Labor Day; 9:30-5, rest of year. Closed Jan. 1, Thanksgiving and Dec. 25. Admission $9; ages 5-11, $5.50. DS, MC, VI. Phone (501) 623-5836.

MAGIC SPRINGS & CRYSTAL FALLS is 2 mi. e. at 1701 US 70E. This theme and water park offers more than 25 rides, including the Arkansas Twister, a 100-foot-high, 3,500-foot-long out-and-back-style wooden roller coaster; The Gauntlet, a suspended looping coaster 110 feet high and 2,260 feet long; and the X-Coaster, a corkscrewing drop from 150 feet at 65 miles per hour. The water park offers a wave pool, a lazy river, four slides and an interactive splash zone.

Allow 3 hours minimum. Magic Springs open Mon.-Thurs. 11-7, Fri. 11-9, Sat. 11-10, Sun. noon-7, Memorial Day weekend through mid-June; Mon.-Thurs. 11-9, Fri.-Sat. 11-10, Sun. noon-8, late June to mid-Aug.; Sat. 11-7, Sun. noon-7, second Sat. in Apr.-Sun. before Memorial Day weekend and mid-Aug. through last Sun. in Sept. Crystal Falls open Mon.-Thurs. 11-6, Fri. 11-8, Sat. 11-9, Sun. noon-6, Memorial Day weekend to mid-Aug.; Sat. 11-6, Sun. noon-6 second Sat. in May-Sun. before Memorial Day weekend and mid-Aug. through Labor Day. Schedule may vary before Memorial Day and in Sept.; phone ahead. Gates open 1 hour before attractions.

Admission $39.99, over age 65 and children under 52 inches tall $29.99. Parking $8. Phone to verify prices and schedules. MC, VI. Phone (501) 624-0100. *See color ad.*

MID-AMERICA SCIENCE MUSEUM is on SR 227, 1 mi. n. of US 270 at 500 Mid-America Blvd. This museum offers participatory exhibits that explore such subjects as perception, energy, sound, light and gravity. Visitors can launch a hot-air balloon, generate electricity and create rivers and mountains in a land model. The museum also offers a laser show and virtual reality simulator.

Food is available. Allow 2 hours minimum. Daily 9:30-6, Memorial Day weekend-Labor Day; Tues.-Sun. 10-5, rest of year. Closed Jan. 1, Thanksgiving and Dec. 24-25. Admission $7; over 61 and ages 4-12, $6. Pricing may vary with special events. Laser show $2 additional. Virtual reality simulator $3 additional. MC, VI. Phone (501) 767-3461.

MOUNTAIN VALLEY WATER SPRING VISITOR CENTER is at 150 Central Ave. The center offers samples, self-guiding tours and exhibits. Built beginning in 1910, this historically restored building also houses a museum and the mineral water company's headquarters. Allow 30 minutes minimum. Mon.-Fri. 9-4:30, Sat. 10-4, Sun. noon-4; closed Jan. 1, Thanksgiving and Dec. 25. Free. Phone (501) 623-6671 or (800) 643-1501.

TINY TOWN is at 374 Whittington Ave. The handiwork of one family, this miniature village consists of animated replicas at one-quarter scale. Settings include a farm, sawmill, American Indian village, Wild West town, blacksmith shop and park. Mon.-Sat. 10-3, Mar.-Nov. Admission $4; ages 4-12, $2. Phone (501) 624-4742.

◆ HOT SPRINGS NATIONAL PARK (D-2)

Elevations in the park range from 600 ft. at the corner of Central and Reserve aves. to 1,420 ft. at Music Mountain. Refer to AAA maps for additional elevation information.

Hot Springs National Park, in western Arkansas, can be reached from the north and south via scenic SR 7, as well as via US 70 from the east and US 270 from both the east and west.

In the picturesque Ouachita (WASH-i-taw) Mountains, Hot Springs differs sharply from the country's other scenic national parks in that portions of it are nearly surrounded by a sizable city. Its 5,839 acres occupy the slopes of Hot Springs, Music, North, West, Sugarloaf and Indian mountains.

The thermal water that flows from the springs is naturally sterile. It begins as rainwater, is absorbed into the mountains northeast of the park and is carried 4,000-8,000 feet underground, where the earth's extreme heat raises its temperature to 143 F. The purified water makes its way back to the surface through cracks and pores in the rock in the form of hot springs. The entire process takes about 4,000 years.

The first European to visit the hot springs is believed to have been Hernando de Soto in 1541. According to legend, the beneficial qualities of the water were known to the American Indians long before the Spaniards arrived. It is said that they declared this area neutral ground, available to all on peaceful terms.

In 1832, because of tourism brought on by the water's perceived medicinal properties, the federal government set aside the springs and surrounding area as the country's first park-type federal reservation. In 1921 Hot Springs became a national park, the country's eighteenth. Numerous bathhouses, eight of which still stand along a portion of Central Avenue known as Bathhouse Row, catered to thousands of health seekers. The popularity of the springs began to decrease in the 1950s, but the springs still attract many visitors.

General Information and Activities

The springs are found along the west slope of Hot Springs Mountain. Within about 10 acres there are 47 springs with a daily flow that varies from 750,000 to 950,000 gallons. The water is collected into one central system and distributed to bathhouses and the drinking and jug fountains near the

corner of Central and Reserve. The standard tub baths can be taken by applying at any of the bathhouses. Options, at no extra cost, include showers, sitz tubs, vapor cabinets and hot packs.

Prescription baths may be taken only by application to a registered physician. Three bathhouses, the Buckstaff, Fordyce and the Libbey Memorial Physical Medicine Center, operate within the park; the latter has pools and specialized equipment and offers pool baths and prescribed physical therapy. Other bathhouses in the park are managed in connection with city hotels; prices vary according to equipment and available accommodations.

The park has 10 miles of good mountain roads for sightseeing by car, as well as extensive walking and horse trails for outdoor enthusiasts; the trails are open daily year-round. Interpretive programs are presented from mid-June to mid-August; phone for schedule. **Note:** Because of sharp switchbacks, vehicles more than 30 feet long cannot negotiate Hot Springs Mountain Drive.

Fall and spring offer displays of flowering trees, shrubs and colorful foliage. Limited programs are available at these times. Nearby Catherine, Hamilton and Ouachita lakes offer fishing. *See Recreation Chart and the AAA South Central CampBook.*

ADMISSION to the park is free.

PETS are permitted in the park only if they are leashed, crated or otherwise physically restricted at all times.

ADDRESS inquiries to the Park Superintendent, P.O. Box 1860, Hot Springs National Park, AR 71902; phone (501) 624-3383.

Points of Interest

DISPLAY HOT WATER SPRINGS is behind Maurice Bathhouse at 369 Central Ave. These are the two thermal springs in Hot Springs National Park from which water still issues in open view. A thermal water cascade is on the Arlington Lawn at the north end of Bathhouse Row. Daily 24 hours. Free.

HOT SPRINGS MOUNTAIN OBSERVATION TOWER is off Fountain St. at 401 Hot Springs Mountain Dr. This 216-foot tower provides scenic views of the park, city and vicinity. Several towers have stood on the site, including the original wooden fire tower that was destroyed by lightning.

Note: Because of sharp switchbacks, vehicles more than 30 feet long cannot negotiate Hot Springs Mountain Drive. Allow 30 minutes minimum. Daily 9-9, Memorial Day-Labor Day; 9-6, Mar. 1-day before Memorial Day and day after Labor Day-Oct. 31; 9-5, rest of year. Closed Jan. 1, Thanksgiving and Dec. 24-25. Admission $6; over 54, $5; ages 5-11, $3. DS, MC, VI. Phone (501) 623-6035.

HOT SPRINGS NATIONAL PARK VISITOR CENTER is on Bathhouse Row. Housed in the historic Fordyce Bathhouse, the center offers displays about area history. The 1915 Spanish Renaissance-style

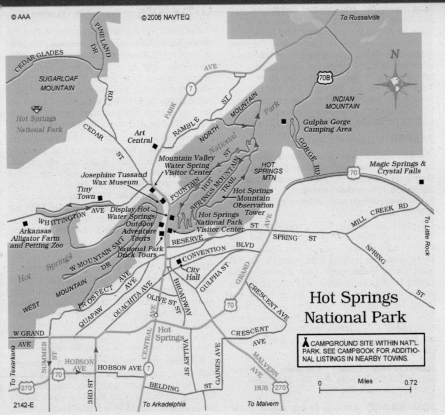

building has marble and mosaic tile floors, stained-glass ceilings and ceramic fountains. Self-guiding and limited 45-minute guided tours are available. A movie is shown every 20 minutes. Open daily 9-5; closed Jan. 1 and Dec. 25. Guided tours are given by volunteers; phone ahead for an appointment/reservation. Free. Phone (501) 624-2701.

NATIONAL PARK DUCK TOURS depart 418 Central Ave., across from Historic Bath House Row in downtown. A 75-minute narrated sightseeing tour aboard amphibious vehicles takes visitors around St. John's Island and Lake Hamilton. Allow 1 hour minimum. Daily 9:30-6, Mar.-Oct. (also 6-7:30 p.m., Memorial Day-Labor Day); as weather permits, rest of year. Fare $14; ages 3-12, $8. DS, MC, VI. Phone (501) 321-2911.

OUTDOOR ADVENTURE TOURS depart 350 Central Ave. across from Bathhouse Row; pick-up also is available from local lodgings. The 90-minute guided van tours cover the historic district of Hot Springs, the national park, Bathhouse Row and area mountains. Other city excursions are available, as are canoeing, hiking and biking trips. Historic tour departs daily at 10, noon, 2 and 4. Fare $30; over 54, $27; ages 5-12, $15. Reservations are recommended. AX, CB, DC, DS, MC, VI. Phone (501) 525-4457.

JACKSONPORT (B-5) pop. 235, elev. 229'

Once a river port for paddlewheelers from New Orleans, Memphis and St. Louis, Jacksonport is just below the confluence of the White and Black rivers. Although the venerable paddlewheelers no longer dock at Jacksonport, the town remains a river port.

JACKSONPORT STATE PARK is .8 mi. n. at 310 Adams St., between SR 69 and the White River. Camping, picnicking, swimming, boating, hiking and fishing are permitted. Daily 8-8. Free. Phone (870) 523-2143. *See Recreation Chart and the AAA South Central CampBook.*

Jacksonport Courthouse Museum is in Jacksonport State Park, .8 mi. n. between SR 69 and the White River. This building dates from 1872. Museum tours offer a look back in history at the steamboat town of Jacksonport. Artifacts and exhibits interpret the use and operation of the courthouse in the 1800s as well as the life of the local citizens.

Tues.-Sat. 8-5, Sun. 1-5, during DST; Wed.-Sat. 8-5, rest of year. Admission $3; ages 6-12, $1.50. Combination ticket with *Mary Woods No. 2* Sternwheel Paddleboat, $5; ages 6-12, $2.75. DS, MC, VI. Phone (870) 523-2143.

Mary Woods No. 2 Sternwheel **Paddleboat** is in Jacksonport State Park, .8 mi. n. of Jacksonport, between SR 69 and the White River. This 1930s vessel moved barges of lumber to mills along the lower White River. Now a floating museum, it features exhibits and furnished cabins and common areas that tell the story of the working crew. Open Tues.-Thurs. 10-5, Fri.-Sat. 9-5, Sun. 1-5, Apr.-Oct. Admission $3; ages 6-12, $1.50. Combination ticket with Jacksonport Courthouse Museum $5; ages 6-12, $2.75. DS, MC, VI. Phone (870) 523-2143.

JASPER (B-2) pop. 498, elev. 834′

Jasper, 4 miles south on the Little Buffalo River, an offshoot of the scenic Buffalo River, took its name from the jasper-green color of the waters of that stream. Passing through town, SR 7 is a Scenic Byway from Harrison north of Jasper to Hot Springs National Park.

In 1972 the Buffalo River, which travels 150 miles through bluffs as high as 440 feet and past wooded hillsides and cultural sites dating back 10,000 years, was designated the country's first National River. Waters range from relatively slow-moving to white-water upriver of Pruitt; the upriver section is generally floatable only in winter and spring. The many hiking trails along the river range from short day-use trails to routes for which a guide is suggested. Canoe rentals are available in Jasper. *See Recreation Chart and the AAA South Central CampBook.*

Jasper/Newton County Chamber of Commerce: 204 North Spring, P.O. Box 250, Jasper, AR 72641; phone (800) 670-7792.

JONESBORO (B-5) pop. 55,515, elev. 302′

More than 15,000 students attend Jonesboro's Arkansas State University. The school's 79,000-square-foot Fowler Center houses a 975-seat concert hall noted for its acoustics, a 344-seat theater and the 5,200-square-foot Bradbury Gallery of art.

ARKANSAS STATE UNIVERSITY MUSEUM is 2 mi. e. in the center of campus off Aggie Rd. at 110 Cooley Dr. Extensive displays relate to Arkansas' prehistory, native cultures, wildlife, pioneer era and military history. The museum also displays decorative glassware and changing exhibits. A historical library and reading room are open to visitors and the 10,000 students. Allow 1 hour, 30 minutes minimum. Mon.-Fri. 9-4, Sat.-Sun. 1-5; closed major holidays and the week of Dec. 25. Free. Phone (870) 972-2074.

FORREST L. WOOD CROWLEY'S RIDGE NATURE CENTER is 3.5 mi. s. on SR 141 to 600 E. Lawson Rd. Opened in 2004, this center focuses on the natural history of the 200-mile-long Crowley's Ridge, and the wildlife that inhabits it. Trails explore wetlands, forest and prairie areas. Allow 30 minutes minimum. Tues.-Fri. 8:30-4:30, Sat. 9-6, Sun. 1-5; closed Jan. 1, Thanksgiving and Dec. 24-25. Free. Phone (870) 933-6787. *See also Crowley's Ridge State Park p. 61.*

LITTLE ROCK (D-3) pop. 183,133, elev. 300′

The profusion of roses in its residential areas has earned Little Rock, capital of Arkansas, the nickname "City of Roses." Settled in 1814 on a rocky bluff overlooking the Arkansas River, Little Rock became the seat of territorial government in 1821 when its population was less than 20. Except for a period during the Civil War when Federal troops under Gen. Fredrick Steele captured the city, it has remained the capital. It also is the state's largest city.

The oldest section of Little Rock is known as the Quapaw Quarter, a 9-square-mile area encompassing the city's central business district and adjacent residential neighborhoods. It includes many examples of Victorian and antebellum architectural styles. Of particular interest is the 1881 English-Gothic-style Cathedral of St. Andrew on the corner of Sixth and South Louisiana streets, with its stained-glass windows by the New York branch of Mayer of Munich; phone (501) 374-2794 for hours of accessibility.

Although no longer open to the public, the Villa Marre at 1321 S. Scott St. can be viewed as part of a driving or walking tour. Built in 1881 this combination Second Empire- and Italianate-style house gained fame in the 1980s when television producers and former Arkansas residents Harry Thomason and Linda Bloodworth-Thomason used the house's exterior to portray the Sugarbaker design firm on the CBS television series "Designing Women."

Riverfront Park comprises 17 acres containing walkways, terraces, plazas, recreation space, a 1,200-seat amphitheater, an activity center and a historical pavilion. The "little rock" for which the city was named is marked by a bronze plaque. Murray Lock and Dam and Murray Park are among the other popular riverbank attractions. The Henry Moore sculpture "Knife's Edge" graces a public plaza downtown at Main and Capitol streets. River Rail Streetcars connect Little Rock and North Little Rock, with eight stops along the way. Stops include the Historic Arkansas Museum, the Museum of Discovery and the two chambers of commerce.

There are a variety of recreational offerings in the Little Rock area. A notable city event is Riverfest, held Friday through Sunday of Memorial Day weekend. Little Rock's visitor information center is in a historic antebellum building, circa 1842, called the Walters-Curran-Bell home but is commonly known as Curran Hall.

The Little Rock Visitor Information Center at Historic Curran Hall: 615 E. Capitol Ave., Little Rock, AR 72203; phone (501) 370-3290 or (877) 220-2568.

Self-guiding tours: A brochure describing three self-guiding walking tours of historic areas of Little Rock is available from the visitor information center. Highlights of the MacArthur Park neighborhood, the downtown riverfront district and the governor's mansion area are covered in the tours, each of which can be completed in less than an hour.

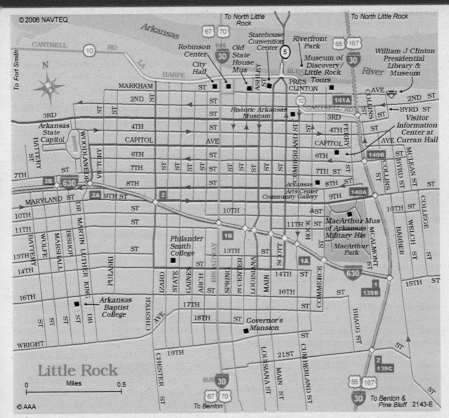

© 2006 NAVTEQ

© AAA

Little Rock

Miles

0   0.5

Shopping areas: Park Plaza Shopping Center on University Avenue is anchored by Dillard's. The River Market District, on President Clinton Avenue, offers visitors an array of diverse shops, galleries, eateries and nightlife entertainment venues.

AEROSPACE EDUCATION CENTER is at 3301 E. Roosevelt at the Little Rock National Airport. In addition to an IMAX theater, the center features a NASA-sponsored exhibit, several historical aircraft and an aerospace library. Tues.-Thurs. 9-3, Fri. 9 a.m.-10 p.m., Sat. 11-10, Sun. 11-6; closed Dec. 25. Phone for titles and times of films. Inclusive admission $7.50; over 59, $6.50; under 13, $5.50. IMAX Fri. at 7 p.m., 8 p.m. and 9 p.m. $5.50 (includes popcorn and soda). AX, CB, DS, MC, VI. Phone (501) 371-0331.

ARKANSAS ARTS CENTER is in MacArthur Park at 9th and Commerce sts. The center contains nine galleries, a children's theater, a museum school and a decorative arts museum. Permanent exhibits include American and European paintings, drawings and sculpture from the 16th century to the present. Food is available 11-2. Center open Tues.-Sat. 10-5, Sun. 11-5; closed major holidays. Free. Phone (501) 372-4000.

Arkansas Arts Center Community Gallery is at 7th and Rock sts. Changing exhibits in this restored 1839 house feature works in various styles and media by local and regional artists and students. Allow 1 hour minimum. When exhibitions are mounted the gallery is open Tues.-Sat. 10-5, Sun. 11-5; closed major holidays and between exhibitions. Donations. Phone (501) 372-4000, ext. 357, to verify the gallery is open.

ARKANSAS STATE CAPITOL is on W. Capitol Ave. Made of Arkansas white marble and granite, the building is patterned after the U.S. Capitol in Washington, D.C. An information desk is on the first floor. Exhibits include a mineral display; videotape programs are available. Guided tours are available. Open Mon.-Fri. 8-5, Sat.-Sun. and holidays 10-3. Guided 1-hour tours are given by appointment Mon.-Fri. 9-4. Free. Phone (501) 682-5080.

CENTRAL HIGH SCHOOL NATIONAL HISTORIC SITE is at 2125 Daisy L. Gatson Bates Dr. In 1957, while Little Rock was in the process of desegregating its public schools, Central High was the scene for events considered pivotal in national Civil Rights history. Across the street is a museum and visitor center featuring an interactive exhibit andtwo audiovisual presentations related to the integration crisis. A commemorative garden is on site. Mon.-Sat. 9-4:30, Sun. 1-4:30; closed major holidays. Free. Phone (501) 374-1957.

HISTORIC ARKANSAS MUSEUM is at 200 E. Third St. at Cumberland St.; from I-30 take exit 141. Of the five restored early-19th-century buildings, four are open to the public. Among the offerings in the 51,000-square-foot museum are galleries devoted to a collection of items by artists and artisans of Arkansas, a contemporary Arkansas Artists' Gallery and a Children's Hands-on Gallery. This is the main center of interpretation about the state's frontier period.

Mon.-Sat. 9-5, Sun. 1-5; closed Jan. 1, Easter, Thanksgiving and Dec. 24-25. One-hour guided tours are given on the hour (except noon). Last tour begins 1 hour before closing. Admission free. Guided tour $2.50; over 64, $1.50; under 18, $1; free to all first Sun. of the month. Phone (501) 324-9351.

Brownlee House is in the Historic Arkansas Museum at 200 E. Third St. The house was built in the 1840s by Scottish stonemason Robert Brownlee for his brother, James. The builder recuperated in the house from a mining accident before leaving for the California gold rush. The marbleized mantels are of particular interest.

Hinderliter Grog Shop is in the Historic Arkansas Museum at 200 E. Third St. Built of logs in the late 1820s, the shop was an important social institution—the settlement tavern where men gathered to talk, drink and gamble. Jesse Hinderliter and his family lived upstairs until 1834 in this, the oldest house in Little Rock. Legend has it that the last Territorial Legislature convened in the large log structure in 1835.

McVicar House is in the Historic Arkansas Museum at 200 E. Third St. Built in the 1840s by James McVicar, warden of the state prison, the house exemplifies the smaller Southern house of its time. The house is held together by white oak pegs and is furnished in period.

Woodruff Print Shop is in the Historic Arkansas Museum at 200 E. Third St. The site includes a house built in 1824 by William E. Woodruff, founder of the *Arkansas Gazette,* the oldest newspaper west of the Mississippi River. A reproduction 1820s print shop includes original furniture and a replica of the press Woodruff rafted up the Arkansas River.

SAVE **LITTLE ROCK TOURS** departs 500 President Clinton Ave. As the bus travels through historic sections of Little Rock, the narrator entertainingly provides information about each landmark. Allow 2 hours minimum. Departures daily at 1; closed Jan. 1, Easter and Dec. 25. Fare $25; over 64 and students with ID $22; ages 6-12, $10. AX, DC, MC, VI. Phone (501) 868-7287.

LITTLE ROCK ZOO is off I-630 exit 4 at 1 Jonesboro Dr. The zoo displays more than 600 native and exotic animals on 40 acres. Highlights include ape, big cat and tropical rain forest exhibits. Pets are not permitted. The 1924 Arkansas Carousel, a rare over-the-jumps antiquity, has been restored as the centerpiece of the zoo's visitor center. Daily 9-5, Oct.-Apr.; 9-4:30, rest of year. Closed Jan. 1, Thanksgiving and Dec. 25. Admission $6; ages 1-12, $4. Under 13 must be with an adult. MC, VI. Phone (501) 666-2406.

MacARTHUR MUSEUM OF ARKANSAS MILITARY HISTORY is at 503 E. 9th St. The museum is housed in the Little Rock Arsenal and contains military items from the Civil War and World Wars I and II. Built in the mid-1800s, the arsenal is the birthplace of Gen. Douglas MacArthur. Exhibits include weapons, uniforms and items relating to the impact of transportation during warfare. Another room has displays depicting the history of the Boy Scouts of America.

Allow 30 minutes minimum. Tues.-Sat. 10-4 (also Memorial Day and Veterans' Day), Sun. 1-4; closed Jan. 1, Thanksgiving and Dec. 24-25. Donations. Phone (501) 376-4602.

MUSEUM OF DISCOVERY is at 500 President Clinton Ave., Suite 150, in the historic riverfront district. Science and history displays are featured in such exhibit areas as Bug Zoo, Arkansas Indians, Passport to the World, Health Hall, Imagination Station, World of the Forest and Zoom Zone. Changing exhibits also are offered. Mon.-Sat. 9-5 (also first Fri. of the month 5-7 p.m.), Sun. 1-5; closed Jan. 1, Easter, Thanksgiving and Dec. 24-25. Admission $7; over 64 and ages 1-12, $6; free to all first Fri. of the month 5-7 p.m. DS, MC, VI. Phone (501) 396-7050 or (800) 880-6475.

OLD STATE HOUSE MUSEUM is at 300 W. Markham at Center St. One of the finest examples of Doric architecture in the South, the house includes two chambers once used by the state legislature and supreme court. Designed by Gideon Shryock, it was begun in 1833 and completed in 1842; additions were made in 1885. When Arkansas became a state in 1836, the building served as the capitol. Displayed are items of state historical interest.

Mon.-Sat. 9-5, Sun. 1-5; closed Jan. 1, Thanksgiving and Dec. 24-25. Free. Phone (501) 324-9685.

 WILLIAM J. CLINTON PRESIDENTIAL LIBRARY AND MUSEUM is at 1200 President Clinton Ave., just e. of I-30 exit 141A. This dramatic glass building cantilevers over the Arkansas River, representing a "bridge to the 21st century." State-of-the-art exhibits chronicle 8 years of the Clinton Administration.

Included in the 20,000 square feet of exhibition space are video stations, interactive displays, a collection of gifts the Clintons received in the White

House and full-scale reproductions of the Oval Office and the Cabinet Room. The former president often stays in the modern penthouse suite above the museum.

Food is available. Allow 3 hours minimum. Mon.-Sat. 9-5, Sun. 1-5; closed Jan. 1, Thanksgiving and Dec. 25. Admission $7; over 61, retired military and college students with ID $5; ages 6-17, $3; active-duty military with ID free. AX, MC, VI. Phone (501) 374-4242.

LONOKE (D-4) pop. 4,287, elev. 242'

JOE HOGAN STATE FISH HATCHERY is 1 mi. s. on US 70 at 23 Joe Hogan Ln. Considered the largest state-owned warm-water fish hatchery in the country, the facility has 56 ponds producing nearly 4 million fish annually for stocking public lakes and streams. The main species are largemouth bass, black and white crappie, bluegill and channel catfish. Spawning season is April through July. A visitor center features an aquarium and an observation platform.

Allow 1 hour minimum. Daily 8-4:30. Free. Phone (501) 676-6963.

MAMMOTH SPRING (A-4)
pop. 1,147, elev. 515'

Named for its size, Mammoth Spring is the outlet of a subterranean river beginning far to the north. American Indian legend has it that the spring erupted as a chief dug a grave for his son, who had died searching for water. The Spring River, formed by the underground spring, is a popular spot for trout fishing and rafting.

MAMMOTH SPRING STATE PARK is on US 63 at jct. SR 9. The park contains Mammoth Spring, one of the nation's larger single springs. Water flow is estimated at 9 million gallons per hour. Some of the flow is stored in a nearby scenic lake. A restored 1886 train depot houses railroad memorabilia and local historical artifacts. Outside the depot stands a Frisco Railroad caboose. Paddleboat rides are available for a fee.

Park open daily 8-dusk. Visitor information center open daily 8-6, Memorial Day weekend-Labor Day; 8-5, rest of year. Depot open Tues.-Sun.; closed Jan. 1 and Dec. 25. Phone to verify depot schedule. Park free. Depot $2.50; ages 6-12, $1.50. Paddleboats $4 for 30 minutes, $6 for 1 hour; fees are per boat, not per person. Phone (870) 625-7364. *See Recreation Chart.*

Mammoth Spring National Fish Hatchery and Aquarium is at 302 Fish Hatchery Ln. in Mammoth Spring State Park at jct. US 63 and SR 9. Established in 1903, the federal hatchery is one of the oldest in the country. The aquarium displays fish and marine life indigenous to the state, including paddlefish, sturgeon, Gulf Coast striped bass, rainbow trout and freshwater mussels. Daily 7-3:30. Free. Phone (870) 625-3912.

MENA (B-1) pop. 5,637, elev. 1,145'

Bordering the Ouachita National Forest, Mena owes its growth to a resort built on Rich Mountain in 1896 by the Kansas City, Pittsburgh and Gulf Railroad. The resort and nearby Lake Wilhelmina were named after Queen Wilhelmina in honor of the railroad's Dutch ownership.

Talimena Scenic Drive begins in Mena and follows the high ridges of the Ouachita Mountains 54 miles west to Talihina, Okla. A number of overlooks along the route afford panoramas of the area.

Mena/Polk County Chamber of Commerce: 524 Sherwood Ave., Mena, AR 71953; phone (479) 394-2912.

JANSSEN PARK is at 7th St. and Janssen Ave. The 10-acre park has two spring-fed lakes and a deer enclosure. Highlights include an 1851 log cabin. Daily dawn-dusk. Free.

MENA DEPOT CENTER is at 524 Sherwood Ave. The restored rail station houses a variety of artifacts and displays. Highlights include railroad memorabilia and arts and crafts exhibits. Mon.-Sat. 9-4; closed major holidays. Free. Phone (479) 394-2912.

QUEEN WILHELMINA STATE PARK is 13 mi. n.w. on SR 88. At 2,681 feet, the park occupies one of the highest elevations in the state. The Arkansas Native Plant & Wildlife Center affords visitors the

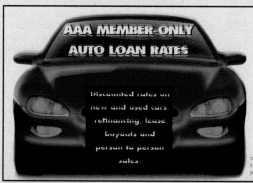

opportunity to view such native wildlife as black bears, cougars, coyotes and wolves as well as small mammals, birds and amphibians in a natural setting. The center also provides information and education about indigenous plants.

Food is available. The park is open daily dawn-10 p.m. The center is open daily 9-6, Memorial Day weekend-Labor Day weekend. Park free. Center $4; under 11, $3.50. Phone (479) 394-2863 for park information, or (800) 264-2477 for reservations, or (479) 437-3750 for the center. *See Recreation Chart and the AAA South Central CampBook.*

MORRILTON (C-3) pop. 6,550, elev. 367′

Morrilton was built along the Little Rock & Fort Smith Railroad in the 1870s. The town's early trading business expanded after a highway bridge built over the Arkansas River increased Morrilton's accessibility. Local industries include plastics, clothing, food and automotive products.

Morrilton Area Chamber of Commerce: 120 N. Division St., P.O. Box 589, Morrilton, AR 72110; phone (501) 354-2393.

THE MUSEUM OF AUTOMOBILES is 16 mi. s.w. via SRs 9 and 154 on Petit Jean Mountain. More than 50 antique and classic automobiles are displayed. Allow 30 minutes minimum. Daily 10-5; closed Dec. 25. Admission $7; over 65, $6.50; ages 6-17, $3.50; under 6 free when accompanied by an adult. Phone (501) 727-5427.

PETIT JEAN STATE PARK is 9 mi. s. on SR 9, then 12 mi. w. on SR 154 to Petit Jean Mountain Rd. Perched on flat-topped Petit Jean Mountain, the park boasts an array of natural features including 95-foot Cedar Falls, Indian Cave, Bear Cave, Rock House Cave and two gravel scenic drives overlooking Cedar Creek Canyon, Red Bluff Drive and the Palisades. The Seven Hollows region contains the unusual Turtle Rocks, the Grotto and the Petit Jean Natural Bridge.

The mountain's name is taken from the legend of a French girl who disguised herself as a boy and accompanied her sailor sweetheart to America. Many points of interest are reached by foot trails. Food is available.

Park open daily dawn-dusk. Visitor center open daily 8-8, Memorial Day weekend-Labor Day; Sun.-Thurs. 8-5, Fri.-Sat. 8-7, Mar. 1-day before Memorial Day weekend and day after Labor Day-Oct. 31; daily 8-5, rest of year. Closed Dec. 25. Free. Phone (501) 727-5441. *See Recreation Chart and the AAA South Central CampBook.*

MOUNTAIN PINE (D-2) pop. 772, elev. 470′

The town of Mountain Pine is so named because its economy is based on pine trees. The local lumber mill is the major industry.

LAKE OUACHITA STATE PARK is 12 mi. n. via SR 227 and Mountain Pine Rd. This 370-acre recreation area is on the shore of Arkansas' largest manmade body of water, Lake Ouachita. Park and

visitor center open daily 8-8, Memorial Day weekend-Labor Day; 8-5, rest of year. Closed Thanksgiving and Dec. 25. Free. Phone (501) 767-9366. *See Recreation Chart and Hot Springs in the AAA South Central CampBook.*

MOUNTAIN VIEW (B-3)
pop. 2,876, elev. 770′

One of the Ozarks' most active crossroads is Mountain View, whose lively cultural heritage is evident in its community events. The Annual Arkansas Folk Festival and the Southern Regional Mountain and Hammer Dulcimer Workshop and Contest are held in April; mid-September brings the Arkansas Old-Time Fiddlers Association State Championship Competition; and mid-October brings the Fall Harvest Festival.

Mountain View Area Chamber of Commerce: Court Square, P.O. Box 133, Mountain View, AR 72560; phone (870) 269-8068.

BLANCHARD SPRINGS CAVERNS is 15 mi. n.w. on SR 14. Guided tours include three underground passageways. A visitor center has an exhibit hall and shows a 20-minute movie every half-hour.

The half-mile Dripstone Trail tour lasts 1 hour and covers a variety of cave formations in the upper level of the cave. The 1.2-mile Discovery Trail tour lasts 90 minutes and follows a cave stream and water-carved passages into the caverns' middle level. This trail has many steps and is not recommended for those with limited mobility or respiratory problems. For the more adventurous, the strenuous 4-hour, 2-mile Wild Cave Adventure tour explores the undeveloped reaches of the underground system. Cave gear is provided. The caverns are 58 degrees Fahrenheit and damp, and the floors tend to be wet; dress appropriately.

Dripstone Trail tour departs approximately every hour daily 9:30-6. Discovery Trail tour departs approximately every hour daily 9:30-6, Memorial Day weekend-Labor Day. Wild Cave Adventure tour departs daily at 10. Visitor center open daily 9:30-6. Closed Jan. 1, Thanksgiving and Dec. 25.

Fee for trail tours $10; ages 6-15, $5; Golden Age and Golden Access cardholders $5. Fee for Wild Cave tour $65.00. A $25 non-refundable deposit is required. Ages 10-12 must be with an adult. Under 10 are not permitted. Reservations are suggested for the Dripstone Trail and Discovery Trail tours. Reservations are required for the Wild Cave Adventure tour. AX, DS, MC, VI. To make reservations or verify tour times or fees phone (870) 757-2211 or (888) 757-2246.

OZARK FOLK CENTER is 1.5 mi. n. via SRs 9/5/14, then 1 mi. w. on SR 382. The center focuses on the crafts, music, dance and oral history of an existing mountain folk culture. Local artisans demonstrate such skills as weaving and candle-making. Special events take place throughout the year. Live musical concerts begin at 7:30 most days during the season.

Picnicking is permitted. Food is available. Craft demonstrations are featured Wed.-Sat. 10-5, Apr.-Oct. Musical programs are presented in the auditorium at 7:30 p.m. on days when craft demonstrations are featured. The center is open on a limited schedule rest of year for workshops, special events and holiday offerings. Admission to craft area or to musical program $9; ages 6-12, $6. Combination crafts and musical program $15.50; ages 6-12, $8.25; family rate (2 adults and children under 18), $40. MC, VI. Phone (870) 269-3851.

MURFREESBORO (E-1)
pop. 1,764, elev. 655'

Murfreesboro is the seat of Pike County, which was named for Lt. Zebulon M. Pike, who explored the Southwest in the early 1800s. The area's main agricultural pursuits are cattle and poultry raising and egg production.

Murfreesboro Chamber of Commerce: 204 E. Main St., P.O. Box 166, Murfreesboro, AR 71958; phone (870) 285-3131.

CRATER OF DIAMONDS STATE PARK is 2 mi. s.e. on SR 301 at 209 State Park Rd. Called the only diamond-producing site in the world open to the public, the park allows visitors to keep any precious and semiprecious stones they find. More than 70,000 diamonds have been uncovered in this ancient volcanic crater since 1906, including the 16.37-carat Amarillo Starlight. The visitor center displays another find, the 1.1-carat cut Strawn-Wagner Diamond—one of the most perfect diamonds ever certified. The Diamond Springs Water Playground is open in the summer.

Though not necessary, trowels are helpful in digging for stones. Rental equipment is available at the Diamond Discovery Center, which offers an instructional video and identification of finds. Picnicking is permitted. Park open daily 8-8, Memorial Day weekend-Labor Day; 8-5, rest of year. Water playground open daily noon-6, Memorial Day weekend-third weekend in Aug. Sat.-Sun. and Labor Day, fourth weekend in Aug.-Labor Day. Park closed Jan. 1, Thanksgiving and Dec. 25.

Park admission $6; ages 6-12, $3. Water playground admission $5, under 42 inches tall $3.50, under age 2 free (limited to 3 children per paying adult). Under age 11 must be with an adult 18 or older. DS, MC, VI. Phone (870) 285-3113. *See Recreation Chart and the AAA South Central CampBook.*

SAVE **KA-DO-HA INDIAN VILLAGE** is 1.5 mi. n.w. of SR 27 to 1010 Caddo Dr. This excavated location of a Mound Builder village was populated about 1,000 years ago by Kadohadocho Indians. The site includes a trading post and a museum displaying tools, pottery, weapons and jewelry. Self-guiding tours and arrowhead hunting are available. Daily 9-6, Memorial Day weekend-Labor Day; 9-5, rest of year. Closed Thanksgiving and Dec. 25. Admission $4; ages 6-13, $2. MC, VI. Phone (870) 285-3736.

NORTH LITTLE ROCK (E-3)
pop. 60,433, elev. 280'

If one man could be said to have created a city, William C. Faucette created North Little Rock. After he lost the 1903 mayoral election in Little Rock, Faucette and his lawyer friends introduced a bill in the Arkansas General Assembly making the section of Little Rock north of the Arkansas River a separate city. Faucette's bill was passed in 1917, making him a new mayor in a new city.

North Little Rock Advertising and Promotion Commission Visitor Center: 1 Eldor Johnson Dr. in Burns Park, P.O. Box 5511, North Little Rock, AR 72119; phone (501) 758-1424 or (800) 643-4690.

Shopping areas: McCain Mall, McCain Boulevard and US 67, counts Dillard's and Sears among its stores.

ARKANSAS INLAND MARITIME MUSEUM is at 100 Riverfront Park Dr. Guided tours of the USS *Razorback* take visitors to all areas of this Balao-class submarine, which served during World War II and the Vietnam War. The sub was later sold to the Turkish Navy and rechristened the *Murat Reis*.

Tours require a moderate level of physical activity that includes climbing up and down ladders; comfortable walking shoes are advised. Not recommended for children under 6. Allow 30 minutes minimum. Mon. and Thurs.-Sat. 10-6, Sun. 1-6, May 15-Aug. 31; Sat. 10-6, Sun. 1-6, rest of year. Closed holidays. Admission $6; over 65, military with ID and ages 6-12, $4. MC, VI. Phone (501) 371-8320.

BURNS PARK is at jct. I-40 and SR 176 exit 150. The 1,575-acre park offers extensive recreational facilities, including soccer and rugby fields, basketball and bocce courts, fitness trails, disk golf, miniature golf, 18-hole golf courses, a waterslide and a playground. The indoor tennis complex has handball, racquetball and volleyball courts. A visitor center contains information about the park and attractions in North Little Rock and Arkansas.

Park open daily 6 a.m.-midnight. Visitor center open daily 8:30-4:30; closed major holidays. Free. Fees for activities. Admission during Holiday Lights Display in Dec. $5 per private vehicle. Phone (501) 791-8537, or (501) 758-1424 for the visitor center, or (800) 643-4690 out of Ark. *See Recreation Chart and the AAA South Central CampBook.*

THE OLD MILL AT T.R. PUGH MEMORIAL PARK is off Fairway Ave. at 3800 Lakeshore Dr. This picturesque replica of an 1830s gristmill appeared in the opening scene of "Gone With the Wind." It is believed to be the last surviving structure used in the film. Mexican sculptor Dionicio Rodríguez formed wet cement by hand to achieve the look of natural wood. *Faux bois* sculptures in the surrounding park include trees, benches, mushrooms and an ornate "timber" bridge, all crafted from concrete. Picnicking is permitted. Daily 8 a.m.-10 p.m., Apr.-Oct.; 8-7, rest of year. Free. Phone (501) 758-1424 or (800) 643-4690.

WILD RIVER COUNTRY is off I-40 exit 148, then .5 mi. w. to 6810 Crystal Hill Rd. This theme park offers water slides, a wave pool and other water-related amusements. A children's play area and facilities for volleyball and basketball also are provided. Food and lockers are available. Mon.-Sat. 10-8, Sun. noon-8, Memorial Day weekend-Labor Day. Admission $24.99, under 49 inches tall $17.99, over 65 and under age 3 free. Admission after 3 p.m. $15.99. AX, MC, VI. Phone (501) 753-8600.

OUACHITA NATIONAL FOREST

Elevations in the forest range from 360 ft. on the Fourche-LaFave River to 2,681 ft. at Rich Tower. Refer to AAA maps for additional elevation information.

In west-central Arkansas and southeastern Oklahoma, the 1,613,120-acre Ouachita National Forest is known for its mountain scenery, recreational opportunities and varied wildlife. The Ouachita Mountains run east and west, rather than north and south as do most American ranges. The novaculite found in this area is highly valued for making Arkansas whetstones, used for sharpening blade tools.

Talimena Scenic Drive provides 54 miles of mountain views along SRs 88 and 1 from near Mena to near Talihina, Okla. The Ouachita National Recreation Trail is a 186-mile east-west route through the mountains from SR 9 near Little Rock to Talimena State Park in Oklahoma. A nature center and three hiking trails are available at Kerr Arboretum and Nature Center, 19 miles south of Heavener, Okla. The Jessieville Visitor Center is open daily 9-5, March to October, weekdays 8-4:30 the rest of the year. The center is 18 miles north of Hot Springs in Jessieville and features the 1.5-mile Friendship Trail, a paved woodland loop.

Developed facilities are available at Lake Sylvia, south of Perryville off SR 9; Little Pines Recreation Area, 12 miles west of Waldron on SR 248; Shady Lake, 25 miles southeast of Mena; Cedar Lake, 10 miles south of Heavener, Okla., off US 270; Charlton Recreation Area near Lake Ouachita, 20 miles west of Hot Springs; Albert Pike Recreation Area, 6 miles north of Langley off SR 84; and Mill Creek, 5 miles east of "Y" City on US 270.

The forest contains six wilderness areas: Caney Creek, 14,460 acres 25 miles southeast of Mena; Black Fork Mountain, 12,151 acres shared with Oklahoma, 18 miles northwest of Mena; Poteau Mountain, 10,884 acres 35 miles south of Fort Smith; Flatside, 10,105 acres 16 miles southwest of Perryville; Dry Creek, 6,310 acres 12 miles southwest of Booneville; and Upper Kiamichi River, 9,371 acres 25 miles east of Talihina, Okla.

Park admission is free. Information about additional recreation areas within the forest and about camping fees can be obtained from the Forest Supervisor's Office, Ouachita National Forest, 100 Reserve St., P.O. Box 1270, Hot Springs, AR 71902; phone (501) 321-5202. *See Recreation Chart and the AAA South Central CampBook.*

OZARK NATIONAL FOREST

Elevations in the forest range from 420 ft. near the town of New Blaine to 2,753 ft. at Mount Magazine. Refer to AAA maps for additional elevation information.

In the Ozark Highlands and Boston Mountains of northwestern Arkansas, the four principal divisions of the Ozark National Forest total more than a million acres. Recreational activities such as hiking, camping, canoeing, horseback riding, hunting, fishing, mountain bicycle riding, swimming and picnicking can be enjoyed in the rugged beauty of the forest.

Blanchard Springs Caverns Recreation Area, off SR 14 north of Mountain View, features a large spring that gushes 1,200 gallons of water per minute; nearby is Blanchard Springs Caverns (*see Mountain View p. 54*).

Alum Cove Natural Bridge Recreation Area, north of Deer on FR 1206, preserves a 130-foot-long natural arch. Cove Lake, a 160-acre mountain lake southeast of Paris on SR 309 near Mount Magazine offers camping, picnicking, swimming, fishing and boating. The 150-mile-long Ozark Highland Trail affords opportunities for hiking and nature study.

Information about the forest's many other recreation areas is available from the Forest Supervisor's Office, Ozark National Forest, 605 W. Main St., P.O. Box 1008, Russellville, AR 72801; phone (479) 968-2354. *See Recreation Chart and the AAA South Central CampBook.*

PARKIN (C-6) pop. 1,602, elev. 210'

PARKIN ARCHEOLOGICAL STATE PARK is n. at jct. US 64 and SR 184 to 60 SR 184N. Ongoing excavations indicate this 17-acre farming village was occupied 1000-1550 A.D. during the Mississippi Period. Many scholars believe it was the Casqui Indian village visited by Hernando de Soto in the summer of 1541 and recorded in his journals. A large ceremonial mound has been preserved along the St. Francis River. A 12-minute DVD presentation is offered.

Self-guiding tours are available. Allow 1 hour minimum. Tues.-Sat. and Mon. holidays 8-5, Sun. noon-5; closed Jan. 1, Thanksgiving and Dec. 24-25. Admission $2.75; ages 6-12, $1.75; family rate $9. Phone (870) 755-2500.

PEA RIDGE NATIONAL MILITARY PARK (A-1)

On US 62 about 9 mi. n.e. of Rogers, in northwest Arkansas, the 4,300-acre park was the site of the Battle of Pea Ridge, also known to the Confederacy as the Battle of Elkhorn Tavern. A reconstruction of the tavern is on the original site. Largely as a result of this battle, fought March 7-8, 1862, Union forces succeeded in securing the state of Missouri. A 7-mile self-guiding driving tour through the park provides insight into the battle. A small portion of the "Trail of Tears" also is within the park.

Park admission ages 16-61, $3; maximum charge per private vehicle $5. Park open daily 8-5 (driving tour until 4:30); closed Jan. 1, Thanksgiving and Dec. 25. Phone (479) 451-8122.

PEA RIDGE NATIONAL MILITARY PARK VISITOR CENTER is 10 mi. n.e. of Rogers via scenic US 62. Museum exhibits and a 28-minute movie, "Thunder in the Ozarks," provide background on the battle. A driving tour of the battlefield begins at the center and travels to 10 stops, including Elkhorn Tavern, with markers and audio descriptions of key points. Center open daily 8-5; closed Jan. 1, Thanksgiving and Dec. 25. Admission free with park admission. Phone (479) 451-8122, ext. 227.

PINE BLUFF (D-4) pop. 55,085, elev. 215'

The second oldest city in the state, Pine Bluff was founded in 1819 as a trading post by Joseph Bonne, who dealt with the Quapaw Indians. Some of the houses on W. Barraque Street date from the Civil War period.

Alliance/Greater Pine Bluff Chamber of Commerce: 612 W. 5th St., P.O. Box 5069, Pine Bluff, AR 71611; phone (870) 535-0110.

ARKANSAS RAILROAD MUSEUM is at 1720 Port Rd. Old repair shops of the Cotton Belt Railway house a steam locomotive and 14 vintage railroad cars, as well as such railroad memorabilia as photographs and train parts. Mon.-Sat. 9-2; closed holidays. Donations. Phone (870) 535-8819.

THE BAND MUSEUM is at 423 Main St. Displays of musical instruments dating from the early 1700s relate the history of American bands and band music. Also in this 1880s building is a working soda fountain. Allow 1 hour minimum. Mon.-Fri. 10-4, Sat.-Sun. by appointment; closed holidays. Free. Phone (870) 534-4676.

DELTA RIVERS NATURE CENTER is at 1400 Black Dog Rd. Located within the Pine Bluff Regional Park on 130 acres of woodlands, this center features exhibits that depict the natural history of Arkansas' Delta region. Nature trails provide viewing opportunities of the area's vegetation and wildlife. A 20,000-gallon freshwater outdoor aquarium contains native fish species, snakes, turtles and alligators. Interactive displays also are offered.

Picnicking is permitted. Tues.-Sat. 8:30-4:30 (also Fri.-Sat. 4:30-7:30, Memorial Day-Labor Day), Sun. 1-5; closed Jan. 1 and Dec. 24-25. Fish feeding time at the aquarium is Tues.-Fri. at 11, Sat.-Sun. at 3. Free. Phone (870) 534-0011.

JEFFERSON COUNTY HISTORICAL MUSEUM is at 201 E. 4th St. Displays in the Union Station train depot chronicle historical events that shaped the county's development. Mon.-Fri. 9-4, Sat. 10-2; closed major holidays. Free. Phone (870) 541-5402.

SOUTHEAST ARKANSAS ARTS AND SCIENCE CENTER is at 701 S. Main St. Permanent and changing exhibits include paintings, sculpture and other works by local and international artists. Mon.-Fri. 10-5, Sat.-Sun. 1-4; closed holidays. Free. Phone (870) 536-3375.

POCAHONTAS (A-5) pop. 6,518, elev. 300'

Pocahontas, a historic river port town, overlooks the once traffic-laden Black River. The Old Randolph County Courthouse, an 1872 brick Victorian structure, is in the town square; a 4-foot meteorite that fell nearby in 1859 rests across the street on the lawn of the current courthouse. Boating and fishing for bream, crappie and bass are popular along the river.

Randolph County Chamber of Commerce: Old Randolph County Courthouse on Town Square, P.O. Box 466, Pocahontas, AR 72455; phone (870) 892-3956.

OLD DAVIDSONVILLE STATE PARK is 2 mi. w. on US 62, then 9 mi. s.w. on SR 166 on the Black River. This site preserves the oldest post office, courthouse and land office in the state, built 1817-22. Office open daily 8-5 (also Fri.-Sat. 5-8), Memorial Day weekend-July 4; daily 8-5, rest of year. Closed Jan. 1, Thanksgiving and Dec. 25. Free. Phone (870) 892-4708. *See Recreation Chart and the AAA South Central CampBook.*

POWHATAN (B-4) pop. 50, elev. 290'

POWHATAN HISTORIC STATE PARK is at 4414 SR 25. This restored 1888 two-story brick building houses official records of Lawrence County dating from 1813. Exhibits depict the history of Powhatan. An 1873 restored limestone jail, which contains two original cells, is on the grounds. Tours include the courthouse, jail, restored residences, businesses and the 1854 Powhatan Academy.

Tues.-Sat. 8-5, Sun. 1-5. Guided tours are available. Town site admission $3; ages 6-12, $1.75; family rate $9.75. Single building tour $1.50; ages 6-12, $1; family rate $9.75. Phone (870) 878-0032.

PRAIRIE GROVE (B-1) pop. 2,540, elev. 174'

PRAIRIE GROVE BATTLEFIELD STATE PARK is e. on US 62. Marking the site of a Civil War battle fought on Dec. 7, 1862, the 838-acre park contains a 55-foot monument, 19th-century houses and buildings, a museum and a walking trail. Interpretive programs include living-history presentations. In even-numbered years the battle is re-created. A 55-minute CD provides directions for a self-guiding tour, descriptions and recollections of participants and their families.

Park open daily 8-dusk. Museum open daily 8-5; closed Jan. 1, Thanksgiving, Dec. 24 (noon-5) and Dec. 25. Park free. Museum admission $3; ages 6-12, $2; family rate $10. CD $4. Phone (479) 846-2990.

ROGERS (A-1) pop. 38,829, elev. 1,384'

The first train steamed into the settlement now known as Rogers in 1881, 22 years after the Butterfield Overland Mail established a way station in town. Spanish and French pioneers once walked this territory, as did American Indians forced westward on the "Trail of Tears" and Civil War soldiers. Nearby recreation areas offer outdoor activities.

Rogers Chamber of Commerce: 113 N. 4th St., P.O. Box 428, Rogers, AR 72756; phone (479) 636-1240.

HOBBS STATE PARK-CONSERVATION AREA is 10 mi. e. at 21392 SR 12E. The 11,764-acre park along the southern shores of Beaver Lake is part of the large-scale power and flood control project in the White River Basin. The terrain offers plateaus, ridges, valleys, a forest and streams and harbors abundant wildlife. Its waters offer large- and small-mouth bass, crappie, bream, channel catfish and northern pike.

Campsites are primitive and at the end of a 4-mile hike. Park open daily 24 hours. Trails open daily 7 a.m.-1 hour after dusk. Firing range open daily 8-7, during DST; 8-5, rest of year. Phone (479) 789-2380. *See Recreation Chart and the AAA South Central CampBook.*

THE ROGERS DAISY AIRGUN MUSEUM is at 202 W. Walnut St. The history of air guns and especially Daisy brand air guns is told through exhibits of the guns and their allied advertisements, packaging and promotional premiums. Allow 30 minutes minimum. Tues.-Sat. 10-5; closed holidays. Admission $2, under 17 free. Phone (479) 986-6873.

ROGERS HISTORICAL MUSEUM is at 322 S. 2nd St. This museum provides permanent and changing historical exhibits, including the 1895 Hawkins House, furnished in the Victorian period. Storefront replicas of a bank, barber shop and store make up First Street. The Attic is a hands-on display for children. In nearby Frisco Park the museum's Frisco caboose is open May through October. Allow one hour minimum. Tues.-Sat. 10-4; closed major holidays. Free. Phone (479) 621-1154.

SAVE **WAR EAGLE CAVERN** is 17 mi. e. on SR 12 to 21494 Cavern Dr. Set in the Ozark mountains on the shores of Beaver Lake, the cavern once sheltered American Indians. Guided 1-hour tours reveal stalactites, stalagmites, fossils and an underground stream; a nature trail is on the grounds. The cave also is home to 75,000 Arkansas brown and grey bats. A cave maze challenges participants to find their way out.

Cave temperature is 58 degrees F. Allow 1 hour minimum. Tours daily as needed 9:30-5, mid-Mar. through Oct. 31; Sat.-Sun. by appointment in Nov. Last tour begins 30 minutes before closing. Fee $9.95; ages 4-11, $5.75. MC, VI. Phone (479) 789-2909.

ST. CHARLES (D-5) pop. 261, elev. 200'

During the Civil War battle of June 17, 1862, a cannonball was shot through a porthole of the federal ironclad *Mound City* on the White River at St. Charles. Called by some historians the most destructive single shot of the war, it hit a steam pipe and killed nearly 100 soldiers.

WHITE RIVER NATIONAL WILDLIFE REFUGE is off SR 1 along the White River. The refuge consists of 145,000 acres of actively managed land, largely hardwood forest, with 90 miles of river and 356 lakes. This is a wintering area for large numbers of ducks and Canada geese. The visitor center offers natural history exhibits, films and a wildlife diorama depicting habitats and animals found at the refuge. Camping, hunting and fishing are available by permit. Refuge open daily 24 hours. Visitor center open 8-4, Mon.-Fri., 9-3, Sat.-Sun.; center closed on federal holidays. Free. Phone (870) 282-8200 or (870) 946-1468.

ST. FRANCIS NATIONAL FOREST (D-6)

Elevations in the forest range from 150 ft. on the Mississippi River to 320 ft. at Crowley's Ridge. Refer to AAA maps for additional elevation information.

In east-central Arkansas, St. Francis National Forest covers 20,977 acres at the south end of a 200-mile-long ridge that rises above the surrounding flat farmlands. The forest offers picnicking, camping, fishing, boating, swimming and hiking.

Developed recreation areas are at 625-acre Bear Creek Lake, 8 miles south of Marianna on SR 44, and at 420-acre Storm Creek Lake, 6 miles north of West Helena on SR 44. For additional information contact the Forest Supervisor, St. Francis National Forest, Box 2675, SR 44, Marianna, AR 72360; phone (870) 295-5278. *See Recreation Chart and the AAA South Central CampBook.*

SALESVILLE (A-3) pop. 437, elev. 772'

NORFORK DAM AND LAKE is at 1414 SR 177S. Part of a power and flood control project in the White River Basin, the area comprises a major recreation center offering camping, swimming and other water activities. Trout fishing is popular in the area; a federal trout hatchery just below the dam is open for self-guiding tours. Daily 8-4. Free. Phone (870) 425-2700 for general information, or (870) 499-5255 for the hatchery. *See Recreation Chart and the AAA South Central CampBook.*

SCOTT (D-4) pop. 94, elev. 249'

PLANTATION AGRICULTURE MUSEUM is at jct. US 165 and SR 161. Exhibits in this 1912 general store trace the state's cotton planting heritage and plantation life from statehood in 1836 through World War II, when farm mechanization became the agricultural standard. Allow 1 hour minimum. Tues.-Sat. and Mon. holidays 8-5, Sun. 1-5; closed Jan. 1, Thanksgiving and Dec. 24-25. Admission $3; ages 6-12, $2; family rate $10. Phone (501) 961-1409.

TOLTEC MOUNDS ARCHEOLOGICAL STATE PARK is 4 mi. s.e. off US 165. The park preserves the remains of prehistoric earthworks called the Toltec Mounds. Once believed to be the work of Toltec Indians from Mexico, these large mounds were probably constructed by an early American group of the Plum Bayou culture. Built A.D. 650-1050, the mounds were abandoned by 1400. Some of the 18 mounds were foundations for temples and houses, while others were burial sites.

Self-guiding tours are offered along a .7-mile trail emphasizing site preservation and research. Park and visitor center open Tues.-Sat. and Mon. holidays 8-5, Sun. noon-5. Closed Jan. 1, Thanksgiving and Dec. 24-25. Admission $2.50; ages 6-12, $1.50; family rate $8. Phone (501) 961-9442.

SHERIDAN (D-3) pop. 3,872, elev. 228'

GRANT COUNTY MUSEUM is off SR 46 at 521 Shackleford Rd. Pioneer, American Indian and Civil War artifacts pertain to the county's history. Also featured are log buildings, including a cabin built about 1850. A history research library is available. Tues.-Sat. 9-noon and 1-4; closed major holidays. Free. Phone (870) 942-4496.

SMACKOVER (F-3) pop. 2,005, elev. 120'

French explorers described this heavily wooded area as *sumac couvert*, meaning "covered with sumac." The Anglicized version became Smackover. The name would become famous in 1922 with the discovery of the Smackover oil field, one of the country's largest petroleum reservoirs. The town's population swelled from 90 to 25,000 in months. Though production declined in the 1930s, oil continues to be a mainstay of the local economy.

ARKANSAS MUSEUM OF NATURAL RESOURCES is on the SR 7 bypass. Indoor and outdoor exhibits illustrate drilling methods and production techniques at this museum, which chronicles the history and development of the oil and brine industry and its impact on the area. Films and displays describe the 1920s oil boom. Mon.-Sat. and holidays 8-5, Sun. 1-5; closed Jan. 1, Thanksgiving and Dec. 24-25. Free. Phone (870) 725-2877.

SPRINGDALE (B-1) pop. 45,798, elev. 1,329'

SAVE **ARKANSAS AND MISSOURI RAILROAD** departs from the depot at 306 E. Emma Ave. Travelers ride in comfort aboard restored late 19th- and early 20th-century passenger cars on an 8-hour, 134-mile round-trip train ride through the scenic Boston Mountains to Van Buren. The full-day ride includes a 2.5-hour stopover. Friday and Saturday round-trips from Van Buren to Winslow, and Sunday round-trips from Fort Smith to Winslow also are offered.

Springdale-to-Van Buren trips depart Fri.-Sat. at 8, Apr.-Sept.; Wed., Fri.-Sat. at 8, Oct. 1 through mid-Nov. Springdale-to-Van Buren Apr.-Sept. fare $45-$65; over 64, $41-$59; ages 4-12, $22-$59. Springdale-to-Van Buren Oct. 1 through mid-Nov. fare $60-$80; over 64 and ages 4-12, $54-$72. Reservations are suggested. Phone to confirm schedule and fares. DS, MC, VI. Phone (479) 751-8600 or (800) 687-8600. *See also Van Buren p. 60.*

SHILOH MUSEUM OF OZARK HISTORY is at 118 W. Johnson Ave. This 2-acre regional history museum consists of various displays that focus on those who shaped Ozark history—the past residents of the area. Seven historic buildings, including a log cabin outhouse, an oak barn and the Searcy House, also are on site. Free guided tours of the Searcy House are available. Changing exhibits are offered year-round. Allow 30 minutes minimum. Mon.-Sat. 10-5; closed Jan. 1, Thanksgiving and Dec. 24-25. Donations. Phone (479) 750-8165.

STUTTGART (D-4) pop. 9,745, elev. 228'

Surrounding Stuttgart is the rice-producing section of the Grand Prairie region, also known as one of the finest fishing areas in the country. The rice fields and the many lakes and reservoirs in the area offer excellent feeding and resting places for waterfowl.

Stuttgart hosts the Wings Over the Prairie Festival, featuring the World Championship Duck Calling Contest, in November.

Stuttgart Chamber of Commerce: 507 S. Main St., Stuttgart, AR 72160; phone (870) 673-1602.

MUSEUM OF THE ARKANSAS GRAND PRAIRIE is just n. of the city park at 921 E. 4th St. The museum contains reproductions of an 1880 homestead and an 1890 village as well as a two-thirds scale model of an 1869 church, a 1914 schoolhouse and replicas of a fire station and a newspaper office. Included are exhibits about prairie farming, wildlife, duck hunting and toys.

A videotape shows rice, soybean and fish farming; a mini-theater videotape traces the history of local crop dusting. Allow 1 hour minimum. Tues.-Fri. 8-4, Sat. 10-4; closed holidays. Donations. Phone (870) 673-7001.

TEXARKANA (E-1) pop. 26,448, elev. 290'

The Arkansas-Texas state line runs approximately through the center of the dual municipality of Texarkana, which has a combined population of about 61,000.

For hundreds of years before European settlement in the area, the Great Southwest Trail, the major route between the American Indian villages of the Mississippi Valley and the West and Southwest, crossed the area around what is now Texarkana. The Grand Caddoes, hospitable to explorers and settlers, farmed in the vicinity and maintained six villages along the banks of the Red River.

Shortly after 1840 a permanent settlement was established at Lost Prairie, 15 miles east of Texarkana. A number of mounds and other traces of former American Indian civilizations remain within a 30-mile radius of the town.

During the 1850s the Cairo and Fulton Railroad served portions of Arkansas and by 1874 had crossed the Red River into Texas, establishing direct rail service to St. Louis. The Texas and Pacific Railroad had laid track to the Arkansas boundary, and the place where the two lines met became a town—Texarkana.

The state line runs through the middle of the Texarkana Post Office and Courthouse, said to be the only federal building situated in two states. Built in 1932 of pink granite from Texas and limestone from Arkansas, the post office has two separate zip codes. Residents on both sides of the border enjoy the Perot Theater, 221 Main St., a restored 1924 facility that presents a variety of Broadway-type shows.

Texarkana Chamber of Commerce: 819 State Line Ave., P.O. Box 1468, Texarkana, TX 75504; phone (903) 792-7191.

SAVE **ACE OF CLUBS HOUSE AND MUSEUM** is at 420 Pine St. This 22-sided house was built in 1885 from the winnings of a poker game. The Italianate Victorian-style building has three octagonal wings and one rectangular wing and is furnished in period. A 15-minute videotape presentation is followed by a 1-hour guided tour that is offered as needed. High heels and photography are not permitted. Allow 1 hour, 30 minutes minimum. Tues.-Sat. 10-4. Last tour begins 1 hour before closing. Fee $6; over 60, $5; students with ID $4. MC, VI. Phone (903) 793-4831.

SAVE **DISCOVERY PLACE CHILDREN'S MUSEUM** is at the corner of Pine St. and State Line Ave. at 215 Pine St. Educational and entertaining hands-on exhibits focus on science and history. A theater, lab demonstrations and a 12-foot sound wall sculpture enhance the learning environment. Allow 1 hour minimum. Tues.-Sat. 10-4; closed major holidays. Admission $4.50, under 4 free. Phone (903) 793-4831.

SAVE **MUSEUM OF REGIONAL HISTORY** is 4 blks. s. of US 59/67/71/82 at 219 N. State Line Ave. Housed in an 1879 brick building, this museum traces the region's history from the early Caddo Indians through 20th-century citizens, including early industry, post World War II and the civil rights movement. In addition to the Native American Gallery, the Scott Joplin Gallery is dedicated to the composer's early life and career in Texarkana. Tues.-Sat. 10-4; closed holidays. Admission $5; over 60, $4; students with ID and children over 5, $3.50. MC, VI. Phone (903) 793-4831.

VAN BUREN (B-1) pop. 18,986, elev. 406'

Settled in 1818, Van Buren is one of the oldest settlements in western Arkansas. It was a steamboat landing, a stage stop for the Butterfield Line from St. Louis to California, a main artery for commerce and the border between the Cherokee and Choctaw tribes.

A 10-block downtown area has been restored to its late 19th-century appearance, complete with old-fashioned lamps and period storefronts. Included in the restoration project are the Albert Pike Schoolhouse, Crawford County Courthouse, Mount Olive Church, Fairview Cemetery and the waterfront.

Van Buren Visitor Center: Old Frisco Depot at 813 Main St., P.O. Box 1518, Van Buren, AR 72957; phone (479) 474-6164 or (800) 332-5889.

Self-guiding tours: The Van Buren Walking Tour features 52 stops. A brochure featuring a map of the path and descriptions of the stops is available from the visitor center.

SAVE **ARKANSAS AND MISSOURI RAILROAD** departs from 813 Main in the Old Frisco Depot. A 70-mile round-trip train ride travels through the Boston Mountains. The 2.5-hour ride in restored early late 19th- and early 20th-century passenger cars takes passengers over three trestles, through the Winslow tunnel and offers scenic views of the mountains. An 80-mile, 3-hour trip from Fort Smith to Winslow departs the Old Frisco Depot at 100 Garrison.

Round-trips to Winslow depart Fri.-Sat. at 11, Apr.-Sept.; Wed., Fri.-Sat. at 10:45, Oct.1 through mid-Nov. Round-trips from Fort Smith to Winslow Sun. at 1, May-July. Van Buren to Winslow fare Apr.-Sept. $30-$52; over 64 $27-$48; ages 4-12, $15-$27. Van Buren to Winslow fare Oct. 1 through mid-Nov. $40-$62; over 64 and ages 4-12, $36-$56. Fort Smith to Winslow fare $35-$57; over 64, $32-$52; ages 4-12, $17-$28. Reservations are suggested. Phone to confirm schedules and fares. DS, MC, VI. Phone (479) 751-8600 or (800) 687-8600. *See also Springdale p. 59.*

WALCOTT (B-5) elev. 340'

Paragould-Greene County Chamber of Commerce: 111 E. Poplar St., P.O. Box 124, Paragould, AR 72450; phone (870) 236-7684.

CROWLEY'S RIDGE STATE PARK is at 2092 SR 168. The 270-acre park is in a hardwood forest atop Crowley's Ridge, a rare geological formation extending for some 200 miles from southern Missouri to eastern Arkansas. Composed of deposits of windblown silt, or loess, the ridge is believed to be unique in the Western Hemisphere; another exists in Siberia. A gravesite monument to Benjamin Crowley honors the first settler in the area and a soldier in the War of 1812.

Park open daily 8 a.m.-10 p.m. Visitor center open daily 8-5 (also Fri.-Sat. 5-8, Memorial Day weekend-July 4); closed Jan. 1 and Dec. 25. Free. Phone (870) 573-6751. *See also Forrest L. Wood Crowley's Ridge Nature Center p. 50, Recreation Chart and the AAA South Central CampBook.*

WASHINGTON (E-1) pop. 148, elev. 375'

Founded in 1825, Washington was a crossroads for travelers in every direction during the 1800s. The Southwest Trail, the earliest road across Arkansas, ran from Missouri through Little Rock and Washington to Fulton, near the Texas-border. From 1831 to 1833 more than 3,000 Choctaw Indians, forcibly evicted from Mississippi, passed through Washington on their way to Oklahoma.

Texas frontiersman Sam Houston planned the Texas Revolution of 1835-36 in a Washington tavern in 1834. During the Civil War the town became the Confederate state capital after Little Rock fell to Union forces. In 1875 and again in 1883 fires destroyed much of the business district, and Washington's glory began to fade. In 1938 Hope replaced Washington as Hempstead county seat.

OLD WASHINGTON HISTORIC STATE PARK is at jct. US 278 and SR 195 at 100 S.W. Morrison. This restored village showcases 19th-century buildings and typical lifestyles of southwest Arkansas. More than 30 structures include the 1857 Augustus M. Crouch House and the 1874 Hempstead County Courthouse, which serves as the park visitor center. Various buildings are open for tours, depending on the day's interpretive theme, and docents in period costume greet visitors at each site. Christmas and Candlelight on the first Saturday in December is a highlight.

Note: Some 150 people live in Old Washington in private residences; not all buildings are open to the public. Food is available. Allow 2 hours minimum. Park open daily 8-5. Structures open for guided tours daily 9-noon and 1-5 (also 5-8 the first Sat. in Dec. for Christmas and Candlelight and the Christmas Ball); closed Jan. 1, Thanksgiving and Dec. 25. Tickets must be purchased from the visitor center. Fee $8; ages 6-12, $4. Admission first Sat. in Dec. $10; ages 6-12, $5. DS, MC, VI. Phone (870) 983-2684.

1836 Hempstead County Courthouse is in Old Washington Historic State Park at 409 Franklin St. Washington's schoolhouse from 1875-1914, the building first served as a courthouse and then the seat of Confederate government in Arkansas when Federal troops occupied Little Rock 1863-65.

Blacksmith Shop is in Old Washington Historic State Park at 600 Conway. This reconstruction of a frontier blacksmith shop commemorates the place where James Black reputedly made the first of what came to be known as Bowie knives. Bowie, who lived in Texas, liked Black's design and bought from him.

Block-Catts House is in Old Washington Historic State Park on the n.e. corner of Jay and Conway sts. Abraham Block built this two-story, frame, Federal-style building in 1832 and reared his 12 children in it.

B.W. Edwards Weapons Museum is in Old Washington Historic State Park at 201 Franklin St. More than 700 firearms, knives and swords are displayed in a 1925 bank.

Crouch House is on the corner of Carroll and Morrison sts. in Old Washington Historic State Park. This Greek Revival home was constructed by Augustus Crouch in 1856. Moved to its present site and restored, the house has been set aside for the study of architecture. Displays of tools and building methods reflect the period.

Print Museum is on n.w. corner of Izard and Franklin sts. in Old Washington Historic State Park. This 1915 building once was the town's post office and a bank. The printing and telegraph equipment now displayed dates from the early 1800s. Tour guides relate the history and operation of the apparatus. Allow 30 minutes minimum.

DID YOU KNOW

Sam Houston and friends planned the 1836 Texas Revolution in a tavern in Washington, Ark.

Purdom House is in Old Washington Historic State Park at 202 S.W. Morrison. The restored 1850 house was the residence of Dr. James A.L. Purdom until his death in 1866. Period medical artifacts are displayed.

Royston House is in Old Washington Historic State Park at 105 S.W. Water St. Restored and furnished in period with some original artifacts, the house dates from 1845. It was the home of Gen. Grandison D. Royston, who served in two of the state's constitutional conventions and in the Confederate Congress.

Royston Log Cabin is on n.w. corner Jay and Conway sts. in Old Washington Historic State Park. This 1832 log cabin has furnishings and items commonly used in the early and mid-1800s. A section of the siding has been removed from the back porch to show the construction of the cabin.

Sanders Farmstead is in Old Washington Historic State Park at 105 S.W. Carroll. The Greek Revival structure is restored and furnished in period. Dating from 1849, this was the home of Simon T. Sanders, county clerk for 30 years.

The Tavern Inn is in Old Washington Historic State Park at 4954 SR 278 N. Containing many period pieces, the inn re-creates the atmosphere of 18th-century taverns that served such travelers as Davy Crockett and Jim Bowie, as well as troops en route to the Mexican War.

Trimble House is on the n.e. corner of Southwest Tr./SR 195 and Washington St. in Old Washington Historic State Park. Built in 1847 as the home of Probate Court Judge John D. Trimble, the house interprets the lives of four generations of the Trimble family, the only family to occupy the dwelling.

WEST FORK (B-1) pop. 2,042, elev. 1,339'

DEVIL'S DEN STATE PARK is 17 mi. s.w. on SR 170. The park encompasses 2,000 acres in a rugged, scenic valley of the Ozark Mountains. The park contains Devil's Den Cave and the Devil's Ice Box, where the temperature never rises above 60 degrees Fahrenheit. A videotape presentation is available at the visitor center at the intersection of SRs 170 and 74. Interpretive programs also are offered.

Park open daily 8-dusk. Visitor center open daily 8-5 (also Fri.-Sat. 5-8, Memorial Day weekend-Labor Day). Free. Phone (479) 761-3325. *See Recreation Chart and the AAA South Central CampBook.*

WILSON (B-6) pop. 939, elev. 559'

The town of Wilson owes its success to the prosperity of Robert E. Lee Wilson. An orphan at 15, Wilson was a small-scale farmer who invested his savings wisely in the 1890s and turned a 2,100-acre swamp into one of the largest cotton plantations in the world. The cotton-growing R.E. Lee Wilson Co. and other Wilson-owned businesses became the cornerstone of the town's economy.

HAMPSON ARCHAEOLOGICAL MUSEUM STATE PARK is .2 mi. n. on US 61 at 2 Lake Dr. The museum displays American Indian artifacts unearthed from the Nodena site on the Mississippi River. A farming-based civilization occupied the 15-acre palisaded village from about 1350 to 1600. Picnic facilities are available. Tues.-Sat. and Mon. holidays 8-5, Sun. 1-5; closed Jan. 1, Thanksgiving and Dec. 24-25. Admission $2.50; ages 6-12, $1.50; family rate $8. Phone (870) 655-8622.

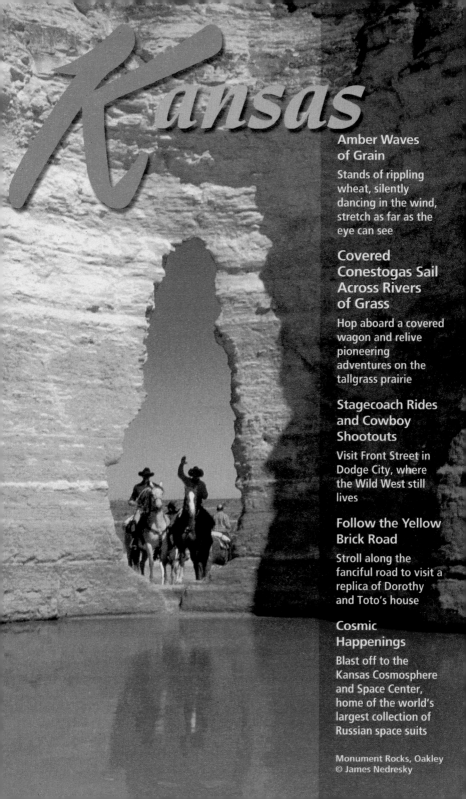

Kansas

Amber Waves of Grain

Stands of rippling wheat, silently dancing in the wind, stretch as far as the eye can see

Covered Conestogas Sail Across Rivers of Grass

Hop aboard a covered wagon and relive pioneering adventures on the tallgrass prairie

Stagecoach Rides and Cowboy Shootouts

Visit Front Street in Dodge City, where the Wild West still lives

Follow the Yellow Brick Road

Stroll along the fanciful road to visit a replica of Dorothy and Toto's house

Cosmic Happenings

Blast off to the Kansas Cosmosphere and Space Center, home of the world's largest collection of Russian space suits

Monument Rocks, Oakley
© James Nedresky

where the wind blows

The Sunflower State. The Jayhawker State. The Wheat State. Midway, U.S.A.

All are fitting nicknames for Kansas, a state where the history is rich and the landscape surprisingly varied.

However, a strong argument could be made for The Pioneer State as an apropos moniker. Indeed, the state has seen its fair share of visionaries and has

been the site of enough famous firsts.

Atchison native Amelia Earhart was the first woman to fly solo across the Atlantic. Frank E. Petersen of Topeka was the first African-American brigadier general in the Marine Corps. Argonian Susan Madora Salter was the first female mayor in the United States.

Kansas was the first state to ratify the amendment that allowed

African-Americans the right to vote. A pair of brothers borrowed $600 to open the first Pizza Hut restaurant. And Independence was the hometown of Miss Able, the first monkey in space.

Kansas entrepreneurs invented the autopilot, the helicopter and the O'Henry candy bar. And native Walter P. Chrysler founded a cornerstone of the American automobile industry: the Chrysler Corporation.

Constant winds stir much more than fields of grain and flowers. They blow in ideas, visions and dreams.

A cyclone rips through the Kansas prairie, flinging the house in which Dorothy and her dog are held captive into "... the midst of a country of marvelous beauty. There were lovely patches of greensward all about, with stately trees bearing rich and luscious fruits. Banks of gorgeous flowers were on every hand, and birds with rare and brilliant plumage sang and fluttered in the trees and bushes."

But author L. Frank Baum needn't have tossed "The Wonderful Wizard of Oz" lead character and supporting canine out of the Jayhawker State to have found a land of similar splendor.

He could have plopped the plucky pair in any number of places in the state and have been able to continue with an interesting story.

Scenario one: The house falls amid the intricate rock formations in the Smoky Hill River Valley, southeast of Oakley. Toto barks fearfully upon encountering the menacing centerpiece of the Chalk Pyramids—Cobra Rock—which rises from the ground to resemble a snake under the spell of its charmer. Meanwhile, Dorothy, upon catching a glimpse of Castle Rock, imagines herself in the role of another fairy tale heroine, Rapunzel.

Scenario two: The house lands in the sprawling fields of the Konza Prairie, south of Manhattan in the Flint Hills. Dorothy opens the front door to find herself face to face with an apprehensive American bison, the state animal. And Toto gets lost in the swaying tall grasses.

Scenario three: The house ends up near Elk Falls. Dorothy takes Toto for a stroll across the Iron Truss Bridge, where she pauses to view the graceful cascades that tumble over rock formations in a canyon on the Elk River.

More Than Just Flatlands

Kansas is all of this and more.

Fields of sunflowers stretch heavenward, their vivid yellow blooms jumping out of a subtle background of azure blue sky. Stalks of wheat bend to and fro as the wind blows fickle over the plains. Ruts of wagon wheels give evidence of a westward migration that rumbled across the Santa Fe Trail.

You can explore sand dunes and irregular hills in the lowlands of the Arkansas River; rugged canyons and rocky bluffs around the lake at Lake Scott State Park, north of Scott City; and salt mines and marshland near Wellington and McPherson.

Exploring the Louisiana Purchase territory, Meriwether Lewis and William Clark camp along the Missouri River.

1804

©Bettmann/Corbis

The Kansas-Nebraska Act is passed, and the Kansas Territory opens for settlement.

1854

The Homestead Act offers individuals federal land for a small filing fee and the promise to live on and improve the land for 5 years.

1862

1899

©Bettmann/Corbis

In Medicine Lodge, prohibitionist Carry Nation begins her crusade against the consumption of liquor.

Kansas Historical Timeline

The state boasts maple forests; the rolling Smoky Hills; Cimarron National Grasslands in its southwesternmost corner; and scores of fence posts cut from rock due to a short supply of timber.

The posts aren't the only rock oddities. Unexplained geological wonders that spring up throughout Kansas give you the chance to let your imagination run wild.

Many of the Mushroom Rocks, near Kanopolis Lake in Ellsworth County, resemble the giant fungus on which Alice found the contemplative, smoking caterpillar in "Alice in Wonderland."

Elephant Rock, near Oberlin, suggests the hulking presence of a pachyderm.

At Rock City, near Minneapolis, the deposits of sandstone boulders—some measuring nearly 30 feet in diameter—are similar enough in shape to cow chips that you might suspect gargantuan cattle once roamed the plains.

A Cast of Characters

Scenic wonders aren't all that make Kansas exceptional. The simple fact that it once was illegal to serve ice cream on cherry pie here certainly sets the state apart. But you wouldn't want to overlook the colorful characters who have left volumes of legend and lore.

During its Wild West days, Kansas embraced a population in an epic struggle of good vs. evil. Peace officers James "Wild Bill" Hickok, Wyatt Earp and William "Bat" Masterson fought valiantly in towns such as Abilene, Dodge City and Wichita to curb the lawless elements—gunslingers, swindlers, brothel keepers and the like.

Meanwhile, outlaws set out to pillage and destroy. Of the three brothers in the notorious Dalton Gang, only Emmett survived a botched bank robbery in Coffeyville; Bob and Grat were shot dead. And Jesse James had a hand in a Lawrence raid that left more than 200 citizens dead and $1.5 million in damages.

Long documented in the annals of mystery is the fate of Atchison native Amelia Earhart, the intrepid aviator whose disappearance during an attempt to fly around the world endures as a puzzle unsolved.

The history and geography of Kansas can appeal to almost anyone. Even Dorothy, after her exotic adventures along the Yellow Brick Road and in the Emerald City, was eager to return to her aunt and uncle back home.

For indeed, there is no place like Kansas.

The Supreme Court decision in Brown vs. The Topeka Board of Education opens the door for school desegregation nationwide.

1954

©Bettmann/Corbis

Kansas becomes the first state to switch its statues displayed in the U.S. Capitol when it replaces a likeness of 19th-century Gov. George W. Glick with one of Dwight D. Eisenhower.

2003

Nancy Landon Kassebaum becomes the first Kansas woman elected to the U.S. Senate.

1978

1953
Dwight D. Eisenhower, who grew up in Abilene, enters the White House.

1917
The demands of World War I bring an agriculture boom to Kansas.

1993
Floods damage or destroy nearly one-fifth of the state's farmland.

©Matthew Mendelsohn/Corbis

1996
Native son Senator Bob Dole unsuccessfully runs for president.

Recreation

If you want to get out and about in Kansas, ask not for whom the wind blows; it blows for thee. You might as well put the blustery gusts to good use.

When the air is moving, grab a sailboard and go **windsurfing.** Short, choppy waves give you a rough, but thrilling, ride on Cheney Lake, west of Wichita. If you like your rides smooth and speedy, head east out of Wichita to Eldorado Lake. Not surprisingly, both lakes also are popular for **sailing.** Another top-notch windsurfing destination is Hillsdale Lake, west of Hillsdale.

If the winds are blowing the same direction as the rivers are flowing, then it's a good day to go **canoeing.** One of the most popular spots is on the Fall River; you can rent a canoe in Eureka. Other waters that beckon to the paddler include the Kansas, Arkansas, Marais des Cygnes, Smoky Hill and Blue rivers.

When the Winds Die Down

Even on the rare occasion that the winds are quiet, there are plenty of other ways to experience the great outdoors.

Swimming, boating and **water skiing** let you keep your cool while playing in the sun. Among the hottest spots are Shawnee Mission Park, northwest of Lenexa; John Redmond Reservoir, northwest of Burlington; and Lake Garnett, in Garnett. Or check out what's going on below the water's surface. Clear water makes for nice **scuba diving** in Crawford Lake, north of Farlington.

Fishing is excellent in the basin below Webster Dam, where catches of trout (during the fall and winter), bass, catfish, crappie and bluegill are common. Lovewell Reservoir, west of Lovewell, is noted for its walleye fishing. If you like a battle, drop a line in Keith Sebelius Reservoir, west of Norton, where trophy wipers—hybrids of white and striped bass—put up a ferocious fight.

Because Kansas lies along the central flyway, the lake margins attract many migrating waterfowl. Bird **hunting** is good near Great Bend at Cheyenne Bottoms, where mallards, pintails and teals nest in the marshes.

In the fall hunters find an abundance of ring-necked pheasants, bobwhites, white-tailed deer and cottontails at Wilson Lake, north of Wilson. Greater prairie chickens are found in the Flint Hills, while lesser prairie chickens inhabit southwestern counties.

Contact the Kansas Department of Wildlife and Parks for information about hunting and fishing regulations and licensing; phone (620) 672-5911.

All Ready to Ride

If you enjoy **bicycling,** the state offers loads of trails to keep you occupied. For a leisurely ride, try the Prairie Spirit Rail Trail, which runs between Ottawa and Welda. Passes are available for a nominal fee at several trail heads along the route. For a more grueling **mountain biking** adventure head to Clinton Lake, southwest of Lawrence, where the 25-mile loop teems with protruding rocks, thick vegetation and soft soil.

To experience Kansas as the pioneers did, saddle up a horse and head to Horsethief Canyon in Kanopolis State Park. The park's 26 miles of multiuse trails are ideal for **horseback riding.** A 22-mile horseback trail follows the south side of Melvern Reservoir, south of Osage City.

Three **hiking** trails wind through the woods in Toronto State Park in Toronto. To traverse the prairie, wander the 6 miles of trails through the grasses at Prairie Center State Park, near Olathe. For a breathtaking panorama, climb atop the red buttes and mesas of the Gypsum Hills in south-central Kansas and gaze upon fields of golden wheat.

Although it won't require much of an expenditure of sweat, an ascent up the state's highest point—4,039-foot Mount Sunflower, near the Colorado border in Wallace County—might provide some comic relief. At the less-than-daunting summit is a sunflower crafted of rail spikes, a rail fence and a mailbox that holds a log in which you can record your impressive feat.

As far as spectator sports go, **greyhound racing** is high on the list with many Kansans. The state is among the primary breeding centers for the sleek dogs. In late April and early October check out National Greyhound Meets.

Recreational Activities

Throughout the TourBook, you may notice a Recreational Activities heading with bulleted listings of recreation-oriented establishments listed underneath. Similar operations also may be mentioned in Destination City recreation sections. Since normal AAA inspection criteria cannot be applied, these establishments are presented only for information. Age, height and weight restrictions may apply. Reservations often are recommended and sometimes are required. Addresses and/or phone numbers are provided so visitors can contact the attraction for additional information.

Fast Facts

POPULATION: 2,688,418.

AREA: 82,264 square miles; ranks 14th.

CAPITAL: Topeka.

HIGHEST POINT: 4,039 ft., Mount Sunflower.

LOWEST POINT: 680 ft., Verdigris River.

TIME ZONE(S): Central/Mountain. DST.

MINIMUM AGE FOR UNRE-STRICTED DRIVER'S LICENSE: 14 years, 6 months.

SEAT BELT/CHILD RESTRAINT LAWS: Seat belts required for driver and front-seat passengers 14 and older. Children ages 8-13, over 80 pounds and over 57 inches are required to be in a seat belt; child restraints are required for under age 8, less than 80 pounds and less than 57 inches.

HELMETS FOR MOTORCY-CLISTS: Required for riders under 18.

RADAR DETECTORS: Permitted.

FIREARMS LAWS: Vary by state and/or county. Contact the Kansas Highway Patrol, 122 S.W. 7th St., Topeka, KS 66603; phone (785) 296-3102.

HOLIDAYS: Jan. 1; Martin Luther King Jr. Day, Jan. (3rd Mon.); Memorial Day, May (last Mon.); July 4; Labor Day, Sept. (1st Mon.); Veterans Day, Nov. 11; Thanksgiving, Nov. (last Thurs.); Christmas, Dec. 25.

TAXES: The Kansas statewide sales tax is 5.3 percent, with local options for an additional increment up to 2 percent. Cities and counties also may levy a tax on lodgings; rates range from 1 to 5 percent.

INFORMATION CENTERS: State welcome centers are at Belle Plaine on I-35N; I-70E Milepost 7 at Goodland; and I-70W Milepost 410 in Kansas City. Most information centers are open daily year-round except holidays.

FURTHER INFORMATION FOR VISITORS:

Kansas Department of Commerce
Travel and Tourism Development Division
1000 S.W. Jackson St., Suite 100
Topeka, KS 66612-1354
(785) 296-2009
TTY (785) 296-3487

RECREATION INFORMATION:

Kansas Department of Wildlife and Parks
512 S.E. 25th Ave.
Pratt, KS 67124-8147
(620) 672-5911

FISHING AND HUNTING REGULATIONS:

Kansas Department of Wildlife and Parks
512 S.E. 25th Ave.
Pratt, KS 67124-9599
(620) 672-5911

ROAD AND WEATHER INFORMATION:

(800) 585-7623 511 inside Kansas

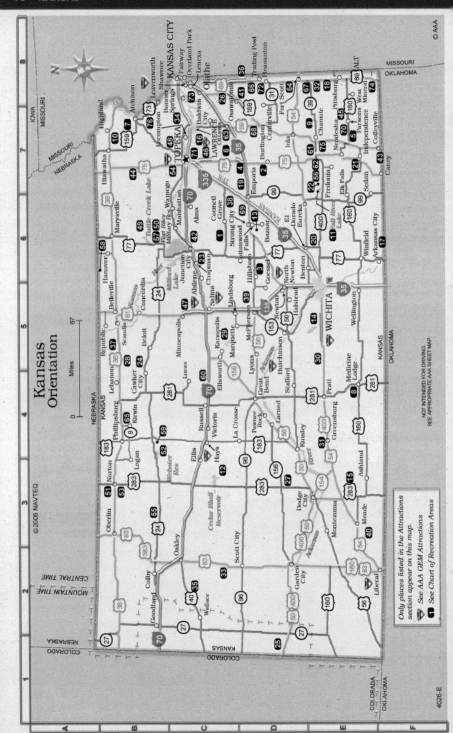

Points of Interest Offering A *Great Experience for Members*®

Abilene (C-5)

EISENHOWER CENTER—The center comprises five buildings: a visitor center, the Eisenhower Home, the Eisenhower Museum, a presidential library and the Place of Meditation. See p. 75.

Hays (C-3)

STERNBERG MUSEUM OF NATURAL HISTORY—One of the world's best collections of fossilized prehistoric flying reptiles is found here, along with life-size animated dinosaurs. Don't miss the fish-within-a-fish fossil. See p. 88.

Hutchinson (D-5)

KANSAS COSMOSPHERE AND SPACE CENTER—Among the center's displays are Apollo, Gemini and Mercury spacecraft; items from NASA missions; satellites; rocket engines; and reportedly the largest collection of Russian space suits in the United States. See p. 90.

Lawrence (C-7)

NATURAL HISTORY MUSEUM AND BIODIVERSITY RESEARCH CENTER—The museum displays birds, fossils and mounted animals primarily from Kansas and the Plains states, including Comanche, a horse that survived Lt. Col. George Custer's Last Stand. See p. 93.

SPENCER MUSEUM OF ART—Strengths of the museum include Renaissance and baroque paintings; American paintings and sculpture; decorative arts; and graphic arts, including photographs and Japanese prints. See p. 93.

Leavenworth (B-8)

FRONTIER ARMY MUSEUM—Exhibits detail the development of Fort Leavenworth; the history of the frontier army; and the Civil, Mexican and Indian wars. Included is the carriage in which Abraham Lincoln rode while visiting the town. See p. 94.

Liberal (E-2)

MID-AMERICA AIR MUSEUM LIBERAL, KANSAS—World War II fighters and bombers, experimental and golden age aircraft, and planes used in the Korean and Vietnam wars are characteristic of the aerospace and aviation exhibits. See p. 95.

North Newton (D-6)

KAUFFMAN MUSEUM—Historic buildings on the 5-acre site include a late 19th-century homesteader's log cabin, an 1886 barn and a Kansas farmstead with an 1875 house. See p. 100.

Salina (C-5)

ROLLING HILLS WILDLIFE ADVENTURE—Situated on 95 acres of Kansas prairie, this center presents some 80 species of rare or endangered animals in re-created natural habitats. See p. 103.

Topeka (C-7)

KANSAS HISTORY MUSEUM AND LIBRARY—Western and Kansas historical topics are presented through an extensive collection of artifacts, exhibits and research materials. See p. 105.

STATE CAPITOL—Built of native limestone in the French Renaissance style, the Capitol boasts an impressive collection of artwork, including murals by John Steuart Curry, David H. Overmyer and Lumen Martin Winter. See p. 106.

Wichita (E-5)

EXPLORATION PLACE—Catch a planetarium show or explore exhibits relating to flight, health, imagination and the environment. See p. 109.

MUSEUM OF WORLD TREASURES—Crown jewels, dinosaur skeletons, mummies, Civil War relics—find all these and more at this treasure trove. See p. 109.

SEDGWICK COUNTY ZOO—In addition to habitats for elephants, baboons, giraffes, lions and reptiles, the zoo offers the 12-acre North American Prairie and its resident bears, wolves and bison. See p. 109.

RECREATION AREAS

	MAP LOCATION	CAMPING	PICNICKING	HIKING TRAILS	BOATING	BOAT RAMP	BOAT RENTAL	FISHING	SWIMMING	PETS ON LEASH	BICYCLE TRAILS	WINTER SPORTS	VISITOR CENTER	LODGE/CABINS	FOOD SERVICE
ARMY CORPS OF ENGINEERS															
Council Grove Reservoir (C-6) 3,280 acres in Council Grove.	1	•	•	•	•	•		•	•	•			•		
John Redmond Reservoir (D-7) 9,400 acres 2 mi. n., then 1 mi. w. of Burlington off US 75. Hunting, water skiing.	2	•	•		•	•		•	•	•			•		
Marion Reservoir (D-6) 6,200 acres 3 mi. n.w. of Marion on the Cottonwood River off US 56.	3	•	•		•	•	•	•	•	•			•		
Melvern Lake (D-7) 6,930 acres 30 mi. e. of Emporia off SR 276.	4	•	•	•	•	•	•	•	•	•	•		•	•	•
Pearson-Skubitz Big Hill Lake (E-7) 1,200 acres 4.5 mi. e. of Cherryvale off county roads.	5	•	•	•	•	•		•	•	•			•		
Pomona Lake (C-7) 4,000 acres 2 mi. n.e. of Vassar on SR 268.	6	•	•	•	•	•	•	•	•	•	•	•	•		•
STATE															
Atchison State Fishing Lake (B-7) 248 acres 3.5 mi. n. and 2 mi. w. of Atchison off SR 7 at 318th St.	7	•	•		•	•		•		•					
Barber State Fishing Lake (E-4) 190 acres .2 mi. n. of Medicine Lodge off US 281.	8	•	•		•	•		•		•					
Bourbon State Fishing Lake (E-7) 380 acres 4 mi. e. of Elsmore off US 59.	9	•	•		•	•		•		•					
Brown State Fishing Lake (B-7) 189 acres 8 mi. s.e. of Hiawatha off US 36.	10	•	•		•			•		•					
Butler State Fishing Lake (E-6) 351 acres 3 mi. n.w. of Latham off a county road.	11	•	•		•	•		•		•					
Cedar Bluff (C-3) 6,869 acres 36 mi. s.w. of Hays off SR 147.	12	•	•		•	•		•	•	•					•
Chase State Fishing Lake (D-6) 492 acres 2 mi. e. of Elmdale in Flint Hills.	13	•	•		•	•		•		•					
Cheney (E-5) 9,238 acres 20 mi. w. of Wichita via US 54 and SR 251.	14	•	•		•	•	•	•	•	•					•
Clark State Fishing Lake (E-3) 1,243 acres 11 mi. s.w. of Kingsdown on SR 94.	15	•	•		•	•		•		•					
Clinton Lake (C-7) 7,000 acres 4 mi. w. of Lawrence off US 40.	16	•	•	•	•	•	•	•	•	•	•	•	•		•
Cowley State Fishing Lake (F-6) 197 acres 13 mi. e. of Arkansas City off US 166.	17	•	•		•			•		•					•
Crawford (E-8) 418 acres 4 mi. n. of Pittsburg off US 69.	18	•	•		•	•		•	•	•					
Douglas State Fishing Lake (D-7) 718 acres n.e. of Baldwin City on US 56.	19	•	•		•	•		•		•					•
El Dorado (E-6) 8,000 acres 3 mi. e., then 2 mi. n. of El Dorado on US 77 off US 54. Nature trail.	20	•	•	•	•	•		•	•	•					
Elk City Reservoir and State Park (E-7) 4,100 acres 7 mi. n.w. of Independence off US 75.	21	•	•	•	•	•		•	•	•	•				
Fall River (E-7) 2,350 acres n.w. of Fall River next to Fall River Reservoir.	22	•	•	•	•	•		•	•	•		•			
Geary State Fishing Lake (C-6) 415 acres 9 mi. s. of Junction City off US 77.	23	•	•		•	•		•		•					
Glen Elder (B-5) 25,100 acres 12 mi. w. of Beloit on US 24.	24	•	•		•	•	•	•	•	•		•	•		
Hamilton State Fishing Lake (D-1) 3 mi. w., then 2 mi. n. of Syracuse off US 50.	25	•	•		•			•		•					
Hillsdale Lake (C-8) 4,580 acres 9 mi. n.w. of Paola off US 169.	26		•	•	•	•		•		•			•		
Hodgeman State Fishing Lake (D-3) 87 acres 2 mi. s. of Jetmore on US 283.	27	•						•		•					
Jewell State Fishing Lake (B-5) 165 acres 10 mi. s.w. of Mankato on a county road.	28	•	•		•	•		•		•					
Kanopolis (C-5) 3,500 acres 12 mi. s.e. of Kanopolis off SR 141.	29	•	•	•	•	•	•	•	•	•		•	•		
Kingman State Fishing Lake (E-5) 4,529 acres 8 mi. w. of Kingman on US 54.	30	•	•	•	•	•		•		•					
Kiowa State Fishing Lake (E-4) 43 acres just n.w. of Greensburg on Bay St.	31	•	•					•		•					

RECREATION AREAS

Recreation Area	MAP LOCATION	CAMPING	PICNICKING	HIKING TRAILS	BOATING	BOAT RAMP	BOAT RENTAL	FISHING	SWIMMING	PETS ON LEASH	BICYCLE TRAILS	WINTER SPORTS	VISITOR CENTER	LODGE/CABINS	FOOD SERVICE
Lake Crawford (E-8) 460 acres 2 mi. n. of Farlington off SR 7.	32	•	•		•	•	•	•	•	•					•
Lake Scott (C-2) 925 acres 12 mi. n. of Scott City via US 83 and SR 95. *(See Scott City p. 104)*	33	•	•	•	•	•	•	•	•	•					•
Leavenworth State Fishing Lake (C-7) 506 acres 3 mi. w. and 1 mi. n. of Tonganoxie on SR 16.	34	•	•		•	•	•	•		•					
Logan State Fishing Lake (C-2) 271 acres 4 mi. n.w. of Russell Springs off SR 25.	35	•	•		•	•		•		•					
Louisburg-Middle Creek State Fishing Lake (D-8) 281 acres 7 mi. s. of Louisburg on Metcalf Rd.	36	•	•		•	•		•		•					
Lovewell (B-5) 5,215 acres 15 mi. n.e. of Mankato off SR 14.	37	•	•		•	•	•	•	•	•			•		•
Lyon State Fishing Lake (C-6) 582 acres 11 mi. n.e. of Emporia on SR 170.	38	•	•		•	•		•		•					
McPherson State Fishing Lake (D-5) 2,560 acres 8 mi. n. of Canton off SR 86.	39	•	•	•	•	•		•		•					
Meade (E-3) 1,240 acres 12 mi. s.w. of Meade off SR 23.	40	•	•			•	•	•	•	•					
Miami State Fishing Lake (D-8) 267 acres 8 mi. e., then 5 mi. s. of Osawatomie off county roads.	41	•	•					•		•					
Milford (C-6) 15,600 acres 4 mi. n.w. of Junction City on SR 57. Nature trails.	42	•	•	•	•	•	•	•	•	•			•	•	•
Montgomery State Fishing Lake (F-7) 408 acres 4 mi. s. of Independence via county road.	43	•	•		•	•		•		•					•
Nebo Watershed State Fishing Lake (B-7) 7 mi. e., then 1 mi. s. of Holton on SR 116.	44	•	•					•		•					
Neosho State Fishing Lake (E-7) 216 acres 7 mi. n.e. of Parsons off US 59.	45	•	•	•	•	•		•		•					
Osage State Fishing Lake (C-7) 506 acres 3 mi. s. of Carbondale off US 75.	46	•	•		•	•		•		•					
Ottawa State Fishing Lake (C-5) 711 acres 8 mi. e. of Minneapolis on SR 93.	47	•	•		•	•		•		•					•
Perry (C-7) 11,100 acres 16 mi. n.e. of Topeka off US 24. ATV area.	48	•	•		•	•	•	•	•	•			•		•
Pottawatomie State Fishing Lake No. 1 (B-6) 190 acres 5 mi. n. of Westmoreland on SR 99.	49	•	•		•	•		•		•					
Pottawatomie State Fishing Lake No. 2 (B-6) 247 acres 4 mi. n. of Manhattan off US 24.	50	•	•		•	•		•		•					
Prairie Dog (B-3) 1,000 acres 4 mi. w. of Norton on US 36. Historical.	51	•	•		•	•	•	•	•	•					
Rooks State Fishing Lake (B-4) 313 acres 5 mi. s.w. of Stockton off US 183.	52	•	•		•	•		•		•					
Sebelius Reservoir (B-3) 700 acres 3 mi. w. of Norton off US 36. Also known as Norton Reservoir.	53	•	•		•	•		•	•	•	•				•
Shawnee State Fishing Lake (C-7) 608 acres 3 mi. n.e. of Silver Lake off US 24.	54	•	•		•	•		•		•					
Sheridan State Fishing Lake (B-3) 335 acres 3 mi. w. of Studley off US 24.	55	•	•	•	•	•		•		•					
Toronto (E-7) 2,660 acres 17 mi. w. of Yates Center off US 54.	56	•	•	•	•	•		•	•	•			•		
Tuttle Creek (B-6) 13,350 acres 5 mi. n. of Manhattan on SR 177.	57	•	•		•	•		•	•	•			•		•
Washington State Fishing Lake (B-6) 463 acres 10 mi. n.w. of Washington off county roads.	58	•	•		•	•		•		•					
Webster (B-4) 7,539 acres 8 mi. w. of Stockton off US 24.	59	•	•	•	•	•		•	•	•	•				•
Wilson Lake (C-4) 18,086 acres 10 mi. n. of Wilson via SR 232.	60	•	•	•	•	•	•	•	•	•	•		•		•
Wilson State Fishing Lake (E-7) 291 acres 1.5 mi. s.e. of Buffalo on US 75.	61	•	•		•	•		•		•					
Woodson State Fishing Lake (E-7) 2,885 acres 10 mi. s.w. of Yates Center off US 54.	62	•	•	•	•	•	•	•		•					•

RECREATION AREAS

	MAP LOCATION	CAMPING	PICNICKING	HIKING TRAILS	BOATING	BOAT RAMP	BOAT RENTAL	FISHING	SWIMMING	PETS ON LEASH	BICYCLE TRAILS	WINTER SPORTS	VISITOR CENTER	LODGE/CABINS	FOOD SERVICE
OTHER															
Forest Park (C-7) 50 acres off Tecumseh and N. Locust sts. at Ottawa on the Marais des Cygnes River.	63		•					•	•						
Gunn Park (D-8) 155 acres on the w. side of Fort Scott. Paddleboats. *(See Fort Scott p. 85)*	64	•	•					•		•					
Kirwin Reservoir (B-4) 3,700 acres 15 mi. s.e. of Phillipsburg on SR 9.	65	•	•		•	•		•	•						
La Cygne Lake (D-8) 2,600 acres 5 mi. e. of La Cygne off US 69.	66	•	•		•	•	•	•	•						
Lake Fort Scott (E-8) 360 acres 4 mi. s.w. of Fort Scott on Lake Rd.	67		•		•	•		•	•						
Lake Garnett (D-7) 55 acres in downtown Garnett. Golf, tennis, water skiing.	68	•	•	•	•	•		•	•						
Lake Kahola (D-6) 405 acres 22 mi. n.w. of Emporia.	69	•	•		•	•		•	•	•					
Lake Parsons (E-7) 2,200 acres 4 mi. n., then 3.5 mi. w. of Parsons on a county road.	70		•	•				•	•						
Lake Shawnee (C-7) 410 acres s.e. of Topeka just outside city limits on E. 29th St.	71		•					•	•						
Marais Des Cygnes Waterfowl Refuge (D-8) 7 mi. n. of Pleasanton off US 69.	72		•	•				•							
Prairie Center (C-8) 300 acres .5 mi. w. of Olathe at 135th and Cedar.	73		•	•				•					•		
Riverside Park (E-8) In downtown Baxter Springs. Golf, tennis; playground.	74	•	•		•	•		•	•						
Santa Fe Park (E-7) 249 acres 2 mi. s. of Chanute on Santa Fe St.	75	•	•			•		•	•						
Warnock Lake (B-7) 2 mi. s.w. of Atchison.	76	•	•					•	•						

Kansas Temperature Averages
Maximum/Minimum
From the records of The Weather Channel Interactive, Inc.

	JAN	FEB	MAR	APR	MAY	JUN	JUL	AUG	SEP	OCT	NOV	DEC
Concordia	37 / 19	42 / 22	51 / 30	64 / 43	74 / 53	85 / 64	92 / 69	90 / 68	81 / 58	70 / 46	52 / 32	42 / 23
Dodge City	42 / 20	47 / 23	54 / 29	66 / 41	76 / 52	87 / 62	93 / 67	92 / 67	83 / 58	71 / 46	55 / 30	46 / 24
Goodland	41 / 14	45 / 17	50 / 23	62 / 34	72 / 45	83 / 55	92 / 61	90 / 60	81 / 50	69 / 38	52 / 24	44 / 17
Topeka	35 / 19	44 / 23	53 / 30	66 / 43	76 / 53	86 / 64	92 / 68	90 / 67	82 / 57	71 / 45	54 / 31	43 / 24
Wichita	42 / 22	47 / 26	56 / 33	68 / 45	77 / 55	88 / 65	92 / 69	93 / 69	84 / 59	72 / 48	55 / 34	45 / 27

Points of Interest

ABILENE (C-5) pop. 6,543, elev. 1,155'

Though its name is of biblical origin, Abilene once was one of the unholiest and wildest towns in the West. Its reputation grew along with the city as hundreds of cowboys came to the town along the historic Chisholm Trail during the late 1800s. Nearly 3 million Texas longhorns passed through Abilene 1867-72 to be shipped east by rail. James "Wild Bill" Hickok, whose deadly accuracy with two pistols was as legendary as his icy willingness to use them, was marshal of the town in 1871.

Still, fame was not quite through with the City on the Plains; Dwight David Eisenhower, first the Supreme Allied Commander during World War II and then the 34th president of the United States, spent his boyhood years in Abilene. As president, he signed a truce to end the Korean War and passed the Federal Aid Highway Act in 1956, which created the present-day interstate highway system.

Eisenhower Park, a 60-acre tract near W. Third and Poplar sts., includes Tom Smith Stadium; a swimming pool; basketball, tennis and sand volleyball courts; picnic grounds; and landscaped gardens. Phone (785) 263-7266.

Glimpses of Abilene's past can be seen at Seelye Mansion, at 1105 N. Buckeye Ave. Great Plains Theatre Festival, a professional regional company, presents Broadway plays June through December in Tietjens Center for the Performing Arts; phone (785) 263-4574. The city also is a major center for greyhound enthusiasts.

Abilene Convention & Visitors Bureau: 201 N.W. Second St., Abilene, KS 67410; phone (785) 263-2231 or (800) 569-5915.

Self-guiding tours: A free brochure detailing a tour past the historic houses of Abilene and Dickinson County is available from the visitors bureau and from Dickinson County Heritage Center and Museum (see attraction listing).

ABILENE & SMOKY VALLEY RAILROAD departs from the 1887 Rock Island Depot at 200 S. 5th St. A 10-mile train ride travels over the rolling flatlands between Abilene and Enterprise. Featured are a restored 1900s wooden dining car, an open-air gondola car, a caboose and a 1945 diesel locomotive.

Allow 1 hour, 30 minutes minimum. Departures Tues.-Sat. at 10 and 2, Sun. at 2, Memorial Day-Labor Day; Sat. at 10 and 2, Sun. at 2, May 1-day before Memorial Day and day after Labor Day-Oct. 31. Fare $12; ages 3-11, $6. DS, MC, VI. Phone (785) 263-0118 or (888) 426-6687.

DICKINSON COUNTY HERITAGE CENTER AND MUSEUM is at 412 S. Campbell St.; the Museum of Independent Telephony (see attraction listing) is in the same building. Early agricultural, cow town, homemaking and industry relics illustrate pioneer life in Dickinson County. The museum also includes an outdoor area featuring an antique carousel, a blacksmith exhibit and a log cabin.

Mon.-Fri. 9-6, Sat. 10-7, Sun. 1-5, Memorial Day-Labor Day; Mon.-Fri. 9-3, Sat. 10-5, Sun. 1-5, rest of year. Closed Jan. 1, Thanksgiving, Sun. after Thanksgiving and Dec. 25. Admission $4; over 61, $3; ages 2-15, $2. Carousel $2. MC, VI. Phone (785) 263-2681.

EISENHOWER CENTER, 2 mi. s. of I-70 on SR 15 at S.E. Fourth St., covers 22 acres of landscaped grounds. The center consists of five buildings, including the visitor center, in which a 23-minute orientation film is shown. Allow 3 hours minimum. Daily 8-5:45, Memorial Day to mid-Aug.; 9-4:45, rest of year. Closed Jan. 1, Thanksgiving and Dec. 25. Visitor center free. Phone (785) 263-6700 or (877) 746-4453.

Eisenhower Home, S.E. Fourth St., was the boyhood home of President Dwight David Eisenhower. Representative of family houses in Kansas during the late 19th century, the frame house is kept as it was in 1946. Free.

Eisenhower Museum, next to the Eisenhower Home, is constructed of Kansas limestone and contains items relating to President Dwight David Eisenhower's life and experiences from boyhood to the post-presidential years. Murals in the lobby depict events from Eisenhower's life and career. Admission $8; over 61, $6; ages 8-15, $1. AX, CB, DC, DS, MC, VI.

Eisenhower Presidential Library, opposite Eisenhower Museum, houses the papers, books and historical materials accumulated by Eisenhower during his term of office. The extensive use of imported marble in the building's interior is offset by the Kansas limestone of the exterior. Free.

Place of Meditation, s. of the visitor center and w. of the library, is the final resting place of Dwight D. and Mamie Doud Eisenhower and their son, Doud Dwight Eisenhower. Daily 8-5:45, Memorial Day weekend to mid-Aug.; 9-4:45, rest of year. Free.

GREYHOUND HALL OF FAME, 2 mi. s. of I-70 via SR 15 to 407 S. Buckeye Ave. (across from Eisenhower Center), has many displays about racing and greyhound dogs from ancient times to the present, including a miniature dog track display. Two resident greyhounds are on the grounds. Highlights include interactive exhibits and a 12-minute orientation film. The Hall of Fame honors legendary greyhounds from around the world as well as pioneers of the sport. Allow 1 hour minimum. Daily

9-5; closed Jan. 1, Thanksgiving and Dec. 25. Donations. Phone (785) 263-3000.

SAVE **LEBOLD MANSION** is at 106 N. Vine St. The imposing Italianate five-story mansion was built in 1880 using native Kansas orange limestone. Each room has been carefully restored and is decorated to reflect different styles of the Victorian era. Guided tours, which focus on the history of the house and its owners, escort guests into public rooms, private family quarters and servants' areas.

Allow 1 hour, 30 minutes minimum. Tues.-Sun. 10-4, day after Easter-Dec. 31; Fri.-Sun. 10-4, rest of year. Closed Jan. 1 and Dec. 25. Admission $10; senior citizens $9; ages 13-18, $5; ages 6-12, $3. Phone (785) 263-4356.

MUSEUM OF INDEPENDENT TELEPHONY is at 412 S. Campbell St., in the same building as Dickinson County Heritage Center and Museum *(see attraction listing)*. The museum relates the history of the telephone and its early independent proprietors since the original patent was issued to Alexander Graham Bell in 1876. Included are interactive exhibits of antique phones, insulators and switchboards. Half-hour guided tours are available by advance request.

Mon.-Fri. 9-5, Sat. 10-8, Sun. 1-5, Memorial Day-Labor Day; Mon.-Fri. 9-4, Sat. 10-5, Sun. 1-5, rest of year. Closed Jan. 1, Thanksgiving and Dec. 25. Admission $4; over 61, $3; ages 2-15, $2. MC, VI. Phone (785) 263-2681.

ALMA (C-6) pop. 797, elev. 1,053'

WABAUNSEE COUNTY HISTORICAL MUSEUM, 227 Missouri St., presents exhibits relating to the county's history. A children's room, dentist's office, general store, textile shop and schoolroom reflect the early 1900s. Displays include American Indian artifacts, a World War II exhibit featuring Kansas native Gen. Lewis Walt, a 1926 Model T car, washing machines, quilts, typewriters and a 1923 Reo fire truck. Genealogy information also is offered. Tues.-Sat. 10-4, Sun. 1-4; closed holidays. Donations. Phone (785) 765-2200.

ARKANSAS CITY (E-6)
pop. 11,963, elev. 1,075'

Arkansas (ar-KAN-sas) City's position, 4 miles north of the present Oklahoma border, made it a logical mustering point for one of the largest land rushes in the history of westward expansion. By the tens of thousands they lined up—eager boomers and homesteaders afoot, on horseback and with every horse-drawn conveyance possible—awaiting the gunshot that would signal the opening of the Cherokee Strip in 1893.

As the West lost its wildness, Arkansas City became what its Arkansas River site promised—a marketing and transportation center. The discovery of oil in the vicinity in the early 20th century added the refineries and other petroleum-related industries that dominated the economy through the middle part of the century.

Arkansas City Area Chamber of Commer and Convention and Visitors Center: 106 Summit, P.O. Box 795, Arkansas City, KS 6700 phone (620) 442-0230 or (620) 442-0236.

CHAPLIN NATURE CENTER, 3 mi. w. via US 16 then 2 mi. n. at 27814 27th Dr., features 5 miles nature trails that meander alongside the Arkans River and through 230 acres of creek, prairie a forest terrain. A visitor center contains a nature brary and educational displays. Events are offer throughout the year. Allow 1 hour minimum. Visit center Tues.-Sat. 9-5, Sun. 1-5, Mar. 15-June 30 a Sept. 1-Nov. 15; Tues.-Fri. 10-2, Sat. 9-5, July-Au Sat. 9-5, Sun. 1-5, rest of year. Closed holiday Trails daily dawn-dusk. Donations. Phone (62 442-4133.

SAVE **CHEROKEE STRIP LAND RUSH MUSEU** 1.5 mi. s. on US 77, depicts the Sept. 1 1893, land run in which 150,000 settlers raced claim more than 6 million acres. An extensive co lection of documents, photographs and other ar facts depicts pioneer life in the area and in t Oklahoma Territory. Tues.-Sat. 10-5; closed ho days. Admission $4.50; over 54, $3.50; ages 6-1 $2. Phone (620) 442-6750.

ASHLAND (E-3) pop. 975, elev. 1,950'

In 1884 a group of Kentuckians decided that town at the junction of two major frontier trails-one from Texas to Fort Dodge, one from Santa F N.M., to Sun City on the Medicine River—woul prove profitable. The community took its name fro Ashland, Ky., and its livelihood from supplying th countless traders, immigrants, soldiers and cowbo who plied these frontier throughways.

Its reputation for unruliness gone with the catt drives, Ashland serves as a center of governme and commerce for the surrounding Red Hills whe farms and cattle ranches. On the east side of th courthouse at 9th and Highland streets, historic trai and other points of interest in Clark County are ind cated on a 20-foot-high engraved relief map.

West of town, northeast of the intersection of U 160 and US 283, lie Big and Little basins. Both ba sins are sinkholes—Kansans call them sinks—cre ated by subsidence as subterranean erosio undermined the surface stratum. Big Basin is 10 feet deep and about a mile wide. Nearby Little Ba sin is marked by St. Jacob's Well, a 125-foot-wid pool that never has been known to dry. It was a vit watering hole for American Indians and pioneers.

Ashland Chamber of Commerce: P.O. Box 37 Ashland, KS 67831; phone (620) 635-2680.

PIONEER-KRIER MUSEUM, w. of Main St. on U 160, displays historical items in late 19th-centur room settings. Among a collection of bridle bits one of Spanish design that is thought to have be longed to a member of Coronado's expedition Other collections include barbed wire, fossilize

ınes, American Indian artifacts and musical instru-
ents. Also featured are memorabilia from track star
es Santee and other notable Kansans.

Allow 1 hour minimum. Mon.-Fri. 10-noon and
5, Sat.-Sun. by appointment; closed Jan. 1,
ıanksgiving and Dec. 25. Donations. Phone (620)
5-2227.

TCHISON (B-7) pop. 10,232, elev. 798′

Independence Park, on the Atchison riverfront,
arks where the Meriwether Lewis and William
ark expedition arrived on July 4, 1804. Five miles
the north lies Independence Creek, so named by
lark to commemorate the first Independence Day
lebrated west of the Mississippi River. Independ-
ıce Creek Lewis and Clark Historic Site at 19917
4th Rd. encompasses a portion of Independence
reek including its confluence with Deer Creek, a
ot Capt. William Clark specifically referred to in
804. A 10-mile hiking and bicycling trail connects
ıe historic site with Independence Park.

Among the city's founders years after Lewis and
lark's travels were Benedictine monks, who estab-
shed an abbey on the north bluffs, and the Ben-
lictine Sisters, who started a convent. Atchison is
nown for the Atchison, Topeka & Santa Fe Rail-
ay, but before the railroad a steady stream of
agon and river traffic fed the infant town.

A marker at the Atchison courthouse commemo-
ites a speech that Abraham Lincoln gave in 1859
nd later delivered in the Cooper Union in New
ork City. The address brought Lincoln the recogni-
on that resulted in his presidential nomination.

Atchison is the birthplace of Amelia Earhart, and
ıonuments to the aviator can be seen at the down-
ıwn pedestrian mall, the International Forest of
riendship and Amelia Earhart Memorial Airport, 3
ıiles west. The Amelia Earhart Birthplace *(see at-
action listing)* overlooks the Missouri River.

The International Forest of Friendship honors
viation and aerospace pioneers. It features trees
presenting the 50 states, U.S. territories and 40
ıreign countries. A "moon tree" grown from a
ycamore seed taken to the moon on *Apollo 14*
ıarks a memorial dedicated to the ill-fated Apollo
nd Challenger crews. Memory Lane winds through
ıe forest and offers tributes to Earhart, Charles
indbergh, the Wright Brothers and others.

The campus of Benedictine College, on the bluffs
f the Missouri River, offers excellent views. Of in-
erest near the campus are St. Benedict's Abbey,
/hich is modeled after Benedictine monasteries of
ıe Middle Ages, and the Abbey Chapel, which has
8 minor altars in its crypt.

Nearby Warnock Lake *(see Recreation Chart)*
eatures swimming, fishing, camping and picnic fa-
ilities. Just 3.5 miles north and 2 miles west of
ıwn on SR 7 to 318th Street is Atchison State Fish-
ıg Lake *(See Recreation Chart and the AAA South
'entral CampBook)*, which also offers camping.

Atchison Convention and Visitors Bureau: 200
S. 10th St., P.O. Box 126, Atchison, KS 66002;
phone (913) 367-2427 or (800) 234-1854.

AMELIA EARHART BIRTHPLACE, overlooking
the Missouri River at Santa Fe and N. Terrace sts.,
is the house where Amelia Earhart was born in 1897
and lived until she was 12. The 1859 Victorian cottage on the bluffs of the Missouri River was owned
by Earhart's grandparents. The house contains photographs, newspaper clippings and some of Earhart's
belongings. Allow 30 minutes minimum. Mon.-Fri.
9-4, Sat. 10-4, Sun. 1-4. Admission $3; under 13,
50c. Phone (913) 367-4217.

**ATCHISON COUNTY HISTORICAL SOCIETY
MUSEUM** is in the 1880s Santa Fe Depot at 200 S.
10th St. Displays explore local history, especially
the Lewis and Clark expedition. Amelia Earhart
memorabilia, railroad artifacts and a 200-piece gun
collection are among the collectibles. Guided tours
are available by request. Mon.-Fri. 8-5, Sat. 9-5,
Sun. 10-5, May 1-Nov. 1; Mon.-Fri. 8-5, Sat. 10-4,
Sun. 11-4, rest of year. Donations. Phone (913)
367-6238.

EVAH C. CRAY HISTORICAL HOME MUSEUM,
805 N. Fifth St., was built in 1882 and resembles a
Scottish castle. The restored three-story house contains 19th-century period rooms filled with antiques
and memorabilia. An 18-minute videotape highlighting Atchison's historic homes and buildings is presented in the carriage house. Allow 1 hour, 30
minutes minimum. Mon.-Sat. 10-4, Sun. 1-4, May-
Oct. and early Dec. to mid-Dec.; Mon. and Fri.-Sat.
10-4, Sun. 1-4, Mar.-Apr.; by appointment rest of
year. Admission $2. Phone (913) 367-3046.

DID YOU KNOW

Aviatrix
Amelia Earhart
hailed from
Atchison.

BALDWIN CITY (C-7) pop. 3,400

Baldwin City, located on the Santa Fe Trail, was the scene of one of many bloody clashes between pro-slavery and anti-slavery factions in the state's territorial days. The battle, which some call one of the first of the Civil War, took place in nearby Black Jack Park in 1856. John Brown and his anti-slavery troops interceded, sending the agitators home and releasing their prisoners.

In the Ivan Boyd Prairie Preserve, wagon ruts carved by Conestogas that traveled west on the trail 1825-75 can be seen. Serving as a more modern path, the town's brick streets were laid in 1925-26 by master craftsman Jim Garfield Brown, an Oneida Indian.

Douglas State Fishing Lake is nearby. *See Recreation Chart and the AAA South Central CampBook.*

Baldwin City Chamber of Commerce: 720 High St., P.O. Box 501, Baldwin City, KS 66006; phone (785) 594-3200.

BAKER UNIVERSITY, 618 Eighth St., is the state's oldest 4-year college and has an enrollment of approximately 900. One of its earliest donations was $100 received in 1864 from Abraham Lincoln. An old English church was reconstructed and is open for viewing at Sixth and Fremont streets. Visitors are welcomed on the campus; tours can be arranged. Phone (785) 594-6451 or (800) 873-4282.

Old Castle, 511 Fifth St. on the Baker University campus, is the oldest college building in the state and now houses a museum with exhibits about early Kansas and the Santa Fe Trail. Mon.-Fri. 8-4:30 and by appointment. Donations. Phone (785) 594-8380.

MIDLAND RAILWAY is off US 56, s. on 11th St., then w. to 1515 W. High St. Presidents William Howard Taft and Theodore Roosevelt visited the 1906 brick and stone Santa Fe Depot, which includes triple-arched windows, a coal fireplace and dual gas/electric lighting systems. Built in 1867, the line was the first railroad south of the Kansas River. Visitors ride on restored 1900s locomotives, coaches and cabooses as they travel through woods and farmland and over a 200-foot-long bridge.

Allow 2 hours minimum. Trains depart for Norwood Thurs. at 10:30, Sat.-Sun. and holidays at 11, last weekend in May-last weekend in Oct. Trains depart for Ottawa Junction Sat.-Sun. at 1 and 3:30, last weekend in May-last weekend in Oct. Fare to Norwood $10; ages 4-12, $5. Fare to Ottawa Junction $15; ages 4-12, $7. Phone (913) 371-3410, (785) 594-6982 or (800) 651-0388.

QUAYLE BIBLE COLLECTION is in the Collins Library on the Baker University campus. Exhibits include rare biblical manuscripts, clay cuneiform tablets dating from 2000 B.C., early English bibles and a leaf from a Gutenberg Bible. Also of interest is an original 17th-century manor room. Allow 30 minutes minimum. Sun.-Mon. and Thurs.-Fri. 1-4,

late Aug.-late May; closed major holidays. Donations. Phone (785) 594-8393.

BAZAAR (D-6) elev. 1,200'

In the late 1800s Bazaar was a busy livestock center that served as a shipping point for cattle raised in the surrounding Flint Hills. Few traces of that early prosperity remain; today it is an ideal place to savor the silence and solitude of the open prairie. On March 31, 1931, that silence was interrupted when beloved Notre Dame football coach Knute Rockne and seven others were killed in a plane crash. A 10-foot-tall monument in the middle of open rangeland marks the remote site.

[SAVE] **FLINT HILLS OVERLAND WAGON TRAIN TRIPS,** which begin at the Bazaar schoolhouse, e. on CR 91 off SR 177, offer 2-day wagon train treks fashioned after those of the 1870s. The hearty pioneer meals and evening campfires are some of the highlights. Inquire about weather and refund policies. Each trip leaves at 9:30 a.m. and returns at noon the following day. Trips are scheduled Sat.-Sun., June-July and in Sept. Fare $160; ages 4-12, $80. Phone (316) 321-6300.

BELLEVILLE (B-5) pop. 2,239, elev. 1,550'

Located in north central Kansas, Belleville was founded in 1869 and named for early resident Anabelle Tutton. A Depression-era building boom, fueled by federal Works Project Administration (WPA) funding, resulted in many fine examples of Art Deco architecture, including the Republic County Courthouse.

A pond that formerly supplied water for Rock Island Railroad steam engines now provides year-round recreation. Rocky Pond Park offers picnicking, fishing and RV camping.

Belleville Chamber of Commerce: 1309 18th St. P.O. Box 280, Belleville, KS 66935; phone (785) 527-5524.

HIGH BANKS HALL OF FAME AND NATIONAL MIDGET AUTO RACING MUSEUM is 1.2 mi. n. of jct. US 36 and US 81 at 1204 H St. The museum preserves racing history and features vintage racecars, uniforms, flags, photographs and other memorabilia relating to midget auto racing. Allow 30 minutes minimum. Tues.-Sun. 10-5. Admission $3, ages 6-14, $2. Phone (785) 527-2526.

REPUBLIC COUNTY HISTORICAL MUSEUM, .75 mi. e. of US 81 on US 36, displays historical clothing, furniture and other relics from the area. On the 4-acre grounds are an 1870s log cabin, an 1872 school, an agriculture building, a caboose from the 1970s and a 1904 church. Allow 1 hour minimum. Mon.-Fri. 1-5, Sun. 1:30-4:30; closed major holidays. Donations. Phone (785) 527-5971.

BELOIT (B-5) pop. 4,019, elev. 1,382'

A trading center and county seat on the Solomon River, Beloit is in the post rock country. Undeterre by the lack of trees, early farmers quarried their fence posts from Greenhorn limestone, which underlies a 200-mile-long, 10- to 40-mile-wide swath of the Smoky Hills region. The stone also was used for construction; Mitchell County Courthouse and St. John's Church are examples of post rock buildings.

A herd of about 450 buffaloes associated with the Butterfield Buffalo Ranch can be seen from the roadway 3 miles west and 2 miles north from the junction of US 24 and SR 14. For more information phone (785) 738-2717. Also of interest is the Little Red Schoolhouse on US 24N. Built in 1871, the schoolhouse has been restored to its 19th-century appearance and contains period textbooks and other historic educational materials.

Fourteen miles west of Beloit on US 24, Glen Elder Dam impounds 12,600-acre Waconda Lake. Glen Elder State Park *(see Recreation Chart and the AAA South Central CampBook)* is a center of recreational activity on the reservoir.

Beloit Area Chamber of Commerce: 123 N. Mill St., P.O. Box 582, Beloit, KS 67420; phone (785) 738-2717.

Self-guiding tours: A walking tour brochure of historic downtown is available from the chamber of commerce.

MITCHELL COUNTY HISTORICAL SOCIETY AND MUSEUM, 1 mi. s. of US 24 at 402 W. Eighth St., houses county historical memorabilia in a renovated four-story building. Displays include period rooms and collections of china, glassware, tools and clothing. Research facilities are available. Allow 1 hour minimum. Mon. and Thurs. 9-4, Tues. 1-5, Fri. 1-4, otherwise by appointment; closed major holidays. Donations. Phone (785) 738-5355.

BENTON (E-6) pop. 827, elev. 1,375′

PRAIRIE ROSE CHUCKWAGON SUPPER AND HOPALONG CASSIDY COWBOY MUSEUM is at 15231 S.W. Parallel Rd. Performers known as the Prairie Rose Wranglers provide western-themed musical entertainment after an all-you-can-eat barbecue

supper. Visitors can wander among the large collection of Hopalong Cassidy memorabilia in the museum, which continuously shows Hopalong movies and television segments in a small theater. Museum open Mon.-Sat. 11-6:30. Dinner shows Thurs.-Sat. at 6:30 p.m. Closed major holidays. Admission $6; senior citizens $5; ages 6-12, $4. Dinner show $25; ages 6-12, $15. Reservations are required for dinner show. MC, VI. Phone (316) 778-2121.

BONNER SPRINGS—

see Kansas City p. 182 in Missouri.

BURLINGTON (D-7) pop. 2,790, elev. 1,035′

COFFEY COUNTY HISTORICAL SOCIETY MUSEUM is 10 blks. w. of US 75 at 1101 Neosho St. Highlights of the museum include a large genealogy library, an impressive collection of guns and American Indian arrowheads, a large veterans display, a doll collection and a series of rooms depicting 19th-century life. On the grounds is a restored 1896 one-room schoolhouse, an 1895 church and a stone gazebo. Mon.-Fri. 10-4, Sat.-Sun. 1-4; closed holidays. Donations. Phone (620) 364-2653 or (888) 877-2653.

CANEY (F-7) pop. 2,092, elev. 770′

SAFARI ZOOLOGICAL PARK is 1.5 mi. e. of US 75 on CR 1425, following signs. The park is home to such animals as alligators, bears, black leopards, jaguars, lions and several white tigers. One-hour guided tours of the park and reptile house offer an educational experience.

Picnicking is permitted. Allow 1 hour minimum. Mon.-Sat. 10-4, Sun. 1-4, Memorial Day weekend-Labor Day; Sat. 10-3, Sun. 1-3, Mar. 1-day before Memorial Day weekend and day after Labor Day-Oct. 31. Hours vary in spring and fall; phone ahead. Admission $7; over 59, $6.50; ages 3-12, $6. Phone (620) 879-2885.

CAWKER CITY (B-4) pop. 521, elev. 1,500′

Visitors can see what is said to be the world's largest ball of twine in downtown Cawker City. The ball currently contains more than 7,051,240 feet of

sisal twine, weighs more than 17,698 pounds and is more than 41 feet in circumference. Community members continue to add to it. The town is on the edge of Waconda Lake, where hunting and fishing are permitted in season.

CENTERVILLE (D-7) elev. 925′

ST. PHILIPPINE DUCHESNE SHRINE AND PARK is on SR 7, 8 mi. n. of jct. SR 7 and SR 52. The shrine preserves the site of a mid-1800s Pottawatomie Indian settlement that was founded with the help of nuns and Jesuit priests. The elderly Sister Rose Philippine Duchesne particularly was devoted to the cause. Several memorials, historical markers and an American Indian burial site are in the 169-acre park, as are nature trails. Picnicking is permitted. Daily dawn-dusk. Donations. Phone (913) 491-9886.

CHANUTE (E-7) pop. 9,441, elev. 930′

Basing its economy on light industries, agriculture, limestone and oil and gas deposits, Chanute is an old railroad town bearing the surname of Octave Chanute, a civil engineer for the LL&G Railway during the early 1870s. His avocation was building and flying heavier-than-air machines. The inventor's designs were used by Orville and Wilbur Wright at Kitty Hawk, N.C.

Nearby recreation sites include Santa Fe Park *(see Recreation Chart)*, on Santa Fe Street; Wilson State Fishing Lake *(see Recreation Chart and Buffalo in the AAA South Central CampBook)*, 12 miles west via SR 39 and US 75 near Buffalo; Fall River State Park *(see Fall River in the AAA South Central CampBook)*, 23 miles west via SR 39; and Pearson-Skubitz Big Hill Lake *(see Cherryvale in the AAA South Central CampBook)*, 25 miles south via US 169.

Chanute Office of Tourism: 21 N. Lincoln Ave., P.O. Box 747, Chanute, KS 66720; phone (620) 431-3350 or (877) 431-3350.

SAVE **MARTIN AND OSA JOHNSON SAFARI MUSEUM**, 111 N. Lincoln Ave., presents the photographs, manuscripts, books, films and various memorabilia of Martin and Osa Johnson, early wildlife photographers and authors. Exhibits feature the couple's trips to the South Seas, Borneo and Africa 1917-36. Other features include West African masks, tribal art and a library containing a 10,000-volume natural history collection. Some of the Johnsons' films are shown by request.

Mon.-Sat. 10-5, Sun. 1-5; closed major holidays. Admission $4; over 64, students with ID and ages 13-18, $3; ages 6-12, $2. DS, MC, VI. Phone (620) 431-2730.

CHAPMAN (C-6) pop. 1,241, elev. 1,115′

KANSAS AUTO RACING MUSEUM is at 1205 Manor Dr. The museum focuses on the history of motor sports in Kansas with displays of restored race cars from various eras, photographs and other

memorabilia. A theater shows race film highlights, and visitors are encouraged to touch the cars. Allow 1 hour minimum. Mon.-Sat. 9-5. Admission $5; over 64 and ages 6-12, $3. MC, VI. Phone (785) 922-6642.

COFFEYVILLE (E-7) pop. 11,021, elev. 736′

Though carefully planned, the simultaneous robbery of Coffeyville's two banks in October 1892 was not executed successfully. Because Eighth Street was being torn up where Bob, Grat and Emmett Dalton and their two confederates intended to tie their horses, they had to leave them in a parallel alley—too far for a safe getaway even under ideal circumstances.

Then, a warning of what was about to happen and a delaying ruse on the part of a bank employee gave townspeople time to arm. The running gun battle that followed left four citizens and all but one of the outlaws dead. Such was the Dalton Raid, one of the most notorious chapters in the annals of Kansas.

One of the banks involved, the Old Condon Bank at 811 Walnut St., has been restored to its original appearance. A replica of the old city jail sits in Death Alley, where the horses were left. The graves of Bob and Gratt Dalton can be seen in Elmwood Cemetery, 2 blocks west of US 169.

Coffeyville once was the home of baseball pitcher Walter Johnson and of 1940 presidential candidate Wendell Willkie, who taught school in the town. A memorial to Johnson is in Walter Johnson Park.

The growth of the town is depicted in 13 murals on downtown walls, sidewalks and stores.

Coffeyville Area Chamber of Commerce: 807 Walnut St., P.O. Box 457, Coffeyville, KS 67337; phone (620) 251-2550 or (800) 626-3357.

SAVE **BROWN MANSION**, 1 mi. s. of jct. US 166 and US 169 on S. Walnut St., is a restored three-story mansion from the early 1900s. Built by one of Coffeyville's wealthiest men, the 16-room house is furnished in period with Tiffany glass accents and items from the United States and Europe. An information center is on the premises.

Allow 1 hour minimum. Guided tours are given on the hour Tues.-Sat. 9-5, Sun. 1-5, June-Aug.; Tues.-Sun. 1-5 in May and Sept.-Oct.; Sat. 9-5, Sun. 1-5, Mar.-Apr. and Nov.-Dec. Closed Easter, Thanksgiving and Dec. 25. Admission $5; ages 13-18, $2; ages 7-12, $1. Combination ticket with the Dalton Defenders Museum $6; ages 13-18, $3. Phone (620) 251-0431.

SAVE **DALTON DEFENDERS MUSEUM**, 113 E. 8th St., contains items pertaining to the Coffeyville bank robberies by the Dalton Gang in 1892. Displayed are photographs, guns used in the holdup and capture, saddles, a bank safe and some of the stolen money bags. Mementos of Wendell Willkie and Walter Johnson also are exhibited.

Daily 9-5, Mar.-Oct.; daily 10-4, Nov.-Dec.; Fri.-Sun. 9-5, rest of year. Closed Easter, Thanksgiving and Dec. 25. Admission $3; ages 13-18, $2. Combination ticket with the Brown Mansion $6; ages 13-18, $3. MC, VI. Phone (620) 251-5944.

COLBY (B-2) pop. 5,450, elev. 3,138'

Colby is a trading and service center for the surrounding wheat- and corn-producing area.

Colby Visitors Center: 2015 S. Range Ave., Colby, KS 67701; phone (785) 460-0076.

Shopping areas: Southwind Plaza, I-70 exit 53, features artwork, Kansas products and Western memorabilia. Shops also line N. Franklin Street downtown.

NORTHWEST RESEARCH EXTENSION CENTER, w. on US 24, conducts horticultural and agricultural studies for Kansas State University. Crop research is conducted on the grounds, which also include several varieties of flower gardens. Guided tours are provided upon request during office hours. Grounds daily 24 hours. Office Mon.-Fri. 8-noon and 1-5; closed holidays. Free. Phone (785) 462-7575.

PRAIRIE MUSEUM OF ART AND HISTORY, 1905 S. Franklin Ave., is a 24-acre complex that includes a restored 1930s house, a sod house, a wooden fan windmill, a country church and a one-room school. Also featured is the 1936 Cooper Barn, which houses a 7,000-square-foot exhibit documenting high plains agriculture 1870-1990. Dolls, toys, ceramics, glass, textiles and furniture make up the collection.

Allow 1 hour minimum. Mon.-Fri. 9-5, Sat.-Sun. 1-5, Apr.-Oct.; Tues.-Fri. 9-5, Sat.-Sun. 1-5, rest of year. Closed holidays. Admission $5; over 64, $4; ages 6-16, $2. AX, DS, MC, VI. Phone (785) 460-4590.

CONCORDIA (B-5) pop. 5,714, elev. 1,363'

Concordia appeals to outdoor enthusiasts. Pheasants and quails are hunted, while the Republican River and area lakes provide good fishing. Concordia maintains five park and playground areas; free camping at Airport Park is popular with tourists traveling in recreational vehicles.

Concordia Chamber of Commerce: 606 Washington St., Concordia, KS 66901; phone (785) 243-4290.

BROWN GRAND THEATRE is on SR 9, 5 blks. w. of US 81 at 310 W. 6th St. Built in 1907, the theater was restored to its original state and reopened in 1980. Once an opera house and movie theater, the building now is a community center for art displays, plays and musical performances. Guided tours featuring the history of the theater and a behind-the-scenes look at the stage are available by request. Allow 30 minutes minimum. Tues.-Fri. 9-noon and 1-3; closed major holidays. Donations. Tours $3. Phone (785) 243-2553.

CLOUD COUNTY HISTORICAL SOCIETY MUSEUM, 635 Broadway, features relics and photographs depicting area history. Of interest is a display about a local prisoner of war camp that housed German soldiers during World War II. Other exhibits contain a Steuben glass collection; a 1928 Lincoln Page airplane; a Norman Rockwell plate and calendar collection; a working, full-size windmill; an antique toy collection; 19th-century farm equipment; musical instruments; and furniture. Allow 1 hour minimum. Tues.-Sat. 1-5; closed major holidays. Donations. Phone (785) 243-2866.

COTTONWOOD FALLS (D-6)
pop. 966, elev. 1,191'

Cottonwood Falls was founded as a busy agricultural and livestock center in the late 1850s. It is home to the French Renaissance-style Chase County Courthouse, built in 1873. Constructed of locally-mined limestone, the courthouse features a mansard roof, dormer windows and a cupola. Still in use, it was designed by John G. Haskell, who also designed the Kansas capitol building in Topeka.

Roniger Memorial Museum displays an extensive collection of American Indian arrowheads and other artifacts discovered during archeological excavations; phone (620) 273-6310.

Chase County Chamber of Commerce: 318 Broadway, Cottonwood Falls, KS 66845; phone (620) 273-8469 or (800) 431-6344.

COUNCIL GROVE (C-6)
pop. 2,321, elev. 1,234'

Expansive maples, elms and oaks shade the streets of Council Grove, much as they did during the meeting between Osage Indian chiefs and U.S. commissioners in the summer of 1825. From that conclave came the treaty by which the government obtained the right-of-way for the Santa Fe Trail as well as the name for this town on the Neosho River.

The remains of Council Oak, under which the agreement was signed, are enshrined at 210 E. Main St. Post Office Oak, a block farther west on Main Street, served as an unofficial post office 1825-47, when Council Grove was one of the most important stations—and the last outfitting point—on the Santa Fe Trail. Letters were left in a stone cache at its foot to be picked up by the next wagon train.

Near Post Office Oak is the "Madonna of the Trail" statue, a 16-foot-tall memorial to the courage of pioneer mothers. The statue also marks the start of the Neosho Riverwalk, a paved, landscaped walkway that begins at Main Street, crosses the Santa Fe Trail and ends a half-mile north at the Kaw Mission State Historic Site.

The massive trunk of Custer Elm is preserved 6 blocks south of Main Street on Neosho Street, near property once owned by Lt. Col. George A. Custer. This once giant tree purportedly marks the site where Custer's 7th Cavalry camped as it guarded the Santa Fe Trail. Among several remaining buildings from the town's pioneer heyday are a 19th-century jail at 502 E. Main St., the 1857 Last

Chance Store at W. Main and Chautauqua streets, and the 1857 Hays House, one of the oldest continuously operated restaurants west of the Mississippi River.

Council Grove/Morris County Chamber of Commerce and Tourism: 212 W. Main St., Council Grove, KS 66846; phone (620) 767-5882 or (800) 732-9211.

Self-guiding tours: A brochure spotting points of historic interest can be obtained from the chamber of commerce and tourism office.

KAW MISSION STATE HISTORIC SITE is at 500 N. Mission St., 5 blks. n. of US 56. Now a museum displaying mission period artifacts, the two-story stone building was erected in 1851 as a school for Kaw Indian children. Exhibits depict the history of the Kaw and the Santa Fe Trail. Allow 30 minutes minimum. Wed.-Sat. 10-5, Sun. 1-5; closed state holidays. Admission $2, students with ID $1, under 5 free. Phone (620) 767-5410.

DODGE CITY (D-3) pop. 26,176, elev. 2,496′

Fittingly called the "Wickedest Little City in America," Dodge City was a wide-open town during the late 1800s. Its infamous Front Street was one of the wildest on the frontier, with one well-stocked saloon for every 20 citizens. Cattlemen, buffalo hunters, soldiers, settlers, gunfighters, railroad men and mule skinners thronged the streets, to the delight and profit of the card sharks, brothel keepers and morticians.

Boot Hill Cemetery is named as such because many of its dead were buried with their boots on. Wyatt Earp and Bat Masterson were among the few able to control the city's lawless elements.

Dodge City began as a stopover on the Santa Fe Trail; wagon wheel ruts still are visible in the sod 9 miles west via US 50. By late 1872 the town was a station on the railroad. Buffalo hunting was intense in the area, and the trading of hides, meat and ultimately bones brought considerable wealth to the town. By the time the buffaloes had nearly become extinct, bellowing herds of Texas cattle had become the primary source of income, and Dodge City became one of the largest cattle markets in the country.

While Dodge City's character has changed, its purpose has not. It remains a major cattle-shipping point and serves as a supply and trade center for a large wheat-growing region.

A look at the city's early days is provided by the mural that adorns the facade of the National Beef Packing Plant, southeast of town on SR 400. It is the work of muralist Stan Herd; another of his depictions can be seen at the Bank of America at 619 N. Second Ave.

Dodge City Convention and Visitors Bureau: 400 W. Wyatt Earp Blvd., Dodge City, KS 67801; phone (620) 225-8186 or (800) 653-9378.

Self-guiding tours: More than 20 points of interest, including churches, monuments and buildings, are described in a free brochure distributed by the convention and visitors bureau. A recorded narrative to accompany the brochure can be rented for $2 or purchased for $5. A driving tour features Fort Dodge.

BOOT HILL AND FRONT STREET is on the original site of Boot Hill Cemetery. Living-history interpreters and exhibits featuring thousands of original historic items depict life in 1876 Dodge City. Visitors can see an Old West gun collection and American Indian artifacts along with buffaloes, cattle and clothing. Included in the complex are Boot Hill Cemetery, Ft. Dodge Jail, a one-room schoolhouse and an 1878 Victorian home once owned by cattle ranchers. A working general store and a saloon are along Front Street.

Food is available in summer. Daily 8-8, Memorial Day weekend-Labor Day; Mon.-Sat. 9-5, Sun. 1-5, rest of year. Closed Jan. 1, Thanksgiving and Dec. 25. Gunfights start at noon and 7 p.m., Memorial Day weekend-Labor Day. Admission Memorial Day weekend-Labor Day $8; over 62 and ages 7-17, $7.50; family rate $25. Admission rest of year $7; over 62 and ages 7-17, $6.50; family rate $20. AX, DS, MC, VI. Phone (620) 227-8188.

CARNEGIE CENTER FOR THE ARTS, Second Ave. and Spruce St., is a community arts center that houses original works by local, regional and national artists. The building, completed in 1907, originally was a Carnegie library and is noted for its unusual architecture. Allow 30 minutes minimum. Tues.-Fri. noon-5, Sat. 11-3, Feb.-Dec.; closed Thanksgiving and Dec. 25. Donations. Phone (620) 225-6388.

DODGE CITY TROLLEY, 400 W. Wyatt Earp Blvd. at the convention and visitors bureau, offers 1-hour tours of Dodge City. Highlights include the original locations of Long Branch Saloon, Front Street and Fort Dodge. Passengers may not exit and re-board the trolley later. Trips depart daily at 9:30, 10:45, 1:30 and 3, Memorial Day to mid-Aug. Fare $6; under 12, $4. Phone (620) 225-8186 or (800) 653-9378.

FORD HOME OF STONE AND MUSEUM, 112 E. Vine St., has 2.5-foot-thick limestone walls that have preserved the structure since 1881. Rooms are furnished in period and contain pioneer memorabilia, antique clothing and household items. Free 45-minute guided tours are offered daily. Mon.-Sat. 9-5, Sun. 2-4, Memorial Day-Labor Day. Donations. Phone (620) 227-6791.

SOLDIERS' HOME AT FORT DODGE is just s. of US 400 at 714 Sheridan St., Unit 28. The fort was a vital Army outpost from 1865, when it was established to protect the Santa Fe Trail from American Indians. Lt. Col. George A. Custer and Union generals Philip Sheridan and Winfield Hancock figured in the fort's history. Original structures were made from sod or adobe, but several 1867 buildings constructed of Kansas sandstone still are in use. A museum and library contain historical and military artifacts.

Museum and library Mon.-Sat. 10-4, Sun. 1-4, May-Sept.; daily 1-4, rest of year. Closed Jan. 1, Easter, Memorial Day, Labor Day, Thanksgiving and Dec. 25. Free. Phone (620) 227-2121.

EDGERTON—
see Kansas City p. 182 in Missouri.

EL DORADO (D-6) pop. 12,057, elev. 1,285'

[SAVE] **BUTLER COUNTY HISTORY CENTER AND KANSAS OIL MUSEUM,** 383 E. Central Ave., chronicles the development of the oil industry in Kansas since 1860. An orientation film about the history of oil is shown at a re-created service station. Outdoor exhibits include an oil derrick, oil field buildings, drilling equipment, a 1930s grocery store, a doctor's office and a restored shotgun house.

Allow 1 hour minimum. Mon.-Sat. 9-5, Sun. 1-5, Memorial Day-Labor Day; Mon.-Sat. 9-5, rest of year. Closed major holidays. Admission $4; senior citizens $3; students with ID and ages 6-18, $2. Phone (316) 321-9333.

COUTTS MEMORIAL MUSEUM OF ART, just n. of jct. US 54 and US 77 at 110 N. Main St., displays paintings, sculptures, prints and drawings by traditional, contemporary, Western and local artists. Antique furnishings and Persian rugs enhance the setting. Of particular interest is the Frederic Remington bronze collection. Allow 1 hour minimum. Mon., Wed. and Fri. 1-5, Tues. and Thurs. 9-noon and 1-5, Sat. noon-4; closed holidays. Donations. Phone (316) 321-1212.

ELK FALLS (E-7) pop. 112, elev. 938'

Once the site of a gristmill, the natural waterfalls for which Elk Falls was named are at the bottom of the Elk River Gorge. Pedestrians can view the waterfalls from the 1893 Iron Truss Bridge. The Prudence Crandall Historical Marker, off SR 160, is dedicated to the famed educator, emancipator and human rights activist who lived in Elk Falls from 1874 until her death in 1890.

ELLIS (C-3) pop. 1,873, elev. 2,117'

ELLIS RAILROAD MUSEUM, 911 Washington St., tracks the history of the railroad in the area. Included are photographs, memorabilia, re-created stations, cars, period clothing and some 1,600 dolls. Train rides aboard a one-third scale streamliner take passengers on a 2-mile track around the museum. Allow 1 hour minimum. Mon.-Sat. 9-5, Sun. 1-5, Apr.-Nov.; daily 11-4, rest of year. Closed Easter, Thanksgiving and Dec. 25. Admission $3; ages 5-12, $2. Train $2; ages 5-12, $1. DS, MC, VI. Phone (785) 726-4493.

[SAVE] **WALTER P. CHRYSLER BOYHOOD HOME AND MUSEUM** is at 102 W. 10th St. The founder of Chrysler Corp. lived in this 1889 house until the age of 22. Early training as a machinist in local railroad yards helped shape his future course. The house is furnished in period and contains Chrysler memorabilia, including the industrialist's corporate desk, which was donated to the museum after his death in 1940.

Tues.-Sat. 10-4, Sun. 1-4, Memorial Day-Labor Day; Tues.-Sat. 11-3, Sun. 1-4, rest of year. Closed Easter, Thanksgiving and Dec. 25. Admission $3; over 62, $2.50; ages 5-15, $1. MC, VI. Phone (785) 726-3636.

ELLSWORTH (C-4) pop. 2,965

[SAVE] **HODGDEN HOUSE MUSEUM COMPLEX,** 104 W. South Main St., houses local memorabilia in various buildings, including the 1873 Hodgden House, a church, livery stable, rural schoolhouse, general store and a log building. A Union Pacific caboose and farm machinery also are on the grounds.

Allow 1 hour minimum. Tues.-Sat. 9-5, Sun. 1-5; closed major holidays. Admission $3; ages 6-12, $1. Admission includes Fort Harker Museum in Kanopolis *(see attraction listing p. 91).* Phone (785) 472-3059.

EMPORIA (D-7) pop. 26,760, elev. 1,135'

Few cities are associated more widely with Kansas' journalistic tradition than Emporia, the home of William Allen White. As the outspoken editor and publisher of the *Emporia Gazette* 1895-1944, his incisive writing influenced national affairs. An essay on free speech, "To an Anxious Friend," won White a Pulitzer Prize in 1922. The William Allen White House State Historic Site, which preserves the stone Tudor-style house where he lived for 45 years, is at 927 Exchange St. and is open weekends; phone (620) 342-2800.

Reminders of the "Sage of Emporia" are numerous. They include the William Allen White Library at the 6,000-student Emporia State University, William Allen White Memorial Drive and a commemorative statue in Peter Pan Park. Not the least of these memorials is the *Emporia Gazette* itself, still published by his family.

In 1953 the city became the first in the nation to observe Veterans Day thanks to the forward thinking of another patriotic citizen. Because Armistice Day honored only World War I veterans, Alvin J. King proposed renaming the holiday in order to include World War II and Korean War veterans. With the endorsement of a fellow Kansan, President Dwight D. Eisenhower, Congress officially changed the name to Veterans Day one year later, and in 2003, Congress declared Emporia its founding city.

The Howe House & Welsh Farmstead, 315 E. Logan Ave., is an 1867 limestone dwelling that reflects period style. Tours may be arranged; phone (620) 340-6310. Recreational facilities are available at several sites, including Peter Pan Park, Randolph and Rural streets, and at Soden's Grove Park, which features the Emporia Zoo *(see attraction listing).*

White Memorial Park, at Sixth and Merchant streets, contains park benches and street lamps in the style of the 1920s. A bust of White's son, William Lindsey White, is the main feature of the park.

Several nearby reservoirs offer fishing, boating and swimming: Lyon, Melvern, Council Grove, Kahola, Pomona and John Redmond lakes *(see Recreation Chart)* all are within a 45-minute drive.

Emporia Convention and Visitors Bureau: Trusler Business Center, 719 Commercial St., P.O. Box 703, Emporia, KS 66801; phone (620) 342-1600 or (800) 279-3730.

Self-guiding tours: Brochures outlining driving tours of Emporia and the Flint Hills as well as a walking tour map of downtown are available from the convention and visitors bureau.

ALL VETERANS MEMORIAL, 933 S. Commercial St., is dedicated to all U.S. war veterans, from the Civil War to Operation Iraqi Freedom and Operation Enduring Freedom. In the small, parklike setting is a World War II army tank surrounded by flags and tributes. A Huey helicopter marks the site of a Vietnam veterans' memorial. Daily dawn-dusk. Free. Phone (620) 342-1803.

EMPORIA ZOO, 75 Soden Rd. in Soden's Grove Park, displays 88 species of native and exotic birds, reptiles and mammals. Some of the exhibits can be seen on a drive-through tour. Walk-through area daily 10-4:30 (also Wed. and Sun. 4:30-8, May-Sept.). Drive-through daily dawn-dusk. Closed Jan. 1, Thanksgiving and Dec. 25. Donations. Phone (620) 342-6558.

LYON COUNTY HISTORICAL MUSEUM, 118 E. Sixth Ave., features local and regional memorabilia, pioneer items, a log cabin furnished in period and rotating exhibits. Tues.-Sat. 1-5; closed holidays. Donations. Phone (620) 340-6310.

NATIONAL TEACHERS HALL OF FAME, 1320 C of E Dr., depicts the heritage of education in America and honors teachers who have been recognized for their commitment and dedication to teaching grades K-12. Mon.-Fri. 8-5, Sat. 9-noon; closed holidays. Donations. Phone (620) 341-5660 or (800) 968-3224.

EUREKA (D-6) pop. 2,914, elev. 1,081′

Eureka allegedly was named for the exclamation of an excited settler who discovered a spring at this site. The area is known for excellent quail, deer and turkey hunting. Recreational opportunities are available at nearby Fall River, Toronto and Woodson state parks *(see Recreation Chart and Fall River and Yates Center in the AAA South Central CampBook)*. Fall River canoe trips can be arranged April through October, and rentals are available; phone (620) 583-6481.

Eureka Area Chamber of Commerce: 309 N. Oak St., P.O. Box 563, Eureka, KS 67045; phone (620) 583-5452.

GREENWOOD COUNTY HISTORICAL SOCIETY MUSEUM, 120 W. Fourth St., has pioneer memorabilia and collections of photographs, local relics and indigenous rocks. The museum also contains a genealogical research center. The Chronicle of Greenwood County facility includes exhibits about fossils, pioneers, ranching, farming and American Indian life. Mon.-Fri. 9-4, Sat. by appointment; closed holidays. Donations. Phone (620) 583-6682.

FORT RILEY (B-6)

Reached from exit 301 off I-70, Fort Riley is the home of the 1st Infantry Division Headquarters. The fort was built in 1853 to protect travelers along the Santa Fe Trail. Originally established as Camp Center, the fort later was named for Gen. Bennett Riley, who led the first military escort down the Santa Fe Trail in 1829. By 1855 the fort was a full dragoon and infantry post, its soldiers credited with helping open the frontier for settlement.

The 101,000-acre, 11,600-personnel military reservation includes camps Forsyth, Funston and Whitside, Marshall Army Air Field and the Custer Hill area. A large historical district offers some 270 stone buildings. The Commanding General's Mounted Color Guard stables are open daily. Tours are available. A valid driver's license or photo ID, along with vehicle registration and proof of insurance are required for entry; phone (785) 239-2737.

CUSTER HOUSE is on Sheridan Ave., Quarters 24A. Built in 1855 of native limestone, the house realistically depicts military life on the western frontier. Though Lt. Col. George A. Custer did not live in the house, it was named to honor him. A 30-minute guided tour explains about furnishings and other items. Mon.-Sat. 10-4, Sun. 1-4, Memorial Day-Labor Day. Schedule may vary; phone ahead. Last tour begins 20 minutes before closing. Donations. Phone (785) 239-2737.

FIRST TERRITORIAL CAPITOL OF KANSAS STATE HISTORIC SITE is 3 mi. from I-70 exit 301, following signs. On the site of Pawnee, a struggling town at the edge of the Fort Riley cavalry post, the 1855 building hosted what became known as the "Bogus Legislature." Anti-slavery arguments here led to the conflict known as the "Bleeding Kansas" period of civil unrest. Restored in 1928, the capitol is now a museum furnished with period items. A self-guiding, .5-mile nature trail features native flora and fauna.

Note: Photo ID, vehicle registration and proof of insurance are required to enter the site. Allow 1 hour minimum. Fri.-Sun. 1-5, Apr.-Oct.; Sat.-Sun. 1-5, rest of year. Closed federal holidays. Trail daily dawn-dusk. Donations. Phone (785) 784-5535, or (785) 238-1666 for tour information.

FORT RILEY 1ST INFANTRY DIVISION MUSEUM, jct. Sheridan and Custer aves. in Bldg. 207, offers a simulated Vietnamese jungle trail. Four major campaigns in which the First Infantry Division fought—World Wars I and II, Vietnam and Operation Desert Storm—are depicted. Allow 30 minutes minimum. Mon.-Sat. 10-4, Sun. 1-4; closed Jan. 1, Easter, Thanksgiving and Dec. 25. Donations. Phone (785) 239-2737.

OLD TROOPER STATUE, on the cavalry parade ground across from the Custer House on Sheridan Ave., is a memorial to the U.S. Cavalry. The statue depicts a horse nicknamed Old Bill and its soldier rider, and is based upon Frederic Remington's pen and ink sketch "Old Bill." Chief, the last cavalry horse, died in 1968 and is buried in front of the memorial.

UNITED STATES CAVALRY MUSEUM is at the jct. of Sheridan and Custer aves. in Bldg. 205. The building, which dates from 1855, originally was a hospital. The museum tells the history of the mounted horse soldier of the U.S. Cavalry 1775-1950. Allow 1 hour minimum. Mon.-Sat. 9-4:30, Sun. noon-4:30; closed Jan. 1, Easter, Thanksgiving and Dec. 25. Donations. Phone (785) 239-2737.

FORT SCOTT (D-7) pop. 8,297, elev. 801'

Formed around a military outpost established in 1842 to keep peace along the American frontier, the town of Fort Scott survived after the fort itself was abandoned and sold in 1855. During this time, pro-slavery versus Free State conflicts were common, and Fort Scott's location 6 miles from the Missouri border made it a frequent scene of violence during the turbulent period known as "Bleeding Kansas."

During the Civil War Fort Scott was divided, with "pro-slavers" living on the east side of town and "free-staters" living on the west side. After the war, the town became a leading city of eastern Kansas and challenged Kansas City's standing as the largest rail center west of the Mississippi River.

The town's many handsome commercial buildings and elegant Victorian residences were built from the 1850s to the 1920s. Narrated "Dolly the Trolley" Tours of historic Fort Scott depart hourly from the visitor information center mid-April to early December.

Fort Scott was the boyhood home and is the final resting place of Gordon Parks, director of the popular 1970s film "Shaft."

Fort Scott Visitor Information Center: 231 E. Wall St., P.O. Box 205, Fort Scott, KS 66701; phone (620) 223-3566 or (800) 245-3678.

Self-guiding tours: A free brochure detailing a historic walking tour of downtown is available from the visitor information center.

FORT SCOTT NATIONAL HISTORIC SITE covers about 17 acres on Old Fort Blvd. on the edge of downtown. Established in 1842, the fort was built on a bluff overlooking the Marmaton River. Twenty fort buildings—which include the post headquarters, officers' quarters, enlisted men's barracks, hospital, bakery, stables, guardhouse, powder magazine and quartermaster's storehouse—have been restored and furnished in period.

Exhibits explain the fort's history, including its role in westward expansion, the Bleeding Kansas era, the Civil War and in protecting the permanent American Indian frontier. Daily 8-5, Apr.-Oct.; 9-5, rest of year. Closed Jan. 1, Thanksgiving and Dec. 25. Guided 1-hour tours are given daily at 1, June-Aug. Admission $3, under 15 free. Phone (620) 223-0310.

GUNN PARK occupies 155 acres along the Marmaton River in the western part of town. Two small lakes offer fishing and paddleboats. Picnicking is permitted. Camping is available. Daily 24 hours. Free. Camping $4-$8. *See Recreation Chart.*

U.S. NATIONAL CEMETERY NO. 1, E. National Ave., covers 21 acres. Established in 1862, it is one of the original 12 national cemeteries designated by President Abraham Lincoln. Daily 8-4:30. Free.

FREDONIA (E-7) pop. 2,600, elev. 866'

STONE HOUSE GALLERY is at 320 N. Seventh St. The gallery, housed in an 1872 building, displays changing exhibits of works by contemporary artists. In addition to monthly art exhibitions, the gallery features theatrical and dance productions as well as vocal and instrumental programs May through December. Allow 30 minutes minimum. Mon.-Fri. 12:30-4:30 and by appointment; closed major holidays. Donations. Phone (620) 378-2052.

GARDEN CITY (D-2) pop. 28,451, elev. 2,830'

Founded in 1879, Garden City's early growth was followed by years of drought and declining population. This cycle continued until dependable irrigation systems were established at the turn of the 20th century.

The Arkansas River makes Garden City one of the state's most extensively irrigated regions; bumper crops of wheat, alfalfa and corn are produced. It also is a major cattle raising and shipping site. South of the city off US 83 a large herd of bison inhabits the nearly 4,000-acre, state-operated Sandsage Bison Range and Wildlife Area. Tours are available by reservation; phone (620) 276-9400.

Finney County Convention and Tourism Bureau: 1511 E. Fulton Terr., Garden City, KS 67846-6165; phone (620) 276-3264 or (800) 879-9803.

FINNUP PARK AND LEE RICHARDSON ZOO is s. on Bus. Rte. 83. The zoo's Wild Asia exhibit features exotic plants, architecture and animals, including snow leopards and red pandas. The Finnup Center for Conservation Education offers interactive learning. Local heritage is preserved at the Finney County Historical Museum. Recreational facilities include a 2.5-million-gallon swimming pool, horseshoe pits, tennis courts, picnic sites and a playground.

Zoo daily 8-7:30, during DST; 8-4:30, rest of year. Conservation center Mon.-Fri. 8-5. Museum

Mon.-Sat. 10-5, Sun. 1-5, Memorial Day-Labor Day; daily 1-5, rest of year. Pool Mon.-Thurs. 1-6, Fri.-Sun. and holidays 1-7, Memorial Day-Labor Day. Closed Jan. 1, Thanksgiving and Dec. 25. Donations. Phone (620) 276-1250 for the park and zoo or (620) 272-3664 for the museum.

GOESSEL (D-6) pop. 565

Goessel was founded in the late 1800s by Russian Mennonites, most of whom were wheat farmers. The town sprang up quickly with the encouragement of the Santa Fe Railroad, which sold land to the farmers at the rate of $2.37 per acre.

SAVE **MENNONITE HERITAGE MUSEUM,** 200 N. Poplar St., includes a replica of the housing resembling barracks built for arriving immigrants. The Turkey Red Wheat Palace displays farm implements and a 6-foot Liberty Bell made from wheat. The Friesen and Krause houses, Schroeder Barn, South Bloomfield and Goessel Preparatory schools, and Goessel State Bank were moved to the museum for preservation.

Allow 1 hour minimum. Tues.-Fri. 10-4:30, Sat.-Sun. 1-4:30, May-Sept.; Tues.-Fri. noon-4, Sat.-Sun. 1-4, Mar.-Apr. and Oct.-Dec. Admission $3; senior citizens $2.50; ages 7-12, $1.50. Phone (620) 367-8200.

GOODLAND (B-2) pop. 4,948, elev. 3,687′

Chosen as the county seat in 1887, the town became known in the 1880s for its rainmaking companies. The idea came from a man who claimed to produce rain by pouring sulfuric acid on zinc to release hydrogen, which would unite with the surrounding oxygen to form water. There was no immediate reaction after Melbourne's experiment, but within a day heavy rains reportedly fell.

Earlier the town had proved equally inventive: In its war with several nearby communities for the

DID YOU KNOW

Kansas was the first state to harvest wheat and continues to be the leader in wheat production.

county seat, residents employed a combination of armed force, false arrest, staged trial and theft to obtain county records. Goodland also can claim that it is the home of America's first patented helicopter.

The brick surface that remains on Main Street and some side streets was laid in 1921 by Jim Brown, an American Indian whose skill was such that he reputedly could lay up to 150 bricks a minute—as fast as five men could supply him—so accurately that no later adjustment to the bricks was necessary.

Twenty miles northeast of Goodland, a historical marker indicates where Lt. Col. George Custer discovered the bodies of the Indian scout, Lt. Lyman Kidder and the 10 cavalrymen felled in the Kidder Massacre of 1867. A map to the site is available at the Sherman County Convention and Visitors Bureau.

Today, the city serves as major retail trade center for northwest Kansas. It also is known as one of the top sunflower producers in the nation; seeds are processed here for confectionery use and for oil. Because of this distinction, Goodland was chosen as one of seven sites worldwide to display giant outdoor reproductions of Vincent van Gogh's sunflower paintings. Visible from I-70, the 80-foot-tall easel and picture is the only one of its kind in the United States.

Sherman County Convention and Visitors Bureau: 925 Main St., P.O. Box 927, Goodland, KS 67735; phone (785) 890-3515 or (888) 824-4222.

Self-guiding tours: The convention and visitors bureau offers maps for walking and driving tours that highlight historic areas.

GOODLAND HIGH PLAINS MUSEUM, 1717 Cherry St., displays a full-size, automated replica of America's first patented helicopter, built in Goodland by Purvis and Wilson in 1910. A 1902 Holsman rope-driven automobile, the Union School House, pioneer and railroad memorabilia, and prehistoric artifacts and fossils also are exhibited. Dioramas depict scenes from Goodland's history.

Allow 1 hour minimum. Mon.-Fri. 9-5, Sat. 9-4, Sun. 1-4, June 1-Aug. 15; Mon.-Fri. 9-5, Sat. 9-4, rest of year. Closed holidays. Donations. Phone (785) 890-4595.

GREAT BEND (D-4) pop. 15,345, elev. 1,843′

While oil is pumped from underground reserves, wheat is harvested from the overlying fields in Great Bend, situated at the apex of the Arkansas River's sweeping arc through central Kansas.

The town was established in 1871 around the shell of Fort Zarah. It guarded the Santa Fe Trail until 1869 when diminished trail traffic and lessened American Indian threat made the post unnecessary. In 1872 the railroad arrived, bringing with it the cattle trade and all the gambling, gunplay and other amusements typical of a cattle railhead. To establish order, state law decreed that the Texas herds could move no closer than a point 30 miles west of town.

Located in Lafayette Park on the historic Santa Fe Trail is the Kansas Quilt Walk. Seven patterns of quilts reflecting the early settlement of the area are etched in the sidewalks around the park. Also noteworthy in town is the Great Bend Mural Project. A collection of outdoor murals created by local artists can be seen on area buildings. Several are located in the Main Street business area.

Fort Zarah Park, 3 miles east of town on US 56, occupies 9 acres. Thirteen miles southwest on US 56, Pawnee Rock *(see place listing p. 101)* looms above the prairie.

In a vast natural sink, 6 miles northeast via US 281 or US 156, lies Cheyenne Bottoms Wildlife Refuge. As one of the nation's largest inland marshes, it is designated as a wetland of international importance. The 41,000-acre reserve attracts great numbers of birds, including the threatened bald eagle.

Great Bend Convention and Visitors Bureau: 3111 10th St., Suite 109, P.O. Box 274, Great Bend, KS 67530-0400; phone (620) 792-2750 or (877) 427-9299.

BARTON COUNTY HISTORICAL SOCIETY MUSEUM AND VILLAGE, on US 281 just s. of the Arkansas River Bridge, is on the historic Santa Fe Trail and comprises 11 buildings, including a schoolhouse, church, pioneer rock house, depot, post office, blacksmith shop and four barns. The museum also has collections of dolls, vintage wedding gowns, military uniforms, unusual farm implements and antique household items. A Grand Army of the Republic display focuses on the post-Civil War period.

Allow 1 hour minimum. Tues.-Fri. 10-5, Sat.-Sun. 1-5, mid-Apr. to mid-Nov.; Wed.-Fri. 10-3, rest of year. Additional hours available by appointment. Admission $2, under 16 free. Phone (620) 793-5125.

BRIT SPAUGH PARK AND ZOO, at Main and 24th sts., offers a zoo, a skate park, baseball diamonds, horseshoe courts and a water park. Zoo highlights include a white Bengal tiger as well as a birds of prey show. Picnicking is permitted. Park daily 6 a.m.-midnight. Zoo daily 9-4:30. Pool Mon.-Fri. 1-7, Sat.-Sun. 1-6, Memorial Day-late Aug. Park and zoo free. Water park $4; under 18, $3. Phone (620) 793-4160 for the zoo or (620) 792-1516 for the pool.

SHAFER MEMORIAL ART GALLERY is 3 mi. n. on US 281, then 2 mi. e. to 245 N.E. 30th Rd. This gallery, on the Barton County Community College campus, features some 770 watercolors, oil paintings, photographs and sculptures. Special emphasis is placed on Kansas artists, particularly the work of bronze sculptor L.E. "Gus" Shafer and painter Charles B. Rogers. The collection also contains works by John James Audubon, Marc Chagall and Pablo Picasso. Allow 30 minutes minimum. Mon.-Fri. 10-5, Sun. 1-4; closed holidays. Free. Phone (620) 792-9342.

GREENSBURG (E-4) pop. 1,574, elev. 2,235′

The speed and dependability with which he drove the stagecoach between Wichita and Dodge City during the 1880s earned D.R. Green his nickname, "Cannonball." Legend has it that while riding as passenger, temperance reformer Carry Nation reached out of the coach, snatched Cannonball's cigar and hurled it onto the road. He drew rein, silently lifted the astounded lady to the roadway and left her to trudge the many remaining miles to town.

Despite Green's prowess, the day came when the Rock Island Railroad won the race against the Santa Fe Railroad, becoming the first rail line through present-day Greensburg and eliminating the need for stagecoach travel.

Greensburg Chamber of Commerce: 315 S. Sycamore St., Greensburg, KS 67054; phone (620) 723-2261.

BIG WELL, 3 blks. s. of US 54, reputedly is the largest hand-dug well in the world. It measures 32 feet in diameter, is 109 feet deep and contains 15 feet of water. It was begun in 1887 by the city and the Santa Fe Railway, which hoped to use the water for its steam-powered engines. The well was completed in 1888 and provided water for the town until 1932. Visitors descend a 105-step stairway to the bottom of the well.

Daily 8-8, Memorial Day weekend-Labor Day; Mon.-Sat. 9-5, Sun. 1-5, rest of year. Closed Thanksgiving and Dec. 25. Admission $2; ages 5-12, $1.50. AX, DS, MC, VI. Phone (620) 723-2261 or (800) 207-7369.

Pallasite Meteorite is displayed in the curios shop. Consisting mainly of iron and stone and weighing more than 1,000 pounds, the meteorite was found on a nearby farm in 1949. This is one of the largest pallasites ever discovered. Free.

HALSTEAD (D-5) pop. 1,873, elev. 1,388′

In 1872 Bernhard Warkentin established a gristmill in Halstead—the first step in what would become one of the largest milling enterprises in the region. More important, however, was his promotion of Turkey Red wheat, the strain responsible for Kansas becoming the "Breadbasket of the Nation" *(see Newton p. 99).* Wheat still is the foundation of Halstead's economy. The Warkentin house and barns, now a landmark, can be seen on the south bank of the Little Arkansas River.

Halstead Chamber of Commerce: P.O. Box 328, Halstead, KS 67056; phone (316) 835-2662.

SAVE **KANSAS LEARNING CENTER FOR HEALTH,** 505 Main St., has displays about the five senses, the various body systems, the heart, nutrition and other topics. Valeda, a talking transparent model of a woman, is the focus of a 15-minute presentation about the body's functions. Visitors learn through interactive exhibits. Allow 1 hour minimum. Mon.-Fri. 10-4; closed holidays. Admission $2; over 64 and ages 5-18, $1.50; family rate $5. Phone (316) 835-2662.

HANOVER (B-6) pop. 653, elev. 1,225'

When G.H. Hollenberg closed his store in Marshall County and moved west to start a ranch near Cottonwood Creek, he knew what he was doing. The site he selected was near the Oregon Trail; the building he erected about 1857-58 served not only as his home but also as a store, tavern, stage station for the Overland Express and finally a station for the Pony Express.

The enterprise flourished, providing food, clothing, animal feed, supplies, repairs, blacksmith services and fresh horses and oxen for the passing wagon trains. The community that developed around the ranch was mainly settled by German immigrants, who named the town after Hollenberg's home in the fatherland.

Hanover Chamber of Commerce: P.O. Box 283, Hanover, KS 66945; phone (785) 337-2252.

HOLLENBERG STATION STATE HISTORIC SITE, 4 mi. n. on SR 148, then 1 mi. e. on SR 243, is the only unaltered Pony Express station remaining in its original location. G.H. Hollenberg built the long frame structure to accommodate his home and the businesses engendered by the traffic on the Oregon Trail.

A museum contains exhibits about the history of the Oregon/California Trail and the Pony Express. A visitor center gallery depicts the evolution of transportation methods. Wed.-Sat. 10-5, Sun. 1-5, Mar.-Nov.; closed holidays. Admission $3, over 59 and students with ID $2, under 5 free. Phone (785) 337-2635.

HAYS (C-3) pop. 20,013, elev. 1,997'

By the early 1860s a rising tide of travelers, settlers and railroad builders was inching across the Kansas plains. American Indians, whose lands were being usurped and whose food staple, the buffalo, was being slaughtered by the intruders, responded with increasing hostility.

For protection, Fort Fletcher was established on the banks of Big Creek on the Smoky Hill Trail. Renamed Fort Hays a year later, it became one of the era's prominent military posts. Unlike other typical frontier military outposts, however, Fort Hays had no stockade. All buildings and quarters were grouped around a parade ground.

At one time William "Buffalo Bill" Cody supplied the fort with buffalo meat. Lt. Col. George Custer's ill-fated 7th Cavalry also was stationed at the fort. By the time Fort Hays was abandoned in 1889, the town had become a thriving railroad and agricultural center.

Deeded to the state, the old military post became the site of 5,500-student Fort Hays State University and a 3,700-acre dryland agricultural research center and park, one of the largest in the world. A small buffalo herd can be seen at Frontier Park across from Fort Hays State Historic Site (see attraction listing).

In summer the Hays Aquatic Park, at 4th and Main streets, provides opportunities for swimming, diving or tubing down a lazy river; phone (785) 623-2650. The Kansas Merci Boxcar Museum, 13th and Canterbury streets, features one of 49 boxcars that arrived in the United States in 1949. Filled with French food and other goods, the gifts expressed the French people's gratitude for American assistance during World War II.

Hays Convention and Visitors Bureau: 1301 Pine St., Suite B, Hays, KS 67601; phone (785) 628-8202 or (800) 569-4505.

Self-guiding tours: A series of 25 markers, beginning downtown at 12th and Fort streets, designates a self-guiding walking tour. Brochures are available at the convention and visitors bureau.

ELLIS COUNTY HISTORICAL SOCIETY MUSEUM, 100 W. Seventh St., is housed in a 19th-century church building. A replica of an early schoolroom and changing exhibits of local settlers' possessions are displayed. A harness shop features saddles from a local historic ranch. Tues.-Fri. 10-5, Sat. 1-5, June-Aug.; Tues.-Fri. 10-5, rest of year. Admission $3; under 12, $1. Phone (785) 628-2624.

Volga-German Haus, on the grounds of the Ellis County Historical Society Museum, is a replica of a typical Volga-German immigrant house of the 1880s. It is filled with period furnishings. House tours are given by appointment; check with the museum. Admission included with museum ticket. Phone (785) 628-2624.

FORT HAYS STATE HISTORIC SITE, 4 mi. s. of I-70 to 1472 US 183 Alt., encompasses the restored buildings of Fort Hays, including the stone guardhouse, blockhouse and officers' quarters. Buildings contain exhibits about military and pioneer history. There is a visitor center on the grounds. Allow 1 hour minimum. Tues.-Sat. 9-5, Sun.-Mon. 1-5; closed holidays. Admission $3, over 59 and students with ID $2, under 5 free. Phone (785) 625-6812.

STERNBERG MUSEUM OF NATURAL HISTORY, off I-70 exit 159, 1 mi. s. on US 183, then following signs, re-creates the late Cretaceous period with dioramas of animated, life-size dinosaurs. The museum, part of Fort Hays State University, also contains one of the world's best collections of fossilized prehistoric flying reptiles and creatures from the Cretaceous sea. One particularly unusual specimen is a fish within a fish.

For children, the Discovery Room contains a giant spider model, computer work stations, live animals and hands-on activities. Changing exhibits are featured throughout the year. Guided tours are available by appointment. Allow 2 hours minimum. Tues.-Sat. 9-7, Sun. 1-7; closed Jan. 1, Thanksgiving and Dec. 25. Discovery Room hours vary; phone

ahead. Admission $6; over 60 and ages 4-12, $4.
MC, VI. Phone (785) 628-5516 or (877) 332-1165.

STONE GALLERY, off Main St. at 107 W. Sixth
St., displays the limestone, wood, clay and plaster
sculptures of Pete Felten, whose public monuments
can be seen throughout the state. Visitors can watch
live demonstrations of the sculpting process. Allow
30 minutes minimum. Mon.-Fri. 9-5. Free. Phone
(785) 625-7619.

HIAWATHA (B-7) pop. 3,417, elev. 1,085′

More than 100 varieties of maple trees, planted
and cultivated by local citizens, line the streets of
Hiawatha. Several city parks offer picnicking and
fishing. A town clock dating from 1891 is at Seventh and Oregon streets.

Hiawatha Chamber of Commerce: 602 Oregon
St., Hiawatha, KS 66434; phone (785) 742-7136.

Self-guiding tours: A brochure outlining a driving
tour of late 19th-century houses is available from
the chamber of commerce.

**BROWN COUNTY HISTORICAL SOCIETY AND
MUSEUM,** in Memorial Auditorium at 611 Utah St.,
depicts the county's history from its settlement in
1854. A doctor's room, general store, Victorian
kitchen and schoolroom are among the displays. Allow 1 hour minimum. Mon.-Fri. 10-3; closed major
holidays. Admission $5; ages 5-12, $2.50. Phone
(785) 742-3330.

DAVIS MEMORIAL, in Mount Hope Cemetery at
the s.e. edge of town, is an unusual memorial commissioned in 1930 by John M. Davis to perpetuate
the memory of his wife, Sarah. Eleven life-size statues depict Mr. and Mrs. Davis at various stages of

their lives. Allow 30 minutes minimum. Daily
8-dusk. Free. Phone (785) 742-7136.

HIGHLAND (B-7) pop. 967, elev. 856′

Highland, founded in 1837, is on what was once
the Iowa Indian Reservation. Highland College, said
to be the state's oldest continuing institution of
higher learning, is an outgrowth of a Presbyterian
mission; phone (785) 442-6000.

**NATIVE AMERICAN HERITAGE MUSEUM
STATE HISTORIC SITE,** 2 mi. e. on Old US 36,
then .2 mi. n. on SR 136, occupies the remaining
portion of the Presbyterian mission building erected
in 1846. The museum recounts the history of the
American Indian, beginning with the forced resettle-
ment of Eastern and Great Lakes natives mandated
by the Indian Removal Act of 1836. Allow 30 minutes minimum. Wed.-Sat. 10-5, Sun. 1-5, Mar.-Nov.;
closed holidays. Admission $3, over 60 and students
with ID $2. Phone (785) 442-3304.

HILLSBORO (D-6) pop. 2,854, elev. 1,426′

The home of Tabor College, Hillsboro was settled
mainly by German-speaking Mennonite immigrants
from Russia and Poland. Arriving in the early
1870s, they are credited with bringing Turkey Red
wheat to the area. Nearby recreation areas include
McPherson State Fishing Lake northwest of Hillsboro and Marion Reservoir to the northeast *(see
Recreation Chart and Canton and Marion in the
AAA South Central CampBook).*

Hillsboro Chamber of Commerce: 109 S. Main
St., Hillsboro, KS 67063; phone (620) 947-3506.

SAVE **THE MENNONITE SETTLEMENT MUSEUM**
is 1 mi. s. of US 56 at 501 S. Ash St. The museum celebrates the immigrant Russian and Polish

Mennonites who settled in western Marion and eastern McPherson Counties in the early 1870s. It includes the historic Peter Paul Loewen House, a traditional Russian Mennonite clay-brick house-barn built in 1876 in the settlement of Hoffnungsthal; the Jacob Friesen Flouring Windmill, a detailed replica of an 1876 flour mill that stood in the settlement of Gnadenau; and the 1886 one-room Kreutziger School House.

Guided tours are available. Allow 1 hour minimum. Tues.-Fri. 10-noon and 1:30-4, Sat.-Sun. 2-4, Mar.-Dec.; closed holidays. Admission $3, students with ID $1, under 5 free with adult. Phone (620) 947-3775.

HUTCHINSON (D-5) pop. 40,787, elev. 1,529′

"Salt of the Earth" has a special meaning in Hutchinson, where the mining and processing of salt has been a major industry since 1888. A bed of salt and salt/shale between 300 and 350 feet thick and some 600 feet below the surrounding wheat fields was discovered in 1887, to the consternation of drillers looking for natural gas.

Even exhausted mines are valuable; they are used by businesses, hospitals and film companies throughout the world for maximum-security storage of their records. Had the gas seekers persevered, they might have found some of the oil that now enriches the city's economy. However, it is the wheat fields themselves rather than the substances extracted from beneath them that support Hutchinson's leading industry. Other economic mainstays include agribusiness, aerospace equipment, health care, specialty vehicle manufacturing, grocery distribution and food processing.

The Fox Theatre has been restored to its 1931 art deco splendor and is open for guided tours, films and live performances; phone (620) 663-5861. Nearly 550 acres of parks provide ample recreational opportunities. In early September the state's agricultural bounty is celebrated when Hutchinson hosts the Kansas State Fair.

Hutchinson Convention and Visitors Bureau: 117 N. Walnut St., P.O. Box 519, Hutchinson, KS 67504-0519; phone (620) 662-3391.

KANSAS COSMOSPHERE AND SPACE CENTER is at 1100 N. Plum St. The facility features the Hall of Space Museum, IMAX Dome Theater, Justice Planetarium, Dr. Goddard's Lab and changing exhibitions. Highlights include an outstanding exhibit of space suits and one of the largest collections of Russian space equipment outside Moscow.

Early space exploration is detailed through exhibits about Germany's V-1 and V-2 rockets and Russia's Sputnik programs. U.S. space artifacts include the actual Apollo 13 command module, *Gemini X* and a full-scale replica of the space shuttle.

IMAX films are shown on a 44-foot screen; the planetarium presents programs about stars and space. Live shows at Dr. Goddard's Lab demonstrate the principles of rocket science.

Allow 3 hours minimum. Mon.-Sat. 9-9, Sun. noon-9, Memorial Day-Labor Day; Mon.-Thurs. 9-6, Fri.-Sat. 9-9, Sun. noon-6, rest of year. Closed Dec. 25. IMAX films, planetarium and laser light shows, and Dr. Goddard's Lab demonstrations are presented daily.

Admission $13; over 59, $12; ages 5-12, $10.50. Single venue (IMAX Dome Theater, Justice Planetarium and Dr. Goddard's Lab) $8; over 59 and ages 5-12, $7.50. AX, DS, MC, VI. Phone (620) 662-2305 or (800) 397-0330.

RENO COUNTY MUSEUM, 100 S. Walnut St., chronicles the history of the county through five exhibits, with topics ranging from settlement to entertainment. Demonstrations are held throughout the year, and changing exhibits and an interactive children's room are featured. Outside is the 1876 Siegrest Claim House, a 1940s windmill, a railroad caboose and locomotive. Tues.-Sat. 9-5, Sun. 1-5; closed holidays. Donations. Phone (620) 662-1184.

INDEPENDENCE (E-7) pop. 9,846, elev. 798′

Formerly the site of the Osage Indian Reservation, the Independence area was opened to settlement in 1870 when the Osage agreed to move to the Indian Territory in what is now Oklahoma. In 1881 natural gas was discovered and Independence grew quickly, as it did again in 1903 with the discovery of oil. Today, with its gas and oil deposits depleted, the city relies on diversified manufacturing and agriculture.

Independence was the boyhood home of Pulitzer Prize winning playwright William Inge whose Midwestern upbringing shaped such dramas as "Splendor in the Grass" and "Come Back, Little Sheba." The William Inge Collection, housed at Independence Community College, contains original manuscripts, documents and memorabilia; phone (620) 331-4100, ext. 4280. Nearby Elk City Reservoir and State Park offers water sports and other recreation *(see Recreation Chart and the AAA South Central CampBook).*

Independence Area Chamber of Commerce: 322 N. Penn, P.O. Box 386, Independence, KS 67301; phone (620) 331-1890 or (800) 882-3606.

THE INDEPENDENCE HISTORICAL MUSEUM, 123 N. 8th St., presents regional history from the 1800s to the present. Housed in a former post office built in 1911, exhibits feature American Indian culture, pioneer artifacts, Civil War military items, an 1884 schoolroom and a furnished log cabin. Guided tours are available by appointment. Allow 1 hour minimum. Wed.-Sat. 10-4, Sun. 1-4; closed holidays. Donations. Phone (620) 331-3515.

LITTLE HOUSE ON THE PRAIRIE, 13 mi. s.w. on US 75, following signs, is a log cabin reconstructed on the site where Laura Ingalls Wilder lived 1869-71. A post office and a one-room schoolhouse are displayed. A hiking trail is available. Mon.-Sat. and holidays 10-5, Sun. 1-5, Mar. 15-Oct. 31. Donations. Phone (620) 289-4238.

RIVERSIDE PARK, 1 mi. n. on US 75, then 2 blks. e. on Oak St., is a 124-acre recreational complex with a swimming pool, water park, tennis courts, a playground, miniature golf, a carousel and train ride. Band concerts are presented Tuesday evenings in summer. Park daily 6 a.m.-midnight. Rides operate Mon.-Sat. 6:30-9:30 p.m., Sun. 1-5:30, Memorial Day weekend-Labor Day. Park free. Miniature golf $1. Train ride 25c. Carousel 5c. Phone (620) 332-2512.

Ralph Mitchell Zoo, on the n. side of Riverside Park, houses a variety of animals, including bears, cougars, birds, reptiles and monkeys. Peacocks roam the grounds. Daily 10-8, Memorial Day-Labor Day; 10-5, rest of year. Free. Phone (620) 332-2512.

IOLA (D-7) pop. 6,302, elev. 962′

In the spring of 1855 a party of pro-slavery men founded a town about a mile and a half southwest of where Iola now stands. They named the town Co-fachique in honor of an American Indian chief, and it became the seat of Allen County. Four years later, area residents decided to establish a new county seat and chose the name Iola after Iola Colborn, wife of the man who built the town's first frame house.

The town expanded rapidly after commercial quantities of natural gas were discovered in 1894, but the boom ended around 1910 after wastefulness depleted the gas deposits. Some factories remained in business, and in the early 1970s Iola saw a new wave of factory building.

Cultural events take place at Bowlus Fine Arts Center, 205 E. Madison Ave.; phone (620) 365-4765.

Iola Area Chamber of Commerce: 208 W. Madison Ave., Iola, KS 66749; phone (620) 365-5252.

ALLEN COUNTY HISTORICAL MUSEUM is at 20 S. Washington Ave. Permanent and changing exhibits describe the history and people of Allen County. The 1869 Old Jail, 203 N. Jefferson, is open for 30-minute guided tours. Tues.-Sat. 12:30-4, Apr.-Oct.; 2-4, rest of year. Jail tours are offered by appointment Donations. Phone (620) 365-3051.

MAJOR GENERAL FREDERICK FUNSTON BOY-HOOD HOME AND MUSEUM is at 14 S. Washington Ave. The 1860 Victorian-style house was moved to its present location, restored and furnished in period to honor Funston and his sterling military career. After enlisting in the Cuban rebel army in 1896, he won a Medal of Honor for his command of a Kansas regiment in the Spanish American War. Allow 1 hour minimum. Tues.-Sat. 12:30-4, May-Oct.; 2-4, rest of year. Donations. Phone (620) 365-6728.

JUNCTION CITY (C-6)
pop. 18,886, elev. 1,080′

Trade has been a major occupation in Junction City since its founding in 1857 at the confluence of the Smoky Hill and Republican rivers. Early commerce was conducted with travelers on the Smoky

Hill Trail and with the Kansa Indians, who often came into town to buy and sell. One notable day in 1867 the wares offered by a Cheyenne war party included some newly acquired scalps.

Although feathers and war paint have since disappeared—Junction City is now a commercial center—many of the military uniforms reminiscent of the hostile 1800s endure at historic Fort Riley (see place listing p. 84), which is just north.

Marking the history of Junction City and surrounding counties is Geary County Historical Society Museum, Sixth and Adams streets. Through the display of artifacts and photographs, the museum traces the progression of inhabitants since the area was settled. The Spring Valley Historic Site, US 18 and Spring Valley Road, contains a restored 1870s schoolhouse, a settler's log cabin and a barn.

Heritage Park contains the Kansas Vietnam Memorial, the 1st Infantry Division Monument, a Desert Storm Memorial and a limestone arch that commemorates participants from both sides of the Civil War. The 9-foot-tall bronze Buffalo Soldier Memorial, 18th Street and Buffalo Soldier Drive, commemorates the African-American soldiers who served in the 9th and 10th horse cavalry regiments during the Civil War.

Popular recreation sites are Milford Lake, Geary County State Fishing Lake and Milford State Park. Milford Lake is the largest blue-water lake in the state. See Recreation Chart and the AAA South Central CampBook.

Geary County Convention and Visitors Bureau: 425 N. Washington St., P.O. Box 1846, Junction City, KS 66441-6846; phone (785) 238-2885 or (800) 528-2489.

MILFORD FISH HATCHERY AND NATURE CENTER, I-70 exit 295, then 5 mi. n. to SR 57 and 2 mi. w., following signs, is on Milford Reservoir and features a fish hatchery where more than 75 million eggs are hatched each April. The nature center offers two dioramas depicting Kansas wildlife, hands-on displays and a hiking trail. Programs are offered by appointment throughout the year. Allow 1 hour minimum. Mon.-Fri. 9-4:30, Sat.-Sun. 1-5, Apr.-Sept. Hatchery tours are given Sat.-Sun. at 1. Donations. Phone (785) 238-5323.

KANOPOLIS (C-5) pop. 543, elev. 1,587′

FORT HARKER MUSEUM is on SR 140. Abandoned in 1872, Fort Harker was used to protect the north central Kansas frontier from hostile American Indians. Featured are a horse-drawn ambulance, military uniforms and equipment from World Wars I and II. A train depot is on the grounds as well as junior officers' quarters.

Allow 30 minutes minimum. Tues.-Sat. 10-5, Sun. 1-5, May-Sept.; Tues.-Fri. and Sun. 1-5, Sat. 10-5 in Apr. and Oct.; Sat. 10-5, Sun. 1-5, rest of year. Closed major holidays. Admission $3; ages 6-12, $1. Admission includes Hodgden House Museum Complex in Ellsworth (see attraction listing p. 83). Phone (785) 472-3059.

KANSAS CITY—

see Kansas City p. 182 in Missouri.

KINSLEY (D-4) pop. 1,658, elev. 2,164'

During the 1870s Kinsley shared in the boom brought by railroad expansion. The *Mercury* newspaper printed 25,000 European editions advertising the town: "Kinsley—The Cynosure Of All Eyes, The Coming Great Metropolis." But when the dust—most of which was caused by a decade of drought—had settled, an 1888 edition of the *Mercury* confessed that the boom was over as nine columns of delinquent tax notices were printed.

Today Kinsley enjoys quieter days as an agricultural center and the seat of Edwards County. The town is noted for being halfway between New York City and San Francisco—1,561 miles from either city—giving it the nickname Midway, U.S.A.

Kinsley Chamber of Commerce: 200 E. 6th St., P.O. Box 332, Kinsley, KS 67547; phone (877) 464-6439.

EDWARDS COUNTY HISTORICAL MUSEUM, jct. US 50 and US 56, features a sod house that includes an explanation of its construction, an 1884 church and blacksmith shop. The "soddy" is furnished with period items. On display are settlers' toys, quilts and clothing as well as Santa Fe Trail memorabilia, including photographs and oxen yokes. Other exhibits feature horse-drawn machinery and an early fire engine. Mon.-Sat. 10-5, Sun. 1-5, May-Sept. Donations. Phone (620) 659-2420.

KIRWIN (B-4) pop. 229, elev. 1,695'

KIRWIN NATIONAL WILDLIFE REFUGE office is 4 mi. w. on SR 9, then 1 mi. s. on E. Xavier Rd. The refuge covers 10,778 acres surrounding Kirwin Reservoir and provides a habitat for various species of migratory waterfowl and grassland nesting birds. The 10-acre Prairie Dog Town allows visitors to view these animals from nature trails. Fishing, birdwatching and seasonal hunting are offered. Regulation information is available at refuge headquarters.

Allow 3 hours minimum. Daily 24 hours. Office Mon.-Fri. 7:30-4. Free. Phone (785) 543-6673.

LA CROSSE (C-4) pop. 1,376, elev. 2,068'

La Crosse, founded in 1876, is a shipping point for wheat and livestock. The town is known as the "Barbed Wire Capital of the World."

Rush County Chamber of Commerce: P.O. Box 716, La Crosse, KS 67548; phone (785) 222-2639.

BARBED WIRE MUSEUM, 120 W. First St., displays some 2,066 types of barbed wire, including the first 1853 patented wire, handmade barbed wire, foreign barbed wire and entanglement wire used in battle since World War I. Many related items also are displayed. Allow 30 minutes minimum. Mon.-Sat. 10-4:30, Sun. 1-4:30, late Apr. to mid-Sept. Donations. Phone (785) 222-9900.

THE POST ROCK MUSEUM is at 202 W. First St. Post rock, a form of limestone common to this region of the state, was used extensively from the late 1870s to the mid-1930s for fence posts and in constructing bridges, houses, churches and other buildings. Displays explain how the rock was found, quarried and used. Allow 30 minutes minimum. Mon.-Sat. 10-4:30, Sun. 1-4:30, May 1 to mid-Sept. Donations. Phone (785) 222-2719.

RUSH COUNTY HISTORICAL MUSEUM, in the old Santa Fe Depot at 201 W. First St., preserves county and period history with a hodgepodge of historical relics. Allow 30 minutes minimum. Mon.-Sat. 10-4:30, Sun. 1-4:30, May 1 to mid-Sept. Donations. Phone (785) 222-2719.

LARNED (D-4) pop. 4,236, elev. 2,002'

Midway along the Santa Fe Trail where Pawnee Creek joins the Arkansas River, the settlement of Larned emerged as the construction of the Santa Fe Railway neared Fort Larned. As the military usefulness of the fort declined, the attractiveness of the fertile agricultural lands became apparent, allowing Larned to develop into the prosperous trading center and county seat it is today.

Central States Scout Museum, 815 Broadway, displays Boy and Girl Scout memorabilia, including uniforms, awards and handbooks; phone (620) 285-8938.

Larned Area Chamber of Commerce: 502 Broadway, Larned, KS 67550; phone (620) 285-6916.

FORT LARNED NATIONAL HISTORIC SITE is 6 mi. w. via SR 156. Established in 1859 to protect mail coaches and commercial wagon trains traveling the Santa Fe Trail, the fort was an important post on the frontier until its deactivation in 1878. The site includes nine original sandstone buildings and a section of wagon-wheel rutted prairie. A visitor center has exhibits and a slide program; living-history programs are held in summer and on major holidays.

Daily 8:30-4:30; closed Jan. 1, Thanksgiving and Dec. 25. Admission $3, under 16 free, family rate $5. Phone (620) 285-6911.

SANTA FE TRAIL CENTER MUSEUM AND LIBRARY, 2 mi. w. on SR 156, depicts the history of one of America's most important frontier pathways as well as the lifestyles of early Kansas pioneers. Permanent displays include a Wichita Indian hunting lodge, a mounted buffalo, a freight wagon, period rooms, a sod house, a limestone cooling house, a one-room schoolhouse, an early African-American church and a dugout house. Changing exhibits also are presented.

Allow 1 hour minimum. Daily 9-5, Memorial Day-Labor Day; Tues.-Sun. 9-5, rest of year. Closed Jan. 1, Thanksgiving and Dec. 25. Admission $4; ages 12-18, $2.50; ages 6-11, $1.50. MC, VI. Phone (620) 285-2054.

LAWRENCE (C-7) pop. 80,098, elev. 822'

Lawrence was at the center of the slavery versus free-state controversy that embroiled Kansas 1855-59. Founded in 1854 by the New England Emigrant Aid Society, the settlement espoused the abolitionist cause.

Although the anti-slavery faction won, the other side ultimately had the last word. In 1863 Confederate guerrilla William Quantrill and 400 raiders swept into Lawrence and attacked the ill-prepared home guard, leaving more than 200 dead and $1.5 million worth of damage.

Modern day Lawrence is a vibrant smaller city with many big-city amenities. Education, transportation, agriculture and light industry provide the basis for a diverse economy. The University of Kansas and Haskell Indian Nations University, the country's only intertribal American Indian college, are focal points for education, arts and culture. Lectures, plays, films, performing arts and concerts are presented year-round at The Lied Center of Kansas; phone the box office at (785) 864-2787. The Lawrence Arts Center, 940 New Hampshire St., hosts visual art, theater and dance events; phone (785) 843-2787.

For recreational pursuits, the city has some 50 parks that offer opportunities for swimming, skateboarding, hiking, tennis, golf, camping and picnicking. Additional information and a map indicating bicycle routes and parks can be obtained at the Parks and Recreation Department, City Hall, Sixth and Massachusetts streets, and at the Lawrence Visitor Information Center, N. Second and Locust streets; phone (888) 529-5267. Clinton Lake State Park *(see Recreation Chart and the AAA South Central CampBook)* is 4 miles west of town.

Downtown Lawrence has a number of historic buildings. The Old West Lawrence Historic District, bounded by Sixth, Eighth, Tennessee and Indiana streets, contains more than 40 Victorian- and Italianate-style residences. The 1912 Liberty Hall, 642 Massachusetts St., was the first motion picture theater west of the Mississippi River.

Lawrence Convention and Visitors Bureau: 734 Vermont St., P.O. Box 586, Lawrence, KS 66044; phone (785) 865-4411 or (888) 529-5267.

Self-guiding tours: Maps for touring the city, its historic district and the University of Kansas campus are available from the convention and visitors bureau.

Shopping areas: The downtown district, running along Massachusetts Street between Sixth and 11th streets, has an eclectic mixture of locally owned shops, cafes and restaurants as well as large national chain stores.

UNIVERSITY OF KANSAS, s. of I-70 exit 202 via US 59, is on Mount Oread, which separates the valleys of the Kansas and Wakarusa rivers. A visitor center, at the corner of 15th and Iowa streets, offers maps and brochures. Guided walking tours of the

1,000-acre wooded campus are available. Of interest is the World War II Memorial Campanile, on Memorial Drive.

Visitor center Mon.-Fri. 8-5, Sat. 9-1; closed university holidays and semester breaks. Phone (785) 864-3911 for tour and general campus information.

Kenneth Spencer Research Library, 1450 Poplar Ln., contains an extensive collection of rare books, manuscripts, old maps and early photographs. Among the specialties are European books printed in the 15th through 17th centuries; books relating to Ireland and 18th-century England; the history of such sciences as botany, ornithology and zoology; and broad collections of Italian, French and English manuscripts of the 11th through 20th centuries. Items in the Kansas Collection pertain to the land encompassed by the Kansas Territory.

Allow 1 hour minimum. Mon.-Fri. 8-5, Sat. noon-4, Sept.-May; Mon.-Fri. 8-5, rest of year. Closed major and university holidays and during semester breaks. Free. Phone (785) 864-4334.

Museum of Anthropology, in Spooner Hall at 1340 Jayhawk Blvd., displays ethnographic materials from North and South America, Africa and the Pacific as well as prehistoric archeological specimens, primarily from the western Plains. Allow 1 hour minimum. Mon.-Sat. 9-5, Sun. 1-5; closed major holidays. Donations. Phone (785) 864-4245.

Natural History Museum and Biodiversity Research Center, in Dyche Hall at 1345 Jayhawk Blvd., displays birds, fossils and mounted animals primarily from Kansas and the Plains states. The main floor features a panorama of North American plants and animals in natural settings and such mounted animals as Comanche, a horse that survived Lt. Col. George Custer's Last Stand. Live snakes, bees and fish comprise other exhibits. Allow 2 hours minimum. Mon.-Sat. 9-5, Sun. noon-5; closed major holidays. Admission $3, children $2. Phone (785) 864-4450.

Robert J. Dole Institute of Politics is off I-70 exit 202, 1.7 mi. s. on Iowa St. (US 59), then w. into University of Kansas via 19th St. to 2350 Petefish Dr. The non-partisan institute contains research and archival materials related to the career of Kansas native Sen. Robert J. Dole. A museum includes interactive exhibits about his early life, military service and political accomplishments.

Memorials to the World Trade Center victims and the state's World War II veterans are included. Allow 1 hour minimum. Mon.-Sat. 9-5, Sun. noon-5; closed holidays. Free. Phone (785) 864-4900.

Spencer Museum of Art is at 1301 Mississippi St.; parking is available next to the university union. The museum, which contains more than 25,000 objects in its permanent collection, ranks among the finest university art museums in the country. Strengths are in Renaissance and baroque painting; American paintings and sculpture; the decorative arts of Europe, America and Asia; and graphic arts, including photographs and Japanese prints.

Permanent and changing exhibits are displayed. Allow 1 hour minimum. Tues.-Sat. 10-5 (also Thurs. 5-9), Sun. noon-5; closed major holidays. Donations. Phone (785) 864-4710.

WATKINS COMMUNITY MUSEUM OF HISTORY, 1047 Massachusetts St., is housed in a restored 1888 bank building. Displays depict area history and include a Victorian parlor, a bicentennial quilt, a 1920 electric car, a horse-drawn surrey, an 1878 playhouse and an 1850s cannon. A children's history room also is offered. Rotating exhibits feature such topics as early settlement, the Underground Railroad and Lawrence resident Dr. James Naismith, originator of the game of basketball. Tues.-Thurs. 10-6 (also Thurs. 6-9 p.m.), Fri. 10-5, Sat. 10-4; closed holidays. Donations. Phone (785) 841-4109.

LEAVENWORTH (B-8) pop. 35,420, elev. 774′

Incorporated in 1854, Leavenworth is the oldest city in Kansas. In 1857 the firm of Russell, Majors & Waddell made the rapidly growing community the headquarters of their vast overland transportation system. In April 1860 the company's other venture, the Pony Express, used lightweight riders on fleet ponies to speed the mail from St. Joseph, Mo., to Sacramento, Calif., in as little as 9 days. Completion of the transcontinental telegraph in October 1861 rendered the service obsolete.

Leavenworth Landing Park, on the Missouri River, commemorates the city's role as "Gateway to the West." It features sculptures of a locomotive and a covered wagon as well as depictions of a railroad roundhouse and paddlewheel steamship.

Leavenworth Convention & Visitors Bureau: 518 Shawnee St., P.O. Box 44, Leavenworth, KS 66048; phone (913) 682-4113 or (800) 844-4114.

Self-guiding tours: Maps featuring area driving and walking tours are available from the convention and visitors bureau.

CARROLL MANSION is at 1128 Fifth Ave. The 16-room Victorian house, built in 1867, was expanded and embellished with fine carved woodwork in 1882. The furnishings illustrate gracious living in the 19th century. Allow 1 hour minimum. Tues.-Sat. 10:30-4:30, Apr.-Nov.; Tues.-Sat. 1-4:30, Dec. 1 to mid-Dec. and mid-Feb. through Mar. 31. Closed holidays. Hours may vary; phone ahead. Admission $5; over 59, $4; ages 5-12, $3. Phone (913) 682-7759 or (800) 844-4114.

FORT LEAVENWORTH is at Seventh St. and US 73. Established in 1827 to guard the Santa Fe and Oregon trails, the fort is the oldest active Army post west of the Mississippi River. It also was an important Army headquarters during the Mexican War 1846-48.

The Santa Fe and Oregon Trail markers, the Fort Leavenworth National Cemetery and the Buffalo

Soldier Monument are of interest. Maps are available for self-guiding tours in the museum. Photo ID is required for all visitors over 16 entering the base. Daily dawn-dusk. Free. Phone (913) 684-5604.

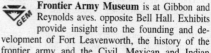 **Frontier Army Museum** is at Gibbon and Reynolds aves. opposite Bell Hall. Exhibits provide insight into the founding and development of Fort Leavenworth, the history of the frontier army and the Civil, Mexican and Indian wars. The museum includes the carriage in which Abraham Lincoln rode while visiting Leavenworth, army carriages and a full-size JN4 "Jenny" biplane.

Also displayed are examples of U.S. military dress and equipment up to World War I as well as several rare Mexican War items. Videotapes about the history of the fort are shown. Mon.-Fri. 9-4, Sat. 10-4; closed federal holidays. Donations. Phone (913) 684-3767 or (913) 684-3186.

RICHARD ALLEN CULTURAL CENTER AND MUSEUM is at 412 Kiowa St. The museum highlights the roles African-Americans have played in the history of Kansas and the West with exhibits about the Buffalo Soldiers, a nickname originally applied to members of the all-black Army regiments created after the Civil War. A restored Buffalo Soldiers home features furnishings and 1920s décor.

Other exhibits include an 1860 tallow light belonging to a runaway slave, a collection of historic photos and memorabilia belonging to former Secretary of State Colin Powell. Guided tours are available. Allow 1 hour minimum. Mon.-Thurs. 1-6:30, Fri. 1-4, Sat. 10-1; closed major holidays. Admission $5; under 13, $2. Phone (913) 682-8772.

LEBANON (B-4) pop. 303, elev. 760′

A stone monument 1 mile northwest marks the historical geographical center of the 48 contiguous United States. A small park, open church, picnic tables and shelter house are at the site.

Lebanon City Office: 404 Main St., P.O. Box 182, Lebanon, KS 66952; phone (785) 389-1141.

LECOMPTON (B-7) pop. 608

Lecompton is on the banks of the Kaw River, in the rolling hills between Topeka and Lawrence. From its founding as Bald Eagle in 1854, until Kansas statehood was granted in 1861, this village was the territorial capital.

CONSTITUTION HALL STATE HISTORIC SITE, 319 Elmore St., is the building in which the controversial Lecompton Constitution for the admittance of Kansas into the Union as a pro-slavery state was written. The document sparked a chain of events that divided the country and eventually climaxed in the Civil War. Displays deal with significant territorial Kansas political and historical events such as the slavery debate. Wed.-Sat. 9-5, Sun. 1-5; closed holidays. Admission $2; grades K-12, $1. Phone (785) 887-6520.

TERRITORIAL CAPITOL-LANE MUSEUM, 609 E. Woodson Rd., was begun in 1855 as the territorial capitol but work was suspended in 1857 when it seemed the capital would be elsewhere. Finally completed in 1882, the building housed Lane University until 1902. Displays include pioneer and American Indian artifacts and an exhibit about President Dwight Eisenhower's parents, who met and married while attending Lane University. Guided 1-hour tours are available upon request. Wed.-Sat. 11-4; Sun. 1-5; closed holidays. Donations. Phone (785) 887-6148.

LENEXA—

see Kansas City p. 183 in Missouri.

LIBERAL (E-2) pop. 19,666, elev. 2,839'

Now used by the Cotton Belt Railroad, the Rock Island Railroad Bridge across the Cimarron River is one of the largest of its kind. Called "Mighty Sampson," it is 1,200 feet long and 100 feet above the riverbed. Support pylons were driven to a depth of 165 feet to resist the shifting quicksand of the river.

Liberal Convention and Tourism Bureau: 1 Yellow Brick Rd., Liberal, KS 67901; phone (620) 626-0170 or (800) 542-3725.

DOROTHY'S HOUSE/ LAND OF OZ /CORONADO MUSEUM is at 567 E. Cedar St. Dorothy's House is a replica of the fictional Kansas farmhouse depicted in the 1939 motion picture, "The Wizard of Oz." A re-creation of the Yellow Brick Road leads to the Land of Oz Museum, which features exhibits about the film as well as related memorabilia. The Coronado Museum contains pictures, documents and historical items pertaining to Seward County and early Kansas.

Allow 1 hour minimum. Guided tours are offered every 30 minutes Mon.-Sat. 9-6, Sun. 1-5, Memorial Day-Labor Day; on the hour Tues.-Sat. 9-5, Sun. 1-5, rest of year. Closed Jan. 1, Easter, Thanksgiving and Dec. 25. Dorothy's House and Land of Oz $5; over 59 and ages 6-18, $3.50. Coronado Museum free. DS, MC, VI. Phone (620) 624-7624.

MID-AMERICA AIR MUSEUM LIBERAL, KANSAS, 2000 W. Second St., is Kansas' largest aviation museum. Collections consist of military and civilian aircraft as well as aerospace aviation exhibits. Visitors can see World War II fighters and bombers, experimental and golden age aircraft and planes used in the Korean and Vietnam wars.

Features include the Liberal Army Airfield, Korean War exhibits, the Col. Tom A. Thomas Jr. Historic Aircraft Collection and a NASA exhibit. More than 100 aircraft are displayed, including such rare planes as the Grumman TBM Avenger, North American B-25, Rutan aircraft, Vought F4U-5N Crusader and the Douglas A-4 Skyhawk. Wind tunnel and hot air balloon exhibits are part of the Aviation Hall of Science.

Allow 1 hour minimum. Mon.-Fri. 8-5, Sat. 10-5, Sun. 1-5; closed Jan. 1, Thanksgiving and Dec. 25. Admission $7; over 62, $5; ages 6-18, $3. DS, MC, VI. Phone (620) 624-5263.

LINDSBORG (C-5) pop. 3,321, elev. 1,335'

The delightful flavor of Scandinavia permeates Lindsborg, founded by a company of Swedish pioneers and farmers in 1869. Many Old World arts and crafts are practiced; studios of several Lindsborg artists feature woodcarvings, ceramics, pottery, metal craft and paintings.

Lindsborg Chamber of Commerce: 104 E. Lincoln St., Lindsborg, KS 67456; phone (785) 227-3706 or (888) 227-2227. *See color ad.*

BIRGER SANDZEN MEMORIAL GALLERY, at 401 N. First St. on the Bethany College campus, features the works of the Swedish-American painter and art teacher. This gallery also displays permanent and changing collections of paintings, prints, ceramics and sculptures in 10 exhibition areas. An outdoor courtyard features a fountain sculpted by the Swedish artist Carl Milles. Tues.-Sun. 1-5. Free. Phone (785) 227-2220.

McPHERSON COUNTY OLD MILL MUSEUM, 5 blks. s. on Main St., then 1 blk. e., includes historic buildings, pioneer exhibits and Swedish costumes. Smoky Valley Roller Mill is one of the earliest water-powered flour mills in the state. The Swedish Pavilion, also on the grounds, originally was part of the 1904 St. Louis World's Fair. A small park and

campground are on the banks of the Smoky Hill River.

Mon.-Sat. 9-5, Sun. 1-5; closed Jan. 1, Thanksgiving and Dec. 25. Admission $2; ages 6-12, $1. DS, MC, VI. Phone (785) 227-3595.

LOGAN (B-3) pop. 603, elev. 1,950'

A farming and oil community on the Solomon River, Logan was established in 1872. Among the founders was a young Dane, Peter Hansen, whose son Dane became an important businessman and a friend and advisor to President Dwight Eisenhower.

DANE G. HANSEN MEMORIAL MUSEUM occupies a square block in the center of town at 110 W. Main St. Oil paintings, a collection of European and Western guns, coins and Oriental art are featured. Traveling exhibits from the Smithsonian Institution and other renowned museums also are presented. Allow 1 hour minimum. Mon.-Fri. 9-noon and 1-4, Sat. 9-noon and 1-5, Sun. and holidays 1-5; closed Jan. 1, Thanksgiving and Dec. 25. Free. Phone (785) 689-4846.

LUCAS (C-4) pop. 436, elev. 1,493'

GARDEN OF EDEN is at Second and Kansas aves. Surrounding a 1907 stone and concrete cabin, the garden features peculiar concrete figures on the ground and perched in trees. By the time he was finished, S.P. Dinsmoor had used more than 113 tons of cement to make statues, which include biblical figures and allegorical characters expressing his social and political beliefs. Dinsmoor's body can be viewed in a glass-covered stone coffin that he built.

Guided tours are available. Daily 10-5, May-Oct.; daily 1-4, Mar.-Apr.; Sat.-Sun. 1-4, rest of year. Admission $5; ages 6-12, $1. Phone (785) 525-6395.

GRASSROOTS ART CENTER, 213 S. Main St., displays one-of-a-kind works by self-taught Kansan folk artists. Sculpture, totem, photography, painting, mosaic and other media are represented in a variety of unusual pieces, including a life-size motorcycle crafted entirely of aluminum can pull-tabs. An outdoor courtyard features limestone carvings.

Guided tours are available. Allow 30 minutes minimum. Mon.-Sat. 10-5, Sun. 1-5, May-Sept.; Mon. and Thurs.-Sat. 10-4, Sun. 1-4, rest of year. Closed major holidays. Admission $5.50; ages 6-12, $1.25. MC, VI. Phone (785) 525-6118.

LYONS (D-5) pop. 3,732, elev. 1,695'

Wheat above ground, oil and salt below—the economy of Lyons has been well-assured since the town was established as the Rice County seat in 1876. The first salt mine opened in 1890; one mine and a processing plant still operate.

In 1541 one of those who accompanied Francisco Vásquez de Coronado on his search for the treasures of Quivira was Father Juan de Padilla. Both men went back to Mexico, but a year later Padilla returned as a missionary to the American Indians. He was attacked and killed, however, and thus became the first Christian martyr on the continent. A large granite cross, 4 miles west on US 56, commemorates his work.

There also is evidence of a prehistoric culture in the area. A 150-foot-long intaglio (impression) resembling a serpent was dug into the earth by the Quivira Indians; it is 5.5 miles north on SR 14, then 5 miles east on a county road. Guided tours to the intaglio can be arranged; phone (620) 257-3941.

Lyons Chamber of Commerce: 116 East Ave. S., P.O. Box 127, Lyons, KS 67554; phone (620) 257-2842.

CORONADO-QUIVIRA MUSEUM, 105 W. Lyon St., displays items from the 16th-century Quiviran Indian culture, including such relics of European contact as chain mail. Other exhibits include items from the pioneer period, especially those relating to the nearby Santa Fe Trail. Allow 1 hour minimum. Mon.-Sat. 9-5, Sun. 1-5; closed major holidays. Admission $2; ages 6-12, $1. MC, VI. Phone (620) 257-3941.

MANHATTAN (C-6) pop. 44,831, elev. 1,019'

Most of its residents having come from northern states, Manhattan maintained a decidedly free-state stance during the "Bleeding Kansas" era. As New England continued to send emigrants to Kansas to cement the abolitionist sympathies, organizations in the East often donated money to the settlers.

The city is nestled in the Flint Hills, so named for their bands of limestone and flint. The region, which remains largely untouched by the plow, includes the Konza Prairie. The Flint Hills are the largest remnants of tallgrass prairie on the continent; uncut or ungrazed, the native bluestem grasses can grow 8 feet high. By appointment, Kansas State University offers guided tours of the tallgrass prairie; phone (785) 587-0441. Three self-guiding trails are open dawn to dusk.

Kansas State Agricultural College, now Kansas State University, opened its doors in 1863; it was one of the first land-grant colleges in the nation. Tours of the 23,000-student campus are offered during the school year; phone (785) 532-6318.

City Park, on Poyntz Avenue between 11th and 14th streets, includes a pioneer log cabin, swimming pool, rose garden and a 30-foot statue of Johnny Kaw, a mythical Kansas wheat farmer. Tuttle Creek State Park offers 13,350 acres for sports and recreation, while Pottawatomie State Fishing Lake No. 2 offers 247 acres (see Recreation Chart and the AAA South Central CampBook).

Manhattan Convention and Visitors Bureau: 501 Poyntz Ave., Manhattan, KS 66502; phone (785) 776-8829 or (800) 759-0134.

Shopping areas: Manhattan Town Center Mall, at Third and Poyntz avenues, features Dillard's, JCPenney and Sears.

MARIANNA KISTLER BEACH MUSEUM OF ART, at 14th St. and Anderson Ave. on the Kansas State University campus, houses some 6,000 pieces with special emphasis given to 20th-century Midwestern artists and photographers. The building's post-modern design is of architectural interest. Allow 30 minutes minimum. Tues.-Fri. 10-5, Sat.-Sun. 1-5; closed major holidays. Free. Phone (785) 532-7718.

RILEY COUNTY HISTORICAL MUSEUM, 2309 Claflin Rd., contains exhibits, changing displays and the Seaton Research Library. Next door is Hartford House, a restored prefabricated cabin brought to Manhattan on a steamboat in 1855. Also on the grounds is the 1870s Randolph Jail. The 1860s Goodnow House State Historic Site contains original furnishings and items belonging to Isaac Goodnow, a leader in the Free State Movement. Tues.-Fri. 8:30-5, Sat.-Sun. 2-5; closed holidays. Library open by appointment. Donations. Phone (785) 565-6490.

SUNSET ZOOLOGICAL PARK, 2333 Oak St., houses more than 220 animals. Among the 104 species are Caribbean flamingos, anteaters, tigers, red pandas and snow leopards. Exhibits include the African Forest Trail, prairie dog plains, a cheetah habitat and the Chimpanzee Habitat. Peacocks roam the grounds. Daily 9:30-5, Apr.-Oct.; noon-5, rest of year. Admission $4; ages 3-12, $2. DS, MC, VI. Phone (785) 587-2737.

MARQUETTE (C-5) pop. 542, elev. 1,388′

KANSAS MOTORCYCLE MUSEUM is at 120 N. Washington St. More than 100 motorcycles of various ages, makes and models fill this museum's two buildings. During his 6-decade-long racing career, the museum's owner won more than 600 trophies, which are on display. Visitors also will see an array of motorcycle memorabilia along with a collection of three- and four-wheeled, open-air vehicles. Guided tours are available. Allow 1 hour minimum. Mon.-Fri. 10-noon and 1-5, Sun. 1-5. Donations. Phone (785) 546-2449.

MARYSVILLE (B-6) pop. 3,271, elev. 1,154′

Marysville, known as the "Black Squirrel City," is one of few known spots in the country in which the black squirrel lives in the wild. The squirrels first came to the city in 1912 as part of a carnival's sideshow to entertain a group of Civil War veterans. Some local youngsters released the squirrels, which scampered from their cages to freedom in the city park, where their descendants still frolic.

Marysville was settled mainly by travelers along the Oregon Trail, seven emigrant trails and the Otoe Indian and Pony Express trails. The town was named for the wife of merchant Frank Marshall, who operated a ferry across the Big Blue River. Several emigrant parties camped near the ferry crossing 1840-60.

The state's first civilian post office was established in Marysville on Nov. 11, 1854. The town also was the home of the first state bank in Kansas.

Marysville and surrounding Marshall County have several national historic landmarks, including old schools, houses and churches dating from the mid-1800s (most of these buildings are not open to the public).

A Union Pacific steam locomotive, schoolhouse, sod house and an 1870 railroad depot sit in Marysville's City Park.

Marysville Chamber of Commerce: 101 N. 10th St., P.O. Box 16, Marysville, KS 66508; phone (785) 562-3101 or (800) 752-3965.

Self-guiding tours: Maps detailing walking and driving tours of Marysville and the surrounding area are available from the chamber of commerce.

HISTORIC COURTHOUSE is at 1207 Broadway. Built in 1891, this beautiful Romanesque structure features marble pillars and an eight-sided tower. Museum displays fill 21 rooms and include items that belonged to German and Czech settlers, baptismal fonts from early churches, farming and blacksmithing tools, a school bell from a rural school, a dentist's office and such medical equipment as an iron lung. The large courtroom has a vaulted ceiling, stained glass windows and original oak furnishings.

Guided tours are available. Allow 1 hour minimum. Daily 1-4, Memorial Day weekend-Sept. 15; Mon.-Fri. 1-4, rest of year. Closed Thanksgiving and Dec. 25. Admission $2, children free. Phone (785) 562-5012.

KOESTER HOUSE MUSEUM, 919 Broadway at US 77 and US 36, is a restored two-story Victorian house built by a local banker about 1874. It is furnished with elegant original pieces. A brick fence designed to prevent flooding encloses the yard. Two statues of lions flank the north gate, while two cast iron dogs guard the east gates. Guided tours are available. Mon.-Sat. 10-noon and 1-4:30, Sun. 1-4:30, Apr.-Nov.; by appointment rest of year. Admission $2.50; ages 5-12, $1. Phone (785) 562-2417 or (785) 562-3101.

ORIGINAL PONY EXPRESS HOME STATION NO. 1 MUSEUM, 106 S. Eighth St., served as an 1859 headquarters for the postal riders before the introduction of the telegraph to the Western territories. The museum displays post office boxes from the state's first civilian post office, established in Marysville in 1854. Mon.-Sat. 10-5, Sun. noon-4, May-Oct. Admission $2; ages 6-12, 50c. Phone (785) 562-3825 or (785) 562-3101.

McPHERSON (D-5) pop. 13,770, elev. 1,490′

McPherson bears the name of Union Civil War general James Birdseye McPherson, who was killed in the Battle of Atlanta in 1864. Although Gen. McPherson never visited the Kansas city named after him, his bronze likeness has watched over the city from its perch in Memorial Park since 1917. The Santa Fe Trail, which crosses just south of McPherson, is a present-day reminder of the area's pioneer heritage.

Most early residents of McPherson were farmers lured to the area by the promise of free land. The discovery of oil in the 1920s largely shielded the local economy from the Great Depression and set the stage for an emerging industrial base.

At 100 N. Maple St. is the historically maintained 1890s McPherson County Courthouse and its 105-foot-high clock tower. The 1888 McPherson Opera House, 221 S. Main St., a Victorian architectural showpiece, is under restoration.

McPherson Convention and Visitors Bureau: 306 N. Main St., P.O. Box 616, McPherson, KS 67460; phone (620) 241-3340 or (800) 324-8022.

Self-guiding tours: Information detailing walking and driving tours is available from the convention and visitors bureau.

McPHERSON MUSEUM, 1130 E. Euclid St., is in a restored 1920s house. Vintage furniture is displayed on the main floor; the other two floors contain antique tools, fossils, American Indian artifacts, farm equipment, pioneer household items, meteorites, gems and minerals along with a children's learning center. Among the highlights is the first man-made diamond. For an additional fee visitors can see six N- and HO-gauge model railroads. Allow 1 hour minimum. Tues.-Sun. 1-5; closed holidays. Donations. Phone (620) 241-8464.

MEADE (E-3) pop. 1,672, elev. 2,500′

Deep artesian wells contribute to the verdancy of Meade's tree-lined streets as well as to that of surrounding farms and ranches. Meade State Park is 12 miles southwest off SR 23 *(see Recreation Chart and the AAA South Central CampBook).*

Meade Economic Development: P.O. Box 238, Meade, KS 67864; phone (620) 873-8795.

DALTON GANG HIDEOUT, ESCAPE TUNNEL AND MUSEUM, 4 blks. s. of US 54 at 502 S. Pearlette St., contains furnishings used in 1887 and an opening to a 95-foot-long tunnel leading to the barn where the gang kept their getaway horses. Mon.-Sat. 9-5, Sun. 1-5; closed Jan. 1, Easter, Thanksgiving

and Dec. 25. Admission $2, under 5 free. Phone (620) 873-2731.

MEADE COUNTY HISTORICAL SOCIETY MUSEUM, 200 E. Carthage, offers a maze of exhibits depicting the area's history. A one-room schoolhouse, church, sod house, general store and blacksmith shop are presented. Also featured is a livery barn with a horse-drawn wicker carriage, a sheepherder's wagon and saddles. Allow 1 hour minimum. Mon.-Sat. 9-5, Sun. 1-5; closed Jan. 1, Easter Thanksgiving and Dec. 25. Admission $2, under 6 free. Phone (620) 873-2359.

MEDICINE LODGE (E-4)
pop. 2,193, elev. 1,468′

Because the Plains tribes believed the wooded valley of the Medicine River to be protected by the Great Spirit, they treated it accordingly, sharing the use of a small lodge where anyone could fast, pray and heal with impunity. Thus it was this spot that the Kiowa, Arapaho, Comanche, Apache and Cheyenne chose for the peace negotiations with representatives of the U.S. government in October 1867.

The list of attendees was impressive: Satanta, great chief of the Kiowa; Black Kettle of the Cheyenne; Ten Bears, the wise Comanche orator; Wolf Sleeve of the Apache; and Little Raven, the Arapaho orator. Government advisers were Gen. William Tecumseh Sherman and S.J. Crawford, governor of Kansas. Covering the event for the St. Louis *Daily Missouri Democrat* was reporter Henry M. Stanley, who, years later in Africa, would utter his query, "Dr. Livingstone, I presume?"

Not far from where it was signed, the treaty is celebrated every three years at Memorial Peace Park with an outdoor pageant re-enacting the event. Barber State Fishing Lake, offering camping, fishing and boating, also is nearby *(see Recreation Chart and the AAA South Central CampBook).*

Medicine Lodge Area Chamber of Commerce: 215 S. Iliff St., P.O. Box 274, Medicine Lodge, KS 67104-1536; phone (620) 886-3417.

CARRY A. NATION HOME is at 211 W. Fowler Ave. at Oak St. Having left her first husband, Dr.

Gloyd, because of his alcoholism, Nation decided that she would become "the John Brown of Prohibition." Her first public demonstration for temperance occurred in Medicine Lodge in 1900. Ultimately her crusade took her, swinging her hatchet and bellowing song and prayer, from Kansas to national renown. Her house, furnished with personal items, now is a museum.

Allow 30 minutes minimum. Daily 10:30-5; closed Jan. 1, Easter, Thanksgiving and Dec. 25. Admission $4; over 55, $3.50; ages 7-14, $2. Admission includes ticket to Medicine Lodge Stockade. Phone (620) 886-3553.

MEDICINE LODGE STOCKADE, in town on US 160, is a reconstruction of the original stockade built on this site in 1874 to protect the early settlers from American Indians. A log house built in 1877 has been moved to the site and furnished in period. The museum contains historical items and records. Allow 1 hour minimum. Mon.-Sun. 10:30-5; closed Jan. 1, Easter, Thanksgiving and Dec. 25. Admission $4; over 55, $3.50; ages 7-14, $2. Admission includes ticket to Carry A. Nation Home. Phone (620) 886-3553.

MINNEAPOLIS (C-5) pop. 2,046, elev. 1,257′

Farming and stockraising in the surrounding Solomon River Valley support Minneapolis. The community's name is an arresting combination of an American Indian word for waters, *minne*, and the Greek word for city, *polis*.

Minneapolis Area Chamber of Commerce: 200 W. Second, Minneapolis, KS 67467; phone (785) 392-3068.

Self-guiding tours: Brochures detailing four tours of the area are offered by the chamber of commerce. Free guided tours are available by appointment.

ROCK CITY, 3.5 mi. s. on SR 106, is a group of about 200 mostly spherical or elliptical sandstone and limestone concretions. Ranging from 8 to 27 feet in diameter, they were formed underground by the precipitation of water-borne calcium carbonate in the spaces of loosely cemented sandstone. Erosion of the surface gradually uncovered the formations. Picnicking is permitted. Allow 30 minutes minimum. Daily dawn-dusk, May 1-Sept. 30; by appointment rest of year. Admission $3; ages 1-15, 50c. Phone (785) 392-2092 or (785) 392-2577.

MONTEZUMA (E-3) pop. 966, elev. 2,785′

Founded in 1912 during an intense land speculation boom, many of Montezuma's early citizens were Mennonites seeking religious freedom and fertile farmland. Wheat and grain still provide the economic mainstay, but fallow fields now yield a more unusual commodity—electricity. With some 170 windmills spread over 205 square miles just east of town, Gray County Wind Farm generates enough energy to power 33,000 homes. A good viewing area lies at the junction of US 56 and CR 17, where an information kiosk explains the operations.

STAUTH MEMORIAL MUSEUM is at 111 N. Aztec St. Displayed are clothing, crafts, decorative arts, ivory carvings, musical instruments, vases and unusual souvenirs collected by Montezuma residents Claude and Donalda Stauth during 40 years of world travel. The Fry Wildlife Collection includes exhibits relating to North American game animals and promotes education and conservation. International traveling exhibits change year-round. Allow 30 minutes minimum. Tues.-Sat. 9-noon and 1-4:30, Sun. 1:30-4:30; closed major holidays. Donations. Phone (620) 846-2527.

NEODESHA (E-7) pop. 2,848, elev. 800′

At the confluence of the Verdigris and Fall rivers, Neodesha (Osage for "meeting of the waters") was a refining center for the area's oil fields. The town now serves as a manufacturing and agricultural center for the region.

Near the town is the grave of Little Bear, one of the great Osage chiefs. According to local legend, American Indians returning to pay homage to their chief found the grave robbed. Angered, they prepared to pillage the white settlement of Neodesha; however, one of the town's doctors pacified them by giving them a skeleton from his office—claiming it was the body of Little Bear.

Neodesha Chamber of Commerce: 100 S. First St., P.O. Box 266, Neodesha, KS 66757; phone (620) 325-2055.

NORMAN NO. 1, First and Main sts., marks the spot where the first successful commercial oil well west of the Mississippi River was drilled in 1892. The rig, now replaced with a replica, was the first to tap the rich Mid-Continental Field, which reached as far as Texas. A museum chronicles local history and features a collection of circus memorabilia donated by retired Barnum and Bailey performers hailing from Neodesha. Museum Tues.-Sat. 10-noon and 1-4. Well daily dawn-dusk. Free. Phone (620) 325-5316.

NEWTON (D-5) pop. 17,190, elev. 1,445′

Newton's history began in 1870 when the site was chosen as a location for a new Atchison, Topeka & Santa Fe Railway terminal. Its position on the Chisholm Trail made the site a logical location. When the railroad pushed on to Dodge City and Wichita, so did Newton's wild and wicked cow town image.

As pressures against their beliefs mounted, Russian Mennonites looked to the North American prairies for a new home. Bernhard Warkentin visited central Kansas in 1872; his favorable reports elicited a wave of immigration. As a result, Newton and the surrounding area constitute the largest Mennonite settlement in the United States.

Mennonite farmers brought with them Turkey Red winter wheat seeds, which had flourished on the central European steppes. Warkentin built a gristmill at nearby Halstead (*see place listing p. 87*) and began promoting the use of this hardy new grain, which was well-suited to conditions in Kansas. His efforts at establishing hard winter wheat helped make Kansas known as the "wheat capital of the world." Warkentin's residence still stands at 211 E. First St.

Newton Convention & Visitors Bureau: 500 N. Main St., Suite 101, Newton, KS 67114; phone (316) 283-7555 or (800) 899-0455.

NORTH NEWTON (D-5)
pop. 1,522, elev. 1,440'

KAUFFMAN MUSEUM is .7 mi. s. of I-135 exit 34 at 27th and N. Main sts., across from Bethel College. The museum is on a 5-acre site that consists of woods and a re-created prairie with native grasses and wildflowers. Indoor exhibits depict the natural history of the Plains, American Indians and the culture and heritage of European Mennonites who immigrated to the Central Plains in the 1870s.

Permanent exhibits include Mennonite Immigrant Furniture and Mirror of the Martyrs. Temporary exhibits are often available. Historic buildings include a late 19th-century homesteader's log cabin, a Kansas farmstead with an 1875 house and an 1886 barn.

Allow 1 hour minimum. Tues.-Fri. 9:30-4:30, Sat.-Sun. 1:30-4:30; closed major holidays. Admission $3; ages 6-16, $1.50. DS, MC, VI. Phone (316) 283-1612.

NORTON (B-3) pop. 3,012, elev. 2,284'

Principally an agricultural community, Norton offers a refreshing glance at national politics. The Gallery of Also Rans, in the First State Bank building at 105 W. Main St., features photographs and biographies of the nation's unsuccessful presidential candidates.

At Prairie Dog State Park, named for a large colony of prairie dogs living there, visitors can see the 1886 Hillmon School and the Adobe House, constructed in the 1890s out of mud and straw. The park is 4 miles west of town on US 36. *See Recreation Chart and the AAA South Central CampBook.*

Norton Area Chamber of Commerce: 104 S. State St., P.O. Box 97, Norton, KS 67654; phone (785) 877-2501.

OAKLEY (C-2) pop. 2,173, elev. 3,049'

At the junction of I-70, US 40 and US 83, Oakley is a busy commercial center. It gained the county seat in the same manner as many early Kansas communities, winning over Russell Springs by only one vote—hardly the plurality required by law. Although the town is not named for the cowgirl entertainer, she did perform nearby with Buffalo Bill's Wild West Show. In tribute, Annie Oakley Park, 600 E. 5th St., offers walking trails, a playground, a swimming pool and picnic facilities.

Oakley Area Chamber of Commerce: 313 Center St., Oakley, KS 67748; phone (785) 672-4862.

FICK FOSSIL AND HISTORY MUSEUM, 700 W. Third St., exhibits fossils, fossil folk art, rocks, minerals, local memorabilia, artwork, a glass collection from the Great Depression and antiques. Other displays include indigenous wildflowers, a sod house and photographs dating from the 1800s. Allow 1 hour minimum. Mon.-Sat. 9-5, Sun. 2-4, May-Sept.; Mon.-Sat. 9-noon and 1-5, rest of year. Closed major holidays. Donations. Phone (785) 672-4839.

MONUMENT ROCKS (CHALK PYRAMIDS) are 20 mi. s. on US 83, then 4 mi. e. on a dirt road. Remnants of layer after layer of Cretaceous seabed, the wind-carved, water-eroded chalk pinnacles rise some 70 feet above the plain. This natural formation served as a landmark for pioneers and American Indians. Weathering has revealed a great variety of marine and reptilian fossils. Chalk bluffs and similar formations are characteristic of the Smoky Hill River Valley from this region east to Cedar Bluff Reservoir. No facilities are available. Free.

PRAIRIE DOG TOWN, off I-70 exit 70 to US 83, features animals common to western Kansas, including buffaloes, donkeys, foxes, goats, pheasants and prairie dogs. Visitors may pet and feed some animals. Animal oddities such as live 5- and 6-legged cows are on the premises. Allow 1 hour minimum. Daily 9-8, Memorial Day weekend-Oct. 31. Admission $6.95; senior citizens $6.25; ages 11-15, $4.95; ages 3-10, $3.95. MC, VI. Phone (785) 672-3100.

OBERLIN (B-3) pop. 1,994, elev. 2,250'

The last American Indian raid on Kansas soil occurred in Oberlin on Sept. 29, 1878. Several days before, Chief Dull Knife and his band of Northern Cheyenne had left Indian Territory heading north in an attempt to regain their homeland in the Dakotas. On Sept. 27 they engaged a detachment of the 19th Infantry from Fort Dodge.

Two days later they raced through Decatur County, killing 19 settlers before fleeing into Nebraska with the 4th Cavalry in hot pursuit. A monument to the unfortunate settlers is in Oberlin Cemetery. Today the town is a trading center for the surrounding High Plains farming country.

Decatur County Area Chamber of Commerce: 104 S. Penn Ave., Oberlin, KS 67749; phone (785) 475-3441.

DECATUR COUNTY LAST INDIAN RAID MUSEUM, 258 S. Penn Ave., is a 14-building complex that includes a sod house, train depot, schoolhouse, land office, livery stable, an 1888 church and a 1930s gas station and grocery store. Period rooms contain pioneer and American Indian artifacts and a quilt collection. Museum Tues.-Sat. 9:30-noon and 1-4:30, Apr.-Nov. Office only open for research Tues.-Thurs. 9:30-noon and 1-4:30, Dec.-Mar. Closed holidays. Admission $5; ages 6-12, $3. Phone (785) 475-2712.

OLATHE—
see Kansas City p. 184 in Missouri.

OSAWATOMIE (C-7) pop. 4,645, elev. 853'

The word Osawatomie (Oh-suh-WAH-tuh-mee) combines the names of the two American Indian tribes who once inhabited the area, the Osage and the Pottawatomie.

As a railroad town, it was the site of pro-slavery and anti-slavery conflicts during the pre-Civil War years. In May 1856 abolitionist John Brown and a small group of followers raided neighboring houses and killed several men as a symbolic warning to the pro-slavery faction.

Several hundred pro-slavers retaliated 3 months later by killing five of Brown's men, including his son, in a raid that became known as the Battle of Osawatomie.

The Old Stone Church, at Sixth and Parker streets, was one of the state's early pioneer churches. Its first pastor was the Rev. Samuel Adair, brother-in-law to John Brown. It may be viewed by appointment; phone (913) 755-4384.

Osawatomie Chamber of Commerce: 628 Main St., P.O. Box 63, Osawatomie, KS 66064; phone (913) 755-4114.

JOHN BROWN STATE HISTORIC SITE, 10th and Main sts., contains a statue of Brown and the log cabin where he sometimes stayed when in Kansas. The cabin, owned by Brown's brother-in-law, the Rev. Samuel Adair, was a station on the Underground Railroad; it contains period furniture. A stone pavilion protects the structure from the elements. The park is built on the site of the 1856 Battle of Osawatomie. A museum interprets the conflict known as "Bleeding Kansas." Wed.-Sat. 11-5, Sun. 1-5 and by appointment; closed holidays. Donations. Phone (913) 755-4384.

OTTAWA (C-7) pop. 11,921, elev. 910'

OLD DEPOT MUSEUM, s.w. of jct. SR 68 and US 59 at 135 W. Tecumseh St., is in a two-story limestone building that originally was a passenger depot on the Santa Fe Railroad. A model train layout depicts local railroading in 1950. Displays focus on area history; changing exhibits are presented. Tues.-Sat. 10-4, Sun. 1-4; closed major holidays. Admission $3, students with ID $1. Phone (785) 242-1250.

OVERLAND PARK—
see Kansas City p. 184 in Missouri.

PARSONS (E-7) pop. 11,514

Parsons' history is closely intertwined with that of the Missouri-Kansas-Texas Railroad, also known as the KATY or MKT. It was home of the diesel shops for the line until it was sold to the Union Pacific in the 1980s.

Buildings of architectural note include the 1920s Carnegie Arts Center, formerly the town's library, and the Parsons Municipal Auditorium, which hosts concerts, theater productions and civic gatherings.

The First Presbyterian Church's turrets and stained-glass windows make it a much photographed structure. Hundreds of Civil War veterans are buried at Oakwood Cemetery, known for its wartime monuments and memorials.

The Parsons Arboretum includes a visitor center, wetlands area, observation deck and an 18-hole disc golf course. Nearby, both Big Hill Lake and Neosho State Fishing Lake *(see Recreation Chart)* offer camping and fishing facilities.

Labette County Convention and Visitors Bureau: 1715 Corning, Parsons, KS 67357; phone (620) 421-6500 or (800) 280-6401.

PAWNEE ROCK (D-4) pop. 356, elev. 1,941'

PAWNEE ROCK STATE HISTORIC SITE, .5 mi. n. off US 56, is a sandstone citadel that was a prominent landmark for travelers on the Santa Fe Trail. American Indians are believed to have met here and used the site as a vantage point to watch for bison herds and wagon trains. Until settlers and the railroad stripped nearly 20 feet of stone from its top, mostly for use in building the Santa Fe Railroad, Pawnee Rock rose nearly 100 feet above the plain. Daily dawn-dusk. Free. Phone (785) 272-8681.

PHILLIPSBURG (B-4) pop. 2,668, elev. 1,939'

Civil War veterans were predominant among those who settled Phillipsburg in 1872 and helped to protect it during its early years. Today the town is known as a trade center and the seat of county government. The Huck Boyd Community Center is a venue for entertainment and civic events. It also houses a railroad museum and a model train layout.

Phillipsburg Area Chamber of Commerce: 270 State St., P.O. Box 326, Phillipsburg, KS 67661; phone (785) 543-2321.

FORT BISSELL, .5 blks. w. on State St./US 36 in City Park, is a reconstruction of an 1872 fort built to protect settlers from Apache Indian raids. Antiques and equipment from an early doctor's office and a barbershop are displayed in the 1878 Glade Depot. Two 1870s log houses depict pioneer lifestyles, one displays a gun collection. A furnished sod house, the original post office, a one-room schoolhouse and an early general store also are on the grounds. Tues.-Sat. 10-noon and 2-6, May-Sept.; by appointment rest of year. Closed July 4. Donations. Phone (785) 543-6212.

PITTSBURG (E-7) pop. 19,243, elev. 922'

Adopting and adapting the name of the Pennsylvania metropolis, Pittsburg was founded in 1876 as a mining camp. Over the years some 200 million tons of coal were excavated here. Pittsburg State University, with an enrollment of 6,500, offers educational and cultural opportunities. Nearby, several reclaimed strip pits provide swimming, fishing and other recreation.

Crawford County Convention and Visitors Bureau: 117 W. Fourth St., P.O. Box 1115, Pittsburg, KS 66762; phone (620) 231-1212.

CRAWFORD COUNTY HISTORICAL MUSEUM, 651 US 69S, contains horse-drawn vehicles, vintage clothing, printing exhibits, items from deep coal-mining operations and farming implements. Also on the grounds are an 1885 schoolhouse, a 1922 Marion steam shovel and a neighborhood grocery store. Thurs.-Sun. noon-5; closed holidays. Donations. Phone (620) 231-1440.

PLEASANTON (D-8) pop. 1,387, elev. 862'

On Oct. 25, 1864, one of the last significant Civil War battles fought west of the Mississippi River occurred along this segment of Mine Creek. Retreating southward before a pursuing Union force, about 7,000 Confederate troops established a defense on the north side of the creek.

When the vanguard of the Union force topped the rise, they faced the muzzles of thousands of pistols and rifles and eight cannons—and charged. A half-hour later the numerically superior Confederates were routed, defeated by the Union's better weapons, position and cavalry. By forcing the Confederates out of Kansas and saving Fort Scott from attack, the Battle of Mine Creek extinguished the South's hope of success in the West.

Pleasanton Chamber of Commerce: 1608 Laural St., Pleasanton, KS 66075; phone the city hall at (913) 352-8257.

LINN COUNTY HISTORICAL MUSEUM is 6 blks. w. of the US 69 bypass at 307 E. Park St. This museum depicts the history of early Linn County through photographs, artifacts, documents, murals, period-room settings, an old general store, a renovated 1880 depot, antique cars, a genealogy library and videotape presentations. Visitors also learn about Civil War events that occurred in the area. The museum distributes pamphlets and maps dealing with Pleasanton and all of Linn County.

Allow 1 hour minimum. Tues. and Thurs. 9-5, Wed. and Sat.-Sun. 1-5; other times by appointment. Closed Jan. 1, Thanksgiving and Dec. 25. Donations. Phone (913) 352-8739.

MINE CREEK BATTLEFIELD STATE HISTORIC SITE is 2 mi. s. on US 69, then .5 mi. w. on SR 52. One of the last significant Civil War battles fought west of the Mississippi River occurred here in 1864. Walking trails, marked with interpretive signs, traverse the 600-acre battlefield site. A visitor center preserves Civil War exhibits, and living history demonstrations are offered. Allow 1 hour minimum. Wed.-Sat. 10-5, Sun. 1-5; closed holidays. Admission $2; ages 5-17, $1. Phone (913) 352-8890.

PRATT (E-4) pop. 6,570, elev. 1,896'

The bounty of the surrounding wheat and cattle ranches and the activity from being a shipping point on the Cotton Belt (Southern Pacific) Railroad sustain Pratt.

Named for Civil War veteran Caleb Pratt, the community was established in 1884 as the railroad pushed westward. Until 1886 the community warred with neighboring Saratoga over the status of county seat. Years after Pratt's victory Saratoga citizens insisted that the Indian scare that had sent them fleeing had been fabricated so that Pratt could win a hastily called election.

During World War II the city served as a training base for crews who flew B-29 bombers. At the municipal airport the B-29 All Veterans Memorial honors these flyers and their contribution to history.

Pratt Area Chamber of Commerce: 114 N. Main St., Pratt, KS 67124; phone (620) 672-5501.

KANSAS STATE FISH HATCHERY, 2 mi. e. on US 54, then 1 mi. s. on SR 64, was one of the first to raise channel catfish. The 187-acre facility includes 87 ponds. A museum and education center feature native birds and animals in their natural habitats and aquariums with every species of fish indigenous to the state. The hatchery also is the operations office of the Kansas Department of Wildlife and Parks. Allow 1 hour minimum. Mon.-Fri. 8-5. Donations. Phone (620) 672-5911.

PRATT COUNTY HISTORICAL MUSEUM, 208 S. Ninnescah, contains six galleries depicting aspects of local history. American Indian artifacts and items relating to area pioneers are displayed, as are period rooms from the late 1800s and sculptures woven from wheat. Old Time Main Street, a reconstructed 19th-century town, includes a general store, post office, bank, jail and icehouse. Daily 2-4; closed major holidays. Donations. Phone (620) 672-7874.

REPUBLIC (B-5) pop. 161, elev. 1,500'

PAWNEE INDIAN VILLAGE STATE HISTORIC SITE, 8 mi. n. of US 36 on SR 266, is on the site of an 1820s Pawnee Indian village. The museum building is constructed over the excavated floor of an earth lodge. Artifacts have been left exactly where they were found. Exhibits and dioramas depict Pawnee life. A nature trail is available. Allow 1 hour minimum. Wed.-Sat. 10-5, Sun. 1-5; closed major holidays. Admission $3, over 59 and students with ID $2, under 5 free. Phone (785) 361-2255.

RUSSELL (C-4) pop. 4,696, elev. 1,826'

Railroad station agents, section hands and military garrisons were the only inhabitants of Fossil Station until 1871, when a colony of some 60 families settled and later changed the name to Russell.

Today Russell is widely associated with former U.S. senator and 1996 presidential nominee Robert Dole, who was born here in 1923; it also is the hometown of Sen. Arlen Specter of Pennsylvania.

Architectural highlights from the city's past include the 1872 Gernon House, 818 Kansas St., and the 1879 Heym-Oliver House, 503 Kansas St. Both dwellings are restored and furnished in period. Guided tours are offered on weekends during summer; phone (785) 483-3637.

Nearby Wilson Lake offers numerous outdoor activities. *See Recreation Chart and Buffalo in the AAA South Central CampBook.*

Russell Convention & Visitors Bureau: 610 N. Main St., Russell, KS 67665; phone (785) 483-6960 or (800) 658-4686.

DEINES CULTURAL CENTER, off I-70 at 820 N. Main St., is a three-story building housing a workshop area and two galleries containing the works of Kansas artists. The wood engravings of E. Hubert Deines are noteworthy. Allow 30 minutes minimum. Tues.-Fri. 12:30-5:30, Sat.-Sun. 1-5; closed holidays. Donations. Phone (785) 483-3742.

FOSSIL STATION MUSEUM, behind Russell County Court House at 331 Kansas St., is housed in a former jailhouse built in 1907. The museum depicts the history of Russell County since the 1860s and features a fossil collection and genealogy information. Allow 1 hour minimum. Mon.-Sat. 11-4, Sun. 1-4, Memorial Day-day before Labor Day. Donations. Phone (785) 483-3637.

OIL PATCH MUSEUM, n.w. of jct. I-70 and US 281, chronicles the history of oil exploration in the area. Old oil derricks, rigs and other equipment can be seen. Allow 1 hour minimum. Daily 4-8, Memorial Day-Labor Day; by appointment rest of year. Donations. Phone (785) 483-6640 or (785) 483-3637.

SALINA (C-5) pop. 45,679, elev. 1,222′

At the junction of I-70 and I-135, Salina is a major trade and distribution center for one of the greatest hard wheat belts in the world. Other agriculture as well as more than 50 diversified manufacturing firms complete the economic portrait of this city on the eastward bend of the Smoky Hill River.

Salina balances industrial growth with educational and cultural expansion. Kansas Wesleyan University and a branch of Kansas State University are important assets. The prize-winning Bicentennial Center in Kenwood Park is the scene of expositions, trade shows, concerts and sporting events.

Salina Area Chamber of Commerce: 120 W. Ash St., P.O. Box 586, Salina, KS 67402-0586; phone (785) 827-9301.

ROLLING HILLS WILDLIFE ADVENTURE is off I-70 exit 244, then 2 mi. s. to 625 N. Hedville Rd. Situated on 95 acres of Kansas prairie, the wildlife center features a zoo with more than 80 species of rare or endangered animals and a museum. Sheltered observation areas permit up-close viewing of animals in natural outdoor settings.

The center's collection includes such endangered species as Indian and white rhinoceroses, tigers, an orangutan and Amur leopards. An indoor reptile house features rare snakes. A children's area allows hands-on interaction with domestic animals. Narrated tram rides operate seasonally.

Picnicking is permitted. Food is available. Allow 2 hours minimum. Daily 8-5, Memorial Day-Labor Day; 9-5, rest of year. Closed Jan. 1 and Dec. 24-25. Admission $8.95; over 64, $7.95; ages 3-12, $4.95. Combination ticket for both zoo and museum $15.95; over 64, $13.95; ages 3-12, $7.95. Tram rides $3. AX, DS, MC, VI. Phone (785) 827-9488.

SAVE **Rolling Hills Wildlife Adventure Museum** is at 625 N. Hedville Rd. The museum leads visitors through elaborate dioramas representing seven distinct environments. Realistic robots, representing peoples from around the world, carry on a dialogue with visitors and each other about the delicate balance between man and nature. The museum also features a 360-degree, domed movie theater, an interactive children's gallery filled with hands-on displays and an area for traveling exhibits.

Allow 1 hour minimum. Daily 8-5, Memorial Day-Labor Day; 9-5, rest of year. Closed Jan. 1 and Dec. 24-25. Admission $8.95; over 64, $7.95; ages 3-12, $4.95. Combination ticket for both zoo and museum $15.95; over 64, $13.95; ages 3-12, $7.95. MC, VI. Phone (785) 827-9488.

SMOKY HILL MUSEUM is at 211 W. Iron Ave. Housed in a 1938 art deco building, the museum's collection features some 20,000 items. Exhibits include a full-size replica of a pioneer sod dugout, a general store and One Keeper's Place, where children investigate historical events. Permanent and changing exhibits are presented. Tues.-Fri. noon-5, Sat. 10-5, Sun. 1-5; closed holidays. Free. Phone (785) 309-5776.

YESTERYEAR MUSEUM, I-70 exit 252 to 1100 W. Diamond Dr., contains a vast collection of historic items related to agricultural and rural life, including farm machinery and implements; steam engines; harvesting machinery; a one-room schoolhouse; a barber shop; a general store; a post office; a small church; and a filling station. Allow 1 hour minimum. Tues.-Sat. 9-5, early Jan.-late Dec.; closed major holidays. Admission $4, under 12 free. Phone (785) 825-8473.

SCANDIA (B-5) pop. 436, elev. 1,450′

Named by the Swedish and Norwegian settlers who first arrived in the 1860s, Scandia maintains close ties to its cultural heritage. Downtown shops display many Swedish wares, including handcrafted items created by local artisans.

THE SCANDIA MUSEUM, jct. Main and Grant sts., is a tribute to the area's Norwegian and Swedish ancestors. Highlights include original artwork, a working loom, antique horse-drawn carriages, a soda fountain and family memorabilia. Wood-carved depictions of a wagon train attack and a Dodge City street scene also are presented. Allow 1 hour minimum. Mon.-Sat. 2-4, May 15-Labor Day. Donations. Phone (785) 335-2506.

SCOTT CITY (C-2) pop. 3,855, elev. 2,971'

Nearby Lake Scott, part of Lake Scott State Park, is fed by underground springs that have eroded the countryside into canyons, green hills and rough terrain—a visual oasis on the flat Kansas topography. South of Scott City lies White Woman Basin, where the surface flow of White Woman Creek disappears. The stream, which rises in Colorado, completes its journey to the Arkansas River below ground.

Scott City Chamber of Commerce: 113 E. Fifth St., Scott City, KS 67871; phone (620) 872-3525.

LAKE SCOTT STATE PARK, 12 mi. n. via US 83 and SR 95, is the site of El Cuartelejo, the ruined pueblo occupied in the late 1600s by Taos and Picurie Indians who fled Spanish occupation in New Mexico. Plains Apache Indians as well as Spanish explorers and French traders camped at the pueblo. Also within the park is the Herbert and Eliza Steele Home. Their original 1888 dugout house was expanded to a four-room house using sandstone from the surrounding bluffs.

Camping is permitted. Daily dawn-dusk, Apr.-Sept.; limited facilities available rest of year. Schedule may vary; phone ahead. Admission Apr.-Sept. $7 per private vehicle. Admission rest of year $6.50 per private vehicle. Phone (620) 872-2061. *See Recreation Chart and the AAA South Central CampBook.*

SEDAN (E-7) pop. 1,342, elev. 862'

Nestled in the Chautauqua Hills, Sedan once relied on oil production to sustain its economy. A yellow-brick road featuring more than 11,000 inscribed bricks runs between buildings, which were constructed from native sandstone and limestone in the late 1800s. Emmett Kelly, the clown known as Weary Willy, was born in Sedan in 1898.

Sedan Chamber of Commerce: P.O. Box 182, Sedan, KS 67361; phone (620) 725-4033.

EMMETT KELLY MUSEUM, 204 E. Main St., displays memorabilia of this Sedan native who became a world-renowned clown. Exhibits also include a large decanter collection. Tues.-Sat. 10-4, May-Oct. Donations. Phone (620) 725-3470.

SHAWNEE—

see Kansas City p. 184 in Missouri.

STAFFORD (D-4) pop. 1,161, elev. 1,858'

QUIVIRA NATIONAL WILDLIFE REFUGE is 6 mi. n. on Main St., 6 mi. e. on 70th St., following signs, then 1 mi. n. to headquarters. The refuge covers 22,135 acres that encompass the Big and Little salt marshes, a portion of Rattlesnake Creek and several other wetlands. Bald eagles, endangered whooping cranes and various other species of migratory waterfowl find refuge here. The best seasons for wildlife viewing are spring and fall. Enjoy hiking and fishing year-round. Picnicking is permitted. Allow 1 hour minimum. Daily dawn-dusk. Free. Phone (620) 486-2393.

STRONG CITY (C-6) pop. 584, elev. 1,182'

At one time prairie grass blanketed a 400,000-square-mile swath of North America, stretching from the Rocky Mountains to east of the Mississippi River, and from Texas north to Saskatchewan. A small portion of this original grassland survives here. Limestone just beneath the sod helped build Strong City's economy as well as countless public and private buildings throughout the west.

TALLGRASS PRAIRIE NATIONAL PRESERVE is .75 mi. w. on US 50, then 2 mi. n. on US 177. This 10,861-acre site protects a remnant of the continent's once vast tallgrass prairie. Guided tours of the 1881 Spring Hill Ranch include the restored Victorian ranch house, a massive three-story limestone barn, a carriage house and a one-room schoolhouse. Via bus, rangers conduct 90-minute prairie tours, which focus on natural history and ecology.

Nature trails are available, and living-history programs are offered during summer. Daily 9-4:30; closed Jan. 1, Thanksgiving and Dec. 25. House tours are offered every hour 9:30-3:30. Bus tours depart at 11, 1 and 3, late Apr.-late Oct. Free. Bus tour $5; ages 5-18, $3. MC, VI. Phone (620) 273-8494.

TOPEKA (C-7) pop. 122,377, elev. 940'

Topeka was founded in 1854 when nine anti-slavery settlers met on the banks of the Kansas River, near the spot where Oregon Trail travelers made their first major river crossing on their journey to the West. The city was incorporated in 1857, and Cyrus K. Holliday, the founder of the Atchison, Topeka & Santa Fe Railway, was among the city's leaders.

When the railway began to extend its tracks westward 1854-69, Topeka defeated Tecumseh for county seat, became the state capital in 1861, survived the mayhem of the "Bleeding Kansas" era, suffered drought and withstood the fringes of the Civil War. In fact, Topeka flourished.

Almost 100 years after Topeka saw clashes between abolitionists and pro-slavery factions, it was the setting for the landmark 1954 Supreme Court ruling *Brown vs. The Topeka Board of Education,* the case that opened the door for school desegregation across the country.

Ten Favrile glass windows designed in 1911 by Louis Comfort Tiffany illuminate the First Presbyterian Church at 817 Harrison St. Tiffany's use of cobalt, gold and copper additives give the Favrile glass remarkably deep colors. The windows may be viewed weekdays. Guided tours are available by appointment; phone (785) 233-9601.

Lake Shawnee, E. 29th Street and West Edge Road, and Perry State Park, 16 miles northeast, offer water sports and other outdoor recreation (*see Recreation Chart and the AAA South Central CampBook*). Heartland Park Topeka, 4 miles south on US 75, is host to national motor sports events April through October; phone (800) 437-2237.

Visit Topeka Inc.: 1275 S.W. Topeka Blvd., Topeka, KS 66612-1852; phone (785) 234-1030 or (800) 235-1030.

Shopping areas: West Ridge Mall, 1 mile south of I-70 on Wanamaker Road between 17th and 21st streets, features Dillard's, JCPenney, Jones and Sears.

BROWN V. BOARD OF EDUCATION NATIONAL HISTORIC SITE is at 1515 S.E. Monroe St. The site commemorates the May 17, 1954, Supreme Court ruling that stated "separate educational facilities are inherently unequal," forcing desegregation of public schools in 21 states. The site consists of the Monroe Elementary School, one of the four segregated elementary schools for African-American children in Topeka, and its grounds. A visitor center contains interpretive exhibits. Allow 1 hour minimum. Daily 9-5; closed Jan. 1, Thanksgiving and Dec. 25. Free. Phone (785) 354-4273.

[SAVE] **COMBAT AIR MUSEUM** is on J Street, hangar 602, along the flight line of Topeka Airport Forbes Field. This museum exhibits examples of aeronautical technology from all U.S. military conflicts from the early 1900s to the present, including aircraft and memorabilia. Among the many displays are an EC-121 Super Constellation, a Blue Angels F-11F Tiger, a Beech RU-8D and Meyers OTW, an F-14 Tomcat and JN4 "Jenny" biplanes. Another exhibit re-creates a German prisoner of war barracks.

Allow 1 hour, 30 minutes minimum. Mon.-Sat. 9-4:30, Sun. noon-4:30; closed Jan. 1, Easter, Thanksgiving and Dec. 25. Last admission 1 hour before closing. Admission $6; over 59, $5; military with ID and ages 6-17, $4. MC, VI. Phone (785) 862-3303.

GAGE PARK occupies 160 acres between W. Sixth Ave. and Tenth St. on Gage Blvd. A conservatory and a miniature train are among its attractions; recreational facilities include a swimming pool, tennis courts and a playground. Across from the Reinisch Rose Garden in the park, a restored 1908 carousel with a Wurlitzer organ is open to the public.

Picnicking is permitted. Park open daily 6 a.m.-11 p.m. Train and carousel operate mid-Apr. through Labor Day (weather permitting). Days and hours vary; phone ahead. Park free. Train $1. Carousel 75c. Phone (785) 368-3838.

Reinisch Memorial Rose and Rock Garden, W. Sixth Ave. and Gage Blvd. in Gage Park, covers 3 acres with many varieties of roses growing amid rock gardens and pools. The blooming season is early spring through late fall. Daily 6 a.m.-11 p.m. Free.

Topeka Zoological Park, 635 S.W. Gage Blvd., is entered from Sixth Ave. or 10th St. Beneath a dome, the Tropical Rain Forest habitat contains animals, birds and plants. Other zoo residents include nocturnal animals, lions, tigers, bears, zebras and gorillas. A children's zoo and playground also are featured.

Food is available. Daily 10-5. Last admission is 1 hour before closing. Closed Jan. 1 and Dec. 25. Admission $4.50; over 64, $3.50; ages 3-12, $3. AX, MC, VI. Phone (785) 368-9180.

THE GREAT OVERLAND STATION is at 701 N. Kansas Ave. In 2004, a local preservation group completed restoration of North Topeka's neglected Union Pacific passenger depot, returning it to its 1927 splendor. The station's grand waiting room features 34-foot-high ornamented ceilings, large windows and impressive 12-foot-wide, 120-bulb chandeliers. A former storage room houses exhibits about Topeka's history and railroad heritage. Outside the station, flags of the 50 states flank a flame-shaped sculpture, the centerpiece of the All Veterans Memorial.

Guided tours are available. Allow 1 hour minimum. Tues.-Sat. 10-4, Sun. 1-4; closed major holidays. Last ticket sold 45 minutes before closing. Admission $4; over 62, $3; ages 3-12, $2. MC, VI. Phone (785) 232-5533.

KANSAS HISTORY MUSEUM AND LIBRARY is at 6425 S.W. Sixth Ave. Home of the Kansas State Historical Society, this complex set on 80 acres of woodlands and prairie features the Center for Historical Research, a library with a vast collection of historic documents and manuscripts; the Potawatomi Mission, an 1847 boarding school for the Potawatomi Indians; the Stach School, a 1910 one-room schoolhouse accessible by appointment; and the Kansas Museum of History.

The Kansas History Center Nature Trail winds 2.5 miles through native grassland, along creek banks and into a wooded area. Accessible to physically impaired visitors, the East Trail portion is a .25-mile loop with interpretive signs that describe the area's natural and cultural histories. While exploring the North Trail section, visitors might see red-tailed hawks, white-tailed deer and wild turkeys.

Allow 1 hour, 30 minutes minimum. Tues.-Sat. 9-5, Sun. 1-5; closed state holidays. Admission $5; over 59, $4; students with ID $3. Phone (785) 272-8681.

Center for Historical Research is at 6425 S.W. Sixth Ave. Headquarters of the Kansas State Historical Society, the center offers extensive resources for genealogists and researchers of Kansas history and the West. Allow 1 hour minimum. Tues.-Sat. 9-4:30; closed state holidays. Free. Phone (785) 272-8681, ext. 117.

Kansas Museum of History is at 6425 S.W. Sixth Ave. Exhibits at the complex detail state history from its earliest days to the present and include displays about American Indian history, forts and trails, Civil War settlement, frontier life, the arrival of the railroad, fast food, African-American history and Kansas families. In the Discovery Place children experience history firsthand by dressing in frontier costumes and visiting a Plains Indian teepee.

Allow 1 hour minimum. Museum Tues.-Sat. 9-5, Sun. 1-5. Discovery Place Tues.-Sat. 1-5. Closed state holidays. Admission $5; over 59, $4; students with ID $3. Phone (785) 272-8681.

Potawatomi Mission is at 6425 S.W. Sixth Ave. Built in 1847 as a boarding school for Potawatomi Indian children, the historic stone building stands at its original location. Exhibits on the first floor include a crucifix and shards of crockery from the original mission. A period room features a hearth and school desks. Allow 30 minutes minimum. Tues.-Fri. 10-4 (also Sat. 10-4, Sun. 1-4, third weekend of the month); closed major holidays. Donations. Phone (785) 272-8681.

OLD PRAIRIE TOWN AT WARD-MEADE HISTORIC SITE, 124 N.W. Fillmore St., offers 2.5 acres of botanical gardens surrounding the Prairie Mansion. Built about 1870, the house is furnished with period pieces and is used as a museum. Also on the grounds are a log cabin, a late 1800s schoolhouse, a church, a general store, a railroad depot, a livery stable and a drugstore.

Self-guiding and guided tours are available; building interiors can only be seen on guided tours. Food is available. Grounds and gardens daily 8 a.m.-dusk. Drugstore and general store Mon.-Sat. 10-4, Sun. noon-4. Guided tours are offered Mon.-Fri. at 10, noon and 2, Sat.-Sun. at noon and 2. Self-guiding tour free. Guided tours $4.50; over 54, $4; ages 6-12, $2. MC, VI. Phone (785) 368-3888.

STATE CAPITOL, on Capitol Sq. between Jackson and Harrison sts. facing 10th St., contains murals by Kansas native John Steuart Curry as well as artists David H. Overmyer and Lumen Martin Winter. Other interesting works include the "Pioneer Mother" and a bronze of Abraham Lincoln by Merrill Gage.

The capitol, built in the French Renaissance style with native limestone, dates from 1866. Atop the dome is the 22-foot-high statue of Ad Astra, a Kansa Indian warrior, after whose tribe the state was named. Visitors can enjoy sweeping views of the city from the outer dome's balcony by climbing the 296 steps to the top as part of a 45-minute guided dome tour.

Mon.-Fri. 8-5. Guided 40-minute tours are given Mon.-Fri. at 9, 10, 11, 1, 2 and 3, Jan.-May; at 9, 11, 1 and 3, rest of year. Tour times may vary in summer; phone ahead. Dome tours are given Tues.-Sat. at 10:30, 11:30, 12:30 and 1:30. Free. Tour reservations are recommended Mar.-May. Phone (785) 296-3966.

WASHBURN UNIVERSITY, 1700 S.W. College Ave., is named for Ichabod Washburn, a New England church deacon and philanthropist who donated $25,000 to the school in 1868. His generous spirit lives on in the likeness of "Ichabod," the school mascot. Some 7,000 students are enrolled in liberal arts, business, nursing and applied studies programs.

The university also is noted for its law school. Phone (785) 670-1030 for campus tours.

Mulvane Art Museum, on campus at 17th and Jewell sts., showcases works from the mountain plains region as well as changing exhibits. Kansas and international artists are featured. Wed.-Fri. noon-5, Sat.-Sun. 1-4; closed holidays and during exhibit installations. Hours may vary; phone ahead. Free. Phone (785) 670-1124.

TRADING POST (D-8) elev. 810′

TRADING POST MUSEUM, on US 69 at mile marker 96, displays artifacts reflecting the history of the area. Represented are the American Indian period before settlement, the fur trade era, the early settlement, the Border War and the Civil War. Tues.-Sat. 9-5, Sun. 11-5, Apr.-Nov. Donations. Phone (913) 352-6441.

VICTORIA (C-4) pop. 1,208, elev. 1,929′

Victoria began as two separate settlements in the 1870s. North of the present town site, Volga-German immigrants founded Herzog, while just south of it was the English colony of Victoria. Local history recounts that the young Englishmen, who had brought fine cattle, sheep and horses with them, were more interested in saloons and dance halls than in raising livestock.

Within 5 years Victoria Colony had folded, unlike the settlement to the north, which had grown and prospered through the hard work of the Volga-German farmers. In 1913 the abandoned colony was absorbed, and Herzog was renamed Victoria, honoring the area's English heritage.

CATHEDRAL OF THE PLAINS, 1 mi. s. of I-70 at 900 Cathedral Ave., was erected 1908-11 mostly by hand labor. Officially named St. Fidelis Roman Catholic Church, the Romanesque cathedral is constructed of native limestone and features 141-foot spires and stained-glass windows imported from Munich, Germany. Allow 30 minutes minimum. Daily dawn-dusk. Donations. Phone (785) 735-2777.

WALLACE (C-2) pop. 67, elev. 3,310′

Founded in 1869 by the Union Pacific Railroad, Wallace soon was bursting at the seams as one of the most important shipping centers in the region. Its importance began to decline with the coming of such other railroads as the Santa Fe and the Burlington. The 1882 closing of the nearby frontier military post, Fort Wallace, cut trade even further. Several years of drought in the early 1890s convinced most of the remaining townspeople to leave, reducing Wallace to its small size.

Some of the original houses and buildings still stand. Markers and headstones in nearby Wallace Cemetery, originally Fort Wallace Cemetery, graphically describe the fates of some of the area's early settlers. A memorial honoring Custer's 7th Cavalry is at this site.

FORT WALLACE MUSEUM, .5 mi. e. on US 40 at a rest area, displays articles used by early settlers

and the garrisoned troops as well as an area depot and a Butterfield Overland Dispatch Stage station. Allow 30 minutes minimum. Mon.-Sat. 9-5, Sun. 1-5, May-Sept.; otherwise varies. Donations. Phone (785) 891-3564.

WAMEGO (B-6) pop. 4,246

A silo featuring a mural depicting scenes of the Oregon Trail is just east of town on Oregon Trail Road.

Wamego Area Chamber of Commerce: 529 Lincoln Ave., P.O. Box 34, Wamego, KS 66547-0034; phone (785) 456-7849.

THE COLUMBIAN THEATRE, MUSEUM AND ART CENTER, 521 Lincoln Ave., features a collection of 1893 paintings from the Chicago World's Fair that depict life in late 19th-century America. A 284-seat theater offers diverse musical and dramatic performances as well as children's theater. The gallery displays regional artwork. Allow 1 hour minimum. Tues.-Sat. 10-5; closed major holidays. Admission $3. Phone (785) 456-2029 or (800) 899-1893.

OLD DUTCH MILL AND WAMEGO MUSEUM COMPLEX, SR 99 s. to 4th St., then e. to Wamego City Park, features a reconstructed 1870s mill that was used as a custom grinder for feed and flour. Wamego Museum, a prairie village, displays local memorabilia. The park also contains the White Chapel School, a jail, general store, log cabin and a playground. Children's train rides can be scheduled by appointment.

Picnicking is permitted. Allow 30 minutes minimum. Daily 10-4, Apr.-Oct.; 1-4, rest of year. Admission (includes museum and all buildings) $4; ages 6-12, $2. Phone (785) 456-2040.

SAVE **THE OZ MUSEUM** is at 511 Lincoln Ave. The museum houses one of the largest private collections of Oz memorabilia, owned by a Wamego native. More than 2,000 items relate to the 1939 "Wizard of Oz" movie and Frank L. Baum's classic children's story. Four galleries, eight alcoves and 20 display cabinets are filled with books, toys, photographs, pages from scripts, posters, clothing and a sequin from Dorothy's original pair of ruby slippers.

Allow 30 minutes minimum. Mon.-Sat. 10-5, Sun. noon-5; closed Easter, Thanksgiving and Dec. 25. Admission $7; ages 4-12, $4. Phone (785) 458-8686.

WELLINGTON (E-5) pop. 8,647, elev. 1,189′

Located in the heart of the Kansas prairie, Wellington was named for the Duke of Wellington. The town's eight original settlers selected the present site in April 1871 because it was just north of the Indian Territory boundary line, which made it a gateway for homesteaders heading south. Wellington is the county seat for Sumner County, which calls itself "Wheat Capital of the World."

Wellington Area Chamber of Commerce: 207 S. Washington Ave., Wellington, KS 67152; phone (620) 326-7466.

CHISHOLM TRAIL MUSEUM, 502 N. Washington Ave., depicts the changing way of life in Kansas since the state was settled. While some of the displays emphasize the agricultural livelihood of the wheat belt, others depict the growth of the region resulting from the establishment of the Chisholm Trail and the railroad. Period furniture is displayed as well as an extensive collection of dolls and local memorabilia. Daily 1-5, June-Oct.; Sat.-Sun. 1-5, Apr. 15-May 31 and in Nov.; by appointment rest of year. Donations. Phone (620) 326-3820.

WEST MINERAL (E-8) pop. 243, elev. 893′

BIG BRUTUS, 6 mi. w. of SRs 7 and 102, then .5 mi. s., once was the world's second-largest electric mining shovel. The 11-million-pound shovel, used in strip mining to remove dirt and rocks, ceased operation in 1974. Visitors can climb into the operator's seat of the 16-story machine. Both the visitor center and Big Brutus contain exhibits explaining the machine's history.

Camping and picnicking are permitted. Allow 1 hour minimum. Daily 9-8, Memorial Day-Labor Day; 9-5, Apr. 1-day before Memorial Day; 10-4, Jan.-Mar. Hours may vary; phone ahead. Admission $5; over 64, $4.50; ages 6-12, $3.50. MC, VI. Phone (620) 827-6177.

WICHITA (E-5) pop. 344,284, elev. 1,397′

For 11,000 years Wichita served as a trading center and meeting place for nomadic people, but it wasn't until 1863 that the first permanent settlement of Wichita Indians was recorded. Shortly after, J.R. Mead became the first white settler when he opened a trading post and established the area as a base for the Chisholm Trail.

By 1870 Wichita, now incorporated as a city, had become a destination for cattle drives from Texas, hence the city's nickname, "Cowtown." When the cattle trade moved west to take advantage of new rail lines, Wichita fell on hard times. The city bounced back in the 1890s as commerce centered on grain began to surpass the wealth once brought by cattle.

The population of Wichita nearly doubled in 1918 after a great oil reserve was discovered nearby. In turn, the oil money allowed local entrepreneurs Lloyd Stearman, Walter Beech and Clyde Cessna to invest in the up-and-coming airplane industry. During World War II Wichita was the major manufacturing center for airplanes needed in the war effort, and today Wichita produces 70 percent of U.S. general aviation aircraft.

Lake Afton Public Observatory is southwest of downtown Wichita in Goddard at 25000 W. 39th St. S. Telescopes are available and astronomy exhibits are displayed in a museum; phone (316) 978-7827.

A lively cultural life centers on the city's symphony orchestra, several other music and theatrical organizations and three institutions of higher learning: Friends University, with 3,200 students; Kansas Newman College; and Wichita State University, with an enrollment of 14,500.

Recreation is as much a part of the city's life as industry and culture. Some 70 municipal parks offer golf, swimming and other pastimes. Information can be obtained from the Park Board; phone (316) 268-4638. For racing enthusiasts, Wichita Greyhound Park offers dog races Wednesday through Sunday year-round at its facility north of the city at I-135 exit 16; phone (316) 755-4000 or (800) 872-2894.

Note: Policies concerning admittance of children to pari-mutuel betting facilities vary. Phone for information.

The Greater Wichita Convention and Visitors Bureau: 100 S. Main St., Suite 100, Wichita, KS 67202; phone (316) 265-2800 or (800) 288-9424.

Shopping areas: Towne East Square, US 54 at Rock Road, features Dillard's, JCPenney, Sears and Von Maur. Towne West Square, on US 54 at Tracy Street, features Dillard's, JCPenney and Sears. Sheplers, 6501 W. Kellogg, specializes in western wear. The Coleman Factory Outlet Store, 239 N. St. Francis, offers outdoor gear and displays of vintage Coleman products.

In the heart of downtown, renovated 19th-century warehouses are the setting for Oldtown Market, which features some 100 trendy urban shops, galleries and restaurants.

[SAVE] **BOTANICA, THE WICHITA GARDENS,** 701 Amidon St., presents a diversity of flowers and plants in various settings on a 9.5-acre site. Theme gardens include the aquatic collection; the woodland walk; the woodland glade; the teaching garden; and the Shakespearean, rose, butterfly, wildflower and sensory gardens. In the Butterfly House hundreds of free-flight butterflies put on a colorful show June through September.

Guided tours are available. Allow 1 hour minimum. Mon.-Sat. 9-5 (also Tues. 5-8, June-Sept.), Sun. and holidays 1-5, Apr.-Nov.; Mon.-Fri. 9-5, rest of year. Closed Jan. 1, Thanksgiving weekend and Dec. 24-25. Admission $6; over 62, $5; students with ID $3; under 5 free; family rate (two parents and all minor children) $12. Phone (316) 264-0448.

EDWIN A. ULRICH MUSEUM OF ART is e. on 17th St. to 1845 Fairmount Ave., on the Wichita State University campus. The museum, which focuses on contemporary art, features 65 modern sculptures displayed throughout the campus. Barbara Hepworth, Henry Moore and Auguste Rodin are among the artists represented. The museum also houses 6,500 pieces, including a large marble and glass mosaic created by Joan Miró. Allow 1 hour minimum. Tues.-Fri. 11-5, Sat.-Sun. 1-5; closed major holidays. Free. Phone (316) 978-3664.

EXPLORATION PLACE, at 300 N. McLean Blvd., has hands-on exhibits exploring flight, health, Kansas and imagination. Exploring Flight and Design traces aviation history since the Wright brothers' historic 1903 accomplishment, and visitors can examine the internal and external forces affecting their lives at Exploring Human Life.

Exploring Our Only Home looks at the state's geography, beginning with its prehistoric days. A miniature display about mid-1900s Kansas architecture and exhibits about tornados and meteorology are other highlights. A three-story stone castle in the Kids Explore area sparks the imagination of children.

Planetarium shows are presented in the CyberDome Theater. Miniature golf, a playground, picnic grove and recreation paths are offered at the outdoor Exploration Park during summer.

Food is available. Allow 1 hour, 30 minutes minimum. Tues.-Sat. 10-5, Sun.-Mon. noon-5, Memorial Day-Labor Day; Tues.-Sat. 10-5, Sun. noon-5, rest of year. Closed Thanksgiving and Dec. 24-25. Admission $8; over 64, $7.50; ages 5-15, $6; ages 2-4, $3. Admission to either CyberDome Theater or miniature golf $5; over 64, $4.50; ages 5-15, $4. Combination tickets are available. AX, DS, MC, VI. Phone (316) 263-3373 or (877) 904-1444.

KANSAS AVIATION MUSEUM, 5 mi. s. of US 54 on Oliver, then 1 mi. e. to 3350 George Washington Blvd., displays planes, aircraft engines and models. A mural of Charles A. Lindbergh's 1927 flight decorates the building's facade. Allow 1 hour minimum. Tues.-Fri. 9-5, Sat. 1-5; closed Thanksgiving and Dec. 25. Admission $5; ages 6-12, $1. Phone (316) 683-9242.

THE MID-AMERICA ALL-INDIAN CENTER, 650 N. Seneca St., depicts North American Indian heritage, traditions and cultures of the past and present. "Keeper of the Plains," a 44-foot-high sculpture by Blackbear Bosin, stands on the grounds. The Gallery of Nations displays tribal flags. Allow 1 hour minimum. Tues.-Sat. 10-4; closed holidays. Admission $7; over 55, $5; ages 6-12, $3. MC, VI. Phone (316) 262-5221.

MUSEUM OF WORLD TREASURES is at 835 E. 1st St. in Old Town. A variety of exhibits contains pieces from forty collectors. The Hall of the Ancients has 3,000-year-old mummies, rare bones and fossils from prehistoric animals, including a Triceratops skull. Among the museum's 10 dinosaurs is a Tyrannosaur Albertosaurus skeleton. Crown Royal jewels dating from 1200 can be seen in the Hall of Royalty, which depicts the grandeur of European monarchs.

The Hall of Americas presents an extensive collection of weapons and uniforms from the Revolutionary War through the Vietnam War, while the Karpeles Historic Manuscript Library features historic letters and documents. Other exhibits contain frontier-era, music, sports and celebrity memorabilia.

Allow 2 hours minimum. Mon.-Sat. 10-5, Sun. noon-5. Admission $7.95; over 59, $6.95; ages 4-12, $5.95. DS, MC, VI. Phone (316) 263-1311.

OLD COWTOWN MUSEUM, 1871 Sim Park Dr., consists of restorations and reproductions of more than 40 buildings dating 1865-80. Among them is the Darius Munger House, the city's first residential structure, Wichita's first jail, a general store, newspaper shop, carpenter shop, drugstore, school, a saloon and a railroad depot. Many are furnished in period. A 5-acre working farm depicts agricultural history.

Guided tours are available. Food is available. Allow 1 hour minimum. Mon.-Sat. 10-5, Sun. noon-5, Apr.-Oct. Admission $7.75; over 62, $6.50; ages 12-17, $6; ages 4-11, $5.50. MC, VI. Phone (316) 264-0671 or (316) 264-6398.

SEDGWICK COUNTY ZOO, near I-235 exit 10, at 5555 Zoo Blvd., contains 247 acres with more than 2,500 animals representing 500 species. Exhibit areas include the Children's Farm; the Amphibian & Reptile Building; the Jungle, presenting tropical sights, sounds and animals; re-created habitats of Africa with elephants, baboons, giraffes and lions; and one of the largest outdoor, walk-through aviaries representing the wild regions Australia and South America.

A close-up look at primates is offered at the Koch Orangutan and Chimpanzee Habitat. A suspension bridge takes visitors out of the village atmosphere of Nganda Island and into the Downing Gorilla Forest of Africa. An elevated boardwalk traverses the 12-acre exhibit of North America, which features native plants, bears, bison, eagles, otters and wolves.

Allow 3 hours minimum. Daily 8:30-5, Mar.-Oct.; 10-5, rest of year. Admission $9; over 62, $7; ages 4-11, $5. AX, DS, MC, VI. Phone (316) 660-9453.

SOCIETY OF DECORATIVE PAINTERS, 393 N. McLean Blvd., is home to the international society's headquarters. The Decorative Arts Collection Museum features an extensive collection of painted objects, watercolors, furniture, toys and antique items from Russia, Japan and the United States. Tours are available. Allow 30 minutes minimum. Mon.-Fri. 8:30-4; otherwise by appointment. Closed major holidays. Admission $3, under 12 free. Phone (316) 269-9300.

WICHITA ART MUSEUM is at 1400 W. Museum Blvd. An extensive exhibit of American art includes works by Mary Cassatt, Arthur Dove, Edward Hopper, Charles M. Russell and others. Art glass sculptures by Dale Chihuly also are featured. Changing exhibits are presented. Food is available. Allow 1 hour minimum. Tues.-Sun. 10-5; closed major holidays. Admission $5; over 55 and students with ID $4; ages 5-17, $2; free to all Sat. MC, VI. Phone (316) 268-4921.

WICHITA CENTER FOR THE ARTS, 9112 E. Central, is on 15 landscaped acres. The building, which has Oriental overtones, houses four galleries, an art school and a professional theater. Sculptures on the grounds give the area a parklike setting. Stage plays, family shows and special productions are scheduled year-round. Allow 30 minutes minimum. Tues.-Sun. 1-5; closed major holidays. Galleries free. Phone (316) 634-2787.

[SAVE] **WICHITA-SEDGWICK COUNTY HISTORI-CAL MUSEUM,** 204 S. Main St., is in the renovated 1892 former city hall building. Area history from frontier times to the early 20th century is presented. Collections include 1890s patterned glass, hand-painted china, fashions and children's toys. A Victorian house, a 1910 drugstore and a 1920s garage with automotive memorabilia are presented. Tues.-Fri. 11-4, Sat.-Sun. 1-5; closed holidays. Admission $4; ages 6-12, $2. Phone (316) 265-9314.

WICHITA STATE UNIVERSITY is at N. Hillside and 17th sts. Highlights of the 330-acre campus include the Corbin Education Center, designed by Frank Lloyd Wright, and a collection of outdoor sculptures from the university's Edwin A. Ulrich Museum of Art *(see attraction listing).* The student body consists of about 11,500 undergraduates and 3,500 graduate students. More than 350 fine arts performances are held on campus.

Free maps detailing the sculptures' sites are available at the museum. Campus tours are offered. Phone (316) 978-3085.

Wichita State University Libraries—Department of Special Collections, 1845 Fairmount St., contain the university's archives, rare books and manuscripts, including a Japanese prayer scroll dating from A.D. 770 and a 1662 Blaeu Atlas of the Americas. Collections about aviation, abolition, and state and local history are available. The library contains numerous historic Kansas photographs and maps as well as more than 300 digitized state maps. Changing exhibits are presented. Mon.-Fri. 8-5; closed holidays. Free. Phone (316) 978-3590.

WINFIELD (E-6) pop. 12,206, elev. 1,127′

Local legend has it that Spanish explorer Francisco Vásquez de Coronado camped in the area during his 16th-century trek west in search of the Seven Golden Cities of Cíbola. More than 3 centuries later the land was occupied by the Osage Indians, with the first European settlers arriving during the 1860s.

Present day Winfield remembers soldiers of all wars in Memorial Park at Ninth and Fuller streets. The Vietnam War Memorial, a replica of the memorial wall in Washington, D.C., is among the monuments in the park. A directory lists the names of the 777 Kansans who lost their lives during that war.

Winfield Convention and Tourism: P.O. Box 640, Winfield, KS 67156; phone (620) 221-2421 or (877) 729-7440.

Self-guiding tours: Brochures distributed by the convention and tourism office detail driving tours highlighting the town's murals, architecture and historic homes.

THE GALLERY AT BADEN SQUARE, 1 mi. e. to 700 Gary St., displays works by local and regional artists. Changing exhibits present pottery, oil paintings, quilts and sculpture. Children's art also is displayed on occasion. Allow 30 minutes minimum. Mon.-Fri. 8-5; closed holidays. Donations. Phone (620) 221-2161.

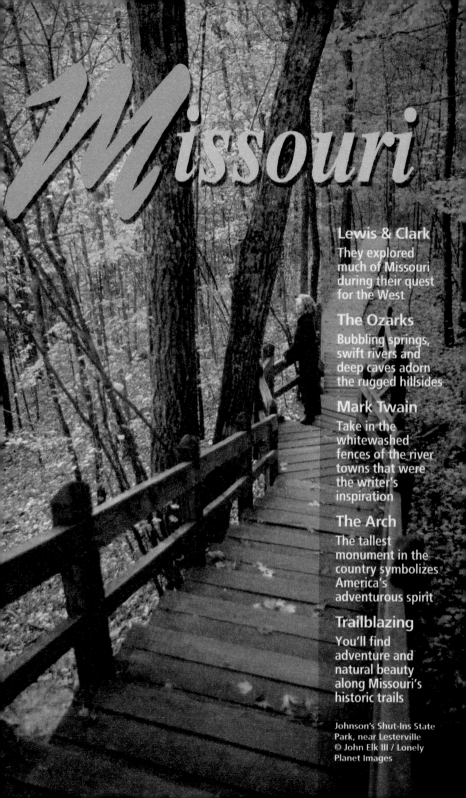

Missouri

Lewis & Clark
They explored much of Missouri during their quest for the West

The Ozarks
Bubbling springs, swift rivers and deep caves adorn the rugged hillsides

Mark Twain
Take in the whitewashed fences of the river towns that were the writer's inspiration

The Arch
The tallest monument in the country symbolizes America's adventurous spirit

Trailblazing
You'll find adventure and natural beauty along Missouri's historic trails

Johnson's Shut-Ins State Park, near Lesterville
© John Elk III / Lonely Planet Images

on the trail to adventure

Alley Spring Mill, west of Eminence / © Tom Algire Photography

Missouri has always provided an open door to adventure, from the footpaths blazed by Lewis and Clark to historic Route 66. Travel one of Missouri's legendary trails to discover the state's delightful mix of frontier heritage and scenic treasures.

Your journey could begin in cosmopolitan St. Louis, wandering thecobblestone streets of Laclede's Landing. Explore the converted warehouses along the Mississippi riverfront, now filled with restaurants and clubs. A brief stroll south is rewarded with a nighttime view of the Gateway Arch.

Then, like the pioneers before you, head westward. Running beside the Missouri River is the Katy Trail, a monumental rails-to-trails conversion.

The whistles of the trains and the rumble along the tracks have been replaced by the crunch of gravel beneath your feet or your bicycle's wheels.

After you pass the striking capitol building in Jefferson City, leave the trail and follow the river's path to Independence and Kansas City. Once trailheads for the Santa Fe and Oregon trails, these cities have maintained their rich history and Western sensibilities.

And don't forget a side trip to Branson. Immerse yourself in the excitement of this vacation mecca before heading to the peaceful wooded hills of the Ozarks.

So start at the Arch, the symbol of our country's pioneering spirit, and create your own trail to adventure.

When Meriwether Lewis and William Clark returned to St. Louis with tales of their discoveries in the West, they sparked a wave of national expansion. The burgeoning towns of Independence and Kansas City became trailheads for the long and arduous journey into the unknown. But many pioneers felt they had gone far enough to find their promised land. These settlers learned what is now well known: You don't need to leave Missouri to find adventure.

Gateway to the West

Steamboats once stopped at the blossoming river towns of Hannibal and St. Charles on their way to St. Louis, the largest city west of the mighty Mississippi. These ships were loaded with supplies for settlers building the communities that would eventually shape the country. The railroad came to Kansas City, and its stockyards provided a natural cattle marketing hub for the vast Western territory.

Today, the leisurely pace of the steamboat is more suited to sightseeing excursions or gambling. The stockyards of Kansas City and the whitewashed picket fences of the river towns have given way to subdivisions and shopping malls. But The Gateway Arch, rising majestically above St. Louis' modern skyline,

remains a symbol of Missouri's early role as a gateway to a new frontier.

Today's explorers can retrace the Santa Fe, Oregon and California trails, following in the footsteps of people who dared to go in search of a better life or a new beginning. They reveal many stories, from the sad steps of the Cherokees along the Trail of Tears near Cape Girardeau to the hoofbeats of the short-lived Pony Express, once headquartered in St. Joseph.

There is still more to be discovered between the rich green of the bottomland forests and the shimmering gold of the tallgrass prairie. St. Louis is a good starting point of exploration. Bicycle paths wind through Forest Park, originally the site of the 1904 St. Louis World's Fair. Today the park is home to the city's art, history and science museums as well as the St. Louis Zoo.

While known for its jazz and barbecue, Kansas City has much more to offer. The city harbors some pretty big surprises, from the 322-foot-wide waterfall beyond the right field fence of Kauffman Stadium to the 18-foot shuttlecocks on the lawn of The Nelson-Atkins Museum of Art. The sparkling, modernistic Crown Center contrasts with the sun-warmed tiles of the Spanish-inspired Country Club Plaza.

A French trading post is established at present-day St. Louis.
1764

The Lewis and Clark expedition departs from St. Charles.
1804

©Bettmann/Corbis

A compromise admits Missouri to the Union as a slave state while prohibiting slavery in the remaining Louisiana Territory.
1820

1811
The New Madrid earthquakes rock the Mississippi Valley.

Missouri Historical Timeline

Library of Congress

1835
Samuel Langhorne Clemens, better known as Mark Twain, is born in the town of Florida.

Sounds of shoppers haggling in the City Market fade with the sunlight into the smooth blues of the historic 18th and Vine District.

In the minds of many (including those who have never been there), Branson equals music theaters. But while the sheer number and variety of live entertainment offerings are indeed noteworthy, this southwestern Missouri town also lies in the heart of Ozarks country. Deep blue springs—some mere trickles, others roaring past well-worn bluffs—flow through the lushly forested hills and valleys of this recreational paradise. After fishing, boating or camping in the midst of such gorgeous scenery, you might well ask yourself why anyone would want to journey elsewhere.

Dreamers and Doers

The state's pioneering spirit does not just apply to those who ventured west. Missouri has been more than a gateway out; it has been a stepping stone up. Mark Twain based the adventures of Tom Sawyer and Huckleberry Finn on his own childhood in Hannibal, while Walt Disney modeled the "Main Street USA" portion of Disneyland after Marceline, his hometown.

A former slave, George Washington Carver took the knowledge that sprouted in his garden in Diamond and used it to revolutionize agriculture in the southern United States. And longtime Independence resident and former Kansas City Automobile Club employee Harry S. Truman steered our country out of World War II, paving the way for postwar prosperity.

Ragtime composer Scott Joplin, rock 'n' roller Chuck Berry, and jazz greats Duke Ellington and Miles Davis are just a few of the musical pioneers who started out in the saloons and clubs of St. Louis and Kansas City. These Missourians didn't wait for anyone to "show them": They led the way with breakthrough performances.

Missouri also has had its share of industrial visionaries. In 1860 Eberhard Anheuser, a successful St. Louis businessman, saw potential in a struggling local brewery. With the help of his son-in-law, Adolphus Busch, he tapped into the national beer market to create Anheuser-Busch Inc., the world's largest brewer. Nebraska teenager Joyce C. Hall got off the train in Kansas City in 1910 with an idea to sell picture postcards. His mail-order business evolved into Hallmark Cards Inc., a $3.5 billion corporation. Both companies are the undisputed leaders in their respective industries.

And where else but in forward-thinking Missouri would you find Branson? This small town,

The Pony Express begins its run from St. Joseph to Sacramento.

1860

©Bettmann/Corbis

Flooding on the Missouri and Mississippi rivers causes billions of dollars in damage across the state.

1993

The Gateway Arch is dedicated in St. Louis.

1966

1945

Missouri native and former AAA sales representative Harry S. Truman becomes the 33rd U.S. president.

Library of Congress

2000

Gov. Mel Carnahan is elected to the U.S. Senate 3 weeks after his death in a plane crash; his widow accepts the seat.

1904

The St. Louis World's Fair attracts 20 million visitors.

tucked into the wooded hills of the Ozarks, is a rather unique hybrid—one part Las Vegas flash, several parts down-home friendliness. Neon and nature combine seamlessly here, with the razzle dazzle of a myriad live entertainment shows matched by the breathtaking sunsets at nearby Table Rock Lake.

Recreation

To experience all the adventure Missouri has to offer, you have to get out of your car. Follow scenic trails up wooded hillsides; jump in spring-fed rivers and shimmering lakes; and explore at least one of the state's more than 5,500 caves. To keep you close to the outdoor action, **campsites** at most state parks operate year-round.

Still Waters Run Deep

South-central Missouri is a water lover's paradise. Surrounded by spectacular rolling hills, Lake of the Ozarks' 54,000 acres of water beckon **boaters, water skiers**, and those who want to enjoy the area's tranquil beauty. Farther south, the crystal clear waters of Table Rock Lake offer **scuba divers** unparalleled views of an underwater forest. **Parasailing** is a leading activity at both lakes, and for those who like to skim the surface, **jet ski** rentals are available at many of the local marinas.

A laid-back afternoon of **rafting** is a wonderful way to enjoy an Ozark river. Whether out for an hour or all day, you'll never feel more relaxed. Alley Spring on the Jacks Fork River and Pulltite, Round and Big springs on the Current River are major starting points. The upper stretches of these rivers are often more challenging during spring; water levels dip in summer.

Canoeing on the Meramec River in eastern Missouri is a tranquil retreat. Meramec State Park near Sullivan features miles of picturesque riverbank scenery, bubbling springs and more than 40 caves. Paddle your way past open glades dotted with Indian paintbrush and fern-covered ravines. Canoes, rafts and inner tubes may be rented at the park, and transportation to one of several launching points is included.

Fishing is the classic pastime in Missouri. The cold water of Lake Taneycomo near Branson is a trout haven year-round. Other lakes throughout the state are teeming with small- and large-mouth bass, goggle-eye, walleye, channel cat and bluegill. Don't forget to pick up a state fishing license ($12 yearly for residents, $5.50 a day or $35 yearly for nonresidents, plus $7 for special "trout tags") before you start reeling them in.

The oak and hickory forests and tall prairie grass that surround all this water provide myriad **hunting** opportunities. Migrating ducks and geese rest at Swan Lake and Mingo national wildlife refuges, near Brookfield and Poplar Bluff, respectively. Quails, wild turkeys, squirrels, rabbits, raccoons and deer are plentiful throughout the state. Hunting seasons vary depending on your prey and permits are required; contact the Missouri Department of Conservation at (573) 751-4115.

Take a Walk on the Scenic Side

In 1986 the Missouri-Kansas-Texas Railroad (the "Katy") stopped running between Sedalia and St. Charles, opening the door for one of the largest rails-to-trails conversions in history. Ten years later, the Katy Trail opened to **hikers** and **bicyclists**.

The trail starts at the restored M-K-T Depot in St. Charles and runs west between towering bluffs and the curvaceous Missouri River. Trailheads with facilities are spaced about every 10 miles. While there aren't many rest stops in between, ripening mulberries beside the trail in summer may tide you over. Favorite pit stops along the 225-mile trek include the Stone Hill Winery in Hermann and the charming bistros and cafes of Rocheport, originally settled by French immigrants.

Another popular hiking route across the state is the still-evolving Ozark Trail, a series of trails that will one day form a continuous route from St. Louis to northern Arkansas. The Taum Sauk section, generally regarded as the trail's most rugged and scenic stretch, winds over sculpted ridges and mossy glades, ascends the summit of Taum Sauk Mountain (the highest in the state) and takes in Mina Sauk Falls.

For **rock climbers**, Missouri has many small cragging areas, mainly south of I-70. Johnson's Shut-In State Park offers some of the oldest exposed rock in the nation, a good practice area for novices. The park is open to climbing from September through May; registration at park headquarters is required.

Recreational Activities

Throughout the TourBook, you may notice a Recreational Activities heading with bulleted listings of recreation-oriented establishments listed underneath. Similar operations also may be mentioned in Destination City recreation sections. Since normal AAA inspection criteria cannot be applied, these establishments are presented for information only. Age, height and weight restrictions may apply. Reservations are often recommended and sometimes required. Visitors should phone or write the attraction for additional information, and the address and phone number are provided for this purpose.

Fast Facts

POPULATION: 5,595,211.

AREA: 69,686 square miles; ranks 19th.

CAPITAL: Jefferson City.

HIGHEST POINT: 1,772 ft., Taum Sauk Mountain.

LOWEST POINT: 230 ft., St. Francis River.

TIME ZONE(S): Central. DST.

MINIMUM AGE FOR UNRESTRICTED DRIVER'S LICENSE: 18.

MINIMUM AGE FOR GAMBLING: 21.

SEAT BELT/CHILD RESTRAINT LAWS: Seat belts required for driver and front seat passengers 16 and older. Children ages 8 through 15, weighing at least 80 pounds and more than 57 inches tall are required to be in a seat belt; child restraints are required for children under 8, under 80 pounds and under 57 inches tall.

HELMETS FOR MOTORCYCLISTS: Required for all riders.

RADAR DETECTORS: Permitted.

FIREARMS LAWS: Vary by state and/or county. Contact the Missouri State Highway Patrol, Attn.: Public Information, P.O. Box 568, Jefferson City, MO 65102; phone (573) 751-3313.

HOLIDAYS: Jan. 1; Martin Luther King Jr. Day, Jan. (3rd Mon.); Lincoln's Birthday, Feb. 12; Presidents Day, Feb. (3rd Mon.); Truman Day, May 8; Memorial Day, May (last Mon.); July 4; Labor Day, Sept. (1st Mon.); Columbus Day, Oct. (2nd Mon.); Veterans Day, Nov. 11; Thanksgiving; Christmas, Dec. 25.

TAXES: Missouri's statewide sales tax is 4.23 percent. Cities may impose an additional increment of up to 2.5 percent; cities not located in counties may impose up to 1.38 percent. Counties also may add increments to the sales tax. Cities may levy lodging taxes of up to 5.5 percent and up to 1.75 percent on food and beverages.

INFORMATION CENTERS: State welcome centers are 2 miles east of the Missouri-Oklahoma state line on I-44 near Joplin; in north St. Louis on Dunn Road off I-270 (Riverview exit); on I-55 at the Marston Rest Area about 40 miles north of the Missouri-Arkansas state line south of New Madrid; west of I-29, a half-mile south of junction with US 136 near Rock Port; in Hannibal, east of US 61, 2 miles south of junction with US 36; and in Kansas City, on the grounds of the Truman Sports Complex off I-70 at the Blue Ridge Cut-Off.

The centers are open daily 8-5, Mar.-Nov.; Mon.-Sat. 8-5, rest of year. The Missouri Division of Tourism office in the Truman State Office Building, 301 W. High St., second floor, Jefferson City, provides travel information Mon.-Fri. 8-5.

FURTHER INFORMATION FOR VISITORS:

Missouri Division of Tourism
P.O. Box 1055
Jefferson City, MO 65102

(573) 751-4133
(800) 519-2300
See color ad inside front cover

RECREATION INFORMATION:

Missouri Department of Natural Resources
Division of Parks
P.O. Box 176
Jefferson City, MO 65102
(800) 334-6946

FISHING AND HUNTING REGULATIONS:

Missouri Department of Conservation
P.O. Box 180
Jefferson City, MO 65102
(573) 751-4115

NATIONAL FOREST INFORMATION:

Mark Twain National Forest
401 Fairgrounds Rd.
Rolla, MO 65401
(573) 364-4621
(877) 444-6777 (reservations)

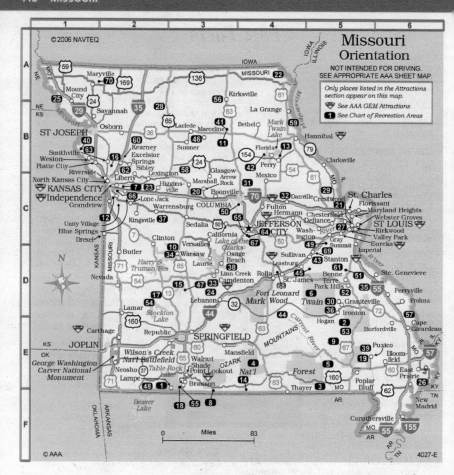

© 2006 NAVTEQ

Missouri
Orientation

NOT INTENDED FOR DRIVING.
SEE APPROPRIATE AAA SHEET MAP.

Only places listed in the Attractions
section appear on this map.

▼ See AAA GEM Attractions

1 See Chart of Recreation Areas

IOWA

Miles   0   83

© AAA

4027-E

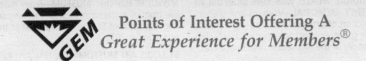

Points of Interest Offering A *Great Experience for Members*®

Branson (E-3)

CELEBRATION CITY—Thrill seekers are sure to be satisfied at this family-oriented amusement park, where the roller coasters are designed to keep riders on the edge of their seats. See p. 137.

MARVEL CAVE—One of the Ozarks' oldest attractions, the cave is known not only for its subterranean features but also as the origin of Silver Dollar City. See p. 139.

SHEPHERD OF THE HILLS HOMESTEAD—Explore the sights described in Harold Bell Wright's prize-winning novel. See p. 138.

THE SHEPHERD OF THE HILLS OUTDOOR THEATRE—This gripping tale of the  struggles faced by Ozark mountaineers offers music, drama and heartfelt emotion. See p. 139.

SILVER DOLLAR CITY—Crafts, rides and family entertainment are on tap at an amusement park that above all celebrates the heritage of the Ozarks. See p. 139.

THE WORLD'S LARGEST TITANIC MUSEUM ATTRACTION—All things *Titanic* are on display at this impressive re-creation of the world-famous ocean liner. See p. 140.

Camdenton (D-3)

BRIDAL CAVE—Breathtaking onyx formations have created the perfect surroundings for a record number of underground weddings. See p. 154.

Carthage (E-1)

PRECIOUS MOMENTS INSPIRATION PARK—Biblical murals, stained-glass windows and a bronze fountain feature inspirational artist Sam Butcher's beloved characters. See p. 155.

Collinsville, Ill.

CAHOKIA MOUNDS STATE HISTORIC SITE—This 2,200-acre site contains 65 preserved American Indian mounds that represent the Mississippian culture that flourished in the area A.D. 900-1500. See p. 213.

Eureka (C-6)

SIX FLAGS ST. LOUIS—Themed areas showcase a variety of shows, rides and attractions; don't miss the musical extravaganzas in Miss Kitty's Saloon and the Palace Music Hall. See p. 209.

Fulton (C-4)

WINSTON CHURCHILL MEMORIAL AND LIBRARY—Tour an 800-year-old London church reassembled at the site of Churchill's "Iron Curtain" speech. See p. 158.

Hannibal (B-5)

MARK TWAIN BOYHOOD HOME AND MUSEUM—Cross the threshold of this mid-1800s home filled with Twain memorabilia and be transported back to the time of Tom Sawyer and Huck Finn. See p. 159.

Independence (C-1)

TRUMAN PRESIDENTIAL MUSEUM & LIBRARY—Documents and furnishings from Truman's life and career are interspersed with other presidential portraits and memorabilia. See p. 179.

Jefferson City (C-4)

MISSOURI STATE CAPITOL—The state museum plus murals by Thomas Hart Benton and N.C. Wyeth are housed in this handsome building of Carthage stone. See p. 162.

Kansas City (C-1)

ARABIA STEAMBOAT MUSEUM—The preserved cargo of a sunken steamship provides insight into pre-Civil War America. See p. 169.

THE NATIONAL WORLD WAR ONE MUSEUM AT THE LIBERTY MEMORIAL—With its comprehensive collection of artifacts and first-rate exhibits, this is the country's only museum dedicated solely to the history of the first World War. See p. 172.

THE NELSON-ATKINS MUSEUM OF ART—While a collection of Asian art is a highlight indoors, a 17-acre sculpture garden on the landscaped grounds is home to works by modern masters. See p. 172.

TOY AND MINIATURE MUSEUM OF KANSAS CITY—Antique toys and scale miniatures include 80 furnished doll houses that will bring out the child in you. See p. 173.

Leasburg (D-4)

ONONDAGA CAVE STATE PARK—One of Missouri's hidden treasures, this cave is known for the size and intricacy of its formations. See p. 187.

St. Louis (C-6)

FOREST PARK—A city landmark, this 1,293-acre park is home to major cultural institutions and provides countless recreational opportunities. See p. 203.

THE GATEWAY ARCH—This symbol of America's pioneer spirit is the tallest man-made monument in the national park system. See p. 205.

MISSOURI BOTANICAL GARDEN—Pick up some tips for your own garden while visiting one of the most beautiful spots in the city. See p. 206.

MISSOURI HISTORY MUSEUM—From hardscrabble frontier settlement to vital 21st-century city, the true spirit of St. Louis is captured at this museum. See p. 203.

ST. LOUIS ART MUSEUM—The Fine Arts Palace of the 1904 World's Fair still contains fabulous collections ranging from ancient to contemporary. See p. 204.

ST. LOUIS SCIENCE CENTER—Exhibits about technology, environment and humanity as well as planetarium shows and an OMNIMAX theater educate, entertain and enlighten. See p. 204.

ST. LOUIS ZOO—This 90-acre zoo in Forest Park showcases natural habitat areas as well as an innovative children's zoo. See p. 204.

Springfield (E-3)

FANTASTIC CAVERNS—Marvel at limestone configurations and underground wildlife from the comfort of Jeep-drawn trams. See p. 216.

WONDERS OF WILDLIFE ZOOQUARIUM—Join in the celebration of our nation's abundant natural resources and its hunting and fishing heritage through interactive exhibits, aquariums and native habitats. See p. 216.

Stanton (D-5)

MERAMEC CAVERNS—Beneath the picturesque scenery of the Meramec Valley, this fascinating cave has generated spectacular mineral formations as well as some colorful history. See p. 218.

RECREATION AREAS

	MAP LOCATION	CAMPING	PICNICKING	HIKING TRAILS	BOATING	BOAT RAMP	BOAT RENTAL	FISHING	SWIMMING	PETS ON LEASH	BICYCLE TRAILS	WINTER SPORTS	VISITOR CENTER	LODGE/CABINS	FOOD SERVICE
NATIONAL FORESTS *(See place listings)*															
Mark Twain 1,500,000 acres. Southern Missouri.		•	•	•	•	•	•	•	•	•		•	•		
Big Bay (E-2) 680 acres 1 mi. s.e. of Shell Knob on SR 39, then 3 mi. s.e. on CR YY.	**1**	•	•		•	•		•	•	•					
Crane Lake (E-5) 99 acres 12 mi. s. of Ironton off SR 49 and CR E.	**2**		•	•	•	•	•		•			•	•		
Fourche Lake (E-5) 40 acres 18 mi. w. of Doniphan on US 160.	**3**		•	•	•	•			•			•	•		
Noblett Lake (E-4) 8 acres 8 mi. w. of Willow Springs on SR 76, then 1.5 mi. s. on SR 181, 3 mi. s.e. on CR AP and 1 mi. s.w. on FR 857. Horse trails.	**4**	•	•	•				•		•		•	•		
Pinewoods Lake (E-5) 30 acres 2 mi. w. of Ellsinore on SR 60. Electric motors only.	**5**		•	•	•	•		•	•	•	•	•	•		
Red Bluff (D-5) 133 acres 1 mi. e. of Davisville on CR V, then 1 mi. n. on FR 2011.	**6**	•	•	•				•	•	•					
NATIONAL SCENIC RIVERWAYS *(See place listings)*															
Ozark 134 miles. Southeastern Missouri.		•	•	•	•	•	•	•	•	•			•	•	•
ARMY CORPS OF ENGINEERS															
Blue Springs Lake (C-2) 720 acres .5 mi. e. of I-470 off Bowlin Rd. in Blue Springs. Marina.	**7**	•	•	•	•	•	•	•	•	•					
Bull Shoals Lake (F-3) 45,500 acres s.e. of Branson on the Missouri-Arkansas state line.	**8**	•	•		•	•	•	•	•	•				•	•
Clearwater Lake (E-5) 1,630 acres 7.5 mi. w. of Piedmont. Tennis; exercise trail, marina.	**9**	•	•	•	•	•	•	•	•	•					
Harry S. Truman (D-3) 55,600 acres 1.5 mi. n.w. of Warsaw on the Osage River. Marina.	**10**	•	•	•	•	•	•	•	•	•			•	•	•
Long Branch Lake (B-3) 2,430 acres 1 mi. w. of Macon on US 36. Marina.	**11**	•	•	•	•	•	•	•	•	•					
Longview Lake (C-2) 930 acres 1 mi. s. of I-470 off Raytown Rd. in Kansas City. Golf; marina.	**12**	•	•	•	•	•	•	•	•	•	•				•
Mark Twain Lake (B-4) 18,600 acres 9mi. n. of Perry on CR J. Golf (nine holes); marina. *(See Perry p. 192)*	**13**	•	•	•	•	•	•	•	•	•			•	•	
Norfork Lake (E-4) 22,000 acres at Tecumseh off US 160.	**14**	•	•		•	•		•	•	•					•
Pomme de Terre (D-3) 7,800 acres 3 mi. s. of Hermitage off SR 64. Marina.	**15**	•	•	•	•	•	•	•	•	•		•	•	•	•
Smithville Lake (B-2) 7,200 acres 5 mi. n. of Kansas City on SR DD, then 2 mi. e. of US 169. Marina.	**16**	•	•	•	•	•	•	•	•	•			•		•
Stockton (D-2) 24,900 acres 1 mi. s. of Stockton on SR 32. Marina.	**17**	•	•	•	•	•	•	•	•	•			•	•	•
Table Rock (F-3) 52,300 acres 5 mi. w. of Branson via SRs 76 and 165. Marina.	**18**	•	•		•	•	•	•	•	•				•	•
Wappapello Lake (E-5) 8,900 acres 16 mi. n.e. of Poplar Bluff via US 60 and CR T.	**19**	•	•	•	•	•	•	•	•	•			•	•	•
STATE															
Arrow Rock (C-3) 167 acres 3 blks. n. of SR 41. *(See Arrow Rock p. 124)*	**20**	•	•	•					•				•	•	•
Babler Memorial (C-5) 2,439 acres 20 mi. w. of St. Louis on SR 109. Tennis; horse rental, nature center.	**21**	•	•	•						•	•	•	•		
Battle of Athens (A-4) 401 acres 8 mi. n. of Revere off SR 81. Historic.	**22**	•	•	•	•	•		•		•					
Battle of Lexington (C-2) 106 acres off US 24. Historic. *(See Lexington p. 188)*	**23**		•	•	•	•		•		•			•		
Bennett Spring (D-3) 3,100 acres 12 mi. w. of Lebanon on SR 64. *(See Lebanon p. 187)*	**24**	•	•	•	•			•	•	•			•	•	•
Big Lake (A-1) 407 acres 11 mi. s.w. of Mound City off SR 118 on SR 111.	**25**	•	•		•	•		•	•	•				•	•

RECREATION AREAS

Recreation Area	MAP LOCATION	CAMPING	PICNICKING	HIKING TRAILS	BOATING	BOAT RAMP	BOAT RENTAL	FISHING	SWIMMING	PETS ON LEASH	BICYCLE TRAILS	WINTER SPORTS	VISITOR CENTER	LODGE/CABINS	FOOD SERVICE
Big Oak Tree (E-6) 1,004 acres 2 mi. e. of East Prairie on SR 80, then 10 mi. s. on SR 102.	26		•	•	•	•		•		•			•		
Castlewood (C-5) 1,780 acres 6 mi. e. of Ballwin on Kiefer Creek Rd. off SR 100. Horse trails.	27		•	•	•	•		•		•	•	•			
Crowder (B-2) 1,912 acres 4 mi. w. of Trenton on SR 146.	28	•	•	•				•	•	•					
Cuivre River (C-5) 6,350 acres 3 mi. e. of Troy off SR 47. Horse trails.	29	•	•	•	•			•	•	•	•				
Elephant Rocks (D-5) 129 acres off SR 21. Interpretive trails. *(See Graniteville p. 158)*	30		•	•				•		•					
Finger Lakes (C-4) 1,132 acres 10 mi. n. of Columbia on US 63.	31	•	•	•		•		•		•			•		
Graham Cave (C-4) 357 acres 2 mi. w. of I-70 and CR TT. *(See Danville p. 157)*	32	•	•	•						•					
Ha Ha Tonka (D-3) 2,953 acres 5 mi. s.w. of Camdenton off US 54 on CR D. Scenic; historic ruins.	33		•	•				•		•					
Harry S. Truman (D-3) 1,440 acres 5 mi. w. of Warsaw off SR 7 on CR UU. Marina.	34	•	•	•	•	•	•	•	•	•					
Hawn (D-5) 4,805 acres 14 mi. s.w. of Ste. Genevieve off SR 32 on SR 144.	35	•	•	•						•					
Johnson's Shut-Ins (D-5) 8,470 acres 8 mi. n. of Lesterville on CR N. Scenic.	36	•	•	•				•	•	•					
Knob Noster (C-2) 3,549 acres 2 mi. s. of Knob Noster off US 50 on SR 132. Horse trails.	37	•	•	•	•			•		•	•		•		
Lake of the Ozarks (D-3) 17,213 acres. Caverns, horse rental, marina.	38	•	•	•	•	•	•	•	•	•			•		
Lake Wappapello (E-5) 1,854 acres 16 mi. n. of Poplar Bluff on US 67 and 9 mi. e. on SR 172. Marina.	39	•	•	•	•	•	•	•	•	•				•	
Lewis and Clark (B-1) 121 acres 21 mi. s.w. of St. Joseph via US 59 and SR 45 on SR 138.	40	•	•		•	•		•	•	•					
Long Branch (B-3) 1,834 acres 2 mi. w. of Macon on US 36. Marina.	41	•	•		•	•		•	•	•					
Mark Twain (B-4) 2,775 acres .5 mi. s. of Florida on SR 107. Playground.	42	•	•	•	•	•		•	•	•					
Meramec (D-5) 6,896 acres 4 mi. e. via SR 185. Scenic. *(See Sullivan p. 218)*	43	•	•	•	•	•	•	•		•			•	•	•
Montauk (D-4) 1,353 acres 21 mi. s.w. of Salem via SR 119.	44	•	•	•				•		•				•	•
Onondaga Cave (D-4) 1,317 acres 5 mi. s. on CR H. Scenic. *(See Leasburg p. 187)*	45	•	•	•	•	•	•	•	•	•			•		•
Pershing (B-3) 2,909 acres 2 mi. w. of Laclede off US 36 on SR 130.	46	•	•	•				•	•	•					
Pomme de Terre (D-3) 734 acres 5 mi. s. of Hermitage via SR 64. Marina.	47	•	•	•	•	•	•	•	•	•					
Roaring River (E-2) 3,403 acres 7 mi. s. of Cassville on SR 112. Horse rental.	48	•	•	•				•	•	•			•	•	•
Robertsville (C-5) 1,212 acres 15 mi. s.w. of Eureka off I-44.	49	•	•	•	•			•		•					
Rock Bridge (C-3) 2,238 acres 7 mi. s. of Columbia on SR 163. Horse trails.	50		•	•				•		•	•	•			
Saint Francois (D-5) 2,735 acres 4 mi. n. of Bonne Terre on US 67. Horse trails.	51	•	•	•	•			•	•	•					
Saint Joe (D-5) 8,238 acres 3 mi. s. of Flat River off CR B via SR 32. Horse trails.	52	•	•	•	•			•	•	•					
Sam A. Baker (E-5) 5,164 acres 6 mi. n. of Patterson via SRs 34 and 143. Nature center, horse trails.	53	•	•	•	•	•		•	•	•			•	•	•
Stockton (D-2) 2,176 acres 8 mi. s.e. of Stockton on SR 215. Marina.	54	•	•	•	•	•	•	•	•	•				•	•
Table Rock (F-3) 356 acres 5 mi. w. of Branson on SR 165. Marina.	55	•	•	•	•	•	•	•	•	•					

RECREATION AREAS

	MAP LOCATION	CAMPING	PICNICKING	HIKING TRAILS	BOATING	BOAT RAMP	BOAT RENTAL	FISHING	SWIMMING	PETS ON LEASH	BICYCLE TRAILS	WINTER SPORTS	VISITOR CENTER	LODGE/CABINS	FOOD SERVICE
Thousand Hills (A-3) 3,215 acres 4 mi. w. of Kirksville off SR 6 on SR 157. Marina.	56	•	•	•	•	•	•	•	•	•				•	•
Trail of Tears (D-6) 3,415 acres 10 mi. n. on SR 177. Horse trails. *(See Cape Girardeau p. 155)*	57	•	•	•	•	•		•	•	•			•		
Van Meter (B-3) 983 acres 12 mi. n.w. of Marshall via SRs 41 and 122. Nature trails. *(See Marshall p. 189)*	58	•	•	•				•		•					
Wakonda (B-4) 1,050 acres 3 mi. s. of La Grange off US 61.	59	•	•	•	•	•		•	•	•				•	
Wallace (B-2) 502 acres 6 mi. s. of Cameron on SR 121.	60	•	•	•	•			•	•	•					
Washington (D-5) 1,822 acres 9 mi. s.w. of De Soto off SR 21.	61	•	•	•				•		•				•	•
Watkins Mill (B-2) 818 acres 6 mi. n. of Excelsior Springs off SR 92 on CR RA.	62	•	•	•	•	•		•	•	•	•		•		
Weston Bend (B-1) 1,133 acres 1 mi. s. of Weston on SR 45.	63	•	•	•				•			•	•			
OTHER															
Binder (C-4) 650 acres off US 50W in Jefferson City.	64	•	•	•	•	•		•							•
Cole County (C-4) 80 acres off Country Club Dr. in Jefferson City.	65		•							•	•				
Fleming Park (C-2) 4,814 acres e. of Kansas City on US 40 and Woods Chapel Rd. *(See Blue Springs p. 178)*	66	•	•	•	•	•	•	•	•	•					•
Hough (C-4) On Mississippi St. in Jefferson City. Golf (18-hole).	67	-	•	•				•							
Little Prairie Lake (D-4) More than 300 acres e. of Rolla on I-44 to CR V, then 2 mi. e. on N. Outer Rd.	68		•			•		•	•	•					•
Meramec Caverns (D-5) 110 acres 3 mi. s. of Stanton off I-44.	69	•	•			•		•	•	•	•			•	•
Mozingo Lake (A-2) 3,000 acres 3 mi. e. of Maryville on US 136. Golf.	70	•	•	•	•	•		•		•					

Missouri Temperature Averages
Maximum/Minimum
From the records of The Weather Channel Interactive, Inc.

	JAN	FEB	MAR	APR	MAY	JUN	JUL	AUG	SEP	OCT	NOV	DEC
Columbia	39 / 21	43 / 24	52 / 32	65 / 44	75 / 54	84 / 64	90 / 68	88 / 66	81 / 58	70 / 47	53 / 33	43 / 25
Kansas City	39 / 22	44 / 26	53 / 33	66 / 45	75 / 55	85 / 66	91 / 71	89 / 69	82 / 60	71 / 49	54 / 35	43 / 27
St. Joseph	37 / 17	41 / 21	51 / 29	65 / 42	75 / 53	85 / 63	91 / 68	88 / 66	81 / 56	70 / 45	52 / 31	41 / 22
St. Louis	40 / 24	44 / 26	53 / 33	66 / 45	76 / 55	86 / 65	90 / 69	88 / 67	81 / 59	70 / 48	54 / 35	43 / 27
Springfield	43 / 24	47 / 27	55 / 33	66 / 45	75 / 54	85 / 64	90 / 67	90 / 67	83 / 58	72 / 47	56 / 34	46 / 27

Points of Interest

ARROW ROCK (C-3) pop. 79

Arrow Rock, first settled in 1810, became an important trading center that served both farmers and westward expeditions along the Santa Fe Trail. Although the settlement was rechristened Philadelphia, it soon reverted to the name given by early explorers for the flint outcroppings in the surrounding limestone bluffs, a material that was used to make arrow points.

Artist George Caleb Bingham made his home in Arrow Rock in the early 19th century, painting scenes of frontier life on the Missouri River. Dr. John Sappington, another nearby resident, engaged in large-scale farming and the marketing of Sappington Anti-fever Pills. Two of his sons-in-law and one of his grandsons became governors of the state. The Friends of Arrow Rock offers a guided tour of Sappington's 1849 Greek Revival mansion by appointment; phone (660) 837-3231.

An 1872 Baptist church has been converted and refurbished to house the Arrow Rock Lyceum Theatre. Matinee performances are given Wed. and Sat.-Sun. at 2, evening performances at 8 p.m., June-Oct.; phone (660) 837-3311.

ARROW ROCK STATE HISTORIC SITE is 3 blks. n. of SR 41. A town founded in 1829 is preserved at the site. Located where the Santa Fe Trail met the Missouri River, the settlement thrived, with 1,000 residents by the 1860s.

Guided 1-hour walking tours conducted by the Friends of Arrow Rock visit the 1837 home of George C. Bingham, the old courthouse and jail, the Huston Tavern and the Sappington Museum.

Picnic areas and campsites are nearby. Grounds open daily 7 a.m.-10 p.m. Visitor center open daily 10-5, June-Aug.; daily 10-4, March-May and Sept.-Nov.; Fri.-Sun. 10-4, rest of year. Visitor center closed Jan. 1, Thanksgiving and Dec. 25. Guided tours (offered by the Friends of Arrow Rock) Mon.-Sat. at 10, 11:30, 1:30, 3 and 4, Sun. at 1:30, 3 and 4, June-Aug.; Sat. at 10, 11:30, 1:30, 3 and 4, Sun. at 1:30, 3 and 4, Apr.-May and Sept.-Oct.

Grounds and visitor center free. Walking tours $5; under 12, $1.50. Phone (660) 837-3330, or (660) 837-3231 for tour reservations. *See Recreation Chart and the AAA South Central CampBook.*

Friends of Arrow Rock Guided Tours is at off I-70 exit SR 41, then 13 mi. n. to the museum on Main St. Tours visit the 1837 home of George C. Bingham, the old courthouse and jail, the Huston Tavern and the Sappington Museum; a second tour includes the Lodge Hall, the print shop and the J.P. Sites Gun Shop and home. Allow 1 hour minimum. Hours. Admission $5; under 12, $1.50. DS, MC, VI. Phone (660) 837-3231.

BETHEL (B-4) pop. 121

Bethel was founded in 1844 when Wilhelm Keil led settlers of German ancestry from Pennsylvania and began a communal religious colony that shared work and property but permitted private earnings. The community numbered about 650 in 1855 when Keil led part of the group west to Oregon; about 340 residents remained at Bethel. Both colonies were disbanded in 1879. More than 30 of Bethel's original buildings remain, and three houses with 1840s furnishings can be visited.

From May through October the Bethel Colony School of Arts offers classes ranging from folk arts to fine arts.

Bethel German Colony: P.O. Box 127, Bethel, MO 63434; phone (660) 284-6493.

Self-guiding tours: Walking tours with a taped narration describing the history of Bethel and various historic houses depart from the Bethel Colony Gift Shop, First and Main streets, daily 10-3, May-Nov.; phone (660) 284-6493.

BLOOMFIELD (E-6) pop. 1,952, elev. 497'

MISSOURI STATE VETERANS CEMETERY is about 3.5 n. off SR 25 from jct. US 60 at 17377 Stars and Stripes Way. A white rail fence with stone pillars encompasses this cemetery for Missouri war veterans and their spouses. A walking trail traverses the landscaped grounds, which include a lake, fountain and columbarium wall. Each burial area is sectioned off alphabetically. Allow 30 minutes minimum. Daily 8 a.m.-dusk. Free. Phone (573) 568-3871.

STARS AND STRIPES MUSEUM/LIBRARY is at 17377 Stars and Stripes Way, adjacent to the Missouri State Veterans Cemetery. It preserves the legacy of a newspaper that has bridged servicemen and women and their families through five major wars. Ten Union soldiers from Illinois, using the vacated press of *The Bloomfield Herald,* published the first issue of *The Stars and Stripes*—which they named after the American flag—on Nov. 9, 1861.

One of those original editions can be seen, along with military memorabilia and displays pertaining to the many notable journalists who have served as "Stripers." Allow 30 minutes minimum. Mon. and Wed.-Fri. 10-4, Sat. 10-2, Sun. 1-4; closed Jan. 1, Easter, Thanksgiving and Dec. 25. Free. Phone (573) 568-2055.

BLUE SPRINGS—*see Kansas City p. 178.*

BONNE TERRE (D-5) pop. 4,039

SAVE **BONNE TERRE MINE TOURS** is on SR 47 at Park St. and Allen St. Visitors explore the lead and silver mines that operated 1870-1962. Tours through the caverns, which are larger than the town of Bonne Terre, pass old mining tools, a flower garden, ore cars and a billion-gallon underground lake popular with scuba divers. A museum on the surface displays old mining equipment and ore samples.

Allow 1 hour minimum. Daily 10-4, Apr.-Oct.; Fri.-Sun. 9-5, rest of year. Boat tours are available in conjunction with walking tours on Sat.-Sun. and by prior arrangement other days. Closed Dec. 25. Walking tour $12.50; over 65, $11.50; ages 5-11, $6.50. Combined boat/walking tour $17.50. DS, MC, VI. Phone (573) 358-2148.

BOONVILLE (C-3) pop. 8,202, elev. 579′

Boonville, on the Missouri River, was an early distribution center from which wagon trains with provisions started over the old Santa Fe Trail to the Southwest. The first battle of the Civil War in Missouri was fought in Boonville on June 17, 1861, when Union troops under Gen. Nathaniel Lyon defeated state troops led by Gov. Claiborne Jackson.

Many houses and public buildings dating from the early to mid-19th century distinguish the town, which has seven historic districts. Steeped in history are such structures as the 1836 Hain House and the renovated 1848 Old Cooper County Jail.

Thespian Hall, built in 1855, is one of the oldest surviving theater buildings west of the Alleghenies. Its exterior is restored to its 1857 appearance and the interior recalls 1901. The hall is open for tours and is the site of spring and fall concerts. The chamber of commerce is located in the restored Katy Depot, which also houses a caboose museum.

Boonville Area Chamber of Commerce: 320 First St., Boonville, MO 65233; phone (660) 882-2721.

BOONE'S LICK STATE HISTORIC SITE is 10 mi. n. off SR 87. Two salt springs, or licks, were used at the site by Daniel Boone's sons Daniel and Nathan and two partners 1806-14 to produce salt. The salt was made by heating brine in large iron pots over a furnace; 300 gallons of brine would yield 60 pounds of salt. The licks turned out 500 pounds of salt a day and required four furnaces and up to 20 workers. Picnic facilities are available. Daily dawn-dusk. Free. Phone (660) 837-3330.

CASINOS

- **Isle of Capri**, 100 Isle of Capri Blvd. Sun.-Thurs. 8 a.m.-5 a.m., Fri.-Sat. 24 hours. Phone (800) 843-4753.

Branson

City Population: 6,050	Elevation: 722 ft.

Editor's Picks:

"The Strip" / © Michael London

Branson's enormous popularity as a vacation destination is a delightfully unlikely success story. That a small southwestern Missouri town with a population of less than 10,000 would be visited by millions of people every year would be unlikely enough. That it is tucked deep into the hills and hollows of the Ozarks, relatively isolated from big cities and major interstates, only makes it more unlikely. But Branson's beginnings are inextricably tied to its location, and it is the Ozark Mountains that give this little community with big appeal its own very special character.

The Ozark Plateau on which Branson sits is a nature lover's feast of rocky hillsides, rivers, lakes, streams, waterfalls, caves, grasslands and dense hardwood forests. One of the region's more intriguing geological features are the glades, often referred to as "balds" by locals, found on the south- and west-facing slopes of hills. Their typically sparse appearance is the result of prolonged sun exposure and fires—caused by lightning as well as intentional burning by Native Americans and early white settlers—that kept them free of the rolling stands of oak and hickory trees that otherwise characterize the terrain.

These Ozark hills were settled by farmers who migrated to the area from the mountains of the Carolinas, Tennessee and Kentucky—themselves descendants of farmers from England, Scotland and Ireland. Staunch individualists, they were used to eking a living from small farms, but the row crops they planted on the steep hillsides quickly eroded the thin soil. By the last decades of the 19th century this region's economic history had become a series of attempts to supplement meager incomes, from lead mining, logging and harvesting mussel shells for the button industry to the production of moonshine.

The ravages of the Civil War also were devastating, particularly along the Arkansas-Missouri border. Outlaws lured by the region's inaccessibility turned it into a no man's land of violence, taking advantage of the clash between pro- and anti-slavery advocates and ruthlessly preying on women and children while men were off fighting. In the vacuum of authority following war's end justice was virtually nonexistent. As thievery became commonplace and murder after murder went unpunished, vigilante groups organized to impose law and order—and in the process continued the reign of lawlessness.

The hillside balds became meeting spots for such gangs as the Bald Knobbers, who roamed Taney County in the 1880s meting out their own brutal brand of justice. Their tactics fell out of favor as time slowly healed the wounds resulting from the rift between Yankee and rebel, but the name ironically lives on in one of Branson's most beloved country music shows.

Founded in 1903, Branson was initially planned as an industrial center that would handle trainloads of logs, lumber and manufactured products. When incorporated on Apr. 1, 1912, it had 1,200 residents. Shortly thereafter the idea of turning the industrial community into a tourist resort took shape. After

man-made Lake Taneycomo was created in 1913 by impounding the waters of the White River, a soft drink bottling plant, a candy factory and an ice cream factory opened near the waterfront.

Long before the twinkling lights of show theaters lit up the evening sky, three humble hotels began catering to vacationers, and local businesses were encouraged to stack their lumber and bricks to present a tidier appearance. The Sammy Lane Resort—the first vacation cabins in the area—was built just upstream from downtown; they stood on stilts anchored with cables to prevent floods from washing them away.

By the 1930s Lake Taneycomo had a reputation as an inexpensive vacation spot easily accessible by car or train. Rolling green hills and the lake setting made Branson a scenic backdrop for street fairs, boat races and picnics. Following World War II the area began attracting artists and craftspeople along with returning servicemen and retirees. One local artist conceived the idea of displaying a Nativity scene on the bluff of Mount Branson, which rises above the downtown business district from the opposite shore of Lake Taneycomo. Local carpenters created the figures, some up to 28 feet tall. The annual lighting ceremonies—inaugurated in December 1949 before an awestruck crowd of thousands—continued a local tradition of parades and community events.

Another early catalyst in the development of tourism was the 1907 publication of Harold Bell Wright's second novel "The Shepherd of the Hills." A best-selling author of fiction, nonfiction and essays, Wright was the New York-born son of a Civil War lieutenant and a mother who encouraged his interest in art. He became a painter and later a minister in Missouri, Kansas and California.

Dolly Parton's Dixie Stampede Dinner and Show
Missouri Division of Tourism

Said to be the first American novel to sell a million copies, "The Shepherd of the Hills" told the inspirational story of a former pastor who chose to live and share his life with the citizens of rural Mutton Hollow. It offered a spiritual message based on a life lived in simplicity, and although Wright was critically maligned in his day he maintained that his intention was never to create great literature but to instead speak to ordinary citizens. Four different movies have been adapted from the novel, most notably a 1941 film starring John Wayne that made glorious use of Technicolor.

More importantly, though, the novel's Ozark Mountains setting sparked interest in Branson as a place to visit. In 1959 the play "The Shepherd of the Hills" was first presented in the Old Mill Theater on the Shepherd of the Hills farm, perched high on a ridge just west of Dewey Bald. The farm later became a tourist attraction, the Shepherd of the Hills Homestead (see attraction listing p. 138). The actors who performed opening night and in the play's early years came from the surrounding communities, and

Destination Branson

*A*lthough Branson first made a name for itself with live country music shows, tourist attractions have always been a large part of its appeal as well. Longtime favorites like Marvel Cave, the Shepherd of the Hills Homestead and Silver Dollar City are still popular today.

*N*ew attractions keep popping up, though, and one of the most impressive is the painstaking re-creation of the *Titanic* that towers above 76 Country Boulevard.

Branson/Lakes Area Chamber of Commerce & CVB

The World's Largest Titanic Museum Attraction, Branson.
From the half-scale exterior of the world's most famous ocean liner to the wealth of fascinating exhibits inside, this museum is a state-of-the-art presentation of all things "Titanic." (See listing page 140)

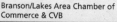

Branson/Lakes Area Chamber of Commerce & CVB

Branson Variety Theater, Branson.
"Broadway! The Star-Spangled Celebration" brings a touch of Big Apple excitement to Branson's ever-expanding live entertainment offerings. (See mention page 150)

*P*laces included in this AAA Destination City:

Ride the Ducks, Branson.
All aboard! Part bus
and part amphibious
vehicle, this duck takes
you on an informative
and entertaining tour
of Branson's Strip and
Table Rock Lake. It's a
quacking good time.
(See listing page 141)

Branson/Lakes Area Chamber of
Commerce & CVB

Branson/Lakes Area Chamber of
Commerce & CVB

Dutton Family Theater, Branson.
The Duttons are one of several
talented performing families in
Branson, and their show—full of
rousing singing, dancing and
country music—is fine family
entertainment. (See mention page
151)

See Vicinity map page 134

The Informed Traveler

Sales Tax: The Branson/Lakes area levies general retail sales, tourism sales and food and beverage sales taxes based on three different jurisdictions: Branson Landing/downtown, citywide and Branson Hills. General retail sales taxes range from 8.6 to 9.6 percent; sales that include a tourism sales tax range from 11.6 to 12.6 percent; food and beverage sales taxes range from 8.975 to 9.975 percent.

WHOM TO CALL

Emergency: 911

Police (non-emergency): (417) 334-3300

Time and Temperature: (417) 336-5000

Hospitals: Lester E. Cox Medical Center-South (Springfield), (417) 269-6000; St. John's Hospital (Springfield), (417) 885-2000; Skaggs Community Health Center, (417) 335-7000.

WHERE TO LOOK

Newspapers

Branson is served by the *Branson Daily News,* a morning newspaper. *Discover Branson* is a free monthly guide published April through December that has information about area attractions, theaters, shopping and recreation. *The Shepherd of the Hills Gazette,* a free newspaper published five times a year, also has attraction, show and visitor information.

Radio

Branson radio station KRZK (106.3 FM) plays country music; KSMU (90.5 FM), affiliated with Missouri State University in Springfield, is a member of National Public Radio.

Visitor Information

Branson/Lakes Area Chamber of Commerce and CVB: P.O. Box 1897, Branson, MO 65615; phone (417) 334-4084 or (800) 214-3661. *See color ad p. 136.*

TRANSPORTATION

Air Travel

Springfield-Branson National Airport is about 45 miles north of Branson via US 65. From Branson, take I-44 exit 82 off US 65 and proceed west about 5 miles to the West Bypass/Willard/airport exit. Take the exit and turn left at the top of the ramp, following the highway south as it loops back over I-44. Turn right at the first traffic signal (W. Kearney Street) and proceed west to the airport. The drive takes 45 minutes to an hour, depending on traffic. Domestic airlines serving the airport include American, Delta, Northwest and United.

Several shuttle and limousine services transport passengers to and from Branson and the airport, including Branson Shuttle, (417) 335-4466 or (800) 237-4466; Julie's Limousine Service, (417) 334-6882; and Tri-Lakes Shuttle, (417) 339-4888 or (800) 841-2313.

Rental Cars

Hertz offers discounts to AAA members; phone (417) 865-1681 or (800) 654-3080.

Buses

Gray Line Branson/Springfield, (800) 542-6768, provides chartered motorcoach service to Branson and one-way transfers to and from Branson and Springfield-Branson National Airport. This is the only transportation company with a service counter in the airport terminal.

Taxis

Cab companies include Jerry's Shuttle Service & Taxi, (417) 348-1419, and Yellow Cab (Springfield), (417) 862-5511.

Public Transport

Unless you're part of a motorcoach tour, getting around Branson is much easier if you have your own vehicle. One convenient alternative to driving is the Branson Looper. This hop-on, hop-off bus service makes more than 40 stops along three color-coded routes that together cover downtown, the SR 76 corridor, and Shepherd of the Hills Expressway and SRs 165 and 265 on the west side of town.

The Looper operates daily 10-10, Apr. 1-Dec. 15 (weather permitting); closed Thanksgiving. A one-day pass that includes unlimited travel on one loop route is $10; ages 3-12, $5. A 1-day gold pass that includes unlimited travel on all three loops is $20; ages 3-12, $10. Two-day, 3-day, 4-day and family passes also are available. For more information phone (417) 339-1033.

many of their children and grandchildren went on to become involved in both the play and the development of Branson's tourism industry.

Winding through the valleys and hollows of the Ozark Mountains from Branson to Eureka Springs, Ark., invitingly blue Table Rock Lake was a natural paradise waiting to be enjoyed. The harnessing of its waters for outdoor recreational use was another step in the region's development. Designed, built and operated by the U.S. Army Corps of Engineers, Table Rock Dam was completed in 1958, paving the way for fishing, boating and other activities.

In 1959 brothers Bill, Jim, Lyle and Bob Mabe set up folding chairs in Branson's City Hall and put on a show. Taking their name from the previous century's vigilante groups, they played banjo, dobro and washtub bass, with an old washboard and the jawbone of a mule providing rhythm, and were an immediate hit with fishermen and the tourists who had begun trickling in. As their popularity grew the Mabes moved their show to an old skating rink, in the process creating Branson's first live music theater. They moved again in 1968 to the present Baldknobbers Music Theatre *(see p. 148)* on SR 76 (later to be known as the Strip), where the Baldknobbers Jamboree continues to pack in the crowds.

The following year saw the opening of a park that has in some ways come to define Branson. Silver Dollar City *(see attraction listing p. 139)* rose from the site of a subterranean cavern known to the Osage Indians and first explored in 1869 by one Henry T. Blow, a St. Louis lead-mining magnate. The exploration party found no lead, but named the geological feature Marble Cave based on their belief that one of the chambers was composed of marble.

The marble turned out to be limestone, and mining efforts didn't pan out. The cave was first opened to sightseers in 1894 and eventually renamed Marvel Cave, but it wasn't until Hugo Herschend, a Chicago vacuum cleaner salesman, purchased a 99-year lease from the owners in the 1950s that its potential as a tourist attraction began to be realized. The Herschends and their two sons made their own improvements, including a tunnel and track for a train that hauled visitors 218 feet up from the cavern's depths.

Looking for ways to increase business, the family decided to build a replica of an Ozark frontier town on the lushly wooded acreage surrounding the cave, figuring it would give visitors waiting for the next tour something else to do. Silver Dollar City opened in 1960 with five shops, a church, a log cabin and a re-enactment of the feud between the Hatfields and the McCoys. Within its first year of operation Silver Dollar City was attracting four times as many visitors as the cave, which remains one of the park's attractions.

National exposure came when several episodes of "The Beverly Hillbillies"—one of the most popular television shows in the country at the time—were filmed at Silver Dollar City in 1969. Brothers Jack and Pete Herschend still own this beautifully landscaped theme park, which is known for its family-friendly atmosphere and values, a dedicated

Dick Clark's American Bandstand Theater / Missouri Division of Tourism

commitment to the preservation of Ozarks heritage and a working colony of artisans who create exquisitely crafted works of art.

The Presley family followed the pioneering Mabes in Branson's fledgling live music industry. Ozarks natives who first established their reputation underground—putting on shows in the caverns of southwestern Missouri—the Presleys opened the Strip's first country music theater in 1967. Forty years later, four generations of Presleys are still playing and singing the country and gospel music they grew up with at the Presleys' Country Jubilee (*see p. 148*).

After the Missouri Pacific Railroad curtailed all passenger service on its White River line in 1960 the number of tourists coming to Branson by automobile grew even greater. To alleviate traffic congestion on winding, two-lane US 65, the highway was shortened and straightened by dynamiting through the limestone hills between Branson and Springfield. In the mid-1970s, following construction of two interchanges that routed traffic away from the congested downtown business district, a few shops and music theaters began to spring up along SR 76.

By the 1980s motels, restaurants and 16 theaters were scattered along a 3-mile stretch of the highway. Branson, however, remained pretty much a well-kept regional secret until the early 1990s. In 1991 the program "60 Minutes" did a feature on the town, proclaiming it "the live country music capital of the universe." The publicity catapulted Branson into its first boom period. Established names like Andy Williams, the Osmond family, Ray Stevens and Jim Stafford were soon headlining shows along SR 76, which became (and still is) known as 76 Country Boulevard.

From the beginning an emphasis was put on entertainment that was wholesome, all-American and family-friendly. And that has not wavered, even as the performance palette has broadened considerably in recent years to embrace lavish Broadway-style productions, heartthrob magicians, Vegas-inspired spectaculars, baby boomer favorites and concert appearances by rock and pop stars. The loyal Branson fan still comes for traditional country and gospel music, homespun comedy and heartfelt displays of patriotic pride—and Branson delivers on all three counts.

A second Branson boom was inaugurated in 2006, when three major attractions that are likely to bring many new visitors to town were unveiled. Foremost was the late May opening of the first phase of Branson Landing (*see p. 143*), at $420 million the most costly and ambitious development the city has yet undertaken.

A shopping, dining and entertainment complex in the heart of the historic downtown district, Branson Landing extends for 1.5 miles along the scenic Lake Taneycomo waterfront. Its shops and restaurants appeal to everyone from kids to retirement-age vacationers, but the Landing also targets a younger, more affluent crowd with a pedestrian-oriented urban streetscape ideal for strolling and nightlife that includes a spectacular choreographed water fountain display.

A terraced, centrally located "town square" slopes down to the waterfront, providing a big open area for concerts, festivals and other entertainment events. The boardwalk that follows the lakeshore is perfect for an evening stroll, and several restaurants have outdoor seating overlooking the water. The complex also includes upscale condominiums and a Hilton boutique hotel. Already a big success, Branson Landing has even entered the local lexicon: "Meet you at the Landing!" is an oft-heard exclamation. Still to come is a new convention center, scheduled to open some time in 2007.

The World's Largest Titanic Museum Attraction (*see attraction listing p. 140*) had its grand opening—presided over by talk show host Regis Philbin—in April. You can't miss the half-scale recreation of the ocean liner that tragically sank in the Atlantic on its maiden voyage; it towers over Country Music Boulevard. The museum's state-of-the-art displays set a new level for Branson attractions.

Dick Clark's American Bandstand Theater (*see p. 148*) is a showcase for popular 1950s and '60s musical artists—namely Bill Medley of the Righteous Brothers, Paul Revere & the Raiders, Gary Lewis & the Playboys and the Comets—as well as revues celebrating the popular music of those two epochal decades. The first new theater to open in nearly a decade, it marks a continuing expansion of Branson's entertainment offerings. And classic car fans will feel like they've died and gone to '57 Heaven (*see attraction listing p. 133*) when they see the theater's collection of vintage automobiles.

Branson, to a degree, sells nostalgia—a longing for a simpler time in America when people could leave their doors unlocked, every family had two parents and terrorists weren't a daily part of the evening news. But what also sets it apart is a sense of genuine friendliness, which feels neither forced nor fabricated. Visitors are made to feel welcome; you'll probably be called "darlin'" or "hon" more than a couple of times. And don't be surprised if a total stranger happens to greet you with a smile, a handshake and a warm "Welcome to the heart of the Ozarks!" Branson really is that kind of place.

Getting There

By Car

Branson receives more than 7 million visitors annually, and more than 85 percent of them drive. This can present a challenge to the existing road network, which was never meant to accommodate the number of vehicles that arrive throughout the year. More than $200 million spent on new highway construction has, however, helped lessen the bottleneck conditions that can occur in summer, the busiest season.

I-44 funnels traffic to Springfield from St. Louis and points east, and from Tulsa, Oklahoma City and points west. South from Springfield or north from Little Rock and Harrison, Ark., the main approach is via US 65, which is four lanes from Springfield south to Branson, facilitating access into town. US 65 is in the process of being widened to four lanes from Hollister, just across Lake Taneycomo from Branson, south to the Arkansas border.

More locally, the Ozark Mountain Highroad (SR 465) runs east-west for 8 miles between US 65 and SR 76 just west of the Shepherd of the Hills Homestead, offering a relaxed and less-traveled route to the Silver Dollar City and Celebration City theme parks and other attractions on the west side of town. North-south SR 13, which branches off SR 76, and east-west SR 86, which branches off US 65 south of Hollister, are easy ways to get to the Table Rock Lake recreational area. For a delightfully scenic day trip from Branson to popular Eureka Springs, Ark., take US 65 south to US 62, then US 62 west.

Getting Around

Street System

Historic downtown Branson, just east of US 65 via US 65 Business Route/Veterans Boulevard, forms a small, compact grid of streets running about six blocks north-south and east-west. East-west Main Street, the eastward extension of SR 76, and north-south Commercial Street are the main thoroughfares. Main Street runs into Branson Landing Boulevard, which fronts Branson Landing and beyond, Lake Taneycomo.

Branson's main drag is, of course, SR 76W, more commonly known as 76 Country Music Boulevard or simply "the Strip." The 5-mile stretch within the city limits, a two-lane highway with a center turning lane, is the heart of many Branson activities, winding past a seemingly endless procession of music theaters, attractions, shopping centers, hotels, motels and restaurants.

The other major roads are SR 248/Shepherd of the Hills Expressway, Gretna Road and Green Mountain Drive. SR 248 branches west off US 65, providing a northerly route that eventually intersects with SR 265 west of SR 76 via Shepherd of the Hills Expressway. Several popular theaters and attractions are along this stretch. Gretna Road, between SR 248 and SR 76, is lined with shopping complexes. Green Mountain Drive runs south of and parallel to SR 76.

Traffic is frequently congested along much of SR 76, particularly so before and after evening performances at the theaters, and major intersections—for example, SR 76 and Gretna Road—can become gridlocked at times. But fortunately, driving the Strip is a choice and not a necessity, thanks to three east-west "relief routes" that can be timesaving options.

Two routes are north of SR 76, and one is south. The Red Route is SR 248 from US 65 west to Shepherd of the Hills Expressway and Shepherd of the Hills Expressway west to SR 265. The Blue Route is Roark Valley Road from SR 76 to Gretna Road and Gretna Road back to SR 76. The Yellow Route is Fall Creek Road to Wildwood Drive, Wildwood Drive to Green Mountain Drive and Green Mountain Drive to SR 76.

Red, blue and yellow route signs are posted regularly along the respective roads. The Yellow Route is the most crowded of the three, so consider using the Blue or Red routes instead. Once you become familiar with these routes, however, getting around Branson is pretty much a snap. You can pick up a Time-Saver road map (created by the Branson/Lakes Area Chamber of Commerce and CVB) showing these routes as well as the location of many theaters and attractions from just about any local hotel or restaurant.

Parking

Finding a place to park in Branson is rarely a problem. Almost all of the theaters have their own large lots, and parking for most shopping centers and restaurants is plentiful. You may have to hunt for a space downtown on weekends. However, the opening of Branson Landing has made this search largely unnecessary, since the Landing's parking garage and two lots (one at each end of the complex) are within easy walking distance of downtown's shops and restaurants.

What To See

'57 HEAVEN is at 1600 SR 76W in Dick Clark's American Bandstand Theater. This is said to be the world's largest collection of vintage 1957 automobiles. Every major American manufacturer from that year is represented, including Buick, Chevrolet, Ford, Cadillac, DeSoto, Hudson, Nash, Studebaker and Packard. Among the beautifully restored rarities are three different makes of Chevrolet's El Morocco, a pink and beige Rambler station wagon and an amethyst-colored Biarritz Cadillac.

Also on display are a Mack fire truck and a Herter boat complete with fins, a popular vehicle accessory that year. The lifestyle exhibits—including a re-created drive-in movie theater setting, fire station, gas station, barber shop, Cadillac dealership and General Electric kitchen—are replete with sunburst clocks, kidney-shaped coffee tables and other 1950s memorabilia.

Allow 1 hour minimum. Mon.-Sat. 9-9, Sun. and holidays 1-9, Mar.-Dec. Admission $15, under 6 free. AX, DS, MC, VI. Phone (417) 332-1957 or (877) 588-1957.

DID YOU KNOW

There are more theater seats in Branson than there are on Broadway in New York City.

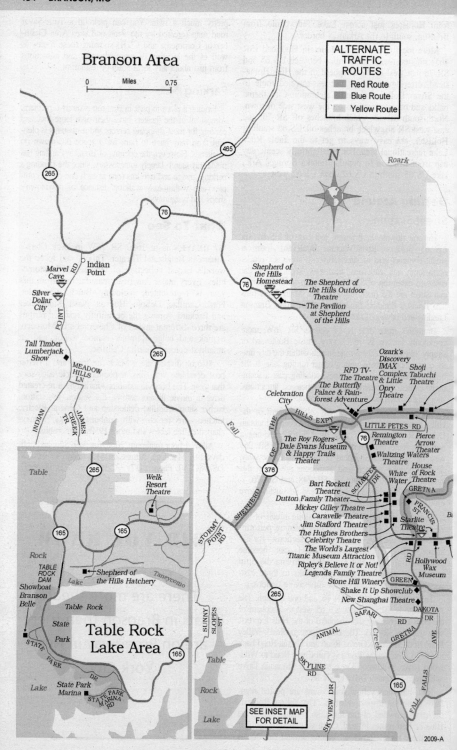

Branson Area

Miles
0   0.75

SEE INSET MAP FOR DETAIL

ALTERNATE TRAFFIC ROUTES
- Red Route
- Blue Route
- Yellow Route

N

Roark

Marvel Cave

Indian Point

Silver Dollar City

Tall Timber Lumberjack Show

MEADOW HILLS LN

JAMES CREEK TR

Shepherd of the Hills Homestead

The Shepherd of the Hills Outdoor Theatre

The Pavilion at Shepherd of the Hills

Ozark's Discovery IMAX Complex & Little Opry Theatre

Shoji Tabuchi Theatre

RFD TV-The Theatre

The Butterfly Palace & Rainforest Adventure

Celebration City

Remington Theatre

Pierce Arrow Theatre

The Roy Rogers-Dale Evans Museum & Happy Trails Theater

Waltzing Waters Theatre

White Water

House of Rock Theatre

Bart Rockett Theatre

Dutton Family Theater

Mickey Gilley Theatre

Caravelle Theatre

Jim Stafford Theatre

The Hughes Brothers Celebrity Theatre

Starlite Theatre

The World's Largest Titanic Museum Attraction

Ripley's Believe It or Not!

Legends Family Theatre

Hollywood Wax Museum

Stone Hill Winery

Shake It Up Showclub

New Shanghai Theatre

LITTLE PETES RD

GRETNA

FRANCIS ST

GREEN

DAKOTA DR

SAFARI

ANIMAL

SKYLINE RD

Creek

GRETNA

FALL FALLS AVE

SKYVIEW DR

Table Rock Lake Area

Table

Welk Resort Theatre

Rock

TABLE ROCK DAM

Showboat Branson Belle

Shepherd of the Hills Hatchery

Taneycomo

Table Rock

State Park

State Park Marina

STATE PARK MARINA RD

STATE PARK DR

Lake

Table Rock Lake

STORMY POINT RD

SHEPHERD

SUNNY SLOPES ST

Table

Fall

THE HILLS EXPY

OF THE HILLS

SCHAEFER DR

2009-A

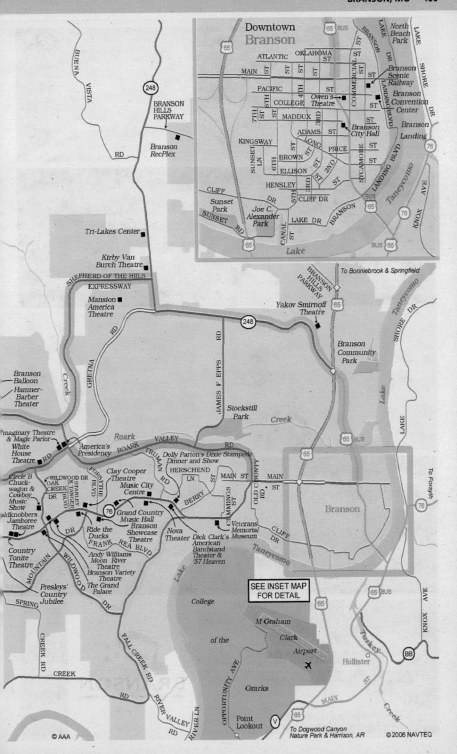

Downtown Branson

North Beach Park

Atlantic St
Oklahoma St
Main St
Pacific St
College St
Owen's Theatre
Maddux St
Adams St
Branson City Hall
Kingsway
Price St
Sunset Ln
Brown St
Ellison St
Hensley St
Cliff Dr
Cliff Dr
Sunset Park
Joe C. Alexander Park
Lake Dr
Canal St
Lake
Branson Scenic Railway
Branson Convention Center
Branson Landing
Landing Blvd
Taneycomo

To Bonniebrook & Springfield

Branson Hills Parkway

Buena Vista Rd
Branson Hills Parkway
Branson RecPlex
Tri-Lakes Center
Kirby Van Burch Theatre
Shepherd of the Hills Expressway
Mansion America Theatre
Yakov Smirnoff Theatre
Branson Community Park
Gretna Rd
James F Epps Rd
Stockstill Park
Creek
Lake Shore Dr
Taneycomo
Branson Balloon
Hamner-Barber Theater
Roark Valley Rd
Imaginary Theatre & Magic Parlor
White House Theatre
America's Presidency
Dolly Parton's Dixie Stampede Dinner and Show
Herschend Ln
Main St
Main St
Branson
Circle B Chuckwagon & Cowboy Music Show
Baldknobbers Jamboree Theatre
Wildwood Dr
Oak Creek Dr
Stanley K Tanger Blvd
Forsythe Blvd
Clay Cooper Theatre Music City Centre
Truman Rd
Berry St
Cummings St
Old County Rd
To Forsyth
Grand Country Music Hall Branson Showcase Theatre
Ride the Ducks
Frank Dr
Nova Theater
Dick Clark's American Bandstand Theater & '57 Heaven
Veterans Memorial Museum
Cliff Dr
Country Tonite Theatre
Andy Williams Moon River Theatre
Branson Variety Theatre
The Grand Palace
Mountain Dr
Wildwood Dr
Rea Blvd
Lake
Taneycomo
SEE INSET MAP FOR DETAIL
Presleys' Country Jubilee
Spring Creek Rd
Fall Creek Rd
College
of the
Ozarks
M Graham Clark Airport
Hollister
Turkey Creek
Knox Ave
Creek Rd
River Valley Rd
River Ln
Opportunity Ave
Point Lookout
To Dogwood Canyon Nature Park & Harrison, AR
Main St

© AAA

© 2006 NAVTEQ

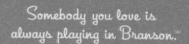

BONNIEBROOK—*see Walnut Shade p. 153.*

THE BUTTERFLY PALACE & RAINFOREST ADVENTURE is at 4106 SR 76W across from Celebration City. This new, state-of-the-art facility features a climate-controlled environment where various tropical butterfly species flit among flowering plants. Other six-legged critters (plus a few four-legged tree frogs) reside at an insect zoo. Visitors also can watch a 3-D film about the life cycle of a butterfly and navigate their way through the Emerald Forest Mirror Maze.

Allow 1 hour minimum. Daily 9-5. Admission $16.95; over 54, $14.95; ages 4-12, $12.95. MC, VI. Phone (417) 332-2231.

 CELEBRATION CITY is at 1383 SR 376, just w. of the jct. with SR 76W. This amusement park has a backdrop of nostalgia, celebrating the America of the 20th century. The theme is apparent at the park entrance, Celebration Street, where a vintage-style carousel operates. Among the more than 30 rides and attractions are Ozark WildCat, an eight-story wooden roller coaster that reaches speeds of 45 mph, and the Accelerator, an 80-foot tower that allows passengers to experience back-to-back positive and negative G-forces.

The themed rides, shops and restaurants in the Route 66 section of the park salute a simpler time of shiny automobiles and drive-in diners, while the Electric Boardwalk's carnival atmosphere offers opportunities galore to play games for prizes. The evening show Ignite the Night is an extravaganza complete with flashing lasers and fireworks accompanied by iconic images and music.

Food is available. Allow a full day. Daily 3-10, late May-late Aug.; Fri.-Sat. 3-10, early to late May and late Aug. to late Sept. Schedule may vary; phone ahead to confirm. Admission $24; over 61 and ages 4-11, $19. Phone ahead to confirm rates. AX, DS, MC, VI. Phone (800) 831-4386. *See color ad card insert.*

COLLEGE OF THE OZARKS—
see Point Lookout p. 153.

DOGWOOD CANYON NATURE PARK—
see Lampe p. 152.

SAVE **DOLLY PARTON'S DIXIE STAMPEDE DINNER AND SHOW** is at 1525 SR 76W. Trick horseback riding, buffaloes and other live animals, singing, dancing and audience participation are all part of the entertainment at this dinner theater.

Allow 2 hours minimum. Show times daily at 5:30 and 8 p.m., June 1 to mid-Aug.; daily at 5:30, mid-Aug. to Aug. 31 and Sept.-Oct.; Sun.-Fri. at 5:30, Sat. at 5:30 and 8 p.m., in May; Sun. and Wed.-Thurs. at 5:30, Fri.-Sat. at 5:30 and 8 p.m., in Apr.; Tues.-Sun. at 5:30, Nov.-Dec.; Wed.-Sat. at 5:30, in Mar. Schedule may vary Mar.-Apr. and Oct.-Dec.; phone ahead to confirm dates and show times. Closed Dec. 24-25. Admission $42.29; ages 4-11, $24.29; under 4 on lap free. Phone ahead to confirm rates. AX, DS, MC, VI. Phone (417) 336-3000 or (800) 520-5544. *See color ad card insert.*

HOLLYWOOD WAX MUSEUM is at 3030 SR 76W. More than 170 lifelike wax celebrities from movies, sports and television are represented, including John Wayne, Tom Cruise, Mark McGwire, Keanu Reeves and Red Skelton. There also are scenes from such popular films as the original "King Kong," "The Wizard of Oz," "Titanic," "The Matrix" and "Pirates of the Caribbean."

Allow 1 hour minimum. Daily 8 a.m.-midnight, Mar. 15-Nov. 15; 8-6, rest of year. Admission $13.95; over 64, $12.95; ages 4-11, $7.95. AX, DS, MC, VI. Phone (417) 337-8277.

OZARKS DISCOVERY IMAX COMPLEX is just e. of SR 76 at 3562 Shepherd of the Hills Expwy. This family-oriented entertainment center features several different larger-than-life IMAX adventures (including "Mysteries of the Nile" and "Ozarks Legacy & Legend") shown on a screen six stories tall and 83 feet wide. The center also has a three-screen movie theater, gift shops, a food court and a restaurant. The Little Opry Theatre presents live musical shows with an emphasis on traditional country and bluegrass.

Allow 2 hours minimum. IMAX box office opens daily at 8:30 a.m.; film screenings daily 9-9. Little Opry Theatre performance times vary; Hank Williams Gospel Hour Sun. at 9 a.m. Stores open Sun.-Thurs.

8:30-8:30, Fri.-Sat. 8:30 a.m.-9:15 p.m. IMAX admission $8.75; ages 4-12, $5.25. Live show tickets $20-$24; Hank Williams Gospel Hour free. AX, DS, MC, VI. Phone (417) 335-4832 or (800) 419-4832.

SAVE **RIPLEY'S BELIEVE IT OR NOT!** is at 3326 SR 76W. More than 400 odd and unusual exhibits from around the world are featured inside creatively themed galleries. Visitors can learn about the world's tallest man, see such pranks of nature as a two-headed cow and witness optical illusions. Interactive displays explore entrepreneur and anthropologist Robert Leroy Ripley's obsession with the strange and unusual.

Allow 1 hour minimum. Daily 9 a.m.-11 p.m., Mar. 15-Dec. 15; 9-7, rest of year. Admission $14.95; over 61, $13.95; ages 4-12, $7.95. AX, DS, MC, VI. Phone (417) 337-5300 or (800) 998-4418.

THE ROY ROGERS-DALE EVANS MUSEUM & HAPPY TRAILS THEATER is at 3950 Green Mountain Dr. across from Celebration City. A larger-than-life statue of Rogers' horse Trigger rears up on its hind legs in front of the museum. Among the exhibits are TV sidekick Pat Brady's jeep "Nellybelle" and memorabilia associated with the Sons of the Pioneers, a cowboy music group formed by Rogers. Hands-on activities are available for children.

The Happy Trails Theater presents a live music show starring Roy "Dusty" Rogers Jr. Video clips of interviews with Rogers, Evans and members of their family are shown, and audiotapes provide explanations of museum exhibits in the words of the husband-and-wife motion picture and television stars.

Allow 2 hours minimum. Mon.-Sat. 9-5:30; live shows Tues.-Sat. at 10 and 2. Closed Easter, Thanksgiving, and Dec. 24-25 and 31. Museum admission $15, under 17 free. Theater admission $27, under 17 free. Combination museum and theater $38. AX, CB, DC, DS, MC, VI. Phone (417) 339-1900 or (866) 769-7643.

SHEPHERD OF THE HILLS HATCHERY is 6 mi. s.w. of downtown Branson via SRs 76W and 165, at the n. end of Table Rock Dam. Rainbow and brown trout are raised at this cold-water facility, which typically produces more than 1,100,000 catchable

fish annually; it also supplies eggs and fingerlings to other trout production facilities. A visitor center features aquarium displays and exhibits that describe the trout spawning cycle and the process of fish rearing. Four hiking trails wind through wooded terrain near the Lake Taneycomo shoreline.

Visitor center open daily 9-6, Memorial Day-Labor Day; 9-5, rest of year. Guided tours Mon.-Fri. at 10, 11, 1 and 2, Memorial Day-Labor Day. Closed Jan. 1, Thanksgiving and Dec. 25. Free. Phone (417) 334-4865.

GEM **SHEPHERD OF THE HILLS HOMESTEAD** is 2 mi. w. at 5586 SR 76W. This working homestead evokes the farm featured in Harold Bell Wright's novel "The Shepherd of the Hills." Jeep-driven guided tours take visitors past Old Matt's Cabin, home of the leading characters, which contains most of its original furnishings. Also on the site are a gristmill, sawmill, smithy, wheelwright shop and a reconstructed church similar to those in which Wright preached during his years in the Ozarks. The Backstage Tour offers a behind-the-scenes look at "The Shepherd of the Hills" outdoor show.

Stone statues of the book's characters stand on Inspiration Point, where the author lived. Inspiration Tower, standing 230 feet high, affords panoramic views of the hills and valleys surrounding the homestead. Old-fashioned wagon rides pulled by Clydesdale horses are available. The Sons of the Pioneers perform May through October in a chuckwagon dinner show. The Trail of Lights, which has more than 80 festive drive-through displays, takes place nightly in November and December.

Homestead open daily 9-5:30, late Apr. to mid-Aug.; 9-4:30, mid-Aug. to late Oct. Guided tours depart on the hour beginning at 10. Last tour begins 30 minutes before closing. Tower open daily at 8 a.m., Apr.-Dec.; at 9 a.m., rest of year. Closing time varies from 5 to 8 p.m. (midnight when the tower is lighted for the holidays). Chuckwagon dinner

showtime 4:15. Admission (includes homestead tour, evening theater performance, Inspiration Tower and applicable taxes) $39; over 54, $35; ages 4-16, $19. Phone (417) 334-4191 or (800) 653-6288. *See color ad.*

The Shepherd of the Hills Outdoor Theatre is at 5586 SR 76W. The story of "The Shepherd of the Hills" is dramatized in this outdoor amphitheater. Kids can participate in bullfrog races Memorial Day-Labor Day. Evening performances Mon.-Sat. at 8:30 p.m., late Apr. to mid-Aug.; at 7:30, mid-Aug. to late Oct.

SILVER DOLLAR CITY is 5 mi. w. on SR 76W to Indian Point Rd., then about half a mile s. to the park entrance. This theme park combines the atmosphere of an 1880s Ozark pioneer village with 21st-century rides and thrills. The Powderkeg roller coaster explosively launches riders from 0 to 53 mph in 2.8 seconds. Other rides include the multi-looping Wildfire! and Thunderation, a runaway mine train. The Geyser Gulch children's area includes a giant treehouse and Splash Harbor, a water cannon play area.

The Grand Exposition is the park's newest themed area and its biggest expansion ever. Modeled after such elegant late 19th-century European amusement parks as Tivoli Gardens in Copenhagen, the exposition's 10 rides—including Elephant March, Royal Tea Party, Wings of Wonder and the Grand Exposition Coaster—were designed to be enjoyed by the entire family.

In addition to rides, visitors can see music and comedy shows in the 4,000-seat Echo Hollow Amphitheater. Numerous other performances take place daily on stages throughout the park. Artisans at various park locations demonstrate such traditional skills as woodcarving, blacksmithing, leatherwork, pottery making, basket weaving and glassblowing, and many of their beautifully handcrafted creations are for sale. Silver Dollar City also has a well-deserved reputation for serving up some of the tastiest theme park food in the country.

Allow a full day. Daily 9:30-7, May 12-Aug. 19; days open as well as opening and closing times vary, Mar.-Apr. and Sept.-Dec. Phone ahead to confirm schedule. Admission $46; over 61, $44; ages 4-11, $36. Phone ahead to confirm rates. AX, DS, MC, VI. Phone (800) 831-4386. *See color ad card insert.*

Marvel Cave lies 500 ft. below Silver Dollar City. This wet limestone cave includes 3 miles of explored passageways and a cathedral room 400 feet long and 20 stories high. The 1-hour tour includes more than 600 stairs and is considered strenuous. A cable railway train returns visitors to the surface. Fee included in Silver Dollar City admission.

TALKING ROCKS CAVERN is 5 mi. s. on SR 13 in Marvel Cave Park. Drapery helictites, musical stalactites and a 100-foot-tall formation called the Cathedral can be seen in the cave, which has approximately 140 steps to climb; concrete walks and railings are provided. A 5-minute sound and light presentation and a 400-acre nature area with walking trails also are featured. Allow 1 hour minimum. Daily 9:30-6, Feb.-Dec. Admission $16.95; ages 4-12, $6.95. Phone (417) 272-3366 or (800) 600-2283.

SAVE **VETERANS MEMORIAL MUSEUM** is 1 mi. w. of US 65 at 1250 SR 76W. The veterans of American wars and military conflicts are honored at this museum, which has collections of uniforms and art as well as artifact exhibits. The focal point is a 70-foot-long bronze sculpture depicting 50 soldiers storming a beach. Each life-size figure represents a U.S. state and is modeled after an actual combat veteran.

Allow 1 hour minimum. Mon.-Sat. 8 a.m.-9 p.m., Sun. 8-8. Admission $13.50; veterans $10; ages 6-12, $5. AX, DS, MC, VI. Phone (417) 336-2300.

WALTZING WATERS THEATRE is at 3617 SR 76W. These musical fountain shows feature 40,000 gallons of water action synchronized with lighting effects and a wide variety of recorded music. Food is available. Allow 1 hour minimum. Shows daily on the hour 10-6; closed Dec. 25. Admission $6; ages 3-11, $3. AX, DS, MC, VI. Phone (417) 334-4144 or (800) 276-7284.

WHITE WATER is 3.7 mi. w. on SR 76W. The water park's rides and attractions include the 500,000-gallon Surfquake wave pool; waterslides, including Tropical Twister, Bermuda Triangle and a 207-foot triple-drop slide called Caribbean Plunge; a Lazy River for inner tubing; the Splash Island children's play area; and RainTree Island.

Daily 10-8, June 10-Aug. 13; 10-6, May 26-June 9, Aug. 14-20 and 26-27, and Sept. 2-4. Schedule may vary; phone ahead to confirm. Admission $31; ages 4-11, $26; over 61, $15. Phone ahead to confirm rates. AX, DS, MC, VI. Phone (800) 831-4386. *See color ad card insert.*

▼ **THE WORLD'S LARGEST TITANIC MUSEUM ATTRACTION** is at jct. SRs 76W and 165 (Gretna Rd.). Built at half-scale to SAVE the original vessel as far back as the second smokestack, this walk-through experience focuses on the passengers and crew aboard the RMS *Titanic* when it sank after hitting an iceberg on Apr. 14, 1912.

Highlights include a replica of the ship's Grand Staircase and a 26-foot-long scale model of the vessel's underwater bow section as seen in the 1997 blockbuster film. Among other exhibits are a regenerating "live" iceberg, re-creations of a first-class stateroom and third-class cabin, an interactive captain's bridge and gallery rooms with displays of personal and historical artifacts.

Each visitor receives a boarding pass with the name and history of a passenger who was on the ill-fated ocean liner's maiden voyage. Allow 1 hour, 30 minutes minimum. Daily 9 a.m.-10 p.m., May 22-Dec. 17; 9-9, Mar. 16-May 21; 9-6, Jan. 1-Mar. 15; 10-6, rest of year. Closed Dec. 25. Admission $20 Jan.-May, $21 rest of year; ages 5-12, $11.15. AX, DS, MC, VI. Phone (417) 334-9500, or (800) 381-7670 for ticket information. *See color ad & card insert.*

WINERIES

• **Stone Hill Winery**, 2 blks. s. of SR 76W on SR 165. Tours and tastings Mon.-Sat. 8:30 a.m.-dusk, Sun. 11-6; closed Jan. 1, Thanksgiving and Dec. 25. Phone (417) 334-1897.

What To Do
Sightseeing
Boat Tours

SHOWBOAT *BRANSON BELLE* departs from White River Landing on SR 165, 6 mi. s. of jct. SR 76W. This turn-of-the-20th-century-style paddlewheeler is 278 feet long and holds 700 passengers. A scenic cruise on Table Rock Lake includes lunch or dinner and a show starring a troupe of seasoned Branson entertainers.

Two-hour cruises departing at noon, 4 and 8 p.m. are available most days, Mar. 31-Dec. 31. Additional

cruises on selected days are available in Mar. Schedules and rates may vary; phone ahead. Boarding begins 1 hour before departure. Noon lunch cruise $39; ages 4-11, $19.50. Four and 8 p.m. early dinner and evening dinner cruises $46 Sun.-Thurs., $49 Fri.-Sat.; ages 4-11, $23 Sun.-Thurs., $24.50 Fri.-Sat. Reservations are recommended. AX, DS, MC, VI. Phone (417) 336-7171 or (800) 227-8587. *See color ad card insert.*

Bus Tours

SAVE Gray Line Branson/Springfield offers sightseeing tours of the Tri-Lakes area as well as nearby Eureka Springs, Ark.; phone (800) 542-6768.

RIDE THE DUCKS departs from 2320 SR 76W, just w. of Green Mountain Dr. (across from the Clay Cooper Theatre). This 80-minute tour aboard a restored World War II amphibious vehicle known as a duck cruises down Country Music Boulevard to SR 165, heads south to Table Rock Dam and climbs off-road to the top of 1,325-foot Baird Mountain for a panoramic view of Table Rock Lake before entering the water where the Showboat *Branson Belle* is docked.

Each ducks driver gives his or her own individual narration during the trip, making this a highly entertaining as well as informative Branson overview. **Note:** It can get quite windy as the open-sided vehicle travels along the road; hold onto your hat.

Departures approximately every 20 minutes daily 8-7, July-Aug.; 8-6, May-June; 9-5, Sept.-Oct.; 9-4, in Apr.; 10-3, first Fri. in Mar.-Mar. 31; 9-2, Nov. 1-Dec. 17; closed Thanksgiving. Fare $17.95; over 61, $16.95; ages 3-12, $10; boarding passes required for under 3. AX, DS, MC, VI. Phone (417) 266-7600 or (877) 887-8225. *See color ad.*

Hot Air Ballooning

SAVE BRANSON BALLOON is 2.5 mi. w. of jct. US 65 and SR 248 (Shepherd of the Hills Expwy.) at 3218 Shepherd of the Hills Expwy. This 200,000-cubic-foot balloon, said to be the largest tethered helium balloon in the United States, stands more than 10 stories tall and has become something of a local landmark. It accommodates up to 30 passengers for a 15-minute ride that ascends to an altitude of 500 feet. The balloon is lighted at night.

Allow 30 minutes minimum. Daily 7 a.m.-11 p.m. (weather permitting); phone ahead to confirm departures. Admission $19.95; over 59 and ages 3-12, $14.95. AX, CB, DC, DS, JC, MC, VI. Phone (417) 336-6060.

Rail Tours

BRANSON SCENIC RAILWAY departs from the depot at 206 E. Main St. Passengers enjoy a narration of the history of the area and the railroad as the 1940s and '50s rolling stock embarks on a 40-mile round trip of the scenic Ozark foothills, crossing bridges and passing through two tunnels.

Food is available. Allow 2 hours minimum. Departures Mon.-Fri. at 9, 11:30, 2 and 4:30, Sat. at 9, 11:30, 2 and 5, June-Aug. and in Oct.; Mon.-Fri. at 9, 11:30 and 2, Sat. at 9, 11:30, 2 and 5, Mar.-May, Sept. and Nov.-Dec. Fare $22.10; ages 3-12, $12.10. Dinner train departs at 5, Apr.-Dec. Hours vary; phone ahead. DS, MC, VI. Phone (417) 334-6110 or (800) 287-2462.

Sports and Recreation

You could quite easily spend a week in Branson doing nothing but seeing shows, visiting attractions and going shopping. You would, however, be missing out on one of the area's most delightful assets: the great outdoors. The recreational opportunities that attracted Branson's first vacationers still abound.

Branson's location in the midst of Table Rock Lake, Bull Shoals Lake and Lake Taneycomo makes what is known as the Tri-Lakes area a terrific place for **boating, fishing** and **camping.** All kinds of activities can be enjoyed at Table Rock Lake and Dam, which was created by the U.S. Army Corps of Engineers to control floods and generate hydroelectric power. The deep-blue lake teems with bass, bluegill, crappie and catfish, making it rewarding for both novice and serious anglers. With nearly 800 miles of shoreline to explore, Table Rock also is a good location for **swimming** and **scuba diving.**

Table Rock State Park, 5272 SR 165 at the south end of Table Rock Dam, has a public marina offering easy lake access and a full range of boat rentals, including WaveRunners and fishing, pontoon and jet ski boats. Two camping areas shaded by oak and hickory trees are located along the winding shoreline, and picnic sites are scattered throughout the park. *See Recreation Chart.*

The Dewey Short Visitor Center has natural history exhibits and shows a fascinating 20-minute film that details the construction of Table Rock Dam. Be sure to walk the Table Rock Lakeshore Trail, which begins at the visitor center and runs south 2.2 miles to the park marina. The scenic views of the lake are heightened in the spring by flowering dogwood and redbud trees and in the fall by a display of colorful foliage. The trail is open daily dawn-dusk. The visitor center is open daily 9-5, Apr.-Oct.; phone (417) 334-4704.

Indian Point, at the south end of Indian Point Road past the entrance to Silver Dollar City, has campgrounds, a marina and a variety of lakeside resorts. The port of Kimberling City, on SR 13 south of Branson West, proclaims itself "The Bass Fishing Capital of the Ozarks." A center for boat rentals, fishing and camping, it has several waterside restaurants—including local favorite The Bearded Clam—that offer courtesy docking.

Due to its proximity to Branson, the area around Table Rock Dam has the greatest concentration of recreation facilities. But the lake spreads out far beyond the dam in a meandering series of arms and inlets, and some nature lovers prefer its western end,

which has equally good fishing along with a more remote, primitive atmosphere. Cape Fair Park, in a lovely wooded setting on Table Rock's James River Arm, is a favorite with both campers and fishermen. There are prime angling spots below Virgin Bluff and across the channel from the park's boat launch ramp. For information phone (417) 538-2220.

Also administered by the U.S. Army Corps of Engineers is Bull Shoals Lake. Although it extends into southern Missouri, most of its area is in northern Arkansas. Less crowded than Table Rock Lake, Bull Shoals offers many of the same activities. The 1,050-mile shoreline is indented with coves ideal for boating, fishing, swimming and water sports. This is a deep, clean lake and the water is very clear—which makes it just about unbeatable for landing crappie, bluegill, walleye and largemouth, smallmouth, white and striped bass. *See Recreation Chart.*

Hikers can trek Bull Shoals' 4-mile Wildwood Trail. The trailhead and parking area is on CR 635, which branches south off US 160 just east of Theodosia. The trail follows the lakeshore south of the Theodosia Marina. Deer outnumber people in these parts, so you're likely to spot a few.

In between these two lakes stretches 22-mile-long Lake Taneycomo. Created by the impounding of the White River, Taneycomo was a warm-water lake from 1913 until the completion of Table Rock Dam in 1958. Virtually overnight it was turned into a cold-water fishery due to the temperature of the water flowing through the dam's power generators. The Missouri Department of Conservation took advantage of this change, constructing the Shepherd of the Hills Hatchery *(see attraction listing p. 138)* at the foot of the dam.

When Table Rock Dam is generating power the water temperature drops, and for all practical purposes Taneycomo becomes a deep, cold, fast-running river. The bracing water makes it one of the best brown and rainbow trout-fishing spots in the Midwest. The lake's headwaters at the foot of Table Rock Dam offer excellent wading and fly rod fishing when power is not being generated. Only flies and hard artificial baits are permitted in this "trophy trout" area, which covers approximately 3 miles from the dam north to the mouth of Fall Creek.

Although officially a lake, serpentine Taneycomo, with its lush green banks, certainly looks more like a river. The Branson Landing Boardwalk offers a pleasant waterside stroll, and you also can walk along the shoreline via N. Lake Drive to North Beach Park, where there is a large covered pavilion and a gazebo.

Dogwood Canyon Nature Park *(see attraction listing p. 152)* has a 6-mile, round-trip paved path that is popular for **hiking** and **bicycling.** The gently sloping trail traverses wooded terrain along the canyon floor, passing waterfalls, burbling streams and stone bridges created by local stonemasons from native dolomite rock. Points of interest along the way include the Glory Hole, a 16-foot-deep, blue-green pool of water inhabited by rainbow and brown trout, and a huge sycamore tree estimated to be more than 250 years old.

Although fishing and boating still rule in the Tri-Lakes area, Branson also is gaining a reputation for **golf**. The backdrop of Ozark Mountains scenery is certainly a big part of what makes golf so appealing in Branson, in addition to the mild weather that allows practically year-round play. Two new courses—Murder Rock Golf & Country Club and the Payne Stewart Tribute Golf Course—are scheduled to open in 2007 and 2008, respectively.

Area courses include the Branson Creek Golf Club, off US 65 about 4 miles south of SR 76; the Holiday Hills Golf Club, about 3 miles east of downtown Branson via SR 76E; the Ledgestone Golf Course, just north of the junction of SR 76W and SR 265; the Pointe Royale Golf Course, on SR 165 3 miles south of SR 76W; the Thousand Hills Golf Course, on Wildwood Drive just south of SR 76W; and the nine-hole, par-3 Top of the Rock Golf Course, off US 65 just north of the junction with SR 86.

Geocaching is becoming more and more popular as a family or group activity. Simply put, this is a scavenger hunt using high-tech equipment—a satellite tracking device that utilizes sophisticated global positioning technology (GPS) to determine an individual's location anywhere on Earth within a distance of approximately 6 to 20 feet. More than a dozen caches, or treasure locations, are scattered throughout the Branson/Tri-Lakes area. For additional information contact the Branson/Lakes Area Chamber of Commerce and CVB.

If you feel like catching a **baseball** game, head up to Springfield and cheer on the Springfield Cardinals AA minor league team *(see p. 215)*. And if you need some exercise, the Branson RecPlex, half a mile east of SR 248 on Branson Hills Parkway,

has a fitness center, track and basketball courts. Guest memberships are available; phone (417) 335-2368.

Shopping

Loads of people come to Branson to shop, and it's easy to see why: with a historic downtown that could almost double for Mayberry, a new waterfront shopping and dining complex at downtown's doorstep and specialty stores and centers practically everywhere you turn, the opportunities are legion.

The big news in 2006 was the opening of Branson Landing. This shopping "village," which has lovely Lake Taneycomo as a backdrop, is divided into six different districts, each with its own style of architecture. Anchors Belk Department Store and Bass Pro Shops are augmented by more than 100 additional stores and shops, including national retailers like Brookstone, Caché and the Discovery Channel Store that are new to the Branson area. Eateries include both fast-food outlets and popular franchises like Famous Dave's Bar-B-Q and Joe's Crab Shack.

Branson's first Bass Pro Shops outlet isn't as large as the flagship store in Springfield but the atmosphere is similar, right down to the beautifully done nature dioramas and freshwater trout aquarium. Be sure to look up as you wander around; some of the most interesting things are above eye level. There's also a floating restaurant and a marina where boats and fishing equipment can be tested.

The town square at the center of the Landing is an open space with terraces that slope down to a waterfront boardwalk. Free concerts take place on Saturday nights. The square also is the site of daily shows incorporating 186 water jet fountains and 15 cannons blasting fireballs, choreographed to special lighting and a variety of music. The dancing water display is most impressive in the evening, especially

when seen from the vantage point of the boardwalk. And since Branson is famous for live performances, the Landing also features street entertainment in the form of jugglers, cloggers, clowns, magicians, musicians and singers from country and bluegrass to jazz and gospel—and even a highland piper in full Scottish regalia.

Branson Landing is a stone's throw from downtown Branson, which offers a much more downhome experience. The vintage flavor of these brick sidewalk-lined streets, adorned with Victorian-style lampposts, is maintained by the Downtown Branson Main Street Association *(see color ad p. 143)*. As a mercantile district the downtown area dates back more than a century, and strolling the streets here does seem like a step back in time.

Browsers will love Dick's Oldtime 5 & 10, at 103 W. Main St. The narrow aisles of this classic "dime store" are crammed with more than 55,000 nostalgic items. You'll see more miniature figurines and key chains than you ever thought possible, but Dick's also carries practical items like kitchen dish towels and jars of homemade jam. Bee Discount, 106 W. Main St., also stocks "a little bit of everything," including gifts and souvenirs.

Branson Bill's Emporium, 110 W. Main St., has NASCAR and Coca-Cola collectibles in addition to gift items. Brier Rose, 117 E. Main St., features antiques, quilts and crocheted accessories, while the House of 1,000 Clocks, 105 S. Veterans Blvd., carries custom-made Bavarian clocks in all shapes and sizes.

Reish Shoes, 120 S. Commercial St., is downtown Branson's oldest business. Owner Joe Reish provides custom fitting, just like the good old days. For elegant girls' and women's clothing as well as home accessories and Victorian-style furnishings, wander through Rebecca's Victorian Boutique, 110 S. Commercial St., or Patricia's Victorian House, 101 W. Main St.

All sorts of specialty shopping complexes are along Country Music Boulevard. The Engler Block, 1335 SR 76 (close to Dolly Parton's Dixie Stampede), offers 30 shops in an indoor mall where you also can observe Ozarks artisans do their thing. Branson wood carver Steve Engler started the tradition, creating his signature hand-carved Santas while customers watched. Browse for Swarovski crystal figurines, cuckoo clocks, stained and blown glass, enameled brass, handcrafted musical instruments and hand-stitched quilts, among other treasures.

If you love Christmas, by all means visit The Grand Village, next to The Grand Palace. This collection of clothing, craft and specialty stores also includes no less than six Kringle's Christmas Shops, where you can search for angels, ornaments, stockings, nutcrackers, candle holders, fiber-optic Christmas trees and a host of other seasonal decorations. There also are shops specializing in art, wood crafts and handmade lace, all in an open-air setting of winding cobblestone lanes, fountains and flowers.

The Victorian Village, on Shepherd of the Hills Expressway next to the Hamner-Barber Theater, offers a variety of collectibles, including candles, gifts, jewelry, quilts and dolls, along with circus memorabilia and reproductions of paintings by inspirational artist Thomas Kinkade. About a mile west are the shops in the Ozarks Discovery IMAX theater complex, where you can grab a bite to eat at the food court while shopping for toys, jewelry, collectibles and souvenirs.

The Branson Mill Craft Village on Gretna Road is a combination specialty retail shopping center and working craft village where glass blowers, silversmiths, wood carvers, scrimshaw crafters, stained- and etched-glass makers and other artisans demonstrate their skills. You'll find everything from wind chimes, pottery, gift baskets and custom picture frames to pewter items, carved walking sticks and hand-painted gourds.

Fans of outlet shopping have three different centers to explore. The 90 stores at Factory Merchants Branson, off SR 76 on Pat Nash Drive (look for the red roofs), include Nautica, Pfaltzgraff and Reebok. The mall has two tree-shaded courtyards and an open-air food area.

The SAVE Tanger Outlet Center, on SR 76 in the middle of the Strip, offers discounted bargains on men's, women's and children's clothing from retailers like Liz Claiborne, Ralph Lauren and Polo, plus shoes, housewares and fashion accessories. The Shoppes at Branson Meadows, 4562 Gretna Rd. near the Branson Mill Craft Village, has a Victorian-style look and discount retailers like Casual Male, Dress Barn, Van Heusen and Wrangler. There are other stores here as well (the House of Lloyd has gifts you won't see elsewhere in town) and a movie multiplex to keep restless kids happy.

If you don't like crowds, shop the outlet malls in January and February. The weekend following Thanksgiving, when holiday specials go on sale, is the year's busiest.

Last but certainly not least are the ubiquitous gift shops at the music theaters. Every theater has one, and some are ostentatious indeed. The Shoji Tabuchi Theatre has several separate shops in an ornate lobby filled with potted palms and Art Deco furniture, while the gift shop at the Andy Williams Moon River Theatre is notable because it is so discreet (more like a boutique).

Show DVDs and tapes, performer CDs and cassettes, and cast posters are uniformly big sellers, but you also can purchase many other keepsakes, from a Jim Stafford "cow patti" to a Baldknobbers ball cap. The most personal, of course, is an autograph, so if you happen to own an old Paul Revere & the Raiders, Righteous Brothers or Mickey Gilley album, bring it along for a personal signature—Branson's stars are very obliging of their fans.

Entertainment

For many visitors, the No. 1 reason to visit Branson is to sample the incredible variety of live entertainment. The city has long outgrown its tag "the country music capital of the universe" that was bestowed by "60 Minutes" back in the early 1990s: Today you can choose from approximately 120 different shows at nearly 50 venues. And while country is still king, it is by no means the only game in town.

There's still plenty of traditional country music, of course, in shows like "Hank Williams Revisited," "The Jim Owen Show" and "Keepin' It Country," as well as shows starring generation-spanning families (Baldknobbers Jamboree Show, Presleys' Country Jubilee, the Duttons). Then there are the old reliables—familiar names like Andy Williams, Jim Stafford, Mickey Gilley and Yakov Smirnoff.

But you also can choose from shows devoted to the 1950s ("Lost in the '50s," "'50s at the Hop"), baby boomer favorites (Bill Medley, Paul Revere & the Raiders, "The Legendary Tops and Temps Show"), tributes galore ("Legends in Concert," "Elvis and the Superstars," "#1 Hits of the '60s," "Charley Pride Tribute"), prestidigitators (Shoji Tabuchi, Kirby Van Burch, Darren Romeo, Bart Rockett) and flashy glitz ("Broadway! The Star-Spangled Celebration," "Neil Goldberg's Cirque"). There's even a world-class acrobatic extravaganza (the New Shanghai Circus) that brings some welcome diversity to town. In short, the array of talent on any given night is truly impressive.

Performances take place year-round, with the majority occurring March through December. Top-name artists like Andy Williams, Jim Stafford, Bobby Vinton, Mickey Gilley and Pam Tillis who headline their own shows appear in Branson at least part of the year. Show schedules are subject to change; new theaters open, old theaters close and existing theaters occasionally change names. Fortunately, in Branson you're never more than a few steps away from a rack of brochures or a free newspaper, many of which publish current schedules. If you want to see a certain show at a particular time, your best bet is to call ahead.

Most evening shows start at 8 p.m.; matinees usually begin at 3 p.m. There also are several popular morning shows usually beginning at 10 a.m., including the Brett Family Singers at the Legends Family Theatre, the Platters at the Starlite Theatre, the "Red Skelton Tribute" at Music City Centre and "Smoke on the Mountain" at the Little Opry Theatre.

Adult ticket prices range from about $20-$50; children's ticket prices range from free to about $31. Tickets can be purchased at the theater box office or through various ticket agencies in the area. Free show guide brochures and coupon sheets, available for the taking at most area hotels, restaurants, theaters and attractions, offer a bewildering assortment of special offers; diligently collecting and sorting through these deals can end up saving you quite a bit of money. AAA members also can purchase discounted theater tickets at any AAA Missouri branch office.

While the humor at some Branson shows can be a bit on the bawdy side, this is still a conservative town, and conservative values are emphasized. Flag-waving patriotism and pro-military sentiments are often expressed in production numbers, and evangelical Christian themes are presented at some shows. Most shows also include a merchandising spiel during intermission, encouraging customers to buy CDs, DVDs, autographed posters and sundry other memorabilia. Many of the performers generously share their time with the audience, coming out during intermission to meet fans and signing autographs in the lobby after the show.

It would literally take weeks to see every single performance in town, and few visitors have that luxury of time. The following rundown of major Branson theaters—in no particular order but collectively offering proven longevity and popularity, long-running and hot new acts, appearances by big-name stars and sheer variety—can help you make the difficult choice of who and what to see during your stay.

Note: In some theater parking lots the rear slopes sharply; visitors with limited mobility or special needs should be dropped off at the main entrance.

Recording artist and TV personality Andy Williams presides at the **Andy Williams Moon River Theatre.** Williams was the first major non-country entertainer to take up permanent residence in Branson, and his theater on SR 76 (next to The Grand Palace) exudes good taste, with warm woodwork, sophisticated art, very comfortable seats and a koi-stocked pond (the "moon river") next to the building. Williams usually appears several months out of the year, singing his hits and performing with guest stars like Glen Campbell and Petula Clark.

Mickey Gilley and his band provide slick, mainstream entertainment at the **Mickey Gilley Theatre,** on SR 76 next to the White Water theme park. Gilley, of course, gained fame after his Texas watering hole with that bucking mechanical bull, Gilley's Bar, was the setting for scenes in the 1980 film "Urban Cowboy" starring John Travolta and Debra Winger. A segment of his show reprises the movie and Gilley's cover version of Ben E. King's "Stand By Me." Jerry Lee Lewis' cousin sings other hits like "Room Full of Roses" and does some funny, seemingly ad-libbed comedy bits with sidekick Joey Riley, who headlines his own show at the **Caravelle Theatre** across the street.

Another crowd-pleaser is Jim Stafford, a Branson mainstay for more than 15 years. At the **Jim Stafford Theatre** (next to the Caravelle) the man who doesn't like "Spiders and Snakes" sings, plays classical guitar and creates heartwarming comedy from everyday life. Stafford's musically accomplished son and daughter are part of the act, making this a great show for families. The theater also presents the rock 'n' rolling musical revue "'50s at the Hop."

Branson Theaters

- **ANDY WILLIAMS MOON RIVER THEATRE**
  (417) 334-4500 or (800) 666-6094

- **BALDKNOBBERS MUSIC THEATRE**
  (417) 334-4528 or (888) 734-1935

- **BART ROCKETT THEATRE**
  (417) 348-0888

- **BRANSON SHOWCASE THEATRE**
  (417) 339-3939 or (417) 339-1960

- **BRANSON VARIETY THEATER**
  (417) 334-2500 or (888) 462-7267

- **CARAVELLE THEATRE**
  (417) 334-5100

- **CIRCLE B CHUCKWAGON & COWBOY MUSIC SHOW**
  (417) 336-3540 or (800) 678-6179

- **CLAY COOPER THEATRE**
  (417) 332-2529 or (888) 222-8910

- **COUNTRY TONITE THEATRE**
  (417) 337-9333 or (877) 336-7827

- **DICK CLARK'S AMERICAN BANDSTAND THEATER**
  (417) 332-1960 or (877) 588-1957

- **DOLLY PARTON'S DIXIE STAMPEDE**
  (417) 336-3000 or (800) 520-5544

- **DUTTON FAMILY THEATER**
  (417) 332-2772 or (888) 388-8661

- **GRAND COUNTRY MUSIC HALL**
  (417) 335-2484

- **THE GRAND PALACE**
  (417) 336-1220 or (800) 884-4536

- **HAMNER-BARBER THEATER**
  (417) 334-4363 or (888) 335-2080

- **HAPPY TRAILS THEATER**
  (417) 339-1925 or (866) 769-7643

- **HOUSE OF ROCK THEATRE**
  (417) 334-9330

- **THE HUGHES BROTHERS CELEBRITY THEATRE**
  (417) 334-0076 or (800) 635-3688

- **IMAGINARY THEATRE & MAGIC PARLOR**
  (417) 332-1911 or (888) 422-3566

- **JIM STAFFORD THEATRE**
  (417) 335-8080 or (417) 335-5300

- **KIRBY VAN BURCH THEATRE**
  (417) 337-7140

- **LEGENDS FAMILY THEATER**
  (417) 335-7827 or (800) 374-7469

- **LITTLE OPRY THEATRE**
  (417) 335-4832

- **MANSION AMERICA THEATRE**
  (417) 239-1333 or (866) 707-4100

- **MICKEY GILLEY THEATRE**
  (417) 334-3210 or (800) 334-1936

- **MUSIC CITY CENTRE**
  (417) 336-1600 or (877) 225-3165

- **NEW SHANGHAI THEATRE**
  (417) 336-8888 or (877) 212-4462

- **NOVA THEATER**
  (417) 334-6806 or (877) 446-6824

- **OWEN'S THEATRE**
  (417) 336-2112 or (800) 358-4795

- **PIERCE ARROW THEATER**
  (417) 336-8742 or (877) 687-4241

- **PRESLEYS' COUNTRY JUBILEE**
  (417) 334-4874 or (800) 335-4874

- **REMINGTON THEATRE**
  (417) 336-1220 or (800) 884-4536

- **RFD TV—THE THEATRE**
  (417) 332-2282

- **SHAKE IT UP SHOWCLUB**
  (417) 335-2700

- **THE SHEPHERD OF THE HILLS OUTDOOR THEATRE**
  (417) 334-4191 or (800) 653-6288

- **SHOJI TABUCHI THEATRE**
  (417) 334-7469

- **SHOWBOAT *BRANSON BELLE***
  (417) 336-7171 or (800) 227-8587

- **SILVER DOLLAR CITY**
  (417) 336-7100 or (800) 952-6626

- **STARLITE THEATRE**
  (417) 337-9333 or (877) 336-7827

- **TALL TIMBER LUMBERJACK SHOW**
  (417) 338-2957 or (866) 338-2957

- **TRI-LAKES CENTER**
  (417) 336-0219

- **WALTZING WATERS THEATRE**
  (417) 334-4144 or (800) 276-7284

- **WELK RESORT THEATRE**
  (417) 337-7469 or (800) 505-9355

- **WHITE HOUSE THEATRE**
  (417) 335-2396 or (877) 487-2386

- **YAKOV SMIRNOFF THEATRE**
  (417) 336-6542 or (800) 336-6542

More giggles await at the **Yakov Smirnoff Theatre,** where the Russian-born comic offers his philosophical insights on men and women, family and life in the United States. Juggler Slim Chance provides daring thrills and more comedy, and a troupe of Russian dancers twist, twirl and leap all over the stage. Smirnoff delivers humor from the heart, and his popular show is another family favorite. The theater is just off US 65 on SR 248.

"Cool cars and rock stars" sums up **Dick Clark's American Bandstand Theater,** on SR 76 across from Dolly Parton's Dixie Stampede. Headliners Bill Medley of the Righteous Brothers and Paul Revere & the Raiders (with Medley's son Darren filling in for original singer Mark Lindsay) each offer up a feast of classic '60s nuggets, from "You've Lost That Lovin' Feeling" and "Unchained Melody" to "Kicks" and "Hungry." Fellow '60s stars Gary Lewis & the Playboys (remember "This Diamond Ring"?) and rock 'n' roll originators the Comets (minus Bill Haley) play morning shows. Fans of classic, beautifully restored '57 Chevys and memory-invoking 1950s memorabilia should not miss the Patch Collection of automobiles on display at '57 Heaven *(see attraction listing p. 133).*

The **Welk Resort Theatre** *(see color ad card insert)* on SR 165 (3 miles south of the SR 76/Gretna Road intersection) presents musical stars from the Lennon Sisters and Gatlin Brothers to Pam Tillis and the multi-instrumental Lowe Family. Other artists perform concerts here as well—everyone from B.B. King to Lynyrd Skynyrd. In-house illusionist Darren Romeo, protege of Siegfried & Roy, makes NASCAR driver Jeff Gordon's race car disappear and also sings. Wunnerful!

One of the flashiest shows in town is at the **Shoji Tabuchi Theatre** on Shepherd of the Hills Expressway (near the Ozarks Discovery IMAX theater complex). Tabuchi—who has a Moe Stooge pudding bowl haircut—his wife, daughter, a troupe of dancers and a band of superbly talented professional musicians put on a show that encompasses practically every style of popular music, from swing and big band to gospel, Dixieland jazz and Broadway show tunes.

Tabuchi plays everything from "Flight of the Bumblebee" to "Over the Rainbow" on his fiddle,

and the production numbers feature top-notch choreography and cool laser special effects. If nothing else, you must see this show just to experience the ladies' powder room or gentlemen's lounge; the rich wood paneling, potted palms, chandeliers, beveled glass wall tiles, onyx sinks, fresh orchids and hand-carved mahogany billiard table are all the last word in lavish.

The **New Shanghai Theatre** (on SR 165 about half a mile south of the SR 76/Gretna Road intersection) is an equally eye-popping show, but in a completely different way. Here the rather utilitarian theater is merely a backdrop for a fast-paced, colorful and thrilling procession of athletic feats. The Acrobats of China—all from Shanghai and ranging in age from 13 to 24—display jaw-dropping strength, outrageous flexibility and amazing balance as they juggle, leap, contort and cavort across the stage. And whether balancing on precariously stacked chairs, artfully piling onto a constantly moving bicycle one by one (that's nine bodies, one bike) or performing a breathtaking aerial ballet, these gifted young people make it all look like a walk in the park.

The Mabe family is still going strong. "Branson's first show," the "Baldknobbers Jamboree," entertains audiences at the **Baldknobbers Music Theatre** *(see color ad card insert)* on SR 76 (next to the Country Tonite Theatre). Garrett, Denton and Brandon Mabe are the latest members carrying forward the family show-business tradition, following in the footsteps of their fathers and grandfathers. The Baldknobbers show has a little bit of everything—broad hillbilly humor (courtesy of Stub Meadows and Droopy Drawers), classic country (including a blazing "Orange Blossom Special"), roof-raising gospel music and a rousing patriotic finale.

The Presley family stars in another longtime Branson favorite at the **Presleys' Country Jubilee** *(see color ad card insert)* theater, on SR 76 next to the Hollywood Wax Museum. Four generations of this talented family appear on stage. It's a fast-paced show, with one musical number after another. There's impassioned Southern gospel singing, classic country tunes and even a bit of "new country" (i.e., current hits). Herkimer and Cecil provide the

Show-Me Springfield

The views from Interstate 44 and Highway 65 may deceive you, but Springfield, Missouri, is a city with a metropolitan area population topping 350,000. The city is host to the metropolitan amenities you expect without the hassles you dread of really large cities. There is enough variety of attractions, shopping, sports, theater, arts and dining to entertain you for days.

The original and largest **Bass Pro Shops Outdoor World** is the granddaddy of all outdoor stores. Explore the 300,000-square-foot showroom loaded with unique features including art gallery, barber shop, waterfalls, aquariums, restaurants, and, of course, the best in outdoor gear. Your adventure starts here.

Wonders of Wildlife Museum & Aquarium will entertain you with an eye-opening world of nature. Sounds of gushing water and birds calling greet guests amid breathtaking views of lush trees, rock outcroppings, 700,000 gallons of gurgling waterfalls and aquariums and more than 225 species of live animals in natural habitats.

Hear the crack of the bat up-close-and-personal with the 2006 World Championship St. Louis Cardinals double-A affiliate **Springfield Cardinals**. Meet tomorrow's big league players today in a stadium reminiscent of the majors.

Leap back in time to the site of the first major Civil War battle west of the Mississippi River and where the first Union general to die in combat— **Wilson's Creek National Battlefield.**

FAST FACTS

- *Birthplace of* **Route 66**
- *Site of first recorded shootout with* **"Wild Bill" Hickok**
- *More than* **800 dining options**
- *A quick 30 miles from* **Branson**

For more information contact the
Convention & Visitors Bureau
1-800-678-8767
show-me-springfield.com

07AAA

comic relief, which is downright silly. You'll laugh anyway.

Celebrity impersonations are always fun to see, and the stars are out in force at **Legends Family Theater,** on SR 76 across from the looming *Titanic.* "Legends in Concert" began as a 2-week engagement in Las Vegas but has grown into a franchise with more than 100 rotating acts. In Branson you'll naturally see country stars like Toby Keith and Kenny Rogers, along with everyone from Celine Dion to the Beatles to Tina Turner and of course, Elvis. Video screens flanking both sides of the stage show footage of the real-life legend, which can invite comparisons both favorable and unfavorable. The good news: no lip syncing. There's also a crack house band. The singing Brett Family performs morning shows at the theater.

At 4,000 seats, **The Grand Palace** (on SR 76 next to the Andy Williams Moon River Theatre) is Branson's biggest theater. If you want to see a big-name concert, this is the place. The domed lobby, with two winding grand staircases and a huge crystal chandelier, sets the tone. The Grand Palace lineup includes well-known country stars (the Oak Ridge Boys, Merle Haggard, Tanya Tucker), superstars like Loretta Lynn who play limited engagements, and plenty of non-country names as well (Tony Bennett, Mannheim Steamroller, comic Jeff Foxworthy). The "Grand Old Gospel Hour" Sunday mornings at 10 is free.

Another roadhouse with a varied entertainment menu is the **Branson Variety Theater,** on SR 76 across from Andy Williams and The Grand Palace. New York razzle-dazzle is provided by "Broadway! The Star-spangled Celebration," with highlights from various Broadway hits performed by an energetic cast and guest star Merrill Osmond (of that famous family). This also is the Branson home of the international music and dance revue "Spirit of the Dance." The theater's guest star concert series includes the likes of Bobby Vinton, Debbie Reynolds and Frankie Avalon, while the Osmonds host the annual holiday show "Spirit of Christmas."

Music City Centre, a short distance down SR 76 from Dolly Parton's Dixie Stampede, features a salute to Red Skelton, as veteran performer Tom Mullica reacquaints audiences with Clem Kadiddlehopper, Freddy the Freeloader and other fondly remembered Skelton characters. For teen appeal there's the singing, dancing, fiddling Haygoods, seven brothers and one sister who previously packed 'em in at Silver Dollar City. And some say the best Elvis tribute in town—from the vocals to those gyrating hips—is Tony Roi's turn as the king of rock 'n' roll.

For a Las Vegas-style show, head to the **Remington Theatre** on SR 76 (next to the Waltzing Waters Theatre), where "Neil Goldberg's Cirque" will take you to a world of fanciful creatures, showcasing an international cast that does pretty amazing things both on the stage and in the air. The outrageous costumes alone are worth the price of admission.

That's more than enough to satisfy most show fans, but Branson boasts a number of other venues. **Owen's Theatre,** the only theater downtown, not only has a resident Elvis but a Saturday night contest for Presley performers, along with musical tributes to country legends Hank Williams and Patsy Cline. Williams also gets his due at the **Little Opry Theatre,** on Shepherd of the Hills Expressway in the Ozarks Discovery IMAX movie complex. "Hank Williams Revisited" and "New's Country Band" are two of the four live shows here, and each one is a must for fans of traditional country and bluegrass music.

The five talented Hughes brothers take the stage at **The Hughes Brothers Celebrity Theatre** (*see color ad card insert*) on SR 76 (across from Jim Stafford). They present both morning (featuring wives and kids) and evening (just the brothers) shows. The brothers' bond shines both vocally and during moments of good-natured banter, which recalls the brothers Smothers. An all-around entertainer (since age 10) is Bart Rockett; his show at the **Bart Rockett Theatre** on SR 76 (near the Dutton Family Theater) features comedy, dancing, music, ventriloquism and illusions.

Another illusionist, Kirby Van Burch, performs "How did he do that?" feats at the **Kirby Van Burch Theatre,** on SR 248 just north of Shepherd

of the Hills Expressway. The props employed by the "Prince of Magic" include a real helicopter that seemingly appears out of thin air. And another family, the Duttons, display their multiple talents at the **Dutton Family Theater** on SR 76 (next to the Caravelle). With a repertoire that manages to include both Pachelbel's "Canon in D major" and the raveup surf instrumental "Wipeout," the Duttons obviously have music in their genes.

The **Starlite Theatre,** on SR 76 across from the Hollywood Wax Museum, presents the Platters (of "The Great Pretender" and "Smoke Gets in Your Eyes" fame). The **Country Tonite Theatre** features "Country Tonite," a toe-tappin' mix of music and comedy hosted by longtime Branson entertainer Clay Cooper. Cooper also headlines his own show at the **Clay Cooper Theatre,** on SR 76 across from Ride the Ducks.

Last but not least, the **Hamner-Barber Theater** on Shepherd of the Hills Expressway (across from the **Pierce Arrow Theater**) offers two different shows: the country, bluegrass and award-winning gospel sounds of the "Braschler Music Show" and the "Hamner-Barber Variety Show," co-starring comedian and ventriloquist Jim Barber and the Hamner family's exotic illusions (which incorporate a bevy of colorful macaws and cockatoos).

As if all this weren't enough to keep visitors busy, many theaters also present their own special Christmas shows during November and December, and many people come to Branson during these two months to celebrate an old-fashioned holiday season. Contact the individual theaters for details.

More theaters are on tap in Branson's future; the Sight & Sound Millennium Theatre, which will present elaborate live theatrical and musical performances based on Bible stories, is scheduled to open in summer 2008. *For a list of current theaters, see Branson Theaters on p. 147.*

Special Events

For many years Branson was traditionally a summer destination, and tourist activities pretty much shut down during the winter. But these days the "season" is all year. Branson's down time (January through March) is known as Hot Winter Fun. These 3 months means fewer crowds, and there's still plenty to do.

Theaters that stay open during all or part of Hot Winter Fun include the Baldknobbers Music Theatre, the Bart Rockett Theatre, Dick Clark's American Bandstand Theater, the House of Rock Theatre, The Hughes Brothers Celebrity Theatre, the Jim Stafford Theatre, Legends Family Theater, the Mansion America Theatre and the Remington Theatre. The Hot Winter Fun Big Show at the Jim Stafford Theatre in mid-February brings a slew of Branson performers together on one stage.

One of the most happening places in town is Silver Dollar City, where a bunch of fun festivals are celebrated spring through fall. World-Fest starts things off, taking place the entire month of April into mid-May.

Next up is the Bluegrass & BBQ Festival, which runs from mid-May to early June. Hundreds of bluegrass performances feature both up-and-coming artists and big-name headliners. The singing and fiddling is complemented by a lip-smackin' lineup of barbecue—pit-cooking demonstrations highlight everything from Texas smoked beef brisket to St. Louis-style ribs and Memphis dry-rubbed meats, which can be doused with all kinds of different barbecue sauces.

National Kids' Fest takes place mid-June to late August. This festival presents special shows and exhibits ranging from extreme sports demonstrations to appearances by exotic animals. The rousing Southern Gospel Picnic brings together the rich harmonies of top-name gospel vocal groups along with another Southern tradition—an old-fashioned picnic spread featuring chicken and all the fixings plus a tempting array of desserts. This family-style music celebration runs from late August to around Sept. 10.

Artisans from around the country gather for the Festival of American Music and Craftmanship, held mid-September to late October. And Silver Dollar City celebrates an Old Time Christmas in November and December.

Branson kicks off spring in early April with BransonFest, a weeklong celebration of food, fun and entertainment. The daily concert schedule showcases a "Branson's greatest hits" lineup of musical performers and production shows—the Lennon Sisters, Jim Stafford, the Acrobats of China and "Broadway! The Star-Spangled Celebration," to name a few. More live entertainment, celebrity meet-and-greets and pavilions representing area businesses, Branson artists and local restaurants round out the festival, which takes place at the Welk Resort Theatre complex on SR 165.

Also in April, Kewpiesta honors Ozarks artist Rose O'Neill, creator of the kewpie doll. In late September the Autumn Daze Craft Festival takes place.

Branson pulls out the stops for the holidays. Beginning Nov. 1 and lasting through December, more than 5 million twinkling lights adorn the streets during the Branson Area Festival of Lights. The Branson Adoration Parade rolls through the streets of the historic downtown area in early December. This nighttime parade is a joyful expression of small-town pride and a faith-based celebration of Christmas, with lighted floats, high school marching bands, musicians and singers all ringing in the season.

The parade coincides with the lighting of the enormous Nativity Scene on Mount Branson, a tradition that goes back almost 60 years. Incorporating 40-foot-tall figures, it is lit from the first Sunday in December through Jan. 1. Branson's music theaters also get into the spirit, presenting literally dozens of special holiday-themed productions in November and December.

The Branson Vicinity

LAMPE (E-2) elev. 1,316'

DOGWOOD CANYON NATURE PARK is s. on SR 13 to jct. SR 86, then w. about 3 mi. on SR 86 following signs to the park turnoff. From Branson, take US 65 s. to jct. SR 86, then w. on SR 86 about 16 mi. to the park turnoff, following signs. Dogwood Canyon is a private refuge encompassing some 10,000 acres of Ozark wilderness. The terrain of ridges, hollows and limestone bluffs is honeycombed with caves and provides a backdrop for waterfalls, meandering streams and woodlands dominated by oaks, pines and cedars.

Activities include walking, hiking or biking along a 6-mile round-trip paved trail, trout fishing and horseback riding. A 2-hour wildlife tram tour winds along the canyon floor before crossing the Arkansas border to encounter herds of Texas longhorn cattle, American bison and elk that live in the park.

All recreational activities are subject to weather conditions and availability. Food is available. Allow 2 hours minimum. Park open daily 8-6 (weather permitting), Mar. 21-Oct. 31; 8-4 rest of year. Most activities offered Mar.-Nov. Closed Jan. 1 and Dec. 25. Fees for individual activities vary. Wildlife tram tour $23.95; ages 3-11, $9.95. One-day Adventure Pass combining various activities $34.95; ages 3-11, $19.95. AX, CB, DC, DS, MC, VI. Phone (417) 779-5983.

POINT LOOKOUT (E-3) elev. 928´

COLLEGE OF THE OZARKS is 2 mi. s. on US 65 to CR V. This liberal arts college is maintained largely by students as one way of defraying the cost of education. Highlights include The College of the Ozarks Greenhouses, containing a collection of more than 7,000 orchids; the neo-Gothic Williams Memorial Chapel, which has impressive stained-glass windows; and the SAVE Ralph Foster Museum, which displays items related to the Ozarks as well as the original vehicle used in the TV series "The Beverly Hillbillies." Also on the grounds is Edwards

Mill, a water-powered mill that produces whole-grain meal.

Food is available. Allow 1 hour, 30 minutes minimum. Museum Mon.-Sat. 9-4:30; closed Thanksgiving week and mid-Dec. through Jan. 31. Museum admission $4.50; over 61, $3.50; under 18 free. Phone (417) 334-6411.

WALNUT SHADE (E-3) elev. 755´

BONNIEBROOK is at 485 Rose O'Neill Rd. This three-story house was the favorite retreat of Rose O'Neill, novelist, artist and creator of the kewpie doll. Her restored home contains family furnishings as well as period items. A museum of O'Neill's works includes books, photographs, illustrations and original dolls. Walkways meander through the wooded grounds, past flower gardens and brooks.

Allow 1 hour minimum. Guided tours are given Mon.-Sat. 9-4, April 1-Dec. 1; closed major holidays. Last tour begins 1 hour before closing. Admission $7, under 12 free. AX, MC, VI. Phone (417) 561-1509 or (800) 539-7437.

© Roy Rogers-Dale Evans Museum & Happy Trails Theater / Branson/Lakes Area Chamber of Commerce & CVB

This ends listings for the Branson Vicinity.
The following page resumes the alphabetical listings of cities in Missouri.

BURFORDVILLE (E-5)

BOLLINGER MILL STATE HISTORIC SITE is .5 mi. e. of SR 34. This turbine-powered mill was first built in 1799 and reconstructed twice during the 19th century. One of only four covered bridges in Missouri is on the grounds. Picnic facilities are available. Tours of the four-story mill are given on the half-hour Mon.-Sat. 10-4, Sun. noon-4; closed holidays. Tour $2.50; ages 6-12, $1.50. Phone (573) 243-4591 or (800) 334-6946.

BUTLER (D-2) pop. 4,209, elev. 850′

BATES COUNTY MUSEUM is on Elks Dr., just off Mill St. and old US 71. Eight themed rooms trace the county's history from early pioneer days through the 1970s. Exhibits feature Osage Indian artifacts, items associated with the 1821 Harmony Mission, Civil War and World War II memorabilia and a Bates County timeline.

Allow 1 hour minimum. Mon.-Sat. 10-4, May-Oct.; closed July 4 and Labor Day. Admission $3, over 64 and students with ID $1. Phone (660) 679-0134.

CALIFORNIA (C-3) pop. 4,005, elev. 889′

BURGER'S SMOKEHOUSE, 3 mi. s. on SR 87, offers a videotape presentation detailing the country ham curing process. The visitor center features a two-and-one-half-story diorama depicting an Ozark landscape during various seasons. Mon.-Fri. 8-4. Free. Phone (573) 796-3134.

CAMDENTON (D-3) pop. 2,779, elev. 1,000′

Camdenton, the seat of Camden County, is in south-central Missouri. Osage and Delaware Indians inhabited this area prior to the onset of white settlement in the 1820s. Houseboat rentals are popular along nearby Lake of the Ozarks.

DID YOU KNOW

The Gateway Arch is the tallest man-made monument in the United States.

Camdenton Area Chamber of Commerce: 611 N. SR 5, P.O. Box 1375, Camdenton, MO 65020; phone (573) 346-2227 or (800) 769-1004.

BRIDAL CAVE is 2 mi. n. on SR 5, then 1.5 mi. w. on Lake Rd. 5-88. Guided 1-hour tours follow concrete walks through the cave, which is known for its massive onyx formations and colorful mineral deposits. The stalactite-adorned Bridal Chapel is a popular site for weddings. On the grounds are picnic facilities, a visitor center, a boat dock and nature trails. Daily 9-6, Memorial Day weekend-Labor Day; 9-4, rest of year. Admission $13; ages 5-12, $6.50. Phone (573) 346-2676.

CAPE GIRARDEAU (E-6)
pop. 35,349, elev. 350′

Named after Jean Baptiste Girardot, who established a trading post here in 1733, Cape Girardeau was settled by Spanish immigrants drawn to the area by Spain's offer of inexpensive, tax-exempt land. Flourishing river trade characterized the town before the Civil War. Cape Girardeau experienced an industrial resurgence in the 1880s with the establishment of new railroad lines.

A look at area heritage and culture is available at the Cape River Heritage Museum, 538 Independence St.; phone (573) 334-0405. The city contains many scenic parks. Court House Park overlooks the Mississippi River, while Capaha Park boasts notable rose gardens. A scenic portion of I-55 runs 57 miles north from Cape Girardeau to St. Mary.

Cape Girardeau Convention and Visitors Bureau: 100 Broadway, P.O. Box 617, Cape Girardeau, MO 63702; phone (573) 335-1631 or (800) 777-0068.

Self-guiding tours: A pamphlet outlining a walking tour of historic downtown Cape Girardeau is available from the convention and visitors bureau.

CAPE ROCK is 2 mi. n.e. via SR 177 and E. Cape Rock Dr. Views of the Mississippi River are particularly scenic from this bluff, said to be the site of Jean Baptiste Girardot's 1733 trading post. Nothing remains of the original settlement. Picnic facilities are available.

SOUTHEAST MISSOURI STATE UNIVERSITY MUSEUM is .3 mi. n. on Pacific, then .2 mi. n.w. on Circle Dr. to 1 University Plaza in the heart of the campus. Of special interest is the museum's extensive collection of Mississippian and Mound Builder pottery. Pieces in the fine arts, archeological and historical collections are displayed on a rotating basis. Monthly art exhibitions include works by regional artists as well as touring national and international exhibitions.

Parking is limited; additional museum parking spaces are reserved behind Academic Hall on University Plaza. Allow 1 hour minimum. Mon.-Fri. 9-4, Sat.-Sun. noon-4; closed school holidays. Free. Phone (573) 651-2260.

TRAIL OF TEARS STATE PARK is 10 mi. n. on SR 177. The 3,415-acre park contains a portion of the Trail of Tears, the route used by the Cherokees on their forced march to Oklahoma. This tract consists of wooded hills and valleys and high bluffs overlooking the Mississippi River. Deer, turkeys, hawks and foxes live year-round in the park; bald eagles come for the winter. Phone (573) 334-1711. *See Recreation Chart and the AAA South Central Camp-Book.*

CARTHAGE (E-1) pop. 12,668, elev. 1,008′

Virtually destroyed during the Civil War, Carthage was subsequently rebuilt largely with marble quarried from the surrounding area. The city's historic square contains several Victorian houses built with the local stone, which also was used in the construction of the Missouri State Capitol in Jefferson City.

Another marble building is the castle-like Jasper County Courthouse, 302 S. Main St., which bristles with turrets and a tall clock spire. Inside, the mural "Forged in Fire" by Lowell Davis depicts the history of Carthage from the time of its first settlers, the Osage Indians, through the Civil War to the present.

Myra Belle Shirley—later to become Belle Starr, infamous Confederate spy and outlaw—was in her teens when the war forced her family to move from the area. Other residents were Annie Baxter, the first woman in the United States to hold elected office; ragtime musician and composer James Scott; and zoologist and lecturer Marlin Perkins, who is honored with a bronze statue in Central Park.

During the Civil War the Battle of Carthage was fought July 5, 1861. Different stages of the battle are shown by markers that begin on Civil War Road, at the baseline 8 miles north of town, and extend to Carter Park on River Street in Carthage. The Battle of Carthage State Historic Site on Chestnut Street provides an interpretive shelter that depicts the history of the battle. For further information about the battle markers contact the convention and visitors bureau.

The Powers Museum at 1617 W. Oak St. recounts the history of Carthage and the surrounding region during the late 19th and early 20th centuries. Art-Central at 1110 E. 13th St. displays the works of local artists; phone (417) 358-4404.

Carthage Convention and Visitors Bureau: 402 S. Garrison, Carthage, MO 64836; phone (417) 359-8181 or (866) 357-8687. *See color ad.*

Self-guiding tours: A historical drive about 4 miles long is defined by green street markers posted throughout the business and residential districts, both of which are distinguished by Victorian architecture.

PRECIOUS MOMENTS INSPIRATION PARK is at 4321 Chapel Rd. Conceived and designed by artist Samuel J. Butcher, the chapel features 30 stained-glass windows and dozens of murals covering the walls and ceiling. Butcher first began drawing teardrop-eyed children called "Precious Moments" to convey messages to family and friends. He further developed his signature style by depicting biblical events. The east gallery displays a large collection of porcelain figurines and some of Butcher's early artistic work to present the history of Precious Moments.

"Fountain of Angels" is a show of water, lights and music set amid 250 bronze sculptures. Also on the 3,000-acre grounds are a visitor center, a museum and a Victorian Wedding Island on a 40-acre lake.

Daily 9-6, Apr. 22-Nov. 3; Sun.-Thurs. 9-6, Fri.-Sat. 9-8, Nov. 4-Dec. 31; daily 9-5, Mar. 11-Apr. 21; daily 9-5 (chapel only), rest of year. Closed Jan. 1, Thanksgiving and Dec. 25. Schedule may vary; phone ahead. Chapel free. All-inclusive admission to "Fountain of Angels" show and changing exhibit $12; over 49, $11; ages 4-12, $5. Phone (800) 543-7975.

CARUTHERSVILLE (F-5) pop. 6,760

CASINOS

- **Casino Aztar**, 777 E. 3rd St. Sun.-Thurs. 9 a.m.-3 a.m., Fri.-Sat. 9 a.m.-5 a.m. Phone (573) 333-1000.

CARVER NATIONAL MONUMENT—
see *George Washington Carver National Monument p. 158.*

CHESTERFIELD—see *St. Louis p. 209.*

CLARKSVILLE (B-5) pop. 490, elev. 456'

Founded in 1816, Clarksville became known for the huge quantities of apples shipped from the area each fall, prompting rivermen to dub the village Appletown. It offers the first opportunity north of St. Louis to view the Mississippi River—up close—at Lock and Dam 24. At the north end of town on US 79 is the Riverlands Association Visitor Center, which offers more views of the river as well as exhibits detailing its history; phone (573) 242-3132.

CLINTON (C-2) pop. 9,311

HENRY COUNTY MUSEUM AND CULTURAL ARTS CENTER is at 203 W. Franklin St. A reconstructed 1800s village includes storefronts and replicas of a drugstore, a soda fountain, a pharmacy, a doctor's office with a collection of medical tools and devices, a barber shop, a schoolhouse, a general store and a blacksmith shop. A log cabin also is displayed across the street from the museum. Allow 1 hour minimum. Mon.-Sat. 10-4, Apr.-Dec.; closed most major holidays. Admission $3, under 12 free. Phone (660) 885-8414.

COLUMBIA (C-3) pop. 84,531, elev. 738'

Columbia began in 1819 as Smithton; it was renamed and made the seat of Boone County in 1821. After Boone's Lick Trail was rerouted south through Columbia, the town became a prosperous outfitting station for westbound emigrants, some of whom chose to remain.

Columbia's residents responded to the competition to secure the appointment for a state university with the fervor of a political campaign. As a result of door-to-door canvassing and torchlight parades, a subscription of $117,000 was raised by 900 patrons, some of whom sold their houses and farms to meet their pledges. The University of Missouri, the first public university west of the Mississippi River, opened its doors in 1839.

MU is Missouri's national flagship university, with more than 265 degree programs and the largest library collection in the state. Its school of journalism, founded in 1908, is distinguished as the world's first. As one of only six universities in the country with medicine, veterinary medicine and law on one campus, MU also plays a significant rule in professional education.

"Mizzou" is a member of the Big 12 Conference and features the state's only Division 1-A athletic program. For sports event schedules and ticket information phone (800) 228-7297.

Columbia College and Stephens College confirm Columbia's identity as a college town, though the insurance industry and medical services reinforce its economic base. The Davis Art and Curved Entrance galleries at Stephens College mount exhibits throughout the year; phone (573) 442-2211.

The 8.2-mile M-K-T Trail connects downtown Columbia to the Katy Trail, a rails-to-trails conversion that crosses the state. At the Stadium Boulevard trailhead is the Martin Luther King Jr. Memorial Garden. Trail maps are available from the convention and visitors bureau.

Columbia Convention & Visitors Bureau: 300 S. Providence Rd., Columbia, MO 65203; phone (573) 875-1231 or (800) 652-0987.

Self-guiding tours: Brochures outlining a driving tour of publicly accessible art are offered by the convention and visitors bureau.

SHELTER INSURANCE GARDENS is off I-70 exit 124, s. on Stadium Blvd., then e. to 1817 W. Broadway St., behind the insurance company's headquarters. Tucked behind stone and wrought-iron gates at the home office complex of Shelter Insurance Companies are 5 acres planted with more than 300 varieties of native trees and shrubs, along with a number of annuals and perennials. Rose, shade, rock, conifer and desert gardens as well as a garden for the blind are all tagged for identification.

Picnicking is permitted. Allow 30 minutes minimum. Daily dawn-dusk; closed Dec. 25. Free. Phone (573) 445-8441.

UNIVERSITY OF MISSOURI-COLUMBIA is on Eighth St., 3 blks. s. of Broadway St. "Mizzou," the oldest state university west of the Mississippi, has 28,000 students and 12,000 faculty and staff. A number of buildings on the 1,358-acre campus are listed on the National Register of Historic Places. Six Ionic columns on Francis Quadrangle are all that remains of Academic Hall, destroyed by fire in 1892. Thomas Jefferson's original tombstone is on the quadrangle.

On Friday visitors can watch the mid-morning feeding of reptiles in Room 202 of Stewart Hall; phone (573) 884-7279.

With more than 5,000 trees and 650 varieties of plants, the MU grounds have been officially designated as a botanic garden. Campus walking tours are given Mon.-Fri. at 10:45, 12:15 and 2:15 during the chool year; Mon.-Fri. at 10:45 and 1:45, mid-May) mid-Aug., unless otherwise arranged. Two weeks' dvance notice is recommended. For further infor- ation contact the Office of Visitor Relations; hone (573) 882-6333 or (800) 856-2181.

George Caleb Bingham Gallery is in the Fine Arts Building at 125A Hitt St. Changing exhibits of art- work by faculty and students as well as artists of na- ional and international stature are mounted. Mon.- ri. 10-4; closed campus holidays and between emesters. Free. Phone (573) 882-3555.

Museum of Anthropology is in room 100 in Swal- ow Hall. Exhibits related to the anthropological his- ory of man are displayed on a rotating basis. Allow 0 minutes minimum. Mon.-Fri. 9-4; closed holi- lays. Free. Phone (573) 882-3573.

Museum of Art and Archaeology is in Pickard Hall at jct. Ninth St. and University Ave. The mu- eum contains a collection of ancient Egyptian, Greek and Roman art; American artworks; and Eu- opean paintings, drawings, prints and sculpture rom the 15th century to the present. Other exhibits eature Asian, African and pre-Columbian art. The Cast Gallery displays plaster casts of Greek and Ro- nan sculptures. Tues.-Fri. 9-4, Sat.-Sun. noon-4; losed holidays. Free. Phone (573) 882-3591.

State Historical Society of Missouri is on the ground floor of the Ellis Library in Lowry Mall, at ct. Ninth St. and Conley Ave. Missouri newspapers, books and publications about state history and gene- logy are part of an extensive collection that in- ludes political cartoons and paintings by John J. Audubon, Thomas Hart Benton, George Caleb Bing- am, Karl Bodmer and contemporary Missouri art- sts. Tours are given by appointment. Mon.-Fri. 8-4, Sat. 9-4:30. Free. Phone (573) 882-7083.

WALTERS-BOONE COUNTY HISTORICAL MU- EUM is 3 mi. s. of jct. I-70/SR 63 at 3801 Ponde- osa St. (Historic Ashland Pike). The history of the rea is presented through historical photographs, ar- ifacts, living-history displays and rotating exhibits. Also in the museum is the Genealogical Society of Central Missouri Library. Adjoining the museum is he Montminy Gallery, which houses the works of ocal artists and professors Tracy and Pierre Montminy.

Allow 1 hour minimum. Tues.-Fri. noon-4, Sat.- Sun. 1-5, Apr.-Oct.; Wed. and Fri. noon-4, Sat.-Sun. -5, rest of year. Admission $3; under 13, $1. Phone 573) 443-8936.

CRESTWOOD—
ee St. Louis p. 209

DANVILLE (C-4)

GRAHAM CAVE STATE PARK is 2 mi. w. off I-70 and CR TT. Archeological profiles of the sandstone ave at the 357-acre park indicate it was occupied about 8000 B.C. Daily 24 hours. Free. Phone (573) 564-3476. *See Recreation Chart and the AAA South Central CampBook.*

DEFIANCE—*see St. Louis p. 209.*

DREXEL (C-1) pop. 1,090, elev. 997′

The Frontier Military Museum, 1 mile east of Drexel on SR 18, displays uniforms, saddles, boots, weapons and other items associated primarily with the Civil War and World Wars I and II. Guided tours are available by appointment only; phone (816) 657-3346.

EAST PRAIRIE (E-6) pop. 3,227

BIG OAK TREE STATE PARK is 2 mi. e. on SR 80, then 10 mi. s. on SR 102. A 1.2-mile boardwalk winds through forests of virgin bottomland hard- woods, enabling visitors to see small wildlife. The trees are notable for their size and provide a habitat for more than 140 species of birds. A free booklet interprets the 10 stations along the trail. Daily 6 a.m.-10 p.m. Free. Phone (573) 649-3149. *See Rec- reation Chart.*

EUREKA—*see St. Louis p. 209.*

EXCELSIOR SPRINGS—
see Kansas City p. 178.

FLORIDA (B-4) pop. 9

John Clemens moved from Tennessee to the new village of Florida in 1835, where he became a part- ner in an in-law's store and set up a law practice. His son, Samuel Langhorne Clemens, was born here and later, as Mark Twain, created some of America's early classic literature. Four years after Twain's birth the family moved to Hannibal, which served as the model for St. Petersburg, the fictional home of Huckleberry Finn and Tom Sawyer.

MARK TWAIN BIRTHPLACE AND MUSEUM STATE HISTORIC SITE is .5 mi. s. on SR 107 in Mark Twain State Park *(see Recreation Chart and the AAA South Central CampBook).* The birthplace of Samuel Clemens is preserved within a steel, glass and stone building. The museum exhibits a hand- written manuscript of "The Adventures of Tom Sawyer" and memorabilia associated with Twain's life and times.

A reading room is available. Allow 1 hour mini- mum. Daily 10-5, Apr. 2-Oct. 31; Wed.-Sun. 10-5, rest of year. Closed Jan. 1, Thanksgiving and Dec. 25. Admission $2.50; ages 6-12, $1.50. Phone (573) 565-3449.

FLORISSANT—*see St. Louis p. 210.*

FORT LEONARD WOOD (D-4) pop. 13,666

Fort Leonard Wood, in the Ozark foothills 2 miles south of I-44 from the Fort Wood exit, is a major U.S. Army training center and headquarters of the Army Engineer School. Established in 1940, the fort is named for the general who helped organize the 1st U.S. Cavalry, The Rough Riders.

MAHAFFEY MUSEUM COMPLEX is at 495 S. Dakota Ave. The complex contains four museums: The U.S. Army Chemical Corps Museum, the U.S. Army Engineer Museum, the U.S. Army Military Police Corps Museum and the Fort Leonard Wood Museum. Walk-through dioramas and artifacts from each corps are featured. The Fort Leonard Wood Museum is a group of World War II-era buildings with items portraying daily military life at the fort. Allow 1 hour minimum. Mon.-Fri. 8-4, Sat. 10-4. Free. Phone (573) 596-0780.

FROHNA (D-6) pop. 192

Frohna was one of several settlements founded in 1839 by a group of 700 German Saxon Lutherans. Eight years later these immigrants founded the Lutheran Church-Missouri Synod. Off CR C on Saxon Memorial Drive is the Saxon Lutheran Memorial, which includes a visitor center, a log parish schoolhouse and an early log and frame house built by one of the original settlers.

FULTON (C-4) pop. 12,128, elev. 813′

Fulton was the birthplace of musician, poet, novelist and reviewer Henry Bellamann, who published three books of poetry and seven novels 1920-45. His best-known novel, "King's Row," depicts life in a small Midwestern town 1890-1910.

Kingdom of Callaway Chamber of Commerce: 409 Court St., Fulton, MO 65251; phone (573) 642-3055.

[SAVE] **AUTO WORLD MUSEUM** is at 200 Peacock Dr. Rare cars, fire trucks and tractors are showcased, many dating from the turn of the 20th century. Cars representing every decade of the 20th century are displayed, along with antique tools. Allow 1 hour minimum. Mon.-Sat. 10-4, Sun. 12:30-4, Apr.-Nov. Admission $5.50; senior citizens and military with ID $4.50; ages 6-12, $2. Phone (573) 642-2080.

WINSTON CHURCHILL MEMORIAL AND LIBRARY is at Westminster and W. 7th sts. The Westminster College Gymnasium was the site of Churchill's prophetic "Iron Curtain" speech on Mar. 5, 1946. To commemorate that visit, the college acquired London's historic Church of St. Mary the Virgin, Aldermanbury, which was slated for demolition, and reassembled it on the campus as a memorial.

The church stood in London's Old City for 800 years. Destroyed by the Great Fire in 1666, it was rebuilt by Sir Christopher Wren. Three hundred years later, the tons of stone walls and columns remaining after the 1940 London blitz were shipped to Fulton. The church has been reconstructed, and the bombed-out portions have been replaced.

Allow 1 hour minimum. Daily 10-4:30; closed Jan. 1, Thanksgiving and Dec. 25. Admission $6; over 60, $5; students 12-18, $4; ages 6-12, $3. MC, VI. Phone (573) 592-5369.

GEORGE WASHINGTON CARVER NATIONAL MONUMENT (E-1)

George Washington Carver National Monument is southeast of Joplin and 2.5 miles southwest of Diamond on CR V. The 210-acre park preserves the birthplace of the noted scientist. Carver developed more than 300 byproducts from the peanut and more than 100 from the sweet potato, as well as new uses for cotton, soybeans, cowpeas and other crops.

Displays in the visitor center pertain to Carver's life and work in the field of botany and his career as a teacher of scientific agriculture. The Discovery Center gives visitors the chance to try hands-on experiments.

A self-guiding, .7-mile trail winds through woods and fields Carver walked as a boy. Sites along the trail include the birthplace site, the "Boy Carver" statue by Robert Amendola and the Carver family cemetery. Allow 1 hour minimum. Daily 9-5; closed Jan. 1, Thanksgiving and Dec. 25. Free. Phone (417) 325-4151.

GLASGOW (B-3) pop. 1,263, elev. 650′

GLASGOW COMMUNITY MUSEUM is at 402 Commerce St. Housed in an 1861 church building, the museum displays many items from the church as well as other artifacts and photographs from the 1800s and early 1900s. Allow 1 hour minimum. Wed.-Sun. 2-5, May 15-Oct. 15. Donations. Phone (660) 338-2377.

GRANDVIEW—see Kansas City p. 178.

GRANITEVILLE (D-5)

ELEPHANT ROCKS STATE PARK is on SR 21. The park's name is derived from Elephant Rock, which is 27 feet tall, 35 feet long, 17 feet wide and weighs about 680 tons. Geologists estimate the granite rock to be approximately 1.2 billion years old. The 1-mile Elephant Rocks Braille Trail, a national recreation trail, describes the park's natural features. Daily 8-8. Free. Phone (573) 697-5395. *See Recreation Chart.*

GRAY SUMMIT (C-5) pop. 2,640, elev. 632′

PURINA FARMS is 2 blks. n. on SR 100 to CR MM, then 1 mi. n. The complex offers a variety of educational displays along with a hands-on experience with pets and farm animals. Young visitors can romp in the hayloft, learn how many people equal the weight of one hog and attend a multimedia presentation about man's relationships with domestic animals. Tues.-Sun. 9:30-3, Memorial Day-Labor Day; Wed.-Fri. 9:30-1, Sat.-Sun. 9:30-3, mid-Mar. through day before Memorial Day and day after Labor Day to mid-Nov. Reservations are required. Free. Phone (314) 982-3232.

TourBookMark

Lodging Listing Symbols

Member Values (see pgs. 12-13)

AAA Official Appointment

SAVE Offers lowest public rate or minimum 10% discount

ASK May offer discount

S Offers senior discount

fyi Informational listing only

Member Services

Airport transportation

Pets allowed

Restaurant on premises

Restaurant off premises (walking distance)

24-hour room service

Cocktail lounge

Child care

Accessibility Features

Accessibility features

Roll-in showers

Hearing impaired equipment

Leisure Activities

Full service casino

Pool

Health club on premises

Health club off premises

Recreational activities

In-Room Amenities

Non-smoking rooms

VCR

Movies

Refrigerator

Microwave

Coffee maker

No air conditioning

No TV

No cable TV

No telephones

Safety Features (see page 24)
(Mexico and Caribbean only)

S Sprinklers

D Smoke detectors

Call property for detailed information about fees & restrictions relating to the lodging listing symbols.

CHOICE HOTELS
INTERNATIONAL

Your trip across America starts here.

CHOICE HOTELS
INTERNATIONAL

choicehotels.com
800.228.1222

We'll see you there.

SHAW NATURE RESERVE is at jct. SR 100 and I-44. The reserve protects some 2,500 acres of natural Ozark landscape and offers 14 miles of hiking trails through such habitats as a floodplain forest, oak-hickory woods, glades, bluffs, a tall-grass prairie, savanna and wetlands. The People and the Land exhibit in the 1879 Joseph H. Manor House deals with environmental and conservation themes.

Reserve open daily 7 a.m.-dusk. Visitor center Mon.-Fri. 8-4:30, Sat.-Sun. 9-5; closed major holidays. Admission $3; over 64, $2; under 12 free. Phone (636) 451-3512.

HANNIBAL (B-5) pop. 17,757, elev. 470′

Samuel Clemens (Mark Twain) lived in Hannibal as a boy and later used the town as the setting for incidents in "The Adventures of Huckleberry Finn" and "The Adventures of Tom Sawyer." Another Hannibal resident was Margaret Tobin, who, after being encouraged by Clemens to tap the wealth in the Rocky Mountains, went West and became adored by Denver society. She married and later was dubbed the Unsinkable Molly Brown after rowing passengers to safety from the sinking *Titanic*.

The Garth Woodside Mansion, on Warren Barrett Drive, was the 20-room home of Col. John H. Garth, a close friend of Clemens. The 1871 Victorian mansion contains a three-story flying staircase—one with no visible means of support—ornate woodwork and hand-carved mantels of Italian marble. Much of the furniture, wall hangings, draperies and carpets belonged to the Garths. In December the mansion is adorned with Victorian holiday decorations; phone (573) 221-2789.

Already imbued with a distinctly American character through its association with Mark Twain, Hannibal also is the southern migration destination for bald eagles that live on the high Mississippi River bluffs. Many of the majestic birds can be seen at the dam at Saverton, about 9 miles south of Hannibal on SR 79.

Hannibal is at the northern end of the scenic portion of SR 79 that runs 86 miles south to St. Peters, following the Mississippi River much of the way. Tom Sawyer look-alikes descend upon Hannibal yearly to compete in the fence-painting contest during National Tom Sawyer Days, held the week of July 4.

Hannibal Convention & Visitors Bureau: 505 N. 3rd St., Hannibal, MO 63401; phone (573) 221-2477.

"ADVENTURES OF TOM SAWYER" DIORAMAS is at 323 N. Main St. Hand-carved miniature figures depict scenes from the novel. Allow 30 minutes minimum. Wed.-Sat. 10-5, Tues. noon-9, Mon. noon-5, Sun. by appointment; closed Thanksgiving and Dec. 25. Admission $3, under 17 free when accompanied by an adult, family rate $6. Phone (573) 221-3525.

HANNIBAL COMPANY TROLLEY RIDE departs from 227 N. Main St. Trolley tours go to the Mark Twain Cave, Sawyer's Creek, Rockcliffe Mansion, Molly Brown's Birthplace, the Welshman Home, the *Mark Twain* Riverboat and the Mississippi River. Trips depart daily every hour and 20 minutes 9-5, mid-Apr. through Oct. 31. Fare $8.50; over 55, $8; ages 5-12, $4. MC, VI. Phone (573) 221-1161.

 MARK TWAIN BOYHOOD HOME AND MUSEUM is at 208 Hill St. The complex consists of several historic buildings and museums related to Hannibal's most famous resident. The home where Samuel Clemens lived between the ages of 7 and 18 was built by his father in 1843. The restored two-story frame house is decorated with period furnishings and also contains interpretive displays. The museum collection includes such Twain memorabilia as first editions of his books, photographs, original manuscripts and the desk where he wrote "The Adventures of Tom Sawyer."

The Mark Twain Museum Gallery, 2 blocks south on Main Street, features 16 Norman Rockwell oil paintings that were used as illustrations in special editions of "The Adventures of Tom Sawyer" and "The Adventures of Huckleberry Finn"; sketches for the paintings were done by Rockwell in Hannibal 1935-36.

Allow 1 hour minimum. Daily 8-6, June-Aug.; daily 8-5, in May; daily 9-5, Apr. and Sept.-Oct.; Mon.-Sat. 9-4, Sun. noon-4, in Mar.; Mon.-Sat. 10-4, Sun. noon-4, rest of year. Closed Jan. 1, Easter, Thanksgiving and Dec. 25. Admission (includes all museum buildings) $8; over 60, $6.50; ages 6-12, $4. Phone (573) 221-9010.

Pilaster House is at Hill and Main sts. This old drugstore was the home of Dr. Orville Grant, a close Clemens family friend. The family moved into Dr. Grant's house after losing their own home. Open same hours as Mark Twain Boyhood Home and Museum. Free with paid admission to Mark Twain Boyhood Home and Museum. Phone (573) 221-9010.

MARK TWAIN CAVE is 2 mi. s.e. on SR 79. Samuel Clemens immortalized this underground labyrinth in "The Adventures of Tom Sawyer" as the cave in which Tom and Becky Thatcher were lost. The cave has dry, lighted passageways and a constant temperature of 52 F. Guided 1-hour tours depart every 15 minutes daily 8-8, June-Aug.; 9-5, Apr.-May and Sept.-Oct.; 10-4, rest of year. Closed Thanksgiving and Dec. 25. Last tour begins 1 hour before closing. Admission $14; ages 5-12, $7. Combination ticket with Cameron Cave $24; ages 5-12, $14. Phone (573) 221-1656.

Cameron Cave is 2 mi. s.e. on SR 79. Visitors carry lanterns during the 90-minute tour of this cave, which has been left in a nearly natural state. Tours depart from the Mark Twain Cave visitor center daily at 10, noon, 1:30 and 3, Memorial Day-Labor Day; by appointment rest of year. Admission $15; ages 5-12, $8. Combination ticket with Mark Twain Cave $24; ages 5-12, $14. Phone (573) 221-1656.

MARK TWAIN **RIVERBOAT** docks at the foot of Center St. This triple-deck riverboat offers narrated sightseeing cruises on the Mississippi River. A 2-hour Dixieland band dinner cruise also is available. One-hour trips depart daily at 11, 1:30 and 4, Memorial Day-Labor Day; otherwise varies Apr.-May and Sept.-Oct. Fare $12; ages 5-12, $9. Phone (573) 221-3222.

RIVERVIEW PARK occupies 400 acres on the bluffs of the Mississippi River. A statue of Samuel Clemens overlooks the river at Inspiration Point. Picnic facilities are available. Daily 6 a.m.-10 p.m. Free. Phone (573) 221-0154.

ROCKCLIFFE MANSION is at 1000 Bird St. Considered one of the finest river estates in the country, the 30-room 1898 mansion has been restored to preserve its *art nouveau* decor. Daily 9-4, Memorial Day-Labor Day; 10-3, rest of year. Closed Jan. 1, Easter, Thanksgiving and Dec. 25. Admission $12.50; senior citizens and ages 5-11, $7.50. Phone (573) 221-4140.

SAWYER'S CREEK FUN PARK is on SR 79S. This amusement park features bumper boats, a shooting gallery, miniature golf and other games. Food is available. Allow 1 hour minimum. Daily 10-dusk, Apr.-Sept. Park free. Rides and activities are priced individually. Phone (573) 221-8221.

TOM AND HUCK MONUMENT is at the foot of Cardiff Hill. In Twain's writings the hill was called Holliday Hill, the rendezvous of Tom Sawyer and his playmates. Life-size figures of Tom Sawyer and Huck Finn, sculpted in 1926, stand on the spot.

SAVE **TWAINLAND EXPRESS SIGHTSEEING TOURS** departs from 400 N. 3rd St. Narrated 1-hour excursions travel through historic Hannibal. Tours are offered daily 10-2:30, June-Aug.; Sat.-Sun. 10-2:30 in May and Sept.-Oct. Fare $8.25; over 55, $7.75; ages 5-16, $5.50. Phone (573) 221-5593 or (800) 786-5193.

HERMANN (C-4) pop. 2,674, elev. 515'

Dissatisfied with life in Philadelphia and intent on preserving their culture, German immigrants moved to Hermann in 1836. Except during Prohibition, Hermann has been a winemaking town. Along with wineries, local industries include metalworking, plastics and shoe factories.

A legacy of fine craftsmanship is remembered at the Deutsche Schule, held in the German School of Arts and Crafts at 4th and Schiller streets, where such artisans as a basket maker, leather craftsman, potter, quilter and weaver can be seen at work. Other craft shops as well as a number of antique shops are located in town. Traditional German festivals are held in May and October.

The Deutschheim State Historic Site, 109 W. 2nd St., includes the Pommer-Gentner House and the Strehly House, both fine examples of Hermann's German heritage. Tours are available daily; phone (573) 486-2200.

Hermann Area Chamber of Commerce: 207A Schiller St., Hermann, MO 65041; phone (573) 486-2313.

HISTORIC HERMANN MUSEUM is at 4th and Schiller sts. The museum, in the 1871 German School Building, has displays about steamboats and river history and exhibits late 19th-century furniture, early Hermann memorabilia and a piece of the Berlin wall. Allow 30 minutes minimum. Tues.-Sat. 10-4, Sun. noon-4, Apr.-Oct. Admission $2; ages 6-12, $1. Phone (573) 486-2017.

WINERIES

• **Hermannhof Winery**, 330 E. 1st St., 2.5 blks. e. of the Mississippi River Bridge on SR 100. Mon.-Sat. 10-5, Sun. 11-5; closed holidays. Phone (573) 486-5959.

• **Stone Hill Winery**, 1110 Stone Hill Hwy., .2 mi. s.w. of jct. SRs 19 and 100. Mon.-Sat. 8:30-dusk, Sun. 10-6; closed Jan. 1, Thanksgiving and Dec. 25. Guided tour $1.50; ages 6-12, 50c. Phone (800) 909-9463.

HIGGINSVILLE (C-2) pop. 4,682, elev. 835'

CONFEDERATE MEMORIAL STATE HISTORIC SITE is 1 mi. n.w. at jct. SRs 13 and 20. This 108-acre park contains a cemetery and monuments commemorating Confederate dead. Picnic facilities and a fishing lake are available. Daily dawn-dusk. Free. Phone (660) 584-2853.

HOGAN (E-5) elev. 853'

Hogan lies at the foot of Taum Sauk Mountain, the highest peak in the state. According to American Indian lore the mountain's rugged face is attributed to the unhappiness of Mina Sauk, daughter of Taum Sauk, chief of the Piankishaws.

Having witnessed her new Osage husband thrown off the mountain in punishment for their improper marriage, the maiden leaped off the peak. The spot where she landed is considered the origin of Mina Sauk Falls, with waters cascading nearly 200 feet over granite ledges. The falls are visible from a path that is halfway up the peak's summit.

IMPERIAL (D-5) pop. 4,373

MASTODON STATE HISTORIC SITE is off I-55 exit 186 at 150 Museum Dr. The Kimmswick Bone Bed, an area rich in Pleistocene fossils and bones, is preserved at the site. Discovered in the early 19th century, this fossil bed yielded more than 60 mastodon skeletons. The visitor center recounts the history of the bone bed through a slide show and relics found on the site. Several trails cross the park.

Grounds open daily 8-dusk. Visitor center Mon.-Sat. 9-4:30, Sun. noon-4:30, Mar.-Nov.; Mon. and Thurs.-Sat. 11-4, Sun. noon-4, rest of year. Closed Jan. 1, Easter, Thanksgiving and Dec. 25. Admission $2.50, under 15 free. Phone (636) 464-2976.

INDEPENDENCE—*see Kansas City p. 178.*

IRONTON (D-5) pop. 1,471, elev. 920'

Ironton, in the picturesque Arcadia Valley of the Ozark Mountain region, was once the headquarters of Gen. Ulysses S. Grant. St. Paul's Episcopal Church, 106 N. Knob St., epitomizes 1871 neo-Gothic architecture in Missouri. Lake Killarney is 3.5 miles east of town on SR 72; to the southwest is Taum Sauk Mountain.

FORT DAVIDSON STATE HISTORIC SITE is n. on SR 21 and e. on CR V. A Union post on this site near Pilot Knob was defended by 1,450 men under Brig. Gen. Thomas Ewing Jr. when it was attacked Sept. 26-27, 1864, by Maj. Gen. Sterling Price and 12,000 Confederate troops. The siege on the earthen fort cost Price more than 1,000 men and ended his march on St. Louis. A visitor center features exhibits and a diorama of the Battle of Pilot Knob.

Visitor center open Mon.-Sat. 10-4, Sun. 11-5. Free. Phone (573) 546-3454.

SILVER MINE DAM is 3.5 mi. s. of SR 72 on CR D to FR 2510, on the St. Francis River in Mark Twain National Forest. At the dam site the river flows between two sheer walls of granite, the remains of the stone dam. The riverbed is strewn with huge boulders. A hiking trail leads to an old silver mine. Camping is permitted April through October, and picnic facilities are available. Daily 24 hours. Parking $2; a fee is charged for camping. Phone (573) 783-7225.

JEFFERSON CITY (C-4) pop. 39,636

The first building denoting Missouri's capital city, completed in 1826, was destroyed by fire in 1837; a new one begun the same year burned after it was

struck by lightning in 1911. The present structure was built in 1918. The Governor's Residence was built in 1871 on the site of the original Capitol. Guided tours of the residence can be arranged through the governor's office; phone (573) 751-4141.

Jefferson Landing State Historic Site, on the river at the end of Jefferson Street, preserves three buildings that were the center of Jefferson City's 19th-century river trade: The 1839 Lohman Building, the 1854 Christopher Maus House and the 1855 Union Hotel. A visitor center in the Lohman Building offers a small museum and an audiovisual presentation about the history of the landing and Jefferson City.

Also of interest is the Safety Education Center and Law Enforcement Museum at the Missouri State Highway Patrol, 1510 E. Elm St. Exhibits include law enforcement antiques and five completely equipped patrol cars dating from 1931 to the present. Phone (573) 526-6149 Mon.-Fri. 8-5.

Stretching more than 200 miles from St. Charles to beyond Sedalia, Katy Trail State Park follows the former route of the Missouri-Kansas-Texas Railroad. Running parallel to the Missouri River, the trail takes hikers and bicyclists through open fields, forests and wetlands and past towering bluffs, and winds through such historic towns as Augusta, Boonville, Columbia, Defiance, Franklin and Marthasville as well as St. Charles and Jefferson City. For further information contact the Department of Natural Resources, P.O. Box 176, Jefferson City, MO 65102-0176; phone (573) 751-2479 or (800) 334-6946.

Jefferson City Convention & Visitors Bureau: 213 Adams St., P.O. Box 2227, Jefferson City, MO 65102-2227; phone (573) 632-2820 or (800) 769-4183.

Self-guiding tours: Visitor guides and maps describing Jefferson City's historic attractions are available at the Jefferson City Convention & Visitors Bureau Mon.-Fri. 8-5.

MISSOURI STATE CAPITOL is at 201 W. Capitol Ave. Built of Carthage stone, the building contains paintings by Thomas Hart Benton, Frank Brangwyn, N.C. Wyeth and other artists who have captured the state's legends, history and landscapes. The State Museum has exhibits interpreting Missouri's natural and cultural heritage on display in the History and Resources halls. Daily 8-5. Tours are given Mon.-Sat. on the hour 8-11 and 1-4, Sun. at 10, 11, 2 and 3; closed Jan. 1, Easter, Thanksgiving and Dec. 25. Free. Phone (573) 751-4127.

MISSOURI VETERINARY MUSEUM is at 2500 Country Club Dr. The museum contains more than 2,500 items and medical instruments relating to the veterinary profession—some extremely rare and many more than 100 years old. Videotapes about pet care and diseases can be viewed. Allow 30 minutes minimum. Mon.-Fri. 9-4, Sat. by appointment. Donations. Phone (573) 636-8737.

RUNGE CONSERVATION NATURE CENTER is .5 mi. n. of jct. US 50 and US 63 on SR 179. Exhibits and nature trails depict varied Missouri habitats, including wetlands, rivers, farms, prairies, glades, forests and caves. A 2,400-gallon aquarium holds indigenous fish. Allow 1 hour minimum. Mon.-Sat. 8-5, Sun. noon-5; closed Jan. 1, Thanksgiving and Dec. 25. Free. Phone (573) 526-5544.

JOPLIN (E-1) pop. 45,504, elev. 1,002'

Following the Civil War, mining companies that had established smelters along the Joplin Creek Valley engaged in fierce rivalry, splitting the town into two factions controlled by competing companies. The valley endured a reign of terror until the state general assembly came to the rescue in 1873 and reincorporated the two towns as the city of Joplin.

Once peace was established in Joplin, the railroad arrived and stimulated development of the zinc industry. Small plots produced great fortunes in zinc, which soon overtook lead production. Joplin's boom stabilized as smelters moved to new deposits outside town, and the more sedate industry of buying and selling ore developed. A railroad center by 1900, the city consequently attracted a number of industrial and wholesale companies.

Joplin is the home of Missouri Southern State College, which offers tours of its 310-acre campus. Noteworthy is a 2,500-piece collection of art reference material, focused on English architecture and furniture of the 16th and 17th centuries, in the Post Memorial Art Reference Library at 300 Main St.; phone (417) 782-7678.

Joplin Area Chamber of Commerce: 320 E. Fourth St., Joplin, MO 64802-1178; phone (417) 624-4150.

JOPLIN MUNICIPAL BUILDING is at 303 E. Third St. The last mural by Thomas Hart Benton, "Joplin at the Turn of the Century," graces the lobby. Mon.-Fri. 8-5. Free. Phone (417) 624-0820.

JOPLIN MUSEUM COMPLEX is in Schifferdecker Park at Seventh St. and Schifferdecker Ave. The history of Joplin and its mining past are the focus of two museums. Tues.-Sat. 10-5 (also Tues. 5-7), Sun. 2-5; closed holidays. Admission $2, under 5 free; free to all Tues. and Fri. Phone (417) 623-1180.

Dorothea Hoover Historical Museum on the park grounds features a miniature animated circus, antique dolls, an 18th-century tavern, photographs and other displays recalling the Joplin of the 1870s. Phone (417) 623-1180.

Tri-State Mineral Museum on the park grounds displays local minerals and scale models of lead-mining apparatus. Antique mining equipment also is exhibited. Phone (417) 623-1180.

When planning your next trip, make it a point to visit aaa.com

Get the BEST price on aaa.com

Start with our #1 rated aaa.com TripTik®. It's more than just lefts and rights; it's your link to the best restaurants, attractions and destinations. And you get the lowest prices at AAA Approved and Diamond rated hotels.

There's more, it's the only travel Web site backed by more than 1,000 AAA offices throughout the USA and Canada, with dedicated travel professionals ready to help with any of your travel needs.

Always Available,
Always AAA.

aaa.com

Kansas City

City Population: 441,545   **Elevation:** 1,005 ft.

Editor's Picks:

Arabia Steamboat Museum.......*(see p. 169)*

The Nelson-Atkins Museum
 of Art ....*(see p. 172)*

Truman Presidential Museum
 & Library...........................*(see p. 179)*

© Richard Cummins / SuperStock

Although it ranks first in the nation as a farm distribution center and hard wheat market, Kansas City is no prairie cow town. With a horizon punctuated by skyscrapers, it seems a mirage in a patchwork landscape of farms and pastures. An exemplary model of urban planning, the city has been carefully shaped into one of the nation's most progressive.

As the heart of America, Kansas City is not confined by state boundaries: Kansas City, Kan., is divided from Kansas City, Mo., merely by a street named State Line Road. Although the larger Kansas City lies in Missouri, its metropolitan core spreads into seven counties in both Missouri and Kansas. The two politically separate cities, which form the Greater Kansas City area, meld into one economic complex.

A trading post established by François Chouteau on the bluffs of the Missouri River in 1821 comprised the initial settlement. The post grew as it accommodated an increasing flow of overland trade and steamboat activity. During the great westward migration, the town, known then as Westport Landing, was a terminus and outfitting point for the Santa Fe and Oregon trails as well as for the California gold rush.

An economic slump ensued when westward movement was halted in the 1850s by the bloody struggle between abolitionists and advocates of slavery for control of the territory of Kansas. Recovery was assured by 1869 when the Hannibal and St. Joseph Railroad linked Kansas City with Chicago and other eastern markets. Within the next decade the city became the nation's primary cattle trading center, and, soon after, a leading grain market.

Modern Kansas City accommodates nearly 200 of the nation's largest industrial firms, including auto assembly, steel and metal fabrication and food processing plants. Commercial expansion has literally penetrated the core of the city. One of the country's foreign trade zones is found 140 feet underground in limestone caverns: Amid a 6-mile network of roads and railroad tracks, foreign goods are stored, free of import duty, by manufacturers and merchants from all over the world.

An ongoing campaign for civic improvement has left an architectural legacy that prompted French author André Maurois to describe Kansas City as "one of the loveliest cities on Earth." In the 1920s J.C. Nichols imported millions of dollars' worth of statues, many centuries old, to line Kansas City's 140 miles of boulevards and parkways. He also developed Country Club Plaza, a tile-roofed, Moorish-style complex that houses the nation's first shopping center amid Italian fountains and lush greenery.

Union Station, a city icon and the country's second-largest train station, regained its 1914 elegance by way of a massive $250 million restoration. Half of all GIs deployed in World War II passed through the soaring arches of the Grand Hall; today an interactive science museum, theaters and restaurants attract a new generation of visitors.

In testimony to an ambitious building program are the architecturally revolutionary Kansas City International Airport and the Harry S. Truman Sports

Getting There — *starting on p. 165*

Getting Around — *starting on p. 165*

What To See — *starting on p. 169*

What To Do — *starting on p. 175*

Where To Stay — *starting on p. 452*

Where To Dine — *starting on p. 454*

Complex, with its twin stadiums for professional baseball and football. Crown Center, an ultramodern city within a city near the heart of downtown, is one of the largest private urban renewal projects in the country. Developed by Hallmark Cards Inc., the 85-acre, $400 million facility encompasses a hotel as well as a shopping, dining and entertainment complex.

The architectural distinction of Kansas City is not limited to public landmarks: Loose Memorial Park and its adjoining residential districts represent Kansas City's older community. Across the border, modern architecture graces the suburb of Mission Hills, Kan.

A constant stream of new ideas emanates from the city's major institutions of higher education—the University of Missouri-Kansas City and Rockhurst College. If early civic leaders were able to see present-day Kansas City, they would be relieved that their chosen name of Possum Trot did not stick. As the song from Rodgers and Hammerstein's "Oklahoma" goes, "Ev'rythin's up to date in Kansas City."

Getting There

By Car

From the north, Kansas City is approached by two major controlled-access highways, I-35 and I-29, which merge into I-29/35, or US 71, and cross the Missouri River before leading into the downtown area via 13th Street. Running into Kansas City, Kan., from the south, I-35 provides direct controlled access to downtown via Washington Avenue and 12th Street.

On the Missouri side the fastest southern approach is via US 71, which connects with the I-435

Crown Center / Missouri Division of Tourism

bypass. The bypass circles the city and can be taken north to I-70. Beginning in St. Louis, I-70 bisects the state and enters Kansas City via the 13th Street exit. I-70 also is the controlled-access route from the west to downtown.

Getting Around

Street System

The Greater Kansas City area follows a basic grid pattern, slightly complicated by the Kansas and Missouri rivers. North Kansas City and Kansas City, Mo., are separated by the Missouri River, from which cross streets are numbered in ascending order well into the suburbs. The reference point for the east-west block designation in downtown Kansas City, Mo., is Main Street. Conversely, numbered streets in Kansas City, Kan., run on a north-south axis, paralleling the abrupt S-curve of the Missouri River.

State Line Road separates the Missouri and Kansas sides of the city. The street systems of both are

Destination Kansas City

Kansas City wears its progress well. Once a river-bend trading post, the city evolved into a sizable commercial center that nevertheless has kept its small-town appeal intact.

Museums and historic districts celebrate varied cultural influences. A restored village stays in touch with simpler times. And a racing roller coaster fills the bill for plain old-fashioned fun.

Missouri Division of Tourism

Kansas City Zoo. A pachyderm whiles away the afternoon in the Okavango Elephant Sanctuary, one of several animal habitats at the Kansas City Zoo. (See listing page 172)

© Richard Cummins / Lonely Planet Images

Kansas City Museum.
All things Kansas City are exhibited at this namesake museum, which emphasizes the city's role in the nation's great 19th-century westward expansion and gives visitors a glimpse of life on the Great Plains. (See listing page 170)

Arabia Steamboat Museum, Kansas City. Two hundred tons of cargo sank along with the steamboat *Arabia* in 1856, only to be recovered from the Missouri River more than 130 years later and exhibited at this fascinating museum. (See listing page 169)

© John Elk III / Lonely Planet Images

© Andre Jenny

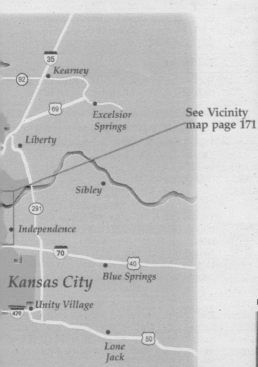

35
Kearney

92

69
Excelsior
Springs

Liberty

Sibley

291

Independence

70

40

Kansas City   Blue Springs

Unity Village

470

Lone
Jack

50

See Vicinity
map page 171

The Nelson-Atkins Museum of Art, Kansas City. An upside-down shuttlecock is one of the more whimsical installations in the sculpture garden on the grounds of Kansas City's premier art museum. (See listing page 172)

Missouri Division of Tourism

Negro Leagues Baseball Museum, Kansas City. A future champion practices his delivery. This museum remembers a baseball era before Jackie Robinson became the first African American signed by the major leagues. (See listing page 171)

The Informed Traveler

Sales Tax: The sales tax rate in the city of Kansas City is 7.55 percent. The city's lodging tax is 11.98 percent and there is a rental car tax of $4 per day.

WHOM TO CALL

Emergency: 911

Police (non-emergency): (816) 234-5000

Time: (913) 831-4141

Temperature: (816) 540-6021

Hospitals: Baptist-Lutheran Medical Center, (816) 276-7000; Saint Joseph Health Center, (816) 942-4400; Saint Luke's Hospital, (816) 932-2000; Saint Luke's Northland (816) 891-6000; Truman Medical Center-Hospital Hill, (816) 404-1000.

WHERE TO LOOK

Newspapers

The major daily newspaper in Kansas City is the *Kansas City Star.*

Radio

Kansas City radio station KCMO (810 AM) is an all news/weather station; KCUR (89.3 FM) is a member of National Public Radio.

Visitor Information

Convention and Visitors Bureau of Greater Kansas City: 1100 Main St., Suite 2550, Kansas City, MO 64105; phone (816) 221-5242 or (800) 767-7700.

In City Center Square, the Convention and Visitors Bureau of Greater Kansas City distributes free brochures Mon.-Fri. 8:30-5; closed Jan. 1, Memorial Day, July 4, Labor Day, Thanksgiving, day after Thanksgiving and Dec. 25. The bureau also operates an information booth in the Crown Center Mall at 2450 Grand Blvd.

Missouri Information Center: 4010 Blue Ridge Cut-Off, Kansas City, MO 64133; phone (816) 889-3330.

The center is off I-70 and Blue Ridge Cut-Off at the Harry S. Truman Sports Complex; it is open daily 9-5.

TRANSPORTATION

Air Travel

Kansas City International Airport (KCI) is 17 miles northwest of downtown. Taxi fare into the city is about $45. Many larger hotels offer airport limousine service.

Rental Cars

Hertz, at the airport, offers discounts to AAA members; phone (816) 243-5765 or (800) 654-3080.

Rail Service

The Amtrak station, (816) 421-3622 or (800) 872-7245, is at 23rd and Main streets.

Buses

Greyhound Lines Inc., (800) 231-2222, is at 1101 Troost St. Other major carriers to Kansas City are Great Southern, Illini-Swallow, Jefferson Lines, Sunnyland and Gulf Transport.

Taxis

Yellow Cab is the city's major taxi service; phone (816) 471-5000. Cabs are deregulated, so fares vary widely. Rates are posted on each cab; you are not required to take the first cab in a line. Up to five people can share a ride for a single fare.

Public Transport

The Metro bus system serves all Greater Kansas City counties except Johnson. The exact-change fare minimum is $1.25 ($3 for an all-day pass) and varies by distance; phone (816) 221-0660.

Route maps are available Mon.-Fri. 8:30-5 from the Convention and Visitors Bureau of Greater Kansas City.

peculiar to their own states, although several streets continue across the border unchanged. The main east-west artery over the Kansas River connecting the twin cities is I-70, which leads into US 24/40, the main route through downtown Kansas City, Kan.

I-70 also intersects other major thoroughfares that travel through and around town. The Southwest Trafficway provides rapid access into the central part of Kansas City, Mo.

Generally downtown speed limits are 25 mph or as posted. Right turns on red are permitted unless otherwise posted. Avoid rush hours, from about 6:30 to 8:30 a.m. and 3:30 to 6 p.m.

Parking

On-street parking is controlled by meters, but finding an empty space in the right spot can be difficult. Numerous commercial lots and garages are concentrated around Central and Grand avenues, between 9th and 14th streets, and at the southern edge of town. Rates average 90c per half-hour, with a maximum of $5.

Parking also is available for $8 around the Harry S. Truman Sports Complex and for $6-$15 at Kemper Arena. Several major downtown hotels are connected to the Kansas City Convention Center by an underground concourse.

What To See

AIRLINE HISTORY MUSEUM is at 201 N.W. Lou Holland Dr. The museum is housed inside the 40,000-square-foot Hangar 9, which once held aviation operations for major airlines. Of particular interest is a 1959 Lockheed Super Constellation, or "Connie," which is easily recognized by its triple tail and tip tanks on the wings. Other highlights are artifacts, photographs, uniforms and navigation instruments. Guided tours are available. Allow 1 hour minimum. Mon.-Sat. 10-4, Sun. noon-4; closed Jan. 1, Thanksgiving and Dec. 25. Admission $7; over 65, $6; ages 6-13, $3. AX, DS, MC, VI. Phone (816) 421-3401 or (800) 513-9484.

AMERICAN ROYAL MUSEUM & VISITORS CENTER is 1 mi. w. from jct. 12th St. and Broadway, then .5 mi. s. on Genesee St. to 1701 American Royal Ct. Interactive displays relate to the agriculture and livestock industries. The museum offers many hands-on exhibits for children and a film about the history of Kansas City.

Food is available. Allow 1 hour minimum. Tues.-Fri. 10-4, Sat.-Sun. by appointment; closed major holidays. Admission $3; over 54, $2.50; ages 3-12, $2. AX, DS, MC, VI. Phone (816) 221-9800.

ARABIA STEAMBOAT MUSEUM is at 400 Grand Ave. in the River Market area. The *Arabia* sank in the Missouri River in 1856 with a 200-ton cargo. This museum displays a vast collection of frontier supplies and personal belongings recovered from the steamboat in 1989, including clothing and shoes, medicines, guns, bottled fruits and vegetables, jewelry and perfume. The 6-ton stern and a paddlewheel are preserved

18th and Vine Historic District / Missouri Division of Tourism

with a full-size reproduction of the main deck. Guided tours include a theater presentation describing the excavation effort, and visitors may view a working preservation lab.

Food is available. Allow 1 hour, 30 minutes minimum. Mon.-Sat. 10-5:30, Sun. noon-5; closed Jan. 1, Easter, Thanksgiving and Dec. 24-25. Tours depart every 30 minutes. Last admission is 1 hour, 30 minutes before closing. Admission $12.50; over 60, $11.50; ages 4-12, $4.75. MC, VI. Phone (816) 471-1856. *See color ad.*

HALLMARK VISITORS CENTER is on 25th St. off Pershing in the Crown Center Complex. Twelve major exhibits relate the Hallmark story and the steps involved in the production of Hallmark products. Some exhibits feature Hallmark employees at work. Tues.-Fri. 9-5, Sat. 9:30-4:30; closed early to mid-Jan., Thanksgiving and Dec. 25. Free. Phone (816) 274-5672.

HARLEY-DAVIDSON ASSEMBLY PLANT AND VISITORS CENTER is at 11401 N. Congress. This is one of two Harley-Davidson motorcycle final assembly plants in the United States. The tour includes a videotape presentation and a chance to see the actual production line where the Sportster and V-Rod models are assembled. Audio headsets and safety glasses are provided.

Tour participants must wear completely enclosed shoes. Cameras are permitted in the tour center, but not on the plant tour. Allow 1 hour minimum. Center open Mon.-Fri. 8-3; closed holidays and during model change periods. One-hour guided tours are given Mon.-Fri. 8-1. Free. A valid photo ID is required for entry; under 12 are not permitted on the plant tour. Reservations are recommended. Phone (816) 270-8488 or (877) 883-1450.

JOHN WORNALL HOUSE MUSEUM is at 61st Terr. and Wornall Rd. This restored 1858 Greek Revival plantation house is furnished in period. A formal herb garden is on the grounds. Tues.-Sat. 10-4, Sun. 1-4; closed major holidays. Admission $4; ages 5-12, $3. Phone (816) 444-1858.

KANSAS CITY MUSEUM is at 3218 Gladstone Blvd. in Kessler Park. Artifacts and displays relate to the development of life on the plains and Kansas City's role in the country's westward expansion. Exhibits depicting rivers, lands, Osage Indians, explorers, trappers and a 1910 corner drugstore with a working soda fountain are featured in Corinthian Hall, a 50-room mansion. A natural history hall and a planetarium also are part of the complex.

Food is available. Allow 1 hour minimum. Tues.-Sat. 9:30-4:30, Sun. noon-4:30; closed Jan. 1, Thanksgiving and Dec. 25. Museum admission $2.50; over 65 and ages 3-17, $2. Planetarium admission $4, under 5 free. Phone (816) 483-8300.

KEMPER MUSEUM OF CONTEMPORARY ART is just e. of 45th and Main sts. at 4420 Warwick Blvd. Georgia O'Keeffe, Robert Mapplethorpe and William Wegman are among the artists represented in a permanent collection of diverse, modern works. Food is available. Allow 1 hour minimum. Tues.-Sat. 10-4 (also Fri.-Sat. 4-9), Sun. 11-5; closed major holidays. Free. Phone (816) 561-3737 or (816) 753-5784.

LINDA HALL LIBRARY adjoins the University of Missouri-Kansas City campus on Rockhill Rd. Devoted exclusively to science and technology, it is a repository for all American, British and Canadian atomic energy publications and other technical journals, some dating from the 17th century. An

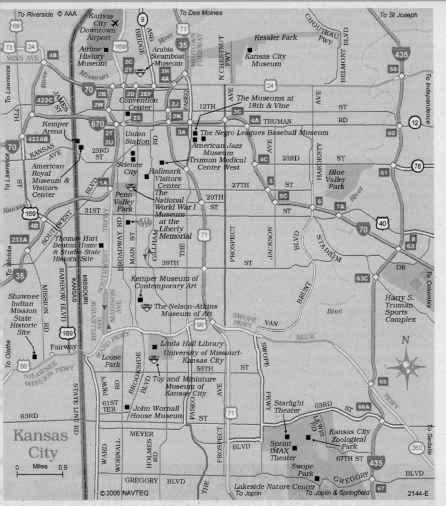

enormous ornamental Russian bowl of carved malachite graces the main floor. Mon.-Fri. 9-5 (also Mon. 5-8:30), Sat. 10-4. Free. Phone (816) 363-4600.

THE MUSEUMS AT 18TH AND VINE are .3 mi. s. off I-70 Paseo exit, then e. to 1616 E. 18th St. This complex, in the heart of one of the country's most celebrated jazz and blues districts, encompasses the American Jazz Museum and the Negro Leagues Baseball Museum. The Horace M. Peterson III Visitor Center offers a brief videotape celebrating the African-American community that thrived at 18th and Vine for more than 40 years.

Museums and visitor center open Tues.-Sat. 9-6, Sun. noon-6; closed holidays. Visitor center free. Phone (816) 474-8463.

American Jazz Museum, 1616 E. 18th St., recalls jazz greats Louis Armstrong, Duke Ellington, Ella Fitzgerald, Charlie Parker and others through listening stations, photographs, videos and memorabilia. Allow 1 hour minimum. Admission $6; ages 5-11, $2.50. Combination ticket with the Negro Leagues Baseball Museum $8; ages 5-11, $4. AX, DS, MC, VI. Phone (816) 474-8463.

Negro Leagues Baseball Museum, 1616 E. 18th St., recounts the formation and history of the Negro Baseball League prior to 1945, the year Jackie Robinson was signed by the Brooklyn Dodgers. Displays include pennants, autographed baseballs, photographs, biographies and an 8-minute videotape about the league narrated by former CNN anchorman Bernard Shaw. Allow 30 minutes minimum. Admission $6; ages 5-11, $2.50. Combination ticket with the American Jazz Museum $8; ages 5-11, $4. AX, DS, MC, VI. Phone (816) 221-1920 or (816) 474-8463.

THE NATIONAL WORLD WAR ONE MU-SEUM AT THE LIBERTY MEMORIAL is at Pershing and Main sts., just s. of downtown in Penn Valley Park. Dedicated to collecting, preserving and interpreting the history of and artifacts associated with the first World War, this complex has undergone a significant expansion. The museum has outstanding displays and interactive exhibits—everything from posters, photographs, uniforms, archival films and vintage audio broadcasts to airplanes, artillery, weaponry, cannons, caissons, a 1917 model Harley-Davidson army motorcycle and a simulated World War I trench.

Exhibit Hall contains a new exhibit, "War Art." Chronological displays and firsthand accounts from diaries trace the history of the war from its beginning to the armistice of Nov. 11, 1918. Visitors also can take an elevator to an open-air observation deck at the top of the 217-foot-tall memorial tower, which has a frieze on one wall. Several fountains grace the landscaped grounds.

Picnicking is permitted. Allow 1 hour minimum. Tues.-Sun. 10-5; closed major holidays except Memorial Day, July 4, Labor Day and Veterans Day. Last admission is 45 minutes before closing. Museum $8; over 65, $7; ages 6-11, $3. Tower $4; ages 6-11, $3. Combination ticket for museum and tower $10; ages 6-11, $5. Active duty military in uniform or with ID free; museum free to all Memorial Day and Veterans Day. AX, CB, DC, DS, MC, VI. Phone (816) 784-1918. *See color ad.*

THE NELSON-ATKINS MUSEUM OF ART is 4.5 mi. s. on US 56 at 45th and Oak sts. The museum contains more than 20,000 items, including an outstanding Asian art collection. The building's 58 galleries and 11 period rooms contain such collections as Egyptian, Greek and Roman sculpture; paintings by American artists and European masters; and a display of English pottery. Works by modern artists are displayed in the 17-acre Kansas City Sculpture Park, said to hold the country's largest collection of monumental bronzes by English sculptor Henry Moore.

Food is available. Tues.-Fri. 10-4 (also Fri. 4-9), Sat. 10-5, Sun. noon-5; closed holidays. Guided tours are given Tues.-Sat. at 11 and 1, Sun. at 1:30 and 2:30. Free. Garage parking $3. Phone (816) 751-1278.

OCEANS OF FUN—*see Worlds of Fun p. 173.*

PENN VALLEY PARK is at 31st and Main sts. Designer George E. Kessler transformed the 176-acre Penn Valley site from a slum area known as Vinegar Hill into this attractive retreat, the prototype for the city's park system. The park contains the American Indian memorial "The Scout," the statue "Pioneer Mother," a lake and scenic drives. Daily dawn-dusk. Free. Phone (816) 784-5030.

SWOPE PARK is s.e. of downtown at Meyer Blvd. and Swope Pkwy. This 1,772-acre park contains golf courses, tennis courts, picnic grounds and a swimming pool. A lagoon offers fishing, boating and ice skating.

The park's Lakeside Nature Center houses native Missouri wildlife, has educational displays and offers nature trails. The center's staff rehabilitates injured wildlife. Swope Park open daily 24 hours. Lakeside Nature Center open Tues.-Sat. 9-5, Sun. noon-4. Free. Phone (816) 513-8960.

Kansas City Zoological Park is at 6700 Zoo Dr. This 200-acre zoo exhibits animals in the Great Ape House, the Tropical Habitat Building and the Okavango Elephant Sanctuary. Africa, Australian Outback, Great Cat Walk, Wolf Pack Woods, Gibbon

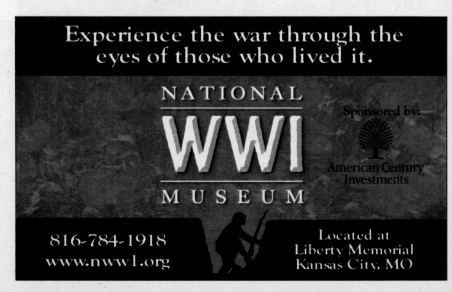

sland, a dairy barn and a children's petting zoo are among the other exhibits. A narrow-gauge railroad and tram carry visitors to major points of interest.

Allow a full day. Daily 9:30-5, Mar.-Oct.; 10-4, rest of year. Closed Jan. 1, Thanksgiving and Dec. 25. Admission $8.50; over 55, $7.50; ages 3-11, $5.50; $5 for all Tues. AX, DS, MC, VI. Phone 816) 513-5700. *See color ad.*

THOMAS HART BENTON HOME & STUDIO STATE HISTORIC SITE is at 3616 Belleview Ave. Missouri's noted 20th-century artist lived here from 1939 until his death in 1975. The Victorian-style home and carriage house studio contain many of Benton's belongings. Allow 30 minutes minimum. Mon.-Sat. 10-4, Sun. noon-5, Apr. 15-Oct. 31; Mon.-Sat. 10-4, Sun. 11-4, rest of year. Closed Jan. 1, Thanksgiving and Dec. 25. Admission $2.50; ages 6-12, $1.50. Phone (816) 931-5722.

TOY AND MINIATURE MUSEUM OF KANSAS CITY is at 5235 Oak St. An extensive collection of antique toys, dolls and trains covers 33,000 square feet and 33 rooms. More than 80 furnished dollhouses—including modern exact-to-scale miniatures made by master crafts-men—are displayed. Special rooms focus on particular types of toys, such as teaching kitchens and farm toys. Allow 1 hour minimum. Wed.-Sat. 10-4, Sun. 1-4; closed major holidays and the first 2 weeks of Sept. Admission $6; senior citizens and students with ID $5; ages 5-12, $4. Phone (816) 333-2055.

UNION STATION is at 30 W. Pershing Rd. More than 79,000 trains passed through this terminal at its peak in 1917, and half of all GIs deployed in World War II traveled under its great clock. Restored in 1999, the station is home to a science museum, theaters and restaurants. The Grand Hall features 95-foot ceilings with ornate plaster ornaments. The Theater District includes the five-story Extreme Screen, live performances on City Stage, and City Dome planetarium and laser-light shows.

Audio tours are available. Union Station open daily 6 a.m.-midnight. Phone for performance schedules. Station free. Extreme Screen movies $5.95. AX, DS, MC, VI. Phone (816) 460-2222.

Science City is in Union Station. A sports stadium, medical center, TV station and construction site are among the more than 50 hands-on neighborhoods where visitors can produce a newscast, dig for fossils and explore the city's underground water and power systems. Tues.-Sat. 10-6, Sun. noon-6, Memorial Day-Labor Day; Tues.-Sat. 10-5, Sun. noon-5, rest of year. Closed Thanksgiving and Dec. 25. Museum admission $8.95; combination ticket good for all venues $13.95. AX, DS, MC, VI. Phone (816) 460-2020.

SAVE **WORLDS OF FUN** is 13.5 mi. n.e. at I-435 exit 54 (Parvin Rd.). This 235-acre entertainment complex combines an amusement park and a tropical water park. Worlds of Fun offers 175 acres of rides, shows and attractions in five internationally themed areas. Featured are MAMBA, one of the tallest, longest and fastest coasters in the world; Timber Wolf, a world-class wooden coaster; and ThunderHawk, a tumble and spin ride.

Park opens daily at 10, mid-May to late Aug. and Labor Day weekend; Sat.-Sun. at 10, early Apr. to mid-May and day after Labor Day weekend-late Oct. Closing times vary. Admission $36.95; over 61, $9.95; over age 2 and under 48 inches tall, $9.95. Twilight rate (Fri. after 6 p.m., Sat. after 4 p.m. and Sun. after 3 p.m.) $19.95. Rates may vary; phone ahead. Combination tickets with Oceans of Fun are available. Parking $9. AX, DS, MC, VI. Phone (816) 454-4545. *See color ad p. 174.*

Oceans of Fun is off I-435 exit 54. This 60-acre tropical-themed water park features the Surf City Wave Pool, a million-gallon pool with 4-foot waves; Hurricane Falls, an eight-story-high family raft ride; and a variety of other water slides. Special areas of the park are designed specifically for children and for adults. Water park opens daily at 10, Memorial Day weekend-late Aug. and Labor Day weekend. Closing time varies. Admission $25.95; over 61, $9.95; over age 2 and under 48 inches tall, $9.95. Admission after 4 p.m. $19.95. Combination tickets with Worlds of Fun are available. Parking $9. AX, DS, MC, VI. Phone (816) 454-4545.

CASINOS

- **Ameristar Casino**, 3200 N. Ameristar Dr. Sun.-Thurs 8 a.m.-5 a.m., Fri.-Sat. 24 hours. Phone (816) 414-7000 or (800) 499-4961.
- **Isle of Capri Casino**, 1800 E. Front St. Sun.-Thurs. 8 a.m.-5 a.m., Fri.-Sat. 24 hours. Phone (816) 855-7777 or (800) 843-4753.

What To Do

Sightseeing

Driving Tours

"Day Tours from Kansas City," a 40-page booklet detailing eight trips within a day's drive, is available to AAA/CAA members free at any AAA service office in Missouri. *See AAA Offices.*

Sports and Recreation

Major league all the way, Kansas City offers a wide range of professional sports. Following their teams with a passionate involvement, Kansas City fans pile into the 118,000-seat Harry S. Truman Sports Complex, with its outstanding stadiums for **baseball** and **football.**

Baseball draws a loyal following April through September to Kauffman Stadium to watch the Kansas City Royals; phone (816) 921-8000. Football is a passion for the die-hard fans of the National Football League's Kansas City Chiefs, who play to capacity crowds in Arrowhead Stadium; phone (816) 920-9400. The Big Eight Conference games draw devoted fans from the universities of Missouri and Kansas.

College **basketball** is popular during the winter months. Major league **soccer's** Kansas City Wizards place their spell over fans at Arrowhead Stadium April through October; phone (816) 920-9300 for schedule and ticket information.

Kansas City's 302 public parks provide opportunities for a variety of recreational pursuits, including **boating, hiking** and **picnicking.** Three parks in particular are known for their natural beauty and developed facilities: Loose Memorial Park, 51st Street and Wornall Road; Swope Park *(see attraction listing p. 172)*, Meyer Boulevard and Swope Parkway; and Fleming Park *(see Recreation Chart and attraction listing p. 178)*, off SR 291 at Blue Springs, in eastern Jackson County.

Opportunities for **golf** are available in Swope Park, which has two of the oldest and most difficult 18-hole courses in the city. The Minor Park Golf Center, Red Bridge and Holmes roads, is a challenging course. Considered by some to be the city's best course, River Oaks is just south of the Kansas City limits at 14204 St. Andrews Dr. in Grandview.

Courses outside Kansas City, Mo., include Chapel Ridge Golf Club, SR 291 and Woods Chapel Road in Lee's Summit; Rockwood Golf Course, 2400 S. Maywood Ave. in Independence; and Shamrock Hills, S. SR 291 in Lee's Summit.

Courses outside Kansas City, Kan., include Overland Park Golf Club, 12501 Quivira Rd. in Overland Park; St. Andrews Golf Club, 11099 W. 135th St. in Overland Park; and Tomahawk Hills, 17501 Midland Dr. in Shawnee.

More than 200 public **tennis** courts are within the Kansas City metropolitan area. Most are free and available on a first-come, first-served basis. The Parks and Recreation Department, (816) 513-7500, will supply locations. Swope Park has courts at the picnic area north of the Starlight Theatre.

The following parks have at least four courts: Concourse, at Anderson and Bellefontaine; King Square, at Swope Parkway and Woodland; Loose Memorial Park, at 52nd Terrace and Summit; Mill Creek Park, at 47th Street and J.C. Nichols Parkway; and Plaza, at 47th and Main streets.

Bicycling is popular on the trails in Swope Park; bicycles can be rented at Shelter House One at the park entrance.

In the winter Kansas City's parks draw visitors for **cross-country skiing.** The lagoon in Loose Memorial Park is a favorite **ice skating** pond, as is the Ice Terrace, the outdoor ice skating rink at Crown Center, 2450 Grand Ave.

Kansas Speedway at I-70 and I-435 draws **motorsports** fans for the NASCAR Winston Cup series, Busch Series racing and additional events; phone (913) 328-7223. **Horse racing** and **dog racing** are offered seasonally at Woodlands, 99th Street and Leavenworth Road off I-435 in Kansas City, Kan.; phone (913) 299-9797.

Note: Policies concerning admittance of children to pari-mutuel betting facilities vary. Phone for information.

DID YOU KNOW

The Kansas City Monarchs were the first baseball team to light the ball field for night games.

Shopping

Ever since pioneers bound for the Santa Fe Trail stopped in Westport to stock their wagon trains, the tradition of shopping in Kansas City has been enthusiastically upheld by its residents. Its identity as an active emporium was permanently secured in 1922 when J.C. Nichols financed the construction of Country Club Plaza, the first totally planned shopping center in the United States.

This extensive Spanish- and Moorish-style complex at 47th Street and J.C. Nichols Parkway has more than 150 shops, restaurants and nightclubs in a 15-block area. National chain stores include FAO Schwarz and Saks Fifth Avenue, and there are specialty retailers as well.

Crown Center, 2450 Grand Ave., is a hotel, shopping, dining and entertainment complex that surrounds the international headquarters of Hallmark Cards, Inc. As the $400 million brainchild of founder Joyce Hall, this 85-acre city within a city includes three levels of specialty shopping, with more than 70 shops and restaurants offering everything from antiques to packaged gourmet foods. Hall's Crown Center is the major department store.

More shops and restaurants can be found along Walnut Street. City Market, the area bounded by 3rd, 6th, Grand and Wyandotte streets, features small shops and areas where farmers sell their produce in much the same way it was done more than a century ago.

Other area shopping malls are Antioch Center, Antioch and Vivion roads; Benjamin Plaza, Bannister and Hillcrest roads; Blue Ridge Mall, 4200 Blue Ridge Blvd.; Independence Center, I-70 and SR 291 in Independence; Indian Springs Marketplace, 4601 State Ave.; Metcalf South Shopping Center, 9635 Metcalf Ave. in Overland Park, Kan.; Metro North Mall, 400 N.W. Barry Rd.; Mission Center Mall, 4801 Johnson Dr. in Mission, Kan.; Oak Park Mall, 11461 W. 95th St. in Overland Park, Kan.; Three Trails Town Center (Bannister Mall), 5600 E. Bannister Rd.; and Ward Parkway, 8600 Ward Pkwy.

Antiques hunters can visit the 45th & State Line Antique, Art & Design Center, an enclave of antique shops 7 blocks west of Country Club Plaza. Lovers of Americana will find shops filled with furniture and accessories.

Shoppers in a nostalgic frame of mind might also wish to visit Westport Square, between Westport Road and Pennsylvania Avenue in the heart of Westport. Many of the old buildings at this former Santa Fe Trail outfitting station have been renovated into shops, galleries, specialty stores, restaurants and bars.

Performing Arts

Kansas City has a rich cultural heritage. The Lyric Opera of Kansas City performs at the Lyric Theater, 11th and Central streets; for information or tickets to its three fall and two spring presentations phone (816) 471-7344. The Kansas City Ballet mounts productions of "The Nutcracker" at the Midland Theater in December, and the Lyric Theater presents performances of the Kansas City Symphony October through May. Phone (816) 931-2232 for ballet schedule information, or (816) 471-0400 for symphony information and tickets.

A tremendous reconstruction effort has turned the once-dilapidated 1912 Gem Theater, 1615 E. 18th St. in the 18th and Vine Historic District, into a center for multicultural arts, entertainment and education programming. Phone (816) 474-6262 or (816) 474-8463 for information about upcoming performances and exhibitions.

The University of Missouri-Kansas City's Conservatory of Music, 4949 Cherry St., draws patrons from within as well as outside the university. Concert series also are sponsored by the Harrington Arts Program at William Jewell College.

In summer Washington Square Park provides a natural setting for the Blue Sunday concert series sponsored by the Parks and Recreation Department; phone (816) 513-7500.

The university-based equity company of the Missouri Repertory Theater stages classic and modern productions in the on-campus Spencer Theater September through June; phone (816) 235-2700. Musical comedy productions, light opera and concerts of all types are on the bill at Swope Park's Starlight Theatre, the nation's second largest outdoor amphitheater. Top stars perform during the mid-June through September season; phone (816) 333-9481.

In late June or early July a work by the Bard of Avon is presented in Southmoreland Park during the Heart of America Shakespeare Festival; phone (816) 531-7728. The Theatre League brings the national touring companies of Broadway musicals to the Music Hall, 301 W. 13th St.; phone (816) 421-7500.

The Folly Theater, W. 12th and Central streets, is a restored turn-of-the-20th-century burlesque house that now presents a variety of entertainment, from children's theater to jazz concerts; phone (816) 842-5500. The Gorilla Theatre, 517 E. 18th St., stages original and avant-garde works as well as classic dramas; phone (816) 510-3372. The Martin City Melodrama and Vaudeville Co., (913) 642-7576, presents performances Thursday through Sunday evenings at 9635 Metcalf Ave. in Overland Park, Kan. The New Theatre Restaurant at 9229 Foster St. in Overland Park, (913) 649-7469, offers evening performances Tuesday through Sunday, and matinees on Sundays.

Other area theaters include the American Heartland Theatre on the third level of the Crown Center, (816) 842-9999; the Coterie Theatre on the center's first level, (816) 474-6552; Comedy City at 300 Charlotte St., (816) 842-2744; the Quality Hill Playhouse at 303 W. 10th St., (816) 421-1700; Theatre for Young America at 30 W. Pershing Rd., (816) 460-2083; the Unicorn Theatre at 3820 Main St., (816) 531-7529; and the Verizon Wireless Amphitheatre at 130th Street and State Avenue in Bonner Springs, Kan., (913) 721-3400.

The events section of the *Kansas City Star* carries current information about the city's performing arts offerings.

Special Events

As winter begins to wane, things heat up in Kansas City with the Home, Flower, Lawn and Garden Show in mid-March and the National Association of Intercollegiate Athletics (NAIA) National Track and Field Competition during late March.

Also in March is the St. Patrick's Day parade, which threads through downtown. The 3-hour parade launches festivities that continue throughout the city well into the night. Around mid-March is the NAIA Basketball Tournament, which includes some of the best men's and women's college basketball teams in the country.

Fiesta in the Heartland is held in early May at the Crown Center, 2450 Grand Blvd. The event commemorates the anniversary of the Battle of Puebla in Mexico. The battle, which occurred in 1862, allowed members of the Mexican government—including president Benito Juárez—to escape capture by the French and eventually free Mexico from French control.

The Crown Center also sponsors free outdoor Summer on the Square activities, including the Kansas City Symphony's Radio Day in May, the Trinity Hospital Hill Run in June and the Noon Tunes on the Square entertainment series on Fridays in July.

Over the July 4th weekend the city pays tribute to its Western roots with the 2-day Jaycee's Pro Rodeo held at Benjamin Ranch, off I-435 at the E. 87th Street exit; phone (816) 761-5055.

In July Kansas City celebrates its musical heritage with the Kansas City Blues and Jazz Festival, recalling the days when 12th and Vine streets were the hangout of celebrated African-American jazz musicians in the 1920s and '30s. The festival's events are held at Liberty Memorial in Penn Valley Park.

The third full weekend of August brings the Ethnic Enrichment Festival to Swope Park, where the world's cultures are celebrated with live music and dance performances, craft exhibitions and a tempting lineup of food booths. Events include Scottish Highland games and the colorful pageantry of the Parade of Nations.

Penn Valley Park is filled with national and regional entertainers during the Spirit Festival, held Labor Day weekend; phone (816) 513-7500. Also in September, Kansas City's Hispanic community commemorates Mexico's independence from Spain with the Fiesta Hispana; phone (816) 452-4712.

Thanksgiving evening marks the Country Club Plaza Christmas lighting ceremony, which illuminates the center's fanciful towers with miles of tiny, colored lightbulbs; phone (816) 753-0100. The day after Thanksgiving, a nearly 100-foot Christmas tree is illuminated during a ceremony at Crown Center Square. The Mayor's Christmas Tree, decorated with more than 900 red and gold ornaments and white lights, stands as the symbol of a citywide charity drive to help people in need during the holidays.

Sports and cultural events occur all year; for details, contact the Convention and Visitors Bureau of Greater Kansas City.

The Kansas City Vicinity

BLUE SPRINGS (C-1) pop. 48,080, elev. 962'

Blue Springs was organized in 1827 near springs used by wagon trains as watering holes. In 1878 the town moved to its present site when the Chicago and Alton Railroad built a station.

Blue Springs Chamber of Commerce: 1000 Main St., Blue Springs, MO 64015; phone (816) 229-8558.

BURR OAK WOODS CONSERVATION NATURE CENTER is 1.2 mi. n. of jct. I-70 and SR 7 exit 20 to 1401 N.W. Park Rd. Nature trails traverse the 1,071-acre nature center, which features natural history exhibits that include a 3,000-gallon aquarium and a wildlife viewing area. Allow 30 minutes minimum. Conservation area open daily 8-8, early Apr.-late Oct.; 8-5, rest of year. Center open Mon.-Sat. 8-5, Sun. noon-5; closed Jan. 1, Thanksgiving and Dec. 25. Free. Phone (816) 228-3766.

FLEMING PARK is at US 40 and Woods Chapel Rd. Recreational activities include hiking, boating and fishing. The 100-acre native hoofed animal enclosure houses bison, elk and whitetail deer. Daily 6 a.m.-dusk; closed Jan. 1 and Dec. 25. Free. Phone (816) 503-4800. *See Recreation Chart.*

MISSOURI TOWN 1855 is within Fleming Park. This collection of original mid-19th-century structures, which depict a typical Midwestern antebellum community, were relocated to the site from a number of locations. Living-history interpreters explain and portray the daily routines of village residents. Old-fashioned events are held year-round. Allow 1 hour minimum. Tues.-Sun. 9-4:30, Mar. 1-Nov. 15; Sat.-Sun. 9-4:30, rest of year. Admission $5; over 62 and ages 5-13, $3. Phone (816) 524-8770.

EXCELSIOR SPRINGS (B-2)
pop. 10,847, elev. 939'

Saline, soda, calcium and iron manganese mineral waters have made Excelsior Springs a well-known spa. The Hall of Waters, operated by the city, has bath facilities for men and women as well as a Hall of Springs, where the waters are dispensed for drinking and for bottling at a plant.

Excelsior Springs Chamber of Commerce: 101 E. Broadway, Excelsior Springs, MO 64024; phone (816) 630-6161.

WATKINS WOOLEN MILL STATE HISTORIC SITE is off I-35 exit SR 92, 7 mi. e. to CR RA, then 1.5 mi. n. to the park entrance. This 1861 woolen mill no longer operates but is still equipped with spinners, twisters and looms. The site, a national landmark, also includes a gristmill, house and other outbuildings, as well as a museum and visitor center.

Allow 1 hour minimum. Mon.-Sat. 10-4, Sun. 11-4; closed Jan. 1, Thanksgiving and Dec. 25. Admission $2.50; ages 6-12, $1.50. Phone (816) 580-3387 or (800) 334-6946. *See Recreation Chart.*

GRANDVIEW (C-1) pop. 24,881, elev. 1,070'

HARRY S. TRUMAN FARM HOME is off US 71, then .7 mi. w. to 12301 Blue Ridge Blvd. Part of the Harry S. Truman National Historic Site *(see attraction listing p. 179)*, this 1894 farmstead was the home of Harry S. Truman's grandparents. Truman lived and worked on the farm 1906-17. The house is filled with photographs of Truman family members. Several outbuildings also are on the grounds.

Allow 30 minutes minimum. Tours are given on the half-hour Fri.-Sun. 9:30-4, Memorial Day weekend-Labor Day. Admission $4, under 17 free. Phone (816) 254-2720.

INDEPENDENCE (C-1)
pop. 113,288, elev. 1,012'

The hometown of President Harry S. Truman, Independence is one of the state's most historic cities. It was the beginning of the Santa Fe Trail in 1821 and of the Oregon and California trails in the 1840s. During the Civil War it was occupied by both Union and Confederate armies.

The Union Pacific Station, also known as the Truman Depot, is at 1111 W. Pacific St. It played an important role in Truman's career and his 1948 whistle stop presidential campaign. The Harry S. Truman Historic District, where Truman lived, includes a number of interesting Civil War era and Victorian houses.

The Little Blue Trace Trail, accessible from the Hartman Heritage Center, I-70 and Little Blue River Road, runs north for 11 scenic miles along the Blue River and is used by walkers, runners and cyclists. For additional information phone Jackson County Parks and Recreation, (816) 503-4800.

Self-guiding tours: The Missouri Mormon Walking Trail, which begins at Walnut and River streets across from the Community of Christ Auditorium, is a 1-mile trail with 14 plaques commemorating early Mormon sites. The Truman Walking Trail, beginning at the Harry S Truman National Historic Site ticket office at Main Street and Truman Road, meanders 2.7 miles through the Truman neighborhood, with 44 plaques embedded in sidewalks along the way.

Independence Department of Tourism: 111 E. Maple St., Independence, MO 64050; phone (816) 325-7111 or (800) 748-7323.

SAVE **1859 JAIL, MARSHAL'S HOME & MUSEUM** is at 217 N. Main St. This restored Civil War-era jail held such notorious characters as Frank James, William Quantrill and the Youngers. Also in the complex are the marshal's house, a local history museum and a one-room schoolhouse.

Allow 30 minutes minimum. Mon.-Sat. 10-4, Sun. 1-4, Apr.-Oct. and in Dec.; Tues.-Sat. 10-4, Sun. 1-4, day after Thanksgiving-Nov. 30. Christmas tours given day after Thanksgiving-Dec. 22 and Dec. 26-30. Closed Dec. 23-25. Admission $5; over 55, $4; ages 6-16, $2. Combination ticket with Bingham-Waggoner Estate and Vaile Mansion $12. Phone (816) 252-1892.

BINGHAM-WAGGONER ESTATE is at 313 W. Pacific St. The 22-room mansion was the 1864-70 home of Missouri artist George Caleb Bingham and his wife. Having seen two Civil War battles nearby, Bingham painted his controversial work "Order Number Eleven" to protest the infamous 1863 directive that drove thousands of border residents from their property if they did not swear allegiance to the Union.

Guided tours are available. Allow 1 hour minimum. Mon.-Sat. 10-4, Sun. 1-4, Apr.-Oct. and day after Thanksgiving-Dec. 30; closed Dec. 23-25. Admission $5; senior citizens $4.50; ages 6-16, $2. Combination ticket with 1859 Jail, Marshal's Home & Museum and Vaile Mansion $12. Phone (816) 325-7111 or (816) 461-3491.

COMMUNITY OF CHRIST WORLD HEADQUARTERS is at River and Walnut sts. Formerly known as the Reorganized Church of Jesus Christ of Latter Day Saints, the organization's headquarters features a 6,334-pipe organ in the auditorium's main conference chamber. A museum is in the 1994 temple across the street. The temple's ceiling resembles a cross section of the shell of a chambered nautilus.

Guided tours are given every half-hour Mon.-Sat. 9-11:30 and 1-4:30, Sun. 1-5; closed Jan. 1, Easter, Thanksgiving and Dec. 24-25. Recitals are given daily at 3, June-Aug.; Sun. at 3, rest of year. Free. Phone (816) 833-1000, ext. 3030.

Children's Peace Pavilion is at 1001 W. Walnut St. Hands-on activities and exhibits are designed to teach children the museum's four concepts of peace: "Peace for Me" explains how to deal with one's feelings; "Peace for Us" places emphasis on the importance of relationships; "Peace for Everyone" is geared toward understanding the diversity of the human race; and "Peace for the Planet" encourages taking care of the Earth. A rain forest display includes a cave for children to explore.

Allow 30 minutes minimum. Tues.-Sat. 9:30-4; closed Jan. 1, Thanksgiving and Dec. 25. Free. Phone (816) 521-3033.

HARRY S. TRUMAN COURTROOM AND OFFICE is in the Jackson County Courthouse on Independence Sq. The multimedia feature "The Man from Independence" focuses on the 33rd president's youth and retirement years in Independence. The 30-minute sound and light show, shown by request, is presented in the restored courtroom Truman used while serving as a county judge. A tour of his adjoining office is included. Allow 30 minutes minimum. Mon.-Fri. 10-3:30. Admission $2; over 59 and ages 5-13, $1. Phone (816) 252-7454.

HARRY S TRUMAN NATIONAL HISTORIC SITE is on Delaware St. off Truman Rd.; a visitor center is at 223 N. Main St. This is the house in which President and Mrs. Truman, when not in Washington, D.C., lived from their marriage in 1919 until their deaths. The Victorian home is crowded with their furnishings and other possessions.

The visitor center distributes tickets on a first-come, first-served basis beginning at 8:30 a.m. for each day's tours; visitors must sign for their own ticket in person. There are no reservations; tours may sell out. The center offers a short audiovisual program. Parking at the historic site is limited. House open daily 9-5, Memorial Day-Labor Day; Tues.-Sun. 9-5, rest of year. Admission to the house is by guided tour, and each tour is limited to eight people. Center open daily 8:30-5. Closed Jan. 1, Thanksgiving and Dec. 25. House tours depart every 15 minutes. Admission $4, under 15 free. Phone (816) 254-9929.

MORMON VISITORS' CENTER is at 937 W. Walnut St. Exhibits, artifacts and works of art chronicle religious leader Joseph Smith, Jr.'s pilgrimage from Ohio to Independence and the role of Mormon followers in the early history of Independence. Guided tours are available. Daily 9-9. Free. Phone (816) 836-3466.

SAVE **NATIONAL FRONTIER TRAILS MUSEUM** is at 318 W. Pacific Ave. The museum researches, interprets and preserves the history of the pioneers and the Santa Fe, Oregon and California trails, all of which began at or near Independence. Exhibits include an 18-minute videotape presentation about the trails. Covered wagon rides are offered seasonally (weather permitting).

Mon.-Sat. 9-4:30, Sun. 12:30-4:30; closed Jan. 1, Thanksgiving and Dec. 25. Admission $5; over 61, $4.50; ages 6-17, $3. Museum and wagon ride $11; ages 6-17, $8. Phone (816) 325-7575.

PUPPETRY ARTS INSTITUTE is at 11025 E. Winner Rd. in Englewood Plaza. The institute has a museum featuring puppets and puppet-related items. Hazelle and Woody Rollins, the owners of one of the country's most renowned puppet and marionette factories, have the remaining inventory from their factories displayed here. Guests also can create their own puppets. Allow 1 hour minimum. Tues.-Sat. 10-5; closed Jan. 1, Thanksgiving and Dec. 25. Admission $3; under 16, $1.50. Phone (816) 833-9777.

GEM **TRUMAN PRESIDENTIAL MUSEUM & LIBRARY** is on the n.e. edge of US 24 at Delaware St. The focal point of the museum, an exhibit about the Missouri native's presidential years, features a film tracing Truman's life from childhood to his swearing in as the 33rd president of the United States. In addition, audiovisual presentations dealing with difficult decisions Truman was faced with during his presidency are shown in two theaters. Other exhibits examine topics such as the challenges faced in the post-World War II years, the beginning of the Cold War and the status of the nation as Truman left office in 1952.

Also displayed are a replica of Truman's office in the White House with the original "The Buck Stops Here" sign, the table on which the United Nations charter was signed and exhibits about the history of the presidency.

Allow 2 hours minimum. Mon.-Sat. 9-5 (also Thurs. 5-9, May-Sept.), Sun. noon-5; closed Jan. 1, Thanksgiving and Dec. 25. Admission $7; over 62, $5; ages 6-18, $3. Phone (816) 268-8200.

VAILE MANSION is at 1500 N. Liberty St. The 30-room home of local entrepreneur and mail contractor Harvey Merrick Vaile was hailed by Kansas City newspaper reporters as "the most princely house and the most comfortable home in the entire West" during its construction in the early 1880s. The restored mansion is furnished in period.

Guided tours are available. Allow 1 hour minimum. Mon.-Sat. 10-4, Sun. 1-4, Apr.-Oct. Admission $5; senior citizens $4.50; ages 6-16, $2. Combination ticket with 1859 Jail, Marshal's Home & Museum and Bingham-Waggoner Estate $12. Phone (816) 325-7111 or (816) 325-7430.

KEARNEY (B-2) pop. 5,472, elev. 829'

JESSE JAMES MUSEUM is about 1.5 mi. e. on SR 92, then 1.5 mi. n. to 21216 Jesse James Farm Rd., following signs. This historic site was the birthplace and home of Jesse James, who grew up in the house with his brother Frank. The 1822 house has been restored with period furnishings; guides relate facts and stories about the outlaws. Daily 9-4, May-Sept.; Mon.-Sat. 9-4, Sun. noon-4, rest of year. Closed Jan. 1, Thanksgiving and Dec. 25. Admission $7; over 62, $6; ages 8-15, $3.75. Phone (816) 628-6065.

LIBERTY (C-2) pop. 26,232, elev. 852'

CLAY COUNTY MUSEUM AND HISTORICAL SOCIETY is at 14 N. Main St. A restored 19th-century drugstore displays patent medicines, pioneer farm tools and other artifacts of 19th-century life in Missouri. The second-floor dining room and parlor are furnished to reflect the style of the 1880s. Allow 30 minutes minimum. Mon.-Sat. 1-4, Feb.-Dec.; closed major holidays. Admission $1; under 13, 50c. Phone (816) 792-1849.

HISTORIC LIBERTY JAIL is at 216 N. Main St. This is a restored version—in cutaway form—of the 1833 jail in which Mormon prophet Joseph Smith was confined for 4 months beginning in 1838, and where he is said to have received several revelations concerning doctrines of the Mormon Church. Allow 30 minutes minimum. Daily 9-9. Free. Phone (816) 781-3188.

JESSE JAMES BANK MUSEUM is at 103 N. Water St. on Liberty Square. The nation's first bank robbery carried out during daylight hours was at this site, committed by the James gang Feb. 13, 1866. The 1858 building houses Jesse James memorabilia, period furnishings and antebellum-era banking displays. Guided tours are available. Allow 30 minutes minimum. Mon.-Sat. 10-4. Admission $5; over 62, $4.50; ages 8-15, $3. Phone (816) 781-4458.

THE WILLIAM JEWELL COLLEGE LIBRARY is on Jewell St. between Kansas and Mississippi aves. The collection includes Elizabethan and Puritan literature, archival records of Missouri history, 16th-century Anabaptist pamphlets and original illustrations by children's author Lois Lenski. Allow 30 minutes minimum. Mon.-Fri. 8-5 (extended hours during school terms). Free. Phone (816) 781-7700, ext. 5468.

LONE JACK (C-2) pop. 528

The Battle of Lone Jack, one of the bloodiest Civil War battles in Missouri, occurred Aug. 16, 1862. Five days earlier Confederate troops had captured Independence and its Union garrison. Joined by reinforcements a few days later, the Confederates moved to Lone Jack, where they clashed with Union troops in hand-to-hand combat for 5 hours until the Union troops retreated.

LONE JACK CIVIL WAR MUSEUM is at jct. SR 150 and US 50. Local Civil War activity is depicted through exhibits, dioramas and an electronic map. Soldiers' Cemetery and a remnant of hedgerows that figured in the battle can be seen. Wed.-Sat. 10-4, Sun. 1-4, Apr.-Oct.; Sat. 10-4, Sun. 1-4, rest of year. Closed Jan. 1, Thanksgiving and Dec. 25. Hours may vary; phone ahead. Admission $3, under 13 free. Phone (816) 697-8833.

NORTH KANSAS CITY (C-1) pop. 4,714

CASINOS

• **Harrah's North Kansas City**, 1 Riverboat Dr. Sun.-Thurs. 8 a.m.-5 a.m., Fri.-Sat. 24 hours. Phone (816) 472-7777 or (800) 427-7247.

PLATTE CITY (B-1) pop. 3,866, elev. 850'

When Missouri became part of the Union in 1821, the northwestern corner of the state was still part of the Indian Territory. It was not until the Platte Purchase of 1836 that this area was bought from the Iowa, Sac and Fox Indians.

Platte County-KCI Area Convention and Visitors Bureau: 409 Third St., P.O. Box 105, Platte City, MO 64079; phone (816) 270-3979.

BEN FERREL PLATTE COUNTY MUSEUM is at Third and Ferrel sts. This restored 1882 Victorian house is furnished in period. The museum contains historical items pertaining to the county and surrounding areas. County records and genealogical histories are contained in the archives and library. Allow 30 minutes minimum. Thurs.-Sat. noon-4, Apr.-Oct. Admission $3; ages 5-18, 50c. Phone (816) 431-5121.

RIVERSIDE (B-1) pop. 2,979, elev. 440'

CASINOS

- *Argosy* **Casino**, e. of jct. I-635 and US 9 on US 9, following signs. Gaming sessions depart Mon.-Fri. every 2 hours 8 a.m.-5 a.m., Fri.-Sat. 24 hrs. Phone (816) 746-7711 or (800) 270-7711.

SIBLEY (B-2) pop. 347

FORT OSAGE is at US 24 and CR BB (Sibley Rd.). The fort is a restoration of the first U.S. outpost in the Louisiana Purchase Territory. The 1808 factory—originally an American Indian trading house—contains original furnishings from the early 1800s. A museum illustrates the trading post's operation, the role of the fort and the lifestyle of the Osage Indian tribe. A 19th-century blacksmith shop and a trade shop with typical early 1800s goods are featured.

Tues.-Sun. 9-4:30, Mar. 1-Nov. 15; Sat.-Sun. 9-4:30, rest of year. Closed Jan. 1 and Dec. 25. Admission $5; over 62 and ages 5-13, $3. Phone (816) 503-4860, ext. 1260.

SMITHVILLE (B-1) pop. 5,514

THE JERRY L. LITTON VISITOR CENTER is at 16311 N. CR DD, at the end of Smithville Lake *(see Recreation Chart)*. Named for the late Missouri congressman, the center highlights his life and has displays and audiovisual presentations about the Smithville Lake area and the history of water management and control by the Army Corps of Engineers. Allow 1 hour minimum. Daily 8-4, Memorial Day-Labor Day; Mon.-Fri. 8-4, rest of year. Free. Phone (816) 532-0174.

UNITY VILLAGE (C-1) pop. 140, elev. 950'

UNITY VILLAGE is at SR 350 and Colbern Rd. The world headquarters of the Unity School of Christianity features historic Mediterranean-style buildings set amid 1,400 acres of woodlands, lakes, fountains and formal rose gardens. A library contains a collection of metaphysical material as well as archives. The Unity Village Chapel is open to visitors. Food is available. Allow 1 hour, 30 minutes minimum. Self-guiding tours can be taken Mon.-Thurs. 9-5, Fri.-Sun. 10-2. Chapel services Sun. at 10:30. Free. Phone (816) 524-3550, ext. 3000.

WESTON (B-1) pop. 1,631, elev. 775'

The pride of Weston is its more than 100 antebellum houses and buildings, similar in appearance to the Classical Revival and Federal-style houses of early 19th-century Virginia and Kentucky.

Founded along the Missouri River, Weston was visited by Meriwether Lewis and William Clark in 1804. Although the Missouri changed its course in the early 20th century, leaving docks perched along a dry riverbed, the town's Main Street tobacco warehouses are still kept full. Tobacco is grown locally and sold at auctions held from mid-November to February.

RECREATIONAL ACTIVITIES

Skiing

- **Snow Creek Ski Area**, 5 mi. n.w. on SR 45 at 1 Snow Creek Dr., Weston, MO 64098. Mon.-Fri. noon-9, Sat. and holidays 9-9, Sun. 9-8, mid-Dec. to mid-Mar. (also Fri.-Sat. 10 p.m.-3 a.m., Jan. 1 to mid-Mar.); closed Dec. 25. Phone (816) 640-2200.

Nearby Kansas

BONNER SPRINGS pop. 6,768, elev. 795'

Most of the year Bonner Springs, just west of the Kansas City metropolitan area, concentrates on light industry and the marketing of agricultural products. On weekends from late August to mid-October, however, the town exhibits a touch of 16th-century Europe when the popular Renaissance Festival of Kansas City is held. From May through September the Verizon Wireless Amphitheater offers outdoor concerts featuring major rock, hip-hop and country artists; phone (913) 721-3400.

Bonner Springs-Edwardsville Area Chamber of Commerce: 205 E. 2nd St., P.O. Box 403, Bonner Springs, KS 66012; phone (913) 422-5044.

SAVE **NATIONAL AGRICULTURAL CENTER AND HALL OF FAME** is 1 mi. n.e. off I-70 at 630 N. 126th St. The center is devoted to achievements in the field of agriculture. Three display buildings house a diverse collection of past, present and future machinery and implements. A small steam train operates on weekends in summer. Mon.-Sat. 9-5, Sun. 1-5, mid-Mar. through Nov. 30; closed major holidays. Admission $7; over 62, $6; ages 5-16, $3. Phone (913) 721-1075.

WYANDOTTE COUNTY MUSEUM is at 631 N. 126th St. in Wyandotte County Park. The museum contains artifacts depicting the area's heritage. Aspects of county history portrayed range from emigrant American Indian tribes to the arrival of Europeans and the development of local industry. Mon.-Sat. 10-4; closed holidays. Free. Phone (913) 721-1078.

EDGERTON pop. 1,440, elev. 835'

LANESFIELD SCHOOL HISTORIC SITE is at jct. 187th St. and Dillie Rd. Built in 1869, the Lanesfield School is a one-room schoolhouse in which grades 1-8 were taught by a single teacher until its consolidation by the school district in 1963. A costumed teacher leads a tour of the building and conducts a lesson students received circa 1904. Allow 30 minutes minimum. Tues.-Sun. 1-5; closed major holidays. Free. Phone (913) 893-6645.

FAIRWAY pop. 3,952

SHAWNEE INDIAN MISSION STATE HISTORIC SITE is n. of US 56 at jct. Mission Rd. and W. 53rd St. A manual labor training school was established here in 1839 on Shawnee land—although its doors were open to 23 different tribes—and operated until 1862. The orientation video "Crossroads of Culture" recounts the mission's history and its role in westward expansion as well as such divisive eras as "Bleeding Kansas," when the Kansas territory became a battleground between pro and antislavery factions, and the Civil War.

The East Building has two floors of exhibits that bring the mission's stories to life. The West and North buildings are the other two remaining structures of the original 16 that once stood on the site's more than 2,000 acres. Regularly scheduled living-history programs take place in the North Building. The West Building is still undergoing renovations.

Tues.-Sat. 9-5, Sun. 1-5, Mar.-Nov.; by appointment rest of year. Admission $3; over 60, $2; students grades kindergarten through college $1. Phone (913) 262-0867.

KANSAS CITY pop. 146,866, elev. 763'

The town of Wyandotte, established in 1858, was located in what is now the downtown area of present-day Kansas City. By the 1870s, railroads and stockyards were contributing to robust growth. Four municipalities—Armourdale, Armstrong, Kansas City and Wyandotte—consolidated in 1886 to form what today is the Kansas portion of the greater Kansas City metropolitan area.

Among those who migrated to Kansas looking for a better life in the latter part of the 19th century were African Americans known as Exodusters. Free blacks who could read, were economically able to buy property and whose self-esteem had been bolstered by military service in the Civil War, they pursued dreams of owning land and escaping the oppressive segregationist policies of Southern states, a legacy that remained despite the civil rights gains introduced by Reconstruction.

Their de facto leader was Benjamin "Pap" Singleton, who was born a slave in Tennessee, escaped to freedom in Detroit and returned to his native state after emancipation. An admirer of abolitionist John Brown's crusade against slavery in Kansas, he chose the state as a destination for the creation of organized African-American "colonies."

Singleton recruited impoverished blacks from throughout the South. Under his leadership, several Exoduster communities took shape in Wyandotte County beginning in the early 1870s, including Hoggstown, Mississippi Town, Quindaro and Rattlebone Hollow, all later incorporated into Kansas City. Quindaro—today a neighborhood on the city's northern edge—was founded by freed African Americans and abolitionists; it was a stop on the Underground Railroad and remained a thriving town until the early 20th century.

Although the organized movement to Kansas later became an unplanned rush (so much so that in 1880 Singleton was called before a U.S. Senate committee to explain the "alarming exodus" of blacks from the South), many who remained were indeed able to better their lives. But Singleton, dismayed with the racial prejudice he continued to encounter, eventually abandoned his efforts to establish African-American colonies in the United States.

These days you can find an exodus of racing fans heading to Kansas City. Grand National and NASCAR events rev up the crowds at Lakeside Speedway, 1 mile west of I-435 exit 18 at 5615 Wolcott Dr., on Friday nights from April through September; phone (913) 299-2040. At the Woodlands Race Track, 99th Street and Leavenworth Road, Thoroughbred racing takes place November to mid-August, and greyhound racing occurs mid-August through October; phone (913) 299-9797 or (800) 695-7223.

Note: Policies concerning admittance of children to pari-mutuel betting facilities vary. Phone for information.

KANSAS SPEEDWAY is off I-70 exit 410 (110th St.) at jct. I-435/I-70. The 1,200-acre complex plays host to NASCAR and Indy races twice a year on its tri-oval track. The Fan Walk, accessed by separate admission on race days, is an interactive area in the infield. Guests have access to a working garage as well as to Autograph Alley, where fans can mingle with drivers. Track tours depart from the guard booth at Speedway Blvd. and Michigan Dr.

NASCAR Craftsman Truck Series, ARCA RE/MAX Series and IRL IndyCar Series racing roars over July 4 weekend, while NASCAR NEXTEL Cup Series and NASCAR Busch Series racing takes place the second weekend in Oct. Walk-up tours Thurs. at 4, Mar.-Nov. Tours $10; under 13, $5. Race tickets are sold in annual packages. Phone (866) 460-7223 for race information and tickets, or (913) 328-3375 for tour information.

© International Speedway Corporation
AAA is the Official Auto Club of Kansas Speedway.

AAA and Motorsports

AAA, a pioneer in the development and growth of auto racing during the first half of the 20th century, has returned to the racetrack. Today the association is the "Official Auto Club" and "Official Roadside Assistance Provider" of 11 tracks owned and operated by the International Speedway Corporation (ISC), which hosts the NASCAR NEXTEL Cup Series and Indy Racing League (IRL) events.

As part of an agreement with ISC, AAA's widely recognized logo appears on track safety and recovery vehicles as well as on track signs, in racing programs and at other promotional venues. ISC, a leading promoter of motorsports activities in the United States, conducts more than 100 events annually. ISC/AAA facilities include California Speedway in Fontana, Calif.; Darlington Raceway in Darlington, S.C.; Daytona International Speedway in Daytona Beach, Fla.; Homestead-Miami Speedway in Homestead, Fla.; Kansas Speedway in Kansas City, Kan.; Martinsville Speedway in Martinsville, Va.; Michigan International Speedway in Cambridge Junction, Mich.; Phoenix International Raceway in Phoenix, Ariz.; Richmond International Raceway in Richmond, Va.; Talladega Superspeedway in Talladega, Ala.; and Watkins Glen International in Watkins Glen, N.Y.

© International Speedway Corporation

LENEXA pop. 40,238, elev. 1,052′

Na-Nex-Se, the wife of a Shawnee Indian chief, lent her name to the Kansas City suburb of Lenexa in 1869. The community attracted German, Swiss and Belgian farmers by the early 1900s, and in the 1930s was known for its prolific spinach crops.

Shawnee Mission Park, on Renner Boulevard, has one of the largest lakes in the area and offers archery, fishing, hiking trails, horseback riding, sailboats and canoes, swimming, tennis, water skiing and windsurfing. The outdoor Theater in the Park presents plays and musicals.

Lenexa Convention & Visitors Bureau: 11180 Lackman Rd., Lenexa, KS 66219; phone (913) 888-1414 or (800) 950-7867.

LEGLER BARN MUSEUM is in 53-acre Sar-Ko-Par Trails Park at 14907 W. 87th St. Pkwy. The limestone Legler barn was built on the Santa Fe Trail in 1864 by Swiss immigrant Adam Legler. Moved to its present site and restored, the barn houses pioneer relics and a prairie schooner. A restored 1912 railroad depot and a Northern Pacific caboose are nearby. Allow 30 minutes minimum. Tues.-Fri. 10-4, Sat.-Sun. 1-4; closed holidays. Donations. Phone (913) 492-0038.

OLATHE pop. 92,962, elev. 1,023′

In 1856 Dr. John T. Barton, appointed physician to the Shawnee Indians, staked a claim to land to which the Shawnees were giving up tribal title and named the land after the Shawnee word for beautiful, *Olathe*. Shortly after Olathe was established, it replaced the settlement of Shawnee as the county seat.

After Kansas was admitted to the Union as a free state in 1861, the town became an easy target for Confederate guerilla commander William Quantrill and his raiders, who invaded and destroyed much of the settlement. Once the Civil War ended, however, Olathe began to rebuild. The rich farmland and a railroad brought new settlers to the area.

Olathe Area Chamber of Commerce: 128 S. Chestnut, P.O. Box 98, Olathe, KS 66051; phone (913) 764-1050.

SAVE **MAHAFFIE STAGECOACH STOP AND FARM HISTORIC SITE** is w. of jct. I-35 and SR 150, at 1100 Kansas City Rd. In 1857 Indiana farmer J.B. Mahaffie arrived in Olathe with his wife and five children to purchase land for farming; by 1865 he reputedly had the largest farm and livestock herd in Olathe township. From 1865 to 1869 Mahaffie's farmstead was used as a stagecoach stop, and the basement of the house served as a dining room for travelers.

Tours are available. Allow 1 hour minimum. Wed.-Sat. 10-4, Sun. noon-4, Apr.-Oct.; closed major holidays. Admission $3.25; ages 5-11, $2. Phone (913) 971-5111.

OVERLAND PARK pop. 149,080

One of the largest cities in the state, Overland Park is the leading business and commercial center for the Johnson County portion of the Kansas City metropolitan area.

Overland Park Convention & Visitors Bureau: 9001 W. 110th, Suite 100, Overland Park, KS 66210; phone (913) 491-0123 or (800) 262-7275.

DEANNE ROSE CHILDREN'S FARMSTEAD is at 13800 Switzer Rd.; from jct. US 69 and US 150 (135th St.), travel .7 mi. w. on US 150 to Switzer Rd., then .2 mi. s. A miniature farm with a barn and silo, the farmstead has horses, rabbits, sheep, chickens, ducks, goats and other barnyard animals that children can pet and feed. The birds of prey exhibit features eagles, owls and hawks.

Picnic facilities and a playground also are available. Daily 9-8, Memorial Day weekend-Labor Day; 9-5, Apr. 1-day before Memorial Day weekend and day after Labor Day-Oct. 31. Free. Phone (913) 897-2360.

OVERLAND PARK ARBORETUM AND BOTANICAL GARDENS is .5 mi. w. of US 69 at jct. 179th St. and Antioch Rd. Multiple gardens and ecosystems cover 300 acres. The Erikson Water Garden features bird and butterfly plants and ornamental grasses. Marder Woodland Garden has regional flora, wood and stone arbors, and a koi pond. The willow trees and annuals in the Monet Garden are similar to their namesake gardens in France.

A children's garden as well as an environmental education and visitor center are available. Allow 1 hour minimum. Daily 8-7:30, mid-Apr. to late Sept.; 8-5, rest of year. Closed Dec. 25. Free. Phone (913) 685-3604.

SHAWNEE pop. 47,996

Behind its modern-day suburban facade—the city is on the southwest edge of the Kansas City metropolitan area—Shawnee is part of a recorded history that dates back to 1724.

In subsequent years the settlement, first called Gum Springs, saw the opening of the Santa Fe Trail, the arrival of the Shawnee Indians from the East, the establishment of the Shawnee Mission and finally a raid by Civil War guerrilla William Quantrill. Shawnee was the largest town in the territory until it lost the title of county seat to Olathe in 1858.

Shawnee Convention & Visitors Bureau: 15100 W. 67th St., Suite 202, Shawnee, KS 66217-9344; phone (913) 631-6545 or (888) 550-7282.

SAVE **THE 1950s ALL-ELECTRIC HOUSE** is off I-435 exit 6A, 1.5 mi. e. on Shawnee Mission Pkwy., then n. to 6305 Lackman Rd. The house was built in 1954 by Kansas City Power and Light as a showcase of modern electric innovations. Pink laminate kitchen counter tops, a remote controlled coffee maker and push-button lights are featured.

The bathroom has traditional lighting, along with a germ-killing light and a tanning lamp. Allow 30 minutes minimum. Guided tours are given every half-hour Tues.-Sun. 1-4; closed major holidays. Last tour departs 30 minutes before closing. Admission $2; under 13, $1. Phone (913) 715-2550.

JOHNSON COUNTY MUSEUM OF HISTORY is off I-435 exit 6A, 1.5 mi. e. on Shawnee Mission Pkwy., then n. to 6305 Lackman Rd. The Seeking the Good Life exhibit has more than 500 artifacts and explores three time periods in Johnson County. These eras are 1820-1880: Settling the Land; 1880-1945: Building the Suburbs; and 1945-present: Developing an Edge City. Interactive displays also highlight the county's history.

A research library also is available. Allow 30 minutes minimum. Tues.-Sat. 10-4:30, Sun. 1-4:30; closed major holidays. Free. Phone (913) 631-6709.

OLD SHAWNEE TOWN is at the jct. of 57th and Cody sts. Two log cabins, a jail, home, barn, smokehouse and schoolhouse are original 1800s structures relocated from around the area. Reproductions include a bank, general store, undertaker/cabinet shop and sod house. All are furnished with antiques. Tues.-Sat. 10-4:30. Admission $1; ages 6-12, 50c. Phone (913) 248-2360.

SAVE **WONDERSCOPE CHILDREN'S MUSEUM** is off I-35 exit 229 (Johnson Dr.), then w. 1.4 mi. to 5705 Flint St. Hands-on activities encourage learning about art, communications, ecology, health, nature, science and space. Allow 1 hour minimum. Tues.-Sat. 10-5, Sun. noon-5 (also Mon. 10-5, Mar.-Aug.); closed major holidays. Admission $6; over 63, $5; under 3, $3. Phone (913) 268-8130.

© Gibson Stock Photography

This ends listings for the Kansas City Vicinity.
The following page resumes the alphabetical listings of cities in Missouri.

KEARNEY—*see Kansas City p. 180.*

KINGSVILLE (C-2) pop. 257, elev. 904′

POWELL GARDENS is at 1609 N.W. US 50, just e. of jct. with SR W. Visitors may walk or take a trolley to the Perennial Garden, featuring more than 500 varieties of plants; the Rock and Waterfall Garden; the Wildlife Meadow; and the Majorie Powell Allen Chapel. A 1-mile nature trail also traverses the 835-acre park. Horticultural displays are located in the Visitor Education Center.

Food is available. Allow 1 hour minimum. Daily 9-6, Apr.-Oct.; 9-5, rest of year. Closed Jan. 1, Thanksgiving and Dec. 25. Admission Apr.-Oct. $8; senior citizens $7; ages 5-12, $3. Admission rest of year $6; senior citizens $5; ages 5-12, $2. AX, CB, DC, DS, JC, MC, VI. Phone (816) 697-2600.

KIRKSVILLE (A-3) pop. 16,988, elev. 965′

Founded in 1841 as the seat of Adair County, Kirksville was named for Jesse Kirk, who exchanged a turkey dinner for the right to name the town after himself. Truman State University and the Kirksville College of Osteopathic Medicine have transformed this former farming community into an important educational center.

The area's rural character still can be enjoyed in such nearby areas as Big Creek and Sugar Creek state forests and at the larger Thousand Hills State Park *(see Recreation Chart and the AAA South Central CampBook).* Thousand Hills offers a petroglyph and the recreational facilities of Forest Lake.

Kirksville Area Chamber of Commerce: 219 S. Franklin, Kirksville, MO 63501; phone (660) 665-3766.

STILL NATIONAL OSTEOPATHIC MUSEUM is 1 mi. w. of US 63 in the Tinning Education Center of the Kirksville College of Osteopathic Medicine, 800

DID YOU KNOW

Harry S. Truman had no middle name —just the letter S.

W. Jefferson St. This museum traces the roots of osteopathic medicine beginning with its founder, Dr. Andrew Taylor Still, and his establishment of the first osteopathic medical school in 1892.

Still's medical approach was based on the belief that the keys to healing lay within the body itself. The museum's collections of photographs, documents and artifacts span more than 120 years.

Allow 1 hour minimum. Mon.-Thurs. 10-4 (also Thurs. 4-7), Sat. noon-4; closed holidays. Schedule may vary; phone ahead. Free. Phone (660) 626-2359.

KIRKWOOD—*see St. Louis p. 210.*

LACLEDE (B-3) pop. 415, elev. 784′

The 1868 Locust Creek Covered Bridge, 3 miles west off US 36, is one of only four covered bridges in Missouri.

GEN. JOHN J. PERSHING BOYHOOD HOME STATE HISTORICAL SITE is 3 blks. e. of SR 5. This shrine to the leader of America's forces in World War I houses antique furnishings and personal effects. Also on the grounds is the one-room Prairie Mound School, where Pershing once taught. Mon.-Sat. 8-4, Sun. noon-6, Apr. 15-Oct. 15; Mon.-Sat. 8-4, Sun. noon-5, rest of year. Closed Jan. 1, Easter, Thanksgiving and Dec. 25. Admission $2.50; ages 6-12, $1.50. Phone (660) 963-2525.

LA GRANGE (B-4) pop. 1,000

La Grange was named for the country home of the Marquis de Lafayette. Founder William Wright recorded the town plat a few years after the French general visited the United States in 1825. An early steamboat landing, the city was incorporated by the Missouri legislature in 1853, the same year St. Louis, Kansas City and St. Joseph were granted charters.

CASINOS

- **Mark Twain Casino**, 104 Pierce St. Sun.-Thurs. 8 a.m.-2 a.m., Fri.-Sat. 8 a.m.-4 a.m. Phone (573) 655-4770 or (866) 454-5825.

LAKE OF THE OZARKS (C-3)

The Bagnell Dam was built on the Osage River in 1931 to form Lake of the Ozarks, Missouri's largest inland body of water and the largest man-made lake in the world at the time of its creation. Fishing, boating and swimming are popular pastimes on the 54,000-acre reservoir, which offers 1,150 miles of shoreline—more than the length of the California coast.

Osage Indians once hunted in the woods surrounding the lake, and it is said they left directions by bending and tying oak saplings. Hundreds of years later, examples of these strangely bent "thong trees" can still be seen.

The Community Bridge, completed in 1998, links the east and west sides of the lake. The toll bridge runs from Lake Ozark to Shawnee Bend.

The following towns on the Lake of the Ozarks are listed separately under their individual names: Camdenton, Linn Creek, Osage Beach and Warsaw *(see place listings)*.

Lake of the Ozarks Convention & Visitor Bureau: P.O. Box 1498, Osage Beach, MO 65065; phone (573) 348-1599. *See color ad.*

LAMAR (D-2) pop. 4,452, elev. 940′

HARRY S. TRUMAN BIRTHPLACE STATE HISTORIC SITE is at 1009 Truman St., near jct. US 71 and US 160. This six-room house, in which President Truman was born and lived the first year of his life, contains many of the original furnishings. Allow 30 minutes minimum. Mon.-Sat. 10-4, Sun. noon-4; closed Jan. 1, Easter, Thanksgiving and Dec. 25. Free. Phone (417) 682-2279.

LAMPE—*see Branson p. 152.*

LAURIE (D-3) pop. 663, elev. 965′

NATIONAL SHRINE OF MARY, MOTHER OF THE CHURCH is 1 mi. n. on SR 5. A 14-foot stainless steel sculpture of the Virgin Mary stands in a terraced amphitheater, surrounded by landscaped fountains and pools. The Mother's Wall displays memorials engraved in black granite. An Avenue of Flags represents the home countries of visitors. Picnicking is permitted. Daily 24 hours; lights are turned off after 11 p.m. Mass is offered Sat. at 8:30 p.m., Sun. at 8:30 a.m., Memorial Day-Labor Day. Donations. Phone (573) 374-6279.

LEASBURG (D-4) pop. 323, elev. 1,019′

ONONDAGA CAVE STATE PARK is 5 mi. s. on CR H. One of the largest lighted caves in Missouri, Onondaga features formations ranging from lacy patterns to massive pieces of onyx. The temperature is always 57 F. Concrete walks wind through the interior. Guided tours are offered. Allow 1 hour minimum. Daily 9-5, Mar.-Oct. Admission $10; over 64, $8; ages 6-12, $5. Phone (573) 245-6576 or (800) 334-6946. *See Recreation Chart and the AAA South Central CampBook.*

LEBANON (D-3) pop. 12,155, elev. 1,265′

Originally named after the Wyota Indians, Lebanon was later renamed after Lebanon, Tenn. In the late 1800s residents discovered that the city's water contained magnetic properties. People flocked to the Gasconade Hotel to bathe in water that was said to contain healing qualities.

Bennett Spring State Park is located 12 miles west on SR 64. The 3,100-acre park offers nature programs and guided tours; phone (417) 532-4338 or (800) 334-6946. *See Recreation Chart.*

Jigsaw puzzles galore can be found at Nancy Ballhagen's Puzzles, about 5 miles east of Lebanon off I-44 exit 135 at 25211 Garden Crest Rd. More than 3,200 different puzzles, ranging from 100 to 18,000 pieces, are in stock. Visitors also can observe the "cutting room" where hand-cut wooden puzzles are created; phone (417) 286-3837.

Lebanon Chamber of Commerce: 500 E. Elm St., Lebanon, MO 65536; phone (417) 588-3256.

BARRELS OF FUN is at 1100 S. Jefferson Ave. This is a tour of Independent Stave Co., a barrel manufacturer founded in 1912. Their wooden barrels utilize the wood of the white oak that grows in Ozark forests. The company supplies more than 50 percent of the barrels made worldwide. Visitors learn how wine barrels are made on the tour. Wine and bourbon tastings are available afterward. A videotape is shown, and a cooperage museum depicts the history of the trade.

Allow 1 hour minimum. Tours are given Mon.-Fri. at 9:15, 10:15, 12:15, 1:15 and 2:15 during wine production in late summer and early fall; phone ahead to verify. Admission $4; under 12, $1. AX, CB, DC, DS, MC, VI. Phone (417) 532-7700.

LEXINGTON (B-2) pop. 4,453, elev. 698′

Lexington was founded in 1822 by settlers from Lexington, Ky. The location they chose on a bluff overlooking the Missouri River helped the city develop into a booming river port by the mid-19th century. In the 1830s and '40s Lexington was a terminus for overland trade; from here, pack mules and ox teams departed for such southwestern destinations as Santa Fe, N.M.

Lexington held strategic importance during the Civil War. The pro-South sentiment felt by many residents was reinforced when Union troops seized nearly $1 million from the Farmers' Bank of Lexington in early September 1861. On Sept. 20, the 3-day Battle of Lexington ended in a victory for the Confederates under Maj. Gen. Sterling Price. Lodged in the east column of the courthouse is a cannonball fired during the battle.

Masonic College, the headquarters of Col. James Mulligan's Union troops, has the added distinction of being the first college sponsored by the Masons. A scale model of the college occupies its original site, now in Central College Park.

During the school year the public may attend the formal dress parade of the nationally acclaimed Wentworth Military Academy Band, which performs Sunday at 2 in the large field house or on the parade grounds. The academy campus, founded in 1880, can be toured; phone (660) 259-2221.

Lexington Area Chamber of Commerce: 1029 Franklin Ave., Lexington, MO 64067; phone (660) 259-3082.

Self-guiding tours: Walking and driving tours encompass many sites in Lexington, including the Madonna of the Trail statue, antebellum houses, old churches and the Pony Express site. Brochures outlining these routes can be obtained at the Lexington Historical Museum *(see attraction listing)* or at the tourism center of the chamber of commerce.

BATTLE OF LEXINGTON STATE HISTORIC SITE is off US 24 exit SR 13, then 4 mi. n. to Main St. The site of the Civil War conflict called the Battle of the Hemp Bales was so named for the bales the Confederate soldiers used as movable breastworks. Original earthworks and trenches are visible. Allow 1 hour minimum. Mon.-Sat. 9-5, Sun. 10-6, Apr. 15-Oct. 31; Wed.-Sat. 9-5, Sun. 10-5, rest of year. Closed Jan. 1, Thanksgiving and Dec. 25. Free. Phone (660) 259-4654. *See Recreation Chart.*

Anderson House is n. on SR 13, overlooking the battlefield. Soldiers engaged in skirmishes around the house, which served as a field hospital and changed from Union to Confederate hands several times. The house is preserved and furnished in period; a museum contains war items. Guided 45-minute tours are offered on the hour Mon.-Sat. 10-4, Sun. noon-5, Mar.-Oct.; Mon.-Sat. 9-4, Sun. noon-5, rest of year. Closed Thanksgiving and Dec. 25. Admission $2.50; ages 6-12, $1.50.

LEXINGTON HISTORICAL MUSEUM is at 112 S. 13th St. The former 1846 Cumberland Presbyterian Church contains photographs of historic Lexington and exhibits focusing on Lexington's Civil War battle and Pony Express station. Mon.-Fri. 1-4:30, Sat. 10-4, Sun. 1-4, June-Oct. Admission $2; under 13, $1. Phone (660) 259-6313 or (660) 259-3817.

LIBERTY—*see Kansas City p. 180.*

LINN CREEK (D-3) pop. 280

(SAVE) **BIG SURF** is at jct. US 54 and SR Y. This 22-acre landscaped water park offers waves, white-water rapids, flumes and a lazy river ride. Food is available. Daily 10-7, late June to mid-Aug.; daily 11-6, mid-Aug. through Labor Day; Mon.-Fri. 11-6, Sat. 10-7, Memorial Day weekend-late June. Admission $23.99; ages 4-10, $18.99; over 60, $9.99; reduced rates after 3. Next-day admission (with paid receipt from the previous day) $10; ages 4-10, $8. AX, DS, MC, VI. Phone (573) 346-6111.

LONE JACK—*see Kansas City p. 180.*

MANSFIELD (E-3) pop. 1,349, elev. 1,488'

In 1894 Laura Ingalls Wilder, her husband and small daughter moved from the prairies of the Dakota Territory to Mansfield, where they purchased a small farm on which the couple lived the rest of their lives. It was on this farm that Laura wrote the "Little House" books, favorites of children and the basis of a popular television series.

LAURA INGALLS WILDER-ROSE WILDER LANE HOME AND MUSEUM is 1 mi. e. of town square on CR A. The 1894 house contains Wilder's furniture and decorative items as they were during her occupancy. A museum contains articles about the "Little House" books, family pictures, clothing and other memorabilia associated with Wilder and her daughter Rose Wilder Lane, also a distinguished author. Mon.-Sat. and holidays 9-5, Sun. 12:30-5:30, March 1 to mid-Nov.; closed Easter. Admission $8; over 65, $6; ages 6-18, $4. Phone (417) 924-3626.

MARCELINE (B-3) pop. 2,558, elev. 863'

Marceline, 3 miles south of US 36 on CR 5, was the boyhood home of beloved film producer, animator, theme park innovator and philanthropist Walter Elias Disney. Disney was born in Chicago, but the family moved to a farm near Marceline when Walt was five, and he later recalled those formative years as the best of his life. When Disney was developing his first theme park in California he had the fictitious Main Street modeled after his hometown; today the two-story brick buildings and cast-iron street lamps along Main Street USA (formerly Kansas Avenue) are reminiscent of the idealized American streetscape Disney incorporated into his parks.

Reminders of one of the 20th century's most influential individuals are scattered throughout town. E.P. Ripley Park is named after Santa Fe Railroad president E.P. Ripley. Disney—whose fondness for trains began as a child in Marceline, where he put his ear to the tracks to listen for their approach—named the first train to operate at Disneyland for Ripley. An original Santa Fe steam locomotive stands in the park, along with a gazebo built in 1898.

Walt's Barn, on the site of the Disney family farm, is a reconstruction of the barn Disney and his younger sister Ruth used to play in; today visitors are encouraged to sign their names and add a message to the walls of "Walt's Happy Place." Also on the site is the Dreaming Tree, a large cottonwood under which the young Disney spent time observing nature (a practice he referred to as "belly botany").

The Uptown Theatre, 104. N. Main St. USA, has hosted two Disney film premieres—"The Great Locomotive Chase" and "The Spirit of Mickey." The Walt Disney Post Office, 120 E. Ritchie Ave., a branch of the U.S. Post Office officially renamed in 2004, is the only federal building named after Disney.

Disney often returned to Marceline not only for personal renewal but to soak up the pastoral setting, which he incorporated into many of his films. Walt Disney's Hometown Toonfest, held in mid-September, brings internationally known cartoonists and animators to town. The festivities include a parade down Main Street USA, a Princess Tea Party for children, an apple pie-eating contest, art and craft booths and speaker presentations at the Uptown Theatre.

Marceline Area Chamber of Commerce: 209 N. Main St. USA, Marceline, MO 64658; phone (660) 376-2332.

WALT DISNEY HOMETOWN MUSEUM is downtown at 120 E. Santa Fe St. in the restored Santa Fe Railroad Depot. Exhibits focus on the Disney family's years in Marceline, Walt Disney's childhood and the family members, friends and associates who supported him in his creative pursuits. Memorabilia on display includes family letters and personal belongings, Mickey Mouse dolls and a Midget Autopia car, donated by Disney and his brother Roy, that was part of an amusement park ride at Disneyland.

Tues.-Sat. 10-4, Sun. 1-4, Apr.-Oct. Admission $5; ages 6-10, $2.50. Phone (660) 376-3343.

MARK TWAIN NATIONAL FOREST

Elevations in the forest range from 230 ft. at the boothill drainage ditches to 1,772 ft. on Taum Sauk Mountain.

In southern and central Missouri, Mark Twain National Forest encompasses 1.5 million acres in 29 counties. Scenic drives, hunting, camping, fishing, canoeing and hiking are among the many activities available in nine wilderness areas. Pinewoods Lake Recreation Area near Ellsinore features a 1.5-mile trail around the lake. A more challenging 5-mile national recreation trail skirts 99-acre Crane Lake, approximately 12 miles south of Ironton off SR 49 and CR E.

Big Bay Recreation Area, southeast of Shell Knob on SR 39, offers swimming, boating and fishing. Swimming in the Huzzah River is available at Red Bluff Recreation Area, east of Davisville on CR V. Activities at Noblett Lake Recreation Area, west of Willow Springs, include hiking, boating, camping and picnicking. Also within the forest is 49-acre Fourche Lake, about 18 miles west of Doniphan on SR 142, then 1 mile south on SR 160.

Skyline Scenic Drive, a 4-mile automobile loop, is 2 miles south of Van Buren on SR 103 and features views of the Ozark countryside. The 8-mile Sugar Camp Scenic Drive, off SR 112 near Cassville, also offers a drive through the Ozarks. Near I-70 is the 35-mile Cedar Creek Trail System. Glade Top Trail Scenic Drive, southeast of Springfield near SR 125, offers 23 miles through open glades.

Information about the forest's many national recreation areas can be obtained from the Forest Supervisor, 401 Fairgrounds Rd., Rolla, MO 65401; phone (573) 364-4621. *See Recreation Chart and the AAA South Central CampBook.*

MARSHALL (C-3) pop. 12,433, elev. 790'

VAN METER STATE PARK is 12 mi. n.w. on SR 122 via SR 41. Remains of ancient cultures dating from 10,000 B.C. have been found. Remnants include burial sites and ceremonial mounds. Mon.-Fri. 8-4, Sat.-Sun. 8:30-5. Free. Phone (660) 886-7537. *See Recreation Chart and the AAA South Central CampBook.*

MARYLAND HEIGHTS—*See St. Louis p. 210.*

MARYVILLE (A-1) pop. 10,581, elev. 1,034'

Maryville is named for Mary Graham, the first woman of European descent to settle in the village. She and her husband Amos built the first house in Maryville in 1844.

Mozingo Lake, 3 miles east on US 136, offers fishing, boating and hiking trails as well as camping and picnic areas. *See Recreation Chart.*

Maryville Chamber of Commerce: 423 N. Market St., Maryville, MO 64468; phone (660) 582-8643.

Self-guiding tours: The Nodaway County Historical Society publishes a driving tour of more than 30 historic buildings and 20 houses in Maryville. Brochures are available from the chamber of commerce.

NODAWAY COUNTY HISTORICAL SOCIETY MUSEUM is at 110 N. Walnut St. Asian artifacts, horse racing memorabilia, a collection of military uniforms and an interactive children's area are offered. A restored 1883 schoolhouse is on the grounds. Allow 1 hour minimum. Tues.-Sat. 1-4, mid-Feb. to Dec. 1. Donations. Phone (660) 582-8176.

MEXICO (C-4) pop. 11,320, elev. 818'

Many Mexico residents share a love of championship horses. Located near the Salt River in Missouri's upland prairie region and established in 1837, early Mexico was encircled by racetracks. These tracks were the scene of Saturday afternoon events well attended by the locals. The trotting and pacing races at Mexico's fair in 1908 were purportedly the first in the nation to offer purses of as much as $1,500.

In the early 20th century Mexico was the center of one of the world's most important fireclay manufacturing areas. The refractories and brick factories here once held a virtual monopoly on the production of many types of fireclay products.

Rated by the Department of the Army and the Department of Education as one of the nation's top military schools, the Missouri Military Academy is the home of the Fusiliers, a national champion drill team. The public is invited to watch the battalion march in review on Sundays at 1:40 from September through May. Campus tours are available daily during the same months; phone (573) 581-1776 or (888) 564-6662.

Mexico Area Chamber of Commerce: 111A N. Washington, Mexico, MO 65265; phone (573) 581-2765.

AUDRAIN COUNTY HISTORICAL SOCIETY AND AMERICAN SADDLE HORSE MUSEUM is at 501 Muldrow St. Gen. Ulysses S. Grant visited the 1857 Graceland house during the early days of the Civil War. The house's second owner, Colby T. Quisenberry, brought the first saddle horses into Audrain County from Kentucky. Rooms are furnished in period. The museum traces the role played by Audrain County in the development of the saddle horse.

Tues.-Sat. 10-4, Sun. 1-4, Feb.-Dec.; closed holidays. Admission $3; under 12, $1. Phone (573) 581-3910.

MOUND CITY (A-1) pop. 1,193, elev. 877'

SQUAW CREEK NATIONAL WILDLIFE REFUGE is s. on CR E to US 159, then .5 mi. w. Some 268 species of birds—including up to half a million waterfowl during migrations—inhabit the 7,200-acre refuge on the east edge of the Missouri River flood plain. Nearly 200 bald eagles winter in the refuge, which has hiking trails, observation towers, a wayside exhibit and a 10-mile auto tour route. Information leaflets are available at the office headquarters. Refuge open daily dawn-dusk (weather permitting). Headquarters open Mon.-Fri. 7:30-4. Free. Phone (660) 442-3187.

NEOSHO (E-2) pop. 10,505, elev. 1,019'

Neosho was named for the Osage word describing the clear water of a large spring near the center of town. The community was the boyhood home of artist Thomas Hart Benton, whose bold caricature-like paintings and murals portrayed the nation's ideas of life west of the Mississippi River in the early 1800s.

Neosho Area Chamber of Commerce: 308 W. Spring, Neosho, MO 64850; phone (417) 451-1925.

NATIONAL FISH HATCHERY is at 520 E. Park St. Lake Taneycomo and military reservations are stocked with rainbow trout by the hatchery, which also produces millions of 3-inch rainbow trout for transfer to federal hatcheries in Arkansas. Picnic facilities are available. Mon.-Fri. 8-4:30. Free. Phone (417) 451-0554.

NEVADA (D-1) pop. 8,607, elev. 862'

In the 1850s Nevada found itself in the middle of the violent border warfare between proponents of slavery and abolitionists in the Kansas Territory. The situation worsened after the outbreak of the Civil War, when Kansas gangs called Jayhawkers ravaged the Missouri border counties between Nevada and Kansas City.

In response to the attacks, Confederate partisans banded together to fight behind Union lines. Considered outlaws by Unionists and heroes by border residents, the guerrilla fighters were called Bushwhackers, and Nevada was deemed the Bushwhacker Capital for its strategic position during the conflict. Bushwhackers from Nevada included Frank James and James A. "Dick" Liddil, another James gang member.

Nevada-Vernon County Chamber of Commerce: 201 E. Cherry, Suite 204, Nevada, MO 64772; phone (417) 667-5300.

BUSHWHACKER MUSEUM entrance is at 212 W. Walnut St. This museum chronicles the history of Vernon County and displays artifacts from the Bushwhacker Jail, the county jail for a century (1860-1960). Also displayed are furnished rooms from the historic Hornback House as well as Civil War memorabilia relating to the Bushwhackers.

The jail is located in the same block as the museum; guided tours are available. Allow 1 hour minimum. Mon.-Sat. 10-4, May-Oct.; by appointment rest of year. Admission $3; ages 12-17, $2; under 12, $1. Phone (417) 667-9602.

NEW MADRID (F-6) pop. 3,334, elev. 225'

New Madrid is at the tip of New Madrid Bend, an almost 360-degree curve at one of the widest points on the Mississippi River. In 1811 the river city's growth halted when its terrain was reshaped by one of the strongest earthquakes felt in North America. This was followed by a series of quakes and tremors that occurred regularly for almost 2 years.

By the time of the Civil War, New Madrid occupied a position offering control of the Mississippi River. On Mar. 13, 1862, after a day of heavy fighting, Brig. Gen. John Pope and his Union troops forced Confederate commodore George Hollins and his men to withdraw.

The New Madrid Observation Deck at the end of Main Street offers a good view of New Madrid Bend.

New Madrid Chamber of Commerce: 560 Mott St., New Madrid, MO 63869; phone (573) 748-5300.

HIGGERSON SCHOOL HISTORIC SITE is at Main and Motts sts. The interior of this one-room schoolhouse is preserved as it was in 1948, when the white clapboard building accommodated one teacher and

32 students in eight grades. Wed.-Sat. 10-4, Memorial Day-Labor Day; by appointment rest of year. Admission $2; over 55, $1.50; ages 6-12, $1. Phone (573) 748-5716.

HUNTER-DAWSON STATE HISTORIC SITE is on Dawson Rd., just e. of Main St. Built in Greek Revival and Italianate styles, this restored 15-room house is furnished as it might have looked in the mid-19th century. Guided tours are available. Mon.-Sat. 10-4, Sun. noon-4; closed Jan. 1, Easter, Thanksgiving and Dec. 25. Admission $2.50; ages 6-12, $1.50. Phone (573) 748-5340 or (800) 334-6946.

NEW MADRID HISTORICAL MUSEUM is at Main and Water sts. Exhibits at the museum reflect the region's rich history, from Mississippian Indian culture to the early 20th century. Rooms are devoted to the 1811-12 earthquakes and the riverbend community's Civil War history. A collection of antique quilts also is displayed. Allow 1 hour minimum. Mon.-Sat. 9-5, Sun. noon-5, Memorial Day-Labor Day; Mon.-Sat. 9-4, Sun. noon-4, rest of year. Admission $2.50; over 55, $2; under 12, $1.50. AX, DS, MC, VI. Phone (573) 748-5944.

NORTH KANSAS CITY—

see Kansas City p. 180.

OSAGE BEACH (D-3) pop. 3,662

Osage Beach's location on Lake of the Ozarks makes it a popular vacation site. Music and comedy shows take place at the Main Street Music Hall, on Main Street at Blair's Landing.

Lake Area Chamber of Commerce: 1000 City Pkwy., Osage Beach, MO 65065; phone (573) 348-2730.

OZARK CAVERNS is s. on US 54 to CR A, 7.5 mi. e. to CR A33, then 1.2 mi. n. on a gravel road in Lake of the Ozarks State Park *(see Recreation Chart)*. The Angels' Shower formation can be viewed on 1-hour tours. Two-hour specialty tours and tours for children are periodically offered in the summer; phone for schedule. A visitor center presents displays about the caverns.

Picnic facilities are available. Allow 1 hour minimum. Tours depart daily at 11, 12:30, 2 and 4, June 1-Aug. 15; daily at 12:30 and 2, Aug. 16-31; Sat.-Sun. at 11, 1 and 3, Apr. 15-May 31 and Sept. 1-Oct. 15. Admission $6; ages 13-18, $5; ages 6-12, $4. Phone (573) 346-2500.

OSBORN (B-2) pop. 455, elev. 1,035'

SHATTO MILK CO. is at 9406 N. CR 33, 8 mi. n. of the jct. with CR 116. This working dairy farm offers guided tours of its operations. Visitors can milk a cow and pet baby calves. Food is available. Picnicking is permitted. Mon.-Fri. 8-6, Sat. 8-4, Sun. 9-4; closed Jan. 1, Thanksgiving and Dec. 25. Farm free. Guided tours $4. Phone (816) 930-3862.

OZARKS AND OZARK NATIONAL SCENIC RIVERWAYS

Stretching across southern Missouri, the Ozark Mountains rise from the Ozark Plateau. One of the oldest mountain ranges in North America, the eroded tableland extends from west of the Mississippi River in northern Arkansas to southern Missouri and northeast Oklahoma, ending in southern Illinois. The hardwood forests that blanket the Ozarks conceal approximately 4,000 caves, giving Missouri its reputation as the cave state.

Immortalized for their exceptional beauty in Harold Bell Wright's novel "The Shepherd of the Hills," the Ozarks are rich in folklore and tradition. The mountains were settled after the Civil War by Scottish mountaineers and homesteaders from Kentucky, Virginia, the Carolinas and Tennessee.

In the isolation of the hills and hollows, indigent farmers tended their moonshine stills and produced from their fiddles the first strains of what came to be known as country music.

The Ozark National Scenic Riverways embrace portions of the Current and Jacks Fork rivers. Land along both sides of the rivers is protected. Forests, with many varieties of trees, shrubs and wildflowers, cover three-fourths of the riverways. Wildlife is abundant; hunting is permitted in season.

The riverways area is noted for its many springs—more than 60 in all. Big Spring, south of Van Buren on US 60 and then 4 miles east on SR 103, is one of the nation's largest springs. Flowing from a collapsed cave, it emits an average of 286 million gallons of water a day. A two-story historic roller mill, 6 miles west of Eminence via SR 106, is preserved at Alley Spring, one of the riverways' largest springs.

Flashlight tours of Round Spring Cavern near Round Spring are offered by park interpreters during the summer. Recreational facilities in the park include camping and picnic areas. Several outfitters offer float trips on the Current and Jacks Fork rivers.

For information about seasonal interpretive programs, craft demonstrations and other activities, visit park headquarters in Van Buren, on the Current River, or write Ozark National Scenic Riverways, P.O. Box 490, Van Buren, MO 63965; phone (573) 323-4236. *See Recreation Chart and the AAA South Central CampBook.*

Towns in the Ozarks region listed in this book under their own descriptions are Branson, Defiance, Hermann, Hogan, Ironton, Jefferson City, New Madrid, Osage Beach, Rolla, St. James and Warsaw *(see place listings)*.

PARK HILLS (D-5) pop. 7,861

MISSOURI MINES STATE HISTORIC SITE is off US 67, 1.8 mi. w. on SR 32, then .9 mi. s. on Park Hills Rd. This 25-acre site encompasses the original buildings of a former lead mine that operated 1906-72. A museum features mining equipment and geology exhibits as well as an extensive mineral collection. A short videotape presentation provides an introduction to the lead mining process.

Allow 1 hour, 30 minutes minimum. Tours of the site are given Mon.-Sat. 10-4, Sun. noon-6, Memorial Day-Labor Day; Mon.-Sat. 10-4, Sun. noon-5, rest of year. Closed Jan. 1, Easter, Thanksgiving and Dec. 25. Fee $2.50; ages 6-12, $1.50. Phone (573) 431-6226 or (800) 334-6946.

PERRY (B-4) pop. 666

CLARENCE CANNON DAM AND MARK TWAIN LAKE are 9 mi. n. on CR J. The 285-mile shoreline of this 18,600-acre site provides 12 recreation areas with facilities for a variety of activities, including boating, fishing, swimming, camping, hiking and hunting. Summer campfire programs about the natural and cultural history of the area are presented at two amphitheaters. The nearby Clarence Cannon Powerhouse Exhibit has hands-on displays about hydroelectric power generation.

Powerhouse open Sat.-Sun. 10-5, late Mar.-late Oct. Free. Phone (573) 735-4097. *See Recreation Chart.*

PERRYVILLE (D-6) pop. 7,667

The Kings Highway, which the Spanish extended from New Madrid to St. Louis in 1789, once ran through the present site of Perryville. The rolling barrens of Perry County were named for the geographically similar small plains areas of southwestern Kentucky.

Perryville Chamber of Commerce: 2 W. St. Maries St., Perryville, MO 63775; phone (573) 547-6062.

NATIONAL SHRINE OF OUR LADY OF THE MIRACULOUS MEDAL is 1.5 mi. n. on W. St. Joseph St., then .2 mi. w. on CR T. The walls and ceilings of St. Mary's of the Barrens Church and the shrine depict religious scenes and the history of the Vincentian order. On the grounds is the Marian Grotto.

Church, shrine and grounds open daily dawn-dusk. Tours of the church and shrine are given Mon.-Fri. at 10 and 1, Sat.-Sun. at 1 and 3. Tours are not offered on holy days and holidays. Free. Phone (573) 547-8344 or (573) 547-8343.

PLATTE CITY — *see Kansas City p. 180.*

POINT LOOKOUT — *see Branson p. 153.*

POPLAR BLUFF (E-5) pop. 16,651, elev. 344′

After the formation of Butler County a site was needed to serve as county seat. The low poplar-covered bluffs lining the Black River were chosen, and in 1850 Poplar Bluff was founded. Poplar Bluff grew slowly until 1873, when the Iron Mountain Railroad spurred commerce and the development of the lumber industry.

When the supply of timber became depleted in the early 20th century, residents turned to farming and the storing and shipping of farm products. Railroads and highways helped make Poplar Bluff a wholesale and retail center for southeastern Missouri and northeastern Arkansas.

Greater Poplar Bluff Area Chamber of Commerce: 1111 W. Pine, Poplar Bluff, MO 63901; phone (573) 785-7761.

THE MARGARET HARWELL ART MUSEUM is at 421 N. Main St. It presents traveling exhibits in addition to monthly changing displays from a permanent collection of works by contemporary Missouri artists, executed in a wide range of media. Allow 30 minutes minimum. Tues.-Fri. noon-4, Sat.-Sun. 1-4; closed major holidays. Museum may close when exhibits are being changed. Free. Phone (573) 686-8002.

PUXICO (E-6) pop. 1,145, elev. 370′

MINGO NATIONAL WILDLIFE REFUGE is 1 mi. n. on SR 51. This 21,676-acre region of swampy bottomlands and wooded uplands is a haven for wintering and migrating waterfowl and other species. Fishing and limited hunting are allowed in season. Write Refuge Manager, Mingo National Wildlife Refuge, 24279 SR 51, Puxico, MO 63960.

Allow 1 hour minimum. Visitor center open Mon.-Fri. 8-4, Sat. 9-4, Sun. noon-4, Mar.-June and Sept.-Nov.; Mon.-Fri. 8-4, rest of year. Closed major holidays. Admission $3 per private vehicle. Phone (573) 222-3589.

REPUBLIC (E-2) pop. 8,438

WILSON'S CREEK NATIONAL BATTLEFIELD MUSEUM is 10 mi. s.w. via SR 60, .7 mi. s.e. on Republic Rd., then 7 mi. s. on CR ZZ. The museum features a collection of Civil War memorabilia from west of the Mississippi River, including flags, photographs, uniforms, weapons and other artifacts. Allow 30 minutes minimum. Daily 9-5. Admission $5, under 16 free, $10 per private vehicle. MC, VI. Phone (417) 732-1224.

RIVERSIDE — *see Kansas City p. 181.*

ROLLA (D-4) pop. 16,347, elev. 1,095′

Rolla was founded in 1855 when a group of railroad contractors built an office and a few warehouses near the farm of John Webber. The prospect of the railroad attracted 600 people within the following 6 months, and in 1857 a search for a town name began.

Webber, who had farmed in the area, wanted to call the town Hardscrabble. A railroad official wanted to call it Phelps Center. The suggestion of a nostalgic North Carolinian who wanted to call it Raleigh was finally approved, but the new name was spelled as the Southerner had pronounced it.

Rolla is the home of the Mid-Continent Mapping Center, National Mapping Division, US Geological Survey. The center, 1400 Independence Rd., offers tours; phone (573) 308-3850 or (573) 308-3500.

St. Patrick, the patron saint of engineers, is honored every March by students attending the University of Missouri at Rolla (UMR), who are dubbed knights in the Order of St. Patrick. Other festivities include a parade, a beard competition and painting Main Street a shade of green.

On the UMR campus near US 63 and State Street is UMR-Stonehenge, a partial replica of the ancient megaliths in England. The stone circle has apertures that allow the date to be told by the position of the sun's rays and permit the viewing of the North Star, features not present in the original construction. The replica is an official triangulation point in the National Geodetic Survey's North American Triangulation Network.

Rolla Area Chamber of Commerce: 1301 Kingshighway, Rolla, MO 65401; phone (573) 364-3577.

ED CLARK MUSEUM OF MISSOURI GEOLOGY is on Fairground Rd. in Buehler Park, .5 mi. e. of I-44 exit 184 at the Missouri Department of Natural Resources, Division of Geology and Land Survey. The museum displays minerals and fossils found in the state. Allow 30 minutes minimum. Mon.-Fri. 8-5. Free. Phone (573) 368-2100.

SAVE **MEMORYVILLE, U.S.A.** is 1 mi. n.e. at jct. I-44 and US 63N. Cars from 1907 to exotic late models, an automobile restoration shop, early 20th-century storefronts and an art gallery are featured. Allow 1 hour minimum. Mon.-Fri. 8-6, Sat.-Sun. 9-5:30; closed Thanksgiving and Dec. 25. Admission $4.75; over 54 and military $3.50; ages 6-12, $2. MC, VI. Phone (573) 364-1810.

ST. CHARLES—*see St. Louis p. 210.*

STE. GENEVIEVE (D-6)
pop. 4,476, elev. 397'

The first permanent settlement in Missouri, founded between 1725 and 1750, Ste. Genevieve is in the region that was once part of Upper Louisiana. French traditions are still evident in the festivals and the residential architecture of a town that once rivaled St. Louis in size and importance.

Great River Road Interpretive Center: 66 S. Main St., Ste. Genevieve, MO 63670; phone (573) 883-7097 or (800) 373-7007.

Self-guiding tours: Information about self-guiding walking tours is available from the interpretive center daily 9-4.

BOLDUC HOUSE is at 125 S. Main St. The home of Louis Bolduc, a wealthy merchant, planter and miner, is one of the few surviving examples of 18th-century French Colonial Mississippi Valley architecture. The restored 1785 house and grounds include the sill and stone foundation, massive trussed roof, 18th-century garden, enclosing *galerie* and stockade fence. The parlor, dining room and bedroom contain period French Canadian furnishings.

Allow 30 minutes minimum. Mon.-Sat. 10-4, Sun. 11-5, Apr.-Oct.; closed Easter. Admission (including Bolduc-LeMeilleur House) $4, students through high school with ID $2. Phone (573) 883-3105.

BOLDUC-LEMEILLEUR HOUSE is at Main and Market sts. This restored 1820 house is an example of combined French and American architectural influences. Allow 30 minutes minimum. Mon.-Sat. 10-4, Sun. 11-5, Apr.-Oct.; closed Easter. Admission (including Bolduc House) $4, students through high school with ID $2. Phone (573) 883-3105.

CHURCH OF STE. GENEVIEVE is on DuBourg Pl. near Merchant St. Although the congregation was established in 1759, the present church was not built until 1876. A religious painting dating from 1663 hangs inside. Daily 6-6. Free. Phone (573) 883-2731.

FELIX VALLE HOUSE STATE HISTORIC SITE is at Second and Merchant sts. In contrast to the vertical log houses erected by French and Spanish colonists, this 1818 house was constructed from stone in the American Federal style. Its two entrances let the building serve as both home and office for its owners. The house is furnished in period. Mon.-Sat. 10-4, Sun. noon-5; closed Mon. Dec.-Feb., Jan. 1, Easter, Thanksgiving and Dec. 25. Admission $2.50; ages 6-12, $1.50. Phone (573) 883-7102.

The Amoureux House is .25 mi. s. on Main St. to 327 St. Mary's Rd. This 1792 French Colonial vertical log home is one of three in the United States built using only vertical logs for its foundation. An exhibit room with information about the community's architectural history and a diorama room with a model of Ste. Genevieve circa 1832 are highlights. Guided tours are available. Allow 30 minutes minimum. Daily 10-4, June-Aug.; Sat.-Sun. 10-4, Apr.-May and Sept.-Oct. Admission $1.50; ages 6-12, 75c. Phone (573) 883-7102.

LA MAISON GUIBOURD-VALLE is at 1 N. Fourth St. Built in the French style by Spanish soldiers in 1784, the house was bought in 1799 by Jacques Jean René Guibourd, a French settler. The restored residence is of vertical log construction and has elegant 18th- and 19th-century French furnishings. Hand-hewn oak beams secured by wooden pegs and a Norman truss form the large attic.

Costumed guides conduct tours. Allow 30 minutes minimum. Tours are given daily 10-5, May-Sept.; daily 10-4, Oct. 1-first weekend in Dec. and in Apr.; Sat.-Sun. 10-4, in Mar. Admission $4; over 60, $3.50; grades K-12, $2. Phone (573) 883-7544.

STE. GENEVIEVE MUSEUM is at Merchant and Third sts. Displays include American Indian relics, Civil War items, old coins, rare documents and birds mounted by John James Audubon during his residence in Ste. Genevieve. Mon.-Sat. 10-4, Sun. 11-4, Apr.-Oct.; daily noon-4, rest of year. Closed Jan. 1,

Easter, Thanksgiving and Dec. 24-25 and 31. Admission $2, students 50c. Phone (573) 883-3461.

ST. JAMES (D-4) pop. 3,704, elev. 1,087'

MARAMEC SPRING PARK is 6 mi. s. on SR 68, then 2 mi. s. on SR 8. The site of the first successful ironworks west of the Mississippi River, the park contains the Ozark Agriculture Museum, the Maramec Museum and the Maramec Nature Center. Picnicking, hiking and trout fishing facilities are available March through October. Daily dawn-dusk. Park admission $3 per private vehicle. Phone (573) 265-7387.

Maramec Museum, 21880 Maramec Dr., depicts the operation of the Maramec Iron Works 1826-76. A taped tour describes working exhibits. Remains of the original facility are on the grounds. Daily 11-5, June-Aug.; Mon.-Fri. 10-3, Sat.-Sun. noon-4 in May; Wed.-Fri. 10-3, Sat.-Sun. noon-4 in Apr. and Sept.-Oct. Free. Phone (573) 265-7124.

ST. JOSEPH (B-1) pop. 73,990, elev. 823'

St. Joseph was founded in 1826 by Joseph Robidoux, who established a fur trading post in the Blacksnake Hills. The mass migrations following the discovery of gold in California in 1848 and Colorado in 1858 transformed the frontier town into a major wagon train staging area and supply depot. In 1859 Robidoux drove the last spike on the Hannibal

and St. Joseph Railroad, which made St. Joseph the westernmost railroad terminal.

The Pony Express launched its famous mail service on Apr. 3, 1860, from St. Joseph to Sacramento, Calif. Riders traveled the 10-day route twice a week.

Notorious outlaw Jesse James lived quietly with his family in St. Joseph, where he was known as the mild-mannered, respected Mr. Howard. He was killed in 1882 by fellow gang member Bob Ford, whose brother Charles claimed the $10,000 reward.

The Buchanan County Courthouse, 411 Jules St., originally was constructed at Fifth and Felix streets in 1873. During the Centennial Exhibition of 1876, the classical Renaissance building was called one of the most outstanding buildings in the country. Its exterior is lighted at night; the interior houses county offices.

St. Joseph Convention and Visitors Bureau: 109 S. 4th St., P.O. Box 445, St. Joseph, MO 64502; phone (816) 233-6688 or (800) 785-0360. See color ad.

THE ALBRECHT-KEMPER MUSEUM OF ART is 2 mi. w. of I-29 at 2818 Frederick Ave. Housed in the 1935 former Albrecht Mansion, the museum displays American art from the 18th century to the present as well as special exhibits. Tues.-Fri. 10-4, Sat.-Sun. 1-4; closed major holidays. Admission $5; over 64, $2; students with ID and ages 7-17, $1. Phone (816) 233-7003.

DOLL MUSEUM is at 1115 S. 12th St. Old dolls in original handmade clothes are displayed. Among the changing exhibits are miniature dishes, toys, buggies and a Missouri farmhouse complete in every detail. Mon.-Sat. 11:30-4:30, June-Sept. Admission $2.50; over 62, $2; ages 5-12, 75c. Phone (816) 233-1420.

THE GLORE PSYCHIATRIC MUSEUM is at 3406 Frederick Ave. It surveys the portrayal and treatment of mental illness over the years, including exhibits of antique ward furniture and such primitive early equipment as lobotomy instruments, a hydrotub, a tranquilizing chair, a restraint cage and wet sheet packs. The museum also recounts the history of a facility once known as "State Lunatic Asylum No. 2."

Allow 1 hour minimum. Mon.-Sat. 10-5, Sun. 1-5; closed major holidays. Admission (includes The Black Archives of St. Joseph and the St. Joseph Museum) $3; ages 7-18, $1. Phone (816) 232-8471 or (800) 530-8866.

The Black Archives of St. Joseph, 3406 Frederick Ave. on The Glore Psychiatric Museum grounds, has exhibits depicting the history and cultural heritage of the African-American community in St. Joseph. Mon.-Sat. 10-5, Sun. 1-5; closed major holidays. Phone (816) 232-8471.

St. Joseph Museum, 3406 Frederick Ave. on The Glore Psychiatric Museum grounds, contains displays of Native American clothing, pottery, weapons and jewelry as well as exhibits chronicling the travels of explorers Meriwether Lewis and William Clark, Civil War history and St. Joseph's role in the nation's westward expansion. Mon.-Sat. 10-5, Sun. 1-5; closed major holidays. Phone (816) 232-8471. *See color ad.*

SAVE **JESSE JAMES HOME** is at 12th and Penn sts. on the grounds of the Patee House Museum *(see attraction listing)*. The outlaw's residence was the scene of his death at the hands of members of his gang. A bullet hole in the wall was made Apr. 3, 1882, when James was killed. The restored house is furnished with original and period pieces. Tape recordings explain the significance of events that occurred in each room. Mon.-Sat. 10-5, Sun. 1-5, Apr.-Oct.; Mon.-Fri. 10-4, Sat. 10-5, Sun. 1-5, rest of year. Admission $2; over 59, $1.50; students with ID $1. Phone (816) 232-8206.

KRUG PARK is at the n. end of the city on St. Joseph Ave. Visitors can view American bison, Texas longhorn cattle, burros, deer, ducks and geese at the park, which encompasses a natural bowl that forms an open-air amphitheater with a seating capacity of 20,000. A 26-mile scenic parkway system and a 9.5-mile greenbelt extend from Krug Park to Hyde Park. Daily 6 a.m.-midnight. Free. Phone (816) 271-5500.

NATIONAL MILITARY HERITAGE MUSEUM is w. off I-29 at 701 Messanie St. Exhibits pay homage to the five branches of the U.S. military. War artillery, personal effects of soldiers, a model of the battleship USS *Missouri*, a diorama depicting two landing ship tanks (LSTs) at Iwo Jima and a collection of military vehicles are displayed. There also is a replica of the Vietnam Veterans Memorial wall in Washington, D.C. Allow 1 hour minimum. Mon.-Fri. 9-5, Sat. 9-1; closed major holidays. Admission $2, children 50c. Phone (816) 233-4321.

PATEE HOUSE MUSEUM is at 12th and Penn sts. One of the finest hotels west of the Mississippi when it opened in 1858, it also was the headquarters of the Pony Express. The museum contains recreated Hannibal and St. Joseph Railroad and Pony Express offices, a wood-burning locomotive and mail car from the 1860s era, a street with models of St. Joseph buildings from the early 1900s, and antique transportation and communications collections.

Mon.-Sat. 10-5, Sun. 1-5, Apr.-Oct.; Sat. 10-5, Sun. 1-5, rest of year. Admission $4; over 59, $3.50; under 18, $2.50. Phone (816) 232-8206.

PONY EXPRESS NATIONAL MEMORIAL is at 914 Penn St. This was the original site of the business venture that developed from the War Department's demand for speedy communications with California. Riders routinely made the 1,966-mile trip between St. Joseph and Sacramento, Calif., in 10 days. The museum houses exhibits about the creation, operation and demise of the Pony Express. Mon.-Sat. 9-5, Sun. 1-5; closed Jan. 1, Thanksgiving and Dec. 24-25 and 31. Admission $4; senior citizens $3; ages 7-18, $2. Phone (816) 279-5059.

ROBIDOUX ROW MUSEUM is at Third and Poulin sts. City founder Joseph Robidoux built this row of seven connected houses 1840-50 as temporary housing for newly arrived settlers. Four restored units remain of the building, including Robidoux's personal quarters, furnished with his possessions and period pieces, and a wintering room for westward bound pioneer families.

Tues.-Fri. 10-4, Sat.-Sun. 1-4, May-Sept.; Tues.-Fri. noon-4, Sun. 1-4, rest of year. Closed Jan. 1, Thanksgiving, and Dec. 24-25 and 31. Admission $2; ages 13-18, 50c. Phone (816) 232-5861.

THE WYETH-TOOTLE MANSION is at 11th and Charles sts. Overlooking the Missouri River, this 1879 Gothic sandstone mansion was designed with a north side turret to create a resemblance to European castles. It is one of many turn-of-the-20th-century residences in the city. Guided tours are available. Allow 30 minutes minimum. Wed.-Sat. 10-5, Sun. 1-5; closed major holidays. Admission $2.50; ages 7-18, $1. Phone (816) 232-8471 or (800) 530-8866.

CASINOS

• **St. Jo Frontier Casino**, 777 Winners Cir. Sun.-Thurs. 8 a.m.-2 a.m., Fri.-Sat. 8 a.m.-4 a.m. Phone (816) 279-5514 or (800) 888-2946.

St. Louis

City Population: 348,189   **Elevation:** 585 ft.

Editor's Picks:

The Gateway Arch.................*(see p. 205)*
St. Louis Science Center.......... *(see p. 204)*
St. Louis Zoo........................*(see p. 204)*

The Gateway Arch / © ImageState-Pictor / Jupiter Images

Chosen by Pierre Laclede in 1764, the site of St. Louis answered the needs of the French fur trader. In the midst of country rich in buffaloes, deer, raccoons, bears, otters, red foxes, muskrats and beavers; on a high bluff with the Missouri and Mississippi rivers nearby; convenient to the established town of New Orleans—the settlement was destined for immediate success.

First came New Orleanian settlers, then native and French-Canadian trappers. Explorers followed, notably Capt. Meriwether Lewis, who outfitted the Lewis and Clark expedition to explore and map the Pacific Northwest. The Lewis & Clark Corps of Discovery Monument located in Case Park pays homage to the two explorers.

The 1857 completion of the railroad link to the East Coast brought newly arrived immigrants from Germany, Ireland and other European countries; their skills and crafts enriched and transformed the character of the city.

Having survived the disastrous 1840s, when a flood, cholera and a catastrophic fire conspired to nearly destroy the town, St. Louis citizens rebuilt with renewed effort. By the 1870s the city had a population of 300,000 and thriving industries. In 1904, 200,000 people helped open the great Louisiana Purchase Exposition, which lasted 7 months and gave the world its first ice cream cones, hot dogs and iced tea. The city received its art museum, the Jefferson National Expansion Memorial and a statue of St. Louis the Crusader.

Growth was slowed by World War I, the Great Depression and Prohibition. Residents, however, had the foresight to help finance a young man named Charles A. Lindbergh, who dreamed of flying across the Atlantic Ocean from New York to Paris.

The 10-story, red-brick Wainwright Building, downtown at Chestnut and Seventh streets, was built in 1892 and is considered to be one of the forerunners of the modern skyscraper. Architect Louis Sullivan incorporated a steel skeleton support structure and a delicate floral motif of terra-cotta ornamentation that accentuated the building's height. Named for local financier Ellis Wainwright, who commissioned the design, it now contains Missouri state government offices.

Office skyscrapers, elegant shopping centers and numerous restaurants, hotels and apartment complexes are the results of an extensive 1960s urban renewal project. Busch Stadium and the America's Center convention center are two of the most visible results from that era. Where dilapidated warehouses once stood, the Gateway Arch soars above the riverfront grounds of the Jefferson National Expansion Memorial. And emblematic of the 21st century is a new Busch Stadium, which rose next to the old one and opened in 2006.

St. Louis also is a city of distinctive neighborhoods. Soulard, just south of downtown, was named for a Frenchman who surveyed the land in this area in the late 18th century (when Missouri was part of the Upper Louisiana territory). It is an ethnically diverse enclave noted for red-brick Victorian and Federal-style townhouses and the Soulard Farmers Market at 7th Street and Lafayette Avenue, reputedly the oldest farmers market west of the Mississippi. Open Wednesday through Saturday, the

Getting There — *starting on p. 201*
Getting Around — *starting on p. 201*
What To See — *starting on p. 201*
What To Do — *starting on p. 206*
Where To Stay — *starting on p. 521*
Where To Dine — *starting on p. 525*

market brims with stalls offering local and imported produce, meats, fish, cheeses, fresh baked items and other goodies.

The Hill, St. Louis' Italian neighborhood, is in the southwestern part of the city, bounded by Hampton Avenue and Kingshighway (just south of I-44). Here even the fire hydrants are painted green, white and red, the colors of the Italian flag, and elderly residents play bocce (BOH-chee), or Italian lawn bowling, a game imported from the mother country. Baseball greats Yogi Berra and Joe Garagiola grew up on The Hill. It also is the city's No. 1 destination for primo Italian food, and the streets are chock-ablock with delis, bakeries, pizza parlors and shops selling specialty salamis and numerous other tempting comestibles.

And speaking of culinary wonders, when the weather turns warm the thoughts of practically every St. Louisan turn to Ted Drewes Frozen Custard, a city institution since 1929. The vanilla custard, a formula developed by Drewes' father, comes with all sorts of topping choices and flavors and is sold in cones, sundaes and "concretes"—milkshakes so thick they refuse to leave the cup even when turned upside down. With names like the Crater Copernicus and the Terramizou, these rich treats are as much a part of summer in St. Louis as a Cardinals game. The flagship stand is at 6726 Chippewa St, (Old Route 66); another branch is at 4224 South Grand in South St. Louis.

In 1873 the first continuous public school kindergarten in the United States was started in what is now the Carondelet Historic Center. St. Louis' commitment to education is evident in the area's five universities and 26 colleges. St. Louis University, founded in 1818, was the first Catholic university in

St. Louis Zoo, Forest Park / Missouri Division of Tourism

the Midwest. Washington University is known for its medical school. The two universities have together produced a dozen Nobel Prize laureates.

The universities of Missouri and Southern Illinois have branch campuses in the area. Other institutions of higher learning include Logan Chiropractic College, the St. Louis Conservatory of Music, the St. Louis College of Pharmacy and Webster University.

Chrysler and General Motors plants have made the St. Louis metropolitan area an important manufacturer of motor vehicles. Such major corporations as Anheuser-Busch, Brown Shoe Co., Inc., Emerson and Solutia have their headquarters here. Many local jobs are in retailing, finance, transportation and manufacturing.

In the past St. Louisans soared in balloons and backed Lindbergh in his dream; more recently many helped build the Mercury and Gemini space capsules and military fighter planes. The city also is an important railroad terminal. St. Louis Union Station, at 1800 Market St., was constructed in 1894 and

Destination St. Louis

S t. Louis is chock-full of history. Once the major gateway for pioneers on westward trails, it's also home to the Old Courthouse, where the infamous Dred Scott trial took place.

T he revitalized waterfront, once crammed with cargo, now flaunts attractions galore.

© Richard Cummins / SuperStock

Museum of Transportation, Kirkwood.
All aboard the happy train! Kirkwood's Museum of Transportation has a collection of vehicles that includes more than 70 locomotives. (See listing page 210)

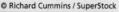
© Richard Cummins / SuperStock

Soldiers' Memorial Military Museum, St. Louis.
The military service of St. Louisans is honored at this museum, which salutes those who fought in World Wars I and II and the Korean and Vietnam conflicts. (See listing page 206)

*P*laces included in this AAA Destination City:

© St. Louis Zoo

St. Louis Zoo.
A trio of zebras seems to be saying, "Bet you can't tell us apart!" They're just a few of the zoo's various animal residents.
(See listing page 204)

© SuperStock

Missouri Botanical Garden, St. Louis.
Tower Grove House, on the grounds of the Missouri Botanical Garden, is furnished in mid-19th century style. (See listing page 206)

See Vicinity map
page 202

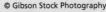
© Gibson Stock Photography

St. Louis Science Center.
Life-size dinosaurs are among the many exhibits at the St. Louis Science Center, where you can even build your own version of the city's signature Gateway Arch. (See listing page 204)

The Informed Traveler

Sales Tax: The sales tax rate in the city of St. Louis is 6.85 percent. The city's lodging tax is 14.1 percent and there is a rental car tax of 5.97 percent.

WHOM TO CALL

Emergency: 911

Police (non-emergency): (314) 444-5555

Time and Temperature: (636) 441-8467 or (314) 321-2222

Hospitals: Barnes-Jewish Hospital, (314) 747-3000; Forest Park Hospital, (314) 768-3000; Missouri Baptist Hospital, (314) 996-5000; Saint Louis University Hospital, (314) 577-8000; St. Anthony's Medical Center, (314) 525-1000; St. John's Mercy Medical Center, (314) 569-6000.

WHERE TO LOOK

Newspapers

St. Louis is served by the *Post-Dispatch*, a morning newspaper.

Radio

St. Louis radio station KMOX (1120 AM) is an all-news/weather station; KWMU (90.7 FM) is a member of National Public Radio.

Visitor Information

St. Louis Visitors Center: 308 Washington Ave., St. Louis, MO 63102; phone (314) 241-1764 daily 9:30-4:30.

St. Louis Convention and Visitors Commission: 701 Convention Plaza, Suite 300, St. Louis, MO 63101; phone (314) 421-2100 for a recorded listing of events, (314) 421-1023 or (800) 916-0092 for general information.

TRANSPORTATION

Air Travel

Lambert-St. Louis International Airport is on I-70 in the northwestern section of the metropolitan area. Taxi fare from the airport is usually about $35. The area's light-rail system, MetroLink, originates at the airport and culminates at Scott Air Force Base in Shiloh, Ill. Trains run daily; schedule varies. Tickets or passes may be purchased; fares vary.

Rental Cars

Hertz offers discounts to AAA members; phone (314) 426-7555 or (800) 654-3080.

Rail Service

The Amtrak terminal, (800) 872-7245, is at 550 S. 16th St.

Buses

The Greyhound Lines Inc. terminal, (800) 231-2222, is at 1450 N. 13th St.

Taxis

Cab companies include County Cab, (314) 991-5300; Laclede, (314) 652-3456; and Yellow, (314) 361-2345. All cabs in St. Louis are on the meter system. Base fare is approximately $2.50 for the first mile, with a rate of $2 per mile. The base fare goes up $1 for each additional passenger. A fuel surcharge of at least $1 also is added to the fare. Taxis can be ordered by phone or hired at cab stands near the large downtown hotels.

Public Transport

Metro, the public transportation system—which includes MetroBus, the MetroLink light-rail train and the Metro Call-A-Ride para-transit van service—routes passengers throughout the St. Louis metropolitan region. The basic bus fare is $1.75; over 64, ages 5-12 and customers with disabilities, 85c. Exact cash fare is required. A MetroLink one-ride ticket is $2; over 64, ages 5-12 and customers with disabilities, $1. Various transfers and multiday passes also are available.

For route information, current fares and hours of system operation contact MetroTransit Information Mon.-Fri. 7-7; phone (314) 231-2345, or (618) 271-2345 in Illinois.

was once the largest and busiest rail passenger terminal in the world. Now a National Historic Landmark and architectural delight, it encompasses a lake, a 539-room hotel and an entertainment, shopping and dining complex.

Getting There

Getting There

As befits the Gateway to the West, a network of major interstate highways flows into St. Louis, bringing goods and people from all points of the compass. From the east come I-55, I-64, I-70 and US 40; all these highways converge at the Poplar Street Bridge to pour into the downtown area and through the western suburbs as I-64/US 40 (the Daniel Boone Expressway).

I-55 approaches from the south and I-44 from the southwest; I-70 enters from the northwest to combine in the downtown area with I-55. A bypass route is formed by I-270, with connections to I-70, I-64, I-55, I-44 and I-170. I-270 becomes I-255 southeast of the city before connecting with I-64 and I-70 to the east in Illinois.

Getting Around

Street System

Streets in downtown St. Louis follow a basic grid pattern complicated by a system of one-way streets. Numbered streets run parallel to the Mississippi River; numbers begin at the river and run westward. The north-south dividing line is Market Street.

After a complete stop, a right turn on red is permitted unless otherwise posted. Driving during rush hours, generally from 7 to 9 a.m. and 4 to 6 p.m., should be avoided.

Parking

On-street parking is controlled by meter, but your chance of finding a space where and when you want one is slight. Many commercial lots and garages are in the downtown business core and around Memorial Plaza; several multilevel garages are in the vicinity of Busch Stadium as well. Rates average $2 per hour for the first 5 hours, $4 for 6 to 13 hours, and $8 for 14 to 24 hours. For stadium events, day or night, the charge is $5-$10.

Rates for the parking garage at the Gateway Arch are 75c for every half-hour, with a $10 maximum charge per day. Additional parking, which costs from $3 to $5 per day, can be found at private lots on the landing.

What To See

ALOE PLAZA faces Market St. between 18th and 20th sts. The 14 bronze figures comprising the "Meeting of the Waters" fountain by Swedish sculptor Carl Milles symbolize the meeting of the Mississippi and Missouri rivers.

AMERICAN KENNEL CLUB MUSEUM OF THE DOG is at 1721 S. Mason Rd., 2 mi. s. of I-64 in Queeny Park. It displays permanent and changing

Jewel Box, Forest Park / © Gibson Stock Photography

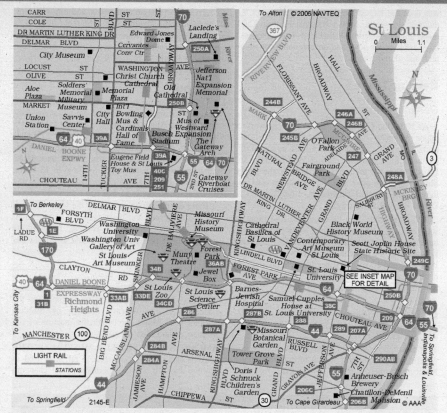

exhibits of fine art, artifacts and literature devoted to dogs. More than 150 informational and instructional videotapes can be viewed in the museum's theater. Use of the library is available by appointment. Museum open Tues.-Sat. 10-4, Sun. 1-5; closed holidays. Admission $5; over 59, $2.50; ages 5-14, $1. Phone (314) 821-3647.

BLACK WORLD HISTORY MUSEUM is at 2505 St. Louis Ave. The museum depicts the lives and contributions of African Americans in the United States from the earliest days of slavery through the 20th century. Life-size wax figures of notable African Americans with a Missouri connection include Dred Scott, Dr. George Washington Carver and Miles Davis. A collection of historical items includes artifacts, documents and a scale model of a slave ship. Allow 1 hour minimum. Tues.-Sat. 10-5; closed Dec. 24-Jan. 1. Admission $5; ages 13-17, $4; over 65, $3.50; under 13, $2.50. MC, VI. Phone (314) 241-7057.

CATHEDRAL BASILICA OF ST. LOUIS is at Lindell Blvd. and Newstead Ave. Combining Romanesque and Byzantine architectural styles, this Catholic cathedral is adorned with more than 41.5 million pieces of glass. Work on the mosaics covering the walls and domed ceilings began in 1912. In

1923 Paul Heuduck took over the task, and in 1988 his son Arno completed it. Grandchildren of both men participated in the project as well. Scenes illustrate the Old and New Testaments and local history. Daily 6-5. Tours are given Sun. at 1. Free. Phone (314) 533-2824 or (314) 373-8243.

SAVE **CHATILLON-DeMENIL MANSION** is at 3352 DeMenil Pl. This three-story Greek Revival mansion was built around 1848. Many of the elegant furnishings and wallpapers came from France. Food is available. Allow 1 hour minimum. Tues.-Sat. 10-4, mid-Feb. through Dec. 31. Admission $5; under 12, $2. Phone (314) 771-5828.

CHRIST CHURCH CATHEDRAL is at 13th and Locust sts. One of the first Protestant churches west of the Mississippi River, this Episcopal cathedral contains noteworthy reredos—ornamental screens behind altars—carved by Harry Hems of Exeter, England. An attractive garden is on the 13th Street side of the cathedral. Mon.-Fri. 9-4. Free. Phone (314) 231-3454.

CITY MUSEUM is at 701 N. 15th St. Built entirely from recycled factory and warehouse materials, the museum's is geared toward children, with exhibits that encourage climbing, sliding and exploring. The mazelike layout takes visitors through an urban phantasmagoria of tunnels, rolling slides, water chutes and labyrinths of twisted metal. Magicians, clowns and acrobats provide additional entertainment.

The rooftop World Aquarium features interactive touch tanks where children can pet sharks and stingrays, pick up a turtle or touch a starfish. Aquatic-themed displays and play spaces are filled with giant seashell columns and spraying jets of water. There also is a Ferris wheel.

Food is available. Allow 2 hours minimum. Museum open Mon.-Fri. 9-5 (also Fri. 5 p.m.-1 a.m.), Sat. 10 a.m.-1 a.m., Sun. 11-5, Memorial Day-Labor Day; Wed.-Fri. 9-5 (also Fri. 5 p.m.-1 a.m.), Sat. 10 a.m.-1 a.m., Sun. 11-5, rest of year. World Aquarium open Mon.-Fri. 9-5 (also Fri. 5-11 p.m.), Sat. 10 a.m.-11 p.m., Sun. 11-5, Memorial Day-Labor Day; Wed.-Fri. 9-5 (also Fri. 5-11 p.m.), Sat. 10 a.m.-11 p.m., Sun. 11-5, rest of year. Closed Easter, Thanksgiving and Dec. 25. Admission $12 ($8 Fri.-Sat. after 5), under 3 free. World Aquarium (available only with City Museum admission) $6, under 3 free. Parking $3 per car, $5 per SUV; additional pay lots and metered street parking available. AX, CB, DC, DS, MC, VI. Phone (314) 231-2489.

CONTEMPORARY ART MUSEUM ST. LOUIS is at 3750 Washington Ave. The museum features art exhibitions by leading contemporary artists as well as performances, lectures and special events. Tues.-Sat. 10-5 (also Thurs. 5-8), Sun. 11-4. Admission $5; over 65, $3; students with ID free; free to all Wed. and Sat. Phone (314) 535-4660.

SAVE **EUGENE FIELD HOUSE AND ST. LOUIS TOY MUSEUM** is at 634 S. Broadway. Antique and collectible toys are displayed at the birthplace and childhood home of children's poet Eugene Field, whose poems included "Little Boy Blue" and "Wynken, Blynken and Nod." The 1845 house was owned by Eugene's father, Roswell Martin Field, the attorney who represented Dred Scott in his 1853 lawsuit for freedom.

Allow 1 hour minimum. Wed.-Sat. 10-4, Sun. noon-4; closed major holidays. Last admission 30 minutes before closing. Admission $4; under 12, 50c. Phone (314) 421-4689.

GEM **FOREST PARK** is bounded by Lindell, Skinker and Kingshighway blvds. and Oakland Ave. Officially opened to the public on June 24, 1876, Forest Park is one of the country's largest urban parks. Beloved by St. Louisans, the park is not only a popular spot for picnicking, jogging and bicycling but also is home to the city's major cultural institutions.

Covering 1,293 acres, Forest Park is located next to the West End residential section in the heart of downtown St. Louis. In addition to the following listed attractions, the park contains the Steinburg Memorial Skating Rink, which offers facilities for ice and roller skating; and the 27-hole Probstein Community Golf Course.

Park open daily 6 a.m.-10 p.m. Free. Phone (314) 289-5300.

Jewel Box is e. of the St. Louis Zoo at Wells and McKinley drs. This Art Deco-style, glass-walled conservatory displays a permanent collection of tropical trees, foliage plants and flowers. Seasonal floral shows take place at Easter, Mother's Day and the Christmas holidays. Allow 30 minutes minimum. Mon.-Fri. 9-4, Sat. 9-11, Sun. 9-2. Admission $1; free to all Mon.-Tues. 9-noon. Phone (314) 531-0080.

GEM **Missouri History Museum,** Lindell Blvd. and DeBaliviere Ave. in Forest Park, can be entered from both the Jefferson Memorial Building and Emerson Center. The museum's interactive galleries include Seeking St. Louis, which takes a look at the lives of St. Louis citizens from the city's earliest days to the present; Lindbergh, an in-depth exploration of the aviator's famed transatlantic flight; and The 1904 World's Fair, a peek into America's future as envisioned from the standpoint of the 20th century's early years.

Other exhibits cover such subjects as the travels of explorers Meriwether Lewis and George Rogers Clark, St. Louis traditions like breweries and baseball, and famed musicians Scott Joplin and Miles Davis. Lectures, concerts and special programs are presented regularly.

Food is available. Allow 1 hour minimum. Daily 10-6 (also Tues. 6-8 p.m.); closed Jan. 1, Thanksgiving and Dec. 25. Free. A fee may be charged for special exhibits. Phone (314) 746-4599. *See color ad p. 203.*

 St. Louis Art Museum is on Art Hill. Built to house the fine arts pavilion at the 1904 World's Fair, this Beaux Arts-style building was designed by famed architect Cass Gilbert. Guarded by the heroic statue of St. Louis the Crusader, it features more than 30,000 works of art covering a spectrum of cultures and periods. Collections include European, Asian and American paintings; African, Oceanic and American Indian art; prints, drawings and photographs; late 19th and early 20th-century American and European decorative arts; 20th-century German art; and Chinese bronzes and porcelains.

The museum also presents changing exhibitions of major touring shows and offers a resource center, library, lectures, films, classes and special events. Food is available. Allow 1 hour minimum. Tues.-Sun. 10-5 (also Fri. 5-9); closed Jan. 1, Thanksgiving and Dec. 25. Tours focusing on particular types of art are conducted Tues.-Sun. at 1:30. Free. Admission is charged for special exhibitions. Phone (314) 721-0072.

St. Louis Science Center is at 5050 Oakland Ave. The center encourages hands-on exploration of such diverse topics as aviation, cosmology, ecology, engineering, medicine and space science. Visitors can program a robot; use a radar gun to clock the speed of traffic passing under a glass bridge above I-64; crawl through a 19th-century coal mine and a modern utility tunnel; and build a replica of the Gateway Arch.

The Discovery Room features imaginative science activities for ages 2-8. Nature, wildlife and adventure films from around the world are shown daily on the four-story OMNIMAX theater. The McDonnell Planetarium features a space station experience and a high-tech view of 9,000 stars in the night sky.

Allow 4 hours minimum. Science center open Mon.-Sat. 9:30-5:30 (also Fri.-Sat. 5:30-9:30), Sun. 11:30-5:30, Memorial Day-Labor Day; Mon.-Sat. 9:30-4:30 (also Fri. 4:30-9:30), Sun. 11:30-4:30, rest of year. Closed Dec. 25. Exhibits gallery free. OMNIMAX theater $8; over 59 and under 18, $7. Discovery Room $3. Tickets should be purchased early in the day. Advance tickets are available. Parking $8. Phone (314) 289-4444 or (800) 456-7572.

St. Louis Zoo is at 1 Government Dr. in Forest Park. About 11,000 animals representing more than 800 species from around the world reside in scenic, natural settings. Among the zoo's highlights is the lushly landscaped Fragile Forest, an outdoor compound home to separate habitats for chimpanzees, orangutans and western lowland gorillas. At Red Rocks, such big cats as lions and tigers coexist peacefully with zebras, giraffes and antelope in natural settings.

Grab your pith helmet for a trek to River's Edge, a 10-acre habitat inhabited by Asian elephants, cheetahs, giant anteaters and viewing areas that provide an opportunity to observe hippos underwater. The Monsanto Insectarium has 100 species of insects and a walk-through butterfly dome. Penguin & Puffin Coast offers a close-up look at these birds, while the Bear Pits are home to black, polar and grizzly bears.

Young visitors to the Children's Zoo can touch animals and play at the playground. The Conservation Carousel features 64 hand-carved wooden animals, each one representing a protected or endangered species. The 1.5-mile Zooline, a miniature railroad, tours the zoo grounds. Sea lion shows take place daily during the summer.

Allow 2 hours minimum. Daily 8-7, Memorial Day weekend-Labor Day; 9-5, rest of year. Closed Jan. 1 and Dec. 25. Zoo free. Children's zoo and train $4 each, under 2 free. Sea lion show $3. Carousel $2. An all-day pass is available. Parking $9. Phone (314) 781-0900.

GRANT'S FARM is on Gravois Rd. at Grant Rd. Ulysses S. Grant built a cabin here in 1856 on land he once farmed. On the 281-acre tract, operated by Anheuser-Busch Inc., are a Clydesdale stable, miniature zoo, animal feeding area and wildlife park. Clydesdales and Dalmatians are featured in a special arena presentation, and there are elephant and bird shows.

Allow 1 hour, 30 minutes minimum. The farm is open and tram tours are offered Tues.-Fri. 9-3:30, Sat. 9-4, Sun. 9:30-4, mid-May through Aug. 13; Wed.-Fri. 9-3, Sat.-Sun. 9-3:30, early Apr. to mid-May; Wed.-Fri. 9:30-2:30, Sat.-Sun. 9:30-3:30, Aug. 14-Oct. 29. Free. Parking $6. Phone (314) 843-1700.

HOLOCAUST MUSEUM AND LEARNING CENTER is at 12 Millstone Campus Dr. in the Kopolow Building. The museum offers a chronological history of the Holocaust. Exhibits revisit personal accounts and memories of survivors who later came to St. Louis. Jewish life in prewar Europe, the rise of Nazism, and events that occurred during the 1933-45 Holocaust and following World War II are depicted through artifacts, audiovisual presentations, photographs and text panels.

Allow 1 hour minimum. Mon.-Thurs. 9:30-4, Fri. 9:30-3, Sun. 10-4; closed Jan. 1, Thanksgiving, Dec. 25 and all major Jewish holidays. Advance reservations are necessary for guided tours. Free. Phone (314) 432-0020.

INTERNATIONAL BOWLING MUSEUM AND CARDINALS HALL OF FAME is at 111 Stadium Plaza. The history and big names of bowling are chronicled through exhibits, a film and an old-fashioned alley with hand-set pins. The St. Louis Cardinals Hall of Fame retraces the history of the major league franchise.

Allow 1 hour minimum. Daily 9-5 (also 5-6:30 on Cardinal home game nights), Apr.-Sept.; Tues.-Sat. 11-4, rest of year. Closed Jan. 1, Thanksgiving, and Dec. 24-25 and 31. Last admission 30 minutes before closing. Admission $7.50; over 65, $7; ages 5-15, $6. MC, VI. Phone (314) 231-6340 or (800) 966-2695.

JEFFERSON BARRACKS HISTORIC PARK is at Grant Rd. and Kingston, about 10 mi. s. via the I-55 S. Broadway exit. Established in 1826, the site was a supply post for troops in the West. A museum in the 1857 powder magazine depicts the history of the barracks, and the Ordnance Building presents changing exhibits.

An overlook provides a view of the Mississippi River. More than 70,000 servicemen are buried in the park, one of the largest national cemeteries in the country. Picnic facilities are available. Allow 1 hour minimum. House and museum open Wed.-Sun. noon-4; closed Jan. 1, Thanksgiving and Dec. 25. Free. Phone (314) 544-5714.

JEFFERSON NATIONAL EXPANSION MEMORIAL is on the riverfront at Market St. This 91-acre national park, which covers the site of the original St. Louis settlement, was established in 1935 to commemorate the westward expansion of the United States during the 19th century. Daily 6 a.m.-11 p.m. Park admission free. Phone (314) 655-1600.

The Gateway Arch is at Memorial Dr. and Market St. This inverted catenary of gleaming stainless steel soars 630 feet above the site of Pierre de Laclede's house and trading post. It commemorates what was the gateway to the West for thousands of 19th-century pioneers. Designed by Eero Saarinen, the memorial is 75 feet higher than the Washington Monument and incorporates 886 tons of stainless steel. Its construction, which took place 1963-65, required specially designed equipment.

The Journey to the Top tram ride experience takes visitors through history on their way to the observation deck; the round trip lasts approximately 60 minutes. Timed tickets are issued every 10 minutes throughout the day. Two movie theaters show three different 45-minute films pertaining to arch construction, the travels of Meriwether Lewis and William Clark, and the settling of the American West.

Ticket center open daily 8 a.m.-10 p.m., Memorial Day-Labor Day; 9-6, rest of year. Closed Jan. 1, Thanksgiving and Dec. 25. Last tram departs 50 minutes before closing. Tram ride $10; ages 13-16, $7; ages 3-12, $3. Individual movie admission $7; ages 13-16, $4; ages 3-12, $2.50. Combination tickets $14-$20; ages 13-16, $11-$17; ages 3-12, $5.50-$7. Phone (314) 655-1700 or (877) 982-1410.

Museum of Westward Expansion is on Market St. at Riverfront beneath the Arch. An extensive collection of artifacts is presented, including exhibits related to the Lewis and Clark expedition. Exhibits depict the social and cultural history of territories west of the Mississippi River, and are presented in concentric semicircles representing interactive timelines. Daily 8 a.m.-10 p.m., Memorial Day-Labor Day; 9-6, rest of year. Closed Jan. 1, Thanksgiving and Dec. 25. Free. Phone (314) 655-1600.

Old Courthouse is at 11 N. Fourth St. Completed in 1862, the courthouse was the site of the Dred Scott slavery trial. Galleries and dioramas depict St. Louis from its French and Spanish occupations through the westward expansion years to the present. Daily 8-4:30; closed Jan. 1, Thanksgiving and Dec. 25. Free. Phone (314) 655-1600.

LACLEDE'S LANDING is on the riverfront between the Eads and Martin Luther King bridges. The renovated turn-of-the-20th-century buildings and cobblestone streets of this nine-block historic district—the site of the city's original settlement—are filled with shops, restaurants and offices.

The Eads Bridge, at the foot of Washington Avenue, was built in 1894. It was the first major railroad bridge across the Mississippi and the first to utilize steel truss construction. This mighty structure carries pedestrian, bicycle, motor vehicle and light rail traffic across the river, offering an unparalleled view of the Gateway Arch en route.

A self-guiding walking tour brochure is available from the St. Louis Visitor Center, at the intersection of Washington and Memorial Drive, daily 9:30-4:30. Phone (314) 241-5875.

LAUMEIER SCULPTURE PARK is s. of I-44 via the Lindbergh Blvd. exit at 12580 W. Rott Rd. The 116-acre park displays contemporary sculpture. Works by such celebrated artists as Vito Acconci, Alice Aycock, Mary Miss, Dennis Oppenheim and Robert Stackhouse grace the expansive lawns, which are surrounded by trees and a natural woodland with hiking trails. A museum houses changing exhibitions of contemporary artwork. Concerts are presented during the summer.

Allow 1 hour minimum. Park open daily 8 a.m.-dusk. Museum Tues.-Fri. 10-5, Sat.-Sun. noon-5. Free. For summer concert schedules phone (314) 821-1209.

SAVE **THE MAGIC HOUSE—ST. LOUIS CHILDREN'S MUSEUM** is at 516 S. Kirkwood Rd. Hands-on exhibits demonstrating science and communications include Children's Village, Math Path, First Impressions and For Baby and Me, a discovery area for children under 2. Allow 1 hour minimum. Mon.-Sat. 9:30-5:30 (also Tues. and Fri. 5:30-9), Sun. 11-5:30, Memorial Day-Labor Day; Tues.-Fri. noon-5:30 (also Fri. 5:30-9), Sat. 9:30-5:30, Sun. 11-5:30, rest of year. Closed Jan. 1, Easter, Thanksgiving and Dec. 25. Admission $7, under 1 free. Phone (314) 822-8900.

MEMORIAL PLAZA is on Market St. between 12th and 15th sts. Developed 1923-60, the plaza honors St. Louis' war dead. On the northern edge is the Soldiers' Memorial and Museum. The plaza is flanked by municipal buildings, including City Hall, modeled after the Hotel DeVille in Paris.

MISSOURI BOTANICAL GARDEN is at 4344 Shaw Blvd. Also known as Shaw's Garden, it features an English woodland garden, Japanese garden, rose and herb gardens and a fragrance garden for the visually impaired. The Kemper Center for Home Gardening is surrounded by 23 thematic residential gardens.

The Climatron, a geodesic dome, houses an assortment of tropical and subtropical plants, including an orchid collection. A camellia collection is featured in the Linnean House. Also noteworthy are the Temperate House, which displays plants from regions of the world with a temperate climate, and the Nanjing Friendship Garden, a reproduction of a garden based on Chinese landscape principles.

A path through the Carver Garden, planted with hydrangeas and sweet potato vines, leads to a fountain and life-size statue of "plant scientist" and native Missourian George Washington Carver. Tower Grove House, the former residence of garden founder Henry Shaw, is a restored mid-19th century residence furnished in period style.

Food is available. Grounds and facilities open daily 9-5 (also Wed. 5-9, Memorial Day-Labor Day); closed Dec. 25. Tower Grove House guided tour Tues.-Sat. 10-4, Sun. 1-4, Mar.-Dec.; closed Jan. 1, Thanksgiving and Dec. 25. Narrated tram tours Mon.-Fri. 10-4, Sat.-Sun. 9-4, Apr.-Oct.; Tues.-Fri. 11-3, Sat. 10-4, Sun. 1-4, Mar. and Nov. Admission (includes Doris I. Schnuck Children's Garden) $8, under 13 free. Tower Grove House tour $4, under 13 free. Tram tours $3, under 3 free if seated in an adult's lap. AX, CB, DC, DS, MC, VI. Phone (314) 577-9400, (314) 577-5100 for Tower Grove House or (800) 642-8842.

Doris I. Schnuck Children's Garden is within the botanical garden. More like a park than a garden, this interactive play space offers rope swings and bridges, a man-made cave, a treehouse and a re-created 19th-century town square complete with a jail, general store, village hall and riverboat. Children also can play in the fountain. A working river runs through the garden. Allow 1 hour minimum. Open same hours as the Missouri Botanical Garden.

OLD CATHEDRAL is at Memorial and Walnut sts. The first church in St. Louis, a Catholic cathedral, was constructed on the site in 1770. This restored structure was begun in 1831 and remains in daily use. A museum contains artifacts and vestments relating to the beginning of the church. Cathedral open daily 6:30-5. Museum open daily 10-3:30. Cathedral and museum free. Phone (314) 231-3250.

SAMUEL CUPPLES HOUSE AT ST. LOUIS UNIVERSITY is on John E. Connelly Mall between Grand Blvd. and Spring Ave. This 42-room Romanesque mansion, complete with 22 fireplaces, was built in 1888 at a cost of $500,000. The exterior boasts gargoyles and ornamental stonework; the interior features Tiffany windows, intricate wood paneling, and displays of fine and decorative arts dating 1400-1920. The Turshin Fine Arts Glass Collection

of American and European Art Glass is displayed on the third floor.

Tues.-Sat. 11-4, Feb.-Dec.; closed holidays. Admission $5, students with ID free. American Sign Language guided tours are available by appointment. Phone (314) 977-3575.

SAPPINGTON HOUSE COMPLEX is .5 mi. e. of I-44 exit Big Bend Rd., then .5 mi. to 1015 S. Sappington Rd. Built in 1808, this two-story brick house is a fine example of Federal architecture. Guides conduct tours of the dwelling and provide information about its period furnishings.

Food is available. Allow 1 hour minimum. Tues.-Fri. 11-2:30, Sat. noon-2:30, Feb.-Dec.; closed Good Friday, July 4, day before Thanksgiving, giving, Dec. 24-25 and 31, and the Sat. before Mon. holidays. Last tour begins 30 minutes before closing. Admission $2.50; ages 6-12, 50c. Phone (314) 822-8171.

SCOTT JOPLIN HOUSE STATE HISTORIC SITE is at 2658A Delmar Blvd. The restored home of this great ragtime composer contains pictures and artifacts of the restoration process as well as narrations and articles about Joplin's life and work. Allow 1 hour minimum. Mon.-Sat. 10-4, Sun. noon-4; closed Jan. 1, Easter, Thanksgiving and Dec. 25. Admission $2.50; ages 6-12, $1.50. Phone (314) 340-5790.

SHAW NATURE RESERVE—
see Gray Summit p. 158.

SIX FLAGS ST. LOUIS—
see Eureka p. 209.

SOLDIERS' MEMORIAL MILITARY MUSEUM is at 1315 Chestnut St. In the central breezeway is a black granite cenotaph bearing the names of 1,075 St. Louis soldiers who died in World War I. Museum exhibits include firearms and other weapons, photographs, medals, uniforms, souvenirs, banners and memorabilia pertaining to St. Louis' military history since 1800. Across the street are memorials to those who died in World War II, Korea and Vietnam. Allow 1 hour minimum. Daily 9-4:30; closed Jan. 1, Thanksgiving and Dec. 25. Free. Phone (314) 622-4550.

CASINOS

• **President Casino on *The Admiral*,** off I-70 6th St. exit, following signs. Sun.-Thurs. 8 a.m.-4 a.m., Fri.-Sat. 24 hours. Phone (314) 622-3000 or (800) 772-3647.

What To Do

Sightseeing

Boat Tours

GATEWAY RIVERBOAT CRUISES departs from the base of the Gateway Arch. Narrated 1-hour trips on the Mississippi River are offered aboard replicas of

19th-century steamboats. Dinner-dance cruises also are available; phone for schedule and reservations.

Sightseeing trips depart daily at 10:30, noon, 1:30, 3 and 4:30 (weather permitting). Fare $10; ages 3-12, $5. AX, MC, VI. Phone (314) 621-4040 or (800) 878-7411.

Bus Tours

SAVE Gray Line, 312 W. Morris, East St. Louis, Ill., provides lecture bus tours about the city's history and major points of interest. Tours lasting 4 and 5 hours are available. Five-hour tour $42; ages 2-14, $21. Four-hour tour $39; ages 2-14, $19. For information and reservations phone (314) 241-1224.

Driving Tours

"Day Tours from St. Louis," a 44-page booklet detailing 10 trips within a day's drive, and a St. Louis points of interest map are available to AAA/CAA members free at any AAA service office in the St. Louis area. *See AAA Offices.*

Helicopter Tours

Fostaire Helicopter Tours covers various sections of St. Louis, focusing on major industries, waterways and other points of interest; phone (314) 421-5440.

Industrial Tours

ANHEUSER-BUSCH BREWERY is at Lynch and 12th sts. Guided 2-hour tours visit the Clydesdale stables, brewhouse, packaging plant and hospitality area. Complimentary samples are offered. The tours involve outside walking and six flights of escalators. Tickets for designated tour times are necessary and are available at the tour center. Mon.-Sat. 9-5, Sun. 11:30-5, June-Aug.; Mon.-Sat. 9-4, Sun. 11:30-4, rest of year. Closed some holidays. Under 18 must be with an adult. Free. Phone (314) 577-2626.

Walking Tours

The city's historical background can be explored in Laclede's Landing, which offers a self-guiding tour of the early settlement of St. Louis *(see attraction listing p. 205).*

The St. Louis Walk of Fame preserves the city's historical and cultural legacy by honoring the accomplishments of individuals with St. Louis connections. A brass star is engraved with the person's name, and an accompanying bronze plaque provides a brief biographical summary.

More than 100 sets of stars and plaques are embedded into the sidewalks of the University City Loop, an area of little shops and cafes along Delmar Boulevard in University City, just outside the St. Louis city limits. Among the veritable who's who of famous honorees are Maya Angelou, Josephine Baker, Chuck Berry, William Burroughs, Miles Davis, Redd Foxx, Joe Garagiola, John Goodman, Ulysses S. Grant, Charles Lindbergh, Agnes Moorehead, Nelly, Marlin Perkins, Joseph Pulitzer, Tina Turner and Shelley Winters.

Sports and Recreation

The 2005 season marked the beloved St. Louis Cardinals' 114th year as a **baseball** franchise and also their final year playing at venerable Busch Stadium, which opened in 1966. Diehard fans had two big reasons to celebrate in 2006: The new Busch Stadium opened on schedule, and the Cardinals won the World Series—their first in 24 years—on the home field against the Detroit Tigers. The improved design of the ballpark offers wider concourses, elevators and escalators between levels and excellent spectator sightlines, as well as dramatic views of downtown and the Gateway Arch. For schedule and ticket information phone (314) 345-9600.

Minor league baseball fun is offered by the Frontier League Western Division's River City Rascals at the Ozzie Smith Sports Complex in O'Fallon, about 35 miles west of downtown St. Louis; phone (636) 240-2287.

The St. Louis Rams play **football** at the Edward Jones Dome at America's Center; phone (314) 982-7267. The arena football season runs from March through June for the Show-Me Believers at St. Charles Family Arena; phone (636) 896-4200.

The St. Louis Blues professional **hockey** team, (314) 622-2500, takes to the ice October through April at the Savvis Center, 14th and Clark streets. The St. Charles Family Arena is the home of the Missouri River Otters minor-league hockey team as well as the St. Louis Steamers indoor **soccer** team; phone (636) 896-4200. The St. Louis Aces, (314) 647-2237, play team **tennis** in July at Dwight Davis Tennis Center in Forest Park.

Gateway International Raceway in nearby Madison, Ill., offers marquee **motorsports** events, including NHRA National, Indy Car Championship, stock and sports car events; phone (618) 482-2400.

Fairmont Park in nearby Collinsville, Ill., offers **Thoroughbred racing** mid-March through October; phone (618) 345-4300.

Note: Policies concerning admittance of children to pari-mutuel betting facilities vary. Phone for information.

There are many **golf** courses throughout the area, including a public course at Ruth Park, 8211 Groby Rd., and three public courses at Forest Park.

Horseback riding is one of many recreational activities available at A.P. Greensfelder Park, north of I-44 on Allenton Road in nearby Pacific. The Wayne C. Kennedy Recreation Complex, on Wells Road, and Edgar M. Queeny Park, between Mason and Weidmann roads, offer **ice skating,** tennis and **swimming.** Ice skating and **roller skating** are popular at the Steinberg Memorial Skating Rink in Forest Park.

Shopping

St. Louis began as a marketplace; furs and food were exchanged for goods from the East and Europe. The embodiment of this role was the city's Union Station, a continental crossroads of mammoth proportions which catered to some 300 trains and tens of thousands of passengers daily.

Passengers no longer throng the vaulted Grand Hall, and trains no longer thunder in the shed. Instead, specialty stores, festive markets and a hotel fill this cavernous space and have restored Union Station as a downtown landmark.

St. Louis also offers such areas as the Central West End's Euclid and McPherson streets. This fashionable neighborhood of townhouses and tree-lined avenues provides a pleasant backdrop for browsing and strolling among a variety of shops and boutiques that sell clothing, antiques and other items. Five minutes south, Cherokee Street Antique Row offers six blocks of antiques and collectibles.

Just west of the city limits at the intersection of I-64 and Brentwood Boulevard is the Saint Louis Galleria; it has 165 stores, including anchors Dillard's and Macy's. Another distinctive mall is West Port Plaza, I-270 and Page Avenue, housing shops that collectively evoke an alpine setting.

Other malls around the city's perimeter are Chesterfield, I-64 and Clarkson Road; Crestwood, Watson and Sappington roads; Jamestown, N. Lindbergh and Old Jamestown Road; Northwest, N. Lindbergh and St. Charles Rock Road; Plaza Frontenac, Lindbergh Boulevard and Clayton Road; South County, S. Lindbergh and Lemay Ferry roads; and West County, I-270 and Manchester Road. Bargain hunters head for St. Louis Mills, SR 370 and St. Louis Mills Boulevard, which features some 200 manufacturers' outlets and specialty retailers, as well as dining and entertainment venues.

Shopping on a smaller scale in nearby Florissant and St. Charles offers historic charm. A couple of craft and gift shops are in the John B. Myers House & Barn, an 1860s Palladian-style house at 180 Dunn Rd. in Florissant. In St. Charles, antiques and crafts fill the shops along Main Street. *See place listing p. 210.*

For outdoor enthusiasts, Bass Pro Shops Outdoor World, 1365 S. 5th St. in St. Charles, features an indoor waterfall and game fish aquarium, wildlife exhibits and sporting demonstrations.

Performing Arts

The St. Louis Symphony, founded in 1880 and one of the oldest symphony orchestras in the nation, performs in Powell Symphony Hall, 718 N. Grand Blvd., from mid-September to mid-May and presents several free outdoor concerts during the summer. The symphony also presents Kinder Koncerts, geared to ages 5 through 8, and Young People's Concerts for ages 9 and up; phone (314) 534-1700 for ticket and schedule information. The acoustically renowned Sheldon Concert Hall, 3648 Washington Ave., presents a variety of concerts; phone (314) 533-9900.

The Muny in Forest Park is a 11,000-seat outdoor amphitheater featuring 7 weeks of Broadway roadshows during the summer. About 1,500 free seats at the top of the house are available on a first-come, first-served basis beginning at 7 p.m.; phone (314) 534-1111. Broadway hits also are performed at the restored 1929 Fox Theatre, 527 N. Grand Blvd. A twin to the Detroit Fox Theatre, the Fox also presents concerts and headlining entertainers in a lavish setting; phone (314) 534-1678.

The UMB Bank Amphitheater is a 20,000-seat venue offering concerts April through September; phone (314) 298-9944.

The Repertory Theatre of St. Louis, 130 Edgar Rd., is the home of St. Louis' regional equity theater as well as the Opera Theatre of St. Louis and Webster University's Conservatory of Theatre Arts; phone (314) 968-4925.

Dance St. Louis regularly gives performances September through April at the Fox Theatre; phone (314) 534-5000. Dance, music and drama are presented at the Edison Theatre on the campus of Washington University; phone (314) 935-6543. Stages St. Louis offers musical theater productions June through October at the Robert G. Reim Theatre at Kirkwood Civic Center; phone (314) 821-2407.

The St. Louis Black Repertory Company offers theater and dance presentations January through June in the Grandel Theatre, 3610 Grandel Sq.; phone (314) 534-3807. Also in the Grandel, the Off-Broadway On Grand Cabaret features Broadway cabaret performers September through December; phone (314) 534-1111.

Special Events

St. Louis warms up to spring with the Storytelling Festival in late April and early May, when both professionals and amateurs celebrate America's tale-telling traditions.

Fourth of July festivities send sparks flying during Fair St. Louis, held near the Gateway Arch and along the St. Louis riverfront. The celebration attracts thousands with big-name entertainment, a family fun village and fireworks. For further information and to verify performance schedule phone (314) 434-3434.

Several events close out the summer, beginning in early September with the Japanese Festival, held at the Missouri Botanical Garden. The Forest Park Balloon Rally is held in mid-September.

Also in September is Bevo Day, an ethnic-themed festival of music, entertainment, arts and crafts, folk dancing and food and drink. The Christmas holiday season kicks off in late November during Winter Wonderland in Tilles County Park, which features thousands of twinkling lights. The St. Louis Convention and Visitors Commission can provide information; phone (314) 421-1023.

The St. Louis Vicinity

CHESTERFIELD (C-5) pop. 46,802

FAUST COUNTY PARK is off I-64 exit 19B, then 1.3 mi. n.e. on Clarkson Rd./Olive Blvd. to 15185 Olive Blvd. A popular spot for picnicking, the 200-acre public park features the preserved home of Missouri's second governor as well as Faust Historical Village, a re-created 19th-century town. The 1920s-era St. Louis Carousel, with some 60 hand-carved animals, is open to the public.

Park open daily 7 a.m.-30 minutes after dusk. Carousel daily 9-5, Memorial Day-Labor Day; Tues.-Sun. 10-4, rest of year. Park free. Carousel $1. Phone (636) 532-7298, or (636) 537-0222 for the carousel.

[SAVE] **Sophia M. Sachs Butterfly House** is off I-64 exit 19B, then 1.3 mi. n.e. on Clarkson Rd./ Olive Blvd. to 15193 Olive Blvd. As many as 100 butterfly species roam freely within this three-story glass conservatory in Faust County Park. A 20-minute film details their life cycle, and a chrysalis exhibit shows caterpillars metamorphosing.

Allow 1 hour minimum. Daily 9-5, Memorial Day weekend-Labor Day; Tues.-Sun. 9-4, rest of year. Closed Jan. 1, Thanksgiving and Dec. 25. Admission $6; over 64, $4.50; ages 4-12, $4. DS, MC, VI. Phone (636) 530-0076.

CRESTWOOD (C-5) pop. 11,863, elev. 621'

ULYSSES S. GRANT NATIONAL HISTORIC SITE is off SR 30 (Gravois Rd.) at 7400 Grant Rd., adjacent to Grant's Farm. The 9.6-acre site includes five historic buildings: the two-story residence, a barn, a chicken house, an icehouse and a summer kitchen. A visitor center is located inside the barn and has exhibits about the Grant family and the residence, also known as White Haven. A videotape presentation is available. Picnicking is permitted. Allow 1 hour minimum. Daily 9-5; closed Jan. 1, Thanksgiving and Dec. 25. Free. Phone (314) 842-3298.

DEFIANCE (C-5) elev. 469'

Daniel Boone, 69 years old and heavily in debt, settled here in 1799 with his wife and some of their children. Defective titles had caused the loss of his land in Kentucky; good reports from one of his sons as well as promises of land grants and honors from the Spanish brought him to Defiance.

Boone received a grant of 845 acres and served 1800-04 as the *syndic* (judge) of the Femme Osage District, a position that gave him control of all civil and military matters. The great explorer died in Defiance a number of years after being forced to sell his land to satisfy his creditors in Kentucky.

Defiance serves as an access point to the Katy Trail, known for its scenery and historic legacy. The trail, which runs almost parallel to the Missouri River, is enjoyed by hikers and bicyclists alike.

[SAVE] **DANIEL BOONE HOME** is 5 mi. w. on CR F.

The frontiersman supervised construction of this four-story, Georgian-style structure, which took 7 years to build, and lived in it until his death in 1820. The house contains many Boone family belongings. Other 19th-century structures on the grounds, including a chapel and schoolhouse, have been restored. Candlelight Christmas Tours are offered the first two Friday and Saturday nights in December.

Guided 1-hour tours of the Boone home and 2-hour tours including the village are offered Mon.-Sat. 9-4:30, Sun. noon-4:30, Apr.-Oct.; Mon.-Sat. 9-2:30, Sun. noon-2:30 in Mar. and Nov. Closed Easter and Thanksgiving. Home tour $7; over 55, $6; ages 4-11, $4. Home and village tour $12; over 55, $10; ages 4-11, $6. Rates and hours may vary; phone ahead. Phone (636) 798-2005.

EUREKA (C-6) pop. 7,676, elev. 465'

Eureka began as a railroad construction camp in 1853. The triumphant name was chosen by a surveyor upon discovering a route through the valley that would eliminate the difficult cutting and grading required by the original route. After the railroad was finished, a town was laid out, and the name remained.

Eureka Chamber of Commerce: 312 N. Central, Eureka, MO 63025; phone (636) 938-6062.

BLACK MADONNA SHRINE AND GROTTOS is s. on SR 109 to CR FF, on CR FF to CR F, then s. on CR F to St. Joseph's Hill Rd., following signs. This site was chosen in 1938 by Franciscan brother Bronislaus for a tribute to the Virgin Mary and to the Black Madonna shrine in his native Poland. He worked for 22 years to complete a cedar chapel and seven grottos of Missouri barite embedded with costume jewelry, rocks and seashells. The chapel later burned and was replaced by an open-air shrine.

A picnic pavilion is available. Daily 9-7, May-Sept.; 9-6 in Apr. and Oct.; 9-4, rest of year. Donations. Phone (636) 938-5361.

[GEM] **SIX FLAGS ST. LOUIS,** off I-44 at Six Flags Rd., has more than 100 rides, shows and attractions. Bugs Bunny National Park includes eight rides, a tree house play structure, an interactive fountain and restaurant, and Superman Tower of Power—a 230-foot drop. Roller coasters include The Boss, Mr. Freeze, Batman The Ride, Ninja, Screamin' Eagle and River King Mine Train. Other rides include Tidal Wave; the Thunder River and Log Flume water rides; The Colossus, an 18-story giant wheel; and Scooby-Doo! Ghostblasters—The Mystery of the Scary Swamp, a water adventure where guests zap targets with "fright lights."

Hurricane Harbor, a 12-acre Caribbean-themed water park, features rides such as a wave pool, an adventure river, a five-story family-themed tree house and Tornado—a thrill ride shaped like a funnel through which four-person rafts spin as they drop 132 feet to the pool below.

The rides are complemented by musical and variety shows at Miss Kitty's Saloon, the Palace Theatre, the Empire Theatre and Sound Stage.

Park open daily, late May to mid-Aug.; Sat.-Sun., Apr. 1-late May and mid Aug. to late Oct. Hurricane Harbor open daily, Memorial Day-Labor Day. Phone ahead to determine hours. Admission $44.99, over 54 and under 49 inches tall $29.99, under 4 free. Hurricane Harbor included with park admission. Parking $10. AAA members save on select services and merchandise. See guest relations for details. AX, DS, MC, VI. Phone (636) 938-4800.

FLORISSANT (C-5) pop. 50,497

In Florissant you'll find houses typical of those built by the French settlers who settled the *fleurissant,* or "flowering," valley in 1786. The Taille de Noyer House, 1 Taille de Noyer Dr., is reached via a driveway on the McCluer High School campus at 1896 S. Florissant Rd. It is believed to be one of the oldest residences in St. Louis County. Prior to a series of expansions and renovations, the 23-room mansion was a simple cabin first used as a fur-trading post in 1790.

Old St. Ferdinand's Shrine, at St. Francois and St. Charles streets, is the oldest Catholic church between the Mississippi River and the Rockies. It is an excellent example of the Federal architectural style applied to a brick building. A convent and historical museum containing religious accouterments adjoin the 1820 church.

Florissant Valley Chamber of Commerce: 420 W. Washington St., Florissant, MO 63031; phone (314) 831-3500.

Self-guiding tours: A brochure describing a walking tour of Florissant is available from the chamber of commerce.

KIRKWOOD (C-6) pop. 27,324

MUSEUM OF TRANSPORTATION is w. off the I-270 Dougherty Ferry Rd. exit at 3015 Barrett Station Rd. Trains, automobiles, buses, streetcars, horse-drawn vehicles, aircraft and boats represent 150 years of American history. The collection includes more than 70 locomotives. Of special interest is Bobby Darin's 1964 dream car, which cost more than $93,000 and took 7 years to build.

Allow 1 hour, 30 minutes minimum. Mon.-Sat. 9-5 (also Thurs. 5-7), Sun. 11-5, May 1-Labor Day; Tues.-Sat. and Mon. holidays 9-4, Sun. 11-4, rest of year. Closed Jan. 1, Thanksgiving and Dec. 25. Admission $4; over 64 and ages 5-12, $2. Phone (314) 965-7998.

POWDER VALLEY CONSERVATION CENTER is off I-44 exit 277B, .5 mi. s. on US 61, .5 mi. w. on Watson Rd., .6 mi. n. on Geyer Rd., then 1.2 mi. w. to 1715 Cragwold Rd. Exhibits include a "tree factory" that explains trees' basic structure and physiology, an active beehive and a 3,000-gallon aquarium. Three paved nature trails wind through 112 acres of forest. Allow 2 hours minimum. Daily 8-8, early Apr.-late Oct.; 8-6, rest of year. Closed Jan. 1, Thanksgiving and Dec. 25. Free. Phone (314) 301-1500.

MARYLAND HEIGHTS (C-5) pop. 25,756

CASINOS

• **Harrah's Hotel & Casino**, 777 Casino Center Dr. Sun.-Thurs. 9 a.m.-5 a.m., Fri.-Sat. 24 hours. Phone (314) 770-8100.

ST. CHARLES (C-5) pop. 60,321, elev. 467'

Founded by French Canadians in 1769, St. Charles was called *Les Petites Cotes*—"the little hills"—for the low bluffs along the Missouri River that form the town's backdrop. Under the Spanish government many American settlers came into the District of San Carlos, which theoretically extended west from the Missouri River to the Pacific Ocean. Among those who flocked to the territory during the 1790s were Daniel Boone and his family.

In 1804 Upper Louisiana was formally transferred from France to the United States, and San Carlos became St. Charles. When Missouri was admitted to the Union on Aug. 10, 1821, St. Charles became the first capital of the state. Although the capital was moved to Jefferson City in 1826, the city continued to grow.

St. Charles was an early center for education west of the Mississippi; the Academy of the Sacred Heart was established in 1818 by Rose Philippine Duchesne, who was canonized in 1988. The St. Charles Historic District embraces nine blocks along S. Main Street, south of the former state capitol.

Lewis and Clark Heritage Days in mid-May commemorate the arrival in St. Charles of William Clark and the Corps of Discovery, where the explorer met up with Meriwether Lewis. A large encampment along the Missouri River is the site for demonstrations of frontier skills, period craft displays and a rousing Fife and Drum Corps muster. In mid-August nearly 300,000 people help St. Charles celebrate Fete des Petites Cotes—Festival of the Little Hills. A 19th-century atmosphere prevails at this summertime event, which offers craft demonstrations, food and entertainment.

Greater St. Charles Convention and Visitors Bureau: 230 S. Main St., St. Charles, MO 63301; phone (636) 946-7776 or (800) 366-2427. *See color ad p. 211.*

FIRST MISSOURI STATE CAPITOL STATE HISTORIC SITE is at 200-214 S. Main St. on the riverfront. These adjoining Federal-style brick buildings were the seat of government 1821-26. The first state

General Assembly met upstairs while the building's owners lived and operated a general store on the first floor. Gov. Alexander McNair's office and a committee room were off the legislative chambers. Several rooms in the 1820 complex have been restored and decorated with period furnishings.

Guided tours are offered. Allow 1 hour minimum. Mon.-Sat. 9-4, Sun. 11-5; closed Jan. 1, Easter, Thanksgiving and Dec. 25. Admission $2.50; ages 6-12, $1.50. Phone (636) 940-3322.

[SAVE] **LEWIS & CLARK BOAT HOUSE AND NATURE CENTER** is at 1050 Riverside Dr. Exhibits relating to the Lewis and Clark expedition and the Missouri River ecosystem are featured. Dioramas, artifacts and sound effects help re-create Lewis and Clark's early 19th-century explorations. Replicas of the three boats used in the expedition are featured on the lower level. The nature center has waterfalls and plant and animal displays.

Allow 30 minutes minimum. Mon.-Sat. 10-5, Sun. noon-5; closed holidays. Admission $2; students with ID and ages 3-17, $1. Phone (636) 947-3199.

CASINOS

- **Ameristar Casino St. Charles**, off I-70 5th St. exit, following signs s. to riverfront. Daily 8 a.m.-4 a.m. Phone (636) 940-4300 or (800) 325-7777.

VALLEY PARK (C-6) pop. 6,518

LONE ELK PARK is w. of SR 141, off N. Outer Rd. The 405-acre landscaped park contains small herds of elk, deer and bison. A lake attracts Canada geese and mallard ducks, while the wooded grounds are home to native wildlife. Animals roam freely through a portion of the park that is set aside as a drive-through area. Nature trails and picnic facilities are available. Daily 8-dusk. Free. Phone (314) 615-7275.

WORLD BIRD SANCTUARY is w. of SR 141 off N. Outer Rd., across from Lone Elk Park. Located on 130 acres, the facility houses a variety of birds and reptiles. More than 250 injured or ill raptors are rehabilitated here each year. There are nature trails and displays featuring birds in their natural habitats. Naturalists are on hand to answer questions. Allow 1 hour minimum. Daily 8-5; closed Thanksgiving and Dec. 25. Free. Phone (636) 861-3225.

WEBSTER GROVES (C-6) pop. 23,230

A parcel of 6,002 acres, once known as "Dry Ridge," was granted to Gregoire Sarpy in 1802 by the last Spanish lieutenant governor of the Louisiana Territory. The land was developed in the late 19th century as an affluent St. Louis suburb. Webster Groves was incorporated in 1896, combining five settlements along the Pacific Railroad line.

[SAVE] **HAWKEN HOUSE** is off I-44 exit 280 (Elm Ave.), 1 mi. s. to Old Watson Rd., then .3 mi. w. to 1155 S. Rock Hill Rd. This Federal-style brick house was the residence of Christopher Hawken of the Hawken Rifle family. Built in 1857 with slave labor, the eight-room home was relocated from its original location in 1970 and is furnished with Victorian antiques.

Guided tours are offered. Allow 1 hour minimum. Tues. and Thurs. 11-3:30, Sun. 1-3:30, Mar.-Dec.; closed holidays. Last tour departs 30 minutes before closing. Admission $4; over 55, $3; under 12 free with adult. Phone (314) 968-1857.

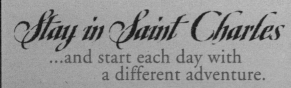

Nearby Illinois

ALTON pop. 30,496, elev. 450'

Just north of the confluence of the Mississippi and Missouri rivers, Alton was founded in the early 19th century. Col. Rufus Easton obtained the land and named the town for his son. The Eagle Packet line of boats, once built in Alton, contributed to local river traffic on the Mississippi. Riverfront Park offers a vantage point for viewing the river.

The issue of slavery found volatile expression in Alton when abolitionist editor Elijah Lovejoy was killed by a proslavery mob in 1837. The Alton Cemetery on Monument Avenue contains Lovejoy's tomb and a monument in his honor. In 1858 the last Lincoln-Douglas debate took place in town. The city's history and river heritage are among themes addressed at the Alton Museum of History and Art, 2809 College Ave.; phone (618) 462-2763.

Perhaps Alton's most renowned native son was Robert Pershing Wadlow; at 8 feet, 11.1 inches he remains the world's tallest known person. A life-size statue of Wadlow can be seen on the campus of Southern Illinois University Dental School. Near the intersection of Broadway and William are the remnants of Alton Prison, where more than 1,300 Confederate soldiers died of various diseases. A portion of the cellblock wall remains.

Alton's Victorian, Federal and Greek Revival 19th-century houses draw attention, particularly in autumn when the trees cloaking the surrounding bluffs are ablaze with fall foliage colors. The Great River Road, which runs north along the Mississippi River, has a bicycle path offering views of the river and bluffs.

Alton Regional Convention and Visitor Bureau Visitors Center: 200 Piasa St., Alton, IL 62002; phone (618) 465-6676 or (800) 258-6645.

Shopping areas: Alton's antique district, in a 3-block area between George and State streets, contains more than 40 shops housed in buildings dating from the 1800s.

NATIONAL GREAT RIVERS MUSEUM is at #2 Lock and Dam Way. Next to the Mississippi River, the museum houses interactive exhibits that describe the river's natural history and its commercial importance. Visitors can view a room-size model of river bluffs that highlights area wildlife and an aquarium that is home to Mississippi River fish species. A Pilot House simulator enables visitors to experience what it is like to steer barges through a lock. Picnicking is permitted. Allow 1 hour minimum. Daily 9-5; closed Jan. 1, Thanksgiving and Dec. 25. Free. Phone (877) 462-6979.

Melvin Price Locks and Dam is at #1 Lock and Dam Way. Part of the Upper Mississippi's flood control and navigation system, the Melvin Price Locks and Dam features two locks through which billions of dollars of goods pass each year. Guided tours of the locks and dam depart from the adjacent museum, where visitors can also see a film about the project. Nearby Esplanade Park has bird-watching platforms from which visitors can often see bald eagles. Tours are given daily at 10, 1 and 3 (weather permitting). Free. Phone (877) 462-6979.

CASINOS

- **Argosy Casino, Alton**, on the riverfront at 219 Piasa St. Daily 8 a.m.-6 a.m. Phone (800) 711-4263.

BELLEVILLE pop. 41,410, elev. 500'

Founded in 1814, Belleville was named by its early French settlers. The discovery of coal in 1828 attracted many German miners. The town retains much of the Teutonic influence in language, song, festivals and architecture. Manufacturers produce a variety of goods, and area coal mines yield more than 3 million tons a year. Scott Air Force Base is nearby.

Belleville Tourism Bureau: 216 E. A St., Belleville, IL 62220; phone (618) 233-6769 or (800) 677-9255.

NATIONAL SHRINE OF OUR LADY OF THE SNOWS is w. on SR 15, just e. of I-255. A 200-acre religious center under direction of the Missionary Oblates of Mary Immaculate, the shrine includes a 2,400-seat amphitheater, a replica of the Lourdes Grotto, prayer gardens and chapels. Food is available. Daily 8-8. Donations. Phone (618) 397-6700. *See color ad p. 212.*

SAVE **ST. CLAIR HISTORICAL SOCIETY** is at 701 E. Washington St. This 1866 Victorian adaptation of a Greek Revival house is furnished in period. The house features changing displays of vintage clothing, toys, quilts and other items. A historical research library also is on the premises. Guided tours are available. Mon.-Fri. 10-2; closed major holidays. Admission $2; ages 6-12, $1. Phone (618) 234-0600.

CAHOKIA pop. 16,391, elev. 401'

Cahokia was founded in 1699 by three missionaries from Québec. Its location along three rivers made it a center of commerce for the region by the mid-1700s. At the end of the French and Indian War in 1763, when this area was ceded to Great Britain, many citizens uneasy about the possibility of a British occupation moved across the Mississippi River and were instrumental in helping found St. Louis.

With the onset of the American Revolution, George Rogers Clark and his troops from Virginia occupied Cahokia, recruited a militia and organized a campaign against British forces at Vincennes, Ind. The settlement remained a British outpost until 1778. The first election for chief magistrates in Illinois was held in Cahokia, which helped establish a sense of peace and order in a territory otherwise characterized by lawlessness.

Jarrot Mansion State Historic Site includes the Jarrot Mansion; completed in 1810, it is one of the oldest brick buildings in the mid-Mississippi River Valley. **Note:** The mansion currently is closed for renovations but is open to the public during special events in March and September; phone (618) 332-1782.

Cahokia Area Chamber of Commerce: 905 Falling Springs Rd., Cahokia, IL 62206; phone (618) 332-1900.

CAHOKIA COURTHOUSE STATE HISTORIC SITE is off I-55/70, just w. of jct. SRs 3 and 157. Built in 1737 as a French residence, the structure was used as a courthouse until 1814. The first U.S. court sessions and elections in the state were held in this building. The visitor center has interactive exhibits that trace the French influence in 18th-century Illinois. Courthouse and visitor center open daily 9-5, Memorial Day-Labor Day; Wed.-Sun. 9-5, rest of year. Closed Jan. 1, Thanksgiving and Dec. 25. Donations. Phone (618) 332-1782.

CHURCH OF THE HOLY FAMILY is 4 mi. s. of I-55/70 at jct. SRs 3 and 157. Said to be the oldest church in Illinois, the 1699 stone and wood building has been in continuous use under French, British

and American rule. Allow 30 minutes minimum. Daily 10-3, June-Aug.; by appointment rest of year. Donations. Phone (618) 337-4548.

COLLINSVILLE pop. 24,707

Horseradishes, log cabins and coal all are a part of Collinsville's heritage, which began when the town's first inhabitant built a log cabin overlooking the Mississippi basin in 1810. The city's name changed from Downing Station to Collinsville in 1825, and it soon became a bustling coal town. Today the area around Collinsville produces most of the world's supply of horseradishes.

Tourism Bureau of Southwestern Illinois: 10950 Lincoln Tr., Fairview Heights, IL 62208; phone (800) 442-1488.

GEM **CAHOKIA MOUNDS STATE HISTORIC SITE** is off I-255 exit 24 (Collinsville Rd.), then w. 1.5 mi. This 2,200-acre site preserves 65 American Indian tribal mounds. Monks Mound, the site's centerpiece, covers more than 14 acres at its base and is 100 feet tall. Evidence of a once flourishing Mississippian civilization—the center of an enormous trade empire distinguished by social and political activity—spans the years A.D. 900-1500. At its peak Cahokia had about 20,000 inhabitants.

An interpretive center houses exhibits about the people who once lived in the region; a 15-minute film documenting the history of Cahokia; and a life-size, re-created Indian village. Hiking trails are on the grounds.

Guided tours are available. Picnicking is permitted. Interpretive center open daily 9-5, Memorial Day-Labor Day; Wed.-Sun. 9-5, rest of year. Closed Jan. 1, Election Day, Nov. 11, Thanksgiving and Dec. 25. Admission $2; under 13, $1. Phone (618) 346-5160.

EAST ST. LOUIS pop. 31,542, elev. 418'

On the Mississippi River opposite St. Louis, East St. Louis was colonized by the French, who built a mission a few miles south at the village of Cahokia in 1699. Capt. James Piggott helped promote permanent settlement of the region when he established a ferry in 1795. Lots in Illinoistown, a village near the ferry, were auctioned off.

River traffic and trade, westward expansion and the development of the area's natural resource, coal, hastened expansion of the site. The coal was pulled by horses over wooden rails along the riverbanks; some note that this means of transporting the mineral constituted claim to the first railroad in the state, and today the East St. Louis area is a railroad center.

The Gateway Geyser, on Front Street at Trendley Avenue, is one of the world's highest fountains, reaching 627 feet. Surrounded by four smaller plumes, the fountain is centered directly across from the Gateway Arch.

Fairmount Park Race Track, in Fairmount City at Collinsville Road and I-255, offers Thoroughbred racing; phone (314) 436-1516 for schedule information.

Note: Policies concerning admittance of children to pari-mutuel betting facilities vary. Phone for information.

Greater East St. Louis Chamber of Commerce: 327 Missouri Ave., Room 602, East St. Louis, IL 62201; phone (618) 271-2855.

CASINOS

- **Casino Queen Hotel & Casino**, directly across from the Gateway Arch at 220 S. Front St. Daily 9 a.m.-6:30 a.m. Phone (618) 874-5000 or (800) 777-0777.

EDWARDSVILLE pop. 21,491, elev. 433′

Edwardsville has two historic areas that provide a glimpse of its past: the St. Louis Street Historic District and the LeClaire Historic District. Southern Illinois University at Edwardsville encompasses a picturesque 2,600-acre campus.

Edwardsville-Glen Carbon Chamber of Commerce: 200 University Park Dr., Suite 260, Edwardsville, IL 62025; phone (618) 656-7600.

MADISON COUNTY HISTORICAL MUSEUM AND ARCHIVAL LIBRARY is at 715 N. Main St. Housed in a restored Federal-style residence built in 1836, the museum contains period furnishings, American Indian and pioneer artifacts, antiques and a variety of changing seasonal exhibits that include quilts, needlework and historic costumes. A history and genealogy reference library is adjacent to the museum. Allow 1 hour minimum. Wed.-Fri. 9-4, Sun. 1-4; closed holidays. Donations. Phone (618) 656-7562.

HARTFORD pop. 1,545, elev. 430′

LEWIS & CLARK STATE HISTORIC SITE is at One Lewis & Clark Tr. near jct. SR 3 and New Poag Rd. At the confluence of the Mississippi and Missouri rivers, the site commemorates Camp River Dubois, the Lewis and Clark Expedition's 1803-04 winter encampment. Costumed guides show visitors around a full-scale log reconstruction of the camp. The interpretive center features a 55-foot replica of a keelboat. Visitors also can watch a 15-minute film detailing the preparations Lewis and Clark made here for their journey west. Picnicking is permitted. Allow 1 hour minimum. Daily 9-5, Memorial Day-Labor Day; Wed.-Sun. 9-5, rest of year. Free. Phone (618) 251-5811.

Missouri Botanical Garden / Missouri Division of Tourism

This ends listings for the St. Louis Vicinity.
The following page resumes the alphabetical listings of cities in Missouri.

SAVANNAH (B-2) pop. 4,762, elev. 1,115'

ANDREW COUNTY MUSEUM AND HISTORICAL SOCIETY is at 202 E. Duncan Dr. at jct. US Bus. Rte. 71 and Duncan Dr. Exhibits depict the history of Andrew County. Featured are kewpie and French doll collections, antique cars and an old general store. Allow 1 hour minimum. Mon.-Sat. 10-4, Sun. 1-4; closed holidays and last weekend of each month. Free. Phone (816) 324-4720.

SEDALIA (C-3) pop. 20,339, elev. 909'

Gen. George R. Smith bought 1,000 acres along the Pacific Railroad right of way for $13 per acre in 1857. He called the town he platted Sedville in honor of his daughter Sarah, whom he affectionately referred to as Sed. Three years later Smith filed a larger plat that included Sedville, naming the new town Sedalia.

In June residents honor one of the best-known composers of ragtime music with the Scott Joplin Ragtime Festival. The products of Missouri's fields and factories are the centerpiece of the State Fair, held in August.

A trailhead leading to Katy Trail State Park, one of the nation's foremost rails-to-trails conversions, is just east of town.

Sedalia Area Chamber of Commerce: 600 E. Third St., Sedalia, MO 65301-4499; phone (660) 826-2222 or (800) 827-5295.

Self-guiding tours: Walking tour brochures of the downtown historic district are available from the chamber of commerce.

BOTHWELL LODGE is 6 mi. n. on US 65 in Bothwell Lodge State Historic Site. The country retreat of lawyer and businessman John Homer Bothwell was built in four sections 1897-1928. The building is furnished much the way Bothwell left it when he died in 1929. A nature trail and picnic facilities are available. Allow 1 hour minimum. Guided tours are offered Mon.-Sat. 10-4, Sun. 11-5. Admission $2.50; ages 6-12, $1.50. Phone (660) 827-0510.

SIBLEY—*see Kansas City p. 181.*

 **SILVER DOLLAR CITY**— *see Branson p. 139.*

SMITHVILLE—*see Kansas City p. 181.*

SPRINGFIELD (E-3) pop. 151,580, elev. 1,292'

The future location of Springfield was designated by John Polk Campbell in 1829, when he carved his initials into an ash tree near the site of four springs. Strategically located at the junction of two important roads, the town flourished during the heavy westward migration of the 1850s. This key location also made the town a target during the Civil War in a battle that took place at what is now Wilson's Creek National Battlefield *(see place listing p. 220).*

Union spy/scout James Butler Hickok, better known as Wild Bill Hickok, stayed in Springfield after the war. Achieving fame as a gunfighter, Hickok made national news in 1865 when he returned fire and killed Dave Tutt in the public square; he was later acquitted for this act.

Westward migration continued to affect Springfield. In 1926 plans for the first paved transcontinental highway in the United States were made. Stretching from the Great Lakes to the Pacific Coast, Route 66 earned the nickname Main Street USA. Traces of the old route are visible along Kearney, Glenstone, College and St. Louis streets.

The past also is evident in the historic houses and buildings along Walnut Street and in the Midtown district. Christ Episcopal Church, 601 E. Walnut St., is said to be the oldest church building in the city. Built in 1870, it features stained-glass windows and ecclesiastical Gothic architecture.

In addition to sightseeing, Springfield offers fishing, boating and picnicking at Fellows, McDaniel and Springfield lakes. Table Rock and Bull Shoals reservoirs also are nearby.

The Frisco Highline Trail, Missouri's second-longest rail trail, connects Springfield and Bolivar along the path of a former railroad line once traveled by Harry S. Truman as a precursor to his famous "Whistle Stop Campaign" in 1948. The 36-mile-long bicycling trail winds through the scenic forest and pasture lands of La Petite Gemme Prairie Natural Area, crossing over 16 trestles along the way (horseback riding is permitted between Willard and Walnut Grove). Trailheads are located in Springfield, Willard, Walnut Grove, Wishart and Bolivar. For more information contact Ozark Greenways, P.O. Box 50733, Springfield, MO 65805; phone (417) 864-2015.

The Springfield Cardinals AA minor league team is a big regional draw during baseball season. Games are played at John Q. Hammons Field, 955 E. Trafficway; phone (417) 863-2143.

Springfield Convention and Visitors Bureau Tourist Information Center: 3315 E. Battlefield Rd., Springfield, MO 65804; phone (417) 881-5300 or (800) 678-8767. *See color ad p. 149 & p. 217.*

Self-guiding tours: For pamphlets about attractions and driving tours of historic downtown Springfield contact the tourist information center.

Shopping Areas: Antique and craft shops abound in Springfield. Ozark Treasures, 1832 S. Campbell St., features more than 100 dealers. The Commercial Street Historical District offers antiques, collectibles and vintage clothing. Contemporary shopping can be found at Battlefield Mall *(see color ad p. 149 & p. 217)*, Battlefield Road and Glenstone Avenue; the more than 170 stores include Dillard's, Famous-Barr, JCPenney and Sears.

Bass Pro Shops Outdoor World, 1935 S. Campbell St., caters to outdoor enthusiasts with a 140,000-gallon game fish aquarium and waterfall, wildlife exhibits and sporting demonstrations. *See color ad p. 149 & p. 217.*

DICKERSON PARK ZOO is off I-44 exit 77, then 1 blk. n. to Norton Rd., following signs to 3043 N. Fort Ave. It features hundreds of different mammals and birds. Tigers and primates live in the Tropical Asia habitat, while gray wolves and mountain lions are among the animals that can be seen at the Missouri Habitats exhibit. Allow 2 hours minimum. Daily 9-5, Apr.-Sept.; 10-4, rest of year (weather permitting). Closed Jan. 1, Thanksgiving and Dec. 25. Admission $6; over 64, $5; ages 3-12, $4. Train rides $2, under 1 free. Phone (417) 864-1800.

DISCOVERY CENTER is off I-44 exit 80A, 3 mi. s. on Glenstone Ave., then 1.5 mi. w. to 438 St. Louis St. Interactive displays include a child-size "town" where visitors can write for a newspaper, anchor a news broadcast, withdraw play money at the bank or shop at the market. Other exhibits explore archeology, energy and anatomy.

Allow 1 hour minimum. Tues.-Fri. 9-5 (also Fri. 5-8), Sat. 10-5, Sun. 1-5; closed Jan. 1, Easter, Thanksgiving and Dec. 25. Admission $7; over 59, $6; ages 3-12, $5. Rates for special exhibits may be higher; phone ahead. MC, VI. Phone (417) 862-9910.

FANTASTIC CAVERNS is 1.5 mi. n. of jct. I-44 and SR 13, then 3 mi. w. on Fantastic Caverns Rd. No walking is necessary on a 1-mile guided tram tour through one of Missouri's largest caves. Fantastic Caverns has a varied history, beginning with its exploration by 12 women in 1867. As a speakeasy in the 1920s the cave was outfitted with a dance floor, gambling tables and a bar. It also served as a meeting place in the 1930s and as a country music theater in the 1960s and early 1970s.

The temperature in the natural limestone cave is a constant 60 F. Daily 8-dusk; closed Thanksgiving and Dec. 24-25. Admission $18; ages 6-12, $10. Phone (417) 833-2010.

THE HISTORY MUSEUM is at 830 Boonville St. Permanent collections on the third floor of the 1894 City Hall Building include regional books and documents and more than 20,000 photographs relating the history of Springfield. Changing exhibits about Ozark and Springfield history also are presented. Tues.-Sat. 10:30-4:30; closed holidays. Admission $3; senior citizens and students with ID $2.50; ages 6-12, $1. Phone (417) 864-1976.

JAPANESE STROLL GARDEN is w. on Battlefield St. to 2400 S. Scenic in Nathanael Greene Park. A tea house and moon bridge are centerpieces of this landscaped 7.5-acre garden, which features bonsai trees and three small lakes with feeding stations for fish and ducks. Allow 1 hour minimum. Thurs.-Mon. 9-7:30, Apr.-Oct. Admission $3, under 12 free. Phone (417) 864-1049.

MISSOURI SPORTS HALL OF FAME is at 5051 Stan Musial Dr. (US 60). Displays of sports memorabilia evoke the memory of legendary Missouri teams and players. Interactive opportunities include

a broadcast booth and a pitching cage where visitors stand behind home plate as major league pitches come in at 100-plus miles per hour. Mon.-Sat. 10-4, Sun. noon-4. Admission $5; senior citizens $4; ages 5-18, $3; family rate $14. DS, MC, VI. Phone (417) 889-3100.

SPRINGFIELD ART MUSEUM is at 1111 E. Brookside Dr. in Phelps Grove Park. Changing exhibits of works by regionally and nationally known artists are featured. Allow 30 minutes minimum. Tues.-Sat. 9-5 (also Thurs. 5-8), Sun. 1-5; closed holidays. Free. Phone (417) 837-5700.

SPRINGFIELD CONSERVATION NATURE CENTER is off US 65 exit US 60W, then .7 mi. following signs to 4600 Chrisman Ave. Among 80 acres of forest, fields and creeks along Lake Springfield, the visitor center has natural history exhibits and offers hunting and fishing permits. Along the nearly 3 miles of trails visitors can spot deer, raccoons, turtles and other wildlife.

Allow 1 hour minimum. Grounds open daily 8 a.m.-9 p.m., Mar.-Oct.; 8-6, rest of year. Visitor center open daily 8-5. Both closed Jan. 1, Thanksgiving and Dec. 25. Free. Phone (417) 888-4237.

SPRINGFIELD LITTLE THEATRE AT THE LANDERS is at 311 E. Walnut St. The baroque Renaissance/Napoleon architecture of this 1909 theater has been carefully preserved and restored. Once the venue for John Philip Sousa and Lillian Russell, the theater offers performances by the Springfield Little Theater troupe, as well as regional ballet and opera companies. Self-guiding tours are available. Mon.-Fri. 11-5, Sept.-June; 11-4, rest of year. Free. Phone (417) 869-3869.

SPRINGFIELD NATIONAL CEMETERY is at 1702 E. Seminole St. The site contains graves of Union and Confederate soldiers as well as veterans from all wars. Five Medal of Honor recipients are buried here; their headstones are engraved in gold. Mon.-Fri. 8-4:30. Free. Phone (417) 881-9499.

WONDERS OF WILDLIFE ZOOQUARIUM is at 500 W. Sunshine St., next to Bass Pro Shops Outdoor World. The museum stresses the importance of conserving natural resources and honors the nation's hunting and fishing heritage. Interactive exhibits with computer simulators, 160 species of live animals and aquariums totaling 700,000 gallons of water depict man's relationship with his surroundings.

The habitats of North America are explored, beginning with Walk in the Woods, where visitors progress through an Ozark woods along a suspended walkway while being serenaded by geese, doves and quails. Galleries on the lower level feature a viewing window providing underwater perspectives of freshwater pond inhabitants. The 225,000-gallon tank in the Out to Sea Gallery has a ceiling-high window separating visitors from various marine creatures.

Show-Me Springfield

The views from Interstate 44 and Highway 65 may deceive you, but Springfield, Missouri, is a city with a metropolitan area population topping 350,000. The city is host to the metropolitan amenities you expect without the hassles you dread of really large cities. There is enough variety of attractions, shopping, sports, theater, arts and dining to entertain you for days.

The original and largest **Bass Pro Shops Outdoor World** is the granddaddy of all outdoor stores. Explore the 300,000-square-foot showroom loaded with unique features including art gallery, barber shop, waterfalls, aquariums, restaurants, and, of course, the best in outdoor gear. Your adventure starts here.

Wonders of Wildlife Museum & Aquarium will entertain you with an eye-opening world of nature. Sounds of gushing water and birds calling greet guests amid breathtaking views of lush trees, rock outcroppings, 700,000 gallons of gurgling waterfalls and aquariums and more than 225 species of live animals in natural habitats.

Hear the crack of the bat up-close-and-personal with the 2006 World Championship St. Louis Cardinals double-A affiliate **Springfield Cardinals**. Meet tomorrow's big league players today in a stadium reminiscent of the majors.

Leap back in time to the site of the first major Civil War battle west of the Mississippi River and where the first Union general to die in combat— **Wilson's Creek National Battlefield.**

FAST FACTS

- *Birthplace of* **Route 66**
- *Site of first recorded shootout with* **"Wild Bill" Hickok**
- *More than* **800 dining options**
- *A quick 30 miles from* **Branson**

For more information contact the
Convention & Visitors Bureau
1-800-678-8767
show-me-springfield.com

07AAA

Picnicking is permitted. Food is available. Allow 1 hour minimum. Daily 9-6. Last admission 1 hour before closing. Admission $10.95; over 65, military and students with ID $8.95; ages 4-11, $6.50. AX, DS, MC, VI. Phone (417) 890-9453 or (888) 521-9497. *See color ad p. 149 & p. 217.*

STANTON (D-5) elev. 871'

Stanton was named after a successful area businessman, Peter Stanton, who owned and operated a powder mill in the area during the 1850s. Stanton is on the scenic portion of I-44 that runs 171 miles west from Gray Summit to Lebanon.

JESSE JAMES MUSEUM is at I-44 exit 230. This museum explores the theory that Jesse James was not killed in 1882 but lived until the age of 103 under an assumed identity. Wax figures of James, his brother Frank, the James gang's cook and J. Frank Dalton, the man who claimed to be Jesse James, help tell the story. Antiques from the late 1800s, many of James' personal belongings and affidavits that testify to the story's authenticity are displayed.

Daily 9-6, June-Aug.; 9-5, Sept.-Oct.; Sat.-Sun. 9-5, Apr.-May. Admission $6; ages 6-11, $2.50. Phone (573) 927-5233.

MERAMEC CAVERNS is off I-44 exit 230, then 3 mi. s. on CR W. Discovered in 1716, the caverns accommodated powder kilns and leaching vats for Union forces during the Civil War.

In 1864 the outlaw band of Confederate William Quantrill's irregulars, of which Jesse James was a member, seized the gunpowder mill. James was so impressed with the cave that he and his gang later used it as a hideout. This colorful history suitably came to a close when a man avowed to be Jesse James held an outlaw reunion in the cave on James' 102nd birthday in 1949.

The caverns feature five floors of colorful mineral formations. At the entrance are a mineral and crystal collection and an ultraviolet rock display. Guided tours take visitors along a mile of lighted concrete walkways; the cave maintains a constant temperature of 60 F. Food is available. Tours depart every 25 minutes daily 8:30-7:30, July 1-Labor Day; 9-7, May-June; 9-5, rest of year. Closed Thanksgiving and Dec. 25. Admission $15; ages 5-11, $8. AX, DS, MC, VI. Phone (573) 468-3166 or (800) 676-6105.

SULLIVAN (D-4) pop. 6,351, elev. 970'

MERAMEC STATE PARK is 4 mi. e. via SR 185. This 6,896-acre park on the Meramec River includes several springs and more than 40 caves. Grounds open daily 7 a.m.-10 p.m., Apr.-Oct.; 7 a.m.-9 p.m., rest of year. Visitor center daily 9-4:30, Apr.-Oct.; daily 8-3:30, Nov.-Dec. and in Mar.; Thurs.-Mon. 8-3:30, rest of year. Fisher Cave tours are given daily at 9:30, 11:30, 1 and 3, June-Aug.; Thurs.-Mon. at 1 and 3, Apr.-May and Sept.-Oct. Grounds

free. Tours $6; ages 13-19, $5; ages 6-12, $4. Phone (573) 468-6072. *See Recreation Chart and the AAA South Central CampBook.*

SUMNER (B-3) pop. 142, elev. 682'

SWAN LAKE NATIONAL WILDLIFE REFUGE is 22 mi. s.w. via US 36 and SR 139; the main entrance is 1 mi. s. of Sumner on CR A. The wintering grounds for one of the largest concentrations of Canada geese in North America, this 10,670-acre refuge also attracts more than 100 bald eagles each winter. Waterfowl concentrations are highest in March, April, October and November. A visitor center features videotapes, exhibits and mounted wildlife.

The refuge also has a .7-mile, self-guiding Habitat Trail and an observation tower. Fishing is permitted. Refuge open daily dawn-dusk, Mar. 1-Oct. 15. Visitor center and office open Mon.-Fri. 7:30-4; closed holidays. Habitat Trail and observation tower open all year. Free. Phone (660) 856-3323.

THAYER (E-4) pop. 2,201

GRAND GULF STATE PARK is about 6 mi. w. on CR W. The 130-foot deep chasm was left when nearly three-quarters of a mile of cavern roof collapsed. Sometimes referred to as the Little Grand Canyon, the 165-acre area includes overlooks, hiking trails and picnic areas. Daily 7 a.m.-dusk. Free. Phone (417) 264-7600.

UNITY VILLAGE — *see Kansas City p. 181.*

VALLEY PARK — *see St. Louis p. 211.*

VERSAILLES (C-3) pop. 2,565, elev. 1,010'

Named after the city in France, Versailles came into being in 1834 when two pioneers donated 36 blocks of land on the condition that it be developed as a settlement. The new town soon became the Morgan County seat. Versailles was a regular stop on the stagecoach line between Jeffersonville and Springfield, and the Martin Hotel (which now houses the Morgan County Historical Museum) was its most welcoming sight, especially for weary passengers.

Versailles Commerce League: P.O. Box 256, Versailles, MO 65084; phone (573) 378-4401 Mon., Wed. and Fri. 10-2.

[SAVE] **JACOB'S CAVE** is 6 mi. s. on SR 5, then e. on CR TT, following signs. One of Missouri's largest caves, Jacob's Cave is known for its depth illusion, reflective pools and ceiling spongework. Along with prehistoric bones and evidence of six ice ages, the cave is said to contain the world's largest geode. Guided tours are available. Allow 1 hour minimum. Daily 9-4. Admission $12; ages 4-12, $6. Phone (573) 378-4374.

[SAVE] **MORGAN COUNTY HISTORICAL MUSEUM** is at 120 N. Monroe St. Occupying the 1853 Martin Hotel, this 28-room museum includes a chapel, children's room, hotel room, doctor's office, tool room, beauty shop, schoolroom and barber shop. Some furnishings are original. Allow 1 hour minimum. Tues.-Fri. 10-3, Sat. 9-noon; closed Thanksgiving and Dec. 25. Admission $4.50; ages 6-12, $1. Phone (573) 378-5530.

WALNUT SHADE — *see Branson p. 153.*

WARRENSBURG (C-2) pop. 16,340

Warrensburg was named for Martin Warren, a blacksmith whose shop along a busy Osage Indian trail was a gathering place for frontier farmers. The town gained fame in 1870 as the site of the "Old Drum" trial, in which Leonidas Hornsby was accused of shooting a hunting dog owned by his brother-in-law, Charles Burden. In his appeal to the jury, Senator G.G. Vest coined the term "man's best friend" to describe the noble dog Drum.

Warrensburg is the home of Central Missouri State University, the third-largest state school in Missouri with an enrollment of 11,500 students.

Greater Warrensburg Area Chamber of Commerce and Visitors Center: 100 S. Holden St., Warrensburg, MO 64093; phone (877) 653-3786.

THE OLD COURTHOUSE is at 302 N. Main St. Site of the "Old Drum" trial, the restored 1838 courthouse includes period furnishings. A monument to the legendary hunting dog stands on the grounds. Tours include the courthouse, a 1913 one-room schoolhouse and the Mary Miller Smiser Heritage Library, which houses artifacts and records dating to the 1860s.

Allow 30 minutes minimum. Mon.-Fri. 1-4; closed major holidays. Admission $3. Phone (660) 747-6480.

DID YOU KNOW

The ice cream cone
was invented at the
1904 World's Fair
in St. Louis.

WARSAW (D-3) pop. 2,070, elev. 708'

Warsaw is a vacation center at the head of Lake of the Ozarks. Parts of the Butterfield Overland Trail, an early stagecoach route, can be hiked within town and the immediate environs. Harry S. Truman State Park *(see Recreation Chart and the AAA South Central CampBook)* offers developed recreational facilities on the Truman Dam's reservoir, formed by the Osage River.

Warsaw Chamber of Commerce: P.O. Box 264, Warsaw, MO 65355; phone (660) 438-5922.

BENTON COUNTY MUSEUM is at 700 Benton St. Exhibits include items from the early 1800s to 1935 as well as mounted native wildlife. Allow 1 hour minimum. Tues.-Sun. 1-5, Memorial Day-Labor Day. Donations. Phone (660) 438-6707.

HARRY S. TRUMAN DAM VISITOR CENTER is 1.5 mi. n. on US 65 to the Truman Dam exit, then 1 mi. w. following signs to Kaysinger Bluff, overlooking the dam. The center has a 23-minute audiovisual presentation about the Ozark Mountains, a photography exhibit documenting the area, a fossil display, a slide presentation about the dam project, a viewing area with telescopes and a self-guiding nature trail. Allow 1 hour minimum. Daily 9-5, Mar.-Oct. Free. Phone (660) 438-2216.

WASHINGTON (C-4) pop. 13,243

Calling itself the corncob pipe capital of the world, Washington was first settled in 1839. Many original buildings along the riverfront and downtown areas have been restored and house restaurants, specialty shops and bed and breakfast inns.

Washington Area Chamber of Commerce: 323 W. Main St., Washington, MO 63090; phone (636) 239-2715.

Self-guiding tours: Guided and self-guiding walking tour information for the historic area is available from the chamber of commerce.

WEBSTER GROVES—*see St. Louis p. 211.*

WESTON—*see Kansas City p. 181.*

WILSON'S CREEK NATIONAL BATTLEFIELD (E-2)

Ten miles southwest of Springfield in the town of Republic, the battlefield is off I-44 exit 70 (CR MM), south on CR MM to US 60, south .5 mile on CR M from US 60 to CR ZZ, then 1.5 miles south on CR ZZ to FM 182 (Elm Street).

The battle of Wilson's Creek took place Aug. 10, 1861. Brig. Gen. Nathaniel Lyon, who commanded the Union forces, was the first Union general to die in battle during the Civil War. A 5-mile, self-guiding automobile tour passes eight wayside exhibits and 12 displays. A .6-mile hiking trail leads to Bloody Hill, the major battle site. The Ray House and Ray Springhouse have been restored to their 1861 appearance. Living-history programs are presented regularly on weekends Memorial Day through Labor Day.

. A visitor center features a film, battle map and museum. For more information write Superintendent, Wilson's Creek National Battlefield, 6424 W. Farm Rd. 182, Republic, MO 65738-0403. Allow 2 hours minimum. Park open daily 8 a.m.-9 p.m., Memorial Day-Labor Day; 8-5, rest of year. Visitor center daily 8-5. Closed Jan. 1, Thanksgiving and Dec. 25. Admission $5 per private vehicle with one adult, maximum charge $10 per private vehicle with more than one adult, under 16 free. Phone (417) 732-2662.

Oklahoma

Cowboys
Step back in time to the Old West at the National Cowboy and Western Heritage Museum

Indians
Festivals, museums and memorials highlight the proud heritage of Oklahoma's tribes

Great Plains
Playful breezes send tall grass waving into a brilliant blue horizon

America's Main Street
You can still get your kicks on Route 66

Blue Waters and Black Gold
Oklahoma, home to drilling rigs and grand lakes, proves oil and water do mix

Tallgrass Prairie Preserve, Pawhuska
© Wolfgang Kaehler

"the land we belong to"

Whether dispossessed American Indians moving in, destitute Dust Bowl farmers moving on or cattle-driving cowboys passing through, the comings and goings of diverse groups of people helped mold the character of Oklahoma. Highway-loving travelers can just take it all in, discovering that the state's position at the nation's crossroads makes it difficult to categorize.

Is it a Southern state? The southeastern corner, with its pine-covered hills and distinctly Southern sensibility, is often called "Little Dixie." On the other hand, undulating acres of wheat and grain elevators thrusting to the sky give northern Oklahoma a Midwestern feel.

Yet the loudest singer in a chorus of voices is that of the great American West. Rodeos from one end of the state to the other both test and show off skills that have been vital to cowboys since the days of the Chisholm Trail. Powwows celebrate and preserve American Indian heritage including the tales of ancestors driven west along the "Trail of Tears." Today more than 30 tribes are headquartered in Oklahoma.

Although most likely somewhat biased, cowboy humorist Will Rogers was not far from the truth when he described his native state as the heart of America's existence.

Before the creation of America's interstate system made driving cross-country a simple matter of zipping between points A and B—before the pleasure of savoring local flavor was sacrificed in the name of progress and expediency—there was Route 66. Affectionately called "The Main Street of America," this 2,400-mile-long ribbon of pavement connected Chicago and Los Angeles on a meandering path through the heart of the nation.

Nowhere is this historic road better preserved than in Oklahoma. Small towns awaiting their first traffic light, neon-lit truck stop cafes, old-fashioned filling stations and vintage motels advertising "air-cooled rooms" still line the remaining stretches of the great highway here. That Route 66 survives in Oklahoma is only appropriate: It was State Highway Commissioner Cyrus Avery who helped plan the route and served as its biggest booster in the 1920s.

Since then US 66, as it was officially labeled, has become intimately connected with the history and character of the state. John Steinbeck dubbed it the "Mother Road" in his opus "The Grapes of Wrath," a novel which dramatized the very real plight of thousands of Depression-era "Okies" who fled the Dust Bowl for California's fertile valleys.

Cowboys and Indians

Route 66 enters the state's northeast corner, an area where the river-laced Ozark foothills meet the prairies, at the town of Quapaw. Here the route intersects with a much older and sadder byway: the "Trail of Tears." Beginning in 1830, native peoples of the southeastern United States were forced to move to the newly created Indian Territory that would later become Oklahoma. The trail takes its name from one infamous march resulting in the death of a quarter of the exiles due to exposure, hunger and fatigue.

Today Oklahoma has one of the largest American Indian populations in the country. Numerous tribal museums, along with powwows such as the Red Earth Native America Cultural Festival held in Oklahoma City, acquaint visitors with the history and ways of life of the 37 tribes represented in the state. Many place names reflect Oklahoma's American Indian heritage.

Near El Reno Route 66 encounters the Chisholm Trail, a historic passage inseparably tied to cowboy legend roughly paralleling

Oklahoma Historical Timeline

Moundbuilders inhabit eastern Oklahoma.
A.D. 500-1300

Spanish explorer Francisco Vasquez de Coronado ventures through the area searching for a city of gold.
1541

Texas ranchers move their cattle along the Chisholm Trail through Oklahoma to reach the railroads in Kansas.
1866-1889

©Legends Archive

1817-1840
The federal government relocates the Five Civilized Tribes—the Cherokee, Chickasaw, Choctaw, Creek and Seminole—from their homes in the southeastern United States to Oklahoma.

1879
Humorist Will Rogers is born in Oologah.

modern US 81. In the late 19th century, thousands of Texas cattlemen drove their herds along the trail to railheads in Kansas for shipment to Eastern markets. Those paid to move the cattle north were called cowboys, and they came to symbolize the rough, rugged, often romanticized image of life in the American West.

You'll find the legacy of this cowboy lifestyle in business offices throughout Oklahoma City and Tulsa, where Stetson hats and glossy leather boots compete with the requisite briefcases and cell phones. And Oklahoma City celebrates the state's cattle-driving past with the National Cowboy and Western Heritage Museum, dedicated to the men and women who pioneered the West.

"The Highway That's the Best"

In 1952, Route 66 was renamed the Will Rogers Memorial Highway after Oklahoma's cowboy humorist and favorite son. It passes through Claremore, where the Will Rogers Memorial Museum overflows with the entertainer's personal items and memorabilia. Claremore also was home to Lynn Riggs, the playwright who penned "Green Grow the Lilacs," upon which the classic musical "Oklahoma!" was based.

Route 66 connects Oklahoma's two biggest cities as well. In Tulsa the highway winds within sight of the Art Deco skyscrapers built during the city's oil boom years. Once known as "The Oil Capital of the World," the city has preserved many of its 1920s and '30s architectural gems.

West of Tulsa, Route 66 rolls through farmland and quaint towns on its way to Oklahoma City, the state capital. Literally built in a day, "OKC"—as it is called locally—materialized on the prairie April 22, 1889, during the most famous in a series of land rushes. Continuing west, remnants of 66 pass through the dry, high plains of western Oklahoma to Texola, near the Texas border.

Those who make the 400-mile trip from Quapaw to Texola on Steinbeck's "Mother Road" will not proceed quickly and may have a hard time finding it in some places—newer, wider I-40 and I-44 bypass Route 66's course through the state and several sections are closed and choked with weeds. Certainly the interstates are faster and more convenient. But by journey's end, those hardy travelers who get their kicks on Route 66 will have enjoyed a thick slice of Americana and in so doing experienced an essential part of Oklahoma.

The first commercial oil well in Oklahoma Territory is discovered at Bartlesville.
1897

Oklahoma celebrates 100 years of statehood.
2007

©Bettmann/Corbis

Oklahoman Wiley Post makes the first successful solo flight around the world.
1933

1889
The unassigned prairie land of the Oklahoma Territory opens for settlement.

Jerry Hymer

1933-1939
Years of plowing and sustained drought dry up the Great Plains region; as farmland becomes useless, hundreds of thousands of people are forced to leave their homes.

2000
An outdoor memorial is dedicated to the 168 people killed in the 1995 bombing of the Alfred P. Murrah Federal Building.

Recreation

A dry Western state evoking images of the Dust Bowl shouldn't have as much water as Oklahoma does. Though the state is naturally blessed with a multitude of rivers, the more than 200 lakes seen today are all products of human ingenuity. Dams built to control flooding have as a fringe benefit created rambling reservoirs, many of which seem purposely designed for outdoor fun. And if you're looking for flat, you'll find it in Oklahoma, but you'll also find rolling foothills and small, ancient mountain ranges in the south and east.

Dust Bowl No More

With all the water splashing behind dams in Oklahoma, **swimming** is popular. At Turner Falls Park near Davis, Honey Creek cascades down a 77-foot waterfall into a lovely natural pool. Swimmers also flock to Arcadia Lake near Edmond and to lakes Ellsworth and Lawtonka near Lawton, both fed by streams from the Wichita Mountains.

Built to control flooding on the Red River, Denison Dam impounds the vast reservoir of Lake Texoma on the Texas-Oklahoma border. The lake's serpentine shoreline is sprinkled with countless secluded coves perfect for **boating,** and numerous charter companies make getting out on the water easy. **Sailing** is particularly enjoyable here, and the swimming, **fishing, water skiing** and **wind surfing** are superb. Lake Thunderbird, near Norman, also is known for its ideal sailing and wind surfing conditions.

Lake Altus-Lugert, near Altus in Quartz Mountain State Park, is great for boating. A 3,600-acre public **hunting** area on the lake's northern shore supports large numbers of quails, turkeys and waterfowl, among other wildlife. In the Ozark foothills, the clear blue water of Grand Lake O' the Cherokees draws boaters and, in the fall, migrating white pelicans. The area around the lake is tailor-made for outdoor recreation; seven of Oklahoma's 51 state parks are scattered along its shores.

Oklahoma's lakes also support a variety of fish, giving anglers a reason to smile. Lakes Hugo, Sardis, Eufaula, John Wells and Clayton, all in the southeast, offer some of the best bass and bluegill catches. The crystal waters of Broken Bow Reservoir teem with trout; Lone Chimney Lake, in central Oklahoma, is home to bass, catfish and crappie. Surrounded by Foss State Park and the Washita National Wildlife Refuge, Foss Lake is a great spot to find walleye, bass and crappie.

Plainly More than Just Plains

While Oklahoma may be "...where the wind comes sweeping down the plain," the landscape varies markedly. Little Sahara State Park, a popular **camping** getaway, takes its name from the sand dunes reaching heights up to 40 feet along the Cimarron River. Rock hounds can dig for rare hourglass selenite crystals in a sea of salt at Great Salt Plains State Park. Lake Hudson boasts myriad bluffs and coves along more than 200 miles of shoreline, so finding an ideal spot to pitch your tent is easy.

In the western panhandle, **hiking** through the rugged landscape of canyons and mesas is a treat for the eyes. Equally rewarding is Boiling Springs State Park, named for the cool springs that bubble up through the sands of the North Canadian River. Colorful gypsum formations distinguish Alabaster Caves State Park; natural springs, old-growth forests and venerable hills characterize the Arbuckle Mountains.

The Wichita Mountains in Oklahoma's southwestern corner offer lakes, streams, canyons and grasslands that attract hikers and **mountain bikers.** Be careful, though; once inside the Wichita Mountains Wildlife Refuge, you might encounter the bison, longhorn cattle, antelopes and elk that have the run of the place. It's wise to let the animals have the right of way. A 3.5-mile paved road inside the refuge leads to one of Oklahoma's highest summits: 2,463-foot Mount Scott.

Oklahoma has more horses per person than any other state, and many recreation areas cater to **horseback riders.** Wilhelmina, McGee Creek and Lake Murray state parks offer a variety of trails. Visitors can rent horses for the day in Robbers Cave State Park, which once served as a hideout for such notorious outlaws as Jesse James and Belle Starr.

Recreational Activities

Throughout the TourBook, you may notice a Recreational Activities heading with bulleted listings of recreation-oriented establishments listed underneath. Similar operations also may be mentioned in Destination City recreation sections. Since normal AAA inspection criteria cannot be applied, these establishments are presented only for information. Age, height and weight restrictions may apply. Reservations often are recommended and sometimes are required. Addresses and/or phone numbers are provided so visitors can contact the attraction for additional information.

Fast Facts

POPULATION: 3,450,654.

AREA: 69,919 square miles; ranks 18th.

CAPITAL: Oklahoma City.

HIGHEST POINT: 4,973 ft., Black Mesa.

LOWEST POINT: 287 ft., Little River.

TIME ZONE(S): Central. DST.

MINIMUM AGE FOR UNRESTRICTED DRIVER'S LICENSE: 16 years, 6 months.

SEAT BELT/CHILD RESTRAINT LAWS: Seat belts required for driver and front-seat passengers 13 and older. Children ages 6 until 13 are required to be in a child restraint or seat belt; child restraints required for under 6.

HELMETS FOR MOTORCYCLISTS: Required for riders under 18.

RADAR DETECTORS: Permitted.

FIREARMS LAWS: Vary by state and/or county. Contact the Bureau of Alcohol, Tobacco and Firearms, 200 N.W. 5th St., Room 103, Oklahoma City, OK 73102; phone (405) 231-5362.

HOLIDAYS: Jan. 1; Martin Luther King Jr. Day, Jan. (3rd Mon.); Washington's Birthday, Feb. (3rd Mon.); Memorial Day, May (last Mon.); July 4; Labor Day; Veterans Day, Nov. 11; Thanksgiving, Nov. (4th Thurs.) and following Fri.; Christmas, Dec. 25.

TAXES: Oklahoma's statewide sales tax is 4.5 percent, with local options for additional increments to be levied by cities and counties. A Tourism Promotion Tax of 0.1 percent is levied on lodgings, restaurants, tour vehicles and amusement admissions.

INFORMATION CENTERS: State welcome centers are near the Oklahoma-Kansas line at I-35 exit 222 in Blackwell; east of Miami at I-44/Will Rogers Turnpike exit 13; at I-44 exit 161 near Catoosa; near the Oklahoma-Arkansas border at I-40 exit 311 at Sallisaw; near the Oklahoma-Texas border on US 69/75 at Colbert; at the Oklahoma-Texas border on I-35 exit 5 at Thackerville; east of the Oklahoma-Texas border near Erick at I-40 exit 11; on US 412/Cherokee Turnpike just west of the Oklahoma-Arkansas border and east of Flint; north of the Oklahoma-Texas border at I-44 exit 20 near Walters; at I-40 exit 157 at Midwest City; at I-35 and N.E. 122nd Street in Oklahoma City; and in the Oklahoma Capitol Building at N.E. 23rd Street and Lincoln Boulevard in Oklahoma City.

With the exception of the center in the Oklahoma Capitol Building, which is open daily 8-4:30 year-round, state information centers are open daily 8:30-5, with longer hours in summer; closed Dec. 25.

FURTHER INFORMATION FOR VISITORS:

Oklahoma Tourism & Recreation Department
P.O. Box 52002
Oklahoma City, OK 73152
(405) 230-8300
(800) 652-6552 out of Okla.

FISHING AND HUNTING REGULATIONS:

Oklahoma Department of Wildlife Conservation
P.O. Box 53465
Oklahoma City, OK 73105
(405) 521-3851

NATIONAL FOREST INFORMATION:

U.S. Forest Service
Southern Region
Regional Office
1720 Peachtree St.
Suite 760S
Atlanta, GA 30309
(404) 347-4177
(877) 444-6777 (reservations)

STATE PARK LODGE AND CABIN RESERVATIONS: For reservations for lodge or cabin accommodations phone
(405) 230-8420 or
(800) 654-8240.

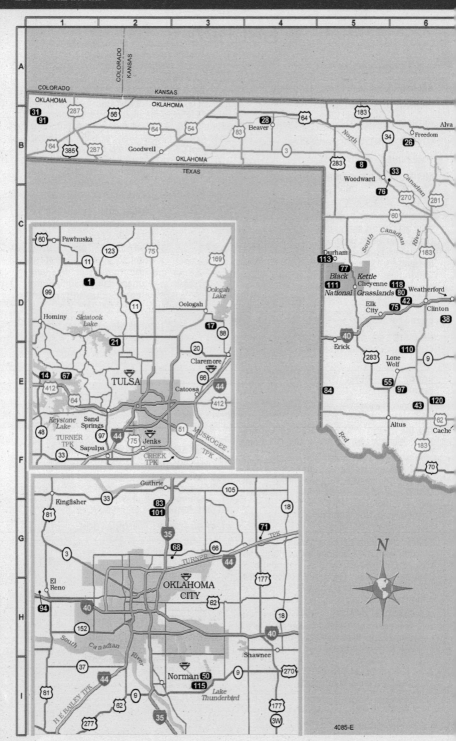

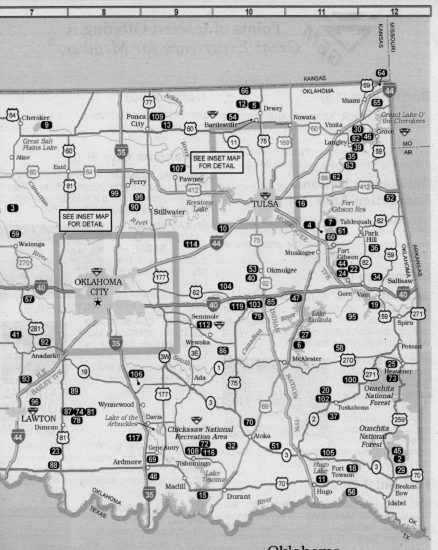

Oklahoma

Orientation

Miles
0 ——————— 49.4

NOT INTENDED FOR DRIVING.
SEE APPROPRIATE AAA SHEET MAP.

Only places listed in the Attractions
section appear on this map.
▽ See AAA GEM Attractions
❶ See Chart of Recreation Areas

© 2006 NAVTEQ

© AAA

Points of Interest Offering A *Great Experience for Members*®

Bartlesville (B-9)

WOOLAROC RANCH, MUSEUM AND WILDLIFE PRESERVE—This attraction's eclectic collection includes artifacts from 40 American Indian tribes and epic Western scenes painted by Frederic Remington, Charles M. Russell and others. See p. 238.

Chickasaw National Recreation Area (F-9)

CHICKASAW NATIONAL RECREATION AREA—Springs, streams and lakes in the forested hills of south-central Oklahoma are the attractions at this recreation area. See p. 240.

Claremore (E-3)

J.M. DAVIS ARMS & HISTORICAL MUSEUM—Davis' collection showcases not only guns but knives, swords, steins, saddles, American Indian artifacts, political buttons, music boxes, World War I posters and more. See p. 275.

WILL ROGERS MEMORIAL MUSEUM—This museum overlooking the Tiawah Valley is home to artifacts and exhibits showcasing Rogers' time  as an actor, author and columnist as well as a rodeo and vaudeville performer. See p. 275.

Fort Sill (F-7)

FORT SILL MILITARY RESERVATION AND NATIONAL HISTORIC LANDMARK—A frontier atmosphere still pervades at this former Indian reservation. See p. 243.

Grove (B-12)

HAR-BER VILLAGE—Reconstructed buildings and timeless collections of glassware, furniture and dolls reflect the lifestyle of early Americans. See p. 244.

Jenks (F-2)

OKLAHOMA AQUARIUM—Undersea creatures of all shapes and sizes swim, float and crawl through the exhibits at this aquarium, which also houses an antique fishing tackle museum. See p. 275.

Norman (I-2)

UNIVERSITY OF OKLAHOMA—Take a tour of this national research university's beautiful 3,000-acre campus. See p. 259.

Oklahoma City (H-2)

MEMORIAL MUSEUM—A chronology of the events surrounding the bombing of the Alfred P. Murrah Federal Building is told through exhibits and personal reminiscences. See p. 254.

MYRIAD BOTANICAL GARDENS & CRYSTAL BRIDGE—A tropical oasis in the city, this translucent conservatory takes you into a world of  waterfalls, palm trees and orchids. See p. 253.

NATIONAL COWBOY AND WESTERN HERITAGE MUSEUM—Exhibits pay tribute to American Indians as well as the pioneers who helped tame the Wild West. See p. 254.

NATIONAL COWBOY & WESTERN HERITAGE MUSEUM

OKLAHOMA CITY NATIONAL MEMORIAL—Victims, rescuers and others whose lives were changed forever as a result of the Alfred P. Murrah Federal Building bombing are honored here. See p. 254.

OKLAHOMA CITY ZOO & BOTANICAL GARDEN—Be on the lookout for more than 2,300 prowling, purring and preening creatures at this zoo. See p. 254.

OKLAHOMA HISTORY CENTER—Relive the excitement of the Oklahoma land runs and the first oil gushers through these extensive exhibits and state archives. See p. 255.

OMNIPLEX—Science and cultural exhibits as well as gardens, a theater and a planetarium comprise this center. See p. 255.

Seminole (D-9)

JASMINE MORAN CHILDREN'S MUSEUM—Shaped like an imaginary town, this museum allows children to role-play dozens of occupations in order to better understand the adult world. See p. 264.

PHILBROOK MUSEUM OF ART—Step into this Italian Renaissance-style villa and delight in American Indian, European, American, African and Asian art collections. See p. 272.

Tulsa (E-2)

GILCREASE MUSEUM—This museum's collection relating to the discovery, expansion and settlement of the Western Frontier includes historical items and artwork by more than 400 artists. See p. 270.

TULSA ZOO AND LIVING MUSEUM—Explore an African savanna, a tropical rain forest and a coral reef without leaving Oklahoma. See p. 272.

ORAL ROBERTS UNIVERSITY—Feel inspiration wash over you as you step out onto the observation deck of the 200-foot Prayer Tower. See p. 271.

RECREATION AREAS

	MAP LOCATION	CAMPING	PICNICKING	HIKING TRAILS	BOATING	BOAT RAMP	BOAT RENTAL	FISHING	SWIMMING	PETS ON LEASH	BICYCLE TRAILS	WINTER SPORTS	VISITOR CENTER	LODGE/CABINS	FOOD SERVICE
NATIONAL FORESTS															
Ouachita (E-12) 1,613,120 acres. West-central Arkansas and southeastern Oklahoma. Horse trails. *(See place listing in Ark. p. 56)*		•	•	•	•	•	•	•	•	•	•	•	•	•	•
NATIONAL GRASSLANDS															
Black Kettle (D-5) 30,710 acres off SR 283 in Cheyenne.		•	•		•	•		•							•
NATIONAL RECREATION AREAS *(See place listings)*															
Chickasaw (F-9) 10,000 acres.		•	•	•	•	•		•	•	•			•		
ARMY CORPS OF ENGINEERS															
Birch Lake (D-1) 3,278 acres 17 mi. s.e. of Pawhuska via SRs 99 and 11. Water skiing; playground.	❶	•	•		•	•		•	•	•			•		
Broken Bow Reservoir (F-12) 28,113 acres 12 mi. n. of Broken Bow off US 259.	❷	•	•	•	•	•		•	•	•			•	•	•
Canton Lake (C-7) 18,901 acres 2 mi. n. of Canton on SR 58A. Recreation areas.	❸	•	•	•	•	•		•	•	•			•		•
Chouteau Lock and Dam (C-11) 7,151 acres 7 mi. n. of Muskogee on US 69, then 3 mi. s.e. on an access road.	❹	•	•	•	•	•		•	•	•			•		
Copan Lake (B-10) 15,952 acres 2 mi. s.w. of Copan off US 75.	❺	•	•		•	•		•	•	•					
Eufaula Lake (E-11) 102,200 acres 6 mi. n. of McAlester on US 69. Horse rental.	❻	•	•	•	•	•	•	•	•	•				•	•
Fort Gibson Lake (C-11) 52,654 acres 15 mi. w. of Tahlequah off SR 51. Hunting; horse rental.	❼	•	•	•	•	•	•	•	•	•					

RECREATION AREAS

	MAP LOCATION	CAMPING	PICNICKING	HIKING TRAILS	BOATING	BOAT RAMP	BOAT RENTAL	FISHING	SWIMMING	PETS ON LEASH	BICYCLE TRAILS	WINTER SPORTS	VISITOR CENTER	LODGE/CABINS	FOOD SERVICE
Fort Supply Lake (B-5) 8,039 acres 2 mi. s. of Fort Supply via US 270 and SR 3.	8	•	•		•	•		•	•	•			•		
Great Salt Plains Lake (B-7) 12,537 acres 3 mi. n. of Jet on SR 38. Water skiing; playground.	9	•	•	•	•	•	•		•	•			•		
Heyburn Lake (C-10) 6,344 acres 4 mi. w. of Kellyville off 151st St. S.	10	•	•		•	•	•	•	•	•			•		
Hugo Lake (F-11) 37,425 acres 8 mi. e. of Hugo on US 70.	11	•	•	•	•	•	•	•	•	•			•		
Hulah Lake (B-10) 21,505 acres 2 mi. w. of Hulah on SR 10.	12	•	•		•	•	•	•	•	•					
Kaw Lake (B-9) 49,963 acres 9 mi. e. of Ponca City on Lake Rd.	13	•	•	•	•	•	•	•	•	•			•		•
Keystone Lake (E-1) 714 acres 16 mi. w. of Tulsa off US 64.	14	•	•		•	•	•	•	•	•				•	•
Lake Texoma (G-9) 202,300 acres on Oklahoma-Texas border off US 75. Horse rental. *(See Durant p. 241)*	15	•	•	•	•	•	•	•	•	•	•		•	•	•
Newt Graham Lock and Dam (C-11) 3,787 acres 8 mi. s.w. of Inola on CR 420.	16	•	•		•	•		•	•	•					
Oologah Lake (D-3) 50,150 acres 8 mi. n. of Claremore via SR 88.	17	•	•	•	•	•	•	•	•	•			•		
Pine Creek Lake (F-11) 26,179 acres 10 mi. n. of Valliant on Pine Creek Rd. Water skiing.	18	•	•		•	•		•	•	•			•		
Robert S. Kerr Lock, Dam and Reservoir (D-12) 56,720 acres 9 mi. s. of Sallisaw off US 59.	19	•	•	•	•	•	•	•	•	•					
Sardis Lake (E-11) 21,564 acres 3 mi. n. of Clayton off SR 2.	20	•	•		•	•		•	•	•					
Skiatook Lake (E-2) 18,911 acres 5 mi. w. of Skiatook off SR 20.	21	•	•		•	•		•	•	•			•		
Tenkiller Ferry Lake (D-11) 30,524 acres 21 mi. s.e. of Muskogee on SR 10, then 7 mi. e. on SR 10A. Recreation areas.	22	•	•	•	•	•	•	•	•	•			•		•
Waurika Lake (F-7) 21,500 acres 6 mi. n.w. of Waurika off SR 5.	23	•	•		•	•		•	•	•			•	•	
Webbers Falls Lock and Dam (D-11) 15,953 acres 3 mi. n.w. of Gore off SR 10.	24	•	•		•	•		•	•	•					
Wister Lake (E-12) 39,170 acres 6 mi. s.w. of Poteau on US 270.	25	•	•		•	•		•	•	•			•	•	
STATE															
Alabaster Caverns (B-6) 200 acres 6 mi. s. of Freedom on SR 50, then .5 mi. e. on SR 50A. Scenic. Playground. *(See Freedom p. 243)*	26	•	•	•				•	•	•			•		
Arrowhead (E-11) 2,459 acres 15 mi. n. of McAlester off US 69. Golf, tennis, water skiing; airstrip, marina, playground.	27	•	•	•	•	•	•	•	•	•				•	•
Beaver Dunes (B-4) 520 acres 1 mi. n. of Beaver on US 270. Golf; dune buggy and motorcycle courses.	28	•	•	•				•		•					
Beavers Bend (F-12) 3,522 acres 10 mi. n.e. of Broken Bow on US 259A. Tennis, water skiing; horse rental, museum, playground.	29	•	•	•	•	•	•	•	•	•			•	•	•
Bernice (B-11) 88 acres .5 mi. e. of Bernice off SR 85A. RV camping only.	30	•	•		•	•		•	•	•					
Black Mesa (B-1) 349 acres 27 mi. n.w. of Boise City off CR 325. Playground.	31	•	•		•	•		•		•					
Boggy Depot (F-10) 630 acres 11 mi. w. of Atoka on SR 7, then 4 mi. s.	32	•	•					•		•			•		
Boiling Springs (B-6) 820 acres 6 mi. n.e. of Woodward on SR 34C. Golf; playground.	33	•	•	•				•	•	•				•	
Brushy Lake (D-12) 90 acres 8 mi. n. of Sallisaw on US 64.	34	•	•		•	•		•	•						
Cherokee (B-11) 43 acres e. of Langley on SR 20. Playground.	35	•	•		•	•		•	•						
Cherokee Landing (C-12) 146 acres about 12 mi. s. of Tahlequah off SR 82. Playground.	36	•	•		•	•		•	•						
Clayton Lake (F-11) 510 acres 30 mi. n.e. of Antlers on US 271.	37	•	•		•	•		•	•						
Crowder Lake (D-6) 10 acres 8 mi. s. of Weatherford on SR 54.	38	•	•		•	•		•							
Disney/Little Blue (B-11) 32 acres e. of Disney on SR 28.	39	•	•		•	•		•	•						

RECREATION AREAS

	Map Location	Camping	Picnicking	Hiking Trails	Boating	Boat Ramp	Boat Rental	Fishing	Swimming	Pets on Leash	Bicycle Trails	Winter Sports	Visitor Center	Lodge/Cabins	Food Service
Dripping Springs (D-10) 420 acres 6 mi. w. of Okmulgee on SR 56.	40	•	•		•	•		•	•	•					
Fort Cobb (E-7) 1,872 acres 5 mi. n.w. of Fort Cobb off SR 9. Golf, water skiing; marina, playground.	41	•	•		•	•	•	•	•	•					
Foss (D-6) 1,749 acres 15 mi. n.w. of Clinton via SRs 73 and 44. Water skiing; playground.	42	•	•		•	•	•	•	•	•					
Great Plains (E-6) 487 acres 6 mi. n. of Snyder on US 183. Water skiing.	43	•	•		•	•		•	•	•					•
Greenleaf (D-11) 565 acres 3 mi. s. of Braggs on SR 10A. Marina, playground.	44	•	•	•	•	•	•	•	•	•			•	•	
Hochatown (F-12) 1,713 acres 7 mi. n.e. of Broken Bow on SR 259A. Golf, water skiing; marina, playground.	45	•	•	•	•	•	•	•	•	•					
Honey Creek (B-12) 30 acres 2 mi. s.w. of Grove on SR 10.	46	•	•		•	•		•	•						
Lake Eufaula (D-11) 2,853 acres 14 mi. s.w. of Checotah via I-40 and SR 150. Golf, tennis, water skiing; airstrip, horse rental, marina, playground.	47	•	•	•	•	•	•	•	•	•			•	•	•
Lake Murray (F-9) 12,496 acres 6 mi. s.e. off US 77. Golf (nine holes), tennis, water skiing; airstrip, horse rental, marina, nature center, playground.	48	•	•	•	•	•	•	•	•	•	•	•	•	•	•
Lake Thunderbird (I-3) 1,834 acres 13 mi. e. of Norman on SR 9. Water skiing; horse rental, playground.	50	•	•	•	•	•	•	•	•	•					•
McGee Creek (F-10) 15,100 acres 18 mi. s.e. of Atoka off US 69. Water skiing.	51	•	•	•	•	•		•	•						
Natural Falls (C-12) 120 acres 3 mi. w. of West Siloam Springs off US 412.	52	•	•	•				•		•					
Okmulgee Lake (D-10) 535 acres 5 mi. w. of Okmulgee on SR 56.	53	•	•		•	•		•					•		
Osage Hills (B-10) 1,199 acres 11 mi. w. of Bartlesville off US 60. Playground.	54	•	•	•	•	•		•	•	•			•		
Quartz Mountain (E-5) 4,284 acres 17 mi. n. of Altus off SR 44A. Golf, tennis, water skiing; playground.	55	•	•	•	•	•	•	•	•	•			•	•	•
Raymond Gary (G-11) 64 acres 16 mi. e. of Hugo on US 70.	56	•	•		•	•		•	•	•					
Red Rock Canyon (D-7) 310 acres s. of Hinton on SR 8. Scenic. Rappelling; playground.	57	•	•	•				•	•	•					
Robbers Cave (E-11) 8,246 acres 4 mi. n. of Wilburton on SR 2. Historic.	58	•	•	•	•	•	•	•	•	•			•	•	•
Roman Nose (C-7) 515 acres 8 mi. n.w. of Watonga via SRs 8 and 8A. Golf, tennis; playground.	59	•	•	•	•	•	•	•	•	•			•	•	•
Sequoyah Bay (C-11) 303 acres 5 mi. s. of Wagoner on SR 16, then 5 mi. e. on Grey Oaks Rd.	60	•	•	•	•	•		•	•	•				•	•
Sequoyah/Western Hills (C-11) 2,876 acres 6 mi. e. of Wagoner on SR 51. Golf, tennis, water skiing; horse rental, marina.	61	•	•	•	•	•	•	•	•	•			•	•	•
Snowdale (C-11) 15 acres 2 mi. w. of Salina on SR 20.	62	•	•		•	•		•	•	•					
Spavinaw (B-11) 35 acres in Spavinaw on SR 20. Playgrounds.	63	•	•		•			•	•	•					
Spring River Canoe Trails (A-12) 35 acres 3 mi. n. of Quapaw off I-44.	64	•	•	•	•			•		•					
Twin Bridges (B-12) 63 acres 6 mi. n.e. of Fairland on US 60.	65	•	•		•	•		•		•					
Wah-Sha-She (A-10) 266 acres 4 mi. w. of Hulah on SR 10. Water skiing; playground.	66	•	•		•	•		•	•	•					
Walnut Creek (E-1) 1,429 acres 15 mi. w. of Tulsa via SR 51 on the n. side of Keystone Reservoir. Water skiing; playground.	67	•	•		•	•		•	•	•				•	
OTHER															
Arcadia Lake (G-3) 5,078 acres 1.5 mi. w. of Arcadia on US 66.	68	•	•	•	•	•		•	•	•			•		
Ardmore City Lake (F-9) 160 acres n. of Ardmore on US 77.	69		•		•	•		•							

RECREATION AREAS

Recreation Area	MAP LOCATION	CAMPING	PICNICKING	HIKING TRAILS	BOATING	BOAT RAMP	BOAT RENTAL	FISHING	SWIMMING	PETS ON LEASH	BICYCLE TRAILS	WINTER SPORTS	VISITOR CENTER	LODGE/CABINS	FOOD SERVICE
Atoka Reservoir (F-10) 6,000 acres 3 mi. n.e. of Atoka on US 69. Water skiing; playgrounds.	70	•	•	•	•	•		•	•						
Bell Cow Lake (G-4) 1,079 acres about 3 mi. n. of Chandler on SR 18.	71	•	•	•	•	•		•	•	•	•				
Blue River Public Hunting and Fishing Area (F-9) 3 mi. n.e. of Tishomingo, then 5 mi. n. of Hunting.	72	•	•					•	•				•		
Cedar Lake (E-12) 90 acres 10 mi. s. of Heavener on US 270, 3 mi. w. on Holson Valley Rd., then 1 mi. n. on FR 269. Horse rental.	73	•	•	•				•	•						
Clear Creek Lake (F-8) 560 acres 13 mi. n.e. of Duncan. Hunting.	74	•	•		•	•		•	•	•					•
Clinton Lake (D-6) 355 acres 14 mi. w. of Clinton on I-40.	75		•		•	•		•		•					
Crystal Beach Park (C-5) s.e. edge of Woodward. Golf (18 holes), miniature golf, tennis; playgrounds, pool with water slide.	76		•	•					•						•
Dead Indian Lake (D-5) 80 acres 10 mi. n. of Cheyenne on US 283. Hunting.	77	•	•		•	•		•	•						
Duncan Lake (F-8) 400 acres 7 mi. n.e. of Duncan.	78	•	•		•	•		•	•						•
Dustin City Lake (D-10) 25 acres 1.5 mi. e. of Dustin.	79	•	•		•			•							
Foss Lake (D-6) 8,800 acres 11 mi. w. of Clinton.	80	•	•		•	•		•							
Fuqua Lake (F-8) 1,500 acres 10 mi. n.e. of Duncan. Hunting.	81	•	•		•	•		•	•	•					
Grand Lake O' The Cherokees (B-11) 59,200 acres off I-44 at Vinita or Afton.	82	•	•		•	•	•	•	•				•	•	•
Guthrie Lake (G-2) 230 acres 4 mi. s. of Guthrie on US 77, then 1 mi. w.	83	•	•		•	•		•	•						
Hall Lake (E-5) 50 acres 11 mi. n. of Hollis.	84	•	•		•	•		•	•						
Henryetta City Lake (D-10) 616 acres 4 mi. e. of Henryetta on New Lake Rd. Water skiing.	85	•	•		•	•		•	•				•		
Holdenville City Lake (E-10) 550 acres 3 mi. s. of Holdenville. Water skiing.	86	•	•		•	•		•		•					•
Humphreys Lake (F-7) 882 acres 12 mi. n.e. of Duncan. Hunting.	87	•	•		•	•		•	•						
Jap Beaver Lake (F-7) 213 acres 4.5 mi. n.w. of Waurika.	88		•	•	•	•		•		•					
J.W. Taylor Lake (E-8) 227 acres 2 mi. s. and 2 mi. e. of Rush Springs.	89	•	•		•			•		•					
Lake Carl Blackwell (C-8) 3,300 acres 8 mi. w. of Stillwater on SR 51.	90	•	•		•	•		•	•	•					
Lake Carl Etling (B-1) 260 acres 26 mi. n.w. of Boise City on SR 325.	91	•	•		•			•						•	
Lake Chickasha (E-7) 1,900 acres 15 mi. n.w. of Chickasha via US 62. Water skiing.	92		•		•	•		•	•						
Lake Ellsworth (E-7) 5,600 acres 14 mi. n.e. of Lawton via I-44.	93	•	•		•	•		•	•	•					
Lake El Reno (H-1) 175 acres at El Reno.	94	•	•	•	•	•		•	•	•	•				
Lake John Wells (D-11) 160 acres 1 mi. s. from Stigler. Water skiing.	95	•	•		•	•		•	•						
Lake Lawtonka (E-7) 1,900 acres 10 mi. n.w. of Lawton via I-44, SR 49 and SR 58. Water skiing.	96	•	•		•	•		•	•	•					
Lake Lugert-Altus (E-6) 17 mi. n. of Altus via US 283.	97	•	•	•	•	•		•	•	•			•	•	•
Lake McMurtry (C-8) 6 mi. n. of Stillwater on US 177.	98	•	•	•	•	•		•		•					
Lake Perry (C-8) 614 acres 1.5 mi. s.w. of Perry on Perry Lake Rd. Water skiing.	99	•	•					•							
Lake Talihina (E-11) 56 acres 3 mi. n.w. of Talihina.	100	•	•					•							
Liberty Lake (G-2) 250 acres 5 mi. s. of Guthrie on US 77, then 2 mi. w.	101	•	•		•	•		•							
Nanih Waiya Lake (E-11) 349 acres 1.5 mi. n.w. of Tuskahoma.	102		•	•	•	•		•							
Nichols Park Lake (D-10) 600 acres 2 mi. s. of Henryetta.	103	•	•		•			•	•						
Okemah Lake (D-10) 730 acres 6 mi. n. of Okemah. Hunting.	104	•	•		•	•		•		•				•	•

RECREATION AREAS

	MAP LOCATION	CAMPING	PICNICKING	HIKING TRAILS	BOATING	BOAT RAMP	BOAT RENTAL	FISHING	SWIMMING	PETS ON LEASH	BICYCLE TRAILS	WINTER SPORTS	VISITOR CENTER	LODGE/CABINS	FOOD SERVICE
Ozzie Cobb Lake (F-11) 457 acres 13 mi. e. of Antlers.	105		•	•	•	•		•							
Pauls Valley (E-8) 750 acres 3 mi. e. of Pauls Valley. Playground.	106	•	•			•		•							
Pawnee City Lake (B-9) 257 acres 1 mi. n. of Pawnee on SR 18. Golf, tennis, water skiing.	107	•	•		•	•		•	•						
Pennington Creek (F-9) in Tishomingo on the 300 block of South Capitol St.	108	•	•		•	•		•	•						
Ponca City Lake (B-9) 900 acres 3 mi. n. of Ponca City via SR 11. Archery, golf, water skiing.	109	•	•	•	•	•		•		•			•		•
Rocky Lake (E-6) 1,205 acres n.w. of Hobart. Playground.	110	•	•		•	•		•	•						
Skip-out Lake (D-5) 60 acres 10 mi. w. of Cheyenne on SR 47. Hunting.	111		•		•	•		•							
Sportsman Lake (D-9) 350 acres 3 mi. e. of Seminole on US 270, then 2 mi. n. and 1.5 mi. e. on county roads. Horseback riding trails, playground.	112	•	•	•	•	•		•		•					
Spring Creek Lake (C-5) 50 acres 21 mi. n.w. of Cheyenne on US 283, then 6 mi. w. on gravel road. Playground.	113	•	•			•			•	•					
Stroud Lake (C-9) 17,600 acres 3 mi. n. of Stroud off SR 99, then 3 mi. e. Water skiing.	114	•	•		•	•		•							
Thunderbird Lake (I-3) 15,000 acres 12 mi. e. of Norman on SR 9. Golf, hunting; playground.	115	•			•	•		•							•
Tishomingo National Wildlife Refuge (F-9) 16,464 acres 3 mi. s. of Tishomingo via an access road off SR 78. *(See Tishomingo p. 265)*	116			•				•							
Turner Falls (F-8) 800 acres 5.2 mi. s. of Davis on US 77. Playground. *(See Davis p. 240)*	117	•	•	•				•	•	•	•			•	•
Washita National Wildlife Refuge (D-6) 8,000 acres 11 mi. w. of Clinton on SR 73, 9 mi. n. on SR 44, 4 mi. w. on SR 33, then .5 mi. n.w. on a county road.	118	•	•	•	•			•					•		
Weleetka City Lake (D-10) 30 acres 1 mi. w. of Weleetka.	119	•						•	•						
Wichita Mountains National Wildlife Refuge (E-6) 59,020 acres 3 mi. n. of Cache on SR 115. *(See Cache p. 239)*	120	•	•	•				•							

Oklahoma Temperature Averages
Maximum/Minimum
From the records of The Weather Channel Interactive, Inc.

	JAN	FEB	MAR	APR	MAY	JUN	JUL	AUG	SEP	OCT	NOV	DEC
Oklahoma City	46 / 27	51 / 30	60 / 37	70 / 48	77 / 58	86 / 67	92 / 70	93 / 70	85 / 62	74 / 51	59 / 37	49 / 30
Tulsa	47 / 28	52 / 31	60 / 37	71 / 48	78 / 58	87 / 67	93 / 71	93 / 71	86 / 63	75 / 53	60 / 39	50 / 31

Points of Interest

ADA (E-9) pop. 15,691, elev. 1,010'

Ada is the seat of Pontotoc County, an area known for oil and gas production as well as cattle raising. Bryd's Mill Spring, south on Cradduck Road following signs to Fittstown, is a popular picnicking site. Opportunities for water skiing and boating are available at Konawa Lake.

Wintersmith Park, on E. 18th Street, contains walking trails, a small zoo, a miniature golf course, children's rides, horseshoe pits and a swimming pool. The park exhibits a restored one-room schoolhouse built in 1907; it is furnished with such items as a potbellied stove and desks that have inkwells.

Ada Chamber of Commerce: 300 W. Main St., P.O. Box 248, Ada, OK 74821; phone (580) 332-2506.

ALINE (B-7) pop. 214, elev. 1,281'

SOD HOUSE, on SR 8, 5.5 mi. n. of US 412, was built in 1894. Typical of many homesteads of the period, the dwelling's timbered, sod-covered roof provided free and renewable shelter for early settlers. Although the house stands on its original site, a large wood structure was built over it in 1964 to prevent weathering.

Antiques and photographs are displayed. An additional building has horse-drawn equipment and period farm implements. Allow 30 minutes minimum. Tues.-Fri. 9-5, Sat.-Sun. 2-5; closed holidays. Free. Phone (580) 463-2441.

ALTUS (F-6) pop. 21,447, elev. 1,388'

Altus is the center of a thriving agricultural region, the result of the 70,000-acre Lugert-Altus irrigation district. Farms produce alfalfa seed, cattle, cotton and wheat. Altus Air Force Base is another major employer. Run by the 97th Air Mobility Wing, the base serves as the Air Force's primary training facility for pilots and flight engineers who handle jumbo jet transports.

For an area that depends on irrigation to prosper, it is ironic that the city's beginnings were marked by a disastrous flood in 1891. Having fled to higher ground, settlers banded together and formed a community to help endure any further hardships the plains might bestow upon them. Altus was the town's chosen name because, according to one of the settlers, it meant "high ground."

Altus Chamber of Commerce: 123 W. Commerce St., Suite 500, P.O. Box 518, Altus, OK 73522; phone (580) 482-0210.

MUSEUM OF THE WESTERN PRAIRIE, 1100 Memorial Dr., depicts the history of Oklahoma's western prairie country from nomadic American Indian inhabitance to urban and agricultural communities. A reconstructed half-dugout (a pioneer house that was built partially underground) is featured. A reference library contains many first-edition publications about the area. Allow 1 hour minimum. Tues.-Sat. 9-5; closed holidays. Donations. Phone (580) 482-1044.

ALVA (B-6) pop. 5,288, elev. 1,332'

Alva is a business center for the surrounding ranching and farming region. The town was named after Santa Fe Railroad lawyer Alva Adams, who later was elected governor of Colorado. As one of four land-office towns for the opening of the Cherokee Outlet in 1893, Alva was an integral part of the settlement of more than 6 million acres, including what later became Woods County.

Alva is home to Northwestern Oklahoma State University, known for its programs in teaching, business, pre-law and pre-medicine.

Alva Area Chamber of Commerce: 410 College Ave., Alva, OK 73717; phone (580) 327-1647.

CHEROKEE STRIP MUSEUM, 901 14th St., contains artifacts from the Cherokee Strip region. Museum displays include medical and dental equipment, Western and American Indian art, farm tools, guns and military items. Period rooms include a chapel, a general store, a barbershop and portions of a 19th-century pioneer house. A one-room schoolhouse exhibits 19th-century relics. Allow 1 hour minimum. Tues.-Sun. 2-5, June-Sept.; Sat.-Sun. 2-5 and by appointment rest of year. Closed holidays. Donations. Phone (580) 327-2030.

ANADARKO (E-7) pop. 6,645, elev. 1,164'

The area in and around Anadarko traditionally served as hunting grounds for three major American Indian tribes. The town was founded in 1901 by white settlers claiming land used by the Kiowa, Comanche and Wichita reservations. Farming and stock raising were the major livelihoods until oil was discovered in 1920 and drilling ensued. Agriculture and oil remain the leading industries.

Local American Indian tribes include the Apache, Caddo, Delaware, Fort Sill Apache, Kiowa and Wichita. The Bureau of Indian Affairs Office is in Anadarko, servicing western Oklahoma and Horton, Kan. Representative of regional American Indian heritage are the striking murals by Kiowa artists in the Federal Building at 120 S. First St.

Colorful sandstone canyons and lakes skirt US 281, which travels 16 miles north of Anadarko to Binger. From Binger a scenic portion of SR 37/152 runs 20 miles east to Minco, where US 81 begins a scenic course through the Canadian River Valley to El Reno at I-40. The Wichita Mountains are southwest of the city.

Anadarko Chamber of Commerce: 516 W. Kentucky Ave., P.O. Box 366, Anadarko, OK 73005; phone (405) 247-6651.

ANADARKO PHILOMATHIC PIONEER MUSEUM, 311 E. Main St. in the former Rock Island depot, contains pioneer artifacts, an American Indian doll collection, American Indian photographs and paintings, a doctor's office and a railroad ticket office. Allow 30 minutes minimum. Tues.-Fri. 10-5, Sat.-Sun. 1-5; closed holidays. Donations. Phone (405) 247-3240.

AAA **INDIAN CITY USA,** 2.5 mi. s. on SR 8, is a re-creation of the once-common Plains Indian villages. Tepees, grass houses, earth lodges and mud huts depict dwellings of the Apache, Caddo, Comanche, Kiowa, Navajo, Pawnee, Pueblo and Wichita tribes. A museum displays items of the southern Plains Indians. Camping and swimming are permitted in the park.

Food is available. Allow 1 hour, 30 minutes minimum. Daily 9-5; closed Jan. 1, Thanksgiving and Dec. 25. Guided tours featuring tribal dances are conducted every 45 minutes. Last tour begins 45 minutes before closing. Admission (including museum) $8.50; ages 6-11, $4.75. AX, CB, DC, DS, MC, VI. Phone (405) 247-5661 or (800) 433-5661.

NATIONAL HALL OF FAME FOR FAMOUS AMERICAN INDIANS, at the e. edge of town on US 62, is a 10-acre tract that preserves the legacies of 42 well-known American Indians in statuary. Bronze busts of each honoree line a .75-mile walkway in an outdoor garden. Allow 1 hour minimum. Visitor center open Mon.-Sat. 9-5, Sun. 1-5; closed Jan. 1, Thanksgiving and Dec. 25. Free. Phone (405) 247-5555.

SOUTHERN PLAINS INDIAN MUSEUM, 715 E. Central Blvd. at SR 8, is operated by the Indian Arts and Crafts Board of the U.S. Department of the Interior. The center emphasizes Southern Plains Indian history and culture through permanent exhibits. Displays include beadwork, featherwork, metalwork, carvings, skin sewing and hide paintings; changing exhibits showcase contemporary American Indian art. Allow 1 hour minimum. Tues.-Sat. 9-5; closed Jan. 1, Thanksgiving and Dec. 25. Free. Phone (405) 247-6221.

ARDMORE (F-8) pop. 23,711, elev. 868′

Ardmore was the site of a track-side tent city, which Santa Fe Railroad officials selected as a permanent townsite in 1887. Named after one official's hometown in Pennsylvania, the land was part of the Roff Brothers' 700 Ranch—the first homeowners in Ardmore. A replica of the ranch house was moved from Fair Park to the Carter County Historical Museum. Ranching is still an important industry, along with oil drilling and refining and tire manufacturing.

Art exhibits and music, dance and theater performances are offered at the Charles B. Goddard Center for the Visual and Performing Arts, First Avenue and D Street S.W., and at The Brass Ring Performing Arts Center, 120 A St. N.E. Two miles east of Ardmore on SR 199, the Samuel Roberts Noble Foundation specializes in medical and agricultural research.

Four municipal lakes—Ardmore City Lake, Lake Jean Neustadt, Mountain Lake, and Rock Creek Reservoir—offer fishing, boating and picnicking opportunities. Southeast of the city, Lake Murray State Park (see Recreation Chart), Oklahoma's largest state park, offers extensive recreational facilities. The Arbuckle Mountains, about 20 miles north of Ardmore, provide another popular recreation area. Ardmore Regional Park has walking and biking trails, a large family picnic area and a softball complex.

Ardmore Chamber of Commerce: 410 W. Main St., P.O. Box 1585, Ardmore, OK 73402; phone (580) 223-7765.

Self-guiding tours: A brochure describing two tours—a self-guiding walking tour of downtown Ardmore's historic sites as well as a driving tour covering sites throughout the city—is available at both the chamber of commerce and at city hall, 23 S. Washington.

An MP3 player is provided for use with the 26-page Historic Downtown Walking Tour booklet. The booklet is available for $12 at the Ardmore Main Street Authority, 9 A St. S.W.

ELIZA CRUCE HALL DOLL COLLECTION MUSEUM, in the Ardmore Public Library at 320 E St. N.W., contains more than 300 dolls, including rare carved wood "Court Dolls" that belonged to Marie Antoinette, 1830s English peddler dolls, "fashion dolls" produced by dressmakers around 1860 and ethnic dolls from all over the world. Also displayed are miniature tea sets. Allow 30 minutes minimum.

DID YOU KNOW

Oklahoma is the state with the highest American Indian population.

Mon.-Thurs. 10-8:30, Fri.-Sat. 10-4, Sun. 1-5; closed major holidays. Free. Phone (580) 223-8290.

GREATER SOUTHWEST HISTORICAL MUSEUM is at 35 Sunset Dr. The museum's main hall features an original 1895 log cabin along with reproductions of a courtroom, law office, school, general store, post office, barbershop, blacksmith shop and doctor's office. One wing exhibits military memorabilia from the American Revolution through Desert Storm. Another wing houses carriages, cameras and a working model of an oil field. Tues.-Sat. 10-5, Sun. 1-5, Memorial Day-Labor Day; Tues.-Sat. 10-5, rest of year. Closed major holidays. Free. Phone (580) 226-3857.

TUCKER TOWER NATURE CENTER is in Lake Murray State Park; from I-35N use exit 24, from I-35S use exit 29 to SR 77S and continue for 7 mi. to the park. Tucker Tower was designed to be a governor's retreat. Instead, this 1933 medieval-style fortress loomed over Lake Murray unfinished and unused until the early 1950s, when it was converted to a museum.

Displays include part of one of the largest meteorites of its type ever discovered as well as fossils, wildlife exhibits and other artifacts. Allow 30 minutes minimum. Daily 9-7. Admission 50c. Phone (580) 223-2109.

ATOKA (F-10) pop. 2,988, elev. 583′

CONFEDERATE MEMORIAL MUSEUM AND CEMETERY is 2 mi. n. on US 69. The museum houses exhibits of domestic furnishings from the early to mid-1900s, a school house display and medical instruments. Civil War-era weapons and uniforms are displayed along with memorabilia about hometown celebrities Reba McEntire and World Champion Bull Rider Lane Frost. The cemetery was used when measles swept through a Confederate camp killing many soldiers. Allow 1 hour minimum. Museum Mon.-Fri. 9-4; closed holidays. Cemetery daily 24 hours. Free. Phone (580) 889-7192.

BARTLESVILLE (B-9) pop. 34,748, elev. 695′

A replica of the first oil well of commercial importance drilled in Oklahoma is in Johnstone Park, which adjoins the Bartlesville city limits. The original well, Nellie Johnstone No. 1, has been reproduced as a memorial to oilmen.

By previous arrangement, tours are available of Prairie Song, a re-created 1800s prairie village 5.5 miles east of the junction of SR 75 and Durham Road. The village features a chapel, general store, homestead cabin, schoolhouse and saloon; phone (918) 534-2662.

Bartlesville Area Convention and Visitors Bureau: 201 S.W. Keeler St., P.O. Box 2366, Bartlesville, OK 74005; phone (918) 336-8708 or (800) 364-8708.

FRANK PHILLIPS HOME is off US 75; take US 60 3 mi. w. to 1107 S. Cherokee Ave. The neoclassic mansion is the restored home of Frank Phillips founder of Phillips Petroleum Co. Built in 1909, the three-level house is noted for its collection of decorative arts and is furnished with family pieces; highlights include Philippine mahogany, handcrafted ceilings and Waterford crystal chandeliers. A permanent exhibit, "Frank and Jane Phillips, Oklahoma Oil Pioneers," is in the garage.

Allow 1 hour minimum. Tours Wed.-Sat. 10-5 Sun. 1-5; closed holidays. Last tour begins 1 hour before closing. Admission $3; ages 6-17, $1. Phone (918) 336-2491.

PRICE TOWER ARTS CENTER is at 510 Dewey Ave. Housed in a Frank Lloyd Wright-designed skyscraper completed in 1956, the arts center features rotating exhibits as well as a permanent collection dedicated to art, architecture and design. A guided tour examines the top two floors, which include the tower's executive offices and some original Frank Lloyd Wright furniture. A short film provides background about Wright and the tower.

Guided tours are available. Allow 1 hour, 30 minutes minimum. Tues.-Sat. 10-5, Sun. noon-5; closed holidays. Admission $4; over 65, $3; under 16 free. Guided tour $8; over 65 and under 16, $5. AX, DS, MC, VI. Phone (918) 336-4949.

WOOLAROC RANCH, MUSEUM AND WILDLIFE PRESERVE is 12 mi. s.w. on SR 123. Covering 3,600 acres of rugged timberland, oilman Frank Phillips' Woolaroc Ranch depicts the culture and legacy of the American West.

Works by Frederic Remington, Charles M. Russell and other Western artists; artifacts from 40 American Indian tribes that lived in Oklahoma; collection of firearms; and exhibits of Western gear are museum highlights. Phillips' elaborate log lodge can be visited. The Oil Patch exhibit, part of a 5-mile driving tour, relates black gold's importance in the state's history.

More than 700 animals reside in the wildlife preserve which can be seen, along with the Oil Patch and an 1840s trader's camp, on the driving tour. Nature trails allow visitors to explore the grounds, and a petting zoo is available in summer. A multimedia show is presented at the Native American Heritage Center.

Allow 3 hours minimum. Tues.-Sun. 10-5, Memorial Day-Labor Day; Wed.-Sun. 10-5, rest of year. Closed Thanksgiving and Dec. 25. Petting zoo open June-Aug. Admission $8; over 64, $6; under 11 free. Phone (918) 336-0307 or (888) 966-5276.

BEAVER (B-4) pop. 1,570

Beaver resides along the banks of the Beaver River and thus received its name. A statue of the town mascot, a giant buck-toothed "Big Beaver," greets visitors. Beaver Dunes State Park (*see Recreation Chart*), just north on US 270, offers nature trails and more than 120 acres of sand dunes suitable for motorcycle riding.

Beaver County Chamber of Commerce: 33 W. 2nd St., Box 878, Beaver, OK 73932; phone (580) 625-4726.

JONES AND PLUMMER TRAIL MUSEUM, s. on US 270 at the Beaver County Fairgrounds, commemorates a trail named for a cattle company and built by fur traders to haul buffalo hides. Displays chronicle the trail's history; exhibits include period handicrafts, clothing, implements and tools, prehistoric fossils, American Indian relics, a ranch buggy and a windmill. There also is a rural schoolhouse. Allow 30 minutes minimum. Tues.-Sat. 1-5; closed Jan. 1, July 4, Thanksgiving and Dec. 25. Donations. Phone (580) 625-4439.

BROKEN BOW (G-12) pop. 4,230

Broken Bow lies in the heart of Oklahoma's timberland region and is the southern terminus of a scenic section of US 259 that runs 62 miles north to the town of Page. Shortleaf and loblolly pine fuel the area's lumber industry, and Oklahoma's state flower, mistletoe, is abundant. Rainbow and brownie trout are stocked biweekly at a fishery that extends from the Broken Bow Dam to the US 70 bridge.

Broken Bow Chamber of Commerce: 113 W. Martin Luther King Dr., Broken Bow, OK 74728; phone (580) 584-3393 or (800) 528-7337.

FOREST HERITAGE CENTER, 7 mi. n. in Beavers Bend State Park *(see Recreation Chart),* focuses on the relationship between man and forest from prehistoric times to the present. Exhibits include trees; petrified logs and tools; forest industry artifacts; 14 dioramas painted by Harry Rossoll, creator of Smokey Bear; wooden sculptures; and carvings.

The seven-sided museum is built around an open courtyard filled with native trees, shrubs and wildflowers. Daily 8-8. Donations. Phone (580) 494-6497.

CACHE (F-6) pop. 2,371, elev. 1,271′

WICHITA MOUNTAINS NATIONAL WILDLIFE REFUGE is 3 mi. n. on SR 115; the refuge headquarters is w. of the visitor center. The 59,020-acre refuge protects buffaloes, longhorn cattle, elk, deer and turkeys. The strangely eroded, often vividly colored mountains form one of the nation's oldest ranges.

The Charons Garden Wilderness Area preserves rugged portions of these mountains. A paved road leads to Mount Scott's summit, and a scenic stretch of SR 49 passes through the refuge. The visitor center has exhibits, an audio driving tour and a video presentation.

Pets are allowed if kept on a leash. Refuge open daily 24 hours. Visitor center Wed.-Mon. 10-5:30. The refuge headquarters offers visitor information Mon.-Fri. 8-4:30. Free. Phone (580) 429-3222. *See Recreation Chart.*

CATOOSA—*see Tulsa p. 275.*

CHEROKEE (B-7) pop. 1,630, elev. 1,175′

Cherokee is in one of the richest farming areas in the state; major products include wheat, alfalfa and livestock. The fertile lands also yield oil and natural gas from the extensive reserves of the Anadarko Basin.

Cherokee Chamber of Commerce: 111 S. Grand Ave., Cherokee, OK 73728; phone (580) 596-3053.

SALT PLAINS NATIONAL WILDLIFE REFUGE is off SR 38, 2 mi. s. of jct. SRs 11 and 38. The 32,000-acre refuge encompasses the Great Salt Plains. The area, once valued for its thin covering of salt, draws visitors who dig for selenite crystals on the salt flats. The Salt River Dam has transformed much of the region into a lake, but the salt flats remain among the Midwest's largest. Migratory birds, beavers, coyotes and deer are residents; a nature trail and a driving tour are available.

Allow 2 hours minimum for the nature trail and 4 hours minimum for the crystal area. Refuge open to vehicle traffic daily dawn-dusk. Crystal digging is permitted Apr. 1-Oct. 15. Headquarters open Mon.-Fri. 7:30-4, Sat. 10-5, Sun. 1-5, Apr. 1-Oct. 15; Mon.-Fri. 7:30-4, rest of year. Free. Visitors must remain in areas designated for public use; driving on the salt flats is prohibited. Phone (580) 626-4794.

CHEYENNE (D-5) pop. 778

Cheyenne was site of the 1868 Battle of the Washita, in which Lt. Col. George A. Custer initiated an attack upon Chief Black Kettle and his people. Also in Cheyenne is Black Kettle National Grasslands *(see Recreation Chart)*, a 30,710-acre area that contains Lake McClellan.

Cheyenne Chamber of Commerce: Cheyenne City Park, P.O. Box 57, Cheyenne, OK 73628; phone (580) 497-3318.

BLACK KETTLE MUSEUM, at US 283 and SR 47, honors those massacred by Lt. Col. George A. Custer's 7th Cavalry in 1868. Relics and Cheyenne Indian artifacts from the nearby battlefield are displayed. A diorama depicts the scene before the battle. Tues.-Fri. 10-4, Sat.-Sun. 9-5. Closed Jan. 1, Thanksgiving and Dec. 25. Donations. Phone (580) 497-3929.

WASHITA BATTLEFIELD NATIONAL HISTORIC SITE, 2 mi. w. on SR 47A, is the site of Lt. Col. George A. Custer's 1868 charge against the sleeping Cheyenne village of Peace Chief Black Kettle. Park rangers give tours and talks departing from the overlook pavilion. This location also is the beginning of a 1.5-mile loop trail.

Daily dawn-dusk. Ranger programs Sat.-Sun. at 9, 10, 11, 2 and 3:30, Memorial Day-Labor Day. Other times are available by request or appointment when staff is available. Free. Phone (580) 497-2143.

▼ CHICKASAW NATIONAL RECREATION AREA (F-9)

Near Sulphur on US 177 and SR 7, the Chickasaw National Recreation Area encompasses 10,000 acres in south-central Oklahoma. Woods and streams with small waterfalls characterize this region, which is known for its mineral waters. Springs within the area have been classified as sulphur, freshwater and bromide.

A small herd of buffalo in a natural setting recalls the vast herds that once roamed the territory. Campfire talks, children's programs and nature walks are summer features. Arbuckle Dam impounds the Lake of the Arbuckles at the confluence of Buckhorn, Guy Sandy and Rock creeks.

Various recreational facilities are offered at specified sites, including six campgrounds. There are several picnic areas, and other facilities are in nearby Sulphur. The 2,350-acre Lake of the Arbuckles offers swimming and boating; a safety inspection for boats is available at launch ramps. A state license is required for fishing; hunting is permitted in season.

The recreation area is split into two districts: The Lake District includes Lake of the Arbuckles, and the Platt District includes Travertine Nature Center and 67-acre Veteran's Lake. Pets are permitted but must be restricted at all times; they are not allowed in swimming areas.

For more information contact the Superintendent, Chickasaw National Recreation Area, 1008 W. 2nd St., Sulphur, OK 73086. Phone (580) 622-3161. *See Recreation Chart and the AAA South Central Camp-Book.*

TRAVERTINE NATURE CENTER is 2 mi. from the park headquarters. Straddling Travertine Creek, the interpretive center exhibits live animals and reptiles native to the surrounding woods, plains and streams. Rangers sometimes carry a live snake for visitors to handle; slides, movies and demonstrations provide further insight into man's relationship with nature.

Nature Center daily 9-6, Memorial Day-Labor Day; 8-5, rest of year. Ranger programs daily at 3, Memorial Day-Labor Day; Sat.-Sun. at 3, rest of year. Closed Jan. 1, Thanksgiving and Dec. 25. Free. Phone (580) 622-3161.

CLAREMORE—*see Tulsa p. 275.*

CLINTON (D-6) pop. 8,833, elev. 1,564'

Clinton is a major shipping center for the area's cotton, wheat and cattle industries. Recreational opportunities are offered at the Washita River. Foss State Park *(see Recreation Chart)* covers 1,749 acres northwest of town, and the Clinton Dam creates a 700-acre lake along the city limits. The nearby 8,000-acre Washita National Wildlife Refuge offers opportunities for wildlife observation and limited hunting and fishing *(see Recreation Chart).*

Clinton Chamber of Commerce: 101 S. 4th St., Frisco Center, Clinton, OK 73601; phone (580) 323-2222.

OKLAHOMA ROUTE 66 MUSEUM is off I-40 exit 65; take I-40 Bus. Rte. w. to 2229 W. Gary Blvd. The museum tells the story of Route 66 and the history of transportation, reflecting American life from the 1920s through the 1970s. Notable are the "World's Largest Curio Cabinet," vintage automobiles and a replica of a roadside diner.

Allow 30 minutes minimum. Mon.-Sat. 9-7, Sun. 1-6, May-Aug.; Mon.-Sat. 9-5, Sun. 1-5, Feb.-Apr. and Sept.-Nov.; Tues.-Sat. 9-5, rest of year. Closed holidays and first week in Jan. Admission $3; over 65, $2.50; ages 6-18, $1. AX, DS, MC, VI. Phone (580) 323-7866.

DAVIS (F-9) pop. 2,610

Near Davis is Turner Falls Park, 5.25 miles south on US 77. In the Arbuckle Mountains, it contains a 77-foot waterfall that has created several natural swimming pools. The park also features camp sites, cabins, caves (too small to enter) and hiking trails. *See Recreation Chart.*

Davis Chamber of Commerce: 100 E. Main St., Davis, OK 73030; phone (580) 369-2402.

ARBUCKLE WILDERNESS, on the access road of I-35 exit 51 (Turner Falls), is a 400-acre wildlife park in the Arbuckle Mountains. A 6.5-mile scenic drive winds through the park where nearly 1,000 exotic animals roam freely. Visitors are permitted to feed the animals from their car, but only with food purchased at the gate. A petting zoo, playground, entertainment, bumper boats, cookouts, go-carts, hayrides and paddleboats are featured.

Sun.-Thurs. 9-6, Fri.-Sat. 9-7, mid-Mar. through Labor Day; daily 9-5, rest of year. Closed Jan. 1, Thanksgiving and Dec. 25. Schedule may vary in winter. Admission $14.99; over 54, $13.99; ages 3-11, $12.99. DS, MC, VI. Phone (580) 369-3383 or (800) 738-7275.

DEWEY (B-10) pop. 3,179

Dewey, named for Adm. George Dewey, was founded by pioneer J.H. Bartles, who also founded Bartlesville. Bartles brought new meaning to the term "traveling salesman" when he decided to move his store from Bartlesville to Dewey because of the railroad stop. After building a road between the two towns, Bartles loaded his store onto large log rollers and hitched it up to a team of oxen. During the 5 months it took to move and resettle the structure, the store remained open for business.

Bartlesville Area Convention and Visitors Bureau—Dewey: 201 S.W. Keeler St., P.O. Box 2366, Bartlesville, OK 74005; phone (918) 336-8708 or (800) 364-8708.

DEWEY HOTEL, 2 blks. w. of US 75 at 801 N. Delaware St., was completed in 1900 as one of the first buildings in the town. Topped by three cupolas, the three-story Victorian structure has been restored and is furnished with turn-of-the-20th-century antiques. Many of the guests who gambled in the hotel's third-story tower room became giants in Oklahoma's oil industry. Mon.-Sat. 10-4, Sun. 1-4, Mar. 1-Dec. 20 Admission $2; under 12 free with adult. Phone (918) 534-0215.

TOM MIX MUSEUM, 2 blks. w. of US 75 at 721 N. Delaware St., exhibits memorabilia about the Western movie star. Originally a rodeo performer in the 101 Ranch's Wild West Show, Tom Mix won fame and fortune during Hollywood's silent film era. His elaborate costumes, guns, saddles, hats and other items are displayed, and his films are shown regularly. Tues.-Sat. 10-4:30, Sun. 1-4:30, Mar.-Dec.; Sat. 10-4:30, Sun. 1-4:30, in Feb. (weather permitting). Closed holidays. Admission $1, children 50c. Phone (918) 534-1555.

DUNCAN (F-7) pop. 22,505

[SAVE] **CHISHOLM TRAIL HERITAGE CENTER** is at 1000 N. Chisholm Trail Pkwy. The history of the Chisholm Trail—the route used to move large herds of cattle between Texas ranches and Kansas railroads—is recounted through paintings, sculptures, a museum and a theater that simulates a 19th-century cattle drive. Interactive displays allow visitors to make trail drive decisions and practice some cowpoke skills. A life-size bronze statue depicting a cattle drive is a museum highlight.

Allow 1 hour minimum. Mon.-Sat. 10-5, Sun. 1-5, Apr.-Sept.; Tues.-Sat. 1-5, rest of year. Closed

Easter and Dec. 25. Admission $6; over 65, $5; ages 5-17, $4. AX, DS, MC, VI. Phone (580) 252-6692.

STEPHENS COUNTY HISTORICAL MUSEUM is off Beech Ave. in Fuqua Park. Housed in the former National Guard Armory, the museum depicts life in rural Oklahoma at the end of the 19th century. Mannequins dressed in period costumes re-create frontier scenes in a blacksmith shop, a log cabin, a pioneer kitchen and other early settings. Gems, antique toys and a Plains Indian exhibit are among other displays. Guided tours are available. Allow 30 minutes minimum. Tues. and Thurs.-Sat. 1-5; closed major holidays. Donations. Phone (580) 252-0717.

DURANT (G-10) pop. 13,549, elev. 643'

The capital of the Choctaw Nation was moved to Durant after Oklahoma became a state in 1907. The Choctaw National Tribal Headquarters is at the intersection of 16th and Locust.

An unusual statue stands on the front lawn of the Durant City Hall. Known as the World's Largest Peanut, the monument is a tribute to Bryan County peanut growers and processors.

Durant Area Chamber of Commerce: 215 N. 4th Ave., Durant, OK 74701; phone (580) 924-0848.

LAKE TEXOMA RECREATION AREA lies along the Oklahoma-Texas border. The 89,000-acre Lake Texoma was created in 1944 with the construction of Denison Dam for flood control along the Red River. The U.S. Army Corps of Engineers' 202,300-acre recreation area offers boating, camping, golf, hiking and swimming. For further information contact the Texoma Project Office, U.S. Army Corps of Engineers, 351 Corps Rd., Denison, TX 75020.

Daily 6 a.m.-10 p.m., Apr.-Oct. Boat ramp fee $3. Beach fee $4 per private vehicle or $1 per person, under 12 free. Phone (903) 465-4990, (877) 444-6777 for campground reservations or (903) 465-1491 for lake level and temperature information. *See Recreation Chart.*

THREE VALLEY MUSEUM is at 401 W. Main St. Housed in a former machine shop, the museum features exhibits about the history of southeastern Oklahoma. The Native American Gallery portrays the cultures of various local tribes including the Caddo, Wichita, Chickasaw and Choctaw. The Transportation room contains antique vehicles, and Small Town, Circa 1900-1930 is filled with historic items donated from area businesses. Guided tours are available. Mon.-Fri. 1-5; closed major holidays. Donations. Phone (580) 920-1907.

DURHAM (C-5) elev. 465'

METCALFE MUSEUM is 1.3 mi. s. on SR 30, 4 mi. e. on SR 33, then 3 mi. s., following signs. "Sagebrush Artist" Augusta Corson Metcalfe's family homestead contains many pieces of her artwork, which depict the Washita Valley's beauty and the struggles of the pioneers who settled there from the late 19th through the mid-20th century.

Also featured are three nature trails, a pioneer house with period furnishings, a saloon with advertisements from that era and buildings with displays and memorabilia. Allow 30 minutes minimum. Tues.-Sat. 10-5 or by appointment, Mar.-Nov. Donations. Phone (580) 655-4467.

ELK CITY (D-5) pop. 10,510, elev. 1,912′

In the late 1800s Elk City was a rest stop for cattlemen driving herds along the Great Western Trail from Texas to Kansas. Oil was discovered in 1947, and the "black gold" flowed until reserves were depleted in the late 1960s. Interests then turned to deep gas exploration in Elk City and the surrounding Anadarko Basin. The town is on historic Route 66.

The quarter horse, which is notable as both a racehorse and the cowboy's mount of choice, is raised in and around Elk City. The breed almost disappeared with the cowboy era but was reintroduced in the 1940s.

Elk City Chamber of Commerce: 1016 E. Airport Industrial Blvd., P.O. Box 972, Elk City, OK 73648; phone (580) 225-0207 or (800) 280-0207.

SAVE **ELK CITY OLD TOWN MUSEUM COMPLEX,** across from the park at jct. Pioneer Rd. and US 66, is a continuous restoration project that re-creates an early Western town. A museum in a late 19th-century Victorian frame house contains detailed period furnishings. The complex also features the Farm and Ranch Museum, the National Transportation Museum, an American Indian tepee, a pioneer doctor's office, the Pioneer Memorial Chapel, a railroad station, a schoolhouse, a Victorian gazebo and a wagon yard.

Mon.-Sat. 9-7, Sun. 1-5, day after Memorial Day-Labor Day; Mon.-Sat. 9-5, Sun. 2-5, rest of year. Closed holidays. Admission $5, senior citizens and students with ID $4, under 6 free. AX, DC, MC, VI. Phone (580) 225-6266.

National Route 66 Museum, at the Elk City Old Town Museum Complex, takes visitors on a trip through the famous route's history with photographs, old signs and vintage automobiles. Mon.-Sat. 9-7, Sun. 1-5, day after Memorial Day-Labor Day; Mon.-Sat. 9-5, Sun. 2-5, rest of year. Closed holidays. Admission (included in Elk City Old Town Museum Complex admission) $5, senior citizens and students with ID $4, under 6 free. Phone (580) 225-6266.

EL RENO—see Oklahoma City p. 258.

ENID (B-7) pop. 47,045, elev. 1,246′

Although some sources hold that the town's name came from Alfred, Lord Tennyson's "Idylls of the King," more colorful stories credit the naming of Enid to cattle drovers who turned the "Dine" sign on the cook's tent upside down.

In an effort to encourage the Rock Island Railroad to stop at Enid rather than its rival North Enid,

an unknown party sawed through the supports on a railroad trestle southeast of town. While attempting to pass through Enid on its usual route, the train fell into a gully, thereby making its first official "stop" at Enid. Enid later was included on the route.

Greater Enid Chamber of Commerce: 210 Kenwood Blvd., P.O. Box 907, Enid, OK 73702; phone (580) 237-2494 or (888) 229-2443.

MR. & MRS. DAN MIDGLEY MUSEUM is 1 blk. s. of jct. US 412 and US 81 at 1001 Sequoyah Dr. In a 1947 house constructed with more than 30 kinds of rock excavated by Dan and Libbie Midgley, displays include family artifacts of these prosperous farmers who were among the state's earliest landowners.

Antique dishes, furniture and farm tools; a fireplace made of petrified wood and fossil stones; a trophy room with hunted animals; and a fluorescent rock collection are shown. Allow 1 hour minimum. Wed.-Fri. 1-5, Sat. 2-5; closed major holidays. Donations. Phone (580) 234-7265.

MUSEUM OF THE CHEROKEE STRIP, 507 S. 4th St., exhibits American Indian and pioneer artifacts depicting the settlement of the area from 1893 to the present. On the museum grounds is the Humphrey Heritage Village, which includes four historic buildings: a one-room schoolhouse, a church, a Victorian house and the original Enid land office. The museum also has a learning center that features video presentations. Allow 1 hour minimum. Tues.-Sat. 9-5; closed holidays. Donations. Phone (580) 237-1907.

RAILROAD MUSEUM OF OKLAHOMA, 702 N. Washington, has a collection of train cars and objects that were used on local trains. China and silver services, steam engine bells, line maps and postcards are among the memorabilia on display; train buffs can peruse a library of railroading books. A room is devoted to model railroads. Rail excursions are offered twice annually. Tues.-Fri. 1-4, Sat. 10-1, Sun. 2-5; closed major holidays. Donations. Phone (580) 233-3051.

ERICK (E-5) pop. 1,023, elev. 2,064′

ROGER MILLER MUSEUM is at jct. Roger Miller Blvd. and Sheb Wooley Ave. Artifacts and memorabilia related to songwriter and entertainer Roger Miller are displayed. The collection includes clothing, handwritten lyrics, instruments, music, photographs and videos. The motorcycle he was riding when he met Elvis Presley is a highlight. Allow 30 minutes minimum. Wed.-Sat. 10-5, Sun. 1-5; closed major holidays. Admission $3; over 62 and ages 12-17, $2. MC, VI. Phone (580) 526-3833.

FORT GIBSON (D-11) pop. 4,054, elev. 534′

Fort Gibson is a rural community near the site of a fort that was established in 1824 as part of a network of garrisons built to maintain peace along the frontier and to quell conflicts with the Osage Indians. The fort also served as a communication and supply center for fur traders and explorers of the Southwest, It was occupied by Union troops during the Civil War and abandoned in 1890.

About a mile from Fort Gibson Historic Site is Fort Gibson National Cemetery, established in 1868. Among the graves in the officers' circle are those of two women: Sam Houston's Cherokee wife, Talihina, and a young woman from Massachusetts named Vivia. Legend states that Vivia disguised herself as a soldier and followed her former lover to Fort Gibson, where she killed him in retaliation for rejecting her. The American Indians were blamed for his death, and Vivia's gender was not discovered until she died.

Fort Gibson Chamber of Commerce: 200 W. Poplar, P.O. Box 730, Fort Gibson, OK 74434; phone (918) 478-4780.

FORT GIBSON HISTORIC SITE is n. of US 62 on SR 80, following signs. The fort, occupied by the U.S. Army 1824-90, includes a visitor center, a reconstructed log fort, walking trails and a museum that houses military relics found in the area. The barracks, stockade and 13 original buildings can be seen. Allow 1 hour minimum. Tues.-Sun. 10-5, Apr.-Sept.; Thurs.-Sun. 10-5, rest of year. Closed Thanksgiving and Dec. 25. Admission $3; over 65, $2.50; ages 6-18, $1. Phone (918) 478-4088.

FORT SILL (F-7)

FORT SILL MILITARY RESERVATION AND NATIONAL HISTORIC LANDMARK, 437 Quanah Rd., is headquarters of the U.S. Army Field Artillery. The Old Post Area, which retains its frontier atmosphere, was established in 1869 by Gen. Philip Sheridan to control local American Indian tribes. The graves of Geronimo and other famous American Indians can be visited.

The Old Stone Corral contains frontier relics, including horse-drawn vehicles, tepees and replicas of a trader's store and blacksmith shop. The Geronimo Guardhouse, where warriors were imprisoned, has exhibits commemorating American Indian Territory days.

Cannon Walk, linking the guardhouse and other exhibit halls, has weapons from battlefields around the world, including Atomic Annie, a 280-millimeter gun that fired the first atomic artillery round. The Quartermaster Warehouse exhibits weapons, uniforms, tools and equipment dating from the 17th century.

Allow 1 hour, 30 minutes minimum. Mon.-Sat. 8:30-4:30, Sun. 12:30-4:30; closed Jan. 1-2 and Dec. 25-26. Gravesites daily dawn-dusk. Free. Phone (580) 442-5123.

Fort Sill Museum, in the Old Post area, preserves the history of the American Indian Territory and of U.S. field artillery. The museum visitor center contains exhibits about Fort Sill history. Allow 2 hours minimum. Mon.-Sat. 8:30-4:30, Sun. 12:30-4:30; closed Jan. 1-2 and Dec. 25-26. Free. Phone (580) 442-5123.

Missile Park, within Fort Sill Military Reservation and National Historic Landmark, contains U.S. Army missiles and rockets that date from 1944 to the present, including a display about Desert Storm artillery. Allow 30 minutes minimum. Mon.-Sat. 8:30-4:30, Sun. 12:30-4:30; closed Jan. 1-2 and Dec. 25-26. Free. Phone (580) 442-5123.

FORT TOWSON (F-11) pop. 611

The town of Fort Towson sprang up as a center of pioneer and American Indian trade after the nearby military fort was established in 1824.

FORT TOWSON HISTORIC SITE is 1 mi. e. on US 70, then .7 mi. n. at sign. The ruins of Fort Towson, built as an outpost to maintain peace and regulate trade between area settlers and American Indians, are preserved at this site. A sutler's store—owned by a peddler who followed an army unit selling items to soldiers—has been reconstructed, and a museum contains items excavated from the site. Allow 30 minutes minimum. Mon.-Fri. 9-5, Sat.-Sun. 1-5; closed holidays. Free. Phone (580) 873-2634.

FREEDOM (B-6) pop. 271

Situated on the Cimarron River, Freedom is known for its granite monument of the Cimarron Cowboy at the intersection of Eagle Pass and Main. A mural titled "Posting the Colors" also is visible from Main Street.

Freedom Chamber of Commerce: 4th and Main, P.O. Box 125, Freedom, OK 73842; phone (580) 621-3276.

ALABASTER CAVERNS STATE PARK is 6 mi. s. on SR 50, then .5 mi. e. on SR 50A. The 200-acre park surrounds a large gypsum cave that contains selenite and alabaster formations. Various species of bats are found within the caverns.

A light jacket and comfortable shoes are recommended. Allow 1 hour minimum. Park open daily 24 hours. Guided cave tours conducted daily 9-5, May-Sept.; 9-4, rest of year. Closed Thanksgiving and Dec. 25. Park free. Cavern tour $8; over 62, $6; ages 6-12, $5. Phone (580) 621-3381. *See Recreation Chart.*

FREEDOM MUSEUM is 2 blks. e. off SR 50 on Main St. Early Oklahoma memorabilia includes antiques, clothing and one of the largest barbed wire collections in the country, containing more than 700 different types of wire. Of special note is the display of prehistoric fossils recovered from archeological digs northwest of Freedom. Tues.-Sun. 2-4, May 1-early Sept. Donations. Phone (580) 621-3533.

GENE AUTRY (F-9) pop. 99, elev. 729'

GENE AUTRY OKLAHOMA MUSEUM, 601 Prairie St., has memorabilia about Western music, film and TV star Gene Autry. Among the items displayed are TV and movie sets, guitars and records; the museum also highlights other Western singing stars. Allow 1 hour minimum. Mon.-Sat. 10-4; closed holidays. Donations. Phone (580) 294-3047.

GOODWELL (B-2) pop. 1,192, elev. 3,286'

Goodwell is within Oklahoma's panhandle, the 34-mile-wide and 168-mile-long strip of land that lies between the borders of Kansas and Texas. Before this area became part of the Oklahoma Territory in 1890 it was known as "No Man's Land" because it was unclaimed. The Rock Island Railroad line helped to establish the town around 1903. Common sense came into play in the naming of Goodwell. During the construction of the railroad, workers were impressed with the soft water they found in a newly drilled well.

NO MAN'S LAND HISTORICAL MUSEUM, on Sewell St. on the campus of Panhandle State University, contains pioneer and American Indian artifacts depicting the development of Oklahoma's "No Man's Land" that later became the heart of the Dust Bowl. There also are alabaster carvings, dinosaur footprints, geological exhibits and mounted animals. Allow 1 hour minimum. Tues.-Fri. 10-noon and 1-3; closed holidays. Free. Phone (580) 349-2670.

GORE (D-11) pop. 850

Gore was the stopping point for Cherokee Indians as they migrated west in 1828. They established a council ground and in 1829 welcomed Sam Houston—who later married a Cherokee—into their tribe. The settlement remained the capital of what became the Cherokee Nation West until the Eastern Cherokees, who were forced to join their Western counterparts via the "Trail of Tears," gained control of the nation and relocated the capital to Tahlequah in 1843.

Gore Chamber of Commerce: 1009 N. Main St., P.O. Box 970, Gore, OK 74435; phone (918) 489-2534.

CHEROKEE COURTHOUSE (TAHLONTEESKEE), 3 mi. e. on US 64/SR 10, is the restored courthouse and council house of the Cherokee Nation West. The tribe named its headquarters Tahlonteeskee after the chief who founded the Western Cherokee Nation. The buildings contain drawings depicting significant events in the tribe's history, along with American Indian artifacts, tools and photographs. Mon.-Sat. 9-5, Sun. 1-5, other times by appointment; closed Thanksgiving and Dec. 25. Free. Phone (918) 489-5663.

GROVE (B-12) pop. 5,131

HAR-BER VILLAGE, 3.5 mi. w. on Har-Ber Rd., is on the shores of Grand Lake O' the Cherokees. This reconstructed 19th-century village encompasses more than 100 log cabin buildings as well as collections of glassware, dolls, china, furniture and farm machinery. Other exhibits include primitives (American Indian pottery or artifacts made before the advent of a spoken language) and arctic animals.

Included among the buildings are a bank, a beauty shop, a courthouse, a dentist's office, a drug store, a jewelry store, a one-room schoolhouse, a post office and stills. A visitor center houses changing exhibits. An ecology center and an herb garden also are on the grounds.

Note: Visitor center scheduled to open early 2007; phone ahead to verify. Allow 3 hours minimum. Mon.-Sat. 9-5, Sun. 12:30-5, Mar. 1-Oct. 14; Mon.-Sat. 9-4, Sun. 12:30-5, Oct. 15-Nov. 15. Admission $3.50; over 62, $2.50; under 14 free. Phone (918) 786-6446.

SAVE LENDONWOOD GARDENS is 1 mi. e. of US 59 at 1310 W. 13th St. The garden features five areas, several with an Oriental theme. The Zen Garden has more than 100 bonsai plants; the Oriental Garden contains a pond and rhododendrons; and the Japanese pond area has conifers, Japanese maples and a tea house. The American Backyard with drought-resistant plants and the English Terrace Garden with dwarf hostas complete the complex. Allow 30 minutes minimum. Daily dawn-dusk. Admission $5, under 13 free. Phone (918) 786-2938.

GUTHRIE—see Oklahoma City p. 258.

HEAVENER (E-12) pop. 3,201

At the base of 1,200-foot-high Poteau Mountain in the Ouachita Range, Heavener was carved out of land known to the Choctaws as the "Prairie of the Tall Grass." It was named for Joe Heavener, a local merchant and owner of the original townsite. The town lies along a scenic section of US 59/270 that runs 26 miles between Poteau and Page.

Heavener Chamber of Commerce: 501 W. 1st St., Heavener, OK 74937; phone (918) 653-4303.

HEAVENER-RUNESTONE STATE PARK, 2.5 mi. e. off US 59 following signs, contains a 12-foot-high, 10-foot-wide stone with runic alphabet carvings believed to have been made by Viking explorers about 750. The stone can be reached via a 100-yard trail. A community building, amphitheater, picnic area and a playground also are available. Allow 1 hour minimum. Park open daily 8-dusk. Interpretive center open daily 8-5. Free. Phone (918) 653-2241.

PETER CONSER HOME, 5 mi. s. on US 59, then 3 mi. w., is the restored house of the leader of the Choctaw Nation. Peter Conser also was a wealthy merchant and captain of the Choctaw Lighthorse, an early law enforcement group. Antiques and photographs are displayed. Wed.-Sat. 10-5, Sun. 1-5; closed holidays. Free. Phone (918) 653-2493.

HOMINY—see Tulsa p. 275.

HUGO (G-11) pop. 5,536, elev. 550'

Known as Circus City, USA, Hugo constitutes the winter headquarters of the five-ring Carson & Barnes and the Kelly-Miller Bros. circuses. Monuments to circus performers can be found in a section of the Mount Olivet Cemetery. Hugo also is home to the 13,500-acre Hugo Lake *(see Recreation Chart)*, where bass and crappie are plentiful.

Hugo Chamber of Commerce: 200 S. Broadway, Hugo, OK 74743; phone (580) 326-7511.

HUGO FRISCO DEPOT MUSEUM is downtown in the 300 block of N. B St. Built in 1914 on the main line from Dallas to St. Louis, the Frisco Depot houses American Indian artifacts, antiques, a miniature train exhibit and railroad memorabilia. Tues.-Sat. 10-4. Donations. Phone (580) 326-6630.

IDABEL (G-12) pop. 6,952, elev. 489′

MUSEUM OF THE RED RIVER is at 812 E. Lincoln Rd. Specializing in American Indian art and artifacts, the museum houses contemporary pottery, beadwork, baskets and crafts.

Archeological findings from the Caddoan Indians as well as historic items of the Choctaw Indians are displayed. A gallery features a complete cast skeleton of an Acrocanthosaurus atokensis, a meat-eating dinosaur that once roamed the area. Allow 1 hour minimum. Tues.-Sat. 10-5, Sun. 11-4; closed Jan. 1, Memorial Day, July 4, Thanksgiving and Dec. 25. Free. Phone (580) 286-3616.

JENKS—*see Tulsa p. 275.*

KINGFISHER (G-1) pop. 4,380, elev. 1,051′

Nicknamed "The Buckle of the Wheat Belt," Kingfisher is among the largest wheat markets in the world. The town was founded during the land run of 1889 and was named after a cattleman called King Fisher, who operated a stagecoach station and line. The Chisholm Trail passed through the area.

Kingfisher Chamber of Commerce: 123 W. Miles, Kingfisher, OK 73750; phone (405) 375-4445.

CHISHOLM TRAIL MUSEUM AND GOVERNOR SEAY MANSION are 5 blks. w. of US 81 at 605 Zellers Ave. The museum has pioneer and American Indian articles as well as a timeline describing the history of the Chisholm Trail. The mansion, across the street at 11th and Overstreet, was built in 1892 and is restored and furnished in period. A late 1890s village located behind the museum features two log cabins, a bank, a schoolhouse and a church. Allow 1 hour minimum for the museum, 30 minutes for the mansion. Tues.-Sat. 9-5, Sun. 1-5; closed holidays. Donations. Phone (405) 375-5176.

LANGLEY (B-11) pop. 669, elev. 760′

PENSACOLA DAM, .5 mi. e. of jct. SRs 28 and 82, impounds 66-mile-long Grand Lake O' The Cherokees, spanning the river between Disney and Langley; the length of the dam and spillways is 6,565 feet. Power plant tours daily 9:30-4, Memorial Day weekend-Labor Day. Free. Phone (918) 782-9594 or (918) 782-3382.

LAWTON (F-7) pop. 92,757, elev. 1,111′

On the morning of Aug. 6, 1901, Lawton was merely a tumbleweed connection on a vast American Indian reservation. By evening it had blossomed into a town of 10,000, the last of the Oklahoma cities to spring up overnight. Lawton was created by a land lottery, in which successful bidders without the cash for immediate payment were allowed 30 minutes in which to get the money before the lot was put up for sale again.

Lawton Chamber of Commerce and Industry: 629 S.W. C Ave., Suite A, P.O. Box 1376, Lawton, OK 73502; phone (580) 355-3541 or (800) 872-4540.

 FORT SILL MILITARY RESERVATION AND NATIONAL HISTORIC LANDMARK—*see Fort Sill p. 243.*

MUSEUM OF THE GREAT PLAINS, in Elmer Thomas Park at 601 Ferris Ave., interprets the relationship between man and the plains environment. Exhibits depict the fur trade and cattle industries, the life of the frontier soldier and technological development on the plains. Replicas of a fur-trading fort and a train depot with a locomotive are displayed as well as a collection of farm machinery. Living-history programs are presented Tuesday through Saturday in the fort's trading post.

Allow 1 hour minimum. Mon.-Sat. 10-5, Sun. 1-5; closed Jan. 1, Thanksgiving and Dec. 25. Admission $5; senior citizens $4; ages 7-11, $2.50. Phone (580) 581-3460.

LONE WOLF (E-6) pop. 500, elev. 1,554′

QUARTZ MOUNTAIN STATE RESORT PARK NATURE CENTER, 10 mi. s. on SR 44, then 1.5 mi. n. on SR 44A, features exhibits about local cultural history, geology, fauna and flora. Ten nature trails are on the grounds; an interpretive trail takes hikers .2 mile along a wooded stream. The second trail, .5 mile in length, climbs 1,500 feet to a mountain summit. A hands-on children's area as well as provisions for boating, camping and picnicking are available. Park open daily 24 hours. Nature center open Wed.-Sun. 8-4. Free. Phone (580) 563-2238. *See Recreation Chart.*

MADILL (F-9) pop. 3,410

Originally supported by surrounding farms and ranches, Madill's economic base changed dramatically in 1945 when Denison Dam was built. The dam flooded the agricultural land and created Lake Texoma *(see Recreation Chart)*, one of Oklahoma's most popular resort areas. To capitalize on its new lakeside location, the town became a recreation center.

Marshall County Chamber of Commerce: P.O. Box 542, Madill, OK 73446; phone (580) 795-2431.

FORT WASHITA, 15 mi. e. on SR 199E, is a 150-acre site containing the well-preserved, partially restored remains of an American Indian fort built in 1842. The Chickasaws and Choctaws used the fort for protection from the Plains Indians, as did pioneers traveling westward. It was last occupied by the Confederate Army during the Civil War. Picnicking is permitted. Allow 1 hour minimum. Mon.-Sat. 9-4:30, Sun. 1-4:30; closed holidays. Donations. Phone (580) 924-6502.

McALESTER (E-11) pop. 17,783, elev. 734'

McAlester began as a tent store owned by J.J. McAlester at the crossroads of the old California Trail and the Texas Road. He later discovered and mined coal in the area.

Because McAlester had married a Choctaw Indian, which made him a member of the Choctaw Nation, the American Indians claimed rights to his newly found wealth. When McAlester protested, the tribal court ruled in his favor; however, the Choctaw chief sentenced him to death in spite of this decision. McAlester made a dramatic escape and later served the state as lieutenant governor.

McAlester Scottish Rite Temple, 2nd and Adams streets, has an auditorium with Egyptian decor. Guided tours are available by reservation; phone (918) 423-6360.

Six miles north is Eufaula Lake *(see Recreation Chart).* The Eufaula Dam's powerhouse, off SR 71, is open for tours by appointment; phone (918) 484-5439.

McAlester Area Chamber of Commerce and Agriculture: 345 E. Adams, McAlester, OK 74502; phone (918) 423-2550.

PIONEER COAL MINER MEMORIAL at 3rd and Chadick sts. in Chadick Park, pays tribute to the thousands of coal miners who worked in the area's mines. The memorial is comprised of a bronze, life-size statue of a miner as well as the Wall of Memories, which contains the names of more than 1,700 miners who died in the profession. Allow 30 minutes minimum. Daily dawn-dusk. Free.

MIAMI (B-11) pop. 13,704, elev. 798'

COLEMAN THEATRE BEAUTIFUL, 103 N. Main St., is a restored 1929 vaudeville movie theater. Guided tours offer visitors a chance to see its mahogany staircases, crystal chandeliers, stained-glass panels and original Wurlitzer pipe organ. Theater performances are given on a regular basis. Allow 1 hour minimum. Tues.-Fri. 10-4, Sat. 10-noon; closed Dec. 25. Donations. Phone (918) 540-2425, ext. 454.

MUSKOGEE (D-10) pop. 38,310, elev. 601'

The town takes its name from the Muscogee tribe of the Creek Nation who moved to Oklahoma in the 1830s. Muskogee also was the home of notable Oklahoma historians Grant and Carolyn Foreman, who wrote a number of books about the Five Civilized Tribes. The couple's residence, the Thomas-Foreman Home, contains their original furniture.

Honor Heights Park, at 40th Street and Park Boulevard, is a 132-acre park with extensive plantings of azaleas, roses and irises surrounding lakes, lily ponds and picnic grounds.

Muskogee Convention and Tourism: 310 W. Broadway, Muskogee, OK 74401; phone (918) 682-2401.

ATALOA LODGE MUSEUM, on the Bacone College campus, displays more than 20,000 American Indian artifacts collected from tribes throughout the country. Mon.-Sat. 8-5, Sun. 1-5. Donations. Phone (918) 781-7283.

SAVE **FIVE CIVILIZED TRIBES MUSEUM,** Agency Hill on Honor Heights Dr., is in the 1875 Union Indian Agency building. Displays and artifacts depict the history and culture of the Cherokee, Chickasaw, Choctaw, Creek and Seminole Indians. An art gallery and a library also are on the premises. Allow 1 hour minimum. Mon.-Sat. 10-5, Sun. 1-5; closed Jan. 1, Thanksgiving and Dec. 25. Admission $3; over 64, $2; students with ID $1.50; under 6 free. Phone (918) 683-1701.

USS *BATFISH* WAR MEMORIAL PARK MUSEUM, Port of Muskogee exit off the Muskogee Turnpike at 3500 Batfish Rd., offers self-guiding tours of the USS *Batfish,* a World War II submarine that sank three enemy submarines and 11 other enemy vessels during battle. Tours include the torpedo room and crew cabins. The museum also contains monuments to other submarines lost during the war and a Walk of Honor that honors all veterans.

Mon. and Wed.-Sat. 9-4, Sun. noon-4, Mar. 15-Oct. 15; closed Easter. Admission $5; over 62, $3; ages 6-15, $2. Phone (918) 682-6294.

NORMAN—*see Oklahoma City p. 259.*

NOWATA (B-11) pop. 3,971

Nowata received its name from a Delaware Indian word, *no-we-ata,* meaning "welcome." The Delaware tribe, called Lenape in their native language, migrated to the Cherokee Nation in 1866, following an agreement set forth by the Cherokee. The pact allowed the newcomers to reside within the Cherokee Nation yet retain their independence as Delaware Indians.

Nowata Chamber of Commerce: 126 S. Maple St., P.O. Box 202, Nowata, OK 74048; (918) 273-2301.

NOWATA COUNTY HISTORICAL SOCIETY MUSEUM, 121 S. Pine St., contains an extensive collection of local memorabilia. Twenty-one rooms display American Indian and cowboy artifacts, period clothing, oil drilling and agricultural equipment, military items, dolls, antique furniture and early household utensils. Tues.-Sat. 1-4. Free. Phone (918) 273-1191.

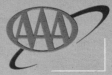

Oklahoma City

City Population: 506,132   Elevation: 1,201 ft.

Editor's Picks:

Bricktown / © Gibson Stock Photography

Born in an afternoon, built over a field of black gold, and redesigned by architect I.M. Pei, Oklahoma City has a history with few plateaus. Between noon and sundown on April 22, 1889, the unassigned prairie lands of the Oklahoma Territory were opened for settlement, and 10,000 land claims surrounding a Santa Fe Railroad station site were made in one afternoon. Oklahoma City literally blossomed overnight.

Established as state capital in 1910, Oklahoma City welcomed thousands of government employees, whose arrival swelled its population to the largest in the state. Manufacturing concerns were established along with the development of natural resources. As it did with many cities, World War I boosted the economy.

On Dec. 4, 1928, what would become a major force in Oklahoma City's economic future surfaced: The first oil well within the city limits struck a gusher. It changed not only the economy but the scenery. Oil derricks sprouted throughout town, adding a familiar silhouette to the city's rapidly changing skyline.

The most renowned strike was the Mary Sudik, which blew in 1930 and lasted for 11 days, spreading oil as far as 15 miles. Producing wells still are found on the Capitol grounds, and more than 2,000 wells are either within or adjacent to the city limits. The pool on which Oklahoma City rests is considered among the richest ever developed in the United States.

Along with the discovery of oil, drilling equipment and petroleum refining industries flourished.

World War II and the postwar years contributed to this economic growth through the establishment of Douglas Aircraft Co. and Tinker Air Force Base, the largest supply and repair depot in the world.

Aviation remains a major industry, with the FAA Aeronautical Center and the Civil Aeromedical Institute making their home at Will Rogers World Airport. "OKC," as the city is affectionately called by its residents, also is the state's leading wholesale and distribution point and ranks among the eight primary livestock markets in the country. More than 855 manufacturing concerns are in operation.

Among Oklahoma City's main public buildings is the Civic Center, which covers six blocks in the heart of downtown. It includes the city hall, county building, police department and Civic Center Music Hall, which seats 3,200. Also a focus in the downtown area is Cox Business Services Convention Center, Broadway and Sheridan. The center includes an arena with a seating capacity of more than 15,000, an exhibition arena and a number of meeting rooms. The nearby Myriad Gardens holds such seasonal events as the Spring Festival of the Arts and Fourth of July activities.

To complement the city's successful commercial growth, Oklahoma City's leaders recommended a

Getting There — *starting on p. 249*

Getting Around — *starting on p. 252*

What To See — *starting on p. 252*

What To Do — *starting on p. 256*

Where To Stay — *starting on p. 595*

Where To Dine — *starting on p. 604*

© Myriad Botanical Gardens & Crystal Bridge

ew look for downtown. In 1964 well-known urban architect I.M. Pei created a master redevelopment plan. Inspired by Copenhagen's Tivoli Gardens, the rejuvenated area includes lakes, water concourses, landscaped hills, an amphitheater and a striking glass and steel botanical bridge containing a greenhouse with exotic plants.

Another innovative addition was the Metro Concourse System of tunnels and skywalks, which connects major hotels, office buildings, conference areas, restaurants and retail establishments within the downtown area.

Despite a sleek and sophisticated appearance, Oklahoma City has not forgotten its pervasive Western and American Indian heritage. It sprang from Indian Territory, and the 39 American Indian tribes still represented in the state hold regular tribal activities in and around the city. Their artwork decorates building interiors and is displayed in local galleries and museums.

The skills of horses and cowboys are revered at many rodeos and horse shows as well as at the National Cowboy and Western Heritage Museum (see attraction listing p. 254). Cowboys still practice their trade at horse and cattle ranches in the surrounding region, and Western wear has withstood the capricious trends of fashion. Heritage has proven a stabilizing influence in a rapidly changing environment.

Getting There

By Car

Transcontinental I-40 is the primary east-west route through the area; it traverses the heart of the city, offering easy interchanges with main streets and other through routes. I-44, a shorter east-west corridor, angles in from the northeast and the southwest, skirting the western side of the city and offering frequent interchanges.

Except for its path through the city, I-44 is a toll highway throughout most of Oklahoma, and its various segments are known as the Will Rogers Turnpike, Turner Turnpike and H.E. Bailey Turnpike. Other east-west routes serving the area mainly accommodate local traffic and include US 62, US 270 and old US 66, which parallels I-44 from the northeast and I-40 from the west.

I-35 bisects both the nation and Oklahoma City, bringing travelers from Lake Superior to the north and from the Mexican border to the south. It courses along the city's east side with frequent interchanges. US 77 closely parallels I-35 and serves mostly local traffic. Also of importance is SR 3, which provides access to Will Rogers and Wiley Post airports as it skirts the city's west side.

I-240 (Southwest Expressway) combines with I-44 and I-35 to form a loop around Oklahoma City, providing a bypass of the downtown area.

Destination Oklahoma City

*I*n Oklahoma City, visitors can find re-created buildings, cowboy and rodeo museums, and other reminders of early days. But don't take it for a one-horse town.

*A*lthough the city's sleek skyscrapers and extensive metro system show that OKC lies firmly in the present, its residents take great pride in its grand, colorful past.

Oklahoma City CVB

Oklahoma City Museum of Art.
A 55-foot-tall glass sculpture created by Dale Chihuly towers above visitors' heads as they enter the museum's atrium. (See listing page 254)

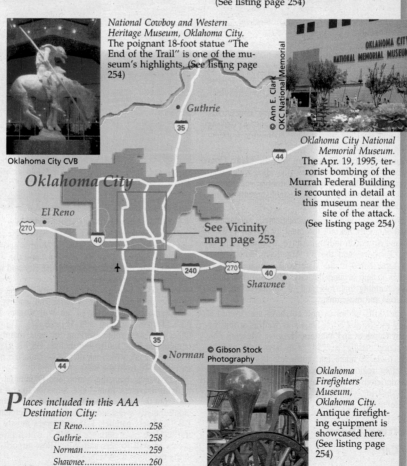

Oklahoma City CVB

National Cowboy and Western Heritage Museum, Oklahoma City. The poignant 18-foot statue "The End of the Trail" is one of the museum's highlights. (See listing page 254)

© Ann E. Clark
OKC National Memorial

Oklahoma City National Memorial Museum. The Apr. 19, 1995, terrorist bombing of the Murrah Federal Building is recounted in detail at this museum near the site of the attack. (See listing page 254)

Oklahoma City

El Reno

Guthrie

See Vicinity map page 253

Shawnee

Norman   © Gibson Stock Photography

Oklahoma Firefighters' Museum, Oklahoma City. Antique firefighting equipment is showcased here. (See listing page 254)

*P*laces included in this AAA Destination City:

The Informed Traveler

Sales Tax: Oklahoma City levies a sales tax of 8.38 percent, a lodging tax of 13.87 percent and a rental car tax of 14.37 percent.

WHOM TO CALL

Emergency: 911

Police (non-emergency): (405) 297-1000

Fire: (405) 297-3439

Time and Temperature: (405) 599-1234

Hospitals: Deaconess Hospital, (405) 604-6000; Integris Baptist Medical Center, (405) 949-3011; Integris Southwest Medical Center, (405) 636-7000; Mercy Health Center, (405) 755-1515; Oklahoma University Medical Center, (405) 271-4700; St. Anthony Hospital, (405) 272-7000.

WHERE TO LOOK

Newspapers

There is one major daily newspaper, the *Daily Oklahoman,* which is distributed in the morning.

Radio

Oklahoma City radio station KTOK (1000 AM) is a news station; KCSC (90.1 FM) is a member of National Public Radio.

Visitor Information

Oklahoma City Convention and Tourism Bureau: 189 W. Sheridan, Oklahoma City, OK 73102; phone (405) 297-8912 or (800) 225-5652.

Visitors guides, maps and brochures are available Mon.-Fri. 8:30-5.

Oklahoma City Chamber of Commerce: 123 Park Ave., Oklahoma City, OK 73102; phone (405) 297-8900.

The chamber dispenses visitor information Mon.-Fri. 8:30-5.

TRANSPORTATION

Air Travel

Fifteen major airlines serve Will Rogers World Airport, 10 miles southwest of downtown. Airport parking costs $4-$8 per day. Cab service averages 20-30 minutes to the downtown area; the average cost is $20. Airport vans depart frequently and provide shuttle service between the airport and downtown; fare is $17 per person.

Buses

Greyhound Lines Inc., Jefferson Lines, MK & O Lines and Oklahoma Transportation Co. are the major bus lines that serve the city. They all operate out of the same terminal at 427 W. Sheridan Ave.; for schedule information phone (405) 235-6425.

Public Transport

Metro Transit operates buses throughout the metropolitan area and includes stops at attractions and shopping centers. The main terminal is on Reno Avenue between Broadway and E.K. Gaylord. The fare is $1.25; ages 6-17, 60c; transfers are free. For schedule and route information phone (405) 235-7433.

Rental Cars

There are several rental car agencies that serve the Oklahoma City area both downtown and at the airport. Hertz, (405) 681-2341 or (800) 654-3080, offers discounts to AAA members.

Taxis

Cab companies include ABC, (405) 232-2402; Safeway, (405) 235-1431; and Yellow, (405) 232-6161. Taxis are metered and charge $1.80 per mile. There is a $1 charge for each additional passenger.

Getting Around

Street System

Except for the area around the Capitol and state office buildings, Oklahoma City is laid out in a grid pattern with streets either running north-south or east-west. The numbered streets run east-west both north and south of Main Street; named north-south streets intersect them. East-west address numbers start at Grand Avenue, and north-south numbers begin at Broadway.

Unless otherwise posted, the speed limit on most streets is 25 to 30 mph. Rush hour traffic, 7:30-9 a.m. and 4-6 p.m., should be avoided.

Parking

Ample parking is available downtown. There are many commercial garages, and most hotels provide parking for guests. Rates are 75c to $1 per hour, or $4 per day.

What To See

45TH INFANTRY DIVISION MUSEUM, .7 mi. w. off I-35 at 2145 N.E. 36th St., traces Oklahoma's military history from 1541 to the present. Exhibited are items from Adolf Hitler's Munich office, uniforms, firearms and a large collection of Bill Mauldin's "Willie and Joe" cartoons. More than 60 military vehicles, aircraft and artillery are outdoors.

A military weapons collection illustrates the development of American military arms from the American Revolution to the Persian Gulf War. Allow 1 hour minimum. Museum Tues.-Fri. 9-4:15, Sat. 10-4:15, Sun. 1-4:15; closed Jan. 1 and Dec. 25. Outdoor military park closes 45 minutes after museum. Free. Phone (405) 424-5313 or (405) 424-5393.

99s MUSEUM OF WOMEN PILOTS is at 4300 Amelia Earhart Rd. at the entrance to Will Rogers World Airport. The 99s were founded in 1929 by a group of female pilots that included Amelia Earhart. Displays trace the history of women in aviation and include exhibits about Earhart, the 1929 Women's Air Derby, World War II, air racing and the space program. The group is named for the number of women who formed the group's original membership.

Allow 1 hour minimum. Mon.-Fri. 9-4, Sat. 10-4; closed major holidays. Admission $5; over 65, $4; ages 3-12, $2. AX, MC, VI. Phone (405) 685-9990.

AMATEUR SOFTBALL HALL OF FAME AND MUSEUM, off I-35 at 2801 N.E. 50th St., presents the history and honors the greats of this popular amateur sport. Allow 30 minutes minimum. Mon.-Fri. 9-4:30, Sat. 10-4, Sun. 1-4, Apr.-Oct.; Mon.-Fri. 8-4:30, rest of year. Closed Jan. 1, Thanksgiving and Dec. 25. Admission $6; ages 6-12, $3. Phone (405) 424-5266, ext. 0.

COLES GARDEN is just n. of I-44 at 1415 N.E. 63rd St. The site features 12 acres of gardens, including a pond with a 75-foot wide waterfall and

© Myriad Botanical Gardens & Crystal Bridge

To Enid · © 2006 NAVTEQ · To Guthrie · © AAA · To Tulsa & Frontier City

Oklahoma City

Will Rogers Park

Oklahoma State Fairgrounds

Oklahoma National Stockyards

Downtown Airpark

Wiley Post Park

Memorial Park

Oklahoma City University

Overholser Mansion

Oklahoma City National Memorial & Memorial Museum

Oklahoma City Museum of Art

Civic Center

Cox Business Svcs Conv Ctr

Wheeler Park

National Cowboy and Western Heritage Museum Omniplex

National Softball Hall of Fame and Museum

Oklahoma Firefighters' Museum

45th Infantry Division Museum

State Capitol

Oklahoma History Center

Harn Homestead and 1889er Museum

Myriad Botanical Gardens & Crystal Bridge

Washington Park

Ford Center

Coles Garden

Oklahoma City Zoo & Botanical Garden

Lincoln Northeast Lake

Park

Douglas Center Park

To Amarillo · To Lawton · To Purcell · To Fort Smith

2146-E

---

many varieties of koi. Visitors enter through the Napoleon Bonaparte gates, hand-forged in France around 1810. Allow 30 minutes minimum. Mon.-Fri. 9-5; closed Jan. 1, Thanksgiving and Dec. 25. Admission $5, ages 1-11 free. Phone (405) 478-1529 or (800) 334-5576.

FRONTIER CITY, 7 mi. n. off I-35 N.E. 122nd St. exit at 11501 N.E. Expressway on the n. I-35 service road, is both a re-created 1880s Oklahoma town and an amusement park. Featured are the vertical thrill ride ErUPtion and roller coasters, which include Diamond Back, Silver Bullet and Wildcat. Gunfights, live shows and musical reviews are staged daily.

Food is available. Allow 1 hour minimum. The 2007 season schedule is Sat. 10:30-8, Sun. noon-7, Mar. 31-May 27; Mon.-Fri. 10:30-8, Sat. 10:30 a.m.-11 p.m., Sun. noon-8, May 28-Aug. 12; Sat.-Sun. noon-8, Aug. 18-Sept. 30; Fri. 6 p.m.-11 p.m., Sat. noon-11, Sun. noon-9, Oct. 5-29. Admission $32.99, over age 62 and under 48 inches tall $24.99, under age 3 free. Parking $10. AX, MC, VI. Phone (405) 478-2412 or (405) 478-2140.

MARTIN PARK NATURE CENTER is 11 mi. w. of I-35 Memorial Rd. exit; enter at 5000 W. Memorial between Meridian and McArthur. The center's 140 acres of woodlands, prairies, creeks and pond provide a natural habitat for armadillos, beavers and more than 200 bird species. The Nature Exhibit Building contains exhibits about wildlife, plants and conservation.

Self-guiding nature trails, some of which are accessible to wheelchairs, traverse the refuge; guided nature hikes are conducted for a fee by reservation. Allow 2 hours minimum. Wed.-Sun. 9-6; closed holidays. Free. Phone (405) 755-0676.

MYRIAD BOTANICAL GARDENS & CRYSTAL BRIDGE, Reno Ave. and Robinson St., is the centerpiece of the Myriad Garden project, which includes 17 acres of rolling hills surrounding a lake in the central business district. The bridge is a 224-foot-long, seven-story glass cylinder containing a botanical conservatory. Featured are tropical gardens—a collection of palm trees, flowers and more than 1,000 species of exotic plants from around the world—and a walkway through a 35-foot series of rock waterfalls to the upper level.

A skywalk affords a panoramic view of palms, cactuses and tiny air plants, including orchids. Lightweight clothing is recommended. Allow 30 minutes minimum. Mon.-Sat. 9-6, Sun. noon-6; closed Jan. 1, Thanksgiving and Dec. 25. Admission $6; over 61 and ages 13-18, $5; ages 4-12, $3. DS, MC, VI. Phone (405) 297-3995.

NATIONAL COWBOY AND WESTERN HERITAGE MUSEUM is .5 mi. w. of I-35 via I-44, at 1700 N.E. 63rd St. This 32-acre memorial to our Western pioneers has an extensive collection of art, historic artifacts and exhibits about American Indian and pioneer life in realistic settings. James Earle Fraser's 18-foot statue "The End of the Trail" and a 33-foot statue of Buffalo Bill are featured.

The Rodeo Hall of Fame has legendary performers' portraits, trophies, saddles and memorabilia. A Western art collection features works by Albert Bierstadt, Frederic Remington and Charles M. Russell as well as contemporary pieces depicting both the historical and the new West.

The Western Performers Gallery shows the idealized West portrayed in motion pictures. Prosperity Junction replicates a circa 1900 western cattle town at dusk with full-size structures, including a saloon, school and church.

Allow 2 hours minimum. Daily 9-5; closed Jan. 1, Thanksgiving and Dec. 25. Admission $8.50; over 62, $7; ages 6-12, $4. AX, DS, MC, VI. (405) 478-2250.

OKLAHOMA CITY MUSEUM OF ART is at 415 Couch Dr. This three-level structure displays artwork from its 3,500-piece permanent collection. As visitors enter the museum's atrium they are greeted by a 55-foot-tall tower of glass created by Dale Chihuly. Galleries feature American, European and Asian art, including portraits, landscapes, modern art, photography, sculpture, abstract art and decorative and fine arts.

Audio tours are available. Allow 1 hour, 30 minutes minimum. Tues.-Sat. 10-5 (also Thurs. 5-9), Sun. noon-5. Admission $9; over 62 and ages 5-18, $7. Audio tours $3. Phone (405) 236-3100 or (800) 579-9278.

OKLAHOMA CITY NATIONAL MEMORIAL, bordered by Robinson and Harvey aves. and 4th and 6th sts., was built in remembrance of the victims, survivors and rescuers of the Alfred P. Murrah Federal Building bombing on Apr. 19, 1995. Twin gates, marking the east and west entrances to the memorial, represent 9:01 and 9:03, the minutes before and after the tragedy.

Each of the 168 lives lost is represented by a chair made of bronze, stone and glass. The plot used for the field of chairs is the same size and configuration as the footprint of the destroyed building. The memorial also has a reflecting pool; a special area for children; and the Survivor Tree, a 60-year-old American elm that miraculously withstood the blast. Daily 24 hours. Free. Phone (405) 235-3313 or (888) 542-4673.

Memorial Museum is at 620 N. Harvey Ave., next to the Oklahoma City National Memorial. In the former Journal Record Building that withstood the bombing of the Murrah Federal Building, the museum's galleries serve as a timeline of that event, beginning with the morning of Apr. 19, 1995. From the first exhibit depicting everyday morning activities in Oklahoma City through the last exhibit about hope for the future, the museum examines various aspects of that act of terrorism.

Audiotape from a hearing being conducted across the street provides the sounds of the explosion and the resulting panic and confusion. Media coverage of the event is shown, as the story moves from rescue and recovery to investigation and capture. Stories told by survivors, family members and rescuers provide personal remembrances of the tragedy. The Gallery of Honor is a tribute to the 168 lives lost.

Allow 2 hours minimum. Mon.-Sat. 9-6, Sun. 1-6; closed Jan. 1, Thanksgiving and Dec. 25. Last admission 1 hour before closing. Admission $8; over 62, $7; college students with ID and ages 6-17, $6. AX, MC, VI. Phone (405) 235-3313 or (888) 542-4673.

OKLAHOMA CITY ZOO & BOTANICAL GARDEN, at Martin Luther King Ave. and Remington Pl., is home to more than 2,300 animals, including 50 endangered or threatened species. Great EscApe features gorillas, orangutans and chimpanzees in a rain forest environment. Cat Forest/Lion Overlook is a naturalistic habitat for wild cats. In the 8-acre Oklahoma Trails exhibit more than 800 animals, including grizzly and black bears, river otters, bobcats and bison, can be seen.

Visitors can hand-feed lorikeets in the aviary. Rides are available on the Endangered Species Carousel, Centennial Choo Choo and the Safari Tram for additional fees.

Picnicking is permitted. Allow 2 hours minimum. Daily 9-6, Memorial Day-Labor Day; 9-5, rest of year. Closed Jan. 1, Thanksgiving and Dec. 25. Admission $7; over 65 and ages 3-11, $4. DS, MC, VI. Phone (405) 424-3344.

Aquaticus, 2101 N.E. 50th St., features marine life from around the world. The Fins and Feathers Show features sea lions Midge and Moe and a group of their bird friends performing in 15- to 20-minute shows. Performances Wed.-Fri. at 11 and 1, Sat.-Sun. at 11, 1 and 3 (weather permitting). Exhibits free. Admission to shows $2; ages 3-11, $1.

OKLAHOMA FIREFIGHTERS' MUSEUM, 2716 N.E. 50th St., contains a collection of antique fire apparatus, tools and machinery used since 1736. Highlights of the collection include an early 20th-century "Metropolitan" steamer and a reconstruction of the first fire station in Oklahoma. Sat.-Thurs.

9-4:30, Fri. 10-4:15, Sun. 1-4:30; closed Jan. 1, Thanksgiving and Dec. 25. Admission $4; over 55, $3; ages 6-12, $2. Phone (405) 424-3440.

OKLAHOMA HISTORY CENTER, 2401 N. Laird Ave., showcases the state's history with its thousands of artifacts and more than 200 interactive exhibits in five galleries. Topics include aviation, commerce, culture, geology, heritage and transportation. Major exhibits depict the history of American Indian tribes living in the state and settler life during the Oklahoma land runs.

Outdoor sculptures, four oil derricks and the .25-mile Red River Journey, which replicates the river valley and its plant life, adorn the grounds. Extensive archives and research materials, including genealogy records and newspapers, are available.

Allow 2 hours minimum. Mon.-Sat. 9-5, Sun. noon-5; closed Jan. 1, Thanksgiving and Dec. 25. Admission $5, senior citizens $4, students with ID $3, under 6 free, family rate $15. MC, VI. Phone (405) 522-5248.

OKLAHOMA NATIONAL STOCKYARDS, 2501 Exchange Ave., was founded in 1910 and is said to be the world's largest cattle market. Guided tours are available; phone for details. Grounds open daily. Cattle are auctioned Mon.-Tues. at 8 a.m. Free. Phone (405) 235-8675 or (405) 235-7267.

OMNIPLEX is at jct. N.E. 52nd St. and Martin Luther King Ave. The science and cultural center, a Smithsonian affiliate, consists of gardens, a planetarium, more than 350 interactive exhibits and a domed theater with a seven-story screen. Science topics portrayed include agriculture, energy, life sciences, light, math, meteorology, nutrition, perception, physics and sound.

Wiley Post and Amelia Earhart are two pioneers showcased in a series of exhibits highlighting the role Oklahomans have played in aviation and space technology. Vintage aircraft, memorabilia and modern spacecrafts can be seen.

Food is available. Allow 2 hours minimum. Mon.-Fri. 9-5, Sat. 9-6, Sun. 11-6; closed Thanksgiving and Dec. 24-25. Admission (including all museums in the center) $9.50; over 64 and ages 3-12, $8.25. Combination rates with the planetarium and domed theater $13.50; over 64 and ages 3-12, $10.25. DS, MC, VI. Phone (405) 602-6664 or (800) 532-7652.

Air Space Museum, 2100 N.E. 52nd St., documents Oklahoma's contributions to aviation—from the Wright brothers to the astronauts—through photographs, films, log books, vintage equipment, memorabilia and models of space capsules. The Oklahoma Aviation and Space Hall of Fame honors Oklahoma natives who have made significant contributions to flight. Phone (405) 424-1443.

Art, Historic and Cultural Galleries, 2100 N.E. 52nd St., are 16 galleries featuring artwork from around the world. The complex includes a section of the Berlin Wall, the Navy Gallery, First Ladies of Oklahoma Gown Collection, State Art Collection,

Oriental Galleries and Sanamu African Gallery. Of special interest is the display of Boehm porcelain and Sutton bird paintings in the Goldman Lecture Room.

International Photography Hall of Fame and Museum, 2100 N.E. 52nd St., displays prints taken by photographers from around the world along with changing exhibits. The hall highlights the world's largest photographic mural, a 360-degree laserscape of the Grand Canyon. Phone (405) 424-4055.

Omniplex Hands-On Science Museum, 2100 N.E. 52nd St., has more than 350 interactive science exhibits such as the Geovator Time Travel Adventure, Energy Quest, Kidspace, Green Arcade and the Crystal Molecule. The Kirkpatrick Planetarium offers free, 45-minute general shows daily. Phone (405) 602-6664.

Red Earth Indian Center, 2100 N.E. 52nd St., examines American Indian cultures and lifestyles through displays of artifacts and art dating from prehistory. A highlight is an extensive collection of cradleboards representing the craftsmanship of Indian tribes from throughout the United States. Phone (405) 427-5228.

OVERHOLSER MANSION, 15th and N. Hudson sts. in Heritage Hills, was the first mansion in Oklahoma City. Home of city founder Henry Overholser, the building exemplifies Victorian residential architecture of the early 20th century. Most of the furnishings, imported from Europe, are original to the house. Allow 30 minutes minimum. Tues.-Sat. 10-3; closed holidays. Guided tours are given on the hour. Last tour begins 1 hour before closing. Fee $3; senior citizens $2.50; ages 6-18, $1. Phone (405) 528-8485.

STATE CAPITOL, 2300 Lincoln Blvd., is an adaptation of classical Greek and Roman architecture. On the grounds is the Capitol Site No. 1 oil well, originally nicknamed Petunia No. 1 because drilling began in November 1941 in the middle of a flower bed. The building is the only Capitol in the world with an oil well beneath it.

At the south entrance is "Statue of a Cowboy," by Constance Warren. A bronze statue of an American Indian caps the dome. Allow 1 hour minimum. Mon.-Fri. 8-4:30. Guided tours of the building are offered on the hour Mon.-Fri. 9-11 and 1-3. Free. Phone (405) 521-3356.

WHITE WATER BAY, 10 mi. w. on I-40 at 3908 W. Reno, is a 20-acre water park with more than 30 water rides, including a giant wave pool, waterslides, body flumes, inner tube courses and activity pools as well as a children's playland.

Picnicking is permitted. Food is available. Allow 2 hours minimum. The 2007 season schedule is Sat. 10:30-8, Sun. 10:30-6, May 19-27; daily 10:30-8, May 28-Aug. 19; Sat. 10:30-7, Sun. and Labor Day 10:30-6, Aug. 25-Sept. 3. Admission $24.99, over age 61 and under 48 inches tall $20.99, under age 3 free. Parking $5. AX, MC, VI. Phone (405) 943-9687.

What To Do

Sports and Recreation

Oklahoma City's parks offer the setting for almost any activity. **Tennis, swimming** and **picnicking** facilities are plentiful at Will Rogers Park, 36th Street and N. Portland. **Boating** and **fishing** are popular at lakes Hefner, Draper and Overholser. Lake Hefner is particularly known for its good **sailing. Water skiing** can be enjoyed at Draper Lake.

Additionally, **jogging** trails are available at Earlywine Park, S.W. 119th and May; Lake Hefner, N. Grand Boulevard between May and Portland; and Memorial Park, 34th and Classen. The Oklahoma City Parks and Recreation Department offers information about all of their facilities; phone (405) 297-2211.

Golf courses are readily available. Public links include nine-hole courses such as Brookside Golf Course, 9016 S. Shields Blvd.; Lakeside Golf Course, 9500 S. Eastern Ave.; and The Links Golf & Athletic Club, 700 N.E. 122nd St. For 18-hole courses offerings include Earlywine Golf Course, 11600 S. Portland Ave; Lake Hefner Golf Course, 4491 S. Lake Hefner Dr.; Lincoln Park Golf Course, 4001 N.E. Grand Blvd.; and Trosper Golf Club, 2301 S.E. 29th St.

Spectator sports also are favorite pastimes. The RedHawks, the Triple A **baseball** farm team of the Texas Rangers, draw fans every spring to SBC Bricktown Ballpark, 2 S. Mickey Mantle Dr.; phone (405) 218-1000. Fall welcomes college **football** as the University of Oklahoma's Sooners, members of the Big Twelve conference, begin their season at Owen Field in Norman; phone (405) 325-2424 or (800) 456-4668.

College **basketball** rounds out the sports year with Oklahoma City University's Stars playing at Freede Center, N.W. 27th and Florida streets; phone (405) 521-5309. The Sooners from the University of Oklahoma compete at Lloyd Noble Center in Norman; phone (405) 325-2424.

State Fair Speedway at 444 Land Rush is the scene of **automobile racing** on Friday nights from late March to mid-September; phone (405) 948-6796. The city also plays host to a number of **rodeos** and **horse shows** throughout the year *(see Special Events)*. The Remington Park pari-mutuel racetrack at US 35 and US 44 offers quarter horse and Thoroughbred **horse racing**; phone (405) 424-1000.

Note: Policies concerning admittance of children to pari-mutuel betting facilities vary. Phone for information.

Shopping

Whether you are looking for Western wear or the latest in high fashion, you can find it in Oklahoma City's department stores and specialty shops.

Establishments that sell cowboy hats, boots and belts are Cattlemen's Western Wear, 1312 S. Agnew Ave.; Langston's Western Wear, 2224 Exchange Ave.; Sheplers Western Wear, 812 S. Meridian; and Tener's, 4320 W. Reno. Other characteristic Oklahoma City purchases are American Indian art and jewelry.

Several enclosed malls are convenient for one-top shopping. To the north is the posh 50 Penn Place, N.W. 50th and Pennsylvania, noted for its exclusive shops. Across the street is Penn Square, one of the largest malls in the area. Also north of the city is Quail Springs, Memorial Road at Penn. To the east is Heritage Park, at S.W. Reno and Air Depot Road in Midwest City. Crossroads Mall, with 130 stores, is south of downtown at I-35 and I-240. Typical anchor stores include Dillard's, Foley's and JCPenney.

Shops, nightclubs and restaurants crowd the historic commercial area known as Bricktown, named for its many turn-of-the-20th-century red brick warehouses. A canal lined with eateries offering outdoor seating winds through Bricktown and links downtown OKC with parks and the North Canadian River.

Performing Arts

Oklahoma City offers a diverse palette of cultural entertainment. Ballet Oklahoma, (405) 843-9898, stages elaborate productions at the Civic Center Music Hall, 201 N. Walker Ave. The music hall also is the home of the Oklahoma City Philharmonic, (405) 232-7575, which performs both classical and pop music. Their seasons run concurrently from September through May. The Chamber Music Series of Oklahoma City, (405) 974-2415, complements the symphony's season with its concerts at Christ the King Church, 8005 Dorset Dr., from October to early April.

Oklahoma City University's music school also contributes to the performing arts scene with six musical performances and vocal and instrumental performances scheduled throughout the year; phone (405) 521-5474 or (800) 633-7242, ext. 5474. The Canterbury Choral Society, (405) 232-7464, performs October through May at the Civic Center Music Hall, 201 N. Walker Ave.

In summer the great outdoors provides a showcase for pop and rock concerts at the amphitheaters at Frontier City and the Oklahoma City Zoo & Botanical Garden. Plenty of guitar playin', banjo pickin' and foot stompin' goes on at Del City's Oklahoma Country-Western Museum and Hall of Fame, 3925 S.E. 29th St., during Blue Grass Music Society performances on the second Saturday of each month from September through May. Country music is the theme Saturday nights at the Oklahoma Opry, 404 W. Commerce; phone (405) 632-8322.

Oklahoma City's theater scene offers several choices. The productions of the Black Liberated Arts Center focus on African American culture and are held at various locations throughout the city; phone (405) 524-3800. A professional summer stock company, the Lyric Theatre, performs musicals from June through August at the Civic Center Music Hall; for ticket information phone (405) 524-9312.

Locals show their talent in a six-play season of musicals and dramas at the Jewel Box Theatre, 3700 N. Walker; phone (405) 521-1786. Concert schedules are provided by the Katt Concert Keeper; phone (405) 840-5160.

Special Events

Home of the National Cowboy Hall of Fame, Oklahoma City also pays tribute to the cowboy's trusted companion, the horse. Six national and international horse shows and at least 20 state and regional competitions are held throughout the year. The major shows take place at the State Fairgrounds Arena at 10th and N. May.

The World Championship Appaloosa Horse Show takes place in July, and the Grand National Morgan Horse Show is held in October. The World Championship Quarter Horse Show is in mid-November. The season ends in December with the Barrel Racing Futurity and the National Reining Futurity. In a similar Western vein, the Chuck Wagon Gathering and Children's Cowboy Festival, held in late May, is a family event featuring chuck wagon cooks from across the country as well as entertainment.

With a large American Indian population, Oklahoma is rich with American Indian culture and tradition. One such tradition is the powwow, when tribe members in full costume gather for days filled with traditional competitions, dance, music and food. These powwows take place throughout the summer, and many are held in Oklahoma City.

One of the largest powwows is the Red Earth Festival; representatives from more than 100 tribes gather during the first weekend in June to celebrate and share their heritage. For more information about this and other events contact the Oklahoma City Convention and Visitors Bureau; phone (405) 297-8912.

The city celebrates the visual and performing arts during April and September art festivals held in area parks; the events feature singers and musicians performing throughout the day as well as artists displaying their works. The activity is enhanced by food stands serving international cuisines. One such show, An Affair of the Heart, takes place in February and October and includes 1,000 art and craft exhibitors.

In September the Oklahoma State Fair transforms the 435-acre State Fairgrounds into a lively happening. One of the largest state fairs in the country, the 17-day event features ice shows, car races, livestock and cooking contests and a rodeo. Closing out the year, the Oklahoma Gas & Electric Garden Lights celebration, held Thanksgiving through January 1 at Myriad Botanical Gardens & Crystal Bridge, glows with thousands of twinkling lights among the trees and trails.

The Oklahoma City Vicinity

EL RENO (H-1) pop. 16,212, elev. 1,360'

El Reno was established in June 1889 when the Rock Island Railroad picked a site on the south bank of the North Canadian River for a depot. Angry citizens of nearby Reno City decided they did not want to be left out of any future railroad riches. They packed their belongings and loaded their houses, stores and even a hotel onto log rollers, forded the river and resettled in the new town of El Reno.

The Heritage Express Trolley transports riders Wednesday through Sunday from Heritage Park through the downtown area. A scenic portion of US 81 runs 12 miles south from El Reno through the Canadian River Valley to Minco.

El Reno Chamber of Commerce: 206 N. Bickford, El Reno, OK 73036; phone (405) 262-1188.

CANADIAN COUNTY HISTORICAL MUSEUM, 300 S. Grand, is housed in the 1906 Rock Island Depot and features American Indian objects, vintage clothing, toys and model trains as well as the depot's original ticket office, a doctor's office and an old fashioned kitchen. Relocated historic buildings on the museum grounds include a 1910 school house, an 1892 hotel, a 1918 Red Cross canteen, a 19th-century jail, a Mennonite church and a restored caboose.

Allow 30 minutes minimum. Wed.-Sat. 10-5, Sun. 1:30-5; closed Jan. 1, July 4, Thanksgiving and Dec. 25. Donations. Phone (405) 262-5121.

HISTORIC FORT RENO, 7107 W. Cheyenne, was a military camp in 1874 and an army remount station 1908-47. It also was a POW camp for captured German soldiers during World War II. Visitors may walk through its chapel and cemetery. A visitors center features historic photographs and other memorabilia. Mon.-Fri. 10-5, Sat.-Sun. 10-4; closed Jan. 1 and Dec. 25. Donations. Phone (405) 262-3987.

GUTHRIE (G-2) pop. 9,925, elev. 961'

As the focal point of the 1889 Oklahoma land rush, Guthrie became a tent city of 15,000 residents by nightfall on April 22, 1889, the day the Unassigned Lands of Oklahoma were officially opened for settlement. Oklahoma was admitted to the Union in 1907, and Guthrie became the first capital of the state. At some point in their lives, Lon Chaney, Tom Mix, Carry Nation and Will Rogers all lived in Guthrie.

Ninety percent of Guthrie's original buildings remain intact; the city has one of the largest districts on the National Register of Historic Places. French architect Joseph Foucart designed most of the town's eclectic Victorian structures.

The Pollard Theater, a renovated early 20th-century opera house at 120 W. Harrison, presents productions performed by Guthrie's resident theater company. Houses dating from Guthrie's territorial and early statehood days line E. Harrison, Oklahoma, Cleveland, Noble and Warner streets. Trolley tours of the historic district depart from the intersection of 2nd and Harrison; phone (405) 282-6000.

Guthrie Convention and Visitors Bureau: 212 W. Oklahoma, P.O. Box 995, Guthrie, OK 73044; phone (405) 282-1947 or (800) 299-1889.

OKLAHOMA SPORTS MUSEUM is at 315 W. Oklahoma Ave. The museum houses a collection of memorabilia honoring athletes, coaches and sports teams with connections to Oklahoma. Sports celebrities and champions highlighted include Troy Aikman, Mickey Mantle, Shannon Miller and Jim Thorpe. Allow 1 hour minimum. Mon.-Sat. 10-5; closed major holidays. Donations. Phone (405) 260-1342.

OKLAHOMA TERRITORIAL MUSEUM, 406 E. Oklahoma Ave., contains exhibits and artifacts pertaining to life in territorial Oklahoma and the land run of 1889. The Carnegie Library, part of the complex, was built 1902-03 and was the site of the inaugurations of the last territorial governor and the first state governor. Allow 1 hour minimum. Tues.-Sat. 9-5; closed holidays. Donations. Phone (405) 282-1889.

SCOTTISH RITE MASONIC TEMPLE, 900 E. Oklahoma Ave., sits on the site originally intended for the state capitol building. The temple bought the land for $1, and a promise to administer "certain improvements," after the state capital relocated to Oklahoma City. These improvements totaled more than $3 million and have created the Gothic, Egyptian, Victorian, Italian and American Indian embellishments found within this Greek Revival building.

Allow 1 hour minimum. Tours are given Mon.-Fri. at 10 and 2; closed holidays and during Masonic functions. Fee $5, students with ID and children free. Students and children must be accompanied by an adult. Phone (405) 282-1281.

STATE CAPITAL PUBLISHING MUSEUM, 301 W. Harrison St., is in a restored 1902 Victorian commercial structure that was the home of the first newspaper published in the Oklahoma Territory. High ceilings, ornate gilt radiators and intricate grillwork and woodwork distinguish the building. The museum contains documents and equipment relating to the history of territorial newspaper publishing and printing in the state. Allow 30 minutes minimum. Thurs.-Sat. 9-5; closed holidays. Donations. Phone (405) 282-4123.

NORMAN (I-2) pop. 95,694, elev. 1,168'

Shortly after its 1889 beginnings and with a population of 500, Norman boasted four churches, two newspapers and 29 businesses. A year later the University of Oklahoma was established.

The Norman and Cleveland County Historical Museum, 508 N. Peters Ave., is in a 1900 Queen Anne-style house once owned by William S. Moore, a Norman businessman. Tours of the house are available; phone (405) 321-0156.

Recreational opportunities in the Norman vicinity are available at Lake Thunderbird State Park (see Recreation Chart).

Norman Convention and Visitors Bureau: 223 E. Main St., Norman, OK 73069; phone (405) 366-8095 or (800) 767-7260.

Shopping areas: Dillard's, JCPenney and Sears are the anchor stores at Sooner Mall, 3301 W. Main St.

LITTLE RIVER ZOO is at 3405 S.E. 120th Ave. More than 400 animals, mostly cast-off pets or rescued wildlife, make their home at this 55-acre refuge. A guided tour includes a petting zoo where visitors can hand-feed animals. Allow 1 hour minimum. Daily 10-5. Admission $6; over 55 and ages 3-11, $4. MC, VI. Phone (405) 366-7229.

UNIVERSITY OF OKLAHOMA, off I-35 Lindsey St. exit, is a national research university with more than 30,000 students and 1,700 faculty members. The 3,000-acre campus houses 13 colleges; seven medical and health-related colleges are at sites in Tulsa and Oklahoma City. The university is a national leader in meteorology and energy-related disciplines. Tours can be arranged at the visitor center in Jacobson Hall, 550 Parrington Oval. Allow 2 hours minimum. Tours are available Mon.-Fri. at 9 and 2, Sat. at 9:30 a.m. Free. Phone (405) 325-2151 or (800) 234-6868.

Fred Jones Jr. Museum of Art, 555 Elm Ave., includes rotating selections of works from Africa, Europe, the Americas and the Orient from its permanent collection as well as temporary exhibitions of contemporary art. An 8-minute video provides an overview of the museum and its collections.

Allow 1 hour, 30 minutes minimum. Tues.-Fri. 10-5 (also Thurs. 5-9), Sun. 1-5, during school year except spring break; Tues.-Sun. noon-4:30, rest of year and during spring break. Closed major holidays. Admission $5; over 64, $4; ages 6-17, $3; free to all Tues. Phone (405) 325-3272.

SAVE **Sam Noble Oklahoma Museum of Natural History**, 2401 Chautauqua Ave. on the University of Oklahoma campus, offers a look back 300 million years at the state's natural history. Visitors can experience hands-on science activities, view dinosaur skeletons and walk through realistic dioramas that depict outdoor settings. Also displayed are artifacts from worldwide civilizations.

Food is available. Allow 1 hour, 30 minutes minimum. Tues.-Sat. 10-5, Sun. 1-5; closed Jan. 1, Thanksgiving and Dec. 25. Admission $5; over 65 and military with ID $4; ages 6-17, $3. MC, VI. Phone (405) 325-4712.

W.B. Bizzell Memorial Library, 401 W. Brooks, has more than 4 million volumes. There are five special collections: the History of Science Collection, with books by Charles Darwin, Galileo and others; the Western History Collection, which includes historical photographs, books and manuscripts; the Bass Business History Collection; the Carl Albert Congressional Archives, which contain congressional papers; and the Nichols Bible Collection.

Allow 30 minutes minimum. Library open Mon.-Sat. at 7:30, Sun. at noon; closing times vary. Closed major holidays. Hours may vary; phone ahead. Free. Phone (405) 325-4142.

SHAWNEE (I-4) pop. 28,692, elev. 1,043′

Shawnee was settled in a matter of minutes after the American Indian Territory of which it was a part was opened to pioneer settlement. Emerging as a bustling railroad town, Shawnee made a bid to become capital of Oklahoma in 1910 but lost the honor to Oklahoma City. The town's fortunes turned, however, with the discovery of oil in 1926. Since then, Shawnee's industry has diversified to include the manufacture of electronic equipment, aircraft parts, clothing and hair dryers.

Shawnee Convention and Visitors Bureau: 131 N. Bell, P.O. Box 1613, Shawnee, OK 74802-1613; phone (405) 275-9780.

MABEE-GERRER MUSEUM OF ART is at 1900 W. MacArthur Dr. on the campus of St. Gregory's University. The museum, which has collections of Renaissance art and antiquities, also sponsors changing contemporary exhibits. African, Greek, American Indian and 19th-century American and European art is displayed at various times throughout the year. Allow 1 hour, 30 minutes minimum. Tues.-Sat. 10-5, Sun. 1-4; closed holidays. Admission $5; over 65, $4; students with ID and ages 6-16, $3. Phone (405) 878-5300.

SANTA FE DEPOT MUSEUM, 614 E. Main St., is in a building that was once the town's train depot. The museum chronicles Shawnee's history with antique automobiles, dolls, furniture, clothing, tools and a pump organ. Also on the grounds is the first house built in Shawnee. Allow 1 hour minimum. Tues.-Sat. 10-4, Sun. 2-4; closed major holidays. Admission $2, students with ID $1. Phone (405) 275-8412.

© National Cowboy and Western Heritage Museum

This ends listings for the Oklahoma City Vicinity.
The following page resumes the alphabetical listings of cities in Oklahoma.

OKMULGEE (D-10) pop. 13,022, elev. 678'

Okmulgee, a Creek word meaning "bubbling water," was capital of the Muscogee Creek Nation a half century before Oklahoma became a state, and it remains the capital.

Dripping Springs State Park, 6 miles west of town on SR 56, offers camping, swimming, fishing and boating; phone (918) 756-5971. *See Recreation Chart.*

Okmulgee Tourism Development: 112 N. Morton, Okmulgee, OK 74447; phone (918) 756-6172.

CREEK COUNCIL HOUSE MUSEUM, 106 W. 6th St., dates from 1878 and was the seat of tribal government until statehood. The museum contains Muscogee Creek Indian craftwork and historical documents and artifacts. Allow 1 hour minimum. Tues.-Sat. 10-4:30; closed Jan. 1, Thanksgiving and Dec. 25. Donations. Phone (918) 756-2324.

OOLOGAH—see Tulsa p. 276.

OUACHITA NATIONAL FOREST—
see place listing in Arkansas p. 56.

PARK HILL (C-12) pop. 3,936, elev. 740'

CHEROKEE HERITAGE CENTER, 21192 S. Keeler Dr., is at the site of the first Cherokee Female Seminary; three columns remain after fire destroyed the building in 1887. The center has an outdoor amphitheater and three sites operated by the Cherokee National Historical Society; in addition, an archives and genealogy center maintain historical records. The outdoor drama "Trail of Tears" is presented Thursday through Saturday evenings, late June through August.

Mon.-Sat. 10-5, Sun. 1-5, Feb.-Dec.; closed Thanksgiving and Dec. 25. Combination admission for Adams Corner Rural Village, Cherokee National Museum and Tsa-La-Gi Ancient Village $8.50; over 55 and college students with ID $7.50; students grades K-12, $5. Drama tickets vary; phone ahead. Combination heritage center and drama tickets are available. AX, DS, MC, VI. Phone (918) 456-6007 or (888) 999-6007.

Adams Corner Rural Village, entered through the Cherokee Heritage Center, is a detailed reconstruction of a small crossroads community dating 1875-90, the final years of the Old Cherokee Nation. A working general store is stocked with handmade items, toys, books and dry goods. Demonstrations include quilting, soap making, woodworking and Cherokee language lessons. A farm features animals typical of this period.

Mon.-Sat. 10-5, Sun. 1-5, Feb.-Dec.; closed Thanksgiving and Dec. 25. Combination admission for Adams Corner Rural Village, Cherokee National Museum and Tsa-La-Gi Ancient Village $8.50; over 55 and college students with ID $7.50; students grades K-12, $5. Drama tickets vary; phone ahead. Combination heritage center and drama tickets are

available. AX, DS, MC, VI. Phone (918) 456-6007 or (888) 999-6007.

Cherokee National Museum, 21672 S. Keeler Dr., uses multimedia exhibits, displays, artifacts and artwork to depict the history of the Cherokees from the white man's arrival in North America to the present. A highlight is the Trail of Tears exhibit. Allow 1 hour minimum. Mon.-Sat. 10-5, Sun. 1-5, Feb.-Dec.; closed Thanksgiving and Dec. 25.

Combination admission for Adams Corner Rural Village, Cherokee National Museum and Tsa-La-Gi Ancient Village $8.50; over 55 and college students with ID $7.50; students grades K-12, $5. Drama tickets vary; phone ahead. Combination heritage center and drama tickets are available. AX, DS, MC, VI. Phone (918) 456-6007 or (888) 999-6007.

Tsa-La-Gi Ancient Village, 515 Willis Rd., is a recreation of a 16th-century Cherokee settlement. Such skills as basket weaving, flint knapping, cooking and pottery making are demonstrated regularly. Allow 1 hour minimum for guided tour. Mon.-Sat. 10-5, Sun. 1-5, Feb.-Dec.; closed Thanksgiving and Dec. 25.

Combination admission for Adams Corner Rural Village, Cherokee National Museum and Tsa-La-Gi Ancient Village $8.50; over 55 and college students with ID $7.50; students grades K-12, $5. Drama tickets vary; phone ahead. Combination heritage center and drama tickets are available. AX, DS, MC, VI. Phone (918) 456-6007 or (888) 999-6007.

MURRELL HOME, 19479 E. Murrell Home Rd., is the restored 1845 residence of George M. Murrell, who married the niece of principal Cherokee chief John Ross. Although looted during the Civil War, the house was the only building in the community to escape destruction. It is furnished with some original pieces. A .7-mile nature trail accommodates wheelchairs. Wed.-Sat. 10-5, Sun. 1-5, Mar.-Oct.; Sat. 10-5, Sun. 1-5, rest of year. Closed state holidays. Donations. Phone (918) 456-2751.

PAWHUSKA—see Tulsa p. 276.

PAWNEE (C-9) pop. 2,230, elev. 822'

More than 30 years before Oklahoma became a state, the original settlers were aided by the Pawnee Indians, a peaceful tribe who inhabited the area for many years. A man who taught among the Pawnees, Gordon W. Lillie, alias Pawnee Bill, also was one of the leaders of the Oklahoma "boomers," a group that pushed for the opening of the territory to settlement in 1889.

Pawnee Bill is best known, however, as a showman who traveled through Europe and America with wife May Manning, performing and preserving scenes from a dying way of life—that of the Wild West cowboys.

Besides the Pawnees, four other tribes remain: the Kaws, the Otoes, the Poncas and the Tonkawas. The Pawnee Indian Agency, American Indian schools and a hospital serve the area.

Pawnee Community Chamber of Commerce: 608 Harrison St., Pawnee, OK 74058; phone (918) 762-2108.

PAWNEE BILL RANCH SITE, .5 mi. w. on US 64 at Blue Hawk Peak, consists of Pawnee Bill's original mansion and several ranch buildings with displays of artifacts, furniture, clothing, weapons and art objects. An additional building houses his personal effects. Buffaloes and longhorn cattle roam the area. Fishing opportunities are available. Picnicking is permitted. Allow 2 hours minimum. Tues.-Sat. 10-5, Sun.-Mon. 1-4, Apr.-Oct.; Wed.-Sat. 10-5, Sun. 1-4, rest of year. Closed holidays. Donations. Phone (918) 762-2513.

PERRY (C-8) pop. 5,230, elev. 989′

Born as a tent city of 25,000 on Sept. 16, 1893, Perry was first known for its large population of sooners, gamblers and ruffians and its 14 saloons. Federal marshals soon brought order, however, and energies turned to farming and building businesses and industries.

Perry Chamber of Commerce: 300 6th St., P.O. Box 426, Perry, OK 73077; phone (580) 336-4684.

CHEROKEE STRIP MUSEUM is .5 mi. e. off I-35 Fir Ave. exit. The museum, which depicts pioneer life on the Cherokee Strip *(see Ponca City),* has a furnished one-room school built in 1895, a tepee, a barn with early farm machinery and sod busting implements. A living-history program is conducted in the schoolhouse during the school year.

Exhibits feature a general store, the office of the seventh governor of Oklahoma and early physician's and dentist's offices. Picnicking is permitted. Allow 1 hour minimum. Tues.-Fri. 9-5, Sat. 10-4; closed holidays and the first 2 weeks in Jan. Donations. Phone (580) 336-2405.

DID YOU KNOW

Oklahoma has more tornados per year than any other state.

PONCA CITY (B-8) pop. 25,919, elev. 1,003′

Ponca City was created in true Oklahoma fashion during the land runs of the late 1800s. On Sept. 16, 1893, homesteaders lined up for a race to claim one of the 160-acre lots in the area surrounding what would soon be Ponca City. Certificates for lots in the business section were sold for $2 each.

Ponca City was built in the midst of the Cherokee Strip, a narrow section of land 50 miles wide that had been reserved for the American Indians as buffalo hunting grounds. President Grover Cleveland instead opened the land to settlement. When oil was discovered in 1910, E.W. Marland, who later became governor of Oklahoma, established Marland Oil, thereby propelling Ponca City into the age of industrialization.

Ponca City Tourism: 420 E. Grand Ave., Ponca City, OK 74601; phone (580) 763-8092.

MARLAND ESTATE MANSION, 901 Monument Rd., was the second home of E.W. Marland, pioneer oilman and 10th governor of Oklahoma. Built in the late 1920s and modeled after the Florentine estates of the Italian Renaissance, the 55-room mansion includes a museum with petroleum exhibits and memorabilia relating to Marland.

Allow 1 hour minimum. Mon.-Sat. 10-5, Sun. 1-5; closed Jan. 1, Easter, Thanksgiving and Dec. 25. Guided tours are available Mon.-Fri. at 1:30, Sat.-Sun. at 1:30 and 3. Admission $7; over 65 and ages 12-17, $5; ages 6-11, $3. MC, VI. Phone (580) 767-0420 or (800) 422-8340.

Bryant Baker Studio, on the grounds of the Marland Estate Mansion, is a replica of the artist's New York studio. Baker, known for his bronze sculpture "The Pioneer Woman," which stands in Ponca City, was the winner of a competition sponsored by E.W. Marland to create a memorial to the courageous women who helped settle this country. The studio contains a collection of plaster and bronze busts created by the sculptor.

MARLAND'S GRAND HOME, 1000 E. Grand Ave., is the 1916 home of E.W. Marland, millionaire oilman and 10th governor of Oklahoma. The building includes three museums. Allow 1 hour minimum. Tues.-Sat. 10-5; closed major holidays. Admission (includes 101 Ranch Room, D.A.R. Memorial Museum and Indian Museum) $3; under 17, $1. Phone (580) 767-0427.

101 Ranch Room, 1000 E. Grand Ave., contains memorabilia from the Miller Brothers 101 Ranch, where E.W. Marland discovered his first oil well. During the early 1900s the ranch spread across four counties and stretched 101,000 miles. Displays include saddles, ropes and photographs from the 101 Ranch Real Wild West Show, which toured the world from 1908 until the Great Depression in 1929.

Tues.-Sat. 10-5; closed major holidays. Admission (includes Marland's Grand Home, D.A.R. Memorial Museum and Indian Museum) $3; under 17, $1. Phone (580) 767-0427.

D.A.R. Memorial Museum, 1000 E. Grand Ave., displays historical books, documents, furnishings and clothing collected by the Daughters of the American Revolution. Of interest is a 13-star U.S. flag taken from a Revolutionary War battlefield. Tues.-Sat. 10-5; closed major holidays. Admission (includes Marland's Grand Home, 101 Ranch Room and Indian Museum) $3; under 17, $1. Phone (580) 767-0427.

Indian Museum, 1000 E. Grand Ave., features artifacts and artwork from more than 30 tribes with special emphasis on local groups such as the Kaw, Osage, Otoe, Ponca, and Tonkawa. Costumes, moccasins, belts and headbands showcase examples of intricate beadwork. Tues.-Sat. 10-5; closed major holidays. Admission (includes Marland's Grand Home, D.A.R. Memorial Museum and 101 Ranch Room) $3; under 17, $1. Phone (580) 767-0427.

[SAVE] **PIONEER WOMAN STATUE AND MUSEUM,** 701 Monument Rd., is a tribute to the women who settled new territory with their families. Exhibits showcase tools, clothing, furniture and personal items that belonged to pioneers; inaugural gowns of Oklahoma's first ladies also are displayed.

The 17-foot-tall bronze statue, commissioned by oilman and 10th governor of Oklahoma E.W. Marland, depicts a pioneer woman and her son. Allow 1 hour minimum. Tues.-Sat. 9-5, Sun. 1-5; closed state holidays. Admission $3; over 65, $2.50; ages 6-18, $1. Phone (580) 765-6108.

POTEAU (E-12) pop. 7,939

Poteau, situated on the banks of the Poteau River, is almost entirely surrounded by mountains. The Winding Stair and Kiamichi mountains are on the southwest horizon, while the Poteau Range dominates the view to the south. Cavanal, said to be the world's highest hill, provides a splendid view of Sugar Loaf Mountain.

The town is an outfitting center for recreation in nearby Ouachita National Forest (see place listing in Arkansas p. 56). Wister Lake (see Recreation Chart) also is in the area. A scenic stretch of US 59/270 extends 25 miles south to the US 259 intersection before the town of Page.

Poteau Chamber of Commerce: 201 S. Broadway, Poteau, OK 74953; phone (918) 647-9178.

ROBERT S. KERR HOME AND MUSEUM is 6 mi. s.w. via US 59, following signs. This former home of U.S. Senator Robert S. Kerr is now a museum with area history exhibits—including rune stones believed to have been carved by Viking explorers; artifacts from the Spiro Indian mound, built 700-1350; Choctaw Nation documents and memorabilia; pioneer items, such as unusual types of barbed wire; and a reproduction of the senator's Washington, D.C., office.

Allow 1 hour minimum. Museum open Mon.-Fri. 9-5, Sat.-Sun. 1-5; closed major holidays. Donations. Phone (918) 647-9579.

SALLISAW (D-12) pop. 7,989, elev. 533'

Sallisaw, surrounded by agricultural land in the northeastern section of the state, is home to Blue Ribbon Downs, the state's first pari-mutuel racetrack. Two miles west of Sallisaw at I-40 and US 64, the track features Thoroughbred and quarter horse racing on weekends February through November. Dwight Mission, about 9 miles northwest, operated as a mission school for the Cherokee for more than a century after its founding in 1828. The town's name is derived from a French word meaning "salt provisions."

Note: Policies concerning admittance of children to pari-mutuel betting facilities vary. Phone for information.

Sallisaw Chamber of Commerce: 301 E. Cherokee Ave., P.O. Box 251, Sallisaw, OK 74955; phone (918) 775-2558.

FOURTEEN FLAGS MUSEUM, jct. US 59/64 at 400 E. Cherokee St., has exhibits that depict the lifestyles of early settlers. A general store, a Union Pacific caboose and several log cabins furnished with homestead artifacts are included. Daily 8-4. Free. Phone (918) 775-2558 for the chamber of commerce.

SEQUOYAH'S HOME SITE is 3 mi. n. on US 59, then 7 mi. e. on SR 101. The 1829 log cabin, one of the state's oldest, was Sequoyah's home before and after the "Trail of Tears" march and contains farm implements he made. The interpretive center describes the Cherokee Nation's history and the Cherokee language syllabus Sequoyah invented. The simplicity of his system enabled the Cherokee to teach and publish within a few years. Picnicking is available. Tues.-Fri. 9-5, Sat.-Sun. 2-5; closed state holidays. Free. Phone (918) 775-2413.

SAND SPRINGS—*see Tulsa p. 276.*

SAPULPA—*see Tulsa p. 277.*

SEMINOLE (D-9) pop. 6,899

Named after the Seminole Indians who previously settled the site, the town reached its peak in 1926 when a large oil pool was tapped. Thousands rushed to the site, and the Seminole post office is reported to have received mail for more than 100,000 people.

JASMINE MORAN CHILDREN'S MUSEUM is 1 mi. w. of jct. SR 9/US 377 at 1714 W. Wrangler Blvd. This hands-on museum is in the form of a child-size town complete with street signs. A courthouse, grocery store, fire station, hospital, television studio and other settings are incorporated into a community just for children.

Exhibits are designed to stimulate the imagination. A child can assume various roles in a community by donning a grocer's apron, dentist's jacket or firefighter's uniform. Other highlights include model trains and airplanes, a doll house with more than 1,000 pieces of furniture, an aquarium, a soap bubble factory, a room of mirrors and computer displays.

A 1936 fire truck, 1921 Model T and 1927 caboose can be explored. Children can enter a soundproof room, use a wheelchair or experiment with braille. Food is available. Allow 1 hour minimum. Tues.-Sat. 10-5, Sun. 1-5; closed major holidays and the 2 weeks following Labor Day. Admission $7; over 60, $6; under 2 free with parent. MC, VI. Phone (405) 382-0950.

SHAWNEE—*see Oklahoma City p. 260.*

SPIRO (D-12) pop. 2,227

Spiro was spawned by the Kansas City Southern Railway in 1895. It adopted most of the citizens of nearby Scullyville, the capital of the Choctaw Indian Agency's northern district and a booming trading post that was decimated by Union troops during the Civil War. All that remains of Scullyville, east on US 271, are the ruins of an American Indian agency building and a church.

Spiro Area Chamber of Commerce: P.O. Box 401, Spiro, OK 74959; phone (918) 962-3816.

SPIRO MOUNDS ARCHEOLOGICAL CENTER is 3 mi. e. on SR 9, then n. 4.2 mi. Oklahoma's only archeological park, comprising 138 acres, has 12 American Indian mounds built 600-1450. The interpretive center displays artifacts and grave goods—valuables buried with the deceased—and explains the symbolism of American Indian artwork and ceremonies.

A trail leads to the mounds and the Spiro Culture House, a reproduction of a type of American Indian dwelling used circa 1000. Picnicking is permitted. Allow 2 hours minimum. Wed.-Sat. 9-5, Sun. noon-5; closed Dec. 25. Free. Phone (918) 962-2062.

STILLWATER (C-9) pop. 39,065, elev. 870′

On April 22, 1889, the town of Stillwater was born with a population of 300. A year later the Oklahoma Agricultural and Mechanical College, now Oklahoma State University, was founded, and Stillwater became one of the Southwest's major educational centers. The city also is known as a center for agribusiness, medical services and industry. Experimental farms can be seen along highways leading into town.

Stillwater is the home of the National Wrestling Hall of Fame, (405) 377-5243, and the Sheerar Cultural and Heritage Center Museum, (405) 377-0359.

Stillwater Convention and Visitors Bureau: 409 S. Main St., Stillwater, OK 74076; phone (405) 743-3697 or (800) 991-6717.

GARDINER ART GALLERY IN THE BARTLETT CENTER FOR STUDIO ARTS is on the Oklahoma State University campus. Once a women's residence hall, the Georgian-style building has been renovated to provide studio space for artists and a setting for their work. In addition, the gallery sponsors touring art exhibitions and houses a permanent collection of works in wood, bronze and print media. Mon.-Fri. 8-5, Sat. 9-1, Sun. 1-5, Sept.-Apr.; Mon.-Fri. 8-5, rest of year. Closed major holidays. Free. Phone (405) 744-6016.

OKLAHOMA MUSEUM OF HIGHER EDUCATION is between Hester and Knoblock sts. n. of University Ave. on the campus of Oklahoma State University. Housed in the 1894 Old Central building, the first permanent building on the university's campus, the museum has exhibits depicting the history of the university and of higher education throughout Oklahoma. Traveling exhibits cover a variety of subjects. Guided tours are available. Open Wed.-Fri. 9-11 and noon-5, Sat. 10-4; closed major holidays. Donations. Phone (405) 744-2828.

TAHLEQUAH (C-11) pop. 14,458, elev. 861′

In a region of lakes within the foothills of the Ozark Mountains, Tahlequah has been the capital of the Cherokee Indian Nation since 1839. Old Cherokee government buildings still standing are the 1844 Supreme Court Building, the 1867 Cherokee Capitol Building and the 1844 Cherokee National Prison.

Designated a scenic highway, SR 10 winds 30 miles northeast from Tahlequah, intersecting with US 412 and US 59 in the town of Kansas. Two miles north of the junction of US 62 and SR 10, Elephant Rock Nature Park offers 120 acres with nature and hiking trails and access to the Illinois River for fishing and swimming.

Tahlequah Area Chamber of Commerce: 123 E. Delaware St., Tahlequah, OK 74464-2817; phone (918) 456-3742 or (800) 456-4860.

Self-guiding tours: City maps, announcements of community activities and brochures outlining self-guiding tours of Tahlequah's historic sites are available at the chamber of commerce.

CHEROKEE HERITAGE CENTER— *see Park Hill p. 261.*

MURRELL HOME—*see Park Hill p. 261.*

TISHOMINGO (F-9) pop. 3,162

Historically significant as the capital of the Chickasaw Nation, Tishomingo is on Lake Texoma. After serving as the last Chickasaw capitol, the granite Victorian Gothic building at N. Fisher and W. 8th streets housed the Johnston County Courthouse 1907-89. Guided tours of the building are available. The restored 1902 Indian Territory Bank of the Chickasaw Nation, a block from Court House Square, houses the Johnston County Museum of History.

Johnston County Chamber of Commerce: 102 S. Capitol, Tishomingo, OK 73460; phone (580) 371-2175.

CHICKASAW COUNCIL HOUSE is on Court House Sq. The museum contains the restored first council house of the Chickasaw Nation as well as photographs and artifacts depicting the history of the Chickasaw tribe before their migration from Mississippi and Alabama to Oklahoma 1838-40. Allow 1 hour minimum. Tues.-Fri. 8-4:30, Sat. 10:30-4; closed holidays. Free. Phone (580) 371-3351.

TISHOMINGO NATIONAL WILDLIFE REFUGE is 3 mi. s. on Refuge Rd.; its headquarters is e. off SR 78. The refuge covers 16,464 acres on the Upper Washita arm of Lake Texoma. It lies in the central flyway and functions primarily as a migratory waterfowl refuge. Eagles, hawks, ducks, geese and pelicans are among the migratory birds found in the refuge; deer, bobcats and beavers also are residents.

Limited fishing and hunting are permitted in designated sections. Allow 1 hour minimum. Refuge open daily dawn-dusk. Headquarters open Mon.-Fri. 7:30-4. Free. Phone (580) 371-2402. *See Recreation Chart.*

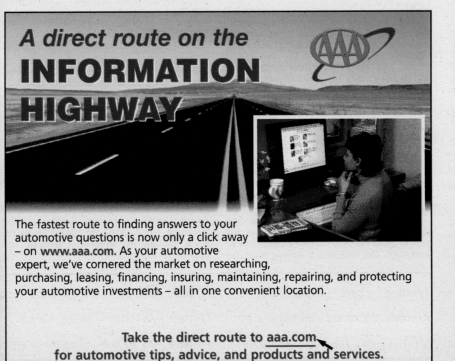

Tulsa

City Population: 393,049 **Elevation: 689 ft.**

Editor's Picks:

Gilcrease Museum ....*(see p. 270)*

Philbrook Museum of Art .... *(see p. 272)*

Tulsa Zoo and Living Museum ... *(see p. 272)*

© Gibson Stock Photography

As Oklahoma's second largest city, Tulsa is the product of an unlikely mixture of oil and water; the development of these two liquid resources spurred the city's rapid economic growth and made Tulsa into the vibrant, bustling community it is today.

Tulsa's beginnings date to 1836 when a band of displaced Creek Indians from Alabama built a council fire under a sturdy oak tree, ending a long, harsh journey over the "Trail of Tears." The name Tulsa is derived from the Creek word "Tullahassee" or "Talahassee," meaning "old town."

While early settlers were attracted to the lush banks of the Arkansas River, the area remained largely undeveloped until a trading post opened in 1846, signaling the beginning of organized commerce in the area. Tulsa became the official name of the town with the creation of the first post office in 1879.

The arrival of the St. Louis-San Francisco Railway provided further impetus for growth. Farmers, ranchers and traders were attracted to the area's increasingly stable system of transportation. One of the first organized groups, a union Sunday school, held class in a tent belonging to a railroad carpenter. By the time Tulsa was incorporated on Jan. 8, 1898, cattle shipping had become the principal industry.

On June 25, 1901, the pace of the town's development quickened. Drillers operating a rig known as Sue Bland #1 struck black gold, creating the state's first commercially important oil well. Eager prospectors swarmed into the area, repeating the frenzy of the land rushes a few years earlier. A second major strike tapped into the large reserves at the Ida Glenn farm in 1905. Oil prices began to climb after pipelines were established to the Gulf of Mexico.

As oil fortunes were literally being made overnight, enterprising Tulsans began an aggressive campaign to attract oilmen to establish themselves in the community. The result was a building boom that also created hotels, office buildings, paved roads, bridges and more railroad links. Train trips organized by civic leaders to promote Tulsa were common at the turn of the 20th century, and humorist Will Rogers was known to accompany these early business boosters. Their vision helped to elevate Tulsa from a dusty cow town in American Indian Territory to a dynamic urban center with a vigorous economy.

Development of water resources has enabled Tulsa to boast the largest number of man-made lakes in the nation. Barge traffic between the Tulsa Port of Catoosa and New Orleans qualifies Tulsa as a major inland harbor. This 445-mile navigation system links Oklahoma with domestic ports in the surrounding five-state area through a complex system of dams, lakes, reservoirs and locks.

While at one time everyone in Tulsa seemed to be involved in some way with the oil business, the city now has a more diversified economy. Although more than 1,000 area firms are still associated with the petroleum business, current industries include aviation, computer technology, financial services, health care, manufacturing and mining. Among the fastest growing are aerospace engineering and telecommunications.

Getting There — *starting on p. 267*

Getting Around — *starting on p. 267*

What To See — *starting on p. 270*

What To Do — *starting on p. 273*

Where To Stay — *starting on p. 628*

Where To Dine — *starting on p. 635*

The area earns its nickname "Green Country" from an abundance of parks and gardens that enhance the city's urban appearance. Many acres of parkland have been preserved despite Tulsa's numerous industries. River Parks, the scene of more than 25 festivals, includes a lake with a floating stage as well as a lengthy trail system on the east and west banks of the Arkansas River.

In Tulsa—a young city mindful of its roots—recreation, cultural arts and industry all come together to form a pleasant setting with a promising future.

Utica Square / Tulsa Metro Chamber of Commerce

Getting There

By Car

Several major highways lead to and from Tulsa. One of the most important is I-44, which approaches the city from the northeast as the Will Rogers Turnpike and from the southwest as the Turner Turnpike. Although I-44 bypasses the downtown area, the city's center is accessible from I-44 by way of numerous interchanges. Martin Luther King Jr. Memorial Expressway (I-244/US 412) is a major access route from I-44 to the heart of Tulsa.

US 75 leads into downtown Tulsa from both the north and the south; the southern segment is known as the Okmulgee Expressway, which becomes the Indian Nation Turnpike farther south.

US 64/412 approaches the city from the west as the Cimarron Turnpike, but becomes the Keystone Expressway before entering the city limits. The Muskogee Turnpike is a major access highway from the southeast. Converging with SR 51, it enters Tulsa as the Broken Arrow Expressway.

East of the city, the Mingo Valley Expressway (US 169) approaches from the north; it is connected to downtown via I-244. Historic Route 66, which at one time carried traffic from Chicago to Southern California, passes through downtown as 11th Street.

Getting Around

Street System

The east-west dividing line is Main Street, while Admiral Boulevard is the city's north-south bisector. Numbered streets run east and west beginning 1 block south of Admiral, unless otherwise designated. A right turn on red is permitted after a complete stop, unless otherwise posted.

Parking

Ample parking is available downtown. There are many commercial garages and lots, and most hotels provide free parking for guests. Rates in the commercial garages are $1.25 per half-hour or $1-$7.50 per day.

Destination Tulsa

Although Tulsa was developed with help from the unlikely mixture of natural resources oil and water, its many lakes, parks and attractions blend nicely to create a beautiful city.

Museums, an amusement park, botanical gardens and a zoo offer Tulsa's visitors an appealing combination of flora, fauna and fun.

© Don Sibley / Tulsa Metro Chamber of Commerce

Boston Avenue United Methodist Church, Tulsa.
A wealth of Art Deco details adorn this landmark downtown church as seen in this close-up of its skyscraperlike tower. (See listing page 270)

Philbrook Museum of Art, Tulsa.
An extensive art collection fills what was once the home of a Tulsa oil man. (See listing page 272)

© Philbrook Museum of Art

Pawhuska

Hominy

See Vicinity map page 271

Tulsa

Oologah

Claremore

Catoosa

Sand Springs

Sapulpa

Jenks

© Wendell Metzen / Index Stock Imagery

Will Rogers Memorial Museum, Claremore.
The museum honors Oklahoma's favorite son with exhibits recounting his life and career. (See listing page 275)

Tulsa Zoo and Living Museum.
In addition to giraffes, the zoo is home to hundreds of other animal species. (See listing page 272)

© Robert A. Chance / Tulsa Zoo

Places included in this AAA Destination City:

The Informed Traveler

Sales Tax: The Tulsa area has a sales tax of 8.52 percent, a lodging tax of 13.52 percent and a rental car tax of 14.51 percent.

WHOM TO CALL

Emergency: 911

Police (non-emergency): (918) 596-7777

Fire: (918) 596-9444

Time and Temperature: (918) 477-1000

Hospitals: Hillcrest Medical Center, (918) 579-1000; Oklahoma State University Medical Center, (918) 587-2561; St. Francis Hospital, (918) 494-2200; St. John Medical Center, (918) 744-2345; SouthCrest Hospital, (918) 294-4000.

WHERE TO LOOK

Newspapers

Tulsa World, the city's daily newspaper, is distributed in the morning.

Radio

Tulsa radio station KRMG (740 AM) is a news station. KWGS (89.5 FM) is a member of National Public Radio.

Visitor Information

Tulsa Metro Chamber of Commerce: Williams Center Tower II, Suite 150, 2 W. 2nd St., Tulsa, OK 74103; phone (918) 585-1201 or (800) 558-3311.

Maps and visitor information are available Mon.-Fri. 8-5.

TRANSPORTATION

Air Travel

With service to most major cities in the United States, Tulsa International Airport is just northeast of downtown and is easily accessible by way of I-244 or US 169. Airport parking costs range from $4-$6 per day. Taxi fare to downtown Tulsa is approximately $22 one way.

Buses

Greyhound Lines Inc. and Jefferson Lines are the major bus lines serving the city. Both operate out of the terminal at 319 S. Detroit Ave.; phone (918) 584-4428 for schedule information.

Public Transport

Tulsa Transit operates buses throughout the metropolitan area and includes stops at attractions and shopping centers. The main terminal is at 319 S. Denver Ave. between Peoria and Utica avenues. Phone (918) 582-2100 for schedules and information.

Rental Cars

Hertz, (800) 654-3080, offers discounts to AAA members. For listings of other agencies check the telephone directory.

Taxis

Cab companies include American Shuttle Service, (918) 744-1111; Checker Cab, (918) 587-6611; Executive Cab Co., (918) 747-8481; and Yellow Cab, (918) 582-6161. Taxis are metered and charge $1.50 plus $1.50-$1.75 for each mile. There is a $1 charge for each additional passenger.

What To See

BELL'S AMUSEMENT PARK, e. of 21st and Harvard sts. at 3901 E. 21st St., has been in operation since 1951. Attractions include a wooden roller coaster, a log flume ride, a children's area, a game arcade and an 18-hole miniature golf course. Mind Melt is a thrill ride that slowly carries passengers to the top of a 141-foot-high tower and then hurls them downward before stopping just short of the ground.

Mon.-Thurs. 6-10 p.m., Fri. 6-11 p.m., Sat. 1-11, Sun. 1-9, Apr.-May and mid-Aug. through Sept. 30; Mon.-Thurs 6-10 p.m., June 1 to mid-Aug. Gate admission $3. Full-day package $17, under 48 inches tall $11.75, over 65 free. Ride tickets $1.25. Mind Melt tickets $3.75. All-day Mind Melt Pass $9. DS, MC, VI. Phone (918) 744-1991.

BIG SPLASH WATER PARK, 4707 E. 21st St., is a water theme park featuring the Motion Ocean wave pool, a water roller coaster, a seven-story waterslide, two speed slides, a lazy river, a kiddie pool for toddlers and a sand volleyball court. Food is available. Allow 4 hours minimum. Mon.-Thurs. 10-6, Fri.-Sat. 10-8, Sun. noon-6, Memorial Day-Labor Day. Admission $17.95; over 60, $11.95; under 3 free. Admission Fri.-Sat. after 4 p.m., $8.95. AX, DS, MC, VI. Phone (918) 749-7385.

BOSTON AVENUE UNITED METHODIST CHURCH, 1301 S. Boston Ave., is an interesting example of modern skyscraper architecture applied to a large church. Completed in 1929, the building is noted for its Art Deco design. Guided tours are available by appointment. Allow 1 hour minimum. Mon.-Fri. 8:30-4:45. Free. Phone (918) 583-5181.

GILCREASE MUSEUM is off US 64/SR 51 at 1400 N. Gilcrease Museum Rd. The museum is known for its comprehensive collection of art of the American West, including works by Albert Bierstadt, Thomas Moran, Frederic Remington and Charles Russell.

Paintings, drawings, prints and sculpture by more than 400 artists from the 18th century to the present are included in the museum's collection. Artists include John James Audubon, John Singleton Copley, Winslow Homer, John Singer Sargent, James McNeill Whistler and N.C. Wyeth. A collection of American Indian art and artifacts, along with historical manuscripts, documents and maps also is featured. Anthropological and archeological collections feature artifacts from North, Central and South American cultures.

Food is available. Allow 3 hours minimum. Daily 10-5; closed Dec. 25. Guided tours are given at 2. Admission $3; family rate $5. An additional fee may be charged for special exhibitions. Phone (918) 596-2700, (888) 655-2278, or (918) 596-1400 for information about special exhibitions and fees.

The Gardens at Gilcrease Museum, on the museum grounds, comprises 23 acres of thematic formal gardens, including Victorian, Colonial, pre-Columbian and Pioneer styles. Paved walking trails allow for exploration, and docent tours are available.

Gilcrease Museum / © Gibson Stock Photography

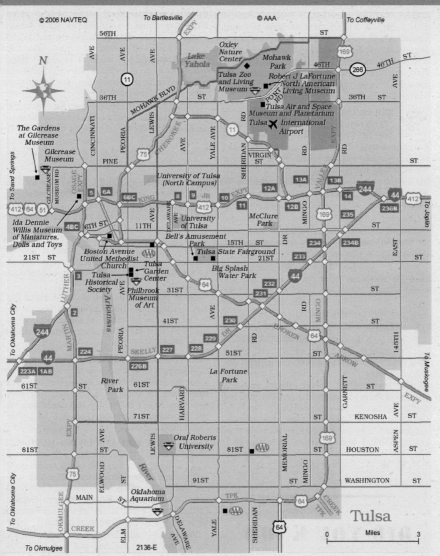

© 2006 NAVTEQ © AAA

Tulsa

Miles

2136-E

Daily dawn-dusk; closed Dec. 25. Donations. Phone (918) 596-2700.

IDA DENNIE WILLIS MUSEUM OF MINIATURES, DOLLS AND TOYS, 628 N. Country Club Dr., is housed in a renovated 1910 Tudor mansion. The museum contains an extensive collection of doll houses, toys, miniatures and more than 2,000 dolls assembled by Ms. Willis over a 30-year period. A collection of American Indian dolls and relics along with an exhibit of ethnic dolls also are available.

Allow 1 hour, 30 minutes minimum. Wed.-Sat. 11-4:30; closed major holidays. Admission $3.50; over 65 and ages 12-17, $3; under 12, $2.50. Phone (918) 584-6654.

ORAL ROBERTS UNIVERSITY, 7777 S. Lewis Ave., has a 200-foot glass and steel prayer tower, seven-story diamond-shaped library and graduate center complex, sports center, symphony hall, chapel, carillon and television production studio. The Prayer Tower Visitor Center offers views of the campus from its observation deck as well as a 20-minute multimedia presentation about the university and a 36-minute presentation about the life of Oral Roberts.

Allow 3 hours minimum. Visitor center open Tues.-Sat. 10-3:30, Sun. 12:30-3:30; closed Jan. 1, Thanksgiving and Dec. 24-25 and 31. Free. Phone (918) 495-6807 for campus tour times.

OXLEY NATURE CENTER, in Mohawk Park at 5701 E. 36th St. N., comprises 800 acres of natural vegetation and walking trails. A visitor center has displays describing unusual local birds and a bee-hive with a see-through panel and entrance tube. Park open daily 7 a.m.-9 p.m. Nature center open daily 8-5. Visitor center open Mon.-Sat. 10-4:30, Sun. noon-4:30. Free. Phone (918) 669-6644.

PHILBROOK MUSEUM OF ART is at 2727 S. Rockford Rd., 1 blk. e. of Peoria Ave. at 27th Pl. This elaborate Italian Renaissance-style villa set on 23 acres of formal and informal gardens was the palatial home of oilman Waite Phillips and his wife Genevieve. Built in the late 1920s, it now houses permanent collections of African, American, American Indian, Asian and European art.

Changing exhibitions, lectures, films, performances and special events are scheduled throughout the year. An audio tour covering the history and architecture of the villa and gardens is available.

Food is available. Allow 2 hours minimum. Tues.-Sat. 10-5 (also Thurs. 5-8), Sun. 11-5; closed major holidays. Admission $7.50; over 64, $5.50; under 12 free. Audio tour $3. AX, MC, VI. Phone (918) 749-7941 or (800) 324-7941.

SAVE **SHERWIN MILLER MUSEUM OF JEWISH ART** is on the Zarrow Campus at 2021 E. 71st St. The museum houses ancient artifacts; Jewish ritual objects and items used in rites of passage; displays comparing a range of societies and their influence on Jewish culture; history exhibits, including accounts of the Jewish experience in Oklahoma; and displays of fine art. An area dedicated to the Holocaust features videotaped interviews with survivors. Another part of the museum contains changing exhibitions. Allow 1 hour minimum. Mon.-Fri. 10-5, Sun. 1-5. Admission $5.50; over 65, $4.50; ages 6-20, $3. MC, VI. Phone (918) 492-1818.

DID YOU KNOW

Billionaire J. Paul Getty began his oil empire in Tulsa.

TULSA AIR AND SPACE MUSEUM AND PLAN-ETARIUM is 6 mi. n.e. off Sheridan Rd. at 3624 N. 74th E. Ave. The museum features several aircraft, historic displays and interactive exhibits. One of the hands-on displays is a model of an aircraft engine that shows its inner workings. Stars and planets can be identified at the planetarium, and an animated show is geared toward children.

Allow 1 hour minimum. Tues.-Sat. 10-5, Sun. 1-5; closed major holidays. Museum or planetarium admission $6; over 61, military and students with ID $5; ages 5-12, $4. Combination ticket $10; over 61, military and students with ID $8; ages 5-12, $6. MC, VI. Phone (918) 834-9900.

TULSA GARDEN CENTER is 1.5 mi. s. of SR 51 at 2435 S. Peoria Ave. in Woodward Park. Included on the grounds are a 21-room mansion, a 3-acre arboretum, a formal sunken garden and a rock garden with flowering annuals and perennials. The five-terraced Italian Renaissance rose garden and the Victorian conservatory are of architectural interest. Also on the grounds are English herb, azalea and iris gardens as well as a test area, where new hybrids of roses are created.

Center open Mon.-Fri. 9-4; closed Memorial Day, July 4, Labor Day, Thanksgiving and Dec. 24-Jan. 1. Docent tours are given by appointment. Woodward Park open daily 7 a.m.-dusk. Donations. Phone (918) 746-5125.

Tulsa Historical Society is at 2445 S. Peoria Ave. in Woodward Park. A room is dedicated to exhibits about the area's oil history and another room features changing exhibits. A 30-minute film about downtown Tulsa's architecture also can be seen. Allow 30 minutes minimum. Thurs.-Sat. 10-2. Free. Phone (918) 712-9484.

TULSA ZOO AND LIVING MUSEUM, 6 mi. n.e. off Sheridan Rd. in Mohawk Park, houses more than 250 animal species on 70 SAVE acres. Some animals reside in grottoes; others, such as the zebras, antelopes and Cape buffaloes, live in the African Savanna section. Chimpanzees cavort in an outdoor playground, while sea lion feedings take place daily at 2.

Visitors can walk through a naturalistic cave in the Eastern Forest building and view a 20,000-gallon shark aquarium and a 10,000-gallon coral reef aquarium in the Southern Lowlands building. The Wetlands exhibit includes an Oklahoma wetlands demonstration area. The Tropical Rainforest exhibit highlights the rain forests of Central and South America and includes nearly 500 animals. A miniature steam train operates daily. Children can ride in a parade of animal figures on the ARVEST Wildlife Carousel.

Allow 2 hours minimum. Zoo and museum daily 9-5; closed third Fri. in June and Dec. 25. Admission (including Robert J. LaFortune North American Living Museum) $6.04; over 54, $4.03; ages 3-11, $3.02. Round-trip train ride $2; one-way $1. Carousel $2. Parking $1. AX, DS, MC, VI. Phone (918) 669-6600.

Robert J. LaFortune North American Living Museum, 5701 E. 36th St. N., contains exhibits describing North American natural history. Displays in each of the four buildings explain the geological and ecological features of four distinct areas through audiovisual demonstrations, live animals, graphics and artifacts. Daily 9-5; closed third Fri. in June and Dec. 25. Admission (included in Tulsa Zoo and Living Museum) $6.04; over 54, $4.03; ages 3-11, $3.02. Round-trip train ride $2; one-way $1. Carousel $2. Parking $1. AX, DS, MC, VI. Phone (918) 669-6600.

What To Do

Sightseeing

Walking Tours

Tulsa's historical business district mirrors the wealth of the oil industry through its opulent Art Deco architecture. Some of the finest examples of zigzag skyscrapers, the streamline style of the 1930s and the classical style popular during the Great Depression are displayed.

Visitors may choose to explore the area on foot; between 2nd and 6th streets and Cincinnati and Cheyenne streets there are approximately 40 Art Deco sites. The Tulsa Union Depot, built in 1931, is on 1st Street; the Philtower, known as the "Queen of the Tulsa skyline," can be found on 5th Street near Boston Street; the Mincks-Adams Hotel, with its terra cotta facade, is at 4th and Cheyenne streets; and the National Bank of Tulsa, containing a lavish lobby, is at 320 S. Boston St.

Sports and Recreation

With hundreds of miles of lakeshore within a 2-hour drive of their city, Tulsans enjoy a variety of water sports. **Fishing, boating** and **water skiing** are popular on any one of the 48 lakes in the Tulsa vicinity including Birch, Eufaula, Fort Gibson, Fountainhead, Greenleaf, Keystone, Skiatook and Tenkiller. Provisions for **swimming** and **picnicking** are plentiful.

Hikers have their choice of trails at nearby Chandler Park and Heyburn, Okmulgee and Oologah lakes, to name a few. A recreation area on one of the largest bodies of water in Oklahoma, Grand Lake o' the Cherokees, is home to 36 holes of year-round **golf.** LaFortune Park in southern Tulsa has a popular three-mile **jogging** track around two 18-hole golf courses and a public swimming pool.

City and county parks are numerous. Among them is Mohawk Park on 36th Street N., one of the largest municipal parks in the nation. Near downtown, the River Parks system offers miles of jogging, walking and **bicycling** trails along the banks of the Arkansas River. Many area parks feature lighted **softball** diamonds.

The Tulsa Drillers, the Double A farm team of **baseball**'s Colorado Rockies, plays in Drillers Stadium on the Tulsa County Fairgrounds. The stadium

is one of the largest minor league stadiums in the country; phone (918) 744-5901 for schedule information. **Ice hockey** fans flock to the Tulsa Convention Center to watch the Tulsa Oilers; phone (918) 632-7825.

At the college level the University of Tulsa Golden Hurricanes and the Oral Roberts University Golden Eagles both field competitive baseball and **basketball** teams. Fans of **football** find plenty of gridiron action every fall at the University of Tulsa's Skelly Stadium; phone (918) 631-4688.

Those who enjoy the thrill of "playing the ponies" can visit Fair Meadows at Expo Square for pari-mutuel Thoroughbred and quarter **horse racing** at various dates during the year; phone (918) 743-7223.

Note: Policies concerning admittance of children to pari-mutuel betting facilities vary. Phone for information.

Shopping

From small, exclusive boutiques to large, bargain-packed malls, Tulsa's shopping centers provide visitors with a wide range of choices. With more than one million square feet of retail floor space, Woodland Hills Mall, 71st Street and Memorial Drive, is said to be the largest in the state. The mall comprises more than 165 stores including Dillard's, Foley's, JCPenney and Sears.

Utica Square, 21st Street S. and Utica Avenue, caters to upscale tastes and also serves as the backdrop for live performances in summer. Centered about a rustic, restored barn at 51st Street S. and Sheridan Avenue, The Farm offers a variety of boutiques in a setting that is reminiscent of a village square.

Among the retailers at Tulsa Promenade, 41st Street and S. Yale Avenue, are Dillard's, Mervyn's, Foley's and JCPenney.

DID YOU KNOW

Oklahoma has more man-made lakes than any other state.

Performing Arts

Early Tulsa settlers included cultured people who brought their appreciation of music with them, thus sowing the seeds for future growth of the arts.

The Tulsa Opera presents a season of internationally renowned productions. The Performing Arts Center (PAC), E. 3rd Street and Cincinnati Avenue in downtown Tulsa, was built with a combination of public and private funds. It serves as the hub of the arts entertainment community in the city. For ticket information phone (918) 596-7111. In addition, Tulsa Ballet performs in Chapman Music Hall at the Tulsa Performing Arts Center; for ticket information phone (918) 749-6006.

The Tulsa Spotlighters present "The Drunkard," a 19th-century melodrama that has been in regular production since 1953. The play, which encourages audience participation, is followed by "The Olio," an old-fashioned variety show. The landmark Richard Mansfield Dickinson Theatre, 1381 Riverside Dr., serves as the play's venue; phone (918) 587-5030.

Special Events

Several events keep Tulsans in touch with their heritage. The Tulsa Indian Art Festival is held in February at Expo Square with more than 35 American Indian tribes participating from across the country. The city celebrates the arts in mid-May with the Tulsa International Mayfest, held in the Main Mall downtown. The Juneteenth Festival in mid-June highlights African-American music traditions with jazz, blues and gospel performances.

The Pinto World Championship Horse Show in June features more than 750 colorful horses and 1,300 riders; the event is held at Expo Square. Following the departure of the pintos, Expo Square is also the site of the Palomino Horse Breeders of America World Championship Horse Show, held in July.

More than 600 exhibitors display arts, crafts, antiques and collectibles during An Affair of the Heart during mid-July at Expo Square.

The Inter-Tribal Indian Club of Tulsa Powwow of Champions held in mid-August attracts dancers from throughout the United States to participate in contests and other cultural activities. Also in August, Jazz on Greenwood showcases nationally known jazz performers.

The Oklahoma Scottish Games and Gathering is held in mid-September at River Parks West, 2105 S. Jackson Ave. The festival includes a Scottish athletic competition for both men and women plus Scottish entertainment. Tents are set up by Scottish clans, food vendors and various Celtic merchants.

The Tulsa State Fair is held at Expo Square in the fall. The fall also brings Oktoberfest, with Austrian and German folk bands, European food, arts and crafts, folk dancers and a children's entertainment tent. The American Bicycle Association Grand Nationals motocross competition draws bicyclists from the U.S. and foreign countries to Expo Square in November.

The Tulsa Vicinity

CATOOSA (E-3) pop. 5,449, elev. 605'

ARKANSAS RIVER HISTORICAL SOCIETY MUSEUM is at 5350 Cimarron Rd., at the Tulsa Port of Catoosa. The museum contains photographs and artifacts relating to the development of the McClellan-Kerr Arkansas River Navigation System.

A videotape explains the system's history; visitors also can see a working scale model of a boat traveling through a lock. A collection of American Indian artifacts found in the Arkansas River Basin also is presented. Allow 30 minutes minimum. Mon.-Fri. 8-4:30; closed holidays. Donations. Phone (918) 266-2291.

CLAREMORE (E-3) pop. 15,873, elev. 608'

Claremore was the home of Lynn Riggs, author of "Green Grow the Lilacs," the play that inspired the musical "Oklahoma!" Northeast of town on SR 28A near Foyil stands what is said to be the world's largest totem pole. Carved of stone and concrete, this 90-foot by 18-foot monument to the American Indian is the center of Totem Pole Park. The park also has a museum and picnic area.

Claremore Area Chamber of Commerce: 419 W. Will Rogers Blvd., Claremore, OK 74017; phone (918) 341-2818.

J.M. DAVIS ARMS & HISTORICAL MUSEUM, 333 N. Lynn Riggs Blvd. (US 66), houses a diverse collection of firearms, swords and knives; Western, Civil War-era and American Indian artifacts; music boxes and musical instruments; steins; political buttons; statues; and World War I posters. A library provides reference works.

More than 20,000 handguns, shotguns and rifles and weapons owned by famous outlaws comprise the firearms collection. The area's Western heritage is remembered by displays of saddles, Stetsons, cattle brands and lariats as well as American Indian pottery and arrowheads.

Antique musical instruments such as Victrolas and banjos are displayed as are 1,200 German beer steins and more than 600 World War I posters. A group of statuary art by late 19th-century sculptor John Rogers depicts vignettes of everyday life. Mon.-Sat. 8:30-5, Sun. 1-5; closed Thanksgiving and Dec. 25. Donations. Phone (918) 341-5707.

WILL ROGERS MEMORIAL MUSEUM, 1 mi. w. on SR 88, is a ranch house-style museum overlooking the Tiawah Valley on the site where Will Rogers planned to build a home. In the foyer is a well-known bronze sculpture of Rogers by Jo Davidson. Among personal items exhibited in nine galleries are an international saddle collection, miniature saddles, riding whips and ropes.

Dioramas highlight Rogers' life and varied stints as a rodeo performer, vaudeville sensation, columnist, author and star of some 70 films. Documentaries and several of Will Rogers' movies are shown continuously; a hands-on children's area specializes in American Indian life. A library and archives are included; the Rogers' family tomb is in a sunken garden. Allow 1 hour minimum. Daily 8-5. Donations. Phone (918) 341-0719 or (800) 324-9455.

HOMINY (D-1) pop. 2,584, elev. 282'

Hominy lies in the center of the former Osage Indian Reservation, composed of different bands of Osage Indians who were relocated from Kansas in 1872. Early residents named the town after the Osage chief Ho Mo I, meaning "night walker."

A series of 40 murals that depict American Indian folklore can be seen on the sides of buildings throughout Hominy. Nearby recreational facilities include Skiatook Lake and Keystone Lake (see Recreation Chart).

Hominy Chamber of Commerce: P.O. Box 99, Hominy, OK 74035; phone (918) 885-4939.

DRUMMOND HOME, 305 N. Price, reflects the lifestyle of Fred and Addie Drummond, who built one of the most successful trading and ranching operations in the area. The Victorian three-story house, completed in 1905, has been painstakingly restored as it appeared in the early 20th century and contains most of its original furnishings. Allow 30 minutes minimum. Wed.-Sat. 9-5, Sun. 1-5; closed state holidays. Last tour begins 30 minutes before closing. Donations. Phone (918) 885-2374.

JENKS (F-2) pop. 9,557

OKLAHOMA AQUARIUM is at 300 Aquarium Dr. Home to more than 4,000 animals from around the world, the aquarium is divided into galleries that include the Shark Adventure, where visitors can walk through a clear acrylic tunnel surrounded by 500,000 gallons of water and schools of sharks. Marvels & Mysteries of the Deep houses seahorses, moon jellies, octopuses, lobster and shrimp. Other unusual sea creatures can be found in the Bio-Diversity gallery, which includes crabs, jellies, sea stars, sea squirts and sponges.

The Adaptation gallery illustrates how animals have adapted to their habitats. A variety of coastal environments are re-created in the Oceans gallery, which also features touch tanks. Visitors can watch divers feed colorful fish at the Coral Reef exhibit, and a museum houses an extensive collection of antique fishing tackle.

Allow 2 hours minimum. Daily 10-6 (also Tues. 6-9 p.m.); closed Jan. 1 and Dec. 25. Last admission 1 hour before closing. Admission $13.95; over 62 and military with ID $11.95; ages 3-12, $9.95. AX, DC, DS, MC, VI. Phone (918) 296-3474.

OOLOGAH (D-3) pop. 883, elev. 657′

WILL ROGERS BIRTHPLACE RANCH is 1.5 mi. n. of SR 88 on an unmarked county road. The 1870 home is on a hill overlooking Oologah Lake and is furnished with family memorabilia and period antiques. Historic videotapes are shown continuously. Daily 8-5. Donations. Phone (918) 341-0719 or (800) 324-9455.

PAWHUSKA (C-1) pop. 3,629, elev. 847′

Pawhuska is capital of the Osage Nation, the wealthiest American Indian tribe in America. The town was named after Pahuiska, chief of the Osage Tribe at the beginning of the 19th century. Pawhuska was later the home of the first Boy Scout troop in America, organized by Rev. John Mitchell in May 1909.

The architectural diversity of Pawhuska's downtown historic district stems from the prosperity that came with the oil strike on Osage land in 1921. Buildings of note include the 1887 Gothic-style Immaculate Conception Catholic Church; the Constantine Theatre and the 1894 City Hall, originally the Osage Agency house.

Pawhuska Chamber of Commerce: 210 W. Main St., Pawhuska, OK 74056; phone (918) 287-1208.

OSAGE COUNTY HISTORICAL SOCIETY MUSEUM, 700 N. Lynn Ave., displays relics of the Old West, the oil industry and the nation's first Boy Scout troop in addition to American Indian artifacts. Mon.-Sat. 9-5; closed Thanksgiving and Dec. 25. Donations. Phone (918) 287-9119.

OSAGE TRIBAL MUSEUM, 819 Grandview Ave., exhibits American Indian regalia and arts and crafts. Mon.-Sat. 8:30-5; closed major holidays. Free. Phone (918) 287-5441.

TALLGRASS PRAIRIE PRESERVE, 18 mi. n. on Kihekah, following signs to preserve headquarters, is a 39,000-acre open range that supports more than 750 species of plants in addition to bison, prairie chickens, bob-white quails, wild turkeys, squirrels and rabbits. The preserve's managers hope to recreate a functioning tallgrass prairie ecosystem at the site. Visitors can take a driving tour along the preserve's gravel roads. Daily dawn-dusk. Free. Phone (918) 287-4803.

SAND SPRINGS (F-1) pop. 17,451

West of downtown Tulsa, Sand Springs is nestled in the steep and wooded hills overlooking the Arkansas River, providing a setting often used as a backdrop in movies. Boating and sailing are available at Keystone Lake (see Recreation Chart).

Sand Springs Area Chamber of Commerce: 121 N. Main St., Sand Springs, OK 74063; phone (918) 245-3221.

[SAVE] DISCOVERYLAND!, 5 mi. s.w. on 41st St., presents the Rogers and Hammerstein play "Oklahoma!" in a 1,500-seat outdoor amphitheater under the stars. Horses and wagons, as well as a real surrey with the fringe on top, are highlights of the production. The frontier musical "Seven Brides for

Seven Brothers" also is presented. A barbecue dinner precedes the shows at an additional cost. Free pony rides for children are available before the show.

Food is available. Inquire about weather policies. Allow 2 hours, 30 minutes minimum. "Oklahoma!" performed Mon.-Wed. and Sat. at 7:30 p.m., "Seven Brides for Seven Brothers" performed Thurs.-Fri. at 7:30 p.m., early June to mid-Aug. Barbecue dinner 6-7:30. Admission $16.95; over 55, $15.95; under 11 free. Barbecue dinner is an additional $9.95; over 55, $9.50; under 11, $6.95. Reservations are recommended. MC, VI. Phone (918) 245-6552.

SAPULPA (F-2) pop. 19,166

The town of Sapulpa was named for Sepulcher, a Creek Indian whose unlikely name evolved over time, thanks to misspellings and mispronunciations, into "Sapuipa." He established a trading post one mile south of the present city around 1850, and in 1886 the Atlantic & Pacific Railroad extended its line from Red Fork to this area and called it Sapulpa Station.

After the 1905 Glen Pool oil discovery 8 miles to the southeast, Sapulpa grew into a city that served the oil industry. The town then developed into an agricultural shipping center and now is supported by glass plants, a pottery factory and several small pipe and steel manufacturing plants.

Frankoma Pottery, 9549 Frankoma Rd., is one of the few potteries in the country that uses local clay to produce its products. The company, which has made handcrafted earthenware pottery since 1933, offers tours of its plant; phone (918) 224-5511.

Sapulpa Area Chamber of Commerce: 101 E. Dewey, Sapulpa, OK 74066; phone (918) 224-0170.

SAPULPA HISTORICAL SOCIETY MUSEUM is at 100 Lee St. Local history is featured on guided tours through the museum exhibits, which showcase Creek and Yuchi Indians, the Glenpool Oil Field and the Frisco Railroad. Late 19th- and early 20th-century appliances depict advances in technology. Allow 2 hours minimum. Mon.-Tues. and Thurs. 10-3, Wed. 10-noon and 1-3; closed major holidays. Donations. Phone (918) 224-4871.

Tulsa Garden Center / © Gibson Stock Photography

This ends listings for the Tulsa Vicinity.
The following page resumes the alphabetical listings of cities in Oklahoma.

TUSKAHOMA (E-11) elev. 582'

Selected by the Choctaw Nation as its capital in 1883, Tuskahoma remained the seat of Choctaw government until after Oklahoma became a state in 1907. The town's name comes from *tushka homma,* which means "red warriors."

CHOCTAW NATION MUSEUM is off US 271N, following signs, in the former capitol building of the Choctaw Nation. The three-story, red-brick structure was completed in 1884 and houses exhibits of pottery, clothing, arrowheads and photographs illustrating the way of life of the Choctaw people. Allow 30 minutes minimum. Tues.-Fri. 9-4:30 (also Sat. 9-4:30 Memorial Day-Labor Day). Free. Phone (918) 569-4465.

VIAN (D-11) pop. 1,362, elev. 550'

SEQUOYAH NATIONAL WILDLIFE REFUGE, off I-40 exit 297, then 3 mi. s. following signs, was established in 1970 to provide a habitat for waterfowl and other migratory birds. The majority of the 20,800-acre refuge is comprised of bottomland and is home to mallards, snow geese, hawks, bobwhite quails and various reptiles. A 6-mile automobile tour winds throughout the refuge, where photograph blinds and observation towers are present. Automobile tour daily dawn-dusk. Refuge headquarters open Mon.-Fri. 7:30-4. Free. Phone (918) 773-5251.

VINITA (B-11) pop. 6,472

Vinita was named by a Cherokee Indian, Col. Elias C. Boudinot, after sculptress Vinnie Ream, whose most renowned work is the pensive statue of Abraham Lincoln at the U.S. Capitol. Boudinot fell in love with the young artist while she was in Washington, D.C., on a commission to create the statue. The first woman to be granted such a federal art commission, Ream's sculpture was unveiled in 1871, the same year Vinita was founded.

Since the days of the longhorn cattle drives from Texas, ranching has been an important industry in Vinita. Early cattlemen, however, would hardly recognize the Brangus, which is a hardy combination of purebred Brahman and Aberdeen-Angus cattle. The breed was created by Raymond Pope, a rancher who lived in the area.

Vinita is an access point for the recreational opportunities on the western shore of Grand Lake O' the Cherokees, created in 1941 with the completion of the Pensacola Dam on the Grand River. *See Recreation Chart.*

Vinita Area Chamber of Commerce: 125 S. Scraper, PSO Building, P.O. Box 882, Vinita, OK 74301; phone (918) 256-7133.

EASTERN TRAILS MUSEUM is inside the Vinita Public Library at 215 W. Illinois St. The museum outlines Oklahoma history through displays of regional American Indian and pioneer artifacts and memorabilia from World Wars I and II. Allow 30 minutes minimum. Mon.-Fri. 1-4, Sat. noon-3. Free. Phone (918) 256-2115.

WATONGA (C-7) pop. 4,658, elev. 1,552'

Founded in 1892, Watonga was named for the Arapaho chief Watonga, or Black Coyote. The town now is a major manufacturer of cheese. Recreational activities abound at nearby Roman Nose State Park *(see Recreation Chart).*

Watonga Chamber of Commerce: P.O. Box 537, Watonga, OK 73772-0357; phone (580) 623-5452.

T.B. FERGUSON HOME is at 519 N. Weigle Ave. The white frame Victorian house was built in 1901 for Thompson Benton Ferguson, the sixth territorial governor of Oklahoma. Prior to serving as governor, Ferguson was the founder and publisher of the *Watonga Republican,* which is still in existence. The home has been restored and is decorated in period. Allow 30 minutes minimum. Wed.-Sat. 10-4; closed state holidays. Donations. Phone (580) 623-5069.

WEATHERFORD (D-6)
pop. 9,859, elev. 1,647'

On the afternoon of April 18, 1892, Oklahoma began its third land run; throngs of men and women gathered at the border of Cheyenne and Arapaho country, waiting for a chance at land ownership. The next morning they rose early, arriving by wagon and on foot to establish the town of Weatherford.

Once a stop on historic Route 66, Weatherford is home to Southwestern Oklahoma State University, known for its school of pharmacy.

Weatherford Area Chamber of Commerce: 522 W. Rainey, Room 224, P.O. Box 857, Weatherford, OK 73096; phone (580) 772-7744 or (800) 725-7744.

GENERAL THOMAS P. STAFFORD AIR AND SPACE CENTER, 3000 Logan Rd. at the Stafford Airport, is a tribute to the Weatherford native's military and aeronautical career. On display are space suits worn by Stafford during four of his space missions, as well as aircraft models, a Gemini capsule seat, Apollo-Soyuz docking collar and photographs from the Apollo 10 mission. Visitors can view such aircraft as an F-16, Mig 21 and a T-38 in addition to a replica of the *Wright Flyer* and *Spirit of St. Louis.*

Mon.-Sat. 9-5, Sun. 1-5; closed Jan. 1, Easter, Memorial Day, July 4, Labor Day, Thanksgiving and Dec. 25. Admission $5, under 19 free. Phone (580) 772-5871.

WEWOKA (E-9) pop. 3,562

The end of the Seminole Indians' "Trail of Tears" journey from Florida, Wewoka became the capital of the Seminole Nation in 1866. Homesteaders appeared at the beginning of the 20th century with the arrival of the Rock Island Railroad. The town became one of the state's leading oil producers overnight with the discovery of the rich Greater Seminole Field in 1926.

The sudden swell in population caused freighting problems for the railroad and stocking problems for local merchants, who were forced to explain to customers that their goods were lost in the "Wewoka Switch." This excuse was used so often that the phrase "caught in a Wewoka Switch" became a popular way of saying that one was caught between a rock and a hard place.

Wewoka Chamber of Commerce: 101 W. Park, Wewoka, OK 74884; phone (405) 257-5485.

SEMINOLE NATION MUSEUM is downtown at 524 S. Wewoka Ave., 1 blk. e. of SR 56. Dioramas, artifacts, crafts, paintings and other exhibits depict the history of the Seminoles and aspects of their culture. Other displays pertain to pioneers and the Oklahoma oil boom. There also is an art gallery. Allow 1 hour minimum. Tues.-Sun. 1-5, Feb.-Dec.; closed major holidays. Donations. Phone (405) 257-5580.

WOODWARD (B-5) pop. 11,853, elev. 1,893′

As were many Oklahoma towns, Woodward was created in a single day. Between noon and sunset on Sept. 16, 1893, when the Cherokee Outlet was opened for homesteading, Woodward became a trade and banking center. It also was on the Western Cattle Trail, which ran from Texas to Dodge City, Kan. The city is a marketing center for a wheat-growing and cattle-raising region.

Woodward Chamber of Commerce: 1006 Oklahoma Ave., P.O. Box 1026, Woodward, OK 73802; phone (580) 256-7411 or (800) 364-5352.

PLAINS INDIANS AND PIONEERS MUSEUM, 2009 Williams Ave., contains historical material pertaining to northwestern Oklahoma. A homesteader's cabin with an attached stable, displays about the area's American Indians and a portrayal of local agricultural development 1880-1950 are among the exhibits presented. Allow 1 hour minimum. Tues.-Sat. 10-5; closed major holidays. Donations. Phone (580) 256-6136.

SOUTHERN PLAINS RANGE RESEARCH STATION, 2000 18th St., is one of the largest agricultural experiment stations in the country. At the 920-acre field station, research is conducted about farming and ranching techniques. A self-guiding tree tour is available. Allow 1 hour minimum. Mon.-Fri. 7:30-4. Free. Phone (580) 256-7449.

WYNNEWOOD (E-8) pop. 2,367, elev. 896′

G.W. EXOTIC ANIMAL PARK is off I-35 exit 64, then 1 blk. e. following signs. This 16-acre sanctuary shelters hundreds of exotic animals, most of which were rescued from cruelty and neglect. Among the animals that visitors can see are bears, bobcats, camels, lions, monkeys and tigers as well as domesticated animals. Plaques for each animal recount the often miserable circumstances in which they were found along with their physical condition at the time.

Allow 1 hour minimum. Daily 7:30-7, early Apr.-late Oct.; 10-5, rest of year. Admission $8; over 64 and ages 3-12, $5. MC, VI. Phone (405) 665-5197.

Where a boy's home is his castle,

no matter what his age.

AAA/CAA Travel offers Disney vacations

with all the special benefits you could wish for.

aaa.com

Only Disney vacations offer the magic and memories that dreams are made of. And only *Walt Disney World* Resort packages offered by *AAA Vacations* offer such special benefits and great values. So call or stop by your AAA/CAA Travel Office today.

Walt Disney World

Because the voyage of your dreams
just happens to be theirs, too.

AAA/CAA Travel adds special
benefits to your Disney dreams.

On a *Disney Cruise Line*®
vacation, you'll find something
enchanting for everyone of
every age—it's the kind of
magic only Disney can create.
And when you book through
AAA/CAA Travel, you'll enjoy
many special benefits! So call
or stop by your AAA/CAA
Travel Office today.

Arkansas

Cossatot River, east of
Vandervoot / Arkansas
Dept of Parks & Tourism
Chuck Haralson

ALMA pop. 4,160

———— WHERE TO STAY ————

COMFORT INN & SUITES   *Book great rates at AAA.com*   **Phone:** (479)632-4141
All Year [ECP]   1P: $59-$109   2P: $59-$109   XP: $5   F17
Location: I-40, exit 13, just n. 439 Hwy 71 N. N 72921 (PO Box 1749). Fax: 479/632-4329. **Facility:** 62 one-
Small-scale Hotel   bedroom standard units, some with whirlpools. 2 stories (no elevator), interior/exterior corridors. *Bath:*
combo or shower only. **Parking:** on-site. **Amenities:** voice mail, irons, hair dryers. **Leisure**
Activities: whirlpool, exercise room. **Guest Services:** coin laundry, wireless Internet. **Business Services:** meeting rooms,
business center. **Cards:** AX, CB, DC, DS, JC, MC, VI.

SOME UNITS

(ASK) (SD) (📷) (🖥) / (✕) (📦) (📼) /

ALTUS pop. 817

———— WHERE TO DINE ————

WIEDERKEHR WEINKELLER
RESTAURANT   **Lunch:** $6-$9   **Dinner:** $12-$28   **Phone:** 479/468-3551
(AAA)   **Location:** I-40, exit 41, 4.5 mi s. SR 186 72821. **Hours:** 11 am-3 & 5-9 pm, Sun 11 am-9 pm. Closed major
holidays. **Reservations:** suggested. **Features:** The wine cellar of this national historic landmark dates to
▽▽▽ ▽▽▽   1880, when J. Wiederkehr built it. Alpine decor enhances the intimate, candlelit atmosphere. Homemade
quiche Lorraine is one outstanding example of the Swiss cuisine. Casual dress; cocktails. **Parking:** on-site.
Ethnic   **Cards:** AX, DC, DS, MC, VI. **Historic**

ARKADELPHIA pop. 10,912

———— WHERE TO STAY ————

BEST WESTERN-CONTINENTAL INN   *Book great rates at AAA.com*   **Phone:** (870)246-5592
(AAA) [SAVE]   5/1-9/15   1P: $69-$99   2P: $70-$99   XP: $6   F18
3/1-4/30 & 9/16-2/29   1P: $67-$99   2P: $69-$99   XP: $6   F18
▽▽▽ ▽▽▽   **Location:** I-30, exit 78, just e. 136 Valley St 71923. Fax: 870/246-3583. **Facility:** 58 one-bedroom standard units.
2 stories (no elevator), exterior corridors. *Bath:* combo or shower only. **Parking:** on-site. **Terms:** pets ($5
Small-scale Hotel   extra charge). **Amenities:** high-speed Internet, voice mail, irons, hair dryers. **Pool(s):** outdoor. **Leisure**
Activities: playground. **Guest Services:** valet and coin laundry. **Cards:** AX, CB, DC, DS, MC, VI.
Free Special Amenities: expanded continental breakfast and preferred room (subject to availability with advance
reservations).

SOME UNITS

(SD) (🛏) (↕🍴) (♿) (🐕) (📷) (📦) (📼) (🖥) / (✕) /
FEE

HAMPTON INN   *Book great rates at AAA.com*   **Phone:** (870)403-0800
▽▽▽▽   All Year   1P: $79-$129   2P: $79-$149
Location: I-30, exit 78, just ne. 108 Mavern Rd 71923. Fax: 870/403-0404. **Facility:** 58 one-bedroom standard
Small-scale Hotel   units, some with whirlpools. 3 stories, interior corridors. *Bath:* combo or shower only. **Parking:** on-site.
Amenities: high-speed Internet, voice mail, irons, hair dryers. **Pool(s):** heated indoor. **Leisure**
Activities: whirlpool, exercise room. **Guest Services:** valet and coin laundry, wireless Internet. **Business Services:** meeting
rooms, business center. **Cards:** AX, DC, DS, MC, VI.

SOME UNITS

(ASK) (SD) (↕🍴) (♿M) (♿) (🐕) (📷) (🖥) / (✕) (📦) (📼) /

SUPER 8 MOTEL
Book great rates at AAA.com

Phone: (870)246-8585

(AAA) [SAVE]

4/1-8/31	1P: $58-$78	2P: $58-$78	XP: $5	F17
12/1-2/29	1P: $48-$78	2P: $48-$78	XP: $5	F17
3/1-3/31 & 9/1-11/30	1P: $48-$68	2P: $48-$68	XP: $5	F17

Small-scale Hotel **Location:** I-30, exit 78, just e. 118 Valley St 71923. **Fax:** 870/246-8585. **Facility:** 48 one-bedroom standard units, some with whirlpools. 1-2 stories (no elevator), exterior corridors. **Parking:** on-site. **Terms:** [CP] meal plan available, pets ($5 fee). **Amenities:** irons, hair dryers. **Pool(s):** outdoor. **Leisure Activities:** whirlpool. **Guest Services:** coin laundry. **Cards:** AX, CB, DC, DS, MC, VI. **Free Special Amenities: continental breakfast and high-speed Internet.**

SOME UNITS

——— WHERE TO DINE ———

FISH NET FAMILY RESTAURANT
Menu on AAA.com

Dinner: $6-$13   **Phone:** 870/246-7885

(AAA)

Seafood **Location:** I-30, exit 78, 2 mi n on SR 7. 5000 Valley St 71923. **Hours:** 4 pm-9 pm, Sun 11 am-8 pm; hours vary off season. Closed: 12/25; also Mon. **Reservations:** suggested. **Features:** The restaurant features casual, relaxed dining in a rustic, nautical theme. The specialty is farm-raised catfish, but they also serve a good selection of steak, chicken and other fresh seafood entrees. The service is friendly and attentive. Casual dress. **Parking:** on-site. **Cards:** DS, MC, VI.

BATESVILLE pop. 9,445

——— WHERE TO STAY ———

BEST WESTERN SCENIC MOTOR INN
Book great rates at AAA.com

Phone: (870)698-1855

(AAA) [SAVE]

All Year [CP]	1P: $64-$95	2P: $67-$95	XP: $8	F12

Motel **Location:** 1.5 mi s on US 167. 773 Batesville Blvd 72501. **Fax:** 870/698-1855. **Facility:** 38 one-bedroom standard units. 2 stories (no elevator), interior corridors. **Parking:** on-site. **Amenities:** high-speed Internet, voice mail, irons, hair dryers. **Pool(s):** outdoor. **Guest Services:** valet laundry. **Cards:** AX, DS, MC, VI. **Free Special Amenities: high-speed Internet.**

SOME UNITS

COMFORT SUITES
Book great rates at AAA.com

Phone: 870/698-1900

All Year	1P: $79-$84	2P: $79-$84	XP: $10	F17

Small-scale Hotel **Location:** 1 mi n on US 167. 1227 N St. Louis St 72501. **Fax:** 870/793-5624. **Facility:** 66 one-bedroom standard units, some with whirlpools. 3 stories, interior corridors. *Bath:* combo or shower only. **Parking:** on-site. **Terms:** [ECP] meal plan available, package plans. **Amenities:** high-speed Internet, voice mail, irons, hair dryers. **Pool(s):** heated indoor. **Leisure Activities:** whirlpool, exercise room. **Guest Services:** valet and coin laundry, wireless Internet. **Business Services:** meeting rooms, business center. **Cards:** AX, DC, DS, JC, MC, VI.

SOME UNITS

HOLIDAY INN EXPRESS
Book at AAA.com

Phone: (870)698-2700

All Year	1P: $69-$89	2P: $75-$99	XP: $6	F11

Small-scale Hotel **Location:** 1 mi n on US 167. 1130 White Dr 72501. **Fax:** 870/698-2700. **Facility:** 65 one-bedroom standard units, some with whirlpools. 3 stories, interior corridors. *Bath:* combo or shower only. **Parking:** on-site. **Terms:** 2 night minimum stay - seasonal, cancellation fee imposed, [CP] meal plan available. **Amenities:** high-speed Internet, dual phone lines, voice mail, irons, hair dryers. **Pool(s):** heated indoor. **Leisure Activities:** whirlpool, exercise room. **Guest Services:** valet and coin laundry. **Business Services:** business center. **Cards:** AX, DS, MC, VI.

SOME UNITS

RAMADA INN OF BATESVILLE
Book at AAA.com

Phone: (870)698-1800

All Year	1P: $64-$148	2P: $70-$149	XP: $6	F17

Small-scale Hotel **Location:** 1 mi n on US 167. 1325 N St Louis St 72501. **Fax:** 870/698-1800. **Facility:** 122 units. 121 one-bedroom standard units, some with whirlpools. 1 one-bedroom suite with whirlpool. 2 stories (no elevator), exterior corridors. **Parking:** on-site. **Terms:** cancellation fee imposed, [BP] meal plan available, small pets only. **Amenities:** high-speed Internet, voice mail, irons, hair dryers. **Pool(s):** outdoor. **Leisure Activities:** whirlpool. **Guest Services:** valet and coin laundry. **Business Services:** meeting rooms. **Cards:** AX, DS, MC, VI.

SOME UNITS

SUPER 8 MOTEL-BATESVILLE
Book at AAA.com

Phone: (870)793-5888

All Year [CP]	1P: $59-$62	2P: $59-$62	XP: $5	F17

Motel **Location:** 1 mi n on US 167. 1287 N St Louis St 72501. **Fax:** 870/793-2422. **Facility:** 49 one-bedroom standard units. 2 stories (no elevator), interior corridors. **Parking:** on-site. **Terms:** pets ($25 fee). **Amenities:** high-speed Internet. **Guest Services:** valet laundry. **Cards:** AX, CB, DC, DS, JC, MC, VI.

SOME UNITS

——— WHERE TO DINE ———

COLTON'S STEAKHOUSE & GRILL
Lunch: $6-$8   **Dinner:** $9-$19   **Phone:** 870/793-7427

Steak House **Location:** 0.4 mi s of jct E Harrison St. 5 Eagle Mountain Dr 72501. **Hours:** 11 am-9 pm, Fri & Sat-10 pm. Closed: 11/22, 12/25. **Features:** A bucket of peanuts on the table, an upbeat Old-West atmosphere and a good selection of steak, chicken and ribs await guests at the casual steakhouse. Casual dress; cocktails. **Parking:** on-site. **Cards:** AX, DC, DS, MC, VI.

BEEBE pop. 4,930

———— WHERE TO STAY ————

DAYS INN *Book great rates at AAA.com*
Phone: (501)882-2008
▼▼▼
All Year   1P: $60-$120   2P: $60-$120   XP: $7   F16
Location: US 67/167, exit 28, just e. 100 Tammy Ln 72012. Fax: 501/882-2018. **Facility:** 40 one-bedroom
Small-scale Hotel standard units. 2 stories (no elevator), exterior corridors. *Bath:* combo or shower only. **Parking:** on-site.
Terms: cancellation fee imposed, package plans, pets ($10 extra charge). **Amenities:** high-speed Internet,
voice mail, irons, hair dryers. **Pool(s):** outdoor. **Guest Services:** coin laundry, wireless Internet. **Cards:** AX, DC, DS, MC, VI.

SOME UNITS

(ASK) (S/D) [🛏️] [¶+] [⛄] [🏊] [🐾] [🖥️] [🖨️] / [✕] /
FEE

BELLA VISTA pop. 16,582

———— WHERE TO STAY ————

———— *The following lodging was either not evaluated or did not* ————
meet AAA rating requirements but is listed for your information only.

VACATION RENTALS BELLA VISTA VILLAGE
Phone: 479/855-1111
[fyi] Not evaluated. **Location:** Jct US 71 and SR 340. 430 Town Center 72714. Facilities, services, and decor characterize
a mid-range property.

BENTON pop. 21,906

———— WHERE TO DINE ————

COLTON'S STEAKHOUSE & GRILL   Lunch: $6-$8   Dinner: $9-$19   Phone: 501/778-6100
▼▼ ◆◆
Location: Just w of jct Congo Rd. 1925 Landers Dr 72015. **Hours:** 11 am-9 pm, Fri & Sat-10 pm. Closed: 11/22,
12/25. **Features:** A bucket of peanuts on the table, an upbeat Old-West atmosphere and a good selection of
Steak House steak, chicken and ribs await guests at the casual steakhouse. Casual dress; cocktails. **Parking:** on-site.
Cards: AX, DC, DS, MC, VI.

[🍽️] [✂️]

DIXIE CAFE   Lunch: $7-$10   Dinner: $7-$10   Phone: 501/315-6200
▼▼
Location: I-30, exit 25. 17306 I-30 72015. **Hours:** 11 am-10 pm. Closed: 11/22, 12/25. **Features:** Southern-style
home cooking-chicken-fried steak, meat loaf, pork chops, turnip greens, mashed potatoes and fresh
Regional American veggies-appeals to families who visit the restaurant's classic "Norman Rockwell" atmosphere. Casual dress.
Parking: on-site. **Cards:** AX, DC, DS, MC, VI.

———— *The following restaurant has not been evaluated by AAA* ————
but is listed for your information only.

WENG'S CHINA BUFFET
Phone: 501/776-0888
[fyi] Not evaluated. **Location:** I-30, exit 118, just s on west service road. 17332 Hwy I-30 72015. **Features:** Set up for
both lunch and dinner, the buffet lines up a wide variety of favorite dishes.

BENTONVILLE pop. 19,730

———— WHERE TO STAY ————

CLARION HOTEL & CONVENTION CENTER   *Book great rates at AAA.com*   Phone: 479/464-4600

Property failed to provide current rates

Small-scale Hotel   **Location:** I-540, exit 85, 1 mi n on US 71B. 211 SE Walton Blvd 72712. Fax: 479/464-4204. **Facility:** 105 units. 99 one-bedroom standard units, some with whirlpools. 6 one-bedroom suites. 3 stories, interior/exterior corridors. *Bath:* combo or shower only. **Parking:** on-site. **Amenities:** video games (fee), high-speed Internet, dual phone lines, voice mail, irons, hair dryers. **Pool(s):** heated indoor. **Leisure Activities:** exercise room. **Guest Services:** valet and coin laundry, wireless Internet. **Business Services:** conference facilities, business center.

SOME UNITS

COMFORT INN   *Book great rates at AAA.com*   Phone: 479/271-9400

All Year   1P: $85-$155   2P: $85-$155

Small-scale Hotel   **Location:** I-540, exit 85, just n on US 71 business route. 3609 Moberly Ln 72712. Fax: 479/271-7222. **Facility:** 64 one-bedroom standard units, some with whirlpools. 2 stories (no elevator), exterior corridors. **Parking:** on-site. **Terms:** cancellation fee imposed. **Amenities:** high-speed Internet, voice mail, irons, hair dryers. **Pool(s):** heated indoor. **Leisure Activities:** whirlpool, limited exercise equipment. **Guest Services:** valet and coin laundry, wireless Internet. **Business Services:** meeting rooms, PC. **Cards:** AX, DC, DS, JC, MC, VI. **Free Special Amenities: expanded continental breakfast and high-speed Internet.**

SOME UNITS

COURTYARD BY MARRIOTT   *Book great rates at AAA.com*   Phone: (479)273-3333

All Year [AP]   1P: $59-$149   2P: $59-$149

Small-scale Hotel   **Location:** US 71, exit 88, just e on SR 72. Located in Beau Terre Office Park. 1001 McClain Rd 72712. Fax: 479/273-3877. **Facility:** Smoke free premises. 90 units. 87 one-bedroom standard units, some with whirlpools. 3 one-bedroom suites. 3 stories, interior corridors. *Bath:* combo or shower only. **Dining:** 6:30-10 am, Sat & Sun 7-11 am. **Amenities:** dual phone lines, voice mail, irons, hair dryers. **Pool(s):** heated indoor. **Leisure Activities:** whirlpool, exercise room. **Guest Services:** valet and coin laundry, wireless Internet. **Business Services:** meeting rooms, business center. **Cards:** AX, CB, DC, DS, JC, MC, VI.

SOME UNITS

HILTON GARDEN INN   *Book great rates at AAA.com*   Phone: (479)464-7300

All Year   1P: $59-$159   2P: $59-$159

Small-scale Hotel   **Location:** I-540, exit 85, just w. 2204 SE Walton Blvd 72712. Fax: 479/464-7377. **Facility:** 133 one-bedroom standard units. 3 stories, interior corridors. *Bath:* combo or shower only. **Parking:** on-site. **Terms:** cancellation fee imposed, package plans. **Amenities:** video games (fee), high-speed Internet, dual phone lines, voice mail, irons, hair dryers. **Pool(s):** heated indoor. **Leisure Activities:** whirlpool, exercise room. **Guest Services:** sundries, valet and coin laundry, wireless Internet. **Business Services:** meeting rooms, business center. **Cards:** AX, CB, DC, DS, JC, MC, VI.

SOME UNITS

LA QUINTA INN & SUITES   *Book great rates at AAA.com*   Phone: 479/271-7555

All Year   1P: $134-$164   2P: $134-$164

Small-scale Hotel   **Location:** I-540, exit 85, 0.7 mi w. 1001 SE Walton Blvd 72712. Fax: 479/271-6262. **Facility:** 107 units. 95 one-bedroom standard units. 12 one-bedroom suites, some with efficiencies. 3 stories, interior corridors. *Bath:* combo or shower only. **Parking:** on-site. **Terms:** weekly rates available, small pets only. **Amenities:** video library, voice mail, irons, hair dryers. *Some:* DVD players. **Pool(s):** heated indoor. **Leisure Activities:** whirlpool, exercise room. **Guest Services:** sundries, valet and coin laundry, wireless Internet. **Business Services:** meeting rooms, business center. **Cards:** AX, DC, DS, MC, VI.

SOME UNITS

SLEEP INN   *Book great rates at AAA.com*   **Phone:** 479/464-4400
▼▼▼   Property failed to provide current rates
                 Location: I-540, exit 85, 1 mi n on US 71B. 215 SE Walton Blvd 72712. **Fax:** 479/464-4188. **Facility:** 103 one-
Small-scale Hotel bedroom standard units. 2 stories, interior corridors. *Bath:* combo or shower only. **Parking:** on-site.
                 Amenities: high-speed Internet, voice mail, irons, hair dryers. **Pool(s):** small heated outdoor. **Guest**
Services: valet and coin laundry. **Business Services:** PC.

SOME UNITS

✈ 🛁 ➤ 🎥 ▣ / ✕ /

SPRINGHILL SUITES BY MARRIOTT   *Book great rates at AAA.com*   **Phone:** (479)464-4777
▼▼▼   All Year [ECP]·   1P: $66-$149   2P: $66-$149   XP: $10   F
                 Location: I-540, exit 85, just w. 2304 SE Walton Blvd 72712. **Fax:** 479/464-4477. **Facility:** Smoke free premises.
Small-scale Hotel 67 one-bedroom standard units. 3 stories, interior corridors. *Bath:* combo or shower only. **Parking:** on-site.
                 Terms: cancellation fee imposed, 13% service charge. **Amenities:** high-speed Internet, dual phone lines,
voice mail, irons, hair dryers. **Pool(s):** heated indoor. **Leisure Activities:** whirlpool, exercise room. **Guest Services:** sundries,
valet and coin laundry, wireless Internet. **Business Services:** meeting rooms, business center. **Cards:** AX, CB, DC, DS, VI.

ASK ❙↑❙ 🐾 ➤ ✕ 🎥 🖥 🖵 ▣

TOWNEPLACE SUITES BY MARRIOTT
BENTONVILLE/ROGERS   *Book great rates at AAA.com*   **Phone:** 479/621-0202
▼▼▼   All Year [CP]   1P: $134-$189   2P: $134-$189
                 Location: I-540, exit 86, just e. 3100 SE 14th St 72712. **Fax:** 479/621-0212. **Facility:** Smoke free premises. 78
Small-scale Hotel units. 65 one-bedroom standard units with kitchens. 9 one- and 4 two-bedroom suites, some with
                 efficiencies or kitchens. 4 stories, interior corridors. *Bath:* combo or shower only. **Parking:** on-site.
Terms: weekly rates available, pets ($75 fee). **Amenities:** video library, DVD players, high-speed Internet, dual phone lines,
voice mail, irons, hair dryers. **Pool(s):** small heated indoor. **Leisure Activities:** exercise room. **Guest Services:** valet and coin
laundry, wireless Internet. **Business Services:** meeting rooms, business center. **Cards:** AX, CB, DC, DS, JC, MC, VI.

ASK 🆂 🐾 🅼 ♿ 🛁 ➤ ✕ 🎥 🖥 🖵 ▣
                                          FEE

----
*The following lodging was either not evaluated or did not
meet AAA rating requirements but is listed for your information only.*

HOLIDAY INN EXPRESS   **Phone:** 479/271-2222
[fyi]   Did not meet all AAA rating requirements for some property operations at time of last evaluation on
                 03/02/2006. **Location:** I-540, exit 85, just w. 2205 SE Walton Blvd 72712. Facilities, services, and decor characterize a
Small-scale Hotel mid-range property.

-------- **WHERE TO DINE** --------

BRIOSO BRAZIL   **Lunch:** $9-$11   **Dinner:** $18-$32   **Phone:** 479/254-9933
▼▼▼   **Location:** I-540, exit 85, just w. 3607 Magelian 72712. **Hours:** 11 am-1:30 & 5-9 pm, Sat from 5 pm. Closed: 1/1,
                 11/22, 12/25; also Sun. **Reservations:** accepted. **Features:** Patrons appreciate the distinctive service and
Brazilian   choice at the sophisticated American churrascaria. Varied side dishes accompany more than 40 choices of
                 protein entrees. Casual dress; beer & wine only. **Parking:** on-site. **Cards:** AX, DC, DS, MC, VI.   ❙Y❙

MONTANA MIKE'S STEAKHOUSE   **Lunch:** $6-$16   **Dinner:** $8-$16   **Phone:** 479/464-8816
▼▼▼   **Location:** Just n of jct SR 72. 301 N Walton Blvd 72712. **Hours:** 11 am-9 pm, Fri & Sat-10 pm. Closed: 11/22,
                 12/25. **Features:** This steakhouse offers a dining experience for the whole family. A rustic look with Western
Steak House   appointments characterizes the dining room. Although it's hard to go wrong with a hearty steak of USDA
                 Choice aged beef, guests also can try smoked, fire-grilled chicken breast, chicken-fried steak, baby back
ribs and other selections. Casual dress; cocktails. **Parking:** on-site. **Cards:** AX, DS, MC, VI.   ❙Y❙ ◣

RIVER GRILLE   **Lunch:** $6-$10   **Dinner:** $20-$38   **Phone:** 479/271-4141
▼▼▼   **Location:** I-540, exit 88, just e. 1003 McClain Rd 72712. **Hours:** 11 am-2:30 & 4:30-9:30 pm, Sat from 5 pm.
                 Closed major holidays; also Sun. **Reservations:** suggested. **Features:** Service is sophisticated and the
American   cuisine of excellent quality at the classy grill. Creative presentation marks the wonderful creme brulee.
                 Dressy casual; cocktails. **Parking:** on-site. **Cards:** AX, CB, DC, DS, JC, MC, VI.   ❙Y❙ ◣

BERRYVILLE pop. 4,433

-------- **WHERE TO STAY** --------

FAIRWAY MOTOR INN   **Phone:** 870-423-3395
AAA [SAVE]   4/22-11/10   1P: $49-$70   2P: $60-$75   XP: $6   D8
                 3/1-4/21, 11/11-12/21 & 1/2-2/29   1P: $37-$50   2P: $42-$65   XP: $6   D8
▼   **Location:** On US 62, 2.5 mi w. Located in a rural area. 577 Hwy 62 W 72616. **Fax:** 870/423-3055. **Facility:** 21 one-
                 bedroom standard units. 2 stories (no elevator), exterior corridors. **Parking:** on-site. **Terms:** open 3/1-12/21
Motel   & 1/2-2/29. **Pool(s):** outdoor. **Leisure Activities:** basketball, horseshoes. **Cards:** DS, MC, VI.
                 Free Special Amenities: local telephone calls.

SOME UNITS

❙↑❙ ➤ 🎥 / ✕ 🖥 /
                                          FEE

BLYTHEVILLE pop. 18,272

──────── WHERE TO STAY ────────

COMFORT INN OF BLYTHEVILLE   *Book great rates at AAA.com*   Phone: 870/763-7081

Small-scale Hotel

All Year   1P: $59-$69   2P: $59-$69   XP: $5   F18
Location: I-55, exit 67, just w. 1520 E Main 72315 (PO Box 1408). Fax: 870/762-5721. **Facility:** 105 one-bedroom standard units. 2 stories (no elevator), exterior corridors. **Parking:** on-site. **Terms:** 7 day cancellation notice, [CP] meal plan available, pets ($15 fee). **Amenities:** irons, hair dryers. **Pool(s):** outdoor. **Guest Services:** valet laundry, wireless Internet. **Business Services:** meeting rooms. **Cards:** AX, DC, DS, MC, VI.

SOME UNITS
ASK SD 🛏 🍴 🏊 📶 🎥 💻 / ✕ 🔒 /
FEE

HAMPTON INN   *Book great rates at AAA.com*   Phone: 870/763-5220

Small-scale Hotel

All Year   1P: $79-$109   2P: $79-$109
Location: I-55, exit 67, just nw. 301 N Access Rd 72315 (PO Box 1408). Fax: 870/762-1397. **Facility:** 87 one-bedroom standard units. 2 stories, exterior corridors. **Terms:** pets ($10 fee). **Amenities:** video games (fee), voice mail, irons, hair dryers. **Pool(s):** small outdoor. **Guest Services:** valet laundry, wireless Internet. **Business Services:** PC. **Cards:** AX, CB, DC, DS, JC, MC, VI.

SOME UNITS
ASK SD 🛏 🍴 🏊 🎥 💻 / ✕ /
FEE

HOLIDAY INN   *Book at AAA.com*   Phone: 870/763-5800

Small-scale Hotel

All Year   1P: $99-$129   2P: $109-$139   XP: $10   F18
Location: I-55, exit 67, just w. 1121 E Main 72315 (PO Box 72316). Fax: 870/763-1326. **Facility:** 152 units. 149 one-bedroom standard units. 3 one-bedroom suites. 2 stories (no elevator), interior/exterior corridors. **Parking:** on-site. **Terms:** small pets only ($15 fee). **Amenities:** video games (fee), dual phone lines, voice mail, irons, hair dryers. **Pool(s):** outdoor, heated indoor. **Leisure Activities:** whirlpool, exercise room. **Guest Services:** valet and coin laundry, wireless Internet. **Business Services:** conference facilities, business center. **Cards:** AX, CB, DC, DS, JC, MC, VI.

SOME UNITS
ASK SD 🛏 🍴 🏊 🎥 🔒 💻 / ✕ /
FEE

SUPER 8 MOTEL-BLYTHEVEILLE   *Book at AAA.com*   Phone: (870)763-2300

Small-scale Hotel

All Year   1P: $57-$62   2P: $62-$69   XP: $5   F18
Location: I-55, exit 67, just nw. 239 N Service Rd 72315. Fax: 870/763-2300. **Facility:** 51 one-bedroom standard units. 3 stories (no elevator), interior corridors. **Parking:** on-site. **Terms:** pets ($5 extra charge). **Amenities:** high-speed Internet, irons, hair dryers. **Guest Services:** valet and coin laundry. **Cards:** AX, DS, MC, VI.

SOME UNITS
ASK SD 🛏 🍴 📶 🎥 💻 / ✕ 🔒 🖨 /
FEE

──────── WHERE TO DINE ────────

OLYMPIA   Lunch: $6-$18   Dinner: $9-$18   Phone: 870/838-1204

Steak & Seafood

Location: I-55, exit 67, just w. I-55 & SR 18 72315. **Hours:** 11 am-9:30 pm, Fri & Sat-10:30 pm. **Closed:** 5/28, 7/4. **Features:** A selection of steak, seafood and pasta dishes is served in a comfortable atmosphere. Casual dress; cocktails. **Parking:** on-site. **Cards:** AX, DS, MC, VI.

🔲

BRINKLEY pop. 3,940

──────── WHERE TO STAY ────────

AMERIHOST INN   *Book at AAA.com*   Phone: 870/734-4300

Small-scale Hotel

Property failed to provide current rates
Location: I-40, exit 216, just n. 1815 N Main St 72021. Fax: 870/734-3579. **Facility:** 60 one-bedroom standard units, some with whirlpools. 2 stories (no elevator), interior corridors. *Bath:* combo or shower only. **Parking:** on-site. **Amenities:** safes, irons, hair dryers. **Pool(s):** heated indoor. **Leisure Activities:** whirlpool, exercise room. **Guest Services:** coin laundry, wireless Internet.

SOME UNITS
🏊 🎥 💻 / ✕ 🔒 🖨 /

BRYANT pop. 9,764

──────── WHERE TO STAY ────────

AMERICAS BEST VALUE INN & SUITES   *Book at AAA.com*   Phone: (501)653-7800

Motel

All Year [CP]   1P: $48-$68   2P: $48-$78   XP: $6   F12
Location: I-30, exit 123, just sw. 407 W Commerce St 72022. Fax: 501/847-8496. **Facility:** 32 one-bedroom standard units, some with whirlpools. 2 stories (no elevator), exterior corridors. **Parking:** on-site, winter plug-ins. **Terms:** pets ($6 extra charge). **Amenities:** voice mail, hair dryers. **Guest Services:** wireless Internet. **Cards:** AX, CB, DC, DS, JC, MC, VI.

SOME UNITS
ASK SD 🛏 🍴 🎥 💻 / ✕ 🔒 🖨 /
FEE

COMFORT INN & SUITES   *Book great rates at AAA.com*   Phone: 501/653-4000

Small-scale Hotel

Property failed to provide current rates
Location: I-30, exit 123, just w. 209 W Commerce St 72022 (PO Box 112, 72089). Fax: 501/653-0973. **Facility:** 78 units. 74 one-bedroom standard units, some with whirlpools. 4 one-bedroom suites. 3 stories, interior corridors. *Bath:* combo or shower only. **Parking:** on-site. **Terms:** pets ($25 extra charge). **Amenities:** high-speed Internet, dual phone lines, voice mail, safes (fee), irons, hair dryers. **Pool(s):** heated indoor. **Leisure Activities:** putting green, exercise room, basketball. **Guest Services:** valet and coin laundry, wireless Internet. **Business Services:** meeting rooms, business center.

SOME UNITS
🛏 🍴 🏊 ✕ 🎥 💻 / ✕ 🔒 🖨 /
FEE

HOLIDAY INN EXPRESS *Book great rates at AAA.com* Phone: (501)847-0900

All Year 1P: $89-$119 2P: $89-$119 XP: $8 F18
Location: I-30, exit 123, just n on west service road. 2915 Main St 72022. Fax: 501/847-3787. **Facility:** 64 one-bedroom standard units, some with whirlpools. 2 stories, interior corridors. *Bath:* combo or shower only. **Parking:** on-site. **Amenities:** high-speed Internet, voice mail, irons, hair dryers. **Pool(s):** outdoor. **Guest Services:** valet and coin laundry. **Business Services:** meeting rooms. **Cards:** AX, CB, DC, DS, MC, VI. **Free Special Amenities:** continental breakfast and high-speed Internet.

Small-scale Hotel

SOME UNITS

SUPER 8 MOTEL *Book at AAA.com* Phone: 501/847-7888

All Year [CP] 1P: $49-$52 2P: $53-$56 XP: $5 F12
Location: I-30, exit 123, just e. 201 Dell Dr 72022. Fax: 501/847-7888. **Facility:** 33 one-bedroom standard units, some with whirlpools. 2 stories (no elevator), exterior corridors. **Parking:** on-site. **Terms:** pets ($5 fee, $20 deposit). **Amenities:** hair dryers. **Cards:** AX, CB, DC, DS, JC, MC, VI.

Motel

SOME UNITS

FEE

—— WHERE TO DINE ——

TA MOLLY'S Lunch: $6-$9 Dinner: $6-$9 Phone: 501/653-2600

Location: I-30, exit 123, just w. 206 W Commerce St 72022. **Hours:** 11 am-9 pm, Fri & Sat-10 pm. Closed: 11/22, 12/25. **Features:** Hearty portions of Mexican cuisine are served promptly in the inviting dining room. Casual dress. **Parking:** on-site. **Cards:** AX, DS, MC, VI.

Mexican

CABOT pop. 15,261

—— WHERE TO STAY ——

SUPER 8 OF CABOT *Book at AAA.com* Phone: (501)941-3748

All Year [CP] 1P: $55-$64 2P: $59-$64 XP: $5 F17
Location: US 67/167, exit 19 (SR 89), just e. 15 Ryeland Dr 72023. Fax: 501/941-5838. **Facility:** 40 one-bedroom standard units. 2 stories (no elevator), exterior corridors. **Parking:** on-site. **Terms:** pets ($5 extra charge). **Amenities:** hair dryers. *Some:* irons. **Pool(s):** outdoor. **Guest Services:** wireless Internet. **Cards:** AX, DC, DS, MC, VI.

Motel
DS, MC, VI.

SOME UNITS

FEE

—— WHERE TO DINE ——

DIXIE CAFE Lunch: $7-$10 Dinner: $7-$10 Phone: 501/843-1700

Location: Just sw of jct Main St. 302 S Rockwood Dr 72023. **Hours:** 11 am-10 pm. Closed: 11/22, 12/25. **Features:** Southern-style home cooking-chicken-fried steak, meat loaf, pork chops, turnip greens, mashed potatoes and fresh veggies-appeals to families who visit the restaurant's classic "Norman Rockwell" atmosphere. Casual dress. **Parking:** on-site. **Cards:** AX, DC, DS, MC, VI.

Regional American

CAMDEN pop. 13,154

—— WHERE TO STAY ——

COMFORT INN *Book great rates at AAA.com* Phone: (870)836-9000

All Year 1P: $90-$100 2P: $90-$100 XP: $10 F12
Location: Just w of jct US 79 and 278. 1 Ridgecrest Dr 71701. Fax: 870/836-9003. **Facility:** 69 one-bedroom standard units, some with whirlpools. 3 stories, interior corridors. *Bath:* combo or shower only. **Parking:** on-site. **Terms:** package plans. **Amenities:** dual phone lines, voice mail, safes (fee), irons, hair dryers. *Some:* high-speed Internet. **Pool(s):** heated indoor. **Leisure Activities:** putting green, exercise room, sports court. **Guest Services:** valet and coin laundry, wireless Internet. **Business Services:** meeting rooms, business center. **Cards:** AX, CB, DC, DS, JC, MC, VI.

Small-scale Hotel

SOME UNITS

HOLIDAY INN EXPRESS *Book at AAA.com* Phone: (870)836-8100

All Year [ECP] 1P: $90-$110 2P: $90-$110
Location: 1 mi w of jct US 79 and 278. 1450 US Hwy 278 W 71701. Fax: 870/837-2300. **Facility:** 64 one-bedroom standard units, some with whirlpools. Interior corridors. *Bath:* combo or shower only. **Parking:** on-site. **Amenities:** high-speed Internet, dual phone lines, voice mail, irons, hair dryers. **Pool(s):** outdoor. **Guest Services:** valet and coin laundry. **Business Services:** meeting rooms, business center. **Cards:** AX, CB, DC, DS, JC, MC, VI.

Small-scale Hotel

SOME UNITS

CLARKSVILLE pop. 7,719

—— WHERE TO STAY ——

BEST WESTERN SHERWOOD INN *Book great rates at AAA.com* Phone: (479)754-7900

All Year [CP] 1P: $42-$74 2P: $42-$74
Location: I-40, exit 58, just n. 1203 S Rogers Ave 72830 (PO Box 146). Fax: 479/754-7900. **Facility:** 53 units. 52 one-bedroom standard units. 1 two-bedroom suite with kitchen. 2 stories (no elevator), exterior corridors. **Parking:** on-site. **Terms:** 10 day cancellation notice. **Amenities:** high-speed Internet, irons, hair dryers. **Pool(s):** small outdoor. **Leisure Activities:** whirlpool. **Guest Services:** coin laundry. **Business Services:** PC. **Cards:** AX, CB, DC, DS, MC, VI. **Free Special Amenities:** continental breakfast and high-speed Internet.

Small-scale Hotel

SOME UNITS

COMFORT INN

(AAA) (SAVE)

⬥⬥⬥⬥

Small-scale Hotel

Book great rates at AAA.com

5/1-10/31   1P: $74-$130   2P: $74-$130   XP: $5   F18
3/1-4/30 & 11/1-2/29   1P: $69-$120   2P: $69-$120   XP: $5   F18

Phone: (479)754-3000

Location: I-40, exit 58, just n. 1167 S Rogers Ave 72830. Fax: 479/754-4131. **Facility:** 51 one-bedroom standard units, some with whirlpools. 2-3 stories (no elevator), exterior corridors. **Parking:** on-site. **Terms:** package plans, pets ($20 extra charge). **Amenities:** high-speed Internet, irons, hair dryers. **Pool(s):** small outdoor. **Guest Services:** valet and coin laundry. **Business Services:** business center. **Cards:** AX, CB, DC, DS, JC, MC, VI. **Free Special Amenities:** expanded continental breakfast and high-speed Internet.

SOME UNITS

[icons] FEE / [icons] /

HAMPTON INN CLARKSVILLE

(AAA) (SAVE)

⬥⬥⬥⬥

Small-scale Hotel

Book great rates at AAA.com

All Year   1P: $70   2P: $82

Phone: (479)754-4444

Location: I-40, exit 55, just n. 2630 W Clark Rd 72830. Fax: 479/754-4447. **Facility:** 62 one-bedroom standard units, some with whirlpools. 2 stories, interior corridors. *Bath:* combo or shower only. **Parking:** on-site. **Terms:** weekly rates available, [ECP] meal plan available. **Amenities:** video games (fee), voice mail, irons, hair dryers. **Pool(s):** heated indoor. **Leisure Activities:** whirlpool. **Guest Services:** coin laundry, wireless Internet. **Business Services:** meeting rooms, business center. **Cards:** AX, CB, DC, DS, MC, VI. **Free Special Amenities:** expanded continental breakfast and newspaper.

SOME UNITS

[icons] FEE / [icons] /

CONWAY pop. 43,167

———— **WHERE TO STAY** ————

DAYS INN

(AAA) (SAVE)

⬥⬥⬥

Small-scale Hotel

Book great rates at AAA.com

All Year [CP]   1P: $59-$119   2P: $59-$119   XP: $8   F18

Phone: (501)450-7575

Location: I-40, exit 127, just n. 1002 E Oak St 72032 (PO Box 1424, 72033). Fax: 501/450-7001. **Facility:** 58 one-bedroom standard units, some with efficiencies and/or whirlpools. 2 stories (no elevator), exterior corridors. *Bath:* combo or shower only. **Parking:** on-site. **Terms:** cancellation fee imposed, pets ($20 fee). **Amenities:** irons, hair dryers. **Pool(s):** small outdoor. **Guest Services:** valet laundry, wireless Internet. **Business Services:** meeting rooms. **Cards:** AX, CB, DC, DS, JC, MC, VI. **Free Special Amenities:** continental breakfast and high-speed Internet.

SOME UNITS

[icons] FEE / [icons] /

HAMPTON INN

(AAA) (SAVE)

⬥⬥⬥

Small-scale Hotel

Book great rates at AAA.com

All Year [BP]   1P: $66-$150   2P: $72-$150   XP: $6   F18

Phone: (501)329-8999

Location: I-40, exit 127, just n. 810 Museum Rd 72032. Fax: 501/327-9388. **Facility:** 75 one-bedroom standard units, some with whirlpools. 3 stories, interior corridors. *Bath:* combo or shower only. **Parking:** on-site. **Amenities:** voice mail, irons, hair dryers. **Pool(s):** outdoor. **Leisure Activities:** exercise room. **Guest Services:** valet and coin laundry, wireless Internet. **Business Services:** meeting rooms. **Cards:** AX, CB, DC, DS, MC, VI. **Free Special Amenities:** expanded continental breakfast and high-speed Internet.

SOME UNITS

[icons] / [icons] /

HOLIDAY INN EXPRESS HOTEL & SUITES

(AAA) (SAVE)

⬥⬥⬥

Small-scale Hotel

Book great rates at AAA.com

All Year [ECP]   1P: $79-$125   2P: $79-$125   XP: $8   F18

Phone: (501)450-9112

Location: I-40, exit 125, just s. 2370 Sanders St 72033 (PO Box 1013). Fax: 501/450-6331. **Facility:** 69 one-bedroom standard units, some with whirlpools. 3 stories, interior corridors. *Bath:* combo or shower only. **Parking:** on-site. **Terms:** 30 day cancellation notice-fee imposed. **Amenities:** high-speed Internet, dual phone lines, voice mail, irons, hair dryers. **Pool(s):** small heated indoor. **Leisure Activities:** exercise room. **Guest Services:** valet and coin laundry, wireless Internet. **Business Services:** meeting rooms, business center. **Cards:** AX, CB, DC, DS, JC, MC, VI. **Free Special Amenities:** newspaper and high-speed Internet.

SOME UNITS

[icons] / [icons] /

QUALITY INN

(AAA) (SAVE)

⬥⬥⬥

Small-scale Hotel

Book great rates at AAA.com

All Year [CP]   1P: $69-$149   2P: $69-$149   XP: $8   F18

Phone: (501)329-0300

Location: I-40, exit 125, just n. 150 Hwy 65 N 72033 (PO Box 88). Fax: 501/329-8367. **Facility:** 60 one-bedroom standard units, some with efficiencies (no utensils) and/or whirlpools. 2 stories (no elevator), exterior corridors. **Parking:** on-site. **Terms:** cancellation fee imposed, pets ($20 fee). **Amenities:** dual phone lines, voice mail, irons, hair dryers. **Pool(s):** outdoor. **Guest Services:** valet laundry, wireless Internet. **Cards:** AX, CB, DC, DS, JC, MC, VI. **Free Special Amenities:** newspaper and high-speed Internet.

SOME UNITS

[icons] FEE / [icons] /

SUPER 8 MOTEL-CONWAY

⬥⬥ ⬥⬥

Small-scale Hotel

Book at AAA.com

All Year   1P: $61-$99   2P: $61-$99   XP: $5   F17

Phone: 501/505-8880

Location: I-40, exit 125. 2430 Sanders St 72032. Fax: 501/505-8884. **Facility:** 64 one-bedroom standard units, some with whirlpools. 2 stories (no elevator), interior corridors. *Bath:* combo or shower only. **Parking:** on-site. **Terms:** [ECP] meal plan available. **Amenities:** hair dryers. **Pool(s):** small heated indoor. **Guest Services:** valet and coin laundry, wireless Internet. **Business Services:** meeting rooms. **Cards:** AX, DC, DS, MC, VI.

SOME UNITS

[icons] / [icons] /

WHERE TO DINE

CHINA TOWN RESTAURANT

Chinese

Lunch: $4-$6   **Dinner:** $7-$9   **Phone:** 501/450-9090

Location: I-40, exit 125, just n; in Conway Towne Center. 201 Hwy 65 N, Suite 60 72032. **Hours:** 11 am-9:30 pm, Fri & Sat-10 pm, Sun-9 pm. Closed: 11/22, 12/25. **Features:** The food is hot, tasty and all-you-can-eat when you dine on the buffet at China Town, which features Mandarin and Cantonese dishes. The popular luncheon buffet is served Monday-Friday 11 am-2 pm and Sunday 11:30 am-3:30 pm and includes veggies and dessert. Casual dress. **Parking:** on-site. **Cards:** MC, VI.

COLTON'S STEAKHOUSE & GRILL

Steak House

Lunch: $6-$8   **Dinner:** $9-$19   **Phone:** 501/329-6454

Location: I-40, exit 127, just s. 120 E Oak 72032. **Hours:** 11 am-9 pm, Fri & Sat-10 pm. Closed: 11/22, 12/25. **Features:** A bucket of peanuts on the table, an upbeat Old-West atmosphere and a good selection of steak, chicken and ribs await guests at the casual steakhouse. Casual dress; cocktails. **Parking:** on-site. **Cards:** AX, DC, DS, MC, VI.

DIXIE CAFE

American

Lunch: $5-$8   **Dinner:** $5-$8   **Phone:** 501/327-4777

Location: I-40, exit 125, 0.5 mi s. 1101 Fendley Dr 72032. **Hours:** 11 am-10 pm. Closed: 11/22, 12/25. **Features:** Southern-style home cooking-chicken-fried steak, meat loaf, pork chops, turnip greens, mashed potatoes and fresh veggies-appeals to families who visit the restaurant's classic "Norman Rockwell" atmosphere. Casual dress. **Parking:** on-site. **Cards:** AX, DC, DS, MC, VI.

MARKETPLACE GRILL

American

Lunch: $8-$23   **Dinner:** $8-$23   **Phone:** 501/336-0011

Location: I-40, exit 125, just nw. 600 Skyline Dr 72032. **Hours:** 11 am-9 pm, Fri & Sat-10 pm. Closed: 1/1, 11/22, 12/25. **Features:** The restaurant is big on menu variety, incorporating freshly made pasta, pizzas, dressings and sauces. Steaks, Cajun dishes and seafood also are served in the spacious, inviting dining room. Casual dress. **Parking:** on-site. **Cards:** AX, CB, DC, DS, MC, VI.

MCALISTER'S DELI

Deli/Subs Sandwiches

Lunch: $4-$7   **Dinner:** $4-$7   **Phone:** 501/513-1311

Location: I-40, exit 125, just se. 2465 Sanders St 72032. **Hours:** 10:30 am-10 pm. **Features:** Patrons can choose from more than 30 sandwiches and 11 ways to have their extra-large baked potatoes served. Kentucky pie is a sinful favorite from the dessert menu. Casual dress. **Parking:** on-site. **Cards:** AX, DC, DS, MC, VI.

EL DORADO pop. 21,530

WHERE TO STAY

COUNTRY INN & SUITES   *Book at AAA.com*

Small-scale Hotel

Phone: (870)881-0455

All Year   1P: $85-$139   2P: $85-$139

Location: Just e of jct US 82 and 82B. 2413 W Hillsboro 71730. Fax: 870/881-9905. **Facility:** 70 units. 64 one-bedroom standard units. 6 one-bedroom suites, some with whirlpools. 3 stories, interior corridors. *Bath:* combo or shower only. **Parking:** on-site. **Terms:** [ECP] meal plan available. **Amenities:** high-speed Internet, voice mail, irons, hair dryers. **Pool(s):** heated indoor. **Leisure Activities:** whirlpool, exercise room. **Guest Services:** valet and coin laundry, wireless Internet. **Business Services:** meeting rooms, business center. **Cards:** AX, CB, DC, DS, JC, MC, VI.

SOME UNITS

HAMPTON INN   *Book great rates at AAA.com*

Small-scale Hotel

Phone: 870/862-1800

Property failed to provide current rates

Location: Just e of jct US 167 and 82B. 2312 Junction City Rd 71730. Fax: 870/862-9797. **Facility:** 69 one-bedroom standard units, some with whirlpools. 3 stories, interior corridors. *Bath:* combo or shower only. **Parking:** on-site. **Amenities:** high-speed Internet, dual phone lines, voice mail, irons, hair dryers. **Pool(s):** outdoor. **Leisure Activities:** whirlpool, exercise room. **Guest Services:** valet and coin laundry. **Business Services:** meeting rooms, business center.

SOME UNITS

LA QUINTA INN EL DORADO   *Book great rates at AAA.com*

Small-scale Hotel

Phone: (870)863-6677

All Year   1P: $55-$65   2P: $65-$75   XP: $5   F14

Location: Just e of jct US 167 and 82B. 2303 Junction City Rd 71730. Fax: 870/863-6677. **Facility:** 70 one-bedroom standard units. 2 stories (no elevator), interior/exterior corridors. *Bath:* combo or shower only. **Parking:** on-site. **Amenities:** high-speed Internet, voice mail, irons, hair dryers. **Pool(s):** outdoor. **Leisure Activities:** exercise room. **Guest Services:** coin laundry. **Business Services:** meeting rooms. **Cards:** AX, CB, DC, DS, JC, MC, VI.

SOME UNITS

EUREKA SPRINGS pop. 2,278

WHERE TO STAY

1881 CRESCENT COTTAGE INN

Historic Bed & Breakfast

Phone: 479/253-6022

All Year   2P: $109-$149

Location: 0.5 mi n on US 62B Historic Loop; downtown. Located in a residential area. 211 Spring St 72632. Fax: 479/253-6234. **Facility:** Known as the first "Painted Lady" in town, the property is located near the Crescent Spring Gazebo. Cozy rooms are decorated with antiques of the era. Smoke free premises. 4 units. 3 one-bedroom standard units with whirlpools. 1 one-bedroom suite with whirlpool. 3 stories (no elevator), interior/exterior corridors. **Parking:** street. **Terms:** age restrictions may apply, 10 day cancellation notice-fee imposed, no pets allowed (owner's pet on premises). **Amenities:** video library. **Cards:** DS, MC, VI.

SOME UNITS

1886 CRESCENT HOTEL & SPA

Book great rates at AAA.com   Phone: (479)253-9766

(AAA) [SAVE]

[VVV VVV]

Historic
Small-scale Hotel

9/29-10/31	1P: $133-$164	2P: $133-$164
5/14-9/28	1P: $119-$153	2P: $119-$153
11/1-2/29	1P: $93-$149	2P: $93-$149
3/1-5/13	1P: $109-$139	2P: $109-$139

Location: 1.3 mi n of jct SR 23 on US 62B Historic Loop. 75 Prospect Ave 72632. Fax: 479/253-5296. **Facility:** Circa 1886 and known as the "Grand Old Lady of the Ozarks"; the lobby and rooms have been restored to their original style of decor. Smoke free premises. 72 units. 64 one-bedroom standard units. 7 one- and 1 two-bedroom suites ($159-$199), some with whirlpools. 5 stories, interior corridors. **Parking:** on-site. **Terms:** 2 night minimum stay - weekends, 3 day cancellation notice-fee imposed, [AP] meal plan imposed, 3% service charge, small pets only ($10 extra charge). **Amenities:** irons, hair dryers. *Some:* high-speed Internet. **Dining:** 2 restaurants, 7 am-10 & 11-9 pm, also, The Crystal Dining Room, see separate listing. **Pool(s):** outdoor. **Leisure Activities:** sauna, hiking trails, spa. *Fee:* country club privileges, victorian wedding court. **Guest Services:** gift shop, area transportation, wireless Internet. **Business Services:** meeting rooms. **Cards:** AX, DS, MC, VI. **Free Special Amenities:** local telephone calls and high-speed Internet. *(See color ad below)*

SOME UNITS
[S/D] [icons] FEE [icons] FEE [icons] / [icons]

1905 BASIN PARK HOTEL

Book at AAA.com   Phone: (479)253-7837

[VV VV]

Historic
Small-scale Hotel

9/29-10/31	1P: $139	2P: $139
5/14-9/28	1P: $119	2P: $119
11/1-2/29	1P: $109	2P: $109
3/1-5/13	1P: $93	2P: $93

Location: 0.7 mi n of jct US 62 via SR 23 N; downtown. 12 Spring St 72632. Fax: 479/253-6985. **Facility:** Built in 1905, some units still have the original furnishings. 61 units. 47 one-bedroom standard units, some with whirlpools. 14 one-bedroom suites ($123-$229), some with whirlpools. 7 stories, interior corridors. *Bath:* combo or shower only. **Parking:** on-site (fee) and valet. **Terms:** 2 night minimum stay - weekends, 3 day cancellation notice-fee imposed, [AP] meal plan available, package plans, pets ($10 extra charge). **Amenities:** irons, hair dryers. *Some:* high-speed Internet. **Dining:** The Balcony Restaurant & Bar, see separate listing. **Pool(s):** small outdoor. **Leisure Activities:** spa. **Guest Services:** area transportation, wireless Internet. **Business Services:** conference facilities. **Cards:** AX, DS, MC, VI.

SOME UNITS
[ASK] [S/D] [icons] FEE [icons] / [icons] /

ANGEL AT ROSE HALL

Phone: 479/253-5405

(AAA) [SAVE]

[VVV VVV]

Bed & Breakfast

All Year [BP]   1P: $175-$185   2P: $175-$185

Location: 1.2 mi n on SR 23, then 0.3 mi sw. 46 Hillside 72632. Fax: 479/253-5405. **Facility:** The house features antique Victorian decor and five units with gas fireplaces. 5 one-bedroom standard units with whirlpools. 2 stories (no elevator), interior corridors. **Parking:** on-site. **Terms:** 2 night minimum stay, age restrictions may apply, 14 day cancellation notice-fee imposed, package plans. **Amenities:** video library, CD players, voice mail, hair dryers. *Some:* DVD players. **Leisure Activities:** gazebo, patio. *Fee:* country club privileges. **Guest Services:** wireless Internet. **Cards:** AX, DS, MC, VI. **Free Special Amenities:** full breakfast and high-speed Internet.

[S/D] [X] [VCR] [icon]

ARSENIC & OLD LACE B&B

Phone: (479)253-5454

[VVV]

Bed & Breakfast

All Year   2P: $139-$249

Location: 1.2 mi n on SR 23, just sw; downtown. Located in a residential area. 60 Hillside Ave 72632. Fax: 479/253-2246. **Facility:** Victorian antiques and stained-glass windows embellish the parlor of this B&B, and the rooms—each with a gas fireplace—vary in theme. 5 one-bedroom standard units with whirlpools. 3 stories (no elevator), interior/exterior corridors. **Parking:** on-site. **Terms:** 2 night minimum stay, age restrictions may apply, 15 day cancellation notice-fee imposed, [BP] meal plan available, package plans, pets (with prior approval, owner's pet on premises). **Amenities:** video library, CD players, irons, hair dryers. **Guest Services:** wireless Internet. **Cards:** AX, DS, MC, VI.

[ASK] [icon] [X] [VCR]

BAVARIAN INN

Phone: 479/253-8128

[VVV VVV]

Small-scale Hotel

Property failed to provide current rates

Location: 1 mi w of jct US 62 and SR 23. 325 W Van Buren St 72632. Fax: 479/253-7896. **Facility:** 21 one-bedroom standard units with whirlpools. 3 stories (no elevator), exterior corridors. **Parking:** on-site. **Terms:** open 3/1-11/27, office hours 8 am-9 pm, pets ($10 extra charge, with prior approval). **Amenities:** irons, hair dryers. *Some:* dual phone lines. **Dining:** restaurant, see separate listing. **Pool(s):** outdoor. **Guest Services:** gift shop. **Business Services:** meeting rooms.

SOME UNITS
[icons] FEE [icons] / [X] [icon]

BEST WESTERN-EUREKA INN

Book great rates at AAA.com

Phone: (479)253-9551

9/14-12/9 [BP]	1P: $69-$139	2P: $69-$139	XP: $8	F17
3/1-8/4 [BP]	1P: $59-$139	2P: $59-$139	XP: $8	F17
8/5-9/13 [BP]	1P: $54-$119	2P: $54-$119	XP: $8	F17
2/14-2/29 [BP]	1P: $49-$109	2P: $49-$109	XP: $8	F17

Small-scale Hotel **Location:** Just w of jct US 62 and SR 23 N. 101 E Van Buren St 72632. Fax: 479/253-9692. **Facility:** 85 one-bedroom standard units, some with whirlpools. 2 stories (no elevator), interior/exterior corridors. **Parking:** on-site. **Terms:** open 3/1-12/9 & 2/14-2/29, [AP] meal plan available, package plans, pets ($6 extra charge). **Amenities:** irons, hair dryers. *Some:* high-speed Internet. **Dining:** The Gazebo Restaurant, see separate listing. **Pool(s):** heated outdoor. **Leisure Activities:** sauna, whirlpool, exercise room. *Fee:* golf privileges. **Guest Services:** wireless Internet. **Business Services:** meeting rooms. **Cards:** AX, CB, DC, DS, MC, VI. **Free Special Amenities:** full breakfast and high-speed Internet.

SOME UNITS

BEST WESTERN INN OF THE OZARKS

Book great rates at AAA.com

Phone: (479)253-9768

6/8-10/27	1P: $69-$129	2P: $69-$129	XP: $6	F18
4/27-6/7	1P: $59-$119	2P: $59-$119	XP: $6	F18
10/28-2/29	1P: $49-$99	2P: $49-$99	XP: $6	F18
3/1-4/26	1P: $49-$89	2P: $49-$89	XP: $6	F18

Small-scale Hotel **Location:** On US 62, 0.5 mi w of jct SR 23. 207 W Van Buren St 72632 (PO Box 431). Fax: 479/253-9768. **Facility:** 122 units. 118 one-bedroom standard units, some with whirlpools. 4 one-bedroom suites ($119-$179). 2 stories (no elevator), exterior corridors. *Bath:* combo or shower only. **Parking:** on-site. **Terms:** 3 day cancellation notice, package plans, small pets only ($7 extra charge). **Amenities:** voice mail, irons, hair dryers. *Some:* high-speed Internet. **Dining:** Myrtie Mae's, see separate listing. **Leisure Activities:** whirlpool, lighted tennis court, table tennis, pavilion, barbecue grills, playground, shuffleboard. *Fee:* miniature golf, game room. **Guest Services:** gift shop, coin laundry, wireless Internet. **Business Services:** conference facilities. **Cards:** AX, CB, DC, DS, MC, VI. **Free Special Amenities:** early check-in/late check-out and room upgrade (subject to availability with advance reservations).

(See color ad below)

SOME UNITS

BRACKENRIDGE LODGE

Phone: 479/253-6803

All Year	1P: $39-$149	2P: $39-$149

Motel **Location:** 1 mi w of jct US 62 and SR 23. 352 W Van Buren St 72632. Fax: 479/253-6986. **Facility:** 12 units. 10 one-bedroom standard units, some with whirlpools. 2 cabins with whirlpools. 1 story, exterior corridors. *Bath:* combo or tub only. **Parking:** on-site. **Terms:** 2 night minimum stay - weekends, 7 day cancellation notice-fee imposed, pets ($10 extra charge). **Amenities:** video library (fee). *Some:* CD players, irons, hair dryers. **Pool(s):** heated outdoor. **Leisure Activities:** whirlpool, basketball. **Cards:** AX, DC, MC, VI.

SOME UNITS

BUDGET HOST INN

Book great rates at AAA.com

Phone: (479)253-7300

3/1-12/10	1P: $42-$65	2P: $48-$88	XP: $6	F6

Location: Just s of jct US 62 and SR 23. 154 Huntsville Rd 72632 (PO Box 527). Fax: 479/253-7304. **Facility:** 29 units. 28 one- and 1 two-bedroom standard units, some with kitchens and/or whirlpools. 2 stories (no elevator), interior/exterior corridors. **Parking:** on-site. **Terms:** open 3/1-12/10, [CP] meal plan available, package plans, small pets only. **Pool(s):** heated outdoor. **Guest Services:** area transportation-trolley stop.

Small-scale Hotel **Cards:** AX, DS, MC, VI. **Free Special Amenities:** continental breakfast and local telephone calls.

SOME UNITS

CLIFF COTTAGE INN-B&B SUITES & COTTAGES

Phone: (479)253-7409

Historic Bed & Breakfast

All Year [BP]   1P: $189-$230   2P: $189-$230   XP: $25
Location: 0.5 mi n of jct US 62 and SR 23, just ne; downtown. Located in the historic district. 42 Armstrong St 72632. **Facility:** Located on the hillside overlooking this popular town, the rooms are cozy and decorated with an eclectic array of Victorian antiques. 8 units. 1 one-bedroom standard unit with whirlpool. 5 one-bedroom suites ($189-$225) with whirlpools. 2 cottages ($230-$240). 1-2 stories (no elevator), interior/exterior corridors. *Bath:* combo, shower or tub only. **Parking:** on-site. **Terms:** 2 night minimum stay - weekends, age restrictions may apply, 10 day cancellation notice-fee imposed, package plans, no pets allowed (owner's pets on premises). **Amenities:** video library, CD players, irons, hair dryers. **Guest Services:** complimentary evening beverages. **Cards:** MC, VI.

COMFORT INN

Book great rates at AAA.com   **Phone:** 479/253-5241

Small-scale Hotel

Property failed to provide current rates
Location: Just w of jct US 62 and SR 23 S. 196 E Van Buren St 72632. Fax: 479/253-6502. **Facility:** 67 one-bedroom standard units, some with whirlpools. 3 stories, interior/exterior corridors. *Bath:* combo or shower only. **Parking:** on-site. **Terms:** pets (with prior approval). **Amenities:** irons, hair dryers. **Pool(s):** outdoor. **Leisure Activities:** *Fee:* massage. **Guest Services:** area transportation (fee), wireless Internet. **Business Services:** meeting rooms. *(See color ad below)*

SOME UNITS

DAYS INN

Book great rates at AAA.com   **Phone:** (479)253-8863

Motel

5/27-10/27 [CP]   1P: $59-$169   2P: $59-$169   XP: $8   F12
3/1-5/26, 10/28-12/8 & 2/8-2/29 [CP]   1P: $49-$109   2P: $49-$109   XP: $8   F12
Location: On US 62, just w of jct SR 23 N. 120 W Van Buren St 72632. Fax: 479/253-7885. **Facility:** 24 one-bedroom standard units, some with whirlpools. 2 stories (no elevator), exterior corridors. **Parking:** on-site. **Terms:** open 3/1-12/8 & 2/8-2/29, 3 day cancellation notice, package plans, small pets only ($15 extra charge). **Amenities:** high-speed Internet, irons, hair dryers. **Pool(s):** small heated outdoor. **Leisure Activities:** basketball. **Guest Services:** wireless Internet. **Cards:** AX, DC, DS, MC, VI.

SOME UNITS

FEE

EVENING SHADE INN

Phone: 479/253-6264

Motel

Property failed to provide current rates
Location: 1.1 mi e of jct US 62 and SR 23. Located in a quiet area. 3079 E Van Buren St 72632. **Facility:** 8 units. 6 one-bedroom standard units with whirlpools. 2 cottages with whirlpools. 1 story, exterior corridors. **Parking:** on-site. **Terms:** office hours 9 am-9 pm, age restrictions may apply. **Amenities:** video library, irons, hair dryers. *Some:* CD players. **Leisure Activities:** hiking trails. **Guest Services:** wireless Internet.

HEARTSTONE INN & COTTAGES

Book great rates at AAA.com   **Phone:** (479)253-8916

Historic Bed & Breakfast

All Year [BP]   1P: $95-$165   2P: $95-$165   XP: $20
Location: On US 62B Historic Loop, just n of jct US 62; downtown. Located in a residential area. 35 Kings Hwy 72632. Fax: 479/253-5361. **Facility:** Cozy rooms and charming decorations are elements of this restored Victorian home. Smoke free premises. 11 units. 9 one-bedroom standard units, some with whirlpools. 2 cottages. 2 stories (no elevator), interior/exterior corridors. **Parking:** on-site. **Terms:** 1-2 night minimum stay - seasonal and/or weekends, age restrictions may apply, 10 day cancellation notice-fee imposed. **Amenities:** video library, DVD players, irons, hair dryers. **Leisure Activities:** golf club & pool privileges. **Guest Services:** gift shop, wireless Internet. **Business Services:** meeting rooms. **Cards:** AX, DS, MC, VI. **Free Special Amenities:** full breakfast and high-speed Internet.

SOME UNITS

HOLIDAY INN EXPRESS   *Book great rates at AAA.com*   Phone: (479)253-5040

(AAA) [SAVE]   5/1-10/31 [ECP]   1P: $89-$139   2P: $89-$139   XP: $10   F19
◆◆◆   3/1-4/30 [ECP]   1P: $79-$129   2P: $79-$129   XP: $10   F19
              11/1-2/29 [ECP]   1P: $69-$119   2P: $69-$119   XP: $10   F19

Small-scale Hotel   **Location:** 0.8 mi e of jct US 62 and SR 23. 3010 E Van Buren St 72632 (PO Box 111). Fax: 479/253-5040. **Facility:** 81 units. 79 one-bedroom standard units. 2 one-bedroom suites ($149-$229) with whirlpools. 2 stories, interior/exterior corridors. *Bath:* combo or shower only. **Parking:** on-site. **Terms:** 3 day cancellation notice, package plans. **Amenities:** high-speed Internet, voice mail, irons, hair dryers. **Pool(s):** heated indoor. **Leisure Activities:** whirlpool. *Fee:* game room. **Business Services:** meeting rooms, PC. **Cards:** AX, DC, DS, MC, VI. **Free Special Amenities:** expanded continental breakfast and high-speed Internet. *(See color ad below)*

SOME UNITS

[S/D] [symbols] / [X] [symbols] /

HOWARD JOHNSON EXPRESS   *Book great rates at AAA.com*   Phone: (479)253-6665

(AAA) [SAVE]   3/1-12/31 & 2/15-2/29   1P: $45-$150   2P: $45-$150   XP: $10   D18
◆◆◆   **Location:** 1.8 mi e of jct US 62 and SR 23. 4042 E Van Buren St 72632 (110 Huntsville Dr). Fax: 479/253-6973. **Facility:** Smoke free premises. 30 one-bedroom standard units. 2 stories (no elevator), exterior corridors. **Parking:** on-site. **Terms:** open 3/1-12/31 & 2/15-2/29, 3-4 night minimum stay - seasonal, small pets only

Small-scale Hotel   ($10 extra charge). **Amenities:** irons, hair dryers. **Pool(s):** outdoor. **Leisure Activities:** whirlpool. **Guest Services:** wireless Internet. **Cards:** AX, CB, DC, DS, MC, VI. **Free Special Amenities:** continental breakfast and local telephone calls.

SOME UNITS

[S/D] [symbols] [X] [symbols] / [symbols] /
FEE

WHAT A DIFFERENCE!

Holiday Inn EXPRESS

- Indoor Pool
- Hot Tub
- FREE Express Start Breakfast
- Trolley Stop
- FREE High-Speed Internet
- Restaurant Adj.
- Dive In Movies

$69.95
AAA Rate
Sun.-Wed.*

Toll Free Reservations **1-800-986-9733** www.eurekaspringsexpress.com
Holiday Inn Express • PO Box 111 • Eureka Springs, Arkansas 72632
* 1-2 persons, subject to availability. Not valid Holidays, Special Events or with any other discount.

Land • O • Nod
Victorian INN

- New Rooms
- Cable TV, HBO • Heated Pool
- Trolley Stop • Central Location
- Continental Breakfast
- Groups Welcome
- Restaurant Adjacent
- Free WI-FI & In-Room Coffee

∞ **Eureka Springs, AR**
1-800-LAND-263
www.landonod.com • Local ph. 479-253-6262 • 109 Huntsville Road

INN AT ROSE HALL

AAA SAVE
Bed & Breakfast

Phone: (479)253-8035

All Year   2P: $129-$179
Location: 1.2 mi n on SR 23, just sw. 56 Hillside 72632 (PO Box 110). **Facility:** The Inn at Rose Hall has a scenic hillside view near historic downtown; Victorian-themed rooms feature fireplaces and whirlpool tubs. 5 one-bedroom standard units with whirlpools. 2 stories (no elevator), interior corridors. *Bath:* combo or tub only. **Parking:** on-site. **Terms:** 2 night minimum stay - weekends, age restrictions may apply, 14 day cancellation notice-fee imposed, [BP] meal plan available, package plans. **Amenities:** video library, irons, hair dryers. *Some:* CD players. **Guest Services:** complimentary evening beverages. **Cards:** AX, DS, MC, VI. **Free Special Amenities: full breakfast and high-speed Internet.**

SOME UNITS

LAND-O NOD-VICTORIAN INN

AAA SAVE
Small-scale Hotel

Phone: (479)253-6262

5/2-11/15	1P: $49-$89	2P: $49-$89	XP: $10 F12
3/15-5/1	1P: $39-$89	2P: $39-$89	XP: $10 F12

Location: Jct US 62 and SR 23 S. 109 Huntsville Rd 72632. Fax: 479/253-9763. **Facility:** 40 units. 37 one- and 3 two-bedroom standard units. 2 stories (no elevator), interior/exterior corridors. *Bath:* combo or shower only. **Parking:** on-site. **Terms:** open 3/15-11/15, office hours 7 am-11 pm, package plans. **Pool(s):** heated outdoor. **Leisure Activities:** playground. *Fee:* golf privileges. **Cards:** AX, DS, MC, VI.

(See color ad p 296)

SOME UNITS

RED BUD VALLEY RESORT

AAA **SAVE**

Vacation Rental Cabin

Phone: (479)253-9028

| 3/1-11/30 | 2P: $99-$160 | XP: $10 | F7 |
| 12/1-2/29 | 2P: $89-$150 | XP: $10 | F7 |

Location: 0.8 mi s of jct US 62 on CR 302 (Rockhouse Rd). Located in a quiet area. 369 CR 340 72632. Fax: 479/253-9373. **Facility:** Log cabins nestled in a serene mountain locale with outstanding views. They range from family to luxury style with a very attractive country decor. 16 cabins ($89-$160), some with whirlpools. 2 stories (no elevator), exterior corridors. *Bath:* combo or shower only. **Parking:** on-site. **Terms:** 2 night minimum stay, 10 day cancellation notice-fee imposed, package plans. **Amenities:** video library (fee), DVD players, hair dryers. *Some:* CD players, irons. **Leisure Activities:** paddleboats, fishing, fishing equipment, hiking trails, playground. *Fee:* picnic pavilion with grills. **Guest Services:** gift shop. **Business Services:** meeting rooms. **Cards:** DS, MC, VI. *(See color ad p 297)*

ROAD RUNNER INN

Motel

Phone: 479/253-8166

| All Year | 1P: $59-$89 | 2P: $59-$89 | XP: $10 | F12 |

Location: On US 62, 4.3 mi w, 3.9 mi s on SR 187, then 3 mi se. 3034 Mundell Rd 72632. **Facility:** Smoke free premises. 12 one-bedroom standard units with efficiencies. 2 stories (no elevator), exterior corridors. *Bath:* shower only. **Parking:** on-site. **Terms:** 4-11 night minimum stay - weekends, 14 day cancellation notice-fee imposed, small pets only ($10 fee, with prior approval). **Cards:** MC, VI.

TRAVELERS INN

Motel

Phone: 479/253-8386

Property failed to provide current rates

Location: On US 62, just e of jct US 62 and SR 23. 2044 E Van Buren St 72632. Fax: 479/253-6980. **Facility:** 59 units. 57 one-bedroom standard units. 2 three-bedroom suites with kitchens. 2 stories (no elevator), exterior corridors. **Parking:** on-site. **Terms:** small pets only ($5 fee). **Pool(s):** heated outdoor. **Guest Services:** wireless Internet. **Business Services:** meeting rooms.

TRAVELODGE

AAA **SAVE**

Small-scale Hotel

Book great rates at AAA.com

Phone: (479)253-8992

| 3/1-12/31 & 2/15-2/29 | 1P: $45-$150 | 2P: $45-$150 |

Location: Jct US 62 and SR 23. 110 Huntsville Dr 72632. Fax: 479/253-8883. **Facility:** 45 one-bedroom standard units, some with whirlpools. 2-4 stories (no elevator), exterior corridors. **Parking:** on-site. **Terms:** open 3/1-12/31 & 2/15-2/29, 3-4 night minimum stay - seasonal, small pets only ($10 extra charge). **Amenities:** irons, hair dryers. **Pool(s):** outdoor. **Leisure Activities:** picnic area. **Guest Services:** area transportation-trolley stop. **Cards:** AX, CB, DC, DS, MC, VI. **Free Special Amenities:** continental breakfast and local telephone calls.

--- **WHERE TO DINE** ---

AUTUMN BREEZE RESTAURANT

Steak & Seafood

Dinner: $10-$40   **Phone:** 479/253-7734

Location: 0.4 mi s of jct US 62 and SR 23. 190 Huntsville Rd 72632. **Hours:** Open 3/2-12/31; 5 pm-9 pm. Closed: 11/22, 12/25; also Sun. **Features:** On the restaurant's eclectic menu are such specialties as coconut beer-battered shrimp, prime rib, rack of lamb, chicken cordon bleu and a fabulous chocolate souffle for dessert. The relaxed and romantic dining room offers a view of the woods and hollow. Dressy casual; beer & wine only. **Parking:** on-site. **Cards:** DS, MC, VI.

THE BALCONY RESTAURANT & BAR

American

Lunch: $6-$17   **Dinner:** $6-$19   **Phone:** 479/253-7837

Location: 0.7 mi n of jct US 62 via SR 23 N; downtown; in 1905 Basin Park Hotel. 12 Spring St 72632. **Hours:** Open 3/1-1/31 & 2/14-2/29; 11 am-10 pm, Sat-11 pm, Sun-8 pm. Closed: 12/25. **Features:** Diners can enjoy varied sandwiches and other American dishes while keeping an eye on the shops and street activity from balcony seats. Casual dress; cocktails. **Parking:** street. **Cards:** AX, DS, MC, VI.

BAVARIAN INN RESTAURANT

German

Dinner: $12-$19   **Phone:** 479/253-7741

Location: 1 mi w of jct US 62 and SR 23; in Bavarian Inn. 325 W Van Buren St 72632. **Hours:** Open 3/5-11/30; 5 pm-9 pm, Sat from 4:30 pm. Closed: 11/22. **Features:** German and Czech foods are prepared to please guests' tastes. The dining room reflects the style of a Swiss chateau. Casual dress; cocktails. **Parking:** on-site. **Cards:** MC, VI.

CHINA BUFFET

Chinese

Lunch: $5-$8   **Dinner:** $6-$8   **Phone:** 479/363-8195

Location: 1.8 mi e of jct US 62 and SR 23. 4032 E Van Buren St 72632. **Hours:** 11 am-9 pm, Fri & Sat-10 pm. Closed: 11/22, 12/25. **Features:** Patrons can order dishes from the menu or do as most do: choose favorites from the buffet. Casual dress. **Parking:** on-site. **Cards:** MC, VI.

THE CRYSTAL DINING ROOM

Steak & Seafood

Lunch: $7-$13   **Dinner:** $15-$45   **Phone:** 479/253-9652

Location: 1.3 mi n of jct SR 23 on US 62B Historic Loop; in 1886 Crescent Hotel & Spa. 75 Prospect Ave 72632. **Hours:** 7-10 am, 11-2 & 5-9 pm, Sun 7-8:30 am, 9:30-2 & 5-9 pm; Sunday brunch. **Reservations:** suggested, evenings & Sunday brunch. **Features:** The formal dining room has tall ceilings and windows, just as when it was built in 1886. A good choice of quality steaks shares menu space with poultry, fish and chicken dishes. Casual dress; cocktails. **Parking:** on-site. **Cards:** AX, DS, MC, VI.

DEVITOS

Italian

Lunch: $7-$11   **Dinner:** $13-$24   **Phone:** 479/253-6807

Location: Center. 5 Center St 72632. **Hours:** Open 3/1-12/31 & 2/14-2/29; 11 am-4 & 5-9 pm. Closed: 11/22, 12/25; also Wed. **Features:** The fresh, grilled trout with lemon and butter sauce is superb at DeVitos. It's their specialty; they raise trout on their family-owned farm. They also serve well-prepared, traditional Italian dishes in a warm and intimate atmosphere. Casual dress; cocktails. **Parking:** street. **Cards:** AX, DS, MC, VI.

ERMILIO'S

Italian

Dinner: $9-$24   **Phone:** 479/253-8806

Location: 2.8 mi nw on US 62B Historic Loop. 26 White St 72632. **Hours:** Open 3/16-2/29; 5 pm-9 pm; call for winter hours. Closed: 1/1, 11/22, 12/25. **Features:** Set in a restored Victorian home, the restaurant provides a warm, friendly atmosphere that's suitable for family dining. Among examples of Italian "home cooking" are such specialties as homemade eggplant parmesan, Italian sausage, meatball lasagna and marinated filet mignon. Casual dress; cocktails. **Parking:** on-site. **Cards:** DS, MC, VI.

THE GAZEBO RESTAURANT

Regional American

Lunch: $4-$9   **Dinner:** $8-$18   **Phone:** 479/253-9551

Location: Just w of jct US 62 and SR 23 N; in Best Western-Eureka Inn. 101 E Van Buren St 72632. **Hours:** Open 3/1-12/31; 7 am-1:30 & 4:30-8 pm. **Reservations:** accepted. **Features:** An attractive 1890s Victorian decor sets the stage at the Gazebo. They feature Ozark fried chicken as a specialty and also offer grilled chicken with pasta, excellent prime rib, catfish and ribs for the area's many visitors. Casual dress; cocktails. **Parking:** on-site. **Cards:** AX, DC, DS, MC, VI.

LOCAL FLAVOR CAFE

American

Lunch: $6-$8   **Dinner:** $9-$20   **Phone:** 479/253-9522

Location: 0.5 mi n of jct US 62 and SR 63; in historic downtown. 73 S Main St 72632. **Hours:** 11 am-9 pm, Sun 8 am-2 & 5-9 pm; to 3 pm, Wed-Sat to 9 pm, Sun 8 am-2 & 5-9 pm off season. Closed: 11/22, 12/24, 12/25. **Features:** The cheerful atmosphere provides a good view of street activity and outdoor dining is available, weather permitting. The creamy tomato soup is delicious, as is the brie plate with homemade bread and fresh fruit. Casual dress; beer & wine only. **Parking:** street. **Cards:** DS, MC, VI.

MYRTIE MAE'S

Regional American

Lunch: $6-$9   **Dinner:** $7-$19   **Phone:** 479/253-9768

Location: On US 62, 0.5 mi w of jct SR 23; in Best Western Inn of the Ozarks. 207 W Van Buren St 72632. **Hours:** 7 am-8:30 pm, Fri & Sat-9 pm. **Reservations:** accepted. **Features:** This locally popular restaurant features country-style cooking such as fried chicken and possum pie (chocolate cream cheese). Myrtie Mae's has a Victorian decor, a casual, family-type atmosphere, and friendly, attentive service. Casual dress; cocktails. **Parking:** on-site. **Cards:** AX, CB, DC, DS, JC, MC, VI. *(See color ad p 294)*

ROGUE'S MANOR AT SWEET SPRING

American

Dinner: $13-$40   **Phone:** 479/253-4911

Location: 0.5 mi n on US 62B Historic Loop; in historic district. 124 Spring St 72632. **Hours:** 5 pm-9 pm. Closed: Mon & Tues 12/1-3/31. **Reservations:** suggested. **Features:** In a Victorian setting, the restaurant prepares such hearty selections as ostrich steak. Casual dress; cocktails. **Parking:** street. **Cards:** AX, DC, DS, MC, VI.

SPARKY'S

American

Lunch: $4-$26   **Dinner:** $4-$26   **Phone:** 479/253-6001

Location: Just e of jct US 62 and SR 23. 147 E Van Buren St 72632. **Hours:** Open 4/1-2/29; 11 am-9 pm. Closed: 12/24, 12/25; also 10/31 & Sun. **Reservations:** not accepted. **Features:** Locals frequent this spot for hanging out in comfort and enjoying casual sandwiches or juicy steak. Casual dress; cocktails. **Parking:** on-site. **Cards:** DS, MC, VI.

FAYETTEVILLE pop. 58,047

—— WHERE TO STAY ——

BEST WESTERN WINDSOR SUITES

Small-scale Hotel

Book great rates at AAA.com   **Phone:** (479)587-1400

All Year   1P: $79-$99   2P: $89-$109   XP: $10   F18

Location: I-540, exit 62, just se. 1122 S Futrall Dr 72701. Fax: 479/587-8630. **Facility:** 68 units. 66 one-bedroom standard units, some with whirlpools. 2 one-bedroom suites with whirlpools. 2 stories (no elevator), exterior corridors. *Bath:* combo or shower only. **Parking:** on-site. **Terms:** small pets only ($10 fee). **Amenities:** high-speed Internet, voice mail, irons, hair dryers. **Pool(s):** heated indoor. **Leisure Activities:** whirlpool, exercise room. **Guest Services:** valet and coin laundry. **Business Services:** meeting rooms, business center. **Cards:** AX, CB, DC, DS, JC, MC, VI. **Free Special Amenities:** expanded continental breakfast and high-speed Internet.

SOME UNITS

CLARION INN

Small-scale Hotel

Book great rates at AAA.com   **Phone:** (479)521-1166

All Year [BP]   1P: $70-$130   2P: $70-$135   XP: $5   F12

Location: I-540, exit 62, just w. 1255 S Shiloh Dr 72701. Fax: 479/521-1204. **Facility:** 197 units. 187 one-bedroom standard units. 10 one-bedroom suites. 2 stories (no elevator), interior/exterior corridors. *Bath:* combo or shower only. **Parking:** on-site. **Amenities:** voice mail, hair dryers. *Some:* high-speed Internet (fee), dual phone lines, irons. **Dining:** 2 restaurants, 6 am-9 pm, cocktails. **Pool(s):** heated indoor. **Leisure Activities:** sauna, whirlpool, limited exercise equipment. **Guest Services:** valet and coin laundry, wireless Internet. **Business Services:** meeting rooms, business center. **Cards:** AX, CB, DC, DS, JC, MC, VI. **Free Special Amenities:** newspaper and high-speed Internet.

SOME UNITS

FAIRFIELD INN BY MARRIOTT

Small-scale Hotel

Book great rates at AAA.com   **Phone:** (479)587-8600

All Year   1P: $85-$105   2P: $90-$110   XP: $5   F18

Location: I-540, exit 67, 1.6 mi e, then just s on US 71B. 720 Millsap Rd 72703. Fax: 479/587-8600. **Facility:** Smoke free premises. 61 one-bedroom standard units. 3 stories, interior corridors. *Bath:* combo or shower only. **Parking:** on-site. **Amenities:** irons, hair dryers. **Pool(s):** heated indoor. **Leisure Activities:** whirlpool. **Guest Services:** valet laundry, wireless Internet. **Cards:** AX, DC, DS, MC, VI.

SOME UNITS

HAMPTON INN   *Book great rates at AAA.com*   Phone: (479)587-8300

All Year   1P: $99-$159   2P: $109-$165   XP: $6   F

Location: I-540, exit 62, just w. 915 Krupa Dr 72704. Fax: 479/587-8301. **Facility:** 95 units. 87 one-bedroom standard units. 8 one-bedroom suites ($149-$225), some with whirlpools. 4 stories, interior corridors. *Bath:* combo or shower only. **Parking:** on-site. **Terms:** 5 day cancellation notice, [ECP] meal plan available, package plans. **Amenities:** high-speed Internet, voice mail, irons, hair dryers. **Pool(s):** heated indoor. **Leisure Activities:** sauna, whirlpool, exercise room. **Guest Services:** sundries, valet and coin laundry, wireless Internet. **Business Services:** meeting rooms, business center. **Cards:** AX, CB, DC, DS, JC, MC, VI.

Small-scale Hotel

SOME UNITS

QUALITY INN   *Book great rates at AAA.com*   Phone: (479)444-9800

All Year   1P: $62-$110   2P: $62-$110   XP: $5   F9

Location: I-540, exit 62, just w. 523 S Shiloh Dr 72704. Fax: 479/521-9006. **Facility:** 58 one-bedroom standard units, some with whirlpools. 2 stories (no elevator), exterior corridors. *Bath:* combo or shower only. **Parking:** on-site. **Terms:** 2-3 night minimum stay - seasonal, cancellation fee imposed, [BP] meal plan available, package plans, small pets only ($15 extra charge). **Amenities:** safes (fee), irons, hair dryers. **Pool(s):** outdoor. **Guest Services:** wireless Internet. **Business Services:** PC. **Cards:** AX, CB, DC, DS, JC, MC, VI.

Small-scale Hotel

Free Special Amenities: expanded continental breakfast and high-speed Internet.

SOME UNITS
FEE

SLEEP INN BY CHOICE HOTELS   *Book great rates at AAA.com*   Phone: (479)587-8700

All Year   1P: $70-$90   2P: $75-$95   XP: $5   F18

Location: I-540, exit 67, 1.6 mi e, then just s on US 71B. 728 Millsap Rd 72703. Fax: 479/587-8700. **Facility:** 62 one-bedroom standard units. 3 stories, interior corridors. *Bath:* combo or shower only. **Parking:** on-site. **Terms:** pets ($5 extra charge). **Amenities:** irons, hair dryers. **Guest Services:** valet laundry, wireless Internet. **Cards:** AX, DC, DS, MC, VI.

Small-scale Hotel

SOME UNITS
FEE

——— *The following lodgings were either not evaluated or did not* ———
meet AAA rating requirements but are listed for your information only.

COMFORT INN   Phone: 479/695-2121

[fyi]

Did not meet all AAA rating requirements for some property operations at time of last evaluation on 08/07/2006. **Location:** I-540, exit 62, just w. 735 Shiloh Dr 72704. Facilities, services, and decor characterize a mid-range property.

Small-scale Hotel

COUNTRY INN & SUITES BY CARLSON   Phone: 479/571-5177

[fyi]

Did not meet all AAA rating requirements for some property operations at time of last evaluation on 07/26/2005. **Location:** I-540, exit 64, just nw. 1234 Steamboat Dr 72704. Facilities, services, and decor characterize a mid-range property.

Small-scale Hotel

**HOLIDAY INN EXPRESS HOTEL &
SUITES-UNVERSITY OF ARKANSAS AREA**   Phone: 479/444-6006

[fyi]

Did not meet all AAA rating requirements for some property operations at time of last evaluation on 08/07/2006. **Location:** I-540, exit 64, just nw. 1251 N Shiloh Dr 72704. Facilities, services, and decor characterize a mid-range property.

Small-scale Hotel

——— **WHERE TO DINE** ———

A Q CHICKEN HOUSE   Lunch: $5-$13   Dinner: $7-$13   Phone: 479/443-7555

Location: I-540, exit 67, 1.6 mi e, then 2.4 mi s on US 71B. 1925 N College Ave 72703. **Hours:** 11 am-9 pm, Fri & Sat-9:30 pm. **Features:** Popular since 1947, the restaurant specializes in pan-fried, grilled, roasted or barbecue chicken dishes. Families love the inviting and cozy atmosphere, and the food is a good value. Casual dress; beer & wine only. **Parking:** on-site. **Cards:** AX, CB, DC, DS, MC, VI.

Regional American

COLTON'S STEAKHOUSE & GRILL   Lunch: $6-$8   Dinner: $9-$19   Phone: 479/973-0876

Location: I-540, exit 67, 1.6 mi e, just s on US 71B, then just w of jct US 71B. 642 E Millsap Rd 72703. **Hours:** 11 am-9 pm, Fri & Sat-10 pm. Closed: 11/22, 12/25. **Features:** A bucket of peanuts on the table, an upbeat Old-West atmosphere and a good selection of steak, chicken and ribs await guests at the casual steakhouse. Casual dress; cocktails. **Parking:** on-site. **Cards:** AX, DC, DS, MC, VI.

Steak House

COLTON'S STEAKHOUSE & GRILL   Lunch: $6-$8   Dinner: $9-$19   Phone: 479/973-0876

Location: I-540, exit 67, 1.6 mi e, just s on US 71B, then just w. 642 E Millsap Rd 72703. **Hours:** 11 am-9 pm, Fri & Sat-10 pm. Closed: 11/22, 12/25. **Features:** A bucket of peanuts on the table, an upbeat Old-West atmosphere and a good selection of steak, chicken and ribs await guests at the casual steakhouse. Casual dress; cocktails. **Parking:** on-site. **Cards:** AX, DC, DS, MC, VI.

Steak House

DIXIE CAFE

Regional American

Lunch: $7-$10   **Dinner:** $7-$10   **Phone:** 501/444-6660

Location: I-540, exit 67, 1.6 mi, then just n on College Ave. 3875 N Shiloh Dr 72703. **Hours:** 11 am-10 pm. Closed: 11/22, 12/25. **Features:** Southern-style home cooking-chicken-fried steak, meat loaf, pork chops, turnip greens, mashed potatoes and fresh veggies-appeals to families who visit the restaurant's classic "Norman Rockwell" atmosphere. Casual dress. **Parking:** on-site. **Cards:** AX, DC, DS, MC, VI.

HOFFBRAU

Steak House

Lunch: $5-$20   **Dinner:** $10-$20   **Phone:** 479/442-4444

Location: Just w of jct US 71B. 31 E Center St 72701. **Hours:** 11 am-10 pm. Closed: 11/22, 12/25; also Sun. **Features:** Diners stop in for a good selection of hand-cut steaks served in a tavern-style dining room. Sharing menu space are sandwiches and some seafood preparations. Casual dress; cocktails. **Parking:** street. **Cards:** AX, CB, DC, DS, JC, MC, VI.

MADAME WU'S CHINESE RESTAURANT

Chinese

Lunch: $5-$7   **Dinner:** $7-$15   **Phone:** 479/251-1818

Location: On SR 265; jct SR 45; in Crossroads Village. 1818 N Crossover Rd 72701. **Hours:** 11 am-2:30 & 5-9 pm, Fri-10 pm, Sat 5 pm-10 pm. Closed: 7/4, 11/22, 12/25. **Features:** This nicely decorated restaurant specializes in "Chinese Country Cooking" with menu offerings from gan shao shrimp & crispy squid to Long Island duckling. The service staff is gracious and welcoming. Casual dress. **Parking:** on-site. **Cards:** AX, DS, MC, VI.

UNCLE GAYLORD'S RESTAURANT & BAR

American

Lunch: $8-$10   **Dinner:** $10-$25   **Phone:** 479/444-0605

Location: Just w of jct US 71B; downtown. 315 W Mountain St 72701. **Hours:** 8 am-1:30 & 5-close, Sun-1:30 pm; Saturday & Sunday brunch. Closed: 11/22, 12/25; also Mon. **Features:** The specialty is Italian pizza at the family-friendly restaurant, which fosters a relaxed atmosphere. Cocktails. **Parking:** on-site. **Cards:** AX, MC, VI.

FORDYCE pop. 4,799

------ WHERE TO STAY ------

DAYS INN   *Book great rates at AAA.com*

Small-scale Hotel

Phone: (870)352-2400

All Year [ECP]   1P: $69-$89   2P: $69-$89   XP: $5   F12

Location: On US 79/167; 1 mi w of center. 2500 W 4th St 71742. **Fax:** 870/352-0220. **Facility:** 47 one-bedroom standard units, some with whirlpools. 2 stories (no elevator), interior/exterior corridors. **Parking:** on-site. **Terms:** pets ($10 fee). **Amenities:** high-speed Internet, irons, hair dryers. *Some:* DVD players, CD players. **Pool(s):** outdoor. **Leisure Activities:** exercise room. **Guest Services:** coin laundry. **Business Services:** PC. **Cards:** AX, CB, DC, DS, JC, MC, VI.

SOME UNITS

ASK SD 🐾 ➿ 📷 🖥 🖃 🍽 / ✕ /
FEE

FORREST CITY pop. 14,774

------ WHERE TO STAY ------

DAYS INN   *Book great rates at AAA.com*

Small-scale Hotel

Phone: (870)633-0777

All Year   1P: $70-$120   2P: $70-$120   XP: $4   F

Location: I-40, exit 241B, just n. 350 Barrow Hill Rd 72335. **Fax:** 870/633-0770. **Facility:** 52 one-bedroom standard units, some with whirlpools. 2 stories (no elevator), exterior corridors. *Bath:* some combo or shower only. **Parking:** on-site. **Terms:** 7 day cancellation notice, pets ($5 extra charge, with prior approval). **Amenities:** hair dryers. *Some:* irons. **Pool(s):** outdoor. **Guest Services:** valet laundry, wireless Internet. **Business Services:** meeting rooms. **Cards:** AX, DC, DS, MC, VI.

SOME UNITS

ASK SD 🐾 🍴 🖥 ➿ 📷 🖃 🍽 / ✕ /
FEE

HAMPTON INN   *Book great rates at AAA.com*

Small-scale Hotel

Phone: 870/630-9000

Property failed to provide current rates

Location: I-40, exit 241B, just n. 300 Holiday Dr 72335. **Fax:** 870/630-0951. **Facility:** 70 one-bedroom standard units, some with whirlpools. 2 stories, interior corridors. *Bath:* combo or shower only. **Parking:** on-site. **Amenities:** high-speed Internet, voice mail, irons, hair dryers. **Pool(s):** outdoor. **Leisure Activities:** exercise room. **Guest Services:** valet laundry, wireless Internet. **Business Services:** meeting rooms, business center.

SOME UNITS

🖥 ➿ 📷 🖃 🍽 / ✕ /

HOLIDAY INN   *Book at AAA.com*

Small-scale Hotel

Phone: 870/633-6300

All Year   1P: $81-$90   XP: $8   F19

Location: I-40, exit 241B, just n. 200 Holiday Dr 72335. **Fax:** 870/633-8512. **Facility:** 79 one-bedroom standard units. 2 stories (no elevator), exterior corridors. **Parking:** on-site. **Terms:** [AP] & [BP] meal plans available, small pets only. **Amenities:** high-speed Internet, voice mail, safes, irons, hair dryers. **Pool(s):** outdoor. **Leisure Activities:** playground, exercise room. **Guest Services:** valet and coin laundry, wireless Internet. **Business Services:** meeting rooms, business center. **Cards:** AX, CB, DC, DS, MC, VI.

SOME UNITS

ASK SD 🐾 🍴 🍸 ➿ 📷 🖥 🖃 🍽 / ✕ /

FORT SMITH pop. 80,268

——— WHERE TO STAY ———

ASPEN HOTEL & SUITES   *Book at AAA.com*   **Phone:** (479)452-9000
▼▼▼▼   All Year [ECP]   1P: $89-$175   2P: $99-$202   XP: $10   F12
         Location: I-540, exit 8B (Rogers Ave), just e. 2900 S 68th St 72903. Fax: 479/484-0551. **Facility:** 57 one-bedroom
Small-scale Hotel standard units, some with whirlpools. 2 stories, interior corridors. **Parking:** on-site. **Amenities:** voice mail,
         irons, hair dryers. **Pool(s):** outdoor. **Leisure Activities:** limited exercise equipment. **Guest Services:** valet
and coin laundry, wireless Internet. **Business Services:** meeting rooms, PC. **Cards:** AX, DC, DS, MC, VI.
                                                                                        SOME UNITS
(ASK) (SD) (✈) (⊁) (📶↑) (⇒) (✕) (🗄) (📠) (💻) / (✕)

BAYMONT INN & SUITES FORT SMITH   *Book at AAA.com*   **Phone:** (479)484-5770
▼▼▼ ▼▼   3/1-10/31 [CP]   1P: $79-$109   2P: $84-$114   XP: $5   F18
         11/1-2/29 [CP]   1P: $69-$99   2P: $74-$104   XP: $5   F18
Small-scale Hotel **Location:** I-540, exit 8A (Rogers Ave), just w. 2123 Burnham Rd 72903. Fax: 479/484-0579. **Facility:** 100 units. 98
one-bedroom standard units, some with kitchens. 2 one-bedroom suites ($119-$144). 3 stories, interior
corridors. **Parking:** on-site. **Terms:** small pets only. **Amenities:** video games (fee), voice mail, irons, hair dryers. **Pool(s):**
outdoor. **Leisure Activities:** exercise room. **Guest Services:** valet and coin laundry, wireless Internet. **Cards:** AX, CB, DC, DS,
MC, VI.
                                                                                        SOME UNITS
(ASK) (🛏) (📶↑) (🌀) (⇒) (✕) (💻) / (✕) (🗄) (📠) /

BELAND MANOR INN   **Phone:** (479)782-3300
▼▼▼▼   All Year [BP]   1P: $89-$150   2P: $89-$185   XP: $15
         Location: I-540, exit 8A (Rogers Ave), 1.3 mi w. 1320 S Albert Pike 72903. Fax: 479/782-7674. **Facility:** A
Country Inn traditional, Colonial-style home. Smoke free premises. 8 one-bedroom standard units, some with whirlpools.
         2 stories (no elevator), interior corridors. **Bath:** combo or shower only. **Parking:** on-site. **Terms:** age
restrictions may apply, 5 day cancellation notice, package plans. **Amenities:** video library, voice mail. *Some:* DVD players, CD
players, high-speed Internet. **Leisure Activities:** limited exercise equipment. **Guest Services:** area transportation, wireless
Internet. **Business Services:** meeting rooms. **Cards:** AX, DC, DS, MC, VI.
                                                                                        SOME UNITS
(⊁) (✕) / (VCR)

COMFORT INN   *Book great rates at AAA.com*   **Phone:** 479/484-0227
▼▼▼▼   Property failed to provide current rates
         Location: I-540, exit 8A (Rogers Ave), just w. 2120 Burnham Rd 72903. Fax: 479/484-5885. **Facility:** 89 one-
Small-scale Hotel bedroom standard units, some with whirlpools. 2 stories (no elevator), interior corridors. **Bath:** combo or
         shower only. **Parking:** on-site. **Terms:** small pets only. **Amenities:** voice mail, safes (fee), irons, hair dryers.
Pool(s): heated indoor. **Leisure Activities:** whirlpool, exercise room. **Guest Services:** valet and coin laundry, wireless Internet.
Business Services: PC.
                                                                                        SOME UNITS
(🛏) (📶↑) (🌀) (⇒) (✕) (🗄) (📠) (💻) / (✕) (VCR)
                                                                                           FEE

**COURTYARD BY MARRIOTT DOWNTOWN FORT
SMITH**   **Phone:** 479/783-2100
[fyi]   All Year   1P: $99-$139   XP: $10   F
         Too new to rate, opening scheduled for November 2006. **Location:** I-540, exit 8, 4.1 mi w; corner of 9th St and
Small-scale Hotel Rogers Ave. 900 Rogers Ave 72901. Fax: 479/783-2103. **Amenities:** 138 units, pets, coffeemakers, pool.
         Cards: AX, DC, DS, MC, VI. *(See color ad below)*

GUESTHOUSE INTERNATIONAL INN   *Book at AAA.com*

◆◆◆◆ ◆◆◆◆
Small-scale Hotel

All Year [ECP]   1P: $69-$74   2P: $74-$79   XP: $5   F18
Phone: (479)646-5100

Location: I-540, exit 12, 0.5 mi s. 3600 Grinnell Ave 72908. Fax: 479/646-4598. **Facility:** 61 one-bedroom standard units. 2 stories (no elevator), interior corridors. **Parking:** on-site. **Terms:** cancellation fee imposed. **Amenities:** irons, hair dryers. *Some:* high-speed Internet. **Pool(s):** small outdoor. **Leisure Activities:** limited exercise equipment. **Guest Services:** valet and coin laundry, wireless Internet. **Cards:** AX, DC, DS.

SOME UNITS
(ASK) (S🄳) 🔲 🛄 📷 🖥 💻 /🗙 📠 /

HAMPTON INN   *Book great rates at AAA.com*

◆◆◆◆ ◆◆◆◆
Small-scale Hotel

Phone: 479/452-2000
Property failed to provide current rates
Location: I-540, exit 8B, just e. 6201-C Rogers Ave 72903 (PO Box 11433, 72917). Fax: 479/452-6668. **Facility:** 178 units. 160 one-bedroom standard units, some with whirlpools. 18 one-bedroom suites. 4 stories, interior corridors. *Bath:* combo or shower only. **Parking:** on-site. **Amenities:** DVD players, high-speed Internet, dual phone lines, voice mail, irons, hair dryers. **Pool(s):** heated indoor, wading. **Leisure Activities:** whirlpool, exercise room, sports court. **Guest Services:** valet and coin laundry, wireless Internet. **Business Services:** meeting rooms, business center.

SOME UNITS
🔲 (🍴) 🔲 🛄 🗙 (VCR) 🖥 💻 /🗙 📠 /

HOLIDAY INN CITY CENTER FORT SMITH   *Book great rates at AAA.com*

(AAA) (SAVE)
◆◆◆◆ ◆◆◆◆
Large-scale Hotel

All Year   1P: $79-$109   2P: $79-$109
Phone: 479/783-1000

Location: Just s of US 64 (Garrison Ave); downtown. 700 Rogers Ave 72901. Fax: 479/783-0312. **Facility:** 255 units. 248 one-bedroom standard units. 7 one-bedroom suites. 9 stories, interior corridors. *Bath:* combo or shower only. **Parking:** on-site and valet. **Terms:** check-in 4 pm, cancellation fee imposed, package plans, pets ($25 fee). **Amenities:** voice mail, irons, hair dryers. **Dining:** 6 am-2 & 5-10 pm, cocktails. **Pool(s):** heated indoor. **Leisure Activities:** sauna, whirlpools, exercise room. **Guest Services:** valet laundry, area transportation, wireless Internet. **Business Services:** conference facilities, business center. **Cards:** AX, CB, DC, DS, JC, MC, VI. **Free Special Amenities:** newspaper and high-speed Internet.

SOME UNITS
(S🄳) 🔲 🐾 (🍴) 🍸 (♿M) 🔲 🛄 🗙 📷 💻 /🗙 🖥 /
FEE

RESIDENCE INN BY MARRIOTT   *Book great rates at AAA.com*

◆◆◆◆ ◆◆◆◆
Small-scale Hotel

All Year [BP]   1P: $109-$149   2P: $109-$149
Phone: 479/478-8300

Location: I-540, exit 8A (Rogers Ave), 0.8 mi e. 3005 S 74th 72903. Fax: 479/478-8302. **Facility:** Smoke free premises. 78 units. 27 one-bedroom standard units. 39 one- and 12 two-bedroom suites. 3 stories, interior corridors. *Bath:* combo or shower only. **Parking:** on-site. **Terms:** cancellation fee imposed, package plans, small pets only ($75 fee). **Amenities:** high-speed Internet, dual phone lines, voice mail, irons, hair dryers. **Pool(s):** heated outdoor. **Leisure Activities:** whirlpool, exercise room, sports court. **Guest Services:** valet and coin laundry. **Business Services:** meeting rooms. **Cards:** AX, CB, DC, DS, JC, MC, VI.

(ASK) (S🄳) 🐾 (🍴) 🔲 🛄 🗙 🗙 📷 🖥 📠 💻
FEE

***The following lodging was either not evaluated or did not
meet AAA rating requirements but is listed for your information only.***

HOLIDAY INN EXPRESS

(fyi)
Small-scale Hotel

Phone: 479/452-7500
Did not meet all AAA rating requirements for some property operations at time of last evaluation on 02/02/2006. **Location:** I-540, exit 8A (Rogers Ave), 0.6 mi e, then 0.5 mi s. 6813 Phoenix Ave 72903. Facilities, services, and decor characterize a mid-range property.

--- **WHERE TO DINE** ---

CALICO COUNTY RESTAURANT

◆◆◆◆ ◆◆
Regional American

Lunch: $5-$9   Dinner: $6-$14   **Phone: 479/452-3299**
Location: I-540, exit 8A (Rogers Ave), 0.3 mi w on SR 22, then just s. 2401 S 56th St 72903. **Hours:** 6:30 am-9 pm, Fri & Sat-10 pm, Sun 7 am-9 pm. Closed: 11/22, 12/25. **Features:** You'll be served hearty portions of good home-style meals at Calico County. This country-style restaurant delivers corn bread, yeast rolls and hot cinnamon rolls with each meal. Their service is attentive and cheerful, and the decor is nostalgic. Casual dress; beer & wine only. **Parking:** on-site. **Cards:** AX, CB, DC, DS, MC, VI.

🔲

CATFISH COVE

◆◆◆
Regional American

Lunch: $9-$11   Dinner: $10-$15   **Phone: 479/646-8835**
Location: I-540, exit 10, 1.5 mi w. 1615 Phoenix Ave 72901. **Hours:** 11 am-2 & 4:30-9 pm, Fri & Sat-9:30 pm, Sun 11 am-8:30 pm. Closed major holidays; also Mon. **Features:** This 29-year-old restaurant has the "best of the best" fried catfish filets, say local newspaper readers. They also offer a buffet, fresh seafood, barbecue ribs, steak and homemade cobbler in a relaxed, rustic-style atmosphere with a hint of the 1880s. Casual dress. **Parking:** on-site. **Cards:** AX, MC, VI.

EL LORITO

◆◆◆ ◆◆
Mexican

Lunch: $4-$13   Dinner: $6-$13   **Phone: 479/782-3820**
Location: I-540, exit 8B, 0.7 mi e, then just s. 3105 S 70th St 72903. **Hours:** 11 am-9 pm. Closed: 4/8, 11/22, 12/25. **Features:** A relaxed service approach and casual decor put diners at ease. The menu lines up a nice selection of traditional Mexican dishes. Casual dress; beer only. **Parking:** on-site. **Cards:** AX, DS, MC, VI.

🔲

MARKETPLACE GRILL

◆◆◆ ◆◆
American

Lunch: $8-$23   Dinner: $8-$23   **Phone: 479/424-1310**
Location: I-540, exit 8, 1.5 mi e, then just s. 8302 Phoenix Ave 72903. **Hours:** 11 am-8:30 pm, Fri & Sat-9:30 pm. Closed: 1/1, 11/22, 12/25. **Features:** The eatery has an large, inviting dining room, and the menu includes a variety of dishes. Many ingredients are made in-house and add to the quality you'll find throughout. Casual dress. **Parking:** on-site. **Cards:** AX, CB, DC, DS, MC, VI.

THE RED BARN STEAK HOUSE **Dinner:** $9-$30 **Phone:** 479/783-4075

Steak House

Location: 4 mi n on US 71B, 1 mi w, then follow signs. 3716 Newlon Rd 72904. **Hours:** 5 pm-11 pm. Closed major holidays; also 12/24, Mon & Sun. **Reservations:** suggested. **Features:** You might be amused at the prospect of dining in a restored old barn at a table situated in a converted horse stall. But you're sure to enjoy the Red Barn dining experience. It features a quaint setting, flavorful steaks and shrimp, and attentive service. Casual dress; cocktails. **Parking:** on-site. **Cards:** AX, DS, MC, VI.

TALIANO'S RESTAURANT **Lunch:** $5-$10 **Dinner:** $13-$35 **Phone:** 479/785-2292

Italian

Location: Just e of US 64 N and 71B; jct N 14th and North B sts. 201 N 14th St 72901. **Hours:** 11 am-1:30 & 5:30-9:45 pm, Mon & Sat from 5:30 pm. Closed major holidays; also Sun. **Reservations:** accepted. **Features:** Taliano's features homemade, handmade pasta and sauce, and lasagna is one of their fine specialties. The restaurant, located in a Victorian home built in 1887, is listed on the National Register of Historic Places. Casual dining in a relaxed atmosphere. Casual dress; beer & wine only. **Parking:** on-site. **Cards:** AX, CB, DC, DS, MC, VI. **Historic**

GENTRY pop. 2,165

——— **WHERE TO STAY** ———

APPLE CREST INN BED & BREAKFAST **Phone:** (479)736-8201

Bed & Breakfast

All Year [BP] 1P: $95-$175 2P: $100-$185 XP: $20 D

Location: On SR 59, 1 mi s. 12758 S Hwy 59 72734 (PO Box 1254). Fax: 479/736-5742. **Facility:** Located in the midst of the Ozark Mountains, this B&B features guest rooms decorated with Victorian furnishings and collectibles from around the world. Smoke free premises. 6 one-bedroom standard units, some with whirlpools. 3 stories (no elevator); interior corridors. **Parking:** on-site. **Terms:** check-in 4 pm, 14 day cancellation notice-fee imposed, pets (with prior approval). **Amenities:** video library. **Leisure Activities:** whirlpool. **Guest Services:** area transportation, wireless Internet. **Business Services:** PC, fax. **Cards:** AX, DS, MC, VI.

SOME UNITS

HARDY pop. 578

——— **WHERE TO STAY** ———

BEST WESTERN VILLAGE INN *Book great rates at AAA.com* **Phone:** (870)856-2176

Motel

DS, MC, VI.

All Year [CP] 1P: $60-$69 2P: $65-$85 XP: $5 F16

Location: 2 mi sw on US 62/412. 3587 Hwy 62/412 72542. Fax: 870/856-2239. **Facility:** 41 one-bedroom standard units. 1-2 stories (no elevator); exterior corridors. **Parking:** on-site. **Terms:** cancellation fee imposed. **Amenities:** irons, hair dryers. *Some:* high-speed Internet. **Pool(s):** outdoor. **Cards:** AX, CB, DC, DS, MC, VI.

SOME UNITS

——— *The following lodging was either not evaluated or did not* ———
meet AAA rating requirements but is listed for your information only.

OLDE STONEHOUSE BED & BREAKFAST INN **Phone:** 870/856-2983

[fyi]

Historic Bed
& Breakfast

Did not meet all AAA rating requirements for some property operations at time of last evaluation on 10/20/2005. **Location:** Center. 108 W Main St 72542. Facilities, services, and decor characterize a mid-range property.

HARRISON pop. 12,152

——— **WHERE TO STAY** ———

COMFORT INN *Book great rates at AAA.com* **Phone:** (870)741-7676

Small-scale Hotel

All Year [ECP] 1P: $65-$89 2P: $85-$105 XP: $10 F18

Location: 1 mi n on US 62/65/412. Located in a commercial area. 1210 Hwy 62/65 N 72601 (PO Box 1158). Fax: 870/741-0827. **Facility:** 93 units. 89 one-bedroom standard units. 4 one-bedroom suites, some with whirlpools. 2 stories (no elevator); interior/exterior corridors. *Bath:* combo or shower only. **Parking:** on-site. **Terms:** pets ($25 fee). **Amenities:** high-speed Internet, irons, hair dryers. **Pool(s):** heated outdoor. **Guest Services:** coin laundry, wireless Internet. **Business Services:** conference facilities. **Cards:** AX, CB, DC, DS, MC, VI.

SOME UNITS

FEE

FAMILY BUDGET INN **Phone:** (870)743-1000

Motel

All Year 1P: $37-$39 2P: $39-$43 XP: $3 F12

Location: 0.7 mi s of jct SR 7. 401 S Main (Hwy 65B S) 72601. Fax: 870/743-1100. **Facility:** 45 one-bedroom standard units. 1 story, exterior corridors. **Parking:** on-site. **Terms:** pets ($5 extra charge). **Pool(s):** outdoor. **Leisure Activities:** playground. *Fee:* miniature golf. **Guest Services:** coin laundry, wireless Internet. **Cards:** AX, DS, MC, VI.

SOME UNITS

FEE

HOLIDAY INN EXPRESS HOTEL & SUITES *Book at AAA.com* Phone: (870)741-3636
All Year [ECP] 1P: $65-$95 2P: $105-$125 XP: $10 F18
Location: Just e from jct US 62/65/412 and SR 43. 117 Hwy 43 E 72601. Fax: 870/741-8222. Facility: 90 one-bedroom standard units, some with whirlpools. 4 stories, interior corridors. Bath: combo or shower only. Small-scale Hotel Parking: on-site. Terms: pets ($25 fee, with prior approval). Amenities: high-speed Internet, dual phone lines, voice mail, irons, hair dryers. Pool(s): heated indoor. Leisure Activities: sauna, whirlpool. Fee: game room. Guest Services: coin laundry, wireless Internet. Business Services: meeting rooms. Cards: AX, CB, DC, DS, MC, VI.

SOME UNITS

WHERE TO DINE

BOTTINI'S RESTAURANT *Menu on AAA.com* Lunch: $8-$15 Dinner: $14-$43 Phone: 870/743-9873
Location: Jct Rush and Main sts. 103 W Rush St 72601. Hours: 11 am-2 & 5-9 pm, Sat from 5 pm; Sunday brunch 10 am-2 pm. Closed: 7/4, 12/24, 12/25; also Mon. Reservations: accepted. Features: Attractive presentation marks the well-prepared dishes, which are served in an upscale environment. Casual dress. Parking: street. Cards: AX, DC, DS, MC, VI.
Mediterranean

COLTON'S STEAK HOUSE & GRILL Lunch: $6-$8 Dinner: $9-$19 Phone: 870/741-1834
Location: Just s of jct US 62/65/412 and SR 43. 820 Hwy 62/65 N 72601. Hours: 11 am-9 pm, Fri & Sat-10 pm. Closed: 11/22, 12/25. Features: A bucket of peanuts on the table, an upbeat Old-West atmosphere and a Steak House good selection of steak, chicken and ribs await guests at the casual steakhouse. Casual dress. Parking: on-site. Cards: AX, DC, DS, MC, VI.

DIAMOND HEAD RESTAURANT Lunch: $6-$8 Dinner: $7-$8 Phone: 870/743-8888
Location: On US 62, 2 mi n. 1408 Hwy 62/65 N 72601. Hours: 11 am-9 pm. Closed: 11/22, 12/25. Features: Guests can select from a variety of traditional dishes or from some steak or seafood choices. Chinese Casual dress. Parking: on-site. Cards: AX, DS, MC, VI.

DIXIE CAFE Lunch: $7-$10 Dinner: $7-$10 Phone: 870/365-0900
Location: Center. 1212 Hwy 62/65 N 72601. Hours: 11 am-10 pm. Closed: 11/22, 12/25. Features: Southern-style home cooking-chicken-fried steak, meat loaf, pork chops, turnip greens, mashed potatoes and fresh Regional American veggies-appeals to families who visit the restaurant's classic "Norman Rockwell" atmosphere. Casual dress. Parking: on-site. Cards: AX, DC, DS, MC, VI.

The following restaurant has not been evaluated by AAA but is listed for your information only.

NEIGHBORS MILL BAKERY & CAFE Phone: 870/741-6455
[fyi] Not evaluated. Location: 1012 Hwy 65 72601. Features: Freshly prepared dinners are served by a friendly staff. Bakery items can be ordered for takeout.

HAZEN pop. 1,637

WHERE TO STAY

SUPER 8 MOTEL *Book great rates at AAA.com* Phone: (870)255-2888
All Year [CP] 1P: $59-$69 2P: $64-$79 XP: $6 F17
Location: I-40, exit 193, just s. 4167 Hwy 63 72064. Fax: 870/255-2887. Facility: 40 one-bedroom standard units. 2 stories (no elevator), exterior corridors. Parking: on-site. Terms: pets ($5 fee). Amenities: hair dryers. Pool(s): small heated indoor. Guest Services: coin laundry, wireless Internet. Cards: AX, CB, DC, Small-scale Hotel DS, MC, VI. Free Special Amenities: continental breakfast and high-speed Internet.

SOME UNITS

HEBER SPRINGS pop. 6,432

WHERE TO STAY

THE ANDERSON HOUSE INN Phone: (501)362-5266
All Year [BP] 1P: $50-$70 2P: $50-$80 XP: $10 F10
Location: On SR 110; center. 201 E Main St 72543. Fax: 501/362-2326. Facility: Built circa 1880, the inn has been restored and features nicely furnished rooms and an inviting parlor. 14 one-bedroom standard units. 2 Historic Bed stories (no elevator), interior/exterior corridors. Bath: combo or shower only. Parking: on-site. & Breakfast Terms: check-in 4 pm, 7 day cancellation notice-fee imposed, package plans. Cards: AX, CB, DC, DS, MC, VI.

SOME UNITS

HELENA pop. 6,323

WHERE TO STAY

EDWARDIAN INN Phone: 870/338-9155
All Year 1P: $80-$100 2P: $90-$125 XP: $20
Location: 2 mi se on US 49B. 317 Biscoe 72342. Fax: 870/338-4215. Facility: This inn, a 1904 Colonial Revival listed on the National Register of Historic Places, features elegant antiques and period pieces. Smoke free Historic Bed premises. 12 one-bedroom standard units. 3 stories (no elevator), interior corridors. Parking: on-site. & Breakfast Terms: [BP] meal plan available. Amenities: high-speed Internet. Some: DVD players. Guest Services: valet laundry. Business Services: meeting rooms. Cards: AX, CB, DC, DS, JC, MC, VI.

SOME UNITS

HOPE pop. 10,616

———— **WHERE TO STAY** ————

BEST WESTERN OF HOPE   *Book great rates at AAA.com*   Phone: (870)777-9222
 (AAA) (SAVE)   All Year [ECP]   1P: $54-$56   2P: $63-$65   XP: $9   F16
▽▽ ▽▽   **Location:** I-30, exit 30, just nw. 1800 Holiday Dr 71801 (PO Box 6611). Fax: 870/777-9077. **Facility:** 74 one-
    bedroom standard units. 2 stories (no elevator), exterior corridors. **Parking:** on-site. **Terms:** package plans.
Small-scale Hotel   **Amenities:** high-speed Internet, voice mail, irons, hair dryers. **Pool(s):** outdoor. **Guest Services:** coin
    laundry, airport transportation-Hope Airport. **Business Services:** meeting rooms. **Cards:** AX, CB, DC, DS,
    JC, MC, VI. **Free Special Amenities: expanded continental breakfast and newspaper.**

SOME UNITS

[icons] /⊠/

HOT SPRINGS pop. 35,750

———— **WHERE TO STAY** ————

BAYMONT INN & SUITES   *Book at AAA.com*   Phone: 501/520-5522
▽▽▽▽   Property failed to provide current rates
    Location: 4 mi s of jct US 270 and SR 7. 5321 Central Ave 71913. Fax: 501/520-4432. **Facility:** 85 units. 81 one-
Small-scale Hotel   bedroom standard units, some with whirlpools. 4 one-bedroom suites. 4 stories, interior corridors. *Bath:*
    combo or shower only. **Amenities:** video games (fee), dual phone lines, voice mail, irons,
hair dryers. **Pool(s):** heated outdoor. **Leisure Activities:** exercise room. **Guest Services:** valet and coin laundry, wireless
Internet. **Business Services:** meeting rooms.

SOME UNITS

[icons] /⊠ [icons] /

BEST WESTERN STAGECOACH INN   *Book great rates at AAA.com*   Phone: (501)624-2531
▽▽▽ ▽▽▽   3/1-4/15 & 1/16-2/29   1P: $80-$95   2P: $80-$95   XP: $10   F17
    4/16-1/15   1P: $70-$90   2P: $70-$90   XP: $5   F17
Small-scale Hotel   **Location:** 1.3 mi n of jct US 270 and SR 7. Located across from Oaklawn Park. 2520 Central Ave 71901.
    Fax: 501/623-0169. **Facility:** 120 one-bedroom standard units. 2 stories (no elevator), exterior corridors.
Parking: on-site. **Terms:** 2-4 night minimum stay - seasonal, 7 day cancellation notice, [ECP] meal plan available, package
plans. **Amenities:** safes, irons, hair dryers. *Some:* high-speed Internet. **Pool(s):** outdoor. **Guest Services:** coin laundry,
wireless Internet. **Cards:** AX, CB, DC, DS, JC, MC, VI.

SOME UNITS

(ASK) [icons] /⊠ [icons] /

CLARION RESORT   *Book great rates at AAA.com*   Phone: (501)525-1391
 (AAA) (SAVE)   All Year   1P: $89-$249   2P: $89-$249   XP: $10   F18
▽▽ ▽▽ ▽▽   **Location:** 5.5 mi s of jct US 270 and SR 7. 4813 Central Ave 71913. Fax: 501/525-0813. **Facility:** 149 units. 147
    one-bedroom standard units, some with whirlpools. 2 one-bedroom suites. 7 stories, interior corridors. *Bath:*
Small-scale Hotel   combo or shower only. **Parking:** on-site. **Terms:** [BP] meal plan available, package plans, pets ($10 extra
    charge). **Amenities:** high-speed Internet, voice mail, irons, hair dryers. *Fee:* video games, safes.
    Dining: 11:30 am-10 pm; hours may vary off season, cocktails. **Pool(s):** outdoor. **Leisure Activities:** boat
dock, fishing, lighted tennis court, playground, horseshoes, volleyball. *Fee:* boats. **Guest Services:** valet and coin laundry,
wireless Internet. **Business Services:** conference facilities. **Cards:** AX, CB, DC, DS, JC, MC, VI. **Free Special Amenities:**
early check-in/late check-out. *(See color ad below)*

SOME UNITS

[icons] FEE [icons] FEE [icons] /⊠ [icons] /

COMFORT INN & SUITES   *Book great rates at AAA.com*   Phone: (501)623-1700
▽▽▽▽   All Year [ECP]   1P: $85-$170   XP: $10   F
    Location: Just n of jct US 270. 3627 Central Ave 71913. Fax: 501/623-1876. **Facility:** 83 one-bedroom standard
Small-scale Hotel   units, some with whirlpools. 3 stories, interior corridors. *Bath:* combo or shower only. **Parking:** on-site.
    Terms: package plans. **Amenities:** high-speed Internet, dual phone lines, voice mail, safes, irons, hair
dryers. **Pool(s):** heated indoor. **Guest Services:** valet and coin laundry, wireless Internet. **Business Services:** meeting rooms.
Cards: AX, CB, DC, DS, JC, MC, VI.

SOME UNITS

(ASK) [icons] FEE [icons] /⊠ [icons] /

EMBASSY SUITES HOT SPRINGS   *Book great rates at AAA.com*   Phone: (501)624-9200

All Year   1P: $129-$179   2P: $129-$179   XP: $10   F18
Location: Just w of jct US 70. 400 Convention Blvd 71901. Fax: 501/624-3225. **Facility:** 246 one-bedroom suites, some with whirlpools. 9 stories, interior corridors. *Bath:* combo or shower only. **Parking:** on-site and valet.
Large-scale Hotel **Terms:** package plans, pets ($25 extra charge). **Amenities:** dual phone lines, voice mail, safes, irons, hair dryers. *Fee:* video games, high-speed Internet. **Dining:** Bistro 400, see separate listing. **Pool(s):** heated indoor. **Leisure Activities:** whirlpool, exercise room, spa. **Guest Services:** gift shop, valet and coin laundry, wireless Internet. **Business Services:** conference facilities, business center. **Cards:** AX, CB, DC, DS, JC, MC, VI.
Free Special Amenities: full breakfast and newspaper. *(See color ad below)*

SOME UNITS

🛏️ 🍽️ 🍸 🖥️ 🐕 📷 🏊 ✕ 🎾 🔌 🖨️ 💻 /✕/
FEE

HAMPTON INN   *Book great rates at AAA.com*   Phone: (501)525-7000

All Year   1P: $90-$109   2P: $90-$109
Location: 1 mi s of jct US 270 and SR 7. Located across from Hot Springs Mall. 151 Temperance Hill Rd 71913.
Small-scale Hotel Fax: 501/525-7626. **Facility:** 82 one-bedroom standard units, some with whirlpools. 4 stories, interior corridors. *Bath:* combo or shower only. **Parking:** on-site. **Amenities:** voice mail, irons, hair dryers. **Pool(s):**
outdoor. **Guest Services:** valet laundry, wireless Internet. **Business Services:** meeting rooms. **Cards:** AX, DC, DS, MC, VI.

SOME UNITS

🆂🅳 🍽️ 🐕 🏊 🛏️ 🎾 🔌 💻 /✕/
FEE

SUPER 8 MOTEL   *Book at AAA.com*   Phone: 501/525-0188

5/16-9/20   1P: $84-$149   2P: $84-$149   XP: $6   F17
3/1-4/16 & 9/21-2/29   1P: $64-$99   2P: $64-$99   XP: $6   F17
4/17-5/15   1P: $64-$74   2P: $64-$74   XP: $6   F17
Small-scale Hotel **Location:** 5 mi s of jct US 270. 4726 Central Ave 71913. Fax: 501/525-7449. **Facility:** 63 one-bedroom standard units. 3 stories, interior corridors. **Parking:** on-site. **Terms:** cancellation fee imposed. **Amenities:** high-speed Internet, irons, hair dryers. **Guest Services:** wireless Internet. **Cards:** AX, DS, MC, VI.

SOME UNITS

ASK 🍽️ 🎾 🔌 💻 /✕ 🖨️/

TRAVELIER INN   Phone: (501)624-4681

3/1-4/15 & 5/25-9/4   1P: $38-$65   2P: $50-$65   XP: $5   F18
4/16-5/24 & 9/5-2/29   1P: $38-$45   2P: $50-$58   XP: $5   F18
Location: 1 mi e of jct US 270B and 70. 1045 E Grand Ave 71901. Fax: 501/624-4684. **Facility:** 56 one-bedroom
Motel standard units, some with efficiencies. 2 stories (no elevator), exterior corridors. **Parking:** on-site. **Pool(s):**
outdoor, wading. **Cards:** AX, CB, DC, DS, JC, MC, VI. **Free Special Amenities: continental breakfast and local telephone calls.**

SOME UNITS

🆂🅳 🛏️ 🍽️ 🏊 🎾 /✕ 🔌 🖨️/

VELDA ROSE RESORT HOTEL & SPA   *Book great rates at AAA.com*   Phone: (501)623-3311

All Year   2P: $79-$95   XP: $5
Location: On US 70B and SR 7; center. 217 Park Ave 71901. Fax: 501/623-8871. **Facility:** 191 one-bedroom standard units. 10 stories, interior corridors. **Parking:** on-site. **Terms:** [AP] & [BP] meal plans available,
Large-scale Hotel package plans, small pets only. **Amenities:** dual phone lines, voice mail, irons, hair dryers. *Some:* safes.
Dining: 6 am-1 & 5-9 pm, Fri & Sat 5 pm-10 pm; hours vary in winter, cocktails, entertainment. **Pool(s):** heated outdoor, wading. **Leisure Activities:** saunas, spa. **Guest Services:** valet laundry. **Business Services:** conference facilities. **Cards:** AX, DS, MC, VI. **Free Special Amenities: local telephone calls and preferred room (subject to availability with advance reservations).**

SOME UNITS

🆂🅳 🛏️ 🍽️ 🍸 🏊 💻 /✕ 🔌/

———— *The following lodgings were either not evaluated or did not* ————
meet AAA rating requirements but are listed for your information only.

DAYS INN HAMILTON RESORT   Phone: 501/525-5666
[fyi]   Did not meet all AAA rating requirements for some property operations at time of last evaluation on
                     01/11/2006. **Location:** 3.8 mi s of jct US 270 and SR 7. Located on Lake Hamilton. 106 Lookout Point 71913.
Small-scale Hotel   Facilities, services, and decor characterize a mid-range property.

EMERALD ISLE RESORT   Phone: 501/525-3696
[fyi]   Not evaluated. **Location:** 6 mi s of jct US 270 and SR 7. 5371 Central Ave 71913. Facilities, services, and decor
                     characterize a mid-range property.

———— **WHERE TO DINE** ————

ANGEL'S ITALIAN RESTAURANT   **Lunch:** $9-$17   **Dinner:** $9-$17   Phone: 501/609-9323
                     Location: 0.6 mi n of jct US 70 and SR 7. 600 Central Ave 71901. **Hours:** 11:30 am-10 pm. Closed: 1/1, 11/22,
Italian   12/25; also Sun. **Features:** In what originally was a bank in the early 1900s, the restaurant exudes
                     character. The dining room affords a street view of downtown. Handmade pizzas are a favorite, but other
                     dishes offer equal flavor and quality. Casual dress; cocktails. **Parking:** street. **Cards:** AX, CB, DC, DS, JC,
MC, VI.

BACK PORCH GRILL   **Dinner:** $10-$38   Phone: 501/525-0885
                     Location: 5.5 mi s of jct US 270 and SR 7. 4810 Central Ave 71913. **Hours:** 4 pm-10 pm. Closed: 11/22, 12/25;
                     also Sun. **Reservations:** suggested. **Features:** An open grill where patrons can observe steaks cooking
Steak & Seafood   from start to finish centers the dining room. Seafood and pasta dishes look as good as they taste. Casual
                     dress; cocktails. **Parking:** on-site. **Cards:** AX, MC, VI.

BELLE ARTI RISTORANTE   **Lunch:** $10-$15   **Dinner:** $10-$35   Phone: 501/624-7474
                     Location: Just s of jct Central Ave and Spring St; downtown. 719 Central Ave 71901. **Hours:** 11:30 am-4 & 5-11 pm.
                     Closed: 12/25. **Reservations:** required, weekends. **Features:** An Old World setting of high ceilings and
Italian   arched doorways sets the stage for excellent cuisine of pasta, steaks and seafood. The filet, with green
                     peppercorns and a creamy cognac sauce, is superb. Locals and visitors alike are drawn to this fine dining
establishment. Casual dress; cocktails. **Parking:** street. **Cards:** AX, MC, VI.

BISTRO 400   **Lunch:** $7-$12   **Dinner:** $17-$30   Phone: 501/321-4421
                     Location: Just w of jct US 70; in Embassy Suites Hot Springs. 400 Convention Blvd 71901. **Hours:** 11 am-2 & 5-10
                     pm. **Reservations:** accepted. **Features:** The upscale yet comfortable setting is enhanced by a good
American   selection of familiar dishes. Casual dress; cocktails. **Parking:** on-site (fee) and valet. **Cards:** AX, DS, JC,
                     MC, VI.

BRICK HOUSE GRILL   **Lunch:** $5-$8   **Dinner:** $9-$21   Phone: 501/321-2926
                     Location: Just n of jct US 70 and SR 7; in Spencer's Corner. 801 Central Ave 71901. **Hours:** 11 am-10 pm, Sun 5
                     pm-9 pm. Closed major holidays. **Features:** Steak and seafood selections are popular for dinner, while
Steak & Seafood   lunch centers primarily on sandwiches and lighter fare. The atmosphere is casual and inviting. Casual dress;
                     cocktails. **Parking:** on-site. **Cards:** AX, CB, DS, MC, VI.

CHEF PAUL'S   **Lunch:** $6-$14   **Dinner:** $15-$40   Phone: 501/520-4187
[AAA]   **Location:** 1 mi s of jct US 270 and SR 7. 4330 Central Ave 71913. **Hours:** 11:30 am-2 & 5:30-9:30 pm, Fri-10 pm,
                     Sat 5:30 pm-10 pm. Closed: Sun. **Reservations:** suggested. **Features:** The mood is intimate in the small
                     but nicely appointed dining room. Meals are individually prepared and have enhanced presentation. Semi-
Continental   formal attire; cocktails. **Parking:** on-site. **Cards:** AX, DC, DS, MC, VI.

COLTON'S STEAKHOUSE & GRILL   **Lunch:** $6-$8   **Dinner:** $9-$19   Phone: 501/623-2110
                     Location: 0.9 mi n of jct US 270 and SR 7. 120 Crawford 71913. **Hours:** 11 am-9 pm, Fri & Sat-10 pm. Closed:
                     11/22, 12/25. **Features:** A bucket of peanuts on the table, an upbeat Old-West atmosphere and a good
Steak House   selection of steak, chicken and ribs await guests at the casual steakhouse. Casual dress; cocktails.
                     Parking: on-site. **Cards:** AX, DC, DS, MC, VI.

COY'S   **Dinner:** $9-$46   Phone: 501/321-1414
                     Location: Just nw of US 70, 1.5 mi e of jct SR 7. 300 Coy St 71902. **Hours:** 5 pm-9 pm, Fri & Sat-10 pm. Closed:
                     11/22, 12/24, 12/25. **Reservations:** accepted. **Features:** This restaurant is popular with local residents and
Steak House   has a long history of having great food served by its warm and considerate staff. Coy's also has a casual
                     and family-type dining atmosphere where the kids are welcome. Casual dress; cocktails. **Parking:** on-site.
Cards: AX, DC, DS, MC, VI.

DIXIE CAFE

Regional American

| Lunch: $6-$9 | Dinner: $6-$9 | Phone: 501/624-2100 |

Location: Just n of jct US 270 and SR 7. 3623 Central Ave 71913. **Hours:** 11 am-10 pm. Closed: 11/22, 12/25. **Features:** Southern-style home cooking-chicken-fried steak, meat loaf, pork chops, turnip greens, mashed potatoes and fresh veggies-appeals to families who visit the restaurant's classic "Norman Rockwell" atmosphere. Casual dress; beer & wine only. **Parking:** on-site. **Cards:** AX, MC, VI.

HOT SPRINGS BRAU HAUS

German

| Dinner: $8-$13 | Phone: 501/624-7866 |

Location: Just n of jct US 70 and SR 7; in Spencer's Corner. 801 Central Ave 71901. **Hours:** 3 pm-10 pm, Fri & Sat-11 pm. Closed major holidays; also Mon. **Features:** German food served in tantalizing combinations dominates the menu. Patrons are all but certain to find their favorites in the re-created brau haus. Casual dress; cocktails. **Parking:** on-site. **Cards:** AX, DS, MC, VI.

LA HACIENDA

Traditional Mexican

| Lunch: $4-$16 | Dinner: $6-$16 | Phone: 501/525-8203 |

Location: SR 7, 1.5 mi s of Oaklawn Race Track. 3836 Central Ave 71913. **Hours:** 11 am-10 pm, Sun 11 am-2 & 5-10 pm. Closed major holidays. **Features:** If you are looking for very good food reminiscent of the Mexican food served much farther west, and large portions, La Hacienda is the place to stop for lunch or dinner. The service is friendly and efficient. Casual dress; cocktails. **Parking:** on-site. **Cards:** AX, DS, MC, VI.

NEW CHINA

Chinese

| Lunch: $6-$6 | Dinner: $7-$8 | Phone: 501/525-8868 |

Location: 1.4 mi s of jct US 270 and SR 7. 4510 Central Ave 71913. **Hours:** 11 am-9:30 pm, Fri & Sat-10 pm. Closed: 11/22. **Features:** The daily buffet lines up a large selection of choices. This place is a favorite among locals. Casual dress. **Parking:** on-site. **Cards:** AX, DS, MC, VI.

HOT SPRINGS VILLAGE pop. 8,397

———— WHERE TO STAY ————

———— *The following lodging was either not evaluated or did not* ————
meet AAA rating requirements but is listed for your information only.

LOS LAGOS

[fyi]

Phone: 501/915-9062

Not evaluated. **Location:** 1 Los Lagos Dr 71909. Facilities, services, and decor characterize a mid-range property.

JACKSONVILLE pop. 29,916

———— WHERE TO STAY ————

COMFORT INN

Small-scale Hotel

Phone: 501/985-4400

All Year | 1P: $50-$125 | 2P: $50-$125

Location: US 67/167, exit 10B southbound; exit 11 northbound. 1500 John Harden Dr 72076. Fax: 501/985-4819. **Facility:** 60 one-bedroom standard units, some with whirlpools. 2 stories (no elevator), interior corridors. *Bath:* combo or shower only. **Parking:** on-site. **Amenities:** voice mail, irons, hair dryers. **Pool(s):** small outdoor. **Leisure Activities:** exercise room. **Guest Services:** coin laundry, wireless Internet. **Business Services:** PC. **Cards:** AX, DC, DS, MC, VI.

SOME UNITS

COMFORT INN

Small-scale Hotel

Book great rates at AAA.com

Property failed to provide current rates

Phone: 501/982-9219

Location: US 67/167, exit 10B southbound; exit 11 northbound. 1850 John Harden Dr 72076. Fax: 501/982-2827. **Facility:** 58 one-bedroom standard units, some with whirlpools. 2 stories (no elevator), exterior corridors. **Parking:** on-site. **Amenities:** high-speed Internet, irons, hair dryers. **Pool(s):** small heated indoor. **Leisure Activities:** whirlpool, exercise room. **Guest Services:** valet and coin laundry, wireless Internet. **Business Services:** meeting rooms, PC.

SOME UNITS

CRANBURY INN & SUITES

Small-scale Hotel

Book great rates at AAA.com

Phone: 501/985-7666

All Year [ECP] | 1P: $79-$99 | 2P: $84-$104

Location: US 67/167, exit 10B southbound; exit 11 northbound. 2110 John Harden Dr 72076. Fax: 501/985-7667. **Facility:** 50 one-bedroom standard units. 3 stories, interior corridors. **Parking:** on-site. **Amenities:** irons, hair dryers. **Pool(s):** small outdoor. **Leisure Activities:** exercise room. **Guest Services:** coin laundry, wireless Internet. **Business Services:** business center. **Cards:** AX, CB, DC, DS, JC, MC, VI. **Free Special Amenities:** expanded continental breakfast and high-speed Internet.

SOME UNITS

JOHNSON pop. 2,319

──── WHERE TO STAY ────

INN AT THE MILL-A CLARION CARRIAGE HOUSE   *Book great rates at AAA.com*   Phone: 479/443-1800

Property failed to provide current rates

▼▼▼ **Location:** I-540, exit 69, just e. 3906 Greathouse Springs Rd 72741 (PO Box 409). Fax: 479/444-6274. **Facility:** 48 units. 46 one-bedroom standard units, some with whirlpools. 2 one-bedroom suites with whirlpools. 2 stories **Small-scale Hotel** (no elevator), interior corridors. **Parking:** on-site. **Amenities:** voice mail, irons, hair dryers. *Some:* high-speed Internet. **Dining:** James At The Mill, see separate listing. **Leisure Activities:** exercise room. **Guest Services:** complimentary evening beverages, valet laundry, wireless Internet. **Business Services:** meeting rooms.

SOME UNITS

🍴 🍸 🐾 🖥 / ✕ /

──── WHERE TO DINE ────

JAMES AT THE MILL   **Lunch:** $8-$13   **Dinner:** $13-$33   Phone: 479/443-1400

▼▼▼ ▼▼▼ **Location:** I-540, exit 69, just e; in Inn at the Mill-A Clarion Carriage House. 3906 Greathouse Springs Rd 72741. **Hours:** 11 am-2 & 5:30-10 pm, Sat from 5:30 pm. Closed: 1/1, 11/22, 12/25; also Sun. **American** **Reservations:** suggested. **Features:** Ozark Plateau cuisine is the claim to fame at the sophisticated restaurant, where entrees are presented with style and panache. Both the food and service are superb, so dining expectations will be more than met. The interesting setting incorporates beautiful outdoor enhancements. Dressy casual; cocktails. **Parking:** on-site. **Cards:** AX, CB, DC, DS, MC, VI.

🚫

JONESBORO pop. 55,515

──── WHERE TO STAY ────

COMFORT INN & SUITES   *Book great rates at AAA.com*   Phone: (870)972-9000

ⒶⒶⒶ (SAVE) **All Year**   1P: $70-$85   2P: $70-$85

▼▼ ▼▼ **Location:** US 63, exit Stadium Blvd/Caraway Rd, just n. 2911 Gilmore Dr 72401. Fax: 870/931-6407. **Facility:** 108 units. 63 one-bedroom standard units, some with whirlpools. 45 one-bedroom suites ($75-$100), some with **Small-scale Hotel** whirlpools. 5 stories, interior corridors. **Parking:** on-site. **Terms:** cancellation fee imposed, package plans, pets ($10 extra charge, with prior approval). **Amenities:** dual phone lines, voice mail, irons, hair dryers. **Pool(s):** outdoor. **Leisure Activities:** exercise room. **Guest Services:** valet laundry, wireless Internet. **Business Services:** meeting rooms, business center. **Cards:** AX, DS, MC, VI. **Free Special Amenities:** expanded continental breakfast and local telephone calls.

SOME UNITS

🆂🅳 🛏 🍴 📞 🛳 🐾 🎬 🖥 / ✕ 🖥
FEE

HAMPTON INN   *Book great rates at AAA.com*   Phone: (870)974-9500

▼▼▼ **All Year**   1P: $76-$135   2P: $89-$145   XP: $5   F18

Location: US 63, exit Stadium Blvd/Caraway Rd, just n. 2900 Phillips Dr 72401. Fax: 870/974-9570. **Facility:** 62 **Small-scale Hotel** one-bedroom standard units, some with whirlpools. 3 stories, interior corridors. *Bath:* combo or shower only. **Parking:** on-site. **Terms:** 7 day cancellation notice, [ECP] meal plan available. **Amenities:** high-speed Internet, voice mail, irons, hair dryers. **Pool(s):** outdoor. **Leisure Activities:** exercise room. **Guest Services:** valet and coin laundry, wireless Internet. **Business Services:** business center. **Cards:** AX, CB, DC, DS, MC, VI.

SOME UNITS

(ASK) 🆂🅳 🍴 📞 🛳 🐾 🖥 / ✕ 🖥 🖥

HOLIDAY INN EXPRESS   *Book at AAA.com*   Phone: 870/932-5554

▼▼▼ **All Year**   1P: $85

Location: US 63, exit Stadium Blvd/Caraway Rd, just n. 2407 Phillips Dr 72401. Fax: 870/932-2586. **Facility:** 102 **Small-scale Hotel** one-bedroom standard units. 4 stories, interior corridors. *Bath:* combo or shower only. **Parking:** on-site. **Amenities:** dual phone lines, voice mail, irons, hair dryers. **Pool(s):** heated outdoor. **Leisure Activities:** exercise room. **Guest Services:** valet and coin laundry, wireless Internet. **Business Services:** meeting rooms, business center. **Cards:** AX, DC, DS, JC, MC, VI.

SOME UNITS

(ASK) 🆂🅳 🛏 🍴 🛳 🐾 🖥 🖥 🖥 / ✕ /

HOLIDAY INN OF JONESBORO   *Book at AAA.com*   Phone: 870/935-2030

Property failed to provide current rates

▼▼▼ **Location:** US 63, exit Stadium Blvd/Caraway Rd, just n. 3006 S Caraway Rd 72401. Fax: 870/935-3440. **Facility:** 179 one-bedroom standard units, some with whirlpools. 2 stories (no elevator), interior/exterior **Small-scale Hotel** corridors. *Bath:* combo or shower only. **Parking:** on-site. **Amenities:** voice mail, irons, hair dryers. **Pool(s):** heated indoor. **Leisure Activities:** whirlpool, exercise room. **Guest Services:** valet and coin laundry, area transportation, wireless Internet. **Business Services:** conference facilities, business center.

SOME UNITS

✈ 🍴 🛳 🐾 🎬 🖥 🖥 🖥 / ✕ /

WEST WASHINGTON GUEST HOUSE   *Book at AAA.com*   Phone: 870/935-9300

Property failed to provide current rates

▼▼▼ **Location:** Just w of jct Main St; downtown. 534 W Washington 72401 (PO Box 69, 72403-0069). **Facility:** This older **Bed & Breakfast** home has all the modern amenities and conviences, but mixed with the charm of yesteryear. 12 units. 11 one-bedroom standard units. 1 one-bedroom suite with whirlpool. 3 stories (no elevator), interior corridors. **Parking:** on-site. **Guest Services:** wireless Internet.

(VCR) 🐾

──── *The following lodging was either not evaluated or did not* ────
meet AAA rating requirements but is listed for your information only.

BAYMONT INN-JONESBORO   Phone: 870/802-2200

[fyi] Did not meet all AAA rating requirements for some property operations at time of last evaluation on 06/15/2006. **Location:** US 63, exit Stadium Blvd/Caraway Rd, just n. 2910 Kazi St 72401. Facilities, services, and **Small-scale Hotel** decor characterize a mid-range property.

——— WHERE TO DINE ———

COLTON'S STEAKHOUSE & GRILL   **Lunch:** $6-$8   **Dinner:** $9-$19   Phone: 870/802-4000

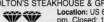
Steak House

Location: US 63, exit Stadium Blvd/Caraway Rd, just s. 2309 E Parker Rd 72401. **Hours:** 11 am-9 pm, Fri & Sat-10 pm. Closed: 11/22, 12/25. **Features:** A bucket of peanuts on the table, an upbeat Old-West atmosphere and a good selection of steak, chicken and ribs await guests at the casual steakhouse. Casual dress; cocktails. **Parking:** on-site. **Cards:** AX, DC, DS, MC, VI.

DIXIE CAFE   **Lunch:** $7-$10   **Dinner:** $7-$10   Phone: 870/932-9400

Regional American

Location: US 63, exit Stadium Blvd/Caraway Rd, 0.5 mi n. 2406 S Caraway Rd 72401. **Hours:** 11 am-10 pm. Closed: 11/22, 12/25. **Features:** Southern-style home cooking-chicken-fried steak, meat loaf, pork chops, turnip greens, mashed potatoes and fresh veggies-appeals to families who visit the restaurant's classic "Norman Rockwell" atmosphere. Casual dress. **Parking:** on-site. **Cards:** AX, DS, MC, VI.

LITTLE ROCK pop. 183,133—See also NORTH LITTLE ROCK.

——— WHERE TO STAY ———

BEST WESTERN GOVERNORS SUITES   *Book great rates at AAA.com*   Phone: (501)224-8051

All Year   1P: $89-$109   2P: $89-$109   XP: $10   F12

Small-scale Hotel

Location: I-430, exit 8, 0.5 mi w, then just s. 1501 Merrill Dr 72211. Fax: 501/224-8051. **Facility:** 49 units. 44 one-bedroom standard units, some with whirlpools. 5 one-bedroom suites ($119-$139). 3 stories, interior corridors. **Parking:** on-site. **Terms:** 7 day cancellation notice, [BP] meal plan available. **Amenities:** high-speed Internet, irons, hair dryers. **Pool(s):** outdoor. **Guest Services:** valet laundry. **Business Services:** meeting rooms. **Cards:** AX, DC, DS, MC, VI. **Free Special Amenities:** full breakfast and early check-in/late check-out. *(See color ad below)*

SOME UNITS

THE CAPITAL HOTEL   Phone: (501)374-7474

All Year   1P: $179-$219   2P: $179-$219   XP: $20

Under major renovation, scheduled to be completed December 2006. **Last rated:** ◆◆◆◆ **Location:** Downtown. 111 W Markham St 72201. Fax: 501/370-7091. **Facility:** Under major renovations, scheduled to be completed July 2006. This 19th century hotel offers 10'-13' high guest room ceilings, fresh flowers and numerous amenities. 123 units. 118 one-bedroom standard units. 5 one-bedroom suites. 4 stories, interior corridors. *Bath:* combo or shower only. **Parking:** on-site (fee) and valet. **Terms:** package plans. **Amenities:** CD players, high-speed Internet, dual phone lines, voice mail, safes, irons, hair dryers. *Some:* DVD players (fee). **Dining:** Ashley's at The Capital, see separate listing. **Guest Services:** gift shop, valet laundry. **Business Services:** meeting rooms, business center. **Cards:** AX, CB, DC, DS, JC, MC, VI. **Free Special Amenities:** newspaper.

Historic
Large-scale Hotel

SOME UNITS
FEE   FEE

COMFORT INN   *Book great rates at AAA.com*   Phone: 501/227-0120

All Year   1P: $68-$89   2P: $72-$93   XP: $4   F

Small-scale Hotel

Location: I-430, exit 6, just e on Markham St, then just n. 300 Markham Center Dr 72205. Fax: 501/227-0120. **Facility:** 70 one-bedroom standard units, some with whirlpools. 3 stories, interior corridors. *Bath:* combo or shower only. **Parking:** on-site. **Terms:** [ECP] meal plan available. **Amenities:** high-speed Internet, irons, hair dryers. **Leisure Activities:** exercise room. **Guest Services:** wireless Internet. **Cards:** AX, CB, DC, DS, JC, MC, VI. **Free Special Amenities:** expanded continental breakfast and high-speed Internet.

SOME UNITS

COMFORT INN & SUITES, DOWNTOWN LITTLE ROCK @ THE CLINTON LIBRARY   *Book great rates at AAA.com*   Phone: (501)687-770

(AAA) (SAVE) 6/1-8/31 [ECP]   1P: $86-$99   2P: $86-$99
▽▽▽   3/1-5/31 & 9/1-2/29 [ECP]   1P: $81-$91   2P: $81-$91
         Location: I-30, exit 140A, just e. 707 I-30 72202. Fax: 501/687-1016. **Facility:** 150 one-bedroom standard unit
Small-scale Hotel 9 stories, interior corridors. **Bath:** combo or shower only. **Parking:** on-site. **Terms:** pets ($25 fee
         Amenities: high-speed Internet, dual phone lines, voice mail, irons, hair dryers. *Fee:* video games, safe
         Pool(s): outdoor. **Leisure Activities:** exercise room. **Guest Services:** sundries, valet and coin laundr
area transportation-within 3 mi, wireless Interent. **Business Services:** conference facilities, business center. **Cards:** AX, C
DC, DS, JC, MC, VI. **Free Special Amenities: expanded continental breakfast and high-speed Internet.**
(See color ad below)

SOME UNITS
[icons] FEE

COURTYARD BY MARRIOTT DOWNTOWN LITTLE ROCK   *Book great rates at AAA.com*   Phone: 501/975-980

▽▽▽   All Year   1P: $99-$179
         Location: I-30, exit 141A. 521 President Clinton Ave 72201. Fax: 501/975-9801. **Facility:** Smoke free premise
Small-scale Hotel 120 one-bedroom standard units, some with whirlpools. 6 stories, interior corridors. **Bath:** combo or showe
         only. **Parking:** on-site (fee). **Terms:** package plans. **Amenities:** high-speed Internet, voice mail, irons, ha
dryers. **Pool(s):** small heated indoor. **Leisure Activities:** whirlpool, exercise room. **Guest Services:** sundries, valet and co
laundry, wireless Internet. **Business Services:** meeting rooms, business center. **Cards:** AX, CB, DC, DS, JC, MC, VI.

(ASK) [icons]

COURTYARD BY MARRIOTT-LITTLE ROCK   *Book great rates at AAA.com*   Phone: (501)227-600

(AAA) (SAVE) All Year   1P: $149-$199   2P: $149-$199
▽▽▽   **Location:** Jct I-430 and 630, exit Shackleford Rd. 10900 Financial Center Pkwy 72211. Fax: 501/227-691
         Facility: Smoke free premises. 149 units. 137 one-bedroom standard units. 12 one-bedroom suites ($19
         $229). 3 stories, interior corridors. **Bath:** combo or shower only. **Parking:** on-site. **Terms:** cancellation fe
Small-scale Hotel imposed, [AP], [BP], [CP], [ECP] & [MAP] meal plans available, package plans. **Amenities:** high-spee
         Internet, voice mail, irons, hair dryers. **Dining:** 6:30-10 am, Sat & Sun 7-11 am. **Pool(s):** heated outdoo
Leisure Activities: whirlpool, exercise room. **Guest Services:** sundries, valet and coin laundry. **Business Services:** meetin
rooms, business center. **Cards:** AX, DC, DS, MC, VI. **Free Special Amenities: high-speed Internet.**

SOME UNITS
[icons]

DOUBLETREE LITTLE ROCK   *Book great rates at AAA.com*   Phone: (501)372-437

▽▽▽   All Year   1P: $99-$179   2P: $99-$179   XP: $10   F1
         Location: Downtown. 424 W Markham St 72201. Fax: 501/372-0518. **Facility:** 287 units. 276 one-bedroo
         standard units. 11 one-bedroom suites, some with whirlpools. 14 stories, interior corridors. **Bath:** combo o
Large-scale Hotel shower only. **Parking:** on-site. **Terms:** cancellation fee imposed. **Amenities:** video games (fee), C
         players, dual phone lines, voice mail, irons, hair dryers. *Some:* high-speed Internet. **Pool(s):** outdoor. **Leisur**
Activities: exercise room. **Guest Services:** gift shop, valet laundry, area transportation, wireless Internet. **Business Services**
conference facilities, business center. **Cards:** AX, CB, DC, DS, MC, VI.

SOME UNITS
(ASK) [icons]

EMBASSY SUITES HOTEL LITTLE ROCK   *Book great rates at AAA.com*   Phone: (501)312-900

(AAA) (SAVE) All Year [BP]   1P: $119-$209   2P: $119-$219   XP: $10   F1
▽▽▽   **Location:** Jct I-430 and 630, just w. 11301 Financial Center Pkwy 72211. Fax: 501/312-9455. **Facility:** 251 one
         bedroom suites, some with whirlpools. 9 stories, interior corridors. **Bath:** combo or shower only. **Parking:**
Large-scale Hotel on-site. **Terms:** package plans, pets ($50 fee). **Amenities:** dual phone lines, voice mail, irons, hair dryers
         Fee: video games, high-speed Internet. **Dining:** 11 am-11 pm, cocktails. **Pool(s):** heated indoor. **Leisur**
Activities: sauna, whirlpool, exercise room. **Guest Services:** gift shop, valet and coin laundry, wireles
Internet. **Business Services:** conference facilities, business center. **Cards:** AX, CB, DC, DS, JC, MC, V
Free Special Amenities: full breakfast and newspaper.

SOME UNIT
[icons] FEE

THE EMPRESS OF LITTLE ROCK BED & BREAKFAST/CONFERENCE CENTER   *Book at AAA.com*

Phone: (501)374-7966

▼▼▼▼
Historic Bed & Breakfast

All Year   1P: $110-$275   2P: $135-$285   XP: $50
Location: I-630, exit 1B, 0.6 mi s. 2120 Louisiana St 72206. Fax: 501/375-4537. **Facility:** Elegant furnishings fill the 1888 Victorian property. 8 one-bedroom standard units, some with whirlpools. 2-3 stories (no elevator), interior corridors. *Bath:* combo or shower only. **Parking:** on-site. **Terms:** office hours 8 am-6 pm, age restrictions may apply, 7 day cancellation notice-fee imposed, package plans, $10 service charge.
Amenities: video library, CD players, high-speed Internet, irons, hair dryers. *Some:* DVD players. **Guest Services:** complimentary evening beverages, valet laundry, wireless Internet. **Business Services:** meeting rooms. **Cards:** AX, MC, VI.

(ASK) (➕➕) (✕) (VCR)
FEE

HAMPTON INN & SUITES   *Book great rates at AAA.com*

Phone: 501/537-3000

▼▼▼▼
Small-scale Hotel

Property failed to provide current rates
Location: I-430, exit 5, just n. 1301 S Shackleford Rd 72211. Fax: 501/537-7070. **Facility:** 126 units. 92 one-bedroom standard units. 34 one-bedroom suites. 5 stories, interior corridors. *Bath:* combo or shower only. **Parking:** on-site. **Amenities:** video games (fee), high-speed Internet, dual phone lines, voice mail, irons, hair dryers. **Pool(s):** heated indoor. **Leisure Activities:** whirlpool, exercise room. **Guest Services:** sundries, valet and coin laundry, wireless Internet. **Business Services:** meeting rooms.

SOME UNITS
(🅼) (♿) (🍽) (⌖) (🐾) (📷) (💻) / (✕) (VCR) (🛄) (📷) /

HAMPTON INN LITTLE ROCK I-30   *Book great rates at AAA.com*

Phone: (501)562-6667

▼▼▼▼
Small-scale Hotel

All Year [CP]   1P: $80-$99   2P: $85-$104   XP: $5   F
Location: I-30, exit 133. 6100 Mitchell Dr 72209. Fax: 501/568-6832. **Facility:** 120 one-bedroom standard units. 4 stories, interior corridors. **Parking:** on-site. **Terms:** cancellation fee imposed, [ECP] meal plan available. **Pool(s):** small outdoor. **Leisure Activities:** exercise room. **Guest Services:** valet and coin laundry, wireless Internet. **Business Services:** meeting rooms. **Cards:** AX, CB, DC, DS, MC, VI.

SOME UNITS
(ASK) (🆂⒟) (🐾) (📷) (💻) / (✕)

HILTON LITTLE ROCK METRO CENTER   *Book great rates at AAA.com*

Phone: (501)664-5020

▼▼▼▼
Small-scale Hotel

All Year   1P: $119-$179   2P: $129-$189   XP: $10   F16
Location: I-630, exit 5 (University Ave), just s. 925 S University Ave 72204. Fax: 501/614-3803. **Facility:** Smoke free premises. 263 one-bedroom standard units, some with whirlpools. 3 stories, interior corridors. *Bath:* combo or shower only. **Parking:** on-site. **Terms:** cancellation fee imposed, weekly rates available, [AP], [BP], [CP] & [ECP] meal plans available, package plans, 4% service charge. **Amenities:** video games (fee), high-speed Internet, dual phone lines, voice mail, irons, hair dryers. **Pool(s):** outdoor, wading. **Leisure Activities:** exercise room. **Guest Services:** gift shop, valet and coin laundry, area transportation, wireless Internet. **Business Services:** conference facilities, business center. **Cards:** AX, DS, MC, VI.

SOME UNITS
(ASK) (🆂⒟) (✈) (🍽) (24🍽) (🍸) (🅼) (♿) (🐾) (✕) (📷) (💻) / (🛄) (📷) /

HOLIDAY INN PRESIDENTIAL CONFERENCE CENTER   *Book at AAA.com*

Phone: 501/375-2100

▼▼▼▼
Small-scale Hotel

All Year   1P: $86-$105
Location: I-30, exit 140B, just w. 600 I-30 72202. Fax: 501/374-9045. **Facility:** 150 units. 146 one-bedroom standard units, some with whirlpools. 4 one-bedroom suites ($159-$289). 8 stories, interior corridors. *Bath:* combo or shower only. **Parking:** on-site. **Terms:** [AP] & [BP] meal plans available, package plans. **Amenities:** dual phone lines, voice mail, irons, hair dryers. **Pool(s):** outdoor. **Leisure Activities:** exercise room. **Guest Services:** valet and coin laundry, area transportation, wireless Internet. **Business Services:** conference facilities, business center. **Cards:** AX, CB, DC, DS, MC, VI.

SOME UNITS
(ASK) (🆂⒟) (✈) (🍽) (🍸) (🐾) (📷) (💻) / (✕) (🛄) (📷) /

HOLIDAY INN SELECT   *Book at AAA.com*

Phone: 501/223-3000

▼▼▼▼
Small-scale Hotel

Property failed to provide current rates
Location: Jct I-430 and 630. 201 S Shackleford Rd 72211. Fax: 501/223-2833. **Facility:** 255 units. 250 one-bedroom standard units, some with whirlpools. 5 one-bedroom suites. 5 stories, interior/exterior corridors. **Parking:** on-site. **Terms:** pets ($100 deposit, $25 extra charge, in designated units). **Amenities:** video games (fee), high-speed Internet, dual phone lines, voice mail, irons, hair dryers. **Pool(s):** heated indoor/outdoor. **Leisure Activities:** whirlpools, exercise room. **Guest Services:** valet and coin laundry, wireless Internet. **Business Services:** conference facilities, business center.

SOME UNITS
(🐾) (🍽) (🍸) (🐾) (📷) (💻) / (✕) (🛄) (📷) /
FEE

LA QUINTA INN   *Book great rates at AAA.com*

Phone: (501)225-7007

▼▼ ▼▼
Small-scale Hotel

6/1-8/15 [CP]   1P: $71-$101   2P: $77-$107   XP: $6   F18
8/16-2/29 [CP]   1P: $69-$99   2P: $75-$105   XP: $6   F18
3/1-5/31 [CP]   1P: $65-$95   2P: $71-$101   XP: $6   F18
Location: I-430, exit 8, just e to Breckenridge Rd, then just s. 1010 Breckenridge Rd 72205. Fax: 501/225-2631.
Facility: 98 units. 95 one-bedroom standard units. 3 one-bedroom suites ($75-$117), some with kitchens. 3 stories, interior corridors. **Parking:** on-site. **Amenities:** video games (fee), high-speed Internet, voice mail, irons, hair dryers. **Guest Services:** coin laundry. **Business Services:** meeting rooms. **Cards:** AX, CB, DC, DS, MC, VI.

SOME UNITS
(ASK) (🐾) (🍸) (📷) (➕➕) (📷) (💻) / (✕) (🛄) (📷) /

LA QUINTA INN LITTLE ROCK (MEDICAL CENTER AREA)   *Book great rates at AAA.com*   **Phone:** (501)664-7000

5/1-2/29	1P: $69-$99	2P: $69-$99
3/1-4/30	1P: $65-$95	2P: $65-$95

Small-scale Hotel   **Location:** I-630, exit 4, just s. 901 Fair Park Blvd 72204-1754. Fax: 501/664-1639. **Facility:** 121 one-bedroom standard units. 2 stories (no elevator), exterior corridors. **Parking:** on-site. **Terms:** small pets only. **Amenities:** video games (fee), high-speed Internet, voice mail, irons, hair dryers. **Pool(s):** outdoor. **Guest Services:** wireless Internet. **Business Services:** meeting rooms. **Cards:** AX, CB, DC, DS, MC, VI.

SOME UNITS

LA QUINTA INN LITTLE ROCK (OTTER CREEK AREA)   *Book great rates at AAA.com*   **Phone:** (501)455-2300

All Year [CP]	1P: $69-$99	2P: $76-$106	XP: $7 F18

Small-scale Hotel   **Location:** I-30, exit 128, just e. 11701 I-30 72209. Fax: 501/455-5876. **Facility:** 145 one-bedroom standard units. 3 stories, exterior corridors. **Parking:** on-site. **Terms:** small pets only. **Amenities:** video games (fee), voice mail, irons, hair dryers. **Pool(s):** small outdoor. **Guest Services:** valet and coin laundry. **Business Services:** meeting rooms. **Cards:** AX, CB, DC, DS, MC, VI.

SOME UNITS

LA QUINTA INN LITTLE ROCK (WEST)   *Book great rates at AAA.com*   **Phone:** (501)224-0900

All Year	1P: $72-$102	2P: $78-$168	XP: $6 F18

Small-scale Hotel   **Location:** I-430, exit 6; I-630, exit Shackleford Rd N; jct I-430 and 630. 200 S Shackleford Rd 72211. Fax: 501/221-7126. **Facility:** 106 one-bedroom standard units. 2 stories (no elevator), exterior corridors. **Parking:** on-site. **Terms:** small pets only. **Amenities:** video games (fee), voice mail, irons, hair dryers. **Pool(s):** small outdoor. **Guest Services:** wireless Internet. **Cards:** AX, CB, DC, DS, MC, VI.

SOME UNITS

THE PEABODY LITTLE ROCK   *Book great rates at AAA.com*   **Phone:** (501)906-4000

All Year	1P: $159-$219	2P: $159-$219	XP: $20 F17

Large-scale Hotel   **Location:** Downtown. 3 Statehouse Plaza 72201. Fax: 501/375-4721. **Facility:** Ducks patrol the waters of an indoor fountain at this upscale hotel, where displays of fine art add a sophisticated ambience to common areas. 418 units. 396 one-bedroom standard units. 20 one- and 2 two-bedroom suites, some with whirlpools. 20 stories, interior corridors. *Bath:* combo or shower only. **Parking:** on-site (fee) and valet. **Terms:** cancellation fee imposed, 4% service charge. **Amenities:** video games (fee), high-speed Internet, dual phone lines, voice mail, irons, hair dryers. **Dining:** Capriccio, see separate listing. **Leisure Activities:** saunas. **Guest Services:** gift shop, valet laundry, area transportation, wireless Internet. **Business Services:** conference facilities, business center. **Cards:** AX, CB, DC, DS, JC, MC, VI. **Free Special Amenities:** newspaper and high-speed Internet.

SOME UNITS   FEE

WINGATE INN   *Book at AAA.com*   **Phone:** (501)227-6800

All Year [CP]	1P: $119-$179	2P: $119-$179	XP: $10 F16

Small-scale Hotel   **Location:** I-430, exit 5, just n. 1212 S Shackleford Rd 72211. Fax: 501/227-6819. **Facility:** 93 units. 87 one-bedroom standard units. 6 one-bedroom suites ($119-$179) with whirlpools. 4 stories, interior corridors. *Bath:* combo or shower only. **Parking:** on-site. **Terms:** package plans. **Amenities:** video games (fee), high-speed Internet, dual phone lines, voice mail, safes, irons, hair dryers. **Pool(s):** heated outdoor. **Leisure Activities:** whirlpool. **Guest Services:** valet laundry, wireless Internet. **Business Services:** meeting rooms, business center. **Cards:** AX, DC, DS, MC, VI.

SOME UNITS   FEE

─────── *The following lodgings were either not evaluated or did not* ───────
meet AAA rating requirements but are listed for your information only.

AIRPORT TRAVELODGE　　　　　　　　　　　　　　　　　　　Phone: 501/490-2200
[fyi]　　Did not meet all AAA rating requirements for some property operations at time of last evaluation on
07/27/2006. **Location:** I-440, exit 5, just n. 7615 Fluid Dr 72206. Facilities, services, and decor characterize a mid-
Small-scale Hotel　range property.

─────── **WHERE TO DINE** ───────

620 RESTAURANT　　　　　　　　　**Dinner:** $9-$24　　　　　　　Phone: 501/221-1620
　　Location: I-430, exit 8, 0.6 mi w on Rodney Parham Rd, then 0.3 mi s. 1620 Market St 72212. **Hours:** 5:30 pm-9 pm,
Fri & Sat-9:30 pm. Closed major holidays; also Sun. **Reservations:** suggested. **Features:** This out-of-the-
Continental　way restaurant has an elegant atmosphere and quiet setting. The eclectic menu selections are
contemporary Continental and very good; they include steak, seafood, chops and pasta. They also have a
large selection of wines. Casual dress; cocktails. **Parking:** on-site. **Cards:** AX, DC, DS, MC, VI.

ASHLEY'S AT THE CAPITAL　　　　**Lunch:** $6-$12　　　　**Dinner:** $16-$33　　　Phone: 501/374-7474
(AAA)　　Under major renovation. **Location:** Downtown; in The Capital Hotel. 111 W Markham St 72201. **Hours:** 6:30-10
[fyi]　　am, 11-2 & 6-11 pm, Sun 11 am-2 pm. **Reservations:** suggested. **Features:** Ashley's elegant and romantic
Continental　atmosphere sets the stage for its superior cuisine of steak and fresh seafood. The smoked corn chowder
soup and baklava cheesecake are excellent. This is fine dining for local residents and visitors. Casual dress;
cocktails. **Parking:** valet. **Cards:** AX, CB, DC, DS, JC, MC, VI.

BENE VITA　　　　　　　　　　**Lunch:** $6-$8　　　　　**Dinner:** $15-$25　　　Phone: 501/666-8482
Location: I-30, exit 141A (Cantrell Rd/SR 10), 3.2 mi w on SR 10. 3701 Cantrell Rd 72202. **Hours:** 11 am-2 & 4:30-9
pm, Fri & Sat-10:30 pm. Closed: 11/22, 12/25. **Features:** Locals love this popular spot for its good variety of
Italian　well-prepared Italian fare. Casual dress; cocktails. **Parking:** on-site. **Cards:** AX, DC, DS, MC, VI.

BEST IMPRESSIONS　　　　　　　　　**Lunch:** $8-$11　　　　　　　　Phone: 501/907-5946
Location: I-30, exit 140A, just w; in Arkansas Arts Center. 501 E 9th St 72202. **Hours:** 11 am-2 pm. Closed: 11/22,
12/25. **Reservations:** suggested. **Features:** Light-colored decor and large windows are a nice match for the
American　attractive dishes and offerings. Dressy casual; cocktails. **Parking:** on-site. **Cards:** AX, DS, MC, VI.

BRAVE NEW RESTAURANT　　　　　**Lunch:** $8-$13　　　　**Dinner:** $20-$30　　　Phone: 501/663-2677
Location: Just n of jct Cottondale Ln. 2300 Cottondale Ln, Suite 105 72202. **Hours:** 11 am-2 & 5-10 pm, Sat from 5
pm. Closed: 11/22, 12/25; also Sun. **Features:** The out-of-the-way restaurant's creative entrees include
American　great preparations of fresh seafood. Waits are common due to this place's popularity. Cocktails. **Parking:**
on-site. **Cards:** AX, DS, MC, VI.

CAJUN'S WHARF　　　　　　　　　　　　　　　　　**Dinner:** $14-$35　　　Phone: 501/375-5354
Location: I-30, exit 141A (Cantrell Rd/SR 10), 2.2 mi w. 2400 Cantrell Rd 72202. **Hours:** 5 pm-10 pm, Fri & Sat-11
pm. Closed: 11/22, 12/25; also Sun. **Features:** Appointed in wharf decor, the rustic restaurant specializes in
Cajun　seafood but also prepares steaks and other dishes. Casual dress; cocktails. **Parking:** on-site. **Cards:** AX,
DS, MC, VI.

CAPRICCIO　　　　　　　　　**Lunch:** $9-$23　　　　**Dinner:** $10-$27　　　Phone: 501/399-8000
Location: Downtown; in The Peabody Little Rock. 3 Statehouse Plaza 72201. **Hours:** 6:30-10:30 am, 11-2 & 6-10
pm. **Reservations:** suggested. **Features:** Preparations of fine Italian cuisine tempt diners who come to
Italian　unwind in an upscale, comfortable setting. Semi-formal attire; cocktails. **Parking:** valet. **Cards:** AX, CB, DC,
DS, MC, VI.

CHI'S CHINESE CUISINE　　　　　**Lunch:** $5-$6　　　　**Dinner:** $7-$19　　　Phone: 501/221-7737
Location: Jct I-430 and 630, 0.5 mi n. 6 Shackleford Rd 72211. **Hours:** 11 am-10 pm, Fri-11 pm. Closed: 7/4,
11/22, 12/25. **Reservations:** accepted. **Features:** Traditional and unusual dishes are served in a pleasant,
Chinese　quiet atmosphere at Chi's. The soft-shell crab, dragon phoenix and lover's shrimp are very good. This 35-
year-old restaurant has been named the area's best Chinese eatery for the past three years. Casual dress;
cocktails. **Parking:** on-site. **Cards:** AX, DS, MC, VI.

COLTON'S STEAKHOUSE & GRILL　　　**Lunch:** $6-$21　　　**Dinner:** $9-$21　　　Phone: 501/562-3273
Location: I-630, exit 5, 2 mi s. Col Glen & University 72204. **Hours:** 11 am-9 pm, Fri & Sat-10 pm. Closed: 11/22,
12/25. **Features:** A bucket of peanuts on the table, an upbeat Old-West atmosphere and a good selection of
Steak House　steak, chicken and ribs await guests at the casual steakhouse. Casual dress; cocktails. **Parking:** on-site.
Cards: AX, DS, MC, VI.

DIXIE CAFE　　　　　　　　　　**Lunch:** $7-$10　　　　**Dinner:** $7-$10　　　Phone: 501/568-6444
　　Location: I-30, exit 16. 10011 Interstate 30 72209. **Hours:** 11 am-10 pm. Closed: 11/22, 12/25.
Features: Southern-style home cooking-chicken-fried steak, meat loaf, pork chops, turnip greens, mashed
Regional American　potatoes and fresh veggies-appeals to families who visit the restaurant's classic "Norman Rockwell"
atmosphere. Casual dress. **Parking:** on-site. **Cards:** AX, DC, DS, MC, VI.

DIXIE CAFE
Regional American
Lunch: $7-$10   **Dinner:** $7-$10   **Phone:** 501/224-372█
Location: I-430, exit 8 (Rodney Parham Rd), just nw; in Pleasant Valley Shopping Center. 10700 N Rodney Parham R█ 72212. **Hours:** 11 am-10 pm. Closed: 11/22, 12/25. **Features:** Southern-style home cooking-chicken-frie█ steak, meat loaf, pork chops, turnip greens, mashed potatoes and fresh veggies-appeals to families wh█ visit the restaurant's classic "Norman Rockwell" atmosphere. Casual dress. **Parking:** on-site. **Cards:** AX█ DC, DS, MC, VI.

DIXIE CAFE
Regional American
Lunch: $6-$9   **Dinner:** $7-$9   **Phone:** 501/663-933█
Location: I-30, exit 141A (Cantrell Rd/SR 10), 3 mi w. 1301 Rebsamen Park Rd 72202. **Hours:** 11 am-10 pm█ Closed: 11/22, 12/25. **Features:** Southern-style home cooking-chicken-fried steak, meat loaf, pork chops█ turnip greens, mashed potatoes and fresh veggies-appeals to families who visit the restaurant's classi█ "Norman Rockwell" atmosphere. Casual dress. **Parking:** on-site. **Cards:** AX, DS, MC, VI.

DONG HAI
Chinese
Lunch: $4-$5   **Dinner:** $5-$10   **Phone:** 501/568-558█
Location: I-30, exit 130, just se. 1001 Mabelvale Plaza 72209. **Hours:** 11 am-9 pm, Fri & Sat-10 pm. Closec█ 11/22. **Features:** Szechuan, Hunan and Cantonese style dishes make up the menu, as well as the buffet█ Friendly servers navigate the comfortable dining room. Casual dress. **Parking:** on-site. **Cards:** DS, MC, V█

DON VICCI'S ITALIAN RISTORANTE
Italian
Lunch: $3-$7   **Dinner:** $9-$22   **Phone:** 501/372-370█
Location: Just e of jct Center St. 211 W Capitol 72201. **Hours:** 10:30 am-3 & 5-9 pm. Closed: 11/22, 12/25; als█ Sun. **Features:** In the heart of downtown, the modestly decorated restaurant builds its menu around Italia█ favorites. Casual dress; cocktails. **Parking:** street. **Cards:** DS, MC, VI.

THE FADED ROSE
Regional Ethnic
Lunch: $4-$8   **Dinner:** $10-$20   **Phone:** 501/224-337█
Location: I-430, exit Shackleford Rd, 0.8 mi w on Markham St, then just n. 400 N Bowman Rd 72211. **Hours:** 11 am█ 11 pm, Sun noon-9:30 pm. Closed: 11/22, 12/25. **Features:** New Orleans decor lends to the sometime█ boisterous atmosphere. Specialties include blackened beef tenderloin topped with sauteed crawfish tails█ trout garnished with crab meat and other Creole dishes. Casual dress; cocktails. **Parking:** on-site █ **Cards:** AX, DC, DS, MC, VI.

FU LIN
Chinese
Lunch: $4-$6   **Dinner:** $7-$17   **Phone:** 501/225-898█
Location: I-430, exit Shackleford Rd, 0.8 mi w on Markham St, then just n. 200 N Bowman Rd 72211. **Hours:** 11 am█ 10 pm, Fri & Sat-11 pm, Sun-9 pm. Closed: 11/22. **Features:** Fu Lin's is very popular with local residents. █ has a wide selection of dishes served in a relaxed, casual, contemporary atmosphere; Sunday buffet is als█ available. The Hunan shrimp, moo goo gai pan and egg fu yong are superb choices. Casual dress█ cocktails. **Parking:** on-site. **Cards:** AX, DC, DS, MC, VI.

GRAFFITI'S
Italian
Dinner: $4-$14   **Phone:** 501/224-907█
Location: I-430, exit 9 (Cantrell Rd), 2 mi e. 7811 Cantrell Rd 72227. **Hours:** 5 pm-9 pm, Fri & Sat-9:30 pm█ Closed major holidays; also Sun. **Features:** Graffiti's is a quaint, little eatery that provides a good dinin█ experience. The restaurant has a colorful and contemporary setting and offers traditional steak, seafoo█ dishes and several "lite bites" low calorie dishes, as well as prompt and attentive service by it█ knowledgeable staff. Casual dress; cocktails. **Parking:** on-site. **Cards:** AX, DC, DS, MC, VI.

GYPSYS GRILL & BAR
New World
Dinner: $15-$26   **Phone:** 501/225-415█
Location: I-430, exit 8, 0.6 mi w. 11401 Rodney Parham Rd 72212-4123. **Hours:** 5 pm-9 pm, Fri & Sat-9:30 pm█ Closed major holidays; also Sun & Mon. **Reservations:** suggested. **Features:** The sophisticated restaurar█ offers pleasurable dining in a refined atmosphere. Appealing presentation adds to the already outstandin█ food, particularly the elegant desserts. Service is prompt and attentive. Casual dress; cocktails. **Parking█ on-site. **Cards:** AX, DC, DS, MC, VI.

HOMER'S RESTAURANT
American
Lunch: $3-$6   **Phone:** 501/374-140█
Location: I-440, exit 3, 0.3 mi n, then 1.5 mi w. 2001 E Roosevelt 72206. **Hours:** 7 am-2 pm. Closed majo█ holidays; also Sat & Sun. **Features:** Don't let the humble exterior deceive, because good home-styl█ dinners, sandwiches and desserts await inside. Casual dress. **Parking:** on-site. **Cards:** AX, DS, MC, VI.

JUANITAS MEXICAN CAFE & CANTINA
Mexican
Lunch: $6-$9   **Dinner:** $7-$14   **Phone:** 501/372-122█
Location: I-630, exit 1A, just s. 1300 Main St 72202. **Hours:** 11 am-2 & 5-9 pm, Fri-10 pm, Sat 11 am-10 pm█ Closed major holidays; also Sun. **Reservations:** accepted. **Features:** Juanita's is a very popular restaurar█ that offers a fun and lively atmosphere and decor. Nightly specials include rib-eye and grilled salmon, th█ San Antonio dinner, and a good selection of tacos and enchiladas. Generous portions and friendly service█ Casual dress; cocktails; entertainment. **Parking:** on-site. **Cards:** AX, CB, DC, DS, MC, VI.

LOCA LUNA
Steak & Seafood
Lunch: $6-$11   **Dinner:** $8-$25   **Phone:** 501/663-466█
Location: I-30, exit 141A (Cantrell Rd/SR 10), 3.3 mi nw. 3519 Old Cantrell 72202. **Hours:** 11 am-2 & 5:30-9 pm█ Fri-10 pm, Sat 5:30 pm-10 pm, Sun 11 am-2:30 & 5:30-9 pm; Sunday brunch. Closed: 11/22, 12/25█ **Features:** Wood-fired brick oven pizzas, steak, seafood and chops are a few of the choices served in█ lively, vibrant atmosphere. Casual dress; cocktails. **Parking:** on-site. **Cards:** AX, DC, DS, MC, VI.

THE PURPLE COW
American
Lunch: $4-$7   **Dinner:** $4-$7   **Phone:** 501/224-443█
Location: 0.6 mi w of jct I-430 and 630. 11602 Chenal Pkwy 72211. **Hours:** 11 am-9:30 pm, Fri & Sat-10 pm, Su█ 10 am-9:30 pm. Closed: 1/1, 11/22, 12/25. **Features:** The '50s-style diner is complete with a soda fountai█ bar and jukebox. The menu consists of favorites from the era, such as well-prepared sandwiches, soup█ and ice cream concoctions. Casual dress. **Parking:** on-site. **Cards:** AX, DC, DS, MC, VI.

THE PURPLE COW

Lunch: $4-$7   **Dinner:** $4-$7   **Phone:** 501/221-3555

American

Location: I-430, exit 9 (Cantrell Rd), 1.8 mi e. 8026 Cantrell Rd 72207. **Hours:** 11 am-9 pm, Fri & Sat-10 pm. Closed: 1/1, 11/22, 12/25. **Features:** Families and children love the restaurant's imaginative retro decor and jukebox music from a 1950s soda-fountain diner. The varied menu of tasty sandwiches, homemade soups and entree salads lends to the relaxed theme and environment. Upbeat servers are friendly and prompt. Casual dress; cocktails. **Parking:** on-site. **Cards:** AX, DC, DS, MC, VI.

ROMANO'S MACARONI GRILL

Lunch: $6-$20   **Dinner:** $8-$20   **Phone:** 501/221-3150

Northern Italian

Location: Jct I-430 and 630, 0.5 mi n on Shackleford Rd, then just w. 11100 W Markham St 72211. **Hours:** 11 am-10 pm, Fri & Sat-11 pm. Closed: 11/22, 12/25. **Features:** Romano's Macaroni Grill has a bright, open dining room with an upscale rustic decor and semi-casual atmosphere. This locally popular restaurant specializes in pizza, pasta, grilled meat and seafood. The fresh baked bread with olive oil is delicious. Casual dress; cocktails. **Parking:** on-site. **Cards:** AX, DC, DS, MC, VI.

SHORTY SMALL'S

Lunch: $6-$17   **Dinner:** $6-$17   **Phone:** 501/224-3344

American

Location: I-430, exit 8, 0.4 mi w. 11100 Rodney Parham Rd 72212. **Hours:** 11 am-10 pm, Fri & Sat-11 pm. **Features:** Focusing on ribs, fried catfish, sandwiches and cheesecake, this restaurant is popular with the locals. The rustic and nostalgic atmosphere is family-oriented, and the feel is casual, hectic and sometimes noisy. Casual dress; cocktails. **Parking:** on-site. **Cards:** AX, DC, DS, MC, VI.

SONNY WILLIAMS' STEAK ROOM

Dinner: $23-$55   **Phone:** 501/324-2999

Steak House

Location: Jct Commerce St. 500 President Clinton Ave 72201. **Hours:** 5 pm-11 pm. Closed: 11/22, 12/25; also Sun. **Reservations:** accepted. **Features:** In the city's Market District, the upscale restaurant serves dishes noteworthy for both their taste and visual appeal. Casual dress; cocktails. **Parking:** on-site. **Cards:** AX, CB, DC, DS, JC, MC, VI.

STAR OF INDIA

Lunch: $7-$8   **Dinner:** $10-$12   **Phone:** 501/227-9900

Indian

Location: Just n of jct Markham St; in West Chase Plaza Shopping Center. 301 N Shackleford Rd 72211. **Hours:** 11 am-3 & 5-10 pm. Closed: 11/22, 12/25. **Features:** The quiet restaurant's blend of outstanding service and magnificent food results in a truly delightful dining experience. The house specialty is lamb with spinach. Stop by at lunchtime for the appealing buffet. Casual dress; beer & wine only. **Parking:** on-site. **Cards:** AX, MC, VI.

TIA'S TEX-MEX

Lunch: $6-$8   **Dinner:** $7-$15   **Phone:** 501/224-9336

Mexican

Location: Jct I-430 and 630, 0.4 mi n. 225 N Shackleford Rd 72211. **Hours:** 11 am-10 pm, Fri & Sat-11 pm. Closed: 11/22, 12/25. **Features:** Tex-Mex and mesquite-grilled dishes are served in a Mexican-style cantina setting comlete with a courtyard dining area. Fresh, hearty portionsmean flavorful choices with burritos, tacos, fajitas, and the chalupa tortilla. Casual dress; cocktails. **Parking:** on-site. **Cards:** AX, DC, DS, MC, VI.

TRIO'S

Lunch: $7-$10   **Dinner:** $11-$20   **Phone:** 501/221-3330

American

Location: I-430, exit 9 (Centrell Rd), 1.7 mi e. 8201 Cantrell Rd, Suite 100 72227. **Hours:** 11 am-2:30 & 5:30-9:30 pm. Closed major holidays; also Sun. **Reservations:** accepted. **Features:** Representative of French, Italian and American dishes are shrimp enchiladas, sea bass and Madagascar beef tenderloin. Casual dress; cocktails. **Parking:** on-site. **Cards:** AX, CB, DC, DS, JC, MC, VI.

LONOKE pop. 4,287

——— WHERE TO STAY ———

DAYS INN

Book great rates at AAA.com   **Phone:** (501)676-5138

	1P: $70-$85	2P: $75-$90	XP: $5	F13
4/2-8/31				
3/1-4/1 & 9/1-2/29	1P: $60-$75	2P: $65-$80	XP: $5	F13

Small-scale Hotel

Location: I-40, exit 175, just n. 105 Dee Dee Ln 72086. Fax: 501/676-5036. **Facility:** 61 one-bedroom standard units, some with whirlpools. 2 stories (no elevator), exterior corridors. *Bath:* combo or shower only. **Parking:** on-site. **Terms:** [CP] meal plan available, pets ($10 extra charge). **Amenities:** hair dryers. **Pool(s):** outdoor. **Guest Services:** coin laundry, wireless Internet. **Cards:** AX, DC, DS, MC, VI. **Free Special Amenities:** continental breakfast and high-speed Internet.

SOME UNITS

HOLIDAY INN EXPRESS HOTEL & SUITES

Book great rates at AAA.com   **Phone:** (501)676-7800

	1P: $109-$119	2P: $109-$119	XP: $10	F16
5/26-9/4				
3/1-5/25 & 9/5-2/29	1P: $99-$109	2P: $99-$109	XP: $10	F16

Small-scale Hotel

Location: I-40, exit 175, just n. 104 Dee Dee Ln 72086. Fax: 501/676-7881. **Facility:** 62 units. 59 one-bedroom standard units. 3 one-bedroom suites ($109-$119). 3 stories, interior corridors. *Bath:* combo or shower only. **Parking:** on-site. **Terms:** [CP] meal plan available, pets ($25 extra charge, with prior approval). **Amenities:** high-speed Internet, voice mail, irons, hair dryers. **Pool(s):** heated indoor. **Leisure Activities:** exercise room. **Guest Services:** valet and coin laundry, wireless Internet. **Business Services:** meeting rooms, business center. **Cards:** AX, DC, DS, MC, VI. **Free Special Amenities:** expanded continental breakfast and high-speed Internet.

SOME UNITS

SUPER 8 MOTEL   *Book great rates at AAA.com*   Phone: (501)676
AAA SAVE   5/23-8/12 [ECP]   1P: $65-$75   2P: $70-$80   XP: $6
                3/1-5/22 & 8/13-2/29 [ECP]   1P: $60-$70   2P: $65-$75   XP: $6
Small-scale Hotel   **Location:** I-40, exit 175, just n. 102 Dee Dee Ln 72086. Fax: 501/676-0630. **Facility:** 46 one-bedroom st
units, some with whirlpools. 2 stories (no elevator), interior corridors. **Parking:** on-site. **Terms:** pe
extra charge). **Amenities:** irons, hair dryers. **Pool(s):** heated indoor. **Guest Services:** wireless I
Cards: AX, CB, DC, DS, JC, MC, VI. **Free Special Amenities: expanded continental breakfa**
high-speed Internet.

SOME U

MAGNOLIA pop. 10,858

——— **WHERE TO STAY** ———

HOLIDAY INN EXPRESS HOTEL & SUITES   *Book at AAA.com*   Phone: 870/234
                                     Property failed to provide current rates
               Location: Just w of jct US 82, 79 and 82B. 1604 E Main 71753. Fax: 870/234-7775. **Facility:** 56 one-be
Small-scale Hotel   standard units, some with whirlpools. 3 stories, interior corridors. *Bath:* combo or shower only. **Parking:** on
site. **Amenities:** voice mail, irons, hair dryers. **Pool(s):** heated indoor. **Leisure Activities:** exercise room
Guest Services: wireless Internet. **Business Services:** meeting rooms, business center.

SOME UNITS

QUALITY INN   *Book great rates at AAA.com*   Phone: 870/234-3612
              All Year   1P: $70-$80   2P: $70-$80   XP: $5
              Location: 1.3 mi w of jct US 79 and 82B. 411 E Main St 71753 (PO Box 1408). Fax: 870/234-2862. **Facility:** 71
Small-scale Hotel   one-bedroom standard units. 2 stories (no elevator), exterior corridors. *Bath:* combo or shower only.
Parking: on-site. **Terms:** package plans. **Amenities:** voice mail, irons, hair dryers. **Pool(s):** outdoor. **Guest**
Services: valet and coin laundry, wireless Internet. **Business Services:** meeting rooms, PC. **Cards:** AX, DC, DS, JC, MC, VI.

SOME UNITS

——— **WHERE TO DINE** ———

CHEN & CHEN   **Lunch:** $5-$8   **Dinner:** $6-$8   Phone: 870/234-3100
              Location: 0.6 mi w of jct US 79 and 82B. 309 N Fredrick St 71753. **Hours:** 11 am-10 pm, Fri & Sat-11 pm. Closed
              11/22, 12/25. **Features:** The menu comprises a wide variety of dishes, but most local patrons choose the
Chinese   buffet offerings for lunch and dinner. Casual dress. **Parking:** on-site. **Cards:** MC, VI.

MALVERN pop. 9,021

——— **WHERE TO STAY** ———

COMFORT INN   *Book great rates at AAA.com*   Phone: 501/467-3300
              6/1-9/15 [CP]   1P: $79-$130   2P: $79-$130   XP: $5   F18
              3/1-5/31 & 9/16-2/29 [CP]   1P: $72-$130   2P: $72-$130   XP: $5   F18
Small-scale Hotel   **Location:** I-30, exit 98A, just e. 2320 Leopard Ln 72104. Fax: 501/467-8827. **Facility:** 51 one-bedroom standard
units, some with whirlpools. 3 stories, interior corridors. *Bath:* combo or shower only. **Parking:** on-site.
Amenities: high-speed Internet, voice mail, irons, hair dryers. **Pool(s):** outdoor. **Guest Services:** coin laundry, wireless
Internet. **Cards:** AX, DC, DS, JC, MC, VI.

SOME UNITS

MARION pop. 8,901

——— **WHERE TO STAY** ———

BEST WESTERN-REGENCY MOTOR INN   *Book great rates at AAA.com*   Phone: (870)739-3278
              All Year [CP]   1P: $55-$65   2P: $65-$75   XP: $5   F18
              Location: I-55, exit 10, just nw. 3635 I-55 72364. Fax: 870/739-3278. **Facility:** 60 one-bedroom standard units. 2
Small-scale Hotel   stories (no elevator), exterior corridors. **Parking:** on-site, winter plug-ins. **Terms:** small pets only
Amenities: high-speed Internet, irons, hair dryers. **Pool(s):** outdoor. **Guest Services:** coin laundry, wireless
Internet. **Cards:** AX, CB, DC, DS, MC, VI.

SOME UNITS

MAUMELLE pop. 10,557

——— **WHERE TO STAY** ———

COMFORT SUITES   *Book great rates at AAA.com*   Phone: (501)851-8444
              All Year   1P: $79-$139   2P: $79-$139   XP: $10   F
              Location: I-40, exit 142, just sw. 14322 Frontier Dr 72113. Fax: 501/851-2525. **Facility:** 52 one-bedroom
Small-scale Hotel   standard units, some with whirlpools. 3 stories, interior corridors. *Bath:* combo or shower only. **Parking:** on-
site. **Terms:** cancellation fee imposed, pets ($20 fee). **Amenities:** voice mail, irons, hair dryers. **Pool(s):**
small outdoor. **Leisure Activities:** exercise room. **Guest Services:** coin laundry, wireless Internet. **Business Services:**
meeting rooms, PC. **Cards:** AX, CB, DC, DS, MC, VI.

SOME UNITS

QUALITY INN-MAUMELLE *Book great rates at AAA.com*   **Phone:** 501/851-3500
Property failed to provide current rates
Location: I-40, exit 142, just sw. 14325 Frontier Dr 72113. **Fax:** 501/851-3045. **Facility:** 55 one-bedroom
Small-scale Hotel   standard units, some with whirlpools. 2 stories (no elevator); exterior corridors. *Bath:* combo or shower only.
Parking: on-site. **Terms:** pets ($10 fee). **Amenities:** video library (fee), irons, hair dryers. **Pool(s):** small
outdoor. **Guest Services:** wireless Internet.

MOUNTAIN HOME pop. 11,012

——— WHERE TO STAY ———

COMFORT INN   *Book great rates at AAA.com*   **Phone:** (870)424-9000
All Year   1P: $60-$150   2P: $60-$150   XP: $8   F17
Location: 1.5 mi e on US 62B. 1031 Highland Cir 72653 (PO Box 345). **Fax:** 870/425-0691. **Facility:** 80 units. 78
one-bedroom standard units, some with whirlpools. 2 one-bedroom suites with whirlpools. 2 stories (no
elevator); interior/exterior corridors. *Bath:* combo or shower only. **Parking:** on-site. **Terms:** [ECP] meal plan
Small-scale Hotel   available, package plans. **Amenities:** high-speed Internet, irons, hair dryers. **Pool(s):** outdoor. **Leisure
Activities:** exercise room. **Guest Services:** valet and coin laundry, wireless Internet. **Business Services:**
meeting rooms. **Cards:** AX, CB, DC, DS, JC, MC, VI. **Free Special Amenities: expanded continental breakfast and high-
speed Internet.**

DAYS INN   *Book great rates at AAA.com*   **Phone:** (870)425-1010
All Year   1P: $65-$70   2P: $65-$70   XP: $6   F18
Location: On US 62B, 2.3 mi e. 1746 E Hwy 62B 72653. **Fax:** 870/425-1115. **Facility:** 53 one-bedroom standard
Small-scale Hotel   units, some with whirlpools. 2 stories (no elevator); interior corridors. *Bath:* combo or shower only. **Parking:**
on-site. **Terms:** small pets only ($8 extra charge, with prior approval). **Amenities:** high-speed Internet,
irons, hair dryers. **Pool(s):** outdoor. **Leisure Activities:** whirlpool. **Guest Services:** valet laundry, wireless Internet. **Business
Services:** PC. **Cards:** AX, DC, DS, MC, VI.

HOLIDAY INN EXPRESS   *Book at AAA.com*   **Phone:** (870)425-6200
5/1-9/15 [CP]   1P: $90-$119   2P: $90-$119   XP: $10   F19
3/1-4/30 & 9/16-2/29 [CP]   1P: $80-$109   2P: $80-$109   XP: $10   F19
Small-scale Hotel   **Location:** 1.4 mi e on US 62B. 1005 Coley Dr 72653. **Fax:** 870/425-6227. **Facility:** 61 one-bedroom
standard units. 3 stories, interior corridors. *Bath:* combo or shower only. **Parking:** on-site. **Terms:** pets ($25 fee).
Amenities: voice mail, irons, hair dryers. **Pool(s):** outdoor. **Leisure Activities:** whirlpool, exercise room. **Guest Services:** valet
laundry, wireless Internet. **Business Services:** meeting rooms, business center. **Cards:** AX, CB, DC, DS, JC, MC, VI.

SUPER 8 MOTEL-MOUNTAIN HOME   *Book at AAA.com*   **Phone:** (870)424-5600
All Year   1P: $46-$59   2P: $51-$65   XP: $5   F12
Motel   **Location:** 1.3 mi e on US 62B. 865 Hwy 62 E 72653. **Facility:** 40 one-bedroom standard units. 2 stories (no
elevator); interior corridors. **Parking:** on-site. **Terms:** cancellation fee imposed, package plans. **Guest
Services:** wireless Internet. **Cards:** AX, DC, DS, MC, VI.

TEAL POINT RESORT   **Phone:** 870/492-5145
5/20-9/7   1P: $95-$379   2P: $95-$379   XP: $6   D16
4/15-5/19   1P: $74-$315   2P: $74-$315   XP: $6   D16
3/1-4/14 & 9/8-2/29   1P: $69-$279   2P: $69-$279   XP: $6   D16
Location: 7 mi on US 62, 0.6 mi n on CR 406, follow signs. 715 Teal Point Rd 72653-7151. **Fax:** 870/492-5215.
Cottage   **Facility:** One- to four-bedroom housekeeping cottages. 19 units. 4 one- and 3 two-bedroom standard units
with kitchens, some with whirlpools. 2 vacation homes ($175-$379) and 10 cottages ($69-$239), some with
whirlpools. 1 story, exterior corridors. *Bath:* combo or shower only. **Parking:** on-site. **Terms:** check-out 9 am, 45 day
cancellation notice-fee imposed, weekly rates available, package plans, pets ($7 extra charge). **Pool(s):** outdoor. **Leisure
Activities:** rental boats, marina, fishing, lawn games, recreation room, playground. *Fee:* bass boats, pontoon boats, ski boats,
game room. **Guest Services:** gift shop, coin laundry, wireless Internet. **Business Services:** meeting rooms. **Cards:** AX, DS,
MC, VI.

——— WHERE TO DINE ———

FRED'S FISH HOUSE   **Lunch:** $6-$17   **Dinner:** $9-$17   **Phone:** 870/492-5958
Location: 4 mi w of jct US 62 business route. Hwy 62 E 72653. **Hours:** 11 am-8 pm, Fri & Sat-9 pm, Sun noon-7
pm. **Closed:** 11/22, 12/25. **Features:** Catfish filets and homemade hush puppies are the specialties at
American   Fred's, which offers a large variety of seafood, steak and chicken in a casual, comfortable setting. Families,
visitors and fishermen will also enjoy the lake view from the outdoor patio. Casual dress; beer & wine only.
Parking: on-site. **Cards:** DS, MC, VI.

——— *The following restaurant has not been evaluated by AAA but is listed for your information only.* ———

DINO'S ITALIAN CUISINE   **Phone:** 870/492-5080
[fyi]   Not evaluated. **Location:** 4628 Hwy 62 E 72653. **Features:** For some years, locals have visited the favored
spot when they crave classic Italian cuisine.

MOUNTAIN VIEW pop. 2,876

——— WHERE TO STAY ———

BEST WESTERN FIDDLERS INN *Book great rates at AAA.com*   Phone: 870/269-2828
▼▼ ▼▼▼   All Year [CP]   1P: $58-$95   2P: $58-$95   XP: $10   F12
Motel   **Location:** 1 mi n on SR 5, 9 and 14. 601 Sylomore 72560. Fax: 870/269-2570. **Facility:** 48 units. 46 one-bedroom standard units. 2 one-bedroom suites ($75-$125) with whirlpools. 2 stories (no elevator), exterior corridors. **Parking:** on-site. **Terms:** package plans, pets (small dogs only, $5 fee). **Amenities:** high-speed Internet, irons, hair dryers. **Pool(s):** heated outdoor. **Cards:** AX, CB, DC, DS, MC, VI.

SOME UNITS
(ASK) [S₀] [🛏] [🍴] [🏊] [💻] / [✕] [🔓]
FEE   FEE

THE INN AT MOUNTAIN VIEW   Phone: (870)269-4200
▼▼ ▼▼▼   All Year [BP]   1P: $68-$140   2P: $83-$140   XP: $18
Bed & Breakfast   **Location:** Center. 307 W Washington St 72560 (PO Box 812). Fax: 870/269-9580. **Facility:** Charming restored historic home circa 1886. Smoke free premises. 12 units. 6 one-bedroom standard units. 5 one-bedroom suites. 1 cottage. 2 stories (no elevator), interior corridors. **Bath:** combo or shower only. **Parking:** on-site. **Terms:** 7 day cancellation notice-fee imposed, package plans. **Business Services:** meeting rooms. **Cards:** AX, CB, DC, DS, MC, VI.

SOME UNITS
[🍴] [✕] [⊘] / [📺] [🔓] [📷] /

OZARK FOLK CENTER DRY CREEK LODGE   Phone: 870/269-3871
▼▼ ▼▼   All Year   1P: $65-$70   2P: $65-$70   XP: $10   F13
Small-scale Hotel   **Location:** 0.8 mi w of jct SR 5, 9 and 14. Located in a secluded area. 1032 Park Ave 72560 (PO Box 500). Fax: 870/269-2909. **Facility:** 60 one-bedroom standard units. 1 story, exterior corridors. **Bath:** combo or shower only. **Parking:** on-site. **Terms:** check-in 4 pm, 2 night minimum stay - seasonal and/or weekends, package plans. **Amenities:** irons, hair dryers. **Pool(s):** outdoor. **Guest Services:** gift shop. **Business Services:** conference facilities. **Cards:** AX, DC, DS, MC, VI.

SOME UNITS
[🏊] [🔓] [💻] / [✕] /

——— WHERE TO DINE ———

OZARK FOLK CENTER SKILLET RESTAURANT   **Lunch:** $4-$7   **Dinner:** $6-$16   Phone: 870/269-3139
▼▼ ▼▼   **Location:** 1 mi nw, 0.8 mi w of jct SR 9 and 14; in Ozark Folk Center. SR 382 72560. **Hours:** Open 4/18-10/31; 7 am-8 pm. **Features:** Families and seniors are catered to at the Ozark Folk Center Restaurant, where the home-style menu features Ozark country-style cooking such as chicken and dumplings and corn bread. The park is dedicated to the preservation of the area's culture. Casual dress. **Parking:** on-site. **Cards:** AX, DS, MC, VI.
American

NORTH LITTLE ROCK pop. 60,433—*See also LITTLE ROCK.*

——— WHERE TO STAY ———

BAYMONT INN & SUITES *Book at AAA.com*   Phone: (501)758-8888
▼▼ ▼▼▼   5/1-2/29   1P: $74-$104   2P: $74-$104
     3/1-4/30   1P: $69-$99   2P: $69-$99
Small-scale Hotel   **Location:** Jct US 67/167, exit 1A northbound; exit 1 southbound. 4100 E McCain Blvd 72117. Fax: 501/758-5055. **Facility:** 122 one-bedroom standard units. 2 stories (no elevator), exterior corridors. **Parking:** on-site. **Terms:** small pets only. **Amenities:** video games (fee), voice mail, irons, hair dryers. **Pool(s):** small outdoor. **Guest Services:** wireless Internet. **Business Services:** meeting rooms. **Cards:** AX, CB, DC, DS, MC, VI.

SOME UNITS
(ASK) [🛏] [🍴] [⊘] [🏊] [🎥] [💻] / [✕] /

COMFORT INN *Book great rates at AAA.com*   Phone: (501)955-9453
▼▼ ▼▼▼   All Year   1P: $69-$96   2P: $69-$96   XP: $5   F18
Small-scale Hotel   **Location:** I-40, exit 157, just s. 5710 Pritchard Dr 72117. Fax: 501/955-9461. **Facility:** 48 one-bedroom standard units, some with whirlpools. 2 stories (no elevator), interior corridors. **Bath:** combo or shower only. **Parking:** on-site, winter plug-ins. **Amenities:** high-speed Internet, irons, hair dryers. *Some:* dual phone lines. **Pool(s):** outdoor. **Leisure Activities:** exercise room. **Guest Services:** coin laundry, wireless Internet. **Business Services:** meeting rooms. **Cards:** AX, DC, DS, MC, VI.

SOME UNITS
(ASK) [S₀] [🏊] [🎥] [🔓] [💻] / [✕] [📷] /

COUNTRY INN & SUITES BY CARLSON *Book at AAA.com*   Phone: (501)758-2002
▼▼ ▼▼▼   All Year [ECP]   1P: $78-$85   2P: $78-$85   XP: $5
Small-scale Hotel   **Location:** I-40, exit 153A, just se. 110 E Pershing Blvd 72114. Fax: 501/758-6755. **Facility:** 55 units. 43 one-bedroom standard units, some with whirlpools. 12 one-bedroom suites ($101-$150). 3 stories, interior corridors. **Bath:** combo or shower only. **Parking:** on-site. **Amenities:** high-speed Internet, voice mail, irons, hair dryers. **Pool(s):** outdoor. **Guest Services:** valet and coin laundry, wireless Internet. **Business Services:** meeting rooms. **Cards:** AX, CB, DC, DS, MC, VI.

SOME UNITS
(ASK) [S₀] [🍴] [♿] [🏊] [🏃] [📷] [🔓] [💻] [💻] / [✕] /

FAIRFIELD INN BY MARRIOTT *Book great rates at AAA.com*   Phone: (501)945-9777
▼▼ ▼▼▼   All Year   1P: $85-$105   2P: $90-$110   XP: $5   F18
Small-scale Hotel   **Location:** I-40, exit 156, just nw. 4120 Healthcare Dr N 72117. Fax: 501/945-9777. **Facility:** Smoke free premises. 86 one-bedroom standard units. 4 stories, interior corridors. **Bath:** combo or shower only. **Parking:** on-site. **Amenities:** voice mail, irons, hair dryers. **Pool(s):** small heated indoor. **Leisure Activities:** whirlpool. **Guest Services:** valet laundry, wireless Internet. **Cards:** AX, DC, DS, MC, VI.

SOME UNITS
(ASK) [S₀] [🍴] [♿] [⊘] [🏊] [✕] [🎥] [💻] / [🔓] [💻] /

HAMPTON INN *Book great rates at AAA.com*   Phone: (501)771-2090

▼▼▼▼ All Year   1P: $89-$109   2P: $99-$119

Small-scale Hotel **Location:** I-40, exit 152. 500 W 29th St 72114. Fax: 501/771-0410. **Facility:** 123 one-bedroom standard units. 4 stories, interior corridors. **Parking:** on-site. **Terms:** [BP] meal plan available, package plans, pets ($35 fee). **Amenities:** video games (fee), voice mail, irons, hair dryers. **Pool(s):** outdoor. **Guest Services:** valet laundry, wireless Internet. **Business Services:** meeting rooms, PC. **Cards:** AX, CB, DC, DS, MC, VI.

SOME UNITS

(ASK) (S🅳) (T📵) (🅟) (🖈) (🔅) (🖥) / (🗙) /
FEE

HAMPTON INN-NORTH LITTLE ROCK/MCCAIN *Book great rates at AAA.com*   Phone: (501)753-8660

▼▼▼ All Year   1P: $99-$149   2P: $109-$159   XP: $10   F18

Small-scale Hotel **Location:** US 67/167, exit 1B (McCain Blvd), just n on west service road. 4801 W Commercial Dr 72116. Fax: 501/753-3433. **Facility:** 62 units. 59 one-bedroom standard units. 3 one-bedroom suites ($130-$149) with whirlpools. 3 stories, interior corridors. *Bath:* combo or shower only. **Parking:** on-site. **Terms:** cancellation fee imposed, [ECP] meal plan available. **Amenities:** high-speed Internet, voice mail, irons, hair dryers. **Pool(s):** outdoor. **Leisure Activities:** exercise room. **Guest Services:** valet and coin laundry, wireless Internet. **Business Services:** meeting rooms. **Cards:** AX, CB, DC, DS, JC, MC, VI.

SOME UNITS

(ASK) (S🅳) (T📵) (🖈) (🔅) (🖥) / (🗙) (🖨)

HOLIDAY INN EXPRESS HOTEL & SUITES *Book great rates at AAA.com*   Phone: (501)945-4800

(AAA) (SAVE) All Year   1P: $95-$140   2P: $95-$140   XP: $10   F17

▼▼▼ **Location:** US 67/167, exit 1A, just e. 4306 E McCain Blvd 72117. Fax: 501/945-4744. **Facility:** 70 one-bedroom standard units. 3 stories, interior corridors. *Bath:* combo or shower only. **Parking:** on-site. **Amenities:** high-speed Internet, dual phone lines, voice mail, irons, hair dryers. **Pool(s):** small heated indoor. **Leisure**

Small-scale Hotel **Activities:** limited exercise equipment. **Guest Services:** valet and coin laundry, wireless Internet. **Business Services:** meeting rooms, business center. **Cards:** AX, CB, DC, DS, MC, VI.

(S🅳) (T📵) (🖈) (🅟) (🔅) (🖥) / (🗙) (🖨) (🖥) /

HOLIDAY INN-NORTH *Book at AAA.com*   Phone: (501)758-1851

▼▼▼ All Year   1P: $89-$99   2P: $89-$99

Small-scale Hotel **Location:** I-40, exit 152 westbound; exit 153A eastbound. 120 W Pershing Blvd 72114. Fax: 501/758-5616. **Facility:** 143 one-bedroom standard units. 4 stories, interior corridors. **Parking:** on-site. **Terms:** 30-day cancellation notice, package plans, pets ($20 fee). **Amenities:** voice mail, irons, hair dryers. **Pool(s):** outdoor. **Leisure Activities:** exercise room. **Guest Services:** coin laundry, wireless Internet. **Business Services:** meeting rooms, business center. **Cards:** AX, DS, MC, VI.

SOME UNITS

(S🅳) (🐕) (T📵) (Y) (🔅) (🖥) / (🗙) /
FEE

LA QUINTA INN & SUITES *Book great rates at AAA.com*   Phone: (501)945-0808

◆◆◆ 5/1-2/29 [CP]   1P: $87-$117   2P: $87-$117

▼▼▼ 3/1-4/30 [CP]   1P: $81-$117   2P: $81-$117

Small-scale Hotel **Location:** US 67/167, exit 1B northbound; exit 1 southbound. 4311 Warden Rd 72116. Fax: 501/945-0393. **Facility:** 98 units. 96 one-bedroom standard units. 2 one-bedroom suites ($121-$157). 3 stories, interior corridors. *Bath:* combo or shower only. **Parking:** on-site. **Terms:** small pets only. **Amenities:** video games (fee), voice mail, irons, hair dryers. **Pool(s):** small outdoor. **Leisure Activities:** exercise room. **Guest Services:** coin laundry, wireless Internet. **Cards:** AX, CB, DC, DS, MC, VI.

SOME UNITS

(ASK) (🐕) (T📵) (🖈) (🅟) (🔅) (🖥) / (🗙) (🖨) (🖥) /

RED ROOF INN *Book great rates at AAA.com*   Phone: (501)945-0080

(AAA) (SAVE) 5/1-8/31   1P: $65   2P: $70   XP: $5   F12

3/1-4/30   1P: $57   2P: $62   XP: $5   F12

▼▼ 9/1-2/29   1P: $55   2P: $60   XP: $5   F12

Small-scale Hotel **Location:** I-40, exit 157, just s. 5711 Pritchard Dr 72117. Fax: 501/945-6039. **Facility:** 52 one-bedroom standard units. 2 stories (no elevator), interior corridors. *Bath:* combo or shower only. **Parking:** on-site. **Terms:** cancellation fee imposed, [CP] meal plan available. **Amenities:** hair dryers. *Some:* high-speed Internet. **Pool(s):** outdoor. **Leisure Activities:** *Fee:* game room. **Guest Services:** coin laundry, wireless Internet. **Cards:** AX, CB, DC, DS, JC, MC, VI. **Free Special Amenities:** continental breakfast and high-speed Internet.

SOME UNITS

(S🅳) (🍽) (🐕) (🔅) (🖨) (🖥) / (🗙) /

RESIDENCE INN BY MARRIOTT-NORTH *Book great rates at AAA.com*   Phone: (501)945-7777

▼▼▼ All Year   1P: $140-$180   2P: $145-$185   XP: $5   F18

Small-scale Hotel **Location:** I-40, exit 156. 4110 Healthcare Dr 72117. Fax: 501/945-7777. **Facility:** Smoke free premises. 96 units. 36 one-bedroom standard units with efficiencies. 44 one- and 16 two-bedroom suites, some with efficiencies or kitchens. 4 stories, interior corridors. *Bath:* combo or shower only. **Parking:** on-site. **Terms:** [BP] meal plan available, pets ($50 fee). **Amenities:** dual phone lines, voice mail, irons, hair dryers. **Pool(s):** heated indoor. **Leisure Activities:** whirlpool, exercise room, sports court. **Guest Services:** valet and coin laundry, wireless Internet. **Business Services:** meeting rooms. **Cards:** AX, DC, DS, MC, VI.

(ASK) (S🅳) (🐕) (T📵) (🖈) (🔅) (🗙) (🖥) (🖨) (🖥) (🖥)
FEE

—— WHERE TO DINE ——

DIXIE CAFE   **Lunch:** $7-$10   **Dinner:** $7-$10   Phone: 501/758-4777

▼▼ **Location:** US 67/167, exit 1. 2724 Lakewood Village Pl 72116. **Hours:** 11 am-10 pm. Closed: 11/22, 12/25. Regional American **Features:** Southern-style home cooking-chicken-fried steak, meat loaf, pork chops, turnip greens, mashed potatoes and fresh veggies-appeals to families who visit the restaurant's classic "Norman Rockwell" atmosphere. Casual dress. **Parking:** on-site. **Cards:** AX, DC, DS, MC, VI.

LAS PALMAS
Mexican

Lunch: $4-$11   **Dinner:** $5-$11   **Phone:** 501/945-8010
Location: US 67/167, exit 1A, just e. 4154 E McCain Blvd 72117. **Hours:** 11 am-9 pm, Fri & Sat-10 pm, Sun 11:30 am-9 pm. **Features:** The locals flock to the comfortable restaurant to find well-prepared Mexican dishes. Service is friendly and efficient. Casual dress; beer only. **Parking:** on-site. **Cards:** AX, CB, DC, DS, MC, VI.

ROYAL BUFFET
Chinese

Lunch: $5   **Dinner:** $7   **Phone:** 501/753-8885
Location: I-40, exit 152, just s. 109 E Pershing Blvd 72114. **Hours:** 11 am-10 pm. Closed: 11/22. **Features:** A good selection of Oriental dishes is always available on the daily buffet. Casual dress. **Parking:** on-site. **Cards:** AX, DS, MC, VI.

SHORTY SMALL'S
American

Lunch: $6-$17   **Dinner:** $6-$17   **Phone:** 501/753-8111
Location: US 67/167, exit 1 southbound; exit 1B northbound. 4317 Warden Rd 72216. **Hours:** 11 am-10 pm, Fri & Sat-11 pm. Closed: 11/22, 12/25. **Features:** Focusing on ribs, fried catfish, sandwiches and cheesecake, this restaurant is popular with the locals. The rustic and nostalgic atmosphere is family-oriented, and the feel is casual, hectic and sometimes noisy. Casual dress; cocktails. **Parking:** on-site. **Cards:** AX, DC, DS, MC, VI.

SIR LOIN'S INN
Steak & Seafood

Dinner: $15-$34   **Phone:** 501/753-1361
Location: I-40, exit 152. 801 W 29th St 72114. **Hours:** 5:30 pm-9:30 pm, Fri & Sat-10 pm. Closed major holidays; also Sun. **Features:** Prime rib and steak are the specialties at this restaurant, which features an Old English-style decor and servers dressed in theme costumes. This out-of-the-way place, with its many small dining rooms, is very popular with local residents. Casual dress; cocktails. **Parking:** on-site. **Cards:** AX, DC, DS, MC, VI.

TIA'S TEX MEX
Mexican

Lunch: $4-$7   **Dinner:** $5-$12   **Phone:** 501/753-8675
Location: US 67/167, exit 1B northbound; exit 1 southbound. 4305 Warden Rd 72116. **Hours:** 11 am-11 pm, Fri & Sat-11 pm. Closed: 11/22, 12/25. **Features:** This locally popular restaurant has a lively atmosphere in a casual-dining setting. The delicious fajitas are the specialty of the house; the pontons platter, freshly made tortillas, praline pecan pie and fried ice cream are also very tasty. Casual dress; cocktails. **Parking:** on-site. **Cards:** AX, DC, DS, MC, VI.

OZARK pop. 3,525

——— WHERE TO STAY ———

OXFORD INN
Motel

All Year   1P: $45   2P: $50   **Phone:** 479/667-1131
XP: $5   F12
Location: I-40, exit 35, 3 mi s on SR 23. 305 N 18th St 72949. Fax: 479/667-4120. **Facility:** 32 one-bedroom standard units. 2 stories (no elevator), exterior corridors. **Parking:** on-site. **Terms:** small pets only ($10 fee). **Pool(s):** outdoor. **Guest Services:** wireless Internet. **Cards:** AX, DS, MC, VI.

SOME UNITS

PARAGOULD pop. 22,017

——— WHERE TO STAY ———

BEST WESTERN RUSTIC INN   *Book great rates at AAA.com*
Small-scale Hotel

All Year [ECP]   1P: $80   2P: $85   **Phone:** (870)239-2161
XP: $5   F17
Location: 2.3 mi w of jct US 412 and 49. 3009 Linwood Dr 72450. Fax: 870/239-2734. **Facility:** 41 one-bedroom standard units, some with whirlpools. 2 stories (no elevator), interior/exterior corridors. **Parking:** on-site. **Amenities:** high-speed Internet, irons, hair dryers. **Pool(s):** outdoor. **Cards:** AX, CB, DC, DS, MC, VI.

SOME UNITS

——— WHERE TO DINE ———

CANDLELITE STEAK HOUSE
Steak & Seafood

Dinner: $9-$21   **Phone:** 870/239-8391
Location: 0.8 mi s of jct US 412 and 49. 1611 Lynwood Dr 72450. **Hours:** 5 pm-10 pm. Closed major holidays; also Sun. **Reservations:** suggested. **Features:** You may be surprised by the intimate, quiet and relaxed atmosphere of Candlelite's fine-dining experience. The restaurant's menu has a good variety of traditional steak, seafood, pasta and chicken dishes. The staff is friendly and attentive. Casual dress; cocktails. **Parking:** on-site. **Cards:** AX, DC, DS, MC, VI.

DIXIE CAFE
Regional American

Lunch: $7-$10   **Dinner:** $7-$10   **Phone:** 870/239-2000
Location: 1.2 mi w of jct US 49. 2904 W Kings Hwy 72450. **Hours:** 11 am-10 pm. Closed: 11/22, 12/25. **Features:** Southern-style home cooking-chicken-fried steak, meat loaf, pork chops, turnip greens, mashed potatoes and fresh veggies-appeals to families who visit the restaurant's classic "Norman Rockwell" atmosphere. Casual dress. **Parking:** on-site. **Cards:** AX, DC, DS, MC, VI.

PINE BLUFF pop. 55,085

──────── WHERE TO STAY ────────

BEST WESTERN PRESIDENTIAL HOTEL   *Book great rates at AAA.com*   Phone: 870/535-6300
▼▼ ▼▼
Property failed to provide current rates
Small-scale Hotel   **Location:** I-530, exit 46, just n. 3104 Market St 71601. Fax: 870/534-2099. **Facility:** 58 one-bedroom standard units, some with whirlpools. 3 stories, interior corridors. *Bath:* combo or shower only. **Parking:** on-site. **Amenities:** high-speed Internet, voice mail, irons, hair dryers. **Pool(s):** indoor. **Leisure Activities:** exercise room. **Guest Services:** coin laundry, wireless Internet. **Business Services:** business center.

SOME UNITS

COMFORT INN   *Book great rates at AAA.com*   Phone: (870)535-5300
▼▼ ▼▼
All Year [CP]   1P: $60-$99   2P: $60-$99   XP: $5   F18
Small-scale Hotel   **Location:** I-530, exit 46, just n. Located across from the Pines Mall. 2809 Pines Mall Dr 71601. Fax: 870/535-1264. **Facility:** 50 one-bedroom standard units, some with whirlpools. 2 stories (no elevator), interior corridors. *Bath:* combo or shower only. **Parking:** on-site. **Terms:** package plans. **Amenities:** high-speed Internet, irons, hair dryers. **Pool(s):** small outdoor. **Guest Services:** valet and coin laundry, wireless Internet. **Business Services:** PC. **Cards:** AX, DC, DS, MC, VI.

SOME UNITS

DAYS INN & SUITES   *Book great rates at AAA.com*   Phone: (870)534-1800
▼▼ ▼▼
All Year   1P: $59-$80   2P: $64-$85   XP: $5   F16
Small-scale Hotel   **Location:** Just n of jct US 65B and 79B. 406 N Blake St 71601. Fax: 870/534-1800. **Facility:** 52 one-bedroom standard units, some with efficiencies (no utensils) and/or whirlpools. 2 stories (no elevator), exterior corridors. *Bath:* combo or shower only. **Parking:** on-site. **Terms:** pets ($25 extra charge). **Amenities:** high-speed Internet, voice mail, irons, hair dryers. **Pool(s):** small outdoor. **Guest Services:** coin laundry. **Business Services:** meeting rooms. **Cards:** AX, DC, DS, MC, VI.

SOME UNITS
FEE

HOLIDAY INN EXPRESS HOTEL & SUITES   *Book at AAA.com*   Phone: (870)879-3800
▼▼ ▼▼
All Year   1P: $85-$150   2P: $85-$150   XP: $10   F
Small-scale Hotel   **Location:** I-530, exit 39, just sw. 3620 Camden Rd 71603. Fax: 870/879-0070. **Facility:** 67 one-bedroom standard units, some with whirlpools. 3 stories, interior corridors. *Bath:* combo or shower only. **Parking:** on-site. **Terms:** cancellation fee imposed, pets ($25 fee). **Amenities:** high-speed Internet, dual phone lines, voice mail, irons, hair dryers. **Pool(s):** outdoor. **Guest Services:** valet and coin laundry. **Business Services:** meeting rooms, business center. **Cards:** AX, CB, DC, DS, MC, VI.

SOME UNITS
FEE   FEE

──────── WHERE TO DINE ────────

COLONIAL STEAKHOUSE   **Dinner:** $15-$27   Phone: 870/536-3488
▼▼ ▼▼
Location: Just w of jct Main St. 111 W 8th Ave 71601. **Hours:** 5 pm-9:15 pm. Closed: Sun & Mon. **Features:** The steakhouse offers a good selection of steaks, which are prepared to the diner's liking. Casual dress; cocktails. **Parking:** on-site. **Cards:** MC, VI.
Steak House

HARBOR OAK'S RESTAURANT   **Lunch:** $5-$6   **Dinner:** $10-$25   Phone: 870/541-9011
▼▼ ▼▼
Location: 1.5 mi n of jct US 65B and Convention Center Dr. 1 Harbor Oaks Dr 71611. **Hours:** 11 am-2:30 & 5-9 pm, Fri & Sat-10 pm. Closed: 12/25; also Sun. **Reservations:** accepted. **Features:** Harbor Oak's is a large restaurant offering a casual and relaxed setting that overlooks an 18-hole golf course. Well-prepared steaks are the specialty of the house. The menu items, which are served in ample portions, are delivered by an attentive staff. Casual dress; cocktails. **Parking:** on-site. **Cards:** AX, DC, DS, MC, VI.
Regional American

POCAHONTAS pop. 6,518

──────── WHERE TO STAY ────────

DAYS INN & SUITES   *Book great rates at AAA.com*   Phone: (870)892-9500
▼▼ ▼▼
All Year   1P: $77   2P: $77   XP: $5   F17
Small-scale Hotel   **Location:** 1.7 mi s. 2805 Hwy 67 S 72455. Fax: 870/892-9500. **Facility:** 58 one-bedroom standard units, some with whirlpools. 3 stories, interior corridors. *Bath:* combo or shower only. **Parking:** on-site. **Terms:** [ECP] meal plan available, small pets only ($25 deposit, $10 extra charge). **Amenities:** voice mail, irons, hair dryers. **Pool(s):** indoor. **Leisure Activities:** whirlpool, exercise room. **Guest Services:** coin laundry, wireless Internet. **Business Services:** meeting rooms, PC. **Cards:** AX, DC, DS, MC, VI.

SOME UNITS
FEE

ROGERS pop. 38,829

──────── WHERE TO STAY ────────

AMERISUITES (ROGERS/BENTONVILLE)   *Book at AAA.com*   Phone: 479/633-8555
▼▼ ▼▼
Property failed to provide current rates
Small-scale Hotel   **Location:** I-540, exit 85, just e. 4610 W Walnut 72756. Fax: 501/633-8333. **Facility:** 104 one-bedroom standard units. 5 stories, interior corridors. *Bath:* combo or shower only. **Parking:** on-site. **Amenities:** video games (fee), high-speed Internet, dual phone lines, voice mail, irons, hair dryers. **Pool(s):** heated outdoor. **Leisure Activities:** exercise room. **Guest Services:** valet and coin laundry. **Business Services:** meeting rooms, business center.

SOME UNITS

CANDLEWOOD SUITES *Book at AAA.com* Phone: (479)636-2783

All Year 1P: $59-$139 2P: $69-$139

Location: I-540, exit 85, 0.5 mi n on 46th St. 4601 W Rozell St 72757. Fax: 479/636-2773. **Facility:** 130 units. 118 one-bedroom standard units with efficiencies. 12 one-bedroom suites with efficiencies. 4 stories, interior corridors. *Bath:* combo or shower only. **Parking:** on-site. **Amenities:** video library, CD players, high-speed Internet, dual phone lines, voice mail, irons, hair dryers. *Some:* DVD players. **Pool(s):** heated indoor. **Leisure Activities:** exercise room. **Guest Services:** valet and coin laundry. **Business Services:** meeting rooms, business center. **Cards:** AX, CB, DC, DS, JC, MC, VI.

Small-scale Hotel

SOME UNITS

(ASK) (S/D) (Ⓣ↑) (🗑) (🏊) (VCR) (🎦) (🗄) (📺) (💻) / (✕) /

COUNTRY INN & SUITES Phone: 479/633-0055

(fyi) Property failed to provide current rates
Too new to rate, opening scheduled for October 2006. **Location:** I-540, exit 85. 4304 W Walnut 72756.
Small-scale Hotel **Amenities:** 110 units, coffeemakers, pool. *(See color ad below)*

EMBASSY SUITES NORTHWEST ARKANSAS *Book great rates at AAA.com* Phone: (479)254-8400

(ⒶⒶⒶ) (SAVE) All Year [BP] 1P: $129-$229 2P: $139-$239 XP: $10 F18

Location: I-540, exit 83, just w, then 0.6 mi s. 3303 Pinnacle Hills Pkwy 72758. Fax: 479/845-2001. **Facility:** 248 one-bedroom suites, some with whirlpools. 9 stories, interior corridors. *Bath:* combo or shower only. **Parking:** on-site. **Terms:** package plans, pets ($75 extra charge). **Amenities:** high-speed Internet, dual phone lines, voice mail, safes, irons, hair dryers. **Dining:** 6-9:30 am, 11-2 & 5-11 pm, Sat & Sun from 7 am. **Pool(s):** heated indoor. **Leisure Activities:** sauna, whirlpool, exercise room. *Fee:* massage. **Guest Services:** gift shop, valet and coin laundry, airport transportation-Northwest Regional Airport, area transportation-within 5 mi. **Business Services:** conference facilities, business center. **Cards:** AX, CB, DC, DS, JC, MC, VI. **Free Special Amenities:** full breakfast and newspaper.

Large-scale Hotel

SOME UNITS

(✈) (🛏) (Ⓣ↑) (📺) (🗑) (🏊) (✕) (🎦) (🗄) (📺) (💻) / (✕) (VCR)
FEE FEE

FAIRFIELD INN & SUITES BY MARRIOTT *Book great rates at AAA.com* Phone: (479)936-5900

All Year [CP] 1P: $59-$149 2P: $59-$149

Location: I-540, exit 85, 0.5 mi n on 46th St. 4611 W Rozell St 72756. Fax: 479/936-5901. **Facility:** Smoke free premises. 99 one-bedroom standard units, some with whirlpools. 3 stories, interior corridors. *Bath:* combo or shower only. **Parking:** on-site. **Terms:** cancellation fee imposed. **Amenities:** high-speed Internet, dual phone lines, voice mail, irons, hair dryers. *Some:* CD players. **Pool(s):** small heated indoor. **Leisure Activities:** whirlpool, exercise room. **Guest Services:** valet and coin laundry, wireless Internet. **Business Services:** meeting rooms, business center. **Cards:** AX, CB, DC, DS, JC, MC, VI.

Small-scale Hotel

SOME UNITS

(ASK) (S/D) (Ⓣ↑) (🗑) (🏊) (✕) (🎦) (💻) / (🗄) (📺) /

HAMPTON INN-BENTONVILLE ROGERS *Book great rates at AAA.com* Phone: (479)986-0500

(ⒶⒶⒶ) (SAVE) All Year 1P: $119-$139 2P: $119-$139 XP: $5 F12

Location: I-540, exit 85, just e. 4501 W Walnut St 72756. Fax: 479/986-9696. **Facility:** 122 one-bedroom standard units, some with whirlpools. 4 stories, interior corridors. *Bath:* combo or shower only. **Parking:** on-site. **Amenities:** video games (fee), dual phone lines, voice mail, irons, hair dryers. **Pool(s):** heated indoor. **Leisure Activities:** whirlpool, exercise room. **Guest Services:** valet and coin laundry, wireless Internet. **Business Services:** meeting rooms, business center. **Cards:** AX, CB, DC, DS, MC, VI.

Small-scale Hotel

(See color ad p 287)

SOME UNITS

(S/D) (Ⓣ↑) (🗑) (🏊) (✕) (🎦) / (✕) (🗄) (📺) /

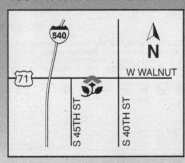

HOMEWOOD SUITES BY HILTON

[fyi]

Property failed to provide current rates
Too new to rate, opening scheduled for November 2006. **Location:** I-540, exit 85. 4302 W Walnut 72756.
Small-scale Hotel Fax: 479/636-5605. **Amenities:** 126 units. *(See color ad p 287)*

Phone: 479/636-5656

RESIDENCE INN BY MARRIOTT

▼▼▼▼

Small-scale Hotel

Book great rates at AAA.com
All Year [BP]   1P: $69-$179   2P: $69-$179
Location: I-540, exit 85, 0.4 mi n on 46th St. 4611 W Locust St 72756. Fax: 479/636-5991. **Facility:** Smoke free premises. 88 units. 28 one-bedroom standard units, some with efficiencies or kitchens. 44 one- and 16 two-bedroom suites ($69-$179), some with efficiencies or kitchens. 4 stories, interior corridors. *Bath:* combo or shower only. **Parking:** on-site. **Terms:** cancellation fee imposed, pets ($75 fee). **Amenities:** video library (fee), DVD players, high-speed Internet, voice mail, irons, hair dryers. **Pool(s):** heated indoor. **Leisure Activities:** whirlpool, sports court. **Guest Services:** sundries, valet and coin laundry, wireless Internet. **Cards:** AX, CB, DC, DS, JC, MC, VI.

Phone: (479)636-5900

(ASK) (SⒹ) 🛏️ (¶¶) (&M) 🍽️ 🏊 💪 ✕ 🎥 🔋 🖥️ 💻
FEE   FEE

——— WHERE TO DINE ———

ABUELO'S MEXICAN FOOD EMBASSY

▼▼▼▼

Mexican

Lunch: $7-$17   **Dinner:** $9-$17   **Phone:** 479/621-0428
Location: I-540, exit 85, just e. 4005 W Walnut St 72756. **Hours:** 11 am-10 pm, Fri & Sat-11 pm. Closed: 11/22, 12/25. **Features:** In addition to a large selection of Mexican dishes, diners will find a 14-ounce rib-eye and beef tenderloin medallions on the menu. Casual dress; cocktails. **Parking:** on-site. **Cards:** AX, CB, DC, DS, JC, MC, VI.

🍽️ 🖊️

BASIL'S CAFE

▼▼▼▼

Mediterranean

Lunch: $6-$10   **Dinner:** $16-$29   **Phone:** 479/464-4190
Location: I-540, exit 83, just w; in Village on the Creek Mall. 5212 Village Pkwy, Suite 12 72758. **Hours:** 11 am-2 & 5-9 pm, Mon from 5 pm. Closed major holidays. **Reservations:** accepted. **Features:** Frequent limited-time specials complement a nice selection of Mediterranean lunches and dinners. In addition to pizza and pasta, the menu lists roasted duck, pine nut-crusted trout and beef tenderloin stir-fry. Casual dress; cocktails.
Parking: on-site. **Cards:** AX, MC, VI.

🍽️

COLTON'S STEAKHOUSE & GRILL

▼▼▼

Steak House

Lunch: $6-$8   **Dinner:** $8-$21   **Phone:** 479/636-3336
Location: I-540, exit 85, 0.4 mi n on 46th St. 4700 W Locust 72756. **Hours:** 11 am-10 pm, Fri-Sun to 11 pm. Closed: 11/22, 12/25. **Reservations:** not accepted. **Features:** A bucket of peanuts on the table, and an upbeat Old-West atmosphere and a good selection of steak, chicken and ribs await guests at the casual steakhouse. Casual dress; cocktails. **Parking:** on-site. **Cards:** AX, DC, DS, MC, VI.

🍽️

CRUMPET TEA ROOM

▼▼

American

DS, MC, VI.

Lunch: $3-$7   **Phone:** 479/636-7498
Location: Jct S 1st St; downtown. 107 W Elm St 72756. **Hours:** 11 am-2 pm. Closed major holidays; also Sun. **Reservations:** suggested. **Features:** The Crumpet Tea Room features a delightful and quaint atmosphere, Victorian dining rooms and decorations, and a very nice selection of quiche, stuffed potatoes, soups, salads, fruits and rolls for lunch. Artwork is also available for purchase. Casual dress. **Parking:** street. **Cards:** AX,

🖊️

DIXIE CAFE

▼▼

Regional American

Lunch: $7-$10   **Dinner:** $7-$10   **Phone:** 501/631-8700
Location: I-540, exit 85, 0.5 mi n on 46th St. 4600 W Rozell St 72756. **Hours:** 11 am-10 pm. Closed: 11/22, 12/25. **Features:** Southern-style home cooking-chicken-fried steak, meat loaf, pork chops, turnip greens, mashed potatoes and fresh veggies-appeals to families who visit the restaurant's classic "Norman Rockwell" atmosphere. Casual dress. **Parking:** on-site. **Cards:** AX, DC, DS, MC, VI.

RIB CRIB BARBECUE

▼▼▼

Barbecue

Lunch: $6-$14   **Dinner:** $6-$14   **Phone:** 479/631-2742
Location: I-540, exit 85, 0.7 mi e. 3604 Walnut St 72756. **Hours:** 11 am-10 pm. Closed: 11/22, 12/25. **Features:** Most guests need extra napkins to tackle the ribs, brisket, ham, pork and chicken selections. The menu also lists sandwiches and wraps, along with tempting sides and large desserts. The decor is decidedly Western. Casual dress; beer only. **Parking:** on-site. **Cards:** AX, DC, DS, MC, VI.

🖊️

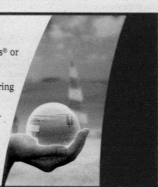

RUSSELLVILLE pop. 23,682

——— WHERE TO STAY ———

BEST WESTERN INN *Book great rates at AAA.com* **Phone:** (479)967-1000
AAA SAVE — All Year [CP] 1P: $60-$71 2P: $65-$71 XP: $4 F14
Location: I-40, exit 81, just s. 2326 N Arkansas Ave 72802. Fax: 479/967-3586. **Facility:** 99 one-bedroom standard units, some with whirlpools. 2 stories (no elevator), exterior corridors. **Parking:** on-site. **Terms:** package plans. **Amenities:** irons, hair dryers. *Some:* high-speed Internet. **Pool(s):** small outdoor.
Small-scale Hotel — **Leisure Activities:** whirlpool, limited exercise equipment. **Guest Services:** valet and coin laundry, wireless Internet. **Business Services:** meeting rooms. **Cards:** AX, DC, DS, MC, VI. **Free Special Amenities:** continental breakfast and high-speed Internet.
SOME UNITS

COMFORT INN *Book great rates at AAA.com* **Phone:** (479)967-7500
All Year 1P: $64 2P: $69 XP: $5 F
Location: I-40, exit 84, just s. 3019 E Parkway Dr 72802. Fax: 479/967-6314. **Facility:** 60 one-bedroom standard
Motel — units, some with whirlpools. 2 stories (no elevator), exterior corridors. **Parking:** on-site. **Terms:** pets ($10 fee). **Amenities:** high-speed Internet, irons, hair dryers. **Pool(s):** small outdoor. **Guest Services:** wireless Internet. **Cards:** AX, DC, DS, MC, VI.
SOME UNITS
FEE

FAIRFIELD INN & SUITES BY MARRIOTT *Book great rates at AAA.com* **Phone:** (479)967-9030
AAA SAVE — All Year 1P: $74 2P: $76
Location: I-40, exit 81, just se. 120 E Harrell Dr 72802. Fax: 479/967-9040. **Facility:** Smoke free premises. 73 units. 70 one-bedroom standard units, some with whirlpools. 3 one-bedroom suites. 3 stories, interior corridors. *Bath:* combo or shower only. **Parking:** on-site. **Terms:** 7 day cancellation notice. **Amenities:** dual
Small-scale Hotel — phone lines, voice mail, irons, hair dryers. *Some:* CD players. **Pool(s):** heated indoor. **Leisure Activities:** whirlpool, exercise room. **Guest Services:** valet and coin laundry, wireless Internet. **Business Services:** meeting rooms, business center. **Cards:** AX, CB, DC, DS, MC, VI. **Free Special Amenities:** expanded continental breakfast and high-speed Internet.
SOME UNITS

HAMPTON INN RUSSELLVILLE *Book great rates at AAA.com* **Phone:** (479)858-7199
AAA SAVE — All Year 1P: $79 2P: $82
Location: I-40, exit 81, just s. 2304 N Arkansas Ave 72802. Fax: 479/858-7198. **Facility:** 83 one-bedroom standard units, some with whirlpools. 2 stories, interior corridors. *Bath:* combo or shower only. **Parking:** on-site. **Terms:** check-in 4 pm, 7 day cancellation notice. **Amenities:** voice mail, irons, hair dryers. **Pool(s):**
Small-scale Hotel — small heated indoor. **Leisure Activities:** whirlpool, exercise room. **Guest Services:** valet and coin laundry, wireless Internet. **Business Services:** meeting rooms, business center. **Cards:** AX, CB, DC, DS, MC, VI. **Free Special Amenities:** expanded continental breakfast and local telephone calls.
SOME UNITS

HOLIDAY INN *Book great rates at AAA.com* **Phone:** (479)968-4300
AAA SAVE — All Year 1P: $74-$89 2P: $74-$89
Location: I-40, exit 81, just s. 2407 N Arkansas Ave 72801 (PO Box 460). Fax: 479/968-4300. **Facility:** 148 units. 146 one-bedroom standard units. 2 one-bedroom suites ($150-$175). 2 stories (no elevator), exterior corridors. **Parking:** on-site. **Terms:** cancellation fee imposed, [BP] meal plan available, package plans, pets
Small-scale Hotel — ($10 extra charge). **Amenities:** irons, hair dryers. **Dining:** Cagle's Mill, see separate listing. **Pool(s):** outdoor. **Leisure Activities:** exercise room. **Guest Services:** valet and coin laundry, airport transportation-Russellville Municipal Airport, wireless Internet. **Business Services:** meeting rooms. **Cards:** AX, CB, DC, DS, MC, VI. **Free Special Amenities:** newspaper and high-speed Internet.
SOME UNITS
FEE FEE FEE

MOTEL 6 RUSSELLVILLE #265 *Book at AAA.com* **Phone:** 479/968-3666
5/25-2/29 1P: $37-$47 2P: $43-$53 XP: $3 F17
3/1-5/24 1P: $34-$44 2P: $40-$50 XP: $3 F17
Motel — **Location:** I-40, exit 81, just n. 215 W Birch St 72802. Fax: 479/890-5207. **Facility:** 79 one-bedroom standard units. 2 stories (no elevator), exterior corridors. *Bath:* shower only. **Parking:** on-site. **Pool(s):** small outdoor.
Guest Services: coin laundry. **Cards:** AX, CB, DC, DS, MC, VI.
SOME UNITS

SUPER 8 MOTEL-RUSSELLVILLE *Book great rates at AAA.com* **Phone:** (479)968-8898
AAA SAVE — All Year 1P: $55-$65 2P: $60-$70 XP: $5 F13
Location: I-40, exit 81, just s. 2404 N Arkansas Ave 72802. Fax: 479/968-8898. **Facility:** 54 one-bedroom standard units. 3 stories (no elevator), interior corridors. **Parking:** on-site. **Terms:** package plans, pets ($10 extra charge). **Guest Services:** wireless Internet. **Cards:** AX, CB, DC, DS, MC, VI.
Small-scale Hotel — **Free Special Amenities:** expanded continental breakfast and high-speed Internet.
SOME UNITS
FEE

——— WHERE TO DINE ———

CAGLE'S MILL **Lunch:** $4-$9 **Dinner:** $7-$17 **Phone:** 479/968-4300
Location: I-40, exit 81, just s. in Holiday Inn. 2407 N Arkansas Ave 72801. **Hours:** 6 am-2 & 4-10 pm, Sun from 7 am. **Features:** Prime rib and possum pie are the specialties at Cagle's Mill, which has an upscale, rustic
Regional American — decor and a warm and hospitable atmosphere. The lunch buffet is very good with several salad varieties. Be certain to leave room for the wonderful desserts. Casual dress. **Parking:** on-site. **Cards:** AX, DC, DS, JC,
MC, VI.

COLTON'S STEAK HOUSE & GRILL **Lunch:** $6-$8   **Dinner:** $9-$19   **Phone:** 479/880-2333
▼▼ ▼▼   **Location:** I-40, exit 81, just s. 2320 N Arkansas 72801. **Hours:** 11 am-10 pm. Closed: 11/22, 12/25. **Features:** A
bucket of peanuts on the table, an upbeat Old-West atmosphere and a good selection of steak, chicken and
Steak House   ribs await guests at the casual steakhouse. Casual dress. **Parking:** on-site. **Cards:** AX, DC, DS, MC, VI.

DIXIE CAFE   **Lunch:** $7-$10   **Dinner:** $7-$10   **Phone:** 501/968-4800
▼▼ ▼▼   **Location:** I-40, exit 81, just se. 105 E Harrell 72801. **Hours:** 11 am-10 pm. Closed: 11/22, 12/25.
Features: Southern-style home cooking-chicken-fried steak, meat loaf, pork chops, turnip greens, mashed
Regional American   potatoes and fresh veggies-appeals to families who visit the restaurant's classic "Norman Rockwell"
atmosphere. Casual dress. **Parking:** on-site. **Cards:** AX, DC, DS, MC, VI.

ITALIAN GARDENS CAFE   **Lunch:** $4-$7   **Dinner:** $6-$12   **Phone:** 479/967-1707
▼▼ ▼▼   **Location:** Center. 315 W Main 72801. **Hours:** 11 am-2 & 5-9 pm. Closed major holidays; also Sun & Mon.
Features: Community residents in the mood for Italian food come to the Main Street cafe. Traditional dishes
Italian   are served in hearty portions. Casual dress. **Parking:** on-site. **Cards:** AX, CB, DC, DS, JC, MC, VI.

MADAME WU'S HUNAN CHINESE RESTAURANT   **Lunch:** $5-$6   **Dinner:** $7-$13   **Phone:** 479/968-4569
▼▼ ▼   **Location:** I-40, exit 81, 2.7 mi s on US 7. 914 S Arkansas Ave 72801. **Hours:** 11 am-2:30 & 4:30-9:30 pm, Fri-10
pm, Sat 4:30 pm-10 pm. Closed major holidays. **Reservations:** accepted. **Features:** You'll have an
Chinese   extensive menu to choose from here. Try the sauteed beef with mushrooms and veggies, crispy sesame
chicken or tasty Hunan shrimp. Madame Wu's has a casually elegant decor. Casual dress. **Parking:** on-site.
Cards: AX, MC, VI.

SEARCY pop. 18,928

———— **WHERE TO STAY** ————

HAMPTON INN   *Book great rates at AAA.com*   **Phone:** (501)268-0654
▼▼ ▼▼   All Year   1P: $99-$109   2P: $99-$109
Location: US 67, exit 46, just w. 3204 E Race Ave 72143. **Fax:** 501/279-2640. **Facility:** 105 units. 104 one-
Small-scale Hotel   bedroom standard units. 1 one-bedroom suite ($125). 2 stories, interior/exterior corridors. **Parking:** on-site.
Terms: pets ($25 extra charge). **Amenities:** video games (fee), voice mail, irons, hair dryers. **Pool(s):**
heated indoor/outdoor. **Leisure Activities:** sauna, whirlpool, exercise room. **Guest Services:** valet and coin laundry, wireless
Internet. **Business Services:** meeting rooms, business center. **Cards:** AX, CB, DC, DS, JC, MC, VI.

SOME UNITS

(ASK) 🆂🅳 🛏 🍴 🍸 🏊 ✖ 📷 💻 / ✖ 🚻 🖥 📠 /
FEE

HOLIDAY INN EXPRESS   *Book at AAA.com*   **Phone:** (501)279-9191
▼▼ ▼▼   All Year   1P: $85-$100   2P: $90-$106   XP: $10   F
Location: US 67, exit 46, just w, then just n. 501 Willow St 72143. **Fax:** 501/279-1320. **Facility:** 71 one-bedroom
Small-scale Hotel   standard units, some with whirlpools. 3 stories, interior corridors. *Bath:* combo or shower only. **Parking:** on-
site. **Terms:** cancellation fee imposed. **Amenities:** high-speed Internet, dual phone lines, voice mail, safes
(fee), irons, hair dryers. **Pool(s):** indoor. **Leisure Activities:** exercise room. **Guest Services:** valet and coin laundry, wireless
Internet. **Business Services:** meeting rooms, business center. **Cards:** AX, CB, DC, DS, JC, MC, VI.

SOME UNITS

(ASK) 🆂🅳 🍴 🐾 🏊 📷 🚻 🖥 💻 / ✖ /

ROYAL INN   *Book great rates at AAA.com*   **Phone:** (501)268-3511
(AAA) (SAVE)   All Year   1P: $45-$60   2P: $55-$70   XP: $5   F12
Location: US 67, exit 46, 1.1 mi w. 2203 E Race Ave 72143. **Fax:** 501/268-3511. **Facility:** 38 one-bedroom
▼   standard units. 1 story, exterior corridors. *Bath:* combo or shower only. **Parking:** on-site. **Terms:** pets ($5
Motel   fee). **Amenities:** *Some:* irons, hair dryers. **Guest Services:** wireless Internet. **Cards:** AX, DS, MC, VI.
Free Special Amenities: continental breakfast and high-speed Internet.

SOME UNITS

🆂🅳 🛏 🍴 🍸 📷 / ✖ 🚻 🖥 💻 /
FEE

———— **WHERE TO DINE** ————

COLTON'S STEAKHOUSE & GRILL   **Lunch:** $6-$21   **Dinner:** $9-$21   **Phone:** 501/268-5777
▼▼ ▼▼   **Location:** US 67, exit 46, 0.5 mi w. 3002 E Race Ave 72143. **Hours:** 11 am-9 pm, Fri & Sat-10 pm. Closed: 11/22,
12/25. **Features:** A bucket of peanuts on the table, an upbeat Old-West atmosphere and a good selection of
Steak House   steak, chicken and ribs await guests at the casual steakhouse. Casual dress; cocktails. **Parking:** on-site.
Cards: AX, DS, MC, VI.

🔧

DIXIE CAFE   **Lunch:** $7-$10   **Dinner:** $7-$10   **Phone:** 501/278-5200
▼▼ ▼▼   **Location:** US 67, exit 46, just sw. 205 S Poplar 72143. **Hours:** 11 am-10 pm. Closed: 11/22, 12/25.
Features: Southern-style home cooking-chicken-fried steak, meat loaf, pork chops, turnip greens, mashed
Regional American   potatoes and fresh veggies-appeals to families who visit the restaurant's classic "Norman Rockwell"
atmosphere. Casual dress. **Parking:** on-site. **Cards:** AX, DC, DS, MC, VI.

SILOAM SPRINGS pop. 10,843

———— **WHERE TO STAY** ————

SUPER 8 MOTEL   *Book at AAA.com*   **Phone:** (479)524-8898
▼▼ ▼▼   All Year   1P: $52-$60   XP: $5   F
Location: Center. 1800 Hwy 412 W 72761. **Fax:** 479/524-5989. **Facility:** 30 one-bedroom standard units. 1
Motel   story, exterior corridors. *Bath:* combo or shower only. **Parking:** on-site. **Terms:** pets (with prior approval).
Amenities: hair dryers. **Pool(s):** outdoor. **Guest Services:** coin laundry, wireless Internet. **Cards:** AX, DS,
MC, VI.

SOME UNITS

(ASK) 🆂🅳 🛏 🍴 🐾 📷 🚻 🖥 💻 / ✖ /

SPRINGDALE pop. 45,798

―――――― **WHERE TO STAY** ――――――

COMFORT SUITES　*Book great rates at AAA.com*　　　　Phone: 479/725-1777

10/19-2/29	1P: $76-$139	2P: $90-$179	XP: $5	F16
5/31-10/18	1P: $100-$101	2P: $101-$110	XP: $5	F16
3/1-5/30	1P: $76-$90	2P: $90-$100	XP: $5	F16

Location: I-540, exit 72, just w. 1099 Rieff St 72764. **Fax:** 479/725-2577. **Facility:** 69 one-bedroom standard units, some with whirlpools. 3 stories, interior corridors. *Bath:* combo or shower only. **Parking:** on-site. **Terms:** [ECP] meal plan available, small pets only. **Amenities:** high-speed Internet, dual phone lines, voice mail, irons, hair dryers. **Pool(s):** small heated indoor. **Leisure Activities:** whirlpool, exercise room. **Guest Services:** sundries, valet and coin laundry, wireless Internet. **Business Services:** meeting rooms, business center. **Cards:** AX, DC, DS, MC, VI. **Free Special Amenities:** expanded continental breakfast and high-speed Internet.

Small-scale Hotel

SOME UNITS

🛎️ 🐾 🍴 ⚒️ ➰ 🎦 🔲 📶 💻 / ☒ /

HAMPTON INN & SUITES　*Book great rates at AAA.com*　　　Phone: (479)756-3500

All Year　　1P: $109-$169

Location: I-540, exit 72, just e. 1700 S 48th St 72762. **Fax:** 479/927-3500. **Facility:** 102 units. 67 one-bedroom standard units. 35 one-bedroom suites ($119-$179) with efficiencies. 3 stories, interior corridors. *Bath:* combo or shower only. **Parking:** on-site. **Terms:** [BP] meal plan available, package plans, small pets only ($50 deposit). **Amenities:** video games (fee), high-speed Internet, voice mail, irons, hair dryers. *Some:* dual phone lines. **Pool(s):** heated outdoor. **Leisure Activities:** exercise room. **Guest Services:** sundries, valet and coin laundry, wireless Internet. **Business Services:** meeting rooms, PC. **Cards:** AX, CB, DC, DS, JC, MC, VI. **Free Special Amenities:** expanded continental breakfast and newspaper. *(See color ad below)*

Small-scale Hotel

SOME UNITS

🐾 🍴 ⚒️ ➰ 🎦 💻 / ☒ 📶 💻 /
FEE

HOLIDAY INN NORTHWEST AR HOTEL &
CONVENTION CENTER　*Book great rates at AAA.com*　　Phone: (479)751-8300

All Year　　1P: $89-$129

Location: I-540, exit 72, just e on US 412. 1500 S 48th St 72762. **Fax:** 479/751-4640. **Facility:** 206 units. 184 one-bedroom standard units. 22 one-bedroom suites ($99-$295), some with whirlpools. 8 stories, interior corridors. *Bath:* combo or shower only. **Parking:** on-site. **Terms:** [BP] & [CP] meal plans available, package plans, small pets only. **Amenities:** video games (fee), high-speed Internet, voice mail, irons, hair dryers. **Dining:** 2 restaurants, 6 am-11 pm, cocktails. **Pool(s):** heated indoor. **Leisure Activities:** sauna, whirlpool, golf privileges, exercise room. **Guest Services:** gift shop, valet and coin laundry, wireless Internet. **Business Services:** conference facilities, business center. **Cards:** AX, CB, DC, DS, JC, MC, VI. **Free Special Amenities:** newspaper. *(See color ad below)*

Large-scale Hotel

SOME UNITS

🛎️ ✈️ 🐾 🍴 🍷 ⚒️ 🎵 ➰ ☒ 🎦 💻 / ☒ 📶 💻 /

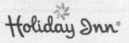

LA QUNITA INN-SPRINGDALE *Book great rates at AAA.com* **Phone:** (479)751-2626
▼▼▼ ▼▼▼
4/29-10/30	1P: $89-$129	2P: $89-$129
3/1-4/28	1P: $82-$129	2P: $82-$129
10/31-2/29	1P: $86-$119	2P: $89-$119

Small-scale Hotel **Location:** I-540, exit 72, just e on US 412. 1300 S 48th St 72764. **Fax:** 479/751-0075. **Facility:** 100 units. 96 one-bedroom standard units. 4 one-bedroom suites ($122-$159). 4 stories, interior corridors. *Bath:* combo or shower only. **Parking:** on-site. **Amenities:** video games (fee), voice mail, irons, hair dryers. **Pool(s):** heated indoor. **Leisure Activities:** whirlpool. **Guest Services:** valet and coin laundry, wireless Internet. **Business Services:** meeting rooms. **Cards:** AX, CB, DC, DS, MC, VI.

SOME UNITS
(ASK) 🐾 ❌ ▥ (●) 🚫 ➰ 🎦 📷 💻 / ⊠ 🔌 🖥 /
FEE

────── *The following lodging was either not evaluated or did not* ──────
meet AAA rating requirements but is listed for your information only.

RESIDENCE INN BY MARRIOTT **Phone:** 479/872-9100
[fyi] Did not meet all AAA rating requirements for some property operations at time of last evaluation on 02/28/2006. **Location:** I-540, exit 72, just e to 48th St, then just s. 1740 S 48th St 72762. Facilities, services, and Small-scale Hotel decor characterize a mid-range property.

────── **WHERE TO DINE** ──────

A Q CHICKEN HOUSE **Lunch:** $5-$6 **Dinner:** $6-$8 **Phone:** 479/751-4633
▼▼▼ ▼▼▼ **Location:** I-540, exit 72, 2.6 mi e on US 412, then 1.4 mi n on US 71B. 1201 N Thompson 72765. **Hours:** 11 am-8:30 pm, Fri & Sat-9 pm, Sun-8 pm. Closed: 11/22, 12/24, 12/25. **Features:** This restaurant has been popular Regional American with local residents since 1947. Its pan-fried chicken is the house specialty, but they offer a good variety of other tasty dishes served in plentiful portions. The servers are cordial and attentive. Casual dress; beer & wine only. **Parking:** on-site. **Cards:** AX, CB, DC, DS, MC, VI.
🖈

MARKETPLACE GRILL **Lunch:** $9-$24 **Dinner:** $9-$24 **Phone:** 479/750-5200
▼▼▼ ▼▼▼ **Location:** I-540, exit 72, just se. 1636 S 48th St 72762. **Hours:** 11 am-9:30 pm, Fri & Sat-10:30 pm. Closed: 1/1, 11/22, 12/25. **Features:** The restaurant is big on menu variety, incorporating freshly made pasta, pizzas, American dressings and sauces. Steaks, Cajun dishes and seafood also are served in the spacious, inviting dining room. Casual dress. **Parking:** on-site. **Cards:** AX, CB, DC, DS, MC, VI.

SUNSET GRILL **Lunch:** $6-$8 **Dinner:** $6-$8 **Phone:** 479/872-9594
▼▼▼ **Location:** I-540, exit 71, 1 mi e. 3418 W Sunset Ave, Suite A 72762. **Hours:** 6 am-2 pm, Fri also 5 pm-8 pm, Sat & American Sun 7 am-2 pm. Closed: 1/1, 4/8, 12/25; also Mon & week of Thanksgiving. **Features:** Guests are offered a choice of traditional home-cooked meals, which are served in good-size portions. Casual dress. **Parking:** on-site. **Cards:** MC, VI.

STAR CITY pop. 2,471

────── **WHERE TO STAY** ──────

SUPER 8 MOTEL-STAR CITY *Book at AAA.com* **Phone:** (870)628-6883
▼▼▼ ▼▼▼ All Year [CP] 1P: $52-$65 2P: $57-$70 XP: $5 F17
Location: Just n on US 425. 1308 N Lincoln St 71667. **Fax:** 870/628-6889. **Facility:** 47 one-bedroom standard Small-scale Hotel units. 2 stories (no elevator), interior corridors. **Parking:** on-site. **Terms:** pets ($10 fee). **Amenities:** high-speed Internet, hair dryers. **Pool(s):** outdoor. **Guest Services:** coin laundry. **Business Services:** meeting rooms. **Cards:** AX, DS, MC, VI.

SOME UNITS
(ASK) 🛏 🐾 ❌ ➰ 🎦 🔌 🖥 💻 / ⊠ /
FEE

STUTTGART pop. 9,745

────── **WHERE TO STAY** ──────

DAYS INN & SUITES **Phone:** 870/673-3616
(AAA) [SAVE] 11/17-2/29 1P: $112-$125 2P: $112-$125 XP: $10 F18
3/1-11/16 1P: $62-$69 2P: $62-$69 XP: $10 F18
▼▼▼ ▼▼▼ **Location:** Just w on US 63/79. 708 W Michigan 72160. **Fax:** 870/673-6920. **Facility:** 40 one-bedroom standard units. 2 stories (no elevator), exterior corridors. **Parking:** on-site. **Terms:** pets ($5 extra charge). Small-scale Hotel **Amenities:** high-speed Internet, dual phone lines, voice mail, irons, hair dryers. **Pool(s):** outdoor. **Guest Services:** valet and coin laundry, wireless Internet. **Business Services:** meeting rooms. **Cards:** AX, CB, DC, DS, JC, MC, VI. **Free Special Amenities:** continental breakfast and high-speed Internet.

SOME UNITS
🐾 🎦 ➰ 🔌 🖥 💻 / ⊠ /
FEE

TEXARKANA pop. 26,448

———— WHERE TO STAY ————

HOLIDAY INN TEXARKANA   *Book great rates at AAA.com*   **Phone:** (870)774-3521

AAA **SAVE**   All Year   1P: $72-$77   2P: $72-$77

WWWW   **Location:** I-30, exit 223B, just n. 5100 N State Line Ave 71854. **Fax:** 870/772-3068. **Facility:** 210 units. 209 one-bedroom standard units. 1 two-bedroom suite with kitchen (no utensils). 4 stories, interior corridors. *Bath:* combo or shower only. **Parking:** on-site. **Terms:** [BP] meal plan available, package plans, small pets only

Small-scale Hotel   ($25 fee). **Amenities:** high-speed Internet, voice mail, irons, hair dryers. **Dining:** 6:30 am-10 pm, Fri & Sat-11 pm, cocktails. **Pool(s):** indoor. **Leisure Activities:** sauna, whirlpool, indoor recreation area, exercise room. *Fee:* game room. **Guest Services:** valet and coin laundry, airport transportation-Texarkana Municipal Airport, wireless Internet. **Business Services:** meeting rooms, PC. **Cards:** AX, DC, DS, MC, VI. **Free Special Amenities:** local telephone calls and high-speed Internet.

SOME UNITS

FEE   ⊞ 🐾 🍴 ⊤ 🎣 ⋙ ✕ 🐕 🛢 🖥 🖵 /✕/

LA QUINTA INN & SUITES   *Book great rates at AAA.com*   **Phone:** (870)773-1000

WW WW   5/25-9/3 [ECP]   1P: $81-$101   2P: $91-$111   XP: $10   F18

9/4-2/29 [ECP]   1P: $74-$94   2P: $84-$104   XP: $10   F18

Small-scale Hotel   3/1-5/24 [ECP]   1P: $70-$90   2P: $80-$100   XP: $10   F18

Location: I-30, exit 223B, just n. 5102 N State Line Ave 71854. **Fax:** 870/773-5000. **Facility:** 101 units. 98 one-bedroom standard units. 4 stories, interior corridors. **Parking:** on-site. **Terms:** small pets only. **Amenities:** video games (fee), voice mail, irons, hair dryers. **Pool(s):** outdoor. **Leisure Activities:** exercise room. **Guest Services:** coin laundry, wireless Internet. **Cards:** AX, CB, DC, DS, MC, VI.

SOME UNITS

(ASK) 🐾 🍴 🎮 ⋙ 🎥 🖵 /✕ 🛢 🖵 /

———— WHERE TO DINE ————

CATTLEMANS STEAKHOUSE   **Dinner:** $13-$24   **Phone:** 870/774-4481

WW WW   **Location:** I-30, exit 223A, 0.5 mi s. 4018 State Line Ave 72632. **Hours:** 5:30 pm-9:30 pm, Fri & Sat-10 pm. Closed major holidays; also Sun. **Reservations:** accepted. **Features:** This restaurant features the

Steak House   traditional steak dishes with basic presentation and preparation methods, but they also serve a nice variety of chicken and fried, broiled or blackened seafood. You'll find the service friendly and attentive. Casual dress; cocktails. **Parking:** on-site. **Cards:** AX, DC, DS, MC, VI.

🍷

LA CARRETA MEXICAN CAFE   **Lunch:** $5-$12   **Dinner:** $7-$12   **Phone:** 870/774-0075

WW WW   **Location:** I-30, exit 223A, 0.5 mi se. 3908 State Line 71854. **Hours:** 11 am-10 pm, Fri & Sat-11 pm. Closed:

Mexican   11/22, 12/25. **Features:** A large selection of traditional dishes is served in a festive, open dining room. Casual dress; cocktails. **Parking:** on-site. **Cards:** AX, DS, MC, VI.

⊤ 🍷

TEXARKANA, TX

———— WHERE TO STAY ————

BAYMONT INN   *Book at AAA.com*   **Phone:** (903)794-1900
All Year [ECP]   1P: $70-$90   2P: $80-$100   XP: $10   F18
Small-scale Hotel **Location:** I-30, exit 223A, sw of jct US 59 and 71. 5201 State Line Ave 75503. Fax: 903/792-5506. **Facility:** 130 units. 128 one-bedroom standard units. 2 one-bedroom suites. 2 stories (no elevator), exterior corridors. **Parking:** on-site. **Terms:** small pets only. **Amenities:** video games (fee), voice mail, irons, hair dryers. **Pool(s):** outdoor. **Guest Services:** valet laundry, wireless Internet. **Business Services:** fax (fee). **Cards:** AX, CB, DC, DS, MC, VI.

SOME UNITS
ⓐSK ⛺ 🍴⁺ 🛟 🛗⁺ 🎦 💻 / ✕ 🛗 🖥 /

BUDGET HOST NORTHGATE INN   *Book great rates at AAA.com*   **Phone:** (903)793-6565
All Year   1P: $55-$64   2P: $58-$69   XP: $2   F12
Small-scale Hotel **Location:** I-30, exit 223B, on northwest frontage road. 400 W 53rd St 75503. Fax: 903/793-3171. **Facility:** 63 one-bedroom standard units. 2 stories (no elevator), interior corridors. **Parking:** on-site. **Terms:** small pets only ($20 fee). **Amenities:** irons, hair dryers. **Pool(s):** outdoor. **Guest Services:** valet and coin laundry, wireless Internet. **Business Services:** meeting rooms, fax (fee). **Cards:** AX, CB, DC, DS, MC, VI.

SOME UNITS
🅢🄳 🛟 🎦 🖥 🖥 / ✕ VCR /
FEE

CLARION HOTEL   **Phone:** 903/792-3222
Property failed to provide current rates
Small-scale Hotel **Location:** I-30, exit 223B. 5301 N State Line Ave 75503. Fax: 903/793-3930. **Facility:** 149 one-bedroom standard units, some with whirlpools. 6 stories, interior corridors. *Bath:* combo or shower only. **Parking:** on-site. **Terms:** pets ($50 deposit, in designated units). **Amenities:** video games (fee), high-speed Internet, voice mail, irons, hair dryers. *Some:* safes. **Pool(s):** heated indoor. **Leisure Activities:** whirlpool, exercise room. **Guest Services:** valet laundry, area transportation, wireless Internet. **Business Services:** meeting rooms, PC, fax.

SOME UNITS
🔀 🍴⁺ 🍸 ⓜ 🛟 🎦 🖥 🖥 / ✕ /
FEE

COMFORT INN   *Book great rates at AAA.com*   **Phone:** 903/792-6688
All Year   1P: $69   2P: $69
Small-scale Hotel **Location:** I-30, exit 223A, just sw. 5105 State Line Ave 75503. Fax: 903/792-4798. **Facility:** 81 units. 79 one-bedroom standard units, some with whirlpools. 2 one-bedroom suites, some with efficiencies or kitchens. 2 stories (no elevator), exterior corridors. **Parking:** on-site. **Terms:** 14 day cancellation notice-fee imposed, package plans, small pets only ($25 fee). **Amenities:** irons, hair dryers. **Pool(s):** small outdoor. **Guest Services:** valet and coin laundry, wireless Internet. **Business Services:** business center. **Cards:** AX, CB, DC, DS, JC, MC, VI.

SOME UNITS
ⓐSK 🅢🄳 ⛺ 🍴⁺ 🛟 🎦 🖥 / ✕ 🛗 🖥 /
FEE

COMFORT SUITES   *Book great rates at AAA.com*   **Phone:** (903)223-0951
All Year [CP]   1P: $86-$95   2P: $86-$95   XP: $6   F
Small-scale Hotel **Location:** I-30, exit 220B. 215 Richill Dr 75503. Fax: 903/223-0729. **Facility:** 70 units. 68 one- and 2 two-bedroom standard units. 3 stories, interior corridors. *Bath:* combo or shower only. **Parking:** on-site. **Terms:** package plans. **Amenities:** high-speed Internet, dual phone lines, voice mail, safes (fee), irons, hair dryers. **Pool(s):** heated indoor. **Leisure Activities:** putting green, exercise room. **Guest Services:** valet and coin laundry, airport transportation-Texarkana Municipal Airport, area transportation-within 5 mi, wireless Internet. **Business Services:** meeting rooms, PC, fax (fee). **Cards:** AX, CB, DC, DS, JC, MC, VI. **Free Special Amenities:** expanded continental breakfast.

🅢🄳 🔀 🍴⁺ ⓜ 🛟 🖥 🖥 / ✕ /

HAMPTON INN & SUITES   *Book great rates at AAA.com*   **Phone:** (903)832-3499
All Year   1P: $102   2P: $102
Small-scale Hotel **Location:** I-30, exit 220B, 0.4 mi w, on south service road. 4601 Cowhorn Creek Rd 75503. Fax: 903/832-3331. **Facility:** 81 one-bedroom standard units. 4 stories, interior corridors. *Bath:* combo or shower only. **Parking:** on-site. **Terms:** 30 day cancellation notice-fee imposed, [ECP] meal plan available. **Amenities:** video games (fee), high-speed Internet, voice mail, irons, hair dryers. **Pool(s):** small heated indoor. **Leisure Activities:** exercise room. **Guest Services:** sundries, valet and coin laundry, wireless Internet. **Business Services:** meeting rooms, PC. **Cards:** AX, CB, DC, DS, JC, MC, VI.

SOME UNITS
ⓐSK 🅢🄳 🍴⁺ ⓜ 🛟 🎦 🖥 🖥 / ✕ /

HOLIDAY INN EXPRESS   *Book great rates at AAA.com*   **Phone:** (903)792-3366
All Year [CP]   1P: $76-$106   2P: $76-$106   XP: $5
Small-scale Hotel **Location:** I-30, exit 223B, 0.3 mi n on US 71. 5401 N State Line Ave 75503. Fax: 903/792-5649. **Facility:** 120 one-bedroom standard units, some with whirlpools. 3 stories, interior corridors. **Parking:** on-site. **Terms:** cancellation fee imposed, small pets only ($25 fee, $100 deposit). **Amenities:** high-speed Internet, dual phone lines, voice mail, irons, hair dryers. **Pool(s):** outdoor. **Leisure Activities:** whirlpool. **Guest Services:** valet and coin laundry, airport transportation-Texarkana Municipal Airport, area transportation-within 5 mi, wireless Internet. **Business Services:** fax (fee). **Cards:** AX, CB, DC, DS, JC, MC, VI. **Free Special Amenities:** newspaper and high-speed Internet.

SOME UNITS
🅢🄳 🔀 🛟 🍴⁺ 🛟 🎦 🖥 🖥 🖥 / ✕ /
FEE

MOTEL 6 - 201   *Book at AAA.com*   **Phone:** 903/793-1413
2/1-5/24   1P: $38-$48   2P: $44-$64   XP: $3   F17
5/25-1/31   1P: $39-$49   2P: $45-$55   XP: $3   F17
Small-scale Hotel **Location:** I-30, exit 222 (Summerhill Rd). 1924 Hampton Rd 75503. Fax: 903/793-5831. **Facility:** 100 one-bedroom standard units. 2 stories (no elevator), exterior corridors. *Bath:* shower only. **Parking:** on-site. **Pool(s):** outdoor. **Guest Services:** coin laundry. **Business Services:** fax (fee). **Cards:** AX, CB, DC, DS, MC, VI.

SOME UNITS
🅢🄳 ⛺ 🛟 🛟 🎦 / ✕ /

——— WHERE TO DINE ———

BRYCE'S CAFETERIA

American

Lunch: $8-$12   **Dinner:** $8-$12   **Phone:** 903/792-1611
Location: I-30, exit 222 (Summerhill Rd), just s to Mall Dr, then just w. 2021 Mall Dr 75503. **Hours:** 11 am-2 & 5-8 pm, Sat & Sun 11 am-8 pm. Closed: 1/1, 12/25. **Features:** Classic American favorites are offered at the traditional cafeteria, a great place for diners who are looking for generous portions of hearty comfort food. Casual dress. **Parking:** on-site. **Cards:** AX, DS, MC, VI.

DIXIE DINER #2

American

Lunch: $8-$15   **Dinner:** $8-$15   **Phone:** 903/223-0841
Location: I-30, exit 218, just n. 4115 N King Hwy, Suite 120 75503. **Hours:** 7 am-9 pm. Closed: 11/22, 12/25. **Features:** People in the Texarkana area rely on the small chain of restaurants for down-home family favorites. Beef, chicken, pork, fish and vegetable dishes all are made in house. A slice of homemade pie is the perfect finish to a meal. Casual dress. **Parking:** on-site. **Cards:** AX, DS, MC, VI.

GRANDY'S

American

Lunch: $6-$9   **Dinner:** $6-$9   **Phone:** 903/832-5206
Location: I-30, exit 220B, just se on Richard Rd to Kennedy Ln, then just e. 3225 Kennedy Ln 75503. **Hours:** 6 am-9:30 pm, Fri & Sat-10 pm. Closed: 11/22, 12/25. **Features:** Fried chicken and country-fried steak are menu standbys at the restaurant, a regional franchise. The decor is a step up from that of most quick-serve eateries and more resembles that of a conventional restaurant. Some elements of increased service include additional rolls, iced tea refills and tray removal. Casual dress. **Parking:** on-site. **Cards:** CB, DS, MC, VI.

TONTITOWN pop. 942

——— WHERE TO DINE ———

MARY MAESTRI'S

Italian

Dinner: $15-$23   **Phone:** 479/361-2536
Location: On US 412 at SR 112. 956 E Henri De Tonti Blvd 72770. **Hours:** 5:30 pm-9:30 pm. Closed major holidays. **Features:** An area institution since 1923, the fine dining establishment restaurant prepares homemade Italian cuisine. Dressy casual; cocktails. **Parking:** on-site. **Cards:** AX, DC, DS, MC, VI.

TRUMANN pop. 6,889

——— WHERE TO STAY ———

DAYS INN & SUITES   *Book great rates at AAA.com*   **Phone:** (870)483-8383

Small-scale Hotel

All Year   1P: $59-$65   XP: $10   F16
Location: US 63, exit 29, just e. 400 Commerce Dr 72472. Fax: 870/483-8384. **Facility:** 54 one-bedroom standard units. 2 stories, interior/exterior corridors. *Bath:* combo or shower only. **Parking:** on-site. **Terms:** package plans, pets ($10 extra charge). **Amenities:** voice mail, irons, hair dryers. **Pool(s):** outdoor. **Leisure Activities:** exercise room. **Guest Services:** coin laundry, wireless Internet. **Business Services:** meeting rooms, PC. **Cards:** AX, DS, MC, VI. **Free Special Amenities:** continental breakfast and high-speed Internet.

VAN BUREN pop. 18,986

——— WHERE TO STAY ———

COMFORT INN   *Book great rates at AAA.com*   **Phone:** (479)474-2223

Small-scale Hotel

All Year [ECP]   1P: $55-$95   2P: $55-$95   XP: $5   F17
Location: I-540, exit 2A, just s. 3131 Cloverleaf 72956. Fax: 479/474-9049. **Facility:** 48 one-bedroom standard units. 2 stories (no elevator), interior corridors. **Parking:** on-site. **Terms:** pets ($25 fee). **Amenities:** irons, hair dryers. **Pool(s):** outdoor. **Guest Services:** coin laundry, wireless Internet. **Cards:** AX, CB, DC, DS, JC, MC, VI.

HAMPTON INN   *Book great rates at AAA.com*   **Phone:** (479)471-7447

Small-scale Hotel

All Year   1P: $89-$120   2P: $94-$125
Location: I-40, exit 5, just ne. 1916 N 6th St 72956. Fax: 479/471-7764. **Facility:** 64 one-bedroom standard units, some with whirlpools. 3 stories, interior corridors. *Bath:* combo or shower only. **Parking:** on-site. **Terms:** [ECP] meal plan available. **Amenities:** high-speed Internet, voice mail, irons, hair dryers. **Pool(s):** heated indoor. **Leisure Activities:** exercise room. **Guest Services:** valet and coin laundry, wireless Internet. **Business Services:** meeting rooms. **Cards:** AX, CB, DC.

The following lodging was either not evaluated or did not meet AAA rating requirements but is listed for your information only.

BEST WESTERN VAN BUREN INN   **Phone:** 479/474-8100

[fyi]

Small-scale Hotel

Did not meet all AAA rating requirements for some property operations at time of last evaluation on 10/06/2005. **Location:** I-40, exit 5, just n. 1903 N 6th St 72956 (PO Box 6217). Facilities, services, and decor characterize a mid-range property.

-------- WHERE TO DINE --------

EL LORITO
Mexican
Lunch: $5-$7   **Dinner:** $5-$7   **Phone:** 479/410-2463
Location: Just w of jct Main St. 511 Broadway St 72956. **Hours:** 11 am-9 pm. Closed: 11/22, 12/25. **Features:** Ample portions of a nice variety of dishes contribute to the restaurant's popularity with the locals. Casual dress; beer only. **Parking:** on-site. **Cards:** AX, DS, MC, VI.

GRINGO'S TEX-MEX RESTAURANT
Tex-Mex
Lunch: $4-$7   **Dinner:** $5-$12   **Phone:** 479/474-7494
Location: I-40, exit 5, just se. 613 N Plaza Ct 72956. **Hours:** 11 am-9 pm. Closed major holidays. **Features:** On the menu is a nice variety of Mexican dishes. The setting is casual and comfortable. Casual dress; beer only. **Parking:** on-site. **Cards:** AX, DS, MC, VI.

WEST HELENA pop. 8,689

-------- WHERE TO STAY --------

BEST WESTERN INN
AAA SAVE
Small-scale Hotel
Book great rates at AAA.com
Phone: (870)572-2592
All Year [CP]   1P: $64-$125   2P: $64-$125   F
Location: US 49, 3 mi w. 1053 Hwy 49 W 72390. **Fax:** 870/572-7561. **Facility:** 63 one-bedroom standard units, some with whirlpools. 2 stories (no elevator), exterior corridors. **Parking:** on-site. **Terms:** pets ($25 deposit, with prior approval). **Amenities:** voice mail, irons, hair dryers. *Some:* high-speed Internet. **Pool(s):** outdoor. **Leisure Activities:** exercise room. **Guest Services:** coin laundry, wireless Internet. **Cards:** AX, CB, DC, DS, MC, VI. **Free Special Amenities:** continental breakfast and high-speed Internet.

SOME UNITS

WEST MEMPHIS pop. 27,666

-------- WHERE TO STAY --------

HAMPTON INN
Small-scale Hotel
Book great rates at AAA.com
Phone: 870/732-1102
All Year   1P: $74-$82   2P: $82-$90
Location: I-40, exit 279A. 2003 S Service Rd 72301. **Fax:** 870/732-1517. **Facility:** 81 one-bedroom standard units. 2 stories (no elevator), exterior corridors. **Parking:** on-site. **Terms:** 30 day cancellation notice, [CP] meal plan available. **Amenities:** dual phone lines, voice mail, irons, hair dryers. **Pool(s):** outdoor. **Guest Services:** valet and coin laundry, wireless Internet. **Business Services:** PC. **Cards:** AX, CB, DC, DS, MC, VI.

SOME UNITS

HOLIDAY INN-WEST MEMPHIS
Small-scale Hotel
Book at AAA.com
Phone: (870)735-4055
All Year   1P: $110-$140   2P: $120-$150   XP: $10   F18
Location: I-40, exit 279A, just s. 2007 S Service Rd 72301. **Fax:** 870/735-4055. **Facility:** 126 one-bedroom standard units. 4 stories, interior corridors. **Parking:** on-site. **Terms:** 7 day cancellation notice-fee imposed. **Amenities:** dual phone lines, voice mail, irons, hair dryers. **Pool(s):** heated indoor. **Leisure Activities:** exercise room. **Guest Services:** valet and coin laundry, wireless Internet. **Business Services:** conference facilities, PC. **Cards:** AX, CB, DC, DS, JC, MC, VI.

SOME UNITS

QUALITY INN
AAA SAVE
Small-scale Hotel
Book great rates at AAA.com
Phone: (870)702-9000
All Year   1P: $59-$129   2P: $64-$134   XP: $5   F18
Location: I-40, exit 278, just se. 1009 S Service Rd 72301. **Fax:** 870/702-6655. **Facility:** 54 one-bedroom standard units, some with whirlpools. 2 stories (no elevator), interior corridors. *Bath:* combo or shower only. **Parking:** on-site. **Terms:** cancellation fee imposed. **Amenities:** high-speed Internet, irons, hair dryers. *Some:* dual phone lines. **Pool(s):** outdoor. **Leisure Activities:** limited exercise equipment. **Guest Services:** valet laundry, wireless Internet. **Cards:** AX, CB, DC, DS, MC, VI. **Free Special Amenities:** expanded continental breakfast and high-speed Internet.

SOME UNITS

RAMADA LIMITED WEST MEMPHIS
Small-scale Hotel
Book at AAA.com
Phone: (870)735-3232
5/1-11/11   1P: $65-$120   2P: $65-$120   XP: $5   F17
3/1-4/30 & 11/12-2/29   1P: $60-$99   2P: $60-$99   XP: $5   F17
Location: I-40, exit 276 eastbound; exit 278 westbound. 210 W Service Rd 72301. **Fax:** 870/735-3232. **Facility:** 130 units. 120 one-bedroom standard units. 10 one-bedroom suites. 2 stories (no elevator), exterior corridors. *Bath:* combo or shower only. **Parking:** on-site. **Terms:** [ECP] meal plan available. **Amenities:** high-speed Internet, voice mail, irons, hair dryers. **Leisure Activities:** exercise room. **Guest Services:** valet and coin laundry, wireless Internet. **Business Services:** meeting rooms, PC. **Cards:** AX, CB, DC, DS, JC, MC, VI.

SOME UNITS

-------- WHERE TO DINE --------

MARGARITAS MEXICAN RESTAURANT & CANTINA
Mexican
Lunch: $5-$14   **Dinner:** $6-$14   **Phone:** 870/702-7314   [32]
Location: I-40, exit 279A, just s. 1100 1/2 Ingram Blvd 72301. **Hours:** 11 am-10 pm. Closed: 11/22, 12/25. **Features:** Varied well-prepared dishes are served promptly in the quaint but festive restaurant. Casual dress; beer & wine only. **Parking:** on-site. **Cards:** AX, MC, VI.

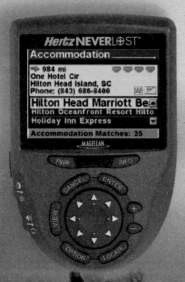

Kansas

Monument Rocks, Oakley
© James Nedresky

ABILENE pop. 6,543

──── WHERE TO STAY ────

BEST WESTERN PRESIDENT'S INN — *Book great rates at AAA.com* — Phone: (785)263-2050

AAA **SAVE**

All Year — 1P: $40-$54 — 2P: $46-$58 — XP: $8 — F16

Small-scale Hotel

Location: I-70, exit 275, just s. 2210 N Buckeye 67410 (PO Box 458). Fax: 785/263-7230. **Facility:** 64 units. 63 one-bedroom standard units. 1 one-bedroom suite. 2 stories (no elevator), exterior corridors. *Bath:* combo or shower only. **Parking:** on-site, winter plug-ins. **Terms:** small pets only. **Amenities:** irons, hair dryers. *Some:* high-speed Internet. **Dining:** 6 am-9 pm, cocktails. **Pool(s):** heated indoor. **Leisure Activities:** whirlpool. **Business Services:** meeting rooms. **Cards:** AX, CB, DC, DS, MC, VI. **Free Special Amenities:** local telephone calls and high-speed Internet.

SOME UNITS

HOLIDAY INN EXPRESS HOTEL & SUITES — *Book at AAA.com* — Phone: 785/263-4049

All Year — 1P: $81 — 2P: $81

Small-scale Hotel

Location: I-70, exit 275, just n. 110 E Lafayette Ave 67410. Fax: 785/263-3201. **Facility:** 61 one-bedroom standard units, some with whirlpools. 2 stories, interior corridors. *Bath:* combo or shower only. **Parking:** on-site. **Terms:** [ECP] meal plan available, pets ($5 fee). **Amenities:** high-speed Internet, dual phone lines, voice mail, irons, hair dryers. **Pool(s):** small heated indoor. **Leisure Activities:** sauna, whirlpool, exercise room. **Guest Services:** valet and coin laundry. **Business Services:** meeting rooms, PC. **Cards:** AX, DC, DS, MC, VI.

SOME UNITS

FEE

SUPER 8 MOTEL — *Book at AAA.com* — Phone: (785)263-4545

All Year — 1P: $50-$70 — 2P: $55-$75 — XP: $5 — F17

Small-scale Hotel

Location: I-70; exit 275, just s. 2207 N Buckeye 67410. Fax: 785/263-7448. **Facility:** 61 one-bedroom standard units. 3 stories (no elevator), interior corridors. **Parking:** on-site. **Terms:** pets ($50 deposit, $10 extra charge). **Business Services:** meeting rooms. **Cards:** AX, CB, DC, DS, MC, VI.

SOME UNITS

FEE

──── WHERE TO DINE ────

BROOKVILLE HOTEL — Lunch: $13 — Dinner: $13 — Phone: 785/263-2244

American

Location: I-70, exit 275, just n, then just e. 105 E Lafayette 67410. **Hours:** 5 pm-8 pm; Sat 11:30 am-2 & 4:30-8 pm, Sun 11:30 am-2:30 & 5-7:30 pm; limited hours 11/1-4/30. Closed major holidays; also Mon. **Reservations:** suggested. **Features:** The historic Brookville Hotel, in the center of town, was built in 1870. The restaurant has been family-owned and operated since 1915. The unique dining experience offers ample portions of the excellent family-style fried chicken. Knowledgeable service. Casual dress; cocktails. **Parking:** on-site. **Cards:** AX, DS, MC, VI. **Historic**

THE KIRBY HOUSE — Lunch: $7-$13 — Dinner: $9-$22 — Phone: 785/263-7336

AAA

American

Location: I-70, exit 275, 1.3 mi s, then just e. 205 NE 3rd St 67410. **Hours:** 11 am-2 & 5-8 pm. Closed: 1/1, 12/25; also Sun. **Reservations:** suggested. **Features:** The Kirby House is located in a restored Victorian home, which was built in 1885 by Thomas Kirby, a local banker. Kirby House features many delicate offerings of steak, seafood, pasta, chicken and pork selections. Save room for the desserts, you won't be disappointed. Casual dress; cocktails. **Parking:** street. **Cards:** AX, DS, MC, VI.

TASTE OF CHINA — Lunch: $4-$13 — Dinner: $4-$13 — Phone: 785/263-4988

Chinese

Location: I-70, exit 275, 0.5 mi s; next to Abilene's Pride Inn. 1709 N Buckeye Ave 67410. **Hours:** 11 am-10 pm. Closed major holidays. **Features:** Patrons can pick and choose from the large all-day buffet or order from the menu, which lists entrees ranging from happy family to seafood delight. A diet menu caters to those who are watching their weight. Casual dress; cocktails. **Parking:** on-site. **Cards:** AX, DS, MC, VI.

ARKANSAS CITY pop. 11,963

──── WHERE TO DINE ────

SIRLOIN STOCKADE — Lunch: $6-$8 — Dinner: $6-$8 — Phone: 620/442-0000

Steak House

Location: On US 77, just n of jct W Bryant Rd/E Windsor Rd. 2825 N Windsor Rd 67005. **Hours:** 11 am-9 pm. Closed major holidays. **Reservations:** not accepted. **Features:** The steakhouse lines up buffet items, including pizza, tacos, soups, salads and desserts, providing both excellent variety and a good value. Rotating theme nights might allow for the sampling of sushi, barbecue and seafood. The buffet also may serve to complement a quality steak. Rolls are baked several times daily. Casual dress. **Parking:** on-site. **Cards:** DS, MC, VI.

ATCHISON pop. 10,232

──── WHERE TO STAY ────

AMERICINN LODGE & SUITES — *Book at AAA.com* — Phone: (913)367-4000

All Year — 1P: $70-$80 — 2P: $70-$80 — XP: $5 — F18

Small-scale Hotel

Location: Just s at US 59 and 73. 500 US 73 66002. Fax: 913/367-9691. **Facility:** 45 units. 42 one-bedroom standard units, some with whirlpools. 3 one-bedroom suites with whirlpools. 2 stories (no elevator), interior corridors. *Bath:* combo or shower only. **Parking:** on-site. **Terms:** cancellation fee imposed, package plans, pets ($50 deposit, $10 extra charge, with prior approval). **Amenities:** high-speed Internet, irons, hair dryers. *Some:* DVD players (fee). **Pool(s):** heated indoor. **Leisure Activities:** sauna, whirlpool. **Guest Services:** valet and coin laundry. **Business Services:** meeting rooms, PC (fee). **Cards:** AX, DS, MC, VI. *(See color ad p 373)*

SOME UNITS

FEE — FEE

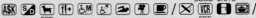

COMFORT INN   *Book great rates at AAA.com*   Phone: 913/367-7666

Property failed to provide current rates

Small-scale Hotel   **Location:** Just s of jct US 59, on US 73. 509 S 9th 66002. Fax: 913/367-7566. **Facility:** 45 one-bedroom standard units. 3 stories (no elevator), interior corridors. **Parking:** on-site. **Amenities:** high-speed Internet, irons, hair dryers. **Leisure Activities:** whirlpool. **Business Services:** meeting rooms.

--------- **WHERE TO DINE** ---------

THE RIVER HOUSE RESTAURANT   **Lunch:** $7-$10   **Dinner:** $11-$20   Phone: 913/367-1010

American   **Location:** Just e of downtown; on Missouri River. 101 Commercial St 66002. **Hours:** 11 am-9 pm. Closed major holidays; also Sun & Mon. **Reservations:** accepted. **Features:** Patrons can appreciate good river views from the renovated, old-style dining room, which has many large windows, and patio. The menu lists traditional and contemporary haute cuisine. This place is popular with the local community. Some favorites include steaks, the veggie sandwich and spinach salad. Casual dress; cocktails. **Parking:** on-site. **Cards:** AX, DS, MC, VI.

BAXTER SPRINGS pop. 4,602

--------- **WHERE TO STAY** ---------

BAXTER INN-4-LESS   Phone: (620)856-2106

All Year   1P: $38-$46   2P: $45-$50   XP: $4   F

Small-scale Hotel   **Location:** On US 69 alternate route, 1 mi s of jct US 166. 2451 Military Ave 66713. Fax: 620/856-2109. **Facility:** 32 one-bedroom standard units. 2 stories (no elevator), interior corridors. **Parking:** on-site. **Terms:** cancellation fee imposed, weekly rates available, package plans. **Cards:** AX, DS, MC, VI.   SOME UNITS

BELLEVILLE pop. 2,239

--------- **WHERE TO STAY** ---------

AMERICAS BEST VALUE INN   *Book at AAA.com*   Phone: (785)527-2231

All Year [CP]   1P: $53-$63   2P: $53-$63

Motel   **Location:** Jct US 81 and 36; northwest corner; just up hill. 215 Hwy 36 66935. Fax: 785/527-2572. **Facility:** 40 units. 38 one-bedroom standard units. 2 one-bedroom suites. 1 story, exterior corridors. **Parking:** on-site. **Terms:** office hours 7 am-10 pm, small pets only (in designated units). **Amenities:** irons, hair dryers. *Some:* high-speed Internet. **Pool(s):** outdoor. **Leisure Activities:** whirlpool. **Guest Services:** coin laundry, wireless Internet. **Cards:** AX, CB, DC, DS, MC, VI.   SOME UNITS

SUPER 8 MOTEL   *Book at AAA.com*   Phone: 785/527-2112

Property failed to provide current rates

Small-scale Hotel   **Location:** On US 36, 0.5 mi e of jct US 81. 1410 28th St 66935. Fax: 785/527-2417. **Facility:** 35 one-bedroom standard units, some with whirlpools. 2 stories (no elevator), interior corridors. **Parking:** on-site, winter plug-ins. **Terms:** office hours 6 am-11 pm, pets (small dogs only, $10 extra charge, in designated units). **Amenities:** hair dryers. **Leisure Activities:** whirlpool. **Guest Services:** coin laundry, wireless Internet.   SOME UNITS   FEE

BELOIT pop. 4,019

--------- **WHERE TO STAY** ---------

SUPER 8 MOTEL-BELOIT   *Book at AAA.com*   Phone: (785)738-4300

All Year   1P: $53-$68   2P: $58-$68   XP: $5   F18

Small-scale Hotel   **Location:** Just e of jct SR 14. 3018 US 24 Hwy 67420. Fax: 785/738-2777. **Facility:** 40 one-bedroom standard units. 2 stories (no elevator), interior/exterior corridors. **Bath:** combo or shower only. **Parking:** on-site, winter plug-ins. **Terms:** [CP] meal plan available, pets (with prior approval). **Amenities:** high-speed Internet, irons, hair dryers. **Guest Services:** coin laundry. **Business Services:** meeting rooms. **Cards:** AX, CB, DC, DS, MC, VI.   SOME UNITS

BONNER SPRINGS —*See Kansas City p. 474.*

BURLINGTON pop. 2,790

--------- **WHERE TO STAY** ---------

COUNTRY HAVEN INN   Phone: (620)364-8260

All Year   1P: $55-$60   2P: $60-$65   XP: $5   F18

Small-scale Hotel   **Location:** Just e of US 75; 1 mi n of center. 207 Cross St 66839. Fax: 620/364-8212. **Facility:** 24 one-bedroom standard units. 2 stories (no elevator), interior corridors. **Parking:** on-site, winter plug-ins. **Terms:** weekly rates available, small pets only ($50 deposit). **Amenities:** voice mail. *Some:* hair dryers. **Guest Services:** wireless Internet. **Business Services:** meeting rooms. **Cards:** AX, CB, DC, DS, MC, VI.   SOME UNITS   FEE

CHANUTE pop. 9,441

─────── **WHERE TO STAY** ───────

CHANUTE SAFARI INN
Phone: 620/431-9460
◈
All Year   1P: $30   2P: $35   XP: $5   F10
Location: US 169, exit 35th St, 1.5 mi e. 3428 S Santa Fe 66720. Fax: 620/431-0923. **Facility:** 41 one-bedroom
Motel   standard units. 1 story, exterior corridors. **Parking:** on-site, winter plug-ins. **Terms:** weekly rates available
              small pets only ($10 extra charge). **Pool(s):** small outdoor. **Guest Services:** coin laundry. **Cards:** AX, DS
MC, VI.
SOME UNITS
(ASK) 🛏 🌊 🛜 📶 🖥 / ⊠ /
FEE

GUEST HOUSE MOTOR INN
Phone: 620/431-0600
◈
All Year   1P: $27   2P: $40   XP: $5   F
Location: US 169, exit 35th St, 2.5 mi ne. 1814 S Santa Fe 66720. Fax: 620/431-2450. **Facility:** 29 one-bedroom
Motel   standard units. 2 stories (no elevator), exterior corridors. **Parking:** on-site. **Terms:** weekly rates available,
              pets ($5 extra charge). **Amenities:** high-speed Internet. **Pool(s):** small outdoor. **Cards:** AX, DS, MC, VI.
SOME UNITS
(ASK) 🛏 🌊 🛜 📶 🖥 / ⊠ /
FEE

CLAY CENTER pop. 4,564

─────── **WHERE TO STAY** ───────

CEDAR COURT MOTEL
Phone: (785)632-2148
◈◈
All Year [CP]   1P: $49-$79   2P: $49-$79   XP: $5
Location: On US 24, just e of jct SR 15. 905 Crawford 67432. Fax: 785/632-5299. **Facility:** 54 one-bedroom
Small-scale Hotel standard units, some with whirlpools. 1-2 stories (no elevator), exterior corridors. *Bath:* combo or shower
              only. **Parking:** on-site. **Terms:** small pets only. **Amenities:** *Some:* dual phone lines, hair dryers. **Pool(s):**
small outdoor. **Business Services:** meeting rooms. **Cards:** AX, DS, MC, VI.
SOME UNITS
(ASK) 🅢 🛏 🍽 👤 🖥 🌊 / ⊠ 🖥 🖳 /

COFFEYVILLE pop. 11,021

─────── **WHERE TO STAY** ───────

APPLETREE INN   *Book great rates at AAA.com*
Phone: (620)251-0002
◇◇◇ (SAVE)
All Year [ECP]   1P: $64-$80   2P: $69-$80   XP: $5   F
◈◈   **Location:** 0.8 mi e of center. 820 E 11th St 67337. Fax: 620/251-1615. **Facility:** 64 units. 63 one-bedroom
Motel   standard units, some with whirlpools. 1 one-bedroom suite ($60-$110). 2 stories (no elevator), interio
              corridors. **Parking:** on-site, winter plug-ins. **Terms:** [CP] meal plan available, pets ($3 extra charge)
              Amenities: high-speed Internet, safes (fee), irons, hair dryers. **Pool(s):** heated indoor. **Leisure**
              Activities: whirlpool, limited exercise equipment. **Guest Services:** valet and coin laundry. **Cards:** AX, DC
DS, MC, VI. **Free Special Amenities:** expanded continental breakfast and high-speed Internet.
SOME UNITS
🅢 🛏 🍽 🌊 📶 🖥 🖳 🖳 / ⊠ (VCR) /
FEE

SUPER 8 MOTEL   *Book great rates at AAA.com*
Phone: (620)251-2250
◇◇◇ (SAVE)
All Year   1P: $51-$58   2P: $57-$64   XP: $6   F18
◈◈   **Location:** On US 169 and 166; center. 104 W 11th St 67337. Fax: 620/251-3846. **Facility:** 91 one-bedroom
Motel   standard units. 2 stories (no elevator), exterior corridors. **Parking:** on-site, winter plug-ins. **Terms:** [CP
              meal plan available, pets (small dogs only, $10 fee). **Amenities:** high-speed Internet, safes (fee). **Pool(s):**
              small outdoor. **Cards:** AX, CB, DC, DS, MC, VI. **Free Special Amenities:** continental breakfast and high-
              speed Internet.
SOME UNITS
🅢 🛏 🍽 🌊 📶 🖥 🖳 / ⊠ /
FEE

─────── **WHERE TO DINE** ───────

SIRLOIN STOCKADE   **Lunch:** $6-$8   **Dinner:** $6-$8   **Phone:** 620/251-8156
◈◈   **Location:** On US 169 and 166; center. 104 W 11th St 67337. **Hours:** 11 am-9 pm. Closed major holidays
              Reservations: not accepted. **Features:** The steakhouse lines up buffet items, including pizza, tacos, soups
Steak House salads and desserts, providing both excellent variety and a good value. Rotating theme nights might allow
              for the sampling of sushi, barbecue and seafood. The buffet also may serve to complement a quality steak
Rolls are baked several times daily. Casual dress. **Parking:** on-site. **Cards:** DS, MC, VI.
⊠

COLBY pop. 5,450

——— WHERE TO STAY ———

COMFORT INN
Book great rates at AAA.com
Phone: (785)462-3833
(AAA) [SAVE]
All Year [BP]   1P: $74-$99   2P: $79-$119   XP: $5   F18
▼▼▼
Location: I-70, exit 53 (SR 25), just s. 2225 S Range 67701 (PO Box 365). **Fax:** 785/462-9704. **Facility:** 77 units.
71 one-bedroom standard units, some with whirlpools. 6 one-bedroom suites ($89-$129). 2 stories (no
elevator), interior corridors. *Bath:* combo or shower only. **Parking:** on-site, winter plug-ins. **Terms:** small
Small-scale Hotel   pets only ($5 extra charge, in designated units). **Amenities:** high-speed Internet, voice mail, safes (fee),
irons, hair dryers. *Some:* dual phone lines. **Dining:** 11 am-2 & 5-10 pm; closed Sun, cocktails. **Pool(s):**
small heated indoor. **Leisure Activities:** whirlpool, exercise room. **Guest Services:** coin laundry, wireless Internet. **Business
Services:** conference facilities. **Cards:** AX, CB, DC, DS, JC, MC, VI. **Free Special Amenities: full breakfast and high-speed
Internet.**

SOME UNITS

DAYS INN
Book great rates at AAA.com
Phone: 785/462-8691
(AAA) [SAVE]
4/2-9/3   1P: $73-$85   2P: $73-$85   XP: $5   F17
▼▼▼ ▼▼
11/3-2/29   1P: $63-$73   2P: $63-$73   XP: $5   F17
9/4-11/2   1P: $59-$68   2P: $59-$68   XP: $5   F17
3/1-4/1   1P: $59-$65   2P: $59-$65   XP: $5   F17
Small-scale Hotel   **Location:** I-70, exit 53 (SR 25), 0.3 mi n. 1925 S Range 67701. **Fax:** 785/462-7732. **Facility:** 45 one-bedroom
standard units. 2 stories (no elevator), interior corridors. **Parking:** on-site. **Terms:** [ECP] meal plan
available, small pets only ($5 extra charge). **Amenities:** irons, hair dryers. **Pool(s):** small heated indoor. **Leisure
Activities:** whirlpool. **Guest Services:** valet laundry, wireless Internet. **Cards:** AX, CB, DC, DS, JC, MC, VI.
Free Special Amenities: expanded continental breakfast and high-speed Internet.

SOME UNITS

HOLIDAY INN EXPRESS HOTEL & SUITES   *Book great rates at AAA.com*
Phone: (785)462-8787
(AAA) [SAVE]
All Year [ECP]   1P: $80-$125   2P: $85-$130   XP: $5   F18
▼▼▼
Location: I-70, exit 53 (SR 25), just ne. 645 W Willow 67701 (PO Box 365). **Fax:** 785/462-2344. **Facility:** 72 units.
69 one-bedroom standard units. 3 one-bedroom suites, some with whirlpools. 3 stories, interior corridors.
Bath: combo or shower only. **Parking:** on-site. **Terms:** small pets only ($10 fee, in designated units).
Small-scale Hotel   **Amenities:** high-speed Internet, dual phone lines, voice mail, irons, hair dryers. **Pool(s):** small heated
indoor. **Leisure Activities:** sauna, exercise room. **Guest Services:** valet and coin laundry. **Business
Services:** meeting rooms. **Cards:** AX, CB, DC, DS, JC, MC, VI. **Free Special Amenities: expanded continental breakfast
and high-speed Internet.**

SOME UNITS

MOTEL 6 #4245   *Book at AAA.com*
Phone: 785/462-8201
▼
Property failed to provide current rates
Location: I-70, exit 53 (SR 25), just n. 1985 S Range 67701. **Fax:** 785/462-9672. **Facility:** 46 one-bedroom
Small-scale Hotel   standard units. 2 stories (no elevator), interior/exterior corridors. **Parking:** on-site, winter plug-ins.
Terms: small pets only. **Guest Services:** coin laundry.

SOME UNITS

QUALITY INN
Book great rates at AAA.com
Phone: (785)462-3933
(AAA) [SAVE]
5/1-8/31   1P: $55-$70   2P: $60-$85   XP: $5   F18
▼▼▼
3/1-4/30   1P: $50-$65   2P: $55-$80   XP: $5   F18
9/1-2/29   1P: $50-$65   2P: $55-$70   XP: $5   F18
Small-scale Hotel   **Location:** I-70, exit 53 (SR 25), just n. 1950 S Range 67701 (PO Box 487). **Fax:** 785/462-7255. **Facility:** 117 one-
bedroom standard units. 2 stories (no elevator), interior/exterior corridors. *Bath:* combo or shower only.
Parking: on-site, winter plug-ins. **Terms:** 7 day cancellation notice, small pets only. **Amenities:** voice mail,
irons, hair dryers. *Some:* high-speed Internet. **Dining:** 11 am-2 & 5-10 pm, Sun-2 pm, cocktails. **Pool(s):** heated indoor, wading.
Guest Services: sundries, valet and coin laundry, wireless Internet. **Business Services:** meeting rooms, PC. **Cards:** AX, CB,
DC, DS, JC, MC, VI. *(See color ad below)*

SOME UNITS

The following lodging was either not evaluated or did not meet AAA rating requirements but is listed for your information only.

SUPER 8 MOTEL
[fyi]
Small-scale Hotel

Phone: 785/462-8248

Did not meet all AAA rating requirements for some property operations at time of last evaluation on 04/22/2005. **Location:** I-70, exit 53 (SR 25), 0.3 mi n, then just w. 1040 Zelfer Ave 67701. Facilities, services, and decor characterize a mid-range property.

—— **WHERE TO DINE** ——

BOURQUIN'S OLD DEPOT RESTAURANT
◆◆
American

Lunch: $6-$8   **Dinner:** $8-$17   **Phone:** 785/462-3300

Location: I-70, exit 54, just n, then 0.5 mi w on I-70 frontage road. 155 E Willow 67701. **Hours:** 11 am-2 & 5-9 pm. Closed: Sun. **Reservations:** accepted. **Features:** Bourquin's features meals "like grandma used to make." Foods and baked items are made from scratch and served in a restored railroad depot, which makes for a unique dining experience. Casual dress; beer & wine only. **Parking:** on-site.

MONTANA MIKE'S STEAKHOUSE
◆◆
Steak House

Lunch: $8-$18   **Dinner:** $8-$18   **Phone:** 785/462-7178

Location: I-70, exit 53 (SR 25), 0.3 mi n, then just e. 1855 S Range 67701. **Hours:** 11 am-9 pm, Fri & Sat-10 pm; seasonal hours vary. Closed: 11/22, 12/25; also Mon. **Features:** This steakhouse offers a dining experience for the whole family. A rustic look with Western appointments characterizes the dining room. Although it's hard to go wrong with a hearty steak of USDA Choice aged beef, guests also can try smoked, fire-grilled chicken breast, chicken-fried steak, baby back ribs and other selections. Casual dress; cocktails. **Parking:** on-site. **Cards:** AX, DS, MC, VI.

[⅏M] [◻]

COLUMBUS pop. 3,396

—— **WHERE TO STAY** ——

MAPLE COMMON   *Book at AAA.com*
◆◆ ◆◆
Small-scale Hotel

Phone: 620/429-3130

All Year   1P: $58-$68   XP: $10   F12
Location: Just e of square; downtown. 120 E Maple 66725. **Fax:** 620/429-3131. **Facility:** 5 one-bedroom standard units. 2 stories (no elevator), interior corridors. **Parking:** street. **Guest Services:** gift shop, valet laundry, area transportation. **Business Services:** meeting rooms. **Cards:** MC, VI.

[✈] [⊓⊢] [✕] [▣]

CONCORDIA pop. 5,714

—— **WHERE TO STAY** ——

HOLIDAY INN EXPRESS HOTEL & SUITES   *Book at AAA.com*
◆◆◆
Small-scale Hotel

Phone: (785)243-2700

All Year   1P: $77
Location: On US 81, 1.5 mi s of center. 2175 Lincoln 66901. **Fax:** 785/243-1255. **Facility:** Smoke free premises. 61 one-bedroom standard units, some with whirlpools. 3 stories, interior corridors. *Bath:* combo or shower only. **Parking:** on-site. **Terms:** [CP] meal plan available. **Amenities:** high-speed Internet, voice mail, irons, hair dryers. **Pool(s):** heated indoor. **Leisure Activities:** whirlpool, exercise room. **Guest Services:** complimentary laundry, wireless Internet. **Business Services:** meeting rooms, business center. **Cards:** AX, DC, DS, MC, VI.

SOME UNITS

[ASK] [S⚡] [⅏M] [⚙] [🖨] [⊳] [✕] [🎥] [▣] / [📞] [🖳] /

SUPER 8 MOTEL-CONCORDIA   *Book great rates at AAA.com*
[AAA] [SAVE]
◆◆ ◆◆
Small-scale Hotel

Phone: (785)243-4200

All Year   1P: $49-$59   2P: $54-$64   XP: $5   F17
Location: On US 81, 1 mi s of center. 1320 Lincoln 66901. **Fax:** 785/243-1246. **Facility:** 44 one-bedroom standard units. 2 stories (no elevator), interior/exterior corridors. **Parking:** on-site, winter plug-ins. **Terms:** [ECP] meal plan available, package plans, pets ($10 fee). **Amenities:** *Some:* irons. **Leisure Activities:** sauna, whirlpool. **Guest Services:** wireless Internet. **Business Services:** PC. **Cards:** AX, DC, DS, MC, VI. **Free Special Amenities:** expanded continental breakfast and high-speed Internet.

SOME UNITS

[S⚡] [🐾] [⊓⊢] [🎥] / [✕] [📞] [🖳] [▣]
FEE

COTTONWOOD FALLS pop. 966

—— **WHERE TO STAY** ——

GRAND CENTRAL HOTEL
[AAA] [SAVE]
◆◆◆ ◆◆◆
Historic
Country Inn

Phone: (620)273-6763

All Year [ECP]   1P: $160-$190   2P: $160-$190   XP: $10   F12
Location: Just w of US 177; center of downtown. 215 Broadway 66845 (PO Box 506). **Fax:** 620/273-8381. **Facility:** The hotel, built in 1884, then renovated in 1995, features rich western flair, oversized guest rooms and large 'spa' style showers. 10 one-bedroom standard units. 2 stories (no elevator), interior corridors. *Bath:* shower only. **Parking:** on-site, winter plug-ins. **Terms:** cancellation fee imposed, pets (with prior approval). **Amenities:** high-speed Internet, hair dryers. **Dining:** Grand Central Grill, see separate listing. **Leisure Activities:** recreation programs. **Guest Services:** valet laundry. **Business Services:** meeting rooms. **Cards:** DS, MC, VI. **Free Special Amenities:** expanded continental breakfast and high-speed Internet.

SOME UNITS

[S⚡] [✈] [🐾] [⊓] [⅏] [VCR] [🖳] / [✕] /

——— WHERE TO DINE ———

GRAND CENTRAL GRILL *Menu on AAA.com*   **Lunch:** $6-$16   **Dinner:** $14-$28   **Phone:** 620/273-6763

American

Location: Just w of US 177; center of downtown; in Grand Central Hotel. 215 Broadway 66845. **Hours:** 11 am-9 pm. Closed: 1/1, 11/22, 12/25; also Sun. **Reservations:** suggested. **Features:** This restaurant features Sterling Silver USDA choice steaks. The menu also offers unique entrees, such as fettuccini portabella, open range kabobs, eggplant parmesan and desserts that are prepared in-house. Save room for the grand creme brulee—you won't be disappointed. Casual dress; cocktails. **Parking:** on-site. **Cards:** AX, DS, MC, VI.

COUNCIL GROVE pop. 2,321

——— WHERE TO STAY ———

THE COTTAGE HOUSE HOTEL & MOTEL   **Phone:** (620)767-6828

Historic
Small-scale Hotel

All Year   1P: $55-$175   2P: $55-$175   XP: $10
Location: Just n of Main St; downtown. 25 N Neosho 66846. Fax: 620/767-6414. **Facility:** Modern comforts in nostalgic surroundings. Some modest motel units. Individually decorated, charming inn rooms. 40 one-bedroom standard units. 1-2 stories (no elevator); interior/exterior corridors. *Bath:* combo or shower only. **Parking:** on-site, winter plug-ins. **Terms:** 7 day cancellation notice, package plans, pets ($10 extra charge). **Amenities:** video library, irons. **Leisure Activities:** sauna, whirlpool. **Guest Services:** gift shop, wireless Internet. **Business Services:** meeting rooms. **Cards:** AX, CB, DC, DS, MC, VI. **Free Special Amenities:** expanded continental breakfast and local telephone calls.

SOME UNITS

——— WHERE TO DINE ———

HAYS HOUSE 1857 RESTAURANT   **Lunch:** $5-$12   **Dinner:** $9-$27   **Phone:** 620/767-5911

American

Location: On US 56; downtown. 112 W Main St 66846. **Hours:** 6:30 am-8 pm, Fri & Sat-9 pm, Sun 6 am-8 pm, Mon 6:30 am-2 pm; hours vary in winter. Closed: 12/25. **Reservations:** suggested, for dinner Sat. **Features:** Listed on the National Register of Historic Places, the restaurant offers a wide variety of home-style cooked foods and beef that is aged on the premises. Aromatic breads and desserts are prepared in house. Casual dress; cocktails. **Parking:** on-site. **Cards:** AX, DS, MC, VI. **Historic**

DERBY pop. 17,807

——— WHERE TO DINE ———

RIB CRIB   **Lunch:** $6-$13   **Dinner:** $6-$13   **Phone:** 316/788-9902

American

Location: SR 15, north side of town. 1440 N Rock Rd 67037. **Hours:** 11 am-10 pm, Fri & Sat-11 pm. Closed major holidays. **Features:** Most guests need extra napkins to tackle the ribs, brisket, ham, pork and chicken selections. The menu also lists sandwiches and wraps, along with tempting sides and large desserts. The decor is decidedly Western. Casual dress; beer only. **Parking:** on-site. **Cards:** AX, DS, MC, VI.

DODGE CITY pop. 26,176

——— WHERE TO STAY ———

COMFORT INN *Book great rates at AAA.com*   **Phone:** (620)338-8700

Small-scale Hotel

All Year [BP]   1P: $85-$95   2P: $105-$125   XP: $5   F17
Location: 1.3 mi w on US 50 business route. 2000 W Wyatt Earp Blvd 67801. Fax: 620/338-8412. **Facility:** 54 one-bedroom standard units. 2 stories (no elevator); interior corridors. **Parking:** on-site. **Terms:** pets ($10 extra charge). **Amenities:** high-speed Internet, voice mail, irons, hair dryers. **Pool(s):** small heated indoor. **Leisure Activities:** whirlpool, exercise room. **Guest Services:** valet laundry, wireless Internet. **Cards:** AX, CB, DC, DS, JC, MC, VI.

SOME UNITS

HOLIDAY INN EXPRESS *Book at AAA.com*   **Phone:** (620)227-5000

Small-scale Hotel

All Year [ECP]   1P: $93-$103   2P: $93-$103   XP: $6   F18
Location: 1.4 mi w on US 50 business route. 2320 W Wyatt Earp Blvd 67801. Fax: 620/225-0499. **Facility:** 63 units. 60 one-bedroom standard units, some with whirlpools. 3 one-bedroom suites ($101-$143) with whirlpools. 2 stories, interior corridors. *Bath:* combo or shower only. **Parking:** on-site. **Terms:** small pets only. **Amenities:** high-speed Internet, voice mail, irons, hair dryers. **Pool(s):** heated indoor. **Leisure Activities:** whirlpool, exercise room. **Guest Services:** valet and coin laundry, wireless Internet. **Business Services:** meeting rooms, business center. **Cards:** AX, CB, DC, DS, MC, VI.

SOME UNITS

SUPER 8 MOTEL *Book at AAA.com*   **Phone:** (620)225-3924

Small-scale Hotel

All Year [CP]   1P: $93-$103   XP: $6   F18
Location: 1.2 mi w on US 50 business route. 1708 W Wyatt Earp Blvd 67801. Fax: 620/225-5793. **Facility:** 64 one-bedroom standard units. 3 stories (no elevator); interior corridors. **Parking:** on-site, winter plug-ins. **Pool(s):** small outdoor. **Guest Services:** valet laundry, wireless Internet. **Cards:** AX, CB, DC, DS, MC, VI.

SOME UNITS

--- **WHERE TO DINE** ---

EL CHARRO RESTAURANT　　Lunch: $5-$15　　Dinner: $5-$15　　Phone: 620/225-0371

Traditional
Mexican

Location: 0.7 mi w on US 50 business route. 1209 W Wyatt Earp Blvd 67801. **Hours:** 11 am-9 pm, Fri & Sat-10 pm. Closed major holidays; also Sun. **Reservations:** accepted. **Features:** This restaurant features large portions of traditional and Tex-Mex offerings, with even a few 'north of the border selections' available. The staff is helpful and the Southwestern style decor is fun. Casual dress; beer only. **Parking:** on-site. **Cards:** AX, DS, MC, VI.

KING'S BUFFET　　Lunch: $5-$9　　Dinner: $6-$9　　Phone: 620/338-8618

Chinese

Location: Center. 1005 W Wyatt Earp Blvd 67801. **Hours:** 11 am-10 pm, Fri & Sat-10:30 pm, Sun 11:30 am-10 pm. **Features:** Although the selections on the lunch and dinner buffets are ample, guests have the option of ordering from a large selection of menu entrees. Casual dress. **Parking:** on-site. **Cards:** MC, VI.

MONTANA MIKE'S STEAKHOUSE　　Lunch: $6-$16　　Dinner: $8-$16　　Phone: 620/408-9551

Steak House

Location: Center. 700 W Wyatt Earp Blvd 67801. **Hours:** 11 am-9 pm, Fri & Sat-10 pm. Closed: 11/22, 12/25. **Features:** This steakhouse offers a dining experience for the whole family. A rustic look with Western appointments characterizes the dining room. Although it's hard to go wrong with a hearty steak of USDA Choice aged beef, guests also can try smoked, fire-grilled chicken breast, chicken-fried steak, baby back ribs and other selections. Casual dress; cocktails. **Parking:** on-site. **Cards:** AX, DS, MC, VI.

EL DORADO pop. 12,057

--- **WHERE TO STAY** ---

BEST WESTERN RED COACH INN　　*Book great rates at AAA.com*　　Phone: (316)321-6900

(AAA) (SAVE)

Small-scale Hotel

| All Year | 1P: $50 | 2P: $55 | XP: $5 | F12 |

Location: I-35, exit 71, 0.5 mi e. 2525 W Central Ave 67042 (PO Box 526, 67042-0526). **Fax:** 316/322-1157. **Facility:** 73 one-bedroom standard units, some with whirlpools. 2 stories (no elevator), exterior corridors. **Parking:** on-site. **Terms:** pets ($15 fee). **Amenities:** irons, hair dryers. **Dining:** 6 am-9 pm, Fri & Sat-10 pm. **Pool(s):** small heated indoor. **Leisure Activities:** sauna, whirlpool. **Guest Services:** wireless Internet. **Business Services:** meeting rooms, PC. **Cards:** AX, DS, MC, VI. **Free Special Amenities:** local telephone calls and high-speed Internet.

SOME UNITS

FEE

SUPER 8 MOTEL-EL DORADO　　*Book at AAA.com*　　Phone: (316)321-4888

Motel

JC, MC, VI.

| All Year [CP] | 1P: $45-$95 | 2P: $45-$95 | XP: $5 | F17 |

Location: I-35, exit 71, 0.5 mi e. 2530 W Central Ave 67042. **Fax:** 316/321-5469. **Facility:** 49 one-bedroom standard units. 2 stories (no elevator), interior corridors. **Parking:** on-site, winter plug-ins. **Amenities:** high-speed Internet, safes (fee). *Some:* hair dryers. **Guest Services:** wireless Internet. **Cards:** AX, CB, DC, DS,

SOME UNITS

ELLIS pop. 1,873

--- **WHERE TO DINE** ---

ARTHUR'S PIZZA & MEXICAN FOODS　　Lunch: $5-$15　　Dinner: $5-$15　　Phone: 785/726-4683

Pizza

Location: I-70, exit 145, 0.6 mi s; corner of Washington and W 9th sts; downtown. 103 W 9th St 67637. **Hours:** 11 am-9 pm, Fri & Sat-10 pm, Sun-8:30 pm; hours may vary in winter. Closed major holidays; also Wed. **Features:** The downtown eatery prepares a combination of Mexican food and pizza in a contemporary setting. Dine-in, take-out and delivery service are available. The food is tasty and well-prepared. Casual dress; beer only. **Parking:** street. **Cards:** DS, MC, VI.

ELLSWORTH pop. 2,965

--- **WHERE TO STAY** ---

BEST WESTERN GARDEN PRAIRIE INN　　*Book great rates at AAA.com*　　Phone: (785)472-3116

(AAA) (SAVE)

Small-scale Hotel

| All Year | 1P: $69-$89 | 2P: $79-$89 | | |

Location: Jct SR 140 and 156. Jct SR 140 & 156 67439 (PO Box 44). **Fax:** 785/472-5703. **Facility:** 36 units. 35 one-bedroom standard units. 1 one-bedroom suite with whirlpool. 1 story, interior/exterior corridors. *Bath:* combo or shower only. **Parking:** on-site, winter plug-ins. **Terms:** [CP] meal plan available. **Amenities:** irons, hair dryers. *Some:* high-speed Internet, dual phone lines. **Pool(s):** small heated indoor. **Leisure Activities:** whirlpool. **Guest Services:** coin laundry. **Business Services:** meeting rooms. **Cards:** AX, DC, DS, MC, VI. **Free Special Amenities:** continental breakfast and local telephone calls.

SOME UNITS

EMPORIA pop. 26,760

--- **WHERE TO STAY** ---

AMERICAS BEST VALUE INN　　*Book great rates at AAA.com*　　Phone: (620)342-7567

(AAA) (SAVE)

Motel

| 3/1-9/30 [CP] | 1P: $47-$57 | 2P: $57-$67 | XP: $5 | F12 |
| 10/1-2/29 [CP] | 1P: $46-$56 | 2P: $56-$66 | XP: $5 | F12 |

Location: I-35, exit 127, 0.8 mi e. 2913 W Hwy 50 66801. **Fax:** 620/343-7374. **Facility:** 46 one-bedroom standard units. 2 stories (no elevator), interior corridors. *Bath:* combo or shower only. **Parking:** on-site, winter plug-ins. **Terms:** package plans, pets (dogs only, $11 fee). **Amenities:** safes (fee). **Guest Services:** coin laundry, wireless Internet. **Cards:** AX, DC, DS, MC, VI. **Free Special Amenities:** continental breakfast and local telephone calls.

SOME UNITS

FEE

BEST WESTERN HOSPITALITY HOUSE   *Book great rates at AAA.com*   **Phone:** (620)342-7587

▼▼ ▼▼
Small-scale Hotel

All Year   1P: $58-$99   2P: $58-$99

Location: I-35, exit 127, just e. 3021 W Hwy 50 66801. Fax: 620/342-9271. **Facility:** 56 units. 53 one-bedroom standard units. 3 one-bedroom suites ($90-$135), some with whirlpools. 1 story, interior/exterior corridors. **Parking:** on-site. **Terms:** [AP] & [BP] meal plans available. **Amenities:** high-speed Internet, irons, hair dryers. **Pool(s):** heated indoor. **Leisure Activities:** whirlpool. **Guest Services:** valet laundry, wireless Internet. **Business Services:** meeting rooms. **Cards:** AX, CB, DC, DS, MC, VI.

SOME UNITS

ASK SD 🛏 ▥ 🍴 ⇔ 🐾 🖨 🖵 / ✕ 🎧 🖼 /

CANDLEWOOD SUITES   *Book at AAA.com*   **Phone:** 620/343-7756

▼▼ ▼▼
Small-scale Hotel

Property failed to provide current rates

Location: I-35, exit 128 (Industrial St), just n, then e. 2602 Candlewood Dr 66801. Fax: 620/343-7762. **Facility:** 60 units. 56 one-bedroom standard units with efficiencies. 4 one-bedroom suites with efficiencies. 3 stories, interior corridors. *Bath:* combo or shower only. **Parking:** on-site, winter plug-ins. **Terms:** pets ($75 extra charge). **Amenities:** video library, CD players, high-speed Internet, dual phone lines, voice mail, irons, hair dryers. **Leisure Activities:** exercise room. **Guest Services:** complimentary and valet laundry. **Business Services:** meeting rooms, business center.

SOME UNITS

🛏 🍴 🖨 🎧 VCR 🖨 🖵 🖼 / ✕ /
FEE

COMFORT INN   *Book great rates at AAA.com*   **Phone:** 620/342-9700

▼▼ ▼▼
Small-scale Hotel

Property failed to provide current rates

Location: I-35, exit 128, just nw. 2836 W 18th Ave 66801. Fax: 620/342-7841. **Facility:** 44 one-bedroom standard units, some with whirlpools. 2 stories (no elevator), interior corridors. *Bath:* combo or shower only. **Parking:** on-site. **Terms:** pets ($10 extra charge). **Amenities:** high-speed Internet, irons, hair dryers. **Pool(s):** heated indoor. **Leisure Activities:** exercise room. **Guest Services:** valet and coin laundry, wireless Internet.

SOME UNITS

🐾 🍴 ⇔ 🎧 🖵 / ✕ 🎧 🖼 /
FEE

FAIRFIELD INN BY MARRIOTT   *Book great rates at AAA.com*   **Phone:** (620)342-4445

▼▼ ▼▼
Small-scale Hotel

All Year [CP]   1P: $89-$99   2P: $99-$109

Location: I-35, exit 128 (Industrial St), just nw. 2930 Eaglecrest Dr 66801. Fax: 620/342-0676. **Facility:** Smoke free premises. 57 one-bedroom standard units. 3 stories, interior corridors. *Bath:* combo or shower only. **Parking:** on-site, winter plug-ins. **Amenities:** irons, hair dryers. **Pool(s):** heated indoor. **Leisure Activities:** whirlpool. **Guest Services:** wireless Internet. **Cards:** AX, DC, DS, MC, VI.

SOME UNITS

ASK SD 🍴 🖨 🎧 ⇔ ✕ 🖨 🖵 / 🎧 🖼 /

─────── *The following lodging was either not evaluated or did not* ───────
meet AAA rating requirements but is listed for your information only.

HOLIDAY INN EXPRESS HOTEL & SUITES   **Phone:** 620/341-9393

[fyi]
Small-scale Hotel

Did not meet all AAA rating requirements for some property operations at time of last evaluation on 04/19/2006. **Location:** I-35, exit 128 (Industrial St), just nw. 2921 W 18th Ave 66801. Facilities, services, and decor characterize a mid-range property.

─────── **WHERE TO DINE** ───────

FOURTH AVENUE DINING COMPANY   **Lunch:** $5-$10   **Dinner:** $6-$15   **Phone:** 620/343-3300

▼▼ ▼▼
American

Location: I-35, exit 130 (Merchant St), 1.2 mi s. 402 Merchant St 66801. **Hours:** 11 am-10 pm. Closed: Sun. **Features:** Quality meals are served in good portion sizes. The dining room is split into several rooms that have an Old Western store appearance. Casual dress; cocktails. **Parking:** on-site. **Cards:** AX, DC, DS, MC, VI.

🍽 🚭

MONTANA MIKE'S STEAKHOUSE   **Lunch:** $6-$16   **Dinner:** $8-$16   **Phone:** 620/343-7481

▼▼ ▼▼
Steak House

Location: I-35, exit 128 (Industrial St), just nw. 3010 Eagle Crest Dr 66801. **Hours:** 11 am-9 pm, Fri & Sat-10 pm. Closed: 11/22, 12/25; also Mon. **Features:** This steakhouse offers a dining experience for the whole family. A rustic look with Western appointments characterizes the dining room. Although it's hard to go wrong with a hearty steak of USDA Choice aged beef, guests also can try smoked, fire-grilled chicken breast, chicken-fried steak, baby back ribs and other selections. Casual dress; cocktails. **Parking:** on-site. **Cards:** AX, DS, MC, VI.

🍽 🚭

FORT SCOTT pop. 8,297

─────── **WHERE TO STAY** ───────

THE COURTLAND HOTEL & DAY SPA   *Book at AAA.com*   **Phone:** 620/223-0098

▼▼ ▼▼
Historic Bed
& Breakfast

All Year   1P: $55-$90   2P: $55-$90   XP: $10   F10

Location: Just w of US 69; downtown. 121 E 1st St 66701. Fax: 620/223-2249. **Facility:** Smaller guest rooms in restored 1906 hotel. Smoke free premises. 16 one-bedroom standard units. 2 stories (no elevator), interior corridors. *Bath:* combo or shower only. **Parking:** on-site. **Terms:** 14 day cancellation notice-fee imposed, [CP] meal plan available, package plans. **Guest Services:** gift shop. **Business Services:** meeting rooms. **Cards:** AX, MC, VI.

SOME UNITS

🍴 ✕ / VCR 🖨 /

FORT SCOTT INN

Phone: (620)223-0100

[AAA] [SAVE]

All Year   1P: $52-$61   2P: $56-$65   XP: $4   F17

Location: On US 69 Bypass, exit US 54 southbound; exit 3rd St northbound. 101 State St 66701. Fax: 620/223-1746. **Facility:** 76 one-bedroom standard units. 2 stories (no elevator), interior/exterior corridors. **Parking:** on-site. **Terms:** small pets only ($10 fee, $1 extra charge). **Amenities:** dual phone lines, voice mail, irons, hair dryers. *Some:* high-speed Internet. **Dining:** 6 am-9 pm, Fri & Sat-10 pm, cocktails. **Pool(s):** small outdoor. **Leisure Activities:** sauna, whirlpool, exercise room. **Guest Services:** coin laundry. **Business Services:** meeting rooms, PC. **Cards:** AX, DC, DS, MC, VI. **Free Special Amenities:** local telephone calls and high-speed Internet.

Small-scale Hotel

SOME UNITS

[icons] FEE

LYONS' VICTORIAN MANSION BED & BREAKFAST AND SPA

Phone: 620/223-3644

Property failed to provide current rates

Location: Jct US 69 and 54 E, 0.3 mi w on Wall St, then 0.6 mi s. 742 S National 66701. Fax: 620/223-0062. **Facility:** The residence is a well-appointed 1876 mansion. Three guest units are located in the guest house in the rear. Smoke free premises. 7 units. 6 one-bedroom standard units, some with whirlpools. 1 two-bedroom suite with whirlpool. 3 stories (no elevator), interior corridors. **Bath:** combo or shower only. **Parking:** on-site. **Amenities:** DVD players, CD players, high-speed Internet, irons, hair dryers. **Leisure Activities:** whirlpool. *Fee:* massage. **Guest Services:** valet laundry. **Business Services:** meeting rooms.

Bed & Breakfast

[icons] FEE

WHERE TO DINE

EL CHARRO

Lunch: $4-$6   **Dinner:** $6-$16   **Phone: 620/223-9944**

Mexican

Location: Downtown. 22 S Main St 66701. **Hours:** 11 am-9 pm, Fri & Sat-10:30 pm, Sun-8 pm. Closed major holidays. **Features:** The restaurant's decor says "Mexico," while its extensive menu centers on traditional favorites, such as chimichangas, fajitas, vegetarian dishes and combination plates. Service is fast and efficient. Casual dress; cocktails. **Parking:** street. **Cards:** AX, DS, MC, VI.

[icon]

GARDEN CITY pop. 28,451

WHERE TO STAY

AMERICINN LODGE & SUITES

Book at AAA.com   **Phone: 620/272-9860**

All Year   1P: $85   2P: $160   XP: $5   F12

Small-scale Hotel

Location: Jct US 50, 83 and SR 156. 3020 E Kansas Ave 67846. Fax: 620/272-0909. **Facility:** 72 units. 71 one-bedroom standard units, some with whirlpools. 1 one-bedroom suite ($140-$160) with whirlpool. 3 stories, interior corridors. *Bath:* combo or shower only. **Parking:** on-site. **Terms:** [ECP] meal plan available, pets ($50 deposit). **Amenities:** high-speed Internet, voice mail, irons, hair dryers. **Pool(s):** small heated indoor. **Leisure Activities:** whirlpool, exercise room. **Guest Services:** valet and coin laundry. **Business Services:** meeting rooms. **Cards:** AX, DC, DS, MC, VI. *(See color ad p 373)*

SOME UNITS

[icons ASK] [icons] FEE [icons]

BEST WESTERN RED BARON HOTEL

Book great rates at AAA.com   **Phone: (620)275-4164**

[AAA] [SAVE]

All Year   1P: $59-$65   2P: $69-$75   XP: $8   F17

Small-scale Hotel

Location: 2.3 mi e on US 50 business route, at US 83 Bypass. 2205 E Hwy 50 67846. Fax: 620/275-6667. **Facility:** 68 one-bedroom standard units. 2 stories (no elevator), exterior corridors. *Bath:* combo or shower only. **Parking:** on-site, winter plug-ins. **Terms:** weekly rates available, [BP] meal plan available. **Amenities:** irons, hair dryers. *Some:* high-speed Internet. **Dining:** Red Baron Restaurant & Lounge, see separate listing. **Pool(s):** heated outdoor. **Leisure Activities:** playground. **Guest Services:** valet and coin laundry. **Cards:** AX, CB, DC, DS, MC, VI. **Free Special Amenities:** full breakfast and high-speed Internet.

SOME UNITS

[icons] [icons] /

BEST WESTERN WHEAT LANDS HOTEL & CONFERENCE CENTER

Book great rates at AAA.com   **Phone: (620)276-2387**

[AAA] [SAVE]

All Year [BP]   1P: $57-$82   2P: $67-$92   XP: $10   F17

Small-scale Hotel

Location: 1 mi e on US 50 business route. 1311 E Fulton 67846. Fax: 620/276-4252. **Facility:** 107 one-bedroom standard units, some with whirlpools. 2 stories (no elevator), exterior corridors. **Parking:** on-site, winter plug-ins. **Amenities:** irons, hair dryers. *Some:* high-speed Internet. **Dining:** The Grain Bin, Wheat Lands Restaurant & Lounge, see separate listings, nightclub. **Pool(s):** heated outdoor. **Leisure Activities:** exercise room. **Guest Services:** valet and coin laundry. **Business Services:** meeting rooms. **Cards:** AX, CB, DC, DS, MC, VI. **Free Special Amenities:** local telephone calls and early check-in/late check-out.

SOME UNITS

[icons] / [icons VCR] [icons] /

COMFORT INN

Book great rates at AAA.com   **Phone: (620)275-5800**

[AAA] [SAVE]

All Year   1P: $60-$149   2P: $60-$149   XP: $10   F17

Small-scale Hotel

Location: Jct US 50, 83 and SR 156. 2608 E Kansas Ave 67846. Fax: 620/276-2204. **Facility:** 62 one-bedroom standard units, some with whirlpools. 3 stories, interior corridors. *Bath:* combo or shower only. **Parking:** on-site. **Terms:** 14 day cancellation notice, [BP] meal plan available, pets ($10 fee). **Amenities:** high-speed Internet, voice mail, irons, hair dryers. **Pool(s):** heated indoor. **Leisure Activities:** whirlpool, steamroom, limited exercise equipment. **Guest Services:** complimentary evening beverages: Mon-Thurs, valet and coin laundry, wireless Internet. **Business Services:** meeting rooms. **Cards:** AX, CB, DC, DS, JC, MC, VI. **Free Special Amenities:** full breakfast and high-speed Internet.

SOME UNITS

[icons] FEE [icons] / [icons]

GARDEN CITY INN *Book at AAA.com* **Phone:** 620/276-7608

Property failed to provide current rates

Small-scale Hotel

Location: Jct Business Rt US 50 W and 83 N. 1202 W Kansas Ave 67846. **Fax:** 620/276-7609. **Facility:** 43 one-bedroom standard units. 2 stories (no elevator), interior corridors. *Bath:* combo or shower only. **Parking:** on-site, winter plug-ins. **Amenities:** irons, hair dryers. *Some:* dual phone lines. **Pool(s):** small heated indoor. **Leisure Activities:** whirlpool. **Guest Services:** valet laundry, area transportation, wireless Internet.

HOLIDAY INN EXPRESS HOTEL & SUITES *Book at AAA.com* **Phone:** (620)275-5900

All Year [ECP]	1P: $95-$105	2P: $95-$105	XP: $6 F18

Small-scale Hotel

Location: Jct US 50, 83 and SR 156. 2502 E Kansas Ave 67846. **Fax:** 620/275-7817. **Facility:** 69 units. 68 one-bedroom standard units. 1 one-bedroom suite ($99-$109) with whirlpool. 3 stories, interior corridors. *Bath:* combo or shower only. **Parking:** on-site, winter plug-ins. **Terms:** check-in 4 pm. **Amenities:** dual phone lines, voice mail, irons, hair dryers. **Pool(s):** small heated indoor. **Leisure Activities:** whirlpool, exercise room. **Guest Services:** valet and coin laundry, wireless Internet. **Business Services:** meeting rooms. **Cards:** AX, CB, DC, DS, MC, VI.

SOME UNITS

——— WHERE TO DINE ———

EL CHARRO RESTAURANT **Lunch:** $5-$15 **Dinner:** $5-$15 **Phone:** 620/275-8399

Traditional
Mexican

Location: 0.5 mi n of US 50 business route. 802 Campus Dr 67846. **Hours:** 11 am-2 & 4:30-9 pm, Fri & Sat-10 pm. Closed: 11/22, 12/25; also Sun. **Reservations:** accepted. **Features:** This restaurant features large portions of traditional and Tex-Mex offerings, with even a few 'north of the border selections' available. The staff is helpful and the Southwestern style decor is fun. Casual dress; beer only. **Parking:** on-site. **Cards:** AX, DS, MC, VI.

THE GRAIN BIN **Dinner:** $11-$20 **Phone:** 620/275-5954

Steak House

Location: 1 mi e on US 50 business route; in Best Western Wheat Lands Hotel & Conference Center. 1301 E Fulton 67846. **Hours:** 6 pm-9 pm, Fri & Sat-10 pm. Closed major holidays; also Sun. **Reservations:** suggested, weekends. **Features:** The Grain Bin's slogan, "Fine foods, fun times," sets the tone for elegant, yet relaxed dining in a fun atmosphere that has a "Clue" game theme. Excellent steaks and prime rib are the specialties here. Young business people like this restaurant. Casual dress; cocktails; entertainment. **Parking:** on-site. **Cards:** AX, CB, DC, DS, MC, VI.

RED BARON RESTAURANT & LOUNGE **Lunch:** $4-$6 **Dinner:** $6-$12 **Phone:** 620/275-1797

American

Location: 2.3 mi e on US 50 business route, at US 83 Bypass; in Best Western Red Baron Hotel. 2205 E Hwy 50 67846. **Hours:** 24 hours. Closed: 12/25. **Reservations:** accepted. **Features:** You'll enjoy visiting with the "Red Baron" in his World War I atmosphere at this restaurant. The menu features flavorful fried chicken, a varied salad bar, and grain-fed beef and T-bone steaks. Families and travelers like the casual, comfortable setting. Casual dress; cocktails. **Parking:** on-site. **Cards:** AX, CB, DC, DS, MC, VI.

WHEAT LANDS RESTAURANT & LOUNGE **Lunch:** $5-$6 **Dinner:** $5-$13 **Phone:** 620/276-2768

American

Location: 1 mi e on US 50 business route; in Best Western Wheat Lands Hotel & Conference Center. 1408 E Fulton 67846. **Hours:** 6 am-9 pm, Sun from 7 am. Closed: 12/25. **Reservations:** accepted. **Features:** The Wheat Lands Restaurant offers nicely prepared steaks, a well-stocked fresh salad bar and blueberry pie made in-house. They also serve a lunch buffet every day except Saturday. The atmosphere is casual, and service is prompt and attentive. Casual dress; cocktails. **Parking:** on-site. **Cards:** AX, CB, DC, DS, MC, VI.

GARDNER —*See Kansas City p. 474.*

GODDARD pop. 2,037

——— WHERE TO STAY ———

EXPRESS INN **Phone:** (316)794-3366

All Year [CP]	1P: $46-$48	2P: $46-$52	XP: $2 F3

Motel

Location: Just se of jct US 54/400 and 199th St. 19941 W Kellogg Dr 67052. **Fax:** 316/794-7692. **Facility:** 35 one-bedroom standard units. 2 stories (no elevator), exterior corridors. **Parking:** on-site, winter plug-ins. **Terms:** cancellation fee imposed, package plans. **Amenities:** high-speed Internet, voice mail. **Guest Services:** valet and coin laundry. **Business Services:** PC. **Cards:** AX, DC, DS, MC, VI. **Free Special Amenities:** continental breakfast and high-speed Internet.

SOME UNITS

GOODLAND pop. 4,948

——— WHERE TO STAY ———

BEST WESTERN BUFFALO INN *Book great rates at AAA.com* **Phone:** (785)899-3621

5/15-9/14	1P: $67	2P: $74	XP: $5 F12
3/1-5/14 & 9/15-2/29	1P: $62	2P: $72	XP: $5 F12

Small-scale Hotel

Location: I-70, exit 17 or 19, n to jct US 24 and SR 27. 830 W Hwy 24 67735. **Fax:** 785/899-5072. **Facility:** 93 units. 90 one- and 2 two-bedroom standard units. 2 stories (no elevator), exterior corridors. **Parking:** on-site, winter plug-ins. **Terms:** 1-5 night minimum stay - seasonal, 5 day cancellation notice, package plans, pets ($25 deposit, in designated units). **Amenities:** irons, hair dryers. *Some:* high-speed Internet. **Dining:** restaurant, see separate listing. **Pool(s):** heated indoor, wading. **Leisure Activities:** whirlpool, playground. **Guest Services:** coin laundry, wireless Internet. **Business Services:** meeting rooms. **Cards:** AX, DC, DS, MC, VI. **Free Special Amenities:** full breakfast and early check-in/late check-out.

SOME UNITS

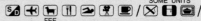
FEE

COMFORT INN · *Book great rates at AAA.com*
Phone: (785)899-7181
AAA SAVE · All Year · 1P: $79-$85 · 2P: $85-$105 · XP: $5 · F
Location: I-70, exit 17, just n. 2519 Enterprise Rd 67735. Fax: 785/899-7183. **Facility:** 49 one-bedroom standard units, some with whirlpools. 2 stories (no elevator), interior corridors. **Bath:** combo or shower only. **Parking:** on-site, winter plug-ins. **Terms:** cancellation fee imposed, pets (small dogs only, $15 fee). **Amenities:** high-speed Internet, voice mail, irons, hair dryers. **Pool(s):** small heated indoor. **Leisure Activities:** whirlpool, exercise room. **Guest Services:** coin laundry, wireless Internet. **Business Services:** PC. **Cards:** AX, CB, DC, DS, JC, MC, VI. **Free Special Amenities:** expanded continental breakfast and high-speed Internet.
Small-scale Hotel

SOME UNITS

SUPER 8 MOTEL-GOODLAND · *Book at AAA.com*
Phone: (785)890-7566
All Year · 1P: $50-$90 · 2P: $56-$100 · XP: $6 · F12
Location: I-70, exit 17 (SR 27), just n. 2520 Commerce Rd 67735. Fax: 785/890-7566. **Facility:** 47 one-bedroom standard units. 2 stories (no elevator), exterior corridors. **Parking:** on-site, winter plug-ins. **Terms:** 14 day cancellation notice, pets ($25 deposit, $5 extra charge). **Amenities:** hair dryers. *Some:* high-speed Internet. **Guest Services:** wireless Internet. **Business Services:** meeting rooms. **Cards:** AX, DC, DS, MC, VI.
Small-scale Hotel

SOME UNITS

——— **WHERE TO DINE** ———

BUFFALO INN RESTAURANT · Lunch: $8-$11 · Dinner: $7-$18 · Phone: 785/890-5057
Location: I-70, exit 17 or 19, n to jct US 24 and SR 27; in Best Western Buffalo Inn. 830 W Hwy 24 67735. **Hours:** 6 am-10 pm; seasonal hours vary. Closed: 12/25. **Features:** Yes, the Buffalo Inn serves genuine buffalo burgers. It also serves very good grain-fed Kansas beef, chicken-fried steak with gravy and other home-cooked meals. The varied menu is complemented by the country-style decor and family atmosphere. Casual dress; beer only. **Parking:** on-site. **Cards:** AX, CB, DC, DS, MC, VI.
American

GREAT BEND pop. 15,345

——— **WHERE TO STAY** ———

BEST WESTERN ANGUS INN · *Book great rates at AAA.com*
Phone: (620)792-3541
AAA SAVE · All Year · 1P: $65 · 2P: $75 · XP: $10 · F18
Location: 0.8 mi w on US 56 and SR 96/156. 2920 10th St 67530. Fax: 620/792-8621. **Facility:** 90 one-bedroom standard units, some with whirlpools. 2 stories (no elevator), interior/exterior corridors. **Parking:** on-site, winter plug-ins. **Terms:** small pets only (with prior approval). **Amenities:** video library, DVD players, dual phone lines, voice mail, irons, hair dryers. **Dining:** 6 am-11 pm, cocktails. **Pool(s):** heated indoor. **Leisure Activities:** sauna, whirlpool, exercise room. *Fee:* game room. **Guest Services:** valet and coin laundry, wireless Internet. **Business Services:** meeting rooms. **Cards:** AX, CB, DC, DS, MC, VI. **Free Special Amenities:** local telephone calls and high-speed Internet.
Small-scale Hotel

SOME UNITS

HIGHLAND HOTEL & CONVENTION CENTER · *Book great rates at AAA.com*
Phone: (620)792-2431
AAA SAVE · All Year · 1P: $71-$85 · 2P: $71-$85 · XP: $10 · F17
Location: 1 mi w on US 56 and SR 96/156. 3017 10th St 67530. Fax: 620/792-5561. **Facility:** 172 one-bedroom standard units. 2 stories (no elevator), interior/exterior corridors. **Bath:** combo or shower only. **Parking:** on-site. **Terms:** cancellation fee imposed, [BP] meal plan available, pets ($10 fee). **Amenities:** *Some:* high-speed Internet. **Dining:** 6 am-1:30 & 5:30-9 pm, cocktails. **Pool(s):** heated indoor. **Leisure Activities:** sauna, whirlpool, steamroom, miniature golf, exercise room. *Fee:* game room. **Guest Services:** valet and coin laundry, wireless Internet. **Business Services:** meeting rooms, PC. **Cards:** AX, DS, MC, VI. **Free Special Amenities:** local telephone calls and high-speed Internet.
Small-scale Hotel

SOME UNITS

——— **WHERE TO DINE** ———

KIOWA KITCHEN · Lunch: $3-$8 · Dinner: $3-$8 · Phone: 620/793-9855
Location: 2 mi e on US 56. 214 E Martin County Rd A 67530. **Hours:** 11 am-9 pm, Sun-3 pm. Closed major holidays; also Mon-Wed. **Features:** The restaurant is a favorite among locals in the mood for Mexican food. The menu incorporates a good variety. Casual dress. **Parking:** on-site. **Cards:** AX, DS, MC, VI.
Mexican

MONTANA MIKE'S STEAKHOUSE · Dinner: $6-$16 · Phone: 620/792-5930
Location: Just s of jct US 56. 906 McKinley 67530. **Hours:** 5 pm-9 pm, Fri & Sat-10 pm. Closed: 11/22, 12/25. **Features:** This steakhouse offers a dining experience for the whole family. A rustic look with Western appointments characterizes the dining room. Although it's hard to go wrong with a hearty steak of USDA Choice aged beef, guests also can try smoked, fire-grilled chicken breast, chicken-fried steak, baby back ribs and other selections. Casual dress; cocktails. **Parking:** on-site. **Cards:** AX, DS, MC, VI.
Steak House

GREENSBURG pop. 1,574

——— **WHERE TO STAY** ———

BEST WESTERN J-HAWK MOTEL · *Book great rates at AAA.com*
Phone: 620/723-2121
All Year · 1P: $69-$72 · 2P: $72-$75 · XP: $3 · F12
Location: Just w on US 54. 515 W Kansas Ave 67054. Fax: 620/723-2650. **Facility:** 30 one-bedroom standard units. 1 story, exterior corridors. **Parking:** on-site, winter plug-ins. **Terms:** small pets only. **Amenities:** high-speed Internet, irons, hair dryers. **Pool(s):** small heated indoor. **Leisure Activities:** whirlpool. **Guest Services:** wireless Internet. **Business Services:** meeting rooms. **Cards:** AX, DC, DS, MC, VI.
Small-scale Hotel

SOME UNITS

HAYS pop. 20,013

——— WHERE TO STAY ———

BEST WESTERN VAGABOND MOTEL
Book great rates at AAA.com **Phone:** (785)625-2511

	5/2-10/15	1P: $62-$72	2P: $62-$76	XP: $4	F12
	10/16-2/29	1P: $54-$63	2P: $58-$67	XP: $4	F12
Motel	3/1-5/1	1P: $53-$63	2P: $57-$67	XP: $4	F12

Location: I-70, exit 159 (US 183), 1 mi s. 2524 Vine St 67601. Fax: 785/625-8879. **Facility:** 92 units. 88 one- and 2 two-bedroom standard units. 2 one-bedroom suites ($89-$150) with whirlpools. 1-2 stories (no elevator), exterior corridors. *Bath:* combo or shower only. **Parking:** on-site. **Terms:** small pets only. **Amenities:** high-speed Internet, irons, hair dryers. **Pool(s):** outdoor. **Leisure Activities:** whirlpools, exercise room. **Guest Services:** valet and coin laundry, wireless Internet. **Business Services:** PC. **Cards:** AX, CB, DC, DS, MC, VI.

SOME UNITS

ASK SD 🐾 🍴 ⚙ 🏊 🎥 🖥 🖥 / ⊠ 📠 /

COMFORT INN
Book great rates at AAA.com **Phone:** (785)628-8008

| | 5/16-9/15 [ECP] | 1P: $55-$80 | 2P: $60-$85 | XP: $5 | F18 |
| | 3/1-5/15 & 9/16-2/29 [ECP] | 1P: $45-$70 | 2P: $50-$75 | XP: $5 | F18 |

Small-scale Hotel **Location:** I-70, exit 159 (US 183), 0.7 mi s. 2810 Vine St 67601. Fax: 785/628-8008. **Facility:** 31 one-bedroom standard units. 2 stories (no elevator), interior corridors. **Parking:** on-site. **Amenities:** irons, hair dryers. **Pool(s):** small heated indoor. **Leisure Activities:** whirlpool. **Guest Services:** wireless Internet. **Cards:** AX, CB, DC, DS, JC, MC, VI.

SOME UNITS

ASK SD 🍴 🏊 🎥 🖥 / ⊠

COMFORT INN & SUITES
Book great rates at AAA.com **Phone:** (785)625-9322

| | 5/16-9/15 [ECP] | 1P: $70-$100 | 2P: $75-$105 | XP: $5 | F18 |
| | 3/1-5/15 & 9/16-2/29 [ECP] | 1P: $60-$85 | 2P: $65-$90 | XP: $5 | F18 |

Small-scale Hotel **Location:** I-70, exit 159 (US 183), just n. 1001 E 41st St 67601. Fax: 785/625-9327. **Facility:** 56 one-bedroom standard units. 3 stories, interior corridors. *Bath:* combo or shower only. **Parking:** on-site, winter plug-ins. **Amenities:** irons, hair dryers. **Pool(s):** small heated indoor. **Leisure Activities:** whirlpool, exercise room. **Guest Services:** coin laundry, wireless Internet. **Business Services:** PC. **Cards:** AX, CB, DC, DS, JC, MC, VI.

SOME UNITS

ASK SD 🍴 ⚙M ⚙ 🎣 🏊 🎥 🖥 / ⊠ 🖥 📠 /

FAIRFIELD INN HAYS
Book great rates at AAA.com **Phone:** (785)625-3344

| | 5/24-9/6 | 1P: $95-$115 | 2P: $95-$115 | |
| | 3/1-5/23 & 9/7-2/29 | 1P: $75-$95 | 2P: $75-$95 | |

Small-scale Hotel **Location:** I-70, exit 159 (US 183), just nw on north service road. 377 Mopar Dr 67601. Fax: 785/625-3322. **Facility:** Smoke free premises. 62 one-bedroom standard units, some with whirlpools. 3 stories, interior corridors. *Bath:* combo or shower only. **Parking:** on-site. **Terms:** 10 day cancellation notice, [CP] meal plan available. **Amenities:** high-speed Internet, irons, hair dryers. **Pool(s):** small heated indoor. **Leisure Activities:** whirlpool, exercise room. **Guest Services:** valet laundry, wireless Internet. **Cards:** AX, CB, DC, DS, JC, MC, VI.

SOME UNITS

ASK SD 🍴 ⚙ 🎣 🏊 ⊠ 🎥 🖥 / 🖥 📠 /

HAMPTON INN
fyi **Phone:** 785/621-4444

| | All Year [BP] | 1P: $74-$99 | 2P: $74-$99 | XP: $4 |

Too new to rate, opening scheduled for February 2007. **Location:** I-70, exit 159. 4002 General Hays Rd 67601.
Small-scale Hotel Fax: 785/621-4442. **Amenities:** 80 units, coffeemakers, pool. **Cards:** AX, CB, DC, DS, JC, MC, VI.

HAMPTON INN-HAYS
Book great rates at AAA.com **Phone:** 785/625-8103

Property failed to provide current rates

Location: I-70, exit 159 (US 183), just sw. 3801 Vine St 67601. Fax: 785/625-3006. **Facility:** 114 one-bedroom standard units, some with whirlpools. 2 stories (no elevator), interior/exterior corridors. *Bath:* combo or shower only. **Parking:** on-site, winter plug-ins. **Terms:** check-in 4 pm. **Amenities:** video games (fee), voice mail, irons, hair dryers. **Guest Services:** valet and coin laundry, wireless Internet.

SOME UNITS

🐾 🍴 ⚙ 🎣 🕹 🎥 🖥 / ⊠ /
FEE

HOLIDAY INN-HAYS
Book at AAA.com **Phone:** (785)625-7371

| | All Year | 1P: $89-$109 | |

Location: I-70, exit 159 (US 183), just s. 3603 Vine St 67601. Fax: 785/625-7250. **Facility:** 191 one-bedroom standard units, some with whirlpools. 2 stories (no elevator), interior/exterior corridors. *Bath:* combo or shower only. **Parking:** on-site, winter plug-ins. **Terms:** 3 day cancellation notice, package plans, small pets only ($20 fee, in designated units). **Amenities:** video games (fee), voice mail, irons, hair dryers. **Pool(s):** heated indoor. **Leisure Activities:** sauna, whirlpool, waterslide, exercise room. **Fee:** game room. **Guest Services:** valet and coin laundry, area transportation, wireless Internet. **Business Services:** conference facilities, PC. **Cards:** AX, DS, MC, VI.

SOME UNITS

ASK SD 🍺 🐾 🍴 🍷 ⚙M ⚙ 🎣 🏊 ⊠ 🎥 🖥 / ⊠ 🖥 📠 /
FEE

SLEEP INN INN & SUITES
Book great rates at AAA.com **Phone:** (785)625-2700

| | 5/16-9/15 [ECP] | 1P: $70-$95 | 2P: $75-$100 | XP: $5 | F18 |
| | 3/1-5/15 & 9/16-2/29 [ECP] | 1P: $60-$80 | 2P: $65-$85 | XP: $5 | F18 |

Small-scale Hotel **Location:** I-70, exit 159 (US 183), just n. 1011 E 41st St 67601. Fax: 785/625-6252. **Facility:** Smoke free premises. 55 one-bedroom standard units. 4 stories, interior corridors. *Bath:* combo or shower only. **Parking:** on-site, winter plug-ins. **Amenities:** voice mail, irons, hair dryers. **Pool(s):** small heated indoor. **Leisure Activities:** whirlpool, exercise room. **Guest Services:** valet and coin laundry, wireless Internet. **Business Services:** business center. **Cards:** AX, CB, DC, DS, JC, MC, VI.

SOME UNITS

ASK SD 🍴 ⚙M ⚙ 🎣 🏊 ⊠ 🎥 🖥 / 🖥 📠 /

SUPER 8 MOTEL-HAYS *Book at AAA.com*
All Year [CP]   1P: $52-$57   2P: $56-$64   XP: $3   F17
Phone: (785)625-8048
Small-scale Hotel **Location:** I-70, exit 159 (US 183), just s. 3730 Vine St 67601. Fax: 785/625-4392. **Facility:** 78 one-bedroom standard units. 3 stories (no elevator), interior corridors. **Parking:** on-site, winter plug-ins. **Amenities:** safes (fee), hair dryers. **Guest Services:** sundries, wireless Internet. **Cards:** AX, CB, DC, DS, JC, MC, VI.

SOME UNITS

(ASK) (S/D) (🛏+) (🍽) (🎥) / (✕) (🛏) (🖨) /

──────── **WHERE TO DINE** ────────

GUTIERREZ MEXICAN RESTAURANT   **Lunch:** $6-$11   **Dinner:** $7-$13   **Phone:** 785/625-4402
Traditional Mexican **Location:** I-70, exit 159 (US 183), 1 mi s, then just e. 1106 E 27th St 67601. **Hours:** 11 am-9 pm, Fri & Sat-10 pm. Closed: 4/8, 11/22, 12/24, 12/25. **Reservations:** accepted. **Features:** Serving Kansans since 1984, the local favorite prepares traditional entrees, including fajitas, burritos, chimichangas and burritos. Dessert selections are interesting and appetizing. Casual dress; cocktails. **Parking:** on-site. **Cards:** AX, DC, DS, MC, VI.

MONTANA MIKE'S STEAKHOUSE   **Lunch:** $8-$18   **Dinner:** $8-$18   **Phone:** 785/628-8786
Steak House **Location:** I-70, exit 159 (US 183), 0.4 mi s. 3216 Vine St 67601. **Hours:** 11 am-9 pm, Fri & Sat-10 pm; seasonal hours vary. Closed: 11/22, 12/25; also Mon. **Features:** This steakhouse offers a dining experience for the whole family. A rustic look with Western appointments characterizes the dining room. Although it's hard to go wrong with a hearty steak of USDA Choice aged beef, guests also can try smoked, fire-grilled chicken breast, chicken-fried steak, baby back ribs and other selections. Casual dress; cocktails. **Parking:** on-site. **Cards:** AX, DS, MC, VI.

(&M)

ROOFTOPS RESTAURANT & LOUNGE   **Lunch:** $6-$9   **Dinner:** $9-$21   **Phone:** 785/628-8631
Steak & Seafood **Location:** Downtown; in Emprise Bank Building, 6th floor. 1200 Main St 67601. **Hours:** 11 am-2 & 5-10 pm, Fri & Sat 5 pm-11 pm. Closed major holidays; also Sun. **Reservations:** suggested. **Features:** Rooftop Restaurant is locally owned and well-known for its excellent view of the city. The dining room is tastefully decorated and the service staff is professional and friendly. You'll find the cuisine flavorful and you might try the baked halibut Italiano or a USDA choice steak. The chicken dijonaise is a favorite and prime rib is offered on Wednesday, Friday and Saturday. You don't want to miss this one. Casual dress; cocktails. **Parking:** on-site. **Cards:** AX, CB, DC, DS, MC, VI.

(Y) (◧)

HESSTON pop. 3,509

──────── **WHERE TO STAY** ────────

AMERICINN LODGE & SUITES-HESSTON *Book at AAA.com*
All Year [ECP]   1P: $64-$99   2P: $64-$99   XP: $6   F
Phone: (620)327-2053
Small-scale Hotel **Location:** I-135, exit 40, just e. 2 Leonard Ct 67062. Fax: 620/327-2083. **Facility:** 42 one-bedroom standard units, some with whirlpools. 2 stories, interior corridors. *Bath:* combo or shower only. **Parking:** on-site. **Terms:** package plans, pets ($50 deposit). **Amenities:** high-speed Internet, hair dryers. *Some:* irons. **Pool(s):** heated indoor. **Leisure Activities:** whirlpool. **Guest Services:** coin laundry. **Business Services:** meeting rooms. **Cards:** AX, DS, MC, VI. *(See color ad p 373)*

SOME UNITS

(ASK) (S/D) (🛏) (🏊) (🛁+) (▣) / (✕) (🛏) (🖨) /
           FEE   FEE

HILLSBORO pop. 2,854

──────── **WHERE TO STAY** ────────

COUNTRY HAVEN INN
All Year [CP]   1P: $52-$60   2P: $60-$65   XP: $5   F18
Phone: (620)947-2929
Small-scale Hotel **Location:** On US 56; center. 804 Western Heights 67063. Fax: 620/947-2922. **Facility:** 24 one-bedroom standard units, some with whirlpools. 2 stories (no elevator), interior corridors. **Parking:** on-site, winter plug-ins. **Terms:** weekly rates available, small pets only ($10 fee, $50 deposit). **Amenities:** voice mail. **Guest Services:** wireless Internet. **Cards:** AX, DS, MC, VI.

SOME UNITS

(ASK) (S/D) (🛒) (🖨) / (✕) (🛏) /
        FEE

HOLTON pop. 3,353

──────── **WHERE TO STAY** ────────

SUPER 8 MOTEL *Book at AAA.com*
Phone: 785/364-1988
Property failed to provide current rates
Small-scale Hotel **Location:** On US 75, just s of jct US 75 and SR 116. 300 S Arizona St 66436. Fax: 785/364-4011. **Facility:** 36 one-bedroom standard units, some with whirlpools. 2 stories (no elevator), interior corridors. *Bath:* combo or shower only. **Parking:** on-site. **Amenities:** high-speed Internet. **Guest Services:** coin laundry.

SOME UNITS

(&M) (&) / (✕) (🛏) (🖨) /
        FEE FEE

HUTCHINSON pop. 40,787

────── WHERE TO STAY ──────

AMERICAS BEST VALUE INN   *Book great rates at AAA.com*   **Phone:** (620)662-6394

(AAA) (SAVE)
♦♦♦♦
Motel

| All Year [CP] | 1P: $56-$76 | 2P: $61-$81 | XP: $5 | F12 |

Location: Just se of jct SR 61. 1315 E 11th Ave 67501. Fax: 620/662-0843. **Facility:** 46 one-bedroom standard units. 2 stories (no elevator), interior corridors. **Parking:** on-site. **Terms:** pets (dogs only, $10 fee). **Amenities:** safes (fee). **Guest Services:** coin laundry. **Cards:** AX, DC, DS, MC, VI. **Free Special Amenities:** continental breakfast and local telephone calls.

SOME UNITS
[icons] FEE

COMFORT INN   *Book great rates at AAA.com*   **Phone:** (620)663-7822

♦♦♦♦ ♦♦♦♦
Small-scale Hotel

6/2-10/1 [BP]	1P: $59-$129	2P: $59-$129	XP: $10	F18
3/1-6/1 [BP]	1P: $55-$99	2P: $55-$99	XP: $10	F18
10/2-2/29 [BP]	1P: $55-$59	2P: $55-$99	XP: $10	F18

Location: Just w of jct SR 61 and N 17th Ave. Located in a commercial area. 1621 Super Plaza 67501. **Facility:** 63 one-bedroom standard units, some with kitchens and/or whirlpools. 3 stories (no elevator), interior corridors. *Bath:* combo or shower only. **Parking:** on-site. **Terms:** pets ($10 fee). **Amenities:** irons, hair dryers. **Pool(s):** outdoor. **Leisure Activities:** whirlpool. **Guest Services:** valet laundry, wireless Internet. **Cards:** AX, CB, DC, DS, JC, MC, VI.

SOME UNITS
[icons] FEE

GRAND PRAIRIE HOTEL & CONVENTION CENTER   *Book great rates at AAA.com*   **Phone:** (620)669-9311

(AAA) (SAVE)
♦♦♦♦ ♦♦♦♦
Large-scale Hotel

| 6/1-8/31 [BP] | 1P: $109-$119 | 2P: $119-$129 | XP: $10 | D21 |
| 3/1-5/31 & 9/1-2/29 [BP] | 1P: $89-$109 | 2P: $99-$119 | XP: $10 | D21 |

Location: Just nw of jct SR 61 and N 11th Ave. 1400 N Lorraine St 67501. Fax: 620/669-9830. **Facility:** 218 units. 216 one-bedroom standard units, some with whirlpools. 2 one-bedroom suites with whirlpools. 2 stories (no elevator), interior/exterior corridors. *Bath:* combo or shower only. **Parking:** on-site. **Terms:** 30 day cancellation notice, weekly rates available, package plans, pets ($35 fee). **Amenities:** irons, hair dryers. **Dining:** 6:30 am-11 pm, Fri & Sat-midnight, Sun-9 pm. **Pool(s):** heated indoor. **Leisure Activities:** whirlpool, waterslide, indoor water park, exercise room. *Fee:* game room. **Guest Services:** valet and coin laundry, wireless Internet. **Business Services:** conference facilities, business center. **Cards:** AX, CB, DC, DS, JC, MC, VI. **Free Special Amenities:** full breakfast and high-speed Internet.

SOME UNITS
[icons] FEE

HAMPTON INN   *Book great rates at AAA.com*   **Phone:** (620)665-9800

♦♦♦ ♦♦♦♦
Small-scale Hotel

| All Year [BP] | 1P: $69-$139 | 2P: $69-$139 | XP: $4 | F18 |

Location: Just se of jct SR 61. 1401 1/2 E 11th Ave 67501. Fax: 620/664-9538. **Facility:** 69 one-bedroom standard units, some with whirlpools. 3 stories, interior corridors. *Bath:* combo or shower only. **Parking:** on-site. **Amenities:** high-speed Internet, voice mail, irons, hair dryers. **Pool(s):** heated indoor. **Leisure Activities:** whirlpool, exercise room. **Guest Services:** valet laundry, wireless Internet. **Business Services:** meeting rooms, PC. **Cards:** AX, CB, DC, DS, JC, MC, VI.

SOME UNITS
[icons]

HOLIDAY INN EXPRESS HOTEL & SUITES   *Book at AAA.com*   **Phone:** (620)669-5200

♦♦♦ ♦♦♦♦
Small-scale Hotel

| All Year [ECP] | 1P: $93-$103 | 2P: $93-$103 | XP: $6 | F18 |

Location: Just w of jct SR 61 and N 17th Ave. 1601 Super Plaza 67501. Fax: 620/664-5454. **Facility:** 69 units. 62 one-bedroom standard units. 7 one-bedroom suites ($120-$149), some with whirlpools. 3 stories, interior corridors. *Bath:* combo or shower only. **Parking:** on-site, winter plug-ins. **Terms:** small pets only. **Amenities:** dual phone lines, voice mail, irons, hair dryers. **Pool(s):** heated indoor. **Leisure Activities:** whirlpool, exercise room. **Guest Services:** valet and coin laundry, wireless Internet. **Business Services:** meeting rooms, business center. **Cards:** AX, CB, DC, DS, MC, VI.

SOME UNITS
[icons]

MICROTEL INN & SUITES   *Book at AAA.com*   **Phone:** (620)665-3700

♦♦
Small-scale Hotel

| All Year [ECP] | 1P: $64-$135 | 2P: $64-$135 | |

Location: Just nw of jct SR 61 and N 11th Ave. 1420 N Lorraine 67501. Fax: 620/663-7282. **Facility:** 67 one-bedroom standard units. 3 stories, interior corridors. *Bath:* combo or shower only. **Parking:** on-site. **Terms:** small pets only. **Amenities:** high-speed Internet, irons, hair dryers. **Guest Services:** valet laundry, wireless Internet. **Cards:** AX, CB, DC, DS, JC, MC, VI.

SOME UNITS
[icons]

────── WHERE TO DINE ──────

ANCHOR INN   **Lunch:** $3-$7   **Dinner:** $5-$7   **Phone:** 620/669-0311

♦♦
Mexican

Location: Center. 128 S Main St 67501. **Hours:** 11 am-2 & 5-9 pm, Sat-9 pm, Sun-4 pm. Closed major holidays. **Features:** The Anchor Inn is a locally popular restaurant operated by the owner/family's third generation. They serve traditional Mexican dishes and a few burger selections in portions that are hearty and satisfying. The older building was recently restored. Casual dress; cocktails. **Parking:** street. **Cards:** AX, DS, MC, VI.

MONTANA MIKE'S STEAKHOUSE   **Lunch:** $6-$16   **Dinner:** $8-$16   **Phone:** 620/669-6886

♦♦♦ ♦♦♦
Steak House

Location: 0.5 mi w of SR 61. 925 E 30th St 67502. **Hours:** 11 am-9 pm, Fri & Sat-10 pm. Closed: 11/22, 12/25. **Features:** This steakhouse offers a dining experience for the whole family. A rustic look with Western appointments characterizes the dining room. Although it's hard to go wrong with a hearty steak of USDA Choice aged beef, guests also can try smoked, fire-grilled chicken breast, chicken-fried steak, baby back ribs and other selections. Casual dress; cocktails. **Parking:** on-site. **Cards:** AX, DS, MC, VI.

[icons]

ROY'S HICKORY PIT BBQ

Barbecue

Lunch: $5-$8

Phone: 620/663-7421

Location: 1 mi w of jct Main St. 1018 W 5th Ave 67501. **Hours:** 11 am-4 pm. Closed major holidays; also Sun & Mon. **Features:** First-timers shouldn't let the outside of this place fool them. Inside is an array of well-prepared barbecue dishes. Locals flock here, as the parking lot tells. Casual dress. **Parking:** on-site.

SIRLOIN STOCKADE

Steak House

Lunch: $6-$8   **Dinner:** $6-$8   **Phone:** 620/663-5951

Location: Just w of jct SR 61. 1526 E 17th Ave 67502. **Hours:** 11 am-9 pm. Closed major holidays. **Reservations:** not accepted. **Features:** The steakhouse lines up buffet items, including pizza, tacos, soups, salads and desserts, providing both excellent variety and a good value. Rotating theme nights might allow for the sampling of sushi, barbecue and seafood. The buffet also may serve to complement a quality steak. Rolls are baked several times daily. Casual dress. **Parking:** on-site. **Cards:** DS, MC, VI.

INDEPENDENCE pop. 9,846

———— WHERE TO STAY ————

APPLETREE INN

Small-scale Hotel

Book at AAA.com

Phone: 620/331-5500

All Year   1P: $75   2P: $85   XP: $5

Location: At 8th and Laurel sts. 201 N 8th St 67301. Fax: 620/331-0641. **Facility:** 64 one-bedroom standard units, some with whirlpools. 2 stories, interior/exterior corridors. *Bath:* combo or shower only. **Parking:** on-site, winter plug-ins. **Terms:** small pets only. **Amenities:** high-speed Internet, voice mail, irons, hair dryers. **Pool(s):** heated indoor. **Leisure Activities:** whirlpools. **Guest Services:** valet laundry. **Cards:** AX, DC, DS, MC, VI.

SOME UNITS

KNIGHTS INN

Small-scale Hotel

Book great rates at AAA.com

Phone: (620)331-7300

All Year   1P: $44-$54   2P: $49-$59   XP: $10   F17

Location: 1.4 mi e of jct US 75 and 160. 3222 W Main St 67301. Fax: 620/331-8740. **Facility:** 41 one-bedroom standard units. 1 story, exterior corridors. **Parking:** on-site, winter plug-ins. **Terms:** cancellation fee imposed, weekly rates available, pets ($10 fee). **Amenities:** high-speed Internet, irons, hair dryers. **Pool(s):** outdoor. **Cards:** AX, DC, DS, MC, VI. **Free Special Amenities:** continental breakfast and local telephone calls.

SOME UNITS

MICROTEL INN & SUITES

Small-scale Hotel

Book great rates at AAA.com

Phone: (620)331-0088

All Year [CP]   1P: $66-$83   2P: $66-$83   XP: $6

Location: 1.2 mi e of jct US 75 and 160. 2917 W Main St 67301. Fax: 620/331-5777. **Facility:** 69 one-bedroom standard units. 3 stories, interior corridors. *Bath:* combo or shower only. **Parking:** on-site, winter plug-ins. **Terms:** pets ($3 fee). **Amenities:** high-speed Internet. *Some:* irons, hair dryers. **Guest Services:** valet laundry. **Cards:** AX, DC, DS, MC, VI. **Free Special Amenities:** continental breakfast and high-speed Internet.

SOME UNITS

SUPER 8 MOTEL

Small-scale Hotel

Book at AAA.com

Phone: (620)331-8288

All Year   1P: $58   2P: $64   XP: $5   F12

Location: 1.3 mi e of jct US 160 and 75. 2800 W Main St 67301. Fax: 620/331-1730. **Facility:** 51 one-bedroom standard units. 2 stories (no elevator), interior corridors. **Parking:** on-site, winter plug-ins. **Terms:** [CP] meal plan available. **Amenities:** high-speed Internet. **Pool(s):** outdoor. **Guest Services:** coin laundry. **Cards:** AX, DS, MC, VI.

SOME UNITS

———— WHERE TO DINE ————

EL PUEBLITO

Mexican

Lunch: $4-$5   **Dinner:** $5-$9   **Phone:** 620/331-5860

Location: 1 mi n on US 75. 1721 N Penn Ave 67301. **Hours:** 11 am-9 pm. Closed major holidays. **Features:** A favorite of area residents, the restaurant serves a variety of freshly prepared Mexican dishes. Casual dress. **Parking:** on-site. **Cards:** AX, DS, MC, VI.

JOHN'S KITCHEN & PUB

American

Dinner: $5-$16   **Phone:** 620/331-4747

Location: Center. 119 W Main St 67301. **Hours:** 5:30 pm-9 pm. Closed major holidays; also Sun, Mon & Thurs. **Features:** Enjoy succulent slabs of smoked ribs in this converted downtown storefront eatery. All beef orders are cut in-house and prepared to your liking. Casual dress; cocktails. **Parking:** on-site. **Cards:** AX, DS, MC, VI.

UNCLE JACKS RESTAURANT & BAR

American

Lunch: $5-$7   **Dinner:** $11-$25   **Phone:** 620/331-5225

Location: Center. 104 N Penn Ave 67301. **Hours:** 11 am-10 pm. Closed major holidays; also Sun. **Reservations:** accepted. **Features:** A New York City-inspired setting greets you in this downtown dining room along with traditional dishes with a trendy twist. Try the buffalo breaded shrimp for an appetizer, then have a juicy, KC strip steak cooked to perfection. Casual dress; cocktails. **Parking:** on-site. **Cards:** AX, DS, MC, VI.

IOLA pop. 6,302

——— WHERE TO STAY ———

BEST WESTERN INN *Book great rates at AAA.com* Phone: (620)365-5161

(AAA) [SAVE]   All Year   1P: $48-$54   2P: $54-$59   XP: $5   F
◇◇ ◇◇   **Location:** Jct US 54 and 169, 1.5 mi w on US 54, then 0.8 mi n. 1315 N State St 66749 (PO Box 169).
Motel   **Fax:** 620/365-6808. **Facility:** 58 one-bedroom standard units. 1 story, exterior corridors. *Bath:* combo or
shower only. **Parking:** on-site. **Terms:** [ECP] meal plan available, small pets only ($5 fee). **Amenities:** high-
speed Internet, voice mail, irons, hair dryers. **Dining:** 6 am-9 pm, Sun 7 am-2 pm, cocktails. **Pool(s):** small
heated outdoor. **Guest Services:** complimentary laundry. **Business Services:** meeting rooms. **Cards:** AX,
DC, DS, MC, VI. **Free Special Amenities:** expanded continental breakfast and high-speed Internet.

SOME UNITS
[icons] /✕/
FEE

SUPER 8 IOLA   *Book at AAA.com*   Phone: (620)365-3030
◇◇ ◇◇   All Year   1P: $61-$71   2P: $69-$79   XP: $5   F17
Small-scale Hotel   **Location:** Jct US 54 and 169. 200 Bills Way 66749. **Fax:** 620/365-6128. **Facility:** 49 one-bedroom standard
units, some with whirlpools. 2 stories, interior corridors. **Parking:** on-site. **Terms:** [ECP] meal plan available,
small pets only. **Amenities:** high-speed Internet, voice mail, hair dryers. **Pool(s):** small heated indoor.
Leisure Activities: whirlpool, exercise room. **Guest Services:** coin laundry. **Business Services:** meeting rooms, PC.
Cards: AX, CB, DC, DS, MC, VI.

SOME UNITS
[ASK] [icons] /✕/

——— WHERE TO DINE ———

EL CHARRO   **Lunch:** $4-$7   **Dinner:** $5-$16   Phone: 620/365-7771
◇◇ ◇◇   **Location:** Downtown. 19 W Madison 66749. **Hours:** 11 am-9 pm, Fri & Sat-10 pm, Sun-8 pm. Closed major
Mexican   holidays. **Features:** The eatery offers a wide variety of authentic Mexican cuisine and fast service. Be
careful; they mean it when they say some dishes are spicy. Casual dress; beer only. **Parking:** street.
Cards: AX, DS, MC, VI.

[icon]

JUNCTION CITY pop. 18,886

——— WHERE TO STAY ———

CANDLEWOOD SUITES BY FLINT HOTELS, LLC
[fyi]   Property failed to provide current rates
          Too new to rate, opening scheduled for February 2007. **Location:** 300 E Chestnut 66441. **Amenities:** 83
Small-scale Hotel   units.

COMFORT INN   *Book great rates at AAA.com*   Phone: (785)238-7887
◇◇ ◇◇   5/16-9/15 [ECP]   1P: $60-$90   2P: $65-$95   XP: $5   F18
Small-scale Hotel   3/1-5/15 & 9/16-2/29 [ECP]   1P: $50-$75   2P: $55-$80   XP: $5   F18
Location: I-70, exit 296, just n. 1214 S Washington St 66441. **Fax:** 785/238-8774. **Facility:** 45 one-bedroom
standard units. 2 stories (no elevator), interior corridors. *Bath:* combo or shower only. **Parking:** on-site.
Amenities: irons, hair dryers. **Pool(s):** small heated indoor. **Leisure Activities:** whirlpool. **Guest Services:** wireless Internet.
Cards: AX, CB, DC, DS, JC, MC, VI.

SOME UNITS
[ASK] [icons] /✕ 🛏 📠/

COURTYARD BY MARRIOTT JUNCTION CITY *Book great rates at AAA.com*   Phone: (785)210-1500
(AAA) [SAVE]   All Year   1P: $94   2P: $94
◇◇ ◇◇   **Location:** I-70, exit 298, just w. 310 Hammons Dr 66441. **Fax:** 785/762-5023. **Facility:** Smoke free premises. 119
Small-scale Hotel   units. 113 one-bedroom standard units. 6 one-bedroom suites ($139-$159). 3 stories, interior corridors.
Bath: combo or shower only. **Parking:** on-site. **Terms:** package plans, pets ($75 fee). **Amenities:** video
games (fee), high-speed Internet, dual phone lines, voice mail, irons, hair dryers. **Pool(s):** heated indoor.
Leisure Activities: whirlpool, exercise room. **Guest Services:** valet and coin laundry, wireless Internet.
Business Services: conference facilities, business center. **Cards:** AX, DS, MC, VI. **Free Special Amenities:** newspaper.
(See color ad below)

SOME UNITS
[icons] /🛏 📠/
FEE

DAYS INN   *Book great rates at AAA.com*   Phone: (785)762-2727
All Year   1P: $55-$75   2P: $55-$75   XP: $5   F18
Location: I-70, exit 296, just n. 1024 N East St 66441. Fax: 785/762-2751. **Facility:** 108 one-bedroom
Small-scale Hotel   standard units. 2 stories (no elevator), interior/exterior corridors. **Parking:** on-site. **Terms:** [CP] & [ECP]
meal plans available, small pets only. **Amenities:** hair dryers. *Some:* irons. **Pool(s):** outdoor, heated indoor.
Leisure Activities: sauna, whirlpool, exercise room. **Guest Services:** valet and coin laundry, wireless Internet. **Business
Services:** meeting rooms, PC. **Cards:** AX, CB, DC, DS, MC, VI.

SOME UNITS

ASK ⓈⒹ 🐾 🍽️ 🍸 📷 🏊 ✕ 💻 / ✕ 🛗 🖥️ /

HOLIDAY INN EXPRESS   *Book at AAA.com*   Phone: 785-762-4200
All Year   1P: $84-$95   2P: $84-$95   XP: $5   F15
Location: I-70, exit 298, just nw. 120 N East St 66441. Fax: 785/762-4219. **Facility:** 60 one-bedroom standard
Small-scale Hotel   units, some with whirlpools. 2 stories (no elevator), interior corridors. **Parking:** on-site. **Terms:** pets ($25
deposit, $5 extra charge). **Amenities:** high-speed Internet, dual phone lines, voice mail, irons, hair dryers.
Pool(s): small heated indoor. **Leisure Activities:** sauna, whirlpool, exercise room. **Guest Services:** valet and coin laundry.
Cards: AX, CB, DC, DS, MC, VI.

SOME UNITS

ASK ⓈⒹ 🐾 🍽️ 🅜 📷 🏊 ✕ 📹 🛗 🖥️ 💻 / ✕ /
FEE

--------- **WHERE TO DINE** ---------

PEKING CHINESE RESTAURANT   **Lunch:** $5-$10   **Dinner:** $8-$12   Phone: 785-238-2336
Location: I-70, exit 296, just n. 836 S Washington St 66441. **Hours:** 11 am-2 & 4-9:30 pm, Sat from 11:30 am.
Closed: 7/4, 11/22, 12/25; also Mon. **Features:** The Peking Chinese Restaurant has friendly service and a
Chinese   varied selection of dishes, including Mongolian beef, and crab rangoon as an appetizer. The atmosphere is
casual and family-style with Asian decorations, and the staff is personable and pleasant. Casual dress.
Parking: on-site. **Cards:** MC, VI.

◥

SIRLOIN STOCKADE   **Lunch:** $6-$8   **Dinner:** $6-$8   Phone: 785-238-1817
Location: I-70, exit 296. 426 Golden Belt Blvd 66441. **Hours:** 11 am-9 pm. Closed: 11/22, 12/25. **Features:** The
steakhouse lines up buffet items, including pizza, tacos, soups, salads and desserts, providing both
American   excellent variety and a good value. Rotating theme nights might allow for the sampling of sushi, barbecue
and seafood. The buffet also may serve to complement a quality steak. Rolls are baked several times daily.
Casual dress. **Parking:** on-site. **Cards:** DS, MC, VI.

◥

--------- *The following restaurant has not been evaluated by AAA* ---------
but is listed for your information only.

FAMILY BUFFET   Phone: 785/762-1882
(fyi)   Not evaluated. **Location:** I-70, exit 298, just nw. 801 E Chestnut St 66441. **Features:** Extensive buffet of Chinese
favorites served for lunch and dinner. Conventional menu also available.

KANSAS CITY —*See Kansas City p. 474.*

LANSING pop. 9,199

--------- **WHERE TO STAY** ---------

ECONO LODGE   *Book great rates at AAA.com*   Phone: (913)727-2777
All Year   1P: $55-$100   2P: $55-$100   Phone: (913)727-2777
Location: I-70, exit 224 (Leavenworth), 10 mi n on US 73 and SR 7. 504 N Main 66043. Fax: 913/727-2777.
Facility: 38 one-bedroom standard units. 2 stories (no elevator), interior corridors. **Parking:** on-site.
Small-scale Hotel   **Terms:** check-in 4 pm, cancellation fee imposed, [CP] meal plan available, pets ($25 deposit, $5 extra
charge). **Amenities:** high-speed Internet. **Cards:** AX, DS, MC, VI. **Free Special Amenities:** continental
breakfast and high-speed Internet.

SOME UNITS

ⓈⒹ 🐾 🍽️ 📹 🛗 🖥️ 💻 / ✕ /
FEE

HOLIDAY INN EXPRESS HOTEL & SUITES   *Book at AAA.com*   Phone: (913)250-1000
All Year [ECP]   1P: $75-$86   2P: $75-$86   XP: $6   F18
Location: I-70, exit 224 (Leavenworth), 10 mi n on US 73 and SR 7. 120 Express Dr 66043. Fax: 913/250-0206.
Small-scale Hotel   **Facility:** 67 units. 52 one-bedroom standard units. 15 one-bedroom suites ($88-$96). 3 stories, interior
corridors. *Bath:* combo or shower only. **Parking:** on-site. **Terms:** pets ($20 fee). **Amenities:** dual phone
lines, voice mail, irons, hair dryers. *Some:* high-speed Internet. **Pool(s):** small heated indoor. **Leisure Activities:** whirlpool,
exercise room. *Fee:* game room. **Guest Services:** valet and coin laundry, wireless Internet. **Business Services:** meeting
rooms. **Cards:** AX, CB, DC, DS, MC, VI.

SOME UNITS

ASK ⓈⒹ 🐾 🍽️ 🅜 🎱 🏊 ✕ 📹 💻 / ✕ 🛗 🖥️ /
FEE

LARNED pop. 4,236

--------- **WHERE TO STAY** ---------

BEST WESTERN TOWNSMAN INN   *Book great rates at AAA.com*   Phone: (620)285-3114
All Year   1P: $59-$69   2P: $59-$69
Location: Jct US 56 and SR 156. 123 E 14th St 67550. Fax: 620/285-7139. **Facility:** 44 one-bedroom standard
units. 1 story, exterior corridors. *Bath:* combo or shower only. **Parking:** on-site, winter plug-ins. **Terms:** [CP]
Small-scale Hotel   meal plan available, small pets only ($10 extra charge, with prior approval). **Amenities:** irons, hair dryers.
Some: high-speed Internet. **Pool(s):** outdoor. **Guest Services:** wireless Internet. **Business Services:**
meeting rooms. **Cards:** AX, CB, DC, DS, MC, VI. **Free Special Amenities:** continental breakfast and
high-speed Internet.

SOME UNITS

ⓈⒹ 🐾 🍽️ 📷 🏊 🎱 💻 / ✕ 🛗 🖥️ /
FEE

LAWRENCE pop. 80,098

——— WHERE TO STAY ———

BAYMONT INN & SUITES
Book great rates at AAA.com

(AAA) [SAVE]
▽▽▽

Small-scale Hotel

Phone: (785)838-4242

4/1-6/30 & 7/1-9/30	1P: $65-$125	2P: $65-$125	XP: $5 F12
10/1-2/29	1P: $55-$85	2P: $55-$85	XP: $5 F12
3/1-3/31	1P: $55-$75	2P: $55-$75	XP: $5 F12

Location: I-70, exit 202, 1 mi s on US 59. 740 Iowa St 66044. **Fax:** 785/838-4343. **Facility:** 65 units. 63 one-bedroom standard units, some with whirlpools. 2 one-bedroom suites ($75-$135) with whirlpools. 3 stories, interior corridors. *Bath:* combo or shower only. **Parking:** on-site. **Terms:** small pets only ($10 extra charge). **Amenities:** high-speed Internet, irons, hair dryers. **Pool(s):** small heated indoor. **Leisure Activities:** whirlpool, exercise room. **Guest Services:** valet and coin laundry, wireless Internet. **Cards:** AX, DC, DS, MC, VI. **Free Special Amenities:** continental breakfast and high-speed Internet.

SOME UNITS

🛎️ [S]/[D] 📶 ⑪♦ 🔳M 🚫 ➿ 📹 🖥️ / ✕ 📱 🖨️ /
FEE

BEST WESTERN LAWRENCE
Book great rates at AAA.com

(AAA) [SAVE]
◈◈

Small-scale Hotel

Phone: (785)843-9100

3/1-10/1 [ECP]	1P: $79-$129	2P: $79-$129	XP: $5 F12
10/2-2/29 [ECP]	1P: $69-$99	2P: $79-$99	XP: $5 F12

Location: On US 59; jct SR 10. Located adjacent to Kansas University. 2309 Iowa St 66046. **Fax:** 785/843-1572. **Facility:** 100 units. 99 one-bedroom standard units, some with whirlpools. 1 one-bedroom suite ($99-$149). 2-3 stories, interior/exterior corridors. *Bath:* combo or shower only. **Parking:** on-site. **Terms:** package plans, pets ($10 fee, must be attended). **Amenities:** voice mail, irons, hair dryers. **Pool(s):** heated indoor. **Leisure Activities:** whirlpool, limited exercise equipment. **Guest Services:** valet and coin laundry, wireless Internet. **Business Services:** meeting rooms, business center. **Cards:** AX, DS, MC, VI. **Free Special Amenities:** expanded continental breakfast and high-speed Internet. *(See color ad below)*

SOME UNITS

🛎️ [S]/[D] 📶 ⑪♦ 🔳M 🚫 ➿ 📹 📱 🖥️ / ✕ 🖨️ /
FEE

CIRCLE S RANCH & COUNTRY INN
◈◈◈◈

Ranch

Phone: (785)843-4124

All Year [BP]	1P: $155-$298	2P: $155-$298	XP: $25 F12

Location: I-70, exit 204, 2.6 mi n on US 59, 5.6 mi n on CR 1045, then 2 mi e on 35th St (gravel road). Located in a rural area. 3325 Circle S Ln 66044. **Fax:** 785/843-4474. **Facility:** Surrounded by scenic views of woods, open range and rolling hills, the ranch is a good spot from which to view buffalo, cows and peacocks. Smoke free premises. 12 one-bedroom standard units, some with whirlpools. 3 stories (no elevator), interior corridors. *Bath:* combo or shower only. **Parking:** on-site. **Terms:** check-in 4 pm, 1-2 night minimum stay - seasonal and/or weekends, 14 day cancellation notice-fee imposed, [CP] & [ECP] meal plans available, package plans. **Amenities:** CD players, hair dryers. **Leisure Activities:** whirlpool, fishing, hiking trails, volleyball. *Fee:* massage. **Guest Services:** wireless Internet. **Business Services:** meeting rooms. **Cards:** DS, MC, VI.

✕ ✕ 📹

ECONO LODGE
Book great rates at AAA.com

(AAA) [SAVE]
▽▽▽

Small-scale Hotel

Phone: (785)842-7030

All Year [BP]	1P: $55-$110	2P: $63-$110	XP: $8 F16

Location: I-70, exit 202, 1 mi s. 2222 W 6th St 66049. **Fax:** 785/842-9668. **Facility:** 108 one-bedroom standard units, some with whirlpools. 3 stories (no elevator), interior corridors. **Parking:** on-site. **Terms:** pets ($10 fee). **Amenities:** voice mail, irons, hair dryers. **Dining:** 6:30 am-1 pm, Wed-Sat also 5 pm-9 pm, cocktails. **Pool(s):** outdoor. **Leisure Activities:** *Fee:* massage. **Guest Services:** valet and coin laundry, wireless Internet. **Business Services:** meeting rooms, PC. **Cards:** AX, DC, DS, MC, VI. **Free Special Amenities:** full breakfast and local telephone calls.

SOME UNITS

🛎️ [S]/[D] 📶 ⑪ 🍸 🚫 ➿ 🔳♦ 📹 🖥️ / ✕ 📱 🖨️ /
FEE   FEE

ELDRIDGE HOTEL *Book great rates at AAA.com*   Phone: (785)749-5011

(AAA) (SAVE) All Year   1P: $125-$350   XP: $10   F12
▼▼▼ **Location:** I-70, exit 204, 1.5 mi s to downtown, on 3rd St. 701 Massachusetts 66044. Fax: 785/749-4512.
Facility: Modern comforts in restored landmark. Many rooms are 2-room suites. Smoke free premises. 48
units. 5 one-bedroom standard units. 43 one-bedroom suites ($125-$350). 5 stories, interior corridors.
Historic **Parking:** valet. **Terms:** check-in 4 pm, cancellation fee imposed, package plans. **Amenities:** voice mail,
Small-scale Hotel irons, hair dryers. **Dining:** Ten Restaurant, see separate listing. **Guest Services:** valet laundry, area
transportation-in town, wireless Internet. **Business Services:** meeting rooms, PC. **Cards:** AX, DC, DS,
MC, VI. **Free Special Amenities: early check-in/late check-out and high-speed Internet.**

SOME UNITS

GOLDEN RULE MOTEL *Book great rates at AAA.com*   Phone: (785)842-5721

(AAA) (SAVE) All Year [CP]   1P: $58-$78   2P: $63-$83   XP: $5   F12
▼▼▼ **Location:** I-70, exit 202, 0.8 mi s, then just w. 515 McDonald Dr 66044. Fax: 785/842-8243. **Facility:** 49 one-
bedroom standard units. 3 stories (no elevator), interior corridors. **Parking:** on-site, winter plug-ins.
Terms: pets (dogs only, $10 fee). **Amenities:** safes (fee). **Guest Services:** coin laundry, wireless Internet.
Small-scale Hotel **Cards:** AX, DC, DS, MC, VI. **Free Special Amenities: continental breakfast and high-speed Internet.**

SOME UNITS

HAMPTON INN *Book great rates at AAA.com*   Phone: (785)841-4994

▼▼▼ All Year [ECP]   1P: $99-$179   2P: $99-$179
Location: I-70, exit 202, 0.8 mi s, then just w. 2300 W 6th St 66049. Fax: 785/841-7997. **Facility:** 89 one-bedroom
Small-scale Hotel standard units, some with whirlpools. 3 stories, interior corridors. *Bath:* combo or shower only. **Parking:** on-
site. **Amenities:** voice mail, irons, hair dryers. *Some:* high-speed Internet. **Pool(s):** small heated indoor.
Leisure Activities: whirlpool, exercise room. **Guest Services:** wireless Internet. **Business Services:** meeting rooms, PC.
Cards: AX, CB, DC, DS, JC, MC, VI.

SOME UNITS

HOLIDAY INN *Book at AAA.com*   Phone: (785)841-7077

▼▼▼ All Year   1P: $79-$119   2P: $79-$119
Location: I-70, exit 202, 0.5 mi s on US 59. 200 McDonald Dr 66044. Fax: 785/841-2799. **Facility:** 192 units. 191
Large-scale Hotel one-bedroom standard units. 1 one-bedroom suite with whirlpool. 4 stories, interior/exterior corridors.
Parking: on-site. **Terms:** package plans, pets ($50 fee). **Amenities:** voice mail, irons, hair dryers. **Pool(s):**
heated indoor. **Leisure Activities:** sauna, whirlpool, miniature golf, exercise room. *Fee:* game room. **Guest Services:** valet and
coin laundry, wireless Internet. **Business Services:** conference facilities. **Cards:** AX, DC, DS, MC, VI.

SOME UNITS

HOLIDAY INN EXPRESS HOTEL & SUITES *Book great rates at AAA.com* **Phone:** (785)749-7555

[AAA] [SAVE]

| | 3/30-8/18 | 1P: $95-$130 | 2P: $95-$130 | XP: $10 | F18 |
| | 3/1-3/29 & 8/19-2/29 | 1P: $85-$117 | 2P: $85-$117 | XP: $10 | F18 |

Location: I-70, exit 197 (SR 10), 8.4 mi e on SR 10 to US 59, then just n. 3411 SW Iowa St 66046 (PO Box 4345). Fax: 785/749-0232. **Facility:** 78 units. 74 one-bedroom standard units, some with whirlpools. 4 one-

Large-scale Hotel bedroom suites. 3 stories, interior corridors. *Bath:* combo or shower only. **Parking:** on-site. **Terms:** cancellation fee imposed. **Amenities:** high-speed Internet, dual phone lines, voice mail, safes, irons, hair dryers. **Pool(s):** small heated indoor. **Leisure Activities:** whirlpool, rental bicycles, hiking trails, exercise room. **Guest Services:** coin laundry, wireless Internet. **Business Services:** meeting rooms, business center. **Cards:** AX, CB, DC, DS, JC, MC, VI. *(See color ad p 354)*

SOME UNITS

[icons] SD TI+ GM ... X ... / X ... /

QUALITY INN *Book great rates at AAA.com* **Phone:** (785)842-5100

[AAA] [SAVE]

All Year 1P: $64-$124 XP: $10 F18

Location: I-70, exit 202, 1 mi s on US 59. 801 N Iowa St 66049. Fax: 785/842-9623. **Facility:** 56 one-bedroom standard units, some with whirlpools. 2 stories (no elevator), interior/exterior corridors. *Bath:* combo or shower only. **Parking:** on-site. **Terms:** pets ($10 fee). **Amenities:** safes (fee), irons, hair dryers. **Pool(s):**

Small-scale Hotel outdoor. **Leisure Activities:** exercise room. **Guest Services:** coin laundry, wireless Internet. **Business Services:** meeting rooms. **Cards:** AX, DS, MC, VI. **Free Special Amenities:** local telephone calls and high-speed Internet.

SOME UNITS

[icons] SD ... TI+ ... ... / X ... /
FEE

WHERE TO DINE

HEREFORD HOUSE **Dinner:** $11-$36 **Phone:** 785/842-2333

American

Location: I-70, exit 202, 1 mi s, then 2 mi w on US 40 (6th St). 4931 W 6th St 66049. **Hours:** 4 pm-9:30 pm, Fri & Sat 3 pm-10 pm, Sun 10 am-9 pm. Closed major holidays. **Features:** The restaurant offers several choices of elegant appetizers such as escargot and shrimp cocktail, and the salads exhibit creativity. Known for their high quality and wide variety of steaks, the restaurant also serves seafood such as lobster tail and broiled trout, as well as numerous specialties including grilled shrimp alfredo. Casual dress; cocktails. **Parking:** on-site. **Cards:** AX, DC, DS, MC, VI.

[icon]

JADE MONGOLIAN BARBEQUE **Lunch:** $6-$15 **Dinner:** $6-$15 **Phone:** 785/865-5233

Chinese

Location: On SR 10 (23rd St), 0.5 mi e of US 59. 1511 W 23rd St 66049. **Hours:** 11 am-10 pm, Fri & Sat-10:30 pm. Closed major holidays. **Features:** Guests can either sample from the large buffet and salad bar or order from the menu. Entrees are prepared to the diner's preference after selections are made from the raw food bar. Choices are plentiful. Casual dress; cocktails. **Parking:** on-site. **Cards:** AX, CB, DC, MC, VI.

[icon]

MONTANA MIKE'S STEAKHOUSE **Lunch:** $6-$16 **Dinner:** $6-$16 **Phone:** 785/749-3005

American

Location: I-70, exit 202, 1.3 mi s. 1015 Iowa St 66044. **Hours:** 11 am-9 pm, Fri & Sat-10 pm. Closed: 11/22, 12/25; also Mon. **Features:** This steakhouse offers a dining experience for the whole family. A rustic look with Western appointments characterizes the dining room. Although it's hard to go wrong with a hearty steak of USDA Choice aged beef, guests also can try smoked, fire-grilled chicken breast, chicken-fried steak, baby back ribs and other selections. Casual dress; cocktails. **Parking:** on-site. **Cards:** AX, DS, MC, VI.

PACHAMAMA'S **Lunch:** $6-$16 **Dinner:** $12-$28 **Phone:** 785/841-0990

Continental

Location: I-70, exit 204, 1 mi s; downtown. 800 New Hampshire St 66044. **Hours:** 11 am-2 & 5-9 pm, Sun from 5 pm. Closed major holidays; also Mon. **Features:** You'll find an International cuisine at Pachamama's, where the menu changes monthly. Its upscale decor features a subtle rain forest decor, open airy spaces and an outstanding view of Alvamar Golf Course. Good selection of wines. Private patio. Dressy casual; cocktails. **Parking:** on-site. **Cards:** AX, DS, MC, VI.

[icons] GM Y

PANDA GARDEN CHINESE RESTAURANT **Lunch:** $5-$13 **Dinner:** $5-$13 **Phone:** 785/843-4312

Chinese

Location: I-70, exit 202, 1 mi s, then 0.5 mi s. 1500 W 6th St 66044. **Hours:** 11 am-9:30 pm, Fri & Sat-10 pm, Sun-9 pm. Closed: Mon. **Features:** Close to many stores, the restaurant employs fast, friendly servers. Patrons can relax in the cozy dining room and browse an extensive menu or choose the buffet, which lines up a small variety of good selections. Casual dress; cocktails. **Parking:** on-site. **Cards:** AX, DS, MC, VI.

[icons] Y

THE PLUM TREE **Lunch:** $5-$6 **Dinner:** $6-$15 **Phone:** 785/841-6222

Chinese

Location: On US 59 (Iowa St), 0.6 mi s of jct SR 10 (23rd St); south side of town. 2620 Iowa St 66046. **Hours:** 11 am-10 pm, Fri & Sat-10:30 pm, Sun 11:30 am-9:30 pm. Closed: Tues. **Features:** The elegant, award-winning restaurant is suited for adults and prepares many gourmet dishes, including lobster, as well as American preparations. Casual dress; beer & wine only. **Parking:** on-site. **Cards:** DS, MC, VI.

[icon]

RUNZA **Lunch:** $4-$6 **Dinner:** $4-$6 **Phone:** 785/841-7044

American

Location: West side of town. 3418 W 6th St 66049. **Hours:** 10:30 am-10 pm. Closed major holidays. **Features:** The restaurant fulfills the need for a quick meal without the frills and expensive prices. Food offerings include the standard burgers and fries, but the real feature is the delicious namesake sandwich, which is dough stuffed with ground beef and spices. Casual dress. **Parking:** on-site. **Cards:** MC, VI.

[icon]

RUNZA **Lunch:** $4-$6 **Dinner:** $4-$6 **Phone:** 785/749-2615

American

Location: Jct US 59 and 27th; south side of town. 2700 Iowa St 66044. **Hours:** 10:30 am-10 pm. Closed major holidays. **Features:** The restaurant fulfills the need for a quick meal without the frills and expensive prices. Food offerings include the standard burgers and fries, but the real feature is the delicious namesake sandwich, which is dough stuffed with ground beef and spices. Casual dress. **Parking:** on-site.

Cards: MC, VI.

TEN RESTAURANT　　　　　**Lunch:** $5-$8　　　　**Dinner:** $12-$22　　　**Phone:** 785/749-5011

American

Location: I-70, exit 204, 1.5 mi s to downtown, on 3rd St; in Eldridge Hotel. 701 Massachusetts St 66044. **Hours:** 7 am-2 & 5-9 pm, Fri & Sat-10 pm, Sun-8 pm. **Features:** Shalor's is located in a historic hotel, lovingly restored to the grandeur of the Civil War era. The restaurant features a good variety of well-prepared entrees including steaks, grilled salmon, pork loin with raspberry maple glaze, and tortellini pasta. Casual dress; cocktails. **Parking:** on-site. **Cards:** AX, DC, DS, MC, VI. **Historic**

LEAWOOD —See Kansas City p. 476.

LENEXA —See Kansas City p. 477.

LIBERAL pop. 19,666

——————— **WHERE TO STAY** ———————

AMERICAS BEST VALUE INN　　*Book great rates at AAA.com*　　　　　**Phone:** 620/624-6203

Motel

All Year　　　　　　1P: $38　　　　　　2P: $48　　　　　XP: $5　　　　　F12
Location: 0.8 w of jct US 54 and 83. 564 E Pancake Blvd 67901. Fax: 620/626-4940. **Facility:** 31 one-bedroom standard units. 1 story, exterior corridors. **Parking:** on-site, winter plug-ins. **Terms:** pets ($3 extra charge). **Pool(s):** outdoor. **Guest Services:** coin laundry, wireless Internet. **Cards:** AX, DS, MC, VI. **Free Special Amenities:** local telephone calls and high-speed Internet.

SOME UNITS
🆂 📶 🛎️ 🛬 📷 🔌 🖨️ 🖵 / ⊗ /
FEE

BLUEBIRD INN BED & BREAKFAST　　　　　　　　　　　　　　**Phone:** (620)624-0720

Bed & Breakfast

All Year　　　　　　1P: $65-$75　　　　2P: $65-$75　　　　XP: $10　　　　F10
Location: Just w of jct US 83 business route (Kansas Ave). 221 W 6th St 67901. Fax: 620/624-2855. **Facility:** One-story stone house on well-maintained and landscaped corner lot. Wood deck at the rear of property is open air with several chairs for guest enjoyment. This is a non-smoking residence; however, smoking is permitted outdoors. The property is frequented by casual travelers, as well as business persons. 4 one-bedroom standard units, some with whirlpools. 1-2 stories, interior corridors. *Bath:* combo or shower only. **Parking:** on-site. **Terms:** check-in 4 pm, weekly rates available, package plans. **Amenities:** video library, DVD players, high-speed Internet, hair dryers. **Cards:** AX, DS, MC, VI. **Free Special Amenities:** full breakfast and high-speed Internet.

SOME UNITS
🆂 ⊗ 🆅🅲🆁 / 🖥 🖨️ 🖵 /

HOLIDAY INN EXPRESS HOTEL & SUITES　　*Book at AAA.com*　　　　　**Phone:** 620/624-9700

Small-scale Hotel

Property failed to provide current rates
Location: 1.5 mi n on US 83 business route. 1550 N Lincoln 67901. Fax: 620/624-0206. **Facility:** 67 units. 61 one-bedroom standard units, some with whirlpools. 6 one-bedroom suites. 3 stories, interior corridors. *Bath:* combo or shower only. **Parking:** on-site. **Amenities:** dual phone lines, voice mail, irons, hair dryers. **Pool(s):** small heated indoor. **Leisure Activities:** whirlpool, exercise room. **Guest Services:** valet and coin laundry, wireless Internet. **Business Services:** meeting rooms, business center.

SOME UNITS
🛗 ♿ 🛬 📷 🖵 / ⊗ 🖥 🖨️ /

LIBERAL INN　　　　　　　　　　　　　　　　　　　　　　**Phone:** (620)624-7254

Small-scale Hotel

All Year　　　　　　1P: $55-$70　　　　2P: $60-$75　　　　XP: $5　　　　F12
Location: 0.5 mi w of jct US 54 and 83. 603 E Pancake Blvd 67901. Fax: 620/624-7254. **Facility:** 124 units. 120 one-bedroom standard units. 4 one-bedroom suites. 2 stories (no elevator), interior corridors. **Parking:** on-site. **Terms:** small pets only. **Amenities:** *Some:* irons. **Dining:** Branding Iron Restaurant, see separate listing. **Pool(s):** heated indoor. **Leisure Activities:** whirlpool. **Guest Services:** valet and coin laundry, wireless Internet. **Business Services:** meeting rooms. **Cards:** AX, CB, DC, DS, MC, VI. **Free Special Amenities:** early check-in/late check-out and high-speed Internet. *(See color ad below)*

SOME UNITS
🆂 ✈️ 🛎️ 🍴 🛬 📷 / ⊗ 🖥 🖨️ 🖵 /

─────── **The following lodgings were either not evaluated or did not** ───────
meet AAA rating requirements but are listed for your information only.

LIBERAL SUPER 8 MOTEL

Phone: 620/624-8880

[fyi]   Did not meet all AAA rating requirements for some property operations at time of last evaluation on
01/25/2006. **Location:** Just w of jct US 54 and 83. 747 E Pancake Blvd 67901. Facilities, services, and decor
Small-scale Hotel   characterize a mid-range property.

RODEWAY INN

Phone: 620/624-5642

[fyi]   Not evaluated. **Location:** 488 E Pancake Blvd 67901. Facilities, services, and decor characterize a basic property.

─────── **WHERE TO DINE** ───────

BRANDING IRON RESTAURANT   **Lunch:** $5-$10   **Dinner:** $5-$18   Phone: 620/624-7254

Location: 0.5 mi w of jct US 54 and 83; in Liberal Inn. 603 E Pancake Blvd (Hwy 54) 67901. **Hours:** 6 am-10:30 pm,
Sun 7 am-10 pm. Closed: 11/22, 12/24, 12/25. **Features:** You'll appreciate the generous portions of
delicious steak, catfish and barbecue ribs at the Branding Iron. The warm, casual atmosphere, home-
cooked foods and friendly, attentive service make this a popular restaurant with just about everyone. Casual
American   dress; cocktails. **Parking:** on-site. **Cards:** AX, CB, DC, DS, MC, VI. *(See color ad p 356)*

CATTLEMANS CAFE II   **Lunch:** $5-$10   **Dinner:** $5-$10   Phone: 620/626-5553

Location: Jct US 54 and 83, just w. 744 E Pancake Blvd 67901. **Hours:** 10:30 am-10:30 pm. Closed: 11/22,
12/25. **Features:** Locals flock to the restaurant for good home cooking and generous portions. Casual
American   dress. **Parking:** on-site. **Cards:** DS, MC, VI.

KING'S BBQ   **Lunch:** $5-$8   **Dinner:** $5-$15   Phone: 620/624-2451

Location: Just e of jct US 54 and 83. 355 Hwy 54 E 67901. **Hours:** 11 am-9 pm. Closed major holidays; also
Sun. **Reservations:** accepted. **Features:** King's hickory-smoked barbecue ribs, chicken and brisket are the
specialties at this casual restaurant. Many items are served family-style and you'll find the 'Wizard of Oz'
Barbecue   memorabilia fun. Casual dress; beer only. **Parking:** on-site. **Cards:** DS, MC, VI.

LA HACIENDA   **Lunch:** $7-$17   **Dinner:** $7-$17   Phone: 620/626-7319

Location: US 54, just e of jct US 83. 339 E Pancake Blvd 67901. **Hours:** 11 am-3 & 5-9 pm, Fri & Sat-10 pm,
Sun-8 pm. Closed major holidays. **Features:** A favorite among locals, the restaurant specializes in Mexican
fare. For those who enjoy seafood prepared in the Mexican tradition, the choices are plentiful. Casual dress;
Mexican   cocktails. **Parking:** on-site. **Cards:** MC, VI.

TASTE OF CHINA   **Lunch:** $6-$9   **Dinner:** $7-$9   Phone: 620/626-7388

Location: Just w of jct US 54 and 83. 741 E Pancake Blvd 67901. **Hours:** 11 am-10:30 pm. Closed: 11/22.
Features: The buffet, which lines up a good array of quality food, is a favorite among many local residents.
Chinese   Casual dress. **Parking:** on-site. **Cards:** AX, DS, MC, VI.

LINDSBORG pop. 3,321

─────── **WHERE TO STAY** ───────

VIKING MOTEL

Phone: 785/227-3336

All Year [CP]   1P: $42-$56   2P: $49-$64   XP: $4

Location: I-135, exit 78, 4 mi sw. Located within easy access to Bethany College. 446 Harrison 67456 (PO Box 227).
Motel   **Facility:** 24 one-bedroom standard units. 2 stories (no elevator), exterior corridors. **Parking:** on-site.
Terms: weekly rates available, small pets only ($5 extra charge). **Pool(s):** outdoor. **Leisure**
Activities: bicycles, horseshoes. **Cards:** AX, CB, DC, DS, MC, VI.

SOME UNITS

MANHATTAN pop. 44,831

─────── **WHERE TO STAY** ───────

BEST WESTERN MANHATTAN INN   *Book great rates at AAA.com*   Phone: 785/537-8300

Property failed to provide current rates

Location: SR 177, 0.4 mi e on US 24 (Frontage Rd). 601 E Poyntz Ave 66502. Fax: 785/537-8303. **Facility:** 45.
Small-scale Hotel   one-bedroom standard units, some with whirlpools. 2 stories (no elevator), interior corridors. *Bath:* combo or
shower only. **Parking:** on-site. **Terms:** pets ($10 extra charge). **Amenities:** high-speed Internet, voice mail,
irons, hair dryers. **Pool(s):** small heated indoor. **Leisure Activities:** exercise room. **Guest Services:** coin laundry. **Business**
Services: meeting rooms.

SOME UNITS

CLARION HOTEL

Phone: (785)539-5311

All Year   1P: $65-$160   2P: $65-$160   XP: $10   F

Location: On SR 18 (Ft. Riley Blvd). 0.3 mi e of jct SR 113. 530 Richards Dr 66502. Fax: 785/539-8368.
Large-scale Hotel   **Facility:** 197 units. 196 one-bedroom standard units. 1 one-bedroom suite ($129-$299). 3 stories,
interior/exterior corridors. *Bath:* combo or shower only. **Parking:** on-site. **Terms:** check-in 4 pm, cancellation
fee imposed, [AP] meal plan available, package plans, small pets only ($20 fee). **Amenities:** video games (fee), voice mail,
irons, hair dryers. **Pool(s):** heated indoor. **Leisure Activities:** sauna, whirlpool, miniature golf, exercise room. *Fee:* game room.
Guest Services: valet and coin laundry, area transportation, wireless Internet. **Business Services:** conference facilities,
business center. **Cards:** AX, DC, DS, MC, VI.

SOME UNITS

COMFORT INN
Book great rates at AAA.com
Phone: (785)770-8000

5/1-2/29	1P: $90-$100
3/1-4/30	1P: $75-$95

Small-scale Hotel **Location:** Jct US 24 (Frontage Rd) and SR 177. 150 E Poyntz Ave 66502. **Fax:** 785/770-8001. **Facility:** 65 one-bedroom standard units, some with whirlpools. 3 stories, interior corridors. *Bath:* combo or shower only. **Parking:** on-site. **Terms:** 7 day cancellation notice-fee imposed, [CP] meal plan available. **Amenities:** voice mail, irons, hair dryers. **Pool(s):** small heated indoor. **Leisure Activities:** whirlpool, exercise room. **Guest Services:** valet and coin laundry, wireless Internet. **Cards:** AX, DC, DS, MC, VI.

SOME UNITS

FAIRFIELD INN BY MARRIOTT
Book great rates at AAA.com
Phone: (785)539-2400

All Year	1P: $95-$155 2P: $95-$155

Small-scale Hotel **Location:** Just w of jct SR 177 and 18 (Ft. Riley Blvd). 300 Colorado St 66502. **Fax:** 785/539-1483. **Facility:** Smoke free premises. 98 one-bedroom standard units. 3 stories, interior corridors. *Bath:* combo or shower only. **Parking:** on-site. **Terms:** [ECP] meal plan available. **Amenities:** dual phone lines, voice mail, irons, hair dryers. **Pool(s):** small heated indoor. **Leisure Activities:** whirlpool, exercise room. **Guest Services:** valet laundry, wireless Internet. **Business Services:** meeting rooms, PC. **Cards:** AX, DC, DS, MC, VI.

SOME UNITS

HAMPTON INN
Book great rates at AAA.com
Phone: (785)539-5000

All Year [CP]	1P: $89-$135 2P: $95-$135

Small-scale Hotel **Location:** SR 177, 0.3 mi e on US 24 (Frontage Rd). 501 E Poyntz Ave 66502. **Fax:** 785/776-6042. **Facility:** 72 units. 71 one-bedroom standard units. 1 one-bedroom suite. 3 stories, interior corridors. *Bath:* combo or shower only. **Parking:** on-site. **Terms:** cancellation fee imposed. **Amenities:** dual phone lines, voice mail, irons, hair dryers. **Pool(s):** heated indoor. **Leisure Activities:** whirlpool, exercise room. **Guest Services:** valet and coin laundry, wireless Internet. **Business Services:** meeting rooms, PC. **Cards:** AX, DS, MC, VI.

SOME UNITS

HOLIDAY INN AT THE CAMPUS
Book at AAA.com
Phone: (785)539-7531

All Year	1P: $79-$149 2P: $89-$169

Small-scale Hotel **Location:** 1 mi n of SR 18 (Ft. Riley Blvd). Located opposite Kansas State University. 1641 Anderson 66502. **Fax:** 785/539-3909. **Facility:** Smoke free premises. 112 units. 111 one-bedroom standard units. 1 one-bedroom suite. 6 stories, interior corridors. **Parking:** on-site. **Terms:** package plans, small pets only ($10 extra charge). **Amenities:** video games, dual phone lines, voice mail, irons, hair dryers. **Dining:** Houlihans, see separate listing. **Pool(s):** outdoor. **Leisure Activities:** exercise room. **Guest Services:** gift shop, valet and coin laundry, area transportation, wireless Internet. **Business Services:** conference facilities, business center. **Cards:** AX, CB, DC, DS, MC, VI.

SOME UNITS

FEE

MOTEL 6 - 152
Book at AAA.com
Phone: 785/537-1022

3/1-9/3	1P: $39-$49	2P: $45-$55	XP: $3 F17
9/4-2/29	1P: $37-$47	2P: $43-$53	XP: $3 F17

Motel **Location:** 0.3 mi ne on US 24 (Frontage Rd) and SR 177. 510 Tuttle Creek Blvd 66502. **Fax:** 785/537-7307. **Facility:** 87 one-bedroom standard units. 2 stories (no elevator), exterior corridors. *Bath:* shower only. **Parking:** on-site. **Terms:** small pets only. **Pool(s):** small heated outdoor. **Guest Services:** coin laundry. **Cards:** AX, CB, DC, DS, MC, VI.

SOME UNITS

SUPER 8 MOTEL-MANHATTAN
Book at AAA.com
Phone: (785)537-8468

All Year [CP]	1P: $59-$125	2P: $65-$125	XP: $5 F

Small-scale Hotel **Location:** Jct US 24 (Frontage Rd) and SR 177. Located across the street from a major mall. 200 Tuttle Creek Blvd 66502. **Fax:** 785/537-9216. **Facility:** 87 one-bedroom standard units. 3 stories (no elevator), interior corridors. **Parking:** on-site. **Amenities:** safes (fee), hair dryers. *Some:* irons. **Leisure Activities:** exercise room. **Guest Services:** valet and coin laundry, wireless Internet. **Business Services:** meeting rooms. **Cards:** AX, CB, DC, DS, JC, MC, VI.

SOME UNITS

—— **WHERE TO DINE** ——

ALL CHINESE BUFFET
Lunch: $6   **Dinner: $8**   **Phone: 785/539-8299**

Chinese **Location:** 0.3 mi e on SR 18 (Ft. Riley Blvd) from jct SR 113, just s. 2304 Stagg Hill Rd 66502. **Hours:** 11 am-9:30 pm, Fri & Sat-10 pm. Closed: 11/22. **Features:** In the evenings, snow crab is included in the large selection on the buffets for a small extra charge. The menu lists an excellent variety of entrees. Casual dress. **Parking:** on-site. **Cards:** AX, MC, VI.

FAMOUS DAVE'S
Lunch: $6-$20   **Dinner: $6-$20**   **Phone: 785/537-2401**

American **Location:** Northeast corner of SR 18 (Ft. Riley Blvd) and CR 113 (Seth Child Rd); southwest side of town; in The Seth Child Shopping Center. 910 Commons Pl 66503. **Hours:** 11 am-10 pm, Fri & Sat-11 pm. Closed: 11/22, 12/25. **Features:** Famous for its legendary pit barbecue, the fun and casual northwoods lodge-style eatery celebrates the many variations of barbecue styles, from Texas beef brisket and Georgian chopped pork to country roast chicken and pit barbecue ribs. Casual dress; cocktails. **Parking:** on-site. **Cards:** AX, DS, MC, VI.

HARRY'S UPTOWN
Lunch: $8-$24   **Dinner: $8-$24**   **Phone: 785/537-1300**

Continental **Location:** Downtown. 418 Poyntz Ave 66502. **Hours:** 11 am-2 & 5-9 pm, Fri & Sat 5 pm-10 pm. Closed: 1/1, 11/22, 12/25; also Sun. **Features:** Enjoy casual fine dining set in the comfortable atmosphere of a historic building at Harry's Uptown. They serve a good variety of creatively prepared chicken, beef and fresh seafood dishes. The server staff is friendly and attentive to your needs. Casual dress; cocktails. **Parking:** street. **Cards:** AX, MC, VI. **Historic**

HOULIHANS

◆◆ ◆◆

American

Lunch: $5-$16   **Dinner:** $8-$16   **Phone:** 785/776-5909

Location: 1 mi n of SR 18 (Ft. Riley Blvd); in Holiday Inn at the Campus. 1641 Anderson Ave 66502. **Hours:** 6:30 am-10 & 11-11 pm, Fri & Sat-midnight. Closed: 12/25. **Features:** Very cozy ambience with intimate booths. Very wide and creative selection of entrees on the menu including steaks, seafood, poultry and pasta. Very friendly and efficient service. Casual dress; cocktails. **Parking:** on-site. **Cards:** AX, DC, DS, MC, VI.

LITTLE APPLE BREWING COMPANY

◆◆ ◆◆

American

Lunch: $5-$29   **Dinner:** $5-$29   **Phone:** 785/539-5500

Location: Off CR 113 (Seth Child Rd); in Westloop Shopping Center. 1110 Westloop Shopping Center 66502. **Hours:** 11 am-10 pm, Fri & Sat-11 pm, Sun-9:30 pm. Closed major holidays. **Features:** Known locally for certified Angus steak and award-winning microbrew, Little Apple has a casual atmosphere with a Western flair. They feature a good selection, fresh ingredients and ample portions of burgers, sandwiches, steaks and Mexican dishes. Casual dress; cocktails. **Parking:** on-site. **Cards:** AX, DS, MC, VI.

SIRLOIN STOCKADE

◆◆ ◆◆

Steak House

Lunch: $6-$8   **Dinner:** $6-$8   **Phone:** 785/776-0516

Location: Center. 325 E Poyntz Ave 66502. **Hours:** 11 am-9 pm. Closed major holidays. **Reservations:** not accepted. **Features:** The steakhouse lines up buffet items, including pizza, tacos, soups, salads and desserts, providing both excellent variety and a good value. Rotating theme nights might allow for the sampling of sushi, barbecue and seafood. The buffet also may serve to complement a quality steak. Rolls are baked several times daily. Casual dress. **Parking:** on-site. **Cards:** DS, MC, VI.

WHISKEY CREEK STEAKHOUSE

◆◆ ◆◆

American

Lunch: $6-$19   **Dinner:** $6-$19   **Phone:** 785/776-7300

Location: On SR 18 (Ft. Riley Blvd), just w of jct SR 177. 200 Manhattan Town Center 66502. **Hours:** 11 am-10 pm, Fri & Sat-11 pm. Closed major holidays. **Features:** Guests can watch as their steak is cooked over a wood-burning fire and throw peanut shells on the floor at this fun, casual steakhouse. The menu's wide variety includes chicken, pasta and barbecue dishes. A rustic theme evokes the wild, wild West. Casual dress; cocktails. **Parking:** on-site. **Cards:** AX, CB, DC, DS, MC, VI.

MANKATO pop. 976

─── WHERE TO DINE ───

BUFFALO ROAM STEAK HOUSE

◆

Steak House

Lunch: $6-$10   **Dinner:** $9-$23   **Phone:** 785/378-3971

Location: 0.5 mi e on US 36 (Pony Express Hwy). 740 E South St 66956. **Hours:** 11 am-1:30 & 5-9 pm, Sat from 5 pm. Closed major holidays; also Sun. **Reservations:** accepted. **Features:** This steak house is a "bring your grandma, kids and mother-in-law" kind of place. The staff is friendly, and their varied menu includes a Friday night Mexican buffet, and a first-Saturday-of-the-month seafood buffet. Casual dress; beer only. **Parking:** on-site. **Cards:** DS, MC, VI.

MARYSVILLE pop. 3,271

─── WHERE TO STAY ───

BEST WESTERN SURF MOTEL

◆◆ ◆◆

Small-scale Hotel

Book great rates at AAA.com

Property failed to provide current rates   **Phone:** 785/562-2354

Location: 1 mi e on US 36 (Pony Express Hwy). 2105 Center St 66508. Fax: 785/562-2354. **Facility:** 52 one-bedroom standard units. 2 stories (no elevator), interior/exterior corridors. *Bath:* combo or shower only. **Parking:** on-site. **Terms:** small pets only ($5 extra charge, in designated units). **Amenities:** irons, hair dryers. *Some:* high-speed Internet. **Leisure Activities:** sauna, whirlpool, exercise room. *Fee:* game room. **Guest Services:** coin laundry. **Business Services:** meeting rooms.

SOME UNITS

OAK TREE INN-MARYSVILLE

◆◆ ◆◆

Small-scale Hotel

Book at AAA.com

All Year   1P: $65   **Phone:** (785)562-1234

Location: 1.6 mi e on US 36 (Pony Express Hwy). 1127 Pony Express Hwy 66508. Fax: 785/562-1100. **Facility:** Smoke free premises. 103 one-bedroom standard units. 2 stories (no elevator), interior corridors. *Bath:* combo or shower only. **Parking:** on-site. **Terms:** check-in 4 pm, pets ($10 fee). **Amenities:** high-speed Internet, irons, hair dryers. **Leisure Activities:** whirlpool, exercise room. **Guest Services:** coin laundry. **Business Services:** meeting rooms. **Cards:** DC, DS, MC, VI.

SOME UNITS

SUPER 8 MOTEL

◆◆ ◆◆

Small-scale Hotel

Phone: (785)562-5588

All Year   1P: $45-$88   2P: $45-$88   XP: $5   F17

Location: 2 mi e on US 36 (Pony Express Hwy). 1155 Pony Express Hwy 66508. Fax: 785/562-2763. **Facility:** 41 one-bedroom standard units, some with whirlpools. 2 stories (no elevator), interior corridors. **Parking:** on-site. **Terms:** pets ($10 fee, in smoking units). **Amenities:** high-speed Internet. **Leisure Activities:** limited exercise equipment. **Guest Services:** coin laundry. **Business Services:** meeting rooms. **Cards:** AX, CB, DC, DS, MC, VI.

SOME UNITS

MCPHERSON pop. 13,770

─── WHERE TO STAY ───

AMERICAS BEST VALUE INN

AAA SAVE

◆◆ ◆◆

Motel

Book great rates at AAA.com

All Year [CP]   1P: $49-$69   2P: $54-$74   XP: $5   F12

Location: I-135, exit 60, just w. 2110 E Kansas Ave 67460. Fax: 620/241-8853. **Facility:** 42 one-bedroom standard units. 2 stories (no elevator), interior corridors. *Bath:* combo or shower only. **Parking:** on-site. **Terms:** pets (dogs only, $10 fee). **Amenities:** safes (fee). **Cards:** AX, DC, DS, MC, VI. **Free Special Amenities:** continental breakfast and local telephone calls.

SOME UNITS

BEST WESTERN HOLIDAY MANOR MOTEL   *Book great rates at AAA.com*   Phone: (620)241-5343

◇◇◇◇   All Year [CP]   1P: $57-$85   2P: $57-$85   XP: $6   F18
Location: I-135, exit 60, just w. 2211 E Kansas Ave 67460 (PO Box 923). Fax: 620/241-8086. **Facility:** 109 one-
Small-scale Hotel   bedroom standard units, some with whirlpools. 2 stories (no elevator), interior/exterior corridors. *Bath:*
combo or shower only. **Parking:** on-site, winter plug-ins. **Terms:** [AP] & [BP] meal plans available, small
pets only ($10 extra charge). **Amenities:** high-speed Internet, voice mail, irons, hair dryers. **Pool(s):** outdoor, small heated
indoor. **Leisure Activities:** whirlpool, exercise room. **Guest Services:** valet laundry. **Business Services:** conference facilities.
Cards: AX, CB, DC, DS, MC, VI.

SOME UNITS
(ASK) [SD] [FEE] [🛏] [🍴] [🍷] [&] [🏊] [🎥] [💻] / [✕] [🔒] [📶] / [FEE]

RED COACH INN   Phone: (620)241-6960
◇◇◇◇   All Year   1P: $49-$150   2P: $54-$150   XP: $5   F12
Location: I-135, exit 60, just w. 2111 E Kansas Ave 67460. Fax: 620/241-4340. **Facility:** 88 units. 87 one-
Small-scale Hotel   bedroom standard units, some with whirlpools. 1 one-bedroom suite ($85-$150) with efficiency (no utensils)
and whirlpool. 2 stories (no elevator), interior/exterior corridors. **Parking:** on-site, winter plug-ins. **Terms:** 30
day cancellation notice, weekly rates available, package plans, small pets only ($15 fee). **Pool(s):** heated indoor. **Leisure
Activities:** sauna, whirlpool, miniature golf, playground. *Fee:* game room. **Business Services:** conference facilities. **Cards:** AX,
DC, DS, MC, VI.

SOME UNITS
(ASK) [SD] [FEE] [🛏] [🍴] [🏊] [✕] [🎥] / [✕] /

MEADE pop. 1,672

——— WHERE TO STAY ———

DALTON'S BEDPOST MOTEL   Phone: 620-873-2131
(AAA) [SAVE]   All Year   1P: $49   2P: $49   XP: $4   F
◇◇◇   **Location:** On US 54. 519 E Carthage 67864 (PO Box 657). Fax: 620/873-2747. **Facility:** 12 one-bedroom
standard units. 1 story, exterior corridors. *Bath:* shower only. **Parking:** on-site, winter plug-ins. **Terms:** [CP]
Motel   meal plan available, small pets only. **Guest Services:** wireless Internet. **Cards:** DS, MC, VI.
Free Special Amenities: continental breakfast and high-speed Internet.

SOME UNITS
[🛏] [🎥] [🔒] / [✕] /

MERRIAM —*See Kansas City p. 478.*

MORAN pop. 562

——— WHERE TO STAY ———

HEDGE APPLE ACRES BED & BREAKFAST   Phone: (620)237-4646
◇◇◇◇   All Year [BP]   1P: $65-$75   2P: $75-$85   XP: $20   D12
Location: Jct US 54 and 59, 2.1 mi e on US 54. Located in a quiet area. 4430 US Hwy 54 66755. **Facility:** Smoke
Bed & Breakfast   free premises. 4 one-bedroom standard units, some with whirlpools. 2 stories (no elevator), interior
corridors. *Bath:* combo or shower only. **Parking:** on-site. **Terms:** 14 day cancellation notice-fee imposed, no
pets allowed (owner's dog on premises). **Leisure Activities:** fishing, hiking trails. **Cards:** AX, DS, MC, VI.

SOME UNITS
[✕] [W] / [☎] /

NEWTON pop. 17,190

——— WHERE TO STAY ———

DAYS INN NEWTON   *Book great rates at AAA.com*
◇◇◇   Property failed to provide current rates   Phone: 316-283-3330
Location: I-135, exit 31, just e. 105 Manchester St 67114. Fax: 316/284-0602. **Facility:** 80 one-bedroom standard
Small-scale Hotel   units. 2 stories, interior corridors. **Parking:** on-site, winter plug-ins. **Terms:** pets ($10 fee). **Amenities:** hair
dryers. *Some:* high-speed Internet, irons. **Pool(s):** small heated outdoor. **Guest Services:** valet laundry,
wireless Internet. **Business Services:** meeting rooms.

SOME UNITS
[🛏] [🍴] [🏊] [🎥] / [✕] [🔒] [📶] [💻] /

OAKLEY pop. 2,173

——— WHERE TO DINE ———

COLONIAL STEAKHOUSE   Lunch: $6-$9   Dinner: $7-$19   Phone: 785-672-4720
(AAA)   **Location:** I-70, exit 70, just s. 464 US 83 67748. **Hours:** 6 am-10 pm; to 9 pm in winter. Closed: 11/22, 12/24,
◇◇◇   12/25. **Reservations:** accepted. **Features:** Hearty, home-style meals are presented in large portions at this
casual, family-style restaurant, which includes an on-premise bakery. On the lengthy menu are USDA
American   choice aged beef, ostrich and buffalo burgers and many comfort foods. Diners won't go away hungry from
the extensive buffet. Casual dress; beer only. **Parking:** on-site. **Cards:** AX, DS, MC, VI.
[🚭]

OBERLIN pop. 1,994

——— WHERE TO STAY ———

FRONTIER MOTEL   Phone: 785/475-2203
◇   Property failed to provide current rates
Location: On US 36, 0.5 mi e of jct US 83. 207 E Frontier Pkwy 67749. Fax: 785/475-3872. **Facility:** 27 units. 25
Motel   one- and 2 two-bedroom standard units. 1 story, exterior corridors. **Parking:** on-site, winter plug-ins.
Terms: office hours 8 am-10 pm. **Pool(s):** outdoor. **Guest Services:** coin laundry, wireless Internet.

SOME UNITS
[🛏] [🍴] [🏊] [🎥] / [✕] [🔒] [📶] /

LANDMARK INN
△△△△ △△△△
Historic
Country Inn

Phone: 785/475-2340

All Year [BP]   1P: $69-$99   2P: $79-$109   XP: $10   F8
Location: Corner of Penn and Hall; downtown. 189 S Penn 67749 (PO Box 162). **Facility:** The inn — located in a restored bank building, circa 1886 — features both antique and replicated antique furnishings and a friendly staff. Smoke free premises. 7 one-bedroom standard units, some with whirlpools. 2-3 stories (no elevator), interior/exterior corridors. **Bath:** combo or shower only. **Parking:** street. **Terms:** office hours 6 am-midnight, cancellation fee imposed, package plans. **Amenities:** video library (fee), voice mail. **Dining:** Teller Room Restaurant, see separate listing. **Leisure Activities:** sauna, limited exercise equipment. **Guest Services:** gift shop, coin laundry, wireless Internet. **Cards:** AX, CB, DC, DS, JC, MC, VI.

ASK SD ✈ ❨❩ ᕼM ✕ VCR

─────── **WHERE TO DINE** ───────

TELLER ROOM RESTAURANT
△△△△ △△△△
American

Lunch: $6-$9   **Dinner:** $12-$18   Phone: 785/475-2340
Location: Corner of Penn and Hall; downtown; in LandMark Inn. 189 S Penn 67749. **Hours:** 11:30 am-1:30 pm, Thurs-Sat also 6:30 pm-8:30 pm. Closed: 4/8, 11/22, 12/25; also Sun. **Reservations:** suggested. **Features:** In a restored circa 1886 bank building, the restaurant treats patrons to a distinctive experience. The dining room has vintage wall coverings, cherry woodwork and reproduction gas lights. The daily changing menu lists a little something for everyone. Save room for one of the scrumptious desserts, all of which are prepared in house. Casual dress. **Parking:** street. **Cards:** AX, CB, DC, DS, MC, VI.

OLATHE —See Kansas City p. 479.

OTTAWA pop. 11,921

─────── **WHERE TO STAY** ───────

BEST WESTERN OTTAWA INN   *Book great rates at AAA.com*
△△△△ △△△△
Small-scale Hotel

Phone: (785)242-2224

All Year   1P: $70-$100   2P: $80-$100   XP: $5   F12
Location: I-35, exit 183 (US 59). 606 E 23rd St 66067. Fax: 785/242-2221. **Facility:** 52 one-bedroom standard units. 2 stories (no elevator), interior/exterior corridors. **Parking:** on-site. **Terms:** [ECP] meal plan available, pets (in smoking units, with prior approval). **Amenities:** high-speed Internet, voice mail, irons, hair dryers. **Pool(s):** small heated indoor. **Leisure Activities:** whirlpool. **Guest Services:** valet and coin laundry. **Business Services:** meeting rooms. **Cards:** AX, CB, DC, DS, MC, VI.

SOME UNITS
ASK SD 🐾 ❨❩ ᕼM ➹ ✹ 🖥 💻 / ✕ 🖥 /

COMFORT INN   *Book great rates at AAA.com*
△△△△ △△△△
Small-scale Hotel

Phone: (785)242-9898

All Year   1P: $79-$159   2P: $79-$159   XP: $10   F18
Location: I-35, exit 183 (US 59), just ne. 2335 S Oak St 66067. Fax: 785/242-7146. **Facility:** 60 one-bedroom standard units, some with whirlpools. 3 stories, interior corridors. **Bath:** combo or shower only. **Parking:** on-site, winter plug-ins. **Terms:** 7 day cancellation notice, [ECP] meal plan available. **Amenities:** video games, high-speed Internet, voice mail, irons, hair dryers. **Pool(s):** heated indoor. **Leisure Activities:** whirlpool, exercise room. **Guest Services:** valet laundry, wireless Internet. **Cards:** AX, DC, DS, MC, VI.

SOME UNITS
ASK SD ❨❩ ᕼM 🄴🄲🄿 ➹ ✹ 🖥 / ✕ 🖥 🖥 /

DAYS INN   *Book great rates at AAA.com*
△△△
Motel

Phone: (785)242-4842

All Year   1P: $48-$70   2P: $54-$90   XP: $6   F12
Location: I-35, exit 183 (US 59), 1 mi n. 1641 S Main 66067. Fax: 785/242-7325. **Facility:** 42 one-bedroom standard units, some with whirlpools. 1-2 stories (no elevator), exterior corridors. **Bath:** combo or shower only. **Parking:** on-site, winter plug-ins. **Terms:** [ECP] meal plan available, small pets only ($15 fee, must be attended). **Amenities:** hair dryers. *Some:* dual phone lines, irons. **Pool(s):** small outdoor. **Guest Services:** coin laundry, wireless Internet. **Cards:** AX, CB, DC, DS, JC, MC, VI.

SOME UNITS
ASK SD 🐾 ᕼM ➹ ✹ 🖥 🖥 / ✕ 🖥 /
FEE

ECONO LODGE   *Book great rates at AAA.com*
AAA [SAVE]
△△△
Small-scale Hotel

Phone: (785)242-3400

All Year   1P: $50-$80   2P: $55-$100   XP: $5   F12
Location: I-35, exit 183 (US 59). 2331 S Cedar Rd 66067. Fax: 785/242-2228. **Facility:** 56 one-bedroom standard units. 2 stories (no elevator), interior corridors. **Parking:** on-site, winter plug-ins. **Terms:** [ECP] meal plan available, small pets only ($10 extra charge, in smoking units, must be attended). **Amenities:** irons, hair dryers. **Pool(s):** small outdoor. **Guest Services:** wireless Internet. **Cards:** AX, DS, MC, VI.

SOME UNITS
SD 🐾 ❨❩ ➹ ✹ 🖥 🖥 🖥 / ✕ /
FEE

TRAVELODGE
△△△
Motel

Phone: 785/242-7000

Property failed to provide current rates
Location: I-35, exit 183 (US 59), just n. 2209 S Princeton Rd 66067. Fax: 785/242-8572. **Facility:** 60 one-bedroom standard units. 2 stories (no elevator), exterior corridors. **Parking:** on-site. **Terms:** small pets only ($10 fee, in smoking units, must be attended). **Amenities:** irons, hair dryers. *Some:* high-speed Internet. **Pool(s):** small outdoor. **Guest Services:** valet and coin laundry, wireless Internet. **Business Services:** meeting rooms.

SOME UNITS
🐾 ❨❩ ➹ ✹ 🖥 🖥 🖥 / ✕ /
FEE

─────── **WHERE TO DINE** ───────

SIRLOIN STOCKADE
△△△
Steak House

Lunch: $6-$8   **Dinner:** $6-$8   Phone: 785/242-4329
Location: I-35, exit 183, just n. 2230 S Princeton St 66067. **Hours:** 11 am-9 pm. Closed major holidays. **Reservations:** not accepted. **Features:** The steakhouse lines up buffet items, including pizza, tacos, soups, salads and desserts, providing both excellent variety and a good value. Rotating theme nights might allow for the sampling of sushi, barbecue and seafood. The buffet also may serve to complement a quality steak. Rolls are baked several times daily. Casual dress. **Parking:** on-site. **Cards:** DS, MC, VI.

◩

OVERLAND PARK —See Kansas City p. 480.

PARK CITY pop. 5,814

──────── WHERE TO STAY ────────

SUPER 8 MOTEL-WICHITA NORTH/PARK CITY   *Book at AAA.com*   Phone: (316)744-2071
All Year [CP]   1P: $45-$85   2P: $45-$85   XP: $4   F17
Location: I-135, exit 14, just sw. 6075 Air Cap Dr 67219. Fax: 316/744-2074. **Facility:** 59 one-bedroom standard
units. 2 stories (no elevator), interior corridors. **Parking:** on-site, winter plug-ins. **Terms:** pets ($10 extra
Small-scale Hotel   charge). **Amenities:** safes (fee). **Guest Services:** coin laundry, wireless Internet. **Cards:** AX, CB, DC, DS,
JC, MC, VI.

SOME UNITS

(A$K) (S/D) 🛏 (†↑†) 🍴 🐾 📺 / ✕ 🔌 📷

FEE

──────── *The following lodging was either not evaluated or did not* ────────
meet AAA rating requirements but is listed for your information only.

COMFORT INN NORTH   Phone: 316/744-7711
[fyi]   Did not meet all AAA rating requirements for some property operations at time of last evaluation on
07/11/2006. **Location:** I-135, exit 14, just ne. 990 Connolly Ct 67219. Facilities, services, and decor characterize a
Small-scale Hotel   mid-range property.

PARSONS pop. 11,514

──────── WHERE TO STAY ────────

SUPER 8 MOTEL-PARSONS   *Book at AAA.com*   Phone: (620)421-8000
All Year [CP]   1P: $59-$79   2P: $59-$79   XP: $5   F17
Location: 1.3 mi e of jct US 59 and 400. 229 E Main 67357. Fax: 620/421-8228. **Facility:** 48 units. 47 one-
bedroom standard units. 1 one-bedroom suite with whirlpool. 2 stories (no elevator), interior corridors.
Small-scale Hotel   **Parking:** on-site, winter plug-ins. **Amenities:** safes (fee), hair dryers. *Some:* irons. **Pool(s):** small heated
indoor. **Leisure Activities:** *Fee:* game room. **Guest Services:** coin laundry, wireless Internet. **Business Services:** meeting
rooms. **Cards:** AX, CB, DC, DS, JC, MC, VI.

SOME UNITS

(A$K) (S/D) 🏊 📺 / ✕ 🔌 📷 📷 /

──────── WHERE TO DINE ────────

SIRLOIN STOCKADE   **Lunch:** $6-$8   **Dinner:** $6-$8   Phone: 620/421-0022
Location: Just e of jct US 59 and 400. 1000 W Main St 67357. **Hours:** 11 am-9 pm. Closed major holidays.
Reservations: not accepted. **Features:** The steakhouse lines up buffet items, including pizza, tacos, soups,
Steak House   salads and desserts, providing both excellent variety and a good value. Rotating theme nights might allow
for the sampling of sushi, barbecue and seafood. The buffet also may serve to complement a quality steak.
Rolls are baked several times daily. Casual dress. **Parking:** on-site. **Cards:** DS, MC, VI.

🔪

PHILLIPSBURG pop. 2,668

──────── WHERE TO STAY ────────

COTTONWOOD INN   Phone: (785)543-2125
All Year   1P: $55-$80   2P: $69-$99   XP: $10
Location: 1 mi e on US 36/183. 1200 State St 67661 (Rt #1, Box 108). Fax: 785/543-5432. **Facility:** 40 one-
bedroom standard units, some with whirlpools. 2 stories (no elevator), exterior corridors. *Bath:* combo or
shower only. **Parking:** on-site, winter plug-ins. **Terms:** office hours 6 am-11 pm, 7 day cancellation notice-
Motel   fee imposed, small pets ok. **Pool(s):** heated outdoor. **Leisure Activities:** exercise room. **Guest Services:**
wireless Internet. **Business Services:** meeting rooms. **Cards:** AX, DS, MC, VI. **Free Special Amenities:**
preferred room (subject to availability with advance reservations) and high-speed Internet.

SOME UNITS

(S/D) 🛏 (†↑†) ♿ 🏊 📺 / ✕

PITTSBURG pop. 19,243

──────── WHERE TO STAY ────────

COMFORT INN & SUITES   *Book great rates at AAA.com*   Phone: (620)231-8800
All Year   1P: $69-$90   2P: $159-$175   XP: $5   F18
Location: 2 mi n on US 69 from jct SR 126. 4009 Parkview Dr 66762. Fax: 620/230-0811. **Facility:** 70 one-
bedroom standard units, some with whirlpools. 3 stories, interior corridors. *Bath:* combo or shower only.
Small-scale Hotel   **Parking:** on-site. **Terms:** [ECP] meal plan available. **Amenities:** high-speed Internet, voice mail, safes
(fee), irons, hair dryers. **Pool(s):** small heated indoor. **Leisure Activities:** whirlpool, exercise room. **Guest Services:** valet and
coin laundry. **Cards:** AX, CB, DC, DS, JC, MC, VI.

SOME UNITS

(A$K) (S/D) (&M) 🐾 🏊 📺 📷 / ✕ (VCR) 🔌 📷

FEE

ECONO LODGE   *Book great rates at AAA.com*   Phone: 620/231-8300
All Year   1P: $45-$70   2P: $49-$89   XP: $6   F12
Location: Jct US 69 and Broadway; south side of town. 2408 S Broadway 66762. Fax: 620/232-2885. **Facility:** 67
units. 66 one-bedroom standard units, some with whirlpools. 1 one-bedroom suite ($69-$109). 1-2 stories,
Small-scale Hotel   exterior corridors. **Amenities:** high-speed Internet, hair dryers. **Pool(s):** small outdoor. **Leisure Activities:** sauna, exercise
room. **Guest Services:** coin laundry. **Cards:** AX, CB, DC, DS, JC, MC, VI. **Free Special Amenities:**
expanded continental breakfast and high-speed Internet.

SOME UNITS

(S/D) 🛏 (†↑†) 🏊 📺 / ✕ 🔌 📷

FEE

HOLIDAY INN EXPRESS   *Book at AAA.com*   Phone: 620-231-8700
All Year   1P: $59-$100   2P: $59-$100   XP: $10   F19
Location: 2.3 mi n on US 69 from jct SR 126. 4020 Parkview Dr 66762 (PO Drawer 1638). Fax: 620/230-0154.
Small-scale Hotel   interior/exterior corridors. **Facility:** 100 units. 99 one-bedroom standard units. 1 one-bedroom suite. 2 stories (no elevator),
Bath: combo or shower only. **Parking:** on-site. **Terms:** weekly rates available.
Amenities: video games, high-speed Internet, voice mail, irons, hair dryers. **Pool(s):** outdoor. **Leisure Activities:** whirlpool,
exercise room. **Guest Services:** valet laundry. **Business Services:** meeting rooms. **Cards:** AX, CB, DC, DS, JC, MC, VI.

SOME UNITS

⊞ 🅜 🖭 📷 🏊 🎥 🖵 / ✕ 📶 🖨 /

SUPER 8 MOTEL-PITTSBURG   *Book at AAA.com*   Phone: (620)232-1881
All Year [CP]   1P: $53-$69   2P: $53-$69   XP: $5   F17
Location: 2.1 mi n on US 69 from jct SR 126. 3108 N Broadway St 66762. Fax: 620/232-1881. **Facility:** 64 one-
Small-scale Hotel   bedroom standard units. 3 stories (no elevator), interior corridors. **Parking:** on-site. **Amenities:** high-speed
Internet, safes (fee). *Some:* irons, hair dryers. **Cards:** AX, CB, DC, DS, JC, MC, VI.

SOME UNITS

🅐🆂🅺 🆂🅳 🍽 📷 🎥 / ✕ 📶 🖨 🖭 /

--------- **WHERE TO DINE** ---------

CHICKEN ANNIE'S ORIGINAL   Dinner: $5-$10   Phone: 620-231-9460
Location: 5 mi n on US 69 from SR 126, 3.5 mi e on rural road, then follow signs. 1143 E 600th Ave 66762. **Hours:** 4
pm-8:30 pm, Sat-9 pm, Sun 11 am-8 pm. Closed: 11/22, 12/25; also Mon. **Reservations:** accepted.
American   **Features:** You'll enjoy the home-style cooking and casual dining of Chicken Annie's, where the featured
dish is, of course, chicken, which is nicely seasoned and perfectly cooked. The German potato salad,
German coleslaw and onion rings are also tasty and fresh. Casual dress; cocktails. **Parking:** on-site. **Cards:** MC, VI.

🍽 🚭

CHICKEN MARYS   Dinner: $5-$12   Phone: 620-231-9510
Location: 5 mi n on US 69, 3.5 mi e on rural road, follow signs. 1133 E 600th Ave 66762. **Hours:** 4 pm-8:30 pm,
Sat-9 pm, Sun 11 am-8 pm. Closed major holidays; also Mon. **Reservations:** accepted. **Features:** Chicken
American   Marys specializes in—what else?—chicken, but it's prepared with a very old, German, family recipe and has
great flavor. Chicken dominates the basic menu of mostly homemade selections. It has a casual
atmosphere and simple decor. Casual dress; beer only. **Parking:** on-site. **Cards:** MC, VI.

🚭

EL CHARRO   Lunch: $4-$6   Dinner: $5-$16   Phone: 620/232-5763
Location: 2 mi n, on US 69 from jct SR 126. 3102 N Broadway 66762. **Hours:** 11 am-9 pm, Fri & Sat-10 pm, Sun-
8 pm. Closed major holidays. **Features:** The eatery offers a wide variety of authentic Mexican cuisine and
Mexican   fast service. Be careful; they mean it when they say some dishes are spicy. Casual dress; cocktails.
Parking: on-site. **Cards:** AX, DS, MC, VI.

🍽 🚭

JIM'S STEAKHOUSE & LOUNGE   Dinner: $6-$25   Phone: 620-231-5770
Location: 2 mi n of jct US 69 and SR 126, on US 69. 1912 N Broadway Ave 66762. **Hours:** 4:30 pm-10 pm. Closed
major holidays; also Sun. **Features:** Most menu items are homemade at Jim's, which is very popular with
American   local residents and has been in business for 60 years. Its casual, family-style atmosphere is comfortable,
lighthearted, quiet and pleasant, plus the server staff is very nice. Casual dress; cocktails. **Parking:** on-site.
Cards: MC, VI.

🍽 🚭

PRAIRIE VILLAGE —*See Kansas City p. 487.*

PRATT pop. 6,570

--------- **WHERE TO STAY** ---------

DAYS INN   *Book great rates at AAA.com*   Phone: (620)672-9465
All Year   1P: $54-$92   2P: $58-$92   XP: $6   F16
Location: 1.7 mi e on US 54. 1901 E 1st St 67124. Fax: 620/672-9468. **Facility:** 45 one-bedroom standard units.
Small-scale Hotel   2 stories (no elevator), exterior corridors. **Parking:** on-site, winter plug-ins. **Terms:** cancellation fee
imposed, pets ($3 extra charge). **Amenities:** high-speed Internet, irons, hair dryers. **Pool(s):** outdoor.
Cards: AX, DC, DS, MC, VI.

SOME UNITS

🅐🆂🅺 🆂🅳 🐾 🏊 🎥 📶 🖨 🖭 / ✕ /
FEE

ECONO LODGE   *Book great rates at AAA.com*   Phone: (620)672-6407
8/1-2/29   1P: $46-$64   2P: $49-$74   XP: $5   F12
4/1-7/31   1P: $46-$54   2P: $49-$64   XP: $5   F12
Small-scale Hotel   3/1-3/31   1P: $42-$54   2P: $46-$56   XP: $5   F12
Location: 1 mi e on US 54. 1336 E 1st St 67124. Fax: 620/672-6707. **Facility:** 40 one-bedroom standard units.
1 story, exterior corridors. **Parking:** on-site, winter plug-ins. **Terms:** [ECP] meal plan available, pets ($5 extra charge).
Amenities: irons, hair dryers. *Some:* high-speed Internet. **Pool(s):** heated outdoor. **Guest Services:** coin laundry. **Business
Services:** meeting rooms. **Cards:** AX, DS, MC, VI.

SOME UNITS

🅐🆂🅺 🆂🅳 🐾 🍽 🏊 🎥 📶 🖨 🖭 / ✕ /
FEE

ECONOMY INN

[AAA] [SAVE]

Motel

Phone: 620/672-5588

All Year | 1P: $32-$42 | 2P: $45-$65 | XP: $8 | F8

Location: 1 mi e on US 54. 1401 E 1st St 67124. Fax: 620/672-1176. **Facility:** 25 units one-bedroom standard units. 1 story, exterior corridors. **Bath:** combo or shower only. **Parking:** on-site. **Terms:** 4 day cancellation notice-fee imposed, pets ($3 extra charge). **Amenities:** hair dryers. **Pool(s):** outdoor. **Guest Services:** coin laundry. **Cards:** AX, DS, MC, VI. **Free Special Amenities: continental breakfast and local telephone calls.**

SOME UNITS

EVERGREEN INN

Motel

DS, MC, VI.

Phone: 620/672-6431

All Year | 1P: $38-$45 | 2P: $50-$65 | XP: $5 | F6

Location: On US 54, 3 mi w. 20001 W US Hwy 54 67124. Fax: 620/672-5766. **Facility:** 16 one-bedroom standard units. 1 story, exterior corridors. **Bath:** combo or shower only. **Parking:** on-site, winter plug-ins. **Terms:** weekly rates available, pets ($5 fee). **Pool(s):** outdoor. **Guest Services:** coin laundry. **Cards:** AX, DS, MC, VI.

SOME UNITS

LEISURE HOTEL *Book at AAA.com*

Small-scale Hotel

wireless Internet.

Phone: (620)672-9433

All Year [ECP] | 1P: $80-$92 | | XP: $10 | F18

Location: On US 54, 2 mi w. 1401 W Hwy 54 67124. Fax: 620/672-2429. **Facility:** 67 one-bedroom standard units. 2 stories (no elevator), interior corridors. **Bath:** combo or shower only. **Parking:** on-site, winter plug-ins. **Amenities:** voice mail, irons, hair dryers. **Pool(s):** small heated indoor. **Guest Services:** valet laundry, wireless Internet. **Business Services:** meeting rooms. **Cards:** AX, CB, DC, DS, MC, VI.

SOME UNITS

SUPER 8 MOTEL OF PRATT *Book at AAA.com*

Small-scale Hotel

Phone: (620)672-5945

3/1-10/1 | 1P: $55-$59 | 2P: $55-$59 | XP: $5 | F17
10/2-2/29 | 1P: $50-$55 | 2P: $50-$55 | XP: $5 | F17

Location: 1.7 mi e on US 54. 1906 E 1st St 67124. Fax: 620/672-2969. **Facility:** 45 one-bedroom standard units. 2 stories (no elevator), interior corridors. **Parking:** on-site, winter plug-ins. **Terms:** small pets only ($5 fee). **Amenities:** high-speed Internet. **Leisure Activities:** whirlpool. **Business Services:** PC. **Cards:** AX, DC, DS, MC, VI.

SOME UNITS

──────── **WHERE TO DINE** ────────

PLAYA AZUL

Mexican

Lunch: $4-$6 | Dinner: $5-$9 | Phone: 620/672-1217

Location: 0.9 mi e on US 54. 1413 E 1st St 67124. **Hours:** 11 am-9:30 pm, Fri & Sat-10:30 pm, Sun-8:30 pm. Closed: 11/22, 12/25. **Features:** A straightforward and basic approach applies to both food presentation and service. Typical Mexican dishes make up the menu. Casual dress. **Parking:** on-site. **Cards:** AX, DS, MC, VI.

RICK'S

American

Lunch: $5-$16 | Dinner: $5-$16 | Phone: 620/672-3681

Location: 3 mi w. 20005 W Hwy 54 67124. **Hours:** 6 am-9 pm. Closed major holidays. **Features:** This locally popular restaurant features a home-style cuisine and a casual atmosphere that's great for birthday celebrations and special occasions. The standard cafe fare offers seafood, beef dishes, pasta and sandwiches. Casual dress. **Parking:** on-site. **Cards:** AX, DS, MC, VI.

RUSSELL pop. 4,696

──────── **WHERE TO STAY** ────────

AMERICINN LODGE & SUITES *Book at AAA.com*

Small-scale Hotel

Phone: (785)483-4200

All Year [ECP] | 1P: $75-$95 | 2P: $75-$95 | XP: $6 | F12

Location: I-70, exit 184 (US 281), just n. 1430 S Fossil St 67665. Fax: 785/483-4249. **Facility:** 54 units. 45 one-bedroom standard units, some with whirlpools. 9 one-bedroom suites ($75-$150), some with whirlpools. 3 stories, interior corridors. **Bath:** combo or shower only. **Parking:** on-site. **Terms:** package plans, pets ($10 extra charge, in limited units). **Amenities:** high-speed Internet (fee), dual phone lines, voice mail, irons, hair dryers. *Some:* DVD players, CD players. **Pool(s):** heated indoor, wading. **Leisure Activities:** sauna, whirlpool, exercise room. **Guest Services:** gift shop, valet and coin laundry. **Business Services:** conference facilities, business center. **Cards:** AX, DC, DS, MC, VI. *(See color ad p 373)*

SOME UNITS

DAYS INN *Book great rates at AAA.com*

Motel

Services: PC.

Phone: 785/483-6660

Property failed to provide current rates

Location: I-70, exit 184 (US 281), just n. 1225 S Fossil St 67665. Fax: 785/483-6660. **Facility:** 49 one-bedroom standard units. 2 stories (no elevator), exterior corridors. **Parking:** on-site, winter plug-ins. **Terms:** pets ($5 extra charge). **Amenities:** hair dryers. **Pool(s):** small outdoor. **Guest Services:** wireless Internet. **Business Services:** PC.

SOME UNITS

MERIDY'S

American

———— WHERE TO DINE ————

Lunch: $6-$10   **Dinner:** $6-$27   **Phone:** 785/483-4300

Location: I-70, exit 184 (US 281), just n. 1220 S Fossil St 67665. **Hours:** 6 am-10 pm. Closed: 11/22, 12/24, 12/25. **Reservations:** accepted. **Features:** This local favorite is known for its down-home cooking and friendly, casual atmosphere. The restaurant proudly serves breakfast, lunch and dinner and features freshly cut steaks and a daily buffet. Casual dress; cocktails. **Parking:** on-site. **Cards:** AX, DS, MC, VI.

SABETHA pop. 2,589

———— WHERE TO STAY ————

The following lodging was either not evaluated or did not meet AAA rating requirements but is listed for your information only.

SABETHA COUNTRY INN   **Phone:** 785/284-2300

[fyi]

Small-scale Hotel

Did not meet all AAA rating requirements for some property operations at time of last evaluation on 09/27/2005. **Location:** US 75, 1 mi s of jct SR 246 and US 75. 1423 S 75 Hwy 66534 (PO Box 44). Facilities, services, and decor characterize a mid-range property.

———— WHERE TO DINE ————

DIECK'S STEAK HOUSE & LOUNGE

American

Lunch: $5-$10   **Dinner:** $10-$15   **Phone:** 785/284-0555

Location: US 75, 1.2 mi s of jct SR 246 and US 75. 1619 S Hwy 75 66534. **Hours:** 11 am-2 & 5-9 pm, Fri & Sat-10 pm. Closed major holidays; also Sun. **Features:** Among choices on the varied menu are several steaks, as well as chicken and seafood preparations. The wait staff is friendly and attentive. Casual dress; cocktails. **Parking:** on-site. **Cards:** DS, MC, VI.

SALINA pop. 45,679

———— WHERE TO STAY ————

AMERICAS BEST INN   *Book at AAA.com*   **Phone:** (785)825-2500

Small-scale Hotel

All Year [CP]   1P: $50-$56   2P: $56-$66   F16

Location: I-70, exit 252, just n. 429 W Diamond Dr 67401. Fax: 785/825-1496. **Facility:** 35 units. 34 one-bedroom standard units. 1 one-bedroom suite. 2 stories (no elevator), interior corridors. **Parking:** on-site. **Terms:** pets ($5 fee). **Amenities:** high-speed Internet. **Guest Services:** coin laundry. **Business Services:** PC. **Cards:** AX, DC, DS, MC, VI.

SOME UNITS

BAYMONT INN & SUITES   *Book at AAA.com*   **Phone:** 785/493-9800

Small-scale Hotel

Property failed to provide current rates

Location: I-135, exit 89 (Schilling Rd), just w. 745 W Schilling Rd 67401. Fax: 785/493-8085. **Facility:** 53 units. 34 one-bedroom standard units. 19 one-bedroom suites, some with whirlpools. 2 stories, interior corridors. *Bath:* combo or shower only. **Parking:** on-site. **Terms:** small pets only ($10 fee). **Amenities:** high-speed Internet, voice mail, irons, hair dryers. **Pool(s):** small heated indoor. **Leisure Activities:** whirlpool, waterslide, limited exercise equipment. **Guest Services:** valet and coin laundry.

SOME UNITS

BEST WESTERN MID-AMERICA INN   *Book great rates at AAA.com*   **Phone:** (785)827-0356

Small-scale Hotel

6/1-10/31   1P: $50-$82   2P: $60-$85   XP: $3   F
3/1-5/31 & 11/1-2/29   1P: $50-$79   2P: $60-$82   XP: $3   F

Location: I-70, exit 252, just s. 1846 N 9th St 67401 (PO Box 132). Fax: 785/827-7688. **Facility:** 108 one-bedroom standard units. 2 stories (no elevator), exterior corridors. *Bath:* combo or shower only. **Parking:** on-site, winter plug-ins. **Terms:** cancellation fee imposed, pets ($50 deposit). **Amenities:** irons, hair dryers. *Some:* high-speed Internet. **Dining:** 5 pm-10 pm, cocktails. **Pool(s):** small outdoor, heated indoor. **Leisure Activities:** whirlpool. **Business Services:** meeting rooms. **Cards:** AX, CB, DC, DS, MC, VI.

SOME UNITS

CANDLEWOOD SUITES   *Book at AAA.com*   **Phone:** (785)823-6939

Small-scale Hotel

All Year   1P: $49-$129   2P: $49-$129

Location: I-135, exit 89 (Schilling Rd), just e to S 9th St, 0.5 mi n to Belmont, then just w. 2650 Planet Ave 67401. Fax: 785/823-9679. **Facility:** 69 one-bedroom standard units with efficiencies. 3 stories, interior corridors. *Bath:* combo or shower only. **Parking:** on-site. **Terms:** cancellation fee imposed, weekly rates available, pets ($20 extra charge). **Amenities:** video library, DVD players, CD players, high-speed Internet, dual phone lines, voice mail, irons, hair dryers. **Leisure Activities:** exercise room. **Guest Services:** valet and coin laundry. **Business Services:** meeting rooms, business center. **Cards:** AX, CB, DC, DS, JC, MC, VI.

SOME UNITS

COMFORT INN   *Book great rates at AAA.com*   **Phone:** (785)826-1711

Small-scale Hotel

All Year   1P: $60-$120   2P: $60-$120

Location: I-135, exit 92, just e. 1820 W Crawford St 67401. Fax: 785/827-6530. **Facility:** 60 one-bedroom standard units. 2 stories (no elevator), interior corridors. **Parking:** on-site. **Terms:** package plans, pets ($10-$20 extra charge). **Amenities:** high-speed Internet, safes (fee), irons, hair dryers. **Pool(s):** small heated indoor. **Leisure Activities:** whirlpool. **Cards:** AX, DS, MC, VI.

SOME UNITS

COUNTRY INN & SUITES BY CARLSON
Book great rates at AAA.com   Phone: (785)827-1271

(AAA) [SAVE]

6/2-8/20 [CP]	1P: $94-$155	2P: $94-$155	XP: $10	F18
8/21-2/29 [CP]	1P: $92-$155	2P: $92-$155	XP: $10	F18
3/1-6/1 [CP]	1P: $89-$150	2P: $89-$150	XP: $10	F18

Small-scale Hotel   **Location:** I-135, exit 89 (Schilling Rd), just e, then 0.3 mi n. 2760 S 9th St 67401. Fax: 785/827-1537. **Facility:** 72 units. 40 one-bedroom standard units, some with whirlpools. 32 one-bedroom suites. 3 stories, interior corridors. *Bath:* combo or shower only. **Parking:** on-site. **Terms:** package plans. **Amenities:** high-speed Internet, dual phone lines, voice mail, irons, hair dryers. *Some:* DVD players. **Pool(s):** small heated indoor. **Leisure Activities:** whirlpool, exercise room. **Guest Services:** valet and coin laundry. **Business Services:** meeting rooms. **Cards:** AX, CB, DC, DS, MC, VI. **Free Special Amenities: newspaper and early check-in/late check-out.**

SOME UNITS

COURTYARD BY MARRIOTT
Book great rates at AAA.com   Phone: (785)309-1300

All Year	1P: $99-$129	2P: $99-$129	XP: $10

Small-scale Hotel   **Location:** I-135, exit 89, just e. 3020 Riffel Dr 67401. Fax: 785/309-1315. **Facility:** Smoke free premises. 80 units. 77 one-bedroom standard units, some with whirlpools. 3 stories, interior corridors. *Bath:* combo or shower only. **Parking:** on-site. **Terms:** [BP] meal plan available, package plans. **Amenities:** high-speed Internet, voice mail, irons, hair dryers. **Pool(s):** small heated indoor. **Leisure Activities:** whirlpool, exercise room. **Guest Services:** valet and coin laundry, wireless Internet. **Business Services:** meeting rooms, business center. **Cards:** AX, CB, DC, DS, JC, MC, VI.

DAYS INN SALINA
Book great rates at AAA.com   Phone: (785)823-9791

6/2-10/1	1P: $44-$94	2P: $49-$99	XP: $5	F17
3/1-6/1 & 10/2-2/29	1P: $39-$69	2P: $44-$74	XP: $5	F17

Small-scale Hotel   **Location:** I-70, exit 252, just n. 407 W Diamond Dr 67401. Fax: 785/823-2211. **Facility:** 45 one-bedroom standard units. 2 stories (no elevator), interior corridors. **Parking:** on-site. **Amenities:** high-speed Internet, hair dryers. **Pool(s):** small heated indoor. **Leisure Activities:** whirlpool. **Cards:** AX, CB, DC, DS, JC, MC, VI.

SOME UNITS

ECONOLODGE
Book great rates at AAA.com   Phone: (785)825-8211

(AAA) [SAVE]

All Year	1P: $55-$65	2P: $60-$70	XP: $5	F12

Small-scale Hotel   **Location:** I-70, exit 252, just s. 1949 N 9th St 67401. Fax: 785/825-1048. **Facility:** 103 one-bedroom standard units, some with whirlpools. 2 stories (no elevator), exterior corridors. **Parking:** on-site, winter plug-ins. **Terms:** small pets only ($10 deposit, $5 extra charge). **Amenities:** voice mail, irons, hair dryers. *Some:* high-speed Internet. **Pool(s):** heated outdoor. **Business Services:** meeting rooms, PC. **Cards:** AX, DC, DS, MC, VI. **Free Special Amenities: continental breakfast and high-speed Internet.**

SOME UNITS

FEE

HAMPTON INN-SALINA
Book great rates at AAA.com   Phone: 785/823-9800

All Year [ECP]	1P: $85-$105	2P: $95-$125	XP: $10	F18

Small-scale Hotel   **Location:** I-135, exit 89 (Schilling Rd), just e. 401 W Schilling Rd 67401. Fax: 785/823-9808. **Facility:** 68 one-bedroom standard units. 3 stories, interior corridors. *Bath:* combo or shower only. **Parking:** on-site. **Amenities:** high-speed Internet, voice mail, irons, hair dryers. **Pool(s):** heated indoor. **Leisure Activities:** whirlpool, exercise room. **Guest Services:** valet and coin laundry. **Business Services:** meeting rooms. **Cards:** AX, DC, DS, MC, VI.

SOME UNITS

HOLIDAY INN EXPRESS HOTEL & SUITES-SALINA
Book at AAA.com   Phone: 785/827-9000

Property failed to provide current rates

Small-scale Hotel   **Location:** I-70, exit 252, just ne. 201 E Diamond Dr 67401. Fax: 785/827-9393. **Facility:** 93 units. 91 one-bedroom standard units, some with whirlpools. 2 one-bedroom suites with whirlpools. 3 stories, interior corridors. *Bath:* combo or shower only. **Parking:** on-site. **Terms:** small pets only ($10 extra charge). **Amenities:** video games, high-speed Internet, voice mail, irons, hair dryers. *Some:* dual phone lines. **Pool(s):** small heated indoor. **Leisure Activities:** exercise room. **Guest Services:** valet and coin laundry. **Business Services:** meeting rooms.

SOME UNITS

FEE

HOLIDAY INN OF SALINA
Book at AAA.com   Phone: 785/823-1739

Property failed to provide current rates

Small-scale Hotel   **Location:** I-135, exit 92, 0.5 mi e. 1616 W Crawford St 67401. Fax: 785/823-1791. **Facility:** 192 units. 183 one-bedroom standard units. 9 one-bedroom suites, some with whirlpools. 3 stories, interior corridors. *Bath:* combo or shower only. **Parking:** on-site. **Terms:** check-in 4 pm, pets ($25 fee). **Amenities:** video games (fee), voice mail, irons, hair dryers. **Pool(s):** heated indoor. **Leisure Activities:** sauna, whirlpool, waterslide, exercise room. *Fee:* game room. **Guest Services:** gift shop, valet and coin laundry, area transportation, wireless Internet. **Business Services:** conference facilities.

SOME UNITS

FEE

RED COACH INN
    Phone: 785/825-2111

3/1-9/16	1P: $59-$99	2P: $69-$109	XP: $8	F12
9/17-2/29	1P: $49-$89	2P: $59-$99	XP: $8	F12

Small-scale Hotel   **Location:** I-135, exit 92, just w. 2110 W Crawford St 67401. Fax: 785/825-6973. **Facility:** 112 one-bedroom standard units, some with whirlpools. 2 stories (no elevator), interior corridors. *Bath:* combo or shower only. **Parking:** on-site. **Terms:** cancellation fee imposed, [CP] meal plan available, package plans, pets ($15 fee, in smoking units). **Amenities:** high-speed Internet, voice mail, irons, hair dryers. **Pool(s):** heated indoor. **Leisure Activities:** sauna, whirlpool, putting green, 2 lighted tennis courts. *Fee:* game room. **Guest Services:** coin laundry. **Business Services:** conference facilities. **Cards:** AX, CB, DC, DS, JC, MC, VI.

SOME UNITS

FEE

SUPER 8 I-70
Book great rates at AAA.com

Phone: 785/823-8808

4/1-2/29 [CP]	1P: $61-$78	2P: $63-$82	XP: $5 F17
3/1-3/31 [CP]	1P: $59-$72	2P: $61-$75	XP: $5 F17

Location: I-70, exit 252, just ne. 120 E Diamond Dr 67401. **Fax:** 785/823-8899. **Facility:** 49 one-bedroom standard units. 2 stories (no elevator), interior corridors. *Bath:* combo or shower only. **Parking:** on-site, winter plug-ins. **Terms:** pets ($5 extra charge). **Amenities:** high-speed Internet, hair dryers. *Some:* irons. **Pool(s):** small heated indoor. **Leisure Activities:** whirlpool. **Guest Services:** coin laundry. **Cards:** AX, DS, MC, VI. **Free Special Amenities:** expanded continental breakfast and high-speed Internet.

Small-scale Hotel

SOME UNITS

The following lodging was either not evaluated or did not meet AAA rating requirements but is listed for your information only.

FAIRFIELD INN
[fyi]
Small-scale Hotel

Phone: 785/823-6900

Did not meet all AAA rating requirements for some property operations at time of last evaluation on 03/08/2006. **Location:** I-135, exit 92, 0.3 mi e. 1740 W Crawford St 67401. Facilities, services, and decor characterize a mid-range property.

WHERE TO DINE

DAIMARU STEAK HOUSE
Japanese

Lunch: $6-$8   **Dinner: $9-$20**   **Phone: 785/820-5500**

Location: I-135, exit 92, 0.5 mi e. 1601 W Crawford St 67401. **Hours:** 11 am-2:30 & 4:30-10 pm, Fri-10:30 pm, Sat noon-10:30 pm, Sun noon-9 pm. Closed major holidays. **Features:** Examples of the many lunch and dinner combinations include lobster and top sirloin or rib-eye and shrimp. Children's selections are available. Sake is worth a try. Casual dress; beer & wine only. **Parking:** on-site. **Cards:** AX, DS, MC, VI.

RUSSELL'S RESTAURANT
American

Lunch: $7-$18   **Dinner: $7-$18**   **Phone: 785/825-5733**

Location: I-135, exit 92, just ne. 649 Westport Blvd 67401. **Hours:** 24 hours. **Reservations:** accepted. **Features:** Russell's casual diner features an extensive, wholesome menu that's appealing to locals and travelers alike. You might try the chicken-fried steak, catfish, or the choice aged Kansas City strip, but be sure to save room for the homemade pies. Casual dress. **Parking:** on-site. **Cards:** AX, DS, MC, VI.

The following restaurant has not been evaluated by AAA but is listed for your information only.

HONG KONG BUFFET
[fyi]

Phone: 785/820-8683

Not evaluated. **Location:** I-135, exit 89, just e to 9th St, then 0.5 mi n. 2445 S 9th St 67401. **Features:** An all-you-can-eat buffet is offered at lunch and dinner along with a long list of dishes on the menu; no MSG and low salt in all cuisine.

SHARON SPRINGS pop. 835

WHERE TO STAY

OAK TREE INN
Book at AAA.com
Small-scale Hotel

Phone: (785)852-4664

All Year [BP]   1P: $73-$79   2P: $73-$79

Location: Jct US 40 and SR 27. 801 N Hwy 27 67758. **Fax:** 785/852-4665. **Facility:** Smoke free premises. 50 one-bedroom standard units. 2 stories (no elevator), interior/exterior corridors. *Bath:* combo or shower only. **Parking:** on-site, winter plug-ins. **Terms:** pets ($5 deposit). **Amenities:** *Some:* irons, hair dryers. **Leisure Activities:** whirlpool, exercise room. **Guest Services:** sundries, coin laundry. **Business Services:** meeting rooms. **Cards:** AX, CB, DC, DS, JC, MC, VI.

SOME UNITS

SHAWNEE —See Kansas City p. 487.

SMITH CENTER pop. 1,931

WHERE TO STAY

U.S. CENTER MOTEL
Motel

Phone: (785)282-6611

3/1-3/31 & 1/1-2/29	1P: $30-$36	2P: $36-$42	XP: $6 F16
4/1-12/31	1P: $36	2P: $42	XP: $6 F16

Location: Jct US 36 and 281. 116 E Hwy 36 66967. **Fax:** 785/282-9116. **Facility:** 21 units. 19 one- and 2 two-bedroom standard units. 1 story, exterior corridors. *Bath:* shower only. **Parking:** on-site, winter plug-ins. **Terms:** office hours 6 am-11 pm, pets ($5 extra charge). **Pool(s):** heated indoor. **Guest Services:** coin laundry, wireless Internet. **Business Services:** PC, fax. **Cards:** AX, DS, MC, VI. **Free Special Amenities:** local telephone calls.

SOME UNITS

TOPEKA pop. 122,377

—— WHERE TO STAY ——

BEST WESTERN CANDLELIGHT INN   *Book great rates at AAA.com*   **Phone:** (785)272-9550

3/1-10/31	1P: $49-$139	2P: $55-$139	XP: $8 F12
11/1-2/29	1P: $49-$79	2P: $55-$79	XP: $8 F12

Motel   **Location:** I-470, exit 3. 2831 SW Fairlawn Rd 66614. **Fax:** 785/272-8242. **Facility:** 97 one-bedroom standard units, some with whirlpools. 2 stories (no elevator), exterior corridors. *Bath:* combo or shower only. **Parking:** on-site. **Terms:** [CP] meal plan available, pets ($8 extra charge). **Amenities:** high-speed Internet, irons, hair dryers. *Some:* DVD players (fee). **Pool(s):** heated outdoor. **Leisure Activities:** whirlpool, playground, exercise room, basketball. **Guest Services:** valet and coin laundry, wireless Internet. **Business Services:** meeting rooms, business center. **Cards:** AX, DC, DS, MC, VI.

SOME UNITS
ASK 🐾 🍽 🖥 🛳 ✕ 🐕 🖥 / ✕ VCR 🔋 📷 /
FEE   FEE

CAPITOL PLAZA HOTEL   *Book great rates at AAA.com*   **Phone:** (785)431-7200

All Year   1P: $99-$114   2P: $99-$114   XP: $10   F18

Large-scale Hotel   **Location:** I-70, exit SE 8th Ave, 1.6 mi s; I-470, exit Topeka Blvd, 2.9 mi n. 1717 SW Topeka Blvd 66612. **Fax:** 785/431-7206. **Facility:** 224 units. 215 one-bedroom standard units. 9 one-bedroom suites, some with whirlpools. 7 stories, interior corridors. *Bath:* combo or shower only. **Parking:** on-site. **Terms:** cancellation fee imposed. **Amenities:** video games, high-speed Internet, voice mail, irons, hair dryers. **Dining:** 6 am-2 & 5-10 pm, cocktails. **Pool(s):** heated indoor. **Leisure Activities:** sauna, whirlpool, exercise room. **Guest Services:** gift shop, valet and coin laundry, area transportation-within city limits, wireless Internet. **Business Services:** conference facilities, business center. **Cards:** AX, DC, DS, MC, VI. **Free Special Amenities:** newspaper.
(See color ad below)

SOME UNITS
✈ 🐾 🍽 🍸 🄼 🖥 🌀 🛳 ✕ 🐕 🖥 / ✕ 🔋 📷 /

CLUBHOUSE INN & SUITES   *Book great rates at AAA.com*   **Phone:** (785)273-8888

All Year [BP]   1P: $109-$125   2P: $109-$125   XP: $10   F19

Small-scale Hotel   **Location:** I-70, exit 356 (Wanamaker Rd). 924 SW Henderson 66615. **Fax:** 785/273-5809. **Facility:** 121 units. 104 one-bedroom standard units. 17 one-bedroom suites, some with whirlpools. 2 stories (no elevator), interior corridors. *Bath:* combo or shower only. **Parking:** on-site. **Terms:** small pets only ($10 extra charge). **Amenities:** high-speed Internet, voice mail, irons, hair dryers. **Pool(s):** small heated outdoor. **Leisure Activities:** whirlpool. **Guest Services:** complimentary evening beverages: Mon-Sat, valet and coin laundry, wireless Internet. **Business Services:** meeting rooms, PC. **Cards:** AX, DC, DS, JC, MC, VI. **Free Special Amenities:** expanded continental breakfast and high-speed Internet. (See color ad below)

SOME UNITS
🄢 🐾 🍽 🖥 🌀 🛳 🐕 🖥 / ✕ 🔋 📷 /
FEE

COMFORT INN BY CHOICE HOTELS — *Book great rates at AAA.com* — Phone: (785)273-5365
WWW WWW All Year 1P: $65-$85 2P: $70-$90 XP: $5 F18
Location: I-470, exit 1 (Wanamaker Rd). 1518 SW Wanamaker Rd 66604. Fax: 785/273-5365. **Facility:** 66 one-bedroom standard units. 2 stories (no elevator), interior corridors. **Parking:** on-site. **Terms:** small pets only ($10 extra charge, in smoking units). **Amenities:** *Some:* irons, hair dryers. **Pool(s):** small heated indoor.
Small-scale Hotel
Leisure Activities: whirlpool. **Guest Services:** wireless Internet. **Cards:** AX, DS, MC, VI.
SOME UNITS

COUNTRY INN & SUITES BY — *Book at AAA.com* — Phone: (785)478-9800
CARLSON-TOPEKA-WEST
WWWWW 1P: $79-$150 2P: $79-$150
Location: I-70, exit 356 (Wanamaker Rd). 6020 SW 10th St 66615 (5707 SW 37th Terrace, 66610).
Small-scale Hotel Fax: 785/478-6812. **Facility:** 58 units. 43 one-bedroom standard units, some with whirlpools. 15 one-bedroom suites, some with whirlpools. 3 stories, interior corridors. *Bath:* combo or shower only. **Parking:** on-site. **Terms:** [ECP] meal plan available, package plans, pets ($10 extra charge, in smoking units). **Amenities:** high-speed Internet, voice mail, irons, hair dryers. **Pool(s):** heated indoor. **Leisure Activities:** whirlpool, exercise room. **Guest Services:** coin laundry, wireless Internet. **Cards:** AX, DC, DS, MC, VI.
SOME UNITS

COURTYARD BY MARRIOTT — *Book great rates at AAA.com* — Phone: (785)271-6165
WWW WWW All Year 1P: $100-$160 2P: $105-$165 XP: $5 F18
Location: I-70, exit 356 (Wanamaker Rd), 1.5 mi s. 2033 SW Wanamaker Rd 66604. Fax: 785/228-9712. **Facility:** Smoke free premises. 90 units. 87 one-bedroom standard units. 3 one-bedroom suites. 3 stories, interior corridors. *Bath:* combo or shower only. **Parking:** on-site. **Amenities:** high-speed Internet, dual phone lines, voice mail, irons, hair dryers. **Pool(s):** heated indoor. **Leisure Activities:** whirlpool, exercise room. **Guest Services:** valet and coin laundry, wireless Internet. **Business Services:** meeting rooms, business center. **Cards:** AX, DC, DS, MC, VI.
SOME UNITS

FAIRFIELD INN BY MARRIOTT — *Book great rates at AAA.com* — Phone: (785)273-6800
WWW WWW All Year 1P: $75-$95 2P: $80-$100 XP: $5 F18
Location: I-470, exit 1 (Wanamaker Rd). 1530 SW Westport Dr 66604. Fax: 785/273-6800. **Facility:** Smoke free premises. 62 one-bedroom standard units. 3 stories, interior corridors. **Parking:** on-site. **Amenities:** irons, hair dryers. **Pool(s):** small heated indoor. **Leisure Activities:** whirlpool. **Guest Services:** valet laundry, wireless Internet. **Cards:** AX, DC, DS, MC, VI.
SOME UNITS

HAMPTON INN-TOPEKA — *Book great rates at AAA.com* — Phone: 785/273-0003
WWW WWW All Year 1P: $71-$110 2P: $75-$120
Location: I-470, exit 1 (Wanamaker Rd), just ne; I-70, exit 356A (Wanamaker Rd), 1 mi s. 1401 SW Ashworth Pl 66604.
Small-scale Hotel Fax: 785/273-3030. **Facility:** 62 one-bedroom standard units. 2 stories (no elevator), exterior corridors. *Bath:* combo or shower only. **Parking:** on-site. **Amenities:** voice mail, irons, hair dryers. **Pool(s):** small outdoor. **Leisure Activities:** whirlpool, exercise room. **Guest Services:** valet laundry, wireless Internet. **Cards:** AX, DC, DS, MC, VI.
SOME UNITS

HOLIDAY INN EXPRESS HOTEL & SUITES — *Book at AAA.com* — Phone: (785)228-9500
WWW WWW All Year 1P: $94
Location: I-70, exit 356 (Wanamaker Rd), just se. 901 SW Robinson Ave 66606. Fax: 785/228-3500. **Facility:** 81 units. 80 one-bedroom standard units, some with whirlpools. 1 one-bedroom suite with whirlpool. 3 stories, interior corridors. *Bath:* combo or shower only. **Parking:** on-site. **Terms:** [ECP] meal plan available. **Amenities:** high-speed Internet, dual phone lines, voice mail, irons, hair dryers. *Some:* CD players. **Pool(s):** small heated indoor. **Leisure Activities:** whirlpool, exercise room. *Fee:* game room. **Guest Services:** valet and coin laundry. **Business Services:** meeting rooms, business center. **Cards:** AX, CB, DC, DS, JC, MC, VI.
SOME UNITS

HOLIDAY INN HOLIDOME — *Book at AAA.com* — Phone: (785)272-8040
WWW WWW All Year 1P: $84-$89 2P: $84-$89 XP: $10 F17
Location: I-70, exit 357A, just sw. 605 Fairlawn Rd 66606. Fax: 785/272-8065. **Facility:** 197 units. 189 one-bedroom standard units, some with whirlpools. 8 one-bedroom suites. 2-4 stories, interior/exterior corridors. *Bath:* combo or shower only. **Parking:** on-site. **Terms:** check-in 4 pm, [BP] meal plan available. **Amenities:** high-speed Internet, dual phone lines, voice mail, irons, hair dryers. **Pool(s):** heated indoor. **Leisure Activities:** sauna, whirlpool, exercise room. *Fee:* game room. **Guest Services:** valet and coin laundry, wireless Internet. **Business Services:** conference facilities, business center. **Cards:** AX, CB, DC, DS, JC, MC, VI.
SOME UNITS

HYATT PLACE TOPEKA/NORTHWEST — *Book great rates at AAA.com* — Phone: (785)273-0066
AAA SAVE All Year [CP] 1P: $79-$149 2P: $79-$149 XP: $10 F17
WWW WWW **Location:** I-70, exit 356 (Wanamaker Rd), just n. 6021 SW Sixth Ave 66615. Fax: 785/273-1423. **Facility:** 128 one-bedroom suites. 6 stories, interior corridors. *Bath:* combo or shower only. **Parking:** on-site.
Small-scale Hotel **Terms:** cancellation fee imposed, small pets only ($10 extra charge). **Amenities:** voice mail, safes (fee), irons, hair dryers. *Some:* high-speed Internet, dual phone lines. **Pool(s):** small heated outdoor. **Leisure Activities:** exercise room. **Guest Services:** complimentary evening beverages: Wed, valet and coin laundry, area transportation-within 5 mi, wireless Internet. **Business Services:** meeting rooms. **Cards:** AX, CB, DC, DS, JC, MC, VI. **Free Special Amenities:** full breakfast and high-speed Internet.
SOME UNITS

QUALITY INN   *Book great rates at AAA.com*

Phone: (785)273-696█

AAA [SAVE]

5/1-10/31	1P: $59-$119	2P: $64-$129	XP: $5	D1█
3/1-4/30	1P: $55-$89	2P: $59-$99	XP: $5	D1█
11/1-2/29	1P: $49-$89	2P: $54-$89	XP: $5	D1█

◇◇◇◇

Small-scale Hotel

Location: I-470, exit 1 (Wanamaker Rd), just ne; I-70, exit 356A (Wanamaker Rd), 1 mi s. 1240 SW Wanamaker Rd 66604. **Fax:** 785-273-6036. **Facility:** 47 one-bedroom standard units. 3 stories, interior corridors. **Parking:** on-site. **Terms:** 5 day cancellation notice-fee imposed, package plans, pets ($5 extra charge). **Amenities:** irons, hair dryers. *Some:* high-speed Internet. **Pool(s):** small heated indoor. **Leisure Activities:** whirlpool. **Guest Services:** valet and coin laundry, wireless Internet. **Business Services:** meeting rooms. **Cards:** AX, DC, DS, MC, VI. **Free Special Amenities:** expanded continental breakfast and high-speed Internet.

SOME UNITS

[icons] S D ⊓ ⑪ ⊘ ⊇ ⊛ 🖵 / ✕ 🛢 📠 / FEE

RAMADA DOWNTOWN HOTEL & CONVENTION CENTER   *Book at AAA.com*

Phone: (785)234-540█

◇◇◇◇

Large-scale Hotel

All Year [BP]   1P: $59-$109   2P: $59-$109

Location: I-70, exit 362B, just e. 420 SE Sixth St 66607. **Fax:** 785/233-0460. **Facility:** 250 units. 226 one-bedroom standard units. 24 one-bedroom suites, some with kitchens and/or whirlpools. 11 stories, interior corridors. *Bath:* combo or shower only. **Parking:** on-site. **Terms:** small pets only. **Amenities:** voice mail, irons, hair dryers. *Some:* CD players, high-speed Internet. **Pool(s):** small outdoor, small heated indoor. **Leisure Activities:** sauna, whirlpool, exercise room. *Fee:* massage, game room. **Guest Services:** gift shop, valet and coin laundry, wireless Internet, beauty shop. **Business Services:** conference facilities, business center. **Cards:** AX, CB, DC, DS, JC, MC, VI.

SOME UNITS

[icons] (ASK) S D ⊓ ⑪ ⊻ ⊑M ⊛ ⊇ ✕ 🖵 / ✕ 🛢 📠 /

RESIDENCE INN BY MARRIOTT   *Book great rates at AAA.com*

Phone: (785)271-890█

◇◇◇

Small-scale Hotel

All Year   1P: $140-$180   2P: $145-$185   F1

Location: I-470, exit 1 (Wanamaker Rd), just se. 1620 SW Westport Dr 66604. **Fax:** 785/271-8903. **Facility:** Smoke-free premises. 66 units. 18 one-bedroom standard units with efficiencies. 36 one- and 12 two-bedroom suites, some with efficiencies or kitchens. 3 stories, interior corridors. *Bath:* combo or shower only. **Parking:** on-site. **Terms:** [BP] meal plan available, pets ($75 fee). **Amenities:** voice mail, irons, hair dryers. *Some:* high-speed Internet. **Pool(s):** small heated indoor. **Leisure Activities:** whirlpool, exercise room, sports court. **Guest Services:** valet and coin laundry, wireless Internet. **Cards:** AX, DC, DS, MC, VI.

[icons] (ASK) S D ⊓ ⑪ ⊑M ⊛ ⊘ ⊇ ✕ ✕ 🖵 🛢 📠 □ / FEE

THE SENATE LUXURY SUITES

Phone: 785/233-505█

◇◇◇

Historic
Small-scale Hotel

All Year   1P: $85-$120

Location: Just w of state capitol; downtown. 900 SW Tyler 66612. **Fax:** 785/233-1614. **Facility:** Contemporary rooms fill this historic hotel, built in 1928. 51 units. 18 one-bedroom standard units. 26 one- and 7 two-bedroom suites, some with whirlpools. 3 stories, interior corridors. **Parking:** on-site. **Terms:** [ECP] meal plan available, package plans, small pets only ($100 deposit, must be in kennel). **Amenities:** voice mail. *Some:* high-speed Internet. **Leisure Activities:** whirlpool, exercise room. **Guest Services:** valet and coin laundry, wireless Internet. **Business Services:** meeting rooms. **Cards:** AX, CB, DC, DS, JC, MC, VI.

SOME UNITS

[icons] (ASK) ⊓ ⑪ ⊻ ⊛ 🖵 / ✕ 🛢 📠 / FEE

SLEEP INN & SUITES
Book great rates at AAA.com

Phone: (785)228-2500

AAA [SAVE]

WWWW

5/1-8/31	1P: $59-$89	2P: $59-$89	XP: $5	F
3/1-4/30 & 9/1-2/29	1P: $49-$79	2P: $49-$79	XP: $5	F

Location: I-70, exit 356 (Wanamaker Rd), just s. 1024 SW Wanamaker Rd 66604. Fax: 785/228-2555. **Facility:** 60 one-bedroom standard units, some with whirlpools. 3 stories, interior corridors. *Bath:* combo or shower only. Small-scale Hotel **Parking:** on-site. **Terms:** pets ($10 extra charge). **Amenities:** high-speed Internet, voice mail, irons, hair dryers. **Pool(s):** small heated indoor. **Leisure Activities:** whirlpool, exercise room. **Guest Services:** coin aundry, wireless Internet. **Business Services:** meeting rooms, business center. **Cards:** AX, CB, DC, DS, JC, MC, VI. **Free Special Amenities:** expanded continental breakfast and high-speed Internet.

SOME UNITS

[icons] FEE / [X] /

SUPER 8 AT FORBES LANDING
Book great rates at AAA.com

Phone: (785)862-2222

AAA [SAVE]

WWWW

6/1-6/17	1P: $70-$140	2P: $70-$140	XP: $7	F17
3/1-5/31 & 6/18-2/29	1P: $70-$100	2P: $70-$100	XP: $7	F17

Location: I-470, exit 6, 2.2 mi s. 5922 S Topeka Blvd 66619. Fax: 785/862-2622. **Facility:** 63 units. 53 one-bedroom standard units, some with whirlpools. 10 one-bedroom suites ($90-$140). 3 stories, interior corridors. *Bath:* combo or shower only. **Parking:** on-site. **Terms:** package plans, pets ($20 fee). **Amenities:** high-speed Internet, voice mail, safes (fee), hair dryers. *Some:* DVD players (fee), irons. **Pool(s):** small heated indoor. **Guest Services:** coin laundry. **Business Services:** meeting rooms, PC. **Cards:** AX, CB, DC, DS, MC, VI. **Free Special Amenities:** expanded continental breakfast and high-speed Internet.

SOME UNITS

[icons] FEE / [X] [VCR] FEE /

──────── **WHERE TO DINE** ────────

ANNIE'S PLACE
Menu on AAA.com **Lunch:** $7-$10 **Dinner:** $7-$16 Phone: 785/273-0848

AAA

WWW

American

Location: I-70, exit 358B (Gage St), 1.5 mi s; in Gage Shopping Center. 4014 Gage Center Dr 66604. **Hours:** 11 am-9 pm. Closed major holidays. **Reservations:** accepted. **Features:** Breads and desserts are prepared in-house at Annie's Place, where the menu offers fresh food and a good variety. The servers are friendly and knowledgeable; the contemporary decor is simple and attractive; and the coconut cream pie tastes great! Casual dress; cocktails. **Parking:** on-site. **Cards:** AX, CB, DC, DS, MC, VI.

[icons]

BLIND TIGER BREWERY & RESTAURANT
Lunch: $6-$9 **Dinner:** $7-$17 Phone: 785/267-2739

WWW

American

Location: I-70, exit 358B, 0.4 mi n on Topeka Blvd, then just e. 417 SW 37th St 66611. **Hours:** 11 am-9 pm, Fri & Sat-10 pm. Closed: 11/22, 12/25. **Features:** Beers brewed on site and hickory-smoked meats are big features at the casual restaurant. You will have fun watching staff work the huge beer tanks, making several award-winning beers. Extensive list of entrees on menu. Relaxing and festive atmosphere in this rustic restaurant. Casual dress; cocktails. **Parking:** on-site. **Cards:** AX, DC, DS, MC, VI.

[icons]

BOSS HAWG'S BARBEQUE
Lunch: $6-$11 **Dinner:** $8-$21 Phone: 785/273-7300

AAA

WWW

American

Location: I-470, exit 3, 1.5 mi e; at Brookwood Shopping Center, on terrace. 2833 SW 29th St 66614. **Hours:** 11 am-9 pm, Fri & Sat-10 pm. Closed: 11/22, 12/25. **Features:** The barbecue eatery features reasonably priced food and a relaxed atmosphere. Service is fast and friendly. A good and wholesome family restaurant. Large list of entrees, including both barbecued items and others without the barbecue. Casual dress; cocktails. **Parking:** on-site. **Cards:** AX, DS, MC, VI.

[icons]

CHINA INN RESTAURANT & CLUB INC
Lunch: $7-$15 **Dinner:** $7-$15 Phone: 785/233-2319

WWW

Chinese

Location: I-70, exit 361A, 2 mi n of jct on Topeka Blvd. 2010 NW Central Ave 66608. **Hours:** 11 am-10 pm, Sat from 5 pm, Sun 11 am-9:30 pm. Closed: 12/20-1/4. **Features:** The China Inn serves an extensive menu of American and Chinese entrees. Generous portions and a relaxed atmosphere create a good dining experience at this restaurant. The chicken chow mein and egg foo yung are good choices. Casual dress; cocktails. **Parking:** on-site. **Cards:** AX, DC, DS, MC, VI.

[icons]

FRITZ CO. GRILLE
Lunch: $6-$17 **Dinner:** $8-$17 Phone: 785/273-7766

WWWW

American

Location: I-70, exit 356 (Wanamaker Rd), 1 mi s. 1717 SW Wanamaker Rd 66604. **Hours:** 11 am-10 pm, Fri & Sat-11 pm. Closed: 11/22, 12/25. **Features:** The eatery's sophisticated and creative dishes include such items as walnut shrimp cocktail, spinach and artichoke dip, espresso crusted New York strip, teriyaki beef kabobs and Sicilian meatloaf. Also offered are pastas, seafood, burgers, and sandwiches, as well as drink specials. Casual dress; cocktails. **Parking:** on-site. **Cards:** AX, CB, DC, DS, JC, MC, VI.

[icons]

PAISANO'S ITALIAN RISTORANTE
Lunch: $6-$9 **Dinner:** $8-$15 Phone: 785/273-0100

WWWW

Italian

Location: I-70, exit 358B (Gage St), 1 mi s; in Fleming Place Shopping Plaza. 4043 SW 10th Ave 66604. **Hours:** 11 am-10 pm, Fri & Sat-11 pm. Closed major holidays. **Features:** Paisano's has a warm and intimate atmosphere as the pleasant backdrop for serving its authentic cuisine. The Marco Polo fettucini Alfredo and lasagna are good choices, as is the primavera pasta for a vegetarian dish. Good beverage selection also. Casual dress; cocktails. **Parking:** on-site. **Cards:** AX, MC, VI.

[icons]

PAT'S PIG

American

Lunch: $4-$13   **Dinner:** $6-$13   **Phone:** 785/862-7427
Location: I-470, exit 6, 2 mi s. 5900 SW Topeka Blvd 66619. **Hours:** 11 am-9 pm, Fri & Sat-10 pm. Closed majo
holidays; also Sun. **Features:** If you're a drag-racing fan, you'll love this place. The walls are adorned with
photos of popular drag-racing stars, all have dined here. The restaurant features authentic hickory-smoke
barbecue in a relaxed atmosphere. Try the ribs served whole—wow! Casual dress; beer only. **Parking:** on
site. **Cards:** AX, DS, MC, VI.

TIMBERLINE STEAKHOUSE & GRILL

American

Lunch: $8-$20   **Dinner:** $8-$20   **Phone:** 785/228-1155
Location: I-70, exit 356 (Wanamaker Rd), 0.5 mi s. 1425 SW Wanamaker Rd 66615. **Hours:** 4 pm-10 pm, Fri-11
pm, Sat 11:30 am-11 pm, Sun 11:30 am-9 pm. Closed: 11/22, 12/25. **Features:** The casual restaurant's
menu features fresh-cut steaks, poultry, pork, ribs and seafood. Casual dress; cocktails. **Parking:** on-site
Cards: AX, DC, DS, MC, VI.

ULYSSES pop. 5,960

——— WHERE TO STAY ———

SINGLE TREE INN   *Book at AAA.com*

Small-scale Hotel

Phone: (620)356-1500
All Year [CP]   1P: $73-$84   XP: $5   F18
Location: 1.5 mi w on US 160. 2033 W Oklahoma St 67880. Fax: 620/356-5562. **Facility:** 43 one-bedroom
standard units, some with whirlpools. 2 stories (no elevator), interior corridors. **Parking:** on-site, winter plug
ins. **Terms:** small pets only ($25 deposit). **Amenities:** irons, hair dryers. **Guest Services:** coin laundry
wireless Internet. **Business Services:** meeting rooms. **Cards:** AX, CB, DC, DS, MC, VI.

SOME UNITS

UNIONTOWN pop. 288

——— WHERE TO STAY ———

WYATT EARP INN & B&B

Small-scale Hotel

Phone: (620)756-4990
11/16-12/15 [AP]   1P: $75-$125   2P: $85-$150   XP: $10   F12
3/1-11/15 & 12/16-2/29   1P: $50-$95   2P: $60-$110   XP: $10   F12
Location: On SR 3; on west side of town. 100 5th St 66779. Fax: 620/756-4994. **Facility:** 26 units. 25 one
bedroom standard units. 1 one-bedroom suite ($125-$200) with efficiency and whirlpool. 1 story, interio
corridors. **Bath:** combo or shower only. **Parking:** on-site. **Terms:** 30 day cancellation notice, seasonal, [AP], [BP], [CP], [ECP] &
[MAP] meal plans available, package plans, pets ($25 deposit, $10 extra charge). **Leisure Activities:** whirlpool. **Business**
Services: meeting rooms. **Cards:** AX, DS, MC, VI.

WAKEENEY pop. 1,924

——— WHERE TO STAY ———

SUPER 8 MOTEL   *Book at AAA.com*

Small-scale Hotel

Phone: (785)743-6442
5/16-9/15 [ECP]   1P: $50-$80   2P: $55-$85   XP: $5   F18
3/1-5/15 [ECP]   1P: $45-$70   2P: $50-$75   XP: $5   F18
9/16-2/29 [ECP]   1P: $40-$65   2P: $45-$70   XP: $5   F18
Location: I-70, exit 128, just n. 709 S 13th St 67672. Fax: 785/743-6628. **Facility:** 43 one-bedroom standard
units. 2 stories (no elevator), interior corridors. **Bath:** combo or shower only. **Parking:** on-site, winter plug-ins
Amenities: *Some:* hair dryers. **Leisure Activities:** whirlpool. **Guest Services:** coin laundry, wireless Internet. **Cards:** AX, CB
DC, DS, JC, MC, VI.

SOME UNITS

WAMEGO pop. 4,246

——— WHERE TO STAY ———

SIMMER MOTEL

Motel

Phone: (785)456-2304
All Year   1P: $39-$80   2P: $44-$90   XP: $5   F8
Location: Jct SR 99, 0.5 mi w. 1215 Hwy 24 W 66547. Fax: 785/456-8255. **Facility:** 34 units. 27 one-bedroom
standard units, some with whirlpools. 7 one-bedroom suites ($60-$160). 1 story, exterior corridors. **Parking:**
on-site. **Terms:** cancellation fee imposed, pets ($5 fee). **Amenities:** voice mail. **Pool(s):** small outdoor
Leisure Activities: playground. **Guest Services:** coin laundry, wireless Internet. **Cards:** AX, DC, DS
MC, VI. **Free Special Amenities:** local telephone calls and high-speed Internet.

SOME UNITS

WELLS

——— WHERE TO STAY ———

TRADER'S LODGE BED & BREAKFAST

Bed & Breakfast

Phone: 785/488-3930
All Year   1P: $65-$85   2P: $70-$90   XP: $10
Location: 2 mi n; stay on blacktop. Located in a quiet rural area. 1392 210th Rd 67467. **Facility:** Smoke free
premises. 4 one-bedroom standard units. 2 stories (no elevator), interior corridors. **Bath:** shower only
Parking: on-site. **Terms:** check-in 5 pm, 7 day cancellation notice. **Amenities:** hair dryers. **Leisure**
Activities: whirlpool, exercise room. **Guest Services:** TV in common area. **Cards:** AX, DS, MC, VI.

WICHITA pop. 344,284

─── **WHERE TO STAY** ───

BEST WESTERN AIRPORT INN & CONFERENCE CENTER *Book great rates at AAA.com* **Phone: (316)942-5600**
⦿ SAVE All Year [CP] 1P: $89-$175 2P: $89-$175 XP: $5 F12
▽▽ **Location:** I-235, exit 7, 0.6 mi w on US 54 (S Frontage Rd). 6815 W Kellogg 67209. Fax: 316/943-1549. **Facility:** 129 units. 128 one-bedroom standard units, some with whirlpools. 1 one-bedroom suite with whirlpool. 2 stories, interior corridors. *Bath:* combo or shower only. **Parking:** on-site. **Terms:** cancellation fee
Small-scale Hotel imposed, package plans, pets ($45 fee). **Amenities:** high-speed Internet, irons, hair dryers. **Dining:** 6 am-2 & 5-10 pm, cocktails. **Pool(s):** heated indoor. **Leisure Activities:** whirlpool, putting green, exercise room, shuffleboard. *Fee:* game room. **Guest Services:** valet laundry, area transportation-within 5 mi. **Business Services:** meeting rooms, PC. **Cards:** AX, CB, DC, DS, MC, VI. **Free Special Amenities: newspaper and high-speed Internet.**

BEST WESTERN GOVERNORS INN & SUITES *Book great rates at AAA.com* **Phone: 316/522-0775**
⦿ SAVE All Year 1P: $59-$69 2P: $69-$79
▽▽ **Location:** I-135, exit 1B, just sw. 4742 S Emporia 67216. Fax: 316/522-1377. **Facility:** 58 one-bedroom standard units, some with whirlpools. 3 stories, interior corridors. *Bath:* combo or shower only. **Parking:** on-site.
Small-scale Hotel **Terms:** small pets only ($20 fee). **Amenities:** irons, hair dryers. *Some:* high-speed Internet. **Pool(s):** heated outdoor. **Leisure Activities:** limited exercise equipment. **Guest Services:** coin laundry, wireless Internet. **Business Services:** meeting rooms. **Cards:** AX, DC, DS, MC, VI. **Free Special Amenities: continental breakfast and high-speed Internet.**

BEST WESTERN HOTEL & SUITES *Book great rates at AAA.com* **Phone: (316)832-9387**
⦿ SAVE 1/1-2/29 1P: $89-$99 2P: $89-$99 XP: $5 F12
▽▽ 3/1-12/31 1P: $75-$89 2P: $75-$89 XP: $5 F12
Location: I-135, exit 13, just w. 915 E 53rd St N 67219. Fax: 316/832-9443. **Facility:** 149 units. 146 one-bedroom standard units, some with whirlpools. 3 one-bedroom suites ($139-$189) with whirlpools. 2 stories
Small-scale Hotel (no elevator), interior/exterior corridors. **Parking:** on-site. **Terms:** [BP] meal plan available, small pets only ($20 fee). **Amenities:** high-speed Internet, irons, hair dryers. **Dining:** 6 am-10 pm. **Pool(s):** small heated indoor. **Leisure Activities:** whirlpool, putting green, indoor recreation area, exercise room, shuffleboard. *Fee:* game room. **Guest Services:** coin laundry. **Business Services:** meeting rooms. **Cards:** AX, DC, DS, MC, VI. **Free Special Amenities: full breakfast and high-speed Internet.**

CANDLEWOOD SUITES — *Book at AAA.com*   Phone: (316)942-0400
All Year   1P: $79-$139   2P: $79-$139
Location: I-235, exit 7, 0.4 mi nw on Dugan Rd. 570 S Julia 67209. Fax: 316/942-3101. **Facility:** 81 units. 69 one-bedroom standard units with efficiencies. 12 one-bedroom suites with efficiencies. 3 stories, interior
Small-scale Hotel   corridors. *Bath:* combo or shower only. **Parking:** on-site. **Terms:** package plans, pets ($75 fee).
Amenities: video library, CD players, high-speed Internet, dual phone lines, voice mail, irons, hair dryers. *Some:* DVD players.
Leisure Activities: exercise room. **Guest Services:** complimentary and valet laundry. **Business Services:** business center.
Cards: AX, DC, DS, MC, VI.

SOME UNITS

COMFORT INN — *Book great rates at AAA.com*   Phone: (316)522-1800
All Year [ECP]   1P: $69   2P: $69   XP: $5   F
Location: I-135, exit 1A/B (47th St S), just e. 4849 S Laura 67216. Fax: 316/522-5273. **Facility:** 114 units. 112 one-bedroom standard units. 2 one-bedroom suites ($90). 2 stories (no elevator), interior corridors. *Bath:*
combo or shower only. **Terms:** weekly rates available, small pets only ($10 fee).
Small-scale Hotel **Amenities:** irons, hair dryers. **Pool(s):** heated outdoor. **Guest Services:** wireless Internet. **Business Services:** meeting rooms, PC. **Cards:** AX, CB, DC, DS, MC, VI. **Free Special Amenities:** expanded continental breakfast and high-speed Internet. *(See color ad below)*

SOME UNITS

COMFORT INN BY CHOICE HOTELS — *Book great rates at AAA.com*   Phone: 316/686-2844
Property failed to provide current rates
Location: I-35, exit 50, just ne. 9525 E Corporate Hills Dr 67207. Fax: 316/686-2844. **Facility:** 58 one-bedroom standard units. 3 stories, interior corridors. *Bath:* combo or shower only. **Parking:** on-site. **Terms:** ($10
Small-scale Hotel   fee). **Amenities:** irons, hair dryers. **Pool(s):** small heated indoor. **Leisure Activities:** whirlpool. **Guest
Services:** valet laundry, wireless Internet.

SOME UNITS

COMFORT SUITES AIRPORT — *Book great rates at AAA.com*   Phone: (316)945-2600
All Year [BP]   1P: $80-$90   2P: $85-$95   XP: $5   F18
Location: Jct I-235 and US 54. Located adjacent to the Towne West Square. 658 Westdale 67209.
Fax: 316/945-5033. **Facility:** 50 one-bedroom standard units. 3 stories, interior corridors. **Parking:** on-site.
Small-scale Hotel **Terms:** 10 day cancellation notice, small pets only ($10 fee). **Amenities:** high-speed Internet, irons, hair
dryers. **Pool(s):** outdoor. **Leisure Activities:** exercise room. **Guest Services:** complimentary evening beverages: Mon-Thurs.,
valet laundry, area transportation. **Business Services:** meeting rooms. **Cards:** AX, CB, DC, DS, JC, MC, VI.

SOME UNITS

COURTYARD BY MARRIOTT — *Book great rates at AAA.com*   Phone: 316/636-4600
Property failed to provide current rates
Location: SR 96, exit Webb Rd, just s. 2975 N Webb Rd 67226. Fax: 316/636-4633. **Facility:** Smoke free
premises. 90 units. 87 one-bedroom standard units, some with whirlpools. 3 one-bedroom suites. 3 stories,
Small-scale Hotel   interior corridors. *Bath:* combo or shower only. **Parking:** on-site. **Amenities:** video games (fee), high-speed
Internet, dual phone lines, voice mail, irons, hair dryers. **Pool(s):** heated indoor. **Leisure Activities:** whirlpool, exercise room.
Guest Services: valet and coin laundry, wireless Internet. **Business Services:** meeting rooms, PC.

SOME UNITS

CRESTHILL SUITES HOTEL   Phone: (316)689-8000
All Year   1P: $129   2P: $129   XP: $10   F12
Location: 1.7 mi e of jct Rock Rd. 12111 E Central Ave 67206. Fax: 316/689-8004. **Facility:** 62 units. 36 one-bedroom standard units with kitchens. 18 one- and 8 two-bedroom suites with kitchens. 2 stories, interior
Small-scale Hotel   corridors. *Bath:* combo or shower only. **Parking:** on-site. **Terms:** package plans, pets ($50 fee).
Amenities: high-speed Internet, dual phone lines, voice mail, irons, hair dryers. **Pool(s):** small outdoor. **Leisure
Activities:** exercise room. **Guest Services:** sundries, complimentary evening beverages: Mon-Thurs, valet and coin laundry.
Business Services: meeting rooms, business center. **Cards:** AX, DS, MC, VI.

SOME UNITS

DAYS INN WEST NEAR AIRPORT   *Book great rates at AAA.com*   **Phone:** (316)942-1717

Motel

All Year   1P: $60-$90   2P: $65-$99   XP: $6   F12
Location: US 54, exit West St, just n, then just w. Located adjacent to a major shopping mall. 550 S Florence 67209. Fax: 316/942-1717. **Facility:** 42 one-bedroom standard units. 2 stories (no elevator), exterior corridors. **Parking:** on-site, winter plug-ins. **Terms:** cancellation fee imposed, package plans. **Amenities:** high-speed Internet, hair dryers. *Some:* irons. **Cards:** AX, CB, DC, DS, MC, VI. **Free Special Amenities: continental breakfast and high-speed Internet.**

SOME UNITS

ECONO LODGE INN & SUITES   *Book great rates at AAA.com*   **Phone:** (316)722-8730

Small-scale Hotel

All Year   1P: $49-$54
Location: I-235, exit 7, 1.1 mi w on US 54. 600 S Holland 67209. Fax: 316/722-8732. **Facility:** 104 units. 103 one-bedroom standard units. 1 one-bedroom suite ($95-$114) with whirlpool. 2 stories (no elevator), interior corridors. **Parking:** on-site. **Terms:** 3 day cancellation notice, package plans, pets ($10 fee). **Amenities:** irons, hair dryers. **Pool(s):** small outdoor. **Leisure Activities:** whirlpool. **Guest Services:** valet and coin laundry, area transportation-within 5 mi, wireless Internet. **Business Services:** meeting rooms, PC. **Cards:** AX, CB, DC, DS, JC, MC, VI. **Free Special Amenities: expanded continental breakfast and high-speed Internet.** *(See color ad below)*

SOME UNITS

FEE

FAIRFIELD INN BY MARRIOTT   *Book great rates at AAA.com*   **Phone:** 316/685-3777

Small-scale Hotel

All Year [CP]   1P: $64-$99   2P: $64-$99
Location: I-35, exit 50, just ne. 333 S Webb Rd 67207. Fax: 316/685-3777. **Facility:** Smoke free premises. 104 one-bedroom standard units. 2 stories (no elevator), interior corridors. **Parking:** on-site, winter plug-ins. **Amenities:** high-speed Internet, irons, hair dryers. **Pool(s):** heated outdoor. **Guest Services:** valet laundry. **Cards:** AX, CB, DC, DS, JC, MC, VI.

FOUR POINTS BY SHERATON WICHITA AIRPORT   *Book great rates at AAA.com*   **Phone:** 316/942-7911

Small-scale Hotel

All Year   1P: $69-$99   2P: $69-$99
Location: I-235, exit 7A, just w. 5805 W Kellogg 67209. Fax: 316/942-0854. **Facility:** 200 one-bedroom standard units, some with whirlpools. 2 stories, interior corridors. **Parking:** on-site. **Terms:** small pets only ($25 fee). **Amenities:** video games (fee), high-speed Internet, dual phone lines, voice mail, safes, irons, hair dryers. **Dining:** Canterbury Restaurant, see separate listing. **Pool(s):** outdoor. **Leisure Activities:** whirlpool, exercise room. **Guest Services:** valet and coin laundry, area transportation-within 5 mi. **Business Services:** conference facilities, business center. **Cards:** AX, CB, DC, DS, MC, VI. **Free Special Amenities: full breakfast and high-speed Internet.**

SOME UNITS

FEE

HAMPTON INN BY HILTON   *Book great rates at AAA.com*   **Phone:** 316/686-3576

Small-scale Hotel

Property failed to provide current rates
Location: I-35, exit 50, just ne. 9449 E Corporate Hills Dr 67207. Fax: 316/686-4604. **Facility:** 81 one-bedroom standard units. 3 stories, interior corridors. *Bath:* combo or shower only. **Parking:** on-site. **Terms:** small pets only. **Amenities:** voice mail, irons, hair dryers. **Pool(s):** small heated indoor. **Leisure Activities:** whirlpool. **Guest Services:** valet laundry, wireless Internet.

SOME UNITS

HAMPTON INN-WEST   *Book great rates at AAA.com*   **Phone:** (316)945-4100

Small-scale Hotel

All Year [ECP]   1P: $89-$200   2P: $89-$200
Location: US 54, exit West St, just e on north service road. 3800 W Kellogg 67213. Fax: 316/945-4611. **Facility:** 121 units. 120 one-bedroom standard units. 1 one-bedroom suite with whirlpool. 4 stories, interior corridors. *Bath:* combo or shower only. **Parking:** on-site. **Amenities:** voice mail, irons, hair dryers. *Some:* dual phone lines. **Pool(s):** outdoor. **Leisure Activities:** exercise room. **Guest Services:** valet laundry, wireless Internet. **Business Services:** meeting rooms, business center. **Cards:** AX, CB, DC, DS, JC, MC, VI.

SOME UNITS

HAWTHORN SUITES AT REFLECTION RIDGE *Book at AAA.com*   **Phone: (316)729-5700**
All Year [BP]   1P: $104-$122
Small-scale Hotel   **Location:** I-235, exit 10, 1.7 mi w on Zoo Blvd/21st St N, then just n. 2405 N Ridge Rd 67205. Fax: 316/773-5471. **Facility:** 52 one-bedroom standard units, some with whirlpools. 2 stories, interior corridors. *Bath:* combo or shower only. **Parking:** on-site. **Terms:** small pets only ($25 fee). **Amenities:** DVD players, voice mail, irons, hair dryers. **Leisure Activities:** exercise room. **Guest Services:** valet and coin laundry, wireless Internet. **Business Services:** meeting rooms. **Cards:** AX, CB, DC, DS, MC, VI.
SOME UNITS

HILTON GARDEN INN-WICHITA *Book great rates at AAA.com*   **Phone: (316)219-4444**
All Year   1P: $99-$149   2P: $99-$149
Small-scale Hotel   **Location:** SR 96, exit Rock Rd, 1.7 mi s, just e. Located in a shopping area. 2041 N Bradley Fair Pkwy 67206. Fax: 316/219-4445. **Facility:** 103 one-bedroom standard units. 3 stories, interior corridors. *Bath:* combo or shower only. **Parking:** on-site. **Terms:** cancellation fee imposed, [BP] meal plan available, package plans. **Amenities:** video games (fee), high-speed Internet, dual phone lines, voice mail, irons, hair dryers. **Pool(s):** small indoor. **Leisure Activities:** whirlpool. **Guest Services:** sundries, valet and coin laundry, area transportation, wireless Internet. **Business Services:** meeting rooms, business center. **Cards:** AX, CB, DC, DS, JC, MC, VI.
SOME UNITS

HOLIDAY INN EXPRESS *Book great rates at AAA.com*   **Phone: 316/529-4848**
All Year   1P: $85-$120   2P: $85-$120
Small-scale Hotel   **Location:** I-35, exit 1B, just ne. 4848 S Laura 67216. Fax: 316/529-8585. **Facility:** 52 one-bedroom standard units. 2 stories, interior corridors. *Bath:* combo or shower only. **Parking:** on-site. **Terms:** [CP] meal plan available, pets ($25 fee). **Amenities:** voice mail, irons, hair dryers. **Pool(s):** small heated indoor. **Leisure Activities:** whirlpool. **Guest Services:** valet laundry, wireless Internet. **Business Services:** PC. **Cards:** AX, CB, DC, DS, JC, MC, VI. **Free Special Amenities:** continental breakfast and high-speed Internet.

HOLIDAY INN EXPRESS-NORTH *Book at AAA.com*   **Phone: (316)634-3900**
All Year   1P: $70-$100   2P: $75-$105   XP: $5   F18
Small-scale Hotel   **Location:** SR 96 E, exit Rock Rd, just sw. 7824 E 32nd St N 67226. Fax: 316/634-3900. **Facility:** 70 one-bedroom standard units. 3 stories, interior corridors. *Bath:* combo or shower only. **Parking:** on-site. **Amenities:** dual phone lines, voice mail, irons, hair dryers. **Pool(s):** heated indoor. **Leisure Activities:** whirlpool. **Guest Services:** valet laundry, wireless Internet. **Cards:** AX, DC, DS, MC, VI.
SOME UNITS

HOLIDAY INN HOTEL & SUITES CONVENTION CENTER *Book at AAA.com*   **Phone: (316)269-2090**
All Year   1P: $84-$129   2P: $89-$149   XP: $5   F17
Small-scale Hotel   **Location:** Just sw of jct US 54/400 and Broadway. 221 E Kellogg 67211. Fax: 316/858-1251. **Facility:** 150 units. 120 one-bedroom standard units. 30 one-bedroom suites. 7 stories, interior corridors. *Bath:* combo or shower only. **Parking:** on-site. **Amenities:** high-speed Internet, voice mail, irons, hair dryers. **Pool(s):** heated outdoor. **Leisure Activities:** sauna, whirlpool, exercise room. **Guest Services:** valet and coin laundry, area transportation. **Business Services:** meeting rooms, business center. **Cards:** AX, CB, DC, DS, JC, MC, VI.
SOME UNITS

HOLIDAY INN SELECT *Book great rates at AAA.com*   **Phone: (316)686-7131**
All Year   1P: $79-$99   XP: $10   F
Small-scale Hotel   **Location:** I-35, exit 50, 0.5 mi w. 549 S Rock Rd 67207. Fax: 316/686-0018. **Facility:** 251 units. 238 one-bedroom standard units. 6 one- and 7 two-bedroom suites ($99-$269), some with whirlpools. 2-9 stories, interior/exterior corridors. *Bath:* combo or shower only. **Parking:** on-site, winter plug-ins. **Terms:** package plans, pets ($25 fee, with prior approval). **Amenities:** dual phone lines, voice mail, irons, hair dryers. *Some:* high-speed Internet. **Dining:** Green Mill, see separate listing. **Pool(s):** heated outdoor, heated indoor. **Leisure Activities:** whirlpool, exercise room. *Fee:* game room. **Guest Services:** valet and coin laundry, area transportation-within 5 mi, wireless Internet. **Business Services:** meeting rooms, business center. **Cards:** AX, CB, DC, DS, MC, VI. **Free Special Amenities:** newspaper and high-speed Internet.
SOME UNITS

HOTEL AT OLD TOWN *Book at AAA.com*   **Phone: (316)267-4800**
All Year [BP]   1P: $189   2P: $199   XP: $10   F12
Small-scale Hotel   **Location:** Just nw of jct First and Mosley sts; center. 830 E First St 67202. Fax: 316/267-4840. **Facility:** 115 units. 103 one-bedroom standard units with efficiencies. 12 one-bedroom suites ($295) with efficiencies and whirlpools. 4 stories, interior corridors. *Bath:* combo or shower only. **Parking:** on-site. **Terms:** package plans. **Amenities:** video library, CD players, high-speed Internet, dual phone lines, voice mail, irons, hair dryers. **Leisure Activities:** exercise room. **Guest Services:** complimentary and valet laundry, wireless Internet. **Business Services:** conference facilities, PC. **Cards:** AX, DC, DS, MC, VI.
SOME UNITS

HYATT REGENCY WICHITA *Book great rates at AAA.com*   **Phone: (316)293-1234**
All Year   1P: $99-$200   2P: $99-$200   XP: $20   F18
Large-scale Hotel   **Location:** Just w of jct Main St and Waterman; downtown. 400 W Waterman 67202. Fax: 316/293-1200. **Facility:** 303 units. 301 one-bedroom standard units. 2 one-bedroom suites. 17 stories, interior corridors. *Bath:* combo or shower only. **Parking:** on-site (fee). **Terms:** cancellation fee imposed. **Amenities:** video games (fee), dual phone lines, voice mail, irons, hair dryers. **Dining:** 4 restaurants, 6:30 am-midnight, cocktails. **Pool(s):** heated indoor. **Leisure Activities:** saunas, whirlpools, steamrooms, exercise room. **Guest Services:** gift shop, valet laundry, area transportation, wireless Internet. **Business Services:** conference facilities, business center. **Cards:** AX, CB, DC, DS, JC, MC, VI. *(See color ad p 377)*
SOME UNITS

INN AT THE PARK Phone: 316-652-0500

(AAA) [SAVE]

Bed & Breakfast

All Year [ECP] 1P: $99-$160 2P: $99-$160
Location: US 54, exit Hillside Ave, 0.4 mi n, then just e. Located in a quiet area. 3751 E Douglas St 67218 (PO Box 20084, 67208). Fax: 316-652-0525. **Facility:** Peaceful surroundings in an upscale area. Suites are well-appointed and the staff is friendly. 12 one-bedroom standard units, some with efficiencies and/or whirlpools. 3 stories (no elevator), interior corridors. **Parking:** on-site. **Terms:** check-in 4 pm, package plans. **Amenities:** DVD players, irons, hair dryers. *Some:* high-speed Internet. **Guest Services:** valet laundry. **Business Services:** meeting rooms, fax. **Cards:** AX, DC, DS, MC, VI. **Free Special Amenities:** expanded continental breakfast and high-speed Internet.

SOME UNITS

LA QUINTA INN & SUITES *Book great rates at AAA.com* Phone: 316-943-2181

Small-scale Hotel

All Year 1P: $72-$81
Location: I-235, exit 7, just w. 5500 W Kellogg 67209. Fax: 316-943-6587. **Facility:** 152 one-bedroom standard units. 5 stories, interior corridors. **Bath:** combo or shower only. **Parking:** on-site. **Terms:** [BP] meal plan available, pets ($25 fee). **Amenities:** video games (fee), voice mail, irons, hair dryers. *Some:* dual phone lines. **Pool(s):** heated indoor. **Leisure Activities:** whirlpool, exercise room. **Guest Services:** valet and coin laundry, area transportation. **Business Services:** meeting rooms, business center. **Cards:** AX, DS, MC, VI.

SOME UNITS

RESIDENCE INN BY MARRIOTT *Book great rates at AAA.com* Phone: 316/686-7331

Small-scale Hotel

Property failed to provide current rates
Location: I-35, exit 50, just ne. 411 S Webb Rd 67207-0000. Fax: 316/686-2345. **Facility:** Smoke free premises. 64 one-bedroom standard units with kitchens. 2 stories (no elevator), exterior corridors. **Parking:** on-site. **Terms:** pets ($75 fee). **Amenities:** high-speed Internet, voice mail, irons, hair dryers. **Pool(s):** outdoor. **Leisure Activities:** whirlpool, sports court. **Guest Services:** valet and coin laundry.

SOME UNITS

RESIDENCE INN BY MARRIOTT AT PLAZZIO *Book great rates at AAA.com* Phone: 316/682-7300

Small-scale Hotel

Property failed to provide current rates
Location: SR 96, exit 13th St, 0.5 mi sw. 1212 N Greenwich 67206. Fax: 316/682-7302. **Facility:** Smoke free premises. 93 units. 54 one-bedroom standard units with kitchens. 32 one- and 7 two-bedroom suites with kitchens. 4 stories, interior corridors. **Bath:** combo or shower only. **Parking:** on-site. **Terms:** pets ($75 fee). **Amenities:** video library (fee), high-speed Internet, voice mail, irons, hair dryers. *Some:* DVD players (fee). **Pool(s):** heated outdoor. **Leisure Activities:** whirlpool, putting green, exercise room, sports court. **Guest Services:** complimentary evening beverages: Mon-Thurs, valet and coin laundry, wireless Internet. **Business Services:** meeting rooms, business center.

SUPER 8 MOTEL-WICHITA/EAST *Book great rates at AAA.com* Phone: 316/686-3888

(AAA) [SAVE]

Motel

All Year 1P: $48-$54 2P: $50-$55 XP: $5 F17
Location: I-35, exit 50, just e. 527 S Webb Rd 67207. Fax: 316/686-1548. **Facility:** 119 one-bedroom standard units. 3 stories (no elevator), interior corridors. **Parking:** on-site, winter plug-ins. **Terms:** cancellation fee imposed, pets ($25 extra charge). **Amenities:** high-speed Internet, safes (fee). *Some:* irons. **Guest Services:** coin laundry, wireless Internet. **Business Services:** meeting rooms. **Cards:** AX, CB, DC, DS, JC, MC, VI. **Free Special Amenities:** continental breakfast and high-speed Internet.

SOME UNITS

TOWNEPLACE SUITES BY MARRIOTT *Book great rates at AAA.com* Phone: 316/631-3773

Small-scale Hotel

All Year 1P: $109 2P: $109
Location: SR 96, exit Webb Rd, just sw. 9444 E 29th St N 67226. Fax: 316/631-3775. **Facility:** Smoke free premises. 82 units. 69 one-bedroom standard units with efficiencies. 13 one-bedroom suites with efficiencies. 3 stories, interior corridors. **Bath:** combo or shower only. **Parking:** on-site. **Terms:** [CP] meal plan available, pets ($75 fee). **Amenities:** video library, voice mail, irons, hair dryers. **Leisure Activities:** whirlpool, exercise room. **Guest Services:** sundries, valet and coin laundry, wireless Internet. **Business Services:** business center. **Cards:** AX, DC, DS, JC, MC, VI.

WESLEY INN

▼▼ ▼▼

Small-scale Hotel

Phone: (316)858-3343

All Year   1P: $55-$65   2P: $55-$65

Location: Just e of jct Hillside. Located across from Wesley Medical Center. 3343 E Central Ave 67208. Fax: 316/858-3352. **Facility:** 74 one-bedroom standard units. 4 stories, interior corridors. *Bath:* combo or shower only. **Parking:** on-site. **Terms:** pets ($25 fee). **Amenities:** video library, voice mail, irons, hair dryers. **Guest Services:** valet and coin laundry, wireless Internet. **Business Services:** PC. **Cards:** AX, DS, MC, VI.

SOME UNITS

[ASK] [S◯] [🛏] [⬚] [⬚] [⬚] [VCR] [⬚] [⬚] [⬚] / [✕] /

WICHITA INN-EAST

[AAA] [SAVE]

▼▼ ▼▼

Small-scale Hotel

Phone: (316)685-8291

All Year   1P: $49-$54   2P: $49-$54   XP: $4   F10

Location: I-35, exit 50, 0.4 mi w. 8220 E Kellogg 67207. Fax: 316/685-0835. **Facility:** 91 one-bedroom standard units. 3 stories, interior corridors. **Parking:** on-site. **Amenities:** video library, voice mail. **Guest Services:** valet and coin laundry. **Cards:** AX, CB, DC, DS, MC, VI. **Free Special Amenities: continental breakfast and high-speed Internet.**

SOME UNITS

[S◯] [VCR] [⬚] [⬚] [⬚] / [✕] /

WICHITA INN-NORTH

▼▼ ▼▼

Small-scale Hotel

Phone: 316/636-2022

Property failed to provide current rates

Location: SR 96, exit Rock Rd, just n. 3741 N Rock Rd 67226. Fax: 316/636-5893. **Facility:** 100 one-bedroom standard units. 3 stories, interior corridors. *Bath:* combo or shower only. **Parking:** on-site. **Amenities:** video library, voice mail, irons, hair dryers. **Guest Services:** valet and coin laundry, wireless Internet.

SOME UNITS

[⬚] [⬚] [VCR] [⬚] [⬚] [⬚] [⬚] / [✕] /

The following lodging was either not evaluated or did not meet AAA rating requirements but is listed for your information only.

DAYS INN WICHITA NORTH

[fyi]

Motel

Phone: 316/832-1131

Did not meet all AAA rating requirements for some property operations at time of last evaluation on 07/13/2006. **Location:** I-135, exit 13, just w. 901 E 53rd St N 67219. Facilities, services, and decor characterize a basic property.

WHERE TO DINE

ABUELO'S MEXICAN FOOD EMBASSY

▼▼ ▼▼

Mexican

Lunch: $7-$17   **Dinner: $9-$17**   **Phone: 316/634-2230**

Location: 1.2 mi w of jct SR 96 and 13th St. 1413 N Waterfront Pkwy 67206. **Hours:** 11 am-10 pm, Fri & Sat-11 pm. Closed: 11/22, 12/25. **Features:** A little extra attention to presentation enhances the traditional Mexican dishes. Distinguishing the casual decor are some upscale touches. Casual dress; cocktails. **Parking:** on-site. **Cards:** AX, CB, DC, DS, JC, MC, VI.

[Y]

ANGELO'S ITALIAN RESTAURANT

▼▼ ▼▼

Italian

Lunch: $4-$9   **Dinner: $7-$17**   **Phone: 316/682-1473**

Location: 1.4 mi s of US 54. 1930 S Oliver 67218. **Hours:** 11 am-10 pm. Closed: 11/22, 12/25; also Mon. **Features:** Established more than 40 years ago, the restaurant is known for its pizza selections and Italian recipes. Portions are plentiful, and the dining room is comfortable and unassuming. Casual dress; cocktails. **Parking:** on-site. **Cards:** AX, CB, DC, DS, JC, MC, VI.

[N]

BG BOLTON'S SPORTS GRILL

▼▼ ▼▼

American

Lunch: $7-$18   **Dinner: $7-$18**   **Phone: 316/558-8600**

Location: Just w of jct SR 96. 11423 E 13th St 67206. **Hours:** 11 am-10 pm, Fri & Sat-11 pm. Closed: 11/22, 12/25. **Features:** Guests can dine in the bar area or in the separate dining room of the nicely decorated sports grill, which prepares a good variety of dishes. Casual dress; cocktails. **Parking:** on-site. **Cards:** AX, DS, MC, VI.

[Y] [N]

CANTERBURY RESTAURANT

▼▼ ▼▼

American

Lunch: $7-$16   **Dinner: $7-$16**   **Phone: 316/942-7911**

Location: I-235, exit 7A, just w; in The Four Points by Sheraton Wichita Airport. 5805 W Kellogg 67209. **Hours:** 6 am-2 & 5-10 pm. **Features:** The restaurant serves traditional dishes in a comfortable, contemporary dining room. Casual dress; cocktails. **Parking:** on-site. **Cards:** AX, DS, MC, VI.

[Y] [N]

CHELSEA BAR & GRILL

[AAA]

▼▼ ▼▼

American

Lunch: $7-$11   **Dinner: $8-$19**   **Phone: 316/636-1103**

Location: 0.5 mi s of jct SR 96. 2949 N Rock Rd 67226. **Hours:** 11 am-10 pm, Fri & Sat-11 pm, Sun 5 pm-9 pm. Closed major holidays. **Features:** At Chelsea's you'll enjoy well-prepared entrees that include beef, chicken, seafood, duck and veal dishes as well as fresh ingredients in all courses. An open grill allows you to watch while the chef prepares your meals. Servers are prompt and friendly. Casual dress; cocktails. **Parking:** on-site. **Cards:** AX, CB, DC, DS, JC, MC, VI.

[Y] [N]

CHESTER'S CHOPHOUSE & WINE BAR

▼▼ ▼▼

Steak House

Lunch: $6-$13   **Dinner: $8-$38**   **Phone: 316/201-1300**

Location: 1.8 mi s of jct SR 96. 1550 N Webb Rd 67206. **Hours:** 11 am-10 pm. Closed: 11/22, 12/25. **Reservations:** suggested. **Features:** Upscale decor and attractive dishes are common observations at the fine-dining restaurant. Dressy casual; cocktails. **Parking:** on-site. **Cards:** AX, DS, MC, VI.

[Y]

CIBOLA
▼▼▼▼
American
MC, VI.

Dinner: $21-$50 Phone: 316/631-3700

Location: SR 96, exit Rock Rd, 2.5 mi s; in Bradley Fair Shopping Center. 1900 N Rock Rd 67206. **Hours:** 5:30 pm-10 pm. Closed major holidays. **Reservations:** suggested. **Features:** Elegance and sophistication distinguish the comfortable dining room, where guests can relax and enjoy a special occasion. Dishes are beautifully presented and exceptionally flavorful. Dressy casual; cocktails. **Parking:** on-site. **Cards:** AX, MC, VI.

GRANITE CITY FOOD & BREWERY
▼▼▼
American

Lunch: $6-$20 **Dinner: $11-$20** Phone: 316/636-5050

Location: Just n of E 21st St. 2244 N Webb Rd 67206. **Hours:** 11 am-1 am, Sun 10 am-midnight. Closed: 11/22, 12/25. **Features:** The popular restaurant and brewery caters to travelers, business professionals, sports enthusiasts and children. The varying menu centers on American fare. Favorites include honey-rosemary filet mignon, barbecue ribs, a nice array of salads and classic sandwiches. Save room for one of the tasty, large-portioned desserts. Five to six beer varieties are brewed on the premises. Casual dress; cocktails. **Parking:** on-site.

GREEN MILL
▼▼▼ ▼▼▼
Italian

Lunch: $6-$20 **Dinner: $6-$20** Phone: 316/687-6455

Location: I-35, exit 50, 0.5 mi w; in Holiday Inn Select. 549 S Rock Rd 67207. **Hours:** 6 am-10 pm, Fri & Sat-11 pm, Sun-9 pm. Closed: 12/25. **Reservations:** accepted. **Features:** Pizza, pasta and calzones, as well as steak, fish and fowl, all are available on the diverse menu. Casual dress; cocktails. **Parking:** on-site. **Cards:** AX, DC, DS, MC, VI.

HOG WILD PIT BAR-B-Q
▼▼
Barbecue

Lunch: $4-$8 **Dinner: $4-$8** Phone: 316/522-7636

Location: I-135, exit 16, just s. 662 E 47th St 67216. **Hours:** 11 am-8 pm. Closed major holidays. **Features:** Tender, flavorful barbecue is ordered via the service line. Those who don't carry out their food have a choice from plenty of seats in the good-sized dining room. Casual dress. **Parking:** on-site. **Cards:** AX, MC, VI.

JIMMIE'S DINER
▼▼
American

Lunch: $4-$8 **Dinner: $4-$8** Phone: 316/636-1818

Location: Just s of jct SR 96. 3111 N Rock Rd 67226. **Hours:** 6 am-9 pm. Closed: 11/22, 12/25. **Features:** The diner's decor, including jukeboxes at each table, harks back to the 1950s. This place hops at breakfast time. Casual dress. **Parking:** on-site. **Cards:** MC, VI.

KWAN COURT
▼▼▼
Asian

Lunch: $6-$12 **Dinner: $7-$22** Phone: 316/634-1828

Location: Just n of 13th St. 1443 N Rock Rd 67206. **Hours:** 11 am-2:30 & 5-10 pm, Fri & Sat-11 pm. Closed major holidays. **Reservations:** accepted. **Features:** An expansive sushi bar complements many traditional Japanese and Chinese dishes. Casual dress; cocktails. **Parking:** on-site. **Cards:** AX, DC, DS, MC, VI.

KYOTO JAPANESE STEAKHOUSE
▼▼▼
Japanese

Lunch: $13-$27 **Dinner: $13-$27** Phone: 316/684-7779

Location: Just nw of jct Center St. 535 N Woodlawn 67208. **Hours:** 11 am-10:30 pm. **Features:** Hibachi cooking done at guests' tables provides entertainment while they dine. Casual dress; cocktails. **Parking:** on-site. **Cards:** AX, DS, MC, VI.

MALAYSIA CAFE
▼▼
Chinese

Lunch: $4-$6 **Dinner: $5-$6** Phone: 316/685-8838

Location: Just w of jct Rock Rd. 7777 E 21st St, Suite 150 67206. **Hours:** 11 am-9:30 pm, Sat & Sun from noon. Closed: 11/22, 12/25. **Features:** Guests order at the register before grabbing a cafe table to enjoy their hearty portions of Malaysian fare. Casual dress. **Parking:** on-site. **Cards:** MC, VI.

OLIVE TREE BISTRO
◈◈◈
▼▼▼ ▼▼▼
Continental

Dinner: $13-$37 Phone: 316/636-1100

Location: 0.5 mi s of jct SR 96. 2949 N Rock Rd 67226. **Hours:** 5:30 pm-9 pm, Fri & Sat-10 pm, Sun 10:30 am-2:30 pm. Closed major holidays. **Reservations:** suggested. **Features:** This bistro features expertly prepared, high-quality foods and fresh ingredients served with presentation. The mushroom soup, a signature item, is delicious. They offer an elegant European atmosphere and attentive, knowledgeable service. Semi-formal attire; cocktails. **Parking:** on-site. **Cards:** AX, CB, DC, DS, MC, VI.

RED, HOT & BLUE
▼▼ ▼▼
Barbecue

Lunch: $5-$7 **Dinner: $6-$14** Phone: 316/630-0600

Location: SR 96, exit Rock Rd, just se. 3320 N Rock Rd 67226. **Hours:** 11 am-9 pm, Fri-Sun to 10 pm. Closed: 11/22, 12/25. **Features:** A nice selection of barbecue selections is matched with such side items as baked beans, potato salad and slaw. Casual dress; cocktails. **Parking:** on-site. **Cards:** AX, DS, MC, VI.

RED ROCK CANYON GRILL
▼▼▼ ▼▼
Steak & Seafood

Dinner: $12-$26 Phone: 316/636-1844

Location: SR 96, exit Rock Rd, 2.6 mi s; in Bradley Fair Shopping Center. 1844 N Rock Rd 67207. **Hours:** 5 pm-10 pm, Fri & Sat-11 pm, Sun 11 am-9 pm. Closed: 11/22, 12/25. **Reservations:** accepted. **Features:** Featuring a wood-fired rotisserie, the restaurant prepares steaks, lamb, pork chops, fresh fish and ribs. The open dining room provides a view of the show kitchen and bar, which centers the room. Casual dress; cocktails. **Parking:** on-site. **Cards:** AX, DC, MC, VI.

RIVER CITY BREWERY CO
▼▼▼ ▼▼
American

Lunch: $7-$15 **Dinner: $7-$15** Phone: 316/263-2739

Location: Just se of jct First and Mosley sts. 150 N Mosley St 67202. **Hours:** 11 am-10 pm, Fri & Sat-11 pm. Closed: 11/22, 12/25. **Features:** The lively diner is likely to make you nostalgic for poodle skirts and sock hops. Kitschy decor and shiny chrome enliven the dining room. Order from the all-day breakfast menu or enjoy old favorites such as burgers, sandwiches and soda fountain treats. Casual dress; cocktails. **Parking:** on-site. **Cards:** AX, DS, MC, VI.

ROLY POLY SANDWICHES

American

Lunch: $4-$7   **Dinner:** $4-$7   **Phone:** 316/682-3920
Location: Just w of jct Rock Rd. 7777 E 21st St 67226. **Hours:** 10 am-8 pm. Closed: 11/22, 12/25; also Sun. **Features:** Slaw, potato salad and other sides complement the eatery's vast selection of wrap sandwiches. Casual dress. **Parking:** on-site. **Cards:** MC, VI.

SCOTCH & SIRLOIN

Steak & Seafood

Lunch: $6-$12   **Dinner:** $9-$28   **Phone:** 316/685-8701
Location: I-35, exit 50, 2.4 mi w. 5325 E Kellogg 67218. **Hours:** 11 am-3 & 5-10 pm, Sat & Sun from 5 pm. Closed major holidays. **Reservations:** suggested. **Features:** The Scotch & Sirloin features an upscale, Tudor-pub atmosphere and a cuisine offering "sterling silver" beef, prime rib and gourmet cheesecake as their specialties. Business travelers and couples enjoy this restaurant. Good service. Casual dress; cocktails. **Parking:** on-site. **Cards:** AX, CB, DC, DS, MC, VI.

STROUD'S RESTAURANT BAR & GRILL

American

Lunch: $6-$11   **Dinner:** $8-$18   **Phone:** 316/838-2454
Location: Just n of jct SR 96. 3661 N Hillside St 67219. **Hours:** 5 pm-9 pm, Fri 11 am-2 & 4-10 pm, Sat from 4 pm, Sun 11 am-9 pm. Closed: 7/4, 12/25. **Features:** Enjoy home-style cooking, a casual family atmosphere and friendly service at Stroud's, which is famous for its succulent pan-fried chicken. They also offer pork chops, chicken-fried steak and seafood. The restaurant is located in a rural area. Casual dress; cocktails. **Parking:** on-site. **Cards:** AX, DS, MC, VI.

TED'S MONTANA GRILL

American

Lunch: $9-$24   **Dinner:** $9-$24   **Phone:** 316/634-8337
Location: Just n of jct SR 96. 3121 N Webb Rd 67226. **Hours:** 11 am-10 pm. Closed: 11/22, 12/25. **Features:** The turn-of-the-20th-century-style Montana saloon has mahogany paneling, Western landscapes, hickory floors, high-back booths and a pressed-tin ceiling. The menu features beef and bison steaks and burgers with fresh-cut French fries, salt-and-pepper onion rings and "flying D" chili side items. Also look for soups, salads, sandwiches, meatloaf, chicken, seafood and assorted blueplate specials. Casual dress; cocktails. **Parking:** on-site. **Cards:** AX, DS, MC, VI.

THAI TRADITION

Thai

Lunch: $6-$8   **Dinner:** $9-$17   **Phone:** 316/687-1500
Location: 1 mi n of US 54, on Edgemoor, just e. 650 N Carriage Pkwy, Suite 120 67208. **Hours:** 11 am-2:30 & 5-10 pm, Fri & Sat-11 pm. Closed major holidays. **Features:** Authentic and well-prepared Thai cuisine is complemented by Chinese and vegetarian selections at this family-owned restaurant. The lemon grass soup bursts with flavor with the addition of kalanga roots. Try this favorite of the locals: savory moonflower roast duck. Casual dress; cocktails. **Parking:** on-site. **Cards:** AX, DS, MC, VI.

WHISKEY CREEK STEAKHOUSE

American

Lunch: $9-$20   **Dinner:** $9-$20   **Phone:** 316/265-0707
Location: Just s of jct E 2nd St N. 233 N Mosley 67202. **Hours:** 11 am-10 pm, Fri & Sat-11 pm. Closed major holidays; also Mon. **Features:** Guests can watch as their steak is cooked over a wood-burning fire and throw peanut shells on the floor at this fun, casual steakhouse. The menu's wide variety includes chicken, pasta and barbecue dishes. A rustic theme evokes the wild, wild West. Casual dress; cocktails. **Parking:** on-site. **Cards:** AX, DS, MC, VI.

WILLIE C'S CAFE & BAR

American

Lunch: $6-$12   **Dinner:** $6-$17   **Phone:** 316/942-4077
Location: US 54, exit West St, just e on north service road. 656 S West St 67213. **Hours:** 11 am-10 pm, Fri & Sat-11 pm. Closed: 11/22, 12/25. **Features:** The border cantina-style decor lends itself to the festive atmosphere at this fun, lively restaurant. Select from a variety of burgers and sandwiches, as well as Tex-Mex, poultry and beef entrees. Dishes are reasonably priced. Casual dress; cocktails. **Parking:** on-site. **Cards:** AX, DC, DS, MC, VI.

YIA YIAS EURO BISTRO

Mediterranean

Lunch: $5-$15   **Dinner:** $7-$25   **Phone:** 316/634-1000
Location: SR 96, exit Rock Rd, 1.7 mi s. 8115 E 21st N 67228. **Hours:** 11 am-10 pm, Fri & Sat-11 pm. Closed: 7/4, 11/22, 12/25. **Features:** The stained-glass lighting sconces cast a warm glow on the perfect setting for entertaining a group or a romantic table for two. The cuisine is European inspired with a few Southwestern twists. Try the succulent grilled beef tenderloin with black pepper-gorgonzola Chianti sauce. And don't forget to save room for one of the delicious desserts. Casual dress; cocktails. **Parking:** on-site. **Cards:** AX, DS, MC, VI.

WINFIELD pop. 12,206

——— **WHERE TO STAY** ———

COMFORT INN

Small-scale Hotel

Book great rates at AAA.com

Phone: (620)221-7529

| All Year | 1P: $91-$179 | 2P: $91-$179 | XP: $10 | F18 |

Location: On US 77, 1 mi s. Hwy 77 at Quail Ridge Dr 67156. Fax: 620/221-0821. **Facility:** 51 one-bedroom standard units, some with whirlpools. 2 stories (no elevator), interior/exterior corridors. **Bath:** combo or shower only. **Parking:** on-site. **Terms:** cancellation fee imposed, package plans, pets ($10 extra charge, with prior approval). **Amenities:** safes, irons, hair dryers. **Pool(s):** small outdoor. **Leisure Activities:** exercise room. **Guest Services:** valet and coin laundry, wireless Internet. **Business Services:** meeting rooms, PC. **Cards:** AX, DC, DS, MC, VI.

SOME UNITS

ECONO LODGE

Motel

Book great rates at AAA.com

Phone: 620/221-9050

Property failed to provide current rates
Location: 0.5 mi s of jct US 77 and 160. 1710 Main St 67156. Fax: 620/221-7062. **Facility:** 29 one-bedroom standard units. 2 stories (no elevator), exterior corridors. **Parking:** on-site. **Terms:** pets ($10 fee). **Guest Services:** wireless Internet.

SOME UNITS

Missouri

Johnson's Shut-Ins State
Park, near Lesterville
© John Elk III / Lonely
Planet Images

Missouri
Orientation
Map To
Destinations

Kansas
City

St. Louis

ALBA pop. 588

―――― **WHERE TO DINE** ――――

OLD MINER'S INN　　　　　　　　**Dinner:** $19-$34　　　　　　　　**Phone:** 417/525-4332

▽▽▽▽

Continental

Location: Just s of jct CR D and O. 208 Main St 64830. **Hours:** 6 pm-9 pm. Closed major holidays; also Sun-Thurs. **Reservations:** required. **Features:** This inn is a little out of the way but its dining experience is well worth the drive. They serve chateaubriand and Dover sole and feature tableside flambe and carving. An extensive wine list, upscale ambience and cordial service complete the meal. Casual dress; cocktails.

Parking: street. **Cards:** MC, VI.

AVA pop. 3,021

―――― **WHERE TO STAY** ――――

AVA SUPER 8　　*Book at AAA.com*　　　　　　　　　　　　　　　　**Phone:** (417)683-1343

▽▽▽▽ ▽▽▽▽

Small-scale Hotel

All Year [CP]　　　　　　　1P: $65-$80　　　　2P: $65-$80　　　　XP: $5　　　　　F13

Location: Jct SR 5 S and 76. 1711 S Jefferson St 65608 (Rt 7, Box 7235). Fax: 417/683-1369. **Facility:** 40 one-bedroom standard units, some with whirlpools. 2 stories (no elevator), interior corridors. **Parking:** on-site. **Terms:** pets ($10 fee, in designated units, with prior approval). **Amenities:** high-speed Internet, voice mail, hair dryers. *Some:* irons. **Guest Services:** coin laundry. **Business Services:** meeting rooms, PC. **Cards:** AX, DS, MC, VI.

SOME UNITS

(ASK) [S🐕] [🛏] [🔲M] [🎦] / [✕] [🔒] [📷] [📺] /
FEE

BALLWIN —*See St. Louis p. 533.*

BELTON pop. 21,730

―――― **WHERE TO STAY** ――――

HOLIDAY INN EXPRESS　　*Book at AAA.com*　　　　　　　　　　**Phone:** (816)322-8700

▽▽▽▽ ▽▽▽▽

Small-scale Hotel

All Year [ECP]　　　　　　1P: $62-$79　　　　2P: $62-$79

Location: Jct US 71 and SR 58, just se. 17205 S US Hwy 71 64012. Fax: 816/318-1532. **Facility:** 50 one-bedroom standard units. 2 stories (no elevator), interior corridors. *Bath:* combo or shower only. **Parking:** on-site. **Amenities:** high-speed Internet, dual phone lines, voice mail, irons, hair dryers. **Pool(s):** outdoor. **Leisure Activities:** exercise room. **Guest Services:** wireless Internet. **Business Services:** PC. **Cards:** AX, DC, DS, MC, VI.

SOME UNITS

(ASK) [S🐕] [🍴] [🔲] [🏊] [📺] / [✕] /

―――― **WHERE TO DINE** ――――

ODEN'S BBQ　　　**Lunch:** $5-$15　　　　**Dinner:** $5-$15　　　**Phone:** 816/322-3072

▽▽▽

American

Location: Just w of jct US 71 and 155th St, 0.8 mi s. 1302 N Scott St 64012. **Hours:** 11 am-9 pm, Fri & Sat-10 pm, Sun-8 pm. Closed major holidays; also Mon. **Features:** Families prefer this spot for casual dining in a rustic, country-style atmosphere. Included in a good offering of sandwich selections are barbecue beef, pork and chicken. Service is friendly and efficient. Casual dress. **Parking:** on-site. **Cards:** AX, MC, VI.

[🚭]

BERKELEY —*See St. Louis p. 533.*

BETHANY pop. 3,087

—— WHERE TO STAY ——

BEST WESTERN BETHANY INN   *Book great rates at AAA.com*   Phone: 660/425-8006

AAA SAVE

5/1-8/31	1P: $60	2P: $65	XP: $5	F12
3/1-4/30	1P: $58	2P: $62	XP: $5	F12
9/1-11/30	1P: $58	2P: $60	XP: $5	F12
12/1-2/29	1P: $55	2P: $60	XP: $5	F12

Small-scale Hotel **Location:** I-35, exit 92, just nw. 496 S 39th St 64424. Fax: 660/425-8010. **Facility:** 50 one-bedroom standard units, some with whirlpools. 3 stories, interior corridors. *Bath:* combo or shower only. **Parking:** on-site. **Terms:** 3 day cancellation notice-fee imposed, pets ($10 fee). **Amenities:** high-speed Internet, irons, hair dryers. **Pool(s):** small heated indoor. **Leisure Activities:** whirlpool, exercise room. **Guest Services:** coin laundry. **Cards:** AX, DC, DS, MC, VI. **Free Special Amenities:** continental breakfast and high-speed Internet.

SOME UNITS
🅂🄳 🛏 🚪 🛗 ♿ 🏊 🐕 🖥 / ✕ 🔌 📶 /
FEE

FAMILY BUDGET INN   Phone: 660/425-7915

AAA SAVE

All Year	1P: $44-$54	2P: $49-$59	XP: $5	F17

Motel **Location:** I-35, exit 92. 4014 Miller St 64424. Fax: 660/425-3697. **Facility:** 78 one-bedroom standard units. 1 story, interior corridors. *Bath:* combo or shower only. **Parking:** on-site, winter plug-ins. **Terms:** weekly rates available, small pets only ($5 extra charge). **Amenities:** high-speed Internet. **Pool(s):** small outdoor. **Business Services:** fax (fee). **Cards:** AX, DS, MC, VI. **Free Special Amenities:** continental breakfast and high-speed Internet.

SOME UNITS
🅂🄳 🛏 ♿ 🏊 🖥 / ✕ 🔌 📶 /
FEE

—— WHERE TO DINE ——

TOOT-TOOT FAMILY RESTAURANT   Lunch: $4-$9   Dinner: $7-$12   Phone: 660/425-7001

AAA

American **Location:** I-35, exit 92, 0.3 mi w on US 136. 3101 Miller St 64424. **Hours:** 6 am-10 pm. **Features:** Most people order the buffet, which is offered for lunch and dinner and is a good value. Full menu available. The good-tasting food is appetizingly presented, the server staff is friendly and helpful, and the decor is rustic Americana. Casual dress. **Parking:** on-site. **Cards:** MC, VI.

BEVIER pop. 723

—— WHERE TO DINE ——

THE PEAR TREE   Dinner: $14-$32   Phone: 660/773-6666

American **Location:** Jct US 63 and 36, 5.4 mi w on US 36, then 1 mi s. 222 N Macon St 63532. **Hours:** Open 3/1-12/31 & 2/1-2/29; 4:30 pm-9:30 pm. Closed: 11/22, 12/24, 12/25; also Sun. **Reservations:** accepted. **Features:** There's much owner pride here, and it's well-deserved. Complementing the outstanding beef and seafood specialties are exceptional onion rings. The luscious cheesecake is on equal footing. The rural, historic setting is worth driving the few extra miles. The atmosphere is suitable for both casual and special occasion dining. Casual dress; cocktails. **Parking:** street. **Cards:** AX, DC, DS, MC, VI.

BLUE SPRINGS —See Kansas City p. 468.

BOONVILLE pop. 8,202

—— WHERE TO STAY ——

BOONVILLE COMFORT INN   *Book great rates at AAA.com*   Phone: (660)882-5317

AAA SAVE

5/1-9/3 [ECP]	1P: $59-$109	2P: $64-$109	XP: $8	F17
3/1-4/30 & 9/4-2/29 [ECP]	1P: $54-$89	2P: $59-$99	XP: $8	F17

Small-scale Hotel **Location:** I-70, exit 101, just sw. 2427 Mid America Industrial Dr 65233. Fax: 660/882-8137. **Facility:** 51 one-bedroom standard units. 2 stories (no elevator), interior corridors. *Bath:* combo or shower only. **Parking:** on-site. **Terms:** small pets only ($10 extra charge). **Amenities:** high-speed Internet, safes (fee), irons, hair dryers. **Pool(s):** heated indoor. **Leisure Activities:** whirlpool. **Guest Services:** coin laundry, wireless Internet. **Cards:** AX, CB, DC, DS, MC, VI. **Free Special Amenities:** expanded continental breakfast and early check-in/late check-out.

SOME UNITS
🅂🄳 🛏 🏊 🖥 / ✕ 🔌 📶 /
FEE

RIVERCENE MANSION BED & BREAKFAST   Phone: (660)848-2497

All Year	1P: $90-$225	2P: $90-$225	XP: $25	

Historic Bed & Breakfast **Location:** I-70, exit 103, 3.6 mi n to CR 463, then just e. Located in a quiet rural area. 127 CR 463 65274. Fax: 660/848-2142. **Facility:** This charming 1869 B&B offers large, antique-filled rooms, and is on the National Register of Historic Places. 9 units. 8 one- and 1 two-bedroom standard units, some with whirlpools. 3 stories (no elevator), interior corridors. *Bath:* combo, shower or tub only. **Parking:** on-site. **Terms:** age restrictions may apply, 7 day cancellation notice-fee imposed, no pets allowed (owner's dog on premises). **Amenities:** high-speed Internet, hair dryers. **Guest Services:** wireless Internet. **Cards:** DS, MC, VI.

SOME UNITS
ASK ✕ 📺 ☎ / 🔌 📶 🖥 /

Destination Branson
pop. 6,050

A lot of people think "shows" when they think of Branson, but there's much more to this southwestern Missouri city.

N estled in the heart of the Ozarks, Branson offers all kinds of outdoor recreation, from boating and fishing to hiking and spelunking. Shopping is another favorite pastime, and Branson Landing is the latest place to do it. This waterfront shopping "village" also features live entertainment and a dancing fountain show.

Showboat Branson Belle, Branson.
Table Rock Lake may not be the mighty Mississippi, but a cruise aboard the *Branson Belle* will take you back to the days when paddlewheelers traveled the nation's waterways. (See listing page 140)

Silver Dollar City, Branson.
Mmmmm, good! At Silver Dollar City you're never more than a few steps away from food that's guaranteed to tempt your taste buds. Bring a hearty appetite. (See listing page 139)

P laces included in this AAA Destination City:

Branson Landing. "See you at the Landing!" It seems like everyone's headed to Branson Landing. Branson's newest and largest shopping, dining and entertainment complex runs along scenic Lake Taneycomo. (See mention page 143)

Branson/Lakes Area Chamber of Commerce & CVB

Missouri Division of Tourism

Fishing at Table Rock. Branson's freshwater lakes are an angler's paradise where you can hook bass, bluegill, crappie and trout against a beautiful Ozarks backdrop.

See Vicinity map page 388 & 389

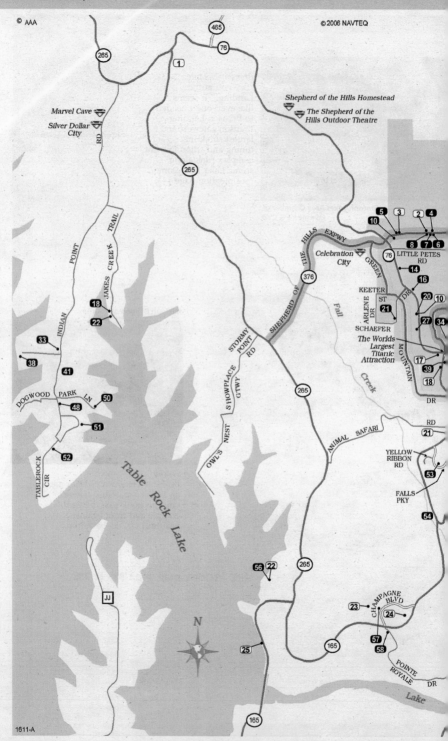

© AAA

© 2006 NAVTEQ

Marvel Cave
Silver Dollar City

Shepherd of the Hills Homestead
The Shepherd of the Hills Outdoor Theatre

Celebration City

LITTLE PETES RD

KEETER ST
ARLENE DR
SCHAEFER

The Worlds Largest Titanic Attraction

MOUNTAIN

YELLOW RIBBON RD

FALLS PKY

Table Rock Lake

DOGWOOD PARK LN

TABLEROCK CIR

JAKES CREEK TRAIL

INDIAN POINT

POINT

SHOWPLACE GTWY

STORMY POINT RD

OWL'S NEST

ANIMAL SAFARI

SHEPHERD OF THE HILLS EXPWY

GREEN

Fall

Creek

CHAMPAGNE BLVD

POINTE ROYALE DR

Lake

N

1611-A

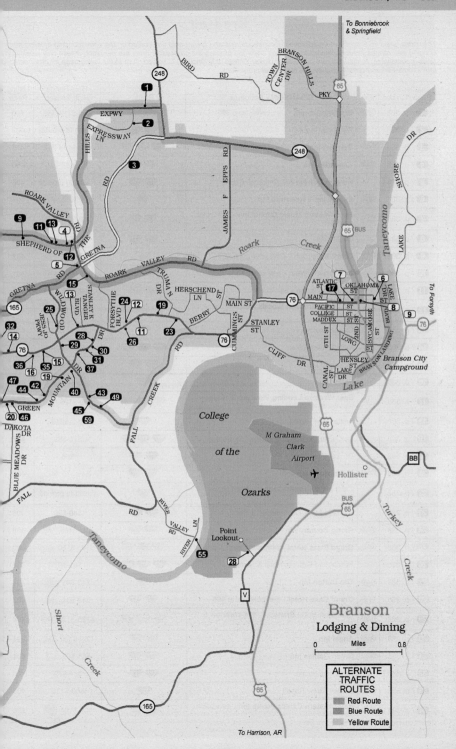

Branson

This index helps you "spot" where approved accommodations and restaurants are located on the corresponding detailed maps. Lodging rate ranges are for comparison only and show the property's high season; rates are per night, unless only weekly (W) rates are available. Restaurant rate range is for dinner, unless only lunch (L) is served. Turn to the listing page for more detailed rate information and consult display ads for special promotions.

Spotter/Map Page Number	OA	BRANSON - Lodgings	Diamond Rating	Rate Range High Season	Listing Page
1 / p. 388	AAA	**Branson Towers** - see color ad p 397	◆◆	$80-$119 SAVE	400
2 / p. 388		Savannah House	◆◆	Failed to provide	409
3 / p. 388	AAA	**Comfort Inn & Suites** - see color ad p 395	◆◆◆	$79-$139 SAVE	401
4 / p. 388	AAA	**Cascades Inn**	◆◆	$65-$85 SAVE	400
5 / p. 388		Honeysuckle Inn & Conference Center	◆◆	Failed to provide	406
6 / p. 388	AAA	**Eagles Inn a Rodeway Inn**	◆	$45-$85 SAVE	402
7 / p. 388	AAA	**Best Western Music Capital Inn** - see color ad p 395	◆◆	$69-$104 SAVE	396
8 / p. 388		Quality Inn	◆◆	$75-$95	408
9 / p. 388	AAA	**Ozark Valley Inn** - see color ad p 407	◆	$65-$115 SAVE	407
10 / p. 388	AAA	**Comfort Inn West** - see color ad p 395	◆◆	$69-$139 SAVE	401
11 / p. 388	AAA	**Scenic Hills Inn** - see color ad p 410	◆◆	$46-$70 SAVE	410
12 / p. 388	AAA	**Westgate Branson Woods Resort** - see color ad p 413	◆◆◆	$59-$139 SAVE	414
13 / p. 388		Classic Motor Inn	◆	Failed to provide	401
14 / p. 388		Hampton Inn-West	◆◆◆	$101-$132	404
15 / p. 388	AAA	**Rosebud Inn**	◆◆	$55-$65 SAVE	409
16 / p. 388	AAA	**Palms Inn**	◆	$33-$49 SAVE	407
17 / p. 388	AAA	**Best Western Landing View Inn & Suites** - see color ad p 394	◆◆◆	$69-$129 SAVE	396
18 / p. 388		Artilla Cove Resort	◆	$92-$240	394
19 / p. 388		La Quinta Inn Branson (Music City Centre)	◆◆◆	$75-$89	407
20 / p. 388		Dockers Inn	◆◆	$65	401
21 / p. 388	AAA	**Mountain Music Inn**	◆◆	$48-$75 SAVE	407
22 / p. 388		Calm Waters Resort, formerly Night Hawk Resort	◆	Failed to provide	400
23 / p. 388		Ramada Inn & Conference Center	◆◆	$40-$90	408
24 / p. 388	AAA	**Grand Country Inn**	◆◆	$99-$109 SAVE	403
25 / p. 388	AAA	**Grand Plaza Hotel** - see color ad p 405	◆◆◆	$105-$150 SAVE	403
26 / p. 388		Holiday Inn Express Hotel & Suites	◆◆◆	$85-$97	406
27 / p. 388	AAA	**The Dutton Inn**	◆	$43-$65 SAVE	401
28 / p. 388	AAA	**Grand Oaks Hotel** - see color ad p 405	◆◆	$49-$94 SAVE	403
29 / p. 388	AAA	**Radisson Hotel Branson** - see color ad p 409	◆◆◆	$125-$135 SAVE	408
30 / p. 388	AAA	**Angel Inn**	◆◆	$69-$129 SAVE	394
31 / p. 388	AAA	**Green Gables Inn**	◆◆	$55-$65 SAVE	404
32 / p. 388		Howard Johnson	◆◆	$64-$79	406
33 / p. 388		Golden Arrow Resort	◆	$60-$130	403
34 / p. 388	AAA	**Best Western Center Pointe Inn** - see color ad p 395	◆◆	$69-$104 SAVE	396

Spotter/Map Page Number	OA	**BRANSON** - Lodgings (continued)	Diamond Rating	Rate Range High Season	Listing Page
35 / p. 388	AAA	**Clarion Hotel at the Palace**	◇◇	$110 SAVE	401
36 / p. 388		Quality Inn & Suites	◇◇	Failed to provide	408
37 / p. 388		Super 8 Motel-Branson	◇	Failed to provide	411
38 / p. 388	AAA	**Still Waters Condominium Resort**	◇◇◇	$59-$375 SAVE	410
39 / p. 388		Fairfield Inn by Marriott	◇◇	$70-$95	402
40 / p. 388	AAA	**Comfort Inn-Thousand Hills** - see color ad p 395	◇◇	$74-$109 SAVE	401
41 / p. 388	AAA	**The Village At Indian Point** - see color ad p 413	◇◇◇	$95-$225 SAVE	413
42 / p. 388		Holiday Inn Express Green Mountain Drive	◇◇	$59-$109	404
43 / p. 388	AAA	**Econo Lodge** - see color ad p 402	◇◇	$53-$67 SAVE	402
44 / p. 388	AAA	**Alpenrose Inn**	◇	$60-$80 SAVE	393
45 / p. 388	AAA	**Thousand Hills Golf Resort** - see color ad p 412, p 397	◇◇	$55-$79 SAVE	411
46 / p. 388	AAA	**Settle Inn Resort & Conference Center** - see color ad p 411	◇◇	$79-$119 SAVE	410
47 / p. 388		Branson's Best	◇	Failed to provide	396
48 / p. 388	AAA	**Eagles's View Cottages & Condos** - see color ad p 406	◇◇	$62-$259 SAVE	402
49 / p. 388		Residence Inn by Marriott	◇◇	$89-$229	409
50 / p. 388	AAA	**Indian Point Lodge** - see color ad p 406	◇◇	$72-$360 SAVE	406
51 / p. 388	AAA	**Trail's End Resort** - see color ad p 406	◇◇	$69-$259 SAVE	411
52 / p. 388		Tribesman Resort	◇◇	$90-$100	412
53 / p. 388	AAA	**Travelodge at the Falls**	◇◇	$63-$95 SAVE	412
54 / p. 388	AAA	**Fall Creek Inn & Suites**	◇◇	$69-$79 SAVE	403
55 / p. 388		Lazy Valley Resort	◇	$59-$64	407
56 / p. 388	AAA	**Chateau on the Lake Resort Spa & Convention Center** - see color ad p 400	◇◇◇◇	$189-$269 SAVE	400
57 / p. 388	AAA	**Welk Resort Branson** - see color ad p 393	◇◇◇	$85-$109 SAVE	414
58 / p. 388	AAA	**Pointe Royale Condominium Resort** - see color ad p 408	◇◇	$117-$198 SAVE	408
59 / p. 388	AAA	**Grand Crowne Resorts**	◇◇◇	$109-$250 SAVE	403
		BRANSON - Restaurants			
1 / p. 388		Zoey's Mediterranean Cuisine	◇◇◇	$18-$25	417
2 / p. 388		Granny's Restaurant	◇◇	$6-$11	415
3 / p. 388		McFarlain's Family Restaurant	◇◇	$6-$14	416
4 / p. 388		B T Bones Steakhouse	◇◇	$9-$29	415
5 / p. 388		The Majestic Steakhouse	◇◇◇	$15-$45	416
6 / p. 388	AAA	**Rocky's Italian Restaurant**	◇◇	$9-$24	416
7 / p. 388		Ruby Lena's Tea Room & Antiques	◇◇	$6-$8(L)	416
8 / p. 388		Farmhouse Restaurant	◇	$6-$10	415
9 / p. 388	AAA	**Candlestick Inn Restaurant & Lounge**	◇◇◇	$17-$48	415
10 / p. 388		The Plantation Restaurant	◇◇	$10	416
11 / p. 388		Outback Steak & Oyster Bar	◇◇	$13-$25	416

Spotter/Map Page Number	OA	**BRANSON** - Restaurants (continued)	Diamond Rating	Rate Range High Season	Listing Page
⑫ / p. 388		Grand Country Buffet	◆◆	$10-$13	415
⑬ / p. 388		Peppercorns Restaurant	◆◆	$11-$18	416
⑭ / p. 388		Charlie's Steak Ribs & Ale	◆◆	$11-$21	415
⑮ / p. 388	AAA	**Buckingham's Restaurant & Oasis Lounge -** see color ad card insert	◆◆◆	$17-$45	415
⑯ / p. 388		Sadie's Sideboard & Smokehouse	◆◆	$7-$21	417
⑰ / p. 388		Acapulco Taco Grill	◆	$5-$7	415
⑱ / p. 388		Uptown Cafe	◆◆	$7-$10	417
⑲ / p. 388		Pasta House	◆◆	$8-$22	416
⑳ / p. 388		Dockers Restaurant	◆◆	$11-$20	415
㉑ / p. 388		Odee's BBQ	◆	$6-$18	416
㉒ / p. 388	AAA	**Chateau Grille**	◆◆◆	$22-$38	415
㉓ / p. 388		Stage Door Restaurant	◆◆	$8-$14	417
㉔ / p. 388		Luigi's Pizza Kitchen South	◆	$5-$14	416
㉕ / p. 388		Billy Gail's Cafe	◆	$5-$8(L)	415
		HOLLISTER - Restaurant			
㉘ / p. 388		Dobyns Dining Room at College of the Ozarks	◆◆◆	$8-$20	419

BRANSON pop. 6,050 (See map and index starting on p. 388)

──── WHERE TO STAY ────

ALPENROSE INN Phone: (417)336-4600 **44**

	11/1-12/17	1P: $60-$80	2P: $60-$80	XP: $5	F15
	9/1-10/31	1P: $55-$75	2P: $55-$75	XP: $5	F15
	5/1-8/31	1P: $50-$65	2P: $50-$65	XP: $5	F15
	3/1-4/30	1P: $40-$50	2P: $40-$50	XP: $5	F15

Motel

Location: Jct SR 76 (Country Music Blvd) and Green Blvd. 2875 Green Mountain Dr 65616. Fax: 417/336-4602. **Facility:** 50 one-bedroom standard units. 2-3 stories (no elevator), exterior corridors. **Parking:** on-site. **Terms:** open 3/1-12/17, office hours 6:30 am-11 pm, [ECP] meal plan available. **Amenities:** video library, hair dryers. *Some:* CD players, irons. **Pool(s):** outdoor. **Leisure Activities:** sun deck. **Guest Services:** gift shop, coin laundry, wireless Internet. **Cards:** AX, DC, DS, MC, VI. **Free Special Amenities:** expanded continental breakfast and high-speed Internet.

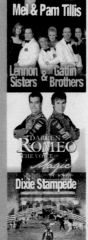

(See map and index starting on p. 388)

ANGEL INN *Book great rates at AAA.com* Phone: (417)334-6500 **30**
AAA SAVE
	8/31-12/9	1P: $69-$129	2P: $69-$129	XP: $5	F11
	5/25-8/30	1P: $59-$119	2P: $59-$119	XP: $5	F11
	3/1-5/24 & 12/10-2/29	1P: $39-$119	2P: $39-$119	XP: $5	F11

Location: 1.5 mi w of jct SR 76 (Country Music Blvd) and US 65, just s. 2350 Green Mountain Dr 65616.
Small-scale Hotel **Fax:** 417/334-6506. **Facility:** 113 one-bedroom standard units, some with whirlpools. 2-4 stories, exterior corridors. *Bath:* combo or shower only. **Parking:** on-site. **Terms:** [ECP] meal plan available, package plans.
Amenities: high-speed Internet, voice mail, irons, hair dryers. **Pool(s):** heated indoor. **Leisure Activities:** whirlpool. **Guest Services:** wireless Internet. **Business Services:** PC. **Cards:** AX, DS, MC, VI. **Free Special Amenities:** expanded continental breakfast and high-speed Internet.

SOME UNITS

ARTILLA COVE RESORT Phone: 417/338-2346 **18**
	5/25-8/18	1P: $92-$240
	8/19-10/20	1P: $72-$165
Vacation Rental	3/1-5/24	1P: $58-$165
Cottage	10/21-2/29	1P: $58-$138

Location: Jct SR 76 and 265, 1 mi s on Indian Point Rd, 1.1 mi e. Located in a quiet area. 1123 Jakes Creek Trail 65616. **Fax:** 417/338-4540. **Facility:** 10 units. 2 one- and 4 two-bedroom suites. with kitchens. 4 cottages. 1 story, exterior corridors. *Bath:* combo or shower only. **Parking:** on-site. **Terms:** office hours 8 am-8 pm, check-out 9:30 am, 3-7 night minimum stay - seasonal, 28 day cancellation notice-fee imposed, package plans. **Amenities:** high-speed Internet. *Some:* DVD players (fee). **Pool(s):** outdoor. **Leisure Activities:** rental boats, rental paddleboats, fishing, hiking trails. *Fee:* boat dock. **Guest Services:** coin laundry. **Cards:** DS, MC, VI.

SOME UNITS

(See map and index starting on p. 388)

BEST WESTERN CENTER POINTE INN · *Book great rates at AAA.com* · **Phone:** (417)334-1894 · [34]

AAA SAVE

9/28-12/15 [ECP]	1P: $69-$104	2P: $69-$104	XP: $5	F17
4/6-9/27 [ECP]	1P: $59-$99	2P: $59-$99	XP: $5	F17
12/16-2/29 [ECP]	1P: $54-$89	2P: $54-$89	XP: $5	F17
3/1-4/5 [ECP]	1P: $54-$74	2P: $54-$74	XP: $5	F17

Small-scale Hotel **Location:** On SR 76 (Country Music Blvd); jct SR 165. 3215 W Hwy 76 65616. **Fax:** 417/334-3437. **Facility:** 164 units. 163 one- and 1 two-bedroom standard units, some with whirlpools. 2-4 stories, interior/exterior corridors. **Parking:** on-site. **Terms:** package plans. **Amenities:** voice mail, irons, hair dryers. *Some:* high-speed Internet. **Pool(s):** outdoor, small heated indoor. **Leisure Activities:** sauna, whirlpools, billiards, exercise room. *Fee:* game room. **Guest Services:** gift shop, coin laundry. **Business Services:** PC. **Cards:** AX, DS, MC, VI. **Free Special Amenities: expanded continental breakfast and high-speed Internet.** *(See color ad p 395)*

SOME UNITS

🆂 🛗 🍴 ♿ 🅿 🏊 ⚒ 🎥 🖥 📺 / 🗙 🛢 🧳 /

BEST WESTERN LANDING VIEW INN & SUITES · *Book great rates at AAA.com* · **Phone:** (417)334-6464 · [17]

AAA SAVE

All Year	1P: $69-$129	2P: $69-$129	XP: $10	F18

Location: 0.3 mi e from SR 76 and US 65. 403 W Main (Hwy 76) 65616. **Fax:** 417/334-6470. **Facility:** 108 units. 102 one-bedroom standard units. 6 one-bedroom suites ($99-$199), some with whirlpools. 2-4 stories (no elevator), exterior corridors. **Parking:** on-site. **Terms:** pets ($10 extra charge). **Amenities:** DVD players, Small-scale Hotel high-speed Internet, irons, hair dryers. **Pool(s):** heated indoor. **Leisure Activities:** sauna, whirlpool. *Fee:* game room. **Guest Services:** coin laundry. **Business Services:** meeting rooms, fax (fee). **Cards:** AX, DS, MC, VI. **Free Special Amenities: continental breakfast and high-speed Internet.** *(See color ad p 394)*

SOME UNITS

🆂 🐾 🍴 🚸 🏊 ⚒ 🎥 🛢 🖥 📺 / 🗙 VCR /
FEE

BEST WESTERN MUSIC CAPITAL INN · *Book great rates at AAA.com* · **Phone:** (417)334-8378 · [7]

AAA SAVE

9/28-12/15 [ECP]	1P: $69-$104	2P: $69-$104	XP: $5	F17
4/6-9/27 [ECP]	1P: $59-$99	2P: $59-$99	XP: $5	F17
12/16-2/29 [ECP]	1P: $54-$89	2P: $54-$89	XP: $5	F17
3/1-4/5 [ECP]	1P: $54-$74	2P: $54-$74	XP: $5	F17

Small-scale Hotel **Location:** 0.3 mi e from jct SR 76 (Country Music Blvd). 3257 Shepherd of the Hills Expwy 65616. **Fax:** 417/334-8855. **Facility:** 93 one-bedroom standard units, some with whirlpools. 3-4 stories, interior corridors. *Bath:* combo or shower only. **Parking:** on-site. **Terms:** package plans. **Amenities:** high-speed Internet, voice mail, irons, hair dryers. **Pool(s):** heated indoor. **Leisure Activities:** sauna, whirlpool, pool table, exercise room. **Guest Services:** gift shop, coin laundry. **Business Services:** PC, fax. **Cards:** AX, DS, MC, VI. **Free Special Amenities: expanded continental breakfast and high-speed Internet.** *(See color ad p 395)*

SOME UNITS

🆂 🍴 🚸 🅼 ♿ 🏊 ⚒ 🎥 📺 / 🗙 🛢 🧳 /

BRANSON'S BEST · *Book at AAA.com* · **Phone:** 417/336-2378 · [47]

♦ Motel

Property failed to provide current rates

Location: 3 mi w from jct US 65 and SR 76 (Country Music Blvd), just s. Located in Thousand Hills. 3150 Green Mountain Dr 65616. **Fax:** 417/336-5846. **Facility:** 66 units. 65 one-bedroom standard units. 1 one-bedroom suite with kitchen. 2-3 stories (no elevator), exterior corridors. **Parking:** on-site. **Terms:** open 3/1-12/15. **Amenities:** high-speed Internet, irons, hair dryers. **Pool(s):** outdoor. **Guest Services:** wireless Internet. **Business Services:** PC (fee).

SOME UNITS

🏊 / 🗙 🛢 🧳 /

Did you know...

You can also trust AAA to provide you with insurance protection. Most[1] AAA clubs provide a variety of insurance products for all phases of your life, at competitive rates from leading companies in their markets. Visit us on aaa.com or call your local AAA office today.

AAA Insurance

Insure With Someone You Trust®

[1]Due to state regulations and local restrictions, insurance is not available through all AAA clubs.

COME SEE US IN

(See map and index starting on p. 388)

BRANSON TOWERS

Phone: 417/336-4500 **1**

	10/1-12/10	1P: $80-$119	2P: $80-$119	XP: $5	F12
	6/1-9/30	1P: $75-$100	2P: $75-$100	XP: $5	F12
	3/1-5/31	1P: $60-$80	2P: $60-$80	XP: $5	F12
	12/11-2/29	1P: $50-$70	2P: $50-$70	XP: $5	F12

Small-scale Hotel **Location:** Jct US 65, 2.2 mi nw on SR 248, just w. 236 Shepherd of the Hills Expwy 65616. **Fax:** 417/334-6838. **Facility:** 208 units. 202 one-bedroom standard units, some with whirlpools. 6 one-bedroom suites ($89-$169), some with whirlpools. 3 stories, interior corridors. **Parking:** on-site. **Terms:** cancellation fee imposed. **Amenities:** irons, hair dryers. **Dining:** 4 am-8 pm; closed 12/31-3/15. **Pool(s):** heated indoor. **Leisure Activities:** whirlpool. *Fee:* air hockey, game room. **Guest Services:** gift shop, valet and coin laundry. **Business Services:** meeting rooms, fax (fee). **Cards:** AX, DC, DS, MC, VI. **Free Special Amenities: continental breakfast and local telephone calls.** *(See color ad p 397)*

SOME UNITS

CALM WATERS RESORT, FORMERLY NIGHT HAWK RESORT

Phone: 417/338-8963 **22**

Vacation Rental Cottage

Property failed to provide current rates

Location: Jct SR 76 and 265, 0.6 mi w, 1 mi s on Indian Point Rd, then 1 mi e. 1043 Jakes Creek Tr 65616 (1043 Jakes Creek Trail). **Fax:** 417/338-5843. **Facility:** 16 units. 4 one-bedroom standard units with efficiencies. 2 two-bedroom suites with efficiencies. 1 vacation home and 9 cottages. 1 story; exterior corridors. *Bath:* combo or shower only. **Parking:** on-site. **Terms:** open 3/1-12/31, office hours 8 am-10 pm, check-out 9:30 am. **Pool(s):** outdoor. **Leisure Activities:** rental boats, rental paddleboats, fishing. *Fee:* boat dock. **Guest Services:** coin laundry. **Business Services:** fax.

SOME UNITS

CASCADES INN

Phone: 417/335-8424 **4**

	10/1-12/10	1P: $65-$85	2P: $65-$85	XP: $5	F
	3/1-9/30	1P: $59-$75	2P: $59-$75	XP: $5	F
	12/11-1/1	1P: $59-$65	2P: $59-$65	XP: $5	F

Small-scale Hotel **Location:** Jct SR 76, just e. 3226 Shepherd of the Hills Expwy 65616. **Fax:** 417/334-1927. **Facility:** 159 units. one-bedroom standard units, some with whirlpools. 2 one-bedroom suites ($75-$150). 4 stories, interior corridors. *Bath:* combo or shower only. **Parking:** on-site. **Terms:** open 3/1-1/1, [ECP] meal plan available, package plans. **Amenities:** high-speed Internet, irons, hair dryers. **Pool(s):** heated indoor. **Leisure Activities:** sauna, whirlpool, exercise room. *Fee:* billiards, massage, game room. **Guest Services:** sundries, coin laundry. **Business Services:** meeting rooms. *Fee:* PC, fax. **Cards:** AX, DC, DS, MC, VI. **Free Special Amenities: expanded continental breakfast and high-speed Internet.**

SOME UNITS

CHATEAU ON THE LAKE RESORT SPA & CONVENTION CENTER

Book great rates at AAA.com

Phone: (417)334-1161 **56**

	5/25-8/18	1P: $189-$269	2P: $189-$269	XP: $25	F17
	8/19-12/8	1P: $139-$269	2P: $139-$269	XP: $25	F17
	3/1-5/24	1P: $119-$249	2P: $119-$249	XP: $25	F17
	12/9-2/29	1P: $109-$199	2P: $109-$199	XP: $25	F17

Resort
Large-scale Hotel **Location:** Just n of jct SR 165 and 265. 415 N State Hwy 265 65616. **Fax:** 417/339-5566. **Facility:** An exceptional property offering elegance and many unique features, including a mixture of Ozark hospitality and sophisticated service. 301 units. 244 one-bedroom standard units. 57 one-bedroom suites ($229-$699), some with whirlpools. 10 stories, interior corridors. *Bath:* combo or shower only. **Parking:** on-site and valet. **Terms:** check-in 4 pm, 3 day cancellation notice-fee imposed, [AP] meal plan available, package plans, small pets only ($25 extra charge). **Amenities:** dual phone lines, voice mail, irons, hair dryers. *Fee:* video games, high-speed Internet. *Some:* DVD players, CD players. **Dining:** 3 restaurants, 6:30 am-10 pm, cocktails, also, Chateau Grille, see separate listing. **Pool(s):** heated outdoor, heated indoor. **Leisure Activities:** sauna, whirlpools, rental boats, canoeing, paddleboats, fishing, 2 lighted tennis courts, recreation programs, 52-seat theater, nature trail, hiking trails, playground, exercise room, spa. *Fee:* marina, waterskiing, scuba diving, charter fishing, personal watercraft, pontoon boats. **Guest Services:** gift shop, valet and coin laundry. **Business Services:** conference facilities, administrative services (fee), fax. **Cards:** AX, DC, DS, MC, VI. **Free Special Amenities: newspaper.** *(See color ad below)*

SOME UNITS

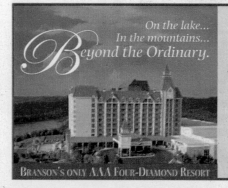

(See map and index starting on p. 388)

CLARION HOTEL AT THE PALACE *Book great rates at AAA.com* Phone: (417)334-7666 **35**

AAA SAVE	5/25-12/31	1P: $110	2P: $110	XP: $10	F18
▼▼▼	5/1-5/24	1P: $95	2P: $95	XP: $10	F18
	3/1-4/30	1P: $80	2P: $80	XP: $10	F18
	1/1-2/29	1P: $70	2P: $70	XP: $10	F18

Small-scale Hotel **Location:** On SR 76 (Country Music Blvd), 3 mi w of jct US 65. 2820 W Hwy 76 65615 (PO Box 6004, 65616). Fax: 417/334-7720. **Facility:** 166 units. 164 one-bedroom standard units, some with whirlpools. 2 two-bedroom suites ($130-$230), some with kitchens. 5-7 stories, interior/exterior corridors. *Bath:* combo or shower only. **Parking:** on-site. **Terms:** [ECP] meal plan available, package plans, $75 service charge. **Amenities:** high-speed Internet, voice mail, irons, hair dryers. **Dining:** Buckingham's Restaurant & Oasis Lounge, see separate listing. **Pool(s):** heated outdoor, heated indoor. **Leisure Activities:** sauna, whirlpools, exercise room. *Fee:* massage. **Guest Services:** valet and coin laundry, airport transportation-Point Lookout Airport, area transportation-within 5 mi. **Business Services:** conference facilities, PC, fax. **Cards:** AX, CB, DC, DS, MC, VI.

SOME UNITS
🆂🅳 ⊀ 🍽 🖥 ➣ ✕ 🎥 🔋 🖨 🖵 / ✕ VCR /

CLASSIC MOTOR INN Phone: 417/334-6991 **13**

▼ Property failed to provide current rates

Small-scale Hotel **Location:** From jct SR 76 and 376 (Shepherd of the Hills Expwy), 1.2 mi e; from SR 76 and Roark Valley Rd, 2.1 mi nw, then just w. 2384 Shepherd of the Hills Expwy 65616. Fax: 417/336-4468. **Facility:** 62 one-bedroom standard units. 2-3 stories, exterior corridors. *Bath:* combo or shower only. **Parking:** on-site. **Terms:** office hours 6 am-midnight. **Amenities:** irons, hair dryers. **Pool(s):** outdoor. **Guest Services:** coin laundry, wireless Internet. **Business Services:** meeting rooms.

SOME UNITS
🍽 🖥 ➣ / ✕ /

COMFORT INN & SUITES *Book great rates at AAA.com* Phone: (417)335-4731 **3**

AAA SAVE	9/28-12/15 [ECP]	1P: $79-$139	2P: $79-$139	XP: $5	F
▼▼▼	4/6-9/27 [ECP]	1P: $69-$139	2P: $69-$139	XP: $5	F
	3/1-4/5 & 12/16-1/2 [ECP]	1P: $64-$104	2P: $64-$104	XP: $5	F

Small-scale Hotel **Location:** 2.9 mi n of jct SR 76 (Country Music Blvd). 5150 Gretna Rd 65616. Fax: 417/335-3697. **Facility:** 102 units. 101 one-bedroom standard units, some with whirlpools. 1 cottage with whirlpool. 1-4 stories, interior/exterior corridors. *Bath:* combo or shower only. **Parking:** on-site. **Terms:** open 3/1-1/2. **Amenities:** high-speed Internet, voice mail, safes (fee), irons, hair dryers. **Pool(s):** heated indoor. **Leisure Activities:** sauna, whirlpool, walking trail, billiards, exercise room, horseshoes. *Fee:* game room. **Guest Services:** gift shop, coin laundry. **Business Services:** meeting rooms, fax (fee). **Cards:** AX, DS, MC, VI. **Free Special Amenities:** expanded continental breakfast and high-speed Internet. *(See color ad p 395)*

SOME UNITS
🆂🅳 🖥 ➣ ✕ 🎥 🖵 / ✕ 🔋 🖨 /

COMFORT INN-THOUSAND HILLS *Book great rates at AAA.com* Phone: (417)335-4727 **40**

AAA SAVE	9/28-12/15 [ECP]	1P: $74-$109	2P: $74-$109	XP: $5	F17
▼▼▼	4/6-9/27 [ECP]	1P: $64-$104	2P: $64-$104	XP: $5	F17
	3/1-4/5 & 12/16-2/29 [ECP]	1P: $59-$99	2P: $59-$99	XP: $5	F17

Small-scale Hotel **Location:** Jct US 65, 2 mi w on SR 76 (Country Music Blvd), then just s. 203 S Wildwood Dr 65616. Fax: 417/335-4748. **Facility:** 108 units. 105 one- and 3 two-bedroom standard units, some with whirlpools. 3-4 stories, interior corridors. *Bath:* combo or shower only. **Parking:** on-site. **Terms:** package plans. **Amenities:** high-speed Internet, voice mail, irons, hair dryers. **Pool(s):** heated indoor. **Leisure Activities:** sauna, whirlpool, exercise room. *Fee:* game room. **Guest Services:** gift shop, coin laundry. **Business Services:** meeting rooms, PC, fax. **Cards:** AX, DS, MC, VI. **Free Special Amenities:** expanded continental breakfast and high-speed Internet. *(See color ad p 395)*

SOME UNITS
🆂🅳 🍽 🖥 📷 ➣ ✕ 🎥 🖵 / ✕ 🔋 🖨 /

COMFORT INN WEST *Book great rates at AAA.com* Phone: (417)334-8694 **10**

AAA SAVE	9/28-12/23 [ECP]	1P: $69-$139	2P: $69-$139	XP: $5	F17
▼▼▼	4/6-9/27 [ECP]	1P: $59-$139	2P: $59-$139	XP: $5	F17
	3/1-4/5 [ECP]	1P: $54-$99	2P: $54-$99	XP: $5	F17

Small-scale Hotel **Location:** Just e of jct SR 76 (Country Music Blvd). 3601 Shepherd of the Hills Expwy 65616. Fax: 417/334-1037. **Facility:** 87 units. 79 one-bedroom standard units. 8 one-bedroom suites ($79-$159), some with whirlpools. 2-3 stories, exterior corridors. **Parking:** on-site. **Terms:** open 3/1-12/23, package plans. **Amenities:** high-speed Internet, irons, hair dryers. **Pool(s):** heated indoor. **Leisure Activities:** whirlpool. **Guest Services:** coin laundry. **Business Services:** PC, fax (fee). **Cards:** AX, DS, MC, VI. **Free Special Amenities:** expanded continental breakfast and high-speed Internet. *(See color ad p 395)*

SOME UNITS
🆂🅳 🍽 ➣ 🎥 🖵 / ✕ 🔋 🖨 /

DOCKERS INN Phone: (417)334-3600 **20**

▼▼ ▼▼	9/1-12/15	1P: $65	XP: $10	F18
	4/1-8/31	1P: $54	XP: $10	F18

Motel **Location:** SR 376, 0.7 mi e on SR 76 (Country Music Blvd), just s. 3060 Green Mountain Dr 65616. Fax: 417/334-8166. **Facility:** 78 one-bedroom standard units. 3 stories (no elevator), exterior corridors. **Parking:** on-site. **Terms:** open 4/1-12/15, office hours 6:30 am-11 pm, check-in 4 pm, package plans. **Pool(s):** outdoor. **Business Services:** meeting rooms, PC, fax. **Cards:** AX, DS, MC, VI.

SOME UNITS
ASK 🆂🅳 🍽 ➣ 🖵 / ✕ /

THE DUTTON INN Phone: (417)334-8873 **27**

AAA SAVE	3/1-12/16 & 12/27-2/29	1P: $43-$65	2P: $43-$65	XP: $5	F12
▼				

Location: 0.7 mi e of jct SR 376, just s. 3454 W Hwy 76 65616. Fax: 417/336-2350. **Facility:** 78 one-bedroom standard units. 2-3 stories, exterior corridors. **Parking:** on-site. **Terms:** open 3/1-12/16 & 12/27-2/29, office hours 7 am-midnight, package plans. **Amenities:** high-speed Internet, voice mail. **Business Services:** Small-scale Hotel meeting rooms, fax. **Cards:** DS, MC, VI. **Free Special Amenities:** full breakfast and high-speed Internet.

SOME UNITS
🍽 🖵 / ✕ 🔋 🖨 /

(See map and index starting on p. 388)

EAGLES INN A RODEWAY INN   *Book great rates at AAA.com*   Phone: (417)336-2666   **6**
AAA SAVE   4/1-12/15   1P: $45-$85   2P: $45-$85   XP: $5   F18
Location: 0.3 mi e of jct SR 76. 3221 Shepherd of the Hills Expwy 65616. Fax: 417/334-7358. **Facility:** 66 one-bedroom standard units. 2-4 stories (no elevator), exterior corridors. *Bath:* combo or shower only. **Parking:** on-site. **Terms:** open 4/1-12/15, office hours 6:45 am-11 pm, pets ($10 extra charge). **Amenities:** hair dryers. *Some:* irons. **Pool(s):** small heated outdoor. **Guest Services:** coin laundry. **Business Services:** fax (fee). **Cards:** AX, DS, MC, VI. **Free Special Amenities: continental breakfast and high-speed Internet.**
Small-scale Hotel

SOME UNITS
[S D] [🛏] [📶] [🍽] [📺] / [⨉] [🔒] [📶] /
FEE

EAGLES'S VIEW COTTAGES & CONDOS   Phone: (417)338-2227   **48**
AAA SAVE   6/1-8/21   1P: $62-$259   2P: $62-$259   XP: $7
   3/1-5/31 & 8/22-12/31   1P: $45-$165   2P: $45-$165   XP: $7
   1/1-2/29   1P: $39-$125   2P: $39-$125   XP: $7
Resort Condominium   **Location:** Jct SR 265, 0.6 mi w on SR 76, 2.9 mi s on Indian Point Rd, then just e. 71 Dogwood Park Trail 65616. Fax: 417/338-3507. **Facility:** Roadside units, some with lake view. 48 units with fireplaces; some with washer and dryer. 94 units. 44 one-bedroom standard units, some with kitchens and/or whirlpools. 15 one-, 20 two- and 1 three-bedroom suites ($45-$259) with whirlpools, some with efficiencies or kitchens. 14 cottages ($39-$239). 1-3 stories (no elevator), exterior corridors. *Bath:* combo or shower only. **Parking:** on-site. **Terms:** office hours 8 am-9 pm, check-in 4 pm, 1-4 night minimum stay - seasonal, 21 day cancellation notice-fee imposed, package plans. **Amenities:** video library (fee). *Some:* DVD players, irons. **Pool(s):** outdoor, wading. **Leisure Activities:** whirlpool, rental boats, paddleboats, marina, scuba diving, snorkeling, fishing, pontoon and deck boats, badminton, tetherball, nature trail, playground, horseshoes, shuffleboard, volleyball. *Fee:* waterskiing, charter fishing, personal watercraft, game room. **Guest Services:** complimentary laundry. **Business Services:** fax (fee). **Cards:** AX, CB, DC, DS, MC, VI. **Free Special Amenities: local telephone calls.** *(See color ad p 406)*

SOME UNITS
[S D] [🚤] [📶] [⨉] [🔒] [📶] [📺] / [VCR]
FEE

ECONO LODGE   *Book great rates at AAA.com*   Phone: (417)336-4849   **43**
AAA SAVE   5/1-10/31   1P: $53-$67   2P: $53-$67   XP: $5   F18
   11/1-2/29   1P: $40-$67   2P: $40-$67   XP: $5   F18
   4/1-4/30   1P: $49-$57   2P: $49-$57   XP: $5   F18
   3/1-3/31   1P: $40-$45   2P: $40-$45   XP: $5   F18
Small-scale Hotel   **Location:** 2 mi w on SR 76 (Country Music Blvd), just s. 230 S Wildwood Dr 65616. Fax: 417/336-4862. **Facility:** 63 units. 62 one-bedroom standard units, some with whirlpools. 1 one-bedroom suite with whirlpool. 2-3 stories (no elevator), exterior corridors. *Bath:* combo or shower only. **Parking:** on-site. **Terms:** cancellation fee imposed, [ECP] meal plan available. **Amenities:** high-speed Internet. **Pool(s):** outdoor. **Leisure Activities:** whirlpool. **Guest Services:** coin laundry, airport transportation-Clark Airport. **Business Services:** fax (fee). **Cards:** AX, DC, DS, MC, VI. **Free Special Amenities: expanded continental breakfast and high-speed Internet.** *(See color ad below)*

SOME UNITS
[S D] [✈] [📶] [♿ M] [🚤] [📺] / [⨉] [🔒] [📶] [📺] /

FAIRFIELD INN BY MARRIOTT   *Book great rates at AAA.com*   Phone: (417)336-5665   **39**
   All Year   1P: $70-$90   2P: $75-$95   XP: $5   F18
Small-scale Hotel   **Location:** US 65, 3.8 mi w on SR 76 (Country Music Blvd), just s. 220 SR 165 S 65616. Fax: 417/336-5665. **Facility:** Smoke free premises. 100 one-bedroom standard units. 4 stories, interior corridors. *Bath:* combo or shower only. **Parking:** on-site. **Amenities:** high-speed Internet, irons, hair dryers. **Pool(s):** small heated indoor. **Leisure Activities:** whirlpool. *Fee:* game room. **Guest Services:** valet laundry. **Business Services:** fax (fee). **Cards:** AX, DC, DS, MC, VI.

SOME UNITS
[ASK] [S D] [📶] [♿] [🔇] [🚤] [⨉] [📺] [📺] / [🔒] [📶] /

(See map and index starting on p. 388)

FALL CREEK INN & SUITES

AAA SAVE

Small-scale Hotel

10/26-12/8 [ECP]	1P: $69-$79	XP: $5	F16
5/18-10/25 [ECP]	1P: $64-$69	XP: $5	F16
3/1-5/17 [ECP]	1P: $50-$60	XP: $5	F16
12/9-2/29 [ECP]	1P: $44-$49	XP: $5	F16

Phone: (417)348-1683 **54**

Location: Jct SR 76 (Country Music Blvd), 1.5 mi s on SR 165. 995 Hwy 165 65616. Fax: 417/239-3944. **Facility:** 101 units. 97 one-bedroom standard units, some with whirlpools. 4 one-bedroom suites ($100-$190) with whirlpools. 3 stories (no elevator), exterior corridors. **Parking:** on-site. **Terms:** package plans, small pets only ($50 deposit, $7 extra charge). **Amenities:** high-speed Internet (fee). *Some:* hair dryers. **Pool(s):** outdoor. **Leisure Activities:** horseshoes. **Guest Services:** coin laundry. **Business Services:** fax (fee). **Cards:** AX, DS, MC, VI. **Free Special Amenities:** continental breakfast and high-speed Internet.

SOME UNITS

GOLDEN ARROW RESORT

Motel

5/25-8/19	1P: $60-$130	2P: $60-$130	XP: $6	F4
8/20-12/15	1P: $42-$90	2P: $42-$90	XP: $6	F4
3/1-5/24	1P: $33-$72	2P: $33-$72	XP: $6	F4

Phone: 417/338-2245 **33**

Location: Jct SR 76 and 265, 0.6 mi w, then 2.8 mi s. 2869 Indian Point Rd 65616. Fax: 417/338-2885. **Facility:** 21 units. 2 one-bedroom standard units. 9 one-, 8 two- and 2 three-bedroom suites ($54-$95), some with efficiencies or kitchens. 1 story, exterior corridors. **Parking:** on-site. **Terms:** open 3/1-12/15, 21 day cancellation notice-fee imposed, package plans. **Pool(s):** outdoor. **Leisure Activities:** whirlpool, playground, basketball, horseshoes, shuffleboard. **Guest Services:** coin laundry. **Cards:** AX, DS, MC, VI.

SOME UNITS

GRAND COUNTRY INN

AAA SAVE

Small-scale Hotel

5/27-8/13	2P: $99-$109	XP: $8	F
8/14-2/29	2P: $69-$99	XP: $8	F
3/1-5/26	2P: $69-$89	XP: $8	F

Phone: (417)335-3535 **24**

Location: Jct US 65, 1.9 mi w. Located adjacent to the mall; 76 Music Hall Theater on premises. 1945 W 76 Country Blvd 65616. Fax: 417/334-1647. **Facility:** 319 one-bedroom standard units. 2-3 stories (no elevator), exterior corridors. *Bath:* combo or shower only. **Parking:** on-site. **Terms:** package plans. **Amenities:** irons, hair dryers. **Dining:** 3 restaurants, 6:30 am-8 pm; from 7 am off season. **Pool(s):** 2 outdoor, heated indoor. **Leisure Activities:** whirlpool, indoor/outdoor water park. *Fee:* miniature golf, game room. **Guest Services:** gift shop, coin laundry. **Business Services:** meeting rooms. **Cards:** AX, DS, MC, VI. **Free Special Amenities:** local telephone calls and high-speed Internet.

SOME UNITS

GRAND CROWNE RESORTS

AAA SAVE

Condominium

All Year	1P: $109-$250	2P: $109-$250

Phone: (417)332-8330 **59**

Location: just sw of jct Wildwood Dr. 300 Golfview Dr 65616. Fax: 417/332-8371. **Facility:** 130 one-bedroom suites with kitchens, some with whirlpools. 5 stories, exterior corridors. *Bath:* combo or shower only. **Parking:** on-site. **Terms:** check-in 4 pm, cancellation fee imposed, package plans. **Amenities:** voice mail, irons, hair dryers. *Some:* DVD players. **Pool(s):** heated indoor. **Leisure Activities:** whirlpool, grills, playground, exercise room. **Guest Services:** complimentary and valet laundry. *(See color ad p 404)*

SOME UNITS

GRAND OAKS HOTEL

AAA SAVE

Small-scale Hotel

Book great rates at AAA.com

3/1-1/1 & 2/1-2/29 [ECP]	1P: $49-$94	2P: $49-$94	XP: $10	F17

Phone: (417)336-6423 **28**

Location: Jct US 65, 1.5 mi w on SR 76 (Country Music Blvd), then just s. 2315 Green Mountain Dr 65616 (PO Box 2290, KIRBYVILLE). Fax: 417/334-6264. **Facility:** 201 one-bedroom standard units, some with whirlpools. 3-4 stories, interior corridors. *Bath:* combo or shower only. **Parking:** on-site. **Terms:** open 3/1-1/1 & 2/1-2/29, 3 day cancellation notice-fee imposed, package plans. **Amenities:** voice mail, irons, hair dryers. **Pool(s):** outdoor, heated indoor. **Leisure Activities:** whirlpools. *Fee:* exercise room, game room. **Guest Services:** coin laundry, wireless Internet. **Business Services:** meeting rooms, PC. **Cards:** AX, DS, MC, VI. **Free Special Amenities:** expanded continental breakfast and local telephone calls. *(See color ad p 405)*

SOME UNITS

GRAND PLAZA HOTEL

AAA SAVE

Small-scale Hotel

Book great rates at AAA.com

9/3-12/15	1P: $105-$150	2P: $105-$150	XP: $5	F18
4/16-9/2	1P: $95-$140	2P: $95-$140	XP: $5	F18
3/1-4/15	1P: $80-$125	2P: $80-$125	XP: $5	F18
12/16-2/29	1P: $72-$117	2P: $72-$117	XP: $5	F18

Phone: (417)336-6646 **25**

Location: 2.5 mi w of jct US 65. 245 N Wildwood Dr 65616. Fax: 417/337-5535. **Facility:** 200 one-bedroom standard units, some with whirlpools. 9 stories, interior corridors. *Bath:* combo or shower only. **Parking:** on-site. **Amenities:** video games (fee), high-speed Internet, irons, hair dryers. **Dining:** 3 pm-10 pm; closed Sun, cocktails. **Pool(s):** small heated indoor. **Leisure Activities:** whirlpool, exercise room. *Fee:* game room. **Guest Services:** coin laundry. **Business Services:** meeting rooms, PC, fax (fee). **Cards:** AX, CB, DC, DS, MC, VI. **Free Special Amenities:** expanded continental breakfast and high-speed Internet. *(See color ad p 405)*

SOME UNITS

(See map and index starting on p. 388)

GREEN GABLES INN
Phone: 417/336-3400   **31**

AAA SAVE

10/1-12/15 [CP]	1P: $55-$65	2P: $55-$65	XP: $5	F12
8/1-9/30 [CP]	1P: $46-$52	2P: $46-$52	XP: $5	F12
5/1-7/31 [CP]	1P: $44-$50	2P: $44-$50	XP: $5	F12
3/1-4/30 [CP]	1P: $41-$46	2P: $41-$46	XP: $5	F12

Small-scale Hotel **Location:** Jct US 65, 2 mi w on SR 76 (Country Music Blvd), then just s. 2400 Green Mountain Dr 65616. Fax: 417/336-3486. **Facility:** 54 one-bedroom standard units. 2-3 stories (no elevator), exterior corridors. *Bath:* combo or shower only. **Parking:** on-site. **Terms:** open 3/1-12/15, office hours 6:30 am-11 pm. **Amenities:** *Some:* high-speed Internet. **Pool(s):** outdoor. **Business Services:** fax. **Cards:** AX, DS, MC, VI. **Free Special Amenities: continental breakfast and high-speed Internet.**

SOME UNITS

HAMPTON INN-WEST   *Book great rates at AAA.com*
Phone: 417/337-5762   **14**

10/1-2/29	1P: $101-$132	2P: $101-$132
5/1-9/30	1P: $91-$122	2P: $91-$122
3/1-4/30	1P: $81-$105	2P: $81-$105

Small-scale Hotel **Location:** 0.3 mi s of jct SR 76 (Country Music Blvd) and Shepherd of the Hills Expwy. Located at the entrance to Remington Theater. 3695 W Hwy 76 65616. Fax: 417/337-8733. **Facility:** 109 one-bedroom standard units, some with whirlpools. 5 stories, interior corridors. *Bath:* combo or shower only. **Parking:** on-site. **Terms:** cancellation fee imposed, [ECP] meal plan available. **Amenities:** high-speed Internet, voice mail, irons, hair dryers. **Pool(s):** heated indoor. **Leisure Activities:** whirlpool, exercise room. **Guest Services:** coin laundry, wireless Internet. **Business Services:** meeting rooms. **Cards:** AX, CB, DC, DS, MC, VI.

SOME UNITS

HOLIDAY INN EXPRESS GREEN MOUNTAIN DRIVE   *Book at AAA.com*
Phone: (417)336-2100   **42**

All Year	1P: $59	2P: $109	XP: $10	F18

Location: 2 mi w on SR 76 (Country Music Blvd), just s on Wildwood Dr, then just w. 2801 Green Mountain Dr 65616. Fax: 417/336-6319. **Facility:** 120 units. 118 one-bedroom standard units, some with whirlpools. 2 one-bedroom suites ($79-$169) with efficiencies and whirlpools. 5 stories, interior corridors. *Bath:* combo or shower only. **Parking:** on-site. **Amenities:** high-speed Internet, voice mail, irons, hair dryers. **Pool(s):** outdoor. **Leisure Activities:** whirlpool. **Guest Services:** coin laundry, wireless Internet. **Cards:** AX, CB, DC, DS, JC, MC, VI.

SOME UNITS

(See map and index starting on p. 388)

HOLIDAY INN EXPRESS HOTEL & SUITES *Book at AAA.com*   Phone: (417)336-1100   26

All Year [ECP]   1P: $85-$97   2P: $85-$97   XP: $6   F18

Small-scale Hotel   **Location:** 1.8 mi w of jct SR 76 (Country Music Blvd) and US 65. 1970 W Hwy 76 (Country Music Blvd) 65616. Fax: 417/336-1122. **Facility:** 144 one-bedroom standard units, some with kitchens and/or whirlpools. 5 stories, interior corridors. *Bath:* combo or shower only. **Parking:** on-site. **Terms:** pets ($25 extra charge). **Amenities:** high-speed Internet, voice mail, irons, hair dryers. **Pool(s):** heated outdoor. **Leisure Activities:** whirlpool, exercise room. **Guest Services:** coin laundry. **Business Services:** PC. **Cards:** AX, CB, DC, DS, MC, VI.

SOME UNITS

HONEYSUCKLE INN & CONFERENCE CENTER   Phone: 417/335-2030   5

Property failed to provide current rates

Small-scale Hotel   **Location:** Just e of jct SR 76 (Country Music Blvd). 3598 Shepherd of the Hills Expwy 65616. Fax: 417/335-2039. **Facility:** 210 one-bedroom standard units, some with whirlpools. 2-3 stories (no elevator), exterior corridors. *Bath:* combo or shower only. **Parking:** on-site. **Amenities:** voice mail, hair dryers. **Pool(s):** outdoor, small indoor. **Leisure Activities:** whirlpool. **Guest Services:** coin laundry. **Business Services:** meeting rooms, fax (fee).

SOME UNITS

HOWARD JOHNSON *Book at AAA.com*   Phone: (417)336-5151   32

5/26-12/16   1P: $64-$79   2P: $64-$79   XP: $6   F17
3/1-5/25   1P: $59-$64   2P: $59-$64   XP: $6   F17

Small-scale Hotel   **Location:** On SR 76 (Country Music Blvd), 3.5 mi w of jct US 65. 3027-A W Hwy 76 65616. Fax: 417/337-7007. **Facility:** 344 units. 343 one-bedroom standard units. 1 one-bedroom suite with whirlpool. 3-4 stories, exterior corridors. **Parking:** on-site. **Terms:** open 3/1-12/16, package plans, pets ($10 extra charge). **Amenities:** irons, hair dryers. *Some:* high-speed Internet. **Pool(s):** outdoor, 2 wading. **Leisure Activities:** whirlpools, playground. **Guest Services:** coin laundry. **Business Services:** meeting rooms, fax (fee). **Cards:** AX, DS, MC, VI.

SOME UNITS

INDIAN POINT LODGE *Book great rates at AAA.com*   Phone: (417)338-2250   50

6/1-8/21   1P: $72-$360   2P: $72-$360   XP: $7
3/1-5/31 & 8/22-12/31   1P: $55-$240   2P: $55-$240   XP: $7
1/1-2/29   1P: $45-$190   2P: $45-$190   XP: $7

Resort Condominium   **Location:** Jct SR 265, 0.6 mi w on SR 76, 2.9 mi s on Indian Point Rd, then just e. 71 Dogwood Park Trail 65616. Fax: 417/338-3507. **Facility:** On lakefront with variety of appointments. All condominium units with fireplaces; some with washer and dryer. 48 units. 6 one-bedroom standard units with efficiencies. 11 one-, 26 two- and 5 three-bedroom suites ($59-$360), some with efficiencies, kitchens and/or whirlpools. 1-3 stories (no elevator), exterior corridors. **Parking:** on-site. **Terms:** office hours 8 am-9 pm, check-in 4 pm, 1-7 night minimum stay - seasonal, 21 day cancellation notice-fee imposed, package plans. **Amenities:** video library (fee). *Some:* irons. **Pool(s):** outdoor, wading. **Leisure Activities:** whirlpool, rental boats, paddleboats, marina, scuba diving, snorkeling, fishing, badminton, tetherball, nature trail, playground, horseshoes, shuffleboard, volleyball. *Fee:* waterskiing, charter fishing, personal watercraft, game room. **Business Services:** fax (fee). **Cards:** AX, CB, DC, DS, MC, VI. **Free Special Amenities:** local telephone calls. *(See color ad below)*

SOME UNITS

(See map and index starting on p. 388)

LA QUINTA INN BRANSON (MUSIC CITY CENTRE) *Book great rates at AAA.com* **Phone:** (417)336-1600 **19**

▼▼▼▼ 7/1-11/30   1P: $75-$89
       3/27-6/30   1P: $60-$70
Small-scale Hotel 3/1-3/26 & 12/1-2/29   1P: $50-$65
Location: 1.6 mi w of jct US 65. 1835 W Hwy 76 65616. Fax: 417/332-2975. **Facility:** 99 one-bedroom standard units, some with whirlpools. 2-3 stories, interior/exterior corridors. *Bath:* combo or shower only. **Parking:** on-site. **Terms:** [ECP] meal plan available, package plans. **Amenities:** high-speed Internet, voice mail, irons, hair dryers. *Some:* dual phone lines. **Pool(s):** heated indoor. **Leisure Activities:** sauna, whirlpool, exercise room. **Guest Services:** gift shop, coin laundry. **Business Services:** meeting rooms, PC, fax. **Cards:** AX, CB, DC, DS, MC, VI.

SOME UNITS
(ASK) 🔊 🐾 ⫟ 🍴 ⊘ 🛄 ⊠ 💻 / ⊠ 🛁 📶 /

LAZY VALLEY RESORT   **Phone:** 417/334-2397 **55**

▼▼▼ All Year   1P: $59-$64   2P: $59-$64   XP: $6   D17
Motel **Location:** 1 mi w of US 65 on SR 76, 2.5 mi s on Fall Creek Rd, follow signs. 285 River Ln 65616. Fax: 417/334-2397. **Facility:** 16 units. 8 one- and 3 two-bedroom standard units with efficiencies. 4 two-bedroom suites ($75-$98), some with efficiencies or kitchens. 1 vacation home ($200). 1 story, exterior corridors. *Bath:* combo or shower only. **Parking:** on-site. **Terms:** 3 night minimum stay - seasonal and/or weekends, 30 day cancellation notice-fee imposed, weekly rates available. **Pool(s):** outdoor. **Leisure Activities:** fishing, basketball. *Fee:* boats, marina.

SOME UNITS
🛶 ⊠ 🎿 🛁 💻 / ⊠ 📶 /

MOUNTAIN MUSIC INN   *Book great rates at AAA.com*   **Phone:** (417)335-6625 **21**

(AAA) (SAVE) 3/1-12/10   1P: $48-$75   2P: $48-$75   XP: $5   F16
▼▼▼ **Location:** Jct SR 376, 0.5 mi e on SR 76 (Country Music Blvd), then 0.5 mi w. 300 Schaefer Dr 65616.
Small-scale Hotel Fax: 417/335-8465. **Facility:** 140 one-bedroom standard units, some with whirlpools. 2-3 stories, interior/exterior corridors. *Bath:* combo or shower only. **Parking:** on-site. **Terms:** open 3/1-12/10, office hours 7 am-11 pm. **Pool(s):** outdoor, heated indoor. **Leisure Activities:** whirlpool, exercise room. **Guest Services:** coin laundry. **Business Services:** meeting rooms. **Cards:** AX, DS, MC, VI.
Free Special Amenities: expanded continental breakfast and local telephone calls.

SOME UNITS
🛶 / ⊠ 📶 /

OZARK VALLEY INN   **Phone:** 417/336-4666 **9**

(AAA) (SAVE) 11/1-12/15   1P: $65-$115   2P: $65-$115   XP: $5   F15
            5/1-10/31   1P: $55-$105   2P: $55-$105   XP: $5   F15
▼▼▼   3/1-4/30   1P: $45-$100   2P: $45-$100   XP: $5   F15
Motel **Location:** Jct SR 76 (Country Music Blvd), 0.9 mi e. 2693 Shepherd of the Hills Expwy 65616. Fax: 417/336-4750. **Facility:** 65 one-bedroom standard units, some with whirlpools. 2-3 stories (no elevator), exterior corridors. **Parking:** on-site. **Terms:** open 3/1-12/15, office hours 7 am-11 pm, [ECP] meal plan available, package plans, pets ($5 extra charge). **Amenities:** hair dryers. *Some:* high-speed Internet. **Pool(s):** small outdoor. **Leisure Activities:** whirlpool. *Fee:* game room. **Guest Services:** coin laundry. **Business Services:** fax. **Cards:** AX, DS, MC, VI.
Free Special Amenities: expanded continental breakfast and high-speed Internet. *(See color ad below)*

SOME UNITS
🐾 🛶 💻 / ⊠ 📶 📶 /
FEE   FEE FEE

PALMS INN   **Phone:** (417)335-7600 **16**

(AAA) (SAVE) All Year [CP]   1P: $33-$49   2P: $33-$49
▼▼▼ **Location:** 0.7 mi w of jct SR 165 (Gretna Rd). 3514 Hwy 76 W 65616. Fax: 417/335-7677. **Facility:** 72 one-bedroom standard units. 3 stories (no elevator), exterior corridors. **Parking:** on-site. **Terms:** 21 day
Motel cancellation notice-fee imposed. **Amenities:** high-speed Internet (fee). **Pool(s):** small outdoor. **Leisure Activities:** sauna. **Guest Services:** coin laundry. **Business Services:** fax (fee). **Cards:** DS, MC, VI.

SOME UNITS
🔊 ⫟ 🛶 / ⊠ 📶 📶 💻 /

(See map and index starting on p. 388)

POINTE ROYALE CONDOMINIUM RESORT   *Book great rates at AAA.com*   Phone: (417)334-5614   58

(AAA) [SAVE]

6/1-12/31	1P: $117-$126	2P: $117-$198	XP: $6	F12
4/1-5/31	1P: $113-$121	2P: $113-$188	XP: $6	F12
3/1-3/31 & 1/1-2/29	1P: $92-$101	2P: $92-$148	XP: $6	F12

Vacation Rental
Condominium

Location: On SR 165, 2.9 mi s of jct SR 76 (Country Music Blvd). 158A Pointe Royale Dr 65616. Fax: 417/334-5620. **Facility:** 180 units. 55 one-, 95 two- and 30 three-bedroom suites ($92-$395) with kitchens, some with whirlpools. 2-3 stories (no elevator), exterior corridors. **Parking:** on-site. **Terms:** office hours 7 am-midnight, check-in 4 pm, 14 day cancellation notice-fee imposed, weekly rates available, package plans. **Amenities:** DVD players, high-speed Internet (fee), voice mail, irons, hair dryers. **Dining:** 7 am-8 pm; hours may vary, cocktails. **Pool(s):** 2 outdoor, heated indoor, wading. **Leisure Activities:** whirlpool, fishing, 2 lighted tennis courts, pavilion, grill, hiking trails, playground, exercise room, basketball. *Fee:* golf-18 holes, massage. **Guest Services:** complimentary laundry. **Business Services:** meeting rooms, business center. **Cards:** AX, DS, MC, VI. **Free Special Amenities: local telephone calls and preferred room (subject to availability with advance reservations).** *(See color ad below)*

SOME UNITS

[S▪D] [📶] [🍴] [▽] [🏊] [✕] [🛗] [🖥] [🖨] / [✕] [VCR] /

QUALITY INN   *Book great rates at AAA.com*   Phone: (417)335-6776   8

10/1-12/15 [ECP]	1P: $75-$95	2P: $75-$95	XP: $5	F18
6/1-9/30 [ECP]	1P: $55-$80	2P: $55-$80	XP: $5	F18
3/1-5/31 & 12/16-2/29 [ECP]	1P: $45-$70	2P: $45-$70	XP: $5	F18

Small-scale Hotel   **Location:** 0.3 mi e of jct SR 76 (Country Music Blvd). 3269 Shepherd of the Hills Expwy 65616. Fax: 417/335-6762. **Facility:** 213 one-bedroom standard units, some with whirlpools. 2-4 stories, interior/exterior corridors. *Bath:* combo or shower only. **Parking:** on-site. **Terms:** [BP] meal plan available, pets ($10 extra charge, with prior approval). **Amenities:** high-speed Internet, irons, hair dryers. **Pool(s):** outdoor, heated indoor. **Leisure Activities:** whirlpool, exercise room. *Fee:* game room. **Guest Services:** coin laundry. **Business Services:** meeting rooms, fax (fee). **Cards:** AX, DC, DS, MC, VI.

SOME UNITS

[ASK] [S▪D] [🛏] [🍴] [▽] [🌀] [🏊] [✕] [🖥] / [✕] [🛗] [🖨] /
    FEE   FEE FEE

QUALITY INN & SUITES   *Book great rates at AAA.com*   Phone: 417/334-1194   36

Property failed to provide current rates

Small-scale Hotel   **Location:** Jct US 65, 2 mi w. 2834 W Hwy 76 65616. Fax: 417/334-6670. **Facility:** 113 units. 109 one- and 4 two-bedroom standard units, some with whirlpools. 2-4 stories, exterior corridors. **Parking:** on-site. **Amenities:** high-speed Internet, irons, hair dryers. **Pool(s):** outdoor, small heated indoor. **Leisure Activities:** whirlpool. **Guest Services:** coin laundry. **Business Services:** meeting rooms, fax.

SOME UNITS

[🍴▪] [🏊] [📹] [🖥] / [✕] [🛗] [🖨] /

RADISSON HOTEL BRANSON   *Book great rates at AAA.com*   Phone: (417)335-5767   29

(AAA) [SAVE]

5/24-12/15	1P: $125-$135	2P: $125-$135	XP: $5	F18
5/1-5/23	1P: $110-$120	2P: $110-$120	XP: $5	F18
3/1-4/30 & 12/16-2/29	1P: $100-$110	2P: $100-$110	XP: $5	F18

Large-scale Hotel   **Location:** Jct US 65, 2 mi w on SR 76 (Country Music Blvd), then just s. 120 S Wildwood Dr 65616. Fax: 417/335-7979. **Facility:** 472 units. 445 one-bedroom standard units. 27 one-bedroom suites with whirlpools. 10 stories, interior corridors. *Bath:* combo or shower only. **Parking:** on-site. **Terms:** [BP] meal plan available, package plans. **Amenities:** voice mail, irons, hair dryers. *Some:* high-speed Internet. **Dining:** 6:30 am-midnight, cocktails. **Pool(s):** heated indoor/outdoor. **Leisure Activities:** sauna, whirlpool, exercise room. *Fee:* game room. **Guest Services:** valet laundry. *Fee:* airport transportation-Springfield Airport, area transportation-Branson area. **Business Services:** conference facilities, fax (fee). **Cards:** AX, CB, DC, DS, JC, MC, VI. **Free Special Amenities: full breakfast and newspaper.** *(See color ad p 409)*

SOME UNITS

[S▪D] [✈] [🍴] [▽] [🏋M] [🥃] [🌀] [🏊] [✕] [📹] [🖥] / [✕] [🛗] [🖨] /
    FEE

RAMADA INN & CONFERENCE CENTER   *Book at AAA.com*   Phone: (417)334-1000   23

3/1-12/8	1P: $40-$90	2P: $40-$90	XP: $5	F

Small-scale Hotel   **Location:** Jct SR 76 (Country Music Blvd) and US 65, 1.5 mi w. 1700 Hwy 76 W 65616. Fax: 417/339-3046. **Facility:** 296 one-bedroom standard units. 2-6 stories, exterior corridors. *Bath:* combo or shower only. **Parking:** on-site. **Terms:** open 3/1-12/8, pets ($20 fee). **Amenities:** irons, hair dryers. *Some:* DVD players, high-speed Internet. **Pool(s):** 2 heated outdoor. **Leisure Activities:** playground, horseshoes, shuffleboard, volleyball. **Guest Services:** coin laundry. **Business Services:** meeting rooms, PC. **Cards:** AX, DC, DS, JC, MC, VI.

SOME UNITS

[ASK] [S▪D] [🛏] [🍴] [🥃] [🏊] [✕] [🖥] / [✕] [VCR] [🛗] [🖨] /
                            FEE   FEE FEE

(See map and index starting on p. 388)

RESIDENCE INN BY MARRIOTT
Book great rates at AAA.com   **Phone:** (417)336-4077   **49**

◆◆ ◆◆ All Year   1P: $89-$229   2P: $89-$229

Small-scale Hotel **Location:** 2 mi w on SR 76 (Country Music Blvd), just s. 280 Wildwood Dr S 65616. Fax: 417/336-5837. **Facility:** Smoke free premises. 85 units. 21 one-bedroom standard units with efficiencies. 49 one- and 15 two-bedroom suites with efficiencies or kitchens. 3 stories, interior corridors. *Bath:* combo or shower only. **Parking:** on-site. **Terms:** pets ($75 fee). **Amenities:** high-speed Internet, voice mail, irons, hair dryers. **Pool(s):** small heated indoor. **Leisure Activities:** whirlpool, exercise room, sports court. **Guest Services:** coin laundry. **Cards:** AX, CB, DC, DS, JC, MC, VI.

[ASK] [S/D] [🛏] [🍴] [&M] [🛎] [🍽] [🛒] [🏊] [🏋] [✦] [📶] [🖥] [📺]
FEE

ROCK VIEW RESORT
      Phone: 417/334-4678

◆ Property failed to provide current rates

Resort Motel **Location:** Jct US 65, 4.4 mi w on SR 165, 0.3 mi s via Dale Dr, then 0.7 mi w. 1049 Park View Dr 65672. Fax: 417/334-1808. **Facility:** Lakeside setting with excellent views on gravel beach. Housekeeping units. 12 units. 7 one- and 2 two-bedroom standard units with efficiencies. 3 one-bedroom suites with efficiencies. 1-2 stories (no elevator), exterior corridors. *Bath:* combo or shower only. **Parking:** on-site. **Terms:** office hours 8 am-6 pm, pets ($7 extra charge, must remain caged). **Pool(s):** small outdoor. **Leisure Activities:** rental boats, fishing, playground, basketball, horseshoes, volleyball. *Fee:* paddleboats, boat dock.

[🐂] [🛒] [🏊] [🏋] [📶] [🖥] [📺]
FEE

ROSEBUD INN
      Phone: 417/336-4000   **15**

AAA [SAVE]   10/1-12/15 [ECP]   1P: $55-$65   2P: $55-$65   XP: $5   F12

◆◆ ◆◆   8/1-9/30 [ECP]   1P: $46-$52   2P: $46-$52   XP: $5   F12

     5/1-7/31 [ECP]   1P: $44-$50   2P: $44-$50   XP: $5   F12

     3/1-4/30 [ECP]   1P: $41-$46   2P: $41-$46   XP: $5   F12

Small-scale Hotel **Location:** Jct US 65, 2 mi nw on SR 248, then 1.7 mi sw via Gretna Rd. 1415 Roark Valley Rd 65616. Fax: 417/336-4919. **Facility:** 65 one-bedroom standard units. 2-3 stories, interior/exterior corridors. *Bath:* combo or shower only. **Parking:** on-site. **Terms:** open 3/1-12/15. **Amenities:** high-speed Internet. **Pool(s):** outdoor. **Guest Services:** sundries. **Cards:** AX, DS, MC, VI. **Free Special Amenities:** expanded continental breakfast and high-speed Internet.

SOME UNITS
[S/D] [&] [🛒] / [X] /

SAVANNAH HOUSE
      Phone: 417/336-3132   **2**

◆◆ ◆◆ Property failed to provide current rates

Small-scale Hotel **Location:** SR 248 and Shepherd of the Hills Expwy, just w. 165 Expressway Ln 65616. Fax: 417/336-4540. **Facility:** 99 units. 93 one-bedroom standard units. 4 one- and 2 two-bedroom suites with whirlpools, some with kitchens. 3-4 stories, interior corridors. *Bath:* combo or shower only. **Parking:** on-site. **Terms:** open 3/1-12/15. **Amenities:** high-speed Internet, voice mail, irons, hair dryers. **Pool(s):** small outdoor. **Business Services:** fax.

SOME UNITS
[🍴] [🛒] / [X] [📶] [🖥] [📺] /

(See map and index starting on p. 388)

SCENIC HILLS INN
Phone: 417/336-8855 **11**

AAA (SAVE)

10/1-12/23 [ECP]	2P: $46-$70	XP: $5	F16
5/1-7/31 [ECP]	2P: $46-$56	XP: $5	F16
8/1-9/30 [ECP]	2P: $46-$55	XP: $5	F16
3/1-4/30 [ECP]	2P: $43-$46	XP: $5	F16

Small-scale Hotel **Location:** Jct SR 76 (Country Music Blvd), 1.1 mi e. 2422 Shepherd of the Hills Expwy 65616. Fax: 417/336-1346. **Facility:** 66 one-bedroom standard units, some with whirlpools. 3-4 stories, interior corridors. *Bath:* combo or shower only. **Parking:** on-site. **Terms:** open 3/1-12/23, office hours 7 am-11 pm, package plans, pets ($7 extra charge). **Amenities:** high-speed Internet (fee). *Some:* irons, hair dryers. **Pool(s):** outdoor. **Leisure Activities:** whirlpool. **Guest Services:** gift shop, coin laundry. **Cards:** AX, DS, MC, VI. **Free Special Amenities:** expanded continental breakfast and local telephone calls. *(See color ad below)*

SOME UNITS

SETTLE INN RESORT & CONFERENCE CENTER
Book great rates at AAA.com   Phone: (417)335-4700 **46**

AAA (SAVE)

9/1-12/15 [CP]	1P: $79-$119	2P: $79-$119
6/1-8/31 [CP]	1P: $69-$99	2P: $69-$99
3/1-5/31 & 12/16-2/29 [CP]	1P: $59-$99	2P: $59-$99

Small-scale Hotel **Location:** Jct SR 76 (Country Music Blvd) and US 65, 3 mi w on SR 76, 0.8 mi s. 3050 Green Mountain Dr 65616. Fax: 417/335-3906. **Facility:** 298 units. 294 one- and 4 two-bedroom standard units, some with efficiencies (no utensils) and/or whirlpools. 3-4 stories, interior corridors. *Bath:* combo or shower only. **Parking:** on-site. **Terms:** [BP] meal plan available, small pets only ($10 extra charge, in designated units). **Amenities:** voice mail, irons, hair dryers. *Some:* high-speed Internet. **Dining:** 11 am-midnight; hours vary off season, cocktails. **Pool(s):** 2 heated indoor. **Leisure Activities:** whirlpools, limited exercise equipment. *Fee:* game room. **Guest Services:** gift shop, valet and coin laundry. **Business Services:** meeting rooms, fax (fee). **Cards:** AX, DS, MC, VI. *(See color ad p 411)*

SOME UNITS

STILL WATERS CONDOMINIUM RESORT
Phone: (417)338-2323 **38**

AAA (SAVE)

5/26-8/18	1P: $59-$375	2P: $59-$375	XP: $8	F5
8/19-2/29	1P: $49-$375	2P: $49-$375	XP: $8	F5
3/1-5/25	1P: $49-$289	2P: $49-$289	XP: $8	F5

Resort Condominium **Location:** Jct SR 265, 0.6 mi w on SR 76, then 2 mi s on Indian Point Rd. 21 Stillwater Tr 65616 (21 Stillwater Trail). Fax: 417/338-8630. **Facility:** This sprawling resort offers guests a wide variety of room types and a vast array of recreational activities, both of which center on Table Rock Lake. Some units with fireplaces and washer/dryers. 182 units. 15 one-bedroom standard units with efficiencies, some with whirlpools. 26 one-, 121 two- and 20 three-bedroom suites with kitchens and whirlpools. 1-4 stories, exterior corridors. *Bath:* combo or shower only. **Parking:** on-site. **Terms:** office hours 8 am-10 pm, check-in 4 pm, 2-4 night minimum stay - seasonal, 21 day cancellation notice-fee imposed, package plans. **Amenities:** video library (fee), DVD players, high-speed Internet, voice mail, irons, hair dryers. **Dining:** 7 am-2 pm seasonal. **Pool(s):** 3 outdoor, 3 wading. **Leisure Activities:** whirlpools, waterslide, paddleboats, fishing, kayak, recreation programs in season, badminton, board games, pavilion, bicycles, hiking trails, playground, basketball, horseshoes, volleyball. *Fee:* boats, canoes, boat dock, waterskiing, fishing guides, personal water craft, game room. **Guest Services:** gift shop, complimentary laundry. **Business Services:** fax (fee). **Cards:** AX, DC, DS, MC, VI.

SOME UNITS

(See map and index starting on p. 388)

SUPER 8 MOTEL-BRANSON *Book at AAA.com*   Phone: 417/334-8880   **37**

Property failed to provide current rates

Small-scale Hotel

Location: 1.5 mi w of jct SR 76 (Country Music Blvd) and US 65, just s. 2490 Green Mountain Dr 65616. Fax: 417/335-3177. **Facility:** 73 one-bedroom standard units, some with whirlpools. 2-3 stories (no elevator), interior corridors. **Parking:** on-site. **Amenities:** high-speed Internet, hair dryers. **Pool(s):** outdoor. **Guest Services:** wireless Internet. **Business Services:** meeting rooms, PC.

SOME UNITS

THOUSAND HILLS GOLF RESORT *Book great rates at AAA.com*   Phone: (417)336-5873   **45**

Resort Condominium

All Year   1P: $55-$79   2P: $55-$79

Location: Jct US 65, 3 mi w on SR 76 (Country Music Blvd), then 0.5 mi s. 245 S Wildwood Dr 65616. Fax: 417/337-5740. **Facility:** Expansive grounds and facilities are featured at this property offering individually decorated rooms, some overlooking the golf course. 310 units. 95 one-bedroom standard units. 60 one-, 77 two- and 50 three-bedroom suites ($119-$169) with kitchens and whirlpools. 28 cabins ($132-$538) with whirlpools. 1-4 stories, exterior corridors. *Bath:* combo or shower only. **Parking:** on-site. **Terms:** office hours 6:30 am-10 pm, check-in 4 pm, cancellation fee imposed, weekly rates available, package plans. **Amenities:** high-speed Internet, voice mail, irons, hair dryers. *Some:* DVD players, CD players, safes. **Pool(s):** 5 outdoor, 2 heated indoor. **Leisure Activities:** whirlpool, lighted tennis court, badminton, sports court, shuffleboard. *Fee:* golf-18 holes, exercise room. **Business Services:** meeting rooms, business center. **Cards:** AX, DS, MC, VI. **Free Special Amenities:** local telephone calls and high-speed Internet. *(See color ad p 412 & p 397)*

SOME UNITS

TRAIL'S END RESORT   Phone: (417)338-2633   **51**

Vacation Rental Cabin

6/1-8/21	1P: $69-$259	2P: $69-$259	XP: $7
3/1-5/31 & 8/22-12/31	1P: $49-$159	2P: $49-$159	XP: $7
1/1-2/29	1P: $45-$125	2P: $45-$125	XP: $7

Location: Jct SR 265, 0.6 mi w on SR 76, 2.9 mi s on Indian Point Rd, then just e. 71 Dogwood Park Tr 65616 (71 Dogwood Park Trail). Fax: 417/338-3507. **Facility:** 30 units. 5 one-bedroom standard units with efficiencies. 4 one- and 3 two-bedroom suites ($45-$259) with efficiencies. 18 cabins ($65-$259). 1 story, exterior corridors. *Bath:* combo or shower only. **Parking:** on-site. **Terms:** office hours 8 am-9 pm, check-in 4 pm, 1-4 night minimum stay - seasonal, 21 day cancellation notice-fee imposed, package plans. **Amenities:** video library (fee). **Pool(s):** outdoor, wading. **Leisure Activities:** whirlpool, rental boats, paddleboats, marina, scuba diving, snorkeling, fishing, badminton, tetherball, nature trail, playground, horseshoes, shuffleboard, volleyball. *Fee:* waterskiing, charter fishing, personal watercraft, game room. **Business Services:** fax (fee). **Cards:** AX, CB, DC, DS, MC, VI. **Free Special Amenities:** local telephone calls. *(See color ad p 406)*

SOME UNITS

FEE   FEE

(See map and index starting on p. 388)

TRAVELODGE AT THE FALLS — *Book great rates at AAA.com* — Phone: (417)336-3255   **53**

AAA SAVE	9/1-2/29	1P: $63-$95	2P: $63-$95	XP: $5 F18
▼▼ ▼▼	5/1-8/31	1P: $56-$95	2P: $56-$95	XP: $5 F18
	3/1-4/30	1P: $46-$95	2P: $46-$95	XP: $5 F18

Small-scale Hotel **Location:** Jct SR 76 (Country Music Blvd), 0.9 mi s on SR 165. 3245 Falls Pkwy 65616. Fax: 417/336-3709. **Facility:** 118 units. 117 one-bedroom standard units. 1 one-bedroom suite ($55-$95) with kitchen. 2-3 stories (no elevator), exterior corridors. *Bath:* combo or shower only. **Parking:** on-site. **Terms:** [ECP] meal plan available. **Amenities:** safes (fee), hair dryers. **Pool(s):** outdoor. **Business Services:** fax (fee). **Cards:** AX, CB, DC, DS, MC, VI. **Free Special Amenities:** expanded continental breakfast and local telephone calls.

SOME UNITS

🆘 📶 🏊 📺 💻 / ✖ VCR 🔌 🖨 /

TRIBESMAN RESORT — Phone: 417/338-2616   **52**

▼▼ ▼▼	5/21-8/20	1P: $90-$100	2P: $90-$100	XP: $10 F4
	8/21-2/29	1P: $80-$90	2P: $80-$90	XP: $10 F4
Resort Cabin	3/1-5/20	1P: $70-$90	2P: $70-$90	XP: $10 F4

Location: Jct SR 265, 0.6 mi w on SR 76 (Country Music Blvd), 3 mi s. 416 Cave Ln on Indian Point Rd 65616. Fax: 417/338-5063. **Facility:** Wooded grounds. Some contemporary condo-style units. Extensive facilities. Smoke free premises. 61 units. 14 one-, 9 two- and 2 three-bedroom suites, some with efficiencies or kitchens. 36 cottages ($100-$300). 1-2 stories (no elevator), exterior corridors. *Bath:* combo or shower only. **Parking:** on-site. **Terms:** office hours 8 am-9 pm, check-in 4 pm, 3-5 night minimum stay, 21 day cancellation notice-fee imposed. **Amenities:** irons. *Some:* high-speed Internet. **Pool(s):** 3 outdoor, small outdoor, heated indoor. **Leisure Activities:** whirlpools, rental boats, rental canoes, rental paddleboats, marina, fishing, recreation programs in summer, hiking trails, shuffleboard. *Fee:* waterskiing, game room. **Guest Services:** complimentary laundry. **Business Services:** meeting rooms, PC. **Cards:** AX, DS, MC, VI.

SOME UNITS

🏊 ✖ 🔌 🖨 💻 / ✖ /

(See map and index starting on p. 388)

THE VILLAGE AT INDIAN POINT   **Phone:** (417)338-8800 **41**

AAA SAVE   All Year   1P: $95-$225   2P: $95-$225   XP: $5   F14

▼▼▼   **Location:** 2.5 mi s of jct SR 76 on Indian Point Rd. 24 Village Tr 65616. Fax: 417/338-8801. **Facility:** Nestled on
Condominium lush, wooded acreage, this resort offers fully-equipped cabin-like units which are handsomely furnished. All
units with stone wood-burning fireplaces. 72 two-bedroom suites with kitchens, some with whirlpools. 3
stories (no elevator), exterior corridors. **Parking:** on-site. **Terms:** check-in 3:30 pm, 2 night minimum stay -
seasonal, 14 day cancellation notice-fee imposed, pets ($10 extra charge). **Amenities:** high-speed Internet.
Some: DVD players, CD players, irons, hair dryers. **Pool(s):** heated outdoor, wading. **Leisure Activities:** boat dock, fishing,
tetherball, hiking trails, playground, limited exercise equipment, basketball, horseshoes. *Fee:* game room. **Guest Services:**
complimentary laundry. **Business Services:** meeting rooms, fax. **Cards:** AX, DS, MC, VI. **Free Special Amenities:** local
telephone calls and high-speed Internet. *(See color ad below)*   SOME UNITS

(See map and index starting on p. 388)

WELK RESORT BRANSON *Book great rates at AAA.com*   **Phone:** (417)336-3575   57

(AAA) (SAVE)	11/1-12/31	1P: $85-$109	2P: $85-$109	XP: $10 F17
▽▽▽	8/31-10/31	1P: $79-$99	2P: $79-$99	XP: $10 F17
	5/25-8/30	1P: $69-$89	2P: $69-$89	XP: $10 F17
	3/2-5/24	1P: $59-$79	2P: $59-$79	XP: $10 F17

Small-scale Hotel   **Location:** 2.9 mi s of jct SR 76 (Country Music Blvd). 1984 SR 165 65616. Fax: 417/339-3176. **Facility:** 160 one-bedroom standard units. 4 stories, interior corridors. *Bath:* combo or shower only. **Parking:** on-site. **Terms:** open 3/2-12/31, 3 day cancellation notice-fee imposed, [AP] & [BP] meal plans available, package plans. **Amenities:** high-speed Internet (fee), voice mail, irons, hair dryers. **Dining:** Stage Door Restaurant, see separate listing. **Pool(s):** heated outdoor. **Leisure Activities:** whirlpool, miniature golf, board games, cards, outdoor games, playground, exercise room. *Fee:* game room. **Guest Services:** gift shop, valet and coin laundry. **Business Services:** meeting rooms, business center. **Cards:** AX, DS, MC, VI. **Free Special Amenities:** newspaper and early check-in/late check-out. *(See color ad p 393)*

SOME UNITS
🆂ⓓ 🍴 ⚕ 🛎 ✖ 💻 / ✖ 📶 🖥 /

WESTGATE BRANSON WOODS RESORT *Book great rates at AAA.com*   **Phone:** (417)334-2324   12

(AAA) (SAVE)	All Year	1P: $59-$139	2P: $59-$139

▽▽▽   **Location:** US 65, exit SR 248 (Shepherd of the Hills Expwy), 3.7 mi w, just n. 2201 Roark Valley Rd 65616 (2801 Old Winter Garden Rd, OCOEE, FL, 34761). Fax: 417/334-0834. **Facility:** A quiet location and wooded setting for all units, which have a log cabin look. Spacious units with attractive decor and furnishings. 225 units. 83 one-bedroom standard units. 82 one-bedroom suites with kitchens, some with whirlpools. 60 cabins with

Resort
Condominium   whirlpools. 1-2 stories (no elevator), exterior corridors. **Parking:** on-site. **Terms:** check-in 4 pm, 7 day cancellation notice, pets ($50 deposit, in designated unit). **Amenities:** video library (fee), voice mail, irons, hair dryers. *Some:* DVD players, CD players, high-speed Internet. **Pool(s):** 2 outdoor, heated indoor. **Leisure Activities:** whirlpool, exercise room. *Fee:* massage. **Guest Services:** complimentary laundry. **Business Services:** meeting rooms, fax (fee). **Cards:** AX, DS, MC, VI. *(See color ad p 413)*

SOME UNITS
🆂ⓓ 🐾 ⚕ ✖ 🎥 📶 🖥 💻 / ✖ 📼 /
FEE

***The following lodgings were either not evaluated or did not
meet AAA rating requirements but are listed for your information only.***

FOXBOROUGH INN   **Phone:** 417/335-4369

(fyi)   Did not meet all AAA rating requirements for some property operations at time of last evaluation on 07/21/2006. **Location:** US 65, exit Shepherd of the Hills Expwy, 2.3 mi w, just sw. 235 Expressway Ln 65616.
Small-scale Hotel   Facilities, services, and decor characterize a mid-range property.

HORIZONS BY MARRIOTT AT BRANSON   **Phone:** 417/348-3000

(fyi)   Not evaluated. **Location:** 2921 Green Mountain Dr 65616. Facilities, services, and decor characterize a mid-range property.

SOUTHERN OAKS INN   **Phone:** 417/335-8108

(fyi)   Did not meet all AAA rating requirements for some property operations at time of last evaluation on 07/19/2006. **Location:** Jct SR 76 (Country Music Blvd), 0.3 mi e. 3295 Shepherd of the Hills Expwy 65616. Facilities,
Small-scale Hotel   services, and decor characterize a mid-range property.

(See map and index starting on p. 388)

———— WHERE TO DINE ————

ACAPULCO TACO GRILL Lunch: $5-$7 Dinner: $5-$7 Phone: 417/239-0074 17

Mexican

Location: Jct SR 76 (Country Music Blvd) and 165, just s. 3310 W Hwy 76, Suite H 65616. **Hours:** 11 am-9 pm, Sun-5 pm. **Closed:** 1/1, 12/25. **Features:** Colorful and cozy, the restaurant uses fresh ingredients that call up the flavors found at taco stands along the coast of Mexico. Casual dress. **Parking:** on-site. **Cards:** AX, DS, MC, VI.

BILLY GAIL'S CAFE Lunch: $5-$8 Phone: 417/338-8883 25

American

Location: Jct SR 76, 0.5 mi s. 5291 State Hwy 265 65616. **Hours:** Open 3/1-12/31 & 2/1-2/29; 7 am-2 pm. **Features:** The laid-back cafe gives diners a real taste of the Ozarks. Parking is near the gas pumps, and guests walk through a consignment shop with the ambience of a garage sale before reaching the rustic dining room. Locals frequent the place for its food and atmosphere, as well as for the company they enjoy from their neighbors. Casual dress. **Parking:** on-site.

B T BONES STEAKHOUSE Lunch: $7-$29 Dinner: $9-$29 Phone: 417/335-2002 4

Steak House

Location: Jct SR 76 (Country Music Blvd), 1.3 mi e. 2280 Shepherd of the Hills Expwy 65616. **Hours:** 11 am-close. **Reservations:** accepted. **Features:** The atmosphere is casual and rustic in the spacious dining room. Steaks feature prominently on the diverse menu. This place tends to become lively at night. Dressy casual; cocktails. **Parking:** on-site. **Cards:** DS, MC, VI.

BUCKINGHAM'S RESTAURANT &
OASIS LOUNGE *Menu on AAA.com* Dinner: $17-$45 Phone: 417/337-7777 15

American

Location: On SR 76 (Country Music Blvd), 3 mi w of jct US 65; in Clarion Hotel at the Palace. 2820 W Hwy 76 65616. **Hours:** Open 3/1-1/31; 5 pm-9 pm. **Closed:** 12/25; also Sun. **Reservations:** suggested. **Features:** Buckingham's offers a fine-dining experience with an unusual African-safari atmosphere. Beef, wild-game meats, seafood and pasta are featured on the menu, and some meals are cooked tableside. Locals enjoy this place. Casual dress; cocktails. **Parking:** on-site. **Cards:** AX, DC, DS, MC, VI.

CANDLESTICK INN RESTAURANT &
LOUNGE Dinner: $17-$48 Phone: 417/334-3633 9

Steak & Seafood

Location: 1.5 mi e on SR 76 E, 0.3 mi w of road sign. 127 Taney St 65616. **Hours:** 5 pm-9 pm, Wed & Thurs also 11 am-3 pm, Fri 11 am-3 & 5-10 pm, Sat 5 pm-10 pm. **Closed:** 12/25. **Reservations:** suggested. **Features:** Since 1962, the casually intimate restaurant has specialized in angus beef strip steaks, tenderloin and filets, as well as such fresh seafood dishes as salmon and trout. Nestled on a hilltop, the upscale dining room overlooks downtown. Dressy casual; cocktails. **Parking:** on-site. **Cards:** AX, DS, MC, VI.

CHARLIE'S STEAK RIBS & ALE Lunch: $5-$10 Dinner: $11-$21 Phone: 417/334-6090 14

American

Location: 2.5 mi w of jct SR 76 (Country Music Blvd) and US 65. 3009 W Hwy 76 65616. **Hours:** Open 3/1-1/31 & 2/1-2/29; 11 am-9 pm; to 11 pm in season. **Closed:** 4/8, 11/22, 12/25. **Features:** The menu centers on steaks and barbecue specialties, but daily lunch and dinner specials also are popular. A rustic theme weaves through the casual atmosphere. Nightly entertainment from Tuesday through Saturday helps contribute to a mood that can get lively in the evening hours. Casual dress; cocktails. **Parking:** on-site. **Cards:** AX, DS, MC, VI.

CHATEAU GRILLE Lunch: $10-$15 Dinner: $22-$38 Phone: 417/334-1161 22

American

Location: Just n of jct SR 165 and 265; in Chateau on the Lake Resort Spa & Convention Center. 415 N State Hwy 265 65616. **Hours:** 6:30 am-10 pm. **Reservations:** suggested. **Features:** The fine-dining establishment affords beautiful views of the lake. Service is polished and the food innovative. Dressy casual; cocktails. **Parking:** on-site and valet. **Cards:** AX, CB, DC, DS, JC, MC, VI.

DOCKERS RESTAURANT Lunch: $7-$20 Dinner: $11-$20 Phone: 417/332-0044 20

American

Location: SR 165, just e. 3100 Green Mountain Dr 65616. **Hours:** Open 4/1-12/15; 7 am-2 & 4-9 pm; closing hours may vary off season. **Features:** When you get near this restaurant, you should have no trouble recognizing it: it's built to look like a riverboat. You'll walk across a faux dock to enter the dining room where you'll find a casual atmosphere and a bountiful buffet. Casual dress; cocktails. **Parking:** on-site. **Cards:** AX, CB, DC, DS, JC, MC, VI.

FARMHOUSE RESTAURANT Lunch: $5-$7 Dinner: $6-$10 Phone: 417/334-9701 8

American

Location: Just e of jct US 65 and SR 76; downtown. 119 W Main St 65616. **Hours:** 7 am-9 pm; Fri & Sat-11 pm in season. **Closed:** 11/22, 12/25. **Features:** Guests are urged to try the chicken-fried steak dinner. For dessert, go for the blackberry cobbler or an apple dumpling with cinnamon sauce and cinnamon ice cream or homemade cherry pie. The list of temptations goes on and on. Casual dress. **Parking:** street. **Cards:** AX, DS, MC, VI.

GRAND COUNTRY BUFFET Lunch: $7-$13 Dinner: $10-$13 Phone: 417/335-2434 12

American

Location: 1.9 mi w of jct US 65; in 76 Music Hall & Grand Ladies Complex. 1945 W 76 Country Blvd 65616. **Hours:** 6 am-midnight. **Features:** Friendly country charm exudes from the cozy restaurant. Many homemade selections, including tasty sweet corn pops, line a tempting buffet. Casual dress. **Parking:** on-site. **Cards:** AX, DS, MC, VI.

GRANNY'S RESTAURANT Lunch: $5-$8 Dinner: $6-$11 Phone: 417/334-7700 2

American

Location: Jct SR 76 (Country Music Blvd), 0.4 mi e. 3292 Shepherd of the Hills Expwy 65616. **Hours:** Open 3/15-12/19; 7 am-8 pm; hours may vary. **Reservations:** accepted. **Features:** This country-garden-style restaurant with a relaxed ambience serves homemade, freshly prepared meals and desserts. Try the chicken-fried steak, prime rib, shrimp, pork chops or pasta, or sample from the ample buffet. Breakfast and lunch are superb also. Casual dress. **Parking:** on-site. **Cards:** DS, MC, VI.

(See map and index starting on p. 388)

LUIGI'S PIZZA KITCHEN SOUTH   Lunch: $5-$14   Dinner: $5-$14   Phone: 417/334-3344   [24]

Italian

Location: On SR 165, 2.9 mi s of jct SR 76 (Country Music Blvd); in Marketplace Center Shopping Plaza. 1972-P State Hwy 165 65616. **Hours:** 11 am-10 pm, Fri & Sat-midnight; to 9 pm 1/1-3/30. Closed: 11/22, 12/25; also Mon & Tues 1/1-3/30. **Features:** This casual pizzeria is in a small shopping center adjacent to the Welk Theater and Hotel. As with most pizzerias, the emphasis is on good food, prepared quickly and served promptly. Casual dress. **Parking:** on-site. **Cards:** AX, DS, MC, VI.

THE MAJESTIC STEAKHOUSE   Lunch: $6-$9   Dinner: $15-$45   Phone: 417/334-8655   [5]

Steak House

Location: From SR 76, 1.9 mi nw on Roark Valley Rd; at Gretna and Roark Valley rds. 2849 Gretna Rd 65616. **Hours:** 11:30 am-3 & 4:30-10 pm, Sun 11 am-9 pm. Closed major holidays. **Reservations:** suggested. **Features:** The distinctive and spacious facility blends elements of both casual and fine dining. Superior steaks share menu space with other delectables. This place is suitable for family gatherings, as well as special occasions. Casual dress; cocktails. **Parking:** on-site. **Cards:** AX, CB, DC, DS, JC, MC, VI.   [Y]

MCFARLAIN'S FAMILY RESTAURANT   Lunch: $6-$14   Dinner: $6-$14   Phone: 417/336-4680   [3]

American

Location: Jct SR 76 (Country Music Blvd); just e; in Imax Entertainment Complex. 3562 Shepherd of the Hills Expwy 65616. **Hours:** 7:30 am-8:15 pm, Fri & Sat-9:15 pm; to 9:15 pm, Fri & Sat-10:15 pm 6/1-9/2; 11 am 8:15 pm 12/16-3/14. Closed: 12/24. **Features:** The restaurant serves Ozark cookin' at its best. Fried green tomatoes, chicken pot pie and blackberry cobbler are among the favorites here. The atmosphere is lively and fun. This is the type of place where guests can bring the whole family. Casual dress. **Parking:** on-site. **Cards:** AX, DS, MC, VI.   [M]

ODEE'S BBQ   Lunch: $5-$10   Dinner: $6-$18   Phone: 417/348-1130   [21]

American

Location: Jct SR 76 (Country Music Blvd), 0.5 mi s. 752 Hwy 165 65616. **Hours:** 11 am-9 pm, Fri & Sat-10 pm; hours may vary off season. Closed: 12/25. **Features:** Down-home with an edge, the casual roadside diner features live rhythm and blues on the deck on Sundays, weather permitting. Casual dress; cocktails. **Parking:** on-site. **Cards:** MC, VI.   [N]

OUTBACK STEAK & OYSTER BAR   Lunch: $6-$19   Dinner: $13-$25   Phone: 417/334-6306   [11]

Steak & Seafood

Location: US 65, 1.5 mi w; in Outback Roadhouse Motel & Suites. 1914 W Hwy 76 65616. **Hours:** 11 am-10 pm, Fri & Sat-11 pm; to 9 pm 1/1-3/30. **Features:** Hearty portions of grilled steaks and seafood are served in a casually rustic, Australian atmosphere. Diners can enjoy live music and outdoor dining with a view of bungee jumping in season. Alligator tail and oysters are popular menu items. Casual dress; cocktails. **Parking:** on-site. **Cards:** AX, DS, MC, VI.   [Y] [N]

PASTA HOUSE   Lunch: $6-$8   Dinner: $8-$22   Phone: 417/337-9882   [19]

Italian

Location: Jct US 65, 2 mi w on SR 76 (Country Music Blvd), just s. 2690 Green Mountain Dr 65616. **Hours:** 11 am-11 pm. Closed: 12/25. **Features:** The restaurant reflects the Old World in a contemporary and comfortable atmosphere. The menu centers on traditional favorites. Try pecan chocolate cake for dessert. Casual dress; cocktails. **Parking:** on-site. **Cards:** AX, DS, MC, VI.   [N]

PEPPERCORNS RESTAURANT   Lunch: $5-$8   Dinner: $11-$18   Phone: 417/335-6699   [13]

American

Location: Jct US 65 and SR 76 (Country Music Blvd), 2 mi w. 2421 W Hwy 76 65616. **Hours:** Open 3/1-12/15; 7 am-8 pm; hours may vary. **Features:** A bright and cheerful, family atmosphere is the setting for Peppercorns, which features a daily buffet during breakfast, lunch and dinner. The menu provides other options. Casual dress. **Parking:** on-site. **Cards:** DS, MC, VI.

THE PLANTATION RESTAURANT   Lunch: $10   Dinner: $10   Phone: 417/334-7800   [10]

American

Location: Jct SR 165, 1.2 mi nw. 3460 W Hwy 76 65616. **Hours:** 7 am-1:30 & 3:30-8 pm; hours vary off season. **Features:** This is casual family dining with lunch and dinner buffet offering all-you-can-eat chicken, catfish, ribs and roast beef. The food is hot and well-prepared and the service is friendly and prompt with good followup. Casual dress; cocktails. **Parking:** on-site. **Cards:** AX, DS, MC, VI.   [N]

RIB CRIB BARBECUE   Lunch: $6-$16   Dinner: $6-$16   Phone: 417/337-7427

Barbecue

Location: 1.6 mi w of jct US 65. 1855 W Hwy 76 65616. **Hours:** 11 am-10 pm; Fri & Sat-11 pm 5/1-9/30. Closed: 11/22, 12/25. **Features:** Most guests need extra napkins to tackle the ribs, brisket, ham, pork and chicken selections. The menu also lists sandwiches and wraps, along with tempting sides and large desserts. The decor is decidedly Western. Casual dress; beer only. **Parking:** on-site. **Cards:** AX, CB, DC, DS, MC, VI.   [M]

ROCKY'S ITALIAN RESTAURANT   Lunch: $6-$10   Dinner: $9-$24   Phone: 417/335-4765   [6]

AAA

Italian

Location: Just n of Main St. 120 N Sycamore 65616. **Hours:** 11 am-9 pm. Closed major holidays; also Sun. **Features:** Rocky's comes highly recommended by local residents, who like its exceptional food and casual, warm atmosphere. They say the shrimp, lasagna and chicken picata are excellent choices. The building is a restored feedmill built at the turn-of-the-century. Casual dress; cocktails. **Parking:** on-site. **Cards:** AX, CB, MC, VI.   [Y] [N]

RUBY LENA'S TEA ROOM & ANTIQUES   Lunch: $6-$8   Phone: 417/239-2919   [7]

American

Location: On SR 76 (Main St); downtown. 224 W Main St 65616. **Hours:** Open 3/1-12/31; 11 am-3 pm. Closed: 1/1, 12/25; also Sun. **Reservations:** accepted. **Features:** Although this place is definitely a ladies' lunch establishment, gentlemen are welcomed as well. Menu selections are limited but delightful. Casual dress. **Parking:** on-site. **Cards:** MC, VI.

(See map and index starting on p. 388)

SADIE'S SIDEBOARD & SMOKEHOUSE   **Lunch:** $7-$21   **Dinner:** $7-$21   **Phone:** 417/334-3619   ⑯
▼▼ ▼▼   **Location:** 3.5 mi w on SR 76 (Country Music Blvd) from jct US 65. 2830 W Hwy 76 65616. **Hours:** Open 3/1-12/31;
                 7 am-8 pm, Fri & Sat-9 pm. **Features:** The casual, family-oriented establishment lays out a buffet with a
Regional American   good variety of down-home country comfort food for breakfast, lunch and dinner. Features include barbecue,
                 beef, pork, chicken, catfish and smoked ham. Casual dress; beer & wine only. **Parking:** on-site. **Cards:** AX,
DS, MC, VI.

SHORTY SMALL'S OF BRANSON   **Lunch:** $6-$19   **Dinner:** $6-$19   **Phone:** 417/334-8797
▼▼ ▼▼   **Location:** Jct SR 76 (Country Music Blvd) and SR 165, 1 mi s; near Tony Orlando Theater. 3270 Yellow Ribbon Rd
                 65616. **Hours:** 11 am-10 pm, Fri & Sat-11 pm; hours vary in winter. Closed: 12/24, 12/25.
American   **Features:** Focusing on ribs, fried catfish, sandwiches and cheesecake, this restaurant is popular with the
                 locals. The rustic and nostalgic atmosphere is family-oriented, and the feel is casual, hectic and sometimes
noisy. Casual dress; cocktails. **Parking:** on-site. **Cards:** AX, DC, DS, MC, VI.

STAGE DOOR RESTAURANT   **Lunch:** $6-$10   **Dinner:** $8-$14   **Phone:** 417/336-3575   ㉓
▼▼ ▼▼   **Location:** 2.9 mi s of jct SR 76 (Country Music Blvd); in Welk Resort Branson. 1984 SR 165 65616. **Hours:** 7 am-8
                 pm. **Reservations:** accepted. **Features:** The dining room features a large window overlooking a lifesize
American   statue of Lawrence Welk. The food tends to be traditional American fare. Casual dress; cocktails. **Parking:**
                 on-site. **Cards:** AX, DS, MC, VI.

UPTOWN CAFE   **Lunch:** $5-$10   **Dinner:** $7-$10   **Phone:** 417/336-3535   ⑱
▼▼ ▼▼   **Location:** Jct SR 76 (Country Music Blvd), just s. 285 SR 165 65616. **Hours:** 7:30 am-8 pm; to 11 pm, Fri & Sat-
                 midnight after Memorial Day; hours may vary. Closed: 11/22, 12/25. **Features:** The Uptown Cafe
American   nostalgically replicates a 1950s-style Route 66 diner, complete with jukebox music, art deco ambience, and
                 soda fountain treats. They specialize in steakburgers, meatloaf, country-fried chicken, banana splits and hot
fudge sundaes. Casual dress. **Parking:** on-site. **Cards:** MC, VI.

ZOEY'S MEDITERRANEAN CUISINE   **Dinner:** $18-$25   **Phone:** 417/338-6511   ①
▼▼▼▼   **Location:** Jct SR 76, 0.4 mi s. 5378 SR 265 65616. **Hours:** Open 3/1-12/30; 4:30 pm-9 pm. Closed: Sun & Mon.
                 Reservations: suggested, weekends. **Features:** The comfortable atmosphere reflects a hint of Old World
Mediterranean   sophistication. Entrees are served with fresh Greek house salad, homemade bread and roasted garlic in
                 olive oil. Casual dress; cocktails. **Parking:** on-site. **Cards:** AX, CB, DC, DS, JC, MC, VI.

———— *The following restaurants have not been evaluated by AAA* ————
but are listed for your information only.

DANNA'S BAR B QUE AND BURGERS   **Phone:** 417/337-5527
[fyi]   Not evaluated. **Location:** SR 165, 1.5 mi s of jct SR 165 and SR 76. 963 Hwy 165 65615. **Features:** Cheerfully
                 unadorned, the restaurant invites patrons to bring the family for burgers and BBQ, and while they're at it, a
root beer float. This place epitomizes an authentic roadside burger joint.

LUIGI'S PIZZA KITCHEN NORTH   **Phone:** 417/339-4544
[fyi]   Not evaluated. **Location:** Jct SR 248 and James Epps Rd, just sw; in Cedar Ridge Center. 1447 State Hwy 248, Suite
                 F 65616. **Features:** The casual pizzeria is in a small shopping center. The emphasis is on good food,
prepared quickly and served promptly.

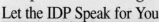

The Branson Vicinity

BRANSON WEST pop. 408

─── WHERE TO STAY ───

BEST WESTERN BRANSON INN & CONFERENCE CENTER *Book great rates at AAA.com*   Phone: (417)338-2141

AAA SAVE

Small-scale Hotel

5/21-12/15		2P: $65-$85	XP: $5	F16
3/1-5/20 & 12/16-2/29		2P: $49-$69	XP: $5	F16

Location: Jct SR 265, 1.1 mi w on SR 76. 8514 State Hwy 76 65737. Fax: 417/338-8320. **Facility:** 145 one-bedroom standard units, some with whirlpools. 3 stories, interior corridors. **Parking:** on-site. **Terms:** package plans, small pets only ($5 extra charge, in designated units). **Amenities:** high-speed Internet, irons, hair dryers. **Pool(s):** heated indoor, wading. **Leisure Activities:** whirlpool, 2 lighted tennis courts, pool table, air hockey. *Fee:* game room. **Guest Services:** coin laundry, area transportation-Silver Dollar City. **Business Services:** meeting rooms, business center. **Cards:** AX, CB, DC, DS, MC, VI. **Free Special Amenities:** early check-in/late check-out and preferred room (subject to availability with advance reservations).** *(See color ad p 394)*

SOME UNITS

LAKEVIEW INN *Book great rates at AAA.com*   Phone: 417/272-8195

AAA SAVE

Small-scale Hotel

6/1-12/31 [BP]	1P: $45-$50	2P: $50-$55	XP: $6	F12
3/1-5/31 [BP]	1P: $35-$50	2P: $40-$55	XP: $6	F12
1/1-2/29 [BP]	1P: $30-$50	2P: $35-$55	XP: $6	F12

Location: 2 mi w of jct SR 76 and 265. 10930 W Hwy 13 & 76 65737 (PO Box 2072). Fax: 417/272-8271. **Facility:** 66 one-bedroom standard units. 2-3 stories (no elevator), exterior corridors. **Parking:** on-site. **Amenities:** *Some:* high-speed Internet. **Pool(s):** outdoor. **Guest Services:** coin laundry. **Business Services:** meeting rooms. **Cards:** AX, DS, MC, VI. **Free Special Amenities: expanded continental breakfast and high-speed Internet.**

SOME UNITS

SHADY ACRE MOTEL   Phone: 417/338-2316

Motel

All Year	2P: $42

Location: Jct SR 265, 1.3 mi w. Located in a quiet area. 8722 Hwy 76 65737. Fax: 417/338-2316. **Facility:** 16 one-bedroom standard units, some with efficiencies. 1-2 stories (no elevator), exterior corridors. **Parking:** on-site. **Terms:** office hours 8 am-9:30 pm, pets (small dogs only, $10 fee, must remain caged). **Pool(s):** small outdoor. **Leisure Activities:** *Fee:* charter fishing. **Business Services:** fax (fee). **Cards:** AX, DS, MC, VI.

SOME UNITS

STONEBRIDGE NIGHTLY RENTALS   Phone: (417)332-1373

AAA SAVE

Resort Condominium

All Year	1P: $199-$389

Location: 1.9 mi w of jct SR 76 and 265. 50 Stonebridge Pkwy 65737. Fax: 417/332-2540. **Facility:** The property offers 3,200 acres of wooded hillsides and streams to be enjoyed from porches and decks and tastefully appointed guest units. 207 units. 42 one-bedroom standard units with whirlpools. 75 one- and 30 two-bedroom suites with kitchens and whirlpools. 60 vacation homes with whirlpools. 1-3 stories (no elevator), exterior corridors. **Parking:** on-site. **Terms:** office hours 7 am-10 pm, check-in 4 pm, 2-3 night minimum stay - seasonal and/or weekends, weekly rates available, package plans. **Amenities:** DVD players, high-speed Internet, voice mail, irons, hair dryers. **Dining:** 7 am-11 pm; hours may vary. **Pool(s):** 2 outdoor. **Leisure Activities:** 3 lighted tennis courts, driving range, hiking trails, playground, exercise room. *Fee:* golf-18 holes. **Business Services:** meeting rooms, business center. **Cards:** AX, CB, DC, DS, JC, MC, VI. **Free Special Amenities: local telephone calls and high-speed Internet.** *(See color ad p 412 and card insert)*

SOME UNITS

——— WHERE TO DINE ———

MICHEL'S RESTAURANT

Regional American

MC, VI.

Lunch: $4-$6   **Dinner:** $6-$12   **Phone:** 417/272-8126
Location: Jct SR 13 and 76. SR 76 & 13 65737. **Hours:** 7 am-8 pm, Sun 8 am-2 pm, Mon 7 am-2 pm. Closed: 12/22-1/7. **Features:** You'll appreciate the food quality, local conversation and outdoor scenes on the walls at Michel's. This eatery offers steak, chicken and fresh seafood as well as homemade soup and dessert. Its relaxed atmosphere is comfortable for families and seniors. Casual dress. **Parking:** on-site. **Cards:** AX,

WOODEN NICKEL RESTAURANT

Steak & Seafood

DC, DS, MC, VI.

Dinner: $10-$30   **Phone:** 417/338-2737
Location: On SR 76, 1 mi w of Silver Dollar City. 8847 State Hwy 76 65737. **Hours:** Open 3/15-12/31; 4:30 pm-8 pm, Fri & Sat-9 pm; to 9 pm, Fri & Sat-10 pm in season. **Reservations:** accepted. **Features:** You'll appreciate the rustic atmosphere at the Wooden Nickel. This restaurant offers seafood, and prime rib and steaks from the choicest beef. The ambience has a very casual flair. Table tops are hammered copper and the salad bar is constructed around a tree which is in the dining room. Casual dress; cocktails. **Parking:** on-site. **Cards:** AX,

CAPE FAIR

——— WHERE TO DINE ———

KOPPIE'S DINER

American

Lunch: $5-$10   **Dinner:** $5-$10   **Phone:** 417/538-4312
Location: Jct SR 76 and 173. 9215 St Hwy 173 65624. **Hours:** 11 am-9 pm, Sun-7 pm. **Reservations:** not accepted. **Features:** A cheerful soda fountain theme characterizes the restaurant, which serves Chicago's Vienna Beef hot dogs, burgers, sandwiches, soup and salads. Ice cream shakes, malts and sundaes are among desserts. Fishermen's lunch boxes are available. Casual dress. **Parking:** on-site. **Cards:** MC, VI.

HOLLISTER pop. 3,867   (See map and index starting on p. 388)

——— WHERE TO STAY ———

RED BUD COVE B & B SUITES

Resort Bed & Breakfast

6/8-10/31 [BP]	1P: $109-$154	2P: $109-$154	XP: $15	F3
3/1-6/7 & 11/1-2/29 [BP]	1P: $98-$144	2P: $98-$144	XP: $15	F3

Phone: (417)334-7144

Location: From jct US 65 and SR 265, 1.6 mi s on US 65; jct SR 265, 2.5 mi w on Graham Clark Dr (CR 65-180). Located in a rural area; lakeside. 162 Lakewood Dr 65672. Fax: 417/337-8823. **Facility:** Located on the south side of Table Rock Lake, the property has very attractive grounds; all units are multi-room suites, some with fireplaces. 8 units. 7 one- and 1 two-bedroom suites ($98-$154), some with efficiencies, kitchens and/or whirlpools. 3 stories (no elevator), interior/exterior corridors. **Parking:** on-site. **Terms:** 2 night minimum stay - seasonal and/or weekends, age restrictions may apply, 14 day cancellation notice, package plans. **Amenities:** DVD players, CD players, high-speed Internet, irons, hair dryers. **Leisure Activities:** whirlpool, boat dock, fishing. **Guest Services:** gift shop. **Business Services:** fax. **Cards:** DS, MC, VI.

SOME UNITS

——— WHERE TO DINE ———

DOBYNS DINING ROOM AT COLLEGE OF THE OZARKS

American

Lunch: $8-$20   **Dinner:** $8-$20   **Phone:** 417/239-1900   [28]
Location: Jct SR 76, 2 mi s on US 65, 0.8 mi w on CR V; in Mabee Lodge, at College of the Ozarks. 1 Opportunity Way 65726. **Hours:** 10:30 am-8 pm, Sun 10 am-2 pm; 7 am-8 pm bakery. Closed: 12/25. **Reservations:** suggested, Sun. **Features:** Friendly service is the hallmark of this restaurant, which features Ozark country cooking and a casual atmosphere where children are welcomed. The Sunday buffet is good. The College of the Ozarks owns and operates this place as a part of the work program required of all students. Casual dress. **Parking:** on-site. **Cards:** AX, CB, DC, DS, JC, MC, VI.

KIMBERLING CITY pop. 2,253

——— WHERE TO STAY ———

——— *The following lodging was either not evaluated or did not* ———
meet AAA rating requirements but is listed for your information only.

WATERS EDGE ON TABLE ROCK LAKE CABIN AND RV RESORT

[fyi]

Phone: 417/739-5377

Not evaluated. **Location:** From SR 13, 0.3 mi n on Kimberling Blvd, just e on Bass Ave, then just s. 72 Marina Way 65686 (PO Box 397). Facilities, services, and decor characterize a basic property.

——— WHERE TO DINE ———

THE BEARDED CLAM

Seafood

Lunch: $5-$9   **Dinner:** $10-$21   **Phone:** 417/739-4440
Location: On SR 13, 0.3 mi n of bridge. Hwy 13 St 65686. **Hours:** 11 am-10 pm, Fri & Sat-11 pm; hours vary in winter. Closed: 12/25. **Reservations:** accepted. **Features:** Expect prompt and cordial service in this seat-yourself casual eatery. Give the special of the day its due consideration, but if it doesn't set your tastebuds clamoring, try the chicken and dumplings. Of course, the children are welcome. Casual dress; cocktails.
Parking: on-site. **Cards:** AX, DS, MC, VI.

PIER RESTAURANT   **Dinner:** $13-$36   **Phone:** 417/739-4311

Regional
Continental

Location: On SR 13; in Kimberling Inn Resort & Conference Center. Hwy 13 65686. **Hours:** 5 pm-10 pm, Fri & Sat-9 pm. **Closed:** 12/25; also Sun & Mon; Tues-Thurs 12/1-5/31. **Reservations:** suggested. **Features:** The Pier's Continental cuisine—with a French flair—features steak, veal and seafood. The restaurant's casually elegant and cozy dining room offers a beautiful view of Table Rock Lake. The service here is cordial and professional. Superb bananas Foster. Casual dress; cocktails. **Parking:** on-site. **Cards:** AX, DS, MC, VI.

REEDS SPRING pop. 465

—— WHERE TO DINE ——

PAPOULI'S   **Lunch:** $6-$11   **Dinner:** $9-$20   **Phone:** 417/272-8243

Greek

Location: On SR 248; jct Reeds Spring. **Hours:** 3 pm-9 pm, Fri-9:30 pm, Sat & Sun 11 am-9:30 pm. **Closed:** Mon-Wed. **Reservations:** accepted. **Features:** Papouli's features friendly, family-style dining and many delicious and flavorful specialties. An enclosed garden with bird feeders and assorted plants enhances the relaxed and enjoyable meal you'll experience here. It's well worth the drive. Casual dress; cocktails. **Parking:** on-site. **Cards:** MC, VI.

RIDGEDALE

—— WHERE TO STAY ——

—— The following lodging was either not evaluated or did not ——
meet AAA rating requirements but is listed for your information only.

BIG CEDAR LODGE   **Phone:** 417/335-2777

[fyi]   Not evaluated. **Location:** Hwy 86 65672 (612 Devil's Pool Rd). Facilities, services, and decor characterize a mid-range property.

Roy Rogers-Dale Evans Museum & Happy Trails Theater / Branson/Lakes Area Chamber of Commerce & CVB

This ends listings for the Branson Vicinity.
The following page resumes the alphabetical listings of cities in Missouri.

BRANSON WEST —See Branson p. 418.

BRENTWOOD —See St. Louis p. 533.

BRIDGETON —See St. Louis p. 534.

BROOKSIDE

──────── WHERE TO DINE ────────

──────── *The following restaurant has not been evaluated by AAA* ────────
but is listed for your information only.

FRONDIZI'S   **Phone: 816/931-3322**
(fyi)   Not evaluated. **Location:** Just s of Country Club Plaza. 4558 Main St 64113. **Features:** Offerings include a
wonderful selection of salads and freshly baked breads. An extensive wine list complements traditional
favorites. The setting is cozy and intimate.

BUTLER pop. 4,209

──────── WHERE TO STAY ────────

SUPER 8 MOTEL - BUTLER   *Book at AAA.com*   **Phone: 660/679-6183**
[diamond]   All Year   1P: $35-$60   2P: $40-$85   XP: $5   F12
Motel   **Location:** Just e of jct US 71 and SR 52. 1114 W Fort Scott St 64730. Fax: 660/679-6185. **Facility:** 48 one-
bedroom standard units. 1-2 stories (no elevator), exterior corridors. **Parking:** on-site, winter plug-ins.
Terms: small pets only ($5 extra charge, with prior approval). **Amenities:** hair dryers. **Guest Services:** coin
laundry, wireless Internet. **Business Services:** PC. **Cards:** AX, CB, DC, DS, JC, MC, VI.

SOME UNITS
(ASK) (S/D) [icons] / [icons] /
FEE

──────── *The following lodging was either not evaluated or did not* ────────
meet AAA rating requirements but is listed for your information only.

DAYS INN   **Phone: 660/679-4544**
(fyi)   Did not meet all AAA rating requirements for some property operations at time of last evaluation on
06/07/2006. **Location:** Just e of jct US 71 and SR 52. 100 S Fran Ave 64730. Facilities, services, and decor
Small-scale Hotel characterize a mid-range property.

CAMDENTON pop. 2,779

──────── WHERE TO STAY ────────

SLEEP INN & SUITES   *Book great rates at AAA.com*   **Phone: (573)346-4501**
(AAA) (SAVE)   5/20-9/10   1P: $99-$115   2P: $99-$115
[diamonds]   3/1-5/19 & 9/11-11/30   1P: $89   2P: $89
          12/1-2/29   1P: $79   2P: $79
Small-scale Hotel **Location:** On US 54. 1390 E Hwy 54 65020 (PO Box 267). Fax: 573/346-7845. **Facility:** 62 units. 60 one-
bedroom standard units, some with whirlpools. 2 one-bedroom suites ($114-$150) with whirlpools. 4 stories,
interior corridors. *Bath:* combo or shower only. **Parking:** on-site. **Amenities:** high-speed Internet, voice mail,
irons, hair dryers. *Some:* safes (fee). **Pool(s):** small heated outdoor, heated indoor. **Leisure Activities:** whirlpool, gazebo, patio,
exercise room. **Guest Services:** valet and coin laundry, wireless Internet. **Business Services:** meeting rooms, PC. **Cards:** AX,
CB, DC, DS, JC, MC, VI. **Free Special Amenities: expanded continental breakfast and high-speed Internet.**

SOME UNITS
(S/D) [icons] / [icons] /

CAMERON pop. 8,312

──────── WHERE TO STAY ────────

BEST WESTERN ACORN INN   *Book great rates at AAA.com*   **Phone: (816)632-2187**
(AAA) (SAVE)   All Year   1P: $72-$80   2P: $75-$85   XP: $5   F17
[diamonds]   **Location:** I-35, exit 54, 0.3 mi e. 2210 E US 36 64429 (PO Box 436). Fax: 816/632-2523. **Facility:** 40 one-
Motel   bedroom standard units. 1 story, exterior corridors. *Bath:* combo or shower only. **Parking:** on-site, winter
plug-ins. **Terms:** [ECP] meal plan available, small pets only. **Amenities:** high-speed Internet, irons, hair
dryers. **Pool(s):** small outdoor. **Guest Services:** valet laundry, area transportation. **Cards:** AX, CB, DC, DS,
JC, MC, VI. **Free Special Amenities: expanded continental breakfast and high-speed Internet.**

SOME UNITS
[icons] / [icons] /
FEE FEE FEE

COMFORT INN   *Book great rates at AAA.com*   **Phone: (816)632-5655**
[diamonds]   All Year   1P: $74-$159   2P: $79-$164   XP: $8   F18
Small-scale Hotel **Location:** I-35, exit 54, just e. 1803 Comfort Ln 64429. Fax: 816/632-3436. **Facility:** 60 one-bedroom standard
units, some with whirlpools. 2 stories, interior corridors. **Parking:** on-site. **Terms:** [ECP] meal plan available,
pets (in kennel). **Amenities:** high-speed Internet, safes (fee), hair dryers. *Some:* irons. **Pool(s):** small
heated indoor. **Leisure Activities:** whirlpool. **Guest Services:** valet and coin laundry. **Cards:** AX, CB, DC, DS, JC, MC, VI.

SOME UNITS
(ASK) (S/D) [icons] / [icons] /

ECONO LODGE   *Book great rates at AAA.com*   Phone: (816)632-6571

AAA SAVE

Motel

All Year   1P: $45-$59   2P: $49-$69   XP: $5   F12
Location: I-35, exit 54, 0.5 mi w on US 36, then just s on US 69. 220 E Grand 64429. Fax: 816/632-6571. **Facility:** 36 one-bedroom standard units. 2 stories (no elevator), exterior corridors. **Bath:** combo or shower only. **Parking:** on-site. **Terms:** small pets only ($5 fee). **Pool(s):** small outdoor. **Cards:** AX, DS, MC, VI.
Free Special Amenities: continental breakfast and high-speed Internet.

SOME UNITS

HOLIDAY INN EXPRESS   *Book at AAA.com*   Phone: (816)632-6666

Small-scale Hotel

All Year   1P: $59-$125   2P: $59-$125   XP: $10   F18
Location: I-35, exit 54, 0.5 mi w on US 36. 601 E Bryan Rd 64429. Fax: 816/632-6666. **Facility:** 47 one-bedroom standard units. 2 stories (no elevator), interior corridors. **Bath:** combo or shower only. **Parking:** on-site, winter plug-ins. **Amenities:** irons, hair dryers. **Pool(s):** small heated indoor. **Guest Services:** wireless Internet. **Cards:** AX, DC, DS, MC, VI.

SOME UNITS

SUPER 8 MOTEL   *Book at AAA.com*   Phone: (816)632-8888

Small-scale Hotel

All Year   1P: $53-$78   2P: $60-$78   XP: $5   F12
Location: I-35, exit 54, 0.5 mi w on US 36. 1710 N Walnut St 64429. Fax: 816/632-8888. **Facility:** 41 one-bedroom standard units, some with whirlpools. 2 stories (no elevator), interior corridors. **Bath:** combo or shower only. **Parking:** on-site, winter plug-ins. **Terms:** [CP] meal plan available, pets ($10 fee, in smoking units, with prior approval). **Amenities:** high-speed Internet, irons, hair dryers. *Some:* CD players. **Pool(s):** small heated indoor. **Leisure Activities:** whirlpool. **Guest Services:** wireless Internet. **Business Services:** PC. **Cards:** AX, CB, DC, DS, JC, MC, VI.

SOME UNITS

CANTON pop. 2,557

—— WHERE TO STAY ——

COMFORT INN CANTON   *Book great rates at AAA.com*   Phone: 573/288-8800

Small-scale Hotel

Property failed to provide current rates
Location: US 61, exit CR P, just e. 1701 Oak St 63435. Fax: 573/288-8820. **Facility:** 60 one-bedroom standard units, some with whirlpools. 3 stories, interior corridors. **Bath:** combo or shower only. **Parking:** on-site. **Terms:** pets ($12.50 extra charge, with prior approval). **Amenities:** high-speed Internet, voice mail, safes (fee), irons, hair dryers. **Pool(s):** small heated indoor. **Leisure Activities:** whirlpool. *Fee:* game room. **Guest Services:** coin laundry, wireless Internet. **Business Services:** meeting rooms, business center.

SOME UNITS

CAPE FAIR —*See Branson p. 419.*

CAPE GIRARDEAU pop. 35,349

—— WHERE TO STAY ——

BELLEVUE BED AND BREAKFAST   Phone: (573)335-3302

Historic Bed
& Breakfast

All Year   1P: $85-$110   2P: $85-$110   XP: $10   D12
Location: Between Lorimier and Fountain sts. Located in a quiet residential area. 312 Bellevue St 63701. Fax: 573/332-7752. **Facility:** A restored 1891 Victorian home close to downtown which features period detail and decor including ceilings with extensive hand-stenciled decoration. 4 one-bedroom standard units, some with whirlpools. 2 stories (no elevator), interior corridors. **Bath:** combo or shower only. **Parking:** on-site. **Terms:** check-in 4 pm, 7 day cancellation notice, package plans, no pets allowed (owner's dogs on premises). **Amenities:** video library, hair dryers. *Some:* CD players, high-speed Internet, irons. **Guest Services:** complimentary evening beverages, wireless Internet. **Business Services:** PC. **Cards:** AX, DS, MC, VI.

SOME UNITS

DRURY LODGE-CAPE GIRARDEAU   *Book at AAA.com*   Phone: (573)334-7151

Small-scale Hotel

All Year [BP]   1P: $75-$120   2P: $85-$130   XP: $10   F18
Location: I-55, exit 96 (William St), just e. 104 S Vantage Dr 63701. Fax: 573/334-7151. **Facility:** 139 one-bedroom standard units. 2 stories (no elevator), interior/exterior corridors. **Parking:** on-site. **Amenities:** high-speed Internet, voice mail, irons, hair dryers. **Dining:** Cedar Street, see separate listing. **Pool(s):** outdoor, wading. **Leisure Activities:** exercise room. **Guest Services:** sundries, complimentary evening beverages, valet and coin laundry, wireless Internet. **Business Services:** conference facilities, PC. **Cards:** AX, CB, DC, DS, MC, VI.

SOME UNITS

DRURY SUITES-CAPE GIRARDEAU   *Book at AAA.com*   Phone: (573)339-9500

Small-scale Hotel

All Year [BP]   1P: $86-$126   2P: $96-$136   XP: $10   F18
Location: I-55, exit 96 (William St), just w. Located in a commercial area. 3303 Campster Dr 63701. Fax: 573/339-9500. **Facility:** 87 units. 8 one-bedroom standard units. 79 one-bedroom suites ($90-$142), some with efficiencies. 5 stories, interior corridors. **Bath:** combo or shower only. **Parking:** on-site, winter plug-ins. **Amenities:** video library, high-speed Internet, voice mail, irons, hair dryers. **Pool(s):** heated indoor. **Leisure Activities:** whirlpool, exercise room. **Guest Services:** complimentary evening beverages, valet and coin laundry, wireless Internet. **Business Services:** meeting rooms, PC. **Cards:** AX, CB, DC, DS, MC, VI.

SOME UNITS

HAMPTON INN-CAPE GIRARDEAU · *Book great rates at AAA.com*
Phone: (573)651-3000
All Year [BP] 1P: $104-$134 2P: $114-$144 XP: $10 F18
Location: I-55, exit 96 (William St), 0.3 mi sw. Located in a commercial area. 103 Cape W Pkwy 63701.
Small-scale Hotel Fax: 573/651-0882. **Facility:** 81 units. 79 one-bedroom standard units. 2 one-bedroom suites ($124-$144).
3 stories, interior corridors. *Bath:* combo or shower only. **Parking:** on-site, winter plug-ins. **Amenities:** high-speed Internet, voice mail, irons, hair dryers. **Leisure Activities:** exercise room. **Guest Services:** valet laundry, wireless Internet. **Cards:** AX, CB, DC, DS, MC, VI.

SOME UNITS
(ASK) 🐕 🕹️ &M 🅔 📷 📺 🖥️ / ✕ 🗄️ 🖨️ /

HOLIDAY INN EXPRESS HOTEL & SUITES *Book at AAA.com*
Phone: (573)334-4491
All Year 1P: $85-$175 2P: $85-$175
Location: I-55, exit 96 (William St), just e. 3253 William St 63701. Fax: 573/334-4261. **Facility:** 102 one-bedroom
Small-scale Hotel standard units, some with whirlpools. 4 stories, interior corridors. *Bath:* combo or shower only. **Parking:** on-site. **Amenities:** high-speed Internet, dual phone lines, voice mail, irons, hair dryers. **Pool(s):** heated indoor.
Leisure Activities: whirlpool, exercise room. *Fee:* game room. **Guest Services:** valet and coin laundry, wireless Internet.
Business Services: meeting rooms, PC. **Cards:** AX, CB, DC, DS, JC, MC, VI.

(ASK) S/D 🍴 &M 🅔 📷 🏊 ✕ 📺 🗄️ 🖨️ 🖥️

PEAR TREE INN BY DRURY-CAPE GIRARDEAU *Book at AAA.com*
Phone: (573)334-3000
All Year [ECP] 1P: $60-$100 2P: $70-$110 XP: $10 F18
Location: I-55, exit 96 (William St), just e. 3248 William St 63701. Fax: 573/334-3000. **Facility:** 78 one-bedroom
Small-scale Hotel standard units. 3 stories, interior corridors. **Parking:** on-site. **Terms:** small pets only. **Amenities:** high-speed
Internet, irons, hair dryers. **Pool(s):** outdoor, wading. **Guest Services:** valet laundry, wireless Internet.
Cards: AX, CB, DC, DS, MC, VI.

SOME UNITS
(ASK) 🐕 🍴 🏊 📺 🖥️ / ✕ /

VICTORIAN INN & SUITES *Book at AAA.com*
Phone: (573)651-4486
All Year 1P: $69-$109 2P: $69-$109
Location: I-55, exit 96 (William St), just e. 3265 William St 63701. Fax: 573/651-3970. **Facility:** 133 units. 128
one-bedroom standard units. 4 one- and 1 two-bedroom suites with whirlpools. 2 stories (no elevator),
Small-scale Hotel interior/exterior corridors. *Bath:* combo or shower only. **Parking:** on-site, winter plug-ins. **Terms:** small pets
only ($50 deposit). **Amenities:** high-speed Internet, dual phone lines, voice mail, irons, hair dryers. **Pool(s):** small heated
indoor, wading. **Leisure Activities:** whirlpool, exercise room. *Fee:* game room. **Guest Services:** complimentary evening
beverages: Mon, valet and coin laundry, wireless Internet. **Business Services:** meeting rooms, PC. **Cards:** AX, DS, MC, VI.

SOME UNITS
(ASK) S/D 🐕 🍴 &M 🅔 📷 🏊 ✕ 📺 🗄️ 🖨️ 🖥️ / ✕ /
FEE

——— **WHERE TO DINE** ———

BELLA ITALIA
Lunch: $6-$15 **Dinner:** $6-$15 **Phone:** 573/332-7800
Location: 2 blks w of Mississippi River; in historic downtown. 20 N Spanish St 63701. **Hours:** 11 am-9 pm, Fri &
Sat-10 pm, Sun-8 pm. Closed major holidays. **Reservations:** not accepted. **Features:** The popular
Italian storefront restaurant treats patrons to thoughtful service and fine food, including sandwiches, calzones,
salads, pasta dishes, pizza and Old World favorites. Casual dress; cocktails. **Parking:** street. **Cards:** AX,
DS, MC, VI. **Historic**
🖊️

BG'S OLDE TYME DELI & SALOON
Lunch: $5-$8 **Dinner:** $5-$8 **Phone:** 573/335-8860
Location: I-55, exit 96 (William St), 1.8 mi e. 205 S Plaza Way 63703. **Hours:** 11 am-10 pm, Fri & Sat-11 pm.
Closed: 1/1, 11/22, 12/25. **Features:** The popular restaurant prepares home-style dinners and smokes
American barbecue pork on the premises. Among offerings are Mexican dishes, catfish and chicken and dumplings
soup, as well as a large selection of sandwiches. Casual dress; cocktails. **Parking:** on-site. **Cards:** AX, DS,
MC, VI.
🍸 🖊️

CEDAR STREET
Lunch: $5-$10 **Dinner:** $8-$18 **Phone:** 573/332-7427
Location: I-55, exit 96 (William St), just w; in Drury Suites-Cape Girardeau. 104 S Vantage Dr 63701. **Hours:** 6 am-9
pm, Sat 7 am-10 pm, Sun 7 am-9 pm. Closed: 12/25. **Reservations:** accepted. **Features:** Patrons can
American unwind in a pleasant atmosphere to sample ribs, steaks and fajitas. Flowerpot bread with flavored butters is
enjoyable. Casual dress; cocktails. **Parking:** on-site. **Cards:** AX, CB, DC, DS, JC, MC, VI. &M 🍸

CHAN'S RESTAURANT
Lunch: $5-$14 **Dinner:** $5-$14 **Phone:** 573/651-4455
Location: I-55, exit 99, 3 mi e. 1159 N Kingshighway 63701. **Hours:** 11 am-9 pm, Fri & Sat-10 pm, Sun 11:30 am-
9 pm. Closed major holidays; also Mon. **Reservations:** accepted. **Features:** You'll enjoy the menu
Chinese selections of sweet and sour shrimp or fish, plus the lo mein shrimp or chicken at Chan's Restaurant. The
Canton-style cuisine is served in an intimate and relaxed atmosphere that's ideal for business people or
families. Casual dress; beer & wine only. **Parking:** on-site. **Cards:** MC, VI.
🖊️

DEXTER BAR-B-QUE
Lunch: $6-$12 **Dinner:** $6-$12 **Phone:** 573/334-9600
Location: I-55, exit 96 (William St), 1.2 mi w to Broadview, then just nw. 236 S Broadview 63701. **Hours:** 11 am-9
pm. Closed major holidays; also Sun. **Features:** The attractive physical facility is casual inside, with
American primarily self-service and really good barbecue. Casual dress. **Parking:** on-site. **Cards:** AX, CB, DC, DS,
JC, MC, VI.

LOGAN'S ROADHOUSE
Lunch: $5-$15 **Dinner:** $5-$15 **Phone:** 573/651-4142
Location: I-55, exit 96 (William St), just e. 3012 William St 63703. **Hours:** 11 am-10 pm, Fri & Sat-11 pm. Closed:
11/22, 12/25. **Reservations:** not accepted. **Features:** Although guests can throw their peanut shells on the
American floor, they'll want to hold onto those large portions of steaks, chops and ribs. Homemade yeast rolls are
included with all entrees. Casual dress; cocktails. **Parking:** on-site. **Cards:** AX, DC, DS, MC, VI.
🖊️

MOLLIE'S CAFE & BAR

Dinner: $13-$25   Phone: 573/339-1661

Northern Continental

Location: I-55, exit 96 (William St), 4.5 mi e, then just n. 11 S Spanish St 63703. **Hours:** 5 pm-10 pm, Fri & Sat-11 pm. Closed major holidays; also Sun. **Reservations:** suggested, weekends. **Features:** The restaurant features a good variety of seafood, beef and pork specialty selections that showcase the chef's unusual and creative methods. Meals are prepared with fresh ingredients and served in a Continental art nouveau dining room that can seem stark to those expecting soft textures and warm colors. Casual dress; cocktails. **Parking:** street. **Cards:** AX, DS, MC, VI.

PAGODA GARDENS

Lunch: $6   Dinner: $8-$18   Phone: 573/334-8931

Chinese

Location: I-55, exit 96 (William St), 1.5 mi e, then just s. 329 S Kingshighway 63703. **Hours:** 11 am-9 pm, Fri & Sat-10 pm. Closed major holidays. **Reservations:** accepted. **Features:** The menu lists a good selection of Oriental dishes, as well as American-style steaks, chicken and seafood. Hot and sour soup with a bouquet of flavors is excellent, and beef skewers are served with a hibachi so diners can finish the cooking. Casual dress; cocktails. **Parking:** on-site. **Cards:** AX, CB, DC, DS, JC, MC, VI.

ROYAL N'ORLEANS RESTAURANT

Dinner: $13-$26   Phone: 573/335-8191

Northern Creole

Location: Center. 300 Broadway St 63703. **Hours:** 5 pm-10 pm, Fri & Sat-11 pm. Closed major holidays; also Sun. **Reservations:** suggested. **Features:** Good meals are prepared with a Creole flair and served in inviting, appealing French Quarter-style dining rooms. The fresh seafood and desserts—such as bananas Foster and cherries jubilee, which are prepared flambe tableside—are excellent. The friendly staff is knowledgeable and attentive. The wine list is impressive and selective. Dressy casual; cocktails; entertainment. **Parking:** street. **Cards:** AX, DC, DS, MC, VI. **Historic**

CARROLLTON pop. 4,122

———— WHERE TO STAY ————

SUPER 8 MOTEL-CARROLLTON

Book at AAA.com

Small-scale Hotel

| All Year | 1P: $55 | 2P: $60 | XP: $5 | F18 |

Phone: (660)542-2988

Location: Jct US 65 and 24, 1.4 mi n. 1408 N Hwy 65 64633. Fax: 660/542-2985. **Facility:** 34 one-bedroom standard units. 2 stories (no elevator), interior corridors. **Parking:** on-site. **Terms:** cancellation fee imposed, weekly rates available, [AP] & [CP] meal plans available, package plans, $59 service charge. **Amenities:** high-speed Internet, irons, hair dryers. **Guest Services:** wireless Internet. **Cards:** AX, CB, DC, DS, JC, MC, VI.

SOME UNITS

CARTHAGE pop. 12,668

———— WHERE TO STAY ————

BEST WESTERN PRECIOUS MOMENTS HOTEL   Book great rates at AAA.com

Small-scale Hotel

| All Year | 1P: $69-$130 | 2P: $69-$130 | XP: $5 | F18 |

Phone: (417)359-5900

Location: Just e of jct US 71 and SR HH. 2701 Hazel St 64836. Fax: 417/359-5240. **Facility:** 122 one-bedroom standard units, some with whirlpools. 2 stories, interior corridors. **Bath:** combo or shower only. **Parking:** on-site. **Terms:** check-in 4 pm, package plans, pets ($10 fee). **Amenities:** high-speed Internet, voice mail, irons, hair dryers. **Pool(s):** heated indoor. **Leisure Activities:** exercise room. **Guest Services:** gift shop, coin laundry. **Cards:** AX, DC, DS, MC, VI. **Free Special Amenities:** early check-in/late check-out and room upgrade (subject to availability with advance reservations).** (See color ad below & p 396)

SOME UNITS

ECONO LODGE   *Book great rates at AAA.com*   Phone: 417/358-3900
▼▼ ▼▼   All Year   1P: $58-$139   2P: $58-$139   XP: $5   F18
         Location: On SR 96; jct US 71. 1441 W Central 64836. Fax: 417/358-6839. **Facility:** 83 units. 82 one-bedroom
Small-scale Hotel   standard units. 1 one-bedroom suite. 2 stories (no elevator), interior/exterior corridors. *Bath:* combo or
         shower only. **Parking:** on-site. **Terms:** weekly rates available, pets ($10 fee). **Amenities:** safes (fee).
Pool(s): heated indoor. **Leisure Activities:** whirlpool. **Guest Services:** wireless Internet. **Business Services:** meeting rooms.
Cards: AX, DS, MC, VI.

SOME UNITS

(ASK) (S₀) (🐾) (🍴) (🖥️) (🏊) (📷) / (✕) (🛄) (📠) /
FEE

SUPER 8 MOTEL   *Book at AAA.com*   Phone: (417)359-9000
▼▼ ▼▼   All Year   1P: $57   XP: $5   F18
         Location: Just e of jct US 71 and SR HH. 416 W Fir Rd 64836. Fax: 417/359-9099. **Facility:** 56 one-bedroom
Small-scale Hotel   standard units. 2 stories (no elevator), interior corridors. **Parking:** on-site. **Terms:** cancellation fee imposed,
         weekly rates available, package plans, pets ($5 fee). **Amenities:** hair dryers. **Leisure Activities:** whirlpool.
Guest Services: coin laundry, wireless Internet. **Cards:** AX, CB, DC, DS, JC, MC, VI.

SOME UNITS

(ASK) (S₀) (🐾) (🍴) (📷) / (✕) (🛄) (📠) /
FEE

────── WHERE TO DINE ──────

BAM-BOO GARDENS   Lunch: $4-$8   Dinner: $4-$8   Phone: 417/358-1611
▼   **Location:** 1 mi e of jct US 71 and SR 96. 102 N Garrison 64850. **Hours:** 11 am-9 pm, Fri-10 pm, Sun-8 pm.
         Closed: 11/22, 12/25. **Features:** Many locals enjoy the buffet offerings, but patrons can order from the menu
Chinese   as well. Casual dress. **Parking:** on-site. **Cards:** MC, VI.   (✎)

SIRLOIN STOCKADE   Lunch: $6-$8   Dinner: $6-$8   Phone: 417/358-1765
▼▼ ▼▼   **Location:** On SR 96, just e of jct US 71 and SR 96. 1027 W Central 64836. **Hours:** 11 am-9 pm. Closed major
         holidays. **Reservations:** not accepted. **Features:** The steakhouse lines up buffet items, including pizza,
Steak House   tacos, soups, salads and desserts, providing both excellent variety and a good value. Rotating theme nights
         might allow for the sampling of sushi, barbecue and seafood. The buffet also may serve to complement a
quality steak. Rolls are baked several times daily. Casual dress. **Parking:** on-site. **Cards:** DS, MC, VI.   (✎)

CARUTHERSVILLE pop. 6,760

────── WHERE TO DINE ──────

CORKY'S RIBS & BBQ   Lunch: $7-$14   Dinner: $7-$14   Phone: 573/333-6081
▼▼ ▼▼   **Location:** Downtown; in Casino Aztar Complex. 777 E Third St 63830. **Hours:** 11 am-9:30 pm, Fri & Sat-12:30 am.
         Reservations: accepted. **Features:** Patrons can admire plenty of Hollywood memorabilia while savoring
American   Memphis-style hickory-smoked ribs. Among good accompaniments are fried pickles, loaded spuds and
         delicious pecan pie. Casual dress; cocktails. **Parking:** on-site. **Cards:** AX, CB, DC, DS, JC, MC, VI.   (✎)

CASSVILLE pop. 2,890

────── WHERE TO STAY ──────

SUPER 8 MOTEL   Phone: 417/847-4888
▼   All Year [CP]   1P: $55-$64   2P: $59-$69   XP: $5   F8
         Location: Just s of jct SR 76, 86 and 37 business route. 101 S Hwy 37 65625. Fax: 417/847-4888. **Facility:** 44
Small-scale Hotel   one-bedroom standard units, some with whirlpools. 2 stories (no elevator), interior corridors. **Parking:** on-
         site. **Terms:** pets ($20 deposit, $5 extra charge, with prior approval). **Amenities:** high-speed Internet, irons.
Pool(s): small outdoor. **Cards:** AX, DC, DS, MC, VI.

SOME UNITS

(ASK) (S₀) (🐾) (🛁M) (🏊) (🛗) (📷) / (✕) (🛄) (📠) /
FEE

────── WHERE TO DINE ──────

THE RIB   Lunch: $6-$10   Dinner: $7-$20   Phone: 417/847-3600
▼▼ ▼▼   **Location:** Jct SR 112 and 248. Hwy 112 S 65625. **Hours:** 11:30 am-1:30 & 5-9 pm, Fri & Sat 5 pm-10 pm.
         Closed: 1/1, 12/25; also Sun & Mon. **Reservations:** accepted. **Features:** Near Roaring River State Park,
American   the cozy, rustic restaurant offers something for everyone. Steaks and ribs, as well as fresh seafood, are
         superb. All steaks are cut on the premises and meats are slow-smoked over a hickory-wood pit. Casual
dress; cocktails. **Parking:** on-site. **Cards:** AX, DS, MC, VI.   (🍽️) (✎)

CHAMP —*See St. Louis p. 534.*

CHARLESTON pop. 4,732

────── WHERE TO STAY ──────

COMFORT INN   *Book great rates at AAA.com*   Phone: (573)683-4200
(AAA) (SAVE)   3/1-9/15 [BP]   1P: $64-$90   2P: $70-$100   XP: $6   F17
         9/16-2/29 [BP]   1P: $60-$85   2P: $64-$90   XP: $6   F17
▼▼ ▼▼   **Location:** I-57, exit 10, just nw. 102 Drake St 63834. Fax: 573/683-2446. **Facility:** 40 one-bedroom standard
Motel   units. 2 stories (no elevator), exterior corridors. **Parking:** on-site, winter plug-ins. **Terms:** 7 day cancellation
         notice, pets ($15 extra charge). **Amenities:** high-speed Internet, irons, hair dryers. *Some:* DVD players.
         Pool(s): small outdoor. **Guest Services:** wireless Internet. **Business Services:** PC, fax. **Cards:** AX, CB,
DC, DS, MC, VI. **Free Special Amenities:** expanded continental breakfast and high-speed Internet.

SOME UNITS

(S₀) (🐾) (🏊) (🛗) (📷) (🛄) (📠) (💻) / (✕) /
FEE

CHESTERFIELD —See St. Louis p. 534.

CHILLICOTHE pop. 8,968

——— WHERE TO STAY ———

BEST WESTERN INN *Book great rates at AAA.com* Phone: (660)646-0572
▼▼▼ ▼▼▼ All Year 1P: $45-$65 2P: $45-$65 XP: $5 F12
Small-scale Hotel Location: Jct SR 36 and 65 (Washington St). 1020 S Washington St 64601. Fax: 660/646-1274. **Facility:** 58 units. 52 one-bedroom standard units. 6 one-bedroom suites, some with whirlpools. 1-3 stories (no elevator), interior/exterior corridors. *Bath:* combo or shower only. **Parking:** on-site. **Terms:** pets ($10 extra charge). **Amenities:** irons, hair dryers. *Some:* high-speed Internet. **Pool(s):** outdoor. **Leisure Activities:** exercise room. **Guest Services:** coin laundry, wireless Internet. **Business Services:** meeting rooms. **Cards:** AX, CB, DC, DS, MC, VI.

SOME UNITS
(ASK) [SD] 🛏 🍴 [&M] 🏊 🎥 🖥 💻 / ✕ 🖨

CHILLICOTHE SUPER 8 MOTEL *Book at AAA.com* Phone: 660/646-7888
▼▼ Property failed to provide current rates
Small-scale Hotel Location: Jct US 36 and 65 (Washington St), 0.8 mi e. 580 Old Hwy 36 E 64601. Fax: 660/646-2531. **Facility:** 55 one-bedroom standard units. 2 stories (no elevator), interior corridors. **Parking:** on-site, winter plug-ins. **Terms:** pets ($10 extra charge). **Amenities:** high-speed Internet, hair dryers. **Guest Services:** wireless Internet. **Business Services:** PC.

SOME UNITS
🛏 🎥 / ✕ 🖥 🖨

——— WHERE TO DINE ———

BEIJING CHINESE RESTAURANT **Lunch:** $5 **Dinner:** $7-$10 **Phone:** 660/646-4112
▼▼▼ ▼▼▼ Location: 1 mi n on US 65 (Washington St). 327 Washington St 64601. **Hours:** 11 am-2 & 4:30-9:30 pm, Sat 11 am-2:30 & 4:30-9:30 pm. Closed: 11/22, 12/25; also Sun. **Reservations:** accepted. **Features:** The popular spot offers a generous buffet and menu selections of favorites, as well as casual atmosphere, friendly service and a good value. Casual dress; beer & wine only. **Parking:** on-site. **Cards:** AX, DS, MC, VI. 🟦
Chinese

WASHINGTON STREET FOOD & DRINK COMPANY **Lunch:** $6-$15 **Dinner:** $6-$15 **Phone:** 660/646-4058
▼▼▼ ▼▼▼ Location: 1.9 mi n on US 65 (Washington St). 1100 N Washington St 64601. **Hours:** 11 am-10 pm, Fri & Sat-10:30 pm, Sun-9 pm. Closed major holidays. **Features:** The atmosphere is comfortable and relaxed. Good menu selections are topped by a better array of tempting desserts, including hand-mixed chocolate, vanilla or cherry colas and fried cheesecake. Casual dress; cocktails. **Parking:** on-site. **Cards:** AX, DS, MC, VI. 🟦
American

CLAYTON —See St. Louis p. 536.

CLINTON pop. 9,311

——— WHERE TO STAY ———

BEST WESTERN COLONIAL MOTEL *Book great rates at AAA.com* Phone: (660)885-2206
(AAA) [SAVE] All Year 1P: $45-$55 2P: $55-$65 XP: $5 F12
▼▼▼ ▼▼▼ Location: Jct SR 7 and 13. 106 S Baird St 64735. Fax: 660/885-2206. **Facility:** 32 one-bedroom standard units. 1-2 stories (no elevator), exterior corridors. **Parking:** on-site, winter plug-ins. **Terms:** [CP] meal plan available, pets ($10 extra charge, with prior approval). **Amenities:** high-speed Internet, irons, hair dryers. **Pool(s):** small outdoor. **Cards:** AX, DC, DS, MC, VI. **Free Special Amenities:** continental breakfast and high-speed Internet.
Motel

SOME UNITS
[SD] 🛏 🍴 🏊 🎥 💻 / ✕ 🖥 /

HAMPTON INN *Book great rates at AAA.com* Phone: 660/885-4488
▼▼▼ ▼ All Year 1P: $79-$89 2P: $79-$89
Small-scale Hotel Location: Just s of jct SR 7 and 13. 900 Kansas Ave 64735. Fax: 660/885-2946. **Facility:** 65 one-bedroom standard units. 3 stories, interior corridors. *Bath:* combo or shower only. **Parking:** on-site. **Terms:** cancellation fee imposed, [BP] meal plan available, package plans. **Amenities:** high-speed Internet, voice mail, irons, hair dryers. **Pool(s):** heated indoor. **Leisure Activities:** exercise room. **Guest Services:** valet laundry, wireless Internet. **Business Services:** meeting rooms. **Cards:** AX, DC, DS, JC, MC, VI.

SOME UNITS
(ASK) [SD] 🍴 [&M] 🎥 🏊 🖥 💻 / ✕ 🖥 🖨 /

MOTEL USA INN Phone: 660/885-2267
(AAA) [SAVE] All Year [CP] 1P: $35-$50 2P: $39-$69 XP: $10 F6
▼ Location: Jct SR 7 and 13. 1508 N 2nd St 64735. Fax: 660/885-2267. **Facility:** 25 one-bedroom standard units. Motel 1 story, exterior corridors. **Parking:** on-site, winter plug-ins. **Terms:** 2 night minimum stay, cancellation fee imposed, pets ($5 fee). **Cards:** AX, DS, MC, VI. **Free Special Amenities:** continental breakfast and local telephone calls.

SOME UNITS
[SD] 🛏 🍴 🎥 / ✕ 🖥 /

PARKFIELD INN

▽▽▽ ▽▽▽
Small-scale Hotel

Phone: 660/890-6188

All Year   1P: $56-$110   2P: $56-$110   XP: $6   F12
Location: Just s of jct SR 7 and 13. 506 Kansas Ave 64735. Fax: 660/890-6161. **Facility:** 60 units. 59 one-bedroom standard units, some with whirlpools. 1 one-bedroom suite with whirlpool. 2 stories, interior corridors. *Bath:* combo or shower only. **Parking:** on-site, winter plug-ins. **Terms:** [ECP] meal plan available.
Amenities: high-speed Internet, irons, hair dryers. **Pool(s):** small heated indoor. **Leisure Activities:** whirlpool. **Guest Services:** coin laundry. **Business Services:** meeting rooms, PC. **Cards:** AX, CB, DC, DS, MC, VI.

SOME UNITS

(ASK) (S/D) (器) (⊹) (🖘) (🖐) (💻) / (✕) (🛢) (📠) /

COLUMBIA pop. 84,531

——— **WHERE TO STAY** ———

CANDLEWOOD SUITES   *Book at AAA.com*

▽▽ ▽▽
Small-scale Hotel

Phone: 573/817-0525

Property failed to provide current rates
Location: I-70, exit 128A, just s to I-70 Dr SE, 0.3 mi e to Wingate Ct. 3100 Wingate Ct 65201. Fax: 573/815-9825. **Facility:** 80 units. 58 one-bedroom standard units with efficiencies. 22 one-bedroom suites with efficiencies. 3 stories, interior corridors. *Bath:* combo or shower only. **Parking:** on-site.
Terms: office hours 7 am-11 pm, pets ($75 extra charge). **Amenities:** video library, DVD players, high-speed Internet, dual phone lines, voice mail, irons, hair dryers. **Leisure Activities:** exercise room. **Guest Services:** sundries, complimentary and valet laundry, wireless Internet.

(📵) (⅛M) (⊹) (🗋) (🖐) (🛢) (📠) (💻)
FEE

COURTYARD BY MARRIOTT-COLUMBIA   *Book great rates at AAA.com*

▽▽▽ ▽▽▽
Small-scale Hotel

Phone: (573)443-8000

All Year   1P: $109-$139   2P: $109-$139
Location: I-70, exit 128A, s on US 63 to CR/AC exit, just ne. 3301 LeMone Industrial Blvd 65201. Fax: 573/443-8008. **Facility:** Smoke free premises. 133 units. 129 one-bedroom standard units, some with whirlpools. 4 one-bedroom suites ($139-$169). 4 stories, interior corridors. *Bath:* combo or shower only. **Parking:** on-site.
Terms: [BP] meal plan available. **Amenities:** high-speed Internet, dual phone lines, voice mail, irons, hair dryers. **Pool(s):** small heated indoor. **Leisure Activities:** whirlpool, exercise room. **Guest Services:** sundries, valet and coin laundry. **Business Services:** conference facilities, business center. **Cards:** AX, DC, DS, MC, VI.

(ASK) (S/D) (✈) (🖐) (⊹) (🗋) (🖘) (✕) (🖐) (🛢) (📠) (💻)

DRURY INN-COLUMBIA   *Book at AAA.com*

▽▽▽ ▽▽▽
Small-scale Hotel

Phone: (573)445-1800

All Year [BP]   1P: $80-$150   2P: $90-$160   XP: $10   F18
Location: I-70, exit 124 (Stadium Blvd), just s. 1000 Knipp St 65203. Fax: 573/445-1800. **Facility:** 123 units. 119 one-bedroom standard units. 4 one-bedroom suites ($110-$145). 5 stories, interior corridors. **Parking:** on-site. **Terms:** small pets only. **Amenities:** high-speed Internet, dual phone lines, voice mail, irons, hair dryers. **Pool(s):** heated indoor. **Leisure Activities:** whirlpool, exercise room. **Guest Services:** complimentary evening beverages, valet and coin laundry, wireless Internet. **Business Services:** meeting rooms, PC. **Cards:** AX, CB, DC, DS, MC, VI.

SOME UNITS

(ASK) (🐾) (🗋) (🖘) (🖐) (🛢) (📠) (💻) / (✕) /

EXTENDED STAYAMERICA-COLUMBIA-STADIUM BLVD   *Book at AAA.com*

▽▽ ▽▽
Small-scale Hotel

Phone: (573)445-6800

All Year   1P: $55-$140   2P: $60-$145   XP: $5   F17
Location: I-70, exit 124 (Stadium Blvd), just ne. 2000 W Business Loop 70 65203. Fax: 573/445-6801. **Facility:** 95 one-bedroom standard units with efficiencies. 3 stories, interior corridors. *Bath:* combo or shower only. **Parking:** on-site. **Terms:** pets ($25 extra charge). **Amenities:** high-speed Internet, voice mail, irons. **Guest Services:** coin laundry, wireless Internet. **Cards:** AX, CB, DC, DS, MC, VI.

SOME UNITS

(ASK) (S/D) (🐾) (🖐) (🛢) (📠) (💻) / (✕) /
FEE

When you're on the road and get into a jam...

24 hours a day, 7 days a week, AAA Emergency Road Service is there. AAA has rescued stranded members for more than 100 years. So if you get a flat tire, run out of gas, or just can't get your car started, call **800-AAA-HELP** and AAA is at your service.

Hearing Impaired: 800-955-4TDD.

FAIRFIELD INN BY MARRIOTT *Book great rates at AAA.com* Phone: (573)814-2727

(AAA) (SAVE)

3/1-11/15	1P: $79-$159
11/16-2/29	1P: $59-$109

Location: I-70, exit 128A, just nw. 2904 Clark Ln 65202. Fax: 573/814-2828. **Facility:** Smoke free premises. 80 one-bedroom standard units, some with whirlpools. 3 stories, interior corridors. *Bath:* combo or shower only.

Small-scale Hotel **Parking:** on-site. **Amenities:** high-speed Internet, irons, hair dryers. **Pool(s):** small heated indoor. **Leisure Activities:** whirlpool, sun deck, limited exercise equipment. **Guest Services:** valet laundry, wireless Internet. **Cards:** AX, CB, DC, DS, JC, MC, VI. **Free Special Amenities:** full breakfast and newspaper.

SOME UNITS

HAMPTON INN *Book great rates at AAA.com* Phone: 573/886-9392

(AAA) (SAVE)

All Year	1P: $109-$169	2P: $109-$169

Location: I-70, exit 128A, just ne. 3410 Clark Ln 65202. Fax: 573/814-2001. **Facility:** 121 one-bedroom standard units, some with whirlpools. 5 stories, interior corridors. *Bath:* combo or shower only. **Parking:** on-site. **Terms:** [ECP] meal plan available. **Amenities:** video games (fee), high-speed Internet, voice mail, irons, hair dryers. **Pool(s):** heated indoor. **Leisure Activities:** whirlpool, exercise room. **Guest Services:** valet and coin laundry, wireless Internet. **Business Services:** business center. **Cards:** AX, DC, DS, MC, VI.

Small-scale Hotel

Free Special Amenities: expanded continental breakfast and high-speed Internet.

SOME UNITS

HOLIDAY INN SELECT EXECUTIVE CENTER *Book great rates at AAA.com* Phone: (573)445-8531

All Year	1P: $85-$300	2P: $85-$300

Location: I-70, exit 124 (Stadium Blvd), just w. 2200 I-70 Dr SW 65203. Fax: 573/445-7607. **Facility:** 311 units.

Large-scale Hotel 306 one-bedroom standard units, some with whirlpools. 1 one- and 4 two-bedroom suites ($140-$300), some with whirlpools. 6 stories, interior corridors. *Bath:* combo or shower only. **Parking:** on-site. **Terms:** check-in 4 pm, cancellation fee imposed, [BP] meal plan available, $2 service charge, pets ($25 extra charge). **Amenities:** video games (fee), high-speed Internet, voice mail, irons, hair dryers. **Dining:** Churchill's, Spanky's Sports Zone Restaurant & Grill, see separate listings. **Pool(s):** heated outdoor, heated indoor. **Leisure Activities:** whirlpool, exercise room. *Fee:* massage. **Guest Services:** gift shop, valet and coin laundry, wireless Internet, personal trainer. *Fee:* beauty salon, shoe shine. **Business Services:** conference facilities, business center. **Cards:** AX, DC, DS, MC, VI.

SOME UNITS

RED ROOF INN-COLUMBIA *Book at AAA.com* Phone: (573)442-0145

5/25-9/2	1P: $47-$65	2P: $52-$73	XP: $5	F18
9/3-12/31	1P: $46-$58	2P: $52-$64	XP: $6	F18
3/1-5/24 & 1/1-2/29	1P: $44-$55	2P: $50-$63	XP: $6	F18

Motel **Location:** I-70, exit 126 (Providence Rd), just n. 201 E Texas Ave 65202. Fax: 573/449-9588. **Facility:** 108 one-bedroom standard units. 2 stories (no elevator), exterior corridors. *Bath:* combo or shower only. **Parking:** on-site. **Terms:** small pets only. **Amenities:** video games (fee), high-speed Internet, voice mail. **Guest Services:** wireless Internet. **Cards:** AX, CB, DC, DS, MC, VI.

SOME UNITS

STONEY CREEK INN *Book great rates at AAA.com* Phone: (573)442-6400

(AAA) (SAVE)

All Year	1P: $78	2P: $88	XP: $10	F17

Location: I-70, exit 126 (Providence Rd/SR 163), 3 mi s; on west outer road. 2601 S Providence Rd 65203. Fax: 573/442-6414. **Facility:** 180 units. 177 one-bedroom standard units, some with efficiencies and/or whirlpools. 3 one-bedroom suites ($128-$278) with whirlpools. 4 stories, interior corridors. *Bath:* combo or shower only. **Parking:** on-site. **Terms:** [ECP] meal plan available, package plans. **Amenities:** high-speed Internet, voice mail, irons, hair dryers. *Some:* DVD players. **Pool(s):** heated indoor/outdoor. **Leisure**

Small-scale Hotel **Activities:** sauna, whirlpool, exercise room. *Fee:* game room. **Guest Services:** gift shop, valet and coin laundry, airport transportation-Columbia Regional Airport, area transportation-Katy Trail & Greyhound bus station. **Business Services:** conference facilities, business center. **Cards:** AX, DC, DS, MC, VI. **Free Special Amenities:** expanded continental breakfast and local telephone calls.

SOME UNITS

SUPER 8 MOTEL-CLARKE LANE IN COLUMBIA *Book at AAA.com* Phone: (573)474-8488

All Year	1P: $51-$91	2P: $57-$96	XP: $5	F18

Location: I-70, exit 128A, northeast corner. 3216 Clark Ln 65202. Fax: 573/474-4180. **Facility:** 75 units. 71 one-and 3 two-bedroom standard units. 1 one-bedroom suite ($63-$110) with kitchen (no utensils). 3 stories (no

Motel elevator), interior corridors. **Parking:** on-site. **Terms:** [CP] meal plan available, pets ($15 extra charge). **Amenities:** high-speed Internet, hair dryers. **Guest Services:** wireless Internet. **Cards:** AX, CB, DC, DS, MC, VI.

SOME UNITS

----- **WHERE TO DINE** -----

THE 63 DINER **Lunch:** $5-$13 **Dinner:** $5-$13 **Phone:** 573/443-2331

Location: I-70, exit 127 (SR 763), 3 mi n. 5801 N 763 65202. **Hours:** 11 am-9 pm, Sat from 6:30 am, Sun 11 am-

American 8 pm. Closed major holidays; also Mon. **Features:** You'll very much enjoy The 63 Diner with its 1950s decor, memorabilia, neon lights and music. They also serve large portions of good food, including an excellent chef salad and very good chicken vegetable soup. Service is friendly and efficient. Casual dress.

Parking: on-site. **Cards:** MC, VI.

ADDISON'S **Lunch:** $7-$18 **Dinner:** $7-$18 **Phone:** 573/256-1995

Location: Between 7th and 8th sts; downtown. 709 Cherry St 65201. **Hours:** 11 am-midnight. **Closed:** 11/22,

American 12/25. **Reservations:** accepted, weekdays. **Features:** Forget table cloths, uniformed waiters or candlelight dining. Addison's is a downtown eatery which serves sophisticated dishes in a casual atmosphere. Casual dress; cocktails. **Parking:** street. **Cards:** AX, DC, DS, MC, VI.

CHERRY STREET ARTISAN CAFE THEATRE
GALLERY   **Lunch:** $5-$10   **Dinner:** $5-$10   **Phone:** 573/817-3274

American

Location: At 9th and Cherry sts; in lower level of City Centre; downtown. 111 9th St, Suite 10 65201. **Hours:** 6:30 am-11 pm, Thurs & Fri-midnight, Sat 7 am-midnight, Sun 2 pm-11 pm. Closed: Sun 12/15-1/15. **Features:** The cafe features intentionally simple but quality furnishings and decor, live music during lunch weekdays, some small-scale live theatre and poetry reading. In the off hours, it's a place to "hang out"; a little like being in a library, only you can eat, drink, and don't have to whisper, although relaxing is acceptable as well. Casual dress; beer & wine only; entertainment. **Parking:** street. **Cards:** MC, VI.

CHURCHILL'S
Dinner: $19-$37   **Phone:** 573/445-8531

Continental

Location: I-70, exit 124 (Stadium Blvd), just w; in Holiday Inn Select Executive Center. 2200 I-70 Dr SW 65203. **Hours:** 5:30 pm-10 pm. Closed major holidays; also Sun & Mon. **Reservations:** suggested. **Features:** Elegant decor contributes to the restaurant's cozy, intimate ambience. The menu has wonderful variety and several sophisticated dishes; entrees feature excellent taste and presentation. Tableside preparation of some dishes enhances the dining experience. Also offered is a fine selection of imported and domestic wines. Dressy casual; cocktails. **Parking:** on-site. **Cards:** AX, DC, DS, MC, VI.

THE COLOSSEUM BISTRO
Lunch: $6-$13   **Dinner:** $6-$18   **Phone:** 573/256-2087

American

Location: S 4th and Broadway sts. 402 E Broadway St 65201. **Hours:** 11 am-11 pm, Fri & Sat-midnight, Sun-10 pm. Closed: 12/25. **Reservations:** accepted. **Features:** Formerly the Katy Railroad Station, the historic setting has been converted into a comfortable and casual eatery. The menu lists a large selection of favorites. Casual dress; cocktails. **Parking:** on-site. **Cards:** AX, DS, MC, VI.

EL MAGUEY
Lunch: $5-$7   **Dinner:** $5-$10   **Phone:** 573/449-6558

Mexican

Location: I-70, exit Business Loop 70 W, 0.7 mi sw. 504 Business Loop 70 W 65203. **Hours:** 11 am-10 pm, Fri & Sat-10:30 pm. Closed major holidays. **Features:** One of a chain of restaurants, this spot prepares such favorites as tacos, burritos, enchiladas and, of course, chips and salsa. Patrons won't go home hungry. Casual dress; beer & wine only. **Parking:** on-site. **Cards:** AX, MC, VI.

EVERETT'S
Lunch: $6-$10   **Dinner:** $12-$25   **Phone:** 573/443-6200

American

Location: I-70, exit 127 (SR 763), southwest corner on the hill. 1601 Range Line 65201. **Hours:** 11 am-10 pm, Fri & Sat-11 pm. Closed: 7/4, 11/22, 12/25. **Features:** The menu at Everett's features certified Angus beef steak, fresh seafood, ribs, chops, chicken, Mexican and pasta served by an enthusiastic and friendly staff. The restaurant has an upscale, enjoyable decor with many plants and soft lighting, creating a pleasant ambience. Casual dress; cocktails. **Parking:** on-site. **Cards:** AX, CB, DC, DS, JC, MC, VI.

FELINI
Lunch: $7-$15   **Dinner:** $7-$15   **Phone:** 573/256-5025

Mediterranean

Location: Corner of S 7th and E Broadway sts; downtown. 700 E Broadway St 65203. **Hours:** 11 am-11 pm. Closed major holidays. **Reservations:** accepted. **Features:** The pleasing family-owned and operated establishment serves Mediterranean and Kosovar food, as well as calzones and pasta dishes. Beer & wine only. **Parking:** street. **Cards:** AX, DS, MC, VI.

GRAND CRU
Lunch: $6-$18   **Dinner:** $6-$38   **Phone:** 573/443-2600

American

Location: 1.2 mi s of Stadium Blvd, on east outer road. 2600 S Providence Rd 65203. **Hours:** 11 am-9 pm, Thurs-Sat to 10 pm. Closed: 12/25. **Reservations:** suggested. **Features:** Innovative menu items are presented in a comfortable atmosphere. Outside patios and inside fireplaces enhance the mood during all seasons. This place provides a special occasion experience at a reasonable price. Dressy casual; cocktails. **Parking:** on-site. **Cards:** AX, DS, MC, VI.

GREAT WALL CHINESE SUPER
BUFFET   *Menu on AAA.com*   **Lunch:** $5-$6   **Dinner:** $8   **Phone:** 573/446-3888

Chinese

Location: I-70, exit 124 (Stadium Blvd), 0.4 mi s. 2005 W Worley St 65203. **Hours:** 11 am-9:30 pm, Fri & Sat-10:30 pm. Closed: 11/22. **Reservations:** accepted. **Features:** This Chinese restaurant features buffet lines with more than fifty different dishes to choose from plus a Mongolian barbecue area where diners can select from a variety of raw ingredients which are then stir-fried on a domed grill while you watch. Casual dress. **Parking:** on-site. **Cards:** AX, CB, DC, DS, JC, MC, VI.

HARPO'S
Lunch: $5-$7   **Dinner:** $5-$8   **Phone:** 573/443-5418

American

Location: At Cherry and 10th sts; downtown. 29 S 10th St 65201. **Hours:** 11 am-9 pm. Closed: 1/1, 4/8, 12/25. **Features:** Comfortably worn, the college-town restaurant has a warm, casual atmosphere. A stone fireplace enhances the feel of the dining room, and seasonal outdoor seating also can be requested. The burgers are great. Casual dress; cocktails. **Parking:** street. **Cards:** AX, DS, MC, VI.

JACK'S GOURMET RESTAURANT
Dinner: $14-$36   **Phone:** 573/449-3927

Continental

Location: Jct Old US 63, exit 128 westbound; exit 127 eastbound, 0.3 mi s on SR 763, then 0.8 mi e. 1903 I-70 Business Loop E 65201. **Hours:** 4 pm-10 pm. Closed major holidays; also Sun. **Reservations:** suggested. **Features:** Particularly appropriate for special occasions, the atmosphere is just as welcoming for business meals as for romantic evenings. Wines pair with selections from the extensive menu. A pianist performs nightly. Casual dress; cocktails; entertainment. **Parking:** on-site. **Cards:** AX, DC, DS, MC, VI.

MURRY'S
American

Lunch: $5-$16   **Dinner:** $9-$16   **Phone:** 573/442-4969

Location: I-70, exit 126 (Providence St), 3.5 mi s, then just w; in Green Meadows Plaza. 3107 Green Meadows Way 65203. **Hours:** 11 am-midnight. Closed major holidays; also Sun. **Features:** Lending to the lively and fun atmosphere are jazz-related posters, photographs and, at certain times of the week, a piano player. A favorite among locals in the know, this place is busy and popular. The menu lists a nice variety of entrees with good flavor and presentation. Servers are attentive and prompt. A jazz band plays on Saturday nights. Casual dress; cocktails. **Parking:** on-site. **Cards:** AX, DS, MC, VI.

OTTO'S CORNER BAR & GRILL
American

Lunch: $6-$10   **Dinner:** $10-$15   **Phone:** 573/443-6996

Location: Corner of 8th and Walnut sts. 38 N 8th St 65203. **Hours:** 11 am-9:30 pm, Fri-11 pm, Sat 5 pm-11 pm. Closed: 7/4, 11/22, 12/25; also Sun. **Features:** Innovative menu selections are prepared in a warm and comfortable atmosphere. A hint of sophistication is evident. Casual dress; cocktails. **Parking:** street. **Cards:** AX, MC, VI.

THE PASTA FACTORY
Italian

Lunch: $7-$12   **Dinner:** $7-$12   **Phone:** 573/449-3948

Location: Corner of Broadway and Hitt sts; entrance from courtyard on east side of building; downtown. 1020 E Broadway St, Suite F 65201. **Hours:** 11 am-10 pm, Fri & Sat-10:30 pm. Closed major holidays. **Features:** In a late 1800s red-brick factory building, the restaurant has a New Orleans-type courtyard and lots of memorabilia. Pasta dishes are widely varied, and other choices, such as rotisserie chicken, also are offered. Favorite selections are mostaccioli con salsiccia—tubular pasta with Italian sausage—and the traditional chicken marsala. Casual dress; cocktails. **Parking:** street. **Cards:** AX, CB, DC, DS, JC, MC, VI.

SPANKY'S SPORTS ZONE RESTAURANT & GRILL
American

Lunch: $7-$20   **Dinner:** $7-$20   **Phone:** 573/445-8383

Location: I-70, exit 124 (Stadium Blvd), just w; in Holiday Inn Select Executive Center. 2200 I-70 Dr SW 65202. **Hours:** 11 am-11 pm. **Reservations:** accepted. **Features:** Contemporary decor and atmosphere boast the latest in current trends; the eatery offers everything from pizza to steaks, appetizers and, of course, the big screen TV. Casual dress; cocktails. **Parking:** on-site. **Cards:** AX, CB, DC, DS, JC, MC, VI.

TELLERS GALLERY AND BAR
American

Lunch: $5-$8   **Dinner:** $6-$16   **Phone:** 573/441-8355

Location: Corner of 9th and Broadway sts; downtown. 820 E Broadway St 65201. **Hours:** 11 am-10 pm, Fri & Sat-11 pm. Closed major holidays; also Sun. **Features:** Among hints of trendy sophistication are the changing gallery exhibits and menu selections that reflect the same qualities. This place is known for its wonderful salads, but many other offerings also are sure to satisfy. Casual dress; cocktails. **Parking:** street. **Cards:** AX, DC, DS, MC, VI.

TRATTORIA STRADA NOVA
Italian

Dinner: $15-$40   **Phone:** 573/442-8992

Location: Between Broadway and Walnut sts; downtown. 21 N 9th St 65202. **Hours:** 5 pm-10 pm. Closed: 7/4, 12/25; also Sun. **Features:** The restaurant features casual, California-style dining with Northern Italian accents. Excellently prepared and nicely presented items on a menu that changes daily are Mediterranean in theme. Servers are attentive, prompt and friendly. Casual dress; cocktails. **Parking:** street. **Cards:** AX, DS, MC, VI.

W G GRINDERS
American

Lunch: $4-$10   **Dinner:** $4-$10   **Phone:** 573/474-6337

Location: Jct 9th and Walnut sts. 33 N 9th St 65203. **Hours:** 10 am-9 pm, Sun from 11 am. **Reservations:** not accepted. **Features:** It takes longer for guests to decide what they want than it does to receive it. On the menu are grinder sandwiches, baked pasta dishes, salads, soups and desserts. The contemporary atmosphere reflects a nostalgic twist. Casual dress; beer only. **Parking:** street. **Cards:** AX, CB, DC, DS, MC, VI.

CONCORDIA pop. 2,360

——— **WHERE TO DINE** ———

BIFFLE'S SMOKE HOUSE BAR-B-Q
American

Lunch: $4-$20   **Dinner:** $4-$20   **Phone:** 660/463-7232

Location: I-70, exit 58, just se. 103 NE 2nd St 64020. **Hours:** 11 am-10 pm, Fri & Sat-11 pm. Closed: 4/8, 11/22, 12/25; also for dinner 12/24 & 12/31, 2 days 2nd weekend in Sept. **Reservations:** accepted. **Features:** Family-owned and operated for 25 years, the restaurant centers its menu on hickory-smoked meats. Casual dress; beer & wine only. **Parking:** on-site. **Cards:** AX, DS, MC, VI.

CREVE COEUR —See St. Louis p. 539.

CUBA pop. 3,230

——— **WHERE TO STAY** ———

SUPER 8 MOTEL
Motel

Book at AAA.com

All Year   1P: $55-$63   2P: $55-$63   XP: $5   F17

Phone: (573)885-2087

Location: I-44, exit 208 (SR 19), just nw. 28 Hwy P 65453. Fax: 573/885-2089. **Facility:** 58 units. 53 one-bedroom standard units. 5 one-bedroom suites ($108-$114), some with whirlpools. 3 stories, interior/exterior corridors. **Parking:** on-site. **Terms:** pets ($10 extra charge). **Amenities:** high-speed Internet, safes (fee), hair dryers. **Guest Services:** coin laundry. **Business Services:** PC. **Cards:** AX, DC, DS, MC, VI.

SOME UNITS

FEE

DES PERES —See St. Louis p. 540.

DEXTER pop. 7,356

——— WHERE TO STAY ———

——— *The following lodging was either not evaluated or did not* ———
meet AAA rating requirements but is listed for your information only.

AMERICAS BEST VALUE INN   Phone: 573/624-3566
[fyi]   Not evaluated. **Location:** I-60, exit One Mile Rd. 1802 N Outer Rd 63841. Facilities, services, and decor characterize
a basic property.

——— WHERE TO DINE ———

MARBLES RESTAURANT   **Lunch:** $5-$18   **Dinner:** $5-$18   Phone: 573/624-8662
   Location: US 60B; 0.7 mi w; in West Sixty Center. 1612 W Business 60 63841. **Hours:** 11 am-10 pm, Fri & Sat-
midnight. Closed: Sun & Mon. **Reservations:** accepted. **Features:** The restaurant features a unique decor
American   with displays of board games, marbles and current and nostalgic amusements. Casual dress; cocktails.
Parking: on-site. **Cards:** AX, CB, DC, DS, JC, MC, VI.

EDMUNDSON —See St. Louis p. 540.

EUREKA —See St. Louis p. 540.

FENTON —See St. Louis p. 541.

FESTUS pop. 9,660

——— WHERE TO STAY ———

BAYMONT INN & SUITES   *Book at AAA.com*   Phone: 636/937-2888
                        Property failed to provide current rates
   Location: I-55, exit 175, just w. 1303 Veterans Blvd 63028. Fax: 636/937-8877. **Facility:** 95 one-bedroom
Small-scale Hotel   standard units. 3 stories, interior corridors. **Parking:** on-site, winter plug-ins. **Terms:** pets ($50 deposit).
Amenities: voice mail, irons, hair dryers. **Guest Services:** valet and coin laundry, wireless Internet.
Business Services: PC.
SOME UNITS

DRURY INN-FESTUS   *Book great rates at AAA.com*   Phone: (636)933-2400
   All Year [BP]   1P: $65-$103   2P: $75-$113   XP: $10   F18
   Location: I-55, exit 175, just e. Located in a commercial area. 1001 Veterans Blvd 63028. Fax: 636/933-2400.
Small-scale Hotel   **Facility:** 58 one-bedroom standard units. 3 stories, interior corridors. **Parking:** on-site. **Amenities:** high-
speed Internet, voice mail, irons, hair dryers. **Pool(s):** outdoor. **Leisure Activities:** exercise room. **Guest
Services:** complimentary evening beverages, valet and coin laundry, wireless Internet. **Business Services:** PC. **Cards:** AX,
CB, DC, DS, MC, VI.
SOME UNITS

FLORISSANT —See St. Louis p. 542.

FORISTELL —See St. Louis p. 542.

FRONTENAC —See St. Louis p. 542.

FULTON pop. 12,128

——— WHERE TO STAY ———

LOGANBERRY INN BED & BREAKFAST   Phone: 573/642-9229
   All Year [BP]   1P: $89-$149   2P: $99-$189   XP: $15   F6
   Location: 1 mi e of jct US 54 and CR F, n on Westminster, then just e. 310 W 7th St 65251. **Facility:** A typical
Bed & Breakfast   Victorian painted lady, this charming B&B is just a short walk from the campus of Westminster College. 5
one-bedroom standard units, some with whirlpools. 2 stories (no elevator), interior corridors. *Bath:* combo or
shower only. **Parking:** on-site. **Terms:** check-in 4 pm, age restrictions may apply, 14 day cancellation notice-fee imposed,
package plans, pets ($10 extra charge, owner's dog on premises). **Amenities:** video library, DVD players, CD players, high-
speed Internet, hair dryers. *Some:* irons. **Leisure Activities:** whirlpool. **Guest Services:** complimentary evening beverages,
wireless Internet. **Business Services:** PC, fax. **Cards:** AX, DS, MC, VI.
SOME UNITS
FEE

——— WHERE TO DINE ———

SIR WINSTON'S RESTAURANT & PUB   **Lunch:** $6-$18   **Dinner:** $6-$18   Phone: 573/642-7733
   Location: On Business Rt 54, 1 mi s. 1205 S Business Rt 54 65251. **Hours:** 11 am-10 pm. Closed: 11/22, 12/25;
   also Sun. **Reservations:** accepted. **Features:** Among the good variety of appetizing menu selections are
American   barbecue chicken and beef dishes. Although the casual, contemporary atmosphere features many pictures
of Winston Churchill, diners shouldn't be confused by the name. The cuisine is not English, and the setting
is not that of a pub. Casual dress; cocktails. **Parking:** on-site. **Cards:** AX, DC, DS, MC, VI.

HANNIBAL pop. 17,757

—— WHERE TO STAY ——

QUALITY INN & SUITES *Book great rates at AAA.com*   Phone: (573)221-4001
(AAA) (SAVE)

| All Year | 1P: $69-$89 | 2P: $69-$89 | XP: $10 | F |

Small-scale Hotel

Location: 2 mi w on US 36, exit Shinn Ln to south service road. 120 Lindsey Dr 63401. Fax: 573/248-0395. **Facility:** 94 units. 77 one-bedroom standard units, some with whirlpools. 17 one-bedroom suites. 3 stories, interior corridors. *Bath:* combo or shower only. **Parking:** on-site. **Terms:** package plans, pets ($10 extra charge). **Amenities:** high-speed Internet, voice mail, irons, hair dryers. **Pool(s):** heated indoor. **Leisure Activities:** whirlpool, exercise room. *Fee:* game room. **Guest Services:** sundries, valet and coin laundry, wireless Internet. **Business Services:** meeting rooms, PC. **Cards:** AX, CB, DC, DS, JC, MC, VI. **Free Special Amenities:** full breakfast and high-speed Internet.

SOME UNITS

🅂🄳 🛏 🏊 ✖ 🎥 💻 / ✖ 📶 📺 /
FEE

SUPER 8 MOTEL *Book at AAA.com*   Phone: (573)221-5863

| All Year | 1P: $54-$90 | 2P: $56-$90 | XP: $5 | F18 |

Motel

Location: Jct US 36, 1.5 mi s on US 61. 120 Huckleberry Heights 63401. Fax: 573/221-5478. **Facility:** 59 one-bedroom standard units. 3 stories (no elevator), interior corridors. **Parking:** on-site. **Terms:** [CP] meal plan available, pets ($15 extra charge). **Amenities:** high-speed Internet. **Pool(s):** small heated outdoor. **Guest Services:** wireless Internet. **Cards:** AX, CB, DC, DS, MC, VI.

SOME UNITS

(ASK) 🅂🄳 🛏 🏊 🎥 / ✖ 📶 📺 /
FEE

—— WHERE TO DINE ——

FIDDLESTICKS FOOD & SPIRITS CO   Lunch: $6-$17   Dinner: $6-$17   Phone: 573/406-0493

American

Location: Jct W US 61, 2 mi w on US 36 to CR 412, then just sw. 8945 Hwy 36 63401. **Hours:** 10:45 am-10 pm. Closed: 11/22, 12/25. **Features:** On the west edge of the city along busy US 36, the restaurant presents a menu of steak, seafood, sandwiches, pasta and more in a crisp but casual setting. A lighter fare menu is offered after 9 pm. Casual dress; cocktails. **Parking:** on-site. **Cards:** AX, DC, DS, MC, VI.

🚫

LOGUE'S RESTAURANT   Lunch: $5-$10   Dinner: $5-$10   Phone: 573/248-1854

American

Location: On US 36, 1.5 mi s of jct US 36. 121 Huckleberry Dr 63401. **Hours:** 6 am-9 pm, Sun-8 pm. Closed: 1/1, 11/22, 12/25. **Features:** Logue's is a family restaurant with a good menu selection of daily specials: fried chicken, spaghetti, baked turkey and burgers. The server staff is friendly, the atmosphere is casual, and prices are quite reasonable. Casual dress. **Parking:** on-site. **Cards:** MC, VI.

🚫

LULA BELLE'S   Lunch: $6-$10   Dinner: $14-$22   Phone: 573/221-6662

American

Location: Adjacent to the river; in historic district. 111 Bird St 63401. **Hours:** 11 am-3 & 4-9 pm, Sun 11 am-2 pm. Closed major holidays. **Reservations:** accepted. **Features:** Near several attractions, the restaurant serves a limited number of menu selections at lunch but a much larger number at dinner. Attentive, friendly servers complement the casual atmosphere and comfortable setting. Guests can expect an all-you-can-eat family-style menu on Sundays. Casual dress; cocktails. **Parking:** on-site. **Cards:** AX, CB, DC, DS, MC, VI.

🍸 🚫

MARK TWAIN DINETTE & FAMILY RESTAURANT   Lunch: $5-$12   Dinner: $5-$12   Phone: 573/221-5511

American

Cards: MC, VI.

Location: Jct US 36 and SR 79. 400 N 3rd St 63401. **Hours:** 6 am-9 pm, Fri & Sat-10 pm. Closed: 11/22, 12/25. **Features:** There's a little something for everyone in the popular diner, established in 1942. Home-made meals are served in dining room booths or at the counter. Guests can get food to go at the old-time drive up. The eatery is in the historic area, adjacent to Mark Twain Home. Casual dress. **Parking:** on-site.

🚫

THE PIRATE'S COVE   Lunch: $5-$13   Dinner: $10-$30   Phone: 573/406-0505

American

Location: US 36, 1.5 m s on US 61 to Clinic Rd, then just w. 421 Clinic Rd 63401. **Hours:** 11 am-10 pm. Closed major holidays. **Reservations:** accepted. **Features:** This restaurant offers diners the casual comfort of a sports bar and the upscale dining of white linen in one location, just off of US 61 on the south side of town. Casual dress; cocktails. **Parking:** on-site. **Cards:** AX, CB, DC, DS, JC, MC, VI.

TJ'S SUPPER CLUB   Lunch: $3-$6   Dinner: $8-$21   Phone: 573/221-5551

American

Good wine selection.

Location: Jct US 36 and 61, 0.5 mi w on US 36. 211 Munger Ln 63401. **Hours:** 11 am-10 pm, Fri & Sat-11 pm; closing hours may vary. Closed: 7/4, 11/22, 12/25. **Reservations:** accepted. **Features:** Specializing in delicious prime rib, TJ's is also known for its extensive menu of steak, fresh seafood, chicken, pasta and salad. Its very comfortable atmosphere is friendly and relaxed, and Mark Twain historic sites are close by. Casual dress; cocktails. **Parking:** on-site. **Cards:** AX, DS, MC, VI.

🍸 🚫

YEN CHING   Lunch: $6   Dinner: $8   Phone: 573/221-5108

Chinese

Location: Just s of jct US 36 and 61; in Steamboat Bend Shopping Center. 108 McMasters Ave (US 61) 63401. **Hours:** 11 am-9:30 pm. Closed: 11/22. **Reservations:** accepted. **Features:** Diners won't find frills in the modest establishment. However, the generous buffet selections are a local favorite. Casual dress. **Parking:** on-site. **Cards:** AX, MC, VI.

🚫

HARRISONVILLE pop. 8,946

──── WHERE TO STAY ────

HARRISONVILLE INN & SUITES *Book great rates at AAA.com* Phone: (816)884-3200
(AAA) (SAVE) All Year 1P: $55-$98 2P: $59-$99 XP: $6 F12
Motel **Location:** Just n of jct US 71 and SR 291. 2201 Rockhaven Rd 64701. Fax: 816/884-3200. **Facility:** 45 one-bedroom standard units, some with whirlpools. 1-2 stories (no elevator), exterior corridors. **Parking:** on-site, winter plug-ins. **Terms:** 7 day cancellation notice-fee imposed, [CP] meal plan available, package plans, pets ($10 extra charge). **Amenities:** irons, hair dryers. *Some:* high-speed Internet. **Pool(s):** outdoor. **Leisure Activities:** playground. **Guest Services:** coin laundry, wireless Internet. **Cards:** AX, CB, DC, DS, JC, MC, VI. **Free Special Amenities:** continental breakfast and high-speed Internet.

SLUMBER INN MOTEL Phone: (816)884-3100
(AAA) (SAVE) All Year [CP] 1P: $38-$47 2P: $40-$60 XP: $5 F16
Motel **Location:** Jct US 71 and SR 7 S (Clinton exit), just w. Located in a rural area. 21400 E 275th St 64701. Fax: 816/884-3100. **Facility:** 28 one-bedroom standard units. 1 story, exterior corridors. **Parking:** on-site, winter plug-ins. **Terms:** 3 day cancellation notice, pets ($5 fee). **Amenities:** high-speed Internet. **Pool(s):** outdoor. **Leisure Activities:** picnic area. **Guest Services:** coin laundry, wireless Internet. **Cards:** AX, DS, MC, VI. **Free Special Amenities:** continental breakfast and high-speed Internet.

SUPER 8 MOTEL *Book at AAA.com* Phone: 816/887-2999
All Year 1P: $50-$70 2P: $59-$79 XP: $5 F12
Small-scale Hotel **Location:** Just n of jct US 71 and 291. 2400 Rockhaven Rd 64701. Fax: 816/887-5761. **Facility:** 56 one-bedroom standard units. 2 stories (no elevator), interior/exterior corridors. *Bath:* combo or shower only. **Parking:** on-site. **Terms:** cancellation fee imposed, [CP] meal plan available. **Amenities:** hair dryers. **Pool(s):** small heated indoor. **Leisure Activities:** whirlpool. **Guest Services:** coin laundry, wireless Internet. **Cards:** AX, DS, MC, VI.

HAYTI pop. 3,207

──── WHERE TO STAY ────

DRURY INN & SUITES-HAYTI CARUTHERSVILLE *Book at AAA.com* Phone: (573)359-2702
All Year [BP] 1P: $69-$136 2P: $79-$146 XP: $10 F18
Small-scale Hotel **Location:** I-55, exit 19 (US 412/SR 84), just w. 1317 Hwy 84 63851. Fax: 573/359-2702. **Facility:** 99 one-bedroom standard units, some with efficiencies and/or whirlpools. 2-3 stories, interior corridors. **Parking:** on-site, winter plug-ins. **Amenities:** high-speed Internet, dual phone lines, voice mail, irons, hair dryers. **Pool(s):** heated indoor. **Leisure Activities:** whirlpool, exercise room. **Guest Services:** complimentary evening beverages, coin laundry, wireless Internet. **Business Services:** PC. **Cards:** AX, CB, DC, DS, MC, VI.

HAZELWOOD —See St. Louis p. 543.

HERMANN pop. 2,674

──── WHERE TO STAY ────

HERMANN HILL VINEYARD & INN Phone: 573/486-4455
All Year [BP] 1P: $157-$331 2P: $157-$331
Bed & Breakfast **Location:** SR 19 (Market St), just w on W 6th St, just s on Washington St, then 0.3 mi w on W 10th St. 711 Wein St 65041 (PO Box 555). Fax: 573/486-5373. **Facility:** On a bluff surrounded by a vineyard, the inn features richly finished common areas, and spacious, elegant rooms with fireplaces and balconies. 12 units. 7 one-bedroom standard units with whirlpools. 5 cottages. 1-4 stories, interior corridors. **Parking:** on-site. **Terms:** check-in 4 pm, 2 night minimum stay - seasonal, age restrictions may apply, cancellation fee imposed. **Amenities:** video library, DVD players, CD players, irons, hair dryers. *Some:* high-speed Internet. **Leisure Activities:** hiking trails. **Guest Services:** area transportation, wireless Internet. **Cards:** DS, MC, VI.

HERMANN MOTEL Phone: 573/486-3131
(AAA) (SAVE) All Year [CP] 1P: $49-$98 2P: $54-$104 XP: $5 F12
Motel **Location:** S on SR 19 (Market St). 112 E 10th St 65041. Fax: 573/486-5244. **Facility:** 24 one-bedroom standard units. 1-2 stories (no elevator), exterior corridors. *Bath:* combo or shower only. **Parking:** on-site. **Terms:** office hours 8 am-11 pm, check-in 4 pm, 10 day cancellation notice. **Cards:** AX, DS, MC, VI. **Free Special Amenities:** continental breakfast and local telephone calls.

WINE VALLEY INN Phone: 573/486-0706
10/1-10/31 [BP] 2P: $135-$235 XP: $50
3/1-9/30 & 11/1-2/29 [BP] 2P: $107-$185 XP: $25
Historic Bed & Breakfast **Location:** I-70, At Market and 4th sts. 403 Market St 65041. Fax: 573/486-8812. **Facility:** The historic Begemann Building offers two- and three-room suites, all with a kitchenette and dining area, in a warm and relaxed atmosphere. 12 units. 4 one-bedroom standard units. 8 one-bedroom suites, some with whirlpools. 2 stories, interior corridors. *Bath:* combo or shower only. **Parking:** street. **Terms:** check-in 4 pm, age restrictions may apply, 14 day cancellation notice-fee imposed, package plans. **Amenities:** high-speed Internet, hair dryers. *Some:* DVD players, CD players. **Guest Services:** area transportation, wireless Internet. **Business Services:** meeting rooms. **Cards:** AX, DS, MC, VI.

——— WHERE TO DINE ———

SIMON'S ON THE WATERFRONT   **Lunch:** $5-$9   **Dinner:** $7-$15   **Phone:** 573/486-2030

American

Location: 1 blk w of Amtrack station. 4 Schiller St 65041. **Hours:** 11 am-8 pm, Fri & Sat-9 pm. Closed: 9/3, 12/25; also Mon & Tues. **Reservations:** accepted. **Features:** Come on in, there is something for everyone in this spacious and homey spot. Casual burgers to fine steaks and German selections. Try the strudel for dessert. Casual dress; cocktails. **Parking:** street. **Cards:** MC, VI.

VINTAGE RESTAURANT AT STONE HILL WINERY   **Lunch:** $6-$10   **Dinner:** $12-$26   **Phone:** 573/486-3479

Steak & Seafood

Location: SR 19 (Market St), just w on SR 100, follow signs; at Stone Hill Winery. 1110 Stone Hill Hwy 65041. **Hours:** Open 3/1-12/31 & 2/1-2/29; 11 am-4:30 & 5-8:30 pm, Fri-9 pm, Sat-10 pm; hours may vary in winter. Closed: 11/22, 12/24, 12/25; also Wed & Thurs 3/1-4/30 & 11/1-12/31. **Reservations:** suggested, for dinner Sat. **Features:** Casual and vintage charm highlight the cozy restaurant, which occupies a former horse barn. It's not unusual for diners to be seated in what was once a horse stall, next to the original feed trough and hay chute. Cordial, attentive servers explain preparations of traditional German cuisine. Since this place is adjacent to a winery, the wine list fittingly includes a number of local vintages. Casual dress; beer & wine only. **Parking:** on-site. **Cards:** AX, DS, MC, VI. **Historic**

HIGGINSVILLE pop. 4,682

——— WHERE TO STAY ———

SUPER 8 MOTEL-HIGGINSVILLE   *Book at AAA.com*   **Phone:** (660)584-7781

4/1-2/29	1P: $55-$71	2P: $61-$77	XP: $3 F17
3/1-3/31	1P: $55-$66	2P: $61-$72	XP: $3 F17

Small-scale Hotel

Location: I-70, exit 49 (SR 13), just se. 6471 Oakview Ln 64037 (PO Box 306). **Fax:** 660/584-2601. **Facility:** 44 one-bedroom standard units. 2 stories (no elevator), interior corridors. *Bath:* combo or shower only. **Parking:** on-site, winter plug-ins. **Terms:** [CP] meal plan available, pets ($10 deposit, $5 extra charge). **Amenities:** video library (fee). **Leisure Activities:** *Fee:* game room. **Guest Services:** coin laundry. **Cards:** AX, CB, DC, DS, JC, MC, VI.

SOME UNITS

(ASK) (S*D) (🐕) (📶) (📺) / (✕) (VCR)
FEE

HOLLISTER —*See Branson p. 419.*

HOLTS SUMMIT pop. 2,935

——— WHERE TO STAY ———

AMERICAS BEST VALUE INN-JEFFERSON CITY   *Book at AAA.com*   **Phone:** (573)896-8787

All Year [ECP]	1P: $60-$70	2P: $60-$70	XP: $5 F10

Small-scale Hotel

Location: Jct US 54 and CR 00, just w, then just s. 150 City Plaza 65043 (PO Box 549). **Fax:** 573/896-9040. **Facility:** 30 one-bedroom standard units, some with whirlpools. 2 stories (no elevator), interior corridors. **Parking:** on-site. **Terms:** cancellation fee imposed. **Amenities:** high-speed Internet, irons. **Guest Services:** coin laundry, wireless Internet. **Cards:** AX, DS, MC, VI.

SOME UNITS

(ASK) (S*D) (📠) (📶) / (✕) (🔌) (📺) /

INDEPENDENCE —See Kansas City p. 468.

JACKSON pop. 11,947

──────── **WHERE TO STAY** ────────

DRURY INN & SUITES-JACKSON,MO   *Book at AAA.com*   Phone: (573)243-9200
All Year [BP]   1P: $67-$112   2P: $77-$122   XP: $10   F18
Location: I-55, exit 105 (SR 61), 0.3 mi w. Located in a rural area. 225 Drury Ln 63755. Fax: 573/243-9200.
Small-scale Hotel   **Facility:** 80 units. 50 one-bedroom standard units. 30 one-bedroom suites ($107-$132). 4 stories, interior
corridors. *Bath:* combo or shower only. **Parking:** on-site. **Amenities:** high-speed Internet, voice mail, irons,
hair dryers. **Pool(s):** heated indoor. **Leisure Activities:** whirlpool, exercise room. **Guest Services:** sundries, complimentary
evening beverages: Mon-Sat, valet and coin laundry, wireless Internet. **Business Services:** PC. **Cards:** AX, CB, DC, DS,
MC, VI.
SOME UNITS

(ASK) 🛏️ 🍴 🔳 &ᴹ ♿ 🏊 📺 🛗 🖥️ 💳 /✕/

──────── **WHERE TO DINE** ────────

──────── *The following restaurant has not been evaluated by AAA* ────────
but is listed for your information only.

TRACTORS CLASSIC AMERICAN GRILL   Phone: 573/243-0340
[fyi]   Not evaluated. **Location:** 124 S High St 63755. **Features:** The eatery serves traditional American fare,
including some very large burgers.

JAMESPORT pop. 505

──────── **WHERE TO DINE** ────────

GINGERICH DUTCH PANTRY & BAKERY   **Lunch:** $4-$8   **Dinner:** $5-$15   Phone: 660/684-6212
Location: 1 mi s of jct SR 6 and 190. 120 S Broadway 64648. **Hours:** 10:30 am-5 pm, Thurs-3 pm, Sat 7 am-8
American   pm, Mon 10:30 am-8 pm; to 3 pm, Fri 10:30 am-8 pm, Sat 7 am-5 pm 12/1-3/31. Closed: 11/22, 12/25; also
Sun. **Reservations:** accepted. **Features:** There's no pretense here—just delicious, homemade offerings,
right down to the bread and jam. Casual dress. **Parking:** street. **Cards:** DC, MC, VI.
&ᴹ

JANE

──────── **WHERE TO STAY** ────────

BOONESLICK LODGE   Phone: (417)226-1888
All Year   1P: $64-$79   2P: $64-$79   XP: $5   F12
Location: just s on US 71. 21140 US Hwy 71 64856. Fax: 417/226-1895. **Facility:** 45 one-bedroom standard
Small-scale Hotel   units, some with whirlpools. 2 stories (no elevator), interior corridors. *Bath:* combo or shower only. **Parking:**
on-site. **Terms:** pets ($5 extra charge). **Amenities:** high-speed Internet, voice mail, hair dryers. **Pool(s):**
small heated outdoor. **Leisure Activities:** whirlpool. **Guest Services:** coin laundry, wireless Internet. **Cards:** AX, DS, MC, VI.
SOME UNITS

(ASK) 🛏️ 🏊 📺 🛗 🖥️ /✕/
FEE

JEFFERSON CITY pop. 39,636

──────── **WHERE TO STAY** ────────

BEST WESTERN CAPITAL INN   Phone: 573/635-4175
[fyi]   All Year   1P: $79-$82   2P: $79-$82
Too new to rate, opening scheduled for March 2007. **Location:** US 54, exit Ellis Blvd, just se. 1937 Christy Dr
Small-scale Hotel   65101. Fax: 573/635-6769. **Amenities:** 75 units, pets, coffeemakers, microwaves, refrigerators, pool.
Cards: AX, CB, DC, DS, MC, VI.

HOLIDAY INN EXPRESS   *Book great rates at AAA.com*   Phone: (573)634-4040
(AAA) [SAVE]   All Year   1P: $75   XP: $10   F19
Location: US 54, exit Ellis Blvd. 1716 Jefferson St 65109. Fax: 573/634-4200. **Facility:** 70 one-bedroom standard
units, some with whirlpools. 3-4 stories, interior corridors. *Bath:* combo or shower only. **Parking:** on-site.
Amenities: high-speed Internet, irons, hair dryers. **Pool(s):** small heated indoor. **Leisure Activities:** sauna,
Small-scale Hotel   whirlpool, exercise room. **Guest Services:** valet laundry, wireless Internet. **Business Services:** meeting
rooms. **Cards:** AX, CB, DC, DS, JC, MC, VI. **Free Special Amenities:** expanded continental breakfast
and high-speed Internet.
SOME UNITS

SⒹ &ᴹ 🔳 🏊 ✕ 📺 🛗 🖥️ 💳 /✕/

TRUMAN HOTEL & CONFERENCE CENTER   Phone: (573)635-7171
(AAA) [SAVE]   All Year   1P: $62-$80   2P: $62-$80   XP: $5   F
Location: US 54, exit Ellis Blvd, 0.5 mi nw. 1510 Jefferson St 65109 (PO Box 104386, 65110-4396).
Fax: 573/635-8006. **Facility:** 232 units. 228 one-bedroom standard units. 4 one-bedroom suites ($140),
some with whirlpools. 2-3 stories (no elevator), interior/exterior corridors. *Bath:* combo or shower only.
Small-scale Hotel   **Parking:** on-site. **Terms:** cancellation fee imposed, [AP] meal plan available, pets ($10 extra charge).
Amenities: high-speed Internet, voice mail, irons, hair dryers. **Dining:** 6:30 am-2 & 5-10 pm, Sat from 7 am,
Sun 7 am-2 pm, cocktails, entertainment. **Pool(s):** outdoor. **Leisure Activities:** movie theater, picnic area, exercise room.
Guest Services: valet laundry, area transportation-within 5 mi, wireless Internet. **Business Services:** conference facilities.
Cards: AX, CB, DC, DS, MC, VI. **Free Special Amenities:** local telephone calls and high-speed Internet.
SOME UNITS

SⒹ 🕒 🛏️ 🍴 🍸 &ᴹ 🏊 📺 🖥️ /✕ 🛗 🖨️ /
FEE

———— *The following lodgings were either not evaluated or did not* ————
meet AAA rating requirements but are listed for your information only.

COMFORT SUITES   Phone: 573/636-0300

[fyi]   Not evaluated. **Location:** US 50, exit Apache Flats westbound, 5 mi w; exit Truman Blvd eastbound, just n to Country Club Dr, then 1.5 mi w. 4804 Country Club Dr 65109. Facilities, services, and decor characterize a mid-range property.

HAMPTON INN-CAPITAL MALL   Phone: 573/634-7440

[fyi]   Not evaluated. **Location:** US 50, exit Apache Flats westbound, 5 mi w; exit Truman Blvd eastbound, just n to Country Club Dr, then 1.5 mi w. 4800 Country Club Dr 65109. Facilities, services, and decor characterize a mid-range property.

———— WHERE TO DINE ————

ALEXANDRO'S RESTAURANT   Dinner: $13-$35   Phone: 573/634-7740

◆◆◆   **Location:** From US 50, just s on Dixie Rd. 2125 Missouri Blvd 65109. **Hours:** 5 pm-10 pm. Closed major holidays; also Sun. **Reservations:** suggested. **Features:** Highly recommended by locals, the restaurant's atmosphere is suitable for both casual and special occasions. The menu offers a good number of specialty items such as seafood, steak, lamb, veal, some Greek selections and pastas. Casual dress; cocktails. **Parking:** on-site.

American

DAS STEIN HAUS   Lunch: $7-$10   Dinner: $14-$33   Phone: 573/634-3869

◆◆◆   **Location:** US 54, exit Stadium Dr, just sw on frontage road (Jefferson St); behind Ramada Inn. 1436 Southridge Dr 65109. **Hours:** 11 am-1 & 5-9:30 pm, Sat & Sun from 5 pm. Closed major holidays; also 12/24 & Mon. **Reservations:** suggested. **Features:** Das Stein Haus features hearty portions of German, Swiss, French and American dishes in its cuisine. Meals offered include beef rouladen, veal, lamb, chicken, duckling and frog legs. Its four dining rooms have a cozy atmosphere in a German decor. Casual dress; cocktails. **Parking:** on-site. **Cards:** AX, DC, DS, MC, VI.

German

DOMENICO'S   Dinner: $8-$23   Phone: 573/893-5454

◆◆◆   **Location:** 4 mi w on US 50, then 0.3 mi n; in Capitol Plaza West. 3702 W Truman Blvd 65109. **Hours:** 4 pm-10 pm. Closed major holidays; also Sun. **Reservations:** accepted. **Features:** Located in a shopping plaza, Domenico's serves up traditional Italian favorites such as veal parmigiano, chicken marsala and shrimp scampi. a house specialty is steak Arcobasso, named for the family which owns and operates this comfortably upscale restaurant. Casual dress; cocktails; entertainment. **Parking:** on-site. **Cards:** AX, DC, DS, MC, VI.

Italian

EL JIMADOR MEXICAN RESTAURANT   Lunch: $4-$6   Dinner: $6-$10   Phone: 573/636-6228

◆◆◆   **Location:** US 54, exit Ellis Blvd, 1.4 mi e. 512 Ellis Blvd 65101. **Hours:** 11 am-10 pm, Fri & Sat-10:30 pm, Sun-9 pm. Closed: 12/25. **Reservations:** accepted, Sun-Wed. **Features:** With a cheerful decor and atmosphere, this is a local recommendation offering good sized portions for a good value. Casual dress; cocktails. **Parking:** on-site. **Cards:** AX, CB, DC, DS, JC, MC, VI.

Mexican

GARFIELD'S RESTAURANT & PUB   Lunch: $4-$6   Dinner: $6-$14   Phone: 573/634-9099

◆◆◆   **Location:** US 50, 4 mi w; southeast side of Capital Mall. 3600 Country Club Dr 65109. **Hours:** 11 am-10 pm, Sun-8 pm. Closed: 4/8, 11/22, 12/25. **Reservations:** accepted, Mon-Thurs. **Features:** The atmosphere is comfortable and lively in the casual restaurant, where guests can choose from among burgers, Tex-Mex and Cajun dishes and grilled items. Casual dress; cocktails. **Parking:** on-site. **Cards:** AX, CB, DC, DS, JC, MC, VI.

American

MADISON'S CAFE   Lunch: $4-$12   Dinner: $5-$24   Phone: 573/634-2988

◆◆◆   **Location:** Between High St and E Capitol Ave; just e of capitol building. 216 Madison 65101. **Hours:** 11 am-10 pm, Fri-11 pm, Sat 4:30 pm-11 pm. Closed major holidays; also Sun. **Features:** This restaurant is popular with professional business people, who enjoy its large portions of good hot food. The restaurant features homemade pasta and other offerings served in a relaxed atmosphere. It's just down the street from the State Capitol. Casual dress; cocktails. **Parking:** street. **Cards:** AX, CB, DC, DS, MC, VI.

Italian

MEL'S COUNTRY CAFE   Lunch: $4-$10   Dinner: $4-$10   Phone: 573/893-9115

◆◆◆   **Location:** US 50 and SR 179, just e. 2121 Industrial Dr 65109. **Hours:** 6 am-8 pm, Sun-2 pm. Closed: Mon. **Features:** The cafe's name says it all. The house specialty is chicken-fried steak, but there are many other offerings, including all-day breakfast items. Homemade pie is a must for dessert. Casual dress. **Parking:** on-site.

American

JOPLIN pop. 45,504

———— WHERE TO STAY ————

BAYMONT INN & SUITES   *Book great rates at AAA.com*   Phone: (417)623-0000

◆◆◆ [SAVE]   All Year [ECP]   1P: $59-$89   2P: $66-$96   XP: $7   F18
◆◆◆   **Location:** I-44, exit 8B, just n. 3510 S Range Line Rd 64804. Fax: 417/781-1954. **Facility:** 104 one-bedroom standard units, some with whirlpools. 3 stories, interior/exterior corridors. *Bath:* combo or shower only. **Parking:** on-site. **Amenities:** high-speed Internet, voice mail, irons, hair dryers. **Pool(s):** outdoor, small heated indoor. **Leisure Activities:** whirlpool, exercise room. **Guest Services:** valet and coin laundry. **Business Services:** meeting rooms, PC. **Cards:** AX, DS, MC, VI. **Free Special Amenities:** expanded continental breakfast and high-speed Internet.

Small-scale Hotel

SOME UNITS

BEST WESTERN OASIS INN & SUITES   *Book great rates at AAA.com*   Phone: (417)781-6776

All Year [ECP]   1P: $59-$79   2P: $66-$86   XP: $7   F18
Location: I-44, exit 8B, just nw. 3508 S Range Line Rd 64804. Fax: 417/659-8362. Facility: 108 units. 96 one-bedroom standard units, some with whirlpools. 12 one-bedroom suites ($99-$149), some with kitchens and/or whirlpools. 2 stories (no elevator), exterior corridors. Parking: on-site. Terms: pets ($10 extra
Small-scale Hotel   charge). Amenities: irons, hair dryers. Some: high-speed Internet. Pool(s): outdoor. Leisure
Activities: limited exercise equipment. Guest Services: complimentary and valet laundry, wireless Internet.
Cards: AX, DS, MC, VI. Free Special Amenities: continental breakfast and high-speed Internet.

COMFORT INN & SUITES   *Book great rates at AAA.com*   Phone: 417/627-0400

All Year   1P: $68-$79   2P: $74-$99   XP: $10   F18
Location: I-44, exit 8B, just n. 3400 S Range Line Rd 64804. Fax: 417/627-0404. Facility: 82 one-bedroom
Small-scale Hotel   standard units, some with whirlpools. 3 stories, interior corridors. Bath: combo or shower only. Parking: on-site. Terms: 14 day cancellation notice. Amenities: high-speed Internet, irons, hair dryers. Pool(s): heated
indoor. Leisure Activities: whirlpool, exercise room. Guest Services: wireless Internet. Business Services: PC. Cards: AX,
DC, DS, MC, VI.

DRURY INN & SUITES-JOPLIN   *Book at AAA.com*   Phone: (417)781-8000

All Year [BP]   1P: $70-$110   2P: $80-$120   XP: $10   F18
Location: I-44, exit 8B, just ne. 3601 Range Line Rd 64804. Fax: 417/781-8000. Facility: 107 units. 101 one-bedroom standard units. 6 one-bedroom suites ($110-$145). 4 stories, interior corridors. Parking: on-site,
Small-scale Hotel   winter plug-ins. Amenities: high-speed Internet, voice mail, irons, hair dryers. Pool(s): heated indoor.
Leisure Activities: whirlpool, exercise room. Guest Services: complimentary evening beverages, valet and coin laundry.
Business Services: meeting rooms. Cards: AX, CB, DC, DS, MC, VI.

HAMPTON INN-JOPLIN   *Book great rates at AAA.com*   Phone: (417)659-9900

All Year   1P: $84-$99   2P: $89-$104
Location: I-44, exit 8B, just ne. 3107 E 36th St 64804. Fax: 417/659-9901. Facility: 89 units. 88 one-bedroom
standard units. 1 one-bedroom suite ($109-$129). 3 stories, interior corridors. Bath: combo or shower only.
Small-scale Hotel   Parking: on-site. Amenities: high-speed Internet, voice mail, irons, hair dryers. Pool(s): small heated
outdoor. Leisure Activities: exercise room. Guest Services: valet laundry, wireless Internet. Business Services: PC.
Cards: AX, CB, DC, DS, JC, MC, VI.

Travel Shopping Made Easy!

LUGGAGE • TRAVEL ACCESSORIES • BUSINESS CASES
DUFFELS & BACKPACKS

Before your next trip, check out eTravel Store at participating club websites on aaa.com.

eTravel Store offers everything needed to make travel better — quality luggage, handy accessories, business cases, duffels, backpacks and more. All delivered right to your door, quality guaranteed.

HILTON GARDEN INN
[fyi]
Small-scale Hotel
Phone: 417/206-6700
Too new to rate, opening scheduled for September 2006. **Location:** 2644 E 32nd St 64804. **Amenities:** 96 units.

HOLIDAY INN
Book great rates at AAA.com
[AAA] **[SAVE]**
Small-scale Hotel
Phone: (417)782-1000
All Year   1P: $89-$149   2P: $99-$159   XP: $10   F19
Location: I-44, exit 8B, just ne. Located adjacent to the Trade Center. 3615 Range Line Rd 64804. Fax: 417/623-4093. **Facility:** 262 units. 258 one-bedroom standard units. 4 one-bedroom suites ($119-$189). 5 stories, interior corridors. **Parking:** on-site. **Terms:** small pets only ($25 deposit). **Amenities:** high-speed Internet, voice mail, irons, hair dryers. **Dining:** 2 restaurants, 6 am-1 & 5-10 pm, cocktails, entertainment. **Pool(s):** heated outdoor, heated indoor. **Leisure Activities:** sauna, whirlpool, exercise room. **Guest Services:** valet and coin laundry, area transportation-within city limits. **Business Services:** conference facilities, business center. **Cards:** AX, CB, DC, DS, JC, MC, VI. **Free Special Amenities:** newspaper. *(See color ad p 437)*

SOME UNITS

MICROTEL INN & SUITES JOPLIN
Book at AAA.com
Small-scale Hotel
Phone: 417/626-8282
All Year   1P: $44-$49   2P: $47-$53   XP: $4   F16
Location: I-44, exit 8A, just s. 4101 Richard Joseph Blvd 64804. Fax: 417/627-9708. **Facility:** 59 one-bedroom standard units. 2 stories (no elevator), interior corridors. *Bath:* combo or shower only. **Parking:** on-site. **Terms:** cancellation fee imposed, [CP] meal plan available, small pets only. **Pool(s):** heated indoor. **Guest Services:** coin laundry, wireless Internet. **Cards:** AX, CB, DC, DS, JC, MC, VI.

SOME UNITS

RESIDENCE INN BY MARRIOTT-JOPLIN
Book great rates at AAA.com
Small-scale Hotel
Phone: (417)782-0908
All Year   1P: $119-$159   F
Location: I-44, exit 8B, just ne. 3128 E Hammons Blvd 64804. Fax: 417/782-0995. **Facility:** Smoke free premises. 114 units. 28 one-bedroom standard units with kitchens. 75 one- and 11 two-bedroom suites ($149-$169), some with efficiencies or kitchens. 4 stories, interior corridors. *Bath:* combo or shower only. **Parking:** on-site. **Terms:** pets ($75 fee). **Amenities:** video games (fee), high-speed Internet, dual phone lines, voice mail, irons, hair dryers. **Pool(s):** heated outdoor. **Leisure Activities:** whirlpools, exercise room, sports court. **Guest Services:** sundries, valet and coin laundry, wireless Internet. **Business Services:** meeting rooms, business center. **Cards:** AX, CB, DC, DS, JC, MC, VI. *(See color ad p 437)*

SLEEP INN
Book great rates at AAA.com
[AAA] **[SAVE]**
Small-scale Hotel
Phone: 417/782-1212
All Year   1P: $69   2P: $69   XP: $10   F16
Location: I-44, exit 4, just s. I-44 & State Hwy 43 S 64803 (PO Box 2748). Fax: 417/782-3366. **Facility:** 61 one-bedroom standard units. 2 stories (no elevator), interior corridors. *Bath:* combo or shower only. **Parking:** on-site. **Terms:** [CP] meal plan available, pets ($15 fee). **Amenities:** video library (fee), irons, hair dryers. **Guest Services:** coin laundry, wireless Internet. **Cards:** AX, CB, DC, DS, JC, MC, VI. **Free Special Amenities:** continental breakfast and high-speed Internet.

SOME UNITS

─── WHERE TO DINE ───

GREAT WALL RESTAURANT
Chinese
Lunch: $5-$6   **Dinner:** $8   **Phone:** 417/624-3889
Location: I-44, exit 8B, 1 mi n. 2705 Range Line Rd 64804. **Hours:** 11 am-9:30 pm, Fri & Sat-10:30 pm, Sun-9 pm. Closed: 11/22. **Reservations:** accepted. **Features:** A large buffet is set up for lunch and dinner. Mongolian barbecue is a favorite. Casual dress. **Parking:** on-site. **Cards:** DS, MC, VI.

JIM BOB'S STEAKS & RIBS
American
Lunch: $7-$20   **Dinner:** $7-$20   **Phone:** 417/781-3300
Location: I-44, exit 8B, 1.4 mi n on US 71. 2040 Range Line Rd 64804. **Hours:** 11 am-10 pm. Closed: 9/3, 11/22, 12/25; also Sun. **Features:** Peanut shells litter the floor of the popular Texas-style steak house. Its casual, country-themed decor includes some stuffed, mounted wildlife. Barbecue dishes are a favorite among townsfolk. Casual dress; cocktails. **Parking:** on-site. **Cards:** AX, DS, MC, VI.

RED HOT & BLUE
Barbecue
Lunch: $6-$11   **Dinner:** $9-$16   **Phone:** 417/782-7427
Location: I-44, exit 8B, 1.5 mi n. 2601 S Range Line Rd 64804. **Hours:** 11 am-10 pm, Fri & Sat-11 pm, Sun-9 pm. Closed: 4/8, 11/22, 12/25. **Features:** Guests can savor succulent Memphis-style barbecue while listening to the blues. Come hungry because the portions are more than ample. Among choices are preparations of pork, beef, turkey, chicken and even catfish. Casual dress; beer only. **Parking:** on-site. **Cards:** AX, MC, VI.

RIB CRIB BARBECUE
Barbecue
Lunch: $6-$14   **Dinner:** $6-$14   **Phone:** 417/206-7427
Location: I-44, exit 8B, 1.4 mi n. 3015 E 24th St 64804. **Hours:** 11 am-10 pm. Closed: 11/22, 12/25. **Features:** Most guests need extra napkins to tackle the ribs, brisket, ham, pork and chicken selections. The menu also lists sandwiches and wraps, along with tempting sides and large desserts. The decor is decidedly Western. Casual dress; beer only. **Parking:** on-site. **Cards:** AX, DC, DS, MC, VI.

WILDER'S STEAKHOUSE
Steak & Seafood
Dinner: $9-$29   **Phone:** 417/623-7230
Location: Center. 1216 Main St 64801. **Hours:** 5 pm-9:30 pm, Fri & Sat-10 pm. Closed major holidays; also Sun. **Features:** A distinctive 1920s setting—with a large bar, towering ceilings and high-backed privacy booths—characterizes the main dining area. Steak and seafood dishes are well-prepared. Served only on Saturday, prime rib is the house favorite. Casual dress; cocktails. **Parking:** on-site. **Cards:** AX, MC, VI.

Destination Kansas City
pop. 441,545

*far cry from its trading post roots, Kansas City today is laced with skyscrapers but still long on charm.

Penn Valley Park, Kansas City.
Scenic drives wind through pretty Penn Valley Park in downtown Kansas City. "Pioneer Mother" is one of several statues that can be seen in the park. (See listing page 172)

*ead outside to enjoy ice skating, cool jazz and lip-smacking barbecue. Then come back in and wander the 85-acre corporate headquarters, retail complex and visitor center operated by greeting-card giant Hallmark.

Country Club Plaza, Kansas City.
Penguins march down an outdoor concourse at Country Club Plaza in downtown Kansas City, a breezy Spanish-style complex of specialty shops, restaurants and nightlife venues.

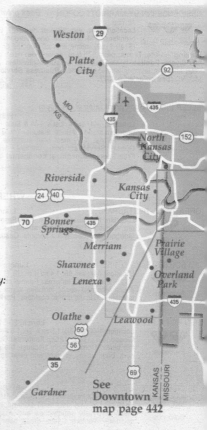

Places included in this AAA Destination City:

See Downtown map page 442

Auto racing.
NASCAR events draw huge crowds to Lakeside Speedway and Kansas Speedway, both in Kansas City, Kans.

© Transtock Inc. / Alamy

Missouri Division of Tourism

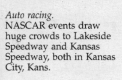

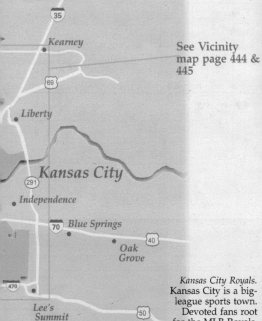

See Vicinity map page 444 & 445

Cinco de Mayo Festival, Kansas City.
Like many other cities across the United States, Kansas City celebrates Cinco de Mayo—or May 5—the anniversary of Mexico's Battle of Puebla. (See mention page 177)

Kansas City Royals.
Kansas City is a big-league sports town. Devoted fans root for the MLB Royals, who play home games in Kauffman Stadium, part of the Harry S. Truman Sports Complex. (See mention page 175)

Missouri Division of Tourism

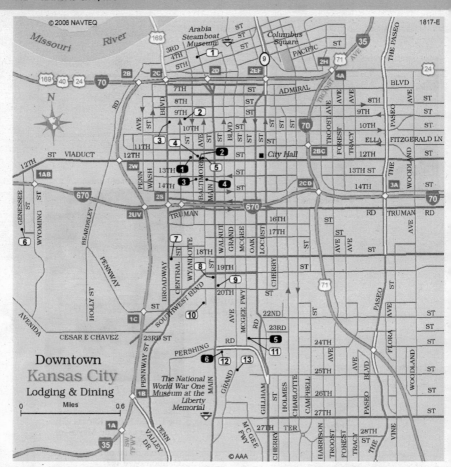

Downtown
Kansas City
Lodging & Dining

Downtown Kansas City

This index helps you "spot" where approved accommodations and restaurants are located on the corresponding detailed maps. Lodging rate ranges are for comparison only and show the property's high season; rates are per night, unless only weekly (W) rates are available. Restaurant rate range is for dinner, unless only lunch (L) is served. Turn to the listing page for more detailed rate information and consult display ads for special promotions.

Spotter/Map Page Number	OA	DOWNTOWN KANSAS CITY - Lodgings	Diamond Rating	Rate Range High Season	Listing Page
❶ / p. 442		Kansas City Marriott Downtown	◈◈◈	$154-$220	453
❷ / p. 442		Hotel Phillips	◈◈◈◈	$99-$264	452
❸ / p. 442	AAA	**Radisson Hotel & Suites Kansas City, City Center**	◈◈◈	$89-$269 SAVE	453
❹ / p. 442		Hilton President Kansas City	◈◈◈	Failed to provide	452
❺ / p. 442	AAA	**Hyatt Regency Crown Center** - see color ad p 452	◈◈◈	$105-$279 SAVE	453
❻ / p. 442	AAA	**The Westin Crown Center** - see color ad p 453	◈◈◈◈	$129-$309 SAVE	454
		DOWNTOWN KANSAS CITY - Restaurants			
① / p. 442		Cafe Al Dente	◈◈	$6-$16	454
② / p. 442	AAA	**Savoy Grill**	◈◈◈	$14-$32	455
③ / p. 442	AAA	**Majestic Steakhouse**	◈◈	$15-$40	455
④ / p. 442		Phillips Chophouse	◈◈◈	$27-$40	455
⑤ / p. 442		12 Baltimore	◈◈◈	$9-$20	454
⑥ / p. 442		The Golden Ox Restaurant	◈◈◈	$9-$39	454
⑦ / p. 442		Jilly's on Broadway	◈	$6-$7	454
⑧ / p. 442		1924 Main	◈◈◈	$20-$38	454
⑨ / p. 442		Hereford House Restaurant	◈◈	$18-$39	454
⑩ / p. 442		Lidia's Kansas City	◈◈◈	$12-$24	454
⑪ / p. 442		Peppercorn Duck Club	◈◈◈	$25-$38	455
⑫ / p. 442		Benton's Steak & Chop House	◈◈◈	$25-$38	454
⑬ / p. 442	AAA	**The American Restaurant at Crown Center**	◈◈◈◈	$36-$80	454

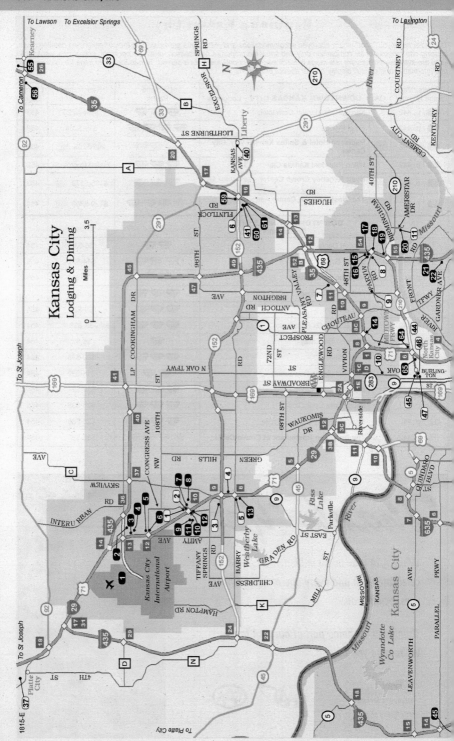

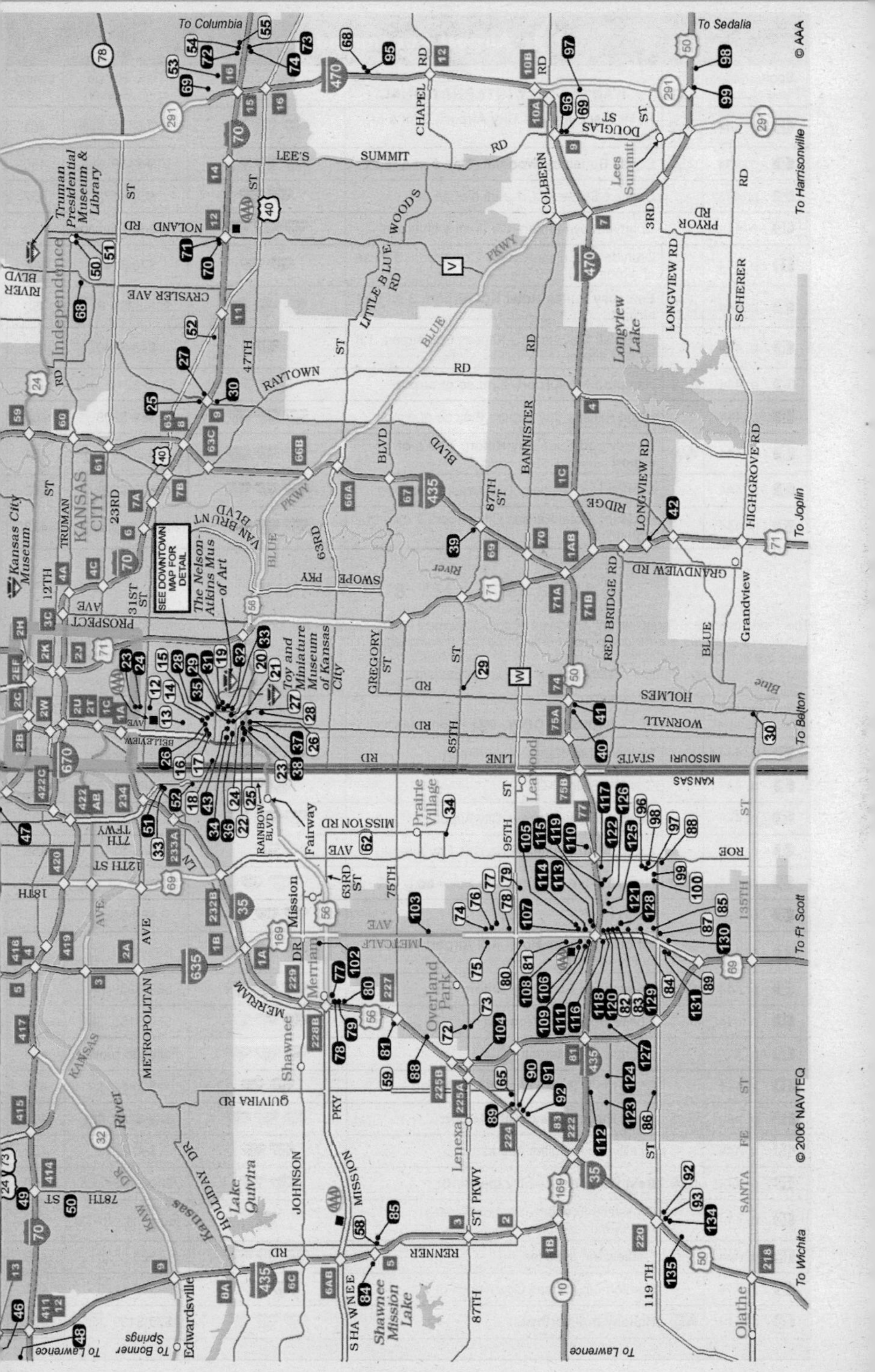

To Columbia
To Sedalia
To Harrisonville
To Joplin
To Belton
To Ft Scott
To Wichita
To Lawrence
To Bonner Springs
Truman Presidential Museum & Library
Independence
Kansas City Museum
KANSAS CITY
The Nelson-Atkins Mus of Art
SEE DOWNTOWN MAP FOR DETAIL
Toy and Miniature Museum of Kansas City
Fairway
Mission
Merriam
Prairie Village
Overland Park
Leawood
Lenexa
Shawnee
Shawnee Mission Lake
Lake Quivira
Edwardsville
Olathe
Grandview
Lees Summit
Longview Lake
Kansas River
Blue River
LEE'S SUMMIT RD
NOLAND RD
RAYTOWN RD
BLUE PKWY
BANNISTER RD
COLBERN RD
LONGVIEW RD
HIGHGROVE RD
RED BRIDGE RD
HOLMES
WORNALL
STATE LINE
MISSOURI
KANSAS
METCALF AVE
MERRIAM DR
METROPOLITAN AVE
QUIVIRA RD
RENNER RD
SANTA FE ST
SHAWNEE MISSION PKY
© AAA
© 2006 NAVTEQ

✈ Airport Accommodations

Spotter/Map Page Number	OA	KANSAS CITY INTERNATIONAL	Diamond Rating	Rate Range High Season	Listing Page
12 / p. 444	AAA	**Hyatt Place Kansas City Airport, 3 mi s of airport**	◇◇◇	$79-$169 SAVE	461
9 / p. 444	AAA	**Chase Suites by Woodfin, 3 mi s of airport**	◇◇◇	$79-$159 SAVE	456
2 / p. 444		Comfort Suites KCI, 1.9 mi e of airport	◇◇	$69-$179	457
10 / p. 444		Courtyard by Marriott-KCI, 4 mi s of airport	◇◇◇	Failed to provide	458
11 / p. 444		Drury Inn & Suites-Kansas City Airport, 3 mi se of airport	◇◇	$70-$140	458
7 / p. 444	AAA	**Embassy Suites Hotel KCI Airport, 3 mi s of airport**	◇◇◇	$99-$239 SAVE	459
4 / p. 444		Extended StayAmerica-Kansas City Airport, 1.8 mi e of airport	◇	$45-$140	459
5 / p. 444	AAA	**Hampton Inn Airport, 2 mi se of airport**	◇◇	$116-$210 SAVE	460
6 / p. 444		Hilton Kansas City Airport, 2 mi se of airport	◇◇◇	$89-$209	460
8 / p. 444	AAA	**Homewood Suites by Hilton, 3 mi s of airport**	◇◇◇	$89-$239 SAVE	461
1 / p. 444		Marriott Hotel-Kansas City Airport, at airport	◇◇◇	$99-$209	462
3 / p. 444		Radisson Hotel Kansas City Airport, 3 mi e of airport	◇◇◇	Failed to provide	463

Kansas City and Vicinity

This index helps you "spot" where approved accommodations and restaurants are located on the corresponding detailed maps. Lodging rate ranges are for comparison only and show the property's high season; rates are per night, unless only weekly (W) rates are available. Restaurant rate range is for dinner, unless only lunch (L) is served. Turn to the listing page for more detailed rate information and consult display ads for special promotions.

Spotter/Map Page Number	OA	KANSAS CITY, MO - Lodgings	Diamond Rating	Rate Range High Season	Listing Page
1 / p. 444		Marriott Hotel-Kansas City Airport	◇◇◇	$99-$209	462
2 / p. 444		Comfort Suites KCI	◇◇	$69-$179	457
3 / p. 444		Radisson Hotel Kansas City Airport	◇◇◇	Failed to provide	463
4 / p. 444		Extended StayAmerica-Kansas City Airport	◇	$45-$140	459
5 / p. 444	AAA	**Hampton Inn Airport - see color ad p 459**	◇◇	$116-$210 SAVE	460
6 / p. 444		Hilton Kansas City Airport	◇◇◇	$89-$209	460
7 / p. 444	AAA	**Embassy Suites Hotel KCI Airport - see color ad p 458**	◇◇◇	$99-$239 SAVE	459
8 / p. 444	AAA	**Homewood Suites by Hilton**	◇◇◇	$89-$239 SAVE	461
9 / p. 444	AAA	**Chase Suites by Woodfin**	◇◇◇	$79-$159 SAVE	456
10 / p. 444		Courtyard by Marriott-KCI	◇◇◇	Failed to provide	458
11 / p. 444		Drury Inn & Suites-Kansas City Airport	◇◇	$70-$140	458
12 / p. 444	AAA	**Hyatt Place Kansas City Airport**	◇◇◇	$79-$169 SAVE	461
13 / p. 444		Quality Inn & Suites Airport	◇◇	$90-$149	462
14 / p. 444	AAA	**Best Western Country Inn-North**	◇◇	$49-$139 SAVE	456
15 / p. 444		Crossland Economy Studios Kansas City-Worlds of Fun	◇	Failed to provide	458
16 / p. 444		Fairfield Inn & Suites	◇◇◇	$95-$120	459
17 / p. 444		Comfort Inn Kansas City/Worlds of Fun	◇◇	$85-$125	457
18 / p. 444	AAA	**Holiday Inn-Northeast**	◇◇◇	$79-$139 SAVE	460

Spotter/Map Page Number	OA	KANSAS CITY, MO - Lodgings (continued)	Diamond Rating	Rate Range High Season	Listing Page
19 / p. 444		Red Roof Inn-North	◆◆	$54-$73	463
20 / p. 444	AAA	**Ameristar Hotel & Casino Kansas City**	◆◆◆	$109-$249 [SAVE]	456
21 / p. 444	AAA	**Intrigue Park Place Hotel** - see color ad p 462	◆◆◆	$209-$229 [SAVE]	461
22 / p. 444	AAA	**La Quinta Inn** - see color ad p 463	◆◆◆	$82-$104 [SAVE]	462
23 / p. 444		Residence Inn by Marriott Downtown/Union Hill	◆◆◆	$123-$209	463
24 / p. 444		Fairfield Inn Kansas City/Union Hill	◆◆◆	Failed to provide	459
25 / p. 444		Drury Inn & Suites-Kansas City Stadium	◆◆◆	$70-$130	458
26 / p. 444	AAA	**Quarterage Hotel**	◆◆	$99-$139 [SAVE]	462
27 / p. 444	AAA	**Clarion Hotel Sports Complex-Kansas City**	◆◆	$69-$169 [SAVE]	457
28 / p. 444		Embassy Suites Hotel Kansas City-Plaza	◆◆◆	Failed to provide	459
29 / p. 444	AAA	**Best Western Seville Plaza Hotel**	◆◆◆	$95-$189 [SAVE]	456
30 / p. 444		Holiday Inn-Sports Complex	◆◆◆	$59-$199	460
31 / p. 444		Kansas City Marriott Country Club Plaza	◆◆◆	$99-$259	462
32 / p. 444		Holiday Inn At The Plaza, Kansas City	◆◆◆	Failed to provide	460
33 / p. 444		Homestead Studio Suites Hotel-Kansas City/Country Club Plaza	◆◆	$80-$150	460
34 / p. 444		Hampton Inn & Suites	◆◆◆	$99-$359	460
35 / p. 444		Courtyard by Marriott-Country Club Plaza - see color ad p 457	◆◆◆	Failed to provide	458
36 / p. 444	AAA	**Sheraton Suites Country Club Plaza**	◆◆◆	$299-$309 [SAVE]	464
37 / p. 444		The Raphael	◆◆◆	$199-$249	463
38 / p. 444	AAA	**The InterContinental Kansas City at the Plaza** - see color ad p 461	◆◆◆◆	$119-$359 [SAVE]	461
39 / p. 444	AAA	**Baymont Inn & Suites Kansas City South**	◆◆	$72-$105 [SAVE]	456
40 / p. 444		Courtyard by Marriott	◆◆◆	$129	457
41 / p. 444		Extended StayAmerica-Kansas City South	◆	$50-$145	459
42 / p. 444		Crescent Hotel KC South	◆◆◆	$60-$70	458
43 / p. 444		Residence Inn Kansas City Country Club Plaza	◆◆◆	$139-$259	463
		KANSAS CITY, MO - Restaurants			
1 / p. 444		Smoke Box Bar-B-Que	◆	$6-$15	466
2 / p. 444		Hong Kong Jade Garden	◆◆	$6-$16	465
3 / p. 444		Tomfooleries	◆◆	$8-$15	467
4 / p. 444		Chipotle	◆	$5-$8	464
5 / p. 444		Minsky's Pizza Cafe & Sports Bar	◆◆	$6-$12	466
6 / p. 444		Corner Cafe	◆◆	$5-$15	465
7 / p. 444		Stroud's North	◆◆	$8-$22	466
8 / p. 444		Mama Jo's BBQ	◆	$5-$8	466
9 / p. 444		The Alamo	◆◆	$6-$14	464
10 / p. 444		Cascone's Italian Restaurant	◆◆	$13-$23	464
11 / p. 444		Horizon's Buffet	◆◆	$13-$20	465
12 / p. 444		Gates Bar-B-Q	◆◆	$10-$20	465
13 / p. 444		Chubby's	◆	$6-$7	465

Spotter/Map Page Number	OA	KANSAS CITY, MO - Restaurants (continued)	Diamond Rating	Rate Range High Season	Listing Page
⑭ / p. 444		Harry's Bar & Tables	◆◆	$7-$17	465
⑮ / p. 444		Californos	◆◆◆	$10-$24	464
⑯ / p. 444		Napoleon Bakery	◆◆	$6-$10(L)	466
⑰ / p. 444		PotPie	◆◆	$12-$23	466
⑱ / p. 444		Booze Fish Wine Bar	◆◆	$8-$16	464
⑲ / p. 444		Cafe Sebastienne	◆◆◆	$15-$27	464
⑳ / p. 444		Jardine's Restaurant & Jazz Club	◆◆	$16-$30	465
㉑ / p. 444		Figlio	◆◆	$8-$21	465
㉒ / p. 444		JJ's Restaurant	◆◆◆	$17-$37	465
㉓ / p. 444		Plaza III, The Steakhouse	◆◆◆	$22-$41	466
㉔ / p. 444		Kona Grill	◆◆◆	$9-$24	465
㉕ / p. 444		re:Verse	◆◆◆	$12-$26	466
㉖ / p. 444		The Raphael Restaurant	◆◆◆	$18-$32	466
㉗ / p. 444	AAA	**Bo Lings**	◆◆	$10-$20	464
㉘ / p. 444	AAA	**Osteria Il Centro**	◆◆◆	$9-$16	466
㉙ / p. 444		Stroud's South Restaurant	◆◆	$10-$22	467
㉚ / p. 444	AAA	**Fiorella's Jack Stack Barbecue of Martin City**	◆◆	$9-$26	465
		KANSAS CITY, KS - Lodgings			
㊺ / p. 444		Hampton Inn Village West	◆◆◆	Failed to provide	476
㊻ / p. 444	AAA	**Great Wolf Lodge-Kansas City** - see color ad p 475	◆◆◆	$279-$399 SAVE	474
㊼ / p. 444		Hilton Garden Inn Kansas City Kansas	◆◆◆	$79-$139	476
㊽ / p. 444	AAA	**Chateau Avalon** - see color ad p 475	◆◆◆	$129-$549 SAVE	474
㊾ / p. 444		Microtel Inn & Suites at the Speedway	◆◆	Failed to provide	476
㊿ / p. 444	AAA	**Comfort Inn** - see color ad p 475	◆◆	$71-$250 SAVE	474
(51) / p. 444	AAA	**Best Western Inn and Conference Center**	◆◆	$69-$89 SAVE	474
(52) / p. 444		Sun Inn	◆◆	$66-$70	476
		KANSAS CITY, KS - Restaurants			
㉝ / p. 444		Taqueria Mexico	◆◆	$5-$18	476
㉞ / p. 444		Dragon Inn	◆◆	$8-$11	476
		KEARNEY - Lodgings			
(55) / p. 444		Kearney Super 8 Motel	◆	$60-$110	470
(56) / p. 444		Best Western Kearney Inn	◆◆	$70-$75	470
		LIBERTY - Lodgings			
(59) / p. 444		Hampton Inn-Kansas City/Liberty - see color ad p 456	◆◆◆	$99-$129	471
(60) / p. 444		Holiday Inn Express	◆◆	$105	472
(61) / p. 444	AAA	**Fairfield Inn Kansas City-Liberty**	◆◆	$94-$160 SAVE	471
		LIBERTY - Restaurants			
㊵ / p. 444		Hardware Cafe	◆◆	$7-$15	472
㊶ / p. 444		The Stack	◆◆	$7-$46	472

Spotter/Map Page Number	OA	NORTH KANSAS CITY - Lodgings	Diamond Rating	Rate Range High Season	Listing Page
64 / p. 444		La Quinta Inn & Suites Kansas City North	◈◈	$84-$120	472
65 / p. 444		Quality Inn & Suites	◈◈	$70-$109	472
		NORTH KANSAS CITY - Restaurants			
44 / p. 444		The Buffet	◈◈	$13-$18	472
45 / p. 444		Kelso's	◈◈	$8-$17	473
46 / p. 444		Chappell's Restaurant & Sports Museum	◈◈	$9-$21	472
47 / p. 444		Paul & Jack's Tavern	◈	$8-$20	473
		INDEPENDENCE - Lodgings			
68 / p. 444		Woodstock Inn Bed & Breakfast	◈◈◈	$98-$219	469
69 / p. 444		Fairfield Inn by Marriott	◈◈	$85-$110	468
70 / p. 444	AAA	**Super 8 Motel**	◈◈	$49-$59 SAVE	469
71 / p. 444	AAA	**Best Western Truman Inn** - see color ad p 468	◈◈	$59-$69 SAVE	468
72 / p. 444	AAA	**Hilton Garden Inn Independence**	◈◈◈	$99-$149 SAVE	469
73 / p. 444	AAA	**Holiday Inn Express Hotel & Suites**	◈◈	$79-$169 SAVE	469
74 / p. 444	AAA	**Comfort Suites**	◈◈◈	$64-$129 SAVE	468
		INDEPENDENCE - Restaurants			
50 / p. 444		The Rheinland Restaurant	◈◈	$13-$16	469
51 / p. 444		Ophelia's Restaurant & Inn	◈◈◈	$13-$30	469
52 / p. 444		V's Italiano Ristorante	◈◈	$9-$26	470
53 / p. 444		Smokehouse Bar-B-Que	◈◈	$8-$22	470
54 / p. 444		Hereford House	◈◈◈	$12-$38	469
55 / p. 444		On the Border Mexican Grill & Cantina	◈◈	$8-$14	469
		MERRIAM - Lodgings			
77 / p. 444		Drury Inn-Merriam/Shawnee Mission Parkway	◈◈◈	$70-$120	478
78 / p. 444		Comfort Inn-Merriam	◈◈	$56-$190	478
79 / p. 444		Homestead Studio Suites Hotel-Kansas City-Shawnee Mission	◈◈	$55-$120	478
80 / p. 444	AAA	**Quality Inn**	◈◈	$49-$199 SAVE	478
81 / p. 444		Hampton Inn & Suites	◈◈◈	$103-$114	478
		SHAWNEE - Lodgings			
84 / p. 444		Courtyard by Marriott	◈◈◈	$169-$189	487
85 / p. 444		Hampton Inn-Shawnee	◈◈◈	Failed to provide	488
		SHAWNEE - Restaurants			
58 / p. 444		Barley's Brewhaus	◈◈◈	$11-$20	488
59 / p. 444		El Toro Bar & Grill Mexican Restaurant	◈◈	$6-$15	488
		LENEXA - Lodgings			
88 / p. 444		Extended StayAmerica -Kansas City-Lenexa-87th St	◈◈◈	$65-$130	477
89 / p. 444		La Quinta Inn Kansas City (Lenexa)	◈◈◈	$72-$108	477
90 / p. 444		Radisson Hotel Lenexa-Overland Park	◈◈◈	$89-$209	477
91 / p. 444		Super 8 Motel-Lenexa	◈◈	$60-$70	477
92 / p. 444	AAA	**Comfort Inn**	◈◈	$65-$95 SAVE	477

Spotter/Map Page Number	OA	**LENEXA - Restaurant**	Diamond Rating	Rate Range High Season	Listing Page
⑥⑤ / p. 444		Shogun Sushi & Steak Restaurant	◆◆◆	$9-$23	478
		LEE'S SUMMIT - Lodgings			
⑨⑤ / p. 444	AAA	**Lee's Summit Holiday Inn Express**	◆◆	$90 SAVE	471
⑨⑥ / p. 444		Hampton Inn - see color ad p 456	◆◆◆	Failed to provide	471
⑨⑦ / p. 444		Fairfield Inn by Marriott	◆◆	$80-$105	470
⑨⑧ / p. 444		Super 8 Motel	◆◆	$59-$90	471
⑨⑨ / p. 444		Comfort Inn by Choice Hotels	◆◆	$80-$105	470
		LEE'S SUMMIT - Restaurants			
⑥⑧ / p. 444		Everett's Restaurant	◆◆	$13-$29	471
⑥⑨ / p. 444		Cactus Grill	◆◆	$8-$12	471
		OVERLAND PARK - Lodgings			
⑩② / p. 444		Holiday Inn of Mission-Overland Park	◆◆◆	$99-$139	482
⑩③ / p. 444		White Haven Motor Lodge	◆◆	$50-$60	485
⑩④ / p. 444	AAA	**Holiday Inn Hotel and Suites**	◆◆◆	$79-$119 SAVE	482
⑩⑤ / p. 444	AAA	**Hampton Inn-Kansas City/Overland Park -** see color ad p 481	◆◆◆	$75-$150 SAVE	481
⑩⑥ / p. 444		Homewood Suites	◆◆◆	$149-$169	483
⑩⑦ / p. 444		Embassy Suites Hotel-Overland Park	◆◆◆	Failed to provide	481
⑩⑧ / p. 444		Extended Stay Deluxe Kansas City-Overland Park-Metcalf	◆◆◆	$70-$165	481
⑩⑨ / p. 444		La Quinta Inn & Suites	◆◆◆	$89-$139	484
①①⓪ / p. 444	AAA	**Settle Inn**	◆◆	$54-$129 SAVE	484
①①① / p. 444		Comfort Inn & Suites	◆◆◆	$79-$110	480
①①② / p. 444		Extended StayAmerica-Kansas City-Overland Park	◆◆	$70-$155	481
①①③ / p. 444		Super 8 Motel	◆◆	$45-$109	485
①①④ / p. 444		Wyndham Garden Hotel-Overland Park	◆◆◆	Failed to provide	485
①①⑤ / p. 444		Red Roof Inn-Overland Park	◆◆	$52-$73	484
①①⑥ / p. 444		Overland Park Marriott Hotel	◆◆◆	$89-$229	484
①①⑦ / p. 444	AAA	**Hyatt Place Overland Park Convention Center**	◆◆◆	$89-$169 SAVE	483
①①⑧ / p. 444		Drury Inn & Suites-Overland Park	◆◆◆	$75-$140	481
①①⑨ / p. 444		Holiday Inn Hotel & Suites Convention Center Overland Park	◆◆◆	$145-$165	482
①②⓪ / p. 444		Pear Tree Inn by Drury-Overland Park	◆◆◆	$50-$115	484
①②① / p. 444	AAA	**Chase Suites by Woodfin**	◆◆◆	$89-$152 SAVE	480
①②② / p. 444		Homestead Studio Suites Hotel-Kansas City-Overland Park	◆◆◆	$70-$155	483
①②③ / p. 444		Candlewood Suites	◆◆◆	Failed to provide	480
①②④ / p. 444	AAA	**Holtze Executive Village**	◆◆◆	$62-$269 SAVE	482
①②⑤ / p. 444		Sheraton Overland Park Hotel at the Convention Center	◆◆◆	$99-$299	484
①②⑥ / p. 444		Hilton Garden Inn	◆◆◆	$79-$229	481

Spotter/Map Page Number	OA	**OVERLAND PARK - Lodgings (continued)**	Diamond Rating	Rate Range High Season	Listing Page
127 / p. 444		DoubleTree Hotel	▼▼▼	$89-$279	480
128 / p. 444	◆◆◆	**Hyatt Place Overland Park Metcalf**	▼▼▼	$89-$169 SAVE	483
129 / p. 444		Courtyard by Marriott	▼▼▼	$169	480
130 / p. 444		Residence Inn by Marriott	▼▼▼	$99-$299	484
131 / p. 444		SpringHill Suites By Marriott	▼▼▼	$69-$159	484
		OVERLAND PARK - Restaurants			
72 / p. 444		India Palace	▼▼	$7-$12	486
73 / p. 444		Chien Dynasty	▼▼	$7-$13	485
74 / p. 444	◆◆◆	**Bo Ling's**	▼▼	$8-$15	485
75 / p. 444		Il Trullo	▼▼▼	$9-$25	486
76 / p. 444		The Longbranch Steakhouse	▼▼	$5-$20	487
77 / p. 444		Johnny Cascone's Italian Restaurant	▼▼▼	$8-$24	486
78 / p. 444		China Star Buffet	▼▼	$8	485
79 / p. 444		Sushi Gin	▼▼	$10-$20	487
80 / p. 444	◆◆◆	**Fiorella's Jack Stack Barbecue of Overland Park, Inc**	▼▼	$7-$26	486
81 / p. 444		Jose Peppers Border Grill & Cantina	▼▼	$7-$10	487
82 / p. 444		Dick Clark's American Bandstand Grill	▼▼	$7-$15	486
83 / p. 444		K.C. Masterpiece Barbecue & Grill	▼▼	$7-$25	487
84 / p. 444		J. Alexander's	▼▼▼	$8-$28	486
85 / p. 444		Andy's Wok	▼▼	$9-$14	485
86 / p. 444		Barley's Brewhaus & Restaurant	▼▼	$11-$20	485
87 / p. 444		Copeland's Famous New Orleans Restaurant & Bar	▼▼▼	$9-$22	486
88 / p. 444		40 Sardines	▼▼▼	$17-$28	485
89 / p. 444		W. J. McBride's Irish Pub	▼▼	$7-$17	487
		OLATHE - Lodgings			
134 / p. 444		Hampton Inn	▼▼▼	$74-$199	479
135 / p. 444		Fairfield Inn-Olathe	▼▼▼	$67-$92	479
		OLATHE - Restaurants			
92 / p. 444		Joe's Crab Shack	▼▼	$7-$25	479
93 / p. 444		Kansas Machine Shed Restaurant	▼▼	$9-$14	479
		PLATTE CITY - Restaurant			
37 / p. 444		Shields Manor Bistro	▼▼▼	$22-$42	473
		PRAIRIE VILLAGE - Restaurant			
62 / p. 444		Cafe Provence	▼▼	$16-$29	487
		LEAWOOD - Restaurants			
96 / p. 444		Hereford House	▼▼▼	$12-$25	477
97 / p. 444		Han Shin Japanese Steak House	▼▼▼	$15-$40	476
98 / p. 444		Yahooz	▼▼▼	$9-$32	477
99 / p. 444		On The Border	▼▼	$7-$14	477
100 / p. 444		The Bristol Seafood Grill	▼▼▼	$15-$35	476

DOWNTOWN KANSAS CITY (See map and index starting on p. 442)

—— WHERE TO STAY ——

HILTON PRESIDENT KANSAS CITY *Book great rates at AAA.com* **Phone:** 816/221-9490 **4**
Property failed to provide current rates

Historic
Small-scale Hotel

Location: Between 14th and 15th sts; center. 1329 Baltimore St 64105. Fax: 816/303-1648. **Facility:** Built in the 1920s and recently refurbished and reopened, the hotel combines old-style charm with modern elegance. Frank Sinatra performed here. 213 one-bedroom standard units, some with whirlpools. 13 stories, interior corridors. *Bath:* combo or shower only. **Parking:** on-site (fee) and valet. **Amenities:** high-speed Internet, dual phone lines, voice mail, irons, hair dryers. **Leisure Activities:** exercise room. **Guest Services:** sundries, valet laundry, area transportation, wireless Internet. **Business Services:** meeting rooms, business center.

SOME UNITS

HOTEL PHILLIPS *Book at AAA.com* **Phone:** (816)221-7000 **2**
All Year 1P: $99-$264 2P: $99-$264 XP: $15 F12
Location: Just s of I-70, US 24 and 40. 106 W 12th St 64105. Fax: 816/221-3477. **Facility:** This restored hotel, dating from 1931 is a boutique-style property featuring many original architectural elements. 217 one-bedroom standard units. 20 stories, interior corridors. *Bath:* combo or shower only. **Parking:** on-site (fee) and valet. **Terms:** cancellation fee imposed, package plans, $2 service charge. **Amenities:** high-speed Internet (fee), dual phone lines, voice mail, irons, hair dryers. *Some:* honor bars. **Dining:** 12 Baltimore, Phillips Chophouse, see separate listings. **Leisure Activities:** exercise room. **Guest Services:** sundries, valet laundry. **Business Services:** meeting rooms, business center. **Cards:** AX, CB, DC, DS, JC, MC, VI.

SOME UNITS

(See map and index starting on p. 442)

HYATT REGENCY CROWN CENTER *Book great rates at AAA.com* Phone: (816)421-1234 **5**
All Year 1P: $105-$279 2P: $105-$279 XP: $25 F18
Location: In Crown Center area. 2345 McGee St 64108. Fax: 816/435-4190. **Facility:** 731 one-bedroom standard units. 40 stories, interior corridors. *Bath:* combo or shower only. **Parking:** on-site (fee) and valet.
Large-scale Hotel **Terms:** cancellation fee imposed. **Amenities:** high-speed Internet (fee), voice mail, honor bars, irons, hair dryers. *Some:* CD players, safes. **Dining:** 8 restaurants, 6 am-11 pm, cocktails, also, Peppercorn Duck Club, see separate listing. **Pool(s):** heated outdoor. **Leisure Activities:** saunas, whirlpool, steamrooms, board games. **Guest Services:** gift shop, valet laundry, area transportation-downtown. **Business Services:** conference facilities, business center. **Cards:** AX, CB, DC, DS, JC, MC, VI. *(See color ad p 452)*

KANSAS CITY MARRIOTT DOWNTOWN *Book great rates at AAA.com* Phone: (816)421-6800 **1**
All Year 1P: $154-$220 2P: $154-$220 XP: $20 F17
Location: Just s of I-70, US 24 and 40. 200 W 12th St 64105. Fax: 816/855-4418. **Facility:** Smoke free premises.
Large-scale Hotel 983 units. 979 one-bedroom standard units. 4 one-bedroom suites, some with kitchens (no utensils). 18-22 stories, interior corridors. *Bath:* combo or shower only. **Parking:** on-site (fee) and valet. **Terms:** cancellation fee imposed, pets ($25 fee). **Amenities:** high-speed Internet (fee), voice mail, irons, hair dryers. **Pool(s):** lap. **Leisure Activities:** sauna. *Fee:* massage. **Guest Services:** gift shop, valet laundry, wireless Internet. **Business Services:** conference facilities, business center. **Cards:** AX, CB, DC, DS, JC, MC, VI.

RADISSON HOTEL & SUITES KANSAS CITY, CITY CENTER *Book great rates at AAA.com* Phone: (816)474-6664 **3**
All Year 1P: $89-$269 2P: $89-$269 XP: $20 F18
Location: Just s of I-70, US 24 and 40. 1301 Wyandotte St 64105. Fax: 816/474-0192. **Facility:** 388 units. 289 one-bedroom standard units. 99 one-bedroom suites ($139-$289). 28 stories, interior corridors. *Bath:* combo or shower only. **Parking:** on-site (fee) and valet. **Terms:** cancellation fee imposed, pets ($15 fee).
Small-scale Hotel **Amenities:** video games (fee), high-speed Internet, voice mail, irons, hair dryers. *Some:* dual phone lines. **Dining:** 6:30 am-2 & 5:30-10 pm, cocktails. **Pool(s):** heated outdoor. **Leisure Activities:** exercise room. **Guest Services:** gift shop, valet laundry. **Business Services:** conference facilities. **Cards:** AX, DC, DS, MC, VI. **Free Special Amenities:** early check-in/late check-out and high-speed Internet. *(See color ad p 452)*

(See map and index starting on p. 442)

THE WESTIN CROWN CENTER — *Book great rates at AAA.com* — Phone: (816)474-4400 — **6**

AAA SAVE — All Year — 1P: $129-$309 — 2P: $129-$309 — XP: $25 — F18
Location: 0.5 mi s. 1 E Pershing Rd 64108. Fax: 816/391-4438. **Facility:** 16 "guest office" suites with fax and other business equipment. Smoke free premises. 729 units. 724 one-bedroom standard units. 5 one-bedroom suites ($350-$1300). 18 stories, interior corridors. *Bath:* combo or shower only. **Parking:** on-site (fee) and valet. **Terms:** cancellation fee imposed, small pets only. **Amenities:** dual phone lines, voice mail, safes, honor bars, irons, hair dryers. *Fee:* video games, high-speed Internet. *Some:* DVD players, CD players, fax. **Dining:** 2 restaurants, 6 am-11 pm, cocktails, also, Benton's Steak & Chop House, see separate listing. **Pool(s):** heated outdoor. **Leisure Activities:** sauna, whirlpool, 2 lighted tennis courts, jogging, sports court. *Fee:* massage. **Guest Services:** gift shop, valet laundry. **Business Services:** conference facilities, business center. **Cards:** AX, CB, DC, DS, JC, MC, VI. *(See color ad p 453)*

Large-scale Hotel

[icons] FEE / VCR /

------- **WHERE TO DINE** -------

12 BALTIMORE — Lunch: $8-$14 — Dinner: $9-$20 — Phone: 816/346-4410 — **5**
American — **Location:** Just s of I-70, US 24 and 40; in Hotel Phillips. 12th and Baltimore 64105. **Hours:** 6:30 am-1 am, Sun-11 pm. **Features:** The casual but sophisticated establishment's dining room sometimes bustles with activity from the lunch and after-work crowds. Casual dress; cocktails. **Parking:** on-site (fee) and valet. **Cards:** AX, CB, DC, DS, JC, MC, VI.

1924 MAIN — Lunch: $17-$20 — Dinner: $20-$38 — Phone: 816/472-1924 — **8**
American — **Location:** 0.8 mi s. 1924 Main St 64108. **Hours:** 11 am-2 & 5-10 pm. Closed: 12/25; also Sun & Mon. **Reservations:** suggested, weekends. **Features:** Nestled in a restored older building with live entertainment and a variety of innovative menu choices, 1924 hits all the right notes. Large wine list to choose from and don't miss the Panzanella Salad. Casual dress; cocktails; entertainment. **Parking:** on-site. **Cards:** AX, CB, DC, DS, JC, MC, VI.

THE AMERICAN RESTAURANT AT CROWN CENTER — Lunch: $15-$30 — Dinner: $36-$80 — Phone: 816/545-8001 — **13**
American — **Location:** On top floor of Halls Department Store; in Crown Center area. 200 E 25th St, Suite 400 64108. **Hours:** 11:30 am-2 & 6-9:30 pm, Fri & Sat-10 pm. Closed major holidays; also Sun. **Reservations:** suggested. **Features:** The recipient of several awards for the quality of its food, the restaurant presents imaginative dishes with superior flavors. Adding to the dining experience are impeccable service, a refined dining room with unusual, washed-oak accents and an impressive wine selection of nearly 1,400 bottles. Semi-formal attire; cocktails; entertainment. **Parking:** on-site and valet. **Cards:** AX, CB, DC, DS, MC, VI.

BENTON'S STEAK & CHOP HOUSE — Dinner: $25-$38 — Phone: 816/474-4400 — **12**
American — **Location:** 0.5 mi s; in The Westin Crown Center. 1 E Pershing Rd 64108. **Hours:** 5:30 pm-10 pm, Sun 10 am-2 pm. Closed: Mon. **Reservations:** suggested. **Features:** Featuring great steak, chops and seafood, Benton's offers a panoramic view from 20 stories above the city. The restaurant displays original artwork by Thomas Hart Benton. Weekly wine promotions. Casual dress; cocktails. **Parking:** on-site and valet. **Cards:** AX, DC, DS, MC, VI.

CAFE AL DENTE — Lunch: $6-$10 — Dinner: $6-$16 — Phone: 816/472-9444 — **1**
Italian — **Location:** At Delaware and 5th sts; in Historic River Market. 412 D Delaware 64105. **Hours:** 11 am-10 pm. Closed: Sun. **Reservations:** accepted. **Features:** Popular with both tourists and locals, the cafe serves prepared-to-order selections. The pleasant location invites relaxation. Casual dress; cocktails. **Parking:** on-site and street. **Cards:** AX, CB, DC, DS, MC, VI.

THE GOLDEN OX RESTAURANT — Lunch: $6-$30 — Dinner: $9-$39 — Phone: 816/842-2866 — **6**
Steak House — **Location:** 1 mi w on I-670, just s; next to stockyards. 1600 Genessee 64102. **Hours:** 11 am-10 pm, Sat 4 pm-10:30 pm, Sun 4 pm-9 pm. Closed: 1/1, 12/25. **Reservations:** accepted. **Features:** Since 1949, the restaurant has carried on the tradition of providing a good place to dine. It is known for its steaks. Casual dress; cocktails. **Parking:** on-site. **Cards:** AX, DC, DS, MC, VI.

HEREFORD HOUSE RESTAURANT — Lunch: $7-$17 — Dinner: $18-$39 — Phone: 816/842-1080 — **9**
American — **Location:** 1 mi s; corner of Main and 20th sts. 2 E 20th St 64108. **Hours:** 11 am-9 pm, Fri-10 pm, Sat 4 pm-10 pm, Sun 4 pm-9 pm. Closed major holidays. **Reservations:** suggested. **Features:** Many people say Hereford House is THE place to have steak in Kansas City. They also have a good variety of chicken and seafood, featuring an award-winning wine list, dessert prepared by a pastry chef, a professional server staff and an open, cozy ambience. Casual dress; cocktails. **Parking:** on-site. **Cards:** AX, DC, DS, MC, VI.

JILLY'S ON BROADWAY — Lunch: $6-$7 — Dinner: $6-$7 — Phone: 816/221-4977 — **7**
American — **Location:** At 19th St; in Crossroads District. 1744 Broadway 64108. **Hours:** 11 am-1:30 am. Closed: Sun. **Features:** Named after Frank Sinatra's favorite hangout, which he sings about in "Me and My Shadow," the genuine joint is dedicated to serving quality entrees and promoting local musical talent. Casual dress; cocktails. **Parking:** on-site. **Cards:** AX, DS, MC, VI.

LIDIA'S KANSAS CITY — Lunch: $10-$14 — Dinner: $12-$24 — Phone: 816/221-3722 — **10**
Northern Italian — **Location:** Corner of Baltimore Ave. 101 W 22nd St 64108. **Hours:** 11 am-2 & 5:30-9 pm, Fri & Sat 11 am-2 & 5-10 pm, Sun 11 am-2 & 5 pm-9 pm; Saturday & Sunday brunch. Closed major holidays. **Reservations:** suggested. **Features:** An old railroad freight building is now home to the popular restaurant, which nestles in beside other trendy eateries. Beautifully redone, the interior sports contemporary design and decor blends dramatically with the original vaulted ceilings and brick walls. Homemade Italian food is prepared with flair. Dressy casual; cocktails. **Parking:** on-site. **Cards:** AX, DC, DS, MC, VI.

(See map and index starting on p. 442)

MAJESTIC STEAKHOUSE   Lunch: $7-$20   Dinner: $15-$40   Phone: 816/471-8484   ③

Location: 0.4 mi n of Truman. 931 Broadway 64105. **Hours:** 11:30 am-9:30 pm, Fri-10:30 pm, Sat 5 pm-10:30 pm, Sun 4 pm-9 pm. Closed major holidays. **Reservations:** suggested. **Features:** A historic landmark downtown featuring classic steaks and seafood, set to a background of jazz. Casual dress; cocktails; entertainment. **Parking:** on-site. **Cards:** AX, DC, DS, MC, VI.

Steak & Seafood

PEPPERCORN DUCK CLUB   Lunch: $15-$18   Dinner: $25-$38   Phone: 816/435-4199   ⑪

American

Location: In Crown Center area; in Hyatt Regency Crown Center. 2345 McGee St 64108. **Hours:** 11:30 am-2 & 5:30-9 pm, Fri-10 pm, Sat 5:30 pm-10 pm, Mon 5:30 pm-9 pm. Closed: Sun. **Reservations:** suggested. **Features:** The upscale restaurant nurtures a relaxing ambience. After feasting on the chef's specialty rotisserie duck, patrons can salivate over the fabulous chocolate dessert bar, which is laden with elaborate meal-enders. Dressy casual; cocktails. **Parking:** on-site and valet. **Cards:** AX, CB, DC, DS, MC, VI.

PHILLIPS CHOPHOUSE   Dinner: $27-$40   Phone: 816/221-7000   ④

American

Location: Just s of I-70, US 24 and 40; in Hotel Phillips. 106 W 12th St 64105. **Hours:** 5:30 pm-10 pm, Fri & Sat-11 pm. Closed: Sun. **Reservations:** suggested. **Features:** Sophistication marks the chophouse's atmosphere, service and menu. Patrons enjoy the pampering and the well-prepared dishes. Dressy casual; cocktails. **Parking:** on-site (fee) and valet. **Cards:** AX, CB, DC, DS, JC, MC, VI.

SAVOY GRILL   Lunch: $5-$16   Dinner: $14-$32   Phone: 816/842-3890   ②

Seafood

Location: Just s of I-70, US 24 and 40. 219 W 9th St 64105. **Hours:** 11 am-11 pm, Fri & Sat-midnight, Sun 4 pm-10 pm. Closed: 12/25. **Reservations:** suggested. **Features:** This restaurant, well-established since 1903, specializes in fresh seafood and prime beef prepared with excellent flavors and presentations. The ambience is turn-of-the-century elegance and is enhanced by the dignified, professional service. Conveniently located downtown within a short walk of several hotels. High-back booths give a feeling of coziness and intimacy. Casual dress; cocktails. **Parking:** on-site. **Cards:** AX, CB, DC, DS, JC, MC, VI.

The following restaurants have not been evaluated by AAA but are listed for your information only.

THE BLUE BIRD BISTRO   Phone: 816/221-7559

[fyi]

Not evaluated. **Location:** 1700 Summit 64108. **Features:** A Blue Bird blue-plate special is offered daily for lunch. Organic beef tenderloin, bison and free-range chicken, veggie burgers, hummus and pasta are some of the offerings.

LE FOU FROG   Phone: 816/474-6060

[fyi]

Not evaluated. **Location:** 400 E 5th St 64108. **Features:** The intimate yet energetic atmosphere brims with the tastes and flavors of old coastal Marseilles.

KANSAS CITY pop. 441,545   (See map and index starting on p. 444)

——— WHERE TO STAY ———

AMERISTAR HOTEL & CASINO KANSAS CITY
Phone: (816)414-7000   20

(AAA) (SAVE)
All Year   1P: $109-$249
◆◆◆   **Location:** I-435, exit 55B, 1.2 mi e on SR 210, then just s. 3200 N Ameristar Dr 64161. **Fax:** 816/414-7225.
Large-scale Hotel   **Facility:** 184 units. 172 one-bedroom standard units. 12 one-bedroom suites. 11 stories, interior corridors.
Bath: combo or shower only. **Parking:** valet. **Terms:** cancellation fee imposed. **Amenities:** video games (fee), high-speed Internet, voice mail, safes, irons, hair dryers. *Some:* honor bars. **Dining:** 7 restaurants, 8 am-5 pm, Fri & Sat 24 hours, cocktails, also, Horizon's Buffet, see separate listing. **Leisure Activities:** 18 movie theater screens. *Fee:* game room. **Guest Services:** gift shop, valet laundry. **Business Services:** conference facilities, fax (fee). **Cards:** AX, CB, DC, DS, JC, MC, VI.

SOME UNITS

BAYMONT INN & SUITES KANSAS CITY SOUTH   *Book great rates at AAA.com*   **Phone:** 816/822-7000   39

(AAA) (SAVE)
5/29-9/10 [CP]   1P: $72-$99   2P: $78-$105   XP: $6   F18
◆◆ ◆◆◆   9/11-2/29 [CP]   1P: $69-$95   2P: $75-$101   XP: $6   F18
3/1-5/28 [CP]   1P: $65-$86   2P: $71-$92   XP: $6   F18
Small-scale Hotel   **Location:** I-435, exit 69 (87th St). 8601 Hillcrest Rd 64138. **Fax:** 816/822-8488. **Facility:** 102 units. 99 one-bedroom standard units, some with kitchens and/or whirlpools. 3 one-bedroom suites. 4 stories, interior corridors. *Bath:* combo or shower only. **Parking:** on-site, winter plug-ins. **Terms:** small pets only (in smoking units). **Amenities:** video games (fee), voice mail, irons, hair dryers. **Leisure Activities:** exercise room. **Guest Services:** valet and coin laundry. **Business Services:** meeting rooms, business center. **Cards:** AX, CB, DC, DS, MC, VI. **Free Special Amenities:** continental breakfast and high-speed Internet.

SOME UNITS

BEST WESTERN COUNTRY INN-NORTH   *Book great rates at AAA.com*   **Phone:** (816)459-7222   14

(AAA) (SAVE)
9/1-10/31   1P: $49-$139   2P: $49-$139   XP: $5   F12
◆◆ ◆◆◆   6/1-8/31   1P: $62-$109   2P: $62-$109   XP: $5   F12
3/1-5/31 & 11/1-2/29   1P: $49-$79   2P: $49-$79   XP: $5   F12
Motel   **Location:** I-35, exit 8C (Antioch Rd), just s on SR 1, then just e. 2633 NE 43rd St 64117. **Fax:** 816/459-7222.
Facility: 44 one-bedroom standard units. 2 stories (no elevator), exterior corridors. **Parking:** on-site. **Terms:** [CP] meal plan available, pets (with prior approval). **Amenities:** high-speed Internet, irons, hair dryers. **Pool(s):** small outdoor. **Guest Services:** coin laundry, wireless Internet. **Business Services:** fax (fee). **Cards:** AX, CB, DC, DS, MC, VI. **Free Special Amenities:** continental breakfast and high-speed Internet.

SOME UNITS

BEST WESTERN SEVILLE PLAZA HOTEL   *Book great rates at AAA.com*   **Phone:** (816)561-9600   29

(AAA) (SAVE)
All Year   1P: $95-$189   2P: $95-$189   XP: $10   F16
◆◆ ◆◆◆   **Location:** 43rd and Main sts, just se. 4309 Main St 64111. **Fax:** 816/561-4677. **Facility:** 77 one-bedroom standard units, some with whirlpools. 4 stories, interior corridors. **Parking:** on-site. **Terms:** cancellation fee imposed, pets (dogs only, $20 fee). **Amenities:** high-speed Internet, voice mail, irons, hair dryers. *Some:* Small-scale Hotel   CD players. **Leisure Activities:** exercise room. **Guest Services:** valet laundry, area transportation-within 2 mi, wireless Internet. **Business Services:** meeting rooms, business center. **Cards:** AX, CB, DC, DS, MC, VI. **Free Special Amenities:** expanded continental breakfast and high-speed Internet.

SOME UNITS

FEE   FEE

CHASE SUITES BY WOODFIN   *Book great rates at AAA.com*   **Phone:** (816)891-9009   9

(AAA) (SAVE)
All Year [ECP]   1P: $79-$159   2P: $79-$159   XP: $10   F
◆◆ ◆◆◆   **Location:** I-29, exit 10. 9900 NW Prairie View Rd 64153. **Fax:** 816/891-8623. **Facility:** 112 units. 84 one-bedroom standard units with kitchens. 28 one-bedroom suites ($119-$189) with kitchens. 2 stories (no elevator), exterior corridors. *Bath:* combo or shower only. **Parking:** on-site. **Terms:** cancellation fee imposed, small Small-scale Hotel   pets only ($50 fee, $5 extra charge). **Amenities:** voice mail, irons, hair dryers. *Fee:* video library, high-speed Internet. *Some:* CD players. **Pool(s):** heated outdoor, wading. **Leisure Activities:** whirlpool, gazebo with grill, exercise room, sports court. **Guest Services:** sundries, complimentary evening beverages: Mon-Thurs, valet and coin laundry, area transportation-within 5 mi. **Business Services:** meeting rooms, business center. **Cards:** AX, DC, DS, MC, VI. **Free Special Amenities:** expanded continental breakfast and newspaper.

SOME UNITS

FEE

(See map and index starting on p. 444)

CLARION HOTEL SPORTS COMPLEX-KANSAS CITY
Book great rates at AAA.com

Phone: (816)737-0200 — 27

All Year 1P: $69-$169 2P: $69-$169 XP: $10 F18

Location: I-70, exit 9 (Blue Ridge Cutoff), just ne. Across from Truman Sports Complex and Chiefs and Royals Stadiums. 9103 E 39th St 64133. Fax: 816/737-4713. **Facility:** 374 units. 366 one-bedroom standard units. 8 one-bedroom suites ($279-$500), some with whirlpools. 15 stories, interior corridors. **Parking:** on-site.

Large-scale Hotel **Terms:** cancellation fee imposed, [BP] & [CP] meal plans available, package plans. **Amenities:** high-speed Internet, voice mail, irons, hair dryers. **Dining:** 7 am-1 am, cocktails. **Pool(s):** heated outdoor, heated indoor. **Leisure Activities:** saunas, whirlpool, exercise room. **Guest Services:** valet and coin laundry, area transportation-stadiums, wireless Internet. **Business Services:** conference facilities, business center. **Cards:** AX, CB, DC, DS, MC, VI. **Free Special Amenities:** newspaper and high-speed Internet.

SOME UNITS

🛎📶 🍽 🍸 🎾 🏊 ✕ 🎥 💳 / ✕ 🛗 🖥 📺 /

COMFORT INN KANSAS CITY/WORLDS OF FUN
Book great rates at AAA.com

Phone: (816)454-3500 — 17

6/1-9/5	1P: $85-$125	2P: $85-$125	XP: $8	F18
9/6-10/31	1P: $65-$125	2P: $65-$125	XP: $8	F18
3/1-5/31	1P: $65-$100	2P: $65-$100	XP: $8	F18
11/1-2/29	1P: $65-$95	2P: $65-$95	XP: $8	F18

Small-scale Hotel

Location: I-435, exit 54, follow signs. 7300 NE Parvin Rd 64117. Fax: 816/455-3147. **Facility:** 86 one-bedroom standard units, some with whirlpools. 3 stories, interior corridors. *Bath:* combo or shower only. **Parking:** on-site. **Terms:** 21 day cancellation notice, [ECP] meal plan available, $2 service charge. **Amenities:** high-speed Internet, voice mail, irons, hair dryers. **Pool(s):** small heated indoor. **Leisure Activities:** whirlpool, exercise room. **Guest Services:** valet laundry. **Cards:** AX, CB, DC, DS, MC, VI.

SOME UNITS

[ASK] 🛎📶 🚭♿ 🛗 🎾 🏊 🎥 💳 / ✕ 🛗 🖥 📺 /

COMFORT SUITES KCI
Book great rates at AAA.com

Phone: (816)464-5500 — 2

All Year 1P: $69-$169 2P: $79-$179 XP: $10 F17

Location: I-29, exit 13, just e. 11951 NW Ambassador Dr 64153. Fax: 816/464-5383. **Facility:** 73 one-bedroom standard units, some with whirlpools. 2 stories, interior corridors. *Bath:* combo or shower only. **Parking:** on-site. **Terms:** cancellation fee imposed, weekly rates available. **Amenities:** high-speed Internet, voice mail, irons, hair dryers. **Pool(s):** small heated indoor. **Leisure Activities:** whirlpool, exercise room. **Guest Services:** valet laundry, area transportation. **Business Services:** meeting rooms, PC. **Cards:** AX, CB, DC, DS, JC, MC, VI.

SOME UNITS

[ASK] 🛎📶 ✈ 🚭♿ 🛗 🎾 🏊 🎥 🛗 🖥 📺 / ✕ /

COURTYARD BY MARRIOTT
Book great rates at AAA.com

Phone: (816)941-3333 — 40

All Year 1P: $129 2P: $129

Location: I-435, exit 74 (Holmes St), just w. 500 E 105th St 64131. Fax: 816/941-7971. **Facility:** Smoke free premises. 149 units. 138 one-bedroom standard units. 11 one-bedroom suites ($149). 3 stories, interior corridors. *Bath:* combo or shower only. **Parking:** on-site. **Terms:** [BP] meal plan available. **Amenities:** high-speed Internet, dual phone lines, voice mail, irons, hair dryers. **Pool(s):** heated indoor. **Leisure Activities:** whirlpool, exercise room. **Guest Services:** valet and coin laundry, area transportation. **Business Services:** meeting rooms, business center. **Cards:** AX, CB, DC, DS, JC, MC, VI.

SOME UNITS

🍽 🚭♿ 🛗 🎾 🏊 ✕ 🎥 💳 / 🛗 📺 /

(See map and index starting on p. 444)

COURTYARD BY MARRIOTT-COUNTRY CLUB PLAZA *Book great rates at AAA.com*   **Phone:** 816/285-9755   **35**

Property failed to provide current rates

Small-scale Hotel   **Location:** Center of downtown. 4600 J C Nichols Pkwy 64112. **Facility:** Smoke free premises. 123 one-bedroom standard units. 6 stories, interior corridors. *Bath:* combo or shower only. **Parking:** on-site. **Amenities:** high-speed Internet, voice mail, irons, hair dryers. *Some:* CD players. **Pool(s):** outdoor. **Leisure Activities:** whirlpool, exercise room. **Guest Services:** sundries, valet and coin laundry, wireless Internet. **Business Services:** meeting rooms, business center. *(See color ad p 457)*

COURTYARD BY MARRIOTT-KCI   *Book great rates at AAA.com*   **Phone:** 816/891-7500   **10**

Property failed to provide current rates

Small-scale Hotel   **Location:** I-29, exit 10, just w. 7901 NW Tiffany Springs Pkwy 64153. Fax: 816/891-8855. **Facility:** Smoke free premises. 149 units. 138 one-bedroom standard units. 11 one-bedroom suites. 3 stories, interior corridors. *Bath:* combo or shower only. **Parking:** on-site. **Amenities:** high-speed Internet, dual phone lines, voice mail, irons, hair dryers. **Pool(s):** heated indoor. **Leisure Activities:** whirlpool, exercise room. **Guest Services:** valet and coin laundry, area transportation. **Business Services:** meeting rooms, PC, fax (fee).

SOME UNITS

CRESCENT HOTEL KC SOUTH   **Phone:** (816)765-4100   **42**

5/1-8/31	1P: $60	2P: $70
3/1-4/30	1P: $55	2P: $60
9/1-2/29	1P: $50	2P: $60

Small-scale Hotel   **Location:** I-435, exit 71A (US 71), 0.5 mi s on US 71 to exit Longview Rd. 5701 Longview Rd 64137. Fax: 816/765-6399. **Facility:** 123 units. 117 one-bedroom standard units, some with whirlpools. 6 one-bedroom suites ($149). 7 stories, interior corridors. **Parking:** on-site. **Terms:** weekly rates available, package plans, 18% service charge. **Amenities:** video games, voice mail, irons, hair dryers. *Some:* high-speed Internet. **Pool(s):** small heated indoor/outdoor. **Leisure Activities:** exercise room. **Guest Services:** valet and coin laundry, wireless Internet. **Business Services:** conference facilities, business center. **Cards:** AX, DS, MC, VI.

SOME UNITS

CROSSLAND ECONOMY STUDIOS KANSAS CITY-WORLDS OF FUN   **Phone:** 816/413-0060   **15**

Property failed to provide current rates

Motel   **Location:** I-435, exit 5A, just w. 4301 N Corrington Ave 64117. Fax: 816/413-8121. **Facility:** 134 one-bedroom standard units with kitchens. 3 stories, exterior corridors. *Bath:* combo or shower only. **Parking:** on-site. **Terms:** office hours 7 am-11 pm, small pets only ($25 extra charge). **Guest Services:** coin laundry, wireless Internet.

SOME UNITS

FEE

DRURY INN & SUITES-KANSAS CITY AIRPORT   *Book at AAA.com*   **Phone:** (816)880-9700   **11**

All Year [BP]   1P: $70-$130   2P: $80-$140   XP: $10   F18

Location: I-29, exit 10, just w. 7900 NW Tiffany Springs Pkwy 64153-2310. Fax: 816/880-9700. **Facility:** 123 units. 107 one-bedroom standard units. 16 one-bedroom suites ($110-$160). 5 stories, interior corridors. *Bath:* Small-scale Hotel   combo or shower only. **Parking:** on-site. **Terms:** small pets only. **Amenities:** high-speed Internet, voice mail, irons, hair dryers. **Pool(s):** heated indoor/outdoor. **Leisure Activities:** whirlpool, exercise room. **Guest Services:** complimentary evening beverages: Mon-Sat, valet and coin laundry. **Business Services:** meeting rooms, PC. **Cards:** AX, CB, DC, DS, MC, VI.

SOME UNITS

DRURY INN & SUITES-KANSAS CITY STADIUM   *Book at AAA.com*   **Phone:** (816)923-3000   **25**

All Year [BP]   1P: $70-$120   2P: $80-$130   XP: $10   F18

Small-scale Hotel   **Location:** I-70, exit 9 (Blue Ridge Cutoff), just nw. Across from Truman Sports Complex and Chiefs and Royals Stadiums. 3830 Blue Ridge Cutoff 64133. Fax: 816/923-3000. **Facility:** 123 units. 111 one-bedroom standard units. 12 one-bedroom suites ($100-$140). 5 stories, interior corridors. **Parking:** on-site. **Amenities:** high-speed Internet, voice mail, irons, hair dryers. **Pool(s):** outdoor. **Leisure Activities:** exercise room. **Guest Services:** complimentary evening beverages: Mon-Sat, valet and coin laundry. **Business Services:** meeting rooms, business center. **Cards:** AX, CB, DC, DS, MC, VI.

SOME UNITS

(See map and index starting on p. 444)

EMBASSY SUITES HOTEL KANSAS CITY-PLAZA   *Book at AAA.com*   Phone: 816/756-1720   **28**
▼▼▼   Property failed to provide current rates
Large-scale Hotel   **Location:** At Broadway and 43rd sts; in Country Club Plaza. 220 W 43rd St 64111. Fax: 816/756-3260. **Facility:** 266 one-bedroom suites. 12 stories, interior corridors. *Bath:* combo or shower only. **Parking:** on-site. **Amenities:** voice mail, irons, hair dryers. *Fee:* video games, high-speed Internet. **Pool(s):** heated indoor. **Leisure Activities:** sauna, whirlpool, steamroom, exercise room. **Guest Services:** gift shop, complimentary evening beverages, valet and coin laundry, area transportation, wireless Internet. **Business Services:** meeting rooms, business center.

SOME UNITS

🍽 🍸 🕹 📠 🛜 🏊 ✕ 🎥 🔌 🛏 🖥 💻 / ✕ /

EMBASSY SUITES HOTEL KCI AIRPORT   *Book great rates at AAA.com*   Phone: (816)891-7788   **7**
ⒶⒶ SAVE   All Year   1P: $99-$239   2P: $99-$239   XP: $10   F17
▼▼▼   **Location:** I-29, exit 10, just e. 7640 NW Tiffany Springs Pkwy 64153. Fax: 816/891-7513. **Facility:** 236 one-bedroom suites, some with whirlpools. 8 stories, interior corridors. *Bath:* combo or shower only. **Parking:** on-site. **Terms:** cancellation fee imposed, small pets only. **Amenities:** dual phone lines, voice mail, irons, hair dryers. *Fee:* video games, high-speed Internet. **Dining:** 6-9:30 am, Sat & Sun 7 am-10:30 pm, cocktails. **Pool(s):** heated indoor. **Leisure Activities:** sauna, whirlpool, exercise room. **Guest Services:** sundries, complimentary evening beverages, valet and coin laundry, area transportation, wireless Internet. **Business Services:** conference facilities, business center. **Cards:** AX, DC, DS, MC, VI. **Free Special Amenities: full breakfast and newspaper.**
(See color ad p 458)

SOME UNITS

🔜 🐶 🍽 🍸 🕹 📠 🛜 🏊 ✕ 🎥 🛏 🖥 💻 / ✕ /

EXTENDED STAYAMERICA-KANSAS CITY AIRPORT   Phone: (816)270-7829   **4**
▼▼   All Year   1P: $45-$135   2P: $50-$140   XP: $5   F17
Small-scale Hotel   **Location:** I-29, exit 13, just se. 11712 NW Plaza Cir 64153. Fax: 816/270-3872. **Facility:** 109 one-bedroom standard units with kitchens. 3 stories, interior corridors. *Bath:* combo or shower only. **Parking:** on-site. **Terms:** office hours 7 am-11 pm, small pets only ($25 extra charge). **Amenities:** irons. **Guest Services:** coin laundry, area transportation, wireless Internet. **Cards:** AX, CB, DC, DS, MC, VI.

SOME UNITS

(ASK) (S🐶) 🔜 🕹 📠 🎥 🛏 🖥 💻 / ✕ /
FEE

EXTENDED STAYAMERICA-KANSAS CITY SOUTH   Phone: (816)943-1315   **41**
▼▼   All Year   1P: $50-$140   2P: $55-$145   XP: $5   F17
Small-scale Hotel   **Location:** I-435, exit 74, just s. 550 E 105th St 64131. Fax: 816/943-1322. **Facility:** 119 one-bedroom standard units with kitchens. 3 stories, interior corridors. *Bath:* combo or shower only. **Parking:** on-site. **Terms:** office hours 7 am-11 pm, small pets only ($25 extra charge). **Amenities:** irons, hair dryers. **Guest Services:** coin laundry, wireless Internet. **Cards:** AX, CB, DC, DS, MC, VI.

SOME UNITS

(ASK) (S🐶) 🐶 📠 🏊 🛏 🖥 💻 / ✕ /
FEE

FAIRFIELD INN & SUITES   *Book great rates at AAA.com*   Phone: (816)452-6212   **16**
▼▼▼   All Year   1P: $95-$115   2P: $100-$120   XP: $5   F18
Small-scale Hotel   **Location:** I-435, exit 54 northbound, just w on Parvin Rd; exit southbound, follow service road 1 mi. Located across from large amusement park. 4231 N Corrington Ave 64117. Fax: 816/452-6212. **Facility:** Smoke free premises. 70 units. 41 one-bedroom standard units. 29 one-bedroom suites. 3 stories, interior corridors. *Bath:* combo or shower only. **Parking:** on-site. **Terms:** check-in 4 pm. **Amenities:** high-speed Internet, voice mail, irons, hair dryers. *Some:* CD players. **Pool(s):** small heated indoor. **Leisure Activities:** whirlpool. **Guest Services:** valet and coin laundry, wireless Internet. **Business Services:** fax (fee). **Cards:** AX, DC, DS, MC, VI.

SOME UNITS

(ASK) (S🐶) 🍽 🕹 📠 🛜 🏊 ✕ 🎥 💻 / 🛏 🖥 /

FAIRFIELD INN KANSAS CITY/UNION HILL   *Book great rates at AAA.com*   Phone: 816/931-5700   **24**
▼▼▼   Property failed to provide current rates
Small-scale Hotel   **Location:** Just n of 31st St. 3001 Main St 64108. Fax: 816/931-1791. **Facility:** Smoke free premises. 116 units. 114 one-bedroom standard units, some with whirlpools. 2 one-bedroom suites. 3-4 stories, interior corridors. *Bath:* combo or shower only. **Parking:** on-site. **Amenities:** high-speed Internet, voice mail, irons, hair dryers. **Pool(s):** heated indoor. **Leisure Activities:** whirlpool, exercise room. **Guest Services:** valet laundry, wireless Internet. **Business Services:** meeting rooms, PC, fax (fee).

SOME UNITS

🕹 📠 🛜 🏊 ✕ 🎥 💻 / 🛏 🖥 /

(See map and index starting on p. 444)

HAMPTON INN AIRPORT   *Book great rates at AAA.com*   Phone: (816)464-5454   **5**

All Year — 1P: $116-$200 — 2P: $126-$210 — XP: $10 — F17
Location: I-29, exit 12, just ne. 11212 N Newark Cir 64153. Fax: 816/464-5416. **Facility:** 120 one-bedroom standard units. 4 stories, interior corridors. *Bath:* combo or shower only. **Parking:** on-site. **Terms:** 5 day cancellation notice, [BP] meal plan available. **Amenities:** video games (fee), high-speed Internet, voice
Small-scale Hotel mail, irons, hair dryers. **Pool(s):** outdoor. **Leisure Activities:** exercise room. **Guest Services:** valet and coin laundry, area transportation-within 3 mi, wireless Internet. **Business Services:** meeting rooms, PC, fax (fee). **Cards:** AX, CB, DC, DS, JC, MC, VI. **Free Special Amenities: expanded continental breakfast and high-speed Internet.** *(See color ad p 459)*

SOME UNITS

HAMPTON INN & SUITES   *Book great rates at AAA.com*   Phone: (816)448-4600   **34**

All Year — 1P: $99-$359 — 2P: $99-$359
Location: Just n of 47th St; in Country Club Plaza. 4600 Summit St 64112. Fax: 816/448-4610. **Facility:** 203 units.
Small-scale Hotel 160 one-bedroom standard units. 43 one-bedroom suites ($159-$359), some with efficiencies and/or whirlpools. 9 stories, interior corridors. *Bath:* combo or shower only. **Parking:** on-site. **Terms:** check-in 4 pm, cancellation fee imposed. **Amenities:** video games (fee), high-speed Internet, dual phone lines, voice mail, irons, hair dryers. *Some:* DVD players. **Pool(s):** heated indoor. **Leisure Activities:** exercise room. **Guest Services:** sundries, valet and coin laundry. **Business Services:** meeting rooms, business center. **Cards:** AX, CB, DC, DS, MC, VI.

SOME UNITS

HILTON KANSAS CITY AIRPORT   *Book great rates at AAA.com*   Phone: (816)891-8900   **6**

All Year — 1P: $89-$209 — 2P: $89-$209 — XP: $10 — F18
Location: I-29, exit 12, just se. 8801 NW 112th St 64153. Fax: 816/891-8030. **Facility:** 347 one-bedroom standard units. 11 stories, interior corridors. *Bath:* combo or shower only. **Parking:** on-site.
Large-scale Hotel **Terms:** cancellation fee imposed, package plans. **Amenities:** dual phone lines, voice mail, irons, hair dryers. *Fee:* video games, high-speed Internet. **Pool(s):** outdoor, heated indoor/outdoor. **Leisure Activities:** whirlpool, 2 tennis courts (1 lighted), basketball. **Guest Services:** valet and coin laundry, wireless Internet. **Business Services:** conference facilities, business center. **Cards:** AX, CB, DC, DS, JC, MC, VI.

SOME UNITS

HOLIDAY INN AT THE PLAZA, KANSAS CITY   *Book at AAA.com*   Phone: 816/753-7400   **32**

Property failed to provide current rates
Location: In Country Club Plaza. One E 45th St 64111. Fax: 816/753-0359. **Facility:** 241 one-bedroom standard units. 5 stories, interior corridors. *Bath:* combo or shower only. **Parking:** on-site. **Terms:** pets ($25 fee).
Small-scale Hotel **Amenities:** high-speed Internet, dual phone lines, voice mail, irons, hair dryers. **Pool(s):** heated outdoor. **Leisure Activities:** exercise room. **Guest Services:** valet and coin laundry, area transportation, wireless Internet. **Business Services:** conference facilities, business center.

SOME UNITS
FEE

HOLIDAY INN KANSAS CITY INTERNATIONAL AIRPORT   Phone: 816/801-8400

[fyi]   Property failed to provide current rates
Too new to rate, opening scheduled for September 2006. **Location:** I-29, exit 112, e via Ambassador, then n.
Small-scale Hotel 11728 N Ambassador Dr 64153. **Amenities:** 141 units.

HOLIDAY INN-NORTHEAST   *Book great rates at AAA.com*   Phone: (816)455-1060   **18**

All Year — 1P: $79-$139 — 2P: $79-$139 — XP: $10 — F17
Location: I-435, exit 54. Located opposite the Worlds Of Fun Amusement Park. 7333 NE Parvin Rd 64117.
Fax: 816/455-0250. **Facility:** 165 one-bedroom standard units. 3 stories, interior corridors. *Bath:* combo or shower only. **Parking:** on-site. **Terms:** weekly rates available, package plans. **Amenities:** video games
Small-scale Hotel (fee), high-speed Internet, voice mail, irons, hair dryers. **Dining:** 5:30 am-9 & 5-10 pm, Sat & Sun 7-11 am, cocktails. **Pool(s):** heated indoor. **Leisure Activities:** sauna, whirlpool, foosball, table tennis, exercise room.
Fee: game room. **Guest Services:** valet and coin laundry, area transportation-within 5 mi, wireless Internet. **Business Services:** conference facilities. **Cards:** AX, DS, MC, VI. **Free Special Amenities: newspaper and high-speed Internet.**

SOME UNITS

HOLIDAY INN-SPORTS COMPLEX   *Book at AAA.com*   Phone: (816)353-5300   **30**

All Year — 2P: $59-$199
Location: I-70, exit 9 (Blue Ridge Cutoff), just se. Across from Truman Sports Complex and Chiefs and Royals Stadiums. 4011 Blue Ridge Cutoff 64133. Fax: 816/353-1199. **Facility:** 165 one-bedroom standard units. 7
Small-scale Hotel stories, interior corridors. *Bath:* combo or shower only. **Parking:** on-site. **Terms:** pets ($25 fee).
Amenities: video games (fee), high-speed Internet, dual phone lines, voice mail, irons, hair dryers. **Pool(s):** heated indoor.
Leisure Activities: sauna, whirlpool, exercise room. *Fee:* game room. **Guest Services:** valet and coin laundry, wireless Internet. **Business Services:** meeting rooms, PC, fax (fee). **Cards:** AX, DC, DS, MC, VI.

SOME UNITS
FEE   FEE FEE

HOMESTEAD STUDIO SUITES HOTEL-KANSAS CITY/COUNTRY CLUB PLAZA   *Book at AAA.com*   Phone: (816)531-2212   **33**

All Year — 1P: $80-$145 — 2P: $85-$150 — XP: $5 — F17
Location: Just ne of Country Club Plaza. 4535 Main St 64111. Fax: 816/531-5552. **Facility:** 100 one-bedroom standard units with efficiencies. 3 stories, interior corridors. *Bath:* combo or shower only. **Parking:** on-site.
Small-scale Hotel **Terms:** office hours 6:30 am-8 pm, pets ($25-$75 fee). **Amenities:** high-speed Internet (fee), voice mail, irons. **Guest Services:** valet and coin laundry, wireless Internet. **Cards:** AX, CB, DC, DS, MC, VI.

SOME UNITS
FEE   FEE

(See map and index starting on p. 444)

HOMEWOOD SUITES BY HILTON   *Book great rates at AAA.com*   Phone: (816)880-9880   **8**

AAA (SAVE)   All Year   1P: $89-$229   2P: $89-$239   XP: $10   F17
▼▼▼   **Location:** I-29, exit 10, just e. 7312 NW Polo Dr 64153. Fax: 816/880-9461. **Facility:** 117 units. 110 one- and 7
Small-scale Hotel   two-bedroom suites with efficiencies. 3 stories, interior corridors. *Bath:* combo or shower only. **Parking:** on-
site. **Terms:** package plans, pets ($50 extra charge). **Amenities:** high-speed Internet, dual phone lines,
voice mail, irons, hair dryers. *Some:* DVD players. **Pool(s):** heated outdoor. **Leisure Activities:** whirlpool,
exercise room, sports court. **Guest Services:** sundries, complimentary evening beverages: Mon-Thurs,
valet and coin laundry. **Business Services:** meeting rooms, business center. **Cards:** AX, CB, DC, DS, JC, MC, VI.
Free Special Amenities: full breakfast and newspaper.   SOME UNITS

FEE   ⊞ ⊠ ⊠ ⊠ ⊠ ⊠ ⊠ ⊞ ⊠ ⊠ / ⊠ /

HYATT PLACE KANSAS CITY AIRPORT   *Book great rates at AAA.com*   Phone: (816)891-0871   **12**

AAA (SAVE)   All Year [CP]   1P: $79-$169   2P: $79-$169   XP: $10   F17
▼▼▼   **Location:** I-29, exit 10, just sw. 7600 NW 97th Terr 64153. Fax: 816/891-3436. **Facility:** 134 one-bedroom
standard units. 6 stories, interior corridors. **Parking:** on-site. **Terms:** cancellation fee imposed, pets ($10
Small-scale Hotel   extra charge). **Amenities:** high-speed Internet, dual phone lines, voice mail, irons, hair dryers. *Fee:* video
games, safes. **Pool(s):** heated outdoor. **Leisure Activities:** exercise room. **Guest Services:** complimentary
evening beverages: Wed, valet and coin laundry, area transportation-within 5 mi, wireless Internet.
Business Services: meeting rooms. **Cards:** AX, CB, DC, DS, JC, MC, VI. **Free Special Amenities:** full breakfast and high-
speed Internet.   SOME UNITS

FEE   ⊞ ⊠ ⊠ ⊠ ⊠ ⊞ ⊠ ⊠ / ⊠ /

**THE INTERCONTINENTAL KANSAS CITY AT THE
PLAZA**   *Book great rates at AAA.com*   Phone: (816)303-2900   **38**

AAA (SAVE)   All Year   1P: $119-$359   2P: $119-$359
▼▼▼ ▼▼▼   **Location:** Corner of Wornall Rd and Ward Pkwy; in Country Club Plaza. 401 Ward Pkwy 64112. Fax: 816/756-1635.
Facility: Located in a fashionable shopping district with upscale cafes and restaurants, this hotel offers
Large-scale Hotel   spacious rooms and upgraded services and amenities. 366 units. 347 one-bedroom standard units. 19 one-
bedroom suites ($239-$5000). 12 stories, interior corridors. *Bath:* combo or shower only. **Parking:** on-site
(fee) and valet. **Terms:** cancellation fee imposed, package plans, small pets only ($25 extra charge).
Amenities: dual phone lines, voice mail, safes, honor bars, irons, hair dryers. *Fee:* video games, high-speed Internet.
Dining: 6:30 am-midnight, cocktails, entertainment. **Pool(s):** heated outdoor, wading. **Leisure Activities:** saunas, steamrooms.
Fee: massage. **Guest Services:** gift shop, valet laundry, wireless Internet. **Business Services:** conference facilities, business
center. **Cards:** AX, DC, DS, MC, VI. *(See color ad below)*   SOME UNITS

FEE   ⊠ ⊠ ⊞ ⊠ ⊠ ⊠ ⊠ ⊠ ⊠ ⊠ ⊠ / ⊠ ⊞ ⊠ /

INTRIGUE PARK PLACE HOTEL   *Book great rates at AAA.com*   Phone: (816)483-9900   **21**

AAA (SAVE)   5/25-9/3   1P: $209-$229   2P: $209-$229   XP: $10   F6
▼▼▼   1/1-2/29   1P: $189-$209   2P: $189-$209   XP: $10   F6
3/1-5/24 & 9/4-12/31   1P: $179-$199   2P: $179-$199   XP: $10   F6
Small-scale Hotel   **Location:** I-435, exit 57, 0.5 mi w on Front St, then just n. 1601 N Universal Ave 64120. Fax: 816/231-1418.
Facility: 328 one-bedroom standard units. 9 stories, interior corridors. **Parking:** on-site. **Terms:** 7 day
cancellation notice-fee imposed, [BP], [CP], [ECP] & [MAP] meal plans available, package plans.
Amenities: high-speed Internet, voice mail, safes, irons, hair dryers. *Some:* CD players. **Dining:** 6:30 am-10 pm, cocktails.
Pool(s): heated indoor/outdoor. **Leisure Activities:** exercise room. **Guest Services:** sundries, valet and coin laundry, area
transportation-within 20 mi, wireless Internet. **Business Services:** conference facilities, fax (fee). **Cards:** AX, DC, DS, MC, VI.
Free Special Amenities: newspaper and high-speed Internet. *(See color ad p 462)*   SOME UNITS

⊠ ⊞ ⊠ ⊠ ⊠ / ⊠ ⊞ ⊠ /

(See map and index starting on p. 444)

KANSAS CITY MARRIOTT COUNTRY CLUB PLAZA   *Book great rates at AAA.com*   **Phone:** (816)531-3000   **31**
All Year   1P: $99-$259   2P: $99-$259   XP: $10   F18
Location: Just n of US 56, 4.5 mi s of downtown. 4445 Main St 64111. Fax: 816/531-3007. **Facility:** Smoke free premises. 295 units. 293 one-bedroom standard units. 2 one-bedroom suites. 19 stories, interior corridors. *Bath:* combo or shower only. **Parking:** on-site (fee) and valet. **Terms:** cancellation fee imposed. **Amenities:** high-speed Internet (fee), dual phone lines, voice mail, irons, hair dryers. **Pool(s):** lap. **Leisure Activities:** whirlpool. **Guest Services:** valet laundry, area transportation, wireless Internet. **Business Services:** conference facilities, business center. **Cards:** AX, CB, DC, DS, JC, MC, VI.
Small-scale Hotel

SOME UNITS
[ASK] [S/D] [icons] / [icons] /

LA QUINTA INN   *Book great rates at AAA.com*   **Phone:** (816)483-7900   **22**
All Year [CP]   1P: $82-$99   2P: $87-$104
Location: I-435, exit 57, just w to Cambridge Ave, then just s. 1051 N Cambridge Ave 64120. Fax: 816/483-8887. **Facility:** 130 one-bedroom standard units. 2 stories (no elevator), interior corridors. *Bath:* combo or shower only. **Parking:** on-site. **Terms:** package plans, small pets only. **Amenities:** high-speed Internet, voice mail, irons, hair dryers. **Pool(s):** heated outdoor. **Leisure Activities:** whirlpool, exercise room, basketball. **Guest Services:** coin laundry, wireless Internet. **Business Services:** fax (fee). **Cards:** AX, CB, DC, DS, MC, VI. **Free Special Amenities:** expanded continental breakfast and high-speed Internet. *(See color ad p 463)*
Small-scale Hotel

SOME UNITS
[S/D] [icons] / [X] [icons] /

MARRIOTT HOTEL-KANSAS CITY AIRPORT   *Book great rates at AAA.com*   **Phone:** 816/464-2200   **1**
All Year   1P: $99-$209
Location: I-29, exit 13, 1 mi w on Airport exit to Bern St. Located on Kansas City International Airport grounds. 775 Brasilia Ave 64153. Fax: 816/464-5915. **Facility:** Smoke free premises. 382 units. 380 one-bedroom standard units. 2 one-bedroom suites ($300-$600). 6-9 stories, interior corridors. *Bath:* combo or shower only. **Parking:** on-site. **Terms:** 17% service charge. **Amenities:** video games, high-speed Internet (fee), voice mail, irons, hair dryers. **Pool(s):** heated indoor. **Leisure Activities:** whirlpool, exercise room, volleyball. **Guest Services:** gift shop, valet and coin laundry. **Business Services:** conference facilities, business center. **Cards:** AX, DC, DS, MC, VI.
Large-scale Hotel

SOME UNITS
[ASK] [icons] / [icons] /

QUALITY INN & SUITES AIRPORT   *Book great rates at AAA.com*   **Phone:** (816)587-6262   **13**
5/31-9/5   1P: $90-$149   2P: $90-$149
3/1-5/30 & 9/6-2/29   1P: $80-$129   2P: $80-$129
Location: I-29, exit 8. 6901 NW 83rd St 64152. Fax: 816/587-5545. **Facility:** 82 one-bedroom standard units, some with whirlpools. 3 stories, interior corridors. *Bath:* combo or shower only. **Parking:** on-site. **Amenities:** high-speed Internet, voice mail, irons, hair dryers. **Pool(s):** small heated indoor. **Leisure Activities:** exercise room. **Guest Services:** valet laundry, wireless Internet. **Business Services:** meeting rooms, fax (fee). **Cards:** AX, DC, DS, MC, VI.
Small-scale Hotel

SOME UNITS
[ASK] [S/D] [icons] / [X] /

QUARTERAGE HOTEL   *Book great rates at AAA.com*   **Phone:** (816)931-0001   **26**
All Year   1P: $99-$139   2P: $99-$139
Location: 0.4 mi w of jct Main St; in Westport Plaza area. 560 Westport Rd 64111. Fax: 816/931-8891. **Facility:** 123 one-bedroom standard units, some with whirlpools. 4 stories, interior corridors. **Parking:** on-site. **Terms:** [BP] meal plan available, package plans. **Amenities:** high-speed Internet, dual phone lines, voice mail, irons, hair dryers. **Leisure Activities:** sauna, whirlpool. **Guest Services:** complimentary evening beverages: Mon-Sat, valet laundry. **Business Services:** meeting rooms, business center. **Cards:** AX, CB, DC, DS, MC, VI. **Free Special Amenities:** full breakfast and high-speed Internet.
Small-scale Hotel

SOME UNITS
[icons] / [X] [icons] /

(See map and index starting on p. 444)

RADISSON HOTEL KANSAS CITY AIRPORT *Book at AAA.com* **Phone:** 816/464-2423 3
WWW (Property failed to provide current rates)
Location: I-29, exit 13, just se. 11828 NW Plaza Cir 64153. **Fax:** 816/464-2560. **Facility:** 138 units. 130 one-
Small-scale Hotel bedroom standard units. 8 one-bedroom suites. 7 stories, interior corridors. **Parking:** on-site. **Terms:** pets
($10 extra charge). **Amenities:** high-speed Internet, voice mail, irons, hair dryers. **Pool(s):** heated indoor.
Leisure Activities: whirlpool, exercise room. **Guest Services:** valet and coin laundry, area transportation. **Business Services:**
meeting rooms, PC.

SOME UNITS
⊞ 🐾 🍽 🍸 🔥M 🖨 🏊 🎦 💻 / ✕ 🛢 📺 /
FEE

THE RAPHAEL *Book at AAA.com* **Phone:** (816)756-3800 37
WWW All Year 1P: $199-$249 2P: $199-$249 XP: $20 F18
Location: Corner of Wornall Rd; in Country Club Plaza. 325 Ward Pkwy 64112. **Fax:** 816/802-2131. **Facility:** All
Historic units with bathrobes. 123 units. 51 one-bedroom standard units. 72 one-bedroom suites ($239-$299). 9
Small-scale Hotel stories, interior corridors. *Bath:* combo or shower only. **Parking:** on-site. **Terms:** check-in 4 pm, [AP], [BP] &
[CP] meal plans available, package plans. **Amenities:** CD players, high-speed Internet, voice mail, honor
bars, irons, hair dryers. *Some:* safes. **Dining:** restaurant, see separate listing. **Guest Services:** valet laundry. **Cards:** AX, CB,
C, DS, JC, MC, VI.

SOME UNITS
🍽 🔥M 🖨 🖨 🐾 🎦 💻 / ✕ 🛢 /

RED ROOF INN-NORTH *Book at AAA.com* **Phone:** (816)452-8585 19
WW 5/25-9/2 1P: $54-$68 2P: $59-$73 XP: $5 F18
3/1-5/24 & 9/3-2/29 1P: $43-$60 2P: $48-$65 XP: $5 F18
Motel **Location:** I-435, exit 55B northbound; exit 55 southbound, just e on SR 210, then just n. 3636 NE Randolph Rd 64161.
Fax: 816/452-4694. **Facility:** 108 one-bedroom standard units. 2 stories (no elevator), exterior corridors.
Bath: combo or shower only. **Parking:** on-site. **Amenities:** voice mail. *Fee:* video games, high-speed Internet. **Cards:** AX, CB,
C, DS, MC, VI.

SOME UNITS
🐾 🔥M 🖨 🎦 / ✕ /

RESIDENCE INN BY MARRIOTT
DOWNTOWN/UNION HILL *Book great rates at AAA.com* **Phone:** (816)561-3000 23
WWW All Year [BP] 1P: $123-$209
Location: Just n of 31st St. 2975 Main St 64108. **Fax:** 816/931-0967. **Facility:** Smoke free premises. 96 units.
Small-scale Hotel 80 one-bedroom standard units with kitchens. 16 two-bedroom suites with kitchens. 2-3 stories (no
elevator), exterior corridors. *Bath:* combo or shower only. **Parking:** on-site. **Terms:** weekly rates available,
package plans, small pets only ($75 fee). **Amenities:** video games (fee), high-speed Internet, voice mail, irons, hair dryers.
Pool(s): outdoor. **Leisure Activities:** exercise room. **Guest Services:** complimentary evening beverages: Mon-Thurs, valet and
coin laundry, area transportation, wireless Internet. **Business Services:** meeting rooms, business center. **Cards:** AX, CB, DC,
DS, JC, MC, VI.

ASK 🐾 🖨 🖨 🏊 ✕ 🎦 🛢 📺 💻
FEE

RESIDENCE INN KANSAS CITY COUNTRY CLUB
PLAZA *Book great rates at AAA.com* **Phone:** (816)753-0033 43
WWW All Year [BP] 1P: $139-$259 2P: $139-$259
Location: In Country Club Plaza. 4601 Broadway Blvd 64112. **Fax:** 816/753-8033. **Facility:** Smoke free premises.
Small-scale Hotel 106 units. 56 one-bedroom standard units with efficiencies. 38 one- and 12 two-bedroom suites, some with
efficiencies or kitchens. 6 stories, interior corridors. *Bath:* combo or shower only. **Parking:** on-site.
Terms: pets ($75 fee). **Amenities:** video games (fee), high-speed Internet, dual phone lines, voice mail, irons, hair dryers.
Some: DVD players. **Pool(s):** small heated indoor. **Leisure Activities:** whirlpool, exercise room, sports court. **Guest Services:**
valet and coin laundry. **Business Services:** meeting rooms, business center. **Cards:** AX, CB, DC, DS, JC, MC, VI.

SOME UNITS
🐾 🖨 🏊 ✕ ✕ 🎦 🛢 🛢 💻 / VCR /
FEE

(See map and index starting on p. 444)

SHERATON SUITES COUNTRY CLUB PLAZA   *Book great rates at AAA.com*   **Phone:** (816)931-4400
 (AAA) (SAVE)   All Year   1P: $299-$309   2P: $299-$309   XP: $10
Location: Corner of Summit and 47th St; in Country Club Plaza. 770 W 47th St 64112. Fax: 816/561-73
Facility: 257 one-bedroom suites. 18 stories, interior corridors. *Bath:* combo or shower only. **Parking:**
site and valet. **Terms:** $2 service charge. **Amenities:** voice mail, irons, hair dryers. *Fee:* video games, hig
Large-scale Hotel   speed Internet. **Dining:** 6 am-10:30 pm, cocktails. **Pool(s):** heated indoor/outdoor. Leisu
Activities: whirlpool, exercise room. **Guest Services:** sundries, valet and coin laundry. Busine
Services: conference facilities, business center. **Cards:** AX, CB, DC, DS, JC, MC, VI.
SOME UN

The following lodging was either not evaluated or did not
meet AAA rating requirements but is listed for your information only.

HOLIDAY INN EXPRESS WESTPORT   **Phone:** 816/931-10
(fyi)   Did not meet all AAA rating requirements for some property operations at time of last evaluation
08/04/2006. **Location:** In Westport Plaza area. Located in a popular antique shopping area. 801 Westport Rd 641
Small-scale Hotel   Facilities, services, and decor characterize a mid-range property.

WHERE TO DINE

THE ALAMO   **Lunch:** $5-$10   **Dinner:** $6-$14   **Phone:** 816/452-2600
    Location: 1.5 mi w, at N Brighton St. 5010 NE Parvin Rd 64117. **Hours:** 11 am-10 pm, Fri & Sat-11 pm. Clos
major holidays. **Reservations:** accepted. **Features:** Mexican and American favorites are served in
Mexican   inviting dining room. Appetizers, soups, salads, burgers, sandwiches and "pieza" share menu space w
traditional entrees. Casual dress; cocktails. **Parking:** on-site. **Cards:** AX, DC, DS, MC, VI.

BO LINGS   **Lunch:** $7-$10   **Dinner:** $10-$20   **Phone:** 816/753-1718
(AAA)   **Location:** In Country Club Plaza; in Kansas City Board of Trade Building. 4800 Main 64112. **Hours:** 11 am-9:30 p
    Fri & Sat-10:30 pm. Closed: 7/4, 11/22, 12/25. **Features:** The restaurant offers a good variety for lunch a
an even greater number of choices for dinner. Dim sum is the way to go on Saturday and Sunday. Service
Chinese   fast and efficient, and the setting provides comfortable booths in a peaceful ambience. Covered parking
nearby. Casual dress; cocktails. **Parking:** street. **Cards:** AX, DC, DS, MC, VI.

BOOZE FISH WINE BAR   **Dinner:** $8-$16   **Phone:** 816/561-5995
    Location: In Westport Plaza. 1511 Westport Rd 64111. **Hours:** 4:30 pm-10 pm, Fri & Sat-11 pm. Closed: Su
Features: The cozy, attractive bistro presents an imaginative appetizer menu, a selection of light entre
International   and an impressive wine list. Casual dress; cocktails. **Parking:** on-site. **Cards:** AX, CB, DC, DS, J
MC, VI.

CAFE SEBASTIENNE   **Lunch:** $8-$15   **Dinner:** $15-$27   **Phone:** 816/561-7740
Location: In Kemper Museum of Contemporary Art. 4420 Warwick Blvd 64111. **Hours:** 11 am-2:30 pm, Fri & S
also 5:30 pm-9:30 pm. Closed: 1/1, 11/22, 12/25; also Mon. **Reservations:** accepted. **Features:** Located
American   a contemporary art museum, the cafe has a cozy ambience for up to 48 diners. The menu offers ma
creative dishes including alfresco fare, and there's patio seating by the waterfall. Many lively works of
decorate the walls. Dressy casual; cocktails. **Parking:** on-site. **Cards:** AX, MC, VI.

CALIFORNOS   **Lunch:** $8-$12   **Dinner:** $10-$24   **Phone:** 816/531-7878
Location: In Country Club Plaza area. 4124 Pennsylvania Ave 64111. **Hours:** 11 am-3 & 5-10 pm, Fri & Sat-11 p
Closed major holidays; also Sun. **Reservations:** accepted. **Features:** Loads of outdoor seating is availab
American   in season, but inside is also a treat. Fresh-minded and contemporary dishes incorporate flavors of the We
Coast. Dressy casual; cocktails. **Parking:** on-site and valet. **Cards:** AX, DC, MC, VI.

CASCONE'S ITALIAN RESTAURANT   **Lunch:** $7-$12   **Dinner:** $13-$23   **Phone:** 816/454-7977
Location: 3 mi n via SR 9 and 283. 3737 N Oak Trafficway 64116. **Hours:** 11 am-3 & 4-10 pm, Fri & Sat-11 p
Sun noon-9 pm. Closed: 7/4, 11/22, 12/25. **Reservations:** suggested. **Features:** You'll enjoy the gre
Italian   selection of delicious and well-presented pasta dishes at the locally popular Cascone's. You'll
appreciate the romantic ambience and casual decor. The serving staff is friendly, prompt and attentiv
House specialties also include several selections of poultry, veal, pork, beef, and seafood. Many appetizers including calam
fritti and escargot. Dressy casual; cocktails. **Parking:** on-site. **Cards:** AX, DC, DS, MC, VI.

CHIPOTLE   **Lunch:** $5-$8   **Dinner:** $5-$8   **Phone:** 816/746-0050
    Location: I-29, exit 8, just ne; in The Shops at Boardwalk Shopping Center. 8600 N Boardwalk Ave 64154. **Hours:**
am-10 pm. Closed major holidays. **Features:** Strikingly contemporary and minimalist, the restaura
Mexican   promotes a distinctive style of serving tacos and burritos. Served with cilantro-lime rice, varied salsas a
options galore, the food is sure to please. Casual dress; cocktails. **Parking:** on-site. **Cards:** AX, MC, VI.

See map and index starting on p. 444)

HUBBY'S
American

| Lunch: $4-$7 | Dinner: $6-$7 | Phone: 816/931-2482 | [13] |

Location: Just w of 37th St. 3756 Broadway St 64111. **Hours:** 24 hours. Closed major holidays. **Reservations:** accepted. **Features:** Although the '50s-style diner bustles, service is warm and friendly. The menu lists a large selection, including breakfast items served 24 hours a day. Casual dress. **Parking:** on-site.

CORNER CAFE
American

| Lunch: $5-$15 | Dinner: $5-$15 | Phone: 816/415-0050 | [6] |

Location: I-35, exit 16, 0.3 mi nw. 8301 N Flintlock Rd 64157. **Hours:** 5 am-10 pm. Closed: 11/22, 12/25. **Features:** With a bustling atmosphere and interesting decor, the eatery offers a good variety of menu selections; something for everyone. Casual dress. **Parking:** on-site. **Cards:** AX, DS, MC, VI.

IGLIO
Italian

| Lunch: $8-$15 | Dinner: $8-$21 | Phone: 816/561-0505 | [21] |

Location: In Country Club Plaza. 209 W 46th Terrace 64112. **Hours:** 11 am-10 pm, Fri & Sat-11 pm, Sun 10:30 am-10 pm. Closed: 12/25. **Reservations:** accepted. **Features:** Pizza baked in a wood-burning oven and handmade fresh pasta are restaurant favorites. Casual dress; cocktails. **Parking:** on-site. **Cards:** AX, DC, DS, MC, VI.

**MORELLA'S JACK STACK BARBECUE
OF MARTIN CITY**
Barbecue

| Lunch: $6-$15 | Dinner: $9-$26 | Phone: 816/942-9141 | [30] |

Location: I-470, exit 74, 4 mi s to jct Holmes and 135th sts. 13441 Holmes St 64145. **Hours:** 11 am-10 pm, Fri & Sat-10:30 pm, Sun-9 pm. Closed: 11/22, 12/25. **Features:** Guests can savor award-winning barbecue in a cozy and rustic atmosphere with old black-and-white photographs, a fireplace and an outdoor patio. The menu lines up hickory-wood-fired meats, chicken, steaks and seafood, as well as salads and sandwiches. Casual dress; cocktails. **Parking:** on-site. **Cards:** AX, DS, MC, VI.

GATES BAR-B-Q
American

| Lunch: $10-$18 | Dinner: $10-$20 | Phone: 816/753-0828 | [12] |

Location: At Main and Linwood sts. 3205 Main St 64111. **Hours:** 10 am-midnight, Fri & Sat-1 am. Closed: 11/22, 12/25. **Reservations:** not accepted. **Features:** A city original, the family restaurant was established in 1946. Service is fast, and "Hi, may I help you?" is the immediate greeting. Casual dress; cocktails. **Parking:** on-site. **Cards:** AX, DS, MC, VI.

HARRY'S BAR & TABLES
American

| Dinner: $7-$17 | Phone: 816/561-3950 | [14] |

Location: In Westport Plaza area. 501 Westport Rd 64111. **Hours:** 4 pm-2 am, Sat from 5 pm, Sun from 5 pm. **Features:** Occupying a corner location in the popular Westport area, the establishment is an elegant mix of a cigar and martini bar and restaurant. The casual dinner menu lists classic favorites with a twist. Casual dress; cocktails. **Parking:** on-site. **Cards:** AX, CB, DC, DS, MC, VI.

HONG KONG JADE GARDEN
Chinese

| Lunch: $5-$7 | Dinner: $6-$16 | Phone: 816/891-8666 | [2] |

Location: I-29, exit 10, just ne; in Tiffany Springs Shopping Center. 10004 NW Executive Hills Blvd 64153. **Hours:** 11 am-9 pm. Closed major holidays; also Sun. **Features:** The comfortable, casual establishment prepares a large variety of favorites. The buffet is an option for the lunchtime crowd, which includes many business professionals. Casual dress; cocktails. **Parking:** on-site. **Cards:** AX, CB, DC, DS, JC, MC, VI.

HORIZON'S BUFFET
International

| Lunch: $7-$10 | Dinner: $13-$20 | Phone: 816/414-2617 | [11] |

Location: I-435, exit 55B, 1.2 mi e on SR 210, then just s; in Ameristar Hotel & Casino Kansas City. 3200 N Ameristar Dr 64161. **Hours:** 11 am-9:30 pm, Fri & Sat-10:30 pm. **Features:** Guests can wander amid stations named Chinatown, K.C. Country Bar-B-Que, Farmer's Market, Viva Mexico and Mama Mia's, but a visit here is incomplete without a stop at the Sweet Dreams dessert bar. Casual dress. **Parking:** on-site and valet. **Cards:** AX, CB, DC, DS, JC, MC, VI.

JARDINE'S RESTAURANT & JAZZ CLUB
American

| Lunch: $6-$8 | Dinner: $16-$30 | Phone: 816/561-6480 | [20] |

Location: In Westport Plaza area. 4536 Main St 64111. **Hours:** 11 am-3 & 5-10 pm, Fri-midnight, Sat 6 pm-midnight, Mon 11 am-3 pm. Closed major holidays. **Reservations:** suggested, weekends. **Features:** Wonderful navy bean soup stands out at the warm, comfortable and slightly contemporary restaurant. Live jazz every night. Casual dress; cocktails; entertainment. **Parking:** on-site. **Cards:** AX, MC, VI.

JJ'S RESTAURANT
Continental

| Lunch: $7-$12 | Dinner: $17-$37 | Phone: 816/561-7136 | [22] |

Location: Just w of Country Club Plaza; between Belleview Ave and Roanoke Pkwy. 910 W 48th St 64112. **Hours:** 11 am-10 pm, Fri-11 pm, Sat 5 pm-11 pm, Sun 5 pm-10 pm. Closed major holidays; also Super Bowl Sun. **Reservations:** suggested. **Features:** Sitting on a pleasant tree-lined street just west of the Country Club Plaza, the little restaurant is a perfect place for a quiet tete-a-tete or a leisurely business luncheon. An astounding selection of wines complements offerings from the bistro-type menu. Casual dress; cocktails. **Parking:** valet and street. **Cards:** AX, CB, DC, DS, JC, MC, VI.

KONA GRILL
Pacific Rim

| Lunch: $6-$12 | Dinner: $9-$24 | Phone: 816/931-5888 | [24] |

Location: Just w of Wornall Rd; in Country Club Plaza. 444 Ward Pkwy 64112. **Hours:** 11 am-11 pm, Fri & Sat-midnight. Closed: 11/22, 12/25. **Features:** The eclectic menu reflects Pacific influences. In addition to noodle dishes and sushi, it lists specialties of macadamia nut chicken and lemon grass-encrusted swordfish. The dining room has a large aquarium, a private area and a sushi bar. The patio opens during warm weather. Casual dress; cocktails. **Parking:** on-site. **Cards:** AX, CB, DC, DS, JC, MC, VI.

(See map and index starting on p. 444)

MAMA JO'S BBQ
Barbecue

Lunch: $5-$8   **Dinner:** $5-$8   **Phone:** 816/455-3300   8
Location: I-435, exit 54. 7201 NE Parvin Rd 64117. **Hours:** 11 am-5 pm, Thurs-Sat to 8 pm. Closed majo holidays; also Sun. **Features:** We haven't seen Mama, but her food is great; the modest facility offers quick serving of very good barbecue. Casual dress. **Parking:** on-site. **Cards:** AX, MC, VI.

MIMI'S CAFE
American

Lunch: $8-$15   **Dinner:** $8-$15   **Phone:** 816/587-587
Location: I-29, exit 8 (NW Barry Rd); in Zona Rosa Shopping Complex. 8501 NW Prairie View Rd 64153. **Hours:** am-11 pm. **Closed:** 12/25. **Reservations:** accepted. **Features:** Breakfast, lunch and dinner are offere throughout the day at this eclectic and popular eatery. With New Orleans inspired decor and a menu tha features something for everyone, finding a favorite dish should be no problem. Casual dress; cocktails **Parking:** on-site. **Cards:** CB, DC, DS, MC, VI.

MINSKY'S PIZZA CAFE & SPORTS BAR
American

Lunch: $3-$6   **Dinner:** $6-$12   **Phone:** 816/741-2737   5
Location: I-29, exit 8 (NW Barry Rd), just sw. 7007 NW Barry Rd 64153. **Hours:** 11 am-11 pm, Fri & Sat-midnigh **Closed:** 4/8, 11/22, 12/25. **Reservations:** accepted. **Features:** Patrons can choose from a large selection o specialty pizzas, sandwiches, salads and pasta in a comfortably worn atmosphere. Casual dress; cocktails **Parking:** on-site. **Cards:** AX, CB, DC, DS, JC, MC, VI.

NAPOLEON BAKERY
American

Lunch: $6-$10   **Phone:** 816/931-4401   1
Location: In Westport Plaza area. 706 Westport Rd 64111. **Hours:** 7 am-4 pm, Sun-2 pm. Closed major holidays also Mon, Sun before 7/4. **Features:** Busy during the lunch hour, the bakery is a popular spot for goo reason. Guests can expect great food in short order. Casual dress; beer & wine only. **Parking:** on-site an street. **Cards:** AX, MC, VI.

OSTERIA IL CENTRO
Northern Italian

Dinner: $9-$16   **Phone:** 816/561-2369   2
Location: Corner of 51st and Main sts; in Country Club Plaza area. 5101 Main St 64112. **Hours:** 4 pm-10 pm, Fri Sat-11 pm. Closed major holidays; also Sun. **Features:** With its engaging music and colorful, creative deco the trendy bistro exudes relaxed sophistication. Menu options are tempting. Although the dress code casual, dressy casual is the norm. Casual dress; cocktails. **Parking:** on-site. **Cards:** AX, DC, DS, MC, VI.

PLAZA III, THE STEAKHOUSE
Steak House

Lunch: $9-$18   **Dinner:** $22-$41   **Phone:** 816/753-0000   2
Location: On US 56; in Country Club Plaza. 4749 Pennsylvania Ave 64112. **Hours:** 11:30 am-2:30 & 5:30-10 pm Fri 5:30 pm-10:30 pm, Sat 5 pm-10:30 pm, Sun 5 pm-10 pm. Closed major holiday **Reservations:** suggested. **Features:** Tender, melt-in-your-mouth Kansas City steaks, prime rib, salmo chicken, pork with sides of fresh mashed potatoes and vegetables or sauteed mushrooms in butter sauce delicious! A variety of salads and classic appetizers and an assortment of tempting, decadent desserts all served i sophisticated and classic atmosphere by professionally trained staff. It doesn't get any better than this. Extensive wine selectio Dressy casual; cocktails; entertainment. **Parking:** on-site. **Cards:** AX, DC, DS, MC, VI.

POTPIE
American

Lunch: $7-$9   **Dinner:** $12-$23   **Phone:** 816/561-2702   1
Location: In Westport Plaza area. 904 Westport Rd 64111. **Hours:** 11 am-10 pm, Fri-11 pm, Sat 5 pm-11 pm **Closed:** Sun & Mon. **Reservations:** accepted. **Features:** The atmosphere is equal parts cozy, warm an comfortable. Food options, including a terrific rendition of a BLT, range from familiar to more distinctive Casual dress; cocktails. **Parking:** on-site and street. **Cards:** AX, DC, DS, MC, VI.

THE RAPHAEL RESTAURANT
Continental

Lunch: $8-$12   **Dinner:** $18-$32   **Phone:** 816/756-3800   2
Location: Corner of Wornall Rd; in Country Club Plaza; in The Raphael. 325 Ward Pkwy 64112. **Hours:** 6:30-10 am 11-3 & 5-10 pm, Sat 7 am-3 & 5-11 pm, Sun 7-11 am. **Reservations:** suggested. **Features:** The weekl changing menu features selections to please a broad array of tastes. Guests can dine leisurely in any or of the cozy dining rooms. From Thursday through Saturday, the piano bar adds a nice touch to the subdue ambience. Casual dress; cocktails; entertainment. **Parking:** on-site and valet. **Cards:** AX, CB, DC, DS, MC, VI.

RE:VERSE
Mediterranean

Lunch: $6-$10   **Dinner:** $12-$26   **Phone:** 816/931-7811   2
Location: At Jefferson and Ward Pkwy; in Country Club Plaza area. 618 Ward Pkwy 64113. **Hours:** 11 am-11 pm Sat & Sun from 9:30 am. **Closed:** 1/1, 12/25. **Reservations:** suggested. **Features:** In the popular Plaz area, the trendy restaurant maintains and air of casual sophistication. Creativity distinguishes the men Dressy casual; cocktails. **Parking:** on-site (fee). **Cards:** AX, CB, DC, DS, JC, MC, VI.

SMOKE BOX BAR-B-QUE
Barbecue

Lunch: $6-$15   **Dinner:** $6-$15   **Phone:** 816/891-8011   1
Location: I-29, exit 10, just ne. 10020 N Ambassador Dr 64153. **Hours:** 10 am-9 pm. Closed major holidays; als Sun. **Features:** This casual, family-run barbecue restaurant features large and tasty portions of beef, har pork and ribs. There is also a variety of sandwiches available. Casual dress; beer & wine only. **Parking:** o site. **Cards:** AX, DC, DS, MC, VI.

STROUD'S NORTH
American

Lunch: $8-$22   **Dinner:** $8-$22   **Phone:** 816/454-9600   7
Location: I-35, exit 11 (Vivion Rd) southbound to NE Oak Ridge Rd; exit N Brighton northbound, just n to Vivion R then just e to NE Oak Ridge Rd, follow signs. 5410 NE Oak Ridge Rd 64119. **Hours:** 5 pm-9:30 pm, Fri 11 am 10:30 pm, Sat 2 pm-10:30 pm, Sun 11 am-9:30 pm. **Closed:** 11/22, 12/24, 12/25. **Features:** You'll enjoy the the catfish and steak are excellent too. The large portions of food are served family-style by a prompt and attentive server stat Casual dress; cocktails. **Parking:** on-site. **Cards:** AX, DC, DS, MC, VI.

See map and index starting on p. 444)

STROUD'S SOUTH RESTAURANT   **Lunch:** $6-$15   **Dinner:** $10-$22   **Phone:** 816/333-2132   [29]
▼▼▼   **Location:** I-435, exit 74 (Holmes Rd), 2 mi n to 85th St, then 0.3 mi e. 1015 E 85th St 64131. **Hours:** 4 pm-10 pm,
Fri 11 am-11 pm, Sat 2 pm-11 pm, Sun 11 am-10 pm. Closed: 11/22, 12/25. **Features:** This restaurant has
American   been quite popular with local residents since 1933. They specialize in tasty, juicy, appetizing fried chicken
dinners served family-style, but the menu also offers pork, beef and seafood. The servers are friendly, fast
and efficient. Casual dress; cocktails; entertainment. **Parking:** on-site. **Cards:** AX, DC, DS, MC, VI.   [Y]

TOMFOOLERIES   **Lunch:** $8-$15   **Dinner:** $8-$15   **Phone:** 816/746-8668   [3]
▼▼▼   **Location:** I-29, exit 8 (NW Barry Rd); in Zonarosa Shopping Complex. 8680 NW Prairie View Rd 64153. **Hours:** 11
am-3 am. Closed: 11/22, 12/25. **Reservations:** accepted. **Features:** A lively atmosphere prevails in the
American   eclectic and contemporary dining room. Guests' attentions are drawn to the giant plasma TV and the train
circling on an overhead track. The menu blends creative cuisine and some old favorites. Casual dress;
cocktails. **Parking:** on-site. **Cards:** AX, CB, DC, DS, JC, MC, VI.   [⬉]

—————— ***The following restaurants have not been evaluated by AAA*** ——————
but are listed for your information only.

AIXOIS   **Phone:** 816/333-3305
[fyi]   Not evaluated. **Location:** S of Country Club Plaza. 251 E 55th St 64113. **Features:** Guests seating inside the
crowded but intimate bistro or on the patio can sample roasted chicken and duck, trout in lemon butter, beef
tenderloin and creme brulee.

AMERISPORTS BREW PUB   **Phone:** 816/414-7000
[fyi]   Not evaluated. **Location:** I-435, exit 55B, In Ameristar Casino. 3200 N Ameristar Dr 64161. **Features:** Sports fans
can salivate over big burgers, pizza and frosty brews while keeping tabs on the action on 40 TV screens,
including a 56-foot video wall.

ARTHUR BRYANT'S BARBECUE   **Phone:** 816/231-1123
[fyi]   Not evaluated. **Location:** 1727 Brooklyn Ave 64127. **Features:** This eatery is a well-established, very casual
Kansas City barbecue joint featuring huge beef, ham, pork and turkey sandwiches.

ARTHUR BRYANT'S BARBEQUE   **Phone:** 816/414-7474
[fyi]   Not evaluated. **Location:** I-435, exit 55B, 1.2 mi e on SR 210, then just s; in Ameristar Hotel & Casino Kansas City.
3200 N Ameristar Dr 64161. **Features:** An offshoot of a Kansas City institution, this restaurant features slow-
smoked barbecue.

BUGATTI'S LITTLE ITALY CAFE   **Phone:** 816/414-7279
[fyi]   Not evaluated. **Location:** I-435, exit 55B, In Ameristar Casino. 3200 N Ameristar Dr 64161. **Features:** Traditional
and creative Italian cuisine is served in an upscale setting with white linen tablecloths. Patio seating is
another option.

CARMEN'S CAFE   **Phone:** 816/333-4048
[fyi]   Not evaluated. **Location:** Just s of Country Club Plaza. 6307 Brookside Plaza 64113. **Features:** Tapas, salads,
chicken, veal, seafood, steak and pasta are sure to please those seeking Italian-American cuisine.

DELILUX   **Phone:** 816/414-2596
[fyi]   Not evaluated. **Location:** I-435, exit 55B, In Ameristar Casino. 3200 N Ameristar Dr 64161. **Features:** Ideal for a
quick meal or snack, this deli features sandwiches, salads and pies.

THE FALCON DINER   **Phone:** 816/414-7170
[fyi]   Not evaluated. **Location:** I-435, exit 55B, In Ameristar Casino. 3200 N Ameristar Dr 64161. **Features:** The
American diner's menu focuses on classic American favorites, including Kansas City strip steak.

GRAND STREET CAFE   **Phone:** 816/561-8000
[fyi]   Not evaluated. **Location:** In Country Club Plaza. 4720 Grand Ave 64111. **Features:** Martini Monday and nightly
live jazz are draws to the glamorous dining room. Seasonal fare is prepared with flair.

GREAT PLAINS CATTLE COMPANY   **Phone:** 816/414-7420
[fyi]   Not evaluated. **Location:** I-435, exit 55B, In Ameristar Casino. 3200 N Ameristar Dr 64161. **Features:** The menu
lists chargrilled steaks, buffalo rib-eye and, for the adventuresome, fried rattlesnake.

HIBACHI, THE JAPANESE STEAK HOUSE   **Phone:** 816/753-0707
[fyi]   Not evaluated. **Location:** In Country Club Plaza. 4745 Wyandotte St 64112. **Features:** Full teppanyaki dinners
and meals prepared tableside are restaurant features.

PEARL'S OYSTER BAR   **Phone:** 816/414-2047
[fyi]   Not evaluated. **Location:** I-435, exit 55B, In Ameristar Casino. 3200 N Ameristar Dr 64161. **Features:** Raw bar
items, steamers and fresh fish are served in a casual setting overlooking the casino.

STARKER'S RESERVE, PUBLIC & PRIVATE DINING   **Phone:** 816/753-3565
[fyi]   Not evaluated. **Location:** In Country Club Plaza. 201 W 47th St. **Features:** International influences pepper
contemporary dishes, which are complemented by an extensive wine list.

The Kansas City Vicinity

BLUE SPRINGS pop. 48,080

―――― WHERE TO STAY ――――

HAMPTON INN BLUE SPRINGS   Phone: (816)220-3844

All Year   1P: $79-$130   2P: $89-$140

Small-scale Hotel   **Location:** I-70, exit 20, just s to South Outer Rd, then just w. 900 NW South Outer Rd 64015. **Fax:** 816/220-3461 **Facility:** 70 one-bedroom standard units, some with whirlpools. 3 stories, interior corridors. *Bath:* combo o shower only. **Parking:** on-site. **Terms:** [ECP] meal plan available, package plans. **Amenities:** high-spee Internet, voice mail, irons, hair dryers. **Pool(s):** heated indoor. **Leisure Activities:** whirlpool. **Guest Services:** wireless Internet **Business Services:** meeting rooms, PC. **Cards:** AX, DC, DS, MC, VI.

SOME UNITS

ASK 🐾 🍴 🌀 🏊 🏋 🎥 💻 / ✕ 🔒 📶

―――― WHERE TO DINE ――――

ZARDA BAR-B-Q   **Lunch:** $5-$10   **Dinner:** $7-$11   Phone: 816/229-9999

Barbecue   **Location:** I-70, exit 20 (SR 7), 0.7 mi sw. 214 N 7 Hwy 64014. **Hours:** 11 am-10 pm; to 9 pm, Fri & Sat-10 pm in winter. **Closed:** 11/22, 12/25. **Features:** Hickory-smoked ribs are slow-cooked over flames to be savored in the casual, comfortable atmosphere. Casual dress. **Parking:** on-site. **Cards:** AX, DC, DS, MC, VI.

INDEPENDENCE pop. 113,288   (See map and index starting on p. 444)

―――― WHERE TO STAY ――――

BEST WESTERN TRUMAN INN   *Book great rates at AAA.com*   Phone: (816)254-0100   **71**

AAA SAVE   5/25-9/30   1P: $59-$69   2P: $59-$69   XP: $8   F12

3/1-5/24 & 10/1-2/29   1P: $54-$64   2P: $54-$64   XP: $8   F12

Motel   **Location:** I-70, exit 12, just n on Noland Rd, then just w. 4048 S Lynn Court Dr 64055. **Fax:** 816/254-6796 **Facility:** 105 one-bedroom standard units. 2 stories (no elevator), exterior corridors. **Parking:** on-site **Terms:** pets ($8 fee, $30 deposit). **Amenities:** high-speed Internet, irons, hair dryers. **Pool(s):** outdoor **Guest Services:** wireless Internet. **Business Services:** meeting rooms. **Cards:** AX, DC, DS, MC, VI **Free Special Amenities:** early check-in/late check-out and room upgrade (subject to availability with advance reservations). *(See color ad below)*

SOME UNITS

S/D 🐾 🌊 🎥 💻 / ✕ 🔒 📶

FEE

COMFORT SUITES   *Book great rates at AAA.com*   Phone: (816)373-9880   **74**

AAA SAVE   All Year   1P: $64-$129   2P: $64-$129   F18

Location: I-70, exit 17, just s on Little Blue Pkwy, then just w. 19751 E Valley View Pkwy 64057. **Fax:** 816/373-9885 **Facility:** 88 units. 86 one-bedroom standard units. 2 stories, interior corridors. *Bath:* combo or shower only. **Parking:** on-site. **Terms:** cancellation fee imposed. **Amenities:** high-speed Internet Small-scale Hotel   voice mail, irons, hair dryers. **Pool(s):** small heated indoor. **Leisure Activities:** whirlpool, exercise room **Guest Services:** valet and coin laundry, wireless Internet. **Business Services:** meeting rooms, PC **Cards:** AX, CB, DC, DS, JC, MC, VI.

SOME UNITS

S/D 🍴 ♿M 🛗 🌊 🎥 🔒 📶 💻 / ✕ /

FAIRFIELD INN BY MARRIOTT   *Book great rates at AAA.com*   Phone: (816)795-1616   **69**

All Year   1P: $85-$105   2P: $90-$110   XP: $5   F18

Location: I-70, exit 15B (SR 291 N), just e on 39th St, just n on Arrowhead Ave behind Kohl's shopping center. 18700 E Small-scale Hotel   37th Terrace 64057. **Fax:** 816/795-1616. **Facility:** Smoke free premises. 63 one-bedroom standard units. 3 stories, interior corridors. *Bath:* combo or shower only. **Parking:** on-site. **Amenities:** high-speed Internet irons, hair dryers. **Pool(s):** heated indoor. **Leisure Activities:** whirlpool. **Guest Services:** valet laundry, wireless Internet **Cards:** AX, DC, DS, MC, VI.

SOME UNITS

ASK S/D ♿ 🌊 ✕ 🎥 💻 / 🔒 📶

(See map and index starting on p. 444)

HILTON GARDEN INN INDEPENDENCE   *Book great rates at AAA.com*   Phone: (816)350-3000   72

(AAA) [SAVE]   All Year   1P: $99-$149   2P: $99-$149   XP: $10   F18
Location: I-70, exit 17, 0.4 mi nw. 19677 E Jackson Dr 64057. Fax: 816/350-3535. **Facility:** 201 one-bedroom standard units. 6 stories, interior corridors. *Bath:* combo or shower only. **Parking:** on-site. **Terms:** [BP] & [CP] meal plans available. **Amenities:** video games (fee), high-speed Internet, dual phone lines, voice mail,
Small-scale Hotel   irons, hair dryers. **Dining:** 6-11 am, Sat & Sun 7:30-11 am. **Pool(s):** small heated indoor. **Leisure Activities:** whirlpool, exercise room. **Guest Services:** sundries, valet and coin laundry, area transportation-within 5 mi, wireless Internet. **Business Services:** conference facilities, business center. **Cards:** AX, CB, DC, DS, MC, VI.
Free Special Amenities: newspaper and high-speed Internet.
SOME UNITS

HOLIDAY INN EXPRESS HOTEL & SUITES   *Book great rates at AAA.com*   Phone: (816)795-8889   73

(AAA) [SAVE]   All Year   1P: $79-$169   2P: $79-$169
Location: I-70, exit 17 (Little Blue Pkwy), just e, then w on E Valley View Pkwy (Eastland Business Park). 19901 E Valley View Pkwy 64057. Fax: 816/795-1734. **Facility:** 90 one-bedroom standard units. 3 stories, interior corridors. *Bath:* combo or shower only. **Parking:** on-site. **Terms:** cancellation fee imposed. **Amenities:** high-
Small-scale Hotel   speed Internet, dual phone lines, voice mail, irons, hair dryers. **Pool(s):** small heated indoor. **Leisure Activities:** whirlpool, exercise room. **Guest Services:** valet and coin laundry, wireless Internet. **Business Services:** meeting rooms, PC. **Cards:** AX, CB, DC, DS, JC, MC, VI.
SOME UNITS

SUPER 8 MOTEL   *Book great rates at AAA.com*   Phone: (816)833-1888   70

(AAA) [SAVE]   5/25-9/30   1P: $49-$59   2P: $49-$59   XP: $8   F12
3/1-5/24 & 10/1-2/29   1P: $44-$54   2P: $44-$54   XP: $8   F12
Location: I-70, exit 12, just nw. 4032 S Lynn Court Dr 64055. Fax: 816/833-1888. **Facility:** 78 one-bedroom standard units, some with whirlpools. 3 stories (no elevator), interior corridors. **Parking:** on-site.
Small-scale Hotel   **Terms:** pets ($30 deposit, $8 extra charge, in smoking units). **Amenities:** high-speed Internet, safes (fee), hair dryers. **Pool(s):** heated outdoor. **Guest Services:** coin laundry, wireless Internet. **Cards:** AX, DC, DS, MC, VI. **Free Special Amenities:** expanded continental breakfast and local telephone calls.
SOME UNITS
FEE

WOODSTOCK INN BED & BREAKFAST   Phone: (816)833-2233   68

All Year [BP]   1P: $98-$219   2P: $98-$219   XP: $12
Location: I-435, exit 61, 3.1 mi e on 23rd St, then 0.8 mi n on Crysler (through traffic light). 1212 W Lexington Ave
Historic Bed   64050. **Facility:** This B&B is located in an updated, turn-of-the-20th-century building that once housed a doll
& Breakfast   and quilt factory; three units have fireplaces. 11 one-bedroom standard units, some with whirlpools. 2 stories (no elevator), interior corridors. *Bath:* combo or shower only. **Parking:** on-site. **Terms:** check-in 4 pm, 7 day cancellation notice-fee imposed, package plans. **Amenities:** high-speed Internet, voice mail, hair dryers. *Some:* CD players.
Guest Services: wireless Internet. **Cards:** AX, DS, MC, VI.

———— WHERE TO DINE ————

CARRABBA'S ITALIAN GRILL   Dinner: $7-$16   Phone: 816/795-9944

Location: I-70, exit 17, just s, then just w on E Valley View Pkwy; in Eastland Business Park. 19900 Valley View Pkwy
Italian   64057. **Hours:** 4 pm-10 pm, Fri-11 pm, Sat noon-11 pm, Sun noon-9 pm. **Features:** An open kitchen is in full view of guests. The dining room is decorated with Italian artifacts and has a fun and very loud atmosphere. Try the sirloin Marsala with sauteed spinach. The popular tiramisu is a tasty item for dessert. Casual dress; cocktails. **Parking:** on-site. **Cards:** AX, CB, DC, DS, JC, MC, VI.

HEREFORD HOUSE   Lunch: $7-$20   Dinner: $12-$38   Phone: 816/795-9200   54

Location: I-70, exit 17, 0.4 mi e. 19721 E Jackson Dr 64057. **Hours:** 11 am-10 pm, Fri-11 pm, Sat noon-11 pm,
Steak House   Sun 11:30 am-9 pm. Closed: 11/22, 12/25. **Reservations:** accepted. **Features:** An area favorite since 1957, the eatery builds its menu on Midwestern corn-fed beef, which is aged and hand-cut. Kansas City strip and prime rib are house specialties. Guests won't go home hungry. Casual dress; cocktails. **Parking:** on-site.
Cards: AX, DC, DS, MC, VI.

ON THE BORDER MEXICAN GRILL & CANTINA   Lunch: $6-$9   Dinner: $8-$14   Phone: 816/795-6198   55

Location: I-70, exit 17, just nw. 19921 E Jackson Dr 64057. **Hours:** 11 am-10 pm, Fri & Sat-11 pm. Closed:
11/22, 12/25. **Features:** Located in a quickly growing area, the restaurant features a menu offering a good
Southwestern   selection of your favorites, plus some contemporary twists. Casual dress; cocktails. **Parking:** on-site. **Cards:** AX, CB, DC, DS, JC, MC, VI.

OPHELIA'S RESTAURANT & INN   Lunch: $8-$15   Dinner: $13-$30   Phone: 816/461-4525   51

Location: I-435, exit 60, 4 mi e on SR 12 (Truman Rd); in Independence Square; in The Inn at Ophelia's. 201 N Main St
64050. **Hours:** 11 am-9 pm, Fri & Sat-10 pm, Sun-2:30 pm. Closed: 11/22, 12/25. **Reservations:** accepted.
American   **Features:** The restaurant caters to patrons whose palates demand creative cuisine. The atmosphere is casual and trendy. Live light jazz adds to the ambience on Friday and Saturday nights. Wine tastings are held Fridays from 6 to 8 pm. Dressy casual; cocktails. **Parking:** street. **Cards:** AX, MC, VI.

THE RHEINLAND RESTAURANT   Lunch: $7-$16   Dinner: $13-$16   Phone: 816/461-5383   50

Location: In Independence Square. 208 N Main St 64050. **Hours:** 11 am-9 pm, Sun noon-2:30 pm, Mon 11 am-
German   2:30 pm. Closed major holidays. **Reservations:** accepted. **Features:** Menu selections are delightful in the warm and cozy atmosphere. This spot is busy at lunchtime and on fair-weather days, but the wait is worthwhile. Casual dress; beer & wine only. **Parking:** street. **Cards:** AX, CB, DC, DS, JC, MC, VI.

(See map and index starting on p. 444)

ROMANO'S MACARONI GRILL   **Lunch:** $8-$20   **Dinner:** $8-$20   **Phone:** 816/795-661

Italian

Location: I-70, exit 17, just nw. 19821 E Jackson Dr 64057. **Hours:** 11 am-10 pm, Fri & Sat-11 pm. Closed 11/22, 12/25. **Features:** Romano's Macaroni Grill has a bright, open dining room with an upscale rustic decor and semi-casual atmosphere. This locally popular restaurant specializes in pizza, pasta, grilled mea and seafood. The fresh baked bread with olive oil is delicious. Casual dress; cocktails. **Parking:** on-site **Cards:** AX, CB, DC, DS, JC, MC, VI.

SMOKEHOUSE BAR-B-QUE   **Lunch:** $7-$22   **Dinner:** $8-$22   **Phone:** 816/795-5555   53

Barbecue

Location: I-70, exit 17, just nw; at Independence Commons Mall. 19000 E 39th St 64057. **Hours:** 11 am-9:30 pm Sun-9 pm. Closed: 4/8, 11/22, 12/25. **Features:** The casual dining room is decorated traditionally. Patron can nosh on tasty barbecue selections, including sandwiches and dinners of fish, ribs, chicken, beef, pork ham, turkey and sausage. Casual dress; cocktails. **Parking:** on-site. **Cards:** AX, DC, DS, MC, VI.

V'S ITALIANO RISTORANTE   **Lunch:** $7-$13   **Dinner:** $9-$26   **Phone:** 816/353-1241   52

Italian

Location: I-70, exit 11 (US 40), 0.3 mi n. 10819 E Hwy 40 64055. **Hours:** 11 am-9:30 pm, Fri-10:30 pm, Sat 11:3 am-10:30 pm, Sun 10 am-8 pm. Closed major holidays. **Reservations:** suggested. **Features:** Family owne and operated since 1964, the restaurant prepares specialties from Northern and Southern Italy and nurture a cozy, quiet ambience. Casual dress; cocktails. **Parking:** on-site. **Cards:** AX, DC, DS, MC, VI.

KEARNEY pop. 5,472   (See map and index starting on p. 444)

——— **WHERE TO STAY** ———

BEST WESTERN KEARNEY INN   **Phone:** (816)628-5000   56

5/1-8/31	1P: $70	2P: $75	XP: $5	F17
9/1-12/31	1P: $65	2P: $65	XP: $5	F17
3/1-4/30 & 1/1-2/29	1P: $60	2P: $65	XP: $5	F17

Small-scale Hotel

Location: I-35, exit 26, just w. 601 Centerville Ave 64060 (PO Box 1210). Fax: 816/628-6482. **Facility:** 40 one bedroom standard units, some with whirlpools. 2 stories (no elevator), interior corridors. *Bath:* combo or shower only. **Parking:** on-site. **Terms:** 5 day cancellation notice, [CP] meal plan available, package plans. **Amenities:** high-speed Internet, voice mail irons, hair dryers. *Some:* DVD players. **Pool(s):** small heated indoor, small heated indoor/outdoor. **Leisure Activities:** whirlpool **Guest Services:** wireless Internet. **Business Services:** meeting rooms, PC. **Cards:** AX, DC, DS, MC, VI.

SOME UNITS

KEARNEY SUPER 8 MOTEL   *Book at AAA.com*   **Phone:** (816)628-6800   55

All Year [ECP]   1P: $60-$110   2P: $60-$110   XP: $5   F15

Small-scale Hotel

Location: I-35, exit 26, just e on SR 92, then just n. 210 Platte Clay Way 64060. Fax: 816/628-6800. **Facility:** 4 one-bedroom standard units, some with whirlpools. 2 stories (no elevator), interior corridors. **Parking:** on-site. **Terms:** 5 day cancellation notice, pets (dogs only, $10 extra charge). **Amenities:** high-speed Internet hair dryers. **Cards:** AX, DC, DS, MC, VI.

SOME UNITS

——— **WHERE TO DINE** ———

OUTLAW'S BARBEQUE & SALOON   **Lunch:** $5-$10   **Dinner:** $6-$13   **Phone:** 816/628-6500

American

Location: Downtown. 129 E Washington St 64060. **Hours:** 11 am-9 pm, Fri & Sat-10 pm. Closed major holidays also Sun. **Features:** Baby back ribs, chicken, steaks, burgers and sandwiches are just a few of the items served in the comfortable setting, which is appropriate for all occasions. Casual dress; cocktails. **Parking:** street. **Cards:** AX, DS, MC, VI.

LEE'S SUMMIT pop. 70,700   (See map and index starting on p. 444)

——— **WHERE TO STAY** ———

COMFORT INN BY CHOICE HOTELS   *Book great rates at AAA.com*   **Phone:** (816)524-8181   99

All Year [ECP]   1P: $80-$100   2P: $85-$105   XP: $5   F18

Small-scale Hotel

Location: Jct US 50 and SR 291 N. 607 SE Oldham Pkwy 64081. Fax: 816/524-8181. **Facility:** 52 one-bedroom standard units. 2 stories (no elevator), interior corridors. **Parking:** on-site, winter plug-ins. **Terms:** pets ($25 deposit). **Amenities:** high-speed Internet, irons, hair dryers. **Pool(s):** heated indoor. **Leisure Activities:** whirlpool. **Guest Services:** wireless Internet. **Cards:** AX, DC, DS, MC, VI.

SOME UNITS

FAIRFIELD INN BY MARRIOTT   *Book great rates at AAA.com*   **Phone:** (816)524-7572   97

All Year   1P: $80-$100   2P: $85-$105   XP: $5   F18

Small-scale Hotel

Location: I-470, exit 10B, 0.5 mi s on SR 291. 1301 NE Windsor Dr 64086. Fax: 816/524-7572. **Facility:** Smoke free premises. 57 one-bedroom standard units. 3 stories, interior corridors. *Bath:* combo or shower only. **Parking:** on-site. **Amenities:** high-speed Internet, irons, hair dryers. **Pool(s):** heated indoor. **Leisure Activities:** whirlpool. **Guest Services:** valet laundry, wireless Internet. **Cards:** AX, DC, DS, MC, VI.

SOME UNITS

(See map and index starting on p. 444)

AMPTON INN *Book great rates at AAA.com* Phone: 816/347-8600 **96**

Property failed to provide current rates

Small-scale Hotel **Location:** I-470, exit 9, just se. 1751 NE Douglas St 64086. Fax: 816/347-8755. **Facility:** 109 one-bedroom standard units, some with whirlpools. 3 stories, interior corridors. *Bath:* combo or shower only. **Parking:** on-site. **Amenities:** video games (fee), high-speed Internet, dual phone lines, voice mail, irons, hair dryers. **ool(s):** small heated indoor. **Leisure Activities:** whirlpool, exercise room. **Guest Services:** valet and coin laundry, wireless nternet. **Business Services:** meeting rooms, business center. *(See color ad p 456)*

SOME UNITS

LEE'S SUMMIT HOLIDAY INN EXPRESS *Book great rates at AAA.com* Phone: (816)795-6400 **95**

(AAA) (SAVE) All Year 1P: $90 2P: $90

Small-scale Hotel **Location:** I-470, exit 14, just e on Bowlin Rd, then 0.4 mi s. 4825 NE Lakewood Way 64064. Fax: 816/795-8335. **Facility:** 75 one-bedroom standard units, some with whirlpools. 3 stories, interior corridors. *Bath:* combo or shower only. **Parking:** on-site. **Terms:** pets ($25 fee). **Amenities:** high-speed Internet, dual phone lines, voice mail, irons, hair dryers. **Pool(s):** small heated indoor. **Leisure Activities:** whirlpool, exercise room. **Guest Services:** valet laundry, wireless Internet. **Business Services:** meeting rooms. **Cards:** AX, CB, DC, DS, JC, MC, VI. **Free Special Amenities: continental breakfast and local telephone calls.**

SOME UNITS

SUPER 8 MOTEL *Book at AAA.com* Phone: 816/524-8863 **98**

All Year [CP] 1P: $59-$80 2P: $65-$90 XP: $5 F12

Small-scale Hotel **Location:** Jct US 50 and SR 291 (north exit), just s on SR 291, e on Outler Rd, then 0.5 mi on frontage road. 963 SE Oldham Pkwy 64081. Fax: 816/524-8956. **Facility:** 61 units. 60 one-bedroom standard units, some with whirlpools. 1 one-bedroom suite with whirlpool. 3 stories, interior corridors. *Bath:* combo or shower only. **Parking:** on-site. **Amenities:** high-speed Internet, hair dryers. **Pool(s):** heated indoor. **Leisure Activities:** whirlpool, limited exercise equipment. **Guest Services:** wireless Internet. **Cards:** AX, DC, DS, MC, VI.

SOME UNITS

——— **WHERE TO DINE** ———

CACTUS GRILL Lunch: $7-$8 Dinner: $8-$12 Phone: 816/246-9555 **69**

Southwestern **Location:** I-470, exit 9, just se. 1667 NE Douglas Rd 64086. **Hours:** 11 am-10 pm, Fri & Sat-11 pm. Closed: 11/22, 12/25. **Features:** New and traditional selections are listed on the inventive menu. Contemporary decor gives the dining room a lively feel. Casual dress; cocktails. **Parking:** on-site. **Cards:** AX, CB, DC, DS, JC, MC, VI.

EVERETT'S RESTAURANT Lunch: $8-$14 Dinner: $13-$29 Phone: 816/795-5553 **68**

American **Location:** I-470, exit 14, just e on Bowlin Rd, then 0.4 mi s. 4835 NE Lakewood Way 64064. **Hours:** 11 am-10 pm, Fri & Sat-11 pm. Closed: 7/4, 11/22, 12/25. **Reservations:** accepted. **Features:** Baby back ribs and bourbon apple pork chops are two signature dishes on the varied menu. The dining room is appointed in traditional decor. Casual dress; cocktails. **Parking:** on-site. **Cards:** AX, CB, DC, DS, JC, MC, VI.

LIBERTY pop. 26,232 (See map and index starting on p. 444)

——— **WHERE TO STAY** ———

FAIRFIELD INN KANSAS CITY-LIBERTY *Book great rates at AAA.com* Phone: (816)792-4000 **61**

(AAA) (SAVE) 5/25-9/3 1P: $94-$150 2P: $99-$160 XP: $5 F17
3/1-5/24 & 9/4-2/29 1P: $75-$110 2P: $80-$120 XP: $5 F17

Small-scale Hotel **Location:** I-35, exit 16 (SR 152), just w, then s. 8101 N Church Rd 64158. Fax: 816/792-0764. **Facility:** Smoke free premises. 99 one-bedroom standard units. 2 stories (no elevator), interior corridors. **Parking:** on-site. **Terms:** [ECP] meal plan available, pets ($75 deposit). **Amenities:** high-speed Internet, irons, hair dryers. **Pool(s):** heated indoor. **Leisure Activities:** whirlpool. *Fee:* game room. **Guest Services:** valet laundry, airport transportation (fee)-Kansas City International Airport. **Business Services:** meeting rooms, business center. **Cards:** AX, CB, DC, DS, JC, MC, VI. **Free Special Amenities: expanded continental breakfast and local telephone calls.**

SOME UNITS

HAMPTON INN-KANSAS CITY/LIBERTY *Book great rates at AAA.com* Phone: (816)415-9600 **59**

6/1-8/31 [ECP] 1P: $99-$119 2P: $109-$129
3/1-5/31 & 9/1-2/29 [ECP] 1P: $89-$119 2P: $99-$129

Small-scale Hotel **Location:** I-35, exit 16 (SR 152), just nw. 8551 N Church Rd 57351. Fax: 816/415-3232. **Facility:** 122 one-bedroom standard units, some with whirlpools. 4 stories, interior corridors. *Bath:* combo or shower only. **Parking:** on-site. **Terms:** package plans. **Amenities:** video games (fee), high-speed Internet, dual phone lines, voice mail, irons, hair dryers. **Pool(s):** small heated indoor. **Leisure Activities:** whirlpool, exercise room. **Guest Services:** valet and coin laundry, wireless Internet. **Business Services:** meeting rooms, business center. **Cards:** AX, CB, DC, DS, JC, MC, VI. *(See color ad p 456)*

SOME UNITS

(See map and index starting on p. 444)

HOLIDAY INN EXPRESS   *Book at AAA.com*   **Phone:** (816)781-5555   6
▼▼▼ ▼▼▼   4/2-8/31   1P: $105   2P: $105
            3/1-4/1 & 9/1-2/29   1P: $81   2P: $81
Small-scale Hotel **Location:** I-35, exit 16 (SR 152), just w to N Church Rd, then just s. 8230 N Church Rd 64158. **Fax:** 816/781-5152. **Facility:** 71 one-bedroom standard units, some with whirlpools. 3 stories, interior corridors. **Bath:** combo or shower only. **Parking:** on-site. **Terms:** cancellation fee imposed, [ECP] meal plan available. **Amenities:** high-speed Internet, dual phone lines, voice mail, irons, hair dryers. **Pool(s):** small heated indoor. **Leisure Activities:** exercise room. **Guest Services:** valet laundry, wireless Internet. **Business Services:** meeting rooms, business center. **Cards:** AX, CB, DC, DS, MC, VI.

SOME UNITS

(A$K) (ii→) (&) (🖙) (📷) (🖥) (📺) (🖥) / (✕) /

─────── **WHERE TO DINE** ───────

HARDWARE CAFE   **Lunch:** $6-$9   **Dinner:** $7-$15   **Phone:** 816/792-3500   4
▼▼▼ ▼▼▼   **Location:** I-35, exit 16 (SR 152), 2 mi e; on the square. 5 E Kansas Ave 64068. **Hours:** 11 am-9 pm, Fri & Sat-1
American   pm, Sun-2 pm. Closed major holidays. **Features:** Located in a hardware store dating back to 1888, this restaurant has a variety of dessert and homemade pies that are well-known to area residents. Diners enjoy the home-style cooking, casual dining, soda fountain, gift shop and many hardware artifacts. Casual dress; beer & wine only. **Parking:** street. **Cards:** AX, DS, MC, VI.

(🖙)

THE STACK   **Lunch:** $7-$15   **Dinner:** $7-$46   **Phone:** 816/781-7822   4
▼▼▼ ▼▼▼   **Location:** I-35, exit 16 (SR 152), just w to N Church Rd. 8250 N Church Rd 64158. **Hours:** 11 am-9 pm, Fri & Sat-
American   10 pm, Sun noon-9 pm. Closed: 11/22, 12/25. **Reservations:** accepted. **Features:** The restaurant offers what the Kansas City area does best: great barbecue in a casual setting. Patrons can order from all the favorites, as well as such sides as the must-try cheesy corn. Casual dress; cocktails. **Parking:** on-site.
Cards: AX, MC, VI.

(&M) (Y) (🖙)

NORTH KANSAS CITY pop. 4,714   (See map and index starting on p. 444)

─────── **WHERE TO STAY** ───────

LA QUINTA INN & SUITES KANSAS CITY NORTH   *Book great rates at AAA.com*   **Phone:** (816)221-1200   6
▼▼▼ ▼▼▼   5/25-2/29 [CP]   1P: $84-$114   2P: $90-$120   XP: $6   F1
            3/1-5/24 [CP]   1P: $82-$112   2P: $88-$118   XP: $6   F1
Small-scale Hotel **Location:** I-29/35, exit 6A, just e on SR 210, then just n. 2214 Taney Rd 64116. **Fax:** 816/471-6207. **Facility:** 93 units. 90 one-bedroom standard units. 3 one-bedroom suites ($122-$160). 3 stories, interior corridors. **Parking:** on-site. **Amenities:** video games (fee), voice mail, irons, hair dryers. *Some:* high-speed Internet. **Guest Services:** wireless Internet. **Business Services:** fax. **Cards:** AX, CB, DC, DS, MC, VI.

SOME UNITS

(A$K) (🐾) (🏊) (📷) (🖥) / (✕) (🖥)

QUALITY INN & SUITES   *Book great rates at AAA.com*   **Phone:** 816/218-1100   6
▼▼▼ ▼▼▼   All Year [CP]   1P: $70-$109   2P: $70-$109   XP: $5   F1
Small-scale Hotel **Location:** I-29/35, exit 6B, 0.3 mi w on Armour Rd, then just s. 1995 Macon St 64116. **Fax:** 816/218-1110. **Facility:** 74 one-bedroom standard units, some with whirlpools. 3 stories, interior corridors. **Bath:** combo or shower only. **Parking:** on-site. **Terms:** cancellation fee imposed. **Amenities:** high-speed Internet, voice mail, irons, hair dryers. **Pool(s):** small heated indoor. **Leisure Activities:** limited exercise equipment. **Guest Services:** coin laundry. **Business Services:** meeting rooms, PC. **Cards:** AX, DC, DS, MC, VI.

SOME UNITS

(A$K) (S🅳) (ii→) (&) (🖙) (📷) (🖥) / (✕) (🖥) (📺)

─────── *The following lodging was either not evaluated or did not* ───────
meet AAA rating requirements but is listed for your information only.

HARRAH'S NORTH KANSAS CITY CASINO AND
   HOTEL   **Phone:** 816/472-7777
   (fyi)   Did not meet all AAA rating requirements for some property operations at time of last evaluation on 07/24/2006. **Location:** I-29/35, exit 6A, 1.4 mi e on SR 210, then just s on Chouteau Thrwy. One Riverboat Dr 64116. **Facilities,** services, and decor characterize a mid-range property.
Large-scale Hotel

─────── **WHERE TO DINE** ───────

THE BUFFET   **Lunch:** $9   **Dinner:** $13-$18   **Phone:** 816/472-7777   44
♦♦ ♦♦   **Location:** I-29/35, exit 6A, 1.4 mi e on SR 210, then just s on Chouteau Thrwy; in Harrah's North Kansas City Casino. One Riverboat Dr 64116. **Hours:** 7-10:30 am, 11-3 & 4-9:30 pm, Fri & Sat-10:30 pm. **Features:** Diners can make selections from buffet stations titled Heritage, Center Cut, KV's BBQ Pit, Wok & Roll, Tour of Italy and American. It's worth sampling some of each, provided there's some room left at the end for a visit to The Sweet Spot. **Parking:** on-site. **Cards:** AX, CB, DC, DS, JC, MC, VI.

(&)

CHAPPELL'S RESTAURANT & SPORTS MUSEUM   **Lunch:** $7-$10 **Dinner:** $9-$21 **Phone:** 816/421-0002   4
▼▼▼ ▼▼▼   **Location:** I-29, exit 6B, 0.7 mi w. 323 Armour Rd 64116. **Hours:** 11 am-11 pm. Closed major holidays; also for dinner 12/24, 12/31 & Sun. **Reservations:** accepted. **Features:** One of the country's most famous sports bars, this neighborhood establishment is filled with museum-quality memoribilia. Menu features steaks, sandwiches, lite selections, prime rib and Saturday night spiced shrimp. Casual dress; cocktails. **Parking:** street. **Cards:** AX, DC, DS, MC, VI.

(Y) (🖙)

(See map and index starting on p. 444)

KELSO'S
American

Lunch: $7-$15   Dinner: $8-$17   Phone: 816/221-8899   45
Location: I-29, exit 6B, 0.7 mi w. 300 Armour Rd 64116. **Hours:** 11 am-10 pm, Fri & Sat-midnight, Sun noon-6 pm. Closed major holidays. **Features:** A touch of class and sophistication can be enjoyed along with great pizza at this casual eatery in the revitalized Northtown area. Casual dress; cocktails. **Parking:** street. **Cards:** AX, DC, DS, MC, VI.

PAUL & JACK'S TAVERN
American

Lunch: $6-$10   Dinner: $8-$20   Phone: 816/221-9866   47
Location: I-29, exit 6B, 1 mi sw. 1808 Clay 64116. **Hours:** 10:30 am-9:30 pm, Sun-5 pm. Closed: Sun. **Reservations:** accepted. **Features:** The eatery, popular with the locals, presents a small-town atmosphere with ample pub fare selections. Casual dress; cocktails. **Parking:** street. **Cards:** AX, CB, DC, DS, JC, MC, VI.

The following restaurants have not been evaluated by AAA but are listed for your information only.

THE RANGE
[fyi]

Phone: 816/889-7159
Not evaluated. **Location:** I-29/35, exit 6A, in Harrah's North Kansas City Casino. One Riverboat Dr 64116. **Features:** The steakhouse with a Southwestern setting features grilled-to-order steaks, prime rib, seafood and poultry entrees.

TASTY THAI
[fyi]

Phone: 816/584-8801
Not evaluated. **Location:** In K-Mart Shopping Center. 7104 NW Prairie Rd 64116. **Features:** Food flavored with peppers, basil, lemongrass and coconut milk is prepared in generous portions. Among selections are sesame chicken, curry dishes and fragrant soups.

OAK GROVE (JACKSON COUNTY) pop. 5,535

─── **WHERE TO STAY** ───

ECONO LODGE
SAVE
Motel

Book great rates at AAA.com

Phone: (816)690-3681
All Year   1P: $45-$79   2P: $50-$89   XP: $10   F
Location: I-70, exit 28, just s on Broadway St, just e on SE 4th St, then just n. 410 SE 1st St 64075. **Fax:** 816/690-6399. **Facility:** 39 one-bedroom standard units. 2 stories (no elevator), exterior corridors. **Parking:** on-site. **Terms:** [CP] meal plan available, package plans, pets ($10 extra charge). **Amenities:** high-speed Internet, hair dryers. **Guest Services:** wireless Internet. **Cards:** AX, CB, DC, DS, MC, VI. **Free Special Amenities:** continental breakfast and high-speed Internet.

SOME UNITS

PLATTE CITY pop. 3,866   (See map and index starting on p. 444)

─── **WHERE TO DINE** ───

SHIELDS MANOR BISTRO
American

Dinner: $22-$42   Phone: 816/858-5557   37
Location: In historic downtown. 121 Main St 64079. **Hours:** 5:30 pm-close. Closed: Sun-Wed. **Reservations:** required. **Features:** The limited but frequently changing menu centers on steak, seafood, poultry, pasta and fusion cuisine. Weekend nights are suited to romantic candlelight dinners, and patio seating is available in season. Dressy casual; beer & wine only. **Parking:** street. **Cards:** AX, DS, MC, VI.

RIVERSIDE pop. 2,979

─── **WHERE TO DINE** ───

The following restaurant has not been evaluated by AAA but is listed for your information only.

CORNER CAFE
[fyi]

Phone: 816/741-2570
Not evaluated. **Location:** Jct SR 9. 4541 NW Gateway 64150. **Features:** This popular spot and convenient location offers many homemade selections, giving comfort food extra points.

WESTON pop. 1,631

─── **WHERE TO DINE** ───

AMERICA BOWMAN RESTAURANT
Irish

Lunch: $8-$15   Dinner: $8-$15   Phone: 816/640-5235
Location: Center. 500 Welt 64098. **Hours:** 11:30 am-3 pm, Fri-Sun to 9 pm. Closed: 11/22, 12/25; also Mon. **Reservations:** accepted. **Features:** Outfitted with rustic decor that recalls an old Irish pub setting, the restaurant provides a cozy and quaint dining experience. Excellent stew, soups, sandwiches, salads and appetizers are offered. A labyrinth of corridors and tunnels connects six dining rooms, including a three-level lounge and microbrewery 55 feet underground. Casual dress; cocktails. **Parking:** on-site. **Cards:** DS, MC, VI.

Nearby Kansas

BONNER SPRINGS pop. 6,768

------- WHERE TO STAY -------

HOLIDAY INN EXPRESS *Book at AAA.com*
Property failed to provide current rates
Phone: 913/721-5300

▼▼▼
Small-scale Hotel

Location: I-70, exit 224. 13031 Ridge Ave 66012. Fax: 913/721-5445. **Facility:** 63 one-bedroom standard units, some with whirlpools. 3 stories, interior corridors. *Bath:* combo or shower only. **Parking:** on-site. **Amenities:** dual phone lines, voice mail, irons, hair dryers. **Pool(s):** small heated indoor. **Leisure Activities:** whirlpool, exercise room. **Guest Services:** valet laundry, wireless Internet.

SOME UNITS

GARDNER pop. 9,396

------- WHERE TO STAY -------

SUPER 8 MOTEL *Book at AAA.com*
Phone: (913)856-8887

◆◆
Small-scale Hotel

All Year [CP]   1P: $60-$120   2P: $65-$120   XP: $5   F16
Location: I-35, exit 210. 2001 E Santa Fe 66030. Fax: 913/856-8645. **Facility:** 56 one-bedroom standard units, some with whirlpools. 2 stories (no elevator), interior corridors. **Parking:** on-site. **Terms:** 3 day cancellation notice, pets ($10 extra charge). **Amenities:** safes (fee). **Guest Services:** wireless Internet. **Business Services:** meeting rooms. **Cards:** AX, DS, MC, VI.

SOME UNITS
FEE

KANSAS CITY pop. 146,866 (See map and index starting on p. 444)

------- WHERE TO STAY -------

BEST WESTERN INN AND CONFERENCE CENTER *Book great rates at AAA.com* **Phone: (913)677-3060** **51**

CAAD SAVE
▼▼▼
Small-scale Hotel

All Year [ECP]   1P: $69-$79   2P: $79-$89   XP: $10   F18
Location: I-35, exit 234 (7th St), just s. 501 Southwest Blvd 66103. Fax: 913/677-7065. **Facility:** 113 one-bedroom standard units, some with whirlpools. 2 stories (no elevator), interior corridors. **Terms:** [CP] meal plan available, package plans, pets (must be attended). **Amenities:** high-speed Internet, voice mail, irons, hair dryers. *Some:* dual phone lines. **Pool(s):** small heated outdoor. **Leisure Activities:** whirlpool, exercise room. **Guest Services:** valet and coin laundry, area transportation-within 5 mi, wireless Internet. **Business Services:** meeting rooms, PC. **Cards:** AX, CB, DC, DS, JC, MC, VI. **Free Special Amenities: continental breakfast and high-speed Internet.**

SOME UNITS

CHATEAU AVALON *Book great rates at AAA.com* **Phone: (913)596-6000** **48**

CAAD SAVE
◆◆◆
Small-scale Hotel

All Year [BP]   1P: $129-$549   2P: $129-$549
Location: I-435, exit 13B (State Ave), just w to Village West Pkwy, then 0.4 mi sw. 701 Village West Pkwy 66111. Fax: 913/596-0500. **Facility:** Smoke free premises. 62 one-bedroom suites with whirlpools. 3 stories, interior corridors. *Bath:* combo or shower only. **Parking:** on-site. **Terms:** check-in 4 pm, 3 day cancellation notice-fee imposed, package plans. **Amenities:** video library, DVD players, CD players, high-speed Internet, voice mail. **Leisure Activities:** *Fee:* massage. **Guest Services:** gift shop. **Business Services:** meeting rooms. **Cards:** AX, CB, DC, DS, JC, MC, VI. **Free Special Amenities: full breakfast and high-speed Internet.**
(See color ad p 475)

COMFORT INN *Book great rates at AAA.com* **Phone: (913)299-5555** **50**

CAAD SAVE
▼▼▼
Small-scale Hotel

All Year [ECP]   1P: $71-$250   2P: $76-$250   XP: $6   F17
Location: I-70, exit 414 (78th St), just s. 234 N 78th St 66112. Fax: 913/299-5505. **Facility:** 45 one-bedroom standard units, some with whirlpools. 3 stories, interior corridors. *Bath:* combo or shower only. **Parking:** on-site. **Terms:** 7 day cancellation notice. **Amenities:** irons, hair dryers. **Pool(s):** small heated indoor. **Leisure Activities:** whirlpool, limited exercise equipment. **Guest Services:** valet laundry, wireless Internet. **Cards:** AX, CB, DC, DS, JC, MC, VI. **Free Special Amenities: expanded continental breakfast and newspaper.** *(See color ad p 475)*

SOME UNITS

GREAT WOLF LODGE-KANSAS CITY *Book great rates at AAA.com* **Phone: (913)299-7001** **46**

CAAD SAVE
◆◆◆◆
Small-scale Hotel

All Year   1P: $279-$399   2P: $279-$399   XP: $15
Location: I-435, exit 13B (State Ave). 10401 Cabela Dr 66111. Fax: 913/299-7002. **Facility:** Smoke free premises. 281 units. 251 one-bedroom standard units, some with whirlpools. 30 one-bedroom suites. 4 stories, interior corridors. *Bath:* combo or shower only. **Parking:** on-site. **Terms:** check-in 4 pm, 3 day cancellation notice-fee imposed. **Amenities:** video games, voice mail, irons, hair dryers. **Dining:** 6 am-10 pm, cocktails. **Pool(s):** outdoor, heated indoor, 2 wading. **Leisure Activities:** whirlpools, indoor waterpark, exercise room, spa, game room. **Guest Services:** gift shop, coin laundry, wireless Internet. **Business Services:** meeting rooms. **Cards:** AX, DS, MC, VI. **Free Special Amenities: local telephone calls.** *(See color ad p 475)*

SOME UNITS

(See map and index starting on p. 444)

HAMPTON INN VILLAGE WEST   *Book great rates at AAA.com*   Phone: 913/328-1400   **45**
Property failed to provide current rates
Location: I-435, exit 13B (State Ave), just w. 1400 Village W Pkwy 66111. Fax: 913/328-1116. **Facility:** 76 units. 74 one-bedroom standard units. 2 one-bedroom suites, some with whirlpools. 3 stories, interior corridors. *Bath:* combo or shower only. **Parking:** on-site. **Amenities:** high-speed Internet, dual phone lines, voice mail, irons, hair dryers. *Some:* video games. **Pool(s):** heated indoor. **Leisure Activities:** exercise room. **Guest Services:** valet and coin laundry, wireless Internet.
Large-scale Hotel

SOME UNITS

HILTON GARDEN INN KANSAS CITY KANSAS   *Book great rates at AAA.com*   Phone: (913)342-7900   **47**
All Year   1P: $79-$139   2P: $79-$139   XP: $10   F18
Location: I-70, exit 423A (Minnesota Ave/5th St) eastbound; exit Minnesota Ave westbound. 520 Minnesota Ave 66101. Fax: 913/342-7901. **Facility:** 147 units. 146 one-bedroom standard units. 1 one-bedroom suite. 6 stories, interior corridors. *Bath:* combo or shower only. **Parking:** on-site. **Amenities:** video games, high-speed Internet, dual phone lines, voice mail, irons, hair dryers. **Pool(s):** small heated indoor. **Leisure Activities:** whirlpool, exercise room. **Guest Services:** valet and coin laundry. **Business Services:** conference facilities, business center. **Cards:** AX, CB, DC, DS, MC, VI.
Large-scale Hotel

SOME UNITS

MICROTEL INN & SUITES AT THE SPEEDWAY   *Book at AAA.com*   Phone: 913/334-3028   **49**
Property failed to provide current rates
Location: I-70, exit 414 (78th St N), just ne. 7721 Elizabeth St 66112. Fax: 913/334-5983. **Facility:** 78 one-bedroom standard units, some with whirlpools. 3 stories, interior corridors. *Bath:* combo or shower only. **Parking:** on-site. **Amenities:** *Some:* irons, hair dryers. **Pool(s):** small heated indoor. **Leisure Activities:** whirlpool, exercise room. **Guest Services:** coin laundry, wireless Internet. **Business Services:** meeting rooms.
Small-scale Hotel

SOME UNITS

SUN INN   Phone: 913/236-6880   **52**
All Year   1P: $66   2P: $70   XP: $5   F
Location: I-35, exit 234 (7th St), 1.3 mi s. Located opposite the Kansas University Medical Center. 3930 Rainbow Blvd 66103. Fax: 913/236-6880. **Facility:** 82 units. 81 one-bedroom standard units. 1 one-bedroom suite. 2 stories (no elevator), interior corridors. **Parking:** on-site. **Terms:** cancellation fee imposed, [CP] meal plan available, package plans. **Amenities:** hair dryers. **Pool(s):** small outdoor. **Guest Services:** coin laundry, area transportation. **Cards:** AX, DC, DS, MC, VI.
Small-scale Hotel

SOME UNITS

─────── **WHERE TO DINE** ───────

DRAGON INN   **Lunch:** $6   **Dinner:** $8-$11   Phone: 913/381-1688   **34**
Location: I-435, exit 77 (Roe Ave), 3.5 mi n, then just e; across from Corinth Square. 3975 W 83rd St 66208. **Hours:** 11 am-9:30 pm, Fri & Sat-10:40 pm. **Closed:** 7/4, 11/22, 12/25. **Features:** The Dragon Inn has a large menu selection that includes Mandarin and Szechuan selections. Its Oriental decor and friendly atmosphere make it intimate and cozy, and the pleasant eatery remains quite popular with local residents. Casual dress; cocktails. **Parking:** on-site. **Cards:** DS, MC, VI.
Chinese

FAMOUS DAVE'S   **Lunch:** $6-$9   **Dinner:** $8-$19   Phone: 913/334-8646
Location: I-435, exit 13B (State Ave). 1320 Village West Pkwy 66111. **Hours:** 11 am-10 pm, Fri & Sat-11 pm. **Closed:** 11/22, 12/25. **Features:** Famous for its legendary pit barbecue, the fun and casual northwoods lodge-style eatery celebrates the many variations of barbecue styles, from Texas beef brisket and Georgian chopped pork to country roast chicken and pit barbecue ribs. Casual dress; cocktails. **Parking:** on-site. **Cards:** AX, DS, MC, VI.
American

TAQUERIA MEXICO   **Lunch:** $5-$18   **Dinner:** $5-$18   Phone: 913/722-9200   **33**
Location: I-35, exit 234 (7th St), just s. 3300 Rainbow Blvd 66103. **Hours:** 9 am-10 pm. **Features:** The restaurant offers a very large selection of Mexican cuisine. The wide variety of choices of fresh vegetable and meat ingredients include guacamole, bell peppers, many cheeses, marinated chicken and beef strips, sausages and eggs on the weekend. Large portions are common. Casual dress; cocktails. **Parking:** on-site. **Cards:** AX, DS, MC, VI.
Mexican

LEAWOOD pop. 27,656   (See map and index starting on p. 444)

─────── **WHERE TO DINE** ───────

THE BRISTOL SEAFOOD GRILL   **Lunch:** $8-$15   **Dinner:** $15-$35   Phone: 913/663-5777   **100**
Location: I-435, exit 77B, 1.3 mi s on Nall Ave; northeast corner of Nall Ave and 119th St; in Town Center Plaza. 5400 W 119th St 66209. **Hours:** 11 am-10 pm, Fri & Sat-11 pm, Sun 10 am-2 & 4:30-9:30 pm. **Closed:** 12/25. **Reservations:** suggested. **Features:** The restaurant has a lively atmosphere and stylish decor that includes an impressive stained-glass dome. Excellent entrees display creative preparation and presentation methods. They offer flavorful seafood stew, soft-shell crab and mesquite-grilled fish. Casual dress; cocktails. **Parking:** on-site. **Cards:** AX, CB, DC, DS, MC, VI.
Seafood

HAN SHIN JAPANESE STEAK HOUSE   **Lunch:** $6-$21   **Dinner:** $15-$40   Phone: (913)327-1118   **97**
Location: I-435, exit 77A (Roe Ave), 1 mi s, then just sw; in Towne Center Plaza. 4817 W 117th St 66211. **Hours:** 11 am-9:30 pm, Fri & Sat-11 pm, Sun noon-9:30 pm. **Closed:** 11/22, 12/25. **Features:** Small groups of people sit around a large, hot grill where the chef makes his magic and puts on a good show using sharp knives. Daily lunch and dinner specials are among offerings. Casual dress; cocktails. **Cards:** AX, DC, DS, MC, VI.
Japanese

(See map and index starting on p. 444)

HEREFORD HOUSE   **Lunch:** $8-$13   **Dinner:** $12-$25   **Phone:** 913/327-0800   96

American

Location: I-435, exit 77B (Nall Ave), 0.8 mi s, then 0.3 on 117th St; in Town Center Plaza. 5001 Town Center Dr 66211. **Hours:** 11 am-10 pm, Fri-11 pm, Sat 4 pm-11 pm, Sun 4 pm-9 pm. Closed major holidays. **Reservations:** accepted. **Features:** A flair of elegance dresses up the rustic decor at the Hereford House. This restaurant specializes in steak and prime rib entrees as well as a variety of seafood and combination dinners. Wine bottles and Southwestern memorabilia are displayed throughout. Casual dress; cocktails. **Parking:** on-site. **Cards:** AX, CB, DC, DS, MC, VI.

ON THE BORDER   **Lunch:** $6-$8   **Dinner:** $7-$14   **Phone:** 913/327-0400   99

Mexican

Location: I-435, exit 77A (Roe Ave), 1.5 mi s to 119th St, then just w. 5200 W 119th St 66209. **Hours:** 11 am-10 pm, Fri & Sat-11 pm. Closed: 11/22, 12/25. **Features:** Mesquite-grilled buffalo fajitas and a good selection of more traditional offerings such as tacos and enchiladas are featured at this locally popular restaurant. Tempting desserts of Kahlua cream pie and sopapillas are also offered. Superb service. Casual dress; cocktails. **Parking:** on-site. **Cards:** AX, CB, DC, DS, MC, VI.

YAHOOZ   **Lunch:** $7-$15   **Dinner:** $9-$32   **Phone:** 913/451-8888   98

American

Location: I-435, exit 77 (Roe Ave), 1 mi s; southwest corner of 117th and Roe Ave. 4701 Town Center Dr 66211. **Hours:** 11 am-10 pm, Fri & Sat-11 pm, Sun 10 am-9 pm. Closed: 7/4, 11/22, 12/25. **Reservations:** accepted. **Features:** Prime steak, chops and fresh seafood are examples of the restaurant's contemporary cowboy cuisine. Casual dress; cocktails. **Parking:** on-site. **Cards:** AX, DC, DS, MC, VI.

LENEXA pop. 40,238   (See map and index starting on p. 444)

——— WHERE TO STAY ———

COMFORT INN   *Book great rates at AAA.com*   **Phone:** (913)438-6969   92

AAA SAVE

Small-scale Hotel

All Year [ECP]   1P: $65-$85   2P: $70-$95   XP: $5   F18
Location: I-35, exit 224 (95th St), just se. 12601 W 96th Terrace 66215. Fax: 913/438-7218. **Facility:** 67 one-bedroom standard units, some with whirlpools. 3 stories, interior corridors. *Bath:* combo or shower only. **Parking:** on-site. **Amenities:** irons, hair dryers. **Pool(s):** small heated indoor. **Leisure Activities:** whirlpool, exercise room. **Guest Services:** valet and coin laundry, wireless Internet. **Business Services:** PC. **Cards:** AX, CB, DC, DS, JC, MC, VI.

SOME UNITS

EXTENDED STAYAMERICA -KANSAS
CITY-LENEXA-87TH ST   *Book at AAA.com*   **Phone:** (913)894-5550   88

Small-scale Hotel

All Year   1P: $65-$125   2P: $70-$130   XP: $5   F17
Location: I-35, exit 227 (75th St), 1 mi s on east frontage road. 8015 Lenexa Dr 66215. Fax: 913/894-5557. **Facility:** 115 units. 109 one-bedroom standard units with efficiencies. 6 one-bedroom suites with efficiencies. 3 stories, exterior corridors. *Bath:* combo or shower only. **Parking:** on-site. **Terms:** small pets only ($25-$75 fee). **Amenities:** high-speed Internet, dual phone lines, voice mail, irons, hair dryers. **Pool(s):** heated outdoor. **Leisure Activities:** exercise room, basketball. **Guest Services:** valet and coin laundry, wireless Internet. **Business Services:** meeting rooms. **Cards:** AX, CB, DC, DS, MC, VI.

SOME UNITS

LA QUINTA INN KANSAS CITY (LENEXA)   *Book great rates at AAA.com*   **Phone:** (913)492-5500   89

Small-scale Hotel

All Year   1P: $72-$102   2P: $78-$108   XP: $6   F18
Location: I-35, exit 224 (95th St), just ne; entrance left on Monrovia Rd, off 95th St. 9461 Lenexa Dr 66215-3836. Fax: 913/492-2935. **Facility:** 107 units. 104 one-bedroom standard units. 3 one-bedroom suites ($102-$138). 3 stories, interior corridors. *Bath:* combo or shower only. **Parking:** on-site. **Amenities:** video games (fee), voice mail, irons, hair dryers. **Pool(s):** small heated outdoor. **Guest Services:** valet and coin laundry, wireless Internet. **Cards:** AX, CB, DC, DS, MC, VI.

SOME UNITS

RADISSON HOTEL LENEXA-OVERLAND PARK   *Book at AAA.com*   **Phone:** (913)888-6670   90

Large-scale Hotel

All Year   1P: $89-$209   2P: $89-$209
Location: I-35, exit 224 (95th St). 12601 W 95th St 66215. Fax: 913/888-9528. **Facility:** 297 one-bedroom standard units. 4 stories, interior/exterior corridors. **Parking:** on-site. **Amenities:** voice mail, irons, hair dryers. *Some:* high-speed Internet. **Pool(s):** small heated indoor. **Leisure Activities:** whirlpool, exercise room. *Fee:* game room. **Guest Services:** gift shop, valet and coin laundry, wireless Internet. **Business Services:** conference facilities, business center. **Cards:** AX, CB, DC, DS, MC, VI.

SOME UNITS

SUPER 8 MOTEL-LENEXA   *Book at AAA.com*   **Phone:** (913)888-8899   91

Small-scale Hotel

All Year [CP]   1P: $60-$70   2P: $60-$70   XP: $7   F17
Location: I-35, exit 224 (95th St), just se. 9601 Westgate Dr 66215. Fax: 913/888-9204. **Facility:** 101 one-bedroom standard units. 3 stories (no elevator), interior corridors. **Parking:** on-site. **Amenities:** safes (fee). **Guest Services:** valet laundry. **Cards:** AX, CB, DC, DS, JC, MC, VI.

SOME UNITS

(See map and index starting on p. 444)

———— WHERE TO DINE ————

SHOGUN SUSHI & STEAK RESTAURANT   **Lunch:** $7-$10   **Dinner:** $9-$23   **Phone:** 913/438-3888   (65)

▼▼▼▼   **Location:** I-35, exit 224 (95th St), just e; in Oak Park Strip Mall. 12028 W 95th St 66215. **Hours:** 11:30 am-2:30 &
Japanese   5-9:30 pm, Fri-10 pm, Sat noon-10 pm, Sun 5 pm-9 pm. Closed major holidays. **Features:** The sushi bar
lines up a good selection, including many kinds of maki rolls. Guests also can order teriyaki, tempura,
sashimi, teppanyaki and combination Japanese plates. Casual dress; cocktails. **Parking:** on-site.
Cards: DS, MC, VI.

———— *The following restaurant has not been evaluated by AAA* ————
but is listed for your information only.

BO LINGS   **Phone:** 913/888-6618
[fyi]   Not evaluated. **Location:** I-435, exit 82 (Quivira Rd), 1 mi n; across from Oak Park Mall. 9576 Quivira Rd 66215.
Features: The restaurant offers creative dishes — some made to order — and a very good selection of
appetizers and entrees; no MSG in sauces and most dinners.

MERRIAM pop. 11,008   (See map and index starting on p. 444)

———— WHERE TO STAY ————

COMFORT INN-MERRIAM   *Book great rates at AAA.com*   **Phone:** (913)262-2622   78
▼▼▼ ▼▼▼   5/25-10/1   1P: $56-$190   2P: $56-$190   XP: $10   F16
3/1-5/24   1P: $46-$80   2P: $46-$80   XP: $5   F16
Small-scale Hotel 10/2-2/29   1P: $50-$70   2P: $50-$70   XP: $5   F16
Location: I-35, exit 228B (Shawnee Mission Pkwy), just se. 6401 E Frontage Rd 66202. Fax: 913/262-1043.
Facility: 64 one-bedroom standard units. 3 stories, interior corridors. **Parking:** on-site. **Terms:** pets ($10 extra charge, in
smoking units). **Amenities:** irons, hair dryers. **Pool(s):** small outdoor. **Guest Services:** wireless Internet. **Business Services:**
PC. **Cards:** AX, CB, DC, DS, JC, MC, VI.

SOME UNITS
(A$K) (S/D) [🛏] [🍽+] [🌀] [🏊] [🎥] [💻] /[✕] [🔒] [📠] /
FEE

DRURY INN-MERRIAM/SHAWNEE MISSION
PARKWAY   *Book at AAA.com*   **Phone:** (913)236-9200   77
▼▼▼ ▼▼▼   All Year [BP]   1P: $70-$110   2P: $80-$120   XP: $10   F18
Location: I-35, exit 228B (Shawnee Mission Pkwy). 9009 W Shawnee Mission Pkwy 66202. Fax: 913/236-9200.
Small-scale Hotel **Facility:** 111 one-bedroom standard units. 4 stories, interior corridors. **Parking:** on-site. **Terms:** small pets
only (must be attended). **Amenities:** high-speed Internet, voice mail, irons, hair dryers. **Pool(s):** outdoor.
Leisure Activities: exercise room. **Guest Services:** complimentary evening beverages: Mon-Sun, valet and coin laundry,
wireless Internet. **Business Services:** meeting rooms. **Cards:** AX, CB, DC, DS, MC, VI.

SOME UNITS
(A$K) [🛏] [🍽+] [♿M] [🌀] [🏊] [🎥] [🔒] [📠] /[✕]

HAMPTON INN & SUITES   *Book great rates at AAA.com*   **Phone:** (913)722-0800   81
▼▼▼▼   All Year [ECP]   1P: $103-$114   XP: $6   F18
Location: I-35, exit 227, just nw. 7400 W Frontage Rd 66203. Fax: 913/722-0222. **Facility:** 85 units. 56 one-
Small-scale Hotel bedroom standard units. 29 one-bedroom suites ($125-$135) with efficiencies, some with whirlpools. 4
stories, interior corridors. *Bath:* combo or shower only. **Parking:** on-site. **Amenities:** video games, dual
phone lines, voice mail, irons, hair dryers. **Pool(s):** small heated indoor. **Leisure Activities:** whirlpool, exercise room. **Guest
Services:** valet and coin laundry, wireless Internet. **Business Services:** meeting rooms. **Cards:** AX, CB, DC, DS, MC, VI.

SOME UNITS
(A$K) (S/D) [🛏] [♿M] [🌀] [🏊] [🎥] [🔒] [💻] /[✕] [📠]

**HOMESTEAD STUDIO SUITES HOTEL-KANSAS
CITY-SHAWNEE MISSION**   *Book at AAA.com*   **Phone:** (913)236-6006   79
▼▼ ▼▼   All Year   1P: $55-$115   2P: $60-$120   XP: $5   F17
Location: I-35, exit 228B (Shawnee Mission Pkwy), just se. 6451 E Frontage Rd 66202. Fax: 913/236-7343.
Motel   **Facility:** 141 one-bedroom standard units with efficiencies. 2 stories (no elevator), exterior corridors. *Bath:*
combo or shower only. **Parking:** on-site. **Terms:** office hours 6:30 am-10 pm, cancellation fee imposed, pets
($75 fee, limit 1). **Amenities:** voice mail, irons. **Guest Services:** valet and coin laundry, wireless Internet. **Cards:** AX, CB, DC,
DS, MC, VI.

SOME UNITS
(A$K) (S/D) [🛏] [🍽+] [♿M] [🌀] [🏊] [🎥] [🔒] [📠] [💻] /[✕]
FEE   FEE

QUALITY INN   *Book great rates at AAA.com*   **Phone:** (913)262-4448   80
(AAA) (SAVE)   5/1-10/10   1P: $49-$199   2P: $59-$199   XP: $10   F16
3/1-4/30 & 10/11-2/29   1P: $39-$89   2P: $39-$89   XP: $5   F16
▼▼ ▼▼   **Location:** I-35, exit 228A, just ne. 6601 E Frontage Rd 66202 (6601 East Frontage Rd). Fax: 913/262-7204.
Facility: 127 one-bedroom standard units. 3 stories, interior/exterior corridors. *Bath:* combo or shower only.
Small-scale Hotel **Parking:** on-site. **Terms:** pets ($10 extra charge). **Amenities:** irons, hair dryers. **Pool(s):** heated outdoor.
Guest Services: valet laundry, wireless Internet. **Business Services:** meeting rooms. **Cards:** AX, CB, DC,
DS, JC, MC, VI. **Free Special Amenities:** expanded continental breakfast and high-speed Internet.

SOME UNITS
(S/D) [🛏] [♿M] [🌀] [🏊] [🎥] [💻] /[✕] [🔒] /
FEE

OLATHE pop. 92,962   (See map and index starting on p. 444)

—— WHERE TO STAY ——

FAIRFIELD INN-OLATHE
Phone: (913)768-7000   135
WWW
All Year   1P: $67-$92
Location: I-35, exit 220 (119th St), just e to Strang Line Rd, then 0.7 mi s. 12245 Strang Line Rd 66062.
Small-scale Hotel **Fax:** 913/768-1610. **Facility:** Smoke free premises. 85 one-bedroom standard units, some with whirlpools. 3 stories, interior corridors. *Bath:* combo or shower only. **Parking:** on-site. **Terms:** [ECP] meal plan available.
Amenities: video games (fee), voice mail, irons, hair dryers. **Pool(s):** small heated indoor. **Leisure Activities:** whirlpool, exercise room. **Guest Services:** valet laundry, wireless Internet. **Cards:** AX, CB, DC, DS, JC, MC, VI.

SOME UNITS

(ASK) (†1†) (&M) (✉) (🕿) (➤) (✕) (🎥) (⬛) / (🖬) (📠) /

HAMPTON INN   *Book great rates at AAA.com*
Phone: (913)393-1111   134
WWW
All Year [ECP]   1P: $74-$199   2P: $80-$199   XP: $5   F18
Location: I-35, exit 220 (119th St), just sw. 12081 S Strang Line Rd 66062. Fax: 913/393-1110. **Facility:** 78 one-
Small-scale Hotel bedroom standard units, some with whirlpools. 3 stories, interior corridors. *Bath:* combo or shower only. **Parking:** on-site. **Terms:** 3 day cancellation notice, package plans, 14% service charge. **Amenities:** voice mail, irons, hair dryers. **Pool(s):** small heated indoor. **Leisure Activities:** whirlpool, exercise room. **Guest Services:** valet laundry, wireless Internet. **Business Services:** meeting rooms. **Cards:** AX, DC, DS, MC, VI.

SOME UNITS

(ASK) (S🄳) (†1†) (&M) (✉) (🕿) (➤) (🎥) (⬛) / (✕) (🖬) (📠) /

HOLIDAY INN   *Book at AAA.com*
Phone: (913)829-4000
WWW
All Year   1P: $83-$105   XP: $6   F18
Location: I-35, exit 215 (151st St). Located adjacent to Olathe Medical Center. 101 W 151st St 66061.
Small-scale Hotel **Fax:** 913/829-8165. **Facility:** 148 one-bedroom standard units. 2 stories (no elevator), interior corridors. **Parking:** on-site. **Terms:** check-in 4 pm. **Amenities:** video games (fee), voice mail, irons, hair dryers. **Pool(s):** small heated indoor/outdoor. **Leisure Activities:** whirlpools, exercise room. **Guest Services:** valet and coin laundry, wireless Internet. **Business Services:** conference facilities. **Cards:** AX, CB, DC, DS, MC, VI.

SOME UNITS

(ASK) (S🄳) (🛏) (†1†) (☂) (🕿) (➤) (🎥) (⬛) / (✕) (🖬) (📠) /
FEE FEE

MICROTEL INN OLATHE   *Book at AAA.com*
Phone: 913/397-9455
WW
Property failed to provide current rates
Location: I-35, exit 215 (151st St), jct 151st St and CR 7 N, just nw of jct I-35. 1501 S Hamilton Cir 66061.
Small-scale Hotel **Fax:** 913/397-9456. **Facility:** 67 one-bedroom standard units. 3 stories, interior corridors. *Bath:* combo or shower only. **Parking:** on-site. **Pool(s):** small heated indoor. **Leisure Activities:** whirlpool. **Guest Services:** coin laundry, wireless Internet.

SOME UNITS

(&M) (✉) (➤) (🎥) / (✕) /

SLEEP INN   *Book great rates at AAA.com*
Phone: (913)390-9500
(AAA) (SAVE)
WW WW
All Year   1P: $74-$85   2P: $74-$85   XP: $5   F18
Location: I-35, exit 215 (151st St), 0.4 mi sw, follow signs. 20662 W 151st St 66061. Fax: 913/390-6630.
Small-scale Hotel **Facility:** 77 one-bedroom standard units, some with whirlpools. 3 stories, interior corridors. *Bath:* combo or shower only. **Parking:** on-site. **Terms:** [ECP] meal plan available, small pets only ($10 fee). **Amenities:** voice mail, irons, hair dryers. *Some:* high-speed Internet. **Pool(s):** small heated indoor. **Leisure Activities:** whirlpool. **Guest Services:** valet laundry, wireless Internet. **Business Services:** meeting rooms. **Cards:** AX, CB, DC, DS, MC, VI. **Free Special Amenities:** expanded continental breakfast and high-speed Internet.

SOME UNITS

(S🄳) (🛏) (&M) (✉) (🕿) (➤) (†🛏🛏) (🎥) (⬛) / (✕) (VCR) (🖬) (📠) /
FEE   FEE   FEE

—— The following lodging was either not evaluated or did not
meet AAA rating requirements but is listed for your information only. ——

COMFORT SUITES AT OLATHE STATION
Phone: 913/397-0100
(fyi)
Did not meet all AAA rating requirements for some property operations at time of last evaluation on
10/01/2004. **Location:** I-35, exit 220 (119th St), just se. 12070 S Strang Line Rd 66062. Facilities, services, and decor
Small-scale Hotel characterize a mid-range property.

—— WHERE TO DINE ——

JOE'S CRAB SHACK
Lunch: $7-$25   Dinner: $7-$25   Phone: 913/393-2929   92
WW WW
Location: I-35, exit 220 (119th St), just se. 11965 S Strang Line Rd 66062. **Hours:** 11 am-10 pm, Fri & Sat-11 pm.
American Closed: 11/22, 12/25. **Features:** The popular seafood restaurant specializes in a year-round variety of crab: Alaskan king, Dungeness, snow and blue. Among other offerings are fresh shrimp, hearty gumbo, clam chowder and classic steaks and chicken. Casual dress; cocktails. **Parking:** on-site. **Cards:** AX, CB, DC, DS, JC, MC, VI.

(🍽) (✂)

KANSAS MACHINE SHED RESTAURANT
Lunch: $7-$10   Dinner: $9-$14   Phone: 913/780-2697   93
WW WW
Location: I-35, exit 220 (119th St), just se. 12080 S Strang Line Rd 66062. **Hours:** 6 am-10 pm, Sun 7 am-9 pm.
American Closed: 1/1, 11/22, 12/25. **Features:** Country-inspired dining-friendly, great cooking, casual homey atmosphere. Try their specialty, chunky potato soup, delicious acre-size platters of sandwiches and burgers and top it off with tempting dessert including their apple cobbler special, served warm with ice cream if you like. Pick up a memento on your way out in their country gift shop. Casual dress; cocktails. **Parking:** on-site. **Cards:** AX, CB, DC, DS, MC, VI.

(🍽) (✂)

(See map and index starting on p. 444)

NOODLES & COMPANY   Lunch: $3-$8   Dinner: $3-$8   Phone: 913/829-4848
Location: I-35, exit 220 (119th St), just w. 15208 W 119th St 66062. **Hours:** 11 am-9 pm, Fri & Sat-10 pm.
Features: Asian, Mediterranean and American-inspired cuisine makes up the menu at this pleasant, quick-
serve eatery. Entrees include Japanese pan noodles, pesto cavatappi and Wisconsin macaroni and cheese.
Thai   Casual dress; beer & wine only. **Parking:** on-site. **Cards:** AX, DS, MC, VI.

ZIO'S ITALIAN KITCHEN   Lunch: $7-$12   Dinner: $7-$12   Phone: 913/782-2225
Location: I-35, exit 220 (119th St), just se. 11981 S Strang Line Rd 66062. **Hours:** 11 am-10 pm, Fri & Sat-11 pm.
Closed: 11/22, 12/25. **Features:** The warm, comfortable atmosphere and Old World decor complement the
Italian   menu. Meals are a good value, and so is the service. This small chain specializes in Italian cuisine,
including oven-baked pizzas and pasta dishes. Guests are encouraged to get creative with their pizzas by
mixing and matching from a list of 24 toppings. Particularly tempting dishes are Artichoke spinach pasta, chicken parmigiana,
and Shrimp Limone. Casual dress; cocktails. **Parking:** on-site. **Cards:** AX, DC, DS, MC, VI.

OVERLAND PARK pop. 149,080   (See map and index starting on p. 444)

──────── WHERE TO STAY ────────

CANDLEWOOD SUITES   *Book at AAA.com*   Phone: 913/469-5557   **123**
               Property failed to provide current rates
            Location: I-435, exit 82 (Quivira Rd), 0.5 mi s, 0.3 mi w on College Ave, then just n. 11001 Oakmont 66210.
Small-scale Hotel   **Fax:** 913/469-5558. **Facility:** 122 units. 98 one-bedroom standard units with efficiencies. 24 one-bedroom
suites with efficiencies. 3 stories, interior corridors. *Bath:* combo or shower only. **Parking:** on-site.
Terms: office hours 7 am-11 pm, pets ($25-$50 fee). **Amenities:** video library, DVD players, CD players, high-speed Internet,
dual phone lines, voice mail, irons, hair dryers. **Leisure Activities:** exercise room. **Guest Services:** valet and coin laundry.
                                           SOME UNITS

CHASE SUITES BY WOODFIN   *Book great rates at AAA.com*   Phone: (913)491-3333   **121**
     All Year [ECP]   1P: $89-$152   2P: $89-$152   XP: $10   F
Location: I-435, exit 79 (Metcalf Ave/US 169), 0.3 mi s on US 169, 0.5 mi e on College Blvd to Lamar Ave, then just n.
6300 W 110th 66211. Fax: 913/491-1377. **Facility:** Smoke free premises. 112 units. 84 one- and 28 two-
bedroom suites with kitchens. 2 stories (no elevator), exterior corridors. *Bath:* combo or shower only.
Small-scale Hotel   **Parking:** on-site. **Terms:** pets ($250 fee). **Amenities:** high-speed Internet (fee), voice mail, irons, hair
dryers. **Pool(s):** small heated outdoor. **Leisure Activities:** whirlpool, barbecue grill, exercise room, sports
court, basketball. **Guest Services:** complimentary evening beverages: Mon-Thurs, valet and coin laundry, area transportation-
within 5 mi. **Business Services:** meeting rooms, business center. **Cards:** AX, DC, DS, MC, VI. **Free Special Amenities:**
expanded continental breakfast and newspaper.
                                   FEE

COMFORT INN & SUITES   *Book great rates at AAA.com*   Phone: (913)648-7858   **111**
     3/1-11/1   1P: $79-$100   2P: $89-$110   XP: $10   F
     11/2-2/29   1P: $69-$99   2P: $79-$100   XP: $10   F
Small-scale Hotel   **Location:** I-435, exit 79 (Metcalf Ave/US 169), just nw. 7200 W 107th St 66212. Fax: 913/648-1867. **Facility:** 82
units. 80 one-bedroom standard units, some with kitchens. 2 one-bedroom suites ($129-$139). 4 stories,
interior corridors. *Bath:* combo or shower only. **Parking:** on-site. **Terms:** [ECP] meal plan available, pets ($10 extra charge).
Amenities: voice mail, irons, hair dryers. **Pool(s):** outdoor. **Leisure Activities:** exercise room. **Guest Services:** valet and coin
laundry, wireless Internet. **Business Services:** meeting rooms, PC. **Cards:** AX, CB, DC, DS, JC, MC, VI.
                                     SOME UNITS

COURTYARD BY MARRIOTT   *Book great rates at AAA.com*   Phone: (913)339-9900   **129**
     All Year   1P: $169
     Location: I-435, exit 79 (Metcalf Ave/US 169), 0.6 mi s. 11301 Metcalf Ave 66210. Fax: 913/339-6091.
Small-scale Hotel   **Facility:** Smoke free premises. 149 units. 136 one-bedroom standard units. 13 one-bedroom suites. 3
stories, interior corridors. *Bath:* combo or shower only. **Parking:** on-site. **Terms:** [BP] meal plan available,
package plans. **Amenities:** high-speed Internet, voice mail, irons, hair dryers. **Pool(s):** heated indoor. **Leisure
Activities:** whirlpool, exercise room. **Guest Services:** valet and coin laundry. **Business Services:** meeting rooms. **Cards:** AX,
CB, DC, DS, JC, MC, VI.
                                     SOME UNITS

DOUBLETREE HOTEL   *Book great rates at AAA.com*   Phone: (913)451-6100   **127**
     6/1-2/29   1P: $89-$269   2P: $99-$279   XP: $10   F
     3/1-5/31   1P: $89-$269   2P: $99-$259   XP: $10   F
Large-scale Hotel   **Location:** I-435, exit 81 (US 69), 0.5 mi s, then just e. 10100 College Blvd 66210. Fax: 913/451-3873. **Facility:** 356
units. 334 one-bedroom standard units. 22 one-bedroom suites ($175-$675). 18 stories, interior corridors.
Bath: combo or shower only. **Parking:** on-site. **Terms:** cancellation fee imposed, package plans. **Amenities:** video games, CD
players, high-speed Internet, dual phone lines, voice mail, irons, hair dryers. *Some:* DVD players. **Pool(s):** heated indoor.
Leisure Activities: sauna, whirlpool, racquetball court, jogging, exercise room. **Guest Services:** gift shop, valet laundry, area
transportation, wireless Internet. **Business Services:** conference facilities, business center. **Cards:** AX, CB, DC, DS, JC,
MC, VI.
                                     SOME UNITS

(See map and index starting on p. 444)

DRURY INN & SUITES-OVERLAND PARK   *Book at AAA.com*   Phone: (913)345-1500   118
All Year [BP]   1P: $75-$130   2P: $85-$140   XP: $10   F18
Location: I-435, exit 79 (Metcalf Ave/US 169), just se. 10963 Metcalf Ave 66210. Fax: 913/345-1500. **Facility:** 170
Small-scale Hotel   units. 117 one-bedroom standard units. 53 one-bedroom suites ($115-$155). 7 stories, interior corridors.
Bath: combo or shower only. **Parking:** on-site. **Terms:** small pets only (must be attended). **Amenities:** high-
speed Internet, dual phone lines, voice mail, irons, hair dryers. **Pool(s):** small heated indoor/outdoor. **Leisure**
Activities: whirlpool, exercise room. **Guest Services:** complimentary evening beverages, valet and coin laundry. **Business**
Services: meeting rooms. **Cards:** AX, CB, DC, DS, MC, VI.
SOME UNITS
(ASK) 🍽 📶 🛗Ⓜ 🖥 🐾 📷 🛢 🖨 💳 / ⊠ /

EMBASSY SUITES HOTEL-OVERLAND PARK   *Book at AAA.com*   Phone: 913/649-7060   107
Property failed to provide current rates
Location: I-435, exit 79 (Metcalf Ave/US 169), just ne. 10601 Metcalf Ave 66212. Fax: 913/649-9382. **Facility:** 199
Large-scale Hotel   units. 12 one-bedroom standard units. 175 one- and 12 two-bedroom suites. 7 stories, interior corridors.
Parking: on-site. **Amenities:** video games (fee), voice mail, irons, hair dryers. **Pool(s):** small heated indoor.
Leisure Activities: saunas, whirlpool, exercise room. **Fee:** game room. **Guest Services:** gift shop, complimentary evening
beverages, valet and coin laundry, area transportation, wireless Internet. **Business Services:** meeting rooms, PC.
SOME UNITS
🍽 🍴 🛗Ⓜ 🖥 🐾 ⊠ 📷 🛢 🖨 💳 / ⊠ 🖨 /

EXTENDED STAYAMERICA-KANSAS
CITY-OVERLAND PARK   *Book at AAA.com*   Phone: 913/661-9299   112
All Year   1P: $70-$150   2P: $75-$155   XP: $5   F17
Location: I-435, exit 82 (Quivira Rd), just sw. 10750 Quivira Rd 66210. Fax: 913/661-9774. **Facility:** 119 units. 117
Small-scale Hotel   one-bedroom standard units with efficiencies. 2 one-bedroom suites with efficiencies. 3 stories, interior
corridors. **Bath:** combo or shower only. **Parking:** on-site. **Terms:** office hours 7 am-11 pm, pets ($25-$75
extra charge). **Amenities:** voice mail, irons. **Guest Services:** coin laundry, wireless Internet. **Cards:** AX, CB, DC, DS, MC, VI.
SOME UNITS
🍴 🍴 🛗Ⓜ 🖥 📶 📷 🛢 🖨 💳 / ⊠ /
FEE

EXTENDED STAY DELUXE KANSAS
CITY-OVERLAND PARK-METCALF   *Book at AAA.com*   Phone: (913)642-2299   108
All Year   1P: $70-$160   2P: $75-$165   XP: $5   F17
Location: I-435, exit 79 (Metcalf Ave/US 169), just nw. 7201 W 106th St 66212. Fax: 913/642-9199. **Facility:** 133
Small-scale Hotel   units. 100 one-bedroom standard units with efficiencies. 33 one-bedroom suites with efficiencies. 3 stories,
interior corridors. **Bath:** combo or shower only. **Parking:** on-site. **Terms:** small pets only ($25 extra charge).
Amenities: dual phone lines, voice mail, irons, hair dryers. **Leisure Activities:** exercise room. **Guest Services:** valet and coin
laundry, wireless Internet. **Cards:** AX, CB, DC, DS, MC, VI.
SOME UNITS
(ASK) Ⓢ 🐾 🍴 🛗Ⓜ 🖥 📷 🛢 🖨 💳 / ⊠ /
FEE

HAMPTON INN-KANSAS CITY/
OVERLAND PARK   *Book great rates at AAA.com*   Phone: (913)341-1551   105
All Year [BP]   1P: $75-$150   2P: $75-$150
Location: I-435, exit 79 (Metcalf Ave/US 169), 0.3 mi ne. 10591 Metcalf Frontage Rd 66212. Fax: 913/341-8668.
Facility: 134 one-bedroom standard units. 5 stories, interior corridors. **Bath:** combo or shower only.
Parking: on-site. **Amenities:** video games (fee), voice mail, irons, hair dryers. **Pool(s):** small heated
Small-scale Hotel   outdoor. **Leisure Activities:** whirlpool. **Guest Services:** valet and coin laundry, wireless Internet. **Business**
Services: meeting rooms. **Cards:** AX, CB, DC, DS, JC, MC, VI. **Free Special Amenities:** expanded
continental breakfast and high-speed Internet. *(See color ad below)*
SOME UNITS
Ⓢ 🍴 🛗Ⓜ 🖥 📷 🛢 🖨 💳 / ⊠ /

HILTON GARDEN INN   *Book great rates at AAA.com*   Phone: 913/345-2661   126
All Year   1P: $79-$229   2P: $79-$229   XP: $10   F18
Location: I-435, exit 77B (Nall Ave), just sw. 5800 College Blvd 66211. Fax: 913/345-2667. **Facility:** 125 one-
bedroom standard units, some with whirlpools. 4 stories, interior corridors. **Bath:** combo or shower only.
Small-scale Hotel   **Parking:** on-site. **Terms:** [BP] meal plan available, package plans. **Amenities:** video games (fee), high-
speed Internet, dual phone lines, voice mail, irons, hair dryers. **Pool(s):** heated indoor. **Leisure Activities:** whirlpool, exercise
room. **Guest Services:** valet and coin laundry, area transportation, wireless Internet. **Business Services:** meeting rooms,
business center. **Cards:** AX, CB, DC, DS, JC, MC, VI.
🍴 🛗Ⓜ 🖥 🐾 📷 🛢 🖨 💳

(See map and index starting on p. 444)

HOLIDAY INN HOTEL AND SUITES   *Book great rates at AAA.com*   Phone: (913)888-8440   [104]

AAA [SAVE]

Small-scale Hotel

All Year   1P: $79-$119   2P: $79-$119
Location: I-35, exit 225A (87th St), just se. 8787 Reeder Rd 66214. **Fax:** 913/888-3438. **Facility:** 191 units. 154 one-bedroom standard units. 37 one-bedroom suites ($89-$129). 8 stories, interior corridors. *Bath:* combo or shower only. **Parking:** on-site. **Amenities:** video games, dual phone lines, voice mail, irons, hair dryers. **Dining:** 6:30 am-2 & 5-11 pm, Sat 7 am-11 pm, Sun 7 am-noon & 5-10 pm, cocktails, also, Green Mill Restaurant & Bar-Overland Park, see separate listing. **Pool(s):** small heated outdoor. **Leisure Activities:** sauna, whirlpool, exercise room. *Fee:* game room. **Guest Services:** valet and coin laundry, area transportation-within 2 mi, wireless Internet. **Business Services:** conference facilities, PC. **Cards:** AX, CB, DC, DS, JC, MC, VI. **Free Special Amenities:** local telephone calls and high-speed Internet.

SOME UNITS

[icons] / [icons] /

HOLIDAY INN HOTEL & SUITES CONVENTION
CENTER OVERLAND PARK   *Book at AAA.com*   Phone: (913)312-0900   [119]

Small-scale Hotel

All Year   1P: $145-$165   2P: $145-$165
Location: I-435, exit 77B (Nall Ave), just sw. 10920 Nall Ave 66211. **Fax:** 913/312-5995. **Facility:** 121 units. 80 one-bedroom standard units. 41 one-bedroom suites ($155-$195), some with whirlpools. 5 stories, interior corridors. *Bath:* combo or shower only. **Parking:** on-site. **Terms:** [AP], [BP], [CP], [ECP] & [MAP] meal plans available. **Amenities:** high-speed Internet, dual phone lines, voice mail, irons, hair dryers. **Pool(s):** small heated indoor/outdoor. **Leisure Activities:** exercise room. **Guest Services:** complimentary evening beverages: Tues-Thurs, valet and coin laundry, area transportation, wireless Internet. **Business Services:** meeting rooms, business center. **Cards:** AX, CB, DC, DS, JC, MC, VI.

SOME UNITS

(ASK) [icons] / [icons] /

HOLIDAY INN OF MISSION-OVERLAND PARK   *Book at AAA.com*   Phone: (913)262-3010   [102]

Large-scale Hotel

All Year   1P: $99-$139   2P: $99-$139
Location: I-35, exit 228B (Shawnee Mission Pkwy), 1 mi e. 7240 Shawnee Mission Pkwy 66202. **Fax:** 913/262-2326. **Facility:** 195 one-bedroom standard units. 2 stories (no elevator), interior/exterior corridors. *Bath:* combo or shower only. **Parking:** on-site. **Terms:** small pets only ($20 fee). **Amenities:** video games, voice mail, irons, hair dryers. **Pool(s):** heated indoor. **Leisure Activities:** sauna, whirlpool, exercise room, sports court. *Fee:* game room. **Guest Services:** valet and coin laundry, wireless Internet. **Business Services:** conference facilities, PC. **Cards:** AX, CB, DC, DS, JC, MC, VI.

SOME UNITS

(ASK) [icons] FEE / [icons] /

HOLTZE EXECUTIVE VILLAGE   *Book great rates at AAA.com*   Phone: (913)344-8100   [124]

AAA [SAVE]

Small-scale Hotel

All Year [ECP]   1P: $62-$269
Location: I-435, exit 82 (Quivira Rd), 0.5 mi s, then just e. 11400 College Blvd 66210. **Fax:** 913/344-8200. **Facility:** 215 units. 98 one-bedroom standard units. 117 one-bedroom suites ($98-$269) with kitchens, some with whirlpools. 3 stories, interior/exterior corridors. *Bath:* combo or shower only. **Parking:** on-site. **Terms:** cancellation fee imposed, small pets only ($250 deposit, $8 extra charge). **Amenities:** video games (fee), high-speed Internet, voice mail, irons, hair dryers. *Some:* dual phone lines. **Pool(s):** heated outdoor. **Leisure Activities:** whirlpool, exercise room. **Guest Services:** complimentary evening beverages: Mon-Thurs, valet and coin laundry, area transportation-within 5 mi, wireless Internet. **Business Services:** meeting rooms. **Cards:** AX, DC, DS, MC, VI. **Free Special Amenities:** expanded continental breakfast and high-speed Internet.

[icons] FEE

(See map and index starting on p. 444)

HOMESTEAD STUDIO SUITES HOTEL-KANSAS CITY-OVERLAND PARK   Book at AAA.com

Phone: (913)661-7111   122

All Year

| | 1P: $70-$150 | 2P: $75-$155 | | F17 |
| | | | XP: $5 | |

Small-scale Hotel

Location: I-435, exit 77B (Nall Ave), just s. 5401 W 110th St 66211. Fax: 913/661-4744. **Facility:** 127 units. 121 one-bedroom standard units with efficiencies. 6 one-bedroom suites with efficiencies. 3 stories, interior corridors. *Bath:* combo or shower only. **Parking:** on-site. **Terms:** small pets only ($75 fee). **Amenities:** voice mail, irons. **Guest Services:** coin laundry, wireless Internet. **Cards:** AX, CB, DC, DS, MC, VI.

SOME UNITS

HOMEWOOD SUITES   Book at AAA.com

Phone: (913)341-5576   106

5/1-10/31 .... 1P: $149-$169   2P: $149-$169
3/1-4/30 & 11/1-2/29 .. 1P: $129-$149   2P: $129-$149

Small-scale Hotel

Location: I-435, exit 79 (Metcalf Ave/US 169), just nw. 10556 Marty Ave 66212. Fax: 913/341-5573. **Facility:** 92 units. 85 one- and 7 two-bedroom suites ($109-$179) with efficiencies. 4 stories, interior corridors. *Bath:* combo or shower only. **Parking:** on-site. **Terms:** cancellation fee imposed, [BP] meal plan available. **Amenities:** voice mail, irons, hair dryers. *Fee:* video library, video games, safes. **Pool(s):** small heated outdoor. **Leisure Activities:** whirlpool, exercise room, sports court. **Guest Services:** complimentary evening beverages: Mon-Thurs, valet and coin laundry, area transportation, wireless Internet. **Business Services:** meeting rooms, business center. **Cards:** AX, CB, DC, DS, MC, VI.

SOME UNITS

HYATT PLACE OVERLAND PARK CONVENTION CENTER   Book great rates at AAA.com

Phone: (913)491-9002   117

5/1-10/31 [CP] .... 1P: $89-$169   2P: $89-$169   XP: $10   F17
3/1-4/30 & 11/1-2/29 [CP] 1P: $79-$149   2P: $79-$149   XP: $10   F17

Small-scale Hotel

Location: I-435, exit 77B (Nall Ave), just se. 5001 W 110th St 66211. Fax: 913/491-9003. **Facility:** 135 one-bedroom suites. 6 stories, interior corridors. *Bath:* combo or shower only. **Parking:** on-site. **Terms:** cancellation fee imposed. **Amenities:** dual phone lines, voice mail, irons, hair dryers. *Fee:* video games, safes. *Some:* high-speed Internet. **Pool(s):** small heated outdoor. **Leisure Activities:** exercise room. **Guest Services:** valet and coin laundry, area transportation-within 5 mi, wireless Internet. **Business Services:** meeting rooms. **Cards:** AX, CB, DC, DS, JC, MC, VI. **Free Special Amenities:** full breakfast and high-speed Internet.

SOME UNITS

HYATT PLACE OVERLAND PARK METCALF   Book great rates at AAA.com

Phone: (913)451-2553   128

5/1-10/31 [CP] .... 1P: $89-$169   2P: $89-$169   XP: $10   F17
3/1-4/30 & 11/1-2/29 [CP] 1P: $79-$149   2P: $79-$149   XP: $10   F17

Small-scale Hotel

Location: I-435, exit 79 (Metcalf Ave/US 169), 0.6 mi s. 6801 W 112th St 66211. Fax: 913/451-3098. **Facility:** 126 one-bedroom standard units. 6 stories, interior corridors. *Bath:* combo or shower only. **Parking:** on-site. **Terms:** cancellation fee imposed, small pets only ($10 extra charge). **Amenities:** dual phone lines, voice mail, safes (fee), irons, hair dryers. **Pool(s):** small heated outdoor. **Leisure Activities:** exercise room. **Guest Services:** valet and coin laundry, area transportation-within 5 mi, wireless Internet. **Business Services:** meeting rooms. **Cards:** AX, CB, DC, DS, JC, MC, VI. **Free Special Amenities:** expanded continental breakfast and high-speed Internet.

SOME UNITS

(See map and index starting on p. 444)

LA QUINTA INN & SUITES — *Book great rates at AAA.com* — Phone: (913)648-5555 **109**
All Year — 1P: $89-$139
Small-scale Hotel — **Location:** I-435, exit 79 (Metcalf Ave/US 169), just nw. 10610 Marty Ave 66212. Fax: 913/648-7130. **Facility:** 143 units. 121 one-bedroom standard units. 22 one-bedroom suites. 3 stories, interior corridors. *Bath:* combo or shower only. **Parking:** on-site. **Amenities:** voice mail, irons, hair dryers. **Pool(s):** small heated outdoor. **Leisure Activities:** whirlpool, exercise room. **Guest Services:** valet and coin laundry, wireless Internet. **Business Services:** meeting rooms, PC. **Cards:** AX, CB, DC, DS, MC, VI.

SOME UNITS

OVERLAND PARK MARRIOTT HOTEL — *Book great rates at AAA.com* — Phone: 913/451-8000 **116**
All Year — 1P: $89-$229 — 2P: $89-$229
Large-scale Hotel — **Location:** I-435, exit 79 (Metcalf Ave/US 169), just sw. 10800 Metcalf Ave 66210. Fax: 913/451-5914. **Facility:** Smoke free premises. 397 units. 390 one-bedroom standard units. 7 one-bedroom suites ($250-$450). 11 stories, interior corridors. *Bath:* combo or shower only. **Parking:** on-site (fee) and valet. **Terms:** cancellation fee imposed, package plans. **Amenities:** dual phone lines, voice mail, safes, irons, hair dryers. *Fee:* video games, high-speed Internet. **Pool(s):** small heated indoor/outdoor. **Leisure Activities:** whirlpool, exercise room. **Guest Services:** gift shop, valet and coin laundry. **Business Services:** conference facilities, business center. **Cards:** AX, CB, DC, DS, MC, VI.

SOME UNITS

PEAR TREE INN BY DRURY-OVERLAND PARK — *Book at AAA.com* — Phone: (913)451-0200 **120**
All Year [BP] — 1P: $50-$105 — 2P: $60-$115 — XP: $10 — F18
Small-scale Hotel — **Location:** I-435, exit 79 (Metcalf Ave/US 169), just se. 10951 Metcalf Ave 66210. Fax: 913/341-0200. **Facility:** 149 one-bedroom standard units. 4 stories, interior corridors. **Parking:** on-site. **Terms:** small pets only (must be attended). **Amenities:** voice mail, irons, hair dryers. **Pool(s):** small heated outdoor. **Leisure Activities:** exercise room. **Guest Services:** complimentary evening beverages: Mon-Thurs, valet and coin laundry, wireless Internet. **Business Services:** meeting rooms, business center. **Cards:** AX, CB, DC, DS, MC, VI.

SOME UNITS

RED ROOF INN-OVERLAND PARK — *Book at AAA.com* — Phone: (913)341-0100 **115**
5/25-9/2 — 1P: $52-$67 — 2P: $58-$73 — XP: $6 — F18
9/3-2/29 — 1P: $45-$57 — 2P: $51-$63 — XP: $6 — F18
3/1-5/24 — 1P: $42-$57 — 2P: $48-$63 — XP: $6 — F18
Motel — **Location:** I-435, exit 79 (Metcalf Ave/US 169), just ne. 6800 W 108th St 66211. Fax: 913/341-2757. **Facility:** 107 one-bedroom standard units. 2 stories (no elevator), exterior corridors. *Bath:* combo or shower only. **Parking:** on-site. **Amenities:** video games (fee), voice mail. **Guest Services:** wireless Internet. **Business Services:** meeting rooms. **Cards:** AX, CB, DC, DS, MC, VI.

SOME UNITS

RESIDENCE INN BY MARRIOTT — *Book great rates at AAA.com* — Phone: (913)491-4444 **130**
All Year [BP] — 1P: $99-$179 — 2P: $179-$299
Small-scale Hotel — **Location:** I-435, exit 79 (Metcalf Ave/US 169), 1.3 mi s. 12010 Blue Valley Pkwy 66213. Fax: 913/345-0644. **Facility:** Smoke free premises. 120 units. 61 one-bedroom standard units with efficiencies. 38 one- and 21 two-bedroom suites, some with efficiencies or kitchens. 3 stories, interior corridors. *Bath:* combo or shower only. **Parking:** on-site. **Terms:** cancellation fee imposed, weekly rates available, pets ($75 fee). **Amenities:** high-speed Internet, dual phone lines, voice mail, irons, hair dryers. **Pool(s):** heated indoor. **Leisure Activities:** putting green, exercise room, sports court. **Guest Services:** complimentary evening beverages: Mon-Thurs, valet and coin laundry. **Business Services:** meeting rooms. **Cards:** AX, DC, DS, MC, VI.

FEE

SETTLE INN — *Book great rates at AAA.com* — Phone: (913)381-5700 **110**
All Year [ECP] — 1P: $54-$129
Small-scale Hotel — **Location:** I-435, exit 77A (Roe Ave), just ne. 4401 W 107th St 66207. Fax: 913/649-6400. **Facility:** 126 one-bedroom standard units. 3 stories, interior/exterior corridors. *Bath:* combo or shower only. **Parking:** on-site. **Terms:** cancellation fee imposed, package plans. **Amenities:** irons, hair dryers. **Pool(s):** small heated outdoor. **Guest Services:** wireless Internet. **Cards:** AX, DC, DS, MC, VI. **Free Special Amenities:** expanded continental breakfast and high-speed Internet.

SOME UNITS

SHERATON OVERLAND PARK HOTEL AT THE CONVENTION CENTER — *Book great rates at AAA.com* — Phone: (913)234-2100 **125**
All Year — 1P: $99-$299 — 2P: $99-$299 — XP: $25 — F16
Large-scale Hotel — **Location:** I-435, exit 79 (Metcalf Ave/US 169), just s to College Blvd, then 0.6 mi e. 6100 College Blvd 66211. Fax: 913/234-2110. **Facility:** 412 units. 393 one-bedroom standard units. 19 one-bedroom suites. 20 stories, interior corridors. *Bath:* combo or shower only. **Parking:** on-site. **Terms:** cancellation fee imposed, small pets only. **Amenities:** high-speed Internet (fee), dual phone lines, voice mail, irons, hair dryers. *Some:* safes. **Pool(s):** heated indoor. **Leisure Activities:** whirlpool, exercise room. **Guest Services:** gift shop, valet laundry. **Business Services:** conference facilities, business center. **Cards:** AX, CB, DC, DS, JC, MC, VI.

SOME UNITS

SPRINGHILL SUITES BY MARRIOTT — *Book great rates at AAA.com* — Phone: (913)491-0010 **131**
All Year — 1P: $69-$159 — 2P: $69-$159
Small-scale Hotel — **Location:** I-435, exit 79 (Metcalf Ave/US 169), 1.3 mi s. Located in a busy retail area. 12000 Blue Valley Pkwy 66213. Fax: 913/491-9242. **Facility:** Smoke free premises. 102 one-bedroom standard units. 4 stories, interior corridors. *Bath:* combo or shower only. **Parking:** on-site. **Terms:** cancellation fee imposed. **Amenities:** high-speed Internet, dual phone lines, voice mail, irons, hair dryers. **Pool(s):** small heated indoor. **Leisure Activities:** whirlpool, exercise room. **Guest Services:** valet and coin laundry, wireless Internet. **Business Services:** PC. **Cards:** AX, CB, DC, DS, JC, MC, VI.

(See map and index starting on p. 444)

SUPER 8 MOTEL   *Book at AAA.com*   Phone: (913)341-4440   113
▼▼ ▼▼
Small-scale Hotel
MC, VI.

All Year   1P: $45-$99   2P: $50-$109   XP: $5   F17
Location: I-435, exit 79 (Metcalf Ave/US 169), just n to 107th St, then just e. 10750 Barkley St 66211. **Fax:** 913/341-9040. **Facility:** 94 one-bedroom standard units. 3 stories, interior corridors. *Bath:* combo or shower only. **Parking:** on-site. **Terms:** pets ($25 fee). **Amenities:** voice mail. **Cards:** AX, CB, DC, DS, JC,

SOME UNITS

(A$K) (S☎) (🛏) (📶) (🔊M) (🔊) / (⊠) (🖥) (🖨) /
FEE

WHITE HAVEN MOTOR LODGE   Phone: 913/649-8200   103
▼▼ ▼▼
Motel

All Year   1P: $50-$52   2P: $58-$60   XP: $2   F3
Location: I-435, exit 79 (Metcalf Ave/US 169), 3.5 mi n. 8039 Metcalf Ave 66204. **Fax:** 913/901-8199. **Facility:** 77 units. 69 one-bedroom standard units. 6 one- and 2 two-bedroom suites ($92-$94). 1-2 stories (no elevator), exterior corridors. *Bath:* combo or shower only. **Parking:** on-site. **Terms:** weekly rates available, [CP] meal plan available, small pets only (must be attended). **Amenities:** voice mail. *Some:* high-speed Internet, dual phone lines. **Pool(s):** small outdoor. **Guest Services:** valet laundry, wireless Internet. **Business Services:** PC. **Cards:** AX, DS, MC, VI.

SOME UNITS

(🛏) (📶) (🔊) (🏊) (🔊) (🖥) / (⊠) (🖨) /

WYNDHAM GARDEN HOTEL-OVERLAND PARK   *Book at AAA.com*   Phone: 913/383-2550   114
▼▼ ▼▼
Small-scale Hotel

Property failed to provide current rates
Location: I-435, exit 79 (Metcalf Ave/US 169), just ne. 7000 W 108th St 66211-1163. **Fax:** 913/383-2099. **Facility:** 180 one-bedroom standard units. 2 stories (no elevator), interior corridors. *Bath:* combo or shower only. **Parking:** on-site. **Amenities:** voice mail, irons, hair dryers. *Fee:* video games, high-speed Internet. **Pool(s):** small heated outdoor. **Leisure Activities:** exercise room. **Guest Services:** complimentary evening beverages: Wed, valet laundry, wireless Internet. **Business Services:** conference facilities, PC.

SOME UNITS

(🍽) (🍸) (🔊M) (🔊) (📷) (🏊) (📷) (🖥) / (⊠) (🖨) (🖨) /

─── WHERE TO DINE ───

40 SARDINES   Lunch: $8-$16   Dinner: $17-$28   Phone: 913/451-1040   88
▼▼ ▼▼ ▼▼
American
Location: I-435, exit 77A (Roe Ave), 1.2 mi s; in Hawthorne Plaza. 11942 Roe Ave 66212. **Hours:** 11 am-2 & 5-10 pm, Fri-11 pm, Sat 5 pm-11 pm, Sun 5 pm-9 pm. Closed major holidays. **Reservations:** suggested. **Features:** This contemporary restaurant features globally influenced cuisine and an excellent wine list. Casual dress; cocktails. **Parking:** on-site. **Cards:** AX, DC, DS, MC, VI.   (🍸)

ANDY'S WOK   Lunch: $6-$10   Dinner: $9-$14   Phone: 913/469-6788   85
▼▼ ▼▼
Chinese
Location: I-435, exit 79 (Metcalf Ave/US 169), 2 mi s, then just e. 6357 W 119th St 66209. **Hours:** 11 am-9:30 pm, Fri & Sat-10:30 pm. **Features:** Andy's serves a good variety of Cantonese and Mandarin dishes, and the spicier, peppery dishes native to the Hunan and Szechuan provinces are well-prepared and nicely presented. Business people frequently dine here for lunch. Comfortable ambience. Casual dress; cocktails.
Parking: on-site. **Cards:** AX, CB, DC, DS, MC, VI.   (🍸) (📥)

BARLEY'S BREWHAUS & RESTAURANT   Lunch: $8-$12   Dinner: $11-$20   Phone: 913/663-4099   86
▼▼ ▼▼
American
Location: I-435, exit 82 (Quivira Rd), 1 mi s. 11924 W 119th St 66213. **Hours:** 11 am-midnight. Closed major holidays; also Sun. **Features:** Guests can select from 99 varieties of beer to complement aged Kansas City strip steak and sausage, which is cut in house, as well as barbecue back ribs, tasty Hawaiian chicken and many creative sandwiches. Soups, dressings and sauces are made from scratch. Casual dress; cocktails; entertainment. **Parking:** on-site. **Cards:** AX, CB, DC, DS, JC, MC, VI.   (🍸) (📥)

BO LING'S   Lunch: $6-$8   Dinner: $8-$15   Phone: 913/341-1718   74
(AAA)
▼▼ ▼▼
Chinese
Location: I-435, exit 79 (Metcalf Ave/US 169), 2 mi n; in Gateway 2000 Plaza Shopping Center. 9055 Metcalf Ave 66212. **Hours:** 11 am-9:30 pm, Fri & Sat-10:30 pm. Closed: 7/4, 11/22, 12/25. **Reservations:** accepted. **Features:** This is a locally popular establishment offering good selections served in a light and airy atmosphere. The Beijing duck, dim sum and cream caramel custard are very good. The dinner menu is extensive and offers large portions with good presentation. Casual dress; cocktails. **Parking:** on-site. **Cards:** AX, DC, DS, MC, VI.   (🍸)

CHIEN DYNASTY   Lunch: $4-$6   Dinner: $7-$13   Phone: 913/888-3000   73
▼▼ ▼▼
Chinese
Location: I-35, exit 225A, 1 mi e. 9921 W 87th St 66212. **Hours:** 11 am-9:30 pm, Fri & Sat-10:30 pm, Sun 11:30 am-9 pm. Closed: 11/22. **Reservations:** accepted. **Features:** The restaurant offers a large selection and wide variety of Chinese dishes with very fast and friendly service; many Chinese decorations lends to the relaxed atmosphere. Casual dress; cocktails. **Parking:** on-site. **Cards:** AX, DS, MC, VI.   (🍸) (📥)

CHINA STAR BUFFET   Lunch: $6   Dinner: $8   Phone: 913/381-8882   78
▼▼ ▼▼
Chinese
Location: I-435, exit 79 (Metcalf Ave/US 169), 1 mi n. 9421 Metcalf Ave 66212. **Hours:** 11 am-9:30 pm, Fri & Sat-10:30 pm. Closed: 11/22. **Features:** Several buffet tables are set up with an ample variety of entrees, appetizers and salads. The dining room is large, modern and well-illuminated. The pleasant owner/manager seats guests and makes them feel welcomed. Casual dress. **Parking:** on-site. **Cards:** AX, DS, MC, VI.   (📥)

(See map and index starting on p. 444)

COPELAND'S FAMOUS NEW ORLEANS
RESTAURANT & BAR   **Lunch:** $7-$12   **Dinner:** $9-$22   **Phone:** 913/663-5290   [87]
American
Location: I-435, exit 79 (Metcalf Ave/US 169), 1.2 mi s, then just se. 11920 Metcalf Ave 66213. **Hours:** 11 am-9 pm, Fri & Sat-10 pm. Closed: 7/4, 11/22, 12/25. **Features:** The extensive menu focuses on Cajun cuisine, including 28-day-aged steaks prepared New Orleans style. Rich flavors abound. Other good choices include Cajun gumbo ya ya and hot crab claws. Casual dress; cocktails. **Parking:** on-site. **Cards:** AX, DC, DS, MC, VI.

DICK CLARK'S AMERICAN BANDSTAND GRILL   **Lunch:** $5-$7   **Dinner:** $7-$15   **Phone:** 913/451-1600   [82]
American
Location: I-435, exit 79 (Metcalf Ave/US 169), just se. 10975 Metcalf Ave 66210. **Hours:** 11 am-11 pm, Fri & Sat-midnight. Closed: 11/22. **Features:** Dick Clark's features a wide-ranging menu, an upscale ambience and a great deal of musical celebrity memorabilia. The lively atmosphere plays music from decades past and the "American Bandstand" TV program. This is quite a popular place. Casual dress; cocktails. **Parking:** on-site. **Cards:** AX, DC, DS, MC, VI.

ELEPHANT BAR & RESTAURANT   **Lunch:** $5-$15   **Dinner:** $5-$15   **Phone:** 913/663-2654
American
Location: I-435, exit 79 (Metcalf Ave/US 169), 1.2 mi s. 11900 Metcalf Ave 66213. **Hours:** 11 am-10 pm, Fri & Sat-11 pm. Closed major holidays. **Features:** Going on safari was never this much fun. Guests who unwind amid the bright jungle decor can sample fresh California cuisine prepared with Pacific Rim influences. Pizza cooked over a wood fire, sizzling cantina fajitas, wok-seared Shanghai cashew chicken and langoustines, and shrimp and chicken jambalaya are among dishes sure to wake up the taste buds. Service is great, too. Casual dress; cocktails. **Parking:** on-site. **Cards:** AX, DS, MC, VI.

FIORELLA'S JACK STACK BARBECUE
OF OVERLAND PARK, INC   **Lunch:** $6-$15   **Dinner:** $7-$26   **Phone:** 913/385-7427   [80]
AAA
Barbecue
Location: I-435, exit 79 (Metcalf Ave/US 169), 1 mi n to 95th St. 9520 Metcalf Ave 66212. **Hours:** 11 am-10 pm, Fri & Sat-10:30 pm, Sun-9 pm. Closed: 11/22, 12/25. **Features:** The popular, comfortable eatery has a big Hereford mural on the wall and lots of wooden pig sculptures. While hickory-smoked meats and sides are the big draw, diners also can get steaks and seafood. Casual dress; cocktails. **Cards:** AX, DC, DS, MC, VI.

FOX AND HOUND ENGLISH PUB   **Lunch:** $7-$17   **Dinner:** $7-$17   **Phone:** 913/649-1700
American
Location: I-435, exit 79 (Metcalf Ave/US 169), 0.5 mi n. 10428 Metcalf Ave 66212. **Hours:** 11 am-1:30 am. Closed: 11/22, 12/25. **Features:** Not your typical stuffy Old English Pub, sister restaurants, Bailey's and Fox & Hound, are the places to go for fun! Pool tables, darts, shuffleboard, and loads of oversized TVs to watch all the games! Dine with friends choosing from the more than 100 beers, Southern BBQ, and pub fare. Casual dress; cocktails. **Parking:** on-site. **Cards:** AX, DC, DS, MC, VI.

GREEN MILL RESTAURANT & BAR-OVERLAND
PARK   **Lunch:** $7-$18   **Dinner:** $7-$18   **Phone:** 913/888-8440
American
Location: I-35, exit 225A (87th St), just se; in Holiday Inn Hotel and Suites. 8787 Reeder Rd 66214. **Hours:** 6:30 am-2 & 5-10 pm, Sat & Sun-11 pm. Closed: 4/8, 11/22, 12/25. **Features:** The eatery prepares top-notch pizzas; a good variety of appetizers, salads, sandwiches and pasta; and some steaks and seafood. Diablo wings are a great way to start the meal. Casual dress; cocktails. **Parking:** on-site. **Cards:** AX, DS, MC, VI.

IL TRULLO   **Dinner:** $9-$25   **Phone:** 913/341-3773   [75]
Italian
Location: I-435, exit 79 (Metcalf Ave/US 169), 1 mi n; in strip mall, set back to west. 9056 Metcalf Ave 66212. **Hours:** 5 pm-9 pm, Fri & Sat-10 pm. Closed major holidays. **Reservations:** accepted. **Features:** This restaurant offers sophisticated cuisine of the Puglia region. They offer fresh salads, pasta and seafood, and bread baked in an oven set in the dining room's stone/concrete trulli. Excellent service gives the feeling it's a "special occasion" to be here. Casual dress; cocktails. **Parking:** on-site. **Cards:** AX, DC, DS, MC, VI.

INDIA PALACE   **Lunch:** $6-$7   **Dinner:** $7-$12   **Phone:** 913/381-1680   [72]
Ethnic
Location: I-35, exit 225A (87th St), 1 mi e. 9918 W 87th St 66212. **Hours:** 11:30 am-2:15 & 5-9:30 pm, Sat & Sun 11:30 am-2:30 & 4-9 pm. **Reservations:** accepted. **Features:** This restaurant has spicy fare from an enticing menu that is generous in portions and taste. If you're uninitiated, try the lunch buffet before launching into unknown territory. They offer 11 different breads and fiery, well-prepared curries. Casual dress; beer & wine only. **Parking:** on-site. **Cards:** AX, CB, DC, DS, MC, VI.

J. ALEXANDER'S   **Lunch:** $8-$28   **Dinner:** $8-$28   **Phone:** 913/469-1995   [84]
American
Location: I-435, exit 79 (Metcalf Ave/US 169), 1 mi s. 11471 Metcalf Ave 66212. **Hours:** 11 am-10 pm, Fri & Sat-11 pm. Closed: 11/22, 12/25. **Features:** The busy and casual restaurant prepares classic fare—including steak, grilled fish and prime rib—in the open kitchen. The dessert menu is excellent. Casual dress; cocktails. **Parking:** on-site. **Cards:** AX, CB, DC, DS, MC, VI.

JOHNNY CASCONE'S ITALIAN RESTAURANT   **Lunch:** $6-$9   **Dinner:** $8-$24   **Phone:** 913/381-6837   [77]
Italian
Location: On US 169, just e. 6863 W 91st St 66212. **Hours:** 11 am-3 & 4-9 pm, Fri-10 pm, Sat 11 am-10 pm, Sun 4 pm-9 pm. Closed major holidays. **Features:** Johnny Cascone's features beef and seafood selections in addition to a large selection of pasta dishes. The baked lasagna, pasta with fresh asparagus, and chicken spidinni are especially good. You'll appreciate the casual and relaxed ambience. Casual dress; cocktails. **Parking:** on-site. **Cards:** AX, CB, DC, DS, MC, VI.

(See map and index starting on p. 444)

JOSE PEPPERS BORDER GRILL & CANTINA   **Lunch:** $6-$8   **Dinner:** $7-$10   **Phone:** 913/341-5673   ⑧①
Mexican
Location: I-435, exit 79 (Metcalf Ave/US 169), 0.6 mi n; in strip mall, set back to west. 10316 Metcalf Ave 66212. **Hours:** 11 am-10 pm, Fri & Sat-11 pm. Closed: 11/22, 12/25. **Features:** Traditional Mexican entrees offer much in the way of creativity, and several dishes are presented in large portions. You will find your old standbys available, such as fajitas and chimichangas, as well as more creative dishes such as the chili relleno platter and the Pollo Magnifico. You will enjoy the elegant, but casual ambience. Casual dress; cocktails. **Parking:** on-site. **Cards:** AX, DC, DS, MC, VI.

K.C. MASTERPIECE BARBECUE & GRILL   **Lunch:** $6-$9   **Dinner:** $7-$25   **Phone:** 913/345-2255   ⑧③
American
Location: I-435, exit 79 (Metcalf Ave/US 169), just se. 10985 Metcalf Ave 66210. **Hours:** 11 am-10 pm, Fri & Sat-11 pm, Sun-9:30 pm. Closed: 11/22, 12/25. **Features:** Very popular with local residents, this restaurant features a large selection of tasty appetizers and entrees, with many classic barbecue choices. The decor includes celebrity photos, several TV sets, a fun atmosphere and attentive service. Casual dress; cocktails. **Parking:** on-site. **Cards:** AX, DC, DS, MC, VI.

THE LONGBRANCH STEAKHOUSE   **Lunch:** $5-$10   **Dinner:** $5-$20   **Phone:** 913/642-2042   ⑦⑥
Steak House
Location: I-435, exit 79 (Metcalf Ave/US 169), 1.5 mi n. 9095 Metcalf Ave 66212. **Hours:** 11 am-11 pm, Sun 4 pm-10 pm. Closed: 11/22, 12/25. **Features:** This restaurant appears to be a rollicking place no matter what time of day you visit. They serve good burgers, iced coffee if you ask, and other tavern-style fare such as steak, sandwiches and salad. The server staff is friendly and helpful. Casual dress; cocktails. **Parking:** on-site. **Cards:** AX, DC, DS, MC, VI.

MIMI'S CAFE   **Lunch:** $5-$15   **Dinner:** $5-$15   **Phone:** 913/599-5848
American
Location: I-35, exit 224, 1 mi e on 95th St. 11885 95th St 66214. **Hours:** 7 am-11 pm. Closed: 12/25. **Reservations:** accepted. **Features:** Breakfast, lunch and dinner are offered throughout the day at this eclectic and popular eatery. With New Orleans inspired decor and a menu that features something for everyone, finding a favorite dish should be no problem. Casual dress; beer & wine only. **Parking:** on-site. **Cards:** AX, DS, MC, VI.

NOODLES & COMPANY   **Lunch:** $3-$8   **Dinner:** $3-$8   **Phone:** 913/239-8424
Thai
Location: I-435, exit 79 (Metcalf Ave/US 169), 2 mi s. 13412 Metcalf Ave 66213. **Hours:** 11 am-9 pm, Fri & Sat-10 pm. **Features:** Asian, Mediterranean and American-inspired cuisine makes up the menu at this pleasant, quick-serve eatery. Entrees include Japanese pan noodles, pesto cavatappi and Wisconsin macaroni and cheese. Casual dress; beer & wine only. **Parking:** on-site. **Cards:** AX, DS, MC, VI.

SUSHI GIN   **Lunch:** $7-$14   **Dinner:** $10-$20   **Phone:** 913/649-8488   ⑦⑨
Japanese
Location: I-435, exit 77 (Nall Ave), 1 mi n. 9559 Nall Ave 66207. **Hours:** 11:30 am-2 & 5-9:30 pm. Closed major holidays; also Sun. **Reservations:** accepted. **Features:** The extensive menu shows good variety, including 25 appetizers and offerings from the sushi bar. Carry-out and catering services are available. Several combination plates are appealing. The dining room is cozy. Casual dress; cocktails. **Parking:** on-site. **Cards:** DC, DS, MC, VI.

W. J. MCBRIDE'S IRISH PUB   **Lunch:** $7-$17   **Dinner:** $7-$17   **Phone:** 913/451-3100   ⑧⑨
Irish
Location: I-435, exit 79 (Metcalf Ave/US 169), 1.2 mi s to 119th St, then just w; in Pinnacle Village Shopping Center. 12030 Blue Valley Pkwy 66213. **Hours:** 11 am-11 pm, Fri & Sat-midnight. **Features:** This eatery is a traditional pub featuring classic Irish cuisine. Casual dress; cocktails. **Parking:** on-site. **Cards:** AX, CB, DC, JC, MC, VI.

PRAIRIE VILLAGE pop. 22,072   (See map and index starting on p. 444)

——— **WHERE TO DINE** ———

CAFE PROVENCE   **Lunch:** $6-$12   **Dinner:** $16-$29   **Phone:** 913/384-5998   ⑥②
French
Location: Downtown; in Prairie Village Shopping Center. 3936 W 69th Terrace 66208. **Hours:** 11 am-2:30 & 5-10 pm. Closed major holidays; also Sun. **Reservations:** suggested. **Features:** The cozy cafe's food is excellent and elegantly presented. Treat yourself to excellent flavors and textures, including very rich sauces and soups; the bouillabaisse is quite good. Casual dress; cocktails. **Parking:** on-site. **Cards:** AX, DC, DS, MC, VI.

SHAWNEE pop. 47,996   (See map and index starting on p. 444)

——— **WHERE TO STAY** ———

COURTYARD BY MARRIOTT   *Book great rates at AAA.com*   **Phone:** (913)631-8800   ⑧④
Small-scale Hotel
All Year   1P: $169-$189   2P: $169-$189
Location: I-435, exit 5 (Midland Dr), just w. 17250 Midland Dr 66217. Fax: 913/631-8801. **Facility:** Smoke free premises. 90 units. 87 one-bedroom standard units, some with whirlpools. 3 one-bedroom suites. 3 stories, interior corridors. *Bath:* combo or shower only. **Parking:** on-site. **Terms:** 3 day cancellation notice, [BP] meal plan available, package plans. **Amenities:** video games (fee), high-speed Internet, voice mail, irons, hair dryers. **Pool(s):** heated indoor. **Leisure Activities:** whirlpool, exercise room. **Guest Services:** valet and coin laundry, wireless Internet. **Business Services:** meeting rooms, business center. **Cards:** AX, CB, DC, DS, JC, MC, VI.

(See map and index starting on p. 444)

HAMPTON INN-SHAWNEE   *Book great rates at AAA.com*   Phone: 913/248-1900   85
▼▼▼▼   Property failed to provide current rates
                     Location: I-435, exit 5 (Midland Dr), just se. 16555 Midland Dr 66217. Fax: 913/248-8567. **Facility:** 127 one-
Small-scale Hotel   bedroom standard units, some with whirlpools. 4 stories, interior corridors. *Bath:* combo or shower only.
                     Parking: on-site. **Amenities:** high-speed Internet, dual phone lines, voice mail, irons, hair dryers. **Pool(s):**
heated indoor. **Leisure Activities:** whirlpool, exercise room. **Guest Services:** valet laundry. **Business Services:** meeting
rooms, business center.

SOME UNITS

───── WHERE TO DINE ─────

BARLEY'S BREWHAUS   **Lunch:** $7-$11   **Dinner:** $11-$20   Phone: 913/268-5160   58
▼▼▼▼   **Location:** I-435, exit 5 (Midland Dr), just e. 16649 Midland Dr 66217. **Hours:** 11 am-11 pm. Closed: 11/22, 12/25.
                     Features: Nearby microbreweries provide 99 varieties of draft beer at the relaxing restaurant, which is
American   comparable to a sports bar but has a more upscale atmosphere and better offerings of pasta, pizza, steaks,
                     sandwiches and creative salads. Hardwood floors, neon lights and pool tables off to the side add to the
mood. Friendly servers are efficient. A good selection of cigars is available in the full-service bar. Casual dress; cocktails.
Parking: on-site. **Cards:** AX, DC, DS, MC, VI.

EL TORO BAR & GRILL MEXICAN RESTAURANT   **Lunch:** $6-$10   **Dinner:** $6-$15   Phone: 913/631-1877   59
▼▼ ▼▼   **Location:** I-35, exit 227, 1.3 mi w, then just n; in strip mall; in Westbrooke Village Shopping Center. 7329 Quivira Rd
                     66216. **Hours:** 10 am-10 pm, Fri & Sat-10:30 pm. Closed major holidays. **Features:** The extensive selection
Mexican   is likely to please all tastes. Lunch specials complement the many kinds of fajitas, quesadillas, burritos,
                     enchiladas and combination plates. A children's menu is available. Casual dress; cocktails. **Parking:** on-site.
Cards: AX, DS, MC, VI.

© Gibson Stock Photography

This ends listings for the Kansas City Vicinity.
The following page resumes the alphabetical listings of cities in Missouri.

KEARNEY —*See Kansas City p. 470.*

KENNETT pop. 11,260

──────── **WHERE TO DINE** ────────

MI RANCHITO IV MEXICAN RESTAURANT   **Lunch:** $4-$6   **Dinner:** $5-$10   **Phone:** 573/717-7070

Mexican   **Location:** Jct US 412 and SR 25, just w. 1730-A First St 63857. **Hours:** 11 am-9 pm, Fri & Sat-10 pm. **Reservations:** accepted. **Features:** The restaurant features colorful decor and a menu that offers familiar favorites as well as some unique entrees. Casual dress; beer & wine only. **Parking:** on-site. **Cards:** MC, VI.

KIMBERLING CITY —*See Branson p. 419.*

KIMMSWICK pop. 94

──────── **WHERE TO DINE** ────────

BLUE OWL RESTAURANT & BAKERY   **Lunch:** $7-$12   **Phone:** 636/464-3128

American   **Location:** Center. 6116 2nd St 63052. **Hours:** 10 am-3 pm, Sat & Sun-5 pm. Closed major holidays; also Mon. **Features:** Tucked amid a village of antique and craft shops, the restaurant has been delighting palates since 1985. Owner-chef Mary Hostetter prepares quiche, croissants, soups, salads, sandwiches and specials. Save room for the luscious desserts made in the on-premises bakery. More than 25 kinds of pies are served each day, as are widely varied cakes and cookies. Casual dress. **Parking:** on-site. **Cards:** AX, DS, MC, VI.

KIRKSVILLE pop. 16,988

──────── **WHERE TO STAY** ────────

COMFORT INN BY CHOICE HOTELS   *Book great rates at AAA.com*   **Phone:** (660)665-2205

   All Year   1P: $79-$99   2P: $89-$109   XP: $5   F15

Motel   **Location:** US 63 N. 2209 N Baltimore 63501. Fax: 660/665-3790. **Facility:** 46 one-bedroom standard units. 2 stories (no elevator), interior corridors. **Parking:** on-site, winter plug-ins. **Amenities:** high-speed Internet, irons, hair dryers. **Leisure Activities:** whirlpool. **Guest Services:** wireless Internet. **Cards:** AX, CB, DC, DS, JC, MC, VI.

SOME UNITS

(ASK) (SD) (GM) [N] [N] [N] [N] [N] [N] / (X) /

SUPER 8 MOTEL-KIRKSVILLE   *Book at AAA.com*   **Phone:** (660)665-8826

   All Year [CP]   1P: $53-$70   2P: $56-$73   XP: $5   F17

Motel   **Location:** On US 63 and SR 6. 1101 Country Club Dr 63501. Fax: 660/665-2376. **Facility:** 61 one-bedroom standard units. 3 stories (no elevator), interior corridors. **Parking:** on-site, winter plug-ins. **Terms:** pets ($10 extra charge, in smoking units). **Amenities:** high-speed Internet, safes (fee). **Leisure Activities:** limited exercise equipment. **Guest Services:** coin laundry, wireless Internet. **Cards:** AX, CB, DC, DS, JC, MC, VI.

SOME UNITS

(ASK) (SD) [N] [N] [N] / (X) [N] [N] /
     FEE

──────── **WHERE TO DINE** ────────

CHINA PALACE   **Lunch:** $5-$11   **Dinner:** $5-$11   **Phone:** 660/627-8888

Chinese   **Location:** On the Square. 124 N Franklin St 63501. **Hours:** 11 am-9 pm, Fri-10 pm, Sat 11:30 am-10 pm, Sun 11:30 am-9 pm. Closed major holidays. **Reservations:** accepted. **Features:** The locally popular restaurant features a Hunan cuisine in its daily buffet for lunch and dinner. The rice pudding and fried bananas are very good. The relaxed decor has an upscale feel that business people and families enjoy. Beer & wine only. **Parking:** on-site. **Cards:** AX, DS, MC, VI.

IL SPAZIO   **Lunch:** $5-$11   **Dinner:** $6-$21   **Phone:** 660/665-8484

American   **Location:** At Washington and S Main sts. 215 W Washington St 63501. **Hours:** 11 am-10 pm, Sun-9 pm. Closed: 11/22, 12/25. **Reservations:** accepted. **Features:** The comfortably casual restaurant offers a pleasant surprise with its contemporary decor and sophisticated touches. Menu selections are ambitious. Casual dress; cocktails. **Parking:** on-site. **Cards:** AX, DS, MC, VI.

THOUSAND HILLS DINING LODGE   **Lunch:** $5-$9   **Dinner:** $6-$19   **Phone:** 660/665-7119

Continental   **Location:** Jct US 63 N, 3.3 mi w on SR 6; jct SR 157, 2.5 mi s to lake; in Thousand Hills State Park. 20431 State Hwy 157 63501. **Hours:** Open 3/1-12/20; 11 am-9 pm; from 4 pm 3/1-4/30 & 9/1-12/21; call for hours. **Reservations:** suggested. **Features:** This restaurant offers a very pleasant dining experience because of its beautiful view of the scenic lake, valley and surrounding woods. The menu features prime rib, steak and lobster, shrimp, and turtle cheesecake. And you'll enjoy the relaxed ambience. Casual dress; cocktails. **Parking:** on-site. **Cards:** AX, DS, MC, VI.

KIRKWOOD —*See St. Louis p. 543.*

LAKE OZARK pop. 1,489

--- **WHERE TO STAY** ---

THE LODGE OF FOUR SEASONS *Book great rates at AAA.com* Phone: (573)365-3000

AAA SAVE	5/19-9/4	1P: $149-$179	2P: $149-$179	XP: $20	F18
	3/1-5/18	1P: $119-$179	2P: $119-$179	XP: $20	F18
▽▽▽▽	9/5-10/31	1P: $109-$169	2P: $109-$169	XP: $20	F18
	11/1-2/29	1P: $89-$169	2P: $89-$169	XP: $20	F18

Resort
Large-scale Hotel
Location: US 54B, 2.5 mi to CR HH, then 2.5 mi w. 315 Four Seasons Dr 65049 (PO Box 215). Fax: 573/365-8525. **Facility:** A top golf resort, as well as home of one of the Midwest's top spa facilites. Luscious and expansive grounds. 352 units. 294 one-bedroom standard units. 8 one-, 40 two- and 10 three-bedroom suites ($250-$600) with whirlpools, some with efficiencies or kitchens. 1-4 stories, interior/exterior corridors. **Parking:** on-site and valet. **Terms:** check-in 4 pm, 7 day cancellation notice-fee imposed, package plans. **Amenities:** high-speed Internet, voice mail, irons, hair dryers. *Some:* honor bars. **Dining:** 7 restaurants, 6:30 am-11 pm, cocktails. **Pool(s):** 2 outdoor, heated outdoor, heated indoor/outdoor. **Leisure Activities:** whirlpools, limited beach access, 2 lighted tennis courts, recreation programs in summer, hiking trails, jogging, playground, exercise room, spa, basketball, volleyball. *Fee:* boats, marina, fishing, charter fishing, pontoon, parasailing, golf-63 holes, trap shooting, scenic cruises in-season, cinema with nightly feature film. **Guest Services:** gift shop, valet laundry, airport transportation-Lee C Fine, wireless Internet. **Business Services:** conference facilities, business center. **Cards:** AX, DS, MC, VI.

SOME UNITS

✈ ⑪ ☂ ⚒ ☎ ✕ ⛄ ▣ / ✕ VCR ▤ ▦ /

--- *The following lodgings were either not evaluated or did not meet AAA rating requirements but are listed for your information only.* ---

HOLIDAY SHORES Phone: 573/348-3438
[fyi] Not evaluated. **Location:** 15 Orville Rd 65065. Facilities, services, and decor characterize a mid-range property.

PORT ELSEWHERE Phone: 573/365-4077
[fyi] Not evaluated. **Location:** 100 Elsewhere Dr 65049. Facilities, services, and decor characterize a mid-range property.

--- **WHERE TO DINE** ---

ANDRE'S AT THE LAKE Dinner: $15-$40 Phone: 573/365-2800
AAA **Location:** CR HH, 2 mi w of jct US 54B. Horseshoe Bend Pkwy 65049. **Hours:** 5 pm-9 pm, Fri & Sat-10 pm; Sunday brunch 10 am-2 pm 4/1-10/31. **Reservations:** suggested. **Features:** This fine dining restaurant, serving American/French cuisine, appeals to those looking for a casual, quiet yet elegant experience with a
▽▽▽▽ spectacular view of the lake. High on a bluff overlooking the Lake of the Ozarks, this restaurant incorporates American wood and native stone to blend in with the natural surroundings. The wood and stone theme is continued inside with large glass windows giving an attractive, open atmosphere. Dressy casual; cocktails. **Parking:** on-site. **Cards:** AX, DC, DS, MC, VI.
☂ ◳

BENTLEY'S RESTAURANT *Menu on AAA.com* Dinner: $14-$28 Phone: 573/365-5301
AAA **Location:** On US 54 business route; 2 mi s of Bagnell Dam Blvd. 3100 Bagnell Dam Blvd 65049. **Hours:** 5 pm-10 pm, Fri & Sat-11 pm. Closed: 11/22, 12/25; also Sun. **Reservations:** suggested, weekends. **Features:** The
▽▽▽▽ restaurant's English pub atmosphere makes it a nice spot in which to savor an English-cut prime rib that's good enough to make diners want to return. The casual dining room affords a pleasant view of the forest up
Steak & Seafood close and the lake in the distance. Casual dress; cocktails. **Parking:** on-site. **Cards:** AX, CB, DC, DS, MC, VI.
☂ ◳

J. B. HOOKS Lunch: $7-$11 Dinner: $16-$26 Phone: 573/365-3255
▽▽▽▽ **Location:** On US 54 business route, 0.7 mi w from jct US 54. 2260 Bagnell Dam Blvd 65049. **Hours:** 11 am-9 pm, Fri & Sat-11 pm. Closed: 12/25. **Features:** Community Bridge and the Lake of the Ozarks are clearly visible
Steak & Seafood from the large windows along one wall of the comfortable restaurant's dining room. Casual dress; cocktails. **Parking:** on-site. **Cards:** AX, DC, DS, MC, VI.
☂ ◳

LI'L RIZZO'S Lunch: $6-$20 Dinner: $6-$20 Phone: 573/365-3003
▽▽▽▽ **Location:** On CR HH, 2.1 mi w of jct US 54B. 434 CR HH 65049. **Hours:** 5 pm-10 pm, Sat & Sun from 11 am; 11
Italian am-10 pm, Fri & Sat-11 pm 4/1-10/31. Closed: 11/22, 12/24, 12/25. **Features:** Li'l Rizzo's features a scenic view of the lake, a relaxed atmosphere, and a good selection of pasta, beef and seafood. They also serve domestic and imported beers and wine by the glass. Patio seating is available, weather permitting. Casual dress; cocktails. **Parking:** on-site. **Cards:** DS, MC, VI.
◳

PORT SIDE RESTAURANT & LOUNGE Lunch: $7-$13 Dinner: $7-$34 Phone: 573/365-2334
▽▽▽▽ **Location:** 2.6 mi s of Bagnell Dam, on US 54 business route; in The Resort at Port Arrowhead. 120 Holiday Ln 65049.
American **Hours:** 6:30 am-2 & 5-10 pm; 6:30 am-1 & 5-10 pm 11/1-3/31. Closed: 12/25. **Reservations:** suggested. **Features:** Creative selections are prepared in a pleasant, lakeview setting. Outdoor seating is a seasonal option. Casual dress; cocktails; entertainment. **Parking:** on-site. **Cards:** AX, DS, MC, VI.
☂ ◳

LAMAR pop. 4,452

--- **WHERE TO STAY** ---

SUPER 8 MOTEL-LAMAR *Book at AAA.com* Phone: (417)682-6888

▽▽▽ ▽▽▽	5/1-2/29 [BP]	1P: $54-$64	2P: $59-$72	XP: $5	F17
	3/1-4/30 [BP]	1P: $54	2P: $59-$62	XP: $5	F17

Small-scale Hotel **Location:** Jct US 71 and 160. 45 SE 1st Ln 64759. Fax: 417/682-3510. **Facility:** 57 one-bedroom standard units, some with whirlpools. 2 stories (no elevator), interior corridors. *Bath:* combo or shower only. **Parking:** on-site. **Terms:** [CP] meal plan available. **Pool(s):** heated outdoor. **Leisure Activities:** limited exercise equipment. **Guest Services:** coin laundry, wireless Internet. **Business Services:** meeting rooms, business center. **Cards:** AX, DC, DS, MC, VI.

SOME UNITS

ASK ⑪ ✦ ☎ ⛄ / ✕ ▤ ▦ /

LAURIE pop. 663

------ **WHERE TO DINE** ------

COUSINS
Lunch: $5-$7
Phone: 573/374-0922

American

Location: Jct SR 135, just s. 601 N Hwy 5 65038. **Hours:** 6 am-2 pm. Closed: 11/22; also 12/24-1/4. **Reservations:** accepted. **Features:** This small town restaurant offers popular country comfort foods in a casual setting with cordial and competent waitresses. Try the "super tenderloin platter" of hand-battered, deep-fried pork tenderloin and mashed potatoes smothered in gravy. Or order breakfast, it is served anytime the restaurant is open. Casual dress. **Parking:** on-site.

LEBANON pop. 12,155

------ **WHERE TO STAY** ------

BEST WESTERN WYOTA INN LEBANON   *Book great rates at AAA.com*
Phone: (417)532-6171

All Year	1P: $49-$99	2P: $49-$99	XP: $10 F16

Small-scale Hotel

Location: I-44, exit 130, just nw. 1225 Mill Creek Rd 65536. **Fax:** 417/532-6174. **Facility:** 52 one-bedroom standard units. 1-2 stories (no elevator), exterior corridors. **Parking:** on-site, winter plug-ins. **Terms:** cancellation fee imposed, [BP] meal plan available, small pets only ($10 extra charge, in designated units). **Amenities:** irons, hair dryers. *Some:* high-speed Internet. **Dining:** Andy's 417 Restaurant, see separate listing. **Pool(s):** outdoor. **Guest Services:** valet and coin laundry. **Business Services:** meeting rooms. **Cards:** AX, CB, DC, DS, MC, VI. **Free Special Amenities:** full breakfast and high-speed Internet.

SOME UNITS

HAMPTON INN   *Book great rates at AAA.com*
Phone: (417)533-3100

5/2-9/1	1P: $91-$119	2P: $101-$129
3/1-5/1 & 9/2-2/29	1P: $84-$96	2P: $90-$107

Small-scale Hotel

Location: I-44, exit 127, just sw. 930 Ivy Ln 65536. **Fax:** 417/533-5858. **Facility:** 68 one-bedroom standard units, some with whirlpools. 3 stories, interior corridors. *Bath:* combo or shower only. **Parking:** on-site. **Terms:** cancellation fee imposed. **Amenities:** video games (fee), high-speed Internet, voice mail, irons, hair dryers. **Pool(s):** outdoor. **Leisure Activities:** exercise room. **Guest Services:** valet laundry. **Business Services:** meeting rooms, PC. **Cards:** AX, DC, DS, MC, VI.

SOME UNITS

HOLIDAY INN EXPRESS   *Book at AAA.com*
Phone: (417)532-1111

5/2-2/29	1P: $89-$99	2P: $99-$109	XP: $10 F18
3/1-5/1	1P: $79-$99	2P: $89-$109	XP: $10 F18

Small-scale Hotel

Location: I-44, exit 127, just n. 1955 W Elm St 65536. **Fax:** 417/532-8650. **Facility:** 62 one-bedroom standard units, some with whirlpools. 3 stories, interior corridors. **Parking:** on-site. **Terms:** cancellation fee imposed, pets ($25 fee). **Amenities:** high-speed Internet, dual phone lines, voice mail, irons, hair dryers. **Pool(s):** heated indoor. **Guest Services:** valet laundry. **Business Services:** meeting rooms, PC. **Cards:** AX, CB, DC, DS, MC, VI.

SOME UNITS

------ *The following lodging was either not evaluated or did not* ------
meet AAA rating requirements but is listed for your information only.

SUPER 8 MOTEL
Phone: 417/588-2574

fyi

Not evaluated. **Location:** I-44, exit 127, just nw. 1831 W Elm 65536. Facilities, services, and decor characterize a mid-range property.

------ **WHERE TO DINE** ------

ANDY'S 417 RESTAURANT
Lunch: $5-$7
Dinner: $7-$14
Phone: 417/533-5801

American

Location: I-44, exit 130, just nw; in Best Western Wyota Inn. 1225 Millcreek Rd 65536. **Hours:** 7 am-8 pm, Sun-3 pm. Closed: 1/1, 12/25. **Features:** Guests will find no pretense here, just home-style cooking and friendly service. Breakfast items are served all day. Casual dress. **Parking:** on-site. **Cards:** MC, VI.

CORNERSTONE SUBS & PIZZA
Lunch: $3-$15
Dinner: $3-$15
Phone: 417/588-3616

American

Location: At Jefferson Ave and Hayes St. 399 S Jefferson Ave 65536. **Hours:** 10:30 am-8 pm, Fri-9 pm. Closed major holidays; also Sun. **Features:** Bustling at lunchtime, the establishment prepares tasty pizza and sandwich selections. The atmosphere is decidedly "no frills". Casual dress. **Parking:** on-site. **Cards:** AX, DS, MC, VI.

DOWD'S CATFISH & BBQ
Lunch: $5-$20
Dinner: $8-$20
Phone: 417/532-1777

American

Location: I-44, exit 127, 0.3 mi w. 1760 W Elm St 65536. **Hours:** 11 am-8 pm, Fri & Sat-9 pm; to 9 pm, Fri & Sat-10 pm in summer. Closed: 1/1, 11/22, 12/25. **Reservations:** accepted. **Features:** This locally popular spot features a fishing theme with "hometown country" thrown in for good measure; the menu offers generous portions of a variety of selections. Casual dress. **Parking:** on-site. **Cards:** AX, DC, DS, MC, VI.

LEE'S SUMMIT —See Kansas City p. 470.

LIBERTY —See Kansas City p. 471.

LICKING pop. 1,471

——— WHERE TO STAY ———

SCENIC RIVERS INN
    ◈◈◈ — Motel
Phone: (573)674-4809

All Year [CP]   1P: $45-$50   2P: $50-$55   XP: $5   F18
Location: On US 63. 209 S Hwy 63 65542 (PO Box 468). Fax: 573/674-2718. **Facility:** 51 one-bedroom standard units, some with whirlpools. 2 stories (no elevator), exterior corridors. *Bath:* combo or shower only. **Parking:** on-site. **Terms:** office hours 7 am-11 pm, pets ($5 extra charge). **Amenities:** hair dryers. **Pool(s):** heated indoor. **Leisure Activities:** whirlpool, exercise room. **Guest Services:** coin laundry, wireless Internet. **Cards:** AX, DS, MC, VI.

SOME UNITS
ASK ⑤ᴅ 🐾 🖐 ⚙ 🏊 🎥 / ✕ 🍽 🔲 🖳 🖥 /
FEE

LOUISIANA pop. 3,863

——— WHERE TO STAY ———

RIVER'S EDGE MOTEL
    AAA [SAVE]
    ◈◈◈ — Motel
Phone: (573)754-4522

All Year   1P: $56-$65   2P: $60-$70   XP: $4   F10
Location: On US 54; at Champ Clark Bridge. 201 Mansion St 63353. Fax: 573/754-4522. **Facility:** 30 one-bedroom standard units. 1-2 stories (no elevator), exterior corridors. **Parking:** on-site, winter plug-ins. **Terms:** small pets only ($5 extra charge). **Amenities:** high-speed Internet. *Some:* irons, hair dryers. **Guest Services:** wireless Internet. **Cards:** AX, DC, DS, MC, VI.

SOME UNITS
🖐 🎥 🔲 🖳 🖥 / ✕ /
FEE

——— WHERE TO DINE ———

EAGLE'S NEST
    ◈◈ — American
Lunch: $5-$8   **Dinner:** $10-$25   **Phone:** 573/754-9888
Location: Just s of jct SR 54 and 79; at SR 79 and Georgia St. 221 Georgia St 63353. **Hours:** 8-10 am, 11-3 & 5-9 pm, Sun 9:30 am-2 pm. Closed: 1/1, 11/22, 12/25. **Reservations:** suggested, weekends. **Features:** Good food is offered at this trendy spot in the historic downtown area; coffees, teas, pastries and wines are available in addition to the specialty menu items. Casual dress; cocktails. **Parking:** street. **Cards:** AX, DS, MC, VI.

MACON pop. 5,538

——— WHERE TO STAY ———

BEST WESTERN INN   *Book great rates at AAA.com*
    ◈◈ — Motel
Phone: (660)385-2125

All Year   1P: $57-$69   2P: $59-$69   XP: $5   F12
Location: On Outer Rd S; at US 36 and Long Branch Lake exit. Located in a country area. 28933 Sunset Dr 63552. Fax: 660/385-4900. **Facility:** 46 one-bedroom standard units. 1-2 stories (no elevator), interior/exterior corridors. *Bath:* combo or shower only. **Parking:** on-site, winter plug-ins. **Terms:** small pets only ($20 deposit). **Amenities:** high-speed Internet, irons, hair dryers. **Pool(s):** small outdoor. **Guest Services:** wireless Internet. **Cards:** AX, CB, DC, DS, JC, MC, VI.

SOME UNITS
ASK ⑤ᴅ ✈ 🖐 🐾 🍴 🏊 🎥 🔲 🖳 🖥 / ✕ /
FEE

COMFORT INN   *Book great rates at AAA.com*
    ◈◈◈ — Small-scale Hotel
Phone: (660)395-8000

All Year   1P: $75-$95   2P: $80-$100   XP: $5   F16
Location: Jct US 36 and 63. 1821 N Missouri St 63552. Fax: 660/395-8001. **Facility:** 62 one-bedroom standard units, some with whirlpools. 3 stories, interior corridors. *Bath:* combo or shower only. **Parking:** on-site. **Terms:** package plans. **Amenities:** high-speed Internet, safes (fee), irons, hair dryers. **Pool(s):** small heated indoor. **Leisure Activities:** whirlpool, exercise room. **Guest Services:** coin laundry, wireless Internet. **Business Services:** meeting rooms, business center. **Cards:** AX, DC, DS, MC, VI.

SOME UNITS
ASK ⑤ᴅ ⚙ᴍ 🗝 🐾 🎥 🖐 🖳 🖥 / ✕ /

SUPER 8 MOTEL   *Book at AAA.com*
    ◈◈ — Small-scale Hotel
Phone: (660)385-5788

All Year   1P: $52-$76   2P: $56-$80   XP: $4   F18
Location: Jct US 36 and 63. 203 E Briggs Dr 63552. Fax: 660/385-5788. **Facility:** 59 one-bedroom standard units. 3 stories (no elevator), interior corridors. **Parking:** on-site. **Terms:** [CP] meal plan available, pets ($10 extra charge). **Amenities:** high-speed Internet, safes (fee). *Some:* hair dryers. **Guest Services:** wireless Internet. **Business Services:** PC. **Cards:** AX, DS, MC, VI.

SOME UNITS
ASK 🖐 🎥 🖥 / ✕ 🔲 🖳 /
FEE

——— WHERE TO DINE ———

THE LONG BRANCH RESTAURANT   **Lunch:** $6-$12   **Dinner:** $6-$18   **Phone:** 660/385-4600
    ◈◈ — American
Location: On Outer Rd S; at US 36 and Long Branch Lake exit. 28855 Sunset Dr 63552. **Hours:** 6:30 am-8:30 pm, Fri & Sat-9 pm. Closed: 1/1, 12/25. **Features:** You'll find good home-style family dining at the Long Branch, which offers a daily buffet with several choices of entrees including fried chicken, pork chops, baked stuffed green peppers as well as salad, soup, vegetables and dessert. Friendly service. Casual dress; cocktails. **Parking:** on-site. **Cards:** AX, DC, DS, MC, VI.

🚭

PEAR TREE SUB STOP   **Lunch:** $4-$10   **Dinner:** $4-$10   **Phone:** 660/385-1500
    ◈ — American
Location: Jct US 36 and 63, just s. 1206 N Missouri 63552. **Hours:** 10:30 am-9 pm. Closed major holidays; also Sun. **Features:** Guests unwind in the cozy dining room over a fresh sandwich, pizza or any of a number of "extras". Casual dress. **Parking:** on-site. **Cards:** AX, MC, VI.

MAPLEWOOD —*See St. Louis p. 544.*

MARSHALL pop. 12,433

——— **WHERE TO STAY** ———

COMFORT INN-MARSHALL STATION *Book great rates at AAA.com* **Phone:** (660)886-8080
(AAA) (SAVE) All Year   1P: $73-$125   2P: $78-$130   XP: $5   F18
Location: On US 65, 2 mi w. 1356 W College St 65340. **Fax:** 660/886-8042. **Facility:** 58 one-bedroom standard
units, some with whirlpools. 3 stories, interior corridors. *Bath:* combo or shower only. **Parking:** on-site.
Terms: [ECP] meal plan available. **Amenities:** high-speed Internet, voice mail, irons, hair dryers. **Pool(s):**
Small-scale Hotel   small heated indoor. **Leisure Activities:** whirlpool. **Guest Services:** coin laundry, wireless Internet.
Business Services: meeting rooms. **Cards:** AX, CB, DC, DS, JC, MC, VI. **Free Special Amenities:**
expanded continental breakfast and local telephone calls.

SOME UNITS

MARSHFIELD pop. 5,720

——— **WHERE TO STAY** ———

HOLIDAY INN EXPRESS *Book at AAA.com* **Phone:** (417)859-6000
4/2-9/6   1P: $94-$110   XP: $10   F18
3/1-4/1 & 9/7-2/29   1P: $86-$99   XP: $10   F18
Small-scale Hotel   **Location:** I-44, exit 100 (SR 38), on southeast corner. 1301 Banning St 65706. **Fax:** 417/859-6001. **Facility:** 58
one-bedroom standard units, some with whirlpools. 2 stories (no elevator), interior corridors. **Parking:** on-
site. **Terms:** cancellation fee imposed, pets ($25 fee, with prior approval). **Amenities:** high-speed Internet, irons, hair dryers.
Pool(s): outdoor. **Guest Services:** coin laundry, wireless Internet. **Business Services:** PC. **Cards:** AX, DC, DS, MC, VI.

SOME UNITS

——— **WHERE TO DINE** ———

DANCEY'S   **Lunch:** $6-$12   **Dinner:** $6-$12   **Phone:** 417/859-5421
Location: I-44, exit 100 (SR 38), 0.4 mi s. 1150 Spur Dr, #16 65706. **Hours:** 11 am-9 pm. Closed: 11/22, 12/25.
American   **Reservations:** accepted. **Features:** The atmosphere is relaxed at the family restaurant, which offers steak,
seafood and chicken dishes, as well as a salad bar. Casual dress. **Parking:** on-site. **Cards:** AX, CB, DS,
MC, VI.

MARYLAND HEIGHTS —*See St. Louis p. 544.*

MARYVILLE pop. 10,581

——— **WHERE TO STAY** ———

AMERICA'S BEST INN & SUITES *Book at AAA.com* **Phone:** (660)562-3111
All Year [ECP]   1P: $52-$62   2P: $59-$69
Location: Jct of US 71 Bypass and 136. 1700 E First St 64468. **Fax:** 660/562-2171. **Facility:** 62 one-bedroom
standard units, some with whirlpools. 2 stories, interior corridors. *Bath:* combo or shower only. **Parking:** on-
Small-scale Hotel   site, winter plug-ins. **Amenities:** high-speed Internet, irons, hair dryers. *Some:* dual phone lines. **Business
Services:** meeting rooms. **Cards:** AX, CB, DC, DS, MC, VI.

SOME UNITS

COMFORT INN *Book great rates at AAA.com* **Phone:** (660)562-2002
All Year   1P: $50-$60   2P: $60-$80   XP: $5   F10
Location: On Business Rt US 71; just n of US 71 Bypass. 2817 S Main St 64468. **Fax:** 660/562-2003. **Facility:** 50
one-bedroom standard units. 2 stories (no elevator), interior corridors. **Parking:** on-site, winter plug-ins.
Small-scale Hotel   **Terms:** [CP] meal plan available. **Amenities:** high-speed Internet, voice mail, safes (fee), irons, hair dryers.
Pool(s): heated indoor/outdoor. **Leisure Activities:** sauna, whirlpool. *Fee:* game room. **Guest Services:** valet laundry.
Business Services: meeting rooms, PC. **Cards:** AX, DC, DS, MC, VI.

SOME UNITS

HOLIDAY INN EXPRESS *Book at AAA.com* **Phone:** (660)562-9949
All Year   1P: $68   2P: $68
Location: On Business Rt 71; just n of US 71 Bypass. 2929 S Main St 64468. **Fax:** 660/562-2906. **Facility:** 59
units. 40 one-bedroom standard units. 19 one-bedroom suites ($77), some with whirlpools. 3 stories, interior
Small-scale Hotel   corridors. *Bath:* combo or shower only. **Parking:** on-site. **Terms:** [CP] meal plan available. **Amenities:** high-
speed Internet, voice mail, irons, hair dryers. **Pool(s):** small heated indoor. **Leisure Activities:** whirlpool, exercise room. **Guest
Services:** valet and coin laundry. **Business Services:** meeting rooms. **Cards:** AX, CB, DC, DS, JC, MC, VI.

SOME UNITS

SUPER 8 MOTEL-MARYVILLE *Book at AAA.com* **Phone:** (660)582-8088
All Year   1P: $45-$50   2P: $50-$55   XP: $3   F16
Location: On Business Rt US 71; just n of US 71 Bypass. 222 Summit Dr 64468. **Fax:** 660/582-3162. **Facility:** 32
one-bedroom standard units. 2 stories (no elevator), interior corridors. **Parking:** on-site. **Terms:** [CP] meal
Small-scale Hotel   plan available, pets ($10 deposit). **Amenities:** high-speed Internet, safes (fee), irons, hair dryers.
Cards: AX, DS, MC, VI.

SOME UNITS

──────── **WHERE TO DINE** ────────

A & G RESTAURANT ▽▽▽ ▽▽▽ American
Lunch: $5-$12 **Dinner:** $9-$20 **Phone:** 660/582-4421
Location: On Business Rt US 71, 2.3 mi n of US 71 Bypass; downtown. 208 N Main St 64468. **Hours:** 11 am-10 pm, Fri & Sat-11 pm, Sun-9 pm. **Closed:** 11/22, 12/25. **Features:** Examples of creative dishes include Jack Daniels grilled chicken and fried strawberry cheesecake. Also on the menu are many kinds of steaks, sandwiches, burgers and Italian dishes, as well as jambalaya and Greek moussaka. Casual dress; cocktails. **Parking:** on-site. **Cards:** AX, DC, DS, MC, VI.

MEHLVILLE —*See St. Louis p. 547.*

MEXICO pop. 11,320

──────── **WHERE TO STAY** ────────

AMERIHOST INN-MEXICO *Book at AAA.com* ▽▽▽ ▽▽▽ Small-scale Hotel
Phone: (573)582-0055
All Year 1P: $69-$84 2P: $69-$84 XP: $10 F
Location: Jct Business Rt US 54 S and 54 Bypass. 900 Vance Rd 65265. **Fax:** 573/582-0189. **Facility:** 61 one-bedroom standard units, some with whirlpools. 2 stories (no elevator), interior corridors. *Bath:* combo or shower only. **Parking:** on-site. **Terms:** weekly rates available. **Amenities:** high-speed Internet, safes (fee), irons, hair dryers. **Pool(s):** heated indoor. **Leisure Activities:** whirlpool, exercise room. **Guest Services:** wireless Internet. **Business Services:** meeting rooms. **Cards:** AX, DC, DS, MC, VI.
SOME UNITS

MINER pop. 1,056

──────── **WHERE TO STAY** ────────

DRURY INN-SIKESTON *Book at AAA.com* ▽▽▽ ▽▽▽ Small-scale Hotel
Phone: (573)471-4100
All Year [BP] 1P: $76-$120 2P: $86-$130 XP: $10 F18
Location: I-55, exit 67, just sw. 2602 E Malone 63801. **Fax:** 573/471-4100. **Facility:** 80 units. 78 one-bedroom standard units. 2 one-bedroom suites ($116-$140). 4 stories, interior corridors. *Bath:* combo or shower only. **Parking:** on-site. **Amenities:** high-speed Internet, dual phone lines, voice mail, irons, hair dryers. **Pool(s):** heated indoor/outdoor. **Leisure Activities:** whirlpool, exercise room. **Guest Services:** complimentary evening beverages: Mon-Sat, valet and coin laundry, wireless Internet. **Business Services:** meeting rooms, PC. **Cards:** AX, CB, DC, DS, MC, VI.
SOME UNITS

PEAR TREE INN BY DRURY-SIKESTON *Book at AAA.com* ▽▽ ▽▽ Small-scale Hotel
Phone: (573)471-8660
All Year [ECP] 1P: $50-$100 2P: $60-$110 XP: $10 F18
Location: I-55, exit 67, just sw. 2602 E Malone 63801. **Fax:** 573/471-8660. **Facility:** 67 one-bedroom standard units. 3 stories (no elevator), exterior corridors. **Parking:** on-site, winter plug-ins. **Amenities:** high-speed Internet, irons, hair dryers. **Pool(s):** outdoor. **Guest Services:** wireless Internet. **Cards:** AX, CB, DC, DS, MC, VI.
SOME UNITS

──────── **WHERE TO DINE** ────────

LAMBERT'S CAFE ▽▽ ▽▽ American Casual dress.
Lunch: $8-$16 **Dinner:** $8-$16 **Phone:** 573/471-4261
Location: I-55, exit 67, 1 mi w on US 62. 2305 E Malone 63801. **Hours:** 10:30 am-9 pm. **Closed:** 1/1, 11/22, 12/24, 12/25. **Features:** Diners who settle in at the friendly, energetic and fun cafe can expect their dinner rolls to be thrown to them from almost anywhere in the restaurant. Examples of down-home country food include chicken and dumplings, ribs and seafood. Servers pleasantly bring out seconds, thirds and more. **Parking:** on-site.

MOBERLY pop. 11,945

──────── **WHERE TO STAY** ────────

BEST WESTERN MOBERLY INN *Book great rates at AAA.com* ▽▽▽ ▽▽▽ Small-scale Hotel
Phone: (660)263-6540
All Year 1P: $62-$120 2P: $69-$127 XP: $7 F12
Location: Jct US 24 and 63 business route. 1200 Hwy 24 E 65270. **Fax:** 660/263-0092. **Facility:** 98 units. 88 one-bedroom standard units. 10 one-bedroom suites. 1-2 stories (no elevator), interior/exterior corridors. **Parking:** on-site. **Terms:** 10 day cancellation notice-fee imposed, small pets only ($30 fee). **Amenities:** high-speed Internet, voice mail, irons, hair dryers. **Pool(s):** outdoor. **Guest Services:** valet and coin laundry. **Business Services:** meeting rooms. **Cards:** AX, CB, DC, DS, JC, MC, VI.
SOME UNITS
FEE

MOUNTAIN GROVE pop. 4,574

──────── **WHERE TO STAY** ────────

DAYS INN OF MOUNTAIN GROVE *Book great rates at AAA.com* AAA [SAVE] ▽▽ Small-scale Hotel
Phone: (417)926-5555
All Year [CP] 1P: $46-$60 2P: $54-$65 XP: $5 F17
Location: Jct US 60 and 95, just se. 300 E 19th St 65711. **Fax:** 417/926-5555. **Facility:** 37 units. 35 one- and 2 two-bedroom standard units. 2 stories (no elevator), exterior corridors. **Parking:** on-site. **Terms:** cancellation fee imposed, small pets only ($5 extra charge). **Amenities:** hair dryers. **Pool(s):** outdoor. **Business Services:** meeting rooms. **Cards:** AX, CB, DC, DS, MC, VI. **Free Special Amenities:** continental breakfast and high-speed Internet.
SOME UNITS
FEE

TRAVELODGE   *Book at AAA.com*   Phone: (417)926-3152
▼▼▼   All Year [CP]   1P: $44-$63   2P: $49-$68   XP: $5   F17
Motel   **Location:** Jct US 60 and 95, just s. 111 E 17th St 65711. Fax: 417/926-3014. **Facility:** 50 one-bedroom standard
              units, some with whirlpools. 1 story, exterior corridors. **Parking:** on-site. **Terms:** cancellation fee imposed,
              small pets only ($10 extra charge, in smoking units). **Amenities:** irons, hair dryers. *Some:* high-speed
Internet. **Pool(s):** outdoor. **Guest Services:** wireless Internet. **Cards:** AX, CB, DC, DS, MC, VI.

--------- **WHERE TO DINE** ---------

THE HAYLOFT RESTAURANT   **Lunch:** $5-$7   **Dinner:** $7-$13   Phone: 417/926-6200
▼▼ ▼▼   **Location:** 0.9 mi s on SR 95. 503 N Main St 65711. **Hours:** 10:30 am-8 pm, Fri & Sat-9 pm, Sun-7 pm. Closed
American   major holidays. **Reservations:** accepted. **Features:** Travelers can join the locals in the eatery, which offers
             small-town charm, a pleasant atmosphere and plenty of comfort food. Casual dress. **Parking:** on-site.
             Cards: DS, MC, VI.

NEOSHO pop. 10,505

--------- **WHERE TO STAY** ---------

SUPER 8 MOTEL-NEOSHO   *Book at AAA.com*   Phone: (417)455-1888
▼▼▼ ▼▼▼   All Year [CP]   1P: $60   2P: $60   XP: $5   F17
Small-scale Hotel **Location:** Just s of jct US 60B and 71B. 3085 Gardner/Edgewood Dr 64850. Fax: 417/455-0921. **Facility:** 58 one-
             bedroom standard units, some with whirlpools. 2 stories (no elevator), interior corridors. **Parking:** on-site.
             Terms: pets ($10 extra charge). **Amenities:** safes (fee), hair dryers. **Guest Services:** coin laundry, wireless
Internet. **Cards:** AX, CB, DC, DS, JC, MC, VI.

NEVADA pop. 8,607

--------- **WHERE TO STAY** ---------

COUNTRY INN & SUITES BY CARLSON   *Book at AAA.com*   Phone: (417)667-9292
▼▼▼ ▼▼▼   All Year   1P: $74-$84   2P: $74-$84   XP: $5   D18
Small-scale Hotel **Location:** US 71, exit Camp Clark, just w. 2520 E Austin 64772 (PO Box P). **Facility:** 45 units. 38 one-bedroom
             standard units, some with whirlpools. 7 one-bedroom suites ($84-$104). 2 stories, interior corridors. *Bath:*
             combo or shower only. **Parking:** on-site. **Terms:** [ECP] meal plan available. **Amenities:** voice mail, irons,
hair dryers. **Pool(s):** small heated indoor. **Leisure Activities:** whirlpool, exercise room. **Guest Services:** coin laundry, wireless
Internet. **Business Services:** meeting rooms. **Cards:** AX, CB, DC, DS, MC, VI.

DAYS INN OF NEVADA   *Book great rates at AAA.com*   Phone: (417)667-6777
▼▼ ▼▼   3/1-9/1 [ECP]   1P: $53-$65   2P: $58-$69   XP: $5   F17
             9/2-2/29 [ECP]   1P: $49-$60   2P: $53-$65   XP: $5   F17
Small-scale Hotel **Location:** US 71, exit Camp Clark, just w. 2345 Marvel Rd 64772. Fax: 417/667-6135. **Facility:** 48 units. 45 one-
             bedroom standard units. 2 one- and 1 two-bedroom suites ($90-$95), some with whirlpools. 2 stories (no
elevator), interior/exterior corridors. **Parking:** on-site, winter plug-ins. **Terms:** pets ($5 extra charge). **Amenities:** hair dryers.
Pool(s): small outdoor. **Guest Services:** coin laundry, wireless Internet. **Business Services:** meeting rooms. **Cards:** AX, CB,
DC, DS, MC, VI.

SUPER 8 MOTEL   *Book at AAA.com*   Phone: 417/667-8888
▼▼ ▼▼   All Year   1P: $49-$57   2P: $54-$57   XP: $5   F17
Small-scale Hotel **Location:** US 71, exit Camp Clark, just w. 2301 E Austin Blvd 64772. Fax: 417/667-8883. **Facility:** 58 one-
             bedroom standard units. 2 stories (no elevator), interior corridors. **Parking:** on-site. **Terms:** pets ($5 extra
             charge, with prior approval). **Pool(s):** small heated indoor. **Guest Services:** coin laundry, wireless Internet.
Business Services: meeting rooms. **Cards:** AX, DC, DS, MC, VI.

--------- **WHERE TO DINE** ---------

CASA AZTECA   **Lunch:** $4-$6   **Dinner:** $5-$12   Phone: 417/667-4771
▼▼▼ ▼▼▼   **Location:** Just n of jct US 71 business route and 54. 117 Centennial Blvd 64772. **Hours:** 11 am-10 pm, Fri & Sat-11
Mexican   pm. Closed major holidays. **Features:** Colorful murals depicting lively Mexican scenes cover the walls.
             Hearty portions of favorite dishes fill guests' plates. Casual dress; beer only. **Parking:** on-site.
             Cards: MC, VI.

NEW FLORENCE pop. 764

──────── WHERE TO STAY ────────

DAYS INN BOONESLICK LODGE　*Book great rates at AAA.com*　**Phone:** (573)835-7777

| | 5/16-10/31 [ECP] | 1P: $57-$75 | 2P: $62-$85 | XP: $5 | F18 |
| | 3/1-5/15 & 11/1-2/29 [ECP] | 1P: $49-$64 | 2P: $54-$69 | XP: $5 | F18 |

Small-scale Hotel　**Location:** I-70, exit 175, just w. 403 Booneslick Rd 63363. Fax: 573/835-7710. **Facility:** 47 one-bedroom standard units, some with whirlpools. 2 stories (no elevator), interior corridors. **Parking:** on-site. **Terms:** weekly rates available, pets ($20 deposit, $10 extra charge). **Amenities:** high-speed Internet, voice mail, safes (fee), hair dryers. **Pool(s):** small heated outdoor. **Leisure Activities:** limited exercise equipment. **Guest Services:** coin laundry, wireless Internet. **Cards:** AX, DS, MC, VI.

SOME UNITS
(A$K) (S☐) 🐕 🏊 📷 / ✕ 🛢 🖥 /
FEE

NIXA pop. 12,124

──────── WHERE TO STAY ────────

SUPER 8 MOTEL　*Book at AAA.com*　**Phone:** 417/725-0880

| | All Year | 1P: $47 | 2P: $55 | XP: $12 |

Small-scale Hotel　**Location:** 0.5 mi n of jct SR 14 and 160; US 65, 4.7 mi w on SR 14, then 0.4 mi n on SR 160. 418 Massey Blvd 65714 (PO Box 555). Fax: 417/725-0880. **Facility:** 60 one-bedroom standard units, some with whirlpools. 2 stories (no elevator), interior corridors. *Bath:* combo or shower only. **Parking:** on-site. **Terms:** cancellation fee imposed, [CP] meal plan available. **Amenities:** high-speed Internet. *Some:* irons. **Pool(s):** outdoor. **Leisure Activities:** limited exercise equipment. **Guest Services:** coin laundry. **Business Services:** meeting rooms. **Cards:** AX, CB, DC, DS, MC, VI.

SOME UNITS
(A$K) (S☐) 🤿 🏊 📷 / ✕ 🛢 🖥 /

NORTH KANSAS CITY —*See Kansas City p. 472.*

OAK GROVE (JACKSON COUNTY) —*See Kansas City p. 473.*

O'FALLON —*See St. Louis p. 548.*

OSAGE BEACH pop. 3,662

──────── WHERE TO STAY ────────

BEST WESTERN DOGWOOD HILLS RESORT INN　*Book great rates at AAA.com*　**Phone:** (573)348-1735

(AAA) (SAVE)	4/22-9/2	1P: $81-$116	2P: $81-$116	XP: $8	F18
	9/3-10/13	1P: $81-$100	2P: $81-$100	XP: $8	F18
	3/2-4/21	1P: $52-$100	2P: $52-$100	XP: $8	F18
	10/14-11/4	1P: $52-$59	2P: $52-$59	XP: $8	F18

Small-scale Hotel　**Location:** 0.5 mi n, off US 54. 1252 State Hwy KK 65065. Fax: 573/348-0014. **Facility:** 59 one-bedroom standard units, some with kitchens. 2-3 stories (no elevator), exterior corridors. **Parking:** on-site. **Terms:** open 3/2-11/4, check-in 4 pm, 14 day cancellation notice, weekly rates available, [BP] meal plan available, package plans, pets ($25 extra charge). **Amenities:** irons, hair dryers. *Some:* high-speed Internet. **Dining:** 7 am-2 pm, cocktails. **Pool(s):** outdoor. **Leisure Activities:** whirlpool. *Fee:* golf-18 holes, lighted driving range. **Guest Services:** wireless Internet. **Business Services:** meeting rooms, PC. **Cards:** AX, CB, DC, DS, MC, VI. **Free Special Amenities:** early check-in/late check-out and room upgrade (subject to availability with advance reservations).

SOME UNITS
(S☐) 🛏 🍽 🐕 📷 🖥 / ✕ 🛢 🖥 /
FEE

HOLIDAY INN EXPRESS　*Book at AAA.com*　**Phone:** (573)302-0330

| | All Year | 1P: $92 |

Small-scale Hotel　**Location:** On US 54, just n of Grand Glaize Bridge. 4533 Hwy 54 65065. Fax: 573/302-0484. **Facility:** 60 one-bedroom standard units, some with whirlpools. 3-4 stories, interior corridors. *Bath:* combo or shower only. **Parking:** on-site. **Terms:** 2 night minimum stay - weekends, cancellation fee imposed, [ECP] meal plan available. **Amenities:** high-speed Internet, voice mail, irons, hair dryers. **Pool(s):** small heated indoor. **Leisure Activities:** *Fee:* game room. **Guest Services:** valet laundry, wireless Internet. **Business Services:** meeting rooms, PC. **Cards:** AX, CB, DC, DS, JC, MC, VI.

SOME UNITS
(A$K) (S☐) 🏊 🐕 ✕ 📷 🖥 / 🛢 🖥 /
FEE

LAKE CHATEAU RESORT　**Phone:** 573/348-2791

	5/25-9/3	1P: $85-$139	2P: $85-$139	XP: $8	F18
	9/4-10/31	1P: $63-$125	2P: $63-$125	XP: $8	F18
	3/1-5/24 & 11/1-2/29	1P: $49-$125	2P: $49-$125	XP: $8	F18

Resort Motel　**Location:** Just s of Grand Glaize Bridge. 5066 Hwy 54 65065. Fax: 573/348-1340. **Facility:** Older, well-kept property nestled along Lake Ozark. 51 units. 49 one- and 1 two-bedroom standard units, some with kitchens and/or whirlpools. 1 cabin. 1-3 stories (no elevator), exterior corridors. *Bath:* combo or shower only. **Parking:** on-site. **Terms:** office hours 7 am-11 pm, check-in 4 pm, pets ($10 fee, in designated units). **Pool(s):** 2 outdoor. **Leisure Activities:** fishing, playground. *Fee:* marina. **Guest Services:** coin laundry, wireless Internet. **Cards:** AX, DS, MC, VI.

SOME UNITS
(A$K) (S☐) 🛏 🍽 🏊 ✕ 🖥 / ✕ 🛢 /
FEE

SCOTTISH INNS   *Book great rates at AAA.com*   **Phone:** (573)348-3123

⬩AAA⬩ SAVE
5/1-9/3   1P: $50-$95   2P: $65-$95   XP: $10   F12
3/1-4/30 & 9/4-2/29   1P: $40-$65   2P: $50-$75   XP: $10   F12
▽▽▽
Motel   **Location:** 1 mi w of Grand Glaize Bridge. 5404 Hwy 54 65065. Fax: 573/348-3124. **Facility:** 23 one-bedroom standard units. 2 stories (no elevator), interior/exterior corridors. **Parking:** on-site, winter plug-ins. **Terms:** cancellation fee imposed, small pets only ($5 extra charge, in smoking units). **Pool(s):** outdoor. **Leisure Activities:** picnic tables. **Cards:** AX, DS, MC, VI. **Free Special Amenities:** local telephone calls and room upgrade **(subject to availability with advance reservations).**

SOME UNITS

[S/D] 🐾 🚗 📺 / ⊠ /
       FEE

TAN-TAR-A RESORT GOLF CLUB, MARINA &
    INDOOR WATER PARK   *Book at AAA.com*   **Phone:** (573)348-3131

▽▽▽▽▽
5/24-8/12   1P: $140-$175   2P: $140-$175
3/1-5/23 & 8/13-10/27   1P: $125-$145   2P: $125-$145
Resort   10/28-2/29   1P: $85-$105   2P: $85-$105
Large-scale Hotel   **Location:** US 54, 2 mi w. Located in a secluded area. SR KK 65065 (PO Box 188TT). Fax: 573/348-3206. **Facility:** Expansive grounds surround this rustic resort located on 370 acres on the banks of the Lake of the Ozarks. 899 units. 731 one-bedroom standard units, some with kitchens and/or whirlpools. 141 one-, 26 two- and 1 three-bedroom suites, some with kitchens and/or whirlpools. 1-8 stories, interior/exterior corridors. *Bath:* combo or shower only. **Parking:** on-site. **Terms:** check-in 4 pm, 3 day cancellation notice-fee imposed, package plans. **Amenities:** high-speed Internet, voice mail, irons, hair dryers. *Some:* dual phone lines. **Pool(s):** 2 outdoor, heated indoor, 2 wading. **Leisure Activities:** whirlpools, waterslide, rental boats, rental paddleboats, fishing, recreation programs, jogging, playground, spa, basketball, volleyball. *Fee:* marina, waterskiing, golf-27 holes, miniature golf, 2 lighted tennis courts, horseback riding, game room. **Guest Services:** gift shop, valet and coin laundry, wireless Internet. **Business Services:** conference facilities, business center. **Cards:** AX, CB, DC, DS, JC, MC, VI.

SOME UNITS

[S/D] ✈ 🍴 ▼ 📶 🏋 🚗 ⚒ ⊠ 📺 💻 / ⊠ ▣ 🍽 /

—— WHERE TO DINE ——

THE BRASS DOOR   **Dinner:** $14-$27   **Phone:** 573/348-9229

American   **Location:** On US 54, 0.5 mi w of Grand Glaize Bridge. 5167 US 54 65065. **Hours:** 5 pm-9 pm, Fri & Sat-10 pm. Closed: 11/22, 12/25. **Reservations:** suggested. **Features:** If you're searching for an early-evening sun-drenched dinner or a quiet, romantic supper, you'll find just what you're looking for at this very nice steak and seafood restaurant. Choose the rainbow trout or prime rib—both are delicious. Good service too. Casual dress; cocktails. **Parking:** on-site. **Cards:** AX, DC, DS, MC, VI.

▼ 🚫

MICHAEL'S STEAK CHALET & SWISS VILLAGE   **Dinner:** $19-$38   **Phone:** 573/348-3611

▽▽▽
Steak & Seafood   **Location:** Just w of jct US 54 and SR KK, 1.2 mi n on Swiss Village Rd (Lake Rd 54-59). 1440 Swiss Village Rd 65065. **Hours:** 4:30 pm-9 pm, Fri & Sat-10 pm. Closed major holidays. **Features:** Affording views of the lake, the secluded restaurant prepares a wonderful assortment of steaks and seafood. Casual dress; cocktails. **Parking:** on-site.

▼ 🚫

ON THE RISE BAKERY & BISTRO   **Lunch:** $7-$12   **Phone:** 573/348-4224

▽▽▽
American   **Location:** 1 mi w of Grand Glaize Bridge. 5439 Hwy 54 65065. **Hours:** 7:30 am-3 pm. Closed: 1/1, 11/22, 12/24, 12/25; also Mon & Tues. **Features:** The atmosphere in the contemporary bistro is casual and comfortable. A variety of coffees and teas is served with a good selection of dishes presented in generous portions. Casual dress; beer & wine only. **Parking:** on-site. **Cards:** AX, DS, MC, VI.

PICKLED PET'S SPORTS BAR & GRILL   **Lunch:** $7-$13   **Dinner:** $7-$13   **Phone:** 573/302-8800

▽▽
American   **Location:** 1 mi w of Grand Glaize Bridge. 5276 Hwy 54 65065. **Hours:** 11 am-9 pm, Fri & Sat-10 pm. Closed: 11/22, 12/25. **Features:** The locally popular sports bar/restaurant offers a very good variety of sandwiches, entrees, pastas, soups and salads as well as appetizer favorites including "Fried Pete's," a.k.a. fried pickles! Also featured are an entertainment area and outdoor dining in season. Cocktails. **Parking:** on-site. **Cards:** AX, DS, MC, VI.

THE POTTED STEER   **Dinner:** $23-$32   **Phone:** 573/348-5053

American   **Location:** On US 54, 0.3 mi sw of Grand Glaize Bridge. **Hours:** 5:30 pm-10 pm, Fri & Sat from 5 pm. Closed: Sun & Mon. **Features:** Locals who dine at this restaurant favor the deep-fried lobster, but the salads with fresh ingredients and delicious homemade dressings are so good that you may want to make a meal of the salad. The restaurant also offers a lake view and superb service. Casual dress; cocktails. **Parking:** on-site. **Cards:** AX, CB, DC, DS, JC, MC, VI.

▼ 🚫

VISTA GRANDE   **Lunch:** $4-$7   **Dinner:** $8-$15   **Phone:** 573/348-1231

▽▽
Mexican   **Location:** On US 54, 1 mi e of Grand Glaize Bridge; across from Factory Outlet Village. 4579 Hwy 54 65065. **Hours:** 11:30 am-10 pm; to 9 pm in winter. Closed: 1/1, 11/22, 12/24, 12/25. **Features:** Tasty, hot, generous servings of very good food is what Vista Grande is known for locally. The Spanish menu is complemented with a few American items. The servers are cheerful and competent in this comfortable establishment. Casual dress; cocktails. **Parking:** on-site. **Cards:** AX, DS, MC, VI.

▼

YANKEE PEDDLERS TEA ROOM   **Lunch:** $6-$8   **Phone:** 573/348-5045

American   **Location:** 0.4 mi e of jct US 54 and SR KK. 5831 Hwy 54 65065. **Hours:** 11 am-3 pm. Closed major holidays; also 12/24 & day before Thanksgiving. **Features:** This place offers everything one could want in a tea room. Things are delightfully mismatched and full of whimsy. Among yummy menu selections are the quiche of the day and the "go nuts salad.". Casual dress; beer & wine only. **Parking:** on-site. **Cards:** DS, MC, VI.

🚫

OVERLAND *—See St. Louis p. 549.*

OZARK pop. 9,665

——— WHERE TO STAY ———

BARNAGAIN BED & BREAKFAST
▼▼▼
Bed & Breakfast
All Year [BP]   1P: $89-$99   2P: $109-$129   XP: $15   F12
Phone: (417)581-2276
Location: Jct US 65 and SR 14, 1.3 mi e on US 65 business route. Located in a quiet area. 904 W Church St 65721. **Facility:** A Victorian farmhouse and 1922 era dairy barn have been converted into lodging quarters in a peaceful country setting near a stream and hiking trail. 4 units. 3 one-bedroom standard units, some with whirlpools. 1 two-bedroom suite with kitchen. 1 story, exterior corridors. **Parking:** on-site. **Terms:** check-in 5 pm, age restrictions may apply, 7 day cancellation notice-fee imposed, weekly rates available. **Amenities:** video library, hair dryers. *Some:* whirlpools. **Pool(s):** outdoor. **Leisure Activities:** bicycles, hiking trails, exercise room, horseshoes, game room. **Guest Services:** complimentary laundry. **Cards:** AX, DS, MC, VI.

(ASK) 🛏 ✕ ✕ (VCR) 🐕 ☎ 🖥 💻

SUPER 8   *Book great rates at AAA.com*
(AAA) (SAVE)
▼
Small-scale Hotel
All Year   1P: $47-$59   2P: $52-$64   XP: $5   F17
Phone: (417)581-8800
Location: US 65, exit SR 14, just w to 20th St, then just s. 299 N 20th 65721 (PO Box 280, 65721-7328). Fax: 417/485-8868. **Facility:** 60 units. 59 one-bedroom standard units. 1 one-bedroom suite ($67-$85). 2 stories (no elevator), interior/exterior corridors. **Parking:** on-site. **Terms:** [CP] meal plan available, pets ($10 extra charge, in designated units). **Amenities:** high-speed Internet. **Pool(s):** small outdoor. **Guest Services:** coin laundry. **Cards:** AX, DS, MC, VI. **Free Special Amenities:** expanded continental breakfast and local telephone calls.

SOME UNITS
(S/D) 🛏 🏊 🐕 / ✕ 🖥 💻 /
FEE

——— WHERE TO DINE ———

LAMBERTS CAFE II
▼▼▼
American
Lunch: $8-$17   **Dinner:** $8-$17   **Phone:** 417/581-7655
Location: Jct US 65, CR J and CC. 1800 W Hwy J 65721. **Hours:** 10:30 am-9 pm. Closed: 1/1, 11/22, 12/24, 12/25; also 12/31. **Features:** Lamberts is housed in a rustic building with flags representing the military services adorning the walls. They serve wholesome home-style food in a bustling atmosphere. Servers toss rolls across the room to those brave enough to try this form of delivery! Casual dress. **Parking:** on-site.

RIVERSIDE INN
(AAA)
▼▼▼
American
Dinner: $17-$32   **Phone:** 417/581-7051
Location: US 65, 1 mi e on SR 14, 0.3 mi n on 3rd St, then 1 mi e. 2629 N Riverside Rd 65721. **Hours:** 5:30 pm-9 pm, Fri & Sat-10 pm. Closed: 7/4, 12/24, 12/25; also Sun & Mon. **Reservations:** suggested. **Features:** A fine dining restaurant nestled in the trees and on the banks of a small river, the Riverside Inn appeals to those looking for a wonderful comtemporary dining experience while surrounded by the allure of the past. The restaurant was built in the early 1900s when fried chicken and the trimmings were the only things on the menu. Today fried chicken is still served but many steak, seafood and chicken dishes have been added. Casual dress; cocktails. **Parking:** on-site. **Cards:** AX, DC, DS, MC, VI.

🚫

PACIFIC pop. 5,482   (See map and index starting on p. 511)

——— WHERE TO STAY ———

COMFORT INN   *Book great rates at AAA.com*
(AAA) (SAVE)
▼▼▼
Small-scale Hotel

5/16-9/5	1P: $79-$99	2P: $89-$109	XP: $5
3/1-5/15 & 9/6-10/31	1P: $69-$79	2P: $79-$89	XP: $5
11/1-2/29	1P: $69	2P: $79	XP: $5

Phone: (636)257-4600   [40]
F
F
F
Location: I-44, exit 257, just ne. 1320 Thornton St 63069. Fax: 636/257-4601. **Facility:** 70 one-bedroom standard units, some with whirlpools. 3 stories, interior corridors. *Bath:* combo or shower only. **Parking:** on-site. **Amenities:** high-speed Internet, voice mail, irons, hair dryers. **Pool(s):** heated indoor. **Leisure Activities:** sauna, whirlpool, exercise room. **Guest Services:** coin laundry, wireless Internet. **Business Services:** meeting rooms, business center. **Cards:** AX, CB, DC, DS, JC, MC, VI. **Free Special Amenities:** expanded continental breakfast and newspaper. *(See color ad below)*

SOME UNITS
(S/D) 👤 🏊 ✕ 🐕 🖥 🛢 💻 / ✕ /

(See map and index starting on p. 511)

QUALITY INN NEAR SIX FLAGS   *Book great rates at AAA.com*   **Phone:** (636)257-8400   **41**
Motel
| | 5/1-9/5 | 1P: $69-$99 | 2P: $79-$99 | XP: $5 | F19 |
| | 3/1-4/30 & 9/6-2/29 | 1P: $59-$69 | 2P: $59-$69 | XP: $5 | F19 |

Location: I-44, exit 257, just se. 1400 W Osage St 63069. **Fax:** 636/257-3112. **Facility:** 46 units. 45 one-bedroom standard units. 1 one-bedroom suite. 2-3 stories (no elevator), interior/exterior corridors. *Bath:* combo or shower only. **Parking:** on-site. **Terms:** weekly rates available, [ECP] meal plan available, pets ($15 extra charge). **Amenities:** high-speed Internet, irons, hair dryers. **Pool(s):** small heated indoor. **Guest Services:** wireless Internet. **Business Services:** meeting rooms. **Cards:** AX, CB, DC, DS, JC, MC, VI.

SOME UNITS

PERRYVILLE pop. 7,667

——— WHERE TO STAY ———

SUPER 8 PERRYVILLE, MO   *Book at AAA.com*   **Phone:** (573)517-7888
Small-scale Hotel
| | All Year | 1P: $55-$75 | 2P: $55-$75 | XP: $5 | F18 |

Location: I-55, exit 129 (SR 51), just w, then just s. 1119 Vincent Dr 63775. **Fax:** 573/517-7101. **Facility:** 64 units. 58 one-bedroom standard units, some with whirlpools. 6 one-bedroom suites ($125-$175) with whirlpools. 3 stories, interior corridors. *Bath:* combo or shower only. **Parking:** on-site. **Terms:** [ECP] meal plan available. **Amenities:** high-speed Internet, safes (fee), irons, hair dryers. *Some:* dual phone lines. **Pool(s):** small heated indoor. **Leisure Activities:** whirlpool, exercise room. **Guest Services:** coin laundry, wireless Internet. **Business Services:** PC. **Cards:** AX, DC, DS, MC, VI.

SOME UNITS

——— WHERE TO DINE ———

TRACTORS CLASSIC AMERICAN GRILL   **Lunch:** $4-$9   **Dinner:** $6-$24   **Phone:** 573/547-1868
American
Location: I-55, exit 129 (SR 51), 1 mi n to W St. Joseph St, then 1 mi e; in town square. 15 W St. Joseph St 63775. **Hours:** 11 am-9 pm, Fri & Sat-10 pm. Closed major holidays; also 12/24 & Sun. **Reservations:** not accepted. **Features:** On the town square, the charming establishment is locally popular for its creative yet comfortable menu selections. Casual dress; cocktails. **Parking:** street. **Cards:** AX, DS, MC, VI.

PEVELY pop. 3,768

——— WHERE TO DINE ———

BOBBY TOM'S BAR-B-QUE   **Lunch:** $4-$10   **Dinner:** $4-$10   **Phone:** 636/475-3400
American
Location: I-55, exit 180 (SR Z), just se. 1620 Hwy Z 63070. **Hours:** 11 am-8 pm. Closed major holidays; also Sun & Mon. **Features:** From the wood stacked on the front porch to the tender, flavorful barbecue, guests appreciate the offerings of the tidy, comfortable roadside establishment. Casual dress. **Parking:** on-site. **Cards:** AX, DS, MC, VI.

PLATTE CITY —See Kansas City p. 473.

PLEASANT HILL pop. 5,582

——— WHERE TO STAY ———

MULBERRY HILL BED & BREAKFAST   **Phone:** (816)540-3457
Bed & Breakfast
| | All Year | | 2P: $55-$125 | XP: $15 | |

Location: Jct SR 7, just w on Myrtle St. 226 N Armstrong 64080. **Fax:** 816/540-3457. **Facility:** 5 one-bedroom standard units, some with whirlpools. 3 stories (no elevator), interior corridors. **Parking:** on-site. **Terms:** check-in 4 pm, age restrictions may apply, 7 day cancellation notice-fee imposed. **Amenities:** video library, DVD players, hair dryers. **Leisure Activities:** whirlpool. **Guest Services:** wireless Internet. **Cards:** DS, MC, VI.

POPLAR BLUFF pop. 16,651

——— WHERE TO STAY ———

COMFORT INN   *Book great rates at AAA.com*   **Phone:** (573)686-5200
Small-scale Hotel
| | All Year | 1P: $63 | 2P: $63 | XP: $5 | F18 |

Location: 1.3 mi s from jct US 60 E. 2582 N Westwood Blvd 63901. **Fax:** 573/686-5655. **Facility:** 58 one-bedroom standard units, some with whirlpools. 3 stories, interior corridors. *Bath:* combo or shower only. **Parking:** on-site. **Terms:** cancellation fee imposed, [ECP] meal plan available, pets ($10 extra charge). **Amenities:** high-speed Internet, voice mail, safes (fee), irons, hair dryers. **Pool(s):** small heated outdoor. **Guest Services:** valet and coin laundry, wireless Internet. **Business Services:** meeting rooms, PC. **Cards:** AX, CB, DC, DS, JC, MC, VI.

SOME UNITS

DRURY INN-POPLAR BLUFF   *Book at AAA.com*   **Phone:** (573)686-2451
Small-scale Hotel
| | All Year [BP] | 1P: $66-$110 | 2P: $76-$120 | XP: $10 | F18 |

Location: On US 67, 1.4 mi s from jct US 60 E. 2220 N Westwood Blvd 63901. **Fax:** 573/686-2451. **Facility:** 78 one-bedroom standard units. 3 stories, interior corridors. **Parking:** on-site. **Amenities:** high-speed Internet, dual phone lines, voice mail, irons, hair dryers. **Pool(s):** heated indoor/outdoor. **Leisure Activities:** whirlpool, exercise room. **Guest Services:** complimentary evening beverages: Mon-Sat, valet and coin laundry, wireless Internet. **Business Services:** PC. **Cards:** AX, CB, DC, DS, MC, VI.

SOME UNITS

HOLIDAY INN   *Book at AAA.com*   Phone: 573/776-1200

Property failed to provide current rates

Small-scale Hotel

Location: On US 67. 2781 N Westwood Blvd 63901. **Fax:** 573/776-1201. **Facility:** 117 units. 114 one-bedroom standard units, some with whirlpools. 3 one-bedroom suites. 4 stories, interior corridors. *Bath:* combo or shower only. **Parking:** on-site. **Amenities:** high-speed Internet, voice mail, irons, hair dryers. **Pool(s):** heated indoor. **Leisure Activities:** whirlpool, exercise room, spa. **Guest Services:** valet and coin laundry, salon, wireless Internet. **Business Services:** conference facilities, business center.

SOME UNITS

PEAR TREE INN BY DRURY-POPLAR BLUFF   *Book at AAA.com*   Phone: (573)785-7100

Motel

| All Year | 1P: $45-$80 | 2P: $55-$90 | XP: $10 | F18 |

Location: On US 67, 1.4 mi s from jct US 60 E. 2218 N Westwood Blvd 63901. **Fax:** 573/785-7100. **Facility:** 77 one-bedroom standard units. 3 stories (no elevator), exterior corridors. **Parking:** on-site. **Amenities:** high-speed Internet, irons, hair dryers. **Pool(s):** outdoor. **Guest Services:** complimentary laundry, wireless Internet. **Cards:** AX, CB, DC, DS, MC, VI.

SOME UNITS

SUPER 8   *Book at AAA.com*   Phone: (573)785-0176

Small-scale Hotel

| All Year | 1P: $45-$50 | 2P: $51-$56 | XP: $6 | F15 |

Location: On US 67, 0.8 mi s from jct US 60 E. 2831 N Westwood Blvd 63901. **Fax:** 573/785-2865. **Facility:** 63 one-bedroom standard units. 2 stories (no elevator), interior corridors. **Parking:** on-site. **Terms:** 15 day cancellation notice, [ECP] meal plan available, package plans, pets ($25 extra charge, with prior approval). **Amenities:** voice mail, safes (fee). **Business Services:** PC. **Cards:** AX, DC, DS, MC, VI.

SOME UNITS

FEE

——— WHERE TO DINE ———

EL ACAPULCO AUTHENTIC MEXICAN RESTAURANT   **Lunch:** $4-$6   **Dinner:** $6-$12   **Phone:** 573/776-7000

Mexican

Location: On US 67, 1.4 mi s of jct US 60 E. 2260 N Westwood Blvd 63901. **Hours:** 11 am-10 pm, Fri & Sat-10:30 pm. Closed major holidays. **Reservations:** accepted. **Features:** The pleasing, family-owned-and-operated establishment offers a pleasant atmosphere and Mexican favorites. Casual dress; cocktails. **Parking:** on-site. **Cards:** AX, DS, MC, VI.

——— The following restaurant has not been evaluated by AAA but is listed for your information only. ———

MAYA'S MEXICAN GRILL   Phone: 573/785-7966

[fyi]   Not evaluated. **Location:** 940 S Westwood Blvd 63901. **Features:** Lively and casual atmosphere within a colorful setting. Large menu selection, including vegetarian options.

POTOSI pop. 2,662

——— WHERE TO STAY ———

POTOSI SUPER 8   *Book at AAA.com*   Phone: (573)438-8888

Small-scale Hotel

| All Year | 1P: $56-$65 | 2P: $56-$65 | XP: $5 | F17 |

Location: Jct SR 8 and 21. 820 E High St 63664. **Fax:** 573/438-2190. **Facility:** 49 one-bedroom standard units, some with whirlpools. 2 stories (no elevator), interior/exterior corridors. **Parking:** on-site. **Terms:** pets ($10 extra charge). **Amenities:** high-speed Internet, safes (fee). *Some:* hair dryers. **Guest Services:** coin laundry, wireless Internet. **Business Services:** meeting rooms, PC, fax. **Cards:** AX, DC, DS, MC, VI.

SOME UNITS

FEE

REEDS SPRING —See Branson p. 420.

REPUBLIC pop. 8,438

——— **WHERE TO STAY** ———

AMERICINN LODGE & SUITES OF REPUBLIC   *Book at AAA.com*   **Phone:** (417)732-5335
All Year   2P: $73-$159
Small-scale Hotel   **Location:** I-44, exit 67, 4.4 mi s to SR 174 (flashing red light/4-way stop), then 0.7 mi e to Highland Park Town Center; just nw of jct US 60, SR 413 and 174. 950 Austin Ln 65738 (PO Box 325). Fax: 417/732-5405. **Facility:** 47 units. 45 one-bedroom standard units, some with whirlpools. 2 one-bedroom suites ($135-$159) with whirlpools. 2 stories, interior corridors. *Bath:* combo or shower only. **Parking:** on-site. **Terms:** [ECP] meal plan available, pets ($10 extra charge, in designated units). **Amenities:** high-speed Internet, voice mail, irons, hair dryers. **Pool(s):** heated indoor. **Leisure Activities:** whirlpool, exercise room. **Guest Services:** coin laundry. **Business Services:** meeting rooms, PC. **Cards:** AX, DS, MC, VI. *(See color ad p 566)*

SOME UNITS
ASK ▥ ⬌ ⊶ ⚑ ▣ / ✕ 🖪 🖵 /
FEE

RICH HILL pop. 1,461

——— **WHERE TO STAY** ———

APACHE MOTEL   **Phone:** (417)395-2161
All Year   1P: $35-$37   2P: $38-$42   XP: $4   F12
Motel   **Location:** Just e of jct US 71 and CR B. Located in a rural area. Hwy 71 and B 64779 (Rt 3, Box 309A). Fax: 417/395-4263. **Facility:** 22 one-bedroom standard units. 1 story, exterior corridors. **Parking:** on-site, winter plug-ins. **Terms:** 3 day cancellation notice, small pets only (with prior approval). **Guest Services:** gift shop. **Cards:** AX, DS, MC, VI.

SOME UNITS
ASK ⓈⒹ ⬌ ⊶ 🖵 / ✕ /

RICHMOND HEIGHTS —See St. Louis p. 549.

RIDGEDALE —See Branson p. 420.

RIVERSIDE —See Kansas City p. 473.

ROLLA pop. 16,347

——— **WHERE TO STAY** ———

BEST WESTERN COACHLIGHT   *Book great rates at AAA.com*   **Phone:** (573)341-2511
5/1-8/31 [ECP]   1P: $64-$94   2P: $69-$99   XP: $5   F18
3/1-4/30 & 9/1-2/29 [ECP]   1P: $61-$84   2P: $65-$89   XP: $5   F18
Motel   **Location:** Jct I-44 and Business Rt 44 S, exit 184. 1403 Martin Springs Dr 65401. Fax: 573/368-3055. **Facility:** 88 one-bedroom standard units. 2 stories (no elevator), interior corridors. **Parking:** on-site. **Terms:** cancellation fee imposed, pets ($10 extra charge, in designated units). **Amenities:** high-speed Internet, safes (fee), irons, hair dryers. **Pool(s):** outdoor. **Leisure Activities:** playground. **Guest Services:** coin laundry. **Business Services:** meeting rooms, PC, fax. **Cards:** AX, CB, DC, DS, MC, VI. **Free Special Amenities:** expanded continental breakfast and newspaper.

SOME UNITS
ⓈⒹ ▥ ⊶ ⬌ ⚑ ▣ / ✕ 🖪 🖵 /
FEE

DAYS INN   *Book great rates at AAA.com*   **Phone:** (573)341-3700
5/2-8/31   1P: $59-$69   2P: $69-$79   XP: $5   F17
3/1-5/1 & 9/1-2/29   1P: $49-$59   2P: $59-$69   XP: $5   F17
Motel   **Location:** I-44, exit 184, just s. 1207 Kingshighway 65401. Fax: 573/341-2346. **Facility:** 37 one-bedroom standard units. 2 stories (no elevator), exterior corridors. **Parking:** on-site. **Terms:** cancellation fee imposed, pets ($10 extra charge). **Amenities:** high-speed Internet, safes (fee), hair dryers. **Pool(s):** outdoor. **Cards:** AX, CB, DC, DS, MC, VI.

SOME UNITS
ASK ⓈⒹ ⬌ ⊶ ⬌ ⚑ ▣ / ✕ 🖪 🖵 /
FEE

DRURY INN-ROLLA   *Book at AAA.com*   **Phone:** (573)364-4000
All Year [BP]   1P: $60-$105   2P: $70-$115   XP: $10   F18
Small-scale Hotel   **Location:** I-44, exit 186 (US 63). 2006 N Bishop Ave 65401. Fax: 573/364-4000. **Facility:** 61 one-bedroom standard units. 2 stories (no elevator), interior corridors. **Parking:** on-site. **Terms:** small pets only. **Amenities:** high-speed Internet, voice mail, irons, hair dryers. **Pool(s):** outdoor. **Leisure Activities:** limited exercise equipment. **Guest Services:** complimentary evening beverages: Mon-Sat, valet laundry. **Business Services:** meeting rooms, PC. **Cards:** AX, CB, DC, DS, MC, VI.

SOME UNITS
ASK ▥ ⊶ ⬌ ⚑ ▣ / ✕ 🖪 🖵 /

HAMPTON INN   *Book great rates at AAA.com*   **Phone:** 573/308-1060
Property failed to provide current rates
Small-scale Hotel   **Location:** I-44, exit 186 (US 63), just n. 2201 N Bishop Ave 65401. Fax: 573/308-1441. **Facility:** 70 one-bedroom standard units, some with whirlpools. 3 stories, interior corridors. *Bath:* combo or shower only. **Parking:** on-site. **Amenities:** video games (fee), high-speed Internet, dual phone lines, voice mail, irons, hair dryers. **Pool(s):** heated outdoor. **Guest Services:** valet and coin laundry. **Business Services:** PC.

SOME UNITS
Ⓜ ♿ ⓪ ⬌ ⤸ ⚑ ▣ / ✕ 🖪 🖵 /

HOLIDAY INN EXPRESS HOTEL & SUITES   *Book great rates at AAA.com*   Phone: (573)426-2900

(AAA) (SAVE)   All Year   1P: $89   2P: $89
Location: I-44, exit 184, just nw. 1610 Old Wire Outer Rd 65401. Fax: 573/426-2909. **Facility:** 80 one-bedroom standard units, some with whirlpools. 3 stories, interior corridors. *Bath:* combo or shower only. **Parking:** on-site. **Amenities:** high-speed Internet, dual phone lines, voice mail, irons, hair dryers. *Some:* DVD players
Small-scale Hotel   (fee), video games, CD players. **Pool(s):** small heated indoor. **Leisure Activities:** whirlpool, exercise room. **Guest Services:** valet and coin laundry, wireless Internet. **Business Services:** business center. **Cards:** AX, DC, DS, JC, MC, VI. **Free Special Amenities: expanded continental breakfast and high-speed Internet.**

SOME UNITS

[icons]

──────── **WHERE TO DINE** ────────

GORDOZ   **Lunch:** $6-$7   **Dinner:** $10-$25   **Phone:** 573/364-2780
Location: SR 72 at Salem Ave; in 72 Center Shopping Plaza. 1212 Hwy 72 E 65401. **Hours:** 11 am-2 & 5-9 pm, Fri-9:30 pm, Sat 4:30 pm-9:30 pm. **Closed:** 5/28, 11/22, 12/25; also Sun. **Reservations:** accepted.
American   **Features:** Steaks and seafood are prominent selections and daily specials reflect an Italian flair at this casual eatery, which occupies a shopping plaza setting. Casual dress; cocktails. **Parking:** on-site.
Cards: AX, CB, DC, DS, JC, MC, VI.

JOHNNY'S SMOKE STAK   **Lunch:** $7-$8   **Dinner:** $7-$14   **Phone:** 573/364-4838
Location: 1 mi s on US 63, then 0.3 mi e on SR 72. 201 Hwy 72 W 65401. **Hours:** 11 am-8 pm, Fri & Sat-9 pm.
American   **Closed:** 1/1, 11/22, 12/25. **Reservations:** suggested, weekends. **Features:** Johnny's has an excellent variety of tasty barbecue ham, pork and beef dishes. You simply must try the hickory-smoked ribs—they're so tender they fall off the bone. The great food and friendly servers make for an enjoyable dining experience. Casual dress; cocktails. **Parking:** on-site. **Cards:** AX, MC, VI.

KYOTO JAPANESE RESTAURANT   **Lunch:** $6-$14   **Dinner:** $10-$20   **Phone:** 573/341-2939
Location: At 11th St. 1002 N Bishop Ave 65401. **Hours:** 11 am-2:30 & 4:30-9 pm, Fri & Sat-10 pm. **Closed:** 7/4, 11/22; also Sun. **Reservations:** accepted. **Features:** Crisp, fresh, light and bright are words that may come
Japanese   to mind when entering Kyoto because the dining room is decorated with lots of natural light-colored wood. This observation will be enhanced when you see the food - which is also crisp, fresh, light and bright as is typical for authentic Japanese restaurants. Casual dress; beer & wine only. **Parking:** on-site. **Cards:** AX, DS, MC, VI.

PENELOPE'S PIZZA & STEAK   **Lunch:** $4-$12   **Dinner:** $5-$12   **Phone:** 573/364-8687
Location: 0.5 mi w from US 63. 1049 Kingshighway 65401. **Hours:** Open 3/1-12/24 & 1/15-2/29; 11 am-9 pm, Fri & Sat-9:30 pm, Sun 7 am-2:30 pm. **Closed:** 7/4, 11/22, 12/25; also Mon. **Reservations:** accepted.
American   **Features:** The casual restaurant offers lunch and dinner buffets, as well as meat dishes and pizza. Casual dress; beer & wine only. **Parking:** on-site. **Cards:** AX, DS, MC, VI.

SIRLOIN STOCKADE   **Lunch:** $6-$8   **Dinner:** $6-$8   **Phone:** 573/364-7168
Location: Jct I-44 and Business Rd 44, exit 184. 1401 Martin Springs Dr 65401. **Hours:** 11 am-9 pm. Closed major holidays. **Reservations:** not accepted. **Features:** The steakhouse lines up buffet items, including pizza, tacos, soups, salads and desserts, providing both excellent variety and a good value. Rotating theme nights
Steak House   might allow for the sampling of sushi, barbecue and seafood. The buffet also may serve to complement a quality steak. Rolls are baked several times daily. Casual dress. **Parking:** on-site. **Cards:** DS, MC, VI.

ZENO'S STEAK HOUSE   **Lunch:** $5-$8   **Dinner:** $9-$21   **Phone:** 573/364-1301
(AAA)   **Location:** I-44, exit 184; in Zeno's Motel. 1621 Martin Springs Dr 65402. **Hours:** 7 am-9 pm, Fri & Sat-10 pm. **Closed:** 12/25. **Reservations:** suggested. **Features:** You'll appreciate the comfortable, sophisticated atmosphere at Zeno's. The steaks and prime rib are cooked to perfection. They also offer Italian and
Steak House   seafood dishes. Without reservations you may have to wait, but the food won't disappoint. Casual dress; cocktails. **Parking:** on-site. **Cards:** AX, CB, DC, DS, MC, VI.

──────── *The following restaurant has not been evaluated by AAA* ────────
but is listed for your information only.

PRYORS FRESH PIZZA   **Phone:** 573/364-1293
[fyi]   Not evaluated. **Location:** I-44, exit 186 (US 63), 2 mi s. 100 N Bishop Ave 65401. **Features:** For over 40 years, this eatery has been serving fresh pizza in a down-home style setting. Put some change in the juke box and
enjoy!

ST. ALBANS (See map and index starting on p. 511)

──────── **WHERE TO DINE** ────────

THE GARDENS AT MALMAISON   **Dinner:** $17-$28   **Phone:** 636/458-0131   (31)
Location: Jct SR 100 and CR T, 3.5 mi n to St. Albans entrance, 2 mi to village. 3519 St. Albans Rd 63073. **Hours:** 6 pm-10 pm; hours may vary. **Closed:** Tues & Wed. **Reservations:** suggested. **Features:** The sophisticated
Traditional French   restaurant is known for sustaining French country dining at its dressy casual best with a tempting array of meals and seasonal specialties. Entrees feature classic French cuisine as well as a few Italian favorites. The signature appetizer is a mushroom creation served in a puff pastry treasure chest that looks as good as it tastes. For dessert, the St. Albans ice cream confection is a treat for the eyes as well as the palate. Price-fixe selections available. Dressy casual; cocktails. **Parking:** on-site. **Cards:** AX, DC, DS, MC, VI. **Historic**

ST. ANN —See St. Louis p. 549.

ST. CHARLES —See St. Louis p. 550.

ST. CLAIR pop. 4,390

——— WHERE TO STAY ———

BUDGET LODGING   **Phone: (636)629-1000**
(AAA) [SAVE] All Year [ECP]   1P: $69-$79   2P: $69-$79   XP: $5   F15
▼▼ ▼▼ **Location:** I-44, exit 240, just w. 866 S Outer Rd W 63077. **Fax:** 636/629-1000. **Facility:** 60 units. 59 one-bedroom
Motel standard units, some with whirlpools. 1 one-bedroom suite ($179-$229) with whirlpool. 1-2 stories (no
elevator), interior/exterior corridors. *Some:* DVD players, CD players, dual phone lines, irons. **Leisure**
Terms: weekly rates available, pets ($10 extra charge). **Amenities:** video library (fee), high-speed Internet,
hair dryers. *Some:* DVD players, CD players, dual phone lines, irons. **Pool(s):** outdoor. **Leisure**
Activities: charcoal grill, picnic area. **Guest Services:** coin laundry, wireless Internet. **Business Services:** meeting rooms.
Cards: AX, CB, DC, DS, JC, MC, VI. **Free Special Amenities: expanded continental breakfast and high-speed Internet.**

SOME UNITS
[S][D] [🛏] [🏊] / [✕] [VCR] [🔌] [📶] [🖥] /
   FEE   FEE

STE. GENEVIEVE pop. 4,476

——— WHERE TO STAY ———

MAIN STREET INN B & B   **Phone: (573)883-9199**
▼▼ ▼▼ All Year [BP]   1P: $95-$110   2P: $115-$175
Historic Bed **Location:** Jct Main and Washington sts; in historic downtown. 221 N Main St 63670 (PO Box 307).
& Breakfast **Fax:** 573/883-9911. **Facility:** Originally built in 1882 as a hotel, this B&B features spacious public areas and
rooms enhanced by fine country antiques. 8 one-bedroom standard units, some with whirlpools. 3 stories
(no elevator), interior/exterior corridors. *Bath:* combo or shower only. **Parking:** street. **Terms:** check-in 4 pm,
age restrictions may apply, 7 day cancellation notice-fee imposed, no pets allowed (owner's pet on premises). **Amenities:** video
library. *Some:* DVD players. **Guest Services:** complimentary evening beverages, wireless Internet. **Cards:** AX, DS, MC, VI.

SOME UNITS
[ASK] [S][D] [✕] [📶] / [📺] [VCR] /

MICROTEL INN & SUITES   *Book great rates at AAA.com*   **Phone: (573)883-8884**
(AAA) [SAVE] All Year [CP]   1P: $60   2P: $60   XP: $5   F16
▼▼ ▼▼ **Location:** I-55, exit 150 (SR 32), 3.9 mi e. 21958 Hwy 32 63670. **Fax:** 573/883-8841. **Facility:** 48 one-bedroom
Small-scale Hotel standard units. 2 stories, interior corridors. *Bath:* combo or shower only. **Parking:** on-site.
Terms: cancellation fee imposed, weekly rates available. **Amenities:** high-speed Internet, voice mail, irons.
Guest Services: coin laundry, wireless Internet. **Business Services:** meeting rooms, PC. **Cards:** AX, DC,
DS, MC, VI. **Free Special Amenities: continental breakfast and local telephone calls.**

SOME UNITS
[S][D] [🍴] [&M] [♿] [🍽] [📶] [🔌] [🖨] / [✕] [🖥] /
                        FEE

——— WHERE TO DINE ———

THE ANVIL SALOON   **Lunch:** $5-$7   **Dinner:** $8-$17   **Phone:** 573/883-7323
▼▼ ▼▼ **Location:** In historic downtown. 46 3rd St 63670. **Hours:** 11 am-8 pm, Fri & Sat-9 pm. Closed major holidays.
American **Reservations:** accepted. **Features:** The charming, circa 1850 establishment originally was a hardware
store. Pork chops, fried chicken, burgers and sandwiches, along with homemade desserts, are served daily.
Casual dress; cocktails. **Parking:** street. **Cards:** AX, DS, MC, VI.

OLD BRICK   **Lunch:** $4-$7   **Dinner:** $7-$20   **Phone:** 573/883-2724
▼▼ ▼▼ **Location:** 3rd and Market sts; center. 90 S 3rd St 63670. **Hours:** 8 am-9 pm, Sat 11 am-10 pm, Sun 11 am-7 pm.
American Closed major holidays. **Reservations:** suggested. **Features:** This restaurant is situated in the first brick
structure built west of the Mississippi, circa 1780. It's well-known for its fried chicken, but the baked chicken
au vin and prime rib are also superb. The buffet lunch attracts a loyal following. Business people and visitors
alike enjoy this popular no-frills eatery. Casual dress; cocktails. **Parking:** on-site and street. **Cards:** AX, DC, DS, MC, VI.
Historic
[🚭]

ST. JOSEPH pop. 73,990

——— WHERE TO STAY ———

BEST WESTERN CLASSIC INN   *Book great rates at AAA.com*   **Phone: (816)232-2345**
(AAA) [SAVE] All Year   1P: $59-$84   2P: $69-$89   XP: $5   F12
▼▼ ▼▼ **Location:** I-29, exit 44, just e. 4502 SE US 169 64507. **Fax:** 816/232-2330. **Facility:** 52 one-bedroom standard
Motel units, some with whirlpools. 2 stories (no elevator), exterior corridors. *Bath:* combo or shower only. **Parking:**
on-site, winter plug-ins. **Terms:** cancellation fee imposed, [ECP] meal plan available. **Amenities:** high-
speed Internet, irons, hair dryers. **Pool(s):** outdoor. **Leisure Activities:** sauna, exercise room. **Guest**
Services: wireless Internet. **Cards:** AX, CB, DC, DS, JC, MC, VI. **Free Special Amenities: expanded**
continental breakfast and high-speed Internet.

SOME UNITS
[S][D] [🍴] [&M] [♿] [📷] [🏊] [🍽] [🖥] / [✕] [🔌] [🖨] /

COMFORT SUITES   *Book great rates at AAA.com*   **Phone:** 816/232-6557
▼▼ ▼▼   Property failed to provide current rates
Small-scale Hotel **Location:** I-29, exit 47, just sw. 917 N Woodbine Rd 64506. **Fax:** 816/232-7100. **Facility:** 65 units. 64 one-
bedroom standard units, some with whirlpools. 1 one-bedroom suite with whirlpool. 3 stories, interior
corridors. *Bath:* combo or shower only. **Parking:** on-site. **Amenities:** voice mail, safes (fee), irons, hair
dryers. *Some:* dual phone lines. **Pool(s):** small heated indoor. **Leisure Activities:** whirlpool, exercise room. **Guest Services:**
valet and coin laundry, wireless Internet. **Business Services:** meeting rooms.

SOME UNITS
[🍴] [&M] [♿] [🏊] [📷] [🔌] [🖨] [🖥] / [✕] [VCR] /
                                                          FEE

DAYS INN *Book great rates at AAA.com*
Phone: (816)279-1671
AAA **SAVE**
All Year
1P: $49-$89
2P: $53-$99
XP: $10
F12
Location: I-29, exit 47, just e. 4312 Frederick Blvd 64506. Fax: 816/279-6729. **Facility:** 100 one-bedroom
standard units. 2 stories (no elevator), exterior corridors. **Parking:** on-site. **Amenities:** hair dryers. *Some:*
Motel
irons. **Pool(s):** outdoor. **Guest Services:** wireless Internet. **Business Services:** meeting rooms.
Cards: AX, CB, DC, DS, MC, VI. **Free Special Amenities: expanded continental breakfast and high-
speed Internet.**
SOME UNITS

DRURY INN & SUITES-ST. JOSEPH *Book at AAA.com*
Phone: (816)364-4700
All Year [BP]
1P: $55-$100
2P: $65-$110
XP: $10
F18
Location: I-29, exit 47. 4213 Frederick Blvd 64506. Fax: 816/364-4700. **Facility:** 132 units. 121 one-bedroom
standard units. 11 one-bedroom suites ($95-$130). 4 stories, interior corridors. **Parking:** on-site.
Small-scale Hotel
Terms: small pets only. **Amenities:** dual phone lines, voice mail, irons, hair dryers. **Pool(s):** small heated
indoor. **Leisure Activities:** whirlpool, exercise room. **Guest Services:** complimentary evening beverages: Mon-Sun, valet and
coin laundry, wireless Internet. **Business Services:** meeting rooms, business center. **Cards:** AX, CB, DC, DS, MC, VI.
SOME UNITS

HAMPTON INN BY HILTON *Book great rates at AAA.com*
Phone: (816)390-9300
All Year
1P: $90-$115
2P: $95-$120
XP: $5
F18
Location: I-29, exit 47, just w. 3928 Frederick Blvd 64501. Fax: 816/390-8382. **Facility:** 60 one-bedroom
standard units. 4 stories, interior corridors. *Bath:* combo or shower only. **Parking:** on-site. **Amenities:** voice
Small-scale Hotel
mail, irons, hair dryers. *Some:* high-speed Internet. **Pool(s):** heated indoor. **Leisure Activities:** whirlpool.
Guest Services: valet laundry, wireless Internet. **Cards:** AX, DC, DS, MC, VI.
SOME UNITS

RAMADA INN *Book at AAA.com*
Phone: 816/233-6192
Property failed to provide current rates
Location: I-29, exit 47. 4016 Frederick Blvd 64506. Fax: 816/233-6001. **Facility:** 163 units. 157 one-bedroom
standard units. 6 one-bedroom suites. 2 stories (no elevator), interior corridors. **Parking:** on-site.
Large-scale Hotel
Terms: check-in 4 pm, small pets only ($25 fee). **Amenities:** high-speed Internet, voice mail, safes (fee),
irons, hair dryers. **Pool(s):** heated indoor. **Leisure Activities:** whirlpool, exercise room. *Fee:* game room. **Guest Services:**
valet and coin laundry, wireless Internet. **Business Services:** conference facilities, business center.
SOME UNITS
FEE

ST. JOSEPH HOLIDAY INN-RIVERFRONT *Book great rates at AAA.com*
Phone: (816)279-8000
AAA **SAVE**
All Year
1P: $89-$109
2P: $94-$114
XP: $10
F18
Location: I-229, exit Edmond St northbound; exit Felix St southbound; downtown. 102 S Third St 64501.
Fax: 816/279-1484. **Facility:** 169 units. 164 one-bedroom standard units. 5 one-bedroom suites ($99-$179),
some with whirlpools. 6 stories, interior corridors. *Bath:* combo or shower only. **Parking:** on-site.
Large-scale Hotel
Terms: package plans, pets ($10 fee). **Amenities:** voice mail, irons, hair dryers. *Some:* high-speed Internet.
Dining: 6 am-11 pm, cocktails. **Pool(s):** heated indoor. **Leisure Activities:** sauna, whirlpool, exercise room.
Guest Services: valet and coin laundry, area transportation, wireless Internet. **Business Services:** conference facilities,
business center. **Cards:** AX, DC, DS, MC, VI.
SOME UNITS
FEE
FEE FEE

STONEY CREEK INN *Book great rates at AAA.com*
Phone: (816)901-9600
AAA **SAVE**
All Year
1P: $72
2P: $82
XP: $10
F18
Location: I-29, exit 47, just w to Woodbine Rd. 1201 N Woodbine Rd 64506. Fax: 816/901-9601. **Facility:** 129
units. 127 one-bedroom standard units, some with whirlpools. 2 one-bedroom suites ($150-$200) with
whirlpools. 3 stories, interior corridors. *Bath:* combo or shower only. **Parking:** on-site. **Amenities:** video
Small-scale Hotel
games (fee), high-speed Internet, voice mail, irons, hair dryers. *Some:* dual phone lines. **Pool(s):** heated
indoor/outdoor. **Leisure Activities:** sauna, whirlpool, exercise room. *Fee:* game room. **Guest Services:**
valet and coin laundry, area transportation. **Business Services:** conference facilities, business center. **Cards:** AX, DC, DS,
MC, VI. **Free Special Amenities: expanded continental breakfast and local telephone calls.**
SOME UNITS

—————— **WHERE TO DINE** ——————

BARBOSAS'
Lunch: $4-$11
Dinner: $4-$11
Phone: 816/233-4970
Location: Downtown. 906 Sylvanie 64506. **Hours:** 11 am-9 pm, Fri & Sat-10 pm. Closed major holidays; also
Sun. **Features:** The dining room carries out a Romanesque-Gothic motif. Among creative dishes are
Mexican
chicken mole and chiles rellenos. Other choices include fajitas, burritos, tostadas, enchiladas and fideos, as
well as children's favorites. Casual dress; cocktails. **Parking:** on-site. **Cards:** AX, CB, DC, DS, MC, VI.

FREDRICK INN STEAK HOUSE & LOUNGE
Lunch: $5-$8
Dinner: $8-$23
Phone: 816/364-5151
Location: I-29, exit 47, 2.5 mi w. 1627 Frederick Ave 64501. **Hours:** 11 am-9 pm, Sat 4 pm-10 pm. Closed major
holidays; also Sun. **Reservations:** suggested, weekends. **Features:** The busy lunch crowd at this
American
restaurant testifies to its popularity. They have an excellent variety of choices on the menu, including prime
rib, seafood, fresh veggies, salad and homemade dessert, and very good service by friendly, attentive
servers. Casual dress; cocktails. **Parking:** on-site. **Cards:** AX, CB, DC, DS, MC, VI.

LA DOLCE VITA AT 36TH STREET RESTAURANT   Lunch: $6-$10   Dinner: $9-$25   Phone: 816/364-1565
American
Location: I-29, exit 47, 0.3 mi w to US 169, then 0.3 mi s. 501 N Belt Hwy 64506. Hours: 11 am-10 pm. Closed major holidays; also Sun. Features: Delicious steak and fresh vegetables make an excellent combination for dinner at this restaurant. The upscale, traditional decor creates an inviting, friendly environment. The varied menu including homemade cheesecake completes the dining experience. Casual dress; cocktails.
Parking: on-site. Cards: AX, DS, MC, VI.

LA MESA MEXICAN RESTAURANT   Lunch: $4-$6   Dinner: $7-$12   Phone: 816/232-5853
Mexican
Location: I-29, exit 47, 0.4 mi w, 1.4 mi s on Belt Hwy, then just e. 3730 Mitchell Ave 64507. Hours: 11 am-9 pm, Fri & Sat-10 pm. Closed major holidays. Features: Extensive menu selection, many combinations and specialties. Large portions and spicy, very comfortable seating in mostly booths. Lively atmosphere with Mexican music and loud talking Mexican speaking chefs. Casual dress; cocktails. Parking: on-site.
Cards: AX, DS, MC, VI.

PALMA'S MEXICAN RESTAURANT   Lunch: $5-$6   Dinner: $6-$10   Phone: 816/279-9445
Mexican
Location: I-29, exit 47, 0.5 mi w on Frederick Blvd, then 1.2 mi n. 2715 N Belt Hwy 64506. Hours: 11 am-9 pm, Fri & Sat-10 pm. Closed major holidays; also Mon. Features: This restaurant features an authentic cuisine based on family recipes, and a casual, friendly atmosphere with Mexican and Southwestern decorations. Order the chicken fajitas and listen to them "sizzle" all the way from the kitchen! Very good service. Casual dress; cocktails. Parking: on-site. Cards: AX, DS, MC, VI.

RIB CRIB   Lunch: $6-$13   Dinner: $6-$13   Phone: 816/279-7422
American
Location: I-29, exit 47, just sw. 3704 Faraon St 64506. Hours: 11 am-10 pm, Fri & Sat-11 pm. Closed major holidays. Features: Most guests need extra napkins to tackle the ribs, brisket, ham, pork and chicken selections. The menu also lists sandwiches and wraps, along with tempting sides and large desserts. The decor is decidedly Western. Casual dress; beer only. Parking: on-site. Cards: AX, DS, MC, VI.

WHISKEY CREEK STEAKHOUSE   Lunch: $9-$20   Dinner: $9-$20   Phone: 816/676-1298
American
Location: I-29, exit 47, just w. 4016 Frederick Ave 64501. Hours: 11 am-10 pm, Fri & Sat-11 pm. Closed: 11/22, 12/25. Features: Guests can watch as their steak is cooked over a wood-burning fire and throw peanut shells on the floor at this fun, casual steakhouse. The menu's wide variety includes chicken, pasta and barbecue dishes. A rustic theme evokes the wild, wild West. Casual dress; cocktails. Parking: on-site.
Cards: AX, DS, MC, VI.

Destination St. Louis
pop. 348,189

*L*et the Gateway to the West be your access to excitement.

*B*ike or stroll in expansive Forest Park; cheer on the Cardinals; take the tram to the top of the city's most interesting "arch"-itectural feature, which offers an outstanding view; or check out the entertainment venues at downtown's historic Laclede's Landing.

© Gibson Stock Photography

Laclede's Landing, St. Louis.
A ride in a horse-drawn carriage is one way to explore historic Laclede's Landing, the nucleus of old St. Louis. (See listing page 205)

Missouri Division of Tourism

St. Louis Cardinals.
Everybody loves the city's major league baseball team. The Cardinals opened their 2006 season in a brand-new stadium.

*P*laces included in this AAA Destination City:

Lewis and Clark Heritage Days, St. Charles.
A Fife and Drum Corps snappily parades during this annual celebration commemorating the arrival of explorers Meriwether Lewis and William Clark in Missouri. (See mention page 210)

Missouri Division of Tourism

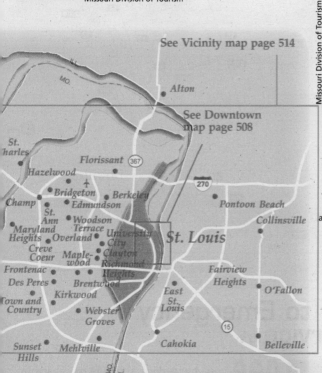

See Vicinity map page 514

See Downtown map page 508

MO.

Alton

St. Charles

Florissant 367

Hazelwood

Bridgeton · Berkeley

Champ · Edmundson 270 Pontoon Beach

St. Ann · Woodson Collinsville

Maryland Terrace University

Heights · Overland · City **St. Louis**

Creve Clayton

Coeur Maple- Richmond

wood Heights

Frontenac · Fairview

Des Peres · Brentwood Heights

Town and Kirkwood East O'Fallon

Country St. Louis

Webster 15

Groves

Sunset Mehlville Cahokia Belleville

Hills

MO. ILL.

Missouri Division of Tourism

St. Louis Storytelling Festival.
The traditional art of tale telling is saluted at this spring festival. Performances are given at locations throughout the city.

The Gateway Arch, St. Louis.
The gleaming stainless steel expanse of The Gateway Arch is St. Louis' most instantly identifiable landmark. (See listing page 205)

© Gateway Arch Riverfront

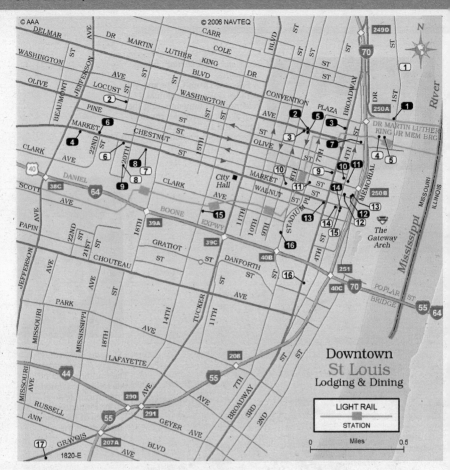

Downtown
St Louis
Lodging & Dining

LIGHT RAIL
STATION

0   Miles   0.5

Your key to Emergency Road Service...

AAA is at your service. Your AAA membership card is the key to obtaining Emergency Road Service. AAA can help when your car stalls, you get a flat tire, you run out of gas and even when you're locked out. Anytime, anywhere, call **800-AAA-HELP** to get going again.

Downtown St. Louis

This index helps you "spot" where approved accommodations and restaurants are located on the corresponding detailed maps. Lodging rate ranges are for comparison only and show the property's high season; rates are per night, unless only weekly (W) rates are available. Restaurant rate range is for dinner, unless only lunch (L) is served. Turn to the listing page for more detailed rate information and consult display ads for special promotions.

Spotter/Map Page Number	OA	DOWNTOWN ST. LOUIS - Lodgings	Diamond Rating	Rate Range High Season	Listing Page
1 / p. 508		Embassy Suites St. Louis Downtown	◆◆◆	$179-$199	523
2 / p. 508		The Renaissance St. Louis Suites Hotel	◆◆◆◆	Failed to provide	524
3 / p. 508		Drury Inn & Suites-St. Louis-Convention Center	◆◆◆	$86-$165	521
4 / p. 508	AAA	Courtyard by Marriott Downtown	◆◆◆	$89-$179 SAVE	521
5 / p. 508	AAA	Renaissance Grand Hotel St. Louis	◆◆◆◆	$229 SAVE	524
6 / p. 508		Hampton Inn-St. Louis/Union Station	◆◆◆	$149-$220	523
7 / p. 508	AAA	Hampton Inn-Gateway Arch	◆◆◆	$109-$169 SAVE	523
8 / p. 508	AAA	Hyatt Regency St. Louis At Union Station - see color ad p 524	◆◆◆◆	$105-$219 SAVE	524
9 / p. 508		Drury Inn-St. Louis/Union Station	◆◆◆	$90-$180	521
10 / p. 508		Hilton-St. Louis Downtown	◆◆◆	$149-$259	524
11 / p. 508	AAA	Crowne Plaza St. Louis Downtown	◆◆◆	$99-$189 SAVE	521
12 / p. 508	AAA	Adam's Mark St. Louis Hotel - see color ad p 521	◆◆◆	$80-$251 SAVE	521
13 / p. 508	AAA	Hilton St. Louis at the Ballpark - see color ad p 523	◆◆◆	$89-$279 SAVE	524
14 / p. 508	AAA	Drury Plaza Hotel-St. Louis At the Arch - see color ad p 522	◆◆◆	$90-$170 SAVE	522
15 / p. 508	AAA	Sheraton St. Louis City Center Hotel & Suites	◆◆◆◆	$399-$529 SAVE	525
16 / p. 508	AAA	The Westin St. Louis	◆◆◆◆	$359 SAVE	525
		DOWNTOWN ST. LOUIS - Restaurants			
1 / p. 508		Al's Restaurant	◆◆◆	$20-$50	525
2 / p. 508		St. Louis Brewery Tap Room	◆	$5-$12	527
3 / p. 508		An American Place	◆◆◆◆	$22-$36	525
4 / p. 508		Hannegan's	◆◆	$8-$23	526
5 / p. 508		Jake's Steaks	◆◆	$12-$40	526
6 / p. 508		Harry's Restaurant & Bar	◆◆◆	$18-$27	526
7 / p. 508		Station Grill	◆◆◆	$13-$32	527
8 / p. 508	AAA	Lombardo's Trattoria	◆◆◆	$15-$25	526
9 / p. 508		Kemoll's Italian Restaurant	◆◆◆	$16-$50	526
10 / p. 508		Dierdorf & Hart's	◆◆◆	$17-$44	526
11 / p. 508	AAA	Mike Shannon's Steaks & Seafood	◆◆◆	$25-$50	527
12 / p. 508		Chestnuts	◆◆◆	$7-$22	525
13 / p. 508	AAA	Faust's	◆◆◆◆	$19-$34	526
14 / p. 508	AAA	Tony's	◆◆◆◆	$20-$40	527
15 / p. 508	AAA	Carmine's Steak House	◆◆◆	$16-$30	525
16 / p. 508		Broadway Oyster Bar	◆	$8-$16	525
17 / p. 508		Hodak's Restaurant & Bar	◆◆	$5-$10	526

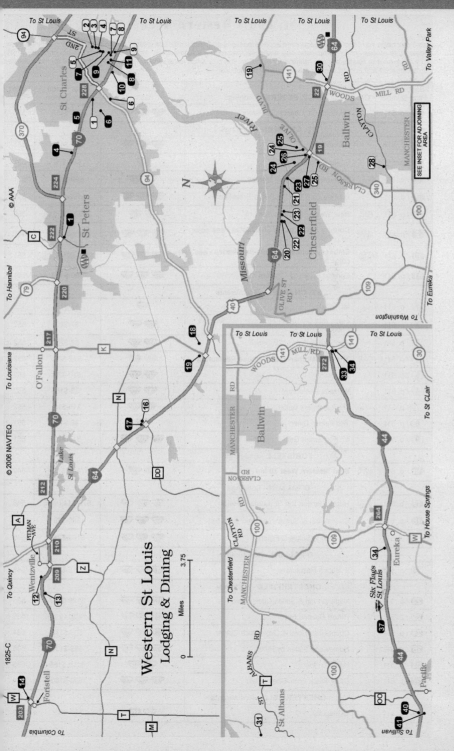

Western St Louis
Lodging & Dining

St. Louis Western Area

This index helps you "spot" where approved accommodations and restaurants are located on the corresponding detailed maps. Lodging rate ranges are for comparison only and show the property's high season; rates are per night, unless only weekly (W) rates are available. Restaurant rate range is for dinner, unless only lunch (L) is served. Turn to the listing page for more detailed rate information and consult display ads for special promotions.

Spotter/Map Page Number	OA	ST. PETERS - Lodgings	Diamond Rating	Rate Range High Season	Listing Page
❶ / p. 511		Drury Inn-St. Charles/St. Peters	◈◈◈	$65-$155	552
		ST. CHARLES - Lodgings			
❹ / p. 511		Hampton Inn	◈◈◈	$89-$114	551
❺ / p. 511		Super 8 Motel	◈	$59-$79	551
❻ / p. 511		TownePlace Suites by Marriott	◈◈	$99-$144	551
❼ / p. 511		Boone's Lick Trail Inn Bed & Breakfast	◈◈◈	$105-$215	550
❽ / p. 511	AAA	**Best Western St. Charles Inn**	◈◈	$79-$109 SAVE	550
❾ / p. 511	AAA	**Country Inn & Suites St. Charles** - see color ad p 550	◈◈	$92-$99 SAVE	551
❿ / p. 511	AAA	**Embassy Suites St. Louis-St. Charles** - see color ad p 550	◈◈◈	$119-$219 SAVE	551
⓫ / p. 511		Comfort Suites-St. Charles	◈◈◈	$90-$130	551
		ST. CHARLES - Restaurants			
① / p. 511		Mr. Steak	◈	$7-$19	552
② / p. 511		Lewis and Clark's An American Restaurant & Public House	◈◈	$7-$20	552
③ / p. 511		Trailhead Brewing Company	◈◈	$8-$20	552
④ / p. 511	AAA	**The New Mother-in-Law House Restaurant**	◈◈	$12-$20	552
⑤ / p. 511		Magpie's	◈◈	$10-$22	552
⑥ / p. 511		Wiliker's Restaurant	◈◈	$8-$15	552
⑦ / p. 511		The Landmark Buffet	◈◈	$15-$18	552
⑧ / p. 511		The Falcon Diner	◈	$8-$15	551
⑨ / p. 511		47 Port Street Grill	◈◈	$15-$25	551
		FORISTELL - Lodgings			
⓮ / p. 511	AAA	**Best Western West 70 Inn**	◈◈	$75-$95 SAVE	542
		O'FALLON - Lodgings			
⓱ / p. 511	AAA	**Hilton Garden Inn St. Louis/O'Fallon**	◈◈◈	$79-$149 SAVE	548
⓲ / p. 511		Country Inn & Suites - see color ad p 548	◈◈◈	$86-$96	548
⓳ / p. 511		Staybridge Suites O'Fallon	◈◈◈	$109-$259	548
		O'FALLON - Restaurant			
⑯ / p. 511		J. Buck's Restaurant	◈◈◈	$15-$26	548
		CHESTERFIELD - Lodgings			
㉒ / p. 511		Hampton Inn & Suites-Chesterfield	◈◈◈	$129-$187	535
㉓ / p. 511	AAA	**Hilton Garden Inn**	◈◈◈	$79-$149 SAVE	535
㉔ / p. 511		DoubleTree Hotel & Conference Center	◈◈◈	$89-$179	534
㉕ / p. 511		Homewood Suites by Hilton	◈◈◈	$89-$139	535
㉖ / p. 511		Hampton Inn	◈◈	$119-$165	535
㉗ / p. 511		Drury Plaza Hotel-Chesterfield	◈◈◈	$90-$160	534
		CHESTERFIELD - Restaurants			
⑲ / p. 511		El Maguey	◈◈	$7-$12	536

Spotter/Map Page Number	OA	CHESTERFIELD - Restaurants (continued)	Diamond Rating	Rate Range High Season	Listing Page
⑳ / p. 511		Villa Farotto Vineyards	◈◈◈	$9-$33	536
㉑ / p. 511		Annie Gunn's	◈◈◈	$8-$38	536
㉒ / p. 511		Fox and Hound Pub & Grille	◈◈	$8-$18	536
㉓ / p. 511		East Coast Pizza	◈	$6-$10	536
㉔ / p. 511		Yia Yia's Euro Cafe	◈◈◈	$10-$25	536
㉕ / p. 511		Aqua Vin Restaurant & Bar	◈◈◈	$13-$30	536
		TOWN AND COUNTRY - Lodgings			
㉚ / p. 511		St. Louis/Maryville Courtyard by Marriott	◈◈◈	$79-$149	553
		VALLEY PARK - Lodgings			
㉝ / p. 511		Hampton Inn-St. Louis Southwest	◈◈◈	$86-$126	554
㉞ / p. 511		Drury Inn & Suites-St. Louis Southwest	◈◈◈	$60-$140	554
		EUREKA - Lodgings			
㉛ / p. 511	ⒶⒶⒶ	**Holiday Inn at Six Flags**	◈◈◈	$159-$239 SAVE	540
		EUREKA - Restaurant			
㉞ / p. 511		Poor Richard's	◈◈	$7-$15	541
		PACIFIC - Lodgings			
㊵ / p. 511	ⒶⒶⒶ	**Comfort Inn** - see color ad p 498	◈◈◈	$79-$109 SAVE	498
㊶ / p. 511		Quality Inn Near Six Flags	◈	$69-$99	499
		WENTZVILLE - Restaurants			
⑫ / p. 511		Stefanina's	◈◈	$8-$15	555
⑬ / p. 511		Ruggeri's Ristorante	◈◈	$7-$22	555
		BALLWIN - Restaurant			
㉘ / p. 511		Charlotte's Rib BBQ	◈◈	$9-$15	533
		ST. ALBANS - Restaurant			
㉛ / p. 511		The Gardens at Malmaison	◈◈◈	$17-$28	502

© AAA

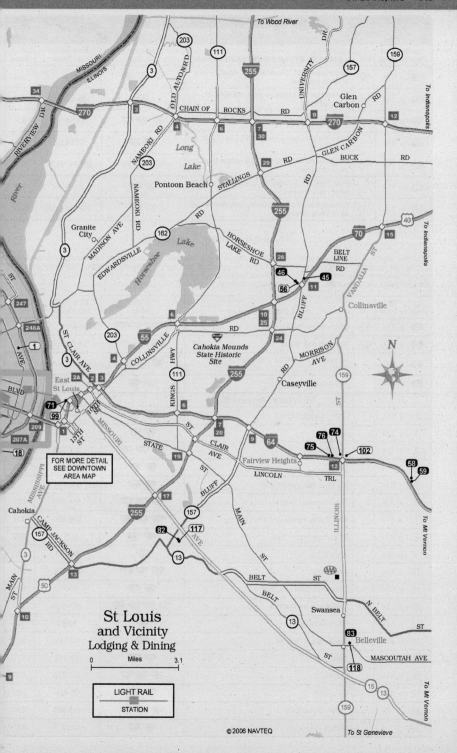

St Louis
and Vicinity
Lodging & Dining

Miles
0   3.1

LIGHT RAIL
STATION

© 2006 NAVTEQ

✈ Airport Accommodations

Spotter/Map Page Number	OA	LAMBERT-ST. LOUIS INTERNATIONAL	Diamond Rating	Rate Range High Season	Listing Page
20 / p. 514	AAA	Renaissance St. Louis Airport Hotel, 1 mi e of main terminal	▽▽▽	$89-$199 SAVE	533
21 / p. 514	AAA	Travelodge St. Louis Airport, 1.5 mi e of main terminal	▽	$69-$79 SAVE	533
25 / p. 514		Embassy Suites St. Louis Airport, 1.5 mi sw from main terminal	▽▽▽	$99-$199	534
17 / p. 514		Drury Inn-St. Louis Airport, 0.5 mi se of main terminal	▽▽	$83-$150	540
16 / p. 514	AAA	St. Louis Airport Marriott, 0.5 mi sw from main terminal	▽▽▽	$89-$179 SAVE	540
28 / p. 514		Pear Tree Inn by Drury-St. Louis Airport, 0.5 mi sw of main terminal	▽▽	$66-$134	549
42 / p. 514	AAA	Holiday Inn Airport Oakland Park Hotel, 1 mi se of main terminal	▽▽	$79-$129 SAVE	555

St. Louis and Vicinity

This index helps you "spot" where approved accommodations and restaurants are located on the corresponding detailed maps. Lodging rate ranges are for comparison only and show the property's high season; rates are per night, unless only weekly (W) rates are available. Restaurant rate range is for dinner, unless only lunch (L) is served. Turn to the listing page for more detailed rate information and consult display ads for special promotions.

Spotter/Map Page Number	OA	ST. LOUIS - Lodgings	Diamond Rating	Rate Range High Season	Listing Page
1 / p. 514	AAA	Chase Park Plaza - see color ad p 528	▽▽▽▽	$229-$1200 SAVE	528
2 / p. 514	AAA	The Parkway Hotel	▽▽▽	$116-$159 SAVE	528
3 / p. 514		Hampton Inn & Suites - St. Louis at Forest Park	▽▽▽	Failed to provide	528
4 / p. 514		The Water Tower Inn	▽▽	$70-$89	529
		ST. LOUIS - Restaurants			
1 / p. 514		Crown Candy Kitchen	▽▽	$4-$7	530
2 / p. 514		Dressel's Pub	▽▽	$7-$14	530
3 / p. 514		Cafe Balaban	▽▽▽	$16-$30	529
4 / p. 514		Duff's	▽▽	$13-$20	530
5 / p. 514		Bar Italia Ristorante-Caffe'	▽▽	$14-$25	529
6 / p. 514		The Tenderloin Room	▽▽▽	$14-$30	531
7 / p. 514		Wild Flower Restaurant and Catering	▽▽▽	$13-$26	531
8 / p. 514		Boathouse Forest Park	▽▽	$7-$15	529
9 / p. 514		Imo's Pizza	▽	$5-$15	530
10 / p. 514		King Louie's	▽▽▽	$17-$28	531
11 / p. 514		Columbo's Cafe and Tavern	▽▽	$4-$10	529
12 / p. 514	AAA	Giovanni's on the Hill	▽▽▽▽	$17-$30	530
13 / p. 514		O'Connell's Pub	▽	$5-$8	531
14 / p. 514		Amighetti's on the Hill	▽	$5-$10	529
15 / p. 514		Zia's	▽▽	$8-$19	531
16 / p. 514		Dominic's	▽▽▽	$18-$35	530
17 / p. 514		Bartolino's	▽▽	$9-$26	529
18 / p. 514		Sidney Street Cafe	▽▽▽	$18-$26	531
19 / p. 514		Mangia Italiano	▽▽	$12-$18	531

Spotter/Map Page Number	OA	**ST. LOUIS - Restaurants (continued)**	Diamond Rating	Rate Range High Season	Listing Page
⑳ / p. 514		King & I Restaurant	▽▽	$9-$13	530
㉑ / p. 514		Pho Grand Vietnamese Restaurant	▽▽	$5-$10	531
㉒ / p. 514		Brazie's Ristorante	▽▽	$9-$24	529
㉓ / p. 514		Frazer's	▽▽	$15-$20	530
㉔ / p. 514		Trattoria Marcella	▽▽▽	$11-$19	531
㉕ / p. 514		Ted Drewe's Frozen Custard	▽	$1-$5	531
		FLORISSANT - Lodgings			
❼ / p. 514	ⒶⒶⒶ	**Hampton Inn-St. Louis Northwest**	▽▽▽	$79-$199 [SAVE]	542
		FLORISSANT - Restaurants			
㉘ / p. 514		Fresh Italy	▽▽	$8-$15	542
㉙ / p. 514		Ruiz Mexican Restaurant	▽▽	$7-$18	542
㉚ / p. 514	ⒶⒶⒶ	**Yacovelli's Restaurant**	▽▽	$15-$20	542
㉛ / p. 514		The Barn Deli	▽▽	$4-$7(L)	542
		CHAMP - Lodgings			
❿ / p. 514		Residence Inn St. Louis Airport/Earth City	▽▽▽	$119-$189	534
		HAZELWOOD - Lodgings			
⓭ / p. 514		La Quinta Inn St. Louis (Airport)	▽▽	$82-$118	543
		HAZELWOOD - Restaurants			
㉞ / p. 514		Village China Wok	▽▽	$6-$10	543
㉟ / p. 514		Pueblo Nuevo Mexican Restaurant	▽	$9-$13	543
		EDMUNDSON - Lodgings			
⓰ / p. 514	ⒶⒶⒶ	**St. Louis Airport Marriott**	▽▽▽	$89-$179 [SAVE]	540
⓱ / p. 514		Drury Inn-St. Louis Airport	▽▽	$83-$150	540
		EDMUNDSON - Restaurant			
㊳ / p. 514		Lombardo's Restaurant	▽▽▽	$15-$20	540
		BERKELEY - Lodgings			
⑳ / p. 514	ⒶⒶⒶ	**Renaissance St. Louis Airport Hotel**	▽▽▽	$89-$199 [SAVE]	533
㉑ / p. 514	ⒶⒶⒶ	**Travelodge St. Louis Airport**	▽	$69-$79 [SAVE]	533
		BRIDGETON - Lodgings			
㉔ / p. 514	ⒶⒶⒶ	**Airport Earth City Courtyard by Marriott**	▽▽	$69-$159 [SAVE]	534
㉕ / p. 514		Embassy Suites St. Louis Airport	▽▽▽	$99-$199	534
		BRIDGETON - Restaurant			
㊶ / p. 514		Berkshire Grill	▽▽	$10-$25	534
		ST. ANN - Lodgings			
㉘ / p. 514		Pear Tree Inn by Drury-St. Louis Airport	▽▽	$66-$134	549
㉙ / p. 514		Hampton Inn-St. Louis Airport	▽▽▽	$99-$165	549
		MARYLAND HEIGHTS - Lodgings			
㉜ / p. 514		Holiday Inn Express/Riverport	▽▽▽	$79-$129	545
㉝ / p. 514		Harrah's St. Louis Casino & Hotel	▽▽▽	$79-$369	545
㉞ / p. 514		Hampton Inn Westport - see color ad p 544	▽▽	$139-$164	544
㉟ / p. 514		Drury Inn & Suites-St. Louis-Westport	▽▽	$66-$130	544

Spotter/Map Page Number	OA	MARYLAND HEIGHTS - Lodgings (continued)	Diamond Rating	Rate Range High Season	Listing Page
36 / p. 514	AAA	Sheraton (West Port) Hotel-Lakeside Chalet - see color ad p 545	▽▽▽	$89-$229 SAVE	545
37 / p. 514	AAA	The Sheraton (West Port) Plaza Tower - see color ad p 545	▽▽▽	$89-$219 SAVE	546
38 / p. 514		DoubleTree Hotel St. Louis at Westport	▽▽▽	Failed to provide	544
39 / p. 514		Staybridge Suites	▽▽▽	Failed to provide	546
		MARYLAND HEIGHTS - Restaurants			
44 / p. 514		Town Square Buffet	▽▽	$13	547
45 / p. 514		Marciano's	▽▽	$9-$19	546
46 / p. 514		Dierdorf & Harts Steakhouse	▽▽▽	$18-$43	546
47 / p. 514		Trainwreck Saloon Westport	▽▽	$7-$15	547
48 / p. 514		Ozzie's Restaurant & Sports Bar	▽▽	$6-$22	546
49 / p. 514		the drunken fish Sushi Bar and Lounge	▽▽	$10-$24	546
		WOODSON TERRACE - Lodgings			
42 / p. 514	AAA	Holiday Inn Airport Oakland Park Hotel	▽▽	$79-$129 SAVE	555
		WOODSON TERRACE - Restaurants			
52 / p. 514		Oakland Park Restaurant	▽▽	$8-$24	555
53 / p. 514		Erio's Restaurant	▽	$6-$10	555
		COLLINSVILLE - Lodgings			
45 / p. 514		Drury Inn-St. Louis/Collinsville	▽▽	$70-$149	557
46 / p. 514		Super 8 Motel-Collinsville	▽	$50-$89	557
		COLLINSVILLE - Restaurant			
56 / p. 514		Zapata's Mexican Restaurant & Cantina	▽▽	$6-$14	557
		CREVE COEUR - Lodgings			
49 / p. 514		Drury Inn & Suites-Creve Coeur	▽▽▽	$80-$150	539
50 / p. 514	AAA	Courtyard by Marriott-Creve Coeur	▽▽▽	$189 SAVE	539
		CREVE COEUR - Restaurants			
67 / p. 514		Balducci's Winefest Restaurant & Bar	▽▽	$5-$11	539
68 / p. 514		Kobe Steak House of Japan	▽▽▽	$13-$27	540
69 / p. 514		Candicci's Restaurant	▽▽▽	$10-$25	539
70 / p. 514		La Bonne Bouchee Westgate Center	▽▽	$8-$10(L)	540
71 / p. 514		Il Bellagio City Place	▽▽▽	$16-$36	539
72 / p. 514		Bristol Bar & Seafood Grill	▽▽▽	$12-$28	539
		CLAYTON - Lodgings			
53 / p. 514	AAA	The Ritz-Carlton, St. Louis	▽▽▽▽	$179-$251 SAVE	537
54 / p. 514	AAA	Crowne Plaza St Louis-Clayton - see color ad p 537	▽▽▽	$139-$209 SAVE	536
55 / p. 514	AAA	Sheraton Clayton Plaza Hotel - see color ad p 537	▽▽▽	$239 SAVE	537
		CLAYTON - Restaurants			
75 / p. 514		Cardwell's in Clayton	▽▽▽	$13-$25	538
76 / p. 514		BARcelona Tapas Restaurant	▽▽▽	$10-$15	538
77 / p. 514		Portabella	▽▽▽	$14-$27	538
78 / p. 514		Cafe De France	▽▽▽	$9-$24	538

Spotter/Map Page Number	OA	CLAYTON - Restaurants (continued)	Diamond Rating	Rate Range High Season	Listing Page
⑦⑨ / p. 514		Luciano's Trattoria	◆◆◆	$8-$22	538
⑧⓪ / p. 514	AAA	**The Grill**	◆◆◆◆	$25-$50	538
⑧① / p. 514		Dominic's Trattoria	◆◆◆	$9-$25	538
⑧② / p. 514		Remy's Kitchen & Wine Bar	◆◆	$6-$20	538
⑧③ / p. 514		Jimmy's On the Park Cafe Bistro & Bar	◆◆◆	$8-$21	538
⑧④ / p. 514		Sasha's Wine Bar & Market	◆◆	$5-$20	538
⑧⑤ / p. 514		Yen Ching	◆◆	$12-$14	539
		O'FALLON - Lodgings			
⑤⑧ / p. 514		Baymont Inn & Suites St. Louis (O'Fallon)	◆◆	Failed to provide	559
⑤⑨ / p. 514		Extended Stay America-O'Fallon Illinois	◆◆		559
		FRONTENAC - Lodgings			
⑥② / p. 514		Hilton St. Louis Frontenac	◆◆◆	Failed to provide	542
		FRONTENAC - Restaurants			
⑧⑧ / p. 514	AAA	**Kreis Restaurant**	◆◆◆	$15-$50	543
⑧⑨ / p. 514		Brio tuscan grille	◆◆◆	$9-$23	543
⑨⓪ / p. 514		Canyon Cafe	◆◆◆	$7-$22	543
		TOWN AND COUNTRY - Lodgings			
⑥⑤ / p. 514	AAA	**St. Louis Marriott West - see color ad p 535**	◆◆◆	$89-$189 [SAVE]	553
		RICHMOND HEIGHTS - Lodgings			
⑥⑧ / p. 514	AAA	**Residence Inn By Marriott-St. Louis Galleria**	◆◆◆	$99-$169 [SAVE]	549
		RICHMOND HEIGHTS - Restaurant			
⑨③ / p. 514		Harvest	◆◆◆	$18-$28	549
		EAST ST. LOUIS - Lodgings			
⑦① / p. 514	AAA	**Casino Queen Hotel**	◆◆◆	$89-$125 [SAVE]	558
		EAST ST. LOUIS - Restaurant			
⑨⑨ / p. 514	AAA	**Royal Table Steakhouse**	◆◆◆	$15-$35	558
		FAIRVIEW HEIGHTS - Lodgings			
⑦④ / p. 514		Drury Inn & Suites-Fairview Heights	◆◆◆	$80-$140	558
⑦⑤ / p. 514		Hampton Inn by Hilton	◆◆◆	$80-$105	558
⑦⑥ / p. 514		Fairfield Inn by Marriott	◆◆	$85-$110	558
		FAIRVIEW HEIGHTS - Restaurant			
⑩② / p. 514		Lotawata Creek Southern Grill	◆◆	$7-$19	558
		KIRKWOOD - Lodgings			
⑦⑨ / p. 514		Best Western Kirkwood Inn	◆◆	$79-$129	543
		KIRKWOOD - Restaurants			
⑪③ / p. 514		Sunset 44	◆◆◆	$12-$25	544
⑪④ / p. 514	AAA	**Citizen Kane's**	◆◆◆	$18-$29	543
		BELLEVILLE - Lodgings			
⑧② / p. 514	AAA	**The Shrine Hotel - see color ad p 212**	◆	$66-$75 [SAVE]	556
⑧③ / p. 514	AAA	**Swans Court Bed & Breakfast**	◆◆◆	$55-$110 [SAVE]	556
		BELLEVILLE - Restaurants			
⑪⑦ / p. 514	AAA	**The Shrine Restaurant - see color ad p 212**	◆◆	$10-$14	557

Spotter/Map Page Number	OA	BELLEVILLE - Restaurants (continued)	Diamond Rating	Rate Range High Season	Listing Page
118 / p. 514		The Pie Pantry	◆	$5-$12(L)	556
		FENTON - Lodgings			
86 / p. 514		Drury Inn & Suites-Fenton	◆◆	$65-$125	541
87 / p. 514		Pear Tree Inn by Drury-Fenton	◆◆	$50-$110	541
88 / p. 514		Fairfield Inn	◆◆	$79-$129	541
89 / p. 514		Holiday Inn Express Hotel & Suites	◆◆◆	$76-$139	541
		SUNSET HILLS - Lodgings			
92 / p. 514	AAA	Holiday Inn-Southwest & Viking Conference Center	◆◆◆	$104-$159 SAVE	553
		SUNSET HILLS - Restaurant			
121 / p. 514		O'Leary's	◆◆	$9-$17	553
		MEHLVILLE - Lodgings			
95 / p. 514		Holiday Inn South County Center	◆◆◆	Failed to provide	547
96 / p. 514		Holiday Inn St. Louis-South I-55	◆◆◆	$89-$175	547
		MEHLVILLE - Restaurant			
124 / p. 514		Gingham's Homestyle Restaurant	◆	$5-$11	547
		OVERLAND - Restaurant			
59 / p. 514		Mandarin House Restaurant	◆◆	$7-$17	549
		UNIVERSITY CITY - Restaurants			
62 / p. 514	AAA	Nobu's Japanese Restaurant	◆◆	$13-$20	554
63 / p. 514		Saleem's	◆◆	$8-$18	554
64 / p. 514		Blueberry Hill	◆◆	$5-$9	553
		BRENTWOOD - Restaurant			
96 / p. 514		Frank Papa's	◆◆◆	$12-$25	533
		MAPLEWOOD - Restaurant			
105 / p. 514		Monarch Restuarant	◆◆◆	$16-$26	544
		WEBSTER GROVES - Restaurants			
108 / p. 514		Zinnia	◆◆◆	$17-$34	554
109 / p. 514		Llywelyn's Pub	◆◆	$6-$12	554
110 / p. 514		Big Sky Cafe	◆◆	$15-$22	554

DOWNTOWN ST. LOUIS (See map and index starting on p. 508)

——— WHERE TO STAY ———

ADAM'S MARK ST. LOUIS HOTEL   *Book great rates at AAA.com*   Phone: (314)241-7400 **12**
(AAA) [SAVE]

4/1-11/17	1P: $80-$251	2P: $80-$251	XP: $20	F17
3/1-3/31 & 11/18-2/29	1P: $62-$215	2P: $62-$215	XP: $20	F17

▽▽▽▽ **Location:** I-70, exit 250B (Stadium/Memorial Dr); at 4th and Chestnut sts. Located across from the Gateway Arch. 315 Chestnut St 63102. Fax: 314/241-6618. **Facility:** 910 units. 880 one-bedroom standard units. 9 one- and 21
Large-scale Hotel two-bedroom suites, some with whirlpools. 18 stories, interior corridors. *Bath:* combo or shower only. **Parking:** on-site (fee) and valet. **Terms:** package plans. **Amenities:** video games (fee), high-speed Internet, voice mail, irons, hair dryers. **Dining:** 6 am-11 pm, cocktails, also, Chestnuts, Faust's, see separate listings, nightclub, entertainment. **Pool(s):** heated outdoor, heated indoor. **Leisure Activities:** saunas, whirlpool, racquetball courts, volleyball. **Guest Services:** gift shop, valet laundry, wireless Internet. **Business Services:** conference facilities, business center. **Cards:** AX, DC, DS, MC, VI. **Free Special Amenities: local telephone calls and high-speed Internet.**
(See color ad below)

SOME UNITS
[icons]

COURTYARD BY MARRIOTT DOWNTOWN   *Book great rates at AAA.com*   Phone: (314)241-9111 **4**
(AAA) [SAVE]
All Year   1P: $89-$179   2P: $89-$179
▽▽▽▽ **Location:** I-64/US 40, exit 39, just n on Jefferson Ave, then just e. 2340 Market St 63103. Fax: 314/241-8113.
Facility: Smoke free premises. 151 units. 139 one-bedroom standard units. 12 one-bedroom suites ($115-$209). 4 stories, interior corridors. *Bath:* combo or shower only. **Parking:** on-site. **Amenities:** high-speed
Small-scale Hotel Internet, voice mail, irons, hair dryers. **Dining:** 6:30-10 am, Sat & Sun 7-11 am. **Pool(s):** small heated indoor. **Leisure Activities:** whirlpool, exercise room. **Guest Services:** sundries, valet and coin laundry. **Business Services:** meeting rooms, business center. **Cards:** AX, CB, DC, DS, JC, MC, VI. **Free Special Amenities: newspaper and high-speed Internet.**

SOME UNITS
[icons]

CROWNE PLAZA ST. LOUIS DOWNTOWN   *Book great rates at AAA.com*   Phone: (314)621-8200 **11**
(AAA) [SAVE]
All Year   1P: $99-$189   2P: $99-$189   XP: $10   F16
▽▽▽▽ **Location:** I-70, exit 250B (Stadium/Memorial Dr); just w; at 4th and Pine sts. 200 N 4th St 63102. Fax: 314/621-8073.
Facility: 440 units. 346 one-bedroom standard units. 79 one- and 15 two-bedroom suites ($129-$239). 29 stories, interior corridors. *Bath:* combo or shower only. **Parking:** on-site (fee) and valet. **Terms:** cancellation
Large-scale Hotel fee imposed, package plans. **Amenities:** video games (fee), high-speed Internet, dual phone lines, voice mail, irons, hair dryers. **Dining:** 6:30 am-2 & 5-10 pm, cocktails. **Pool(s):** outdoor. **Leisure Activities:** exercise room. **Guest Services:** valet and coin laundry, area transportation-within 5 mi. **Business Services:** conference facilities, business center. **Cards:** AX, DC, DS, MC, VI. **Free Special Amenities: newspaper and high-speed Internet.**

SOME UNITS
[icons]

DRURY INN & SUITES-ST. LOUIS-CONVENTION CENTER   *Book great rates at AAA.com*   Phone: (314)231-8100 **3**
▽▽▽▽
All Year [BP]   1P: $86-$155   2P: $96-$165   XP: $10   F18
Location: I-70, exit 250B (Stadium/Memorial Dr), at convention center. 711 N Broadway 63102. Fax: 314/621-6568.
Large-scale Hotel **Facility:** 178 units. 144 one-bedroom standard units. 34 one-bedroom suites ($101-$175). 6 stories, interior corridors. **Parking:** on-site. **Amenities:** high-speed Internet, voice mail, irons, hair dryers. **Pool(s):** small heated indoor. **Leisure Activities:** whirlpool, exercise room. **Guest Services:** complimentary evening beverages, valet and coin laundry. **Business Services:** meeting rooms, PC. **Cards:** AX, CB, DC, DS, MC, VI.

SOME UNITS
[ASK] [icons]

DRURY INN-ST. LOUIS/UNION STATION   *Book great rates at AAA.com*   Phone: (314)231-3900 **9**
▽▽▽▽
All Year [BP]   1P: $90-$170   2P: $100-$180   XP: $10   F18
Location: Just e of Jefferson Ave; between Market St and Clark Ave. 201 S 20th St 63103. Fax: 314/231-3900.
Small-scale Hotel **Facility:** 177 units. 172 one-bedroom standard units. 5 one-bedroom suites ($120-$185), some with kitchens. 7 stories, interior corridors. **Parking:** on-site. **Amenities:** high-speed Internet, voice mail, irons, hair dryers. **Dining:** Lombardo's Trattoria, see separate listing. **Pool(s):** small heated indoor. **Leisure Activities:** whirlpool, exercise room. **Guest Services:** complimentary evening beverages, valet and coin laundry. **Business Services:** meeting rooms, PC. **Cards:** AX, CB, DC, DS, MC, VI.

SOME UNITS
[ASK] [icons]

(See map and index starting on p. 508)

DRURY PLAZA HOTEL-ST. LOUIS AT THE ARCH   *Book great rates at AAA.com*   Phone: (314)231-3003   **14**

AAA SAVE   All Year [BP]   1P: $90-$160   2P: $100-$170   XP: $10   F18
▽▽▽   **Location:** I-70, 250B (Stadium/Memorial Dr), just w on Pine St to Broadway, just s to Walnut St, just e to 4th St, then
Historic   just n. 4th & Market sts 63102. Fax: 314/231-2952. **Facility:** Elaborate public areas featuring crystal
Small-scale Hotel   chandeliers and upscale appointments. Bathrooms with marble walls and large guest units with upscale
design. 355 units. 299 one-bedroom standard units, some with whirlpools. 56 one-bedroom suites ($110-
$290), some with whirlpools. 4-10 stories, interior corridors. **Bath:** combo or shower only. **Parking:** on-site
(fee). **Amenities:** high-speed Internet, dual phone lines, voice mail, irons, hair dryers. **Dining:** Carmine's
Steak House, Max & Erma's, see separate listings. **Pool(s):** heated indoor. **Leisure Activities:** whirlpools, exercise room.
Guest Services: sundries, complimentary evening beverages, valet and coin laundry, wireless Internet. **Business Services:**
meeting rooms, business center. **Cards:** AX, CB, DC, DS, MC, VI. *(See color ad below)*   SOME UNITS

🐕 🍴 ▦ 🍸 (&M) 📶 ⊘ 🏊 📹 📠 ⊟ 🖥 / ✕ /

(See map and index starting on p. 508)

EMBASSY SUITES ST. LOUIS DOWNTOWN — *Book at AAA.com* — Phone: (314)241-4200 — **1**
All Year — 1P: $179-$199 — XP: $20 — F18
Large-scale Hotel — Location: At foot of Martin Luther King Bridge. Located in Laclede's Landing. 901 N 1st St 63102-2548. Fax: 314/241-6513. **Facility:** 297 units. 296 one- and 1 two-bedroom suites, some with kitchens. 8 stories, interior corridors. **Parking:** on-site (fee). **Terms:** check-in 4 pm, cancellation fee imposed, [BP] meal plan available. **Amenities:** voice mail, irons, hair dryers. *Fee:* video games, high-speed Internet. **Pool(s):** small heated indoor, wading. **Leisure Activities:** sauna, whirlpool, exercise room. *Fee:* game room. **Guest Services:** gift shop, complimentary evening beverages, valet and coin laundry, area transportation. **Business Services:** conference facilities, PC. **Cards:** AX, CB, DC, DS, JC, MC, VI.
SOME UNITS
(ASK) (S$_D$) (†¶) (⊤) (≥) (⊠) (⋇) (⊞) (⊡) (⊑) / (⊠) /

HAMPTON INN-GATEWAY ARCH — *Book great rates at AAA.com* — Phone: (314)621-7900 — **7**
(AAA) (SAVE)
3/1-10/31 [ECP] — 1P: $109-$169 — XP: $10 — D18
11/1-2/29 [ECP] — 1P: $89-$129 — XP: $10 — D18
Small-scale Hotel — Location: I-70, exit 250B (Stadium/Memorial Dr), just sw. 333 Washington Ave 63102. Fax: 314/421-6468. **Facility:** 190 one-bedroom standard units. 17 stories, interior corridors. *Bath:* combo or shower only. **Parking:** on-site (fee). **Terms:** 3 day cancellation notice. **Amenities:** video games (fee), high-speed Internet, dual phone lines, voice mail, irons, hair dryers. **Pool(s):** heated indoor. **Leisure Activities:** whirlpool, exercise room. *Fee:* game room. **Guest Services:** gift shop, valet and coin laundry, wireless Internet. **Business Services:** meeting rooms, business center. **Cards:** AX, CB, DC, DS, JC, MC, VI. **Free Special Amenities:** expanded continental breakfast and high-speed Internet.
SOME UNITS
(S$_D$) (≥) (⊠) (⋇) (⊞) (⊑) / (⊠) /

HAMPTON INN-ST. LOUIS/UNION STATION — *Book great rates at AAA.com* — Phone: (314)241-3200 — **6**
All Year [BP] — 1P: $149-$219 — 2P: $159-$220 — XP: $10 — F18
Small-scale Hotel — Location: I-64/US 40, exit 39, just n on Jefferson Ave, then just e. 2211 Market St 63103. Fax: 314/241-9351. **Facility:** 239 units. 229 one-bedroom standard units. 10 one-bedroom suites. 11 stories, interior corridors. **Parking:** on-site. **Terms:** small pets only (in carriers). **Amenities:** high-speed Internet, dual phone lines, voice mail, irons, hair dryers. **Pool(s):** heated indoor. **Leisure Activities:** whirlpool, exercise room. **Guest Services:** valet and coin laundry. **Business Services:** meeting rooms, PC, fax. **Cards:** AX, CB, DC, DS, MC, VI.
SOME UNITS
(ASK) (🛏) (†¶) (≥) (⋇) (⊑) / (⊠) (⊞) (⊡) /

Hilton
St. Louis at the Ballpark
Travel should take you places.™

Hilton St. Louis at the Ballpark presents a dynamic new vision and perspective of lodging, coupled with the legacy of flawless Hilton service.

One South Broadway • St. Louis, Missouri 63102
Phone: 314/421.1776 • Fax : 314/331.9029
www.hiltonstlouis.com

(See map and index starting on p. 508)

HILTON ST. LOUIS AT THE BALLPARK   *Book great rates at AAA.com*   Phone: (314)421-1776   **13**

4/1-10/31   1P: $89-$279   2P: $89-$279
3/1-3/31 & 11/1-2/29   1P: $89-$249   2P: $89-$249

Location: Between Walnut and Market sts. One S Broadway 63102. Fax: 314/331-9029. **Facility:** 675 units. 668 one-bedroom standard units. 6 one- and 1 two-bedroom suites. 22-25 stories, interior corridors. **Bath:** combo or shower only. **Parking:** on-site (fee) and valet. **Terms:** check-in 4 pm, [BP] & [CP] meal plans available, package plans. **Amenities:** high-speed Internet (fee), dual phone lines, voice mail, irons, hair dryers. **Dining:** 3 restaurants, 6:30 am-midnight, cocktails. **Pool(s):** heated indoor. **Leisure Activities:** saunas, whirlpool, exercise room. **Guest Services:** gift shop, valet and coin laundry. **Business Services:** conference facilities, business center. **Cards:** AX, DC, DS, MC, VI. **Free Special Amenities:** early check-in/late check-out and high-speed Internet.

Large-scale Hotel

(See color ad p 523)

SOME UNITS

HILTON-ST. LOUIS DOWNTOWN   *Book great rates at AAA.com*   Phone: (314)436-0002   **10**

All Year [BP]   1P: $149-$249   2P: $159-$259   XP: $10   F18

Location: I-70, exit 249C/251C (Sixth St) to N Broadway to Olive St. 400 Olive St 63102. Fax: 314/436-4252. **Facility:** Located in the Historical Merchants Laclede Building, this hotel has been restored to its turn-of-the-century ambiance. 195 units. 194 one-bedroom standard units, some with whirlpools. 1 one-bedroom suite ($179-$279) with efficiency and whirlpool. 8 stories, interior corridors. **Bath:** combo or shower only. **Parking:** on-site (fee) and valet. **Amenities:** video games (fee), high-speed Internet, dual phone lines, voice mail, irons, hair dryers. **Leisure Activities:** whirlpool. **Guest Services:** sundries, valet laundry. **Business Services:** meeting rooms, business center. **Cards:** AX, CB, DC, DS, JC, MC, VI.

*Historic
Small-scale Hotel*

SOME UNITS

HYATT REGENCY ST. LOUIS AT UNION STATION   *Book great rates at AAA.com*   Phone: (314)231-1234   **8**

All Year   1P: $105-$219   2P: $105-$219   XP: $25   F18

Location: Just e on Jefferson Ave, off US 40 at 18th and Market sts. 1 St. Louis Union Station 63103. Fax: 314/923-3970. **Facility:** Magnificent historical landmark location! Built in 1894, and once the largest/busiest station in the world, history buffs might request a room in the original train track section, as well as take advantage of the guided tours. 538 units. 531 one-bedroom standard units. 7 one-bedroom suites. 5-6 stories, interior corridors. **Bath:** combo or shower only. **Parking:** on-site (fee) and valet. **Terms:** cancellation fee imposed. **Amenities:** high-speed Internet (fee), dual phone lines, voice mail, irons, hair dryers. **Dining:** Station Grill, see separate listing. **Pool(s):** outdoor. **Leisure Activities:** saunas, exercise room. **Guest Services:** sundries, valet laundry. **Business Services:** conference facilities, business center. **Cards:** AX, CB, DC, DS, JC, MC, VI. *(See color ad below)*

*Classic
Large-scale Hotel*

SOME UNITS

RENAISSANCE GRAND HOTEL ST. LOUIS   *Book great rates at AAA.com*   Phone: 314/621-9600   **5**

All Year   1P: $229

Location: Across from America's Center Convention Center. 800 Washington Ave 63101. Fax: 314/621-9601. **Facility:** This stately modernization of the original 1917 hotel embraces both the past and present in elegance. Smoke free premises. 918 units. 894 one-bedroom standard units. 24 one-bedroom suites, some with whirlpools. 23 stories, interior corridors. **Bath:** combo or shower only. **Parking:** on-site (fee) and valet. **Terms:** check-in 4 pm, cancellation fee imposed, package plans, pets ($75 fee). **Amenities:** dual phone lines, voice mail, irons, hair dryers. **Fee:** video games, high-speed Internet. **Dining:** 3 restaurants, 6:30 am-10 pm, cocktails, also, An American Place, see separate listing. **Pool(s):** heated indoor. **Leisure Activities:** whirlpool. **Guest Services:** gift shop, valet laundry. **Business Services:** conference facilities, business center. **Cards:** AX, DC, DS, MC, VI. **Free Special Amenities:** newspaper and early check-in/late check-out.

Large-scale Hotel

FEE

THE RENAISSANCE ST. LOUIS SUITES HOTEL   *Book great rates at AAA.com*   Phone: 314/621-9700   **2**

Property failed to provide current rates

Location: Next to America's Center Convention Center. 827 Washington Ave 63101. Fax: 314/621-9702. **Facility:** The restoration of a 1929 artistic landmark offers the elegance of a boutique style hotel; guest units combine modern luxury with historic charm. Smoke free premises. 165 units. 1 one-bedroom standard unit. 164 one-bedroom suites. 25 stories, interior corridors. **Bath:** combo or shower only. **Parking:** on-site (fee) and valet. **Terms:** check-in 4 pm, pets ($45 extra charge). **Amenities:** CD players, dual phone lines, voice mail, irons, hair dryers. **Fee:** video games, high-speed Internet. **Leisure Activities:** saunas, whirlpool, exercise room. **Guest Services:** sundries, valet laundry. **Business Services:** meeting rooms, business center.

*Historic
Small-scale Hotel*

FEE

See map and index starting on p. 508)

HERATON ST. LOUIS CITY CENTER HOTEL &
SUITES *Book great rates at AAA.com*   Phone: (314)231-5007   **15**

AAA [SAVE]   All Year   1P: $399-$529   2P: $399-$529   XP: $20   F18

Large-scale Hotel   **Location:** I-40, exit 39B (14th St), just ne. 400 S 14th St 63103. Fax: 314/231-5008. **Facility:** 288 units. 144 one-bedroom standard units, some with whirlpools. 137 one- and 7 two-bedroom suites, some with whirlpools. 13 stories, interior corridors. *Bath:* combo or shower only. **Parking:** on-site (fee) and valet. **Terms:** cancellation fee imposed, package plans. **Amenities:** dual phone lines, voice mail, irons, hair dryers. *Fee:* video games, high-speed Internet. *Some:* CD players. **Dining:** 2 restaurants, 6:30 am-midnight, cocktails. **Pool(s):** heated indoor. **Leisure Activities:** whirlpool, sun deck, exercise room. *Fee:* massage, game room. **Guest Services:** gift shop, valet and coin laundry, wireless Internet. **Business Services:** conference facilities, business center. Cards: AX, DC, DS, MC, VI.

SOME UNITS
[icons] FEE

THE WESTIN ST. LOUIS   *Book great rates at AAA.com*   Phone: (314)621-2000   **16**

AAA [SAVE]   All Year   1P: $359   2P: $359   XP: $30   F18

Historic
Large-scale Hotel   **Location:** Just w of Busch Stadium. 811 Spruce St 63102. Fax: 314/552-5700. **Facility:** Rehabilitated warehouse offering strong design elements with luxurious, ultra-modern and upscale appointments. Smoke free premises. 255 units. 240 one-bedroom standard units. 15 one-bedroom suites, some with whirlpools. 5-7 stories, interior corridors. *Bath:* combo or shower only. **Parking:** on-site (fee) and valet. **Terms:** cancellation fee imposed, small pets only. **Amenities:** dual phone lines, voice mail, safes, honor bars, irons, hair dryers. *Fee:* video games, high-speed Internet. *Some:* DVD players, CD players. **Dining:** 6 am-11 pm, Fri-midnight, at 7 am-midnight, Sun 7 am-11 pm, cocktails. **Leisure Activities:** spa. **Guest Services:** valet laundry, wireless Internet. **Business Services:** conference facilities, business center. Cards: AX, CB, DC, DS, JC, MC, VI. **Free Special Amenities:** newspaper and high-speed Internet.

[icons]

──────── *The following lodging was either not evaluated or did not* ────────
meet AAA rating requirements but is listed for your information only.

OMNI MAJESTIC HOTEL   Phone: 314/436-2355

[fyi]   Did not meet all AAA rating requirements for some property operations at time of last evaluation on 07/10/2006. **Location:** Between 10th and 11th sts. 1019 Pine St 63101. Facilities, services, and decor characterize a mid-range property.

Historic
Small-scale Hotel

──────── **WHERE TO DINE** ────────

AL'S RESTAURANT   Dinner: $20-$50   Phone: 314/421-6399   ①

Location: 1.1 mi n from I-44/55/66; just w of Riverfront. 1200 N 1st St 63102. **Hours:** 5 pm-9:30 pm. Closed major holidays; also Sun & 7/1-7/14. **Reservations:** suggested. **Features:** Al's Restaurant offers fine dining with elegant rooms and polished, professional service. The server recites dinner choices and displays meat choices on a chilled silver charger. The filet mignon with peppercorn and cognac, cream sauce is very good.

Continental
Dressy casual; cocktails. **Parking:** on-site and valet. **Cards:** AX, MC, VI.

[icons]

AN AMERICAN PLACE   Dinner: $22-$36   Phone: 314/418-5800   ③

Location: Across from America's Center Convention Center; in Renaissance Grand Hotel St. Louis. 822 Washington Ave 63101. **Hours:** 5 pm-10 pm, Fri & Sat-11 pm. Closed: 11/22, 12/25; also Sun & Mon. **Reservations:** suggested. **Features:** You will find the highest quality throughout this historical and elegant dining room. Many original elements of this former 1917 hotel lobby, including elaborate ceiling, marble walls, large columns, elegant draperies, and glorious potted palms, set the stage for the innovative menu of great American foods; the daily-changing menu lists the farmers, ranchers, fishermen and produce growers that provide excellent use of local and regional market availability. Dressy casual; cocktails. **Parking:** valet. **Cards:** AX, CB, DC, DS, JC, MC, VI.

American

[icon]

BROADWAY OYSTER BAR   Lunch: $8-$16   Dinner: $8-$16   Phone: 314/621-8811   ⑯

Location: I-40, exit 40B, just s. 736 S Broadway St 63102. **Hours:** 11 am-10 pm, Fri & Sat-11 pm. Closed: 11/22, 12/24, 12/25. **Features:** This restaurant is one of a very few restaurants in the downtown area offering Cajun and Creole cuisine. Upon entering, the strong smell of spicy cooking and live music reflect a New Orleans Mardi Gras influence. A courtyard beer garden is available for outdoor dining in the summer season. Casual dress; cocktails; entertainment. **Parking:** street. **Cards:** AX, CB, DC, DS, JC, MC, VI.

Traditional Cajun

CARMINE'S STEAK HOUSE   Dinner: $16-$30   Phone: 314/241-1631   ⑮

AAA   **Location:** I-70, 250B (Stadium/Memorial Dr), just w on Pine St to Broadway, just s to Walnut St, just e to 4th St, then just n; in Drury Plaza Hotel-St. Louis At the Arch. 20 S 4th St 63102. **Hours:** 4 pm-10 pm, Fri & Sat-11 pm, Sun-9 pm. Closed major holidays; also 12/24. **Reservations:** suggested. **Features:** Conveniently close to the Gateway Arch and Busch Stadium, Carmine's Steak House offers beef, aged a minimum of twenty-one days, served in a bright, upscale dining room. Dressy casual; cocktails. **Parking:** on-site. **Cards:** AX, DC, DS, MC, VI.

Steak House

[icons]

CHESTNUTS   Lunch: $7-$22   Dinner: $7-$22   Phone: 314/241-7400   ⑫

Location: I-70, exit 250B (Stadium/Memorial Dr); at 4th and Chestnut sts; in Adam's Mark St. Louis Hotel. 112 N 4th St 63102. **Hours:** 6 am-10 pm. **Reservations:** accepted. **Features:** Patrons can settle into plush and often bustling surroundings in the lobby restaurant. Fresh twists on favorites are served in an eye-appealing style. Casual dress; cocktails. **Parking:** on-site (fee). **Cards:** AX, CB, DC, DS, JC, MC, VI.

American

[icon]

(See map and index starting on p. 508)

DIERDORF & HART'S   Lunch: $7-$16   Dinner: $17-$44   Phone: 314/421-1772   [10]
Steak & Seafood
Location: On ground floor of Gateway One on the Mall building; between Market and Chestnut sts. 701 Market S 63101. **Hours:** 11 am-10 pm, Fri-10:30 pm, Sat 4:30 pm-10:30 pm, Sun 4:30 pm-10 pm. Closed majo holidays. **Reservations:** suggested. **Features:** With beautiful views of the historic "Old Courthouse" framed by the St. Louis Gateway Arch, this classy dining room offers the finest steaks and polished, professiona service in an upscale downtown location. The dining room is decorated with strong masculine colors and dark wood furnishing The wine list maintains an excellent balance between French and California wines. Dressy casual; cocktails. **Parking:** on-site **Cards:** AX, DC, DS, MC, VI.

FAUST'S   *Menu on AAA.com*   Dinner: $19-$34   Phone: 314/342-4690   [13]
American
Location: I-70, exit 250B (Stadium/Memorial Dr); at 4th and Chestnut sts; in Adam's Mark St. Louis Hotel. 112 N 4th S 63102. **Hours:** 5:30 pm-10 pm. Closed: 1/1. **Reservations:** suggested. **Features:** The restaurant offers an elegant atmosphere and creative meal preparation and presentation for true fine dining. The service is polished and attentive. An extensive wine list has been thoughtfully selected to compliment the seasona menu which utilizes the freshest local produce. Dressy casual; cocktails; entertainment. **Parking:** on-site (fee). **Cards:** AX, CB, DC, DS, JC, MC, VI.

HANNEGAN'S   Lunch: $7-$12   Dinner: $8-$23   Phone: 314/241-8877   [4]
American
Location: Just n of Gateway Arch; in Laclede's Landing. 719 N 2nd St 63102. **Hours:** 11 am-10 pm, Fri & Sat-11 pm. Closed: 1/1, 11/22, 12/24, 12/25; also 1st week of Jan. **Reservations:** accepted. **Features:** In a replica of the US Senate dining room, the casual restaurant is splashed in unusual decor. Longtime favorites include the 20-ounce double-rib pork chop with peppercorn sauce and deep-dish blackberry pie. The signature dish is Senate bean soup made from the authentic recipe used in the U.S. Senate dining room. Casual dress; cocktails. **Parking:** street. **Cards:** AX, DC, DS, MC, VI.

HARRY'S RESTAURANT & BAR   Lunch: $10-$15   Dinner: $18-$27   Phone: 314/421-6969   [6]
Continental
Location: Just w of Union Station. 2144 Market St 63104. **Hours:** 11 am-3 & 5-10 pm, Fri-10 pm, Sat 5 pm-10 pm, Sun 5 pm-9 pm. Closed major holidays. **Reservations:** suggested. **Features:** A longtime favorite of the business crowd, the casually sophisticated restaurant is decidedly masculine. Regional produce factors into such dishes as blue crab-encrusted Atlantic salmon and sauteed shrimp linguine. Casual dress; cocktails. **Parking:** on-site. **Cards:** AX, CB, DC, DS, JC, MC, VI.

HODAK'S RESTAURANT & BAR   Lunch: $5-$10   Dinner: $5-$10   Phone: 314/776-7292   [17]
American
Location: I-55, exit 207/290C; at corner of McNair, exit toward Gravois Rd/I-44 W/12th St ramp, then just w. 2100 Gravois Rd 63104. **Hours:** 10 am-10 pm, Fri & Sat-11 pm. Closed major holidays. **Features:** Consider among the city's best, the restaurant's fried chicken packages well in a good-value four-piece platter with fries and coleslaw. Reasonably priced weekday luncheon specials center on everything from hot dogs to rib-eye steak. Casual dress. **Parking:** street. **Cards:** AX, CB, DC, DS, JC, MC, VI.

JAKE'S STEAKS   Lunch: $6-$9   Dinner: $12-$40   Phone: 314/621-8184   [5]
American
Location: In Laclede's Landing. 708 N 2nd St 63102. **Hours:** 11:30 am-10 pm. Closed: 11/22, 12/24, 12/25. **Reservations:** accepted. **Features:** Loaded with character, the historic tavern and restaurant serves a good selection of appetizers, salads, pasta, sandwiches, seafood and, of course, steaks. Casual dress; cocktails. **Parking:** on-site (fee). **Cards:** AX, DC, DS, MC, VI.

KEMOLL'S ITALIAN RESTAURANT   Dinner: $16-$50   Phone: 314/421-0555   [9]
Italian
Location: On Broadway; between Olive and Pine sts; on ground floor of Metropolitan Square Building. 1 Metropolitan Square 63102. **Hours:** 5 pm-10 pm. Closed major holidays; also Sun. **Reservations:** suggested. **Features:** You'll enjoy the fine dining, elegant atmosphere and smooth service at this restaurant, which is a local legend and famous for its fresh artichoke antipasto. Its Old European ambience is accented in each dining room. Extensive wine list is well-balanced in price and variety. Garage parking is off of Pine St. Dressy casual; cocktails. **Parking:** on-site. **Cards:** AX, DC, DS, MC, VI.

LOMBARDO'S TRATTORIA   Lunch: $8-$11   Dinner: $15-$25   Phone: 314/621-0666   [8]
Italian
Location: Just e of Jefferson Ave; between Market and Clark sts; at Drury Inn St. Louis/Union Station. 201 S 20th S 63103. **Hours:** 11 am-10 pm, Fri-11 pm, Sat 5 pm-11 pm, Sun 4 pm-9 pm. Closed major holidays. **Reservations:** suggested. **Features:** A sophisticated atmosphere punctuates the restaurant, which is a nice place for celebrating special occasions. Creative entrees show pleasant presentation. Casual dress; cocktails. **Parking:** valet. **Cards:** AX, CB, DC, DS, JC, MC, VI.

MAX & ERMA'S   Lunch: $8-$12   Dinner: $12-$17   Phone: 314/621-5815
American
Location: I-70, exit 250B (Stadium/Memorial Dr), just w on Pine St to Broadway, just s to Walnut St, just e to 4th St then just n; in Drury Plaza Hotel-St. Louis At the Arch. 316 Market St 63102. **Hours:** 11 am-10 pm, Fri & Sat-11 pm, Sun-9 pm. Closed major holidays. **Features:** Complete with gorgeous stained-glass lamps, turn-of-the-20th century artifacts and a magician, this lively eatery offers up an array of sandwiches. The spicy Tijuana burger or the original garbage burger are favorites. Casual dress; cocktails. **Parking:** on-site (fee). **Cards:** AX, CB, DC, DS, JC, MC, VI.

(See map and index starting on p. 508)

MIKE SHANNON'S STEAKS & SEAFOOD   Lunch: $9-$20   Dinner: $25-$50   Phone: 314/421-1540   ⑪

AAA

Steak & Seafood

Location: Corner of 7th and Chestnut sts. 100 N 7th St 63101. **Hours:** 11 am-11 pm, Sat from 5 pm, Sun 5 pm-10 pm. Closed major holidays. **Reservations:** suggested. **Features:** Sports lovers and others will appreciate the classic decor, solid service and great steaks at Mike Shannon's, two blocks from Busch Stadium. Some of the best beef and fresh seafood in St. Louis, as well as plenty of sports memorabilia, can be found here. Dressy casual; cocktails. **Parking:** street. **Cards:** AX, CB, DC, DS, JC, MC, VI.

ST. LOUIS BREWERY TAP ROOM   Lunch: $5-$10   Dinner: $5-$12   Phone: 314/241-2337   ②

American

Location: On 21st St; between Olive and Locust sts. 2100 Locust St 63103. **Hours:** 11 am-10 pm, Fri & Sat-midnight, Sun noon-9 pm. Closed major holidays. **Features:** As the name might imply, the restaurant's dining room occupies a working brewery. At least 10 fresh beers, which diners can watch being brewed on the premises through a picture window, are on tap at all times. Those interested in tasting more than one house brew should order the Schlafly Sampler, which includes six, five-ounce samples. Casual dress; cocktails. **Parking:** on-site. **Cards:** AX, DC, DS, MC, VI.

STATION GRILL   Lunch: $9-$14   Dinner: $13-$32   Phone: 314/231-1234   ⑦

American

Location: Just e on Jefferson Ave, off US 40 at 18th and Market sts; in Hyatt Regency St. Louis At Union Station. 1 St. Louis Union Station 63103. **Hours:** 6:30 am-2 & 5-10 pm, Fri & Sat-11 pm. **Reservations:** suggested. **Features:** For almost 100 years, many a rail journey began or ended at the historic Union Station in downtown St. Louis. Today, many people enjoy a gastronomic excursion in the warm setting of the Station Grill which is housed in the historic railroad hotel at the entrance to Union Station. There, a variety of meats will be paired with fresh seasonal vegatables and will be offered up to your delight. Traditional desserts will conclude your culinary journey in this memorable restaurant. Dressy casual; cocktails. **Parking:** on-site (fee) and valet. **Cards:** AX, CB, DC, DS, JC, MC, VI.

TONY'S   *Menu on AAA.com*   Dinner: $20-$40   Phone: 314/231-7007   ⑭

AAA

Italian

Location: I-70, exit 250B (Stadium/Memorial Dr), just w on Pine St, just s on Broadway St, then just e. 410 Market St 63102. **Hours:** 5:30 pm-10:30 pm, Sat .5 pm-11 pm. Closed major holidays; also Sun. **Reservations:** suggested. **Features:** Tony's has fine dining in an intimate, candlelit setting. The formal service features tableside finishing of a varied cuisine that incorporates regional and Continental influences. Dishes are often prepared with rich cream sauces. Semi-formal attire; cocktails. **Parking:** valet. **Cards:** AX, CB, DC, DS, MC, VI.

ST. LOUIS pop. 348,189 (See map and index starting on p. 514)

──────── **WHERE TO STAY** ────────

CHASE PARK PLAZA *Book great rates at AAA.com*   Phone: (314)633-3000   **1**
(AAA) (SAVE)   All Year   1P: $229-$1200   2P: $229-$1200   XP: $15   F
▽▽▽▽ ▽▽▽▽   **Location:** I-64/US 40, exit N Kingshighway Blvd; corner of Kingshighway and Lindell blvds. 212-232 N Kingshighway
Historic   Blvd 63108. Fax: 314/633-1144. **Facility:** A legendary hotel offering a contemporary blend of charm and
Large-scale Hotel   sophistication, rising in stately grandeur. Catering to business and leisure travelers. 252 units. 58 one-
bedroom standard units. 178 one-, 15 two- and 1 three-bedroom suites, some with kitchens and/or
whirlpools. 11 stories, interior corridors. *Bath:* combo or shower only. **Parking:** on-site (fee) and valet.
Terms: 3 day cancellation notice-fee imposed, package plans. **Amenities:** video games, CD players, dual
phone lines, voice mail, honor bars, irons, hair dryers. *Fee:* high-speed Internet, safes. **Dining:** 5 restaurants, 6:30 am-11 pm,
cocktails, also, The Tenderloin Room, see separate listing. **Pool(s):** heated outdoor. **Leisure Activities:** spa. *Fee:* cinemas.
Guest Services: gift shop, valet and coin laundry, area transportation (fee)-within 5 mi, wireless Internet, beauty salon, tanning
facilities, barber shop, shoe shine, floral shop. **Business Services:** conference facilities, business center. **Cards:** AX, DC, DS,
MC, VI. *(See color ad below)*

SOME UNITS

[icons]

**HAMPTON INN & SUITES - ST. LOUIS AT FOREST
PARK** *Book great rates at AAA.com*   Phone: 314/655-3993   **3**
     Property failed to provide current rates
▽▽▽   **Location:** I-64/US 40, exit 34C, just se. 5650 Oakland Ave 63110 (5650 Oakland Avenue). Fax: 314/655-3994.
Small-scale Hotel   **Facility:** 126 one-bedroom standard units. 6 stories, interior corridors. *Bath:* combo or shower only.
Parking: on-site. **Amenities:** high-speed Internet, voice mail, irons, hair dryers. **Pool(s):** heated indoor.
Leisure Activities: whirlpool, exercise room. **Guest Services:** sundries, valet laundry, area transportation, wireless Internet.
Business Services: meeting rooms, business center.

SOME UNITS

[icons]

THE PARKWAY HOTEL *Book great rates at AAA.com*   Phone: (314)256-7777   **2**
(AAA) (SAVE)   All Year   1P: $116-$159   2P: $116-$159   XP: $10   F16
▽▽▽▽   **Location:** I-64/US 40, exit 36B (Kingshighway N), 0.6 mi n to Forest Park Blvd. 4550 Forest Park Blvd 63108
  $309). 8 stories, interior corridors. *Bath:* combo or shower only. **Parking:** on-site (fee). **Terms:** check-in 4
Small-scale Hotel   pm. **Amenities:** high-speed Internet, dual phone lines, voice mail, irons, hair dryers. *Some:* CD players.
Dining: 6:30 am-11 pm, Fri & Sat-midnight, cocktails. **Leisure Activities:** exercise room. **Business Services:** business center. **Cards:** AX, DS, MC, VI.
Free Special Amenities: local telephone calls and newspaper.

[icons]

Chase Park Plaza
Saint Louis, Missouri

experience true luxury

WELCOME TO THE CHASE PARK PLAZA HOTEL

The legendary Chase Park Plaza offers guests a contemporary blend of elegance and sophistication. Encompassed in over one million square feet of space are luxurious rooms and suites, five fabulous restaurants and bars, impeccable meeting facilities, five-screen cinema and a well appointed fitness center. We know your will enjoy your stay.

RESERVATIONS ~ 1.877.587.2427
WWW.CHASEPARKPLAZA.COM

Preferred
HOTELS & RESORTS

Four Diamond Award

212 NORTH KINGSHIGHWAY BLVD. ~ ST. LOUIS, MO 63108

(See map and index starting on p. 514)

THE WATER TOWER INN
Phone: 314/977-7500 [4]

All Year [CP]   1P: $70-$89   2P: $70-$89

Small-scale Hotel   **Location:** I-44, exit Grand Ave, just ne; in University Salus Center. Located at St. Louis University. 3545 Lafayette Ave 63104. Fax: 314/977-7505. **Facility:** 62 one-bedroom standard units. 6 stories, interior corridors. *Bath:* combo or shower only. **Parking:** on-site. **Amenities:** high-speed Internet, voice mail, irons, hair dryers. **Leisure Activities:** exercise room. **Guest Services:** valet and coin laundry. **Business Services:** meeting rooms. **Cards:** AX, DS, MC, VI.

SOME UNITS

ASK SD TI ⬚ / ✕ ▯ ▣ /

──────── *The following lodging was either not evaluated or did not* ────────
meet AAA rating requirements but is listed for your information only.

THE FLEUR-DE-LYS MANSION
Phone: 314/773-3500

[fyi]   Did not meet all AAA rating requirements for some property operations at time of last evaluation on 07/14/2006. **Location:** I-44, exit 288 (Grand Ave), just s, then just e. 3500 Russell Blvd 63104. Facilities, services, and

Historic Bed   decor characterize a mid-range property.
& Breakfast

──────── **WHERE TO DINE** ────────

AMIGHETTI'S ON THE HILL   Lunch: $5-$10   Dinner: $5-$10   **Phone: 314/776-2855** [14]

Italian   **Location:** I-44, exit 287 (Kingshighway Blvd), just s to Shaw Ave, just w to Hereford, just s to Wilson Ave, then w. 5141 Wilson Ave 63110. **Hours:** 9 am-7 pm, Sat-5:30 pm. Closed major holidays; also Sun & Mon. **Features:** Simply good food is what diners get at the reliable restaurant, occupying a storefront building in the historic Italian district known as "The Hill." Patrons place orders for traditional Italian dishes with the cashier, pick up the meal when their name is called, and eat off disposable dinnerware. Despite the no-frills approach, the food is consistently fresh and flavorful. Casual dress; beer & wine only. **Parking:** street. **Cards:** MC, VI.

BAR ITALIA RISTORANTE-CAFFE'   Lunch: $7-$12   Dinner: $14-$25   **Phone: 314/361-7010** [5]

Italian   **Location:** 1 mi of I-64, US 40 and Kingshighway Blvd, exit 36B, just e. 13 Maryland Plaza 63108. **Hours:** 11:30 am-10 pm, Fri & Sat-10:30 pm, Sun-9 pm. Closed major holidays; also Mon. **Reservations:** suggested. **Features:** The creative and colorful cuisine of this restaurant is served in a casual, sidewalk-cafe atmosphere. In addition to pasta dishes, they offer fresh seafood, steaks and chicken entrees. Friendly, efficient server staff. Casual dress; cocktails. **Parking:** street. **Cards:** AX, CB, DC, DS, JC, MC, VI.

BARTOLINO'S   Lunch: $9-$13   Dinner: $9-$26   **Phone: 314/644-2266** [17]

Italian   **Location:** I-44, exit 286, 0.5 mi s. 2524 Hampton Ave 63139. **Hours:** 11 am-10:30 pm, Fri-11 pm, Sat 4 pm-11 pm. Closed major holidays; also Sun. **Reservations:** accepted. **Features:** Bartolino's is a locally popular restaurant that has been family-owned and operated for 30 years. Their menu offers traditional Italian fare of veal, fresh seafood, chicken, pasta and homemade desserts. Service and decor are casual and comfortable. Casual dress; cocktails. **Parking:** on-site. **Cards:** AX, CB, DC, MC, VI.

Ⴤ ◥

BOATHOUSE FOREST PARK   Lunch: $7-$10   Dinner: $7-$15   **Phone: 314/367-2224** [8]

American   **Location:** I-64/US 40, exit 34D (Hampton Ave), just n to Concourse Dr, follow signs; in Forest Park. 6101 Government Dr 63110. **Hours:** 11 am-9 pm, Fri 11 am-close, Sat 10 am-close, Sun 10 am-9 pm; seasonal hours vary. Closed: 4/8, 11/22; also Mon in winter. **Reservations:** suggested. **Features:** During warm weather, patrons head to the patio to enjoy cold drinks, live music and beautiful lakeside sunsets. Patrons' dogs are welcomed to take a seat beside patio tables, where they're given their own water bowl and treats. When temperatures drop, guests head inside to enjoy relaxing meals and tasty hot cocoa by the large stone fireplace. Casual dress; cocktails. **Parking:** on-site. **Cards:** AX, MC, VI.

BRAZIE'S RISTORANTE   Lunch: $6-$13   Dinner: $9-$24   **Phone: 314/481-5464** [22]

South Italian   **Location:** I-44, exit 286 (Hampton Ave), 1.4 mi s; in Hampton Plaza. 3453 Hampton Ave 63139. **Hours:** 11 am-2 & 5-9 pm, Fri & Sat-10 pm, Sun 5 pm-9 pm. Closed major holidays. **Reservations:** suggested. **Features:** You'll enjoy this family-owned and operated restaurant featuring traditional fare of sandwiches, pasta, salad and soup that are freshly prepared and imaginatively seasoned. The setting has a pleasant atmosphere, relaxing decor and friendly service. Dressy casual; cocktails. **Parking:** on-site. **Cards:** AX, CB, DC, DS, JC, MC, VI.

◥

CAFE BALABAN   Lunch: $9-$14   Dinner: $16-$30   **Phone: 314/361-8085** [3]

American   **Location:** I-64/US 40, exit 36B (Kingshighway Blvd), 1.1 mi n to McPherson, just e to N Euclid Ave, then n. 405 N Euclid Ave 63108. **Hours:** 11 am-2:30 & 6-10:30 pm, Fri & Sat 5:30 pm-11:30 pm, Sun 11 am-2:30 & 5-10:30 pm. Closed major holidays. **Reservations:** suggested, weekends. **Features:** Open for nearly 30 years, the cafe specializes in fresh seafood and prepares all items in house. Smoked trout with corn pancake and barbecue spiced salmon are two good choices. The bistro atmosphere lends to a lively local following on weekends. Valet service is offered every night. Casual dress; cocktails; entertainment. **Parking:** street. **Cards:** AX, CB, DC, DS, JC, MC, VI.

◥

COLUMBO'S CAFE AND TAVERN   Lunch: $4-$10   Dinner: $4-$10   **Phone: 314/647-2661** [11]

American   **Location:** I-44, exit 287 (Kingshighway Blvd S), 1.6 mi w; at Manchester and Mitchelle rds. 6487 Manchester Rd 63139. **Hours:** 11 am-10 pm. Closed: 11/22, 12/25; also Sun. **Features:** The classic neighborhood establishment serves great pub fare, a large selection of appetizers, cooked-to-order steaks and several chicken dishes. The atmosphere is pleasant. Casual dress; cocktails. **Parking:** on-site. **Cards:** AX, MC, VI.

(See map and index starting on p. 514)

CROWN CANDY KITCHEN Lunch: $4-$7 Dinner: $4-$7 Phone: 314/621-9650 ①
WWWW
American
Location: I-70, exit 249A westbound; exit 248B eastbound, just nw; at St. Louis Ave and N 14th St. 1401 St. Louis Ave 63106. **Hours:** 10:30 am-9 pm, Fri & Sat-10 pm, Sun noon-9 pm; to 10 pm, Sun noon-10 pm 5/28-9/5. Closed major holidays. **Features:** A local tradition, the soda fountain opened in 1913. This place makes all its own ice cream and still practices the confectionery art. Sandwiches, soups, hot dogs and chili are among choices, but the soda fountain is the reason for visiting. Casual dress. **Parking:** street. **Cards:** AX, DS, MC, VI. **Classic Historic**

DOMINIC'S Dinner: $18-$35 Phone: 314/771-1632 ⑯
WWWW
Italian
Location: I-44, exit 287 (Kingshighway Blvd), just s, just w on Shaw Ave, then 2 blks s on Hereford. 5101 Wilson Ave 63110. **Hours:** 5 pm-10 pm, Fri & Sat-11 pm. Closed major holidays; also Sun. **Reservations:** suggested. **Features:** You'll enjoy the elegant dining and sophisticated service with tableside preparation at Dominic's. Their varied menu includes pleasing presentation of chicken, pasta and fresh seafood entrees and an extensive wine list. Prompt, attentive service. Dressy casual; cocktails. **Parking:** valet and street. **Cards:** AX, CB, DC, DS, MC, VI.

DRESSEL'S PUB Lunch: $6-$12 Dinner: $7-$14 Phone: 314/361-1060 ②
WWWW
English
Location: I-64/US 40, exit 36B (Kingshighway Blvd), 1.1 mi n to McPherson, just e to N Euclid Ave, then just n. 419 N Euclid Ave 63108. **Hours:** 11:30 am-11:30 pm, Sat from noon, Sun noon-10:30 pm. Closed major holidays. **Features:** Dressel's, renowned for its stew, soup and homemade deep-fried potato chips, also offers sandwiches and salad. This place appeals to the university crowd and theater-goers. Its intimate, cozy, artistic atmosphere has a sidewalk cafe in season. Casual dress; cocktails. **Parking:** street. **Cards:** AX, DC, DS, MC, VI.

DUFF'S Lunch: $8-$12 Dinner: $13-$20 Phone: 314/361-0522 ④
WWWW
American
Location: I-64/US 40, exit Kingshighway Blvd, 1 mi n to McPherson, just e. 392 N Euclid Ave 63108. **Hours:** 11 am-10 pm, Fri & Sat-10:30 pm, Sun 10 am-2 & 5-10 pm. Closed: 11/22, 12/25; also Mon. **Reservations:** suggested. **Features:** You'll discover festive dining at Duff's, which is quite popular with local residents and business people. They feature creative pasta, chicken, steak, seafood entrees and brunch on Saturday and Sunday. Choose either the rustic indoor area with wood floors and brick walls or the outdoor cafe covered in a canopy of lush foliage in the summer season. Casual dress; cocktails. **Parking:** on-site. **Cards:** AX, CB, DC, DS, JC, MC, VI.

ELEPHANT BAR Lunch: $7-$18 Dinner: $7-$18 Phone: 314/835-0545
WWWW
American
Location: I-270, exit 9 (Manchester Rd), just se; adjacent to West County Mall, southeast side. 1085 W County Center Dr 63131. **Hours:** 11 am-10 pm, Fri & Sat-11 pm. Closed: 11/22, 12/25. **Reservations:** suggested. **Features:** Going on safari was never this much fun. Guests who unwind amid the bright jungle decor can sample fresh California cuisine prepared with Pacific Rim influences. Pizza cooked over a wood fire, sizzling cantina fajitas, wok-seared Shanghai cashew chicken and langoustines, and shrimp and chicken jambalaya are among dishes sure to wake up the taste buds. Service is great, too. Casual dress; cocktails. **Parking:** on-site. **Cards:** AX, CB, DC, DS, JC, MC, VI.

FRAZER'S Dinner: $15-$20 Phone: 314/773-8646 ㉓
WWWW
American
Location: I-55, exit 206C (Arsenal St), just w to Lemp, just n to Pestalozzi St, then just e. 1811 Pestalozzi St 63118. **Hours:** 11 am-2 & 5-10 pm, Fri & Sat 5 pm-11 pm. Closed major holidays; also Sun. **Reservations:** suggested. **Features:** The stylish, creative menu is the star at this restaurant. A nice variety of pasta, pizza, seafood, pork, chicken, beef and sandwiches are the flavorful offerings. All desserts are made in-house. The setting features a relaxed, comfortable dining area. Casual dress; cocktails. **Parking:** street. **Cards:** AX, DC, DS, MC, VI.

GIOVANNI'S ON THE HILL Dinner: $17-$30 Phone: 314/772-5958 ⑫
AAA
WWWWW
Italian
Location: I-44, exit 287 (Kingshighway Blvd) eastbound, just s to Shaw Ave, 0.3 mi w; exit Kingshighway Blvd westbound, follow sign 0.4 mi w to Kingshighway Blvd, just s to Shaw Ave, then 0.3 mi w. 5201 Shaw Ave 63110. **Hours:** 5 pm-11 pm, Sat-midnight. Closed major holidays; also Sun. **Reservations:** suggested. **Features:** In the St. Louis neighborhood, "The Hill," you can discover fine dining in Giovanni's unpretentious yet elegant setting. This restaurant features tableside preparations of its locally renowned and innovative cuisine of pasta, veal, lamb and seafood. Semi-formal attire; cocktails. **Parking:** valet and street. **Cards:** AX, CB, DC, MC, VI.

IMO'S PIZZA Lunch: $5-$15 Dinner: $5-$15 Phone: 314/644-5480 ⑨
WW
Italian
Location: I-64/US 40, exit 34D (Hampton Ave), just se. 1000 Hampton Ave 63110. **Hours:** 10:30 am-midnight, Fri & Sat-1 am. Closed: 1/1, 11/22, 12/25. **Features:** Original St. Louis-style pizza is said to have begun with Ed Imo's distinctive recipe, which includes square-cut pieces of thin crispy crust, tomato sauce and provolone cheese. This place is nothing fancy, but the pizza's hard to beat. **Parking:** on-site. **Cards:** AX, CB, DC, DS, JC, MC, VI.

KING & I RESTAURANT Lunch: $6-$7 Dinner: $9-$13 Phone: 314/771-1777 ⑳
WWWW
Thai
Location: I-44, exit 288 (Grand Ave), 1 mi s. 3157 S Grand Ave 63118. **Hours:** 11 am-2:30 & 5-9:30 pm, Fri-10 pm, Sat noon-3 & 5-10 pm, Sun noon-3 & 5-9:30 pm. Closed: 11/22, 12/25; also Mon & 7/4-7/10. **Reservations:** suggested. **Features:** Authentic and well-prepared Thai cuisine is complemented by Chinese and vegetarian selections at this family-owned restaurant. Specials include pad thai, kai tom kha pork satay and pik seafood. The warm, romantic atmosphere features seating on the floor. Casual dress; cocktails. **Parking:** street. **Cards:** AX, DC, DS, MC, VI.

(See map and index starting on p. 514)

KING LOUIE'S   **Lunch:** $8-$10   **Dinner:** $17-$28   **Phone:** 314/865-3662   ⑩

International

Location: I-70, exit Chouteau Ave, just s; at 39th St. 3800 Chouteau Ave 63110. **Hours:** 11 am-2 & 5-11 pm, Sat-11 pm. Closed major holidays; also Sun. **Reservations:** suggested. **Features:** High-quality dishes on the sophisticated and ever-changing menu are based on market availability. Depending on the season, guests can enjoy the cozy fireplace corner or the outdoor seating. Casual dress; cocktails. **Parking:** valet. **Cards:** AX, CB, DC, DS, JC, MC, VI.

MANGIA ITALIANO   **Lunch:** $5-$10   **Dinner:** $12-$18   **Phone:** 314/664-8585   ⑲

Italian

Location: I-64/US 40, exit Grand Ave, 1.5 mi s. 3145 S Grand Ave 63118. **Hours:** 11:30 am-10 pm, Fri & Sat-10:30 pm, Sun 5 pm-10 pm. Closed: 11/22, 12/25. **Features:** Featuring eclectic decor, casual charm, and a menu offering a number of specialty items, the restaurant is located amongst unique shops and restaurants in a quirky but established south city area. Casual dress; cocktails. **Parking:** street. **Cards:** AX, CB, DC, DS, MC, VI.

O'CONNELL'S PUB   **Lunch:** $5-$8   **Dinner:** $5-$8   **Phone:** 314/773-6600   ⑬

American

Location: I-44, exit 36B (Kingshighway Blvd S), 0.3 mi s, then just e. 4652 Shaw Ave 63110. **Hours:** 11 am-midnight, Sun noon-10 pm. Closed major holidays; also week of 7/4. **Features:** Daily specials might include Reubens, barbecue rib tips or fish and chips. Casual dress; cocktails. **Parking:** on-site. **Cards:** AX, CB, DC, DS, MC, VI.

PHO GRAND VIETNAMESE RESTAURANT   **Lunch:** $5-$10   **Dinner:** $5-$10   **Phone:** 314/664-7435   ㉑

Ethnic

Location: I-44, exit 288, 1.2 mi s. 3195 S Grand Ave 63118. **Hours:** 11 am-9:45 pm, Fri & Sat-10:45 pm. Closed major holidays; also Tues. **Features:** Since 1990, through the medium of food, the Trinh family has been sharing the warmth and tradition of their homeland with a growing circle of friends and fans who are drawn to Pho Grand for a taste of Vietnam. Your taste might include Cha Gio (a deep fried Vietnamese egg roll) and Mi Xao Mem (stir fried soft egg noodles with assorted meats and vegetables) or one of the many aromatic and flavorful soups. Try the robust Cafe Sua Da (iced coffee with sweetened condensed milk). Casual dress; beer & wine only. **Parking:** street. **Cards:** AX, DS, MC, VI.

SIDNEY STREET CAFE   **Dinner:** $18-$26   **Phone:** 314/771-5777   ⑱

Nouvelle American

Location: I-55, exit 208 (7th St), just e to Broadway, 1 mi s to Sidney St, then 0.6 mi w. 2000 Sidney St 63104. **Hours:** 5 pm-9:30 pm, Fri & Sat-10:30 pm. Closed major holidays; also Sun & Mon. **Reservations:** suggested. **Features:** Near the Anheuser-Busch Brewery in the Benton Park residential neighborhood, the fine dining restaurant presents a menu of dishes that fuse contemporary American and Continental cuisine. Parking for guests only is provided in a lot across the street. Dressy casual; cocktails. **Parking:** on-site. **Cards:** AX, CB, DC, DS, MC, VI. **Historic**

TED DREWE'S FROZEN CUSTARD   **Lunch:** $1-$5   **Dinner:** $1-$5   **Phone:** 314/481-2652   ㉕

American

Location: I-44, exit Laclede Station Rd, just e on Wilshusen Ave, just n on Murdoch Ave, just w on Lansdowne Ave, just e on Jamieson Ave, then just ne. 6726 Chippewa St 63109. **Hours:** Open 3/1-1/1 & 2/14-2/28; 11 am-close; seasonal hours vary. Closed: 11/22, 12/25. **Features:** Folks in St. Louis stand in line for the eatery's specialty custard, no matter what the season. Limited parking and standing room only are just a part of the experience that has been a local tradition since 1931. Casual dress. **Parking:** on-site. **Cards:** MC, VI.

THE TENDERLOIN ROOM   **Lunch:** $8-$15   **Dinner:** $14-$30   **Phone:** 314/361-0900   ⑥

Steak House

Location: I-40, I-64/US 40, exit N Kingshighway Blvd; corner of Kingshighway and Lindell blvds; in Chase Park Plaza. 212-232 N Kingshighway Blvd 63108. **Hours:** 11 am-2 & 5-9 pm, Fri-10 pm, Sat 5 pm-10 pm, Sun 5 pm-9 pm. **Reservations:** accepted. **Features:** The restaurant is legendary in the area. The longtime owner-operator gives character to the elegant, Old World dining room. On the menu are steaks, seafood specialties and fresh seasonal salads. Dressy casual; cocktails. **Parking:** valet. **Cards:** AX, CB, DC, DS, JC, MC, VI.

TRATTORIA MARCELLA   **Dinner:** $11-$19   **Phone:** 314/352-7706   ㉔

Italian

Location: I-44, exit 286 (Hampton Ave), 0.5 mi s to Watson Rd, then 1.2 mi s; corner of Watson and Pernod rds. 3600 Watson Rd 63109. **Hours:** 5 pm-10 pm, Fri & Sat-11 pm. Closed major holidays; also Sun & Mon. **Reservations:** suggested. **Features:** The popularity of Trattoria Marcella means you'd better call early for your reservation and then be prepared to be a part of a full house when you dine. The happy chorus of your fellow diners will set a festive tone for your enjoyment of rustic Italian dishes prepared with fresh-picked herbs, crisp vegetables and mushrooms straight-from-the-field, all depending on the time of year. Dressy casual; cocktails. **Parking:** on-site. **Cards:** AX, DC, MC, VI.

WILD FLOWER RESTAURANT AND CATERING   **Lunch:** $5-$12   **Dinner:** $13-$26   **Phone:** 314/367-9888   ⑦

American

Location: Just e of Laclede and Euclid Aves. 4590 Laclede Ave 63108. **Hours:** 11 am-10 pm, Fri & Sat-11 pm, Sun 10:30 am-10 pm. Closed major holidays; also Tues. **Reservations:** accepted. **Features:** Delightful menu items are served in this historic building, which retains many original elements. Casual dress; cocktails. **Parking:** street. **Cards:** AX, DS, MC, VI.

ZIA'S   **Lunch:** $6-$9   **Dinner:** $8-$19   **Phone:** 314/776-0020   ⑮

Italian

Location: I-44, exit 287 (Kingshighway Blvd), just s to Shaw Ave, 0.4 mi w to Wilson Ave, then just s. 5256 Wilson Ave 63110. **Hours:** 11 am-10 pm, Fri & Sat-10:30 pm. Closed major holidays; also Sun. **Features:** In the Italian neighborhood of "The Hill," the restaurant serves reliable Italian food, such as chicken spiedini. Casual dress; cocktails. **Parking:** street. **Cards:** AX, DC, DS, MC, VI.

(See map and index starting on p. 514)

─────── *The following restaurants have not been evaluated by AAA* ───────
but are listed for your information only.

CAFE EAU   Phone: 314/633-3000
[fyi]   Not evaluated. **Location:** I-64/US40, exit N Kingshighway Blvd; corner of Kingshighway and Lindell blvds; in Chase Park Plaza. 212-232 N Kingshighway Blvd 63108. **Features:** Popular with the hip, younger crowd, this eatery features small plates of imaginative American fare.

CAFE NATASHA-KABOB INTERNATIONAL   Phone: 314/771-3411
[fyi]   Not evaluated. **Location:** 3200 S Grand Ave 63118. **Features:** Kebabs dominate a menu of savory and pungent Persian cuisine. The large dining patio opens seasonally.

CUNETTO HOUSE OF PASTA   Phone: 314/781-1135
[fyi]   Not evaluated. **Location:** 5453 Magnolia Ave 63110. **Features:** True to its name, this place serves more than 30 types of pasta in large portions.   [icon]

THE DRUNKEN FISH SUSHI BAR AND LOUNGE   Phone: 314/367-4222
[fyi]   Not evaluated. **Location:** I-64, exit 36B, 1 mi n of I-64/US 40 and Kingshighway Blvd. 1 Maryland Plaza Dr 63108. **Features:** The cozy, contemporary and sophisticated restaurant serves sushi and other Japanese specialties.

EAU BISTRO   Phone: 314/633-3000
[fyi]   Not evaluated. **Location:** I-64/US 40, exit N Kingshighway Blvd; corner of Kingshighway and Lindell blvds; in Chase Park Plaza. 212-232 N Kingshighway Blvd 63108. **Features:** This sophisticated restaurant features imaginative American fare along with an excellent wine list.

KOPPERMAN'S DELICATESSEN   Phone: 314/361-0100
[fyi]   Not evaluated. **Location:** 386 N Euclid Ave 63108. **Features:** The menu features kosher-style fare, including overstuffed sandwiches and imported foods.

MARQUEE CAFE   Phone: 314/633-3000
[fyi]   Not evaluated. **Location:** I-64/US 40, exit N Kingshighway Blvd; corner of Kingshighway and Lindell blvds. 212-232 N Kingshighway Blvd 63108. **Features:** Located in the legendary Chase Park Plaza, this upscale and sophisticated outlet serves breakfast, lunch and dinner.

ZOE PAN-ASIAN CAFE   Phone: 314/361-0013
[fyi]   Not evaluated. **Location:** 4753 McPherson 63108. **Features:** On the menu are five-spice quail and cinnamon beef with bok choy and noodles.   [icon]

The St. Louis Vicinity

BALLWIN pop. 31,283 (See map and index starting on p. 511)

———— WHERE TO DINE ————

CHARLOTTE'S RIB BBQ   Lunch: $6-$8   Dinner: $9-$15   Phone: 636/394-3332   (28)
▽▽▽   **Location:** SR 141, 3.2 mi w; in Claymont Center. 15467 Clayton Rd 63011. **Hours:** 11 am-9 pm, Sun noon-8 pm.
American   Closed: Mon. **Features:** Patrons can sit back and enjoy the Western-themed eatery, which serves appetizers, salads and a wide range of barbecue favorites, including sugar-cured ham, ribs, brisket, catfish and pork steaks, to name a few. Save room for one of the homemade desserts. Casual dress; beer & wine only. **Parking:** on-site. **Cards:** AX, CB, DC, DS, MC, VI.

BERKELEY pop. 10,063 (See map and index starting on p. 514)

———— WHERE TO STAY ————

RENAISSANCE ST. LOUIS AIRPORT HOTEL   *Book great rates at AAA.com*   Phone: (314)429-1100   (20)
AAA (SAVE)   All Year   1P: $89-$199   2P: $89-$199   XP: $20
▽▽▽   **Location:** I-70, exit 237 (Natural Bridge Rd), just n; exit 6 (Natural Bridge Rd), just n. 9801 Natural Bridge Rd 63134.
Large-scale Hotel   Fax: 314/429-3466. **Facility:** Smoke free premises. 393 units. 391 one-bedroom standard units. 2 one-bedroom suites. 12 stories, interior corridors. *Bath:* combo or shower only. **Parking:** on-site (fee) and valet. **Amenities:** dual phone lines, voice mail, irons, hair dryers. *Fee:* video games, high-speed Internet. **Dining:** 6:30 am-2 & 5:30-10 pm, cocktails. **Pool(s):** outdoor, small heated indoor. **Leisure Activities:** saunas, whirlpool, exercise room. **Guest Services:** gift shop, valet laundry. **Business Services:** conference facilities, business center. **Cards:** AX, CB, DC, DS, JC, MC, VI. **Free Special Amenities: preferred room (subject to availability with advance reservations).**

SOME UNITS

TRAVELODGE ST. LOUIS AIRPORT   *Book great rates at AAA.com*   Phone: 314/890-9000   (21)
AAA (SAVE)   3/1-9/5   1P: $69-$79   2P: $69-$79   XP: $10   F12
▽▽   9/6-2/29   1P: $59-$69   2P: $59-$69   XP: $10   F12
Small-scale Hotel   **Location:** I-70 E, exit 237 (Natural Bridge Rd), 0.4 mi e; exit 6 (Natural Bridge Rd), westbound. 9645 Natural Bridge Rd 63134. Fax: 314/890-9111. **Facility:** 43 one-bedroom standard units, some with whirlpools. 2 stories (no elevator), interior corridors. *Bath:* combo or shower only. **Parking:** on-site. **Terms:** 1-7 night minimum stay, [CP] meal plan available. **Amenities:** safes (fee), irons, hair dryers. **Guest Services:** coin laundry. **Cards:** AX, DS, MC, VI. **Free Special Amenities: continental breakfast and local telephone calls.**

SOME UNITS

BRENTWOOD pop. 7,693 (See map and index starting on p. 514)

———— WHERE TO DINE ————

FRANK PAPA'S   Dinner: $12-$25   Phone: 314/961-3344   (96)
▽▽▽   **Location:** I-64, exit 31A westbound, 0.7 mi s; exit 31 eastbound, 0.6 mi s. 2241 S Brentwood Blvd 63144. **Hours:** 5
Italian   pm-10 pm, Fri & Sat-11 pm. Closed major holidays; also 12/24 & Sun. **Reservations:** suggested. **Features:** Attractively priced country Italian fare is dished in generous portions. The casual fine-dining establishment includes a wine cellar. Casual dress; cocktails. **Parking:** on-site. **Cards:** AX, DS, MC, VI.

BRIDGETON pop. 15,550 (See map and index starting on p. 514)

──────── WHERE TO STAY ────────

AIRPORT EARTH CITY COURTYARD BY MARRIOTT *Book great rates at AAA.com* **Phone:** (314)209-1000 **24**
(AAA) (SAVE) All Year 1P: $69-$159 2P: $69-$159
▽▽▽▽ **Location:** I-70, exit 231B (Earth City Expwy), 0.5 mi n to Rider Trail S, then 0.9 mi e. 3101 Rider Trail S 63044 (3101
Rider Tr S). **Fax:** 314/209-1001. **Facility:** Smoke free premises. 121 units. 115 one-bedroom standard units,
Small-scale Hotel some with whirlpools. 6 one-bedroom suites. 3 stories, interior corridors. *Bath:* combo or shower only.
Parking: on-site. **Terms:** package plans. **Amenities:** high-speed Internet, voice mail, irons, hair dryers.
Dining: 6:15-10 am, Sat & Sun 7-11 am. **Pool(s):** small heated indoor. **Leisure Activities:** whirlpool,
exercise room. **Guest Services:** sundries, valet and coin laundry. **Business Services:** meeting rooms, PC. **Cards:** AX, CB,
DC, DS, JC, MC, VI. **Free Special Amenities:** newspaper and high-speed Internet.
SOME UNITS
[icons]

EMBASSY SUITES ST. LOUIS AIRPORT *Book at AAA.com* **Phone:** (314)739-8929 **25**
All Year [BP] 1P: $99-$189 2P: $99-$199 XP: $10 F18
▽▽▽▽ **Location:** I-70, exit 235A (Lindberg Blvd/US 67), just s to Lone Eagle Dr, then just w. 11237 Lone Eagle Dr 63044.
Small-scale Hotel **Fax:** 314/739-6355. **Facility:** 159 one-bedroom suites ($99-$189). 6 stories, interior corridors. *Bath:* combo
or shower only. **Parking:** on-site. **Terms:** cancellation fee imposed, package plans. **Amenities:** voice mail,
irons, hair dryers. *Fee:* video games, high-speed Internet. **Pool(s):** heated indoor. **Leisure Activities:** sauna, whirlpool, exercise
room. **Guest Services:** sundries, complimentary evening beverages, valet and coin laundry, area transportation. **Business
Services:** meeting rooms, PC. **Cards:** AX, CB, DC, DS, JC, MC, VI.
SOME UNITS
[icons]

──────── WHERE TO DINE ────────

BERKSHIRE GRILL **Lunch:** $10-$25 **Dinner:** $10-$25 **Phone:** 314/298-1260 **41**
▽▽ ▽▽ **Location:** I-270, exit 20B (St. Charles Rock Rd), just ne. 12455 St. Charles Rock Rd 63044. **Hours:** 11 am-11 pm,
Fri & Sat-midnight, Sun-10 pm. **Closed:** 11/22, 12/25. **Reservations:** accepted. **Features:** Eclectic, casual
American cuisine is prepared in a comfortable atmosphere. Beef, seafood, chicken and pasta preparations share
menu space. Casual dress; cocktails. **Parking:** on-site. **Cards:** AX, DC, DS, MC, VI.
[icons]

CHAMP (See map and index starting on p. 514)

──────── WHERE TO STAY ────────

RESIDENCE INN ST. LOUIS AIRPORT/EARTH CITY *Book great rates at AAA.com* **Phone:** (314)209-0995 **10**
5/28-10/28 [BP] 1P: $119-$189
▽▽▽▽ 3/1-5/27 [BP] 1P: $104-$169
Small-scale Hotel 10/29-2/29 [BP] 1P: $99-$169
Location: I-70, exit 231B (Earth City Expwy N), just e. 3290 Rider Tr S 63045 (3290 Rider Trail S, EARTH CITY).
Fax: 314/209-0999. **Facility:** Smoke free premises. 104 units. 40 one-bedroom standard units, some with efficiencies or
kitchens. 42 one- and 22 two-bedroom suites, some with efficiencies or kitchens. 4 stories, interior corridors. *Bath:* combo or
shower only. **Parking:** on-site. **Terms:** pets ($75 extra charge). **Amenities:** video games (fee), high-speed Internet, dual phone
lines, voice mail, irons, hair dryers. **Pool(s):** small heated indoor. **Leisure Activities:** whirlpool, exercise room, sports court.
Guest Services: complimentary evening beverages: Mon-Thurs, valet and coin laundry. **Business Services:** PC. **Cards:** AX,
CB, DC, DS, JC, MC, VI.
[icons]
FEE

CHESTERFIELD pop. 46,802 (See map and index starting on p. 511)

──────── WHERE TO STAY ────────

DOUBLETREE HOTEL & CONFERENCE CENTER *Book great rates at AAA.com* **Phone:** (636)532-5000 **24**
All Year 1P: $89-$179 2P: $89-$179 XP: $10 F18
▽▽▽▽ **Location:** I-64, exit 19A (Chesterfield Pkwy), 0.5 mi w. 16625 Swingley Ridge Rd 63017. **Fax:** 636/519-7078.
Small-scale Hotel **Facility:** 223 units. 221 one-bedroom standard units. 2 one-bedroom suites ($129-$279). 12 stories, interior
corridors. *Bath:* combo or shower only. **Parking:** on-site. **Terms:** [AP], [BP] & [CP] meal plans available.
Amenities: high-speed Internet (fee), dual phone lines, voice mail, irons, hair dryers. **Pool(s):** outdoor, heated indoor. **
Leisure Activities:** sauna, whirlpool, 15 tennis courts (9 indoor, 2 lighted), racquetball courts, jogging, basketball, volleyball.
Fee: massage. **Guest Services:** valet laundry, area transportation. **Business Services:** conference facilities, business center.
Cards: AX, CB, DC, DS, JC, MC, VI.
SOME UNITS
[icons]
FEE FEE

DRURY PLAZA HOTEL-CHESTERFIELD *Book great rates at AAA.com* **Phone:** (636)532-3300 **27**
All Year [BP] 1P: $90-$150 2P: $100-$160 XP: $10 F18
▽▽▽▽ **Location:** I-64/US 40, exit 19B (Clarkson Rd/Olive Blvd); jct I-64/US 40 and Clarkson Rd; southwest corner. 355
Small-scale Hotel Chesterfield Center E 63017. **Fax:** 636/733-0554. **Facility:** 275 units. 224 one-bedroom standard units. 51 one-
bedroom suites ($130-$220), some with whirlpools. 10 stories, interior corridors. *Bath:* combo or shower
only. **Parking:** on-site. **Amenities:** high-speed Internet, voice mail, irons, hair dryers. **Pool(s):** outdoor, heated indoor. **Leisure
Activities:** whirlpool, exercise room. **Guest Services:** sundries, complimentary evening beverages, valet laundry, wireless
Internet. **Business Services:** meeting rooms, business center. **Cards:** AX, CB, DC, DS, JC, MC, VI.
SOME UNITS
[icons]

(See map and index starting on p. 511)

HAMPTON INN
Book great rates at AAA.com   Phone: (636)537-2500   26

4/15-9/2   1P: $119-$159   2P: $125-$165
3/1-4/14 & 9/3-2/29   1P: $109-$149   2P: $115-$155

Small-scale Hotel **Location:** I-64, exit 19B (Clarkson Rd/Olive Blvd), just n to Swingley Ridge Rd, then just w. 16201 Swingley Ridge Rd 63017. Fax: 636/537-1234. **Facility:** 92 one-bedroom standard units, some with whirlpools. 3 stories, interior corridors. *Bath:* combo or shower only. **Parking:** on-site. **Terms:** check-in 4 pm, [ECP] meal plan available. **Amenities:** high-speed Internet, voice mail, irons, hair dryers. **Pool(s):** small heated indoor. **Leisure Activities:** whirlpool, exercise room. **Guest Services:** valet laundry. **Business Services:** PC. **Cards:** AX, CB, DC, DS, JC, MC, VI.

SOME UNITS
(ASK) (S)(D) 🏊 📹 💻 / ✕ 📱 🗄 /

HAMPTON INN & SUITES-CHESTERFIELD
Book great rates at AAA.com   Phone: (636)530-0770   22

4/15-9/3   1P: $129-$179   2P: $137-$187
3/1-4/14 & 9/4-2/29   1P: $119-$169   2P: $127-$177

Small-scale Hotel **Location:** I-64/US 40, exit 17 (Boones Crossing), just e. 5 McBride and Son Center Dr 63005. Fax: 636/530-0772. **Facility:** 120 units. 98 one-bedroom standard units. 22 one-bedroom suites ($129-$187) with efficiencies, some with whirlpools. 3 stories, interior corridors. *Bath:* combo or shower only. **Parking:** on-site. **Terms:** check-in 4 pm, [ECP] meal plan available. **Amenities:** high-speed Internet, voice mail, irons, hair dryers. *Some:* DVD players, dual phone lines. **Pool(s):** heated indoor. **Leisure Activities:** whirlpool, exercise room. *Fee:* game room. **Guest Services:** sundries, valet and coin laundry, area transportation. **Business Services:** meeting rooms, PC. **Cards:** AX, CB, DC, DS, JC, MC, VI.

SOME UNITS
(ASK) (S)(D) 🏊 ✕ 📹 📱 🗄 💻 / ✕ /

HILTON GARDEN INN
Book great rates at AAA.com   Phone: (636)532-9400   23

(AAA) (SAVE)   All Year   1P: $79-$149   2P: $79-$149   XP: $10   F18

Location: I-64, exit 19A, 0.5 mi w on N Outer 40 Dr to Chesterfield Pkwy N, 0.8 mi on Chesterfield Airport Rd to Baxter Rd, then 0.3 mi. 16631 Chesterfield Grove Rd 63005. Fax: 636/532-9401. **Facility:** 100 one-bedroom standard Small-scale Hotel units. 4 stories, interior corridors. *Bath:* combo or shower only. **Parking:** on-site. **Terms:** [AP] & [BP] meal plans available, package plans. **Amenities:** high-speed Internet, dual phone lines, voice mail, irons, hair dryers. **Dining:** 6 am-10 pm, Sat & Sun from 7 am. **Pool(s):** small heated indoor. **Leisure Activities:** whirlpool, exercise room. **Guest Services:** sundries, valet and coin laundry, area transportation-within 5 mi. **Business Services:** meeting rooms, business center. **Cards:** AX, DC, DS, MC, VI. **Free Special Amenities:** newspaper and high-speed Internet.

SOME UNITS
(S)(D) 🍽 (&M) (&) 📶 🏊 📹 📱 🗄 💻 / ✕ /

HOMEWOOD SUITES BY HILTON
Book at AAA.com   Phone: (636)530-0305   25

All Year   1P: $89-$139

Location: I-64, exit 20, 1 mi n. 840 Chesterfield Pkwy W 63017. Fax: 636/530-0319. **Facility:** 145 units. 140 one-Small-scale Hotel and 5 two-bedroom suites with efficiencies. 3 stories, interior corridors. *Bath:* combo or shower only. **Parking:** on-site. **Terms:** cancellation fee imposed, weekly rates available, [BP] meal plan available, package plans, pets ($25 fee). **Amenities:** video games (fee), high-speed Internet, dual phone lines, voice mail, irons, hair dryers. *Some:* DVD players. **Pool(s):** heated outdoor. **Leisure Activities:** exercise room. **Guest Services:** sundries, complimentary evening beverages: Mon-Thurs, valet and coin laundry, area transportation. **Business Services:** meeting rooms, business center. **Cards:** AX, DC, DS, MC, VI.

SOME UNITS
(ASK) (S)(D) 🐾 (&) 🏊 (VCR) 📹 📱 🗄 💻 / ✕ /
FEE

(See map and index starting on p. 511)

———— WHERE TO DINE ————

ANNIE GUNN'S Lunch: $8-$38 Dinner: $8-$38 Phone: 636/532-7684 21
▼▼▼ **Location:** I-64, exit 19A (Chesterfield Pkwy), 0.4 mi w to Chesterfield Pkwy, just s to Chesterfield Airport Rd, then 1 mi
Regional American w. 16806 Chesterfield Airport Rd 63005. **Hours:** 11 am-10:30 pm, Fri & Sat-11:30 pm, Sun-9 pm. Closed major
holidays; also Mon. **Reservations:** suggested. **Features:** Traditional barbecue reflects creative gourmet
twists in the laid-back Irish pub. The popular restaurant is often busy—waits for a table are not unusual.
Favorites include smoked pork chops grilled with barbecue glaze and bread pudding. The delightful mixed field green salad is
served with toasted pine nuts. Casual dress; cocktails. **Parking:** on-site. Cards: AX, DC, DS, MC, VI. ◩

AQUA VIN RESTAURANT & BAR Lunch: $7-$12 Dinner: $13-$30 Phone: 636/532-9300 25
▼▼▼ **Location:** US 40, 1 mi nw; next to Chesterfield Mall. 16125 Chesterfield Pkwy W 63017. **Hours:** 11 am-10 pm.
American Closed: 1/1, 12/25; also Sun. **Reservations:** suggested. **Features:** The trendy, contemporary establishment
lines up an intriguing variety of menu selections. Dressy casual; cocktails. **Parking:** on-site. Cards: CB, DC,
DS, MC, VI. ▼ ◩

EAST COAST PIZZA Lunch: $6-$10 Dinner: $6-$10 Phone: 636/536-7888 23
◆◆ **Location:** At Chesterfield Commons Shopping Center. 17304 Chesterfield Airport Rd 63005. **Hours:** 11 am-10 pm,
American Fri & Sat-11 pm, Sun-9 pm. Closed major holidays. **Features:** The family-owned and operated eatery
serves New York pizza with daily made hand-tossed dough and homemade pizza sauce. Philadelphia
cheese steak and other sandwiches, as well as soups and spaghetti, are other delicious options. Casual
dress; beer & wine only. **Parking:** on-site. Cards: AX, DC, DS, MC, VI.

EL MAGUEY Lunch: $5-$6 Dinner: $7-$12 Phone: 314/878-5988 19
◆◆ ◆◆ **Location:** Just e of SR 141; in Woodchase Plaza. 13377 Olive Blvd 63017. **Hours:** 11 am-10:30 pm,
Mexican Tues-10 pm. Closed major holidays. **Reservations:** accepted. **Features:** One of a chain of restaurants, this
place prepares all the favorites, including tacos, burritos, enchiladas and, of course, chips and salsa.
Patrons won't go home hungry. Casual dress; beer only. **Parking:** on-site. Cards: AX, DS, MC, VI. ◔M

FOX AND HOUND PUB & GRILLE Lunch: $8-$18 Dinner: $8-$18 Phone: 636/536-0802 22
◆◆ ◆◆ **Location:** I-64/US 40, exit 19A (Chesterfield Pkwy). 17416 Chesterfield Airport Rd 63005. **Hours:** 11 am-10 pm, Fri
American & Sat-11 pm, Sun-9 pm. Closed major holidays. **Features:** Casual diners visit the popular spot for thin-crust
and traditional pizzas, burgers, sandwiches and appetizers, including "Grand Champion" wings. Casual
dress; cocktails. **Parking:** on-site. Cards: AX, CB, DC, DS, JC, MC, VI. ◩

VILLA FAROTTO VINEYARDS Lunch: $8-$19 Dinner: $9-$33 Phone: 636/519-0048 20
▼▼▼ **Location:** I-64, exit 17, 0.3 mi on Boones Crossing St, then 0.4 mi w. 17417 Chesterfield Airport Rd 63005. **Hours:** 11
Italian am-10 pm, Fri & Sat-11 pm. Closed: 11/22, 12/25. **Reservations:** accepted. **Features:** Contemporary and
classy, this sophisticated trendy spot comes highly recommended by local businesses; you won't be
disappointed. Casual dress; cocktails. **Parking:** on-site. Cards: AX, CB, DC, DS, JC, MC, VI. ◔M ▼

YIA YIA'S EURO CAFE Lunch: $9-$18 Dinner: $10-$25 Phone: 636/537-9991 24
▼▼▼ **Location:** I-64, exit 20 (Chesterfield Pkwy), just ne. 15601 Olive Blvd 63017. **Hours:** 11 am-10 pm, Fri & Sat-11
Northern American pm, Sun 10 am-9 pm. Closed: 7/4, 12/25. **Reservations:** suggested. **Features:** Among examples of
European-style cuisine that reflects a Mediterranean flair are oak-fired pizza, piadini and pasta favorites.
Dressy casual; cocktails. **Parking:** on-site. Cards: AX, DC, DS, MC, VI. ◩

———— *The following restaurants have not been evaluated by AAA* ————
but are listed for your information only.

GIANFABIO RISTORANTE/IL FORNO CAFE Phone: 636/532-6686
fyi Not evaluated. **Location:** 127 Hilltown Village Center 63017. **Features:** The establishment features both
traditional and West Coast-style Italian cuisine.

SPIRO'S RESTAURANT Phone: 314/878-4449
fyi Not evaluated. **Location:** 1054 N Woods Mill Rd 63017. **Features:** Greek food and other Continental specialties
are presented along with daily specials. ▼

CLAYTON pop. 13,900 (See map and index starting on p. 514)

———— WHERE TO STAY ————

CROWNE PLAZA ST LOUIS-CLAYTON *Book great rates at AAA.com* Phone: (314)726-5400 54
(AAA) SAVE All Year 1P: $139-$209 2P: $139-$209 XP: $10 F17
▼▼▼ **Location:** I-64/US 40, exit 31 (Brentwood Blvd), 1.3 mi n, then 0.7 mi e. 7750 Carondelet Ave 63105.
Fax: 314/719-1126. **Facility:** 252 one-bedroom standard units, some with whirlpools. 2-8 stories, interior
corridors. **Bath:** combo or shower only. **Parking:** on-site (fee) and valet. **Terms:** [BP] meal plan available,
Small-scale Hotel pets (with prior approval). **Amenities:** video games (fee), CD players, high-speed Internet, dual phone lines,
voice mail, honor bars, irons, hair dryers. **Dining:** 6:30 am-11 pm, Sun-10 pm, cocktails. **Pool(s):** heated
indoor/outdoor. **Leisure Activities:** sauna, exercise room, game room. **Guest Services:** gift shop, valet and coin laundry, area
transportation-within Clayton & Galleria, wireless Internet. **Business Services:** conference facilities, business center.
Cards: AX, CB, DC, DS, JC, MC, VI. **Free Special Amenities:** newspaper and high-speed Internet. *(See color ad p 537)*
SOME UNITS
✈ ⛺ ⅋ ▼ ⌖ ⊘ ⇌ ✕ ⌤ ▣ /✕ ⊹

(See map and index starting on p. 514)

THE RITZ-CARLTON, ST. LOUIS   *Book great rates at AAA.com*   Phone: (314)863-6300   53

⬜AAA (SAVE)   All Year   1P: $179-$251
▽▽▽▽ ▽▽▽▽   **Location:** I-64, exit 32B, 1.2 mi n on Hanley Rd, then just e. 100 Carondelet Plaza 63105. Fax: 314/863-3525.
Large-scale Hotel   **Facility:** A luxury hotel with elegant public areas paneled in African Makore mahogany with original oil paintings, marble floors and oriental rugs. Smoke free premises. 301 units. 267 one-bedroom standard units. 34 one-bedroom suites, some with whirlpools. 18 stories, interior corridors. *Bath:* combo or shower only. **Parking:** on-site (fee) and valet. **Terms:** check-in 4 pm, cancellation fee imposed, package plans, small pets only ($150 fee). **Amenities:** CD players, dual phone lines, voice mail, safes, honor bars, irons, hair dryers. *Fee:* video games, high-speed Internet. *Some:* DVD players. **Dining:** The Grill, see separate listing, entertainment. **Pool(s):** small heated indoor. **Leisure Activities:** saunas, whirlpool, steamrooms, sun deck. *Fee:* massage. **Guest Services:** gift shop, valet laundry. **Business Services:** conference facilities, business center. **Cards:** AX, CB, DC, DS, JC, MC, VI.
Free Special Amenities: newspaper.

FEE

SHERATON CLAYTON PLAZA HOTEL   *Book great rates at AAA.com*   Phone: (314)863-0400   55

⬜AAA (SAVE)   All Year   1P: $239   2P: $239   XP: $10   F18
▽▽▽▽   **Location:** I-64/US 40, exit 31 (Brentwood Blvd), 1.3 mi n, then 0.7 mi e. 7730 Bonhomme Ave 63105.
Small-scale Hotel   Fax: 314/862-4152. **Facility:** 257 units. 229 one-bedroom standard units. 25 one- and 3 two-bedroom suites, some with kitchens. 16 stories, interior corridors. *Bath:* combo or shower only. **Parking:** on-site (fee) and valet. **Terms:** cancellation fee imposed, [AP], [BP] & [CP] meal plans available, package plans, small pets only. **Amenities:** high-speed Internet (fee), dual phone lines, voice mail, irons, hair dryers. *Some:* fax. **Dining:** 6:30 am-11 pm, Sat & Sun from 7 am, cocktails. **Pool(s):** heated indoor. **Leisure Activities:** whirlpool, outdoor deck, exercise room. **Guest Services:** valet and coin laundry, area transportation-within 5 mi, beauty salon, wireless Internet. **Business Services:** conference facilities, business center. **Cards:** AX, CB, DC, DS, JC, MC, VI.
Free Special Amenities: newspaper and preferred room (subject to availability with advance reservations).
(See color ad below)

SOME UNITS

(See map and index starting on p. 514)

———— **WHERE TO DINE** ————

BARCELONA TAPAS RESTAURANT　　**Lunch:** $10-$15　　**Dinner:** $10-$15　　**Phone:** 314/863-9909　　76
▼▼▼▼　**Location:** Just n of Forsyth Blvd. 34 N Central Ave 63105. **Hours:** 11 am-11 pm, Sun from 5 pm. Closed: 11/22,
　　　　12/25. **Reservations:** accepted. **Features:** At this favorite spot, located in an upscale casual area, be
Spanish　prepared for a high-energy atmosphere and great food. Dressy casual; cocktails. **Parking:** street.
　　　　Cards: AX, CB, DC, DS, JC, MC, VI.

CAFE DE FRANCE　　　　　　　**Lunch:** $9-$12　　　　**Dinner:** $9-$24　　**Phone:** 314/678-0200　　78
▼▼▼▼　**Location:** I-64, exit 32, 1 mi n on Hanley Rd, then just e. 7515 Forsyth 63105. **Hours:** 11:30 am-2 & 5 pm, Fri &
　　　　Sat 5 pm-10:30 pm. Closed major holidays; also Sun. **Reservations:** suggested. **Features:** Diners can
French　expect a distinctive mix of fine and casual dining. Offerings range from bistro fare to more complex choices.
　　　　Casual dress; cocktails. **Parking:** on-site. **Cards:** AX, CB, DC, DS, MC, VI.

CARDWELL'S IN CLAYTON　　　**Lunch:** $6-$13　　　　**Dinner:** $13-$25　　**Phone:** 314/726-5055　　75
▼▼▼▼　**Location:** I-170, exit 1F, 1.5 mi e. 8100 Maryland Ave 63105. **Hours:** 11:30 am-2:30 & 5:30-10 pm, Fri & Sat-10
　　　　pm. Closed major holidays; also Sun. **Reservations:** suggested. **Features:** Cardwell's offers a creative,
American　superb cuisine prepared with a subtle flair. The five-onion soup appetizer and grilled venison are good, as is
　　　　the pumpkin cheesecake. This restaurant has an atmosphere of casual elegance and a very good wine
selection. Dressy casual; cocktails. **Parking:** street. **Cards:** AX, CB, DC, MC, VI.

DOMINIC'S TRATTORIA　　　　**Lunch:** $8-$12　　　　**Dinner:** $9-$25　　**Phone:** 314/863-4567　　81
▼▼▼▼　**Location:** I-64/US 40, exit 31A (Brentwood Blvd), 1.1 mi n to Bonhomme; in Park Tower Building. 200 S Brentwood Blvd
　　　　63105. **Hours:** 11 am-2 & 5-10 pm, Fri-9:45 pm, Sat 5 pm-10:30 pm. Closed major holidays; also Sun.
Italian　**Reservations:** suggested. **Features:** Sophisticated without being stuffy, the restaurant is on the ground
　　　　floor of a multi-story building. Favorite preparations of pasta, veal, chicken, beef and fish all are
complemented by the complete wine list. Service is professional and efficient. Dressy casual; cocktails. **Parking:** valet.
Cards: AX, DC, DS, MC, VI.

THE GRILL　　　　　　　　　　　　**Dinner:** $25-$50　　　　　　　　　　**Phone:** 314/863-6300　　80
ⓐⓐⓐ　**Location:** I-64, exit 32B, 1.2 mi n on Hanley Rd, then just e; in The Ritz-Carlton, St. Louis. 100 Carondelet Plaza 63105.
　　　　Hours: 6 pm-10 pm. **Reservations:** suggested. **Features:** Fresh interpretations of classic cuisine combine
▼▼　▼▼　the finest ingredients with creative techniques. The atmosphere merges refinement with comfort. The
American　signature dish is bison rib-eye, and fresh seafood—delivered daily—is prepared with personal choices of
　　　　distinctive sauce. The dessert menu lists signature souffles and traditional classics. Dressy casual; cocktails.
　　　　Parking: on-site (fee) and valet. **Cards:** AX, CB, DC, DS, JC, MC, VI.

JIMMY'S ON THE PARK CAFE BISTRO & BAR　**Lunch:** $5-$13　　**Dinner:** $8-$21　　**Phone:** 314/725-8585　　83
▼▼▼▼　**Location:** I-64/US 40, exit 34B (Clayton/Skinker), 0.6 mi w to DeMun Ave, then 0.3 mi n. 706 DeMun Ave 63105.
　　　　Hours: 11:30 am-10 pm, Fri & Sat-10:30 pm, Sun 10 am-2 & 5-9 pm, Mon 5 pm-10 pm. Closed major
American　holidays. **Reservations:** suggested. **Features:** The casual restaurant's specialties reflect fine contemporary
　　　　cuisine, including light and tasty flash-fried spinach and tenderloin Anthony. Live jazz fills the air Friday and
Saturday nights, as well as Saturday and Sunday afternoons. Casual dress; cocktails. **Parking:** on-site. **Cards:** AX, CB, DC,
MC, VI.

LUCIANO'S TRATTORIA　　　　**Lunch:** $8-$22　　　　**Dinner:** $8-$22　　**Phone:** 314/863-9969　　79
▼▼▼▼　**Location:** I-64/US 40, exit 32, 1.2 mi n on Hanley Rd, then just e. 172 Carondelet Pl 63105. **Hours:** 11 am-2:30 & 5-
　　　　10:30 pm, Fri & Sat-11 pm, Sun 4 pm-9 pm. Closed major holidays. **Reservations:** suggested. **Features:** A
Italian　touch of jazzy sophistication marks the warm, contemporary atmosphere. From pizza to veal, menu
　　　　creations reflect current spins on old favorites. Dressy casual; cocktails. **Parking:** on-site (fee) and valet.
Cards: AX, CB, DC, DS, JC, MC, VI.

PORTABELLA　　　　　　　　　**Lunch:** $8-$13　　　　**Dinner:** $14-$27　　**Phone:** 314/725-6588　　77
▼▼▼▼　**Location:** I-64, exit 31A (Brentwood Blvd), 1.6 mi n, just e on Maryland, then just s. 15 N Central Ave 63105.
　　　　Hours: 11:30 am-2 & 5:30-10 pm, Fri-10:30 pm, Sat 5:30 pm-10:30 pm, Sun 5 pm-9 pm. Closed: 7/4, 11/22,
Italian　12/25. **Reservations:** suggested. **Features:** Portabella's has enhanced the traditional menu of pasta and
　　　　mushrooms—appetizers and entrees—with light touches and splendid accents. Its atmosphere is
understated elegance, and its wine list is extensive. Valet service is available after 6 pm. Formal attire; cocktails. **Parking:** valet
and street. **Cards:** AX, MC, VI.

REMY'S KITCHEN & WINE BAR　**Lunch:** $6-$10　　　　**Dinner:** $6-$20　　**Phone:** 314/726-5757　　82
▼▼　▼▼　**Location:** Just n of Forest Park Pkwy. 222 S Bemiston Ave 63105. **Hours:** 11:30 am-2 & 5:30-10 pm, Thurs & Fri-
　　　　midnight, Sat 5:30 pm-midnight. Closed major holidays; also Sun. **Reservations:** suggested.
Regional　**Features:** Gourmet cuisine with Mediterranean accents is served in a friendly and energetic atmosphere.
Continental　The tasty grazing selection includes a choice of two soups, pita and hummus, chilled cucumber and grilled
　　　　tenderloin salad. Casual dress; cocktails. **Parking:** on-site. **Cards:** AX, DC, DS, MC, VI.

SASHA'S WINE BAR & MARKET　**Lunch:** $5-$20　　　　**Dinner:** $5-$20　　**Phone:** 314/863-7274　　84
▼▼　▼▼　**Location:** I-64/US 40, exit 34B (Clayton/Skinker), 0.6 mi w to Demun Ave, then 0.3 mi n. 706-C Demun Ave 63105.
　　　　Hours: 11 am-1 am, Sat from 10 am, Sun 10 am-midnight. **Reservations:** accepted. **Features:** Extensive
American　by-the-glass wine selections, delightful food and seasonal sidewalk seating are hallmarks of the trendy
　　　　neighborhood restaurant. Whether seated inside or out, diners are delighted by the meal and the eclectic,
comfortable atmosphere. Casual dress; cocktails. **Parking:** street. **Cards:** AX, CB, DC, DS, JC, MC, VI.

(See map and index starting on p. 514)

YEN CHING
Chinese

Lunch: $5-$10 Dinner: $12-$14 Phone: 314/721-7507 85

Location: I-64/US 40, exit 31A (Brentwood Blvd), 0.4 mi n. 1012 S Brentwood Blvd 63117. **Hours:** 11:30 am-2 & 5-9:30 pm, Fri-10:30 pm, Sat 5 pm-10:30 pm, Sun 4:30 pm-9 pm. Closed: 11/22, 12/25. **Reservations:** suggested, weekends. **Features:** This locally popular restaurant has a casual, relaxed decor and authentic cuisine. Families and business people enjoy this eatery, although it has limited parking. The Yen Ching beef and chicken choices are good, as is the glazed banana dessert. Casual dress; cocktails. **Parking:** on-site. **Cards:** AX, MC, VI.

The following restaurants have not been evaluated by AAA but are listed for your information only.

CAFE' NAPOLI
[fyi]

Phone: 314/863-5731

Not evaluated. **Location:** 7754 Forsyth Blvd 63105. **Features:** Classic Italian dishes are served in large portions.

INDIA'S RASOI
[fyi]

Phone: 314/727-1414

Not evaluated. **Location:** 7923 Forsyth Blvd 63105. **Features:** The owner's mother prepares dishes of traditional Indian cuisine, including lamb in yogurt sauce.

CREVE COEUR pop. 16,500 (See map and index starting on p. 514)

——— WHERE TO STAY ———

COURTYARD BY MARRIOTT-CREVE COEUR *Book great rates at AAA.com* Phone: 314/993-0515 50

Small-scale Hotel

All Year 1P: $189 2P: $189
Location: I-270, exit 14 (Olive Blvd), 0.5 mi e to New Ballas Rd, then just n. 828 N New Ballas Rd 63146. Fax: 314/993-1354. **Facility:** Smoke free premises. 154 units. 141 one-bedroom standard units. 13 one-bedroom suites ($249). 2-4 stories, interior corridors. *Bath:* combo or shower only. **Parking:** on-site. **Terms:** cancellation fee imposed, [BP] meal plan available. **Amenities:** high-speed Internet, voice mail, irons, hair dryers. **Pool(s):** small heated indoor. **Leisure Activities:** whirlpool, exercise room. **Guest Services:** sundries, valet and coin laundry. **Business Services:** meeting rooms, business center. **Cards:** AX, DC, DS, MC, VI. **Free Special Amenities:** high-speed Internet.

SOME UNITS

DRURY INN & SUITES-CREVE COEUR *Book great rates at AAA.com* Phone: (314)989-1100 49

Small-scale Hotel

All Year [BP] 1P: $80-$140 2P: $90-$150 XP: $10 F18
Location: I-270, exit 14 (Olive Blvd). 11980 Olive Blvd 63141. Fax: 314/989-1100. **Facility:** 187 units. 155 one-bedroom standard units. 32 one-bedroom suites ($105-$175). 8 stories, interior corridors. *Bath:* combo or shower only. **Parking:** on-site. **Terms:** small pets only. **Amenities:** high-speed Internet, voice mail, irons, hair dryers. **Pool(s):** small heated indoor. **Leisure Activities:** whirlpool, exercise room. **Guest Services:** complimentary evening beverages, valet and coin laundry. **Business Services:** meeting rooms, business center. **Cards:** AX, CB, DC, DS, MC, VI.

SOME UNITS

——— WHERE TO DINE ———

BALDUCCI'S WINEFEST RESTAURANT & BAR Lunch: $5-$11 Dinner: $5-$11 Phone: 314/576-5024 67
Italian

Location: I-270, exit 16B (Page Ave W), 0.5 mi w to Bennington Pl, then 0.3 mi n. 12527 Bennington Pl 63146. **Hours:** 11 am-9 pm, Fri-10 pm, Sat 5 pm-10 pm, Sun 5 pm-9 pm. Closed major holidays. **Features:** A family tradition since 1887, locally owned and operated, Balducci's is locally popular. Menu offers toasted ravioli, quiche, pasta, pizza and a good selection of salads and sandwiches. Casual dress; cocktails. **Parking:** on-site. **Cards:** AX, DS, MC, VI.

BRISTOL BAR & SEAFOOD GRILL Lunch: $8-$16 Dinner: $12-$28 Phone: 314/567-0272 72
Seafood

Location: I-270, exit 14 (Olive Blvd), 0.5 mi e. 11801 Olive Blvd 63141. **Hours:** 11 am-10 pm, Fri-10:30 pm, Sat 4:30 pm-10:30 pm, Sun 10 am-2 & 4:30-9 pm. Closed major holidays. **Reservations:** suggested. **Features:** All seafood is a great catch, and fresh fish is grilled over a mesquite-wood fire. Because attention is paid to seasonal ingredients, the menu is printed each day. A warm, sophisticated atmosphere draws the local corporate crowd. Casual dress; cocktails. **Parking:** on-site. **Cards:** AX, CB, DC, DS, JC, MC, VI.

CANDICCI'S RESTAURANT Lunch: $6-$10 Dinner: $10-$25 Phone: 314/878-5858 69
Italian

Location: I-270, exit 14 (Olive Blvd), 0.8 mi w; in Dierberg's Heritage Place Shopping Center. 12513 Olive Blvd 63141. **Hours:** 11 am-10 pm, Fri & Sat-11 pm, Sun 4 pm-9 pm. Closed major holidays. **Reservations:** suggested, weekends. **Features:** Langusto suprimo and vitello carciofini are among creative dishes served at the popular restaurant, which blends aspects of casual and fine dining. Service is polite and attentive, and the candlelit atmosphere is cozy and intimate. Casual dress; cocktails. **Parking:** on-site. **Cards:** AX, DC, DS, MC, VI.

IL BELLAGIO CITY PLACE Lunch: $10-$16 Dinner: $16-$36 Phone: 314/994-1080 71
Italian

Location: I-270, exit 14 (Olive Blvd), 0.6 mi e. 11631 Olive Blvd 63141. **Hours:** 11 am-10 pm, Fri & Sat-11 pm. Closed major holidays; also Sun. **Reservations:** accepted. **Features:** Rich contemporary decor characterizes the casual fine-dining atmosphere. Formal service appeals to business, special occasion and casual diners. Dressy casual; cocktails. **Parking:** on-site. **Cards:** AX, CB, DC, DS, JC, MC, VI.

(See map and index starting on p. 514)

KOBE STEAK HOUSE OF JAPAN **Lunch:** $6-$19 **Dinner:** $13-$27 **Phone:** 314/434-2600 ⑥⑧

Japanese **Location:** I-270, 0.7 mi w; in Dierbergs Heritage Place Shopping Center. 12521 Olive Blvd 63141. **Hours:** 11:30 am-2 & 5:30-9 pm, Fri 11:30 am-2 & 5-10 pm, Sat 5 pm-10 pm, Sun 4:30 pm-8:30 pm. **Reservations:** suggested. **Features:** Patrons often visit the popular casual spot for special occasions. The menu focus is on steak, chicken and seafood. Casual dress; cocktails. **Parking:** on-site. **Cards:** AX, DC, DS, MC, VI.

LA BONNE BOUCHEE WESTGATE CENTER **Lunch:** $8-$10 **Phone:** 314/576-6606 ⑦⓪

French **Location:** I-270, exit 14 (Olive Blvd), 0.3 mi w; in Westgate Center. 12344 Olive Blvd 63141. **Hours:** 11 am-3 & 5-9 pm, Sun 8 am-1 pm, Mon 11 am-3 pm. Closed major holidays. **Reservations:** accepted. **Features:** A cafe-like decor sets the stage for casual, quiet dining with fabulous, yet simple, meals. Most days, only one meat and one fish entree are offered. Otherwise, diners opt for salads, quiche, soups, sandwiches and other light fare. The bakery offers many European cakes and fresh pastries. Casual dress; cocktails. **Parking:** on-site. **Cards:** AX, CB, DC, DS, MC, VI.

DES PERES pop. 8,592

———— **WHERE TO DINE** ————

ELEPHANT BAR **Lunch:** $7-$16 **Dinner:** $7-$16 **Phone:** 314/835-0545

American **Location:** I-270, exit Manchester Rd, just e. 1085 W County Center Dr 63131. **Hours:** 11 am-10 pm, Fri & Sat-11 pm. Closed: 12/25. **Features:** Going on safari was never this much fun. Guests who unwind amid the bright jungle decor can sample fresh California cuisine prepared with Pacific Rim influences. Pizza cooked over a wood fire, sizzling cantina fajitas, wok-seared Shanghai cashew chicken and langoustines, and shrimp and chicken jambalaya are among dishes sure to wake up the taste buds. Service is great, too. Casual dress; cocktails. **Parking:** on-site. **Cards:** AX, CB, DC, DS, JC, MC, VI.

EDMUNDSON pop. 840 (See map and index starting on p. 514)

———— **WHERE TO STAY** ————

DRURY INN-ST. LOUIS AIRPORT *Book great rates at AAA.com* **Phone:** (314)423-7700 ⑰

All Year [BP] 1P: $83-$140 2P: $93-$150 XP: $10 F18

Small-scale Hotel **Location:** I-70, exit 236 (Lambert Airport), just se. 10490 Natural Bridge Rd 63134. **Fax:** 314/423-7700. **Facility:** 172 units. 162 one-bedroom standard units. 10 one-bedroom suites ($135-$155). 6 stories, interior corridors. **Bath:** combo or shower only. **Parking:** on-site. **Amenities:** high-speed Internet, voice mail, irons, hair dryers. **Pool(s):** small heated indoor. **Leisure Activities:** whirlpool, exercise room. **Guest Services:** complimentary evening beverages, valet and coin laundry. **Business Services:** meeting rooms, PC, fax. **Cards:** AX, CB, DC, DS, MC, VI.

SOME UNITS

ST. LOUIS AIRPORT MARRIOTT *Book great rates at AAA.com* **Phone:** (314)423-9700 ⑯

All Year 1P: $89-$179 2P: $89-$179

Large-scale Hotel **Location:** I-70, exit 236 (Lambert Airport). 10700 Pear Tree Ln 63134. **Fax:** 314/423-0213. **Facility:** Smoke free premises. 601 units. 598 one-bedroom standard units. 3 one-bedroom suites. 3-9 stories, interior corridors. **Bath:** combo or shower only. **Parking:** on-site (fee). **Terms:** cancellation fee imposed, package plans. **Amenities:** high-speed Internet (fee), voice mail, irons, hair dryers. *Some:* CD players. **Dining:** 6 am-midnight, cocktails. **Pool(s):** outdoor, heated indoor/outdoor. **Leisure Activities:** whirlpool. **Guest Services:** gift shop, valet and coin laundry. **Business Services:** conference facilities, business center. **Cards:** AX, CB, DC, DS, JC, MC, VI. **Free Special Amenities:** early check-in/late check-out and room upgrade (subject to availability with advance reservations).

SOME UNITS

———— **WHERE TO DINE** ————

LOMBARDO'S RESTAURANT **Lunch:** $6-$12 **Dinner:** $15-$20 **Phone:** 314/429-5151 ㊳

Italian **Location:** I-70, exit 236 (Lambert Airport), just se. 10488 Natural Bridge Rd 63134. **Hours:** 11 am-10 pm, Sat from 5 pm. Closed: 11/22, 12/25; also Sun. **Reservations:** accepted. **Features:** A longtime and well-respected restaurant family, the Lombardos have been serving fine food since 1934. Warm and sophisticated decor, fine service and an atmosphere suitable for business and special occasion dining characterize this place. Casual dress; cocktails. **Parking:** on-site. **Cards:** AX, CB, DC, DS, JC, MC, VI.

EUREKA pop. 7,676 (See map and index starting on p. 511)

———— **WHERE TO STAY** ————

HOLIDAY INN AT SIX FLAGS *Book great rates at AAA.com* **Phone:** (636)938-6661 ㊲

5/25-9/2	1P: $159-$239	2P: $159-$239	XP: $5	F17
3/1-5/24	1P: $99-$229	2P: $99-$229	XP: $5	F17
10/28-2/29	1P: $99-$189	2P: $99-$189	XP: $5	F17
9/3-10/27	1P: $119-$169	2P: $119-$169	XP: $5	F17

Small-scale Hotel **Location:** I-44, exit 261 (Allenton Rd). 4901 Six Flags Rd 63025 (PO Box 999). **Fax:** 636/938-4099. **Facility:** 179 units. 166 one-bedroom standard units. 1 one- and 12 two-bedroom suites. 1-3 stories, interior/exterior corridors. **Bath:** combo or shower only. **Parking:** on-site. **Terms:** check-in 4 pm, 3 day cancellation notice-fee imposed, [BP] meal plan available, package plans, small pets only ($10 extra charge). **Amenities:** video games (fee), high-speed Internet, voice mail, irons, hair dryers. **Dining:** 6:30 am-2 & 5-10 pm, cocktails. **Pool(s):** heated indoor, wading. **Leisure Activities:** sauna, whirlpool, putting green, exercise room, shuffleboard. *Fee:* game room. **Guest Services:** valet and coin laundry, area transportation-Six Flags. **Business Services:** meeting rooms, PC. **Cards:** AX, CB, DC, DS, JC, MC, VI. **Free Special Amenities:** newspaper and high-speed Internet.

SOME UNITS

(See map and index starting on p. 511)

———— WHERE TO DINE ————

POOR RICHARD'S   **Lunch:** $6-$9   **Dinner:** $7-$15   **Phone:** 636/938-4666 ㉞
♦♦♦ ♦♦♦   **Location:** I-44, exit 264, 1 mi w; in Hilltop Village Center. 108 A Hilltop Village Center 63025. **Hours:** 11 am-1 am,
American   Sun noon-midnight. Closed: 4/8, 11/22, 12/25. **Features:** Since 1998, the restaurant has served basic pub
               fare, including the ever-popular chicken wings. Casual dress; cocktails. **Parking:** on-site. **Cards:** AX, DS,
               MC, VI.

FENTON pop. 4,360 (See map and index starting on p. 514)

———— WHERE TO STAY ————

DRURY INN & SUITES-FENTON   *Book great rates at AAA.com*   **Phone:** (636)343-7822 ㊏
♦♦♦ ♦♦♦   All Year [BP]   1P: $65-$115   2P: $75-$125   XP: $10   F18
Small-scale Hotel **Location:** I-44, exit 274 (Bowles Ave), just se. 1088 S Highway Dr 63026. **Fax:** 636/343-7822. **Facility:** 141 units.
               129 one-bedroom standard units. 12 one-bedroom suites ($100-$150). 4 stories, interior corridors. **Parking:**
               on-site. **Terms:** small pets only. **Amenities:** high-speed Internet, dual phone lines, voice mail, irons, hair
dryers. **Pool(s):** heated indoor/outdoor, wading. **Leisure Activities:** whirlpool, exercise room. **Guest Services:** complimentary
evening beverages, valet and coin laundry, wireless Internet. **Business Services:** meeting rooms, PC. **Cards:** AX, CB, DC, DS,
MC, VI.
                                                                                          SOME UNITS
(ASK) 🛏 🍴 ⊘ ⊛ ✦ 🖥 📠 ⊟ /✕/

FAIRFIELD INN   *Book great rates at AAA.com*   **Phone:** (636)305-1500 ㊢
♦♦♦ ♦♦♦   All Year [ECP]   1P: $79-$129
Small-scale Hotel **Location:** I-44, exit 275 (E Soccer Park Rd) westbound; exit 274B eastbound to S Highway Dr, just s. Located in a
               commercial area. 1680 Fenton Business Park Ct 63026. **Fax:** 636/305-1900. **Facility:** Smoke free premises. 106
               one-bedroom standard units. 3 stories, interior corridors. *Bath:* combo or shower only. **Parking:** on-site.
Amenities: high-speed Internet, voice mail, irons, hair dryers. **Pool(s):** small heated indoor. **Leisure Activities:** whirlpool,
exercise room. **Guest Services:** valet laundry, wireless Internet. **Business Services:** PC, fax. **Cards:** AX, DC, DS, MC, VI.
                                                                                          SOME UNITS
(ASK) 🅂⊘ ⊛ ✕ ✦ 🖥 /⊟ 📠 /

HOLIDAY INN EXPRESS HOTEL & SUITES   *Book at AAA.com*   **Phone:** (636)349-4444 ㊭
♦♦♦♦♦♦ ♦♦♦   All Year [ECP]   1P: $76-$139   2P: $76-$139
Small-scale Hotel **Location:** I-44, exit 274A (Bowles Ave), just s. Located in a commercial area. 1848 Bowles Ave 63026.
               Fax: 636/305-1234. **Facility:** 76 units. 73 one-bedroom standard units, some with whirlpools. 3 one-
               bedroom suites ($98-$209) with whirlpools. 3 stories, interior corridors. *Bath:* combo or shower only.
Parking: on-site, winter plug-ins. **Amenities:** high-speed Internet, voice mail, irons, hair dryers. *Some:* DVD players, dual
phone lines. **Pool(s):** small heated indoor. **Leisure Activities:** exercise room. **Guest Services:** valet and coin laundry, wireless
Internet. **Business Services:** meeting rooms, PC, fax. **Cards:** AX, CB, DC, DS, JC, MC, VI.
                                                                                          SOME UNITS
(ASK) ⊘ ⊛ ✦ 🖥 📠 🖥 /✕/

PEAR TREE INN BY DRURY-FENTON   *Book great rates at AAA.com*   **Phone:** (636)343-8820 ㊐
♦♦♦ ♦♦♦   All Year   1P: $50-$100   2P: $60-$110   XP: $10   F18
Small-scale Hotel **Location:** I-44, exit 274 (Bowles Ave), just s. 1100 S Highway Dr 63026. **Fax:** 636/343-8820. **Facility:** 101 one-
               bedroom standard units. 3 stories, interior corridors. **Parking:** on-site. **Terms:** small pets only.
               Amenities: high-speed Internet, voice mail, irons, hair dryers. **Pool(s):** outdoor. **Guest Services:** valet
laundry, wireless Internet. **Cards:** AX, CB, DC, DS, MC, VI.
                                                                                          SOME UNITS
(ASK) 🛏 🍴 ⊘ ⊛ 🔼 ✦ 🖥 /✕ ⊟ 📠 /
                    FEE

———— *The following lodging was either not evaluated or did not* ————
meet AAA rating requirements but is listed for your information only.

TOWNEPLACE SUITES BY MARRIOTT   **Phone:** 636/305-7000
[fyi]   Did not meet all AAA rating requirements for some property operations at time of last evaluation on
Small-scale Hotel 05/31/2006. **Location:** I-44, exit 275 westbound; exit 274 eastbound to S Highway Dr, just s. 1662 Fenton Business
               Park Ct 63026. Facilities, services, and decor characterize a mid-range property.

———— WHERE TO DINE ————

———— *The following restaurants have not been evaluated by AAA* ————
but are listed for your information only.

BANDANA'S BAR-B-Q   **Phone:** 636/305-8855
[fyi]   Not evaluated. **Location:** I-44, exit 274 (Bowles Ave), just s. 1160 S Highway Dr 63026. **Features:** The real wood-
               pit smoker produces tasty meats. Try a Southern favorite: hot boiled peanuts on the side.

POOR RICHARD'S   **Phone:** 636/349-3438
[fyi]   Not evaluated. **Location:** I-44, exit 274 (Bowles Ave). 960 Brookwood Center 63026. **Features:** Since 1998, the
               restaurant has been serving basic pub fare, including its ever-popular chicken wings.

FLORISSANT pop. 50,497 (See map and index starting on p. 514)

——— WHERE TO STAY ———

HAMPTON INN-ST. LOUIS NORTHWEST *Book great rates at AAA.com* **Phone:** (314)839-2200 **7**
(AAA) [SAVE]
All Year   1P: $79-$199   2P: $89-$199   XP: $10
Location: I-270, exit 26B (Graham Rd/Hanley Rd), just nw. Located in a commercial area. 55 Dunn Rd 63031.
Fax: 314/830-1878. **Facility:** 126 one-bedroom standard units. 4 stories, interior corridors. **Parking:** on-site.
Amenities: video games (fee), high-speed Internet, voice mail, irons, hair dryers. **Pool(s):** outdoor. **Leisure**
Small-scale Hotel **Activities:** exercise room. **Guest Services:** valet laundry, area transportation-within 3 mi. **Business**
Services: meeting rooms, business center. **Cards:** AX, CB, DC, DS, JC, MC, VI. **Free Special Amenities:**
expanded continental breakfast and high-speed Internet.

SOME UNITS

[icons]

——— WHERE TO DINE ———

THE BARN DELI   **Lunch:** $4-$7   **Phone:** 314/838-3670 **31**
American
Location: I-270, exit 26B (Graham Rd/Hanley Rd), just n on Graham Rd, then just w. 180 Dunn Rd 63031. **Hours:** 11
am-3 pm. Closed major holidays; also Sun. **Reservations:** accepted. **Features:** Built in the early 1870s as
a farm barn, the building has been converted to retail space including this laid-back deli, a hidden treasure.
Lining the menu are taste-tempting soups, salads, sandwiches and sweets. The signature barn nut pie
features pecans on a cheesecake filling in a pie-dough crust. Casual dress; beer & wine only. **Parking:** on-site. **Cards:** AX, DC,
MC, VI.

[icon]

FRESH ITALY   **Dinner:** $8-$15   **Phone:** 314/830-0600 **28**
Italian
Location: I-270, exit 25 (Lindbergh Blvd), 2 mi n; in Florissant Oaks Plaza. 119 Florissant Oaks Plaza 63031. **Hours:** 4
pm-9 pm, Fri & Sat-10 pm, Sun-9 pm. Closed major holidays; also Mon. **Features:** Homemade food makes
the wait worthwhile at the cozy and comfortable neighborhood establishment. Casual dress; beer & wine
only. **Parking:** on-site. **Cards:** AX, DS, MC, VI.

RUIZ MEXICAN RESTAURANT   **Lunch:** $6-$9   **Dinner:** $7-$18   **Phone:** 314/838-3500 **29**
Mexican
Location: I-270, exit 25 (Lindbergh Blvd), 2.1 mi n. 901 N Hwy 67 (Lindbergh Blvd) 63031. **Hours:** 11 am-10 pm, Fri
& Sat-11 pm. Closed major holidays. **Reservations:** accepted. **Features:** The city's oldest Mexican
restaurant is run by the Ruiz family's third generation. Popular with locals, it serves enchiladas, tamales
made from scratch, fajitas with tender rib eye and great margaritas. Casual dress; cocktails. **Parking:** on-
site. **Cards:** AX, CB, DC, DS, MC, VI.

[icons]

YACOVELLI'S RESTAURANT   **Dinner:** $15-$20   **Phone:** 314/839-1000 **30**
(AAA)
Italian
Location: I-270, exit 26B (Graham Rd/Hanley Rd), just n. 407 Dunn Rd 63031. **Hours:** 4 pm-9 pm, Fri & Sat-10
pm, Sun-8 pm. Closed: 11/22, 12/25; also Mon & Tues. **Reservations:** suggested, weekends.
Features: One of the area's oldest names in the restaurant industry, Yacovelli's has been in continuous
operation since 1919. Specializing in a varied cuisine of prime rib, steak, seafood, chicken and Italian
gourmet, this place offers a fine dining experience in a comfortable and relaxed atmosphere. The three
separate dining rooms are small, intimate and romantic. Casual dress; cocktails. **Parking:** on-site.
Cards: AX, DC, DS, MC, VI.

[icon]

FORISTELL pop. 331 (See map and index starting on p. 511)

——— WHERE TO STAY ———

BEST WESTERN WEST 70 INN *Book great rates at AAA.com* **Phone:** (636)673-2900 **14**
(AAA) [SAVE]
5/1-10/31   1P: $75-$95   2P: $75-$95   XP: $5   F17
3/1-4/30 & 11/1-2/29   1P: $62-$82   2P: $62-$82   XP: $5   F17
Location: I-70, exit 203 (CR W), just n. Located near a truck stop. 12 Hwy W 63348. Fax: 636/673-7222.
Facility: 58 one-bedroom standard units. 2 stories (no elevator), interior corridors. **Parking:** on-site.
Small-scale Hotel **Terms:** [CP] meal plan available, package plans, pets ($10 extra charge). **Amenities:** high-speed Internet,
voice mail, irons, hair dryers. **Pool(s):** outdoor. **Leisure Activities:** *Fee:* billiards, game room. **Guest**
Services: coin laundry, wireless Internet. **Cards:** AX, CB, DC, DS, MC, VI. **Free Special Amenities: continental breakfast**
and high-speed Internet.

SOME UNITS

[icons] FEE

FRONTENAC pop. 3,483 (See map and index starting on p. 514)

——— WHERE TO STAY ———

HILTON ST. LOUIS FRONTENAC *Book great rates at AAA.com* **Phone:** 314/993-1100 **62**
Property failed to provide current rates
Location: I-64/US 40, exit 28A (S Lindbergh Blvd), just s. 1335 S Lindbergh Blvd 63131. Fax: 314/993-8085.
Small-scale Hotel **Facility:** 263 units. 224 one-bedroom standard units. 39 one-bedroom suites. 2-3 stories, interior corridors.
Bath: combo or shower only. **Parking:** on-site. **Amenities:** dual phone lines, voice mail, irons, hair dryers.
Fee: video games, high-speed Internet. **Pool(s):** outdoor. **Leisure Activities:** sauna, exercise room. **Guest Services:** gift shop,
valet laundry, wireless Internet, barber shop. **Business Services:** conference facilities, business center.

SOME UNITS

(See map and index starting on p. 514)

——— WHERE TO DINE ———

RIO TUSCAN GRILLE   Lunch: $9-$17   Dinner: $9-$23   Phone: 314/432-4410   89
▼▼▼
Italian
Location: I-64/US 40, exit 28A (S Lindbergh Blvd), just s; at Plaza Frontenac. 1601 S Lindbergh Blvd 63131. **Hours:** 11 am-10 pm, Fri & Sat-11 pm. Closed: 11/22, 12/25. **Reservations:** accepted. While the atmosphere is casual, upscale Tuscan villa-style decor lends a sophisticated touch to the dining experience. Both lunch and dinner offer all the attentiveness a diner expects, and the food is superlative. From the garlic, spinach and artichoke dip starter to beef, chicken, veal, seafood and homemade pasta entrees, there is a selection to satisfy all tastes. Among specialties are home-made mozzarella, crisp flat breads and wood-fired oven-baked pizza, in addition a selection of steaks and chops. Dressy casual; cocktails. **Parking:** on-site. **Cards:** AX, DS, MC, VI.   ⍾

ANYON CAFE   Lunch: $7-$13   Dinner: $7-$22   Phone: 314/872-3443   90
▼▼▼
Southwestern
Location: I-64/US 40, exit 28A (S Lindbergh Blvd), just s; at Plaza Frontenac. 1707 S Lindbergh Blvd, Suite 2 63131. **Hours:** 11 am-10 pm, Fri & Sat-11 pm, Sun-9 pm. Closed: 11/22, 12/25. **Reservations:** suggested. **Features:** On the menu is a good variety of Southwestern favorites. Guests unwind in the lively atmosphere. Dressy casual; cocktails. **Cards:** AX, CB, DC, DS, JC, MC, VI.   ⍾ ⊠

REIS RESTAURANT   Dinner: $15-$50   Phone: 314/993-0735   88
AAA
▼▼▼
Steak & Seafood
Location: I-64/US 40, exit 28B (N Lindbergh Blvd), 0.8 mi n. 535 S Lindbergh Blvd 63131. **Hours:** 5 pm-10:30 pm, Sat-11 pm, Sun 4:30 pm-9:30 pm. Closed major holidays. **Reservations:** suggested. **Features:** A fine dining institution since the 1930s, the restaurant exudes a classic English hunt-club atmosphere with a lively business crowd on weeknights. Known for its prime rib, steak and fresh seafood, this place also prepares German dishes. Dressy casual; cocktails. **Parking:** on-site. **Cards:** AX, CB, DC, DS, MC, VI.   ⍾ ⊠

HAZELWOOD pop. 26,206   (See map and index starting on p. 514)

——— WHERE TO STAY ———

LA QUINTA INN ST. LOUIS (AIRPORT)   *Book great rates at AAA.com*   Phone: (314)731-3881   13
▼▼▼ ▼▼▼
small-scale Hotel

3/1-9/15 [CP]	1P: $82-$112	2P: $88-$118	XP: $6	F18
9/16-2/29 [CP]	1P: $79-$109	2P: $85-$115	XP: $6	F18

Location: I-270, exit 23 (McDonnell Blvd), just s. Located in a commercial area. 5781 Campus Ct 63042. **Fax:** 314/731-1511. **Facility:** 104 units. 103 one-bedroom standard units. 1 one-bedroom suite ($117-$147). 3 stories, interior corridors. **Parking:** on-site. **Terms:** small pets only. **Amenities:** video games (fee), high-speed Internet, voice mail, irons, hair dryers. **Pool(s):** outdoor. **Leisure Activities:** exercise room. **Guest Services:** valet and coin laundry, area transportation. **Business Services:** meeting rooms. **Cards:** AX, DC, DS, MC, VI.
SOME UNITS
(ASK) ✈ 🐾 ☷ ▨ 🛥 🎥 ▦ / ⊠ ▯ ▭ /

——— WHERE TO DINE ———

PUEBLO NUEVO MEXICAN RESTAURANT   Lunch: $5-$7   Dinner: $9-$13   Phone: 314/831-6885   35
▼▼
Mexican
Location: I-270, exit Lindbergh Blvd, 0.5 mi n. 7401 N Lindbergh Blvd 63042. **Hours:** 11 am-9:30 pm, Fri & Sat-10 pm. Closed major holidays; also Sun & 12/23-1/5. **Features:** The cozy neighborhood establishment provides a good selection of traditional dishes. Casual dress; cocktails. **Parking:** on-site. **Cards:** AX, DS, MC, VI.

VILLAGE CHINA WOK   Lunch: $5-$6   Dinner: $6-$10   Phone: 314/838-5995   34
▼▼ ▼▼
Chinese
Location: I-270, exit 25 (US 67/Lindbergh Blvd), 0.6 mi n. 7541 N Lindbergh Blvd 63042. **Hours:** 11 am-9 pm, Fri & Sat-10 pm, Sun noon-9 pm. Closed: 11/22. **Reservations:** accepted. **Features:** The buffet lines up Chinese and international choices ranging from fried rice to pizza. Casual dress; beer & wine only. **Parking:** on-site. **Cards:** AX, DC, DS, MC, VI.   ⌖ᴹ ⊠

KIRKWOOD pop. 27,324   (See map and index starting on p. 514)

——— WHERE TO STAY ———

BEST WESTERN KIRKWOOD INN   *Book great rates at AAA.com*   Phone: (314)821-3950   79
▼▼ ▼▼
small-scale Hotel

5/1-9/30 [CP]	1P: $79-$129	2P: $79-$129	XP: $10	F18
3/1-4/30 & 10/1-2/29 [CP]	1P: $69-$109	2P: $69-$109	XP: $10	F18

Location: I-44, exit 277B (Lindbergh Blvd), just n. Located in a commercial area. 1200 S Kirkwood Rd 63122. **Fax:** 314/984-9798. **Facility:** 113 one-bedroom standard units. 6 stories, interior corridors. **Parking:** on-site. **Terms:** 7 day cancellation notice, pets ($10 extra charge). **Amenities:** high-speed Internet, voice mail, irons, hair dryers. *Fee:* video games, safes. **Pool(s):** heated outdoor, wading. **Leisure Activities:** playground, limited exercise equipment. **Guest Services:** valet laundry, wireless Internet. **Business Services:** meeting rooms. **Cards:** AX, CB, DC, DS, JC, MC, VI.
SOME UNITS
(ASK) ⓢⒹ 🐾 ☷ ⍾ ▨ 🛥 ⊠ 🎥 ▦ / ▯ ▭ /
FEE

——— WHERE TO DINE ———

CITIZEN KANE'S   *Menu on AAA.com*   Dinner: $18-$29   Phone: 314/965-9005   114
AAA
▼▼▼
American
Location: I-44, exit 277B (Lindbergh Blvd), 1.2 mi n, then just w. 133 W Clinton Pl 63122. **Hours:** 5 pm-9 pm, Fri & Sat-10 pm. Closed: 1/1, 11/22, 12/24, 12/25; also Sun & Mon. **Reservations:** suggested. **Features:** Steak reigns so supreme in this house that even the soup selection includes steak soup. However, the menu also offers fish and fowl choices. Entrees come with soup, salad and a vegetable. Professional, polished service avoids being overly personal. Casual dress; cocktails. **Parking:** on-site. **Cards:** AX, DC, DS, MC, VI.

(See map and index starting on p. 514)

SUNSET 44   **Lunch: $6-$10**   **Dinner: $12-$25**   **Phone:** 314/965-6644   (T

American

Location: I-44, exit 277B (Lindbergh Blvd), 1.7 mi n, then just w; in Adams Place Plaza. 118 W Adams Ave 63* **Hours:** 11:30 am-9:30 pm, Fri-10 pm, Sat 5 pm-10 pm, Sun 9 am-1 & 4:30-8 pm, Mon 4 pm-9 pm. Clos 12/25. **Reservations:** suggested. **Features:** The restaurant sustains a casually elegant atmosphere a light, airy decor. Among preparations on the award-winning menu are braised short ribs of beef, Italian b tenderloin, Atlantic salmon and crab cakes. Service is friendly, casual and efficient. Casual dress; cocktails. **Parking:** on-s **Cards:** AX, CB, DC, DS, JC, MC, VI.

MAPLEWOOD pop. 9,228 (See map and index starting on p. 514)

—— **WHERE TO DINE** ——

MONARCH RESTUARANT   **Lunch: $9-$14**   **Dinner: $16-$26**   **Phone:** 314/644-3995   (T

International

Location: At Manchester and Sutton rds; downtown. 7401 Manchester Rd 63143. **Hours:** 11 am-2 & 5-11 pm, I midnight, Sat 5 pm-midnight. Closed: Sun. **Reservations:** suggested. **Features:** International cuisine sho French overtones. The sophisticated establishment offers both bistro and fine-dining experiences. Dre casual; cocktails. **Parking:** on-site and valet. **Cards:** AX, CB, DC, DS, JC, MC, VI.

MARYLAND HEIGHTS pop. 25,756 (See map and index starting on p. 514)

—— **WHERE TO STAY** ——

DOUBLETREE HOTEL ST. LOUIS AT WESTPORT   *Book great rates at AAA.com*   **Phone:** 314/434-0100

Property failed to provide current rates

Small-scale Hotel

Location: I-270, exit 16A (Page Ave), just e to Lackland Rd, then 0.4 mi sw on Lackland and Craigshire rds. 1 Craigshire Rd 63146. **Fax:** 314/434-5067. **Facility:** 327 one-bedroom standard units, some with whirlpools. stories, interior corridors. *Bath:* combo or shower only. **Parking:** on-site. **Terms:** pets ($50 fe **Amenities:** high-speed Internet, dual phone lines, voice mail, irons, hair dryers. *Some:* video games (fee). **Pool(s):** hea indoor. **Leisure Activities:** whirlpool, exercise room. **Guest Services:** valet laundry, area transportation. **Business Servic** conference facilities, business center.

SOME UN

DRURY INN & SUITES-ST. LOUIS-WESTPORT   *Book great rates at AAA.com*   **Phone:** (314)576-9966

All Year [BP]   1P: $66-$120   2P: $76-$130   XP: $10

Small-scale Hotel

Location: I-270, exit 17 (Dorsett Rd), just se. Located in a commercial area. 12220 Dorsett Rd 630 **Fax:** 314/576-9966. **Facility:** 125 units. 119 one-bedroom standard units. 6 one-bedroom suites ($1 $150). 4 stories, interior corridors. **Parking:** on-site. **Terms:** small pets only. **Amenities:** high-spe Internet, voice mail, irons, hair dryers. **Pool(s):** outdoor. **Leisure Activities:** exercise room. **Guest Services:** compliment evening beverages, valet and coin laundry. **Business Services:** meeting rooms, business center. **Cards:** AX, CB, DC, D MC, VI.

SOME UN

HAMPTON INN WESTPORT   *Book great rates at AAA.com*   **Phone:** (314)298-7878

All Year [BP]   1P: $139-$159   2P: $144-$164   XP: $5

Small-scale Hotel

Location: I-270, exit 17 (Dorsett Rd), just ne. Located in a commercial area. 2454 Old Dorsett Rd 630 **Fax:** 314/298-7429. **Facility:** 122 one-bedroom standard units. 4-5 stories, interior corridors. **Parking:** site. **Terms:** cancellation fee imposed, package plans. **Amenities:** high-speed Internet, voice mail, iro hair dryers. **Pool(s):** small outdoor. **Leisure Activities:** exercise room. **Guest Services:** valet laundry, area transportatio wireless Internet. **Business Services:** meeting rooms. **Cards:** AX, CB, DC, DS, JC, MC, VI. *(See color ad below)*

SOME UN

(See map and index starting on p. 514)

HARRAH'S ST. LOUIS CASINO & HOTEL — *Book at AAA.com* — **Phone:** (314)770-8100   33
▼▼✧✧▼ All Year   1P: $79-$369   2P: $79-$369   XP: $20   F17
Location: I-70, exit 231A (Earth City Expwy S), 1 mi s to Casino Center Dr, then 1.2 mi nw. 777 Casino Center Dr
Large-scale Hotel 63043. **Fax:** 314/770-8399. **Facility:** 502 units. 466 one-bedroom standard units. 36 one-bedroom suites
($129-$599), some with whirlpools. 8-11 stories, interior corridors. *Bath:* combo or shower only. **Parking:** on-
site and valet. **Terms:** check-in 4 pm, cancellation fee imposed, [BP] meal plan, package plans. **Amenities:** high-
speed Internet (fee), dual phone lines, voice mail, irons, hair dryers. *Some:* DVD players, CD players, safes. **Dining:** Town
Square Buffet, see separate listing. **Leisure Activities:** exercise room. **Guest Services:** gift shop, valet laundry. **Business
Services:** conference facilities. **Cards:** AX, CB, DC, DS, JC, MC, VI.

SOME UNITS
(ASK) [icons] / X /

HOLIDAY INN EXPRESS/RIVERPORT — *Book at AAA.com* — **Phone:** (314)298-3400   32
▼▼✧✧▼ All Year [CP]   1P: $79-$129   2P: $79-$129
Location: I-70, exit 231A (Earth City Expwy), 0.3 mi s. Located in Riverport Commercial Development. 13735 Riverport
Small-scale Hotel Dr 63043. **Fax:** 314/298-9646. **Facility:** 177 one-bedroom standard units. 6 stories, interior corridors. *Bath:*
combo or shower only. **Parking:** on-site. **Terms:** check-in 4 pm, cancellation fee imposed, [AP] & [BP] meal
plans available. **Amenities:** video games (fee), high-speed Internet, dual phone lines, voice mail, irons, hair dryers.
Dining: Kriegers Pub & Grill, see separate listing. **Pool(s):** small outdoor. **Leisure Activities:** sauna, whirlpool, exercise room.
Guest Services: valet and coin laundry, area transportation. **Business Services:** meeting rooms, business center. **Cards:** AX,
CB, DC, DS, JC, MC, VI.

SOME UNITS
(ASK) (SD) [icons] / X /

SHERATON (WEST PORT) HOTEL-LAKESIDE
CHALET — *Book great rates at AAA.com* — **Phone:** (314)878-1500   36
(AAA) (SAVE)   All Year   1P: $89-$229
▼▼✧✧▼ **Location:** I-270, exit 16A (Page Ave), 0.8 mi e to Lackland Rd exit, just w to Craig Rd, then 0.4 mi n. Located in the
Westport Plaza Shopping Center. 191 Westport Plaza Dr 63146. **Fax:** 314/878-2837. **Facility:** 300 units. 293 one-
Large-scale Hotel bedroom standard units. 7 one-bedroom suites. 4-6 stories, interior corridors. *Bath:* combo or shower only.
Parking: on-site. **Terms:** [AP] & [BP] meal plans available, package plans. **Amenities:** dual phone lines,
voice mail, irons, hair dryers. *Fee:* video games, high-speed Internet. **Dining:** 6:30 am-2 & 5-11 pm,
cocktails. **Pool(s):** small heated outdoor. **Leisure Activities:** exercise room. **Guest Services:** sundries, valet laundry, area
transportation-within 5 mi. **Business Services:** conference facilities, business center. **Cards:** AX, DC, DS, MC, VI.
(See color ad below)

SOME UNITS
[icons] / X /

(See map and index starting on p. 514)

THE SHERATON (WEST PORT) PLAZA TOWER   *Book great rates at AAA.com*   Phone: (314)878-1500

 (SAVE)   All Year   1P: $89-$219
Location: I-270, exit 16A (Page Ave), 0.8 mi e, exit Lackland Rd, just w to Craig Rd, then 0.4 mi n. Located in Westport Plaza Shopping Center. 900 Westport Plaza Dr 63146. **Fax:** 314/434-0140. **Facility:** 210 one-bedro standard units. 12 stories, interior corridors. *Bath:* combo or shower only. **Parking:** on-site. **Terms:** [
Large-scale Hotel   meal plan available, package plans, 14% service charge. **Amenities:** dual phone lines, voice mail, iro hair dryers. *Fee:* video games, high-speed Internet. **Dining:** 6:30 am-2 pm. **Pool(s):** small heated indo
Leisure Activities: sauna, whirlpool, exercise room. **Guest Services:** sundries, valet laundry, area transportation-within 5
Business Services: conference facilities, business center. **Cards:** AX, DC, DS, MC, VI. *(See color ad p 545)*

SOME UNIT

STAYBRIDGE SUITES   *Book at AAA.com*   Phone: 314/878-1555
Property failed to provide current rates
Location: I-270, exit 16A (Page Ave), 0.8 mi e, exit Lackland Rd, 1 mi w, then s via Lackland and Craigshire rds. 18
Small-scale Hotel   Craigshire Rd 63146. **Fax:** 314/878-9203. **Facility:** 106 units. 58 one-bedroom standard units with kitchen
48 two-bedroom suites with kitchens. 2 stories (no elevator), interior/exterior corridors. *Bath:* combo
shower only. **Parking:** on-site. **Terms:** pets ($100 extra charge). **Amenities:** video library (fee), DVD players, CD players, hi
speed Internet, voice mail, irons, hair dryers. *Some:* dual phone lines. **Pool(s):** outdoor. **Leisure Activities:** whirlpool, exerc
room, sports court. **Guest Services:** sundries, complimentary evening beverages: Tues-Thurs, valet and coin laundry, wirele
Internet. **Business Services:** meeting rooms, business center.

SOME UN

FEE

─────── *The following lodging was either not evaluated or did not* ───────
meet AAA rating requirements but is listed for your information only.

COURTYARD BY MARRIOTT-WESTPORT   Phone: 314/997-12
[fyi]   Did not meet all AAA rating requirements for some property operations at time of last evaluation
02/23/2006. **Location:** I-270, exit 16A (Page Ave), 0.8 mi e, exit Lackland Rd, just w to Craig Rd, 0.4 mi n to Westf
Small-scale Hotel   Industrial Dr, then 1.3 mi e. 11888 Westline Industrial Dr 63146. Facilities, services, and decor characterize a mid-ran property.

─────── **WHERE TO DINE** ───────

DIERDORF & HARTS STEAKHOUSE   **Dinner:** $18-$43   Phone: 314/878-1801
Location: I-270, exit 16A (Page Ave), 0.8 mi e to Lackland Rd exit, just w to Craig Rd, then 0.4 mi n; in center
Westport Plaza Shopping Center. 323 Westport Plaza 63146. **Hours:** 4:30 pm-9:30 pm, Fri & Sat-10:30 pm, Sur
East Steak House   pm. Closed major holidays. **Reservations:** suggested. **Features:** Owned by former St. Louis Cardi
football players Dan Dierdorf and Jim Hart, this restaurant proves they know food as well as they kn
football. Prime beef and fresh seafood are of the finest quality—all prepared to perfection and served in a restaurant w
dressy, masculine decor. Service is as highly polished as the glassware and silverware. Dressy casual; cocktails. **Parking:** o
site. **Cards:** AX, CB, DC, DS, MC, VI.

THE DRUNKEN FISH SUSHI BAR AND LOUNGE   **Lunch:** $9-$14   **Dinner:** $10-$24   Phone: 314/275-8300
Location: I-270, exit 16A (Page Ave), 0.8 mi e to Lackland Rd, just n to Craig Rd, then 0.4 mi n; in southwest end
Westport Plaza Shopping Center. 639 Westport Plaza 63146. **Hours:** 11 am-2 & 5-midnight, Sat & Sun 5 pm-
Japanese   pm. Closed: 5/28, 7/4, 12/25. **Reservations:** accepted. **Features:** The cozy, contemporary a
sophisticated restaurant serves sushi and other Japanese specialties. Casual dress; cocktails. **Parking:** o
site. **Cards:** AX, DC, DS, MC, VI.

KRIEGER'S   **Lunch:** $7-$15   **Dinner:** $7-$15   Phone: 314/878-15
Location: I-270, exit 17 (Dorsett Rd), 0.3 mi sw. 12664 Dorsett Rd 63043. **Hours:** 11 am-midnight, Fri & Sat-1 a
Sun-11 pm. Closed major holidays. **Features:** The sports bar and restaurant caters to the business lur
American   crowd and sports enthusiasts. The atmosphere is casual, and the menu variety is good. Among choices
toasted ravioli, thin-crust pizza, burgers and chicken. Casual dress; cocktails. **Parking:** on-site. **Cards:** A
DC, DS, MC, VI.

KRIEGERS PUB & GRILL   **Lunch:** $7-$14   **Dinner:** $7-$14   Phone: 314/292-00
Location: I-70, exit 231A (Earth City Expwy), 0.3 mi s; in Holiday Inn Airport/Riverport. 13735 Riverport Dr 630
Hours: 6:30 am-11 pm. Closed: 1/1, 11/22, 12/25. **Features:** The sports bar and restaurant caters to t
American   business lunch crowd and sports enthusiasts. The atmosphere is casual, and the menu variety is goo
Among choices are toasted ravioli, thin-crust pizza, burgers and chicken. Casual dress; cocktails. **Parkin**
on-site. **Cards:** AX, CB, DC, DS, JC, MC, VI.

MARCIANO'S   **Lunch:** $7-$10   **Dinner:** $9-$19   Phone: 314/878-8180
Location: I-270, exit 16A (Page Ave), 0.8 mi e, exit Lackland Rd, just w to Craig Rd, then 0.4 mi n. 333 Westport Pla
63146. **Hours:** 11 am-10:30 pm, Fri-11 pm, Sat noon-11 pm, Sun 4 pm-9 pm. Closed: 1/1, 11/22, 12/25; a
Italian   Sun. **Reservations:** accepted. **Features:** The casual, colorful mix of old world and light contemporary
popular with the business lunch crowd. Dressy casual; cocktails. **Parking:** on-site. **Cards:** AX, CB, DC, D
JC, MC, VI.

OZZIE'S RESTAURANT & SPORTS BAR   **Lunch:** $6-$22   **Dinner:** $6-$22   Phone: 314/434-1000
Location: 0.8 mi e to Lackland Rd, just n to Craig Rd, then 0.4 mi n; in southwest end of Westport Plaza Shopp
Center. 645 Westport Plaza 63146. **Hours:** 11 am-11 pm, Fri & Sat-midnight, Sun-10 pm. Closed: 12/2
American   **Reservations:** accepted. **Features:** Ozzie's offers a wide variety of salad, grilled chicken, fajitas, pas
appetizers and soup. The sporty, enjoyable atmosphere becomes louder when a popular game is bei
played. Families, business professionals and couples like this place. Casual dress; cocktails. **Parking:** on-site. **Cards:** AX, C
DS, MC, VI.

(See map and index starting on p. 514)

OWN SQUARE BUFFET **Lunch:** $9 **Dinner:** $13 **Phone:** 314/770-8100 **44**
▼▼ ▼▼ **Location:** I-70, exit 231 (Earth City Expwy), 1 mi s to Casino Center Dr, then 1.2 mi nw; in Harrah's St. Louis Casino &
American Hotel. 777 Casino Center Dr 63043. **Hours:** 7-10:30 am, 11-3 & 4:30-10 pm, Sat & Sun 7:30 am-3 & 4:30-10
pm. **Features:** Patrons can choose from a large selection of familiar, well-prepared favorites. The food is a
feast for the eyes and the stomach. Casual dress; beer & wine only. **Parking:** on-site. **Cards:** AX, CB, DC,
S, JC, MC, VI.

RAINWRECK SALOON WESTPORT **Lunch:** $7-$15 **Dinner:** $7-$15 **Phone:** 314/434-7222 **47**
▼▼ ▼▼ **Location:** I-270, exit 16A (Page Ave), 0.8 mi e to Lackland Rd, just n to Craig Rd, then 0.4 mi n; in Westport Plaza
American Shopping Center. 314 Westport Plaza 63146. **Hours:** 11 am-10 pm. Closed major holidays; also Sun.
Features: Diners enjoy this place—from the antique bar to the swinging saloon doors to the running train
om. overhead. Old memorabilia, new satellite-fed TV screens and live music on weekends enliven the dining
om. The menu lists bison and ostrich burgers, salads, steaks and seafood. Try the famous St. Louis salad or sweet potato
es. Outdoor seating available in season. Patrons must be 21 or older after 9 pm. The non-smoking area is 50 percent at
nch, 25 percent at dinner and nonexistent after 10 pm. Casual dress; cocktails. **Parking:** on-site. **Cards:** AX, DS, MC, VI.

MEHLVILLE pop. 28,822 (See map and index starting on p. 514)

——— WHERE TO STAY ———

OLIDAY INN ST. LOUIS-SOUTH I-55 *Book at AAA.com* **Phone:** (314)894-0700 **96**
▼▼▼▼ All Year 1P: $89-$175 2P: $89-$175
Location: I-55, exit 195 (Butler Hill Rd), just se. 4234 Butler Hill Rd 63129. **Fax:** 314/894-0167. **Facility:** 163 units.
Small-scale Hotel 160 one-bedroom standard units. 3 one-bedroom suites. 2 stories (no elevator), interior/exterior corridors.
Bath: combo or shower only. **Parking:** on-site. **Terms:** pets ($50 deposit, with prior approval).
Amenities: video games (fee), high-speed Internet, dual phone lines, voice mail, irons, hair dryers. **Pool(s):** outdoor, heated
door, 2 wading. **Leisure Activities:** whirlpool, exercise room, shuffleboard. **Guest Services:** complimentary evening
everages: Wed, valet and coin laundry. **Business Services:** conference facilities, business center. **Cards:** AX, CB, DC, DS,
C, MC, VI.

SOME UNITS
(ASK) (S) (🐾) (🍴) (Y) (🖥) (📷) (🏊) (✕) (👤) (🖥) / (✕) (🔋) (📠) /
FEE

OLIDAY INN SOUTH COUNTY CENTER *Book at AAA.com* **Phone:** 314/892-3600 **95**
▼▼▼▼ Property failed to provide current rates
Location: I-55, exit 197 (Lindbergh Blvd), just e. Located adjacent to a shopping center. 6921 S Lindbergh Blvd 63125.
Small-scale Hotel Fax: 314/892-2091. **Facility:** 149 one-bedroom standard units. 4 stories, interior corridors. *Bath:* combo or
shower only. **Parking:** on-site. **Amenities:** video games (fee), high-speed Internet, dual phone lines, voice
ail, irons, hair dryers. **Pool(s):** heated indoor. **Leisure Activities:** whirlpool, exercise room. **Guest Services:** valet and coin
undry. **Business Services:** conference facilities, PC.

SOME UNITS
(🍴) (Y) (🖥) (📷) (🏊) (👤) (🖥) / (✕) (🔋) (📠) /

——— WHERE TO DINE ———

INGHAM'S HOMESTYLE RESTAURANT **Lunch:** $4-$7 **Dinner:** $5-$11 **Phone:** 314/487-2505 **124**
▼▼ **Location:** I-55, exit 197 (Lindbergh Blvd), 0.5 mi e. 7333 S Lindbergh Blvd 63125. **Hours:** 24 hours. Closed: 11/22,
American 12/25. **Features:** Enveloped in a country atmosphere, the locally popular restaurant features warm, family-
friendly dining. The menu lists a variety of home-style meals, including pancakes, omelets, burgers,
sandwiches and homemade pies. Seniors love this place. Casual dress. **Parking:** on-site. **Cards:** AX, DS,
C, VI.

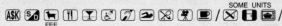

O'FALLON pop. 46,169   (See map and index starting on p. 511)

———— WHERE TO STAY ————

COUNTRY INN & SUITES   *Book great rates at AAA.com*   Phone: (636)300-4844
▼▼▼▼   All Year   1P: $86-$96   2P: $86-$96
       Location: I 64/US 40, exit 9 (CR K), just nw. 1175 Technology Dr 63368. **Fax:** 636/300-4944. **Facility:** 123 un
Small-scale Hotel 83 one-bedroom standard units, some with whirlpools. 40 one-bedroom suites ($96-$140). 4 stories, inte
       corridors. *Bath:* combo or shower only. **Parking:** on-site. **Terms:** small pets only. **Amenities:** high-spe
Internet, voice mail, irons, hair dryers. **Pool(s):** small heated indoor. **Leisure Activities:** whirlpool, exercise room. Gu
Services: valet and coin laundry, area transportation. **Business Services:** meeting rooms, business center. **Cards:** AX, C
DC, DS, MC, VI. *(See color ad below)*

SOME UNITS

HILTON GARDEN INN ST. LOUIS/O'FALLON   *Book great rates at AAA.com*   Phone: (636)625-2700
ⒶⒶⒶ SAVE   All Year   1P: $79-$149   2P: $79-$149   XP: $10
▼▼▼▼   **Location:** I-70, exit 216 (Bryan Rd), 4.2 mi s. 2310 Technology Dr 63368. **Fax:** 636/625-1776. **Facility:** 122 on
       bedroom standard units. 3 stories, interior corridors. *Bath:* combo or shower only. **Parking:** on-s
Small-scale Hotel **Terms:** [AP] & [BP] meal plans available, package plans. **Amenities:** video games (fee), high-spe
Internet, dual phone lines, voice mail, irons, hair dryers. **Dining:** 6:30-10 am, 11-2 & 5-10 pm, Sat & Sun
10 am. **Pool(s):** small heated indoor. **Leisure Activities:** whirlpool, exercise room. **Guest Service
sundries, complimentary evening beverages: Wed, valet and coin laundry. **Business Services:** meeting rooms, busine
center. **Cards:** AX, DC, DS, MC, VI. **Free Special Amenities: newspaper and high-speed Internet.**

SOME UN

STAYBRIDGE SUITES O'FALLON   *Book at AAA.com*   Phone: (636)300-0999
▼▼▼▼   All Year   1P: $109-$259   2P: $109-$259
       Location: I 64/US 40, exit 9 (CR K), just nw. 1155 Technology Dr 63368. **Fax:** 636/300-0998. **Facility:** 97 units.
Small-scale Hotel one-bedroom standard units with efficiencies. 40 one- and 12 two-bedroom suites ($109-$259) w
       efficiencies. 3 stories, interior corridors. *Bath:* combo or shower only. **Parking:** on-site. **Terms:** cancellati
fee imposed, pets ($100 extra charge). **Amenities:** DVD players, high-speed Internet, dual phone lines, voice mail, irons, h
dryers. **Pool(s):** heated outdoor. **Leisure Activities:** exercise room. **Guest Services:** sundries, complimentary eveni
beverages: Tues-Thurs, valet and coin laundry, area transportation. **Business Services:** meeting rooms, business cent
Cards: AX, CB, DC, DS, JC, MC, VI.

SOME UN

———— WHERE TO DINE ————

J. BUCK'S RESTAURANT   **Lunch:** $10-$15   **Dinner:** $15-$26   Phone: 636/329-0070
▼▼▼▼   **Location:** I-64/US 40, exit 9 (CR K), just nw. 1165 Technology Dr 63368. **Hours:** 11 am-10 pm, Fri & Sat-11 p
       Closed: 1/1, 11/22, 12/25; also Sun. **Reservations:** accepted. **Features:** Sophisticated and contempora
American decor distinguishes this sleek setting, which celebrates some of baseball's greats. The menu lines up fre
       and innovative offerings. Casual dress; cocktails. **Parking:** on-site. **Cards:** AX, CB, DC, DS, JC, MC, VI.

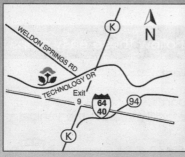

OVERLAND pop. 16,838   (See map and index starting on p. 514)

—— WHERE TO DINE ——

MANDARIN HOUSE RESTAURANT　　**Lunch:** $6-$8　　**Dinner:** $7-$17　　**Phone:** 314/427-8070　59
▼▼▼ **Location:** I-170, exit 4 (Page Ave), just w; in Overland Plaza Shopping Center. 9150 Overland Plaza 63114.
Mandarin　**Hours:** 11:30 am-2 & 5-9 pm, Fri & Sat-10 pm, Sun 11:30 am-2 & 4:30-9 pm. Closed major holidays.
Reservations: accepted. **Features:** Very popular locally, features a dramatic entry with mini-pagoda and
decorative bridge. Pleasant dining in spacious setting. An unexpected treat. Casual dress; cocktails.
Parking: on-site. **Cards:** AX, MC, VI.　　　　　　　　　　　　　　　　　　　　　　　　　　　　　　［N］

RICHMOND HEIGHTS pop. 9,602   (See map and index starting on p. 514)

—— WHERE TO STAY ——

RESIDENCE INN BY MARRIOTT-ST. LOUIS
GALLERIA　*Book great rates at AAA.com*　　　　　　　　　　　　　**Phone:** (314)862-1900　68
(AAA) [SAVE]　All Year　　　　　　1P: $99-$169　　　　2P: $99-$169
▼▼▼　**Location:** I-170, exit 1C (Brentwood Ave) northbound; exit southbound, 0.5 mi e of Galleria via Galleria Pkwy. 1100
McMorrow Ave 63117. **Fax:** 314/862-5621. **Facility:** Smoke free premises. 152 units. 114 one-bedroom
Small-scale Hotel　standard units with kitchens. 38 one-bedroom suites ($119-$199) with kitchens. 2 stories (no elevator),
exterior corridors. *Bath:* combo or shower only. **Parking:** on-site. **Terms:** weekly rates available, [BP] meal
plan available, pets ($75 fee). **Amenities:** video games (fee), high-speed Internet, voice mail, irons, hair
dryers. **Pool(s):** heated outdoor. **Leisure Activities:** whirlpool, exercise room, sports court. **Guest Services:** complimentary
evening beverages: Mon-Thurs, valet and coin laundry, wireless Internet. **Business Services:** meeting rooms, PC. **Cards:** AX,
CB, DC, DS, JC, MC, VI. **Free Special Amenities: full breakfast and high-speed Internet.**

[S/D] [🐾] [📶] [♿M] [♿] [🌀] [🏊] [🍴] [🖼] [📷] [🔌] [💻] [📺]
　　　FEE

—— WHERE TO DINE ——

HARVEST　　　　　　**Dinner:** $18-$28　　　　　　**Phone:** 314/645-3522　93
▼▼▼　**Location:** I-64/US 40, exit 33B, 0.3 mi n. 1059 S Big Bend Blvd 63117. **Hours:** 5:30 pm-9:30 pm, Fri & Sat-10 pm,
Sun 5 pm-9 pm. Closed major holidays; also Mon. **Reservations:** suggested. **Features:** Food is king at the
Nouvelle American　sophisticated restaurant. Executive chef-owner Stephen Gontram delights in using the freshest seasonal
produce to create innovative American cuisine. He starts with the ordinary, then pairs and prepares it in
unusual ways to produce results that are anything but ordinary. The menu changes frequently, but the level of creativity does
not. Dressy casual; cocktails. **Parking:** on-site. **Cards:** AX, DC, DS, MC, VI.
　　　［Y］

ST. ANN pop. 13,607   (See map and index starting on p. 514)

—— WHERE TO STAY ——

HAMPTON INN-ST. LOUIS AIRPORT　　*Book great rates at AAA.com*　　　**Phone:** (314)429-2000　29
▼▼▼　All Year [BP]　　　　　1P: $99-$155　　　　2P: $109-$165　　　　XP: $10　　F18
Location: I-70, exit 236 (Airport Dr), just sw. 10820 Pear Tree Ln 63074. **Fax:** 314/423-7765. **Facility:** 99 one-
Small-scale Hotel　bedroom standard units. 5 stories, interior corridors. *Bath:* combo or shower only. **Parking:** on-site.
Terms: small pets only. **Amenities:** high-speed Internet, voice mail, irons, hair dryers. **Pool(s):** outdoor.
Leisure Activities: exercise room. **Guest Services:** valet laundry. **Business Services:** meeting rooms, business center.
Cards: AX, CB, DC, DS, MC, VI.
　　　　　　　　　　　　　　　　　　　　　　　　　　　　　SOME UNITS
[ASK] [✈] [🐾] [🏊] [🍴] [🔌] [💻] [📺] [✕]

PEAR TREE INN BY DRURY-ST. LOUIS AIRPORT　*Book great rates at AAA.com*　**Phone:** (314)427-3400　28
▼▼▼　All Year [ECP]　　　　　1P: $66-$124　　　　2P: $76-$134　　　　XP: $10　　F18
Location: I-70, exit 236 (Airport Dr), just sw. 10810 Pear Tree Ln 63074. **Fax:** 314/427-3400. **Facility:** 155 one-
Small-scale Hotel　bedroom standard units. 4 stories, interior corridors. **Parking:** on-site. **Amenities:** high-speed Internet, voice
mail, irons, hair dryers. **Pool(s):** outdoor. **Guest Services:** valet laundry. **Business Services:** meeting
rooms. **Cards:** AX, CB, DC, DS, MC, VI.
　　　　　　　　　　　　　　　　　　　　　　　　　　　　　SOME UNITS
[ASK] [✈] [🐾] [🏊] [📷] [💻] [✕] [🔌] [📺]

—— WHERE TO DINE ——

BANDANA'S　　　　**Lunch:** $5-$10　　　**Dinner:** $5-$10　　　**Phone:** 314/426-9955
▼▼▼　**Location:** I-70, exit 236 (Airport Dr), just sw. 10800 Pear Tree Ln 63074. **Hours:** 11 am-9 pm, Fri & Sat-10 pm.
American　Closed: 11/22, 12/25. **Features:** The real wood-pit smoker produces tasty meats. Guests might want to try
hot boiled peanuts, a Southern favorite, as a side item. Casual dress; beer & wine only. **Parking:** on-site.
Cards: AX, DS, MC, VI.
　　　　　　　　　　　　　　　　　　　　　　　　　　　　　　　　　　　　［♿M］［N］

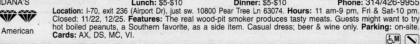

ST. CHARLES pop. 60,321   (See map and index starting on p. 511)

———— WHERE TO STAY ————

BEST WESTERN ST. CHARLES INN   *Book great rates at AAA.com*   Phone: (636)947-5900

(AAA) (SAVE)   5/1-9/30 [CP]   1P: $79-$150   XP: $10   F
▼▼▼▼   3/1-4/30 & 10/1-2/29 [CP]   1P: $79-$109   2P: $79-$109   XP: $10   F
Small-scale Hotel   **Location:** I-70, exit 229B (5th St N), just n to St. Charles Center Dr, then just w. Located in Mark Twain Mall, adjacent
Bass Pro Shop. 1377 S 5th St 63301. Fax: 636/947-7212. **Facility:** 64 one-bedroom standard units, some w
whirlpools. 3 stories, interior corridors. *Bath:* combo or shower only. **Parking:** on-site. **Amenities:** hig
indoor. **Leisure Activities:** exercise room. **Guest Services:** coin laundry. **Business Services:** PC. **Cards:** AX, CB, DC, D
MC, VI. **Free Special Amenities:** expanded continental breakfast and high-speed Internet.

SOME UNITS

BOONE'S LICK TRAIL INN BED & BREAKFAST   Phone: (636)947-7000
▼▼▼▼   All Year   1P: $105-$175   2P: $115-$215   XP: $45   D
Bed & Breakfast   **Location:** Downtown. Located in the historic district. 1000 S Main St 63301. Fax: 636/946-2637. **Facility:**
traditional Federal-style inn built in the 1840s, this brick home is near the Missouri River, within walki
distance of shops and restaurants. 7 units. 6 one-bedroom standard units. 1 cottage ($165-$315) wi
whirlpool. 2-3 stories (no elevator), interior/exterior corridors. *Bath:* combo or shower only. **Parking:** on-site. **Terms:** check-
3:30 pm, 10 day cancellation notice-fee imposed, package plans. **Amenities:** high-speed Internet, voice mail, irons, hair dryer
Some: DVD players, CD players. **Guest Services:** wireless Internet. **Business Services:** PC. **Cards:** AX, CB, DC, DS, J
MC, VI.

SOME UNITS

(See map and index starting on p. 511)

COMFORT SUITES-ST. CHARLES — *Book great rates at AAA.com* — **Phone:** (636)949-0694 — **11**
WWWW — All Year [BP] — 1P: $90-$125 — 2P: $100-$130 — XP: $5 — F18
Small-scale Hotel — **Location:** I-70, exit 229 (5th St), just ne. 1400 S 5th St 63301. Fax: 636/949-0697. **Facility:** 71 units. 69 one- and 1 two-bedroom standard units, some with whirlpools. 1 one-bedroom suite ($150-$250) with whirlpool. 3 stories, interior corridors. *Bath:* combo or shower only. **Parking:** on-site. **Amenities:** high-speed Internet, voice mail, safes (fee), irons, hair dryers. **Pool(s):** small heated indoor. **Leisure Activities:** exercise room. **Guest Services:** complimentary evening beverages: Mon-Thurs, valet and coin laundry. **Business Services:** business center. **Cards:** AX, CB, DC, DS, MC, VI.
SOME UNITS

COUNTRY INN & SUITES ST. CHARLES — *Book great rates at AAA.com* — **Phone:** (636)724-5555 — **9**
(AAA) [SAVE] — All Year — 1P: $92-$99 — 2P: $92-$99 — XP: $8 — F17
WWWW — **Location:** I-70, exit 229A (5th St S), to S Main St, then 0.7 mi ne. 1190 S Main St 63301. Fax: 636/724-5557.
Small-scale Hotel — **Facility:** 86 units. 53 one-bedroom standard units, some with whirlpools. 33 one-bedroom suites ($112-$129). 3 stories, interior corridors. *Bath:* combo or shower only. **Parking:** on-site. **Terms:** 3 day cancellation notice-fee imposed, weekly rates available, package plans, small pets only (with prior approval). **Amenities:** high-speed Internet, dual phone lines, voice mail, irons, hair dryers. **Pool(s):** small heated indoor. **Leisure Activities:** whirlpool, adjacent to Katy Trail, rental bicycles, exercise room. **Guest Services:** valet and coin laundry. **Business Services:** business center. **Cards:** AX, CB, DC, DS, MC, VI. *(See color ad p 550)*
SOME UNITS

EMBASSY SUITES ST. LOUIS-ST. CHARLES — *Book great rates at AAA.com* — **Phone:** (636)946-5544 — **10**
(AAA) [SAVE] — 6/15-2/29 — 1P: $119-$219 — XP: $10 — F18
WWWW — **Location:** I-70, exit 229A (5th St S), just s to Veterans Memorial Pkwy, then just w. Lcoated adjacent to St. Charles Memorial Convention Center. Two Convention Center Plaza 63303. Fax: 636/946-5577. **Facility:** 296 one-bedroom Small-scale Hotel suites ($119-$219), some with whirlpools. 12 stories, interior corridors. *Bath:* combo or shower only. **Parking:** on-site. **Terms:** open 6/15-2/29, cancellation fee imposed. **Amenities:** high-speed Internet (fee), dual phone lines, voice mail, safes, irons, hair dryers. **Dining:** 11 am-10 pm, cocktails. **Pool(s):** small heated indoor. **Leisure Activities:** whirlpool, exercise room, spa. **Guest Services:** gift shop, complimentary evening beverages, valet and coin laundry, area transportation-within 3 mi. **Business Services:** conference facilities, business center. **Cards:** AX, CB, DC, DS, MC, VI. **Free Special Amenities:** full breakfast and newspaper. *(See color ad p 550)*
SOME UNITS

HAMPTON INN — *Book great rates at AAA.com* — **Phone:** (636)947-6800 — **4**
WWWW — All Year — 1P: $89-$114 — 2P: $89-$114
Small-scale Hotel — **Location:** I-70, exit 225 (Cave Springs), 0.5 mi e. 3720 W Clay St 63301. Fax: 636/947-0020. **Facility:** 123 one-bedroom standard units. 4 stories, interior corridors. *Bath:* combo or shower only. **Parking:** on-site, winter plug-ins. **Terms:** [ECP] meal plan available, package plans. **Amenities:** video games (fee), high-speed Internet, voice mail, irons, hair dryers. **Pool(s):** heated indoor. **Leisure Activities:** whirlpool, exercise room. **Guest Services:** valet laundry. **Business Services:** meeting rooms, PC. **Cards:** AX, DC, DS, MC, VI.
SOME UNITS

SUPER 8 MOTEL — *Book at AAA.com* — **Phone:** (636)946-9992 — **5**
WW — 5/1-9/30 — 1P: $59-$75 — 2P: $69-$79 — XP: $5 — F17
— 10/1-11/30 — 1P: $55-$65 — 2P: $65-$75 — XP: $5 — F17
Small-scale Hotel — 3/1-4/30 — 1P: $49-$59 — 2P: $59-$65 — XP: $5 — F17
— 12/1-2/29 — 1P: $45-$59 — 2P: $55-$65 — XP: $5 — F17
Location: I-70, exit 227 (Zumbehl Rd), 0.3 mi w. 3040 W Clay St 63301. Fax: 636/724-1095. **Facility:** 52 one-bedroom standard units. 3 stories, interior corridors. **Parking:** on-site. **Amenities:** high-speed Internet, hair dryers. **Pool(s):** small heated indoor. **Leisure Activities:** whirlpool. **Cards:** AX, DC, DS, MC, VI.
SOME UNITS

TOWNEPLACE SUITES BY MARRIOTT — *Book great rates at AAA.com* — **Phone:** 636/949-6800 — **6**
WWW — 5/1-10/31 — 1P: $99-$144 — 2P: $99-$144
— 3/1-4/30 & 11/1-2/29 — 1P: $89-$134 — 2P: $89-$134
Small-scale Hotel — **Location:** I-70, exit 227 (Zumbehl Rd), 0.6 mi s. 1800 Zumbehl Rd 63303. Fax: 636/949-2121. **Facility:** Smoke free premises. 95 units. 69 one-bedroom standard units with kitchens. 4 one- and 22 two-bedroom suites with efficiencies. 3 stories, interior corridors. *Bath:* combo or shower only. **Parking:** on-site. **Amenities:** high-speed Internet, voice mail, irons, hair dryers. **Dining:** restaurant, see separate listing. **Pool(s):** outdoor. **Leisure Activities:** exercise room, basketball. **Guest Services:** valet and coin laundry. **Business Services:** meeting rooms, PC. **Cards:** AX, DC, DS, JC, MC, VI.

WHERE TO DINE

7 PORT STREET GRILL — **Dinner:** $15-$25 — **Phone:** 636/940-4471 — **9**
WWW — **Location:** I-70, exit 228 (First Capitol), 1.3 mi ne; in Ameristar Casino St. Charles. 1260 S Main St 63301. **Hours:** 5
American — pm-10 pm, Fri & Sat-11 pm. **Reservations:** suggested. **Features:** The restaurant fosters a fine-dining atmosphere in a tasteful, intimate room of cherry wood and etched glass. For starters, try the spring rolls. Valet parking is validated for diners. Casual dress; cocktails. **Parking:** on-site. **Cards:** AX, CB, DC, DS, JC, MC, VI.

THE FALCON DINER — **Lunch:** $5-$10 — **Dinner:** $8-$15 — **Phone:** 636/940-4955 — **8**
WW — **Location:** I-70, exit 228 (First Capitol), 1.3 mi ne; in Ameristar Casino St. Charles. 1260 S Main St 63301. **Hours:** 7
American — am-3 am, Fri & Sat 24 hrs. **Features:** The contemporary, retro-style diner specializes in Midwestern favorites. The menu lists appetizers, soups, salads, barbecue, seafood, pasta, sandwiches, burgers and breakfast items. Casual dress; cocktails. **Parking:** on-site. **Cards:** AX, CB, DC, DS, JC, MC, VI.

(See map and index starting on p. 511)

THE LANDMARK BUFFET **Lunch:** $9-$13   **Dinner:** $15-$18   **Phone:** 636/940-4470 ⑦
▼▼ ▼▼ **Location:** I-70, exit 228 (First Capitol), 1.3 mi ne; in Ameristar Casino St. Charles. 1260 S Main St 63301. **Hours:** 1
American am-2 & 4-9:30 pm, Sat & Sun 9:30 am-3 & 4-9:30 pm. **Features:** Among the generous options onboard th
glittering casino riverboat are prime rib, steak, crab legs and shrimp. The restaurant is popular wit
gamblers, but the international buffet is a good enough draw on its own. Casual dress; cocktails. **Parkin**
on-site. **Cards:** AX, CB, DC, DS, JC, MC, VI.

LEWIS AND CLARK'S AN AMERICAN RESTAURANT
& PUBLIC HOUSE **Lunch:** $7-$20   **Dinner:** $7-$20   **Phone:** 636/947-3334 ②
▼▼ ▼▼ **Location:** In historic Old Town. 217 S Main St 63301. **Hours:** 11 am-10 pm, Fri & Sat-11 pm
American **Reservations:** accepted. **Features:** Located in the Historic Main Street District, Lewis and Clark's feature
a good variety of prime rib, seafood and pasta dishes as well as Mexican and Creole food. The buildin
dates back to the mid-1800s and its third-floor balcony is quite popular. Casual dress; cocktails. **Parkin**
street. **Cards:** AX, CB, DC, DS, MC, VI.

MAGPIE'S **Lunch:** $6-$10   **Dinner:** $10-$22   **Phone:** 636/947-3883 ⑤
▼▼ ▼▼ **Location:** Downtown; in historic Old Town. 903 S Main St 63301. **Hours:** 11 am-3 pm; Fri & Sat-9 pm in seaso
American weather permitting. Closed major holidays. **Features:** The circa 1821 building is cozy and casual. On th
eclectic menu are daily specials, as well as soups, salads, quiche, crepes, sandwiches, steaks, chicken, fis
and homemade desserts. Outdoor seating is available in season. Casual dress; cocktails. **Parking:** stree
Cards: MC, VI. **Historic**

MR. STEAK **Lunch:** $7-$19   **Dinner:** $7-$19   **Phone:** 636/946-7444 ⑦
▼ **Location:** I-70, exit 228 (First Capitol), 1 mi w on service road (Bogey Rd). 2731 Veterans Memorial Pkwy 6330:
American **Hours:** 10:30 am-10 pm, Fri & Sat-11 pm. Closed: 11/22, 12/25. **Features:** The long-time family-owned an
operated business offers no pretentions, just good food in a comfortable atmosphere. Casual dres
Parking: on-site. **Cards:** AX, DC, DS, MC, VI.

THE NEW MOTHER-IN-LAW HOUSE
RESTAURANT *Menu on AAA.com* **Lunch:** $7-$8   **Dinner:** $12-$20   **Phone:** 636/946-9444 ④
ⒶⒶⒶ **Location:** Main St at Tomkins; in historic Old Town. 500 S Main St 63301. **Hours:** 11 am-2:30 & 5:30-9:30 pm
▼▼ ▼▼ Mon-2:30 pm. Closed: 1/1, 11/22, 12/25; also Sun. **Reservations:** suggested, weekend
American **Features:** Regardless of how you feel about going to YOUR mother-in-law's house, you'll enjoy coming t
this one because it is a casual and welcoming place to enjoy house-made comfort foods. An island in th
middle of the dining room is the salad bar featuring over a dozen recipes gathered from family and friends o
owner, Donna Hafer. Casual dress; cocktails. **Parking:** street. **Cards:** DS, MC, VI. **Historic**

TRAILHEAD BREWING COMPANY **Lunch:** $8-$20   **Dinner:** $8-$20   **Phone:** 636/946-2739 ③
▼▼ ▼▼ **Location:** Downtown; in historic Old Town. 921 S Riverside Dr 63301. **Hours:** 11 am-10 pm, Fri & Sat-11 pm
American **Reservations:** accepted. **Features:** Nothing fancy here—just good old-fashioned hamburgers, sandwiche
fries and one of the favorites: chili. Casual dress; cocktails. **Parking:** street. **Cards:** AX, CB, DC, D$
MC, VI.

WILIKER'S RESTAURANT **Lunch:** $6-$15   **Dinner:** $8-$15   **Phone:** 636/947-1441 ⑥
▼▼ ▼▼ **Location:** I-70, exit 228, 0.9 mi s on SR 94, then just e on Friedens Rd; in Country Club Plaza Shopping Center. 150
American Country Club Plaza 63303. **Hours:** 11 am-10 pm, Fri & Sat-midnight, Sun 10 am-9 pm. Closed: 12/2!
Reservations: accepted. **Features:** The popular restaurant nurtures a warm, quiet tavern-type atmospher
Nostalgic decor lends to the mood. The menu centers on pasta, steak and seafood. A brunch buffet is s
up on Sunday. For dessert, try chocolate gooey butter cake. Casual dress; cocktails. **Parking:** on-site. **Cards:** AX, CB, DC, D$
JC, MC, VI.

———— *The following restaurants have not been evaluated by AAA* ————
but are listed for your information only.

AMERISPORTS BAR & GRILL **Phone:** 636/940-493
[fyi] Not evaluated. **Location:** I-70, exit 228 (First Capitol), 1.3 mi ne; in Ameristar Casino St. Charles. 1260 S Main S
63301. **Features:** Guests eat up not only the delicious ribs, which are cooked in a wood-fired oven, but als
the state-of-the-art audio/video system, which features a 34-foot video wall.

PEARL'S OYSTER BAR **Phone:** 636/940-494
[fyi] Not evaluated. **Location:** I-70, exit 228 (First Capitol), 1.3 mi ne; in Ameristar Casino St. Charles. 1260 S Main S
63301. **Features:** Exhibition-style cooking is applied to preparations of fresh, Southern-style seafood, as we
as offerings from the raw bar.

ST. PETERS pop. 51,381 (See map and index starting on p. 511)

———— **WHERE TO STAY** ————

DRURY INN-ST. CHARLES/ST. PETERS *Book great rates at AAA.com*   **Phone:** (636)397-9700
▼▼ ▼▼ ▼ All Year [BP]   **1P:** $65-$145   **2P:** $75-$155   **XP:** $10   F1
Small-scale Hotel **Location:** I-70, exit 222 (Mid Rivers Mall Dr), just se. Located adjacent to the Mid Rivers Mall. 170 Westfield Dr 6337.
Fax: 636/397-9700. **Facility:** 135 units. 129 one-bedroom standard units. 6 one-bedroom suites ($120
$155). 6 stories, interior corridors. *Bath:* combo or shower only. **Parking:** on-site. **Terms:** small pets onl
Amenities: high-speed Internet, voice mail, irons, hair dryers. **Pool(s):** small heated indoor. **Leisure Activities:** whirlpo
exercise room. **Guest Services:** complimentary evening beverages, valet and coin laundry. **Business Services:** meetin
rooms, PC, fax. **Cards:** AX, CB, DC, DS, MC, VI.

SOME UNITS
ⒶⓈⓀ 🛏 🍴 🔊M 🖥 📷 🏊 🎿 💻 ✕ 🔌 📠

(See map and index starting on p. 511)

——— **WHERE TO DINE** ———

RED ROBIN GOURMET BURGERS   **Lunch:** $7-$9   **Dinner:** $7-$12   **Phone:** 636/279-6622
American   **Location:** I-70, exit 222 (Mid Rivers Mall Dr), 0.4 mi s. 317 Mid Rivers Mall Dr 63376. **Hours:** 11 am-10 pm, Fri &
Sat-11 pm. Closed: 11/22, 12/25. **Reservations:** not accepted. **Features:** The "cool" burger joint displays
contemporary and colorful decor that is entertainment in itself. Among offerings of good food are variations
on the traditional burger. Casual dress; cocktails. **Parking:** on-site. **Cards:** AX, DC, DS, MC, VI.

SUNSET HILLS pop. 8,267   (See map and index starting on p. 514)

——— **WHERE TO STAY** ———

HOLIDAY INN-SOUTHWEST & VIKING
CONFERENCE CENTER   *Book great rates at AAA.com*   **Phone:** (314)821-6600   **92**
Small-scale Hotel   **Location:** I-44, exit 277B, just s. 10709 Watson Rd 63127. **Fax:** 314/821-4673. **Facility:** 213 one-bedroom
standard units, some with whirlpools. 4 stories, interior corridors. *Bath:* some combo or shower only.
Parking: on-site. **Terms:** check-in 4 pm, [BP] meal plan available, package plans, pets ($25 extra charge).
Amenities: high-speed Internet, voice mail, irons, hair dryers. *Some:* dual phone lines. **Dining:** 6 am-2 & 5-
10 pm, cocktails, nightclub, entertainment. **Pool(s):** outdoor, small heated indoor. **Leisure**
Activities: whirlpool, exercise room. **Fee:** game room. **Guest Services:** complimentary evening beverages: Tues, valet and
coin laundry, area transportation-within 5 mi. **Business Services:** conference facilities, business center. **Cards:** AX, CB, DC,
DS, JC, MC, VI. **Free Special Amenities: newspaper and high-speed Internet.**   SOME UNITS

——— **WHERE TO DINE** ———

O'LEARY'S   **Lunch:** $7-$9   **Dinner:** $9-$17   **Phone:** 314/842-7678   **121**
American   **Location:** I-44, exit 277A (Lindbergh Blvd), 0.8 mi s. 3828 S Lindbergh Blvd 63127. **Hours:** 11 am-10 pm, Fri & Sat-
11 pm, Sun 10 am-9 pm. Closed major holidays. **Reservations:** accepted. **Features:** Owned in part by
actor John Goodman, the sports-themed restaurant prepares huge salads and grilled meats. Casual dress;
cocktails. **Parking:** on-site. **Cards:** AX, DS, MC, VI.

TOWN AND COUNTRY pop. 10,894   (See maps and indexes starting on p. 511, 514)

——— **WHERE TO STAY** ———

ST. LOUIS MARRIOTT WEST   *Book great rates at AAA.com*   **Phone:** (314)878-2747   **65**
Large-scale Hotel   **Location:** I-64/US40, exit 23 (Maryville Centre Dr), just n. 660 Maryville Centre Dr 63141. **Fax:** 314/878-3005.
Facility: Smoke free premises. 300 units. 299 one-bedroom standard units. 1 one-bedroom suite. 8 stories,
interior corridors. **Parking:** on-site. **Terms:** check-in 4 pm, pets ($75 fee, with prior approval).
Amenities: voice mail, irons, hair dryers. **Fee:** video games, high-speed Internet. *Some:* dual phone lines.
Dining: 6:30 am-11 pm, Sat & Sun from 7 am, cocktails. **Pool(s):** outdoor, heated indoor. **Leisure**
Activities: sauna, whirlpool, hiking trails, jogging, exercise room. **Guest Services:** sundries, valet laundry, area transportation-
within 3 mi. **Business Services:** conference facilities, business center. **Cards:** AX, DC, DS, MC, VI. **Free Special Amenities:**
early check-in/late check-out and room upgrade (subject to availability with advance reservations).
(See color ad p 535)

ST. LOUIS/MARYVILLE COURTYARD BY MARRIOTT   *Book great rates at AAA.com* **Phone:** (314)514-7300   **30**
Small-scale Hotel   All Year   1P: $79-$149   2P: $79-$149
Location: I-64/US 40, exit 23 eastbound; exit 22 westbound (Maryville Center Dr), just n. Located adjacent to Maryville
University. 511 Maryville University Dr 63141. **Fax:** 314/514-1010. **Facility:** Smoke free premises. 122 units. 116
one-bedroom standard units, some with whirlpools. 6 one-bedroom suites. 3 stories, interior corridors. *Bath:*
combo or shower only. **Parking:** on-site. **Terms:** [BP] meal plan available, package plans. **Amenities:** video games (fee), high-
speed Internet, dual phone lines, voice mail, irons, hair dryers. **Pool(s):** small heated indoor. **Leisure Activities:** whirlpool,
exercise room. **Guest Services:** sundries, valet laundry, area transportation, wireless Internet. **Business Services:** meeting
rooms, PC. **Cards:** AX, CB, DC, DS, MC, VI.   SOME UNITS

UNIVERSITY CITY pop. 37,428   (See map and index starting on p. 514)

——— **WHERE TO DINE** ———

BLUEBERRY HILL   **Lunch:** $5-$9   **Dinner:** $5-$9   **Phone:** 314/727-4444   **64**
American   **Location:** I-170, exit 2 (Delmar Blvd), 2.9 mi e. 6504 Delmar in The Loop 63130. **Hours:** 11 am-1:30 am, Sun-
midnight. **Reservations:** accepted. **Features:** The restaurant's mission is to celebrate a bygone era, and it
does so with a walk of fame on which embedded stars honor local notables from Dred Scott to Chuck Berry. It
also has appealing decor. Among decor accents are sheet music, record album covers, old posters and a Wurlitzer jukebox that
plays more than 3,000 tunes. Menu choices include hamburgers, jerk chicken, vegetarian specials, homemade soups, chili,
salads and breakfast items. Casual dress; cocktails; entertainment. **Parking:** street. **Cards:** AX, CB, DC, DS, MC, VI. **Historic**

(See map and index starting on p. 514)

NOBU'S JAPANESE RESTAURANT   Lunch: $6-$11   Dinner: $13-$20   Phone: 314/997-2303   62

Japanese

Location: I-170, exit 3A (Olive Blvd), just e. 8643 Olive Blvd 63132. **Hours:** 11:30 am-2 & 5-9:30 pm, Fri-10 pm, Sat 5 pm-10 pm, Sun 5 pm-9 pm. Closed major holidays; also Mon & week of 7/4. **Reservations:** suggested, weekends. **Features:** Specializing in fresh seafood, the restaurant employs several different techniques in the preparation of their meals. Sushi, sashimi and tempura plus the more common fried and grilled methods are used. You might want to consider a combination dinner which includes miso soup, salad with peanut oil dressing and steamed rice plus the entree of your choice. Dramatic lacquered trays provide the palate on which the food is displayed. Casual dress; beer & wine only. **Parking:** on-site. **Cards:** AX, DC, MC, VI.

SALEEM'S   Lunch: $8-$18   Dinner: $8-$18   Phone: 314/721-7947   63

Lebanese

Location: I-170, exit 2, 3 mi e. 6501 Delmar Blvd 63130. **Hours:** 11:30 am-2:30 & 5-10 pm, Fri & Sat-11 pm. Closed: 7/4, 11/22, 12/25; also Sun. **Reservations:** accepted. **Features:** Delicacies such as chicken and lamb shish kebab, garlic potato dip and baklava have made the restaurant a favorite of Middle Eastern aficionados for 25 years. Specialty lamb dishes are prepared in many ways, almost all with garlic. In fact, the restaurant's slogan is "where garlic is king." The atmosphere is fun and energetic. Smoking is not permitted on weekends. Casual dress; cocktails. **Parking:** street. **Cards:** DS, MC, VI.

The following restaurants have not been evaluated by AAA but are listed for your information only.

MAI LEE RESTAURANT   Phone: 314/993-3754

fyi

Not evaluated. **Location:** 8440 Delmar Blvd 63124. **Features:** More than 280 selections of Vietnamese food are made fresh daily.

SEKI FINE JAPANESE CUISINE & SUSHI BAR   Phone: 314/726-6477

fyi

Not evaluated. **Location:** 6335 Delmar Blvd 63130. **Features:** An extensive list of Japanese favorites includes sushi, sashimi, tempura and udon noodles.

VALLEY PARK pop. 6,518   (See map and index starting on p. 511)

--- WHERE TO STAY ---

DRURY INN & SUITES-ST. LOUIS SOUTHWEST   *Book great rates at AAA.com*   Phone: (636)861-8300   34

Small-scale Hotel

All Year [BP]   1P: $60-$130   2P: $70-$140   XP: $10   F18
Location: I-44, exit 272 (SR 141), just sw. 5 Lambert Drury Pl 63088. Fax: 636/861-8300. **Facility:** 175 units. 145 one-bedroom standard units. 30 one-bedroom suites ($95-$170). 7 stories, interior corridors. *Bath:* combo or shower only. **Parking:** on-site. **Amenities:** high-speed Internet, voice mail, irons, hair dryers. **Pool(s):** heated indoor/outdoor. **Leisure Activities:** whirlpool, exercise room. **Guest Services:** complimentary evening beverages, valet and coin laundry, wireless Internet. **Business Services:** meeting rooms, PC. **Cards:** AX, CB, DC, DS, MC, VI.

SOME UNITS

HAMPTON INN-ST. LOUIS SOUTHWEST   *Book great rates at AAA.com*   Phone: (636)529-9020   33

Small-scale Hotel

All Year [BP]   1P: $86-$111   2P: $96-$126   XP: $10   F18
Location: I-44, exit 272 (SR 141), just sw. 9 Lambert Drury Pl 63088. Fax: 636/529-0808. **Facility:** 92 one-bedroom standard units. 4 stories, interior corridors. *Bath:* combo or shower only. **Parking:** on-site. **Amenities:** high-speed Internet, voice mail, irons, hair dryers. **Pool(s):** outdoor. **Leisure Activities:** exercise room. **Guest Services:** valet laundry, wireless Internet. **Business Services:** PC. **Cards:** AX, CB, DC, DS, MC, VI.

SOME UNITS

WEBSTER GROVES pop. 23,230   (See map and index starting on p. 514)

--- WHERE TO DINE ---

BIG SKY CAFE   Dinner: $15-$22   Phone: 314/962-5757   110

Regional American

Location: I-44, exit 282 (Murdoch Rd/Laclede Station Rd), just n on Murdoch Rd, just w on Big Bend Blvd, then just s. 47 S Old Orchard Ave 63119. **Hours:** 5:30 pm-9:30 pm, Fri & Sat-11 pm, Sun 4:30 pm-9:30 pm. Closed major holidays; also Mon. **Reservations:** suggested. **Features:** The cafe's specialties are dished in large portions. A superb array of mix-and-match dishes is enhanced by delicious mashed potatoes. A grazing menu is presented on Monday nights. The attractive patio allows for outdoor dining amid funky decor. Casual dress; cocktails. **Parking:** on-site. **Cards:** AX, CB, DC, DS, JC, MC, VI.

LLYWELYN'S PUB   Lunch: $6-$12   Dinner: $6-$12   Phone: 314/962-1515   109

Irish

Location: 1 blk n of Lockwood St; between Elm and N Gore sts. 17 W Moody St 63119. **Hours:** 11 am-9 pm, Fri & Sat-10 pm, Sun noon-9 pm. Closed: 7/4, 11/22, 12/25. **Features:** Examples of traditional pub fare include shepherd's pie, Irish stew, fish and chips, Welsh potato chips, Welsh rarebit and pub pretzels. Casual dress; cocktails. **Parking:** on-site. **Cards:** AX, DS, MC, VI.

ZINNIA   Lunch: $7-$10   Dinner: $17-$34   Phone: 314/962-0572   108

Nouvelle American

Location: I-44, exit 282 (Murdoch Rd/Laclede Station Rd), 0.3 mi n to Big Bend Blvd, then 0.3 mi e. 7491 Big Bend Blvd 63119. **Hours:** 11 am-2 & 5:30-9:30 pm, Fri & Sat-10:30 pm, Sun 4:30 pm-9 pm. Closed major holidays; also Mon. **Reservations:** suggested. **Features:** Creative American cuisine exhibits Asian and Californian influences. The emphasis is on fresh seafood and regional products. The bright contemporary surroundings are inviting. Dress is business casual. Casual dress; cocktails. **Parking:** on-site. **Cards:** AX, DC, DS, MC, VI.

WENTZVILLE pop. 6,896   (See map and index starting on p. 511)

——— WHERE TO DINE ———

RUGGERI'S RISTORANTE   **Lunch:** $6-$14   **Dinner:** $7-$22   **Phone:** 636/327-3777   13

Italian

Location: I-70, exit 208 (Pearce Blvd), just s, then just w. 1 Ruggeri Dr 63385. **Hours:** 11 am-10 pm, Sat from 3 pm, Sun 10 am-9 pm. Closed major holidays. **Reservations:** accepted. **Features:** This is a restaurant which is convenient for the passing travelers as well as the locals. Traditional Italian meat dishes like chicken Florentine and veal cutlet Milanese are given pride of place alongside such pasta specials as rigatoni con broccolini. If you have a taste for pasta, you might want to try the farfalle pommodoro, with bow tie pasta in a light tomato cream sauce enhanced with onion, garlic and basil. Casual dress; cocktails. **Parking:** on-site. **Cards:** AX, DC, DS, MC, VI.

STEFANINA'S   **Lunch:** $5-$15   **Dinner:** $8-$15   **Phone:** 636/327-5800   12

Italian

Location: I-70, exit 208 (Pearce Blvd), just n, then 1 mi e. 762 W Pearce Blvd 63385. **Hours:** 11 am-9 pm, Fri-10:30 pm, Sat-10 pm, Sun noon-9 pm. Closed major holidays. **Features:** Since 1995, this casual restaurant on the north frontage road along I-70 has served traditional Italian favorites and a few Sicilian specialties. Pizza is the most popular menu item. Casual dress; cocktails. **Parking:** on-site. **Cards:** AX, DC, DS, MC, VI.

WOODSON TERRACE pop. 4,189   (See map and index starting on p. 514)

——— WHERE TO STAY ———

HOLIDAY INN AIRPORT OAKLAND PARK HOTEL   *Book great rates at AAA.com*   **Phone:** (314)427-4700   42

Small-scale Hotel

All Year   1P: $79-$119   2P: $79-$129   XP: $10   F18
Location: I-70, exit 236 (Lambert Airport), 0.6 mi e on Natural Bridge Rd, then just s. 4505 Woodson Rd 63134. **Fax:** 314/656-1656. **Facility:** 158 one-bedroom standard units. 5 stories, interior corridors. **Bath:** combo or shower only. **Parking:** on-site. **Terms:** package plans. **Amenities:** video games (fee), high-speed Internet, voice mail, irons, hair dryers. **Dining:** Oakland Park Restaurant, see separate listing. **Pool(s):** heated outdoor. **Leisure Activities:** sauna, exercise room. **Guest Services:** valet and coin laundry, area transportation-within 3 mi. **Business Services:** conference facilities, business center. **Cards:** AX, CB, DC, DS, JC, MC, VI. **Free Special Amenities:** newspaper and high-speed Internet.

SOME UNITS

——— WHERE TO DINE ———

ERIO'S RESTAURANT   **Lunch:** $5-$10   **Dinner:** $6-$10   **Phone:** 314/423-1555   53

Italian

Location: I-70, exit 236 (Lambert Airport), 0.6 mi e on Natural Bridge Rd, then just s. 4434 Woodson Rd 63134. **Hours:** 11 am-9 pm, Fri & Sat-10 pm, Sun 4 pm-9 pm. Closed major holidays; also Mon. **Features:** At the longtime family-owned and operated business, there is no pretense but instead just good food in a comfortable atmosphere. Casual dress; beer & wine only. **Parking:** on-site. **Cards:** AX, DC, DS, MC, VI.

OAKLAND PARK RESTAURANT   **Lunch:** $7-$10   **Dinner:** $8-$24   **Phone:** 314/656-1660   52

American

Location: I-70, exit 236 (Lambert Airport), 0.6 mi e on Natural Bridge Rd, then just s; in Holiday Inn Airport Oakland Park Hotel. 4505 Woodson Rd 63134. **Hours:** 6 am-10:30 & 11-1 pm, Sat 6 am-10:30 & 5-10 pm, Sun 6 am-10:30 & 5-9 pm. Closed major holidays. **Reservations:** accepted. **Features:** The Italian chef creates American cuisine with his homeland flair. The restaurant is best known for steaks and ribs. A lunch buffet is available. Casual dress; cocktails. **Parking:** on-site. **Cards:** AX, CB, DC, DS, JC, MC, VI.

——— *The following restaurant has not been evaluated by AAA* ———
but is listed for your information only.

YESTERDAY'S   **Phone:** 314/423-5677

fyi

Not evaluated. **Location:** I-170, exit 6 (Natural Bridge Rd), 1 mi sw. 4412-16 Woodson Rd 63134. **Features:** On the menu is a good selection of appetizers, soups, salads, pizzas and sandwiches, as well as chicken, shrimp, fish and steak entrees.

Nearby Illinois

ALTON pop. 30,496

——— WHERE TO STAY ———

COMFORT INN
Book great rates at AAA.com
All Year [BP]   1P: $85-$99   2P: $85-$99   XP: $5   F18
Phone: (618)465-9999
Location: Off SR 3, jct SR 140. 11 Crossroads Ct 62002. **Fax:** 618/465-0055. **Facility:** 62 one-bedroom standard
Small-scale Hotel   units, some with whirlpools. 3 stories, interior corridors. *Bath:* combo or shower only. **Parking:** on-site.
Terms: pets (with prior approval). **Amenities:** high-speed Internet, safes (fee), irons, hair dryers. **Pool(s):**
small heated indoor. **Leisure Activities:** exercise room. **Guest Services:** coin laundry, wireless Internet. **Business Services:**
business center. **Cards:** AX, CB, DC, DS, MC, VI.
SOME UNITS

SUPER 8 MOTEL
Book at AAA.com
All Year [ECP]   1P: $54-$80   2P: $54-$80   XP: $6   F18
Phone: (618)465-8885
Location: On SR 111, 1.8 mi e of jct US 67. Located in a commercial area. 1800 Homer Adams Pkwy 62002.
Small-scale Hotel   **Fax:** 618/465-8964. **Facility:** 63 one-bedroom standard units. 3 stories (no elevator), interior corridors.
Parking: on-site. **Terms:** small pets only ($50 deposit). **Amenities:** high-speed Internet, safes (fee), hair
dryers. *Some:* irons. **Guest Services:** wireless Internet. **Cards:** AX, CB, DC, DS, MC, VI.
SOME UNITS
FEE

——— WHERE TO DINE ———

CASTELLI'S MOONLIGHT RESTAURANT   **Lunch:** $5-$10   **Dinner:** $5-$20   **Phone:** 618/462-4620
Location: Jct SR 3/140/111, 0.4 mi e, then 1.2 mi n. 3400 Fosterburg Rd 62002. **Hours:** 11:15 am-10 pm, Sat from
4 pm, Sun 11:15 am-2 pm. Closed: 11/22, 12/25; also Mon. **Features:** Since 1937, patrons have enjoyed
Italian   the casual atmosphere and homemade specialties here. The Roman house salad with creamy Italian
dressing and the "talk-n-chic" fried chicken are notable hits in this cozy and friendly eatery convenient for
travelers. Casual dress; cocktails. **Parking:** on-site. **Cards:** AX, DS, MC, VI.

TONY'S RESTAURANT & THIRD ST CAFE   **Dinner:** $10-$25   **Phone:** 618/462-8384
Location: US 67, just n of jct SR 100. 312 Piasa St 62002. **Hours:** 4:30 pm-10 pm, Fri & Sat-11 pm. Closed:
3/23, 12/24, 12/25. **Reservations:** suggested. **Features:** Located at the foot of Piasa Street, close to the
Steak House   banks of the Mississippi River, this eatery occupies a building which once housed a popular department
store. Now, this building is home to a restaurant with several dining rooms, each with different levels of
sophistication and elegance. You will be able to select from pasta, pizza, steak and seafood and a wide variety of cheesecake
desserts. Casual dress; cocktails. **Parking:** on-site. **Cards:** AX, CB, DC, DS, JC, MC, VI.

BELLEVILLE pop. 41,410   (See map and index starting on p. 514)

——— WHERE TO STAY ———

THE SHRINE HOTEL   **Phone:** 618/397-1162   82
All Year [CP]   1P: $66   2P: $75   XP: $10   F18
Location: I-255, exit 17A, 1 mi e on SR 15; in Shrine of Our Lady of the Snows Complex. Located on grounds of
National Shrine. 451 S Demazenod Dr 62223. **Fax:** 618/394-6524. **Facility:** 78 one-bedroom standard units. 2
stories, interior corridors. *Bath:* combo or shower only. **Parking:** on-site. **Terms:** small pets only.
Small-scale Hotel   **Amenities:** high-speed Internet, irons, hair dryers. **Dining:** restaurant, see separate listing. **Leisure**
Activities: hiking trails, playground, exercise room. **Guest Services:** gift shop, coin laundry, wireless
Internet. **Business Services:** conference facilities, PC. **Cards:** AX, CB, DC, DS, JC, MC, VI. **Free Special Amenities:**
expanded continental breakfast and high-speed Internet. *(See color ad p 212)*
SOME UNITS

SWANS COURT BED & BREAKFAST   **Phone:** (618)233-0779   83
All Year   1P: $55-$110   2P: $77-$110   XP: $25
Location: Jct SR 15 and 159, 3.6 mi n to D St, just e to Court St, then just n. Located in a residential area. 421 Court St
62220. **Fax:** 618/277-3150. **Facility:** Second Empire architecture defines this restored 1883 B&B; furnishings
Historic Bed   include period pieces. 4 one-bedroom standard units. 2 stories (no elevator), interior corridors. *Bath:* combo
& Breakfast   shared or private, combo or shower only. **Parking:** on-site. **Terms:** age restrictions may apply, weekly rates
available. **Guest Services:** complimentary laundry. **Cards:** AX, DS, MC, VI. **Free Special Amenities:** full
breakfast and early check-in/late check-out.

——— WHERE TO DINE ———

THE PIE PANTRY   **Lunch:** $5-$12   **Phone:** 618/277-4140   118
Location: I-64, exit 12, 6 mi s on SR 159, then just e. 310 E Main St 62220. **Hours:** 7 am-3 pm, Sun 8 am-2 pm.
Closed major holidays. **Reservations:** accepted. **Features:** The courtyard of this 100-year-old carriage
American   house with a cobblestone floor, antique furniture, large skylights and high beamed ceiling is striking. The pie
is the definite show stopper though, and is an excellent ending to any meal you choose here. Casual dress.
Parking: on-site. **Cards:** MC, VI.

(See map and index starting on p. 514)

THE SHRINE RESTAURANT Lunch: $6-$10 Dinner: $10-$14 Phone: 618/397-6700 (117)

AAA
WWW
American

Location: I-255, exit 17A, 1 mi e on SR 15; in Shrine of Our Lady of the Snows Complex; in The Shrine Hotel. 442 S Demazenod Dr 62223. **Hours:** 11 am-8 pm, Fri & Sat-9 pm, Sun 10 am-8 pm. Closed: 11/22, 12/25. **Features:** Homemade soup and a varied salad bar that includes a pasta station are favorites at the casual family restaurant, which is known for its comfort foods. The setting, on the grounds of the national shrine for which it is named, is beautiful and serene. Casual dress; cocktails. **Parking:** on-site. **Cards:** AX, DS, MC, VI. *(See color ad p 212)*

COLLINSVILLE pop. 24,707 (See map and index starting on p. 514)

——— WHERE TO STAY ———

DRURY INN-ST. LOUIS/COLLINSVILLE *Book at AAA.com* Phone: (618)345-7700 **45**

WWW WWW
Small-scale Hotel

All Year [BP] 1P: $70-$139 2P: $80-$149 XP: $10 F18

Location: I-55/70, exit 11 (SR 157), just n. 602 N Bluff Rd 62234. Fax: 618/345-7700. **Facility:** 123 one-bedroom standard units. 4 stories, interior corridors. **Parking:** on-site. **Amenities:** high-speed Internet, dual phone lines, voice mail, irons, hair dryers. **Pool(s):** small heated indoor. **Leisure Activities:** exercise room. **Guest Services:** complimentary evening beverages, coin laundry, wireless Internet. **Business Services:** meeting rooms, business center. **Cards:** AX, CB, DC, DS, MC, VI.

SOME UNITS

SUPER 8 MOTEL-COLLINSVILLE *Book at AAA.com* Phone: (618)345-8008 **46**

WWW
Small-scale Hotel

All Year [ECP] 1P: $50-$89 2P: $50-$89 XP: $6 F18

Location: I-55/70, exit 11 (SR 157), just n. 2 Gateway Dr 62234. Fax: 618/344-7062. **Facility:** 63 one-bedroom standard units. 3 stories (no elevator), interior corridors. **Parking:** on-site, winter plug-ins. **Amenities:** high-speed Internet, safes (fee), irons, hair dryers. **Guest Services:** wireless Internet. **Cards:** AX, CB, DC, DS, MC, VI.

SOME UNITS

(ASK) (S✦D) (†↑) (✦) (🛏) (📠) (💻) /(✕)/

——— WHERE TO DINE ———

BANDANA'S BBQ Lunch: $5-$12 Dinner: $7-$12 Phone: 618/344-4476

WWW
Barbecue

Location: I-55/70, exit 11 (SR 157), just n. 4 Commerce Dr 62234. **Hours:** 11 am-9 pm, Fri & Sat-10 pm. Closed: 11/22, 12/25. **Features:** The hickory smoke taste in the ribs, pork, chicken, turkey and beef brings patrons back time and again. Of the four basic sauces, the hot Memphis style is for those who prefer spicy. For a different flavor, deep-fried corn on the cob is interesting. Casual dress; beer & wine only. **Parking:** on-site.
Cards: AX, DC, DS, MC, VI.

(✉)

ZAPATA'S MEXICAN RESTAURANT & CANTINA Lunch: $5-$7 Dinner: $6-$14 Phone: 618/343-1337 **56**

WWW
Mexican

Location: I-55/70, exit 11 (SR 157), just nw. 8 Eastport Plaza Dr 62234. **Hours:** 11 am-10 pm, Fri-11 pm, Sat noon-11 pm, Sun noon-10 pm. Closed: 3/23, 11/22, 12/25. **Features:** Authentic Mexican entrees of burritos, fajitas and chile rellenos are sure to please the casual diner. The carmones diablo are a great shrimp offering with a little spice. Casual dress; cocktails. **Parking:** on-site. **Cards:** AX, DC, DS, MC, VI.

(✦M) (🍸) (✉)

EAST ST. LOUIS pop. 31,542   (See map and index starting on p. 514)

——— WHERE TO STAY ———

CASINO QUEEN HOTEL   **Phone: (618)874-5000**   **71**

AAA [SAVE]   4/1-8/31 [CP]   1P: $89-$125   2P: $89-$125   XP: $20   F16
             9/1-3/31 [CP]   1P: $69-$125   2P: $69-$125   XP: $20   F16
▽▽▽   **Location:** I-55, exit 2A, 0.6 mi n on River Park Dr, then just w. Metrolink stop in parking lot. 200 S Front St 62201 (220
Small-scale Hotel S Front St). Fax: 618/874-8404. **Facility:** 157 units. 150 one-bedroom standard units, some with whirlpools. 7
one-bedroom suites ($157-$500) with whirlpools. 7 stories, interior corridors. *Bath:* combo or shower only.
Parking: on-site and valet. **Terms:** cancellation fee imposed, package plans. **Amenities:** video games
(fee), high-speed Internet, dual phone lines, voice mail, irons, hair dryers. **Dining:** 3 restaurants, 24 hours, also, Royal Table
Steakhouse, see separate listing. **Pool(s):** small heated indoor. **Leisure Activities:** exercise room. **Guest Services:** gift shop,
valet laundry, area transportation-shuttle to downtown lodgings, wireless Internet. **Business Services:** conference facilities.
Cards: AX, CB, DC, DS, MC, VI. **Free Special Amenities:** continental breakfast and high-speed Internet.

SOME UNITS

[S/D] [📶] [24↑] [Y] [ᏻM] [🐾] [➔] [📹] [🖥] [📠] / [✕] /

——— WHERE TO DINE ———

ROYAL TABLE STEAKHOUSE   **Dinner: $15-$35**   **Phone: 618/874-5000**   **99**

AAA   **Location:** I-55, exit 2A, 0.6 mi n on River Park Dr, then just w; in Casino Queen Hotel. 200 S Front St 62201. **Hours:** 5
pm-9 pm. Closed: Mon. **Reservations:** required. **Features:** The intimate and elegant atmosphere is just the
▽▽▽   beginning of your dining experience. From aged beef of chateaubriand for two to filet mignon to rack of lamb
American   and fresh seafood selections, you are sure to find a tempting selection. Various pasta and vegetarian dishes
complete the entree selections. Wonderful appetizers and desserts are offered for the start of your meal or
for a great ending. Casual dress; cocktails. **Parking:** on-site and valet. **Cards:** AX, CB, DC, DS, JC,
MC, VI.

[ᏻM] [N]

FAIRVIEW HEIGHTS pop. 15,034   (See map and index starting on p. 514)

——— WHERE TO STAY ———

DRURY INN & SUITES-FAIRVIEW HEIGHTS   *Book at AAA.com*   **Phone: (618)398-8530**   **74**

▽▽▽   All Year [BP]   1P: $80-$130   2P: $90-$140   XP: $10   F18
Location: I-64, exit 12 (SR 159). 12 Ludwig Dr 62208. Fax: 618/398-8530. **Facility:** 142 units. 126 one-bedroom
Small-scale Hotel standard units. 16 one-bedroom suites ($105-$155). 4 stories, interior corridors. *Bath:* combo or shower
only. **Parking:** on-site. **Amenities:** video library (fee), DVD players, high-speed Internet, dual phone lines,
voice mail, irons, hair dryers. **Pool(s):** heated indoor/outdoor. **Leisure Activities:** whirlpool, exercise room. **Guest Services:**
complimentary evening beverages, valet and coin laundry. **Business Services:** meeting rooms, PC. **Cards:** AX, CB, DC, DS,
MC, VI.

SOME UNITS

[A$K] [🐾] [T↑↓] [➔] [📹] [🖥] [📠] [📠] / [✕] /

FAIRFIELD INN BY MARRIOTT   *Book great rates at AAA.com*   **Phone: (618)398-7124**   **76**

▽▽   All Year   1P: $85-$105   2P: $90-$110   XP: $5   F18
Location: I-64, exit 12 (SR 159). 1 mi nw. 140 Ludwig Dr 62208. Fax: 618/398-7124. **Facility:** Smoke free
Small-scale Hotel premises. 63 one-bedroom standard units. 3 stories, interior corridors. *Bath:* combo or shower only.
Parking: on-site, winter plug-ins. **Amenities:** high-speed Internet, irons, hair dryers. **Pool(s):** small heated
indoor. **Leisure Activities:** whirlpool. **Guest Services:** valet laundry. **Cards:** AX, DC, DS, MC, VI.

SOME UNITS

[A$K] [S/D] [T↑↓] [ᏻM] [🐾] [🕹] [➔] [✕] [📹] [📠] / [🖥] [📠]

HAMPTON INN BY HILTON   *Book great rates at AAA.com*   **Phone: (618)397-9705**   **75**

▽▽▽   All Year   1P: $80-$100   2P: $85-$105   XP: $5   F18
Location: I-64, exit 12 (SR 159). 1 mi nw. 150 Ludwig Dr 62208. Fax: 618/397-7829. **Facility:** 62 one-bedroom
Small-scale Hotel standard units. 3 stories, interior corridors. *Bath:* combo or shower only. **Parking:** on-site. **Amenities:** high-
speed Internet, voice mail, irons, hair dryers. **Pool(s):** small heated indoor. **Leisure Activities:** whirlpool.
Guest Services: valet laundry. **Cards:** AX, DC, DS, MC, VI.

SOME UNITS

[A$K] [S/D] [ᏻM] [🐾] [🕹] [➔] [📹] [📠] / [✕] [🖥] [📠]

——— WHERE TO DINE ———

LOTAWATA CREEK SOUTHERN GRILL   **Lunch: $7-$19**   **Dinner: $7-$19**   **Phone: 618/628-7373**   **102**

▽▽ ▽▽   **Location:** I-64, exit 12 (SR 159), just n. 311 Salem Pl 62208. **Hours:** 11 am-10 pm, Fri & Sat-11 pm. Closed:
11/22, 12/25. **Features:** Traditional Southern food served in a casual setting is what you'll find, along with
Regional American lots of country-fried items and blackened Cajun fare. The quality is consistently high, especially among the
hand-cut beef, homemade bread and dessert. Casual dress; cocktails. **Parking:** on-site. **Cards:** AX, CB,
DC, DS, JC, MC, VI.

[Y] [N]

O'FALLON pop. 21,910   (See map and index starting on p. 514)

——— WHERE TO STAY ———

BAYMONT INN & SUITES ST. LOUIS (O'FALLON)   *Book at AAA.com*   **Phone:** 618/632-6668   [58]

Property failed to provide current rates

Small-scale Hotel   **Location:** I-64, exit 14 (US 50), 0.5 mi e. 136 Regency Park Ln. Fax: 618/632-6676. **Facility:** 64 one-bedroom standard units, some with whirlpools. 3 stories, interior corridors. *Bath:* combo or shower only. **Parking:** on-site. **Amenities:** video games (fee), high-speed Internet, voice mail, irons, hair dryers. **Pool(s):** small heated indoor. **Leisure Activities:** whirlpool, exercise room. **Guest Services:** coin laundry.

SOME UNITS

COMFORT INN   *Book great rates at AAA.com*   **Phone:** (618)624-6060

	1P: $89-$149	2P: $89-$149	XP: $10	F18
5/1-9/30 [BP]				
4/1-4/30 & 10/1-3/31 [BP]	1P: $79-$129	2P: $79-$129	XP: $10	F18

Small-scale Hotel   **Location:** I-64, exit 19B (SR 158), 0.5 mi n, then just sw. Located in a semi-rural area. 1100 Eastgate Dr 62269. Fax: 618/624-1753. **Facility:** 96 one-bedroom standard units, some with whirlpools. 2 stories (no elevator), interior corridors. **Parking:** on-site. **Terms:** pets ($50 deposit). **Amenities:** high-speed Internet, irons, hair dryers. **Pool(s):** outdoor. **Leisure Activities:** whirlpool. **Guest Services:** coin laundry. **Business Services:** meeting rooms, PC. **Cards:** AX, CB, DC, DS, JC, MC, VI.

SOME UNITS

FEE

DRURY INN & SUITES-O'FALLON IL   **Phone:** 618/624-2211

| All Year [BP] | 1P: $80-$130 | 2P: $90-$140 | XP: $10 | F18 |

Small-scale Hotel   Too new to rate, opening scheduled for January 2007. **Location:** I-64, exit 16 (Green Mount Rd). 1118 Central Park Dr 62269. **Amenities:** 180 units, pets, coffeemakers, microwaves, refrigerators, pool. **Cards:** AX, CB, DC, DS, MC, VI.

EXTENDED STAY AMERICA-O'FALLON ILLINOIS   **Phone:** 618/624-1757   [59]

Small-scale Hotel   **Location:** I-64, exit 14, just w to Regency Park Dr, then 0.4 mi s. 154 Regency Park Dr 62269. Fax: 618/624-1778. **Facility:** 89 one-bedroom standard units with efficiencies. 3 stories, interior corridors. *Bath:* combo or shower only. **Parking:** on-site. **Terms:** pets ($25 extra charge, limit 1). **Amenities:** high-speed Internet, voice mail, irons. **Guest Services:** coin laundry, wireless Internet.

SOME UNITS

FEE

Missouri Botanical Garden / Missouri Division of Tourism

This ends listings for the St. Louis Vicinity.
The following page resumes the alphabetical listings of cities in Missouri.

ST. PETERS —*See St. Louis p. 552.*

ST. ROBERT pop. 2,760

—— **WHERE TO STAY** ——

BAYMONT INN & SUITES FT. LEONARD WOOD-ST. ROBERT *Book at AAA.com*   **Phone: 573/336-5050**
Property failed to provide current rates
Location: I-44, exit 161, just nw. 139 Carmel Valley Way 65584. Fax: 573/336-5045. **Facility:** 69 one-bedroom standard units, some with whirlpools. 4 stories, interior corridors. *Bath:* combo or shower only. **Parking:** on-site. **Amenities:** high-speed Internet, voice mail, safes (fee), irons, hair dryers. *Some:* DVD players.
Small-scale Hotel
Pool(s): small heated indoor. **Leisure Activities:** whirlpool, exercise room. **Guest Services:** valet and coin laundry. **Business Services:** meeting rooms.

SOME UNITS

COMFORT INN *Book great rates at AAA.com*   **Phone: (573)336-3553**

12/21-2/29 [ECP]	1P: $84-$124	2P: $89-$129	XP: $5 F18
3/1-12/20 [ECP]	1P: $74-$124	2P: $79-$129	XP: $5 F18

Location: I-44, exit 161, just nw. 103 St. Robert Blvd 65584. Fax: 573/336-2939. **Facility:** 70 one-bedroom standard units, some with whirlpools. 3 stories, interior corridors. *Bath:* combo or shower only. **Parking:** on-site. **Amenities:** high-speed Internet, voice mail, safes (fee), irons, hair dryers. *Some:* dual phone lines. **Pool(s):** small heated indoor. **Leisure Activities:** whirlpool, exercise room. **Guest Services:** valet and coin laundry. **Business Services:** PC. **Cards:** AX, CB, DC, DS, JC, MC, VI.
Small-scale Hotel

SOME UNITS

HAMPTON INN ST. ROBERT/FT LEONARD WOOD *Book great rates at AAA.com*   **Phone: 573/336-3355**
Property failed to provide current rates
Location: I-44, exit 161, just nw. 103 St. Robert Blvd 65584. Fax: 573/336-3660. **Facility:** 81 one-bedroom standard units, some with whirlpools. 3 stories, interior corridors. *Bath:* combo or shower only. **Parking:** on-site. **Amenities:** video games (fee), high-speed Internet, voice mail, irons, hair dryers. **Pool(s):** indoor.
Small-scale Hotel
Leisure Activities: exercise room. **Guest Services:** complimentary evening beverages: Thurs, valet and coin laundry. **Business Services:** meeting rooms, PC.

SOME UNITS

HOLIDAY INN EXPRESS-ST. ROBERT *Book at AAA.com*   **Phone: (573)336-2299**
All Year [ECP] 1P: $94 2P: $94 XP: $10 F18
Location: I-44, exit 161, just s, then 0.3 mi e on frontage road. 114 Vickie Lynn Ln 65584. Fax: 573/336-5998. **Facility:** 52 one-bedroom standard units. 2 stories (no elevator), interior corridors. **Parking:** on-site.
Small-scale Hotel
Amenities: video library (fee), high-speed Internet, dual phone lines, voice mail, irons, hair dryers. *Some:* DVD players (fee). **Pool(s):** heated indoor. **Leisure Activities:** exercise room. **Guest Services:** valet and coin laundry, wireless Internet. **Business Services:** business center. **Cards:** AX, CB, DC, DS, MC, VI.

SOME UNITS

MAINSTAY SUITES   *Book great rates at AAA.com*   **Phone:** (573)451-2700
▼▼▼▼   All Year   1P: $90-$100   2P: $90-$100   XP: $5   F
Location: I-44, exit 159, 0.8 mi nw. 227 St. Robert Blvd 65584. Fax: 573/451-2701. **Facility:** 77 units. 50 one-
Small-scale Hotel   bedroom standard units with efficiencies. 24 one- and 3 two-bedroom suites ($110-$170) with efficiencies. 4
stories, interior/exterior corridors. *Bath:* combo or shower only. **Parking:** on-site. **Terms:** weekly rates
available, pets ($10 extra charge). **Amenities:** DVD players, high-speed Internet, voice mail, irons, hair dryers. *Some:* dual
phone lines. **Pool(s):** small outdoor. **Leisure Activities:** exercise room. **Guest Services:** sundries, valet and coin laundry.
Business Services: business center. **Cards:** AX, CB, DC, DS, MC, VI.

SOME UNITS
(A$K) (S⊘) (🛏) (📶⁺) (🛄) (🎥) (🎬) (🔒) (🖥) (💻) / (✕) /
FEE

MICROTEL INN & SUITES   *Book at AAA.com*   **Phone:** (573)336-7705
▼▼▼   All Year   1P: $50-$80   2P: $55-$85   F16
Location: I-44, exit 161 westbound to Business Loop 44/Old Route 66, 0.9 mi w; exit 159 eastbound, 0.4 mi se. 562 Old
Small-scale Hotel   Route 66 65584. Fax: 573/336-7906. **Facility:** 66 one-bedroom standard units, some with whirlpools. 3
stories, interior corridors. *Bath:* combo or shower only. **Parking:** on-site. **Terms:** [CP] meal plan available.
Amenities: high-speed Internet (fee), voice mail. **Leisure Activities:** exercise room. **Guest Services:** gift shop, valet and coin
laundry. **Business Services:** meeting rooms. **Cards:** AX, DS, MC, VI.

SOME UNITS
(A$K) (S⊘) (📶ℳ) (🔒) (🎥) (💻) / (✕) (🔒) (🖥) /

MOTEL 6 #4211   **Phone:** (573)336-3610
(AAA) (SAVE)   All Year   1P: $40-$50   2P: $45-$55   XP: $6   F17
▼   **Location:** I-44, exit 161, just s, then 0.3 mi e on frontage road. 545 Hwy Z 65584. Fax: 573/336-5421. **Facility:** 79
one-bedroom standard units. 3 stories, interior corridors. *Bath:* combo or shower only. **Parking:** on-site.
Terms: small pets only (in smoking units). **Amenities:** video library (fee), high-speed Internet, voice mail.
Small-scale Hotel   *Some:* irons, hair dryers. **Leisure Activities:** *Fee:* dvd player. **Guest Services:** valet and coin laundry,
wireless Internet. **Business Services:** PC. **Cards:** AX, CB, DC, DS, JC, MC, VI. **Free Special Amenities:**
local telephone calls and high-speed Internet.

SOME UNITS
(S⊘) (🛏) (📶ℳ) (🎥) / (✕) (🔒) (🖥) (💻) /
FEE   FEE

─────── **WHERE TO DINE** ───────

ADONIA'S STEAK & SEAFOOD   **Dinner:** $17-$24   **Phone:** 573/336-5110
▼▼ ▼▼   **Location:** I-44, exit 127, 1 mi e on south outer road. 819 Zeigenbein Rd 65584. **Hours:** 4:30 pm-9 pm. Closed:
Steak & Seafood   11/22, 12/25; also Sun-Tues. **Reservations:** accepted. **Features:** A touch of sophistication in this military
town, the establishment sustains a pleasant atmosphere that lends itself to special occasions. Dressy
casual; cocktails. **Parking:** on-site. **Cards:** AX, DC, DS, MC, VI.

(📶ℳ) (🍽)

AUSSIE JACK'S   **Lunch:** $6-$8   **Dinner:** $8-$19   **Phone:** 573/336-2447
▼   **Location:** I-44, exit 161, just nw. 141 St. Robert Blvd 65584. **Hours:** 11 am-10 pm, Fri & Sat-11 pm, Mon & Tues
Australian   from 4 pm. Closed: 1/1. **Features:** An Australian influence punctuates such casually comfortable favorites
as Toowoomba chicken, a charbroiled chicken breast topped with Monterey Jack cheese, bacon and
sauteed mushrooms. Other popular choices include the 12-ounce campfire rib-eye and the decadent
crocodile sundae, which is topped with whipped cream and candied pecans covered in caramel sauce. Casual dress; cocktails.
Parking: on-site. **Cards:** AX, DC, DS, MC, VI.

(🍽) (🗭)

─────── *The following restaurant has not been evaluated by AAA* ───────
but is listed for your information only.

SWEETWATER BAR-B-QUE   **Phone:** 573/336-8830
(fyi)   Not evaluated. **Location:** I-44, exit 163, just se. 14076 Hwy 2 65584. **Features:** A tiny gem of the Ozarks, the
restaurant invites guests to cozy up with real wood-pit-smoked barbecue and fixings.

SALEM pop. 4,854

─────── **WHERE TO STAY** ───────

HOLIDAY INN EXPRESS   *Book at AAA.com*   **Phone:** (573)729-4700
▼▼▼▼   All Year   1P: $76-$85   2P: $76-$85
Location: Jct SR 19 and 32-72. 1200 S Hwy 19 65560. Fax: 573/729-7976. **Facility:** 65 one-bedroom standard
Small-scale Hotel   units. 4 stories, interior corridors. *Bath:* combo or shower only. **Parking:** on-site. **Amenities:** high-speed
Internet, voice mail, irons, hair dryers. **Pool(s):** heated indoor. **Leisure Activities:** whirlpool, exercise room.
Guest Services: valet and coin laundry. **Business Services:** meeting rooms, PC. **Cards:** AX, CB, DC, DS, JC, MC, VI.

SOME UNITS
(A$K) (S⊘) (📶ℳ) (🔒) (🎥) (🛌) (💻) / (✕) (🔒) (🖥) /

SEDALIA pop. 20,339

─────── **WHERE TO STAY** ───────

COMFORT INN SEDALIA STATION   *Book great rates at AAA.com*   **Phone:** (660)829-5050
(AAA) (SAVE)   All Year   1P: $72-$139   2P: $78-$145   XP: $6   F18
▼▼▼▼   **Location:** On US 50, 1 mi w of US 65. 3600 W Broadway 65301. Fax: 660/829-5150. **Facility:** 76 one-bedroom
standard units, some with whirlpools. 3-4 stories, interior corridors. *Bath:* combo or shower only. **Parking:**
Small-scale Hotel   **Terms:** [ECP] meal plan available. **Amenities:** high-speed Internet, irons, hair dryers. **Pool(s):**
heated indoor. **Leisure Activities:** whirlpool. **Guest Services:** valet and coin laundry, wireless Internet.
Business Services: meeting rooms. **Cards:** AX, CB, DC, DS, JC, MC, VI. **Free Special Amenities:**
expanded continental breakfast and high-speed Internet.

SOME UNITS
(S⊘) (📶⁺) (🔒) (🛌) (📶⁺) (🎥) (🔒) (🖥) (💻) / (✕) /

HOTEL BOTHWELL, A CLARION COLLECTION   *Book great rates at AAA.com*   Phone: (660)826-5588

(AAA) (SAVE)

▼▼▼▼

Classic
Small-scale Hotel

5/30-9/1	1P: $84-$234	2P: $84-$234
3/1-5/29 & 9/2-2/29	1P: $70-$184	2P: $70-$184

Location: Corner of 4th and S Ohio sts; downtown. 103 E 4th St 65301. **Fax:** 660/826-0395. **Facility:** A tastefully restored historic hotel which allows guests to enjoy authentic "railroad hotel" rooms all the way up to spacious and elegant suites. 48 units. 45 one- and 3 two-bedroom standard units, some with whirlpools. 7 stories, interior corridors. *Bath:* combo or shower only. **Parking:** on-site. **Terms:** cancellation fee imposed, [CP] meal plan available, small pets only ($25 extra charge). **Amenities:** high-speed Internet, voice mail, irons, hair dryers. **Dining:** 11 am-2 & 5-10 pm; closed Mon, cocktails. **Leisure Activities:** exercise room. **Guest Services:** gift shop, valet and coin laundry, wireless Internet. **Business Services:** meeting rooms, PC. **Cards:** AX, CB, DC, DS, JC, MC, VI. **Free Special Amenities:** expanded continental breakfast and high-speed Internet.

SOME UNITS

[S_D] [⛺] [♨] [▼] [📶] [▣] / [⊠] /
FEE

——— WHERE TO DINE ———

EL TAPATIO MEXICAN RESTAURANT   Lunch: $7-$13   Dinner: $7-$13   Phone: 660/827-5553

▼▼
Mexican

Location: Jct US 50 and 65, just e. 1705 W Broadway 65301. **Hours:** 10 am-10 pm, Fri & Sat-10 pm, Sun-9 pm. Closed: 7/4, 11/22, 12/24, 12/25. **Reservations:** accepted. **Features:** The popular, family-run restaurant nurtures a lively and colorful atmosphere. Live entertainment on weekends. Casual dress; cocktails. **Parking:** on-site. **Cards:** AX, DS, MC, VI.

[&M] [⟍]

GIAVANNI'S   Lunch: $5-$7   Dinner: $7-$20   Phone: 660/826-6066

▼▼▼▼
Italian

Location: Jct US 50 and 65, just w. 1975 W Broadway 65301. **Hours:** 11 am-10 pm. Closed: 11/22, 12/25; also Mon. **Reservations:** accepted. **Features:** Italian favorites, including pizza and sandwiches, are served in a cheerful and comfortable environment. Casual dress; cocktails. **Parking:** on-site. **Cards:** AX, DS, MC, VI.

[&M] [▼] [⟍]

KEHDE'S BARBEQUE   Lunch: $6-$20   Dinner: $6-$20   Phone: 660/826-2267

▼▼▼▼
American

Location: On US 65, 0.7 mi s of jct US 50. 1915 S Limit Ave 65301. **Hours:** 11 am-9 pm. Closed major holidays; also Tues. **Reservations:** accepted. **Features:** Unique inside and out, featuring railroad memorabilia. Expect large portions and friendly hometown service. Casual dress; beer only. **Parking:** on-site. **Cards:** AX, DS, MC, VI.

[⟍]

PATRICIA'S MEXICAN RESTAURANT AND MORE   Lunch: $5-$11   Dinner: $5-$11   Phone: 660/827-4141

▼▼
Mexican

Location: On US 65, 0.5 mi n of jct US 50 and 65. 3000 S Limit 65301. **Hours:** 11 am-9 pm, Fri & Sat-10 pm. Closed major holidays; also Mon. **Reservations:** accepted. **Features:** Patricia's has a rustic decor that is light and airy and offers patio dining in season. The menu features Southwestern meals and sandwiches, and the fruit chimichanga is one of the more unusual desserts. The server staff is friendly and efficient. Casual dress; cocktails. **Parking:** on-site. **Cards:** DS, MC, VI.

[⟍]

SHELBINA pop. 1,943

——— WHERE TO STAY ———

AMERICAS BEST VALUE INN   *Book at AAA.com*   Phone: (573)588-0020

▼▼
Motel

All Year	1P: $51	2P: $55	XP: $4 F12

Location: US 36, exit SR 15, 0.3 mi n. 711 N Hwy 15 63468. **Fax:** 573/588-0045. **Facility:** 20 one-bedroom standard units. 1 story, interior corridors. **Parking:** on-site. **Amenities:** high-speed Internet, hair dryers. **Guest Services:** coin laundry, wireless Internet. **Business Services:** PC. **Cards:** AX, DS, MC, VI.

SOME UNITS

[A$K] [S_D] [⋇] [▣] / [⊠] [🛏] [▤]

SHELL KNOB pop. 1,393

——— WHERE TO DINE ———

THE STEAK INN   Dinner: $8-$25   Phone: 417/858-6814

▼▼
Steak House

Location: 0.3 mi s of bridge. S Hwy 39 65747. **Hours:** 5 pm-9 pm; hours may vary in winter. Closed: 11/22, 12/25, 12/26; also Mon. **Features:** Cedar and etched-glass accents combine with a glossy flagstone floor to evoke a warm, rustic atmosphere. For a touch of spring, the garden room may be just the ticket. Locals frequent this place for its salad bar and because they can watch their steak being grilled. Casual dress; cocktails. **Parking:** on-site. **Cards:** MC, VI.

[▼] [⟍]

SIKESTON pop. 16,992

——— WHERE TO DINE ———

JEREMIAH'S RESTAURANT & LOUNGE   Dinner: $10-$35   Phone: 573/472-4412

▼▼▼▼
American

Location: Corner of E Malone and N Kingshighway sts; downtown. 102 N Kingshighway St 63801. **Hours:** 5 pm-10 pm. Closed: Sun. **Reservations:** suggested. **Features:** The exterior is basic, but the atmosphere inside is pleasant, warm and inviting. On the menu are fine steak, chicken, seafood and pasta selections. Dressy casual; cocktails. **Parking:** on-site. **Cards:** AX, CB, DC, DS, JC, MC, VI.

[▼] [⟍]

© AAA

To Willard   To Clinton & Kansas City   To Sedalia

Sptingfield-
Branson
Regional
Airport

GENERAL AVIATION

Springfield
Lodging & Dining

0   Miles   2.7

© 2006 NAVTEQ

To Nixa & Little Rock   To Little Rock & Poplar Bluff   1741-A

Driving Solutions

From teens to mature operators, AAA offers a variety of in-depth, powerful learning programs to help you stay safe throughout your driving career. You can rely on AAA to meet all of your driver training needs:

- Mature operators
- Online traffic school
- Teaching teen drivers
- Ticket dismissal
- Points reduction
- Insurance discounts

*For more information about **AAA**'s driver training programs, contact a participating **AAA** office or visit www.aaa.com.*

✈ Airport Accommodations

Spotter/Map Page Number	OA	SPRINGFIELD-BRANSON REGIONAL	Diamond Rating	Rate Range High Season	Listing Page
6 / p. 564	⟨AAA⟩	Courtyard by Marriott Airport, 1.8 mi e from main terminal	◈◈◈	$124-$189 [SAVE]	567

Springfield

This index helps you "spot" where approved accommodations and restaurants are located on the corresponding detailed maps. Lodging rate ranges are for comparison only and show the property's high season; rates are per night, unless only weekly (W) rates are available. Restaurant rate range is for dinner, unless only lunch (L) is served. Turn to the listing page for more detailed rate information and consult display ads for special promotions.

Spotter/Map Page Number	OA	SPRINGFIELD - Lodgings	Diamond Rating	Rate Range High Season	Listing Page
1 / p. 564		La Quinta Inn Springfield	◈◈	$72-$92	568
2 / p. 564	⟨AAA⟩	Krystal Aire-A Non-Smoking Hotel - see color ad p 568	◈◈	$65-$99 [SAVE]	568
3 / p. 564	⟨AAA⟩	Holiday Inn North - see color ad p 567	◈◈◈	$99-$249 [SAVE]	568
4 / p. 564		Hampton Inn & Suites	◈◈◈	Failed to provide	567
5 / p. 564		Drury Inn & Suites-Springfield	◈◈◈	$80-$132	567
6 / p. 564	⟨AAA⟩	Courtyard by Marriott Airport	◈◈◈	$124-$189 [SAVE]	567
7 / p. 564		Comfort Inn & Suites	◈◈	$69-$109	567
8 / p. 564	⟨AAA⟩	Holiday Inn Express Hotel & Suites - see color ad p 567	◈◈	$109-$169 [SAVE]	567
9 / p. 564	⟨AAA⟩	Best Western Route 66 Rail Haven	◈◈	$59-$84 [SAVE]	566
10 / p. 564	⟨AAA⟩	University Plaza Hotel and Convention Center	◈◈	$109-$159 [SAVE]	569
11 / p. 564		Comfort Inn	◈◈	$55-$149	566
12 / p. 564	⟨AAA⟩	Quality Inn & Suites	◈◈	$69-$129 [SAVE]	568
13 / p. 564	⟨AAA⟩	Baymont Inn & Suites - see color ad p 566	◈◈	$69-$106 [SAVE]	566
14 / p. 564	⟨AAA⟩	Residence Inn-Springfield	◈◈◈	$134-$229 [SAVE]	568
15 / p. 564		Sleep Inn of Springfield	◈◈	Failed to provide	569
		SPRINGFIELD - Restaurants			
1 / p. 564		the Cafe	◈◈	$7-$20	569
2 / p. 564		Nonna's Italian American Cafe	◈◈	$8-$14	570
3 / p. 564		Gallery Bistro	◈◈	$10-$23	569
4 / p. 564		Anton's Coffee Shop	◈	$6-$7(L)	569
5 / p. 564		Nearly Famous Deli & Pasta House	◈	$6-$15	570
6 / p. 564		Clary's American Grill	◈◈◈	$17-$39	569
7 / p. 564		Hemingway's Blue Water Cafe	◈◈	$8-$16	569
8 / p. 564		Ocean Zen	◈◈◈	$8-$25	570
9 / p. 564		Valentine's	◈◈	$4-$27	570
10 / p. 564		Schultz & Dooley's III	◈◈	$5-$8	570
11 / p. 564		Heritage Cafeteria	◈	$5-$10	569
12 / p. 564		J Parrino's Pasta House & Bar	◈◈	$5-$20	570
13 / p. 564		Metropolitan Grill	◈◈◈	$14-$24	570
14 / p. 564		Pasta Express	◈	$5-$7	570
15 / p. 564		Village Coffee & Sweets	◈◈	$5-$6	570
16 / p. 564		Mr Yen's	◈◈	$7-$14	570
17 / p. 564		The Argentina Steakhouse	◈◈◈	$12-$42	569
18 / p. 564		Churchill Coffee Estate & Cafe	◈	$6-$7	569

SPRINGFIELD pop. 151,580 (See map and index starting on p. 564)

——— WHERE TO STAY ———

BAYMONT INN & SUITES *Book great rates at AAA.com*   Phone: (417)889-8188   **13**
(AAA) (SAVE)   All Year [ECP]   1P: $69-$99   2P: $76-$106   XP: $7   F18
▼▼▼▼   **Location:** On US 60. 3776 S Glenstone Ave 65804. Fax: 417/889-6173. **Facility:** 107 units. 103 one-bedroom standard units, some with whirlpools. 4 one-bedroom suites ($99-$149), some with whirlpools. 4 stories, interior corridors. *Bath:* combo or shower only. **Parking:** on-site. **Terms:** pets ($50 deposit, in designated Small-scale Hotel units). **Amenities:** high-speed Internet, voice mail, irons, hair dryers. **Pool(s):** heated indoor. **Leisure Activities:** whirlpool, exercise room. **Guest Services:** complimentary evening beverages: Wed, valet and coin laundry. **Business Services:** PC. **Cards:** AX, CB, DS, MC, VI. **Free Special Amenities: expanded continental breakfast and high-speed Internet.** *(See color ad below)*

SOME UNITS
(icons) FEE

BEST WESTERN ROUTE 66 RAIL HAVEN   *Book great rates at AAA.com*   Phone: (417)866-1963   **9**
(AAA) (SAVE)   All Year   1P: $59-$79   2P: $64-$84   XP: $5   F18
▼▼▼▼   **Location:** I-44, exit 80A, 3 mi s. 203 S Glenstone Ave 65802. Fax: 417/866-1963. **Facility:** Ask about 50s theme rooms. Historic Route 66 property with contemporary room appointments. 93 units. 88 one-bedroom standard units, some with whirlpools. 5 one-bedroom suites ($99-$149). 1 story, exterior corridors. **Parking:** Classic Historic on-site. **Terms:** small pets only ($10 extra charge). **Amenities:** irons, hair dryers. *Some:* high-speed Motel Internet. **Pool(s):** outdoor. **Leisure Activities:** whirlpool. **Guest Services:** valet laundry. **Business Services:** PC. **Cards:** AX, DS, MC, VI. **Free Special Amenities: continental breakfast and high-speed Internet.**

SOME UNITS
(icons) FEE

COMFORT INN   *Book great rates at AAA.com*   Phone: (417)520-6200   **11**
▼▼▼   All Year   1P: $55-$149   2P: $55-$149   XP: $5   F18
  Location: US 65, exit Battlefield Rd, just w. 3370 E Battlefield Rd 65804. Fax: 417/520-6600. **Facility:** 108 units. Small-scale Hotel   107 one-bedroom standard units, some with whirlpools. 1 one-bedroom suite with whirlpool. 2 stories, interior corridors. *Bath:* combo or shower only. **Parking:** on-site. **Terms:** [BP] meal plan available. **Amenities:** *Some:* high-speed Internet, voice mail, irons, hair dryers. *Fee:* safes. **Pool(s):** outdoor. **Leisure Activities:** whirlpool, exercise room, basketball. **Guest Services:** valet and coin laundry, area transportation. **Business Services:** meeting rooms, business center. **Cards:** AX, CB, DC, DS, JC, MC, VI.

SOME UNITS
(ASK) (icons) FEE

(See map and index starting on p. 564)

COMFORT INN & SUITES   *Book great rates at AAA.com*   Phone: (417)869-8246   **7**

♦♦♦ ♦♦♦

5/1-10/31	1P: $69-$99	2P: $79-$109	XP: $5	F18
3/1-4/30 & 11/1-2/29	1P: $59-$79	2P: $69-$89	XP: $5	F18

Small-scale Hotel   **Location:** I-44, exit 80A, just s. 2815 N Glenstone Ave 65803. Fax: 417/869-3711. **Facility:** 77 one-bedroom standard units. 3-4 stories, interior corridors. **Parking:** on-site. **Terms:** [ECP] meal plan available. **Amenities:** high-speed Internet, voice mail, safes (fee), irons, hair dryers. **Pool(s):** small heated indoor. **Leisure Activities:** whirlpool, exercise room. **Guest Services:** valet and coin laundry. **Business Services:** meeting rooms. **Cards:** AX, CB, DC, DS, JC, MC, VI.

SOME UNITS

(ASK) ⬛ ⬛ ⬛ 🛂 ⬛ 📶 ⬛ / ✕ 📱 ⬛ /

COURTYARD BY MARRIOTT AIRPORT   *Book great rates at AAA.com*   Phone: 417/869-6700   **6**

(AAA) (SAVE)
♦♦♦ ♦♦♦

All Year   1P: $124-$189   2P: $127-$189

Small-scale Hotel   **Location:** I-44, exit 75 (US 160 W Bypass), just se to SR 744, then just w. 3527 W Kearney 65803. Fax: 417/869-9052. **Facility:** Smoke free premises. 142 units. 138 one-bedroom standard units, some with whirlpools. 4 one-bedroom suites ($189). 3 stories, interior corridors. **Bath:** combo or shower only. **Parking:** on-site. **Terms:** [BP] meal plan available. **Amenities:** high-speed Internet, dual phone lines, voice mail, irons, hair dryers. **Dining:** 6-10 am, Sat & Sun 7-11 am. **Pool(s):** small heated indoor. **Leisure Activities:** whirlpool, gazebo, outdoor courtyard, exercise room. **Fee:** in-room workout videos. **Guest Services:** sundries, valet and coin laundry, airport transportation-Springfield Branson Regional Airport. **Business Services:** meeting rooms, PC. **Cards:** AX, CB, DC, DS, JC, MC, VI. **Free Special Amenities:** newspaper.

SOME UNITS

✈ ⬛ 🛂 ⬛ 📶 ⬛ ✕ ✕ ⬛ ⬛ / 📱 ⬛ /

DRURY INN & SUITES-SPRINGFIELD   *Book at AAA.com*   Phone: (417)863-8400   **5**

♦♦♦ ♦♦♦

All Year [BP]   1P: $80-$122   2P: $90-$132   XP: $10   F18

Small-scale Hotel   **Location:** I-44, exit 80A (Glenstone Ave), just s. 2715 N Glenstone Ave 65803. Fax: 417/863-8400. **Facility:** 110 units. 95 one-bedroom standard units, some with whirlpools. 15 one-bedroom suites ($100-$157), some with whirlpools. 5 stories, interior corridors. **Bath:** combo or shower only. **Parking:** on-site. **Terms:** small pets only. **Amenities:** high-speed Internet, voice mail, irons, hair dryers. **Pool(s):** heated indoor/outdoor. **Leisure Activities:** whirlpool, exercise room. **Guest Services:** sundries, complimentary evening beverages, valet and coin laundry. **Business Services:** meeting rooms, business center. **Cards:** AX, CB, DC, DS, MC, VI.

SOME UNITS

(ASK) ⬛ ⬛ 🛂 ⬛ 📶 ⬛ 📶 📱 ⬛ ⬛ / ✕ /

HAMPTON INN & SUITES   *Book great rates at AAA.com*   Phone: 417/869-5548   **4**

♦♦♦ ♦♦♦

Property failed to provide current rates

Small-scale Hotel   **Location:** I-44, exit 80A, just s. 2750 N Glenstone Ave 65803. Fax: 417/869-5551. **Facility:** 89 units. 64 one-bedroom standard units. 25 one-bedroom suites. 3 stories, interior corridors. **Bath:** combo or shower only. **Parking:** on-site. **Amenities:** video games (fee), high-speed Internet, voice mail, irons, hair dryers. **Pool(s):** heated indoor. **Leisure Activities:** whirlpool, exercise room. **Guest Services:** sundries, valet and coin laundry. **Business Services:** meeting rooms, business center.

SOME UNITS

📶 📶 ⬛ / ✕ 📱 ⬛ /

HOLIDAY INN EXPRESS HOTEL & SUITES   *Book great rates at AAA.com*   Phone: (417)862-0070   **8**

(AAA) (SAVE)
♦♦♦ ♦♦♦

All Year [CP]   1P: $109-$169

Small-scale Hotel   **Location:** Just w of National Ave. 1117 E St. Louis St 65806. Fax: 417/862-9149. **Facility:** 120 units. 116 one-bedroom standard units. 4 one-bedroom suites ($129-$169). 4 stories, interior corridors. **Bath:** combo or shower only. **Parking:** on-site. **Terms:** pets ($25 fee). **Amenities:** video games (fee), high-speed Internet, dual phone lines, voice mail, irons, hair dryers. **Pool(s):** heated outdoor. **Leisure Activities:** whirlpools, exercise room. **Guest Services:** sundries, valet and coin laundry. **Business Services:** meeting rooms, business center. **Cards:** AX, CB, DC, DS, JC, MC, VI. **Free Special Amenities:** expanded continental breakfast and newspaper.** *(See color ad below)*

SOME UNITS

⬛ 🛂 ⬛ 📶 ⬛ / ✕ 📱 ⬛ /
FEE

(See map and index starting on p. 564)

HOLIDAY INN NORTH   *Book great rates at AAA.com*   Phone: (417)865-8600   **3**

All Year   1P: $99-$249   2P: $99-$249
Location: I-44, exit 80A, just se. 2720 N Glenstone Ave 65803. Fax: 417/862-9415. **Facility:** 188 units. 164 one- and 2 two-bedroom standard units. 22 one-bedroom suites, some with whirlpools. 6 stories, interior corridors. *Bath:* combo or shower only. **Parking:** on-site. **Terms:** pets ($25 fee). **Amenities:** video games (fee), high-speed Internet, voice mail, irons, hair dryers. **Dining:** 6 am-10:30 & 5:30-10 pm, Sun 6 am-11 & 5:30-9 pm, cocktails. **Pool(s):** heated indoor. **Leisure Activities:** sauna, whirlpool, exercise room. **Guest Services:** valet laundry, area transportation. **Business Services:** conference facilities, business center. **Cards:** AX, CB, DC, DS, MC, VI. **Free Special Amenities:** newspaper. *(See color ad p 567)*

Small-scale Hotel

SOME UNITS

[icons]

KRYSTAL AIRE-A NON-SMOKING HOTEL   *Book great rates at AAA.com*   Phone: (417)869-0001   **2**

All Year   1P: $65-$99   2P: $65-$99
Location: I-44, exit 80A, just sw. 2745 N Glenstone Ave 65803. Fax: 417/869-9146. **Facility:** 102 units. 95 one-bedroom standard units. 7 one-bedroom suites ($79-$119), some with whirlpools. 2-3 stories (no elevator), interior/exterior corridors. **Parking:** on-site. **Terms:** pets (in designated units). **Amenities:** high-speed Internet, voice mail, irons, hair dryers. **Pool(s):** outdoor. **Leisure Activities:** exercise room. **Guest Services:** valet laundry. **Cards:** AX, DC, DS, MC, VI. **Free Special Amenities:** expanded continental breakfast and high-speed Internet. *(See color ad below)*

Small-scale Hotel

SOME UNITS

[icons]

LA QUINTA INN SPRINGFIELD   *Book great rates at AAA.com*   Phone: (417)520-8800   **1**

3/1-10/31 [CP]   1P: $72-$92
11/1-2/29 [CP]   1P: $62-$82
Location: I-44, exit 80A. 1610 E Evergreen 65803. Fax: 417/520-8200. **Facility:** 104 one-bedroom standard units. 3 stories, interior corridors. **Parking:** on-site. **Terms:** [BP] meal plan available, small pets only. **Amenities:** high-speed Internet, voice mail, irons, hair dryers. **Pool(s):** small heated indoor. **Leisure Activities:** whirlpool, exercise room. **Guest Services:** valet and coin laundry. **Business Services:** PC. **Cards:** AX, CB, DC, DS, MC, VI.

Small-scale Hotel

SOME UNITS

[icons]

QUALITY INN & SUITES   *Book great rates at AAA.com*   Phone: (417)888-0898   **12**
F17

All Year   1P: $69-$129   XP: $5
Location: US 60 (James River Expwy), exit Kansas Expwy, just n to Chesterfield Blvd, then just w. Located adjacent to Chesterfield Village. 3930 S Overland Ave 65807. Fax: 417/888-0881. **Facility:** 50 one-bedroom standard units, some with whirlpools. 2 stories (no elevator), interior corridors. *Bath:* combo or shower only. **Parking:** on-site. **Terms:** pets ($10 fee, $30 deposit, in designated units). **Amenities:** high-speed Internet, voice mail, safes (fee), irons, hair dryers. **Pool(s):** small heated indoor. **Leisure Activities:** exercise room. **Guest Services:** valet and coin laundry. **Business Services:** meeting rooms, PC. **Cards:** AX, DS, MC, VI. **Free Special Amenities:** expanded continental breakfast and high-speed Internet.

Small-scale Hotel

SOME UNITS

[icons]

RESIDENCE INN-SPRINGFIELD   *Book great rates at AAA.com*   Phone: (417)890-0020   **14**

All Year [CP]   1P: $134-$229   2P: $134-$229
Location: US 60 (James River Expwy), exit National St, just s, then just e. 1303 E Kingsley St 65804. Fax: 417/890-0055. **Facility:** Smoke free premises. 136 units. 113 one- and 23 two-bedroom suites, some with efficiencies or kitchens. 4 stories, interior corridors. *Bath:* combo or shower only. **Parking:** on-site. **Terms:** weekly rates available, pets ($75 fee). **Amenities:** video games (fee), high-speed Internet, dual phone lines, voice mail, irons, hair dryers. **Pool(s):** small heated outdoor. **Leisure Activities:** whirlpools, lighted tennis court, barbecue grill, patio, exercise room, sports court, basketball. **Guest Services:** sundries, valet and coin laundry. **Business Services:** meeting rooms, PC. **Cards:** AX, CB, DC, DS, JC, MC, VI. **Free Special Amenities:** expanded continental breakfast and newspaper.

Small-scale Hotel

[icons]

(See map and index starting on p. 564)

SLEEP INN OF SPRINGFIELD   *Book great rates at AAA.com*   Phone: 417/886-2464   **15**

Property failed to provide current rates

Small-scale Hotel
Location: US 60 (James River Expwy), exit Campbell Ave, just se. 233 El Camino Alto 65810. Fax: 417/886-4121. **Facility:** 104 one-bedroom standard units, some with whirlpools. 3 stories, interior corridors. *Bath:* combo or shower only. **Parking:** on-site. **Terms:** small pets only ($10 extra charge). **Amenities:** video games (fee), high-speed Internet, voice mail, irons, hair dryers. **Pool(s):** small heated indoor. **Leisure Activities:** whirlpool. **Guest Services:** complimentary evening beverages: Mon-Thurs, valet laundry. **Business Services:** meeting rooms.

SOME UNITS

UNIVERSITY PLAZA HOTEL AND CONVENTION
CENTER   *Book great rates at AAA.com*   Phone: (417)864-7333   **10**

Large-scale Hotel
All Year   1P: $109-$159   2P: $109-$159
Location: 0.5 mi e on St. Louis St. 333 John Q Hammons Pkwy 65806. Fax: 417/831-5893. **Facility:** 271 units. 238 one-bedroom standard units. 33 one-bedroom suites ($134-$184), some with whirlpools. 9 stories, interior corridors. *Bath:* combo or shower only. **Parking:** on-site. **Terms:** pets ($50 extra charge). **Amenities:** dual phone lines, voice mail, irons, hair dryers. *Fee:* video games, high-speed Internet. **Dining:** 6:30 a-m 2 & 5-10 pm, cocktails. **Pool(s):** heated outdoor, small heated indoor. **Leisure Activities:** whirlpool, exercise room. **Guest Services:** sundries, valet and coin laundry, beauty salon. **Business Services:** conference facilities, business center. **Cards:** AX, CB, DC, DS, MC, VI. **Free Special Amenities:** newspaper.

SOME UNITS

--- WHERE TO DINE ---

ANTON'S COFFEE SHOP   **Lunch:** $6-$7   Phone: 417/869-7681   **4**

American
Location: I-44, exit 80A, 3 mi s, at Grand Ave. 937 S Glenstone Ave 65802. **Hours:** 6 am-2 pm, Sun from 8 am. Closed major holidays; also Tues. **Reservations:** not accepted. **Features:** Breakfast served all day has been a tradition since 1974 in the basic, no-frills eatery. Daily chalkboard specials complement an extensive selection of omelets, sandwiches, burgers and salads. Casual dress. **Parking:** on-site and street.

THE ARGENTINA STEAKHOUSE   **Lunch:** $6-$13   **Dinner:** $12-$42   Phone: 417/886-8010   **17**

Argentine
Location: US 60 (James River Expwy), 2.7 mi w. 1410 E Republic Rd 65804. **Hours:** 11 am-2 & 5-9:30 pm, Fri & Sat-10 pm. Closed: 1/1, 12/25; also Sun. **Reservations:** suggested. **Features:** The kitchen staff—all trained and certified chefs from Buenos Aires—cooks many of the steak, chops, chicken, seafood and pasta selections over a parrilla, the traditional Argentinean open fire pit. Dressy casual; cocktails. **Parking:** on-site. **Cards:** AX, DC, MC, VI.

THE CAFE   **Lunch:** $7-$20   **Dinner:** $7-$20   Phone: 417/866-7626   **1**

American
Location: I-44, exit 75 (US 160 W Bypass), just se to SR 744, then just w; adjacent to Courtyard By Marriott Hotel. 3521 W Kearney 65803. **Hours:** 11 am-10 pm, Fri & Sat-11 pm. Closed: 11/22, 12/25. **Features:** The menu lists chicken and pork tenderloins, as well as pasta, steak, seafood, sandwiches and burgers. Casual dress; cocktails. **Parking:** on-site. **Cards:** AX, CB, DC, DS, JC, MC, VI.

CHURCHILL COFFEE ESTATE & CAFE   **Lunch:** $6-$7   **Dinner:** $6-$7   Phone: 417/823-8209   **18**

Deli/Subs
Sandwiches
Location: 1 mi w of US 60 on Business Rt US 65. 1604 E Republic Rd 65804. **Hours:** 7 am-10 pm, Fri & Sat-11 pm. Closed: 4/8, 11/22, 12/25. **Features:** The upscale deli's cozy atmosphere includes wooden table and chair sets and a conversation area of sofas and overstuffed chairs. Soups, salads and sandwiches are served in ample portions. Desserts in the glass display case look scrumptious. Patrons can help themselves to exotic coffees, which are roasted and blended locally and brewed fresh. Casual dress. **Parking:** on-site. **Cards:** AX, DS, MC, VI.

CLARY'S AMERICAN GRILL   **Dinner:** $17-$39   Phone: 417/886-1940   **6**

American
Location: US 65, exit Sunshine Ave, 0.6 mi w; in northeast corner of Southern Hills Shopping Center. 3014-A E Sunshine 65804. **Hours:** 5 pm-10 pm, Fri & Sat-11 pm. Closed major holidays; also Sun. **Reservations:** suggested, weekends. **Features:** Fine dining is the order of the day at this restaurant where soft lights, plants, cool jazz and quiet intimacy all blend to create a sophisticated atmosphere. Creative, artistically presented plates prepared with fresh, high-quality ingredients enhance the air of sophistication. Servers are cordial, accommodating and professional. Casual dress; cocktails. **Parking:** on-site. **Cards:** AX, CB, DC, DS, MC, VI.

GALLERY BISTRO   **Dinner:** $10-$23   Phone: 417/866-0440   **3**

American
Location: Just sw of Jefferson Ave. 221 E Walnut St 65806. **Hours:** 5 pm-10 pm, Fri & Sat-11 pm. Closed major holidays; also Sun. **Reservations:** suggested. **Features:** The restaurant's contemporary cuisine includes a large selection of beef, seafood and pasta entrees. Pan-seared Alaskan halibut with risotto is a nice choice. Creme caramel over fresh berries makes a light, pleasant ending. Casual dress; cocktails. **Parking:** street.

HEMINGWAY'S BLUE WATER CAFE   **Lunch:** $7-$10   **Dinner:** $8-$16   Phone: 417/891-5100   **7**

American
Location: Business Rt US 65, 2 mi w on US 60 (Sunshine St); in south end of Bass Pro Shops Outdoor World. 1935 S Campbell 65807. **Hours:** 7 am-9 pm, Sun 9 am-5 pm. Closed: 12/25. **Reservations:** accepted. **Features:** The restaurant celebrates the sea with an atmosphere inspired by American author and saltwater fishing legend Ernest Hemingway. Buffets are virtual feasts with so many selections that diners could return repeatedly and not duplicate a meal. Casual dress; cocktails. **Parking:** on-site. **Cards:** AX, DS, MC, VI.

HERITAGE CAFETERIA   **Lunch:** $5-$10   **Dinner:** $5-$10   Phone: 417/883-3033   **11**

American
Location: 2.5 mi w of US 65; in Fremont Center. 1364 E Battlefield Rd 65804. **Hours:** 11 am-2 & 4:30-7:30 pm, Fri-8 pm, Sat 11 am-8 pm, Sun 11 am-7 pm. Closed: 12/25. **Reservations:** accepted. **Features:** The Heritage provides cafeteria dining with selections such as fried chicken, roast beef, chicken-fried steak, vegetables and homemade cornbread and muffins. The relaxed atmosphere is complemented by the hand-painted mural showing the Ozarks' four seasons. Casual dress. **Parking:** on-site. **Cards:** AX, DC, DS, MC, VI.

(See map and index starting on p. 564)

J PARRINO'S PASTA HOUSE & BAR Lunch: $5-$20 Dinner: $5-$20 Phone: 417/882-1808 (12)
Italian
Location: US 65, exit Battlefield Rd. 2.8 mi w; in Galleria Shopping Center. 1550 E Battlefield Rd 65804. **Hours:** 11 am-10 pm, Fri & Sat-11 pm, Sun-9 pm. Closed: 1/1, 11/22, 12/25. **Reservations:** suggested, weekends. **Features:** The casual, fresh and delightful cafe offers much to tempt the palate. The menu lists a wide variety of appetizers, with an even wider array of pastas. Specialty entrees also are a satisfying choice. Casual dress; cocktails. **Parking:** on-site. **Cards:** AX, DC, DS, MC, VI.

METROPOLITAN GRILL Lunch: $8-$12 Dinner: $14-$24 Phone: 417/889-4951 (13)
Mediterranean
Location: 0.6 mi w of jct US 65. 2931 E Battlefield Rd 65804. **Hours:** 11 am-10 pm, Fri-11 pm, Sat 5 pm-11 pm, Sun 5 pm-9 pm. Closed major holidays. **Reservations:** accepted. **Features:** Appropriate for both sophisticated and casual meals, the pleasant restaurant delivers a fresh and creative approach both in the food and in the atmosphere. Casual dress; cocktails. **Parking:** on-site. **Cards:** AX, CB, DC, DS, JC, MC, VI.

MR YEN'S Lunch: $6-$14 Dinner: $7-$14 Phone: 417/881-1061 (16)
Chinese
Location: US 60 (James River Expwy), 1.3 mi w of Business Rt US 65, exit National Ave, just s to Kingsley, then just w. 4117 S National Ave 65807. **Hours:** 11 am-10 pm, Fri & Sat-11 pm. **Reservations:** suggested, weekends. **Features:** The visual feast begins upon arrival, when diners gaze around at the red-tile roof, gardens, fountains and striking, pagoda-style architecture. Featured is a variety of Chinese dishes, as well as live lobster that can be selected from a large tank. On weekends from 11 am to 3 pm, diners can select from a dim sum menu with 30 items brought to the table. Casual dress; cocktails. **Parking:** on-site. **Cards:** AX, DS, MC, VI.

NEARLY FAMOUS DELI & PASTA HOUSE Lunch: $6-$15 Dinner: $6-$15 Phone: 417/883-3403 (5)
Italian
Location: Jct CR D and US 65, just w to Kentwood, then just s. 1828 S Kentwood 65804. **Hours:** 11 am-9 pm. Closed major holidays; also Sun. **Features:** Off the beaten path, the quiet, unassuming restaurant has a simple exterior, but it's wise not to judge the book by its cover. Since 1976, this place has served such tasty foods as delicatessen sandwiches, soups, pasta dishes and homemade desserts with beverages ranging from soft drinks and espresso to wine and cocktails. Staff members seem to enjoy what they do, and that attitude carries over into the service they provide. Casual dress; cocktails. **Parking:** on-site. **Cards:** AX, CB, DC, DS, JC, MC, VI.

NONNA'S ITALIAN AMERICAN CAFE Lunch: $5-$7 Dinner: $8-$14 Phone: 417/831-1222 (2)
Italian
Location: At McDaniel; downtown. 306 South Ave 65806. **Hours:** 11 am-10 pm, Sun & Mon-9 pm. Closed major holidays. **Features:** A casual dining room and good food await diners at Nonna's. Traditional pasta dishes, as well as steak and chicken entrees, line the menu. Casual dress; cocktails. **Parking:** on-site. **Cards:** AX, CB, DC, JC, MC, VI.

OCEAN ZEN Lunch: $5-$12 Dinner: $8-$25 Phone: 417/889-9596 (8)
Pacific Rim
Location: On Business Rt US 65, just s of CR D. 2058 S Glenstone Ave 65804. **Hours:** 11 am-3 & 4:30-10 pm, Fri & Sat-11 pm. Closed: 11/22, 12/25. **Reservations:** accepted. **Features:** Upscale casual, upbeat and trendy, this restaurant offers comtemporary Pacific Rim cuisine in a metropolitan atmosphere. Casual dress; cocktails. **Parking:** on-site. **Cards:** AX, CB, DC, DS, JC, MC, VI.

PASTA EXPRESS Lunch: $5-$7 Dinner: $5-$7 Phone: 417/890-1345 (14)
American
Location: US 65, exit Battlefield Rd; in Fox Grape Plaza. 3250 E Battlefield Rd 65804. **Hours:** 11 am-9 pm, Sun-8 pm. Closed major holidays. **Features:** Although the establishment bustles at lunchtime, it manages to prepare tasty dishes in short order. Casual dress. **Parking:** on-site. **Cards:** AX, DS, MC, VI.

RIB CRIB BARBECUE Lunch: $6-$20 Dinner: $6-$20 Phone: 417/866-6677
American
Location: I-44, exit 80A, 2 mi s. 1640 N Glenstone Ave 65804. **Hours:** 11 am-10 pm. Closed: 11/22, 12/25. **Features:** Most guests need extra napkins to tackle the ribs, brisket, ham, pork and chicken selections. The menu also lists sandwiches and wraps, along with tempting sides and large desserts. The decor is decidedly Western. Casual dress; beer only. **Parking:** on-site. **Cards:** AX, DS, MC, VI.

SCHULTZ & DOOLEY'S III Lunch: $5-$8 Dinner: $5-$8 Phone: 417/655-1222 (10)
American
Location: 0.8 mi w of US 65; in Battlefield Tower Shopping Center. 2916 S Lone Pine 65804. **Hours:** 11 am-10 pm, Fri & Sat-11 pm. Closed: 11/22, 12/25. **Features:** The bar and hamburger business focuses on freshness in its ground beef, produce and baked items. Also of note are the old-fashioned milkshakes. The atmosphere is warm and casual. Casual dress; cocktails. **Parking:** on-site. **Cards:** AX, MC, VI.

VALENTINE'S Lunch: $4-$10 Dinner: $4-$27 Phone: 417/891-9700 (9)
American
Location: At Battlefield Rd and Campbell St; in Imperial Plaza. 2902-B S Campbell St 65807. **Hours:** 11 am-10 pm, Fri & Sat-11 pm, Sun 10 am-10 pm. Closed: 11/22, 12/25. **Reservations:** accepted. **Features:** Minimalist decor adds a touch of contemporary sophistication to the casual establishment. On the menu is a good selection of appetizers, salads, steaks, pasta, seafood, chicken and sandwiches. Casual dress; cocktails. **Parking:** on-site. **Cards:** AX, DC, DS, MC, VI.

VILLAGE COFFEE & SWEETS Lunch: $5-$6 Dinner: $5-$6 Phone: 417/890-0303 (15)
American
Location: US 60 (James River Expwy), exit Kansas Expwy, just n to Chesterfield Blvd, then just w. 2132 W Chesterfield 65807. **Hours:** 7 am-7 pm, Fri-10 pm, Sat 8 am-10 pm. Closed: Sun. **Features:** The cozy bistro tempts guests with a dazzling variety of coffees, teas, smoothies and even milkshakes and malts. Selections range from yummy sandwiches, salads and soups to pastry items and fudge. Casual dress. **Parking:** street. **Cards:** AX, DS, MC, VI.

ZIGGIE'S CAFE Lunch: $5-$9 Dinner: $6-$17 Phone: 417/447-1607
American
Location: I-44, exit 80A, 2 mi s on I-44 business route. 853 N Glenstone Ave 65802. **Hours:** 24 hours. **Reservations:** accepted. **Features:** Lending to the warm, cheerful atmosphere is a mix of contemporary decor and memorabilia. Included in a good variety of menu selections are salads, pasta, charbroiled items, burgers and sandwiches. Casual dress; cocktails. **Parking:** on-site. **Cards:** AX, DC, DS, MC, VI.

(See map and index starting on p. 564)

ZIGGIE'S CAFE

◆ American

Lunch: $7-$10   **Dinner:** $7-$15   **Phone:** 417/883-0900
Location: 0.4 mi s from jct S Campbell and W Sunshine sts. 2222 S Campbell St 65807. **Hours:** 24 hours. **Features:** Popular with locals and visitors alike, the restaurant serves breakfast 24 hours a day. Also on the menu is a wide variety of standard Midwestern comfort foods, including wonderful fried chicken. On Wednesdays, dessert is free. Casual dress. **Parking:** on-site. **Cards:** AX, DS, MC, VI.

──────── *The following restaurants have not been evaluated by AAA* ────────
but are listed for your information only.

AUNT MARTHA'S PANCAKE HOUSE

[fyi]

Phone: 417/881-3505
Not evaluated. **Location:** 1700 E Cherokee 65804. **Features:** It's back to the basics in the hometown cafe. Patrons are likely to meet Aunt Martha herself in this popular spot.

GARBO'S PIZZERIA

[fyi]

Phone: 417/883-9010
Not evaluated. **Location:** US 60 (James River Expwy), exit Kansas Expwy, just w; in Chesterfield Village. 2101 W Chesterfield Blvd, Bldg C 65807. **Features:** The pleasant, casual setting offers a variety of selections, including the signature pizzas, which are great.

SCHULTZ & DOOLEY'S CHESTERFIELD VILLAGE

[fyi]

Phone: 417/885-0060
Not evaluated. **Location:** 2210 W Chesterfield Blvd 65807. **Features:** The bar and hamburger business focuses on freshness in its ground beef, produce and baked items. Also of note are the old-fashioned milkshakes. The atmosphere is warm and casual.

SCHULTZ & DOOLEY'S TOO

[fyi]

Phone: 417/886-0200
Not evaluated. **Location:** 3512 S National Ave 65807. **Features:** The bar and hamburger business focuses on freshness in its ground beef, produce and baked items. Also of note are the old-fashioned milkshakes. The atmosphere is warm and casual.

SULLIVAN pop. 6,351

──────── **WHERE TO STAY** ────────

BAYMONT INN

◆◆ Small-scale Hotel

Book at AAA.com
                    Property failed to provide current rates
Phone: 573/860-3333
Location: I-44, exit 225. 275 N Service Rd W 63080. **Fax:** 573/860-3334. **Facility:** 68 one-bedroom standard units, some with whirlpools. 3 stories, interior corridors. *Bath:* combo or shower only. **Parking:** on-site. **Amenities:** high-speed Internet, voice mail, irons, hair dryers. **Pool(s):** heated indoor. **Leisure Activities:** whirlpool. **Guest Services:** valet and coin laundry, wireless Internet. **Business Services:** meeting rooms.

SOME UNITS
[symbols] FEE

COMFORT INN

◆◆ Small-scale Hotel

Book great rates at AAA.com
All Year [CP]   1P: $90   2P: $90   XP: $5   F18
Phone: (573)468-7800
Location: I-44, exit 225, just sw. 736 S Service Rd W 63080. **Fax:** 573/468-7801. **Facility:** 59 one-bedroom standard units, some with whirlpools. 3 stories, interior corridors. *Bath:* combo or shower only. **Parking:** on-site. **Terms:** 1-2 night minimum stay - seasonal, 12 day cancellation notice-fee imposed, package plans. **Amenities:** high-speed Internet, voice mail, irons, hair dryers. **Pool(s):** heated indoor. **Leisure Activities:** exercise room. **Guest Services:** coin laundry, wireless Internet. **Business Services:** meeting rooms, PC. **Cards:** AX, DS, MC, VI.

[symbols]

──────── **WHERE TO DINE** ────────

BUFFALO'S SOUTHWEST CAFE

◆◆◆ Southwestern

Lunch: $4-$7   **Dinner:** $7-$15   **Phone:** 573/860-2233
Location: I-44, exit 226 (SR 185 S), just sw. 320 Park Ridge Rd 63080. **Hours:** 11 am-10 pm, Fri & Sat-11 pm; to 9 pm, Fri & Sat-10 pm in winter. Closed: 4/8, 11/22, 12/25. **Features:** Step back into the Old West to enjoy some of this Southwestern fare. Well known for lip smacking chicken wings that come in a variety of flavors. This fast paced eatery also serves ribs and steak or choose a creative selection from the "outlaw" burger men. Casual dress; cocktails. **Parking:** on-site. **Cards:** AX, DC, DS, MC, VI.

[symbols]

SUNRISE BEACH pop. 368

──────── **WHERE TO STAY** ────────

──────── *The following lodging was either not evaluated or did not*
meet AAA rating requirements but is listed for your information only.

LAKEVIEW RESORT

[fyi]

Phone: 573/374-5555
Not evaluated. **Location:** 11 CR 69, Box 505 65079. Facilities, services, and decor characterize a mid-range property.

SUNSET HILLS —*See St. Louis p. 553.*

SWEET SPRINGS pop. 1,628

—————— WHERE TO STAY ——————

PEOPLE'S CHOICE MOTEL   Phone: (660)335-6315
(AAA) [SAVE]   All Year   1P: $29-$33   2P: $37-$41   XP: $5   F10
Location: I-70, exit 66, just se. 1001 N Locust St 65351 (Rt 2, Box 2A). Fax: 660/335-6315. **Facility:** 29 one-
Motel   bedroom standard units. 1 story, exterior corridors. **Parking:** on-site. **Terms:** pets ($20 deposit). **Cards:** AX,
                 DS, MC, VI. **Free Special Amenities:** local telephone calls and early check-in/late check-out.

                                                                                        SOME UNITS

SUPER 8 MOTEL   *Book at AAA.com*   Phone: 660/335-4888
All Year   1P: $55-$68   XP: $5   F18
                 Location: I-70, exit 66, just se. 208 W 40 Hwy 65351 (RR 2, Box 216 B). Fax: 660/335-0012. **Facility:** 46 one-
Small-scale Hotel bedroom standard units, some with whirlpools. 2 stories (no elevator), interior corridors. *Bath:* combo or
shower only. **Parking:** on-site. **Terms:** weekly rates available, pets ($5 extra charge). **Amenities:** high-
speed Internet, voice mail, hair dryers. **Leisure Activities:** exercise room. **Guest Services:** coin laundry, wireless Internet.
Business Services: PC. **Cards:** AX, DS, MC, VI.

                                                                                        SOME UNITS

—————— WHERE TO DINE ——————

BROWNSVILLE STATION   **Lunch:** $4-$8   **Dinner:** $6-$12   Phone: 660/335-6802
Location: I-70, exit 66, just sw. 102 W Old Hwy 40 65351. **Hours:** 5:30 am-9 pm; to 10 pm in summer.
American   **Features:** Just off busy I-70, the casual restaurant is a convenient place to grab a bite while traveling
                 between St. Louis and Kansas City. The menu focuses strictly on unpretentious comfort food, with an
                 emphasis on economy and large portions. Casual dress. **Parking:** on-site. **Cards:** DS, MC, VI.

TOWN AND COUNTRY —*See St. Louis p. 553.*

TRENTON pop. 6,216

—————— WHERE TO STAY ——————

HYDE MANSION BED & BREAKFAST INN   Phone: 660/359-5631
All Year [ECP]   1P: $65-$100   2P: $75-$110   XP: $20   D12
                 Location: Just e of jct Main and 7th sts, then e from courthouse. Located in a quiet residential area. 418 E 7th St
Bed & Breakfast 64683. Fax: 660/359-5632. **Facility:** Designated smoking area. 6 one-bedroom standard units. 2 stories (no
                 elevator), interior corridors. *Bath:* combo or shower only. **Parking:** on-site. **Terms:** check-in 5 pm.
Amenities: high-speed Internet, hair dryers. *Some:* DVD players. **Leisure Activities:** limited exercise equipment. **Guest
Services:** wireless Internet. **Cards:** MC, VI.

SUPER 8 MOTEL   Phone: 660/359-2988
All Year   1P: $55   2P: $60   XP: $5   F17
                 Location: US 65, 1 mi n of jct SR 6 and US 65. 1845A E 28th St 64683. Fax: 660/359-3869. **Facility:** 34 one-
Small-scale Hotel bedroom standard units. 2 stories (no elevator), interior corridors. *Bath:* combo or shower only. **Parking:** on-
                 site. **Terms:** check-in 4 pm, small pets only ($10 fee, $40 deposit). **Amenities:** high-speed Internet. **Guest
Services:** wireless Internet. **Cards:** AX, DS, MC, VI.

                                                                                        SOME UNITS

TROY pop. 6,737

—————— WHERE TO STAY ——————

SUPER 8 MOTEL-TROY   Phone: 636/528-6888
All Year   1P: $70-$100   2P: $75-$104   XP: $5   F18
                 Location: Jct US 47 and 61, just w. 28 Turnbull Tr 63379. Fax: 636/528-7180. **Facility:** 70 one-bedroom standard
Small-scale Hotel units, some with whirlpools. 3 stories, interior corridors. *Bath:* combo or shower only. **Parking:** on-site.
                 Terms: [ECP] meal plan available. **Amenities:** DVD players, high-speed Internet, dual phone lines, irons,
hair dryers. *Fee:* video library, safes. **Pool(s):** small heated indoor. **Leisure Activities:** whirlpool, exercise room. **Guest
Services:** coin laundry, wireless Internet. **Business Services:** PC. **Cards:** AX, DC, DS, MC, VI.

                                                                                        SOME UNITS

UNION pop. 7,757

—————— WHERE TO STAY ——————

SUPER 8 MOTEL   *Book at AAA.com*   Phone: 636/583-8808
All Year   1P: $65-$85   2P: $65-$85   XP: $8   F17
                 Location: I-44, exit 247 (US 50), 4.7 mi w; just w of jct SR 47. 1015 E Main St 63084. Fax: 636/583-8870.
Small-scale Hotel **Facility:** 50 one-bedroom standard units, some with whirlpools. 3 stories, interior corridors. *Bath:* combo or
                 shower only. **Parking:** on-site. **Terms:** [CP] meal plan available, pets (dogs only, $8 extra charge, with prior
approval). **Amenities:** high-speed Internet, safes (fee), hair dryers. *Some:* irons. **Pool(s):** small heated indoor. **Guest Services:**
coin laundry, wireless Internet. **Cards:** AX, DC, DS, MC, VI.

                                                                                        SOME UNITS

UNIVERSITY CITY —See St. Louis p. 553.

VALLEY PARK —See St. Louis p. 554.

WARRENSBURG pop. 16,340

―――― **WHERE TO STAY** ――――

COMFORT INN   *Book great rates at AAA.com*   **Phone:** (660)429-4848
All Year [ECP]   1P: $76-$140   2P: $81-$145   XP: $5   F18
Location: Jct US 50 and SR 13, just s to Russell Ave, then 0.8 mi e. 609 E Russell Ave 64093. **Fax:** 660/429-4850.
Small-scale Hotel **Facility:** 78 one-bedroom standard units, some with whirlpools. 3-4 stories, interior corridors. *Bath:* combo
or shower only. **Parking:** on-site. **Amenities:** high-speed Internet, voice mail, irons, hair dryers. **Pool(s):**
heated indoor. **Leisure Activities:** whirlpool, exercise room. **Guest Services:** valet and coin laundry, wireless Internet.
Business Services: meeting rooms. **Cards:** AX, CB, DC, DS, JC, MC, VI.
SOME UNITS

HOLIDAY INN EXPRESS   *Book at AAA.com*   **Phone:** 660/747-3000
Property failed to provide current rates
Location: Jct US 50 and SR 13, just s to Russell Ave, then 0.8 mi e. 626 E Russell Ave 64093. **Fax:** 660/747-4167.
Small-scale Hotel **Facility:** 82 one-bedroom standard units. 3 stories, interior corridors. *Bath:* combo or shower only. **Parking:**
on-site. **Amenities:** high-speed Internet, dual phone lines, voice mail, irons, hair dryers. *Some:* DVD
players, CD players. **Pool(s):** small heated indoor. **Leisure Activities:** whirlpool, exercise room. **Fee:** game room. **Guest
Services:** valet and coin laundry, wireless Internet. **Business Services:** meeting rooms, PC.
SOME UNITS

―――― **WHERE TO DINE** ――――

HERO'S RESTAURANT & PUB   **Lunch:** $6-$17   **Dinner:** $6-$17   **Phone:** 660/747-3162
Location: Downtown. 107 W Pine St 64093. **Hours:** 11 am-10 pm, Fri & Sat-11 pm, Sun 10 am-10 pm; Sunday
brunch. **Closed:** 11/22, 12/25; also for dinner 12/24. **Reservations:** accepted. **Features:** Sports, Hollywood
American   and political heroes are central to the wealth of memorabilia. The menu offers something for everyone, with
homemade onion rings and fries being a popular speciality. Casual dress; cocktails. **Parking:** street.
Cards: AX, DC, DS, MC, VI.

PLAYERS RESTAURANT & LOUNGE   **Lunch:** $5-$8   **Dinner:** $6-$17   **Phone:** 660/747-2115
Location: Jct US 50 and SR 13, just s to Russell, then 0.8 mi e. 503E N McGuire 64093. **Hours:** 11 am-10 pm, Fri &
Sat-11 pm. **Closed** major holidays. **Features:** You'll enjoy the sports bar and grill atmosphere and very good
American   selection of menu items at Players. The meals and sandwiches are hot, tasty and appetizingly presented,
and the servers are fast, efficient and friendly. Some Italian and Greek dishes. Casual dress; cocktails.
Parking: on-site. **Cards:** AX, DC, DS, MC, VI.

WARRENTON pop. 5,281

―――― **WHERE TO DINE** ――――

BREWSKIES   **Lunch:** $5-$9   **Dinner:** $7-$13   **Phone:** 636/456-7678
Location: Downtown. 209 E Main St 63383. **Hours:** 11 am-9 pm, Fri-10 pm, Sat noon-10 pm, Mon 11 am-2 pm.
Closed major holidays; also Sun. **Features:** Popular with the local crowd, the downtown restaurant presents
American   a menu that lists something for almost everyone. A warm, lived-in atmosphere prevails. Casual dress;
cocktails. **Parking:** street. **Cards:** AX, MC, VI.

WARSAW pop. 2,070

―――― **WHERE TO STAY** ――――

SUPER 8 MOTEL-WARSAW   **Phone:** 660/438-2882
3/1-10/21   1P: $72   2P: $85   XP: $6   F
10/22-2/29   1P: $70   2P: $85   XP: $6   F
Small-scale Hotel **Location:** US 65 and SR 7, exit Clinton. 1603 Commercial St 65355 (PO Box 1571). **Fax:** 660/438-4045.
Facility: 44 one-bedroom standard units. 2 stories (no elevator), exterior corridors. **Parking:** on-site.
Terms: check-in 4 pm, pets ($5 fee, $20-$40 deposit). **Amenities:** *Some:* DVD players, high-speed Internet. **Pool(s):** small
outdoor. **Leisure Activities:** horseshoes. **Guest Services:** wireless Internet. **Business Services:** PC. **Cards:** AX, DC, DS,
MC, VI.
SOME UNITS
FEE

WASHINGTON pop. 13,243

―――― **WHERE TO STAY** ――――

SLEEP INN & SUITES   *Book great rates at AAA.com*   **Phone:** (636)390-8877
All Year   1P: $89-$149   2P: $89-$149
Location: I-44, exit 251, 8.5 mi w on SR 100 to S Point Rd. 4104 S Point Rd 63090. **Fax:** 636/390-2224.
Facility: 71 one-bedroom standard units. 3 stories, interior corridors. *Bath:* combo or
shower only. **Parking:** on-site. **Terms:** cancellation fee imposed, [CP] meal plan available, package plans,
Small-scale Hotel pets (small dogs only, $25 extra charge). **Amenities:** high-speed Internet, voice mail, safes (fee), irons, hair
dryers. **Pool(s):** small heated indoor. **Leisure Activities:** whirlpool, exercise room. **Fee:** golf privileges.
Guest Services: sundries, valet and coin laundry. **Business Services:** meeting rooms. **Cards:** AX, DC, DS, MC, VI.
Free Special Amenities: expanded continental breakfast and high-speed Internet.
SOME UNITS
FEE

SUPER 8 WASHINGTON   *Book at AAA.com*   **Phone:** (636)390-0088

All Year   1P: $72-$102   2P: $72-$102   XP: $8   F17

Location: I-44, exit 251, 10 mi, w on SR 100; just s of SR 100 and 47. 2081 Eckelkamp Ct 63090 (PO Box 93). Fax: 636/390-2533. **Facility:** 51 one-bedroom standard units, some with whirlpools. 2 stories (no elevator), Small-scale Hotel interior corridors. *Bath:* combo or shower only. **Parking:** on-site. **Terms:** 7 day cancellation notice, weekly rates available, pets (dogs only, $10 fee, $25 deposit). **Amenities:** safes (fee), irons, hair dryers. *Some:* high-speed Internet. **Leisure Activities:** limited exercise equipment. **Guest Services:** coin laundry. **Cards:** AX, CB, DC, DS, MC, VI.

SOME UNITS

———— WHERE TO DINE ————

AMERICAN BOUNTY RESTAURANT   **Lunch:** $8-$15   **Dinner:** $16-$24   **Phone:** 636/390-2150

Location: Jct SR 47 and 100, 0.7 mi w on SR 100, 1.3 mi n on Jefferson St, then 0.4 mi w. 430 W Front St 63090. **Hours:** 5 pm-9 pm, Sat also 11 am-2 pm, Sun noon-7 pm. Closed: 4/8, 11/22, 12/24, 12/25; also Mon. **Reservations:** suggested, weekends. **Features:** In a restored 1858 brick building facing the Missouri River, this treasure of a restaurant prepares sophisticated cuisine, with an emphasis on regional dishes reflecting

Nouvelle   the produce of the Missouri Valley. Plate presentations are a delight. Seafood, pork, lamb and steak
American   selections are prepared with creativity and flair. Service is friendly and energized. Casual dress; cocktails. **Parking:** street. **Cards:** AX, DC, DS, MC, VI. **Historic**

CHICO'S CANTINA   **Lunch:** $5-$8   **Dinner:** $7-$16   **Phone:** 636/390-9393

Location: 0.9 mi e of jct SR 100 and 47; on SR 100; in Phoenix Center. 2000 Phoenix Center Dr 63090. **Hours:** 11 am-10 pm, Fri & Sat-10:30 pm, Sun-9 pm; 11 am-9 pm, Fri & Sat-10:30 pm, Sun-8 pm in winter. Closed

Mexican   major holidays; also 12/24. **Reservations:** accepted. **Features:** The attractive facility allows for sidewalk dining in season. Diners relax in the colorful setting to savor meals prepared with fresh ingredients. Casual dress; cocktails. **Parking:** on-site. **Cards:** AX, DC, DS, MC, VI.

RICHARD'S ON THE RIVERFRONT   **Lunch:** $6-$18   **Dinner:** $6-$18   **Phone:** 636/239-2111

Location: SR 47, 0.7 mi w to Jefferson St, just n to Front St, then 0.3 mi w. 116 W Front St 63090. **Hours:** 11 am-9 pm, Sun 10 am-8 pm. Closed major holidays. **Reservations:** suggested, weekends. **Features:** With a great

Italian   view overlooking the Missouri River, the restaurant presents a menu of traditional appetizers, salads, sandwiches and varied pasta dishes. Servers are attentive. Casual dress; cocktails. **Parking:** street. **Cards:** AX, DS, MC, VI.

WEBSTER GROVES —*See St. Louis p. 554.*

WENTZVILLE —*See St. Louis p. 555.*

WESTON —*See Kansas City p. 473.*

WEST PLAINS pop. 10,866

———— WHERE TO STAY ————

SUPER 8 MOTEL-WEST PLAINS   *Book at AAA.com*   **Phone:** 417/256-8088

All Year [CP]   1P: $55   2P: $55   XP: $5   F17

Location: On US 63B, 0.8 mi s of jct US 63. 1210 Porter Wagoner Blvd 65775. Fax: 417/256-2369. **Facility:** 49 Small-scale Hotel one-bedroom standard units. 2 stories (no elevator), interior corridors. **Parking:** on-site. **Terms:** pets ($25 extra charge, with prior approval). **Amenities:** high-speed Internet, irons, hair dryers. **Guest Services:** wireless Internet. **Cards:** AX, CB, DC, DS, JC, MC, VI.

SOME UNITS

WOODSON TERRACE —*See St. Louis p. 555.*

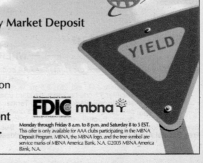

Oklahoma

Tallgrass Prairie Preserve,
Pawhuska
© Wolfgang Kaehler

Oklahoma Orientation

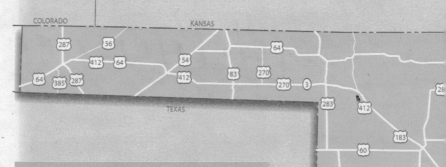

Map To Destinations

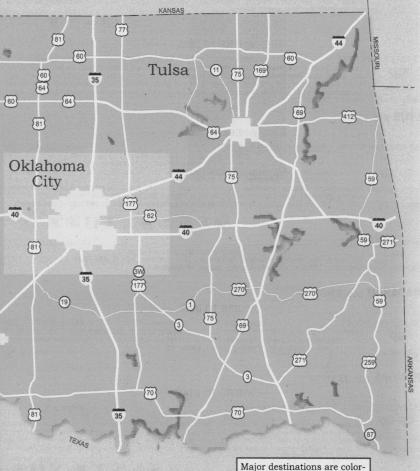

Major destinations are color-coded to index boxes, which display vicinity communities you will find listed within that destination's section of the book.

Cities outside major destination vicinities are listed in alphabetical order throughout the book.

Use the Comprehensive City Index at the back of this book to find every city's listing locations.

ADA pop. 15,691

———— WHERE TO STAY ————

BEST WESTERN RAINTREE MOTOR INN
Phone: (580)332-6262

(AAA) (SAVE)
♦♦♦♦♦

Small-scale Hotel

All Year | 1P: $75-$89 | 2P: $80-$89 | XP: $5 | F12
Location: 1.5 mi n on US 377/SR 99. 1100 N Mississippi Ave 74820. Fax: 580/436-4929. **Facility:** 39 one-bedroom standard units. 2 stories (no elevator), exterior corridors. **Parking:** on-site. **Amenities:** high-speed Internet, irons, hair dryers. **Pool(s):** heated indoor. **Cards:** AX, DC, DS, MC, VI. **Free Special Amenities:** full breakfast and high-speed Internet.

SOME UNITS

🏊 📷 💻 /✕/

———— WHERE TO DINE ————

JD'S CAFE & CAFETERIA
Lunch: $5-$10 | Dinner: $5-$10 | Phone: 580/332-9750

♦♦♦

American

Location: Center. 911 N Broadway 74820. **Hours:** 5 am-8:30 pm; 11 am-2 pm cafeteria. Closed: 11/22, 12/25; also Sun & Mon. **Reservations:** accepted. **Features:** JD's features a good menu selection of family-style meals such as roast beef, mashed potatoes, corn and apple cobbler. The restaurant has a friendly and courteous staff that's attentive to your needs while dining, and a wholesome environment. Casual dress. **Parking:** on-site. **Cards:** AX, CB, DC, DS, MC, VI.

ALTUS pop. 21,447

———— WHERE TO STAY ————

BEST WESTERN ALTUS *Book great rates at AAA.com*
Phone: (580)482-9300

(AAA) (SAVE)
♦♦♦♦♦

Small-scale Hotel

All Year | 1P: $74-$80 | 2P: $76-$80 | XP: $4 | F18
Location: 2 mi n on US 283. 2804 N Main St 73521. Fax: 580/482-2245. **Facility:** 100 one-bedroom standard units. 2 stories (no elevator), exterior corridors. **Parking:** on-site. **Terms:** cancellation fee imposed, package plans, small pets only. **Amenities:** video games (fee), voice mail, irons, hair dryers. **Pool(s):** heated indoor/outdoor. **Leisure Activities:** sauna, whirlpool, exercise room. **Guest Services:** complimentary evening beverages, valet and coin laundry, wireless Internet. **Business Services:** meeting rooms, PC, fax. **Cards:** AX, CB, DC, DS, JC, MC, VI. **Free Special Amenities:** expanded continental breakfast and high-speed Internet.

SOME UNITS

🏠 🛏 🍴 🍽 🏊 ✕ 📷 🛢 💻 /✕/

HAMPTON INN & SUITES
Phone: 580/482-1273

(fyi)

Small-scale Hotel

Property failed to provide current rates
Too new to rate, opening scheduled for February 2007. **Location:** 3601 N Main 73521. Fax: 580/482-1062. **Amenities:** 162 units, coffeemakers, microwaves, refrigerators, pool.

ANADARKO pop. 6,645

———— WHERE TO DINE ————

K.I.G. CUE BAR-B-CUE
Lunch: $5-$13 | Dinner: $8-$13 | Phone: 405/247-2454

♦♦♦

Barbecue

Location: 0.5 mi e of jct SR 8. 1315 E Central Blvd 73005. **Hours:** 11 am-9 pm. Closed: 11/22, 12/25; also Sun & Mon. **Reservations:** accepted. **Features:** Patrons can sample from the daily all-you-can-eat buffet or order from the menu. Casual dress. **Parking:** on-site. **Cards:** DS, MC, VI.

ARDMORE pop. 23,711

———— WHERE TO STAY ————

BEST WESTERN INN *Book great rates at AAA.com*
Phone: 580/223-7525

♦♦ ♦♦

Small-scale Hotel

All Year | 1P: $79 | 2P: $85 | XP: $6 | F12
Location: I-35, exit 31A, just ne. 6 Holiday Dr 73401. Fax: 580/223-7693. **Facility:** 55 one-bedroom standard units, some with whirlpools. 2 stories (no elevator), interior corridors. **Parking:** on-site, winter plug-ins. **Terms:** cancellation fee imposed, [CP] meal plan available, pets ($20 deposit, $6 extra charge). **Amenities:** irons, hair dryers. **Pool(s):** outdoor. **Guest Services:** valet and coin laundry, wireless Internet. **Business Services:** meeting rooms. **Cards:** AX, DC, DS, MC, VI.

SOME UNITS

(ASK) 🛏 🍴 🏊 📷 💻 /✕ 🛢 🖥/
FEE

HAMPTON INN *Book great rates at AAA.com*
Phone: (580)223-6394

♦♦♦ ♦♦♦

Small-scale Hotel

1/1-2/29 [BP] | 1P: $102-$189 | 2P: $107-$189 | XP: $5 | F18
3/1-12/31 [BP] | 1P: $97-$179 | 2P: $102-$179 | XP: $5 | F18
Location: I-35, exit 31A, just se. 410 Railway Express Rd 73401. Fax: 580/223-5898. **Facility:** 82 units. 78 one-bedroom standard units, some with whirlpools. 4 one-bedroom suites ($159-$179). 3 stories, interior corridors. *Bath:* combo or shower only. **Parking:** on-site. **Amenities:** high-speed Internet, voice mail, irons, hair dryers. **Pool(s):** heated indoor. **Leisure Activities:** sauna, whirlpool, exercise room. **Guest Services:** valet and coin laundry, wireless Internet. **Business Services:** meeting rooms, business center. **Cards:** AX, CB, DC, DS, JC, MC, VI.

SOME UNITS

(ASK) 🏠 🍴 🖐 🏊 ✕ 📷 🛢 🖥 💻 /✕/

HOLIDAY INN *Book at AAA.com*
Phone: 580/223-7130

♦♦♦

Small-scale Hotel

Property failed to provide current rates
Location: I-35, exit 31A, just e. 2705 W Broadway 73401. Fax: 580/223-7130. **Facility:** 169 units. 167 one-bedroom standard units, some with whirlpools. 2 one-bedroom suites. 2 stories (no elevator), exterior corridors. **Parking:** on-site, winter plug-ins. **Terms:** pets ($20 fee). **Amenities:** high-speed Internet, voice mail, irons, hair dryers. **Pool(s):** outdoor, wading. **Leisure Activities:** playground, exercise room. **Guest Services:** valet and coin laundry, wireless Internet. **Business Services:** meeting rooms, PC.

SOME UNITS

🛏 🍴 🌀 🏊 📷 💻 /✕ 🛢 🖥/
FEE

LA QUINTA INN ARDMORE

◆◆ ◆◆ *Book great rates at AAA.com* **Phone:** (580)223-7976

Small-scale Hotel

All Year [ECP] 1P: $70-$75 XP: $5 F18
Location: I-35, exit 33, just e. 2432 Veterans Blvd 73401. Fax: 580/223-7393. **Facility:** 64 one-bedroom standard units. 2 stories (no elevator), exterior corridors. **Parking:** on-site, winter plug-ins. **Terms:** small pets only. **Amenities:** high-speed Internet, voice mail, irons, hair dryers. **Pool(s):** small heated outdoor. **Leisure Activities:** whirlpool, exercise room. **Guest Services:** valet and coin laundry, wireless Internet. **Business Services:** PC. **Cards:** AX, DC, DS, MC, VI.

SOME UNITS

ASK ◨ 🐕 🍴 🖧 ⛱ 🎥 🛢 🖨 🖥 / ✕ /

MICROTEL INN & SUITES

◆◆ ◆◆ Property failed to provide current rates **Phone:** 580/224-2600

Small-scale Hotel

Location: I-35, exit 32, just w. 1904 Cooper Dr 73401. Fax: 580/224-9589. **Facility:** 43 units. 42 one-bedroom standard units. 1 one-bedroom suite with kitchen. 2 stories (no elevator), interior corridors. *Bath:* combo or shower only. **Parking:** on-site. **Terms:** pets ($25 deposit). **Amenities:** voice mail. **Guest Services:** coin laundry, wireless Internet.

SOME UNITS

🐕 ⊞ 🖧 🎥 / ✕ 🛢 🖥 🖨 /
FEE

SHILOH MORNING INN

◆◆◆ ◆ *Book at AAA.com* **Phone:** 580/223-9500

Bed & Breakfast

All Year [BP] 1P: $148-$185 2P: $148-$185
Location: 2.1 mi n of jct US 177 and SR 199, 0.8 mi w. Located in a quiet area; gated property. 2179 Ponderosa Rd 73401. Fax: 580/223-9615. **Facility:** A view of the sunrise can be seen from guest room balconies at this inn located in the country. Smoke free premises. 9 units. 8 one-bedroom standard units. 1 cottage ($225-$289). 2 stories (no elevator), interior corridors. *Bath:* combo or tub only. **Parking:** on-site. **Terms:** check-in 4 pm, 2 night minimum stay - weekends, age restrictions may apply, 7 day cancellation notice-fee imposed, no pets allowed (pet on premises). **Amenities:** video library, DVD players, hair dryers. *Some:* voice mail. **Leisure Activities:** hiking trails. **Guest Services:** wireless Internet. **Business Services:** meeting rooms. **Cards:** AX, DS, MC, VI.

SOME UNITS

🖧M VCR 🎥 🛢 🖥 / ✕ 🔲 🖨 /

WHERE TO DINE

BUDRO'S RIB JOINT

◆◆ **Lunch:** $5-$10 **Dinner:** $6-$18 **Phone:** 580/223-2272

Barbecue

Location: I-35, exit 31A, 0.8 mi e. 1606 McLish 73401. **Hours:** 11 am-11 pm. Closed major holidays. **Features:** In addition to barbecue beef and pork dishes, the menu lists a good selection of steak, catfish and chicken. Casual dress; beer only. **Parking:** on-site. **Cards:** AX, CB, DC, DS, JC, MC, VI.

🖊

POLO'S MEXICANO

◆◆ ◆◆ **Lunch:** $5-$12 **Dinner:** $7-$12 **Phone:** 580/226-7656

Mexican

Location: I-35, exit 31A, just e. 2610 W Broadway 73401. **Hours:** 11 am-9 pm. Closed: 11/22, 12/25. **Features:** Traditional preparations are served in ample portions. Fajitas are the signature dish. Casual dress. **Parking:** on-site. **Cards:** AX, CB, DC, DS, JC, MC, VI.

🖊

SIRLOIN STOCKADE

◆◆ ◆◆ **Lunch:** $6-$8 **Dinner:** $6-$8 **Phone:** 580/226-6281

Steak House

Location: On US 77. 1217 N Commerce 73401. **Hours:** 11 am-9 pm. Closed major holidays. **Reservations:** not accepted. **Features:** The steakhouse lines up buffet items, including pizza, tacos, soups, salads and desserts, providing both excellent variety and a good value. Rotating theme nights might allow for the sampling of sushi, barbecue and seafood. The buffet also may serve to complement a quality steak. Rolls are baked several times daily. Casual dress. **Parking:** on-site. **Cards:** DS, MC, VI.

🖊

TWO FROGS GRILL

◆◆ ◆◆ **Lunch:** $6-$12 **Dinner:** $6-$18 **Phone:** 580/226-3764

American

Location: I-35, exit 31A, just se. 2646 W Broadway 73401. **Hours:** 11 am-10 pm, Sun-9 pm. Closed: 12/25. **Features:** Food that will make your mouth water is served in a casual and fun atmosphere. The relaxed feel from the moment you step through the door tells you that this is one place to hop on into and fill your tank. Casual dress; cocktails. **Parking:** on-site. **Cards:** AX, DS, MC, VI.

🍸 🖊

BARTLESVILLE pop. 34,748

―――――― WHERE TO STAY ――――――

HAMPTON INN — *Book great rates at AAA.com* — Phone: 918/333-4051
♦♦♦ 5/1-8/31 [ECP] 1P: $84 2P: $84-$87
♦♦♦ 3/1-4/30 & 9/1-2/29 [ECP] 1P: $82-$84 2P: $84
Small-scale Hotel **Location:** 0.8 mi n of jct US 60 and 75. 130 SE Washington Blvd 74006. Fax: 918/333-0672. **Facility:** 67 one-bedroom standard units. 3 stories, interior corridors. *Bath:* combo or shower only. **Parking:** on-site. **Terms:** cancellation fee imposed, package plans. **Amenities:** high-speed Internet, dual phone lines, voice mail, irons, hair dryers. **Pool(s):** heated indoor. **Leisure Activities:** sauna, whirlpool, exercise room. **Guest Services:** valet and coin laundry, wireless Internet. **Business Services:** meeting rooms, business center. **Cards:** AX, DC, DS, MC, VI.

SOME UNITS
ASK ⬛ 🍴⊹ 📶 ➰ ✕ 📷 🛢 🖥 🖥 / ✕ /

MICROTEL INN & SUITES OF BARTLESVILLE — *Book at AAA.com* — Phone: (918)333-2100
♦♦♦ All Year [CP] 1P: $49-$89 2P: $49-$89 XP: $5 F17
Small-scale Hotel **Location:** 1.4 mi s of jct US 60 E. 2696 SE Washington Blvd 74006. Fax: 918/333-4145. **Facility:** 56 one-bedroom standard units, some with whirlpools. 3 stories, interior corridors. *Bath:* combo or shower only. **Parking:** on-site. **Terms:** 7 day cancellation notice, small pets only ($25 deposit). **Amenities:** voice mail, irons, hair dryers. **Leisure Activities:** limited exercise equipment. **Guest Services:** coin laundry, wireless Internet. **Cards:** AX, DS, MC, VI.

SOME UNITS
ASK ⬛ 🖐 ♿M 📶 ➰ 📷 🖥 / ✕ 🛢 🖥 /
FEE

―――――― WHERE TO DINE ――――――

GOLDIES PATIO GRILL — Lunch: $5-$8 — Dinner: $5-$8 — Phone: 918/335-5507
♦♦ **Location:** 1.1 mi n of jct US 60 and 75. 201 SE Washington 74006. **Hours:** 11 am-9 pm. Closed: 1/1, 11/22, 12/25.
American **Features:** The menu comprises grilled items, chicken, sandwiches and steak, but this place is bests known for its excellent charbroiled burgers. The decor incorporates 1950s and '60s memorabilia. Casual dress. **Parking:** on-site. **Cards:** AX, DS, MC, VI.

MONTANA MIKE'S STEAKHOUSE — Lunch: $6-$16 — Dinner: $8-$16 — Phone: 918/333-2666
♦♦ **Location:** 1 mi n of center. 3825 SE Adams 74006. **Hours:** 11 am-9 pm, Fri & Sat-10 pm. Closed: 11/22, 12/25.
Steak House **Features:** This steakhouse offers a dining experience for the whole family. A rustic look with Western appointments characterizes the dining room. Although it's hard to go wrong with a hearty steak of USDA Choice aged beef, guests also can try smoked, fire-grilled chicken breast, chicken-fried steak, baby back ribs and other selections. Casual dress; cocktails. **Parking:** on-site. **Cards:** AX, DS, MC, VI.

📺 ✕

RIB CRIB BBQ — Lunch: $6-$15 — Dinner: $6-$15 — Phone: 918/333-6200
♦♦ **Location:** 1.4 mi s of jct US 60 and 75. 2077 SE Washington Blvd 74006. **Hours:** 11 am-10 pm. Closed: 11/22,
Barbecue 12/25. **Features:** Most guests need extra napkins to tackle the ribs, brisket, ham, pork and chicken selections. The menu also lists sandwiches and wraps, along with tempting sides and large desserts. The decor is decidedly Western. Casual dress; beer only. **Parking:** on-site. **Cards:** AX, MC, VI.

BIG CABIN pop. 293

―――――― WHERE TO STAY ――――――

SUPER 8 MOTEL-BIG CABIN — *Book at AAA.com* — Phone: (918)783-5888
♦♦ All Year 1P: $44 2P: $49-$58 XP: $5 F14
Motel **Location:** I-44, exit 283, just ne. 30954 S Hwy 69 74301. Fax: 918/783-5887. **Facility:** 62 one-bedroom standard units. 1-2 stories (no elevator), interior/exterior corridors. **Parking:** on-site, winter plug-ins. **Terms:** [ECP] meal plan available, pets ($20 deposit, with prior approval). **Amenities:** hair dryers. **Pool(s):** small heated indoor. **Leisure Activities:** whirlpool. **Guest Services:** coin laundry, wireless Internet. **Cards:** AX, DS, MC, VI.

SOME UNITS
ASK ⬛ 🖐 ➰ 📷 / ✕ 🛢 🖥 /
FEE

BIXBY —*See Tulsa p. 641.*

BLACKWELL pop. 7,668

―――――― WHERE TO STAY ――――――

BEST WESTERN BLACKWELL INN — *Book great rates at AAA.com* — Phone: (580)363-1300
♦♦ ♦♦ All Year [ECP] 1P: $67-$79 2P: $67-$79 XP: $5 F17
Small-scale Hotel **Location:** I-35, exit 222, just ne. 4545 W White Ave 74631. Fax: 580/363-1373. **Facility:** 62 one-bedroom standard units. 3 stories, interior corridors. *Bath:* combo or shower only. **Parking:** on-site. **Terms:** pets ($10 extra charge). **Amenities:** high-speed Internet, voice mail, irons, hair dryers. **Pool(s):** heated indoor. **Leisure Activities:** whirlpool. **Guest Services:** sundries, coin laundry, wireless Internet. **Cards:** AX, CB, DC, DS, JC, MC, VI.

SOME UNITS
ASK ⬛ 🖐 🍴⊹ 📶 ➰ 📷 🛢 🖥 🖥 / ✕ /
FEE

COMFORT INN — *Book great rates at AAA.com* — Phone: (580)363-7000
AAA SAVE All Year [ECP] 1P: $64-$79 2P: $64-$79 XP: $5 F17
♦♦ ♦♦ **Location:** I-35, exit 222, just ne. 1201 N 44th St 74631 (PO Box 888). Fax: 580/363-3849. **Facility:** 60 one-bedroom standard units. 2 stories (no elevator), interior corridors. *Bath:* combo or shower only. **Parking:** on-site. **Terms:** pets ($10 extra charge). **Amenities:** irons, hair dryers. *Some:* high-speed Internet. **Pool(s):** Small-scale Hotel small heated indoor. **Guest Services:** wireless Internet. **Business Services:** meeting rooms. **Cards:** AX, CB, DC, DS, JC, MC, VI. **Free Special Amenities:** expanded continental breakfast and high-speed Internet.

SOME UNITS
⬛ 🖐 🍴⊹ 📶 ➰ 📷 🖥 / ✕ 🛢 🖥 /
FEE

BROKEN ARROW —See Tulsa p. 641.

CATOOSA —See Tulsa p. 643.

CHICKASHA pop. 15,850

——— WHERE TO STAY ———

HOLIDAY INN EXPRESS HOTEL & SUITES *Book at AAA.com* **Phone:** 405/224-8883
◆◆◆ ◆ All Year 1P: $81 2P: $86
Small-scale Hotel **Location:** I-44, exit 80, just se. 2610 S 4th St 73018. Fax: 405/224-8884. **Facility:** 62 one-bedroom standard units, some with whirlpools. 3 stories, interior corridors. *Bath:* combo or shower only. **Parking:** on-site. **Terms:** 14 day cancellation notice-fee imposed, package plans, pets ($25 extra charge). **Amenities:** voice mail, irons, hair dryers. *Some:* high-speed Internet. **Pool(s):** heated indoor. **Leisure Activities:** whirlpool, exercise room. **Guest Services:** valet and coin laundry, wireless Internet. **Business Services:** meeting rooms, business center. **Cards:** AX, CB, DC, DS, MC, VI.

(ASK) (S▢) ⛟ (⛓M) ⬚ ⊃ ⬚ ▣ / ✕ ▤ ⬚ SOME UNITS
FEE

CHOCTAW —See Oklahoma City p. 608.

CLAREMORE —See Tulsa p. 643.

CLINTON pop. 8,833

——— WHERE TO DINE ———

WONG'S RESTAURANT **Lunch:** $4-$6 **Dinner:** $6-$13 **Phone:** 580/323-4588
◆◆◆ **Location:** I-40, exit exit 65A, 0.5 mi n, then just e. 712 Opal Ave 73601. **Hours:** 11 am-10 pm. Closed: 11/22,
Chinese 12/25; also Mon. **Features:** The extensive menu at Wong's features Cantonese and Szechuan selections with many American dishes including pork, beef, shrimp and chicken samplings. The friendly, family-style atmosphere is casual and relaxed. Service is efficient and prompt. Casual dress; beer only. **Parking:** on-site. **Cards:** MC, VI.

(⛓M)

DAVIS pop. 2,610

——— WHERE TO STAY ———

DAVIS MICROTEL INN & SUITES-TREASURE
VALLEY CASINO *Book at AAA.com* **Phone:** (580)369-3223
◆◆◆ ◆◆◆ All Year 1P: $70-$105 2P: $85-$105 XP: $5 F17
Small-scale Hotel **Location:** I-35, exit 55, just e. Rt 1, Box 7C 73030. Fax: 580/369-3227. **Facility:** 55 one-bedroom standard units. 4 one-bedroom suites ($95-$105). 3 stories, interior corridors. *Bath:* combo or shower only. **Parking:** on-site. **Terms:** [CP] meal plan available, pets ($10 extra charge). **Amenities:** high-speed Internet, voice mail, irons, hair dryers. **Pool(s):** heated indoor. **Leisure Activities:** sauna, whirlpool, exercise room. *Fee:* game room. **Guest Services:** coin laundry, wireless Internet. **Business Services:** meeting rooms, PC. **Cards:** AX, DS, MC, VI.

(ASK) ⛟ (¶↑) (⛓M) ⬚ ⊃ 𝄞 ⬚ ✕ ▣ / ✕ ▤ ⬚ ▣ / SOME UNITS
FEE

DEL CITY —See Oklahoma City p. 608.

DUNCAN pop. 22,505

——— WHERE TO STAY ———

CHISHOLM SUITE HOTEL **Phone:** (580)255-0551
◆◆◆ ◆◆ All Year [CP] 1P: $80-$188 2P: $80-$188 XP: $7 F12
Small-scale Hotel **Location:** Center. 1204 N Hwy 81 73533. Fax: 580/470-1023. **Facility:** 60 units. 35 one-bedroom standard units. 23 one- and 2 two-bedroom suites, some with efficiencies, kitchens and/or whirlpools. 4 stories, interior corridors. *Bath:* combo or shower only. **Parking:** on-site. **Terms:** pets ($75 deposit). **Amenities:** DVD players, high-speed Internet, voice mail, irons, hair dryers. **Pool(s):** small outdoor. **Leisure Activities:** exercise room. **Business Services:** meeting rooms, PC. **Cards:** AX, DC, DS, MC, VI.

(ASK) (S▢) ⛟ (¶↑) ⊃ (VCR) ▣ ▤ ⬚ ▣ / ✕ / SOME UNITS
FEE

DURANT pop. 13,549

——— WHERE TO STAY ———

BEST WESTERN MARKITA INN *Book great rates at AAA.com* **Phone:** (580)924-7676
(AAA) (SAVE) All Year 1P: $55-$80 2P: $65-$85 XP: $5 F17
◆◆◆ ◆◆ **Location:** Just w of US 69/75 and 70. 2401 W Main St 74701. Fax: 580/924-3060. **Facility:** 62 units. 61 one-bedroom standard units, some with whirlpools. 1 one-bedroom suite with whirlpool. 2 stories (no elevator),
Small-scale Hotel exterior corridors. *Bath:* combo or shower only. **Parking:** on-site. **Amenities:** high-speed Internet, irons, hair dryers. **Pool(s):** outdoor. **Guest Services:** coin laundry, wireless Internet. **Business Services:** meeting rooms. **Cards:** AX, DC, DS, MC, VI. **Free Special Amenities:** local telephone calls and room upgrade
(subject to availability with advance reservations).

(S▢) (¶↑) ⊃ ▣ ▤ ⬚ / ✕ (VCR) ⬚ / SOME UNITS

HOLIDAY INN EXPRESS HOTEL & SUITES *Book at AAA.com* Phone: 580/924-8881
Property failed to provide current rates

◆◆◆ **Location:** Just e of jct US 75/69 and 70. 2112 W Main St 74701. Fax: 580/924-0955. **Facility:** 62 one-bedroom
Small-scale Hotel standard units, some with whirlpools. 2 stories (no elevator), interior corridors. *Bath:* combo or shower only.
Parking: on-site. **Terms:** pets ($25 fee). **Amenities:** high-speed Internet, irons, hair dryers. **Pool(s):**
outdoor. **Guest Services:** valet and coin laundry, wireless Internet. **Business Services:** meeting rooms.

SOME UNITS
🖼🍴🛋🗇🐾🛎🎬📺/✕🖥📠/
FEE   FEE

EDMOND —*See Oklahoma City p. 608.*

ELK CITY pop. 10,510

—— WHERE TO STAY ——

HOLIDAY INN *Book great rates at AAA.com* Phone: (580)225-6637
🔺🔺 ⓐⓐⓐ SAVE All Year [BP] 1P: $119-$229 XP: $10 F19
Location: I-40, exit 38, just sw. 101 Meadow Ridge Dr 73644. Fax: 580/225-6637. **Facility:** 151 units. 147 one-
◆◆◆◆ bedroom standard units. 4 one-bedroom suites, some with whirlpools. 2 stories (no elevator),
Small-scale Hotel interior/exterior corridors. **Terms:** check-in 4 pm, pets (with prior approval).
Amenities: video games (fee), voice mail, irons, hair dryers. **Dining:** 6 am-11 & 5-10 pm, Sun 6 am-2 & 5-9
pm, cocktails, nightclub. **Pool(s):** heated indoor. **Leisure Activities:** sauna, whirlpool, miniature golf, indoor
recreation area, exercise room. *Fee:* game room. **Guest Services:** valet and coin laundry, wireless Internet. **Business
Services:** meeting rooms. **Cards:** AX, CB, DC, DS, MC, VI. **Free Special Amenities: full breakfast and local telephone
calls.** *(See color ad below)*

SOME UNITS
🖼🍴🗇🛎✕🎬📺/✕🖥📠/
FEE

EL RENO —*See Oklahoma City p. 610.*

ENID pop. 47,045

—— WHERE TO STAY ——

AMERIHOST INN & SUITES ENID *Book great rates at AAA.com* Phone: (580)234-6800
ⓐⓐⓐ SAVE All Year 1P: $67-$130 2P: $67-$130
🔺🔺🔺 **Location:** Just off US 412, 2 mi w of US 81. 3614 W Owen K Garriott Rd 73703. Fax: 580/234-7900. **Facility:** 60
one-bedroom standard units, some with whirlpools. 2 stories (no elevator), interior corridors. *Bath:* combo or
Small-scale Hotel shower only. **Parking:** on-site. **Terms:** cancellation fee imposed, pets ($50 extra charge). **Amenities:** voice
mail, safes (fee), irons, hair dryers. **Pool(s):** heated indoor. **Leisure Activities:** whirlpool, limited exercise
equipment. **Guest Services:** valet laundry. **Business Services:** meeting rooms. **Cards:** AX, DC, DS,
MC, VI. **Free Special Amenities: continental breakfast and local telephone calls.**

SOME UNITS
🐂🍴🛋🗇🛎🎬📺/✕🖥📠/
FEE

HOLIDAY INN EXPRESS HOTEL & SUITES *Book at AAA.com* Phone: 580/237-7722
◆◆◆ Property failed to provide current rates
Location: 2.3 mi w of jct US 81. 4702 W Garriott Rd 73703. Fax: 580/234-0011. **Facility:** 78 units. 75 one-
Small-scale Hotel bedroom standard units, some with whirlpools. 3 one-bedroom suites with whirlpools. 3 stories, interior
corridors. *Bath:* combo or shower only. **Parking:** on-site. **Amenities:** high-
speed Internet, voice mail, safes, irons, hair dryers. *Some:* DVD players. **Pool(s):** heated indoor. **Leisure Activities:** whirlpool,
exercise room. **Guest Services:** valet and coin laundry, wireless Internet. **Business Services:** meeting rooms, business
center.

SOME UNITS
🐂🍴🛎🎬📺/✕🖥📠/
FEE

——— **WHERE TO DINE** ———

RIB CRIB BARBECUE

Barbecue
Lunch: $6-$14   **Dinner:** $6-$14   **Phone:** 580/237-7333
Location: Center. 4901 W Owen K Garriott Rd 73703. **Hours:** 11 am-10 pm. Closed: 11/22, 12/25.
Features: Most guests need extra napkins to tackle the ribs, brisket, ham, pork and chicken selections. The menu also lists sandwiches and wraps, along with tempting sides and large desserts. The decor is decidedly Western. Casual dress; beer only. **Parking:** on-site. **Cards:** AX, DC, DS, MC, VI.

ERICK pop. 1,023

——— **WHERE TO STAY** ———

COMFORT INN
Small-scale Hotel
Book great rates at AAA.com   **Phone:** (580)526-8124
All Year [ECP]   1P: $79-$99   2P: $85-$129   XP: $8   F16
Location: I-40, exit 7, just nw. 1001 N Sheb Wooley 73645 (PO Box 34). **Fax:** 580/526-8127. **Facility:** 50 one-bedroom standard units. 2 stories (no elevator), exterior corridors. **Parking:** on-site. **Terms:** 5 day cancellation notice, small pets only ($6 fee). **Amenities:** high-speed Internet, irons, hair dryers. **Pool(s):** small indoor. **Leisure Activities:** sauna, whirlpool. **Cards:** AX, CB, DC, DS, JC, MC, VI.

FREDERICK pop. 4,637

——— **WHERE TO STAY** ———

SCOTTISH INNS
Motel
Book great rates at AAA.com   **Phone:** (580)335-2129
All Year   1P: $45-$60   2P: $45-$60   XP: $5   F
Location: 1 mi s. 1015 S Main St 73542 (PO Box 98). **Fax:** 580/335-7277. **Facility:** 20 one-bedroom standard units. 2 stories (no elevator), exterior corridors. **Parking:** on-site, winter plug-ins. **Terms:** 2-3 night minimum stay - seasonal and/or weekends, cancellation fee imposed, package plans, small pets only. **Amenities:** Some: irons. **Pool(s):** small outdoor. **Guest Services:** wireless Internet. **Cards:** AX, DS, MC, VI. **Free Special Amenities:** local telephone calls and early check-in/late check-out.

GLENPOOL —See Tulsa p. 644.

GROVE pop. 5,131

——— **WHERE TO DINE** ———

RIB CRIB BARBECUE
Barbecue
Lunch: $6-$14   **Dinner:** $6-$14   **Phone:** 918/786-5400
Location: Center. Main St 74344. **Hours:** 11 am-10 pm. Closed: 11/22, 12/25. **Features:** Most guests need extra napkins to tackle the ribs, brisket, ham, pork and chicken selections. The menu also lists sandwiches and wraps, along with tempting sides and large desserts. The decor is decidedly Western. Casual dress; beer only. **Parking:** on-site. **Cards:** AX, DC, DS, MC, VI.

GUTHRIE —See Oklahoma City p. 610.

GUYMON pop. 10,472

——— **WHERE TO STAY** ———

COMFORT INN & SUITES
Small-scale Hotel
Book great rates at AAA.com   **Phone:** 580-338-0831
Property failed to provide current rates
Location: Just s of jct US 64. 5th St (Hwy 54) 73942. **Fax:** 580/338-0833. **Facility:** 51 units. 49 one-bedroom standard units, some with whirlpools. 2 one-bedroom suites. 3 stories, interior corridors. *Bath:* combo or shower only. **Parking:** on-site. **Amenities:** DVD players, CD players, high-speed Internet, voice mail, irons, hair dryers. **Pool(s):** heated indoor. **Leisure Activities:** whirlpool, exercise room. **Guest Services:** wireless Internet. **Business Services:** meeting rooms.

DAYS INN AND SUITES
Small-scale Hotel
Book great rates at AAA.com   **Phone:** (580)338-8801
3/1-10/31   1P: $60-$99   2P: $68-$110
11/1-2/29   1P: $60-$90   2P: $65-$90
Location: Just s of jct US 64. 620 NE Hwy 54 73942. **Fax:** 580/338-8648. **Facility:** 35 one-bedroom standard units. 1 story, interior corridors. **Parking:** on-site, winter plug-ins. **Terms:** [CP] meal plan available, pets ($10 extra charge). **Amenities:** high-speed Internet, dual phone lines, irons, hair dryers. **Pool(s):** small heated indoor. **Leisure Activities:** whirlpool, limited exercise equipment. **Guest Services:** coin laundry, wireless Internet. **Business Services:** PC. **Cards:** AX, DS, MC, VI. **Free Special Amenities:** expanded continental breakfast and high-speed Internet.

GUYMON SUPER 8
Small-scale Hotel
Book great rates at AAA.com   **Phone:** (580)338-0507
All Year   1P: $51-$75   2P: $51-$75
Location: Jct US 54 and 64. 1201 Hwy 54 E 73942. **Fax:** 580/338-0507. **Facility:** 59 one-bedroom standard units, some with whirlpools. 2 stories (no elevator), interior corridors. *Bath:* combo or shower only. **Parking:** on-site, winter plug-ins. **Terms:** [ECP] meal plan available, pets ($5 extra charge). **Amenities:** Some: irons, hair dryers. **Guest Services:** coin laundry, wireless Internet. **Business Services:** meeting rooms, PC. **Cards:** AX, DC, DS, MC, VI. **Free Special Amenities:** expanded continental breakfast and high-speed Internet.

LODGE U.S.A.

AAA [SAVE]
Motel

All Year   1P: $46   2P: $52   XP: $5   F13   **Phone:** (580)338-5431
Location: Just s of jct US 64. 923 Hwy 54 E 73942. Fax: 580/338-0554. **Facility:** 40 one-bedroom standard units. 1 story, exterior corridors. **Parking:** on-site. **Terms:** [CP] meal plan available, small pets only (with prior approval). **Business Services:** PC. **Cards:** AX, CB, DC, DS, MC, VI. **Free Special Amenities:** continental breakfast and high-speed Internet.

SOME UNITS

WESTERN TOWNSMAN INN

Small-scale Hotel

All Year   1P: $55-$99   2P: $55-$99   XP: $5   F16   **Phone:** (580)338-6556
Location: 0.7 mi s of jct US 64. 212 NE Hwy 54 73942 (PO Box 159). Fax: 580/338-1374. **Facility:** 73 one-bedroom standard units, some with whirlpools. 1-2 stories (no elevator), exterior corridors. *Bath:* combo or shower only. **Parking:** on-site, winter plug-ins. **Terms:** 7 day cancellation notice, weekly rates available, package plans, small pets only (with prior approval). **Amenities:** irons, hair dryers. **Pool(s):** small heated outdoor, small heated indoor. **Leisure Activities:** whirlpool, limited exercise equipment. **Guest Services:** valet laundry, wireless Internet. **Business Services:** meeting rooms. **Cards:** AX, CB, DC, DS, JC, MC, VI.

SOME UNITS

------ **WHERE TO DINE** ------

NAIFEH'S STEAKHOUSE

Steak & Seafood

     Lunch: $5-$15   **Dinner:** $5-$15   **Phone:** 580/338-5355
Location: 0.8 mi n on US 64. 704 NE 12th 73942. **Hours:** 11 am-8:30 pm. Closed major holidays; also Sun & Mon. **Reservations:** suggested, weekends. **Features:** You'll enjoy the relaxed, casual atmosphere, friendly and attentive service, and tasty, family-style food at Naifeh's. Steaks are their specialty, but the catfish, cheesecake and pecan pie are also good. The home-style decor complements the environment. Casual dress. **Parking:** on-site. **Cards:** MC, VI.

HENRYETTA pop. 6,096

------ **WHERE TO STAY** ------

GREEN COUNTRY INN

AAA [SAVE]
Motel

All Year   1P: $38-$41   2P: $42-$48   XP: $5   F   **Phone:** (918)652-9988
Location: I-40, exit 237, just ne. 2004 Old Hwy 75 W 74437. Fax: 918/652-4769. **Facility:** 41 one-bedroom standard units. 1 story, exterior corridors. **Parking:** on-site, winter plug-ins. **Terms:** pets ($5 fee). **Pool(s):** small outdoor. **Cards:** AX, DS, MC, VI.

SOME UNITS
FEE

HINTON pop. 2,175

------ **WHERE TO STAY** ------

MICROTEL INN & SUITES   *Book at AAA.com*

Small-scale Hotel

All Year [CP]   2P: $60-$75   **Phone:** (405)542-6011
Location: I-40, exit 101, just sw. 4800 N Broadway 73047. Fax: 405/542-3534. **Facility:** 44 one-bedroom standard units. 2 stories, interior corridors. *Bath:* combo or shower only. **Parking:** on-site. **Terms:** pets ($10 extra charge). **Amenities:** voice mail. **Pool(s):** heated indoor. **Guest Services:** wireless Internet. **Business Services:** meeting rooms. **Cards:** AX, DS, MC, VI.

SOME UNITS
FEE

IDABEL pop. 6,952

——— WHERE TO STAY ———

COMFORT SUITES   *Book great rates at AAA.com*   Phone: (580)286-9393
(AAA) [SAVE]
All Year   1P: $75-$150   2P: $75-$150   XP: $6   F12
▽▽▽▽   **Location:** Just s of jct US 70 and 259. 400 SE Lincoln Blvd 74745. **Fax:** 580/286-2005. **Facility:** 60 one-bedroom
Small-scale Hotel   standard units, some with whirlpools. 2 stories, interior corridors. *Bath:* combo or shower only. **Parking:** on-site. **Terms:** pets ($15 fee). **Amenities:** voice mail, irons, hair dryers. *Some:* dual phone lines. **Pool(s):** outdoor. **Leisure Activities:** whirlpool, exercise room. **Guest Services:** valet and coin laundry, wireless Internet. **Business Services:** meeting rooms, business center. **Cards:** AX, CB, DC, DS, JC, MC, VI.
Free Special Amenities: expanded continental breakfast and high-speed Internet.

SOME UNITS
[S/D] [🍳] [👥] [🐾] [📷] [📶] [🛗] [🖥] / [✕] /
FEE

MICROTEL INN   *Book at AAA.com*   Phone: (580)286-4466
▽
All Year   1P: $49-$54   2P: $59-$64   XP: $5   F17
Small-scale Hotel   **Location:** 4 mi w on US 70. 2906 NW Texas St 74745. **Fax:** 580/286-9166. **Facility:** 43 one-bedroom standard
MC, VI.   units, some with whirlpools. 2 stories (no elevator), interior corridors. *Bath:* combo or shower only. **Parking:** on-site. **Terms:** [CP] meal plan available. **Guest Services:** coin laundry, wireless Internet. **Cards:** AX, DS, MC, VI.

SOME UNITS
[ASK] [S/D] [👥] [📶] / [✕] [🛗] [🖥] /

JENKS —*See Tulsa p. 644.*

LAWTON pop. 92,757

——— WHERE TO STAY ———

BAYMONT INN & SUITES   *Book great rates at AAA.com*   Phone: (580)353-5581
(AAA) [SAVE]
All Year   1P: $84-$94
▽▽▽▽   **Location:** I-44, exit 39A, 3.7 mi w. 1203 NW 40th St 73505. **Fax:** 580/353-5608. **Facility:** 72 one-bedroom
Small-scale Hotel   standard units, some with whirlpools. 3 stories, interior corridors. *Bath:* combo or shower only. **Parking:** on-site. **Terms:** [CP] meal plan available, pets ($25 deposit). **Amenities:** video games (fee), voice mail, irons, hair dryers. *Some:* fax. **Pool(s):** heated indoor. **Leisure Activities:** exercise room. **Guest Services:** coin laundry, wireless Internet. **Cards:** AX, DC, DS, MC, VI. **Free Special Amenities: expanded continental breakfast and high-speed Internet.**

SOME UNITS
[S/D] [👥] [🍴] [🐾] [📷] [📶] [🛗] [🖥] / [✕] /
FEE

BEST WESTERN HOTEL & CONVENTION CENTER   *Book great rates at AAA.com*   Phone: (580)353-0200
(AAA) [SAVE]
All Year [BP]   1P: $89   2P: $94   XP: $5   F16
▽▽▽▽   **Location:** I-44, exit 37, just e. 1125 E Gore Blvd 73501. **Fax:** 580/353-6801. **Facility:** 145 units. 141 one-bedroom standard units, some with whirlpools. 4 one-bedroom suites ($175-$185). 2 stories, interior/exterior
Small-scale Hotel   corridors. *Bath:* combo or shower only. **Terms:** [AP] meal plan available, package plans, 20% service charge, small pets only ($40 fee). **Amenities:** high-speed Internet, voice mail, irons, hair dryers. **Dining:** 6 am-2 & 5-10 pm, cocktails, nightclub. **Pool(s):** 2 small outdoor, heated indoor. **Leisure Activities:** sauna, lighted tennis court, exercise room. **Guest Services:** valet and coin laundry, area transportation-within 5 mi, wireless Internet. **Business Services:** conference facilities, PC. **Cards:** AX, DC, DS, MC, VI. **Free Special Amenities: full breakfast and high-speed Internet.**

SOME UNITS
[S/D] [✈] [👥] [🍴] [🍸] [🐾] [✕] [📷] [🛗] [🖥] / [✕] /
FEE

FAIRFIELD INN & SUITES BY MARRIOTT   *Book great rates at AAA.com*   Phone: (580)248-5500
▽▽▽▽
2/1-2/29   1P: $79-$169
3/1-1/31   1P: $79-$159
Small-scale Hotel   **Location:** I-44, exit 37, just sw. 201 SE 7th St 73501. **Fax:** 580/248-5501. **Facility:** Smoke free premises. 84 one-bedroom standard units, some with whirlpools. 4 stories, interior corridors. *Bath:* combo or shower only. **Parking:** on-site. **Amenities:** high-speed Internet, voice mail, irons, hair dryers. *Some:* CD players. **Pool(s):** heated outdoor. **Leisure Activities:** whirlpool, exercise room. **Guest Services:** valet and coin laundry, wireless Internet. **Business Services:** meeting rooms, business center. **Cards:** AX, DC, DS, JC, MC, VI.

SOME UNITS
[ASK] [S/D] [🍴] [👤M] [👥] [🐾] [✕] [📷] [🛗] [🖥] /

HOLIDAY INN EXPRESS HOTEL & SUITES   *Book at AAA.com*   Phone: 580/248-4446
▽▽▽▽
Property failed to provide current rates
Small-scale Hotel   **Location:** I-44, exit 37, just sw. 209 SE Interstate Dr 73501. **Fax:** 580/248-4447. **Facility:** 99 one-bedroom standard units. 4 stories, interior corridors. *Bath:* combo or shower only. **Parking:** on-site. **Amenities:** high-speed Internet, voice mail, irons, hair dryers. **Pool(s):** outdoor. **Leisure Activities:** whirlpool, exercise room. **Guest Services:** sundries, valet and coin laundry, wireless Internet. **Business Services:** meeting rooms, business center.

SOME UNITS
[🍴] [👤M] [👥] [🐾] [📷] [🛗] [🖥] / [✕] /

SPRINGHILL SUITES BY MARRIOTT   *Book great rates at AAA.com*   Phone: (580)248-8500
▽▽▽▽
2/1-2/29   1P: $114-$179
3/1-1/31   1P: $109-$169
Small-scale Hotel   **Location:** I-44, exit 37, just w. 3 SE Interstate Dr 73501. **Fax:** 580/248-3256. **Facility:** Smoke free premises. 80 one-bedroom standard units, some with whirlpools. 3 stories, interior corridors. *Bath:* combo or shower only. **Parking:** on-site. **Amenities:** video games (fee), high-speed Internet, voice mail, irons, hair dryers. **Pool(s):** heated indoor. **Leisure Activities:** whirlpool, exercise room. **Guest Services:** sundries, valet and coin laundry, wireless Internet. **Business Services:** meeting rooms, business center. **Cards:** AX, DC, DS, JC, MC, VI.

[👥] [🐾] [✕] [📷] [🛗] [🖥] [🖥]

—————— WHERE TO DINE ——————

GOLDEN CHINA
▽▽▽
Chinese

Lunch: $4-$10   **Dinner:** $6-$10   **Phone:** 580/248-9889
Location: I-44, exit 39A, 2 mi w. 2512 NW Cache Rd 73505. **Hours:** 11 am-2:30 & 4-9:30 pm, Fri & Sat 11 am-10 pm, Sun-9 pm. Closed: 11/22, 12/25. **Features:** All of the expected beef, poultry, pork, vegetable and seafood dishes are served in a casual, relaxed setting. Casual dress. **Parking:** on-site. **Cards:** AX, DS, MC, VI.

LOCUST GROVE pop. 1,366

—————— WHERE TO STAY ——————

——— *The following lodging was either not evaluated or did not* ———
meet AAA rating requirements but is listed for your information only.

HOLIDAY INN EXPRESS HOTEL & SUITES
[fyi]
Small-scale Hotel

Phone: 918/479-8082
Did not meet all AAA rating requirements for some property operations at time of last evaluation on 02/28/2006. **Location:** Just nw of jct US 412 and SR 82. 106 Holiday Ln 74352 (PO Box 1150). Facilities, services, and decor characterize a mid-range property.

LONE WOLF pop. 500

—————— WHERE TO STAY ——————

QUARTZ MOUNTAIN RESORT, ARTS &
CONFERENCE CENTER   *Book at AAA.com*
▼▼ ▼▼
Small-scale Hotel

Phone: 580/563-2424
Property failed to provide current rates
Location: 1.4 mi w of jct SR 44 and 44A. 1.9 mi n. Located in Quartz Mountain State Park. Rt 1, Box 37 73655. **Fax:** 580/563-2422. **Facility:** Smoke free premises. 118 units. 116 one-bedroom standard units. 2 one-bedroom suites with whirlpools. 2 stories, interior corridors. *Bath:* combo or shower only. **Parking:** on-site. **Terms:** check-in 4 pm. **Amenities:** high-speed Internet, dual phone lines, voice mail, hair dryers. **Pool(s):** heated indoor. **Leisure Activities:** whirlpool, exercise room. **Guest Services:** gift shop, wireless Internet. **Business Services:** conference facilities, PC.

SOME UNITS
[⊔¶ 🏊 ✕ 🎦 🖥 / 🖨 /]

MARIETTA pop. 2,445

—————— WHERE TO DINE ——————

DENIM'S RESTAURANT
ⒶⒶⒶ
▽
American

Lunch: $4-$14   **Dinner:** $4-$14   **Phone:** 580/276-3222
Location: I-35, exit 15, 0.3 mi e. Hwy 32 & I-35 73448. **Hours:** 6:30 am-9 pm, Sun-3 pm. Closed major holidays. **Features:** They'll give you a warm, inviting reception at Denim's, where all the food is made from scratch. The chicken-fried steak, ribeye steak and 13 different desserts are superb. The restaurant's atmosphere is very quiet, relaxed, friendly and homey. Casual dress. **Parking:** on-site. **Cards:** AX, DS, MC, VI.

MCGEHEES CATFISH RESTAURANT
▽
Regional American

Dinner: $5-$14   **Phone:** 580/276-2751
Location: I-35, exit 15, 1.5 mi w, follow signs. 407 W Broadway 73448. **Hours:** 5 pm-8:30 pm, Sat & Sun from 1 pm. Closed: 11/22, 12/25; also Wed. **Features:** Of course, this restaurant serves farm-raised and delicious catfish, but they're also well-known for freshly-made coleslaw and hush puppies, and steak and hamburgers as well. The rustic Western decor creates a family-friendly atmosphere. Casual dress. **Parking:** on-site.
Cards: DS, MC, VI.

MCALESTER pop. 17,783

—————— WHERE TO STAY ——————

AMERICINN OF MCALESTER   *Book at AAA.com*
▼▼▼▼
Small-scale Hotel

Phone: (918)426-1300
All Year   1P: $99   2P: $99   XP: $6   F18
Location: 1 mi s on US 69. 609 S George Nigh Expwy 74501. **Fax:** 918/426-1330. **Facility:** 56 units. 55 one-bedroom standard units, some with whirlpools. 1 one-bedroom suite ($169) with whirlpool. 3 stories, interior corridors. *Bath:* combo or shower only. **Parking:** on-site. **Terms:** package plans. **Amenities:** video library, DVD players, high-speed Internet, voice mail, irons, hair dryers. **Pool(s):** heated indoor. **Leisure Activities:** whirlpool, exercise room. **Guest Services:** valet and coin laundry, wireless Internet. **Business Services:** PC, fax. **Cards:** AX, DS, MC, VI.
(See color ad p 595)

[ASK S🅳 ⊔¶ 🄼 🖭 🚼 🛏 🖨 🖥 🖳]

BEST WESTERN INN OF MCALESTER   *Book great rates at AAA.com*
▼▽ ▽▽
Small-scale Hotel

Phone: 918/426-0115
Property failed to provide current rates
Location: 3 mi s on US 69. 1215 George Nigh Expwy 74502 (PO Box 1532). **Fax:** 918/426-3634. **Facility:** 61 one-bedroom standard units. 2 stories (no elevator), exterior corridors. **Parking:** on-site. **Amenities:** high-speed Internet, irons, hair dryers. **Pool(s):** outdoor. **Guest Services:** valet laundry, wireless Internet.

SOME UNITS
[🐑 ⊔¶ 🄯 🛏 🚼 🖨 🖥 🖳 / ✕ /]

HAPPY DAYS HOTEL
▽▽▽
Small-scale Hotel

Phone: (918)429-0910
All Year   1P: $60-$70   2P: $70-$80
Location: 3.3 mi s on US 69. 1400 S George Nigh Expwy 74501. **Fax:** 918/429-0134. **Facility:** 42 units. 41 one-bedroom standard units. 1 two-bedroom suite ($86-$145) with whirlpool. 2 stories (no elevator), interior corridors. *Bath:* combo or shower only. **Parking:** on-site. **Terms:** pets ($20 extra charge). **Amenities:** irons, hair dryers. **Pool(s):** small outdoor. **Guest Services:** coin laundry, wireless Internet. **Business Services:** PC. **Cards:** AX, DC, DS, MC, VI.

SOME UNITS
[ASK S🅳 🐑 🖭 🛏 🚼 🎦 / ✕ / VCR 🖨 🖥 🖳]
FEE   FEE

SUPER 8 MOTEL

Motel
MC, VI.

Phone: 918/426-5400

All Year   1P: $54-$125   2P: $64-$160   XP: $5   F12
Location: Just n of jct US 69. 2400 S Main St 74501. Fax: 918/426-5400. **Facility:** 32 one-bedroom standard units. 1 story, exterior corridors. **Parking:** on-site, winter plug-ins. **Terms:** pets ($20 deposit, with prior approval). **Amenities:** hair dryers. **Guest Services:** coin laundry, wireless Internet. **Cards:** AX, CB, DC, DS,

SOME UNITS

The following lodging was either not evaluated or did not meet AAA rating requirements but is listed for your information only.

HOLIDAY INN EXPRESS HOTEL & SUITES   **Phone:** 918/302-0001
[fyi]   Did not meet all AAA rating requirements for some property operations at time of last evaluation on 06/24/2005. **Location:** 1.2 mi s on US 69. 650 George Nigh Expwy 74501. Facilities, services, and decor characterize
Small-scale Hotel   a mid-range property.

--- **WHERE TO DINE** ---

GIA COMO'S RESTAURANT   Lunch: $10-$16   Dinner: $10-$18   **Phone:** 918/423-2662
Italian
Location: 2 mi e on US 69. 501 S George Nigh Expwy 74501. **Hours:** 11:30 am-9 pm. Closed major holidays; also Sun & Mon. **Reservations:** suggested, weekends. **Features:** This restaurant features well-prepared and generous portions of traditional Italian meals in a friendly, warm, family-style atmosphere. The steaks are also good, and the staff provides pleasant, prompt service. Try the spumoni ice cream. Casual dress; beer only. **Parking:** on-site. **Cards:** DS, MC, VI.

HUNAN CHINESE RESTAURANT   Lunch: $4-$5   Dinner: $5-$9   **Phone:** 918/426-0481
Chinese
Location: 1 mi s on US 69. 618 S George Nigh Expwy 74501. **Hours:** 11 am-2:30 & 4:30-9 pm, Fri-9:30 pm, Sat 11 am-9:30 pm. Closed major holidays; also Sun. **Reservations:** accepted. **Features:** The variety of classic dishes is broad. Also on the menu are such American entrees as rib eye steak. Casual dress; beer only. **Parking:** on-site. **Cards:** DS, MC, VI.

MEDICINE PARK pop. 373

--- **WHERE TO DINE** ---

THE MEERS STORE & RESTAURANT   Lunch: $4-$8   Dinner: $4-$16   **Phone:** 580/429-8051
American
Location: I-44, exit 45, 12 mi nw, follow signs on SR 49 and 17. HC 30 73501. **Hours:** 10:30 am-8 pm. Closed: 11/22, 12/25. **Features:** The down-home barbecue ribs choice is the signature dish at the Meers Store, which is located in a historic grocery store in an old mining town. The burgers are popular too. The atmosphere is rustic and friendly to families. Casual dress; beer only. **Parking:** on-site.

MIAMI pop. 13,704

--- **WHERE TO STAY** ---

MIAMI SUPER 8 MOTEL   *Book at AAA.com*   **Phone:** 918/542-3382
Small-scale Hotel
Internet.
Property failed to provide current rates
Location: I-44, exit 313, just w. 2120 E Steve Owens Blvd 74354. Fax: 918/540-0535. **Facility:** 50 one-bedroom standard units. 2 stories (no elevator), interior corridors. *Bath:* combo or shower only. **Parking:** on-site. **Amenities:** safes (fee). **Pool(s):** heated indoor. **Leisure Activities:** whirlpool. **Guest Services:** wireless

SOME UNITS

MICROTEL INN & SUITES   *Book at AAA.com*   **Phone:** 918/540-3333
Small-scale Hotel
Some: irons, hair dryers. **Pool(s):** heated indoor. **Leisure Activities:** whirlpool, exercise room. **Guest Services:** coin laundry, wireless Internet. **Business Services:** meeting rooms, PC.
Property failed to provide current rates
Location: I-44, exit 313, just w. 2015 E Steve Owens Blvd 74355 (PO Box 1226). Fax: 918/540-3334. **Facility:** 46 one-bedroom standard units, some with whirlpools. 2 stories (no elevator), interior corridors. *Bath:* combo or shower only. **Parking:** on-site. **Terms:** pets ($25 extra charge). **Amenities:** high-speed Internet, voice mail.

SOME UNITS
FEE

--- **WHERE TO DINE** ---

MONTANA MIKE'S STEAKHOUSE   Lunch: $6-$16   Dinner: $8-$16   **Phone:** 918/542-8808
Steak House
Location: Just n of jct 1st St. 840 N Main 74354. **Hours:** 11 am-9 pm, Fri & Sat-10 pm. Closed: 11/22, 12/25. **Features:** This steakhouse offers a dining experience for the whole family. A rustic look with Western appointments characterizes the dining room. Although it's hard to go wrong with a hearty steak of USDA Choice aged beef, guests also can try smoked, fire-grilled chicken breast, chicken-fried steak, baby back ribs and other selections. Casual dress; cocktails. **Parking:** on-site. **Cards:** AX, DS, MC, VI.

MIDWEST CITY —*See Oklahoma City p. 610.*

MOORE —*See Oklahoma City p. 611.*

MUSKOGEE pop. 38,310

─────── **WHERE TO STAY** ───────

COMFORT INN — *Book great rates at AAA.com*   Phone: 918/687-4224
▽▽ ▽▽   All Year   1P: $85   2P: $85   XP: $5   F18
Location: Jct US 62 and 69, just sw. 3133 Azalea Park Dr 74401. Fax: 918/683-4474. **Facility:** 54 one-bedroom
Small-scale Hotel standard units, some with whirlpools. 2 stories (no elevator), interior corridors. *Bath:* combo or shower only.
Parking: on-site. **Terms:** [CP] meal plan available. **Amenities:** high-speed Internet, voice mail, irons, hair
dryers. **Pool(s):** small outdoor. **Leisure Activities:** exercise room. **Guest Services:** coin laundry. **Business Services:** business
center. **Cards:** AX, DC, DS, MC, VI.

SOME UNITS

🅂🅓 🏊 ▦ 🛄 📠 ▭ /✕/

HAMPTON INN — *Book great rates at AAA.com*   Phone: (918)682-2587
▽▽▽▽   All Year   1P: $76-$126   2P: $81-$148
Location: Just se of jct US 62 and 69. 3100 Military Blvd 74401. Fax: 918/683-0249. **Facility:** 64 one-bedroom
Small-scale Hotel standard units, some with whirlpools. 3 stories, interior corridors. *Bath:* combo or shower only. **Parking:** on-
site. **Terms:** [ECP] meal plan available. **Amenities:** high-speed Internet, dual phone lines, voice mail, irons,
hair dryers. **Pool(s):** heated indoor. **Leisure Activities:** sauna, whirlpool, exercise room. **Guest Services:** valet and coin
laundry, wireless Internet. **Business Services:** business center. **Cards:** AX, CB, DC, DS, MC, VI.

SOME UNITS

ASK 🅂🅓 🔇 🏊 ▦ 🛄 📠 ▭ /✕/

─────── *The following lodging was either not evaluated or did not* ───────
meet AAA rating requirements but is listed for your information only.

LA QUINTA INN & SUITES MUSKOGEE   Phone: 918/687-9000
[fyi]   Did not meet all AAA rating requirements for some property operations at time of last evaluation on
01/20/2006. **Location:** Just se of jct US 62 and 69. 3031 Military Blvd 74401. Facilities, services, and decor
Small-scale Hotel characterize a mid-range property.

─────── **WHERE TO DINE** ───────

CHINA KING SUPER BUFFET   **Lunch:** $6-$7   **Dinner:** $6-$8   Phone: 918/686-9888
▽▽ ▽▽   **Location:** 2.2 mi e of jct US 69 and 62. 231 W Shawnee Ave 74401. **Hours:** 11 am-9 pm, Fri & Sat-9:30 pm.
Chinese   Closed: 11/22, 12/25. **Features:** The buffet lines up a large variety of entrees, soups, egg rolls and desserts.
Casual dress. **Parking:** on-site. **Cards:** AX, DS, MC, VI.

🍴

JASPERS   **Lunch:** $5-$20   **Dinner:** $9-$20   Phone: 918/682-7867
▽▽ ▽▽   **Location:** 0.7 mi e of jct US 69. 1702 W Okmulgee 74401. **Hours:** 11 am-10 pm, Sat from 5 pm. Closed major
holidays; also Sun. **Reservations:** suggested, Fri & Sat. **Features:** Family-owned since 1983, Jaspers
Steak & Seafood features a full range of steak, crab legs, sandwiches, hamburgers and great dessert. The home-cooked fare
is served in a quiet, comfortable, low-key atmosphere that includes a "wall of fame" and two banquet rooms.
Casual dress; cocktails. **Parking:** on-site. **Cards:** AX, DC, DS, MC, VI.

🍸 🍴

MAHYLON'S   **Lunch:** $5-$11   **Dinner:** $5-$11   Phone: 918/686-7427
▽▽ ▽▽   **Location:** Off Muskogee Tpke, exit Chandler Rd, 1.2 mi w. 3301 Chandler Rd 74403. **Hours:** 11 am-9 pm. Closed
major holidays; also Sun & Mon. **Features:** This restaurant's rustic, log cabin atmosphere with knotty pine
American   walls and high ceilings is the perfect setting for their hickory-smoked barbecue dishes. They serve good-
sized portions of barbecue chicken, pork and beef in a traditional plate presentation. Casual dress; beer
only. **Parking:** on-site. **Cards:** AX, DC, DS, MC, VI.

🍴

MISS ADDIE'S TEA ROOM   **Lunch:** $4-$9   **Dinner:** $13-$27   Phone: 918/682-1506
▽▽ ▽▽   **Location:** At 9th St and Broadway; downtown. 821 W Broadway 74401. **Hours:** 11 am-9 pm, Sat-9:30 pm;
Saturday brunch. Closed: 1/1, 11/22, 12/24, 12/25; also Sun. **Reservations:** accepted. **Features:** Located
American   in a restored drugstore dating to 1915, Miss Addie's features fresh ingredients, good flavors, pleasant
service, bright ambience and a pianist Friday and Saturday. The ever changing menu offers steak, fresh
salmon, shrimp provencal and Saturday brunch. Casual dress; cocktails. **Parking:** on-site and street. **Cards:** AX, DS, MC, VI.

🍴

SPEEDWAY GRILLE   **Lunch:** $3-$6   **Dinner:** $3-$6   Phone: 918/687-6552
▽   **Location:** 0.6 mi e of jct US 69. 2010 W Okmulgee St 74401. **Hours:** 5:30 am-7 pm, Sat-2:30 pm. Closed major
holidays; also Sun. **Features:** There's nothing fancy here, just good, old-fashioned hamburgers,
American   sandwiches, french fries and one of the favorites, chili. Casual dress. **Parking:** on-site. **Cards:** MC, VI.

🍴

NORMAN —*See Oklahoma City p. 612.*

Destination Oklahoma City
pop. 506,132

The Wild West. American Indians, oil wells, bucking broncos and undaunted cowboys paint a picture of the lives led by those who called the land west of the Mississippi River home.

Today Oklahoma City celebrates its Old West heritage with American Indian festivals, rodeos and a wagonload of national and international horse shows.

Oklahoma City CVB

Ballet Oklahoma, Oklahoma City. Among the city's diverse cultural offerings are such holiday favorites as "The Nutcracker" performed by Ballet Oklahoma. (See mention page 257)

Oklahoma City skyline. OKC's modern skyscrapers are actually built over a field of black gold.

© Gibson Stock Photography

Oklahoma City CVB

Red Earth Festival, Oklahoma City. More than 100 tribes gather to celebrate their heritage during the first weekend in June. (See mention page 257)

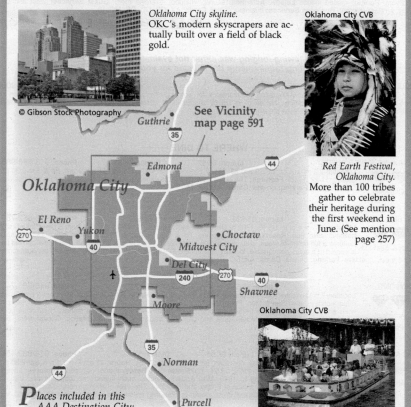

See Vicinity
map page 591

Oklahoma City CVB

Bricktown Canal, Oklahoma City. A water taxi ferries passengers among a host of entertainment venues, shops and restaurants in the city's historic Bricktown district. (See listing page 257)

Places included in this
AAA Destination City:

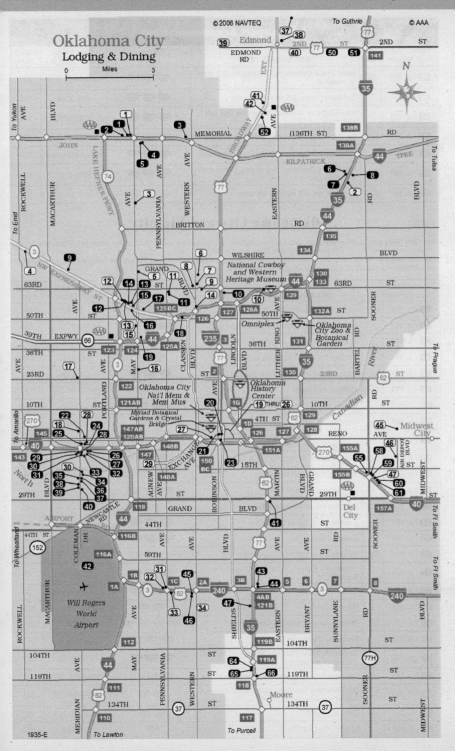

Oklahoma City
Lodging & Dining

0   Miles   3

✈ Airport Accommodations

Spotter/Map Page Number	OA	OKLAHOMA CITY	Diamond Rating	Rate Range High Season	Listing Page
36 / p. 591	AAA	**Hyatt Place Oklahoma City/Airport, 3.5 mi n of terminal**	▼▼▼	$89-$159 [SAVE]	600
35 / p. 591		Embassy Suites, 3.5 mi n of terminal	▼▼▼	$99-$199	598
42 / p. 591		Four Points by Sheraton Oklahoma City, just n of terminal	▼▼▼	$120-$150	598
40 / p. 591	AAA	**Governors Suites Hotel, 2 mi n of terminal**	▼▼▼	$78-$110 [SAVE]	598
37 / p. 591		Hampton Inn OKC Airport, 3.5 mi n of terminal	▼▼▼	Failed to provide	599
39 / p. 591		Holiday Inn Oklahoma City Airport, 3.3 mi n of terminal	▼▼▼	$107-$117	600
38 / p. 591	AAA	**Wingate Inn, 3.5 mi n of terminal**	▼▼▼	$99-$120 [SAVE]	604

Oklahoma City and Vicinity

This index helps you "spot" where approved accommodations and restaurants are located on the corresponding detailed maps. Lodging rate ranges are for comparison only and show the property's high season; rates are per night, unless only weekly (W) rates are available. Restaurant rate range is for dinner, unless only lunch (L) is served. Turn to the listing page for more detailed rate information and consult display ads for special promotions.

Spotter/Map Page Number	OA	OKLAHOMA CITY - Lodgings	Diamond Rating	Rate Range High Season	Listing Page
1 / p. 591		La Quinta Inn and Suites-Quail Springs	▼▼▼	$129	600
2 / p. 591		AmeriSuites (Oklahoma City/Quail Springs)	▼▼▼	$99-$179	595
3 / p. 591		Best Western Memorial Inn & Suites	▼▼▼	$85-$95	595
4 / p. 591		Fairfield Inn by Marriott - Quail Springs	▼▼	$85-$110	598
5 / p. 591		Hampton Inn by Hilton-Quail Springs	▼▼	$75-$100	598
6 / p. 591	AAA	**Comfort Inn North**	▼	$65-$125 [SAVE]	597
7 / p. 591		Quality Inn At Frontier City	▼▼	$50-$70	601
8 / p. 591		Sleep Inn & Suites	▼▼	$74-$84	602
9 / p. 591		La Quinta Inn & Suites Oklahoma City (Northwest Expressway)	▼▼	$89-$149	600
10 / p. 591	AAA	**Best Western Broadway Inn & Suites**	▼▼	$79-$89 [SAVE]	595
11 / p. 591	AAA	**Waterford Marriott Hotel**	▼▼▼▼	$129-$259 [SAVE]	604
12 / p. 591		Oklahoma City Marriott	▼▼▼	$132-$169	600
13 / p. 591	AAA	**Comfort Inn at Founders Tower**	▼▼	$69-$149 [SAVE]	596
14 / p. 591		Country Inn & Suites By Carlson	▼▼▼	Failed to provide	597
15 / p. 591		Crowne Plaza Hotel	▼▼▼	Failed to provide	597
16 / p. 591	AAA	**Hampton Inn NW - see color ad p 599**	▼▼▼	$75-$170 [SAVE]	599
17 / p. 591		Holiday Inn Express Hotel and Suites Penn Square	▼▼▼	$99-$109	599
18 / p. 591		Courtyard by Marriott-NW	▼▼▼	Failed to provide	597
19 / p. 591		Ramada Limited	▼▼	Failed to provide	601
20 / p. 591	AAA	**Renaissance Oklahoma City Hotel**	▼▼▼▼	$169-$309 [SAVE]	601
21 / p. 591	AAA	**Sheraton Oklahoma City**	▼▼▼	$229-$269	602
22 / p. 591		Residence Inn by Marriott-Oklahoma City West - see color ad p 602	▼▼▼	$159-$189	602
23 / p. 591	AAA	**Courtyard by Marriott-Downtown/Bricktown**	▼▼▼	$99-$159 [SAVE]	597
24 / p. 591	AAA	**Best Western Saddleback Inn & Conference Center - see color ad p 596**	▼▼	$99-$129 [SAVE]	595
25 / p. 591	AAA	**Days Inn West**	▼▼	$39-$95 [SAVE]	597
26 / p. 591		Motel 6 West - 1128	▼	$39-$55	600

Spotter/Map Page Number	OA	**OKLAHOMA CITY - Lodgings (continued)**	Diamond Rating	Rate Range High Season	Listing Page
27 / p. 591	AAA	**Comfort Inn**	◇◇	$69-$74 SAVE	596
28 / p. 591		La Quinta Inn Oklahoma City (Airport)	◇◇◇	$79-$114	600
29 / p. 591		Hilton Garden Inn Oklahoma City Airport	◇◇◇	$149-$179	599
30 / p. 591		Clarion Meridian Hotel and Convention Center	◇◇	$69-$79	596
31 / p. 591		Motel 6 Airport - 116	◇	$39-$55	600
32 / p. 591		Courtyard by Marriott Airport	◇◇◇	$89-$179	597
33 / p. 591		Holiday Inn Express Hotel & Suites	◇◇◇	$129-$139	599
34 / p. 591		Candlewood Suites Hotel	◇◇	Failed to provide	596
35 / p. 591		Embassy Suites	◇◇◇	$99-$199	598
36 / p. 591	AAA	**Hyatt Place Oklahoma City/Airport**	◇◇◇	$89-$159 SAVE	600
37 / p. 591		Hampton Inn OKC Airport	◇◇◇	Failed to provide	599
38 / p. 591	AAA	**Wingate Inn**	◇◇◇	$99-$120 SAVE	604
39 / p. 591		Holiday Inn Oklahoma City Airport	◇◇◇	$107-$117	600
40 / p. 591	AAA	**Governors Suites Hotel**	◇◇◇	$78-$110 SAVE	598
41 / p. 591		Super 8 Bricktown	◇	$44-$48	602
42 / p. 591		Four Points by Sheraton Oklahoma City	◇◇◇	$120-$150	598
43 / p. 591		Fairfield Inn by Marriott Crossroads Mall	◇◇	$85-$110	598
44 / p. 591		Residence Inn by Marriott South-Crossroads Mall	◇◇◇	$140-$175	602
45 / p. 591		Holiday Inn Express	◇◇	$75-$100	599
46 / p. 591		Quality Inn	◇◇	$69-$95	601
47 / p. 591		Baymont Inn	◇◇	$75-$111	595
		OKLAHOMA CITY - Restaurants			
1 / p. 591		Abuelo's Mexican Food Embassy	◇◇◇	$9-$17	604
2 / p. 591		Charly's Restaurant	◇	$5-$8	605
3 / p. 591		Papa Dio's Italian Restaurant & Wine Bar	◇◇	$9-$23	607
4 / p. 591		Hunan Wok Restaurant	◇	$6-$11	606
5 / p. 591		La Baguette Bistro Casual Restaurant & Bakery	◇◇	$10-$23	606
6 / p. 591		Newton's	◇◇◇	$11-$33	606
7 / p. 591		House of Hunan-Olie Ave	◇◇	$4-$10	606
8 / p. 591		The Coach House	◇◇◇◇	$22-$40	605
9 / p. 591		Pearls Oyster Bar	◇◇	$9-$18	607
10 / p. 591		The County Line Barbecue	◇◇	$7-$19	605
11 / p. 591		Bellini's Ristorante & Grill	◇◇◇	$10-$48	604
12 / p. 591		Madisons Pancake House	◇◇	$7-$12	606
13 / p. 591		J W's Steakhouse	◇◇◇	$18-$38	606
14 / p. 591		Deep Fork Grill	◇◇	$8-$34	605
15 / p. 591		Ron's Hamburgers & Chili	◇	$4-$6	607
16 / p. 591		Ted's Cafe Escondido	◇◇	$8-$12	607
17 / p. 591	AAA	**Gopuram, Taste of India**	◇◇	$10-$15	606
18 / p. 591	AAA	**Cimarron Steak House**	◇◇	$6-$22	605
19 / p. 591		Mantel Wine Bar & Bistro	◇◇◇	$15-$35	606

Spotter/Map Page Number	OA	OKLAHOMA CITY - Restaurants (continued)	Diamond Rating	Rate Range High Season	Listing Page
20 / p. 591		Abuelo's Mexican Food Embassy	◆◆◆	$9-$17	604
21 / p. 591		Bricktown Brewery	◆◆	$8-$16	604
22 / p. 591		Nonna's Euro-American Ristorante and Bar	◆◆◆	$17-$42	606
23 / p. 591		Mickey Mantle's Steakhouse	◆◆◆	$20-$35	606
24 / p. 591		Chelino's Mexican Restaurant	◆◆	$8-$13	605
25 / p. 591		Coach's BBQ Pizza & Brewery	◆◆	$7-$16	605
26 / p. 591		Bourbon Street Cafe	◆◆	$9-$20	604
27 / p. 591		LaLuna Mexican Cafe	◆◆	$7-$15	606
28 / p. 591	AAA	**Trapper's Fishcamp & Grill**	◆◆	$8-$23	607
29 / p. 591		Cattlemen's Steakhouse	◆◆	$10-$25	605
30 / p. 591		Golden Palace	◆◆	$6-$12	605
31 / p. 591		Pearl's Oyster Bar	◆◆	$9-$18	607
32 / p. 591		Aloha Garden Restaurant	◆◆	$5-$11	604
33 / p. 591		Hunan Chinese Restaurant	◆	$6-$8	606
34 / p. 591		Ted's Cafe Escondido	◆◆	$9-$14	607
EDMOND - Lodgings					
50 / p. 591	AAA	**Best Western Edmond Inn & Suites**	◆◆	$81-$86 SAVE	608
51 / p. 591		Holiday Inn Express Hotel & Suites	◆◆◆	Failed to provide	608
52 / p. 591	AAA	**Sleep Inn & Suites**	◆◆	$86-$139 SAVE	608
EDMOND - Restaurants					
37 / p. 591		Ted's Cafe Escondido	◆◆	$8-$12	609
38 / p. 591		Milano's Pizzeria	◆	$3-$7	609
39 / p. 591		House of Hunan	◆◆	$7-$22	609
40 / p. 591		Alvarado's	◆	$6-$15	609
41 / p. 591		Coach's BBQ, Pizza & Brewery	◆◆	$7-$16	609
42 / p. 591		Portobello's Italian Grill & Wine Bar	◆◆	$8-$20	609
DEL CITY - Lodgings					
55 / p. 591		La Quinta Inn Oklahoma City East (Del City)	◆◆	$75-$111	608
MIDWEST CITY - Lodgings					
58 / p. 591		Holiday Inn Express Hotel & Suites	◆◆◆	$79-$149	611
59 / p. 591	AAA	**Comfort Inn & Suites**	◆◆◆	$84-$89 SAVE	610
60 / p. 591		AmeriSuites (Midwest City/Tinker Air Force Base)	◆◆◆	$94-$124	610
61 / p. 591		Studio 6 #6003	◆	$47-$61	611
MIDWEST CITY - Restaurants					
45 / p. 591		Ron's Hamburgers & Chili	◆	$4-$6	611
46 / p. 591		Chequers Restaurant & Pub	◆◆	$5-$10	611
47 / p. 591		Primo's d' Italia	◆◆	$8-$16	611
MOORE - Lodgings					
64 / p. 591	AAA	**Best Western Green Tree Inn & Suites**	◆◆	$75 SAVE	611
65 / p. 591		Comfort Inn & Suites	◆◆	$69-$109	612
66 / p. 591		Super 8 Motel	◆	Failed to provide	612

OKLAHOMA CITY pop. 506,132   (See map and index starting on p. 591)

——— WHERE TO STAY ———

AMERISUITES (OKLAHOMA CITY/QUAIL SPRINGS)   *Book at AAA.com*   Phone: (405)749-1595   **2**

All Year [ECP]   1P: $99-$179   2P: $99-$179   XP: $10
Location: John Kilpatrick Tpke, exit May Ave, 0.4 mi w on north service road. 3201 W Memorial Rd 73134. Fax: 405/749-1573. **Facility:** 128 one-bedroom standard units. 6 stories, interior corridors. *Bath:* combo or shower only. **Parking:** on-site. **Terms:** package plans, small pets only. **Amenities:** video games (fee), high-speed Internet, voice mail, irons, hair dryers. *Some:* dual phone lines. **Pool(s):** outdoor. **Leisure Activities:** exercise room. **Guest Services:** sundries, valet and coin laundry, wireless Internet. **Business Services:** meeting rooms, PC. **Cards:** AX, CB, DC, DS, JC, MC, VI.

SOME UNITS

(ASK) (SD) 🐾 🍽️ (⛓️) 🏊 📷 🛗 🖥️ 🖨️ / ✕ (VCR) /

BAYMONT INN   *Book at AAA.com*   Phone: (405)631-8661   **47**

5/25-8/17 [CP]	1P: $75-$105	2P: $81-$111	XP: $6 F18
8/18-2/29 [CP]	1P: $72-$102	2P: $78-$108	XP: $6 F18
3/1-5/24 [CP]	1P: $69-$99	2P: $75-$105	XP: $6 F18

Location: I-35, exit 121A (82nd St), just sw. 8315 I-35 S 73149. Fax: 405/631-1892. **Facility:** 121 units. 120 one-bedroom standard units. 1 one-bedroom suite ($99-$141). 2 stories (no elevator), exterior corridors. **Parking:** on-site. **Amenities:** video games (fee), high-speed Internet, voice mail, irons, hair dryers. **Pool(s):** outdoor. **Guest Services:** coin laundry. **Business Services:** meeting rooms. **Cards:** AX, CB, DC, DS, MC, VI.

SOME UNITS

(ASK) 🐾 🍽️ 🔊 🏊 📶 📷 🖨️ / ✕ 🛗 🖥️ /
FEE   FEE FEE

BEST WESTERN BROADWAY INN & SUITES   *Book great rates at AAA.com*   Phone: (405)848-1919   **10**

(AAA) (SAVE)

All Year   1P: $79   2P: $89
Location: I-44, exit 127, just e on 63rd St, then just s. 6101 N Santa Fe 73118. Fax: 405/840-1581. **Facility:** 96 one-bedroom standard units, some with whirlpools. 3 stories, interior corridors. **Parking:** on-site, winter plug-ins. **Terms:** cancellation fee imposed, package plans. **Amenities:** irons, hair dryers. **Pool(s):** outdoor. **Leisure Activities:** whirlpool. **Guest Services:** valet laundry, wireless Internet. **Business Services:** meeting rooms. **Cards:** AX, CB, DC, DS, JC, MC, VI. **Free Special Amenities:** full breakfast and high-speed Internet.

SOME UNITS

🍽️ 🍸 🏊 📶 📷 🖥️ / ✕ 🛗 🖨️ /

BEST WESTERN MEMORIAL INN & SUITES   *Book great rates at AAA.com*   Phone: (405)286-5199   **3**

3/1-9/30	1P: $85-$95	2P: $85-$95
10/1-2/29	1P: $80-$90	2P: $80-$90

Location: John Kilpatrick Tpke, exit Western Ave, just nw. 1301 W Memorial Rd 73114. Fax: 405/286-5198. **Facility:** 60 one-bedroom standard units, some with whirlpools. 3 stories, interior corridors. *Bath:* combo or shower only. **Parking:** on-site. **Terms:** [ECP] meal plan available, pets ($10 extra charge). **Amenities:** high-speed Internet, voice mail, irons, hair dryers. **Pool(s):** heated indoor. **Leisure Activities:** whirlpool, exercise room. **Guest Services:** valet and coin laundry, wireless Internet. **Business Services:** meeting rooms, PC. **Cards:** AX, CB, DC, DS, MC, VI.

SOME UNITS

(ASK) (SD) 🐾 (LM) 🏊 📷 🛗 🖥️ 🖨️ / ✕ (VCR) /
FEE

BEST WESTERN SADDLEBACK INN & CONFERENCE CENTER   *Book great rates at AAA.com*   Phone: (405)947-7000   **24**

(AAA) (SAVE)

All Year [BP]   1P: $99-$129   2P: $99-$129   XP: $10   F17
Location: I-40, exit 145 (Meridian Ave), just ne. 4300 SW 3rd St 73108. Fax: 405/948-7636. **Facility:** 220 one-bedroom standard units. 3 stories, interior/exterior corridors. **Parking:** on-site. **Terms:** package plans, small pets only ($50 deposit). **Amenities:** high-speed Internet, voice mail, irons, hair dryers. *Some:* CD players. **Dining:** 6 am-2 & 5-10 pm, Sun-2 pm, cocktails. **Pool(s):** heated outdoor. **Leisure Activities:** sauna, whirlpool, exercise room. **Guest Services:** gift shop, complimentary evening beverages: Mon-Thurs, valet and coin laundry, area transportation-within 5 mi, wireless Internet. **Business Services:** conference facilities, business center. **Cards:** AX, CB, DC, DS, MC, VI. **Free Special Amenities:** full breakfast and local telephone calls. *(See color ad p 596)*

SOME UNITS

(SD) (⛓️) 🐾 🍽️ 🍸 🔊 🏊 ✕ 📷 🛗 🖥️ / ✕ (VCR) 🖨️ /
FEE

(See map and index starting on p. 591)

CANDLEWOOD SUITES HOTEL   *Book at AAA.com*   Phone: 405/680-8770   **34**

▼▼▼▼   Property failed to provide current rates
Small-scale Hotel   **Location:** I-40, exit 145 (Meridian Ave), 1.1 mi s. 4400 River Park Dr 73108. Fax: 405/680-8779. **Facility:** 122 units. 98 one-bedroom standard units with efficiencies. 24 one-bedroom suites with kitchens. 3 stories, interior corridors. *Bath:* combo or shower only. **Parking:** on-site. **Terms:** pets ($75 fee). **Amenities:** video library, DVD players, CD players, high-speed Internet, voice mail, irons, hair dryers. **Leisure Activities:** exercise room. **Guest Services:** valet and coin laundry.

SOME UNITS

🐶 🛅 📶 ⚙M 👤 VCR 📽 🛢 🖥 ☕ / ✕ /
FEE

CLARION MERIDIAN HOTEL AND CONVENTION CENTER   *Book great rates at AAA.com*   Phone: (405)942-8511   **30**

▼▼▼▼   All Year   1P: $69-$79
Small-scale Hotel   **Location:** I-40, exit 145 (Meridian Ave), just s. 737 S Meridian Ave 73108. Fax: 405/946-7126. **Facility:** 312 units. 228 one-bedroom standard units. 84 one-bedroom suites ($79). 2 stories (no elevator), interior corridors. *Bath:* combo or shower only. **Parking:** on-site. **Terms:** cancellation fee imposed, [ECP] meal plan available, small pets only (with prior approval). **Amenities:** voice mail, irons, hair dryers. **Pool(s):** heated indoor. **Leisure Activities:** exercise room. *Fee:* game room. **Guest Services:** complimentary evening beverages: Mon-Thurs, valet and coin laundry, area transportation, wireless Internet. **Business Services:** conference facilities, PC. **Cards:** AX, CB, DC, DS, JC, MC, VI.

SOME UNITS

ASK S📶 🔌 🐶 🛅 ⚙M 👤 🍽 🛁 📽 ☕ / ✕ 🛢 /

COMFORT INN   *Book great rates at AAA.com*   Phone: 405/943-4400   **27**

🔺🔺🔺 SAVE   All Year   1P: $69   2P: $74   XP: $5   F18
▼▼▼▼   **Location:** I-40, exit 145 (Meridian Ave), just e on south frontage road. 4240 W I-40 Service Rd 73108. Fax: 405/943-2374. **Facility:** 50 one-bedroom standard units. 2 stories (no elevator), interior/exterior corridors. *Bath:* combo or shower only. **Parking:** on-site. **Terms:** small pets only. **Amenities:** high-speed
Small-scale Hotel   Internet, irons, hair dryers. **Pool(s):** outdoor. **Guest Services:** valet and coin laundry, wireless Internet. **Business Services:** PC. **Cards:** AX, CB, DC, DS, JC, MC, VI. **Free Special Amenities:** expanded continental breakfast and high-speed Internet.

SOME UNITS

S📶 🐶 🛅 👤 🍽 🏊 📽 🛢 🖥 ☕ / ✕ /

COMFORT INN AT FOUNDERS TOWER   *Book great rates at AAA.com*   Phone: (405)810-1100   **13**

🔺🔺🔺 SAVE   All Year   1P: $69-$149   2P: $74-$149   XP: $8   F18
▼▼▼▼   **Location:** 0.5 mi e of jct SR 74 and 3. 5704 Mosteller Dr 73112. Fax: 405/810-1106. **Facility:** Smoke free premises. 51 one-bedroom standard units, some with whirlpools. 3 stories, interior corridors. *Bath:* combo or shower only. **Parking:** on-site. **Terms:** [ECP] meal plan available, small pets only (with prior approval).
Small-scale Hotel   **Amenities:** high-speed Internet, dual phone lines, voice mail, irons, hair dryers. **Leisure Activities:** exercise room. **Guest Services:** valet and coin laundry, wireless Internet. **Business Services:** business center. **Cards:** AX, DC, DS, MC, VI. **Free Special Amenities:** expanded continental breakfast and high-speed Internet.

SOME UNITS

S📶 🐶 🛅 👤 ✕ 📽 ☕ / 🛢 🖥 /

(See map and index starting on p. 591)

COMFORT INN NORTH *Book great rates at AAA.com* Phone: (405)478-7282 **6**
AAA SAVE All Year 1P: $65-$110 2P: $69-$125 XP: $5 F16
Location: I-35, exit 137 (122nd St), just sw. 4625 NE 120th 73131. Fax: 405/478-5226. **Facility:** 60 one-bedroom
standard units, some with whirlpools. 2 stories (no elevator), interior corridors. **Bath:** combo or shower only.
Small-scale Hotel **Parking:** on-site. **Terms:** [ECP] meal plan available, small pets only ($5 extra charge). **Amenities:** voice
mail, irons, hair dryers. **Pool(s):** small heated indoor. **Leisure Activities:** whirlpool, exercise room. **Guest
Services:** coin laundry, wireless Internet. **Business Services:** meeting rooms. **Cards:** AX, DC, DS, MC, VI.
Free Special Amenities: expanded continental breakfast and high-speed Internet.
SOME UNITS

COUNTRY INN & SUITES BY CARLSON *Book at AAA.com* Phone: 405/843-2002 **14**
Property failed to provide current rates
Location: 0.4 mi e of jct SR 74 and 3. 3141 Northwest Expwy 73112. Fax: 405/607-4027. **Facility:** 80 units. 68
one-bedroom standard units. 12 one-bedroom suites, some with whirlpools. 10 stories, interior corridors.
Small-scale Hotel **Bath:** combo or shower only. **Parking:** on-site. **Amenities:** high-speed Internet, dual phone lines, voice mail,
irons, hair dryers. **Pool(s):** small outdoor. **Leisure Activities:** exercise room. **Guest Services:** valet and coin laundry.
Business Services: meeting rooms, business center.
SOME UNITS

COURTYARD BY MARRIOTT AIRPORT *Book great rates at AAA.com* Phone: (405)946-6500 **32**
All Year 1P: $89-$159 2P: $109-$179 XP: $10 F
Location: I-40, exit 145 (Meridian Ave), just e on south frontage road. 4301 Highline Blvd 73108. Fax: 405/946-7638.
Small-scale Hotel **Facility:** Smoke free premises. 149 units. 137 one-bedroom standard units. 12 one-bedroom suites ($179-
$199). 3 stories, interior corridors. **Bath:** combo or shower only. **Parking:** on-site. **Terms:** [BP] meal plan
available. **Amenities:** high-speed Internet, dual phone lines, voice mail, irons, hair dryers. **Pool(s):** heated outdoor. **Leisure
Activities:** whirlpool, exercise room. **Guest Services:** valet and coin laundry. **Business Services:** meeting rooms, business
center. **Cards:** AX, CB, DC, DS, JC, MC, VI.
SOME UNITS

**COURTYARD BY
MARRIOTT-DOWNTOWN/BRICKTOWN** *Book great rates at AAA.com* Phone: (405)232-2290 **23**
AAA SAVE All Year [BP] 1P: $99-$149 2P: $109-$159 XP: $10 F
Location: Gaylord and Reno aves; downtown. 2 W Reno Ave 73102. Fax: 405/232-2202. **Facility:** Smoke free
premises. 225 units. 213 one-bedroom standard units, some with whirlpools. 12 one-bedroom suites. 8
stories, interior corridors. **Bath:** combo or shower only. **Parking:** on-site (fee) and valet. **Terms:** 30 day
Small-scale Hotel cancellation notice-fee imposed, package plans, small pets only ($50 extra charge). **Amenities:** video
games (fee), high-speed Internet, dual phone lines, voice mail, safes, irons, hair dryers. **Dining:** 6:30 am-10
& 4-11 pm, Sat & Sun 7 am-11 & 4-11 pm. **Pool(s):** heated indoor. **Leisure Activities:** whirlpool, exercise room. **Guest
Services:** sundries, valet and coin laundry, wireless Internet. **Business Services:** meeting rooms, business center. **Cards:** AX,
DC, DS, MC, VI. **Free Special Amenities: newspaper.**
SOME UNITS

COURTYARD BY MARRIOTT-NW *Book great rates at AAA.com* Phone: 405/848-0808 **18**
Property failed to provide current rates
Location: I-44, exit 125C westbound; exit 125B eastbound, just e. 1515 Northwest Expwy 73118. Fax: 405/848-3113.
Small-scale Hotel **Facility:** Smoke free premises. 122 units. 118 one-bedroom standard units, some with whirlpools. 4 one-
bedroom suites. 4 stories, interior corridors. **Bath:** combo or shower only. **Parking:** on-site. **Terms:** pets
($50 fee). **Amenities:** high-speed Internet, voice mail, irons, hair dryers. **Pool(s):** heated indoor. **Leisure Activities:** whirlpool,
exercise room. **Guest Services:** sundries, valet and coin laundry, wireless Internet. **Business Services:** meeting rooms, PC.
SOME UNITS

CROWNE PLAZA HOTEL *Book at AAA.com* Phone: 405/848-4811 **15**
Property failed to provide current rates
Location: 0.5 mi e of jct SR 74 and 3. 2945 Northwest Expwy 73112. Fax: 405/843-4829. **Facility:** 215 units. 213
one-bedroom standard units. 2 one-bedroom suites, some with whirlpools. 9 stories, interior/exterior
Large-scale Hotel corridors. **Bath:** some combo or shower only. **Parking:** on-site. **Terms:** small pets only ($40 fee).
Amenities: video games (fee), dual phone lines, voice mail, irons, hair dryers. **Pool(s):** heated outdoor. **Leisure
Activities:** whirlpool, exercise room. **Guest Services:** sundries, valet laundry, wireless Internet. **Business Services:** meeting
rooms, PC.
SOME UNITS

DAYS INN WEST *Book great rates at AAA.com* Phone: (405)942-8294 **25**
AAA SAVE All Year 1P: $39-$65 2P: $42-$95 XP: $6 F12
Location: I-40, exit 145 (Meridian Ave), just ne. 504 S Meridian Ave 73108. Fax: 405/947-3529. **Facility:** 133 one-
bedroom standard units. 2 stories (no elevator), exterior corridors. **Parking:** on-site. **Terms:** 30 day
cancellation notice, pets ($10 fee). **Amenities:** hair dryers. *Some:* irons. **Pool(s):** small outdoor. **Guest
Small-scale Hotel **Services:** valet and coin laundry, wireless Internet. **Cards:** AX, DC, DS, MC, VI. **Free Special Amenities:
full breakfast and high-speed Internet.**
SOME UNITS

(See map and index starting on p. 591)

EMBASSY SUITES　　*Book at AAA.com*　　　　　　　　　　Phone: (405)682-6000　[35]
▽▽▽▽　All Year [BP]　　　　　1P: $99-$189　　　2P: $109-$199　　　XP: $10　　F18
Large-scale Hotel　**Location:** I-40, exit 145 (Meridian Ave), 1 mi s. 1815 S Meridian Ave 73108. Fax: 405/682-9835. **Facility:** 236 one-bedroom suites. 6 stories, interior corridors. **Parking:** on-site. **Terms:** cancellation fee imposed, small pets only ($35 fee). **Amenities:** video games (fee), voice mail, irons, hair dryers. **Pool(s):** heated indoor. **Leisure Activities:** sauna, whirlpool, exercise room. *Fee:* game room. **Guest Services:** gift shop, complimentary evening beverages, valet and coin laundry, wireless Internet. **Business Services:** meeting rooms, business center. **Cards:** AX, CB, DC, DS, JC, MC, VI.

SOME UNITS
[✈] [🛏] [♨] [⌖] [➰] [✗] [🎦] [🛄] [🖥] [💻] / [✗] /
FEE

FAIRFIELD INN BY MARRIOTT CROSSROADS MALL　　*Book great rates at AAA.com*　Phone: (405)634-9595　[43]
▽▽▽ ◆◆◆　All Year　　　　1P: $85-$105　　　2P: $105-$110　　　XP: $5　　　F18
Small-scale Hotel　**Location:** I-240, exit 4C eastbound; exit 5 westbound, 0.8 mi w. 1101 E I-240 Service Rd 73119. Fax: 405/634-9595. **Facility:** Smoke free premises. 81 one-bedroom standard units. 3 stories, interior corridors. *Bath:* combo or shower only. **Parking:** on-site. **Amenities:** voice mail, irons, hair dryers. **Pool(s):** heated indoor. **Leisure Activities:** whirlpool. **Guest Services:** valet laundry, wireless Internet. **Cards:** AX, DC, DS, MC, VI.

SOME UNITS
[ASK] [S🐕] [⌖] [➰] [🔧] [✗] [🎦] [🖥] / [🛄] [💻] /
FEE

FAIRFIELD INN BY MARRIOTT - QUAIL SPRINGS　　*Book great rates at AAA.com*　Phone: (405)755-8686　[4]
▽▽▽ ◆◆◆　All Year　　　　1P: $85-$105　　　2P: $90-$105　　　XP: $5　　　F18
Small-scale Hotel　**Location:** John Kilpatrick Tpke, exit May Ave, just e on south frontage road. 13520 Plaza Terrace 73120. Fax: 405/755-8686. **Facility:** Smoke free premises. 63 one-bedroom standard units. 3 stories, interior corridors. *Bath:* combo or shower only. **Parking:** on-site. **Amenities:** high-speed Internet, voice mail, irons, hair dryers. **Pool(s):** heated indoor. **Leisure Activities:** whirlpool. **Guest Services:** valet laundry, wireless Internet. **Cards:** AX, DC, DS, MC, VI.

SOME UNITS
[ASK] [S🐕] [♨] [➰] [🔧] [✗] [🎦] [🖥] / [🛄] [💻] /

FOUR POINTS BY SHERATON OKLAHOMA CITY　　*Book great rates at AAA.com*　Phone: (405)681-3500　[42]
▽▽▽▽　All Year　　　　1P: $120-$150　　　2P: $120-$150
Small-scale Hotel　**Location:** I-40, exit 145 (Meridian Ave), 4 mi s. 6300 Terminal Dr 73159. Fax: 405/682-9090. **Facility:** 117 units. 116 one-bedroom standard units. 1 one-bedroom suite. 2 stories (no elevator), interior corridors. *Bath:* combo or shower only. **Parking:** on-site. **Terms:** [BP] meal plan available, pets ($30 extra charge). **Amenities:** video games (fee), dual phone lines, voice mail, irons, hair dryers. *Some:* fax. **Pool(s):** heated outdoor, wading. **Leisure Activities:** exercise room. **Guest Services:** valet and coin laundry, wireless Internet. **Business Services:** meeting rooms, business center. **Cards:** AX, DC, DS, MC, VI.

SOME UNITS
[ASK] [S🐕] [✈] [🛏] [♨] [🔧] [➰] [🎦] [🖥] / [✗] [🛄] [💻] /
FEE

GOVERNORS SUITES HOTEL　　　　　　　　　　　　　Phone: (405)682-5299　[40]
◐◐◐ [SAVE]　3/1-11/30 [BP]　　　1P: $78-$110　　　2P: $78-$110　　　XP: $7　　F5
　　　　12/1-2/29 [BP]　　　1P: $69-$99　　　2P: $69-$99　　　XP: $7　　F5
▽▽▽▽
Small-scale Hotel　**Location:** I-40, exit 145 (Meridian Ave), 1.2 mi s. 2308 S Meridian Ave 73108. Fax: 405/604-0883. **Facility:** 50 units. 45 one-bedroom standard units. 5 one-bedroom suites ($110-$165) with whirlpools, some with efficiencies (no utensils). 3 stories, interior corridors. **Parking:** on-site. **Terms:** 1-3 night minimum stay - seasonal and/or weekends, package plans. **Amenities:** irons, hair dryers. **Pool(s):** outdoor. **Leisure Activities:** whirlpool, steamroom, exercise room. **Guest Services:** coin laundry, wireless Internet. **Business Services:** meeting rooms. **Cards:** AX, DS, MC, VI. **Free Special Amenities:** full breakfast and high-speed Internet.

SOME UNITS
[S🐕] [♨] [➰] [✗] [🎦] [🛄] [🖥] [💻] / [✗] /

HAMPTON INN BY HILTON-QUAIL SPRINGS　　*Book great rates at AAA.com*　Phone: (405)752-7070　[5]
▽▽▽▽　All Year　　　　1P: $75-$95　　　2P: $80-$100　　　XP: $5　　　F18
Small-scale Hotel　**Location:** John Kilpatrick Tpke, exit May Ave, just e on south frontage road. 13500 Plaza Terrace 73120. Fax: 405/752-7491. **Facility:** 63 one-bedroom standard units. 3 stories, interior corridors. *Bath:* combo or shower only. **Parking:** on-site, winter plug-ins. **Amenities:** voice mail, irons, hair dryers. **Pool(s):** indoor. **Leisure Activities:** whirlpool. **Guest Services:** valet laundry, wireless Internet. **Cards:** AX, DC, DS, MC, VI.

SOME UNITS
[ASK] [S🐕] [♨] [🔧] [➰] [🔧] [🎦] [🖥] / [✗] [🛄] [💻] /
FEE

(See map and index starting on p. 591)

HAMPTON INN NW　　*Book great rates at AAA.com*　　　　　　　**Phone:** (405)947-0953　🔟

⚠️ SAVE　All Year　　　　1P: $75-$160　　　2P: $85-$170
〰️〰️〰️　**Location:** Jct SR 3A and May Ave. 3022 Northwest Expwy 73112. Fax: 405/947-7667. **Facility:** 97 one-bedroom standard units, some with whirlpools. 5 stories, interior corridors. *Bath:* combo or shower only. **Parking:** on-site. **Terms:** 14 day cancellation notice, [BP] meal plan available. **Amenities:** voice mail, irons, hair dryers.
Small-scale Hotel　*Some:* high-speed Internet, dual phone lines. **Pool(s):** indoor. **Leisure Activities:** exercise room. **Guest Services:** valet laundry, wireless Internet. **Business Services:** meeting rooms, PC. **Cards:** AX, CB, DC, DS, MC, VI. **Free Special Amenities:** local telephone calls and newspaper. *(See color ad below)*

SOME UNITS
🆂🅳 🕙 ♿ 🎧 ⊴ 🐾 📷 🖥 🖵 🖳 /🗙/

HAMPTON INN OKC AIRPORT　　*Book great rates at AAA.com*　　　　**Phone:** 405/682-2080　㊲

〰️〰️〰️　　　　　　　　Property failed to provide current rates
　　　　　Location: I-40, exit 145 (Meridian Ave), 1 mi s. 1905 S Meridian Ave 73108. Fax: 405/682-3662. **Facility:** 134 one-
Small-scale Hotel　bedroom standard units. 3 stories, interior corridors. **Parking:** on-site. **Amenities:** video games (fee), high-speed Internet, voice mail, irons, hair dryers. **Pool(s):** small outdoor. **Leisure Activities:** exercise room.
Guest Services: complimentary evening beverages: Tues & Wed, valet laundry, wireless Internet. **Business Services:** meeting rooms, PC.

SOME UNITS
✈️ 🕙 ⊴ 🐾 📷 🖳 /🗙 🖥 🖵/

HILTON GARDEN INN OKLAHOMA CITY AIRPORT　　*Book great rates at AAA.com*　　**Phone:** (405)942-1400　㉙

〰️〰️〰️　All Year　　　　1P: $149-$179　　　2P: $149-$179　　　　　　F18
　　　　　Location: I-40, exit 145 (Meridian Ave), just sw. 801 S Meridian Ave 73108. Fax: 405/942-5088. **Facility:** 161 units.
Small-scale Hotel　137 one-bedroom standard units. 24 one-bedroom suites ($179). 6 stories, interior corridors. *Bath:* combo or shower only. **Parking:** on-site. **Terms:** weekly rates available, [AP] & [BP] meal plans available, 20% service charge. **Amenities:** video games (fee), high-speed Internet, dual phone lines, voice mail, irons, hair dryers. **Pool(s):** small heated outdoor. **Leisure Activities:** whirlpool, exercise room. **Guest Services:** sundries, valet and coin laundry, area transportation, wireless Internet. **Business Services:** meeting rooms, business center. **Cards:** AX, CB, DC, DS, MC, VI.

SOME UNITS
🅰🆂🅺 ✈️ 🍴 🍸 🅼 ♿ 🎧 ⊴ 🐾 📷 🖥 🖵 🖳 /🗙/

HOLIDAY INN EXPRESS　　*Book at AAA.com*　　　　　　　　**Phone:** (405)631-3111　㊺

〰️〰️〰️　All Year　　　　1P: $75-$95　　　2P: $80-$100　　　XP: $5　　　F18
　　　　　Location: I-240, exit 2A, just s. 7601 CA Henderson Blvd 73139. Fax: 405/631-3111. **Facility:** 64 one-bedroom
Small-scale Hotel　standard units. 3 stories, interior corridors. *Bath:* combo or shower only. **Parking:** on-site. **Amenities:** voice mail, irons, hair dryers. **Pool(s):** heated indoor. **Leisure Activities:** whirlpool. **Guest Services:** valet laundry, wireless Internet. **Cards:** AX, DC, DS, MC, VI.

SOME UNITS
🅰🆂🅺 🆂🅳 🕙 ♿ 🎧 🐾 📷 🖵 /🗙 🖥 🖵/

HOLIDAY INN EXPRESS HOTEL & SUITES　　*Book at AAA.com*　　　　**Phone:** (405)948-3366　㉝

〰️〰️〰️　All Year [CP]　　　1P: $129-$139　　　　　　　XP: $10　　　F18
　　　　　Location: I-40, exit 145 (Meridian Ave), just s. 4400 Highline Blvd 73108. Fax: 405/948-3366. **Facility:** 83 units. 81
Small-scale Hotel　one-bedroom standard units. 2 one-bedroom suites. 3 stories, interior corridors. *Bath:* combo or shower only. **Parking:** on-site. **Amenities:** dual phone lines, voice mail, irons, hair dryers. **Leisure Activities:** exercise room. **Guest Services:** valet and coin laundry, wireless Internet. **Business Services:** meeting rooms, business center. **Cards:** AX, CB, DC, DS, MC, VI.

SOME UNITS
🕙 ♿ 📷 🖳 /🗙 🖥 🖵/

HOLIDAY INN EXPRESS HOTEL AND SUITES PENN
　　SQUARE　　*Book at AAA.com*　　　　　　　　**Phone:** (405)848-1500　🔟7

〰️〰️〰️　All Year [CP]　　　1P: $99-$109　　　2P: $99-$109　　　XP: $10　　　F14
　　　　　Location: 0.7 mi e of jct SR 3 and 74. 2811 Northwest Expwy 73112. Fax: 405/848-7474. **Facility:** 76 one-bedroom standard units, some with whirlpools. 3 stories, interior corridors. *Bath:* combo or shower only.
Small-scale Hotel　**Parking:** on-site. **Amenities:** dual phone lines, voice mail, irons, hair dryers. **Pool(s):** heated indoor.
Leisure Activities: exercise room. **Guest Services:** valet and coin laundry, wireless Internet. **Business Services:** meeting rooms, PC. **Cards:** AX, CB, DC, DS, JC, MC, VI.

SOME UNITS
🅰🆂🅺 🆂🅳 🕙 🅼 ♿ 🎧 ⊴ 🐾 🖳 /🗙 🖥 🖵/

(See map and index starting on p. 591)

HOLIDAY INN OKLAHOMA CITY AIRPORT   *Book at AAA.com*   Phone: (405)685-4000   **39**

Small-scale Hotel

All Year — 1P: $107-$117   2P: $107-$117

Location: I-40, exit 145 (Meridian Ave), 1.3 mi s. 2101 S Meridian Ave 73108. Fax: 405/685-0574. **Facility:** 246 units. 236 one-bedroom standard units. 10 one-bedroom suites. 2 stories (no elevator), interior/exterior corridors. *Bath:* combo or shower only. **Terms:** [BP] meal plan available. **Amenities:** video games (fee), voice mail, irons, hair dryers. **Pool(s):** heated indoor. **Leisure Activities:** sauna, whirlpool, exercise room. *Fee:* game room. **Guest Services:** valet and coin laundry, wireless Internet. **Business Services:** meeting rooms, business center. **Cards:** AX, CB, DC, DS, JC, MC, VI.

SOME UNITS

(ASK) (SD) ✈ ⛏ 🍴 ▽ 🕎 ➰ ✕ ♨ 🖥 / ✕ 🔌 /

HYATT PLACE OKLAHOMA CITY/AIRPORT   Phone: (405)682-3900   **36**

(AAA) (SAVE)

Small-scale Hotel

All Year [CP]   1P: $89-$159   2P: $89-$159   XP: $10   F17

Location: I-40, exit 145 (Meridian Ave), 1 mi s. 1818 S Meridian Ave 73108-1718. Fax: 405/682-3977. **Facility:** 128 one-bedroom standard units. 6 stories, interior corridors. *Bath:* combo or shower only. **Terms:** cancellation fee imposed. **Amenities:** dual phone lines, voice mail, irons, hair dryers. *Fee:* video games, safes. **Pool(s):** small heated outdoor. **Leisure Activities:** exercise room. **Guest Services:** valet and coin laundry, wireless Internet. **Business Services:** meeting rooms. **Cards:** AX, CB, DC, DS, JC, MC, VI. **Free Special Amenities:** full breakfast and high-speed Internet.

SOME UNITS

✈ 🍴 🕎 ➰ ✕ (VCR) ♨ 🖥 🖥 🖥 / ✕ /

LA QUINTA INN & SUITES OKLAHOMA CITY
(NORTHWEST EXPRESSWAY)   *Book great rates at AAA.com*   Phone: (405)773-5575   **9**

Small-scale Hotel

3/1-5/1 [CP]   1P: $89-$119   2P: $99-$149   XP: $10   F18
5/2-2/29 [CP]   1P: $95-$125   2P: $105-$135   XP: $10   F18

Location: 1.9 mi w of jct SR 3 and 74. 4829 Northwest Expwy 73132-5215. Fax: 405/773-5655. **Facility:** 119 units. 113 one-bedroom standard units. 6 one-bedroom suites ($129-$175). 6 stories, interior corridors. *Bath:* combo or shower only. **Parking:** on-site. **Terms:** small pets only. **Amenities:** video games (fee), high-speed Internet, voice mail, irons, hair dryers. *Some:* dual phone lines. **Pool(s):** heated outdoor. **Leisure Activities:** whirlpool, exercise room. **Guest Services:** valet and coin laundry, area transportation, wireless Internet. **Business Services:** meeting rooms. **Cards:** AX, CB, DC, DS, MC, VI.

SOME UNITS

(ASK) ✈ ⛏ 🍴 🕎 ➰ ✕ 🖥 / ✕ 🔌 🖥 /

LA QUINTA INN AND SUITES-QUAIL SPRINGS   *Book great rates at AAA.com*   Phone: (405)755-7000   **1**

Small-scale Hotel

All Year [ECP]   1P: $129   2P: $129   XP: $10   F14

Location: John Kilpatrick Tpke, exit May Ave, just nw. 3003 W Memorial Rd 73134. Fax: 405/755-7008. **Facility:** 96 one-bedroom standard units, some with whirlpools. 3 stories, interior corridors. *Bath:* combo or shower only. **Parking:** on-site. **Terms:** pets ($50 extra charge). **Amenities:** high-speed Internet, dual phone lines, voice mail, irons, hair dryers. *Some:* CD players. **Pool(s):** heated indoor. **Leisure Activities:** whirlpool, putting green, exercise room. **Guest Services:** valet and coin laundry, wireless Internet. **Business Services:** meeting rooms, PC. **Cards:** AX, CB, DC, DS, JC, MC, VI.

SOME UNITS

(ASK) (SD) ⛏ 🍴 ♿M ➰ ✕ ♨ 🖥 🖥 🖥 / ✕ /
FEE

LA QUINTA INN OKLAHOMA CITY (AIRPORT)   *Book great rates at AAA.com*   Phone: (405)942-0040   **28**

Small-scale Hotel

3/1-11/16 [CP]   1P: $79-$109   2P: $84-$114   XP: $5   F18
11/17-2/29 [CP]   1P: $76-$106   2P: $81-$111   XP: $5   F18

Location: I-40, exit 145 (Meridian Ave), just se. 800 S Meridian Ave 73108. Fax: 405/942-0638. **Facility:** 168 one-bedroom standard units. 2 stories (no elevator), interior/exterior corridors. *Bath:* combo or shower only. **Parking:** on-site. **Amenities:** video games (fee), voice mail, irons, hair dryers. **Pool(s):** small outdoor, wading. **Leisure Activities:** exercise room. **Guest Services:** valet laundry, wireless Internet. **Business Services:** meeting rooms. **Cards:** AX, CB, DC, DS, MC, VI.

SOME UNITS

(ASK) ✈ ⛏ 🍴 ▽ ➰ ✕ 🖥 / ✕ 🔌 🖥 /

MOTEL 6 AIRPORT - 116   *Book at AAA.com*   Phone: 405/946-6662   **31**

Motel

5/25-2/29   1P: $39-$49   2P: $45-$55   XP: $3   F17
3/1-5/24   1P: $37-$47   2P: $43-$53   XP: $3   F17

Location: I-40, exit 145 (Meridian Ave), just s. 820 S Meridian Ave 73108. Fax: 405/946-4058. **Facility:** 128 one-bedroom standard units. 2 stories (no elevator), exterior corridors. *Bath:* shower only. **Parking:** on-site. **Terms:** small pets only. **Pool(s):** heated outdoor. **Guest Services:** coin laundry. **Cards:** AX, CB, DC, DS, MC, VI.

SOME UNITS

(SD) ⛏ 🍴 ➰ ✕ 🖥 / ✕ /

MOTEL 6 WEST - 1128   *Book at AAA.com*   Phone: 405/947-6550   **26**

Small-scale Hotel

5/25-2/29   1P: $39-$49   2P: $45-$55   XP: $3   F17
3/1-5/24   1P: $38-$48   2P: $44-$54   XP: $3   F17

Location: I-40, exit 145 (Meridian Ave), just e on south frontage road. 4200 I-40 Service Rd 73108. Fax: 405/947-0970. **Facility:** 119 one-bedroom standard units. 3 stories, interior/exterior corridors. *Bath:* combo or shower only. **Parking:** on-site. **Terms:** small pets only. **Pool(s):** small outdoor. **Leisure Activities:** whirlpool. *Fee:* game room. **Guest Services:** coin laundry. **Cards:** AX, CB, DC, DS, MC, VI.

SOME UNITS

(SD) ⛏ 🍴 ➰ ✕ / ✕ 🔌 🖥 /

OKLAHOMA CITY MARRIOTT   *Book great rates at AAA.com*   Phone: (405)842-6633   **12**

Large-scale Hotel

All Year   1P: $132-$169   2P: $132-$169

Location: Just e of jct SR 3 and 74. 3233 Northwest Expressway 73112. Fax: 405/842-3152. **Facility:** Smoke free premises. 354 units. 352 one-bedroom standard units. 2 one-bedroom suites. 16 stories, interior corridors. *Bath:* combo or shower only. **Parking:** on-site. **Terms:** cancellation fee imposed, package plans. **Amenities:** high-speed Internet (fee), voice mail, irons, hair dryers. **Dining:** J W's Steakhouse, see separate listing. **Pool(s):** heated indoor/outdoor. **Leisure Activities:** whirlpool, exercise room. **Guest Services:** sundries, valet and coin laundry. **Business Services:** conference facilities, business center. **Cards:** AX, CB, DC, DS, JC, MC, VI.

SOME UNITS

(ASK) 🍴 ▽ 🕎 ➰ ✕ 🖥 ♨ 🖥 / (VCR) 🖥 🖥 /
FEE

(See map and index starting on p. 591)

QUALITY INN — *Book great rates at AAA.com* — **Phone:** (405)632-6666 — 46

All Year — 1P: $69-$90 — 2P: $75-$95 — XP: $6 — F18

Small-scale Hotel — **Location:** I-240, exit 2A, just s. 7800 CA Henderson Blvd 73139. Fax: 405/632-9717. **Facility:** 149 one-bedroom standard units. 2 stories (no elevator), exterior corridors. *Bath:* combo or shower only. **Parking:** on-site. **Terms:** small pets only ($10 extra charge). **Amenities:** safes (fee), irons, hair dryers. **Pool(s):** outdoor. **Guest Services:** coin laundry, wireless Internet. **Business Services:** meeting rooms. **Cards:** AX, CB, DC, DS, JC, MC, VI.

SOME UNITS

FEE

QUALITY INN AT FRONTIER CITY — *Book great rates at AAA.com* — **Phone:** (405)478-0400 — 7

6/1-7/31 — 1P: $50-$65 — 2P: $60-$70 — XP: $5 — F12
3/1-3/31 — 1P: $45-$60 — 2P: $50-$65 — XP: $5 — F12
8/1-2/29 — 1P: $50-$55 — 2P: $50-$55 — XP: $5 — F12
Small-scale Hotel — 4/1-5/31 — 1P: $40-$50 — 2P: $45-$55 — XP: $5 — F12

Location: I-35, exit 137, just sw. 12001 N I-35 Service Rd 73131. Fax: 405/478-8338. **Facility:** 65 one-bedroom standard units. 2 stories (no elevator), exterior corridors. **Parking:** on-site, winter plug-ins. **Terms:** [CP] meal plan available, small pets only ($7-$10 fee). **Amenities:** irons, hair dryers. **Pool(s):** small outdoor. **Leisure Activities:** basketball. **Guest Services:** coin laundry, wireless Internet. **Cards:** AX, CB, DC, DS, JC, MC, VI.

SOME UNITS

FEE

RAMADA LIMITED — *Book at AAA.com* — **Phone:** 405/948-8000 — 19

Property failed to provide current rates

Small-scale Hotel — **Location:** I-44, exit 124, just n. 2727 W I-44 Service Rd 73112. Fax: 405/946-0899. **Facility:** 57 one-bedroom standard units, some with whirlpools. 3 stories, interior corridors. *Bath:* combo or shower only. **Parking:** on-site. **Terms:** pets ($10 extra charge). **Amenities:** high-speed Internet, voice mail, irons, hair dryers. **Pool(s):** heated indoor. **Leisure Activities:** whirlpool, limited exercise equipment. **Guest Services:** coin laundry, wireless Internet. **Business Services:** meeting rooms.

SOME UNITS

FEE

RENAISSANCE OKLAHOMA CITY HOTEL — *Book great rates at AAA.com* — **Phone:** (405)228-8000 — 20

All Year — 1P: $169-$309 — 2P: $169-$309 — XP: $10 — F18

Large-scale Hotel — **Location:** Sheridan and Broadway aves; downtown. 10 N Broadway Ave 73102. Fax: 405/228-8080. **Facility:** Located in the heart of downtown and within walking distance of Bricktown, this upscale, well-appointed hotel is also near the interstate. Smoke free premises. 311 units. 258 one-bedroom standard units. 53 one-bedroom suites ($259-$309), some with whirlpools. 15 stories, interior corridors. *Bath:* combo or shower only. **Parking:** on-site (fee) and valet. **Terms:** cancellation fee imposed, package plans, small pets only. **Amenities:** video games (fee), high-speed Internet, dual phone lines, voice mail, honor bars, irons, hair dryers. **Dining:** 3 restaurants, 6:30 am-2 & 5-10 pm, cocktails. **Pool(s):** indoor. **Leisure Activities:** sauna, whirlpool, exercise room. *Fee:* massage. **Guest Services:** gift shop, valet and coin laundry, wireless Internet. **Business Services:** conference facilities, business center. **Cards:** AX, CB, DC, DS, MC, VI. **Free Special Amenities:** newspaper.

SOME UNITS

RESIDENCE INN BY MARRIOTT — **Phone:** 405/601-1700

fyi — All Year — Too new to rate, opening scheduled for December 2006. **Location:** I-40, exit 150B or C. 400 E Reno Ave 73104.
Small-scale Hotel — Fax: 405/601-1701. **Amenities:** 151 units, pets, coffeemakers, microwaves, refrigerators, pool, tennis. **Terms:** cancellation fee imposed. **Cards:** AX, CB, DC, DS, MC, VI. (See color ad below)

(See map and index starting on p. 591)

RESIDENCE INN BY MARRIOTT-OKLAHOMA CITY
WEST   *Book great rates at AAA.com*   **Phone:** 405/942-4500   **22**

All Year [BP]   1P: $159-$189

Small-scale Hotel
Location: I-40, exit 145 (Meridian Ave), 0.3 mi n, then just e. 4361 W Reno Ave 73107. **Fax:** 405/942-7777. **Facility:** Smoke free premises. 135 units. 97 one-bedroom standard units. 38 one-bedroom suites ($159-$189). 2 stories (no elevator), exterior corridors. **Parking:** on-site. **Terms:** cancellation fee imposed, pets ($75 fee). **Amenities:** voice mail, irons, hair dryers. **Pool(s):** small outdoor. **Leisure Activities:** whirlpool, exercise room, sports court. **Guest Services:** complimentary evening beverages: Mon-Thurs, valet and coin laundry, area transportation, wireless Internet. **Business Services:** meeting rooms. **Cards:** AX, CB, DC, DS, JC, MC, VI. *(See color ad below)*

SOME UNITS
(ASK) ⊬ 🐾 ⑪ ⊘ ⇌ ✕ 🎥 🖃 🖵 / (VCR)
FEE

RESIDENCE INN BY MARRIOTT
SOUTH-CROSSROADS MALL   *Book great rates at AAA.com*   **Phone:** (405)634-9696   **44**

All Year   1P: $140-$170   2P: $145-$175   XP: $54   F18

Small-scale Hotel
Location: I-240, exit 4C eastbound, 0.4 mi nw; exit 5 westbound, 0.8 mi nw. 1111 E I-240 Service Rd 73149. **Fax:** 405/634-6984. **Facility:** Smoke free premises. 90 units. 37 one-bedroom standard units with efficiencies. 35 one- and 18 two-bedroom suites, some with efficiencies or kitchens. 3 stories, interior corridors. **Bath:** combo or shower only. **Parking:** on-site. **Terms:** [BP] meal plan available, pets ($75 fee). **Amenities:** dual phone lines, voice mail, irons, hair dryers. **Pool(s):** heated indoor. **Leisure Activities:** whirlpool, exercise room. **Guest Services:** valet and coin laundry, wireless Internet. **Business Services:** meeting rooms. **Cards:** AX, DC, DS, MC, VI.

(ASK) (S) 🐾 ⑪ 🐾 ⇌ ✕ 🎥 🖃 🖵 🖵
FEE

SHERATON OKLAHOMA CITY   *Book great rates at AAA.com*   **Phone:** (405)235-2780   **21**

All Year   1P: $229-$269   2P: $229-$269   XP: $30   F17

Large-scale Hotel
Location: Sheridan and Broadway aves; downtown. One N Broadway Ave 73102. **Fax:** 405/232-8752. **Facility:** 395 units. 393 one-bedroom standard units. 2 one-bedroom suites with whirlpools. 15 stories, interior corridors. **Bath:** combo or shower only. **Parking:** on-site (fee) and valet. **Terms:** cancellation fee imposed, pets (dogs only, $50 fee, with prior approval). **Amenities:** voice mail, irons, hair dryers. *Some:* dual phone lines. **Dining:** 6:30 am-2 & 5:30-10 pm, cocktails. **Pool(s):** outdoor. **Leisure Activities:** exercise room. **Guest Services:** gift shop, valet laundry, beauty salon, wireless Internet. **Business Services:** conference facilities, business center. **Cards:** AX, DC, DS, MC, VI.

SOME UNITS
🐾 ⑪ 🍸 🐾 ⊘ ⇌ 🎥 🖵 / ✕ (VCR) 🖃
FEE   FEE   FEE

THE SKIRVIN HILTON   **Phone:** 405/272-3040

(fyi)   Property failed to provide current rates
Too new to rate, opening scheduled for February 2007. **Location:** I-40, exit 150C. 1 Park Ave 73102. Small-scale Hotel **Fax:** 405/272-5160. **Amenities:** 225 units. *(See color ad p 603)*

SLEEP INN & SUITES   *Book great rates at AAA.com*   **Phone:** (405)478-9898   **8**

6/1-9/1   1P: $74-$84   2P: $74-$84   XP: $10   F18
3/1-4/1   1P: $69-$84   2P: $69-$84   XP: $10   F18
4/2-5/31 & 9/2-2/29   1P: $59-$74   2P: $59-$74   XP: $10   F18

Small-scale Hotel
Location: I-35, exit 137 (122nd St), just e. 12024 122nd St 73131. **Fax:** 405/478-9898. **Facility:** 69 one-bedroom standard units, some with whirlpools. 3 stories, interior corridors. **Bath:** combo or shower only. **Parking:** on-site. **Terms:** [ECP] meal plan available, package plans. **Amenities:** high-speed Internet, voice mail, irons, hair dryers. **Pool(s):** heated indoor. **Leisure Activities:** whirlpool, exercise room. **Guest Services:** coin laundry, wireless Internet. **Business Services:** PC. **Cards:** AX, DC, DS, MC, VI.

SOME UNITS
(ASK) (S) ⑪ ⊘ ⇌ 🎥 🖃 🖵 🖵 / ✕ /

SUPER 8 BRICKTOWN   *Book at AAA.com*   **Phone:** 405/677-1000   **41**

All Year   1P: $44-$45   2P: $44-$48   XP: $5   F18

Motel
Location: I-35, exit 124B northbound; exit 125A southbound, just n on service road. 3030 S I-35 73129. **Fax:** 405/677-1000. **Facility:** 101 one-bedroom standard units. 2 stories (no elevator), exterior corridors. **Parking:** on-site. **Amenities:** *Some:* hair dryers. **Cards:** AX, DC, DS, JC, MC, VI.

SOME UNITS
(ASK) (S) ⑪ 🎥 / ✕ 🖵 /

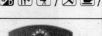

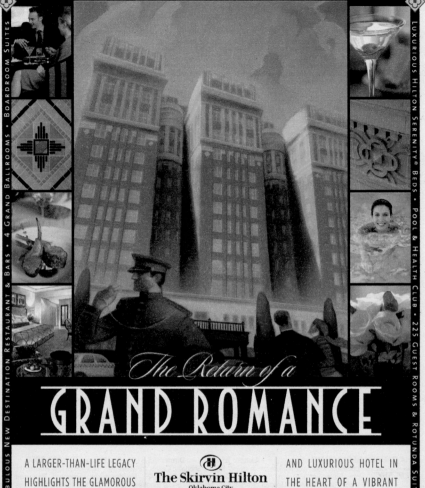

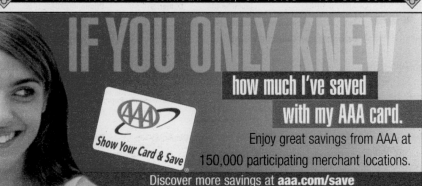

(See map and index starting on p. 591)

WATERFORD MARRIOTT HOTEL *Book great rates at AAA.com*   Phone: (405)848-4782 **11**
(AAA) (SAVE) All Year   1P: $129-$249   2P: $139-$259   XP: $10   F16
▼▼▼ **Location:** I-44, exit 125A, 1.4 mi n. Located in a corporate and residential area. 6300 Waterford Blvd 73118.
Fax: 405/843-9161. **Facility:** Splendid landscaping and elegant public areas characterize this Marriott.
Smoke free premises. 197 units. 196 one-bedroom standard units. 1 one-bedroom suite ($179-$269) with
Large-scale Hotel whirlpool. 9 stories, interior corridors. *Bath:* combo or shower only. **Parking:** on-site and valet.
Amenities: video games (fee), voice mail, irons, hair dryers. *Some:* dual phone lines. **Dining:** 6:30 am-2 &
6-10 pm, cocktails. **Pool(s):** heated outdoor. **Leisure Activities:** saunas, whirlpool, exercise room. *Fee:* massage. **Guest
Services:** valet laundry, wireless Internet. **Business Services:** conference facilities, business center. **Cards:** AX, CB, DC, DS,
JC, MC, VI. **Free Special Amenities:** newspaper.
SOME UNITS

WINGATE INN *Book great rates at AAA.com*   Phone: (405)682-3600 **38**
(AAA) (SAVE) All Year   1P: $99-$120   2P: $99-$120
▼▼▼ **Location:** I-40, exit 145 (Meridian Ave), 1.1 mi s. 2001 S Meridian Ave 73108. Fax: 405/682-1882. **Facility:** 99 one-
bedroom standard units, some with whirlpools. 4 stories, interior corridors. *Bath:* combo or shower only.
Small-scale Hotel **Parking:** on-site. **Terms:** [ECP] meal plan available. **Amenities:** video games (fee), high-speed Internet,
dual phone lines, voice mail, safes, irons, hair dryers. **Pool(s):** small heated indoor. **Leisure
Activities:** sauna, whirlpool, exercise room. **Guest Services:** complimentary evening beverages: Tues,
valet laundry, wireless Internet. **Business Services:** meeting rooms, business center. **Cards:** AX, DC, DS, MC, VI.
Free Special Amenities: expanded continental breakfast and high-speed Internet.
SOME UNITS

──────── *The following lodging was either not evaluated or did not* ────────
meet AAA rating requirements but is listed for your information only.

RED ROOF INN   Phone: 405/947-8777
(fyi)   Did not meet all AAA rating requirements for some property operations at time of last evaluation on
Small-scale Hotel 02/23/2006. **Location:** I-40, exit 145 (Meridian Ave), just n. 309 S Meridian Ave 73108. Facilities, services, and decor
characterize a basic property.

──────── **WHERE TO DINE** ────────

ABUELO'S MEXICAN FOOD EMBASSY   **Lunch:** $6-$17   **Dinner:** $9-$17   Phone: 405/235-1422 **20**
▼▼▼▼ **Location:** Just w of jct Oklahoma Ave. 17 E Sheridan Ave 73104. **Hours:** 11 am-10 pm, Fri & Sat-11 pm; to 9 pm
in winter. Closed: 11/22, 12/25. **Features:** The upscale restaurant's menu incorporates top-quality steaks
Mexican and traditional Mexican dishes. Casual dress; cocktails. **Parking:** on-site (fee). **Cards:** AX, DC, DS,
MC, VI.

ABUELO'S MEXICAN FOOD EMBASSY   **Lunch:** $6-$17   **Dinner:** $9-$17   Phone: 405/755-2680 **1**
▼▼▼▼ **Location:** John Kilpatrick Tpke, exit May Ave, just n. 3001 W Memorial Rd 73134. **Hours:** 11 am-10 pm, Fri & Sat-
11 pm. Closed: 11/22, 12/25. **Features:** Well-prepared dishes include shredded beef burritos, grilled chicken
Mexican and other Mexican favorites. Plenty of attractive plants, murals and statues decorate the upscale dining
room. Casual dress; cocktails. **Parking:** on-site. **Cards:** AX, CB, DC, DS, JC, MC, VI.

ALOHA GARDEN RESTAURANT   **Lunch:** $5-$7   **Dinner:** $5-$11   Phone: 405/686-0288 **32**
▼▼▼ **Location:** I-240, exit 1C, just nw; in Walnut Square Shopping Center. 2219 SW 74th St, #105 73159. **Hours:** 11 am-9
pm, Fri & Sat-9:30 pm, Sun-8 pm. Closed: 7/4, 11/22, 12/25. **Reservations:** accepted. **Features:** The
Chinese locally popular Aloha Garden offers a nice selection on its luncheon and dinner buffet, which includes large
portions and is a good value. You may also order from the menu that offers American dishes in addition to
Chinese offerings. Pleasant, friendly service. Casual dress; cocktails. **Parking:** on-site. **Cards:** AX, CB, DC, DS, MC, VI.

BELLINI'S RISTORANTE & GRILL   **Lunch:** $8-$48   **Dinner:** $10-$48   Phone: 405/848-1065 **11**
▼▼▼ **Location:** I-44, exit 125A, 1.4 mi n. 6305 Waterford Blvd 73118. **Hours:** 11 am-9 pm, Fri & Sat-10 pm. Closed:
11/22, 12/25. **Reservations:** accepted. **Features:** Next to underground parking, the restaurant is appointed
Italian in upscale decor and treats patrons to nicely presented and prepared Italian fare. Dressy casual; cocktails.
Parking: on-site. **Cards:** DS, MC, VI.

BOURBON STREET CAFE   **Lunch:** $6-$9   **Dinner:** $9-$20   Phone: 405/232-6666 **26**
▼▼▼ **Location:** Just n of jct Reno and Oklahoma aves; in Bricktown. 100 E California Ave 73104. **Hours:** 11 am-10 pm, Fri
& Sat-11 pm. Closed: 11/22, 12/25. **Features:** Patrons might think they've stepped into New Orleans, due to
Cajun the lively jazz music and bustling atmosphere. Menu selections include seafood, pasta, chicken and steak,
all prepared in the expected Cajun tradition. Casual dress; cocktails. **Parking:** on-site (fee). **Cards:** AX, CB,
DC, DS, JC, MC, VI.

BRICKTOWN BREWERY   **Lunch:** $6-$16   **Dinner:** $8-$16   Phone: 405/232-2739 **21**
▼▼▼ **Location:** Near downtown; at Sheridan and Oklahoma aves. 1 N Oklahoma Ave 73104. **Hours:** 11 am-10 pm, Fri &
Sat-midnight, Sun noon-8 pm. Closed: 11/22, 12/25. **Features:** Bricktown Brewery is nestled in the city's
American historic, restored-warehouse district. The two-story warehouse was built before statehood (1903) and has a
rustic atmosphere. The menu includes delicious roasted salmon steak, barbecue copperhead and chicken
pot pie. Casual dress; cocktails. **Parking:** on-site. **Cards:** AX, CB, DC, DS, MC, VI.

(See map and index starting on p. 591)

CATTLEMEN'S STEAKHOUSE Lunch: $5-$14   Dinner: $10-$25   Phone: 405/236-0416   ㉙
▼▼▼ ▼▼▼   **Location:** I-40, exit 148A, 0.8 mi s. 1309 S Agnew 73108. **Hours:** 6 am-10 pm, Fri & Sat-midnight. **Closed:** 11/22,
Steak House   12/25. **Features:** Located in the historic stockyards city, Cattlemen's Steakhouse has been an Oklahoma
tradition since 1910. They offer freshly cut beef of the finest grade, cooked to your specification. And you'll
find the server staff friendly and attentive. Casual dress; cocktails. **Parking:** on-site. **Cards:** AX, CB, DC,
DS, MC, VI.

CHARLESTON'S RESTAURANT Lunch: $8-$22   Dinner: $8-$22   Phone: 405/721-0060
▼▼▼ ▼▼▼   **Location:** Just w of jct MacArthur Blvd. 5909 Northwest Expressway 73132. **Hours:** 11 am-9 pm, Fri & Sat-10 pm.
Steak & Seafood   **Closed:** 11/22, 12/25. **Reservations:** accepted. **Features:** This casual dining spot boasts a friendly, club-like
atmosphere. Fine steak and seafood, as well as hardwood-grilled dishes, are at the heart of the menu. The
noteworthy baked potato soup is rich with onions and bacon bits. Casual dress; cocktails. **Parking:** on-site.
Cards: AX, DS, MC, VI.

CHARLESTON'S RESTAURANT Lunch: $8-$22   Dinner: $8-$22   Phone: 405/681-6686
▼▼▼ ▼▼▼   **Location:** I-40, exit 145 (Meridian Ave), 1.1 mi s. 2000 S Meridian Ave 73102. **Hours:** 11 am-10 pm, Fri & Sat-11
American   pm. **Closed:** 11/22, 12/25. **Reservations:** accepted. **Features:** This casual dining spot boasts a friendly,
club-like atmosphere. Fine steak and seafood, as well as hardwood-grilled dishes, are at the heart of the
Parking: on-site.   menu. The noteworthy baked potato soup is rich with onions and bacon bits. Casual dress; cocktails.

CHARLY'S RESTAURANT Lunch: $4-$6   Dinner: $5-$8   Phone: 405/475-9944   ②
▼▼▼   **Location:** I-44, exit 137, just e. 12000 N I-35 73149. **Hours:** 6 am-10 pm. **Features:** A variety of popular
American   American dishes are prepared for lunch and dinner. This place also is a favorite for breakfast. Casual dress.
Parking: on-site. **Cards:** AX, DS, MC, VI.

CHELINO'S MEXICAN RESTAURANT Lunch: $6-$8   Dinner: $8-$13   Phone: 405/235-3533   ㉔
▼▼▼ ▼▼▼   **Location:** Just w of Oklahoma Ave. 15 E California 73104. **Hours:** 11 am-10 pm, Fri & Sat-11 pm, Sun 11 am-9
Mexican   pm. **Closed:** 11/22, 12/25. **Reservations:** not accepted. **Features:** In the Bricktown area, the restaurant
makes seating available on the terrace, as well as in the festive dining room. Casual dress; cocktails.
Parking: on-site (fee). **Cards:** AX, DS, MC, VI.

CIMARRON STEAK HOUSE Lunch: $5-$13   Dinner: $6-$22   Phone: 405/948-7778   ⑱
ⒶⒶⒶ   **Location:** I-40, exit 145 (Meridian Ave), 0.5 mi n. 201 N Meridian Ave 73107. **Hours:** 11 am-10 pm, Fri & Sat-11
▼▼▼ ▼▼▼   pm. **Closed:** 11/22, 12/25. **Reservations:** accepted, Sun-Thurs. **Features:** The steaks served here are
Steak House   naturally aged and cut on the premises, then mesquite-broiled for a good flavor. They also serve ribs, pork
chops and seafood. Pleasant service is provided in a Western decor and atmosphere. Live entertainment
offered Saturday. Casual dress; cocktails. **Parking:** on-site. **Cards:** AX, CB, DC, DS, MC, VI.

THE COACH HOUSE Lunch: $11-$17   Dinner: $22-$40   Phone: 405/842-1000   ⑧
▼▼▼▼ ▼▼▼▼   **Location:** I-44, exit 126, 0.8 mi to Avondale Dr, then just nw. 6437 Avondale Dr 73112. **Hours:** 11:30 am-2 & 6-10
American   pm, Sat from 6 pm. **Closed:** Sun. **Reservations:** suggested. **Features:** This cottage-style restaurant—with
its high, arched windows and stone exterior—is warm and inviting. Rich, dark woods in the interior adds to
the elegance. The artful presentation of skillfully prepared cuisine contributes to a dining extravaganza.
Dressy casual; cocktails. **Parking:** on-site. **Cards:** AX, CB, DC, DS, MC, VI.

COACH'S BBQ PIZZA & BREWERY Lunch: $7-$16   Dinner: $7-$16   Phone: 405/232-6224   ㉕
▼▼▼ ▼▼▼   **Location:** Just n of jct Reno Ave. 20 S Mickey Mantle Dr 73104. **Hours:** 11 am-10 pm, Fri & Sat-11 pm. **Closed:**
Barbecue   11/22, 12/25. **Features:** Baby back ribs, rib-eye, pizza and assorted other dishes make up the menu. Large
windows overlook Bricktown Ball Field, allowing for great views from many tables. A balcony is available by
reservation during events. Casual dress; cocktails. **Parking:** on-site (fee). **Cards:** AX, DS, MC, VI.

THE COUNTY LINE BARBECUE Lunch: $7-$19   Dinner: $7-$19   Phone: 405/478-4955   ⑩
▼▼▼ ▼▼▼   **Location:** I-44, exit 129 (ML King Ave), 0.6 mi w. 1226 NE 63rd St 73111. **Hours:** 11 am-9 pm, Fri & Sat-10 pm.
American   **Closed:** 1/1, 11/22, 12/24, 12/25. **Features:** Slow-smoked barbecue and prime rib dishes are served in the
1930s roadhouse atmosphere of the Oklahoma County Line Restaurant. The interior is decorated with
Western memorabilia, and the server staff is attentive and prompt. The baby back ribs are great. Casual
dress; cocktails. **Parking:** on-site. **Cards:** AX, CB, DC, DS, JC, MC, VI.

DEEP FORK GRILL Lunch: $8-$16   Dinner: $8-$34   Phone: 405/848-7678   ⑭
▼▼▼ ▼▼▼   **Location:** I-44, exit 126, just n. 5418 N Western 73118. **Hours:** 11 am-10 pm, Fri-2 am, Sat 5 pm-2 am, Sun
Continental   10:30 am-10 pm; Sunday brunch. **Closed** major holidays. **Reservations:** suggested, weekends.
Features: The favorites among Deep Fork Grill's good selection are cedar-plank salmon, chili-lacquered
chicken salad, fresh seafood, certified angus beef steak, and housemade desserts. The quiet, intimate,
romantic atmosphere suits business people and couples. Casual dress; cocktails. **Parking:** on-site. **Cards:** AX, CB, MC, VI.

GOLDEN PALACE Lunch: $5-$12   Dinner: $6-$12   Phone: 405/686-1511   ㉚
▼▼▼ ▼▼▼   **Location:** I-40, exit 145 (Meridian Ave), 1 mi s. 1500 S Meridian Ave 73108. **Hours:** 11 am-9:30 pm, Sun-8:30 pm.
Chinese   **Closed:** 1/1, 11/22, 12/25. **Reservations:** not accepted. **Features:** Guests can sample Chinese or
Vietnamese dishes from the menu or buffet or opt for the Mongolian barbecue. The food is enjoyable.
Casual dress; beer only. **Parking:** on-site. **Cards:** AX, DS, MC, VI.

(See map and index starting on p. 591)

GOPURAM, TASTE OF INDIA   *Menu on AAA.com*   **Lunch:** $6-$8   **Dinner:** $10-$15   **Phone:** 405/948-7373   (17)
Indian
Location: I-44, exit 122, 1.3 mi w; in Windsor Hills Shopping Center. 4559 NW 23rd St 73127. **Hours:** 11 am-10 pm. **Features:** Although the exterior, which sits in a strip shopping center, is nondescript, the interior is loaded with charm. Indian cultural decorations set the mood to transfer you to another part of the world. The authentic cuisine and extensive menu are a world diner's delight. Casual dress; cocktails. **Parking:** on-site. **Cards:** AX, DC, DS, JC, MC, VI.

HOUSE OF HUNAN-OLIE AVE   **Lunch:** $4-$10   **Dinner:** $4-$10   **Phone:** 405/840-2332   (7)
Chinese
Location: I-44, exit 126, 0.9 mi n, then just e on 65th St. 6600 N Olie Ave 73116. **Hours:** 11 am-9 pm. Closed: 7/4, 11/22, 12/25. **Features:** You'll enjoy the Belgian crispy shrimp and governor's chicken at the House of Hunan. They offer large servings, low prices and well-prepared foods in a quiet, comfortable, nicely decorated setting. The turtle cheesecake is good too. Friendly service. Casual dress; cocktails. **Parking:** on-site. **Cards:** AX, DC, DS, MC, VI.

HUNAN CHINESE RESTAURANT   **Lunch:** $6-$8   **Dinner:** $6-$8   **Phone:** 405/685-5288   (33)
Chinese
Location: I-240, exit 1A, just se. 1506 SW 74th St 73159. **Hours:** 11 am-9 pm. Closed: 11/22, 12/25. **Features:** The all-you-can-eat buffet, which lines up a nice sampling of dishes, is most diners' preferred method of assembling a meal. Casual dress. **Parking:** on-site. **Cards:** MC, VI.

HUNAN WOK RESTAURANT   **Lunch:** $5-$11   **Dinner:** $6-$11   **Phone:** 405/722-8996   (4)
Chinese
Location: 3.4 mi w of jct SR 3 and 74. 6812 Northwest Expressway 73132. **Hours:** 11 am-10 pm. Closed: 11/22, 12/25. **Features:** Many frequent patrons choose from the buffet or the Mongolian barbecue. Both are equally good and have a nice variety of choices. Casual dress. **Parking:** on-site. **Cards:** AX, DS, MC, VI.

J W'S STEAKHOUSE   **Dinner:** $18-$38   **Phone:** 405/842-6633   (13)
Steak House
Location: Just e of jct SR 3 and 74; in Oklahoma City Marriott. 3233 Northwest Expressway 73112. **Hours:** 6 pm-10 pm, Fri & Sat-11 pm. Closed major holidays; also Sun. **Reservations:** suggested. **Features:** You won't go wrong by choosing the prime rib or garlic filet mignon at J W's. The menu has a very good selection of fresh seafood, pork and beef, and meals are well-prepared. The restaurant has an elegant, intimate atmosphere with Southwestern decor. Dressy casual; cocktails. **Parking:** on-site. **Cards:** AX, CB, DC, DS, JC, MC, VI.

LA BAGUETTE BISTRO CASUAL RESTAURANT &
BAKERY   **Lunch:** $7-$12   **Dinner:** $10-$23   **Phone:** 405/840-3047   (5)
French
Location: I-44, exit 124, 2.3 mi n. 7408 N May Ave 73116. **Hours:** 8 am-10 pm, Fri & Sat-11 pm, Sun 9:30 am-2:30 pm. Closed major holidays. **Reservations:** accepted. **Features:** La Baguette's delicious, creative food belies its modest surroundings. Entrees offered: chicken, duck, pork, beef tenderloin, lamb and seafood—all delicious. The choices from their in-house bakery are also excellent, rich and flavorful. Pleasant service. Casual dress; cocktails. **Parking:** on-site. **Cards:** AX, CB, DC, DS, MC, VI.

LALUNA MEXICAN CAFE   **Lunch:** $6-$15   **Dinner:** $7-$15   **Phone:** 405/235-9596   (27)
Mexican
Location: Just ne of jct Walker Ave. 409 W Reno Ave 73102. **Hours:** 11 am-9 pm, Fri & Sat-9:30 pm. Closed: 1/1, 11/22, 12/25; also Sun. **Features:** Good-size portions and all the expected Mexican standbys are available. Service is relaxed and casual. Casual dress; cocktails. **Parking:** on-site. **Cards:** AX, DS, MC, VI.

MADISONS PANCAKE HOUSE   **Lunch:** $5-$8   **Dinner:** $7-$12   **Phone:** 405/848-5050   (12)
American
Location: 0.4 mi e of jct SR 3 and 74. 3315 Northwest Expressway 73112. **Hours:** 24 hours. **Features:** Hearty portions and a good selection are a couple reasons locals visit the pancake house. As expected, breakfasts are popular. Casual dress. **Parking:** on-site. **Cards:** AX, DS, MC, VI.

MANTEL WINE BAR & BISTRO   **Lunch:** $9-$35   **Dinner:** $15-$35   **Phone:** 405/236-8040   (19)
American
Location: Just ne of jct Mickey Mantle Blvd. 201 E Sheridan 73104. **Hours:** 11 am-10 pm, Fri & Sat-11 pm, Sun 5 pm-9 pm. Closed major holidays. **Reservations:** suggested. **Features:** The upscale restaurant serves attractive dishes that burst with flavor. Reservations are suggested due to space limitations in the dining room and small waiting area. Dressy casual; cocktails. **Parking:** on-site. **Cards:** AX, MC, VI.

MICKEY MANTLE'S STEAKHOUSE   **Dinner:** $20-$35   **Phone:** 405/272-0777   (23)
Steak House
Location: Just n of jct Reno Ave and Mickey Mantle Blvd; in Bricktown. 7 Mickey Mantle Dr 73104. **Hours:** 5 pm-10 pm, Fri & Sat-11 pm. Closed major holidays. **Reservations:** suggested. **Features:** Patrons can expect tender steak selections served amid tasteful memorabilia spanning Mickey Mantle's career. A nice selection of desserts is available to those who save room. Casual dress; cocktails. **Parking:** on-site (fee) and valet. **Cards:** AX, CB, DC, DS, JC, MC, VI.

NEWTON'S   **Dinner:** $11-$33   **Phone:** 405/840-0115   (6)
American
Location: I-44, exit 126, 1.2 mi n. 1025 NW 70th St 73116. **Hours:** 5 pm-9:30 pm, Fri & Sat-10 pm. Closed major holidays; also Sun. **Reservations:** suggested. **Features:** The subdued, yet elegant, dining room is a nice setting in which to savor one of a superb array of tastefully prepared entrees. Diverse selections ensure diners enjoy a memorable experience. Dressy casual; cocktails. **Parking:** on-site. **Cards:** AX, DS, MC, VI.

NONNA'S EURO-AMERICAN RISTORANTE AND BAR   **Lunch:** $10-$13   **Dinner:** $17-$42   **Phone:** 405/235-4410   (22)
American
Location: Just n of jct Reno Ave. 1 Mickey Mantle Dr 73104. **Hours:** 11 am-2 & 5-10 pm. Closed: 11/22, 12/25; also Sun. **Reservations:** suggested. **Features:** You'll find upscale decor and furnishings and a nice selection of Euro-American dishes at the restaurant, which is also known for quality treats from the bakery. Dressy casual; cocktails. **Parking:** valet. **Cards:** AX, DS, MC, VI.

(See map and index starting on p. 591)

PAPA DIO'S ITALIAN RESTAURANT & WINE BAR   **Lunch:** $6-$10   **Dinner:** $9-$23   **Phone:** 405/755-2255   ③

Italian

Location: SR 74, exit Hefner Rd, 0.6 mi e, then just se. 10712 N May Ave 73120. **Hours:** 11 am-2:30 & 4-9:30 pm, Fri-10 pm, Sat 4:30 pm-10 pm, Mon 4:30 pm-9 pm. Closed major holidays; also Sun. **Features:** You'll discover creative and tasty dishes and an upbeat atmosphere at Papa Dio's, which has an upscale side where there is more of a fine-dining atmosphere with soft candlelight. The veal parmigiana, mozzarella sticks and cheesecake are very good. Casual dress; cocktails. **Parking:** on-site. **Cards:** AX, DS, MC, VI.

PEARLS OYSTER BAR   **Lunch:** $6-$8   **Dinner:** $9-$18   **Phone:** 405/848-8008   ⑨

Seafood

Location: 0.6 mi w of jct US 77. 928 NW 63rd St 73116. **Hours:** 11 am-11 pm. Closed: 11/22, 12/25. **Features:** Pearl's features entree selections of seafood such as trout and catfish as well as chicken, pork chops and steak dishes, many with Cajun-style spiciness. The upbeat-tempo atmosphere creates a fun dining experience with pleasant and attentive service. Casual dress; cocktails. **Parking:** on-site. **Cards:** AX, CB, DC, DS, MC, VI.

PEARL'S OYSTER BAR   **Lunch:** $6-$14   **Dinner:** $9-$18   **Phone:** 405/682-1500   ㉛

Cajun

Location: I-240, exit 1C, just w on north frontage road. 2125 W I-240 73159. **Hours:** 11 am-10:30 pm, Fri & Sat-11:30 pm. Closed: 11/22, 12/25. **Features:** Pearl's features entree selections of seafood such as trout and catfish as well as chicken, pork chops and steak dishes, many with Cajun-style spiciness. The upbeat-tempo atmosphere creates a fun dining experience with pleasant and attentive service. Casual dress; cocktails. **Parking:** on-site. **Cards:** AX, CB, DC, DS, MC, VI.

RIB CRIB BARBECUE   **Lunch:** $6-$14   **Dinner:** $6-$14   **Phone:** 405/616-7800

Barbecue

Location: I-240, exit 3B, just n. 401 SW 74th St 73139. **Hours:** 11 am-10 pm. Closed: 11/22, 12/25. **Features:** Most guests need extra napkins to tackle the ribs, brisket, ham, pork and chicken selections. The menu also lists sandwiches and wraps, along with tempting sides and large desserts. The decor is decidedly Western. Casual dress; beer only. **Parking:** on-site. **Cards:** AX, DC, DS, MC, VI.

RIB CRIB BARBECUE   **Lunch:** $5-$8   **Dinner:** $5-$8   **Phone:** 405/917-7400

Barbecue

Location: I-40, exit 145 (Meridian Ave), 0.5 mi s. 1223 S Meridian Ave 73108. **Hours:** 11 am-10 pm. Closed: 11/22, 12/25. **Features:** Most guests need extra napkins to tackle the ribs, brisket, ham, pork and chicken selections. The menu also lists sandwiches and wraps, along with tempting sides and large desserts. The decor is decidedly Western. Casual dress; beer only. **Parking:** on-site. **Cards:** AX, DC, DS, MC, VI.

RON'S HAMBURGERS & CHILI   **Lunch:** $4-$6   **Dinner:** $4-$6   **Phone:** 405/943-7667   ⑮

American

Location: I-44, exit 124, 0.4 mi n. 4723 N May Ave 73112. **Hours:** 10:30 am-8 pm. Closed: 11/22, 12/25; also Sun. **Features:** The restaurant's name gives a strong indication of the strengths—varied hamburgers and the popular chili—but a few surprises also lurk on the menu. Casual dress. **Parking:** on-site. **Cards:** DS, MC, VI.

SHORTY SMALL'S   **Lunch:** $6-$17   **Dinner:** $7-$17   **Phone:** 405/947-0779

Barbecue

Location: I-40, exit 145 (Meridian Ave), just n. 4500 W Reno Ave 73127. **Hours:** 11 am-10 pm, Fri & Sat-11 pm. Closed: 11/22, 12/25. **Reservations:** not accepted. **Features:** Focusing on ribs, fried catfish, sandwiches and cheesecake, this restaurant is popular with the locals. The rustic and nostalgic atmosphere is family-oriented, and the feel is casual, hectic and sometimes noisy. Casual dress; cocktails. **Parking:** on-site. **Cards:** AX, CB, DC, DS, MC, VI.

TED'S CAFE ESCONDIDO   **Lunch:** $8-$14   **Dinner:** $9-$14   **Phone:** 405/635-8337   ㉞

Mexican

Location: I-240, exit 2A, 0.8 mi s. 8324 S Western 73159. **Hours:** 11 am-10 pm, Fri & Sat-10:30 pm. Closed major holidays. **Features:** The Oklahoma City favorite is frequently busy but handles large crowds efficiently to prevent them from being a distraction. Casual dress; beer only. **Parking:** on-site. **Cards:** AX, DS, MC, VI.

TED'S CAFE ESCONDIDO   **Lunch:** $6-$12   **Dinner:** $8-$12   **Phone:** 405/848-8337   ⑯

Mexican

Location: I-44, exit May Ave, 2.4 mi n to 68th St, then just e. 2836 NW 68th St 73116. **Hours:** 10:45 am-10 pm, Fri & Sat-10:30 pm, Sun 11 am-8 pm. Closed major holidays. **Features:** Ted's is a free standing Mexican restaurant with the exterior being a typical stucco fascade. The restaurant is a local family favorite, serving a variety of Mexican dishes. Casual dress; beer only. **Parking:** on-site. **Cards:** AX, DS, MC, VI.

TRAPPER'S FISHCAMP & GRILL   **Lunch:** $7-$23   **Dinner:** $8-$23   **Phone:** 405/943-9111   ㉘

American

Location: I-40, exit 145 (Meridian Ave), 0.3 mi n, then just e. 4300 W Reno 73107. **Hours:** 11 am-10 pm. Closed: 11/22, 12/25. **Features:** Evocative of a rustic lodge, the dining room sports hunting and fishing equipment and some mounted game on the walls. Choices on the menu range from beef to seafood. Casual dress; cocktails. **Parking:** on-site. **Cards:** AX, DS, MC, VI.

ZIO'S ITALIAN KITCHEN   **Lunch:** $6-$12   **Dinner:** $6-$12   **Phone:** 405/680-9999

Italian

Location: I-40, exit 145 (Meridian Ave), 1.2 mi s. 2305 S Meridian Ave 73108. **Hours:** 11 am-10 pm, Fri & Sat-11 pm. Closed: 11/22, 12/25. **Features:** The warm, comfortable atmosphere and Old World decor complement the menu. Meals are a good value, and so is the service. This small chain specializes in Italian cuisine, including oven-baked pizzas and pasta dishes. Guests are encouraged to get creative with their pizzas by mixing and matching from a list of 24 toppings. Particularly tempting dishes are Artichoke spinach pasta, chicken parmigiana, and Shrimp Limone. Casual dress; cocktails. **Parking:** on-site. **Cards:** AX, CB, DC, DS, MC, VI.

The Oklahoma City Vicinity

CHOCTAW pop. 9,377

──── WHERE TO DINE ────

OLD GERMANY RESTAURANT   *Menu on AAA.com*   **Lunch:** $6-$9   **Dinner:** $9-$24   **Phone:** 405/390-8647
(AAA)
German
Location: I-40, exit 166, 3 mi n, then 1 mi e. 15920 SE 29th 73020. **Hours:** 11 am-2 & 5-9 pm. Closed major holidays; also Sun & Mon. **Reservations:** accepted. **Features:** You'll enjoy Old World-style food and environment here. Sit in the Bavarian room, Black Forest Chalet or Wine Cellar and have jager schnitzel (grilled pork loin), wiener schnitzel (breaded veal) or a variety of German sausages. Weekends offer live music. Casual dress; cocktails. **Parking:** on-site. **Cards:** AX, CB, DC, DS, MC, VI.

DEL CITY pop. 22,128   (See map and index starting on p. 591)

──── WHERE TO STAY ────

LA QUINTA INN OKLAHOMA CITY EAST (DEL CITY)   *Book great rates at AAA.com*   **Phone:** (405)672-0067   **55**
Small-scale Hotel

| | 6/18-8/18 [CP] | 1P: $75-$105 | 2P: $81-$111 | XP: $6 | F18 |
| | 3/1-6/17 & 8/19-2/29 [CP] | 1P: $69-$99 | 2P: $75-$105 | XP: $6 | F18 |

Location: I-40, exit 156A (Sooner Rd), just nw. 5501 Tinker Diagonal Rd 73115-4613. **Fax:** 405/670-4739. **Facility:** 105 units. 102 one-bedroom standard units. 3 one-bedroom suites ($94-$151). 3 stories, interior/exterior corridors. *Bath:* combo or shower only. **Parking:** on-site. **Amenities:** video games (fee), high-speed Internet, voice mail, irons, hair dryers. **Pool(s):** small outdoor. **Guest Services:** coin laundry. **Cards:** AX, CB, DC, DS, MC, VI.

SOME UNITS

EDMOND pop. 68,315   (See map and index starting on p. 591)

──── WHERE TO STAY ────

BEST WESTERN EDMOND INN & SUITES   *Book great rates at AAA.com*   **Phone:** (405)216-0300   **50**
(AAA) [SAVE]
Small-scale Hotel

| All Year | 1P: $81 | 2P: $86 |

Location: I-35, exit 141, 1.1 mi w. Located in a quiet area. 2700 E 2nd St 73034. **Fax:** 405/359-9287. **Facility:** 60 one-bedroom standard units, some with whirlpools. 2 stories (no elevator), interior corridors. *Bath:* combo or shower only. **Parking:** on-site. **Terms:** [ECP] meal plan available, pets ($10 fee, with prior approval). **Amenities:** irons, hair dryers. *Some:* high-speed Internet. **Pool(s):** small heated indoor. **Leisure Activities:** whirlpool, exercise room. **Guest Services:** wireless Internet. **Business Services:** meeting rooms, PC. **Cards:** AX, CB, DC, DS, JC, MC, VI. **Free Special Amenities:** expanded continental breakfast and high-speed Internet.

SOME UNITS
FEE

FAIRFIELD INN & SUITES BY MARRIOTT   **Phone:** 405/341-4818
[fyi]
Small-scale Hotel
Property failed to provide current rates
Too new to rate, opening scheduled for November 2006. **Location:** I-35, exit 141, southwest corner of I-35 and Second St. 301 Meline Dr 73034. **Fax:** 405/341-4819. **Amenities:** 90 units, coffeemakers, pool.

HOLIDAY INN EXPRESS HOTEL & SUITES   *Book at AAA.com*   **Phone:** 405/844-3700   **51**
Small-scale Hotel
Property failed to provide current rates
Location: I-35, exit 141, just w. 3840 E 2nd St 73034. **Fax:** 405/844-3710. **Facility:** 80 units. 77 one-bedroom standard units, some with whirlpools. 3 one-bedroom suites. 3 stories, interior corridors. *Bath:* combo or shower only. **Parking:** on-site. **Amenities:** video games (fee), high-speed Internet, dual phone lines, voice mail, irons, hair dryers. **Pool(s):** heated indoor. **Leisure Activities:** whirlpool, exercise room. **Guest Services:** valet and coin laundry, wireless Internet. **Business Services:** meeting rooms, business center.

SOME UNITS

SLEEP INN & SUITES   *Book great rates at AAA.com*   **Phone:** (405)844-3000   **52**
(AAA) [SAVE]
Small-scale Hotel

| All Year | 1P: $86-$136 | 2P: $89-$139 | XP: $3 | F17 |

Location: John Kilpatrick Tpke, 1.5 mi n on US 77. 3608 S Broadway Extension 73013. **Fax:** 405/844-3086. **Facility:** 100 units. 94 one-bedroom standard units, some with whirlpools. 6 one-bedroom suites, some with whirlpools. 3 stories, interior corridors. *Bath:* combo or shower only. **Parking:** on-site. **Terms:** cancellation fee imposed. **Amenities:** voice mail, safes (fee), irons, hair dryers. *Some:* high-speed Internet, dual phone lines. **Pool(s):** small heated indoor. **Leisure Activities:** whirlpool, exercise room. **Guest Services:** coin laundry, wireless Internet. **Business Services:** meeting rooms, PC. **Cards:** AX, DC, DS, MC, VI. **Free Special Amenities:** expanded continental breakfast and high-speed Internet.

SOME UNITS

The following lodging was either not evaluated or did not meet AAA rating requirements but is listed for your information only.

HAMPTON INN   **Phone:** 405/844-3037
[fyi]
Small-scale Hotel
Did not meet all AAA rating requirements for some property operations at time of last evaluation on 11/22/2005. **Location:** I-35, exit 141, just w. 300 Meline Dr 73034. Facilities, services, and decor characterize a mid-range property.

(See map and index starting on p. 591)

———— WHERE TO DINE ————

ALVARADO'S
Mexican

Lunch: $5-$6   Dinner: $6-$15   Phone: 405/359-8860   40
Location: I-35, exit 141, 2.3 mi w. 1000 E 2nd St 73034. **Hours:** 11 am-9 pm, Fri & Sat-10 pm. Closed: 11/22, 12/25; also Sun. **Features:** Traditional Mexican dishes are served in a relaxed setting. The basic decor and seating match the restaurant's theme. Casual dress; beer only. **Parking:** on-site. **Cards:** AX, DS, MC, VI.

CHARLESTON'S RESTAURANT
Steak & Seafood

Lunch: $8-$22   Dinner: $8-$22   Phone: 405/478-4949
Location: John Kilpatrick Tpke, 1.5 mi n on US 77. 3409 S Broadway, Suite 400 73013. **Hours:** 11 am-9 pm, Fri & Sat-10 pm. Closed: 11/22, 12/25. **Reservations:** accepted. **Features:** This casual dining spot boasts a friendly, club-like atmosphere. Fine steak and seafood, as well as hardwood-grilled dishes, are at the heart of the menu. The noteworthy baked potato soup is rich with onions and bacon bits. Casual dress; cocktails. **Parking:** on-site. **Cards:** AX, DS, MC, VI.

COACH'S BBQ, PIZZA & BREWERY
Barbecue

Lunch: $7-$16   Dinner: $7-$16   Phone: 405/359-2222   41
Location: John Kilpatrick Tpke, 1.5 mi n on US 77. 3005 S Broadway 73013. **Hours:** 11 am-10 pm, Fri & Sat-11 pm. Closed: 11/22, 12/25. **Features:** Although gourmet pizza and barbecue dishes get the marquee billing, other dishes here are equally well prepared. Casual dress; cocktails. **Parking:** on-site. **Cards:** AX, DS, MC, VI.

GOLDIES PATIO GRILL
American

Lunch: $5-$8   Dinner: $5-$8   Phone: 405/348-1555
Location: Center. 5 E 9th St 73013. **Hours:** 11 am-9 pm. Closed: 1/1, 11/22, 12/25. **Features:** The menu comprises grilled items, chicken, sandwiches and steak, but this place is bests known for its excellent charbroiled burgers. The decor incorporates 1950s and '60s memorabilia. Casual dress. **Parking:** on-site. **Cards:** AX, DS, MC, VI.

HOUSE OF HUNAN
Chinese

Lunch: $4-$7   Dinner: $7-$22   Phone: 405/330-1668   39
Location: 1.4 mi w of US 77 on 2nd St (Edmond Rd); in Oakbrook Center. 2137 W Edmond Rd 73013. **Hours:** 11 am-9 pm, Fri & Sat-10 pm, Sun noon-9:30 pm. Closed: 7/4, 11/22, 12/25. **Reservations:** accepted. **Features:** The House of Hunan's extensive menu features pork, chicken and shrimp entrees served with vegetables and fried rice. The restaurant offers a casual, family-dining atmosphere. Service is prompt and attentive. They will also deliver meals to motels. Casual dress; cocktails. **Parking:** on-site. **Cards:** AX, DS, MC, VI.

MCALISTER'S DELI
Deli/Subs
Sandwiches

Lunch: $4-$6   Dinner: $4-$6   Phone: 405/340-3354
Location: I-35, exit 141, 2.3 mi w. 1021 E 2nd St 73034. **Hours:** 10:30 am-10 pm. Closed: 11/22, 12/25. **Features:** Patrons can choose from more than 30 sandwiches and 11 ways to have their extra-large baked potatoes served. Kentucky pie is a sinful favorite from the dessert menu. Casual dress. **Parking:** on-site. **Cards:** AX, DS, MC, VI.

MILANO'S PIZZERIA
Pizza

Lunch: $3-$7   Dinner: $3-$7   Phone: 405/330-4999   38
Location: Just n of jct US 77. 119 N University 73034. **Hours:** 11 am-9 pm, Fri & Sat-10 pm. Closed: 11/22, 12/25. **Features:** The restaurant's appearance is modest, but guests come back again and again for good pizza and calzones. Casual dress; beer only. **Parking:** on-site. **Cards:** DS, MC, VI.

PORTOBELLO'S ITALIAN GRILL & WINE BAR
Italian

Lunch: $6-$20   Dinner: $8-$20   Phone: 405/330-9984   42
Location: John Kilpatrick Tpke, 1.8 mi n on US 77. 3300 S Broadway 73013. **Hours:** 11 am-9 pm, Fri & Sat-10 pm. Closed: 11/22, 12/25. **Reservations:** accepted. **Features:** Good-size portions of traditional Italian fare are complemented by a selection of desserts. Casual dress; cocktails. **Parking:** on-site. **Cards:** AX, DS, MC, VI.

RIB CRIB BBQ
Barbecue

Lunch: $6-$9   Dinner: $6-$9   Phone: 405/715-2200
Location: Center. 720 S Broadway 73013. **Hours:** 11 am-10 pm. Closed: 11/22, 12/25. **Features:** Most guests need extra napkins to tackle the ribs, brisket, ham, pork and chicken selections. The menu also lists sandwiches and wraps, along with tempting sides and large desserts. The decor is decidedly Western. Casual dress. **Parking:** on-site. **Cards:** AX, DS, MC, VI.

SHORTY SMALL'S
Barbecue

Lunch: $6-$17   Dinner: $6-$17   Phone: 405/478-1784
Location: John Kilpatrick Tpke, 1.5 mi n on US 77. 3601 S Broadway, Suite 100 73013. **Hours:** 11 am-10 pm, Fri & Sat-11 pm. Closed: 11/22, 12/25. **Features:** Focusing on ribs, fried catfish, sandwiches and cheesecake, this restaurant is popular with the locals. The rustic and nostalgic atmosphere is family-oriented, and the feel is casual, hectic and sometimes noisy. Casual dress; cocktails. **Parking:** on-site. **Cards:** AX, DC, DS, MC, VI.

TED'S CAFE ESCONDIDO
Mexican

Lunch: $6-$12   Dinner: $8-$12   Phone: 405/810-8337   37
Location: 0.6 mi e of jct Broadway. 801 E Danforth 73034. **Hours:** 11 am-9 pm, Fri & Sat-10 pm, Sun-8:30 pm. Closed major holidays. **Features:** Freshly prepared foods are dished in hearty portions. Guests have a choice of ground or shredded beef. Casual dress; beer only. **Parking:** on-site. **Cards:** AX, DS, MC, VI.

EL RENO pop. 16,212

——— **WHERE TO STAY** ———

BEST WESTERN HENSLEY'S　*Book great rates at AAA.com*　　　Phone: (405)262-6490
(AAA) (SAVE)　All Year [BP]　　1P: $65-$95　　2P: $65-$95　　XP: $5　　F12
Location: I-40, exit 123, just s. 2701 S Country Club Rd 73036 (PO Drawer 1089). Fax: 405/262-7642. **Facility:** 60
one-bedroom standard units. 2 stories (no elevator), exterior corridors. **Parking:** on-site, winter plug-ins.
Small-scale Hotel　**Terms:** small pets only ($25 deposit, $5 extra charge). **Amenities:** irons, hair dryers. *Some:* high-speed
Internet. **Pool(s):** outdoor. **Leisure Activities:** playground. **Guest Services:** wireless Internet. **Cards:** AX,
DC, DS, MC, VI. **Free Special Amenities: full breakfast and high-speed Internet.**

SOME UNITS

——— **WHERE TO DINE** ———

MONTANA MIKE'S STEAKHOUSE　　**Lunch:** $6-$16　　**Dinner:** $8-$16　　Phone: 405/422-1100
Location: I-40, exit 123, just ne. 1609 SW 27th 73036. **Hours:** 11 am-9 pm, Fri & Sat-10 pm. Closed: 11/22,
12/25. **Features:** This steakhouse offers a dining experience for the whole family. A rustic look with Western
Steak House　appointments characterizes the dining room. Although it's hard to go wrong with a hearty steak of USDA
Choice aged beef, guests also can try smoked, fire-grilled chicken breast, chicken-fried steak, baby back
ribs and other selections. Casual dress. **Parking:** on-site. **Cards:** AX, DS, MC, VI.

GUTHRIE pop. 9,925

——— **WHERE TO STAY** ———

BEST WESTERN TERRITORIAL INN　*Book great rates at AAA.com*　　　Phone: (405)282-8831
(AAA) (SAVE)　All Year　　1P: $66-$79　　2P: $66-$79
Location: I-35, exit 157, just sw. 2323 Territorial Trail 73044. Fax: 405/282-8831. **Facility:** 84 one-bedroom
standard units. 2 stories (no elevator), interior corridors. *Bath:* combo or shower only. **Parking:** on-site.
Small-scale Hotel　**Terms:** small pets only. **Amenities:** voice mail, irons, hair dryers. **Pool(s):** heated outdoor. **Guest Services:**
wireless Internet. **Business Services:** meeting rooms. **Cards:** AX, CB, DC, DS, MC, VI.
Free Special Amenities: continental breakfast and high-speed Internet.

SOME UNITS

SLEEP INN　*Book great rates at AAA.com*　　　Phone: (405)260-1400
(AAA) (SAVE)　All Year　　1P: $73-$95　　2P: $77-$110　　XP: $5　　F17
Location: I-35, exit 157, just nw. 414 Heather Rd 73044. Fax: 405/260-1000. **Facility:** 78 units. 77 one-bedroom
standard units, some with whirlpools. 1 one-bedroom suite ($95-$140) with whirlpool. 3 stories, interior
corridors. *Bath:* combo or shower only. **Parking:** on-site. **Terms:** [CP] meal plan available. **Amenities:** voice
Small-scale Hotel　mail, safes (fee), irons, hair dryers. **Pool(s):** small heated indoor. **Leisure Activities:** whirlpool, limited
exercise equipment. **Guest Services:** valet and coin laundry, wireless Internet. **Business Services:**
meeting rooms, PC. **Cards:** AX, DC, DS, MC, VI. **Free Special Amenities: expanded continental breakfast and high-speed
Internet.**

SOME UNITS

——— **WHERE TO DINE** ———

STABLES CAFE　　**Lunch:** $5-$15　　**Dinner:** $5-$15　　Phone: 405/282-0893
Location: I-35, exit 157, 1.8 mi w. 223 N Division 73044. **Hours:** 11 am-9 pm, Fri & Sat-10 pm. Closed major
holidays. **Features:** First a livery and feed store when built in 1890, the renovated building now houses a
Barbecue　restaurant that serves great-tasting barbecue and steaks. Nostalgic advertisements for beverages, bread,
soap and the like lend to the decor. Casual dress. **Parking:** on-site. **Cards:** AX, CB, DC, DS, JC, MC, VI.

MIDWEST CITY pop. 54,088　(See map and index starting on p. 591)

——— **WHERE TO STAY** ———

AMERISUITES (MIDWEST CITY/TINKER AIR FORCE
BASE)　*Book at AAA.com*　　　Phone: (405)737-7777　60
　All Year [BP]　　1P: $94-$104　　2P: $104-$124　　XP: $10　　F17
Location: I-40, exit 156A (Sooner Rd), just n. 5701 Tinker Diagonal Rd 73110. Fax: 405/737-7773. **Facility:** 80 one-
Small-scale Hotel　bedroom standard units. 4 stories, interior corridors. *Bath:* combo or shower only. **Parking:** on-site.
Terms: small pets only ($10 extra charge). **Amenities:** video games (fee), high-speed Internet, voice mail,
irons, hair dryers. *Some:* dual phone lines. **Pool(s):** heated indoor. **Leisure Activities:** exercise room. **Guest Services:** valet
and coin laundry. **Business Services:** meeting rooms, business center. **Cards:** AX, CB, DC, DS, JC, MC, VI.

SOME UNITS

COMFORT INN & SUITES　*Book great rates at AAA.com*　　　Phone: (405)733-1339　59
(AAA) (SAVE)　All Year [ECP]　　1P: $84　　2P: $89　　XP: $5　　F11
Location: I-40, exit 156A (Sooner Rd), just n. 5653 Tinker Diagonal Rd 73110. Fax: 405/732-6550. **Facility:** 78
units. 75 one-bedroom standard units. 3 one-bedroom suites ($89-$139) with whirlpools. 4 stories, interior
corridors. *Bath:* combo or shower only. **Parking:** on-site. **Terms:** cancellation fee imposed. **Amenities:** high-
Small-scale Hotel　speed Internet, dual phone lines, voice mail, irons, hair dryers. **Pool(s):** heated indoor. **Leisure
Activities:** exercise room. **Guest Services:** valet and coin laundry. **Business Services:** meeting rooms,
PC. **Cards:** AX, CB, DC, DS, JC, MC, VI. **Free Special Amenities: expanded continental breakfast and high-speed
Internet.**

SOME UNITS

(See map and index starting on p. 591)

HOLIDAY INN EXPRESS HOTEL & SUITES *Book at AAA.com* Phone: (405)736-1000 **58**
All Year 1P: $79-$149 2P: $79-$149 XP: $10 F18
Small-scale Hotel **Location:** I-40, exit 156A (Sooner Rd), just n. 1700 S Sooner Rd 73110. Fax: 405/733-5599. **Facility:** 87 one-bedroom standard units, some with whirlpools. 4 stories, interior corridors. *Bath:* combo or shower only. **Parking:** on-site. **Terms:** [ECP] meal plan available. **Amenities:** high-speed Internet, dual phone lines, voice mail, irons, hair dryers. **Pool(s):** heated indoor. **Leisure Activities:** whirlpool, exercise room. **Guest Services:** valet and coin laundry. **Business Services:** meeting rooms, business center. **Cards:** AX, CB, DC, DS, MC, VI.

SOME UNITS

[ASK] [SD] [🍴] [icons] / [X] /

SHERATON MIDWEST CITY HOTEL AT THE REED
  CONFERENCE CENTER Phone: 405/741-7333
[fyi] Property failed to provide current rates
Small-scale Hotel Too new to rate. **Location:** I-40, exit 156A (Sooner Rd). 5750 Will Rogers Rd 73110. **Amenities:** 151 units, pets, coffeemakers.

STUDIO 6 #6003 *Book at AAA.com* Phone: 405/737-8851 **61**
All Year 1P: $47-$57 2P: $51-$61 XP: $3 F17
Motel **Location:** I-40, exit 156A (Sooner Rd), just ne. 5801 Tinker Diagonal Rd 73110. Fax: 405/737-1627. **Facility:** 68 one-bedroom standard units with efficiencies. 2 stories (no elevator), exterior corridors. *Bath:* combo or shower only. **Parking:** on-site. **Terms:** weekly rates available, pets ($10 extra charge). **Pool(s):** small outdoor. **Guest Services:** coin laundry. **Cards:** AX, CB, DC, DS, MC, VI.

SOME UNITS

[SD] [icons] / [X] /
FEE

──────── *The following lodging was either not evaluated or did not* ────────
meet AAA rating requirements but is listed for your information only.

HAMPTON INN Phone: 405/732-5500
[fyi] Did not meet all AAA rating requirements for some property operations at time of last evaluation on 06/23/2006. **Location:** I-40, exit 156A (Sooner Rd), just ne. 1833 Center Dr 73110. Facilities, services, and decor
Small-scale Hotel characterize a mid-range property.

──────── **WHERE TO DINE** ────────

CHEQUERS RESTAURANT & PUB Lunch: $5-$10 Dinner: $5-$10 Phone: 405/736-6944 **46**
Location: I-40, exit 156B, 1.4 mi n. 1009 S Air Depot 73110. **Hours:** 11 am-10 pm, Fri & Sat-11 pm. Closed: 12/25. **Features:** Menu choices—which include Mexican, pasta, steak and seafood dishes—suit many
American tastes. Casual dress; cocktails. **Parking:** on-site. **Cards:** AX, DC, DS, MC, VI.
[icon]

PRIMOS D' ITALIA Lunch: $8-$16 Dinner: $8-$16 Phone: 405/736-9090 **47**
Location: I-40, exit 156A (Sooner Rd), just ne. 5661 Tinker Diagonal 73110. **Hours:** 10:30 am-10 pm. Closed: 11/22, 12/25. **Reservations:** accepted. **Features:** The extensive menu includes both traditional Italian
Italian dishes and assorted pizzas. Casual dress; cocktails. **Parking:** on-site. **Cards:** AX, DS, MC, VI.
[icons]

RIB CRIB BARBECUE Lunch: $6-$14 Dinner: $6-$14 Phone: 405/737-4500
Location: I-40, exit 159A, 0.7 mi ne. 1821 S Douglas Blvd 73130. **Hours:** 11 am-10 pm. Closed: 11/22, 12/25. **Features:** Most guests need extra napkins to tackle the ribs, brisket, ham, pork and chicken selections. The
Barbecue menu also lists sandwiches and wraps, along with tempting sides and large desserts. The decor is decidedly Western. Casual dress; beer only. **Parking:** on-site. **Cards:** AX, DC, DS, MC, VI.
[icon]

RON'S HAMBURGERS & CHILI Lunch: $4-$6 Dinner: $4-$6 Phone: 405/733-7667 **45**
Location: I-40, exit 156B, 2.3 mi n. 351 N Air Depot, Suite A 73110. **Hours:** 10:30 am-8 pm. Closed: 11/22, 12/25; also Sun. **Features:** The restaurant's name gives a strong indication of the strengths—varied hamburgers
American and the popular chili—but a few surprises also lurk on the menu. Casual dress. **Parking:** on-site. **Cards:** MC, VI.

MOORE pop. 41,138 (See map and index starting on p. 591)

──────── **WHERE TO STAY** ────────

BEST WESTERN GREEN TREE INN & SUITES *Book great rates at AAA.com* Phone: (405)912-8882 **64**
All Year 1P: $75 2P: $75 XP: $5 F12

Location: I-35, exit 118, just n on westbound frontage road. 1811 N Moore Ave 73160. Fax: 405/912-4587. **Facility:** 64 units. 55 one-bedroom standard units. 9 one-bedroom suites ($89-$99), some with efficiencies (no utensils). 3 stories, interior corridors. *Bath:* combo or shower only. **Parking:** on-site. **Terms:** 14 day
Small-scale Hotel cancellation notice-fee imposed, [CP] meal plan available, pets ($10 extra charge). **Amenities:** high-speed Internet, voice mail, irons, hair dryers. **Pool(s):** heated indoor. **Leisure Activities:** whirlpool, exercise room.
Guest Services: coin laundry, wireless Internet. **Business Services:** meeting rooms. **Cards:** AX, DS, MC, VI.
Free Special Amenities: expanded continental breakfast and high-speed Internet.

SOME UNITS

[SD] [icons] / [X] /
FEE

(See map and index starting on p. 591)

COMFORT INN & SUITES   *Book great rates at AAA.com*   Phone: 405/912-1400   **65**
▼▼▼ ▼▼▼   6/1-9/30   1P: $69-$99   2P: $79-$109   XP: $5   F18
    3/1-5/31 & 10/1-2/29   1P: $59-$89   2P: $69-$99   XP: $5   F18
Small-scale Hotel   **Location:** I-35, exit 118, just nw. 1809 N Moore Ave 73160. **Fax:** 405/912-0800. **Facility:** 58 one-bedroom standard units. 3 stories, interior corridors. *Bath:* combo or shower only. **Parking:** on-site. **Amenities:** high-speed Internet, irons, hair dryers. **Pool(s):** small heated indoor. **Leisure Activities:** whirlpool. **Cards:** AX, CB, DC, DS, JC MC, VI.

SOME UNITS
(ASK) (S/D) (▮▮) (☂) (⌨) (≈) (▯) (▮) / (✕) (▮) (▤) /

MICROTEL INN & SUITES   *Book at AAA.com*   Phone: 405/799-8181
▼▼ ▼▼   Property failed to provide current rates
    Location: I-35, exit 116, just s on east service road. 2400 S Service Rd 73160. **Fax:** 405/799-0944. **Facility:** 61
Small-scale Hotel   one-bedroom standard units, some with whirlpools. 2 stories, interior corridors. *Bath:* combo or shower only. **Parking:** on-site. **Terms:** pets ($7 extra charge). **Amenities:** high-speed Internet, irons, hair dryers. **Pool(s):** small outdoor. **Guest Services:** coin laundry.

SOME UNITS
(▮) (▮▮) (⌨) (≈) (⌨) / (✕) (▮) (▤) (▯)
FEE

SUPER 8 MOTEL   *Book at AAA.com*   Phone: 405/794-4030   **66**
▼   Property failed to provide current rates
Motel   **Location:** I-35, exit 118, just ne. 1520 N Service Rd 73160. **Fax:** 405/794-4030. **Facility:** 40 one-bedroom standard units, some with whirlpools. 2 stories (no elevator), exterior corridors. **Parking:** on-site.

SOME UNITS
(⌨) (▮) (▤) / (✕) /

——— **WHERE TO DINE** ———

ROYAL BAVARIA BREWHAUS &
RESTAURANT   *Menu on AAA.com*   **Dinner:** $6-$20   Phone: 405/799-7666
(AAA)   **Location:** I-240, exit 8, 6 mi s. 3401 S Sooner Rd 73165. **Hours:** 5:30 pm-10 pm, Sat from 4 pm, Sun 4 pm-9
▼▼ ▼▼   pm. **Closed:** 11/22, 12/25; also Mon. **Features:** The Royal Bavaria Brewhaus serves great-tasting authentic
German   German cuisine. Casual dress; beer & wine only. **Parking:** on-site. **Cards:** AX, DC, DS, MC, VI.

NORMAN pop. 95,694

——— **WHERE TO STAY** ———

DAYS INN   *Book great rates at AAA.com*   Phone: 405/360-4380
▼▼ ▼▼   3/1-8/31   1P: $48-$58   2P: $48-$58
    9/1-2/29   1P: $45-$55   2P: $45-$55
Small-scale Hotel   **Location:** I-35, exit 110, 0.5 mi s on east service road. 609 N Interstate Dr 73069. **Fax:** 405/321-5767. **Facility:** 75 one-bedroom standard units. 2 stories (no elevator), exterior corridors. **Parking:** on-site. **Terms:** pets ($ extra charge). **Amenities:** hair dryers. **Pool(s):** small outdoor. **Guest Services:** wireless Internet. **Cards:** AX, DC, DS, MC, VI.

SOME UNITS
(ASK) (S/D) (▮) (▮▮) (⌨) (≈) (⌨) (▮) (▤) (▯) / (✕) /
FEE

FAIRFIELD INN BY MARRIOTT   *Book great rates at AAA.com*   Phone: (405)447-1661
▼▼▼ ▼▼▼   All Year   1P: $95-$115   2P: $100-$120   XP: $5   F18
    Location: I-35, exit 109 (Main St), just sw. 301 Norman Center Ct 73072. **Fax:** 405/447-1661. **Facility:** Smoke free
Small-scale Hotel   premises. 76 one-bedroom standard units. 3 stories, interior corridors. *Bath:* combo or shower only. **Parking:** on-site. **Amenities:** voice mail, irons, hair dryers. **Pool(s):** small heated indoor. **Leisure Activities:** whirlpool. **Guest Services:** valet laundry, wireless Internet. **Cards:** AX, DC, DS, MC, VI.

SOME UNITS
(ASK) (S/D) (▮▮) (⌨) (⌨) (≈) (▥) (✕) (⌨) (▯) / (▮) (▤)

HAMPTON INN   *Book great rates at AAA.com*   Phone: (405)366-2100
▼▼▼ ▼▼▼   All Year   1P: $109-$161   XP: $5   F17
    Location: I-35, exit 109 (Main St), just sw. 309 Norman Center Ct 73072. **Fax:** 405/366-6408. **Facility:** 61 one-
Small-scale Hotel   bedroom standard units, some with whirlpools. 2 stories, interior corridors. *Bath:* combo or shower only. **Parking:** on-site. **Amenities:** voice mail, irons, hair dryers. **Pool(s):** small heated indoor. **Leisure Activities:** sauna, exercise room. **Guest Services:** valet laundry, wireless Internet. **Business Services:** meeting rooms, PC. **Cards:** AX, CB, DC, DS, MC, VI.

SOME UNITS
(ASK) (▮▮) (⌨M) (⌨) (≈) (⌨) (▯) / (✕) (▮) (▤)

LA QUINTA INN & SUITES OKLAHOMA CITY
    (NORMAN)   *Book great rates at AAA.com*   Phone: (405)579-4000
▼▼▼ ▼▼   3/1-12/16 [CP]   1P: $96-$126   2P: $102-$132   XP: $6   F18
    12/17-2/29 [CP]   1P: $92-$122   2P: $98-$128   XP: $6   F18
Small-scale Hotel   **Location:** I-35, exit 108B (Lindsey), just nw. 930 Ed Noble Dr 73072. **Fax:** 405/579-4001. **Facility:** 117 units. 113 one-bedroom standard units. 4 one-bedroom suites ($132-$164). 4 stories, interior corridors. *Bath:* combo or shower only. **Parking:** on-site. **Terms:** small pets only. **Amenities:** video games (fee), high-speed Internet, voice mail, irons, hair dryers. *Some:* dual phone lines. **Pool(s):** heated outdoor. **Leisure Activities:** whirlpool, exercise room. **Guest Services:** valet and coin laundry, wireless Internet. **Business Services:** meeting rooms. **Cards:** AX, CB, DC, DS, MC, VI.

SOME UNITS
(ASK) (▮) (▮▮) (⌨) (≈) (⌨) (▯) / (✕) (▮) (▤)

MONTFORD INN

Phone: (405)321-2200

All Year   2P: $95-$169   XP: $25

Bed & Breakfast

Location: I-35, exit 109 (Main St), 2.1 mi e to University Blvd, then just n. 322 W Tonhawa 73069. **Fax:** 405/321-8347. **Facility:** Near downtown shops and restaurants and the University of Oklahoma, the inn offers a porch, flower and herb garden and rooms with fireplaces. Smoke free premises. 16 units. 10 one-bedroom standard units, some with whirlpools. 6 one-bedroom suites with whirlpools. 2 stories (no elevator), interior/exterior corridors. **Parking:** on-site. **Terms:** check-in 4 pm, 5 day cancellation notice-fee imposed. **Amenities:** video library, DVD players, irons, hair dryers. *Some:* CD players. **Guest Services:** valet laundry, wireless Internet. **Business Services:** meeting rooms. **Cards:** AX, DC, DS, MC, VI.

SOME UNITS

QUALITY INN

Book great rates at AAA.com   **Phone:** 405/364-5554

All Year [CP]   1P: $75-$85   2P: $95-$105   XP: $5   F15

Motel

Location: I-35, exit 109 (Main St), just se. 100 SW 26th Dr 73069. **Fax:** 405/364-1671. **Facility:** 44 one-bedroom standard units. 2 stories (no elevator), exterior corridors. **Parking:** on-site, winter plug-ins. **Terms:** pets ($5 extra charge). **Amenities:** irons, hair dryers. **Guest Services:** wireless Internet. **Business Services:** PC. **Cards:** AX, DC, DS, MC, VI.

SOME UNITS

THE RESIDENCE INN BY MARRIOTT

Book great rates at AAA.com   **Phone:** (405)366-0900

All Year [BP]   1P: $129   2P: $189

Small-scale Hotel

Location: I-35, exit 108A, just se. 2681 Jefferson St 73072. **Fax:** 405/360-6552. **Facility:** Smoke free premises. 126 units. 96 one- and 30 two-bedroom standard units with kitchens. 2 stories (no elevator), exterior corridors. *Bath:* combo or shower only. **Parking:** on-site. **Terms:** pets ($75 fee). **Amenities:** high-speed Internet, voice mail, irons, hair dryers. **Pool(s):** outdoor. **Leisure Activities:** whirlpool, exercise room, sports court. **Guest Services:** sundries, complimentary evening beverages: Mon-Thurs, valet and coin laundry. **Business Services:** meeting rooms. **Cards:** AX, CB, DC, DS, JC, MC, VI. **Free Special Amenities:** full breakfast and high-speed Internet.

FEE

—— WHERE TO DINE ——

CHARLESTON'S RESTAURANT

Lunch: $8-$22   **Dinner:** $8-$22   **Phone:** 405/360-0900

Steak & Seafood

Location: I-35, exit 109 (Main St), just sw. 300 Ed Noble Pkwy 73072. **Hours:** 11 am-9 pm, Fri & Sat-10 pm. Closed: 11/22, 12/25. **Reservations:** accepted. **Features:** This casual dining spot boasts a friendly, club-like atmosphere. Fine steak and seafood, as well as hardwood-grilled dishes, are at the heart of the menu. The noteworthy baked potato soup is rich with onions and bacon bits. Casual dress; cocktails. **Parking:** on-site. **Cards:** AX, DS, MC, VI.

COACH'S BBQ, PIZZA & BREWERY

Lunch: $5-$11   **Dinner:** $7-$11   **Phone:** 405/360-5726

American

Location: Downtown. 102 W Main St 73069. **Hours:** 11 am-11 pm. Closed: 11/22, 12/25. **Features:** You'll surely find something to enjoy here. The hickory-smoked barbecue dishes are excellent; the freshly made pizzas are superb too. Plus you can sample several home-brewed beers, view Heisman Trophies on display and watch sports on TV too. Casual dress; cocktails. **Parking:** on-site. **Cards:** AX, DS, MC, VI.

GOLDIES PATIO GRILL

Lunch: $5-$8   **Dinner:** $5-$8   **Phone:** 405/329-6363

American

Location: I-35, exit 108B (Lindsey St), 0.9 mi e. 1808 W Lindsey 73069. **Hours:** 11 am-9 pm. Closed: 1/1, 11/22, 12/25. **Features:** The menu comprises grilled items, chicken, sandwiches and steak, but this place is known for its excellent charbroiled burgers. The decor incorporates 1950s and '60s memorabilia. Casual dress. **Parking:** on-site. **Cards:** AX, DS, MC, VI.

LA BAGUETTE RESTAURANT & BAKERY

Lunch: $3-$10   **Dinner:** $3-$10   **Phone:** 405/329-5822

French

Location: I-35, exit 109 (Main St), 1.6 mi e. 924 W Main St 73069. **Hours:** 7 am-8 pm, Sun 9 am-2 pm. Closed major holidays. **Features:** La Baguette serves an appetizing array of French pastries, fruit tarts and delicious European tortes. The chocolate mousse cake is rich and flavorful. The marble-top coffee bar and artwork are reminiscent of a French bistro with a light, airy atmosphere. Casual dress. **Parking:** on-site. **Cards:** AX, DS, MC, VI.

LEGEND'S RESTAURANT

Lunch: $6-$11   **Dinner:** $11-$22   **Phone:** 405/329-8888

Continental

Location: I-35, exit 108B (Lindsey St), 1 mi e. 1313 W Lindsey St 73069. **Hours:** 11 am-10 pm, Fri & Sat-11 pm, Sun 10 am-10 pm. Closed major holidays. **Features:** A quiet, elegant atmosphere envelops the restaurant, which specializes in a variety of daily-made homemade desserts. Casual dress; cocktails. **Parking:** on-site. **Cards:** AX, CB, DC, DS, MC, VI.

MISAL OF INDIA BISTRO

Lunch: $7-$20   **Dinner:** $7-$20   **Phone:** 405/579-5600

Indian

Location: I-35, exit 109 (Main St), 0.7 mi s on W Service Rd. 580 Ed Noble Pkwy 73072. **Hours:** 11 am-3 & 5-10 pm, Fri & Sat-11 pm. Closed: 11/22, 12/25. **Features:** Lining the popular restaurant's menu is a wide assortment of chicken, lamb, beef and vegetable dishes, many of which are prepared in a tandoor. Casual dress; cocktails. **Parking:** on-site. **Cards:** AX, CB, DC, DS, JC, MC, VI.

RIB CRIB BARBECUE
▼▼ ▼▼
Barbecue

Lunch: $6-$14 **Dinner:** $6-$14 **Phone:** 405/573-7900
Location: I-35, exit 108, just w. 1131 Rambling Oaks Dr 73072. **Hours:** 11 am-10 pm. Closed: 11/22, 12/25.
Features: Most guests need extra napkins to tackle the ribs, brisket, ham, pork and chicken selections. The menu also lists sandwiches and wraps, along with tempting sides and large desserts. The decor is decidedly Western. Casual dress; cocktails. **Parking:** on-site. **Cards:** AX, CB, DC, DS, JC, MC, VI.

TASTE OF CHINA
▼▼▼ ▼▼▼
Chinese

Lunch: $6-$9 **Dinner:** $7-$9 **Phone:** 405/292-8988
Location: I-35, exit 110, just s on west service road. 600 N Interstate Dr 73072. **Hours:** 11 am-10 pm, Fri & Sat-10:30 pm. Closed: 11/22, 12/25. **Features:** Mongolian barbecue is included in the price of the buffet, which lines up a large variety of tried-and-true favorites. Casual dress. **Parking:** on-site. **Cards:** AX, DS, MC, VI.

VAN'S PIG STANDS
▼
Barbecue

Lunch: $3-$11 **Dinner:** $3-$11 **Phone:** 405/364-0600
Location: I-35, exit 110 (Robinson St), 2.5 mi e to US 77 (Porter Ave), then 0.5 mi s. 320 N Porter Ave 73069. **Hours:** 11 am-9 pm, Fri & Sat-10 pm. **Features:** Don't let the modest exterior and seating prevent you from trying this flavorful barbecue that you can watch being prepared; they've been in business since 1930 for a good reason. Casual dress. **Parking:** on-site. **Cards:** AX, DS, MC, VI.

PURCELL pop. 5,571

——— **WHERE TO STAY** ———

ECONO LODGE
⟨AAA⟩ [SAVE]
▼▼
Motel

Book great rates at AAA.com
All Year 1P: $65-$80 2P: $85-$90 XP: $5 D16
Phone: (405)527-5603
Location: I-35, exit 91, just e. 2122 Hwy 74 S 73080. Fax: 405/527-5603. **Facility:** 32 one-bedroom standard units. 2 stories (no elevator), exterior corridors. **Parking:** on-site, winter plug-ins. **Terms:** 5 day cancellation notice, [CP] meal plan available, pets ($5 extra charge). **Amenities:** *Some:* irons, hair dryers. **Guest Services:** wireless Internet. **Cards:** AX, DC, DS, MC, VI. **Free Special Amenities: continental breakfast and high-speed Internet.**

SOME UNITS
[S⊘] [🐾] [🛏] [❄] [🅰] [📷] / [✕] [🔋] /
FEE

SHAWNEE pop. 28,692

——— **WHERE TO STAY** ———

BUDGET INN
▼
Motel

All Year 1P: $45-$50 2P: $55-$65 XP: $5 D5
Phone: 405/275-8430
Location: I-40, exit 181, 2.5 mi s. 14204 Hwy 177 74804. **Facility:** 30 one-bedroom standard units. 1 story, exterior corridors. **Parking:** on-site. **Terms:** cancellation fee imposed. **Cards:** AX, DS, MC, VI.

SOME UNITS
[ASK] [S⊘] / [✕] [🔋] /

DAYS INN-SHAWNEE
⟨AAA⟩ [SAVE]
▼▼ ▼▼
Motel

Book great rates at AAA.com
All Year 1P: $60-$70 2P: $70-$80 XP: $5 F12
Phone: (405)275-6720
Location: I-40, exit 186, just n. 5107 N Harrison 74804. Fax: 405/878-0164. **Facility:** 52 one-bedroom standard units. 2 stories (no elevator), interior corridors. **Parking:** on-site, winter plug-ins. **Terms:** [ECP] meal plan available. **Amenities:** hair dryers. **Guest Services:** valet laundry, wireless Internet. **Cards:** AX, CB, DC, DS, JC, MC, VI. **Free Special Amenities: expanded continental breakfast and high-speed Internet.**

SOME UNITS
[S⊘] [🛏] [❄] [📷] [🔋] [🖥] [📺] / [✕] /

HAMPTON INN BY HILTON
▼▼ ▼▼
Small-scale Hotel

Book great rates at AAA.com
All Year 1P: $85-$105 2P: $90-$110 XP: $5 F18
Phone: (405)275-1540
Location: I-40, exit 185, just se. 4851 N Kickapoo 74801. Fax: 405/275-2065. **Facility:** 64 one-bedroom standard units. 3 stories, interior corridors. *Bath:* combo or shower only. **Parking:** on-site. **Amenities:** voice mail, irons, hair dryers. **Pool(s):** heated indoor. **Leisure Activities:** whirlpool. **Guest Services:** valet laundry, wireless Internet. **Cards:** AX, DC, DS, MC, VI.

SOME UNITS
[ASK] [S⊘] [🛏] [📶] [❄] [🏊] [⛱] [📷] [📺] / [✕] [🔋] [🖥] /

MOTEL 6 - 1236
▼
Motel

Book at AAA.com
5/25-2/29 1P: $49-$59 2P: $55-$65 XP: $3 F17
3/1-5/24 1P: $46-$56 2P: $52-$62 XP: $3 F17
Phone: 405/275-5310
Location: I-40, exit 186, just ne. 4981 N Harrison 74801. Fax: 405/275-6370. **Facility:** 64 one-bedroom standard units. 2 stories (no elevator), interior corridors. *Bath:* combo or shower only. **Parking:** on-site. **Terms:** small pets only. **Pool(s):** small outdoor. **Guest Services:** coin laundry. **Cards:** AX, CB, DC, DS, MC, VI.

SOME UNITS
[S⊘] [🐾] [🛏] [❄] [📷] [🏊] [📺] / [✕] /

——— WHERE TO DINE ———

BILLY BOY BBQ

American

Lunch: $4-$10   Dinner: $4-$10   **Phone:** 405/275-2040

Location: I-40, exit 186, 1.5 mi s to MacArthur St, then 0.7 mi w. 120 W MacArthur St 74801. **Hours:** 11 am-8:30 pm. Closed major holidays; also Sun. **Features:** Family-owned since 1972, Billy Boy's specializes in very good barbecue dishes served in enormous helpings. They also serve shrimp, chicken, steak and sandwiches. This place is a bright, clean and casual restaurant with hometown-style service. Casual dress. **Parking:** on-site. **Cards:** DS, MC, VI.

FRATELI'S ITALIAN RISTORANTE

Italian

Lunch: $6-$16   Dinner: $6-$16   **Phone:** 405/275-6103

Location: I-40, exit 185, 2.1 mi s. 1945 N Kickapoo 74801. **Hours:** 11 am-10 pm. Closed: Sun. **Features:** Varied dishes are served in a quaint setting. Local diners often opt for one of the New York-style pizzas. Casual dress; beer & wine only. **Parking:** on-site. **Cards:** AX, CB, DC, DS, JC, MC, VI.

GARFIELD'S RESTAURANT & PUB

Tex-Mex

Lunch: $5-$7   Dinner: $7-$12   **Phone:** 405/273-3301

Location: I-40, exit 185, just s. 4845 N Kickapoo 74801. **Hours:** 11 am-11 pm, Fri & Sat-midnight, Sun-10 pm. Closed: 11/22, 12/25. **Features:** The atmosphere is comfortable and lively in the casual restaurant, where guests can choose from among burgers, Tex-Mex and Cajun dishes and grilled items. Casual dress; cocktails. **Parking:** on-site. **Cards:** AX, CB, DC, DS, JC, MC, VI.

YUKON pop. 21,043

——— WHERE TO STAY ———

BEST WESTERN INN & SUITES YUKON

Small-scale Hotel

Book great rates at AAA.com

All Year   1P: $84-$89   XP: $5   F18

Phone: (405)265-2995

Location: I-40, exit 138, just sw. 11440 W I-40 Service Rd 73099. Fax: 405/265-2996. **Facility:** 69 units. 68 one-bedroom standard units, some with whirlpools. 1 one-bedroom suite with efficiency. 2 stories, interior/exterior corridors. *Bath:* combo or shower only. **Parking:** on-site. **Terms:** [AP] meal plan available, pets ($25 deposit, $5 extra charge, in designated units). **Amenities:** dual phone lines, voice mail, irons, hair dryers. *Some:* high-speed Internet. **Pool(s):** heated indoor. **Leisure Activities:** whirlpool, exercise room. **Guest Services:** valet and coin laundry, wireless Internet. **Business Services:** meeting rooms, PC. **Cards:** AX, DC, DS, MC, VI. **Free Special Amenities:** full breakfast and high-speed Internet. *(See color ad below)*

SOME UNITS

FEE

HAMPTON INN

Small-scale Hotel

Book great rates at AAA.com

6/1-8/31   1P: $89   2P: $94

3/1-5/31 & 9/1-2/29   1P: $82   2P: $87

Phone: 405/350-6400

Location: I-40, exit 136, just ne. 1351 Canadian Ct 73099. Fax: 405/350-6500. **Facility:** 73 one-bedroom standard units, some with whirlpools. 3 stories, interior corridors. *Bath:* combo or shower only. **Parking:** on-site. **Amenities:** voice mail, irons, hair dryers. *Some:* dual phone lines. **Pool(s):** heated indoor. **Leisure Activities:** exercise room. **Guest Services:** valet and coin laundry, wireless Internet. **Business Services:** meeting rooms, PC. **Cards:** AX, DC, DS, MC, VI. **Free Special Amenities:** expanded continental breakfast and high-speed Internet.

SOME UNITS

——— WHERE TO DINE ———

ALFREDO'S MEXICAN CAFE **Lunch:** $7-$12 **Dinner:** $8-$12 **Phone:** 405/354-4343

Mexican

Location: I-40, exit 136, just se. 1751 Garth Brooks, Suite 110 73099. **Hours:** 11 am-9 pm, Fri & Sat-9:30 pm, Sun-8 pm. Closed: 11/22, 12/25. **Features:** Prompt servers satisfy diners with a good selection of entrees. The popular lunch spot has a well-lit dining room that offers a good window view. Casual dress. **Parking:** on-site. **Cards:** AX, DC, DS, MC, VI.

PRIMO'S D'ITALIA **Lunch:** $6-$15 **Dinner:** $8-$15 **Phone:** 405/350-9090

Italian

Location: I-40, exit 136, just n. 1215 Garth Brooks Blvd, Suite C 73099. **Hours:** 11 am-9 pm, Fri-Sun to 10 pm. Closed: 11/22, 12/25. **Reservations:** suggested. **Features:** Guests can expect freshly-prepared dishes and generous portions. Among selections are prime rib, seafood pasta and pizza. Casual dress; cocktails. **Parking:** on-site. **Cards:** AX, DC, DS, MC, VI.

RIB CRIB BARBECUE **Lunch:** $6-$14 **Dinner:** $6-$14 **Phone:** 405/354-2828

Barbecue

Location: I-40, exit 136, just s. 1750 Garth Brooks Blvd 73099. **Hours:** 11 am-10 pm. Closed: 11/22, 12/25. **Features:** Most guests need extra napkins to tackle the ribs, brisket, ham, pork and chicken selections. The menu also lists sandwiches and wraps, along with tempting sides and large desserts. The decor is decidedly Western. Casual dress; beer only. **Parking:** on-site. **Cards:** AX, DC, DS, MC, VI.

© National Cowboy and Western Heritage Museum

This ends listings for the Oklahoma City Vicinity.
The following page resumes the alphabetical listings of cities in Oklahoma.

OKMULGEE pop. 13,022

———— **WHERE TO STAY** ————

BEST WESTERN OKMULGEE   *Book great rates at AAA.com*   Phone: (918)756-9200
(AAA) [SAVE]   All Year   1P: $89-$109   2P: $99-$119   XP: $10   F18
▽▽▽   Location: Just n of jct US 75 and SR 56. 3499 N Wood Dr 74447 (PO Box 520, GLENPOOL, 74033-0520).
Fax: 918/752-0022. **Facility:** 50 one-bedroom standard units, some with kitchens and/or whirlpools. 2
stories, interior corridors. *Bath:* combo or shower only. **Parking:** on-site, winter plug-ins. **Terms:** [CP] meal
Small-scale Hotel   plan available, small pets only ($50 deposit). **Amenities:** high-speed Internet, voice mail, irons, hair dryers.
Dining: 7 am-9 pm, Fri & Sat-10 pm, Sun-3 pm. **Pool(s):** outdoor. **Leisure Activities:** exercise room.
Guest Services: coin laundry. **Business Services:** meeting rooms. **Cards:** AX, CB, DC, DS, JC, MC, VI.
Free Special Amenities: early check-in/late check-out and high-speed Internet.

SOME UNITS
[S/D] [🛏] [🍴] [Y] [⟨⟩] [🏊] [📷] [🖥] [🖨] [💻] / [✕] /
FEE

———— **WHERE TO DINE** ————

SIRLOIN STOCKADE   Lunch: $6-$8   Dinner: $6-$8   Phone: 918/756-4440
▽▽▽   Location: Between E 6th and E 7th sts. 130 S Wood Dr 74447. **Hours:** 11 am-9 pm. Closed major holidays.
Steak House   **Reservations:** not accepted. **Features:** The steakhouse lines up buffet items, including pizza, tacos, soups,
salads and desserts, providing both excellent variety and a good value. Rotating theme nights might allow
for the sampling of sushi, barbecue and seafood. The buffet also may serve to complement a quality steak.
Rolls are baked several times daily. Casual dress. **Parking:** on-site. **Cards:** DS, MC, VI.
[✎]

OWASSO —*See Tulsa p. 645.*

PAULS VALLEY pop. 6,256

———— **WHERE TO STAY** ————

COMFORT INN & SUITES   *Book great rates at AAA.com*   Phone: (405)207-9730
▽▽▽   5/27-9/5   1P: $90-$109   2P: $90-$109   XP: $5   F12
3/1-5/26 & 9/6-2/29   1P: $80-$99   2P: $80-$99   XP: $5   F12
Small-scale Hotel   **Location:** I-35, exit 72, just e. 103 S Humphrey Blvd 73075. Fax: 405/238-1439. **Facility:** 64 one-bedroom
standard units, some with whirlpools. 3 stories, interior corridors. *Bath:* combo or shower only. **Parking:** on-
site. **Terms:** small pets only. **Amenities:** high-speed Internet, voice mail, irons, hair dryers. **Pool(s):** heated indoor. **Leisure
Activities:** exercise room. **Guest Services:** coin laundry, wireless Internet. **Business Services:** meeting rooms. **Cards:** AX,
DC, DS, JC, MC, VI.

SOME UNITS
[ASK] [S/D] [🛏] [🏊] [📷] [🖥] [🖨] [💻] / [✕] /

DAYS INN   *Book great rates at AAA.com*   Phone: 405/238-7548
(AAA) [SAVE]   All Year   1P: $64-$71   2P: $64-$71   XP: $5   F12
▽▽▽   Location: I-35, exit 72, just e. 2606 W Grant Ave 73075. Fax: 405/238-1262. **Facility:** 53 one-bedroom standard
units. 2 stories (no elevator), interior corridors. **Parking:** on-site. **Terms:** [CP] meal plan available.
Small-scale Hotel   **Amenities:** hair dryers. **Guest Services:** wireless Internet. **Cards:** AX, DS, MC, VI.
Free Special Amenities: continental breakfast and high-speed Internet.

SOME UNITS
[S/D] [🍴] [📷] / [✕] [🖥] [💻] /

PONCA CITY pop. 25,919

———— **WHERE TO STAY** ————

COMFORT INN & SUITES   *Book great rates at AAA.com*   Phone: (580)765-2322
(AAA) [SAVE]   All Year   1P: $89-$159   2P: $89-$159   XP: $10   F18
▽▽▽   Location: I-35, exit 214, 3 mi n on US 77. 3101 N 14th St 74604. Fax: 580/762-1981. **Facility:** 59 units. 58 one-
bedroom standard units, some with whirlpools. 1 one-bedroom suite. 3 stories, interior corridors. *Bath:*
combo or shower only. **Parking:** on-site. **Terms:** [ECP] meal plan available, pets ($10 extra charge).
Small-scale Hotel   **Amenities:** high-speed Internet, voice mail, irons, hair dryers. **Pool(s):** heated indoor. **Leisure
Activities:** whirlpool, exercise room. **Guest Services:** sundries, valet and coin laundry, wireless Internet.
Business Services: meeting rooms, business center. **Cards:** AX, CB, DC, DS, JC, MC, VI. **Free Special Amenities:**
expanded continental breakfast and high-speed Internet.

SOME UNITS
[S/D] [🛏] [🍴] [⟨M⟩] [⟨⟩] [🏊] [📷] [🖥] [🖨] [💻] / [✕] /
FEE

HOLIDAY INN PONCA CITY   *Book at AAA.com*   Phone: 580/762-8311
▽▽   All Year   1P: $79-$92   XP: $8
Location: 2.8 mi n on US 77. 2215 N 14th St 74601. Fax: 580/765-0014. **Facility:** 137 one-bedroom standard
Small-scale Hotel   units. 2 stories (no elevator), exterior corridors. *Bath:* combo or shower only. **Parking:** on-site.
Terms: package plans. **Amenities:** voice mail, irons, hair dryers. **Pool(s):** outdoor. **Leisure
Activities:** exercise room. **Guest Services:** valet laundry, wireless Internet. **Business Services:** meeting rooms. **Cards:** AX,
CB, DC, DS, JC, MC, VI.

SOME UNITS
[ASK] [S/D] [🍴] [Y] [🎬] [🏊] [📷] [💻] / [✕] [🖥] /

———— *The following lodging was either not evaluated or did not* ————
meet AAA rating requirements but is listed for your information only.

FAIRFIELD INN BY MARRIOTT   Phone: 580/765-3000
[fyi]   Did not meet all AAA rating requirements for some property operations at time of last evaluation on 12/20/2005. **Location:** 3.4 mi n on US 77. 3405 N 14th St 74601. Facilities, services, and decor characterize a mid-
Small-scale Hotel   range property.

———— **WHERE TO DINE** ————

HUNAN CHINESE RESTAURANT   **Lunch:** $6   **Dinner:** $8   Phone: 580/765-6716
▼▼▼   **Location:** Just nw of jct 14th and Prospect sts. 2800 N 5th St 74601. **Hours:** 11 am-9:30 pm. Closed major
     holidays. **Features:** Locals enjoy the buffet, which is well stocked with a selection of entrees and side items.
Chinese   Casual dress. **Parking:** on-site. **Cards:** AX, DS, MC, VI.

POTEAU pop. 7,939

———— **WHERE TO STAY** ————

DAYS INN & SUITES   *Book great rates at AAA.com*   Phone: (918)647-3510
▼▼▼   All Year   1P: $72-$89   2P: $79-$89   XP: $7   F17
   Location: Center. 1702 N Broadway 74953. Fax: 918/647-3511. **Facility:** 62 one-bedroom standard units, some
Small-scale Hotel   with whirlpools. 3 stories, interior corridors. *Bath:* combo or shower only. **Parking:** on-site. **Terms:** [ECP]
meal plan available. **Amenities:** high-speed Internet, voice mail, hair dryers. *Some:* irons. **Pool(s):** outdoor.
Leisure Activities: whirlpool, limited exercise equipment. **Guest Services:** valet laundry, wireless Internet. **Business Services:** meeting rooms. **Cards:** AX, CB, DC, DS, JC, MC, VI.

SOME UNITS

(A$K) ▣ ▣ ▤ ▤ ▤ / ✕ /

PRYOR pop. 8,659

———— **WHERE TO STAY** ————

COMFORT INN & SUITES   *Book great rates at AAA.com*   Phone: (918)476-6660
▼▼▼   6/6-6/22 [ECP]   1P: $89-$139   2P: $89-$139   XP: $7   F16
   6/23-2/29 [ECP]   1P: $79-$129   2P: $79-$129   XP: $7   F16
   3/1-6/5 [ECP]   1P: $74-$119   2P: $74-$119   XP: $7   F16
Small-scale Hotel   **Location:** 5 mi s on US 69. 307 Mid America Dr 74362 (PO Box 1111). Fax: 918/476-6915. **Facility:** 64 units. 62 one-bedroom standard units, some with whirlpools. 2 one-bedroom suites ($85-$119) with efficiencies and whirlpools. 3 stories, interior corridors. *Bath:* combo or shower only. **Parking:** on-site. **Terms:** pets ($10 extra charge). **Amenities:** high-speed Internet, voice mail, irons, hair dryers. **Pool(s):** small heated indoor. **Leisure Activities:** whirlpool, exercise room. **Guest Services:** valet and coin laundry, wireless Internet. **Business Services:** meeting rooms, business center. **Cards:** AX, CB, DC, DS, MC, VI.

SOME UNITS

(A$K) ▣ ▣ ▣ ▣ ▣ ▣ ▣ ▣ ▣ / ✕ /
FEE

MICROTEL INN & SUITES   *Book great rates at AAA.com*   Phone: (918)476-4661
(AAA) (SAVE)   All Year   1P: $46-$55   2P: $60-$70   XP: $5   F12
▼▼▼   **Location:** 5.1 mi s on US 69. 315 Mid America Dr 74361 (PO Box 1024, 74362). Fax: 918/476-4662. **Facility:** 58 one-bedroom standard units. 2 stories (no elevator), interior corridors. *Bath:* combo or shower only.
Small-scale Hotel   **Parking:** on-site. **Terms:** pets ($10 extra charge). **Amenities:** *Some:* high-speed Internet. **Leisure Activities:** exercise room. **Guest Services:** valet and coin laundry, wireless Internet. **Business Services:** PC. **Cards:** AX, DS, MC, VI. **Free Special Amenities: expanded continental breakfast and high-speed Internet.**

SOME UNITS

▣ ▣ ▣ ▣ ▣ ▣ / ✕ ▣ ▣ ▣ /
FEE

———— **WHERE TO DINE** ————

GOLDIES PATIO GRILL   **Lunch:** $5-$8   **Dinner:** $5-$8   Phone: 918/825-3313
▼▼▼   **Location:** Jct US 69. 21 SE 8th St 74361. **Hours:** 11 am-9 pm. Closed: 1/1, 11/22, 12/25. **Features:** The menu
   comprises grilled items, chicken, sandwiches and steak, but this place is bests known for its excellent
American   charbroiled burgers. The decor incorporates 1950s and '60s memorabilia. Casual dress. **Parking:** on-site.
   Cards: AX, DS, MC, VI.

PURCELL —*See Oklahoma City p. 614.*

RAMONA pop. 564

———— **WHERE TO DINE** ————

THE WILMINGTON RESTAURANT   **Dinner:** $27-$40   Phone: 918/371-1200
▼▼▼   **Location:** On US 75, 5 mi s; in The Inn at Jarrett Farm. 38009 US Hwy 75 74061. **Hours:** 5 pm-close; Sunday
   brunch 11 am-2 pm. Closed: 4/8, 12/25; also Mon. **Reservations:** required. **Features:** Windows overlooking
American   the swimming pool and landscape provide a great view as guests dine. Dressy casual; cocktails. **Parking:**
   on-site. **Cards:** AX, DC, DS, MC, VI.

ROLAND pop. 2,842

——————— WHERE TO STAY ———————

DAYS INN OF ROLAND　　　　　　　　　　　　　　　　　　　**Phone: 918/427-1000**

Property failed to provide current rates

▼▼ ▼▼　**Location:** I-40, exit 325, just ne. 207 Cherokee Blvd 74954 (Rt 1, Box 126). Fax: 918/427-1000. **Facility:** 44 one-bedroom standard units. 2 stories (no elevator), interior corridors. *Bath:* combo or shower only. **Parking:** on-site. **Terms:** pets ($10 fee). **Amenities:** hair dryers. **Pool(s):** outdoor. **Guest Services:** coin laundry, wireless Internet. **Business Services:** meeting rooms.

Small-scale Hotel

SOME UNITS

[icons] FEE

SALLISAW pop. 7,989

——————— WHERE TO STAY ———————

BEST WESTERN BLUE RIBBON INN　*Book great rates at AAA.com*　　**Phone: 918/775-6294**

(AAA) (SAVE)　All Year　　　　　1P: $69-$79　　　　2P: $79-$89

▼▼ ▼▼　**Location:** I-40, exit 308 (US 59), just n. 706 S Kerr Blvd (US 59) 74955 (PO Box 462). Fax: 918/775-5151. **Facility:** 81 one-bedroom standard units. 2 stories (no elevator), interior/exterior corridors. **Parking:** on-site, winter plug-ins. **Terms:** small pets only ($15 fee). **Amenities:** high-speed Internet, irons, hair dryers. **Pool(s):** outdoor, small heated indoor. **Guest Services:** coin laundry. **Business Services:** meeting rooms, PC. **Cards:** AX, CB, DC, DS, MC, VI. **Free Special Amenities:** expanded continental breakfast and early check-in/late check-out.

Small-scale Hotel

SOME UNITS

[icons] FEE

MICROTEL INN & SUITES　*Book at AAA.com*　　　　　**Phone: (918)774-0400**

▼▼ ▼▼　All Year　　　　　1P: $49-$59　　　2P: $59-$69　　　XP: $5　　　F12

Location: I-40, exit 308 (US 59), just n. 710 S Kerr Blvd 74955. Fax: 918/774-0401. **Facility:** 56 one-bedroom standard units, some with whirlpools. 3 stories, interior corridors. *Bath:* combo or shower only. **Parking:** on-site. **Terms:** weekly rates available, [CP] meal plan available, pets ($10 fee). **Amenities:** high-speed Internet. **Pool(s):** small outdoor. **Business Services:** meeting rooms, business center. **Cards:** AX, DC, DS, MC, VI.

Small-scale Hotel

SOME UNITS

[icons] FEE

——————— WHERE TO DINE ———————

CAPORALES　　　**Lunch:** $5-$9　　　**Dinner:** $6-$9　　　**Phone:** 918/774-0604

▼　**Location:** I-40, exit 308 (US 59), 0.4 mi n. 1600 S Tatham Ave 74955. **Hours:** 11 am-9 pm. Closed: 7/4, 11/22, 12/25; also Sun. **Features:** Dishes with straightforward appeal are served in an open, unadorned dining room. Casual dress; beer only. **Parking:** on-site. **Cards:** AX, DS, MC, VI.

Mexican

——————— *The following restaurant has not been evaluated by AAA* ———————
but is listed for your information only.

SHAD'S CATFISH HOLE RESTAURANT　　　　　　　　　　**Phone: 918/775-5801**

[fyi]　Not evaluated. **Location:** I-40, exit 308 (US 59), 7.2 mi s. Applegate Cove Rd 74955. **Features:** The restaurant is known for hearty portions and flavorful catfish in an area that recognizes good catfish.

SAND SPRINGS —*See Tulsa p. 645.*

SAPULPA —*See Tulsa p. 646.*

SAVANNA pop. 730

——————— WHERE TO STAY ———————

CANDLELIGHT INN & SUITES　　　　　　　　　　**Phone: (918)548-3676**

(AAA) (SAVE)　All Year　　　　　1P: $50-$85　　　2P: $55-$85　　　XP: $8　　　F12

▼▼ ▼▼　**Location:** 1.5 mi sw of jct US 69 and Indian Creek Tpke. Hwy 69 74565 (PO Box 265). Fax: 918/548-3530. **Facility:** 33 one-bedroom standard units. 1 story, interior corridors. *Bath:* combo or shower only. **Parking:** on-site. **Amenities:** high-speed Internet, voice mail, irons, hair dryers. **Guest Services:** coin laundry. **Cards:** AX, DC, DS, MC, VI. **Free Special Amenities:** expanded continental breakfast and high-speed Internet.

Small-scale Hotel

SOME UNITS

[icons]

SAYRE pop. 4,114

——————— WHERE TO STAY ———————

AMERICINN LODGE & SUITES OF SAYRE　*Book at AAA.com*　　**Phone: (580)928-2700**

▼▼ ▼▼　All Year　　　　　1P: $71-$145　　　2P: $71-$145　　　XP: $5　　　F12

Location: I-40, exit 20, just n. 2405 S El Camino Rd 73662. Fax: 580/928-2711. **Facility:** 45 units. 44 one-bedroom standard units, some with whirlpools. 1 one-bedroom suite ($99-$149) with whirlpool. 2 stories (no elevator), interior corridors. *Bath:* combo or shower only. **Parking:** on-site. **Terms:** [ECP] meal plan available, pets ($15 fee). **Amenities:** high-speed Internet, hair dryers. *Some:* irons. **Pool(s):** heated indoor. **Leisure Activities:** sauna, whirlpool. **Guest Services:** coin laundry. **Business Services:** meeting rooms, PC. **Cards:** AX, DC, DS, MC, VI. *(See color ad p 595)*

Small-scale Hotel

SOME UNITS

[icons] FEE

SEMINOLE pop. 6,899

—— WHERE TO DINE ——

THE CATFISH ROUND-UP **Lunch:** $7-$10 **Dinner:** $7-$10 **Phone:** 405/382-7957
Location: I-40, exit 200, just se. Hwy 99 74868. **Hours:** 11 am-9 pm. Closed: 1/1, 11/22, 12/25. **Features:** You'll find prompt and friendly service, a relaxed, casual atmosphere and a good selection of offerings at the Catfish Round-Up, which specializes in fried catfish dishes. Sugar-coated donut balls and hot rolls are included with your selection. Casual dress. **Parking:** on-site. **Cards:** AX, MC, VI.

American

SHAWNEE —See Oklahoma City p. 614.

STILLWATER pop. 39,065

—— WHERE TO STAY ——

BEST WESTERN STILLWATER *Book great rates at AAA.com* **Phone:** (405)377-7010
All Year 1P: $79-$99 2P: $79-$99 XP: $10 F18
Location: 1 mi n on US 177 (Perkins Rd). 600 E McElroy 74075. Fax: 405/743-1686. **Facility:** 122 units. 121 one-bedroom standard units. 1 one-bedroom suite ($115-$135). 4 stories, interior corridors. **Parking:** on-site, winter plug-ins. **Terms:** [BP] meal plan available, small pets only. **Amenities:** video games (fee), voice mail,
Small-scale Hotel irons, hair dryers. **Dining:** 6 am-9 & 5-9 pm, cocktails. **Pool(s):** heated indoor. **Leisure Activities:** sauna, whirlpool. **Guest Services:** valet and coin laundry, wireless Internet. **Business Services:** meeting rooms, business center. **Cards:** AX, CB, DC, DS, MC, VI. **Free Special Amenities:** full breakfast and high-speed Internet.

SOME UNITS
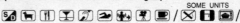

FAIRFIELD INN BY MARRIOTT *Book great rates at AAA.com* **Phone:** (405)372-6300
All Year 1P: $77-$97 2P: $82-$102 XP: $5 F18
Location: Just w of jct US 177 (Perkins Rd). 418 E Hall of Fame Ave 74075. Fax: 405/372-6300. **Facility:** Smoke
Small-scale Hotel free premises. 64 one-bedroom standard units. 3 stories, interior corridors. *Bath:* combo or shower only.
Parking: on-site, winter plug-ins. **Amenities:** irons, hair dryers. **Pool(s):** heated indoor. **Leisure Activities:** whirlpool. **Guest Services:** valet laundry, wireless Internet. **Cards:** AX, DC, DS, MC, VI.

SOME UNITS

HAMPTON INN & SUITES *Book great rates at AAA.com* **Phone:** (405)743-1306
All Year [ECP] 1P: $89-$159 2P: $89-$159
Location: Just e of jct US 177 (Perkins Rd). 717 E Hall of Fame Ave 74075. Fax: 405/743-1382. **Facility:** 81 units. 73 one-bedroom standard units. 8 one-bedroom suites, some with whirlpools. 3 stories, interior corridors.
Bath: combo or shower only. **Parking:** on-site. **Amenities:** video games (fee), high-speed Internet, voice
Small-scale Hotel mail, irons, hair dryers. **Pool(s):** heated outdoor. **Leisure Activities:** whirlpool, exercise room. **Guest Services:** sundries, valet and coin laundry, wireless Internet. **Business Services:** meeting rooms, business center. **Cards:** AX, CB, DC, DS, MC, VI. *(See color ad below)*

SOME UNITS

HOLIDAY INN *Book at AAA.com* **Phone:** (405)372-0800
All Year 1P: $71 2P: $71 XP: $8 F18
Location: 1.8 mi w on SR 51. 2515 W 6th Ave 74074. Fax: 405/377-8212. **Facility:** 139 one-bedroom standard
units, some with whirlpools. 2 stories (no elevator), interior/exterior corridors. *Bath:* combo or shower only.
Small-scale Hotel **Parking:** on-site. **Terms:** [BP] meal plan available, package plans, small pets only. **Amenities:** voice mail,
irons, hair dryers. **Pool(s):** heated indoor. **Leisure Activities:** sauna, whirlpool, putting green, exercise room. *Fee:* game room.
Guest Services: valet laundry, wireless Internet. **Business Services:** meeting rooms. **Cards:** AX, CB, DC, DS, MC, VI.

SOME UNITS

——— WHERE TO DINE ———

GOLDIES PATIO GRILL   **Lunch:** $5-$8   **Dinner:** $5-$8   **Phone:** 405/372-6700

American

Location: Just w of jct US 177 (Perkins Rd). 508 E Hall of Fame 74075. **Hours:** 11 am-9 pm. Closed: 1/1, 11/22, 12/25. **Features:** The menu comprises grilled items, chicken, sandwiches and steak, but this place is bests known for its excellent charbroiled burgers. The decor incorporates 1950s and '60s memorabilia. Casual dress; beer only. **Parking:** on-site. **Cards:** AX, DS, MC, VI.

JOSEPPI'S ITALIAN KITCHEN   **Lunch:** $5-$16   **Dinner:** $7-$16   **Phone:** 405/624-8037

Italian

Location: Just w of jct US 177 (Perkins Rd). 223 E Hall of Fame Ave 74075. **Hours:** 11 am-10 pm, Fri & Sat-11 pm, Sun-9:30 pm. Closed: 11/22, 12/25. **Features:** Italian dishes, pizza and salad are served in the lively, energetic restaurant. Casual dress; cocktails. **Parking:** on-site. **Cards:** AX, DS, MC, VI.

KYOTO JAPANESE RESTAURANT   **Lunch:** $5-$11   **Dinner:** $6-$23   **Phone:** 405/377-8168

Japanese

Location: 1.9 mi n of SR 51. 2021 N Boomer Rd 74075. **Hours:** 11 am-10 pm, Sun-9 pm. Closed: 1/1, 11/22, 12/25; also Mon. **Reservations:** suggested. **Features:** Kyoto's features delightful hibachi-style cooking and a fresh-sushi bar with Japanese chefs. Try the Kyoto dragon roll—it's a unique combination of eel, crabmeat, cucumbers, avocados and shrimp. Two tatami rooms are available for private parties. Casual dress; cocktails. **Parking:** on-site. **Cards:** AX, DS, MC, VI.

MEXICO JOE'S   **Lunch:** $5-$11   **Dinner:** $6-$11   **Phone:** 405/372-1169

Mexican

Location: Just w of jct US 177 (Perkins Rd). 311 E Hall of Fame Ave 74075. **Hours:** 11 am-10 pm, Fri & Sat-11 pm, Sun-9 pm. Closed: 11/22, 12/25. **Features:** The lively, upbeat restaurant presents a menu that lists a nice selection of traditional fare. Casual dress. **Parking:** on-site. **Cards:** AX, DS, MC, VI.

RIB CRIB BARBECUE   **Lunch:** $6-$14   **Dinner:** $6-$14   **Phone:** 405/372-1900

Barbecue

Location: Center. 103 S Perkins Rd 74074. **Hours:** 11 am-10 pm. Closed: 11/22, 12/25. **Features:** Most guests need extra napkins to tackle the ribs, brisket, ham, pork and chicken selections. The menu also lists sandwiches and wraps, along with tempting sides and large desserts. The decor is decidedly Western. Casual dress; beer only. **Parking:** on-site. **Cards:** AX, DC, DS, MC, VI.

SIRLOIN STOCKADE   **Lunch:** $6-$8   **Dinner:** $6-$8   **Phone:** 405/624-1681

Steak House

Location: On US 177, just s of jct E Hall of Fame. 208 N Perkins Rd 74074. **Hours:** 11 am-9 pm. Closed major holidays. **Reservations:** not accepted. **Features:** The steakhouse lines up buffet items, including pizza, tacos, soups, salads and desserts, providing both excellent variety and a good value. Rotating theme nights might allow for the sampling of sushi, barbecue and seafood. The buffet also may serve to complement a quality steak. Rolls are baked several times daily. Casual dress. **Parking:** on-site. **Cards:** DS, MC, VI.

STILWELL pop. 3,276

——— WHERE TO STAY ———

AMERICINN MOTEL & SUITES   *Book at AAA.com*   **Phone:** 918/696-6789

Small-scale Hotel

| All Year | 1P: $62-$125 | 2P: $62-$125 | XP: $5 | F12 |

Location: Jct US 59 and SR 100, just e. US 59 & SR 100 E 74960 (Rt 6, Box 1915). **Fax:** 918/696-5803. **Facility:** 45 units. 42 one-bedroom standard units, some with whirlpools. 3 one-bedroom suites, some with whirlpools. 2 stories (no elevator), interior corridors. *Bath:* combo or shower only. **Parking:** on-site. **Terms:** 3 day cancellation notice-fee imposed. **Amenities:** voice mail, hair dryers. *Some:* irons. **Pool(s):** heated indoor. **Leisure Activities:** whirlpool. **Guest Services:** coin laundry. **Business Services:** meeting rooms, PC. **Cards:** AX, DS, MC, VI.
(See color ad p 595)

SOME UNITS

TAHLEQUAH pop. 14,458

——— WHERE TO STAY ———

COMFORT INN & SUITES   *Book great rates at AAA.com*   **Phone:** (918)431-0600

Small-scale Hotel
All Year [CP]   1P: $69-$100   2P: $69-$100   XP: $10   F16
Location: Just se of jct US 62 and SR 51, 82 and 10. 101 Reasor St 74464. **Fax:** 918/431-0600. **Facility:** 58 one-bedroom standard units, some with whirlpools. 3 stories, interior corridors. **Parking:** on-site. **Terms:** package plans. **Amenities:** high-speed Internet, voice mail, irons, hair dryers. **Pool(s):** heated indoor. **Leisure Activities:** whirlpool, limited exercise equipment. **Guest Services:** coin laundry, wireless Internet. **Business Services:** meeting rooms, business center. **Cards:** AX, CB, DC, DS, JC, MC, VI.

SOME UNITS
(ASK) 🅢 🏊 🎥 🚪 🖨 🖥 / ⊗ /

HOLIDAY INN EXPRESS   *Book at AAA.com*   **Phone:** 918/456-7800
Property failed to provide current rates
Small-scale Hotel
Location: 1.2 mi e on SR 51 from jct US 62. 701 Holiday Dr 74464. **Fax:** 918/456-7806. **Facility:** 62 units. 58 one-bedroom standard units. 4 one-bedroom suites with whirlpools. 2 stories, interior corridors. *Bath:* combo or shower only. **Parking:** on-site. **Terms:** check-in 4 pm. **Amenities:** high-speed Internet, voice mail, irons, hair dryers. **Pool(s):** small heated outdoor. **Leisure Activities:** exercise room. **Guest Services:** valet laundry. **Business Services:** PC.

SOME UNITS
🏊 🎥 🚪 🖨 🖥 / ⊗ /

——— WHERE TO DINE ———

EL ZARAPE   **Lunch:** $3-$11   **Dinner:** $5-$11   **Phone:** 918/456-0708
Mexican
Location: Just w of jct US 62 and SR 82. 701 E Downing St 74464. **Hours:** 11 am-9 pm. Closed major holidays; also Sun. **Features:** A local favorite for Mexican cuisine, the restaurant presents a varied menu of well-prepared choices. Service is prompt. Simple furnishings decorate the dining area. Casual dress; beer only. **Parking:** on-site. **Cards:** AX, DS, MC, VI.

THACKERVILLE pop. 404

——— WHERE TO STAY ———

WINSTAR MICROTEL INN AND SUITES   *Book at AAA.com*   **Phone:** 580/276-4487
Small-scale Hotel
All Year [CP]   1P: $185   2P: $185   XP: $5   F17
Location: I-35, exit 1, 1.2 mi n on E Service Rd. Rt 1, Box 682 73459. **Fax:** 580/276-9127. **Facility:** 100 one-bedroom standard units, some with whirlpools. 3 stories, interior corridors. *Bath:* combo or shower only. **Parking:** on-site. **Terms:** pets ($10 extra charge). **Amenities:** voice mail, irons, hair dryers. **Pool(s):** heated indoor. **Leisure Activities:** whirlpool. **Guest Services:** coin laundry, wireless Internet. **Business Services:** meeting rooms, PC. **Cards:** AX, DS, MC, VI.

SOME UNITS
(ASK) 🛏 🍴 👨 🏊 🎥 🖥 / ⊗ 🚪 🖨
FEE

Destination Tulsa

pop. 393,049

Tulsa, nicknamed "The Green Country," has an abundance of parks where visitors can explore nature trails or eat a picnic lunch.

River Parks is the site of more than 25 annual festivals; Tulsa's spirited shindigs include American Indian powwows, art shows and myriad music festivals featuring bluegrass, blues, gospel, jazz and reggae performers.

The "Golden Driller," Tulsa. Looming 76 feet above Tulsa's Expo Square, the "Golden Driller" statue rests his mighty concrete arm atop an actual oil derrick.

© Don Sibley / Tulsa Metro Chamber of Commerce

© Don Sibley / Tulsa Metro Chamber of Commerce

Indian Powwow, Tulsa. Traditional outfits worn at powwows throughout the year reflect Oklahoma's rich, American Indian heritage.

Art Deco buildings, Tulsa. Thanks to an oil boom in the early 1900s, many of Tulsa's buildings—such as the Warehouse Market—were constructed in the Art Deco style popular at the time.

Tulsa Opera. Colorful costumes and elaborate sets characterize performances by the nationally recognized Tulsa Opera.

Places included in this AAA Destination City:

© Don Sibley / Tulsa Metro Chamber of Commerce

See Vicinity map page 624

© 2006 NAVTEQ

© AAA

Tulsa
Lodging & Dining

✈ Airport Accommodations

Spotter/Map Page Number	OA	TULSA INTERNATIONAL	Diamond Rating	Rate Range High Season	Listing Page
5 / p. 624	AAA	**Best Western Airport, 3.5 mi se of terminal**	▽▽	$69-$89 SAVE	628
2 / p. 624		Hilton Garden Inn, opposite terminal	▽▽▽	$134-$199	631
6 / p. 624	AAA	**La Quinta Inn Tulsa (Airport), 2.5 mi sw of terminal**	▽▽	$82-$105 SAVE	632
1 / p. 624		Radisson Tulsa Airport, opposite terminal	▽▽▽	Failed to provide	634

Tulsa and Vicinity

his index helps you "spot" where approved accommodations and restaurants are located on the corresponding detailed maps. odging rate ranges are for comparison only and show the property's high season; rates are per night, unless only weekly (W) tes are available. Restaurant rate range is for dinner, unless only lunch (L) is served. Turn to the listing page for more detailed te information and consult display ads for special promotions.

Spotter/Map Page Number	OA	TULSA - Lodgings	Diamond Rating	Rate Range High Season	Listing Page
1 / p. 624		Radisson Tulsa Airport	▽▽▽	Failed to provide	634
2 / p. 624		Hilton Garden Inn	▽▽▽	$134-$199	631
3 / p. 624		Country Inn & Suites By Carlson	▽▽	$59-$75	629
4 / p. 624		Holiday Inn-International Airport	▽▽▽	$84	632
5 / p. 624	AAA	**Best Western Airport**	▽▽	$69-$89 SAVE	628
6 / p. 624		La Quinta Inn Tulsa (Airport)	▽▽	$82-$105	632
7 / p. 624	AAA	**Crowne Plaza Tulsa**	▽▽▽	$89-$169 SAVE	629
8 / p. 624		DoubleTree Hotel Downtown Tulsa	▽▽▽	$149-$410	630
9 / p. 624	AAA	**Econo Lodge Airport**	▽▽	$42-$99 SAVE	630
10 / p. 624		Ambassador Hotel	▽▽▽	$157-$193	628
11 / p. 624		McBirney Mansion Bed & Breakfast	▽▽▽	Failed to provide	633
12 / p. 624		Comfort Suites-Tulsa Airport	▽▽	$79-$120	629
13 / p. 624		Microtel Inn & Suites	▽▽	$55-$125	633
14 / p. 624		StudioPLUS Tulsa Central	▽▽	$59-$74	635
15 / p. 624	AAA	**Quality Suites**	▽▽	$75-$125 SAVE	633
16 / p. 624	AAA	**Holiday Inn Express-Tulsa Central**	▽▽▽	$99-$139 SAVE	632
17 / p. 624	AAA	**Best Western Inn & Suites**	▽▽▽	$95-$150 SAVE	628
18 / p. 624		Hampton Inn	▽▽▽	Failed to provide	631
19 / p. 624		Embassy Suites Hotel	▽▽▽	$99-$299	630
20 / p. 624	AAA	**Comfort Suites**	▽▽▽	$89-$115 SAVE	629
21 / p. 624		Sleep Inn & Suites Tulsa Central	▽▽	Failed to provide	635
22 / p. 624		La Quinta Inn Tulsa (East)	▽▽	$75-$111	633
23 / p. 624		Guest House Suites Plus	▽▽▽	Failed to provide	631
24 / p. 624		Radisson Tulsa - see color ad p 634	▽▽▽	Failed to provide	634
25 / p. 624		La Quinta Inn & Suites Tulsa Central	▽▽▽	$89-$109	632
26 / p. 624		Holiday Inn Select	▽▽▽	$79-$99	632

Spotter/Map Page Number	OA	**TULSA** - Lodgings (continued)	Diamond Rating	Rate Range High Season	Listing Page
27 / p. 624		Red Roof Inn	◆◆	$39-$300	634
28 / p. 624	AAA	**Days Inn**	◆◆	$75 SAVE	630
29 / p. 624		Baymont Inn & Suites Tulsa	◆◆	$64-$100	628
30 / p. 624	AAA	**Best Western Trade Winds Central Inn**	◆◆	$55-$79 SAVE	628
31 / p. 624		La Quinta Inn Tulsa (South)	◆◆	$65-$105	633
32 / p. 624		DoubleTree Hotel At Warren Place	◆◆◆	$109-$185	630
33 / p. 624	AAA	**Sleep Inn & Suites Tulsa South**	◆◆	$79-$129 SAVE	635
34 / p. 624	AAA	**Renaissance Tulsa Hotel & Convention Center**	◆◆◆◆	$129-$229 SAVE	634
35 / p. 624		AmeriSuites (Tulsa/Hyde Park)	◆◆	Failed to provide	628
36 / p. 624		Fairfield Inn by Marriott-Tulsa/Woodland Hills	◆◆	$77-$102	631
37 / p. 624		Holiday Inn Express	◆◆	$75-$105	631
38 / p. 624		Tulsa Marriott Southern Hills	◆◆◆	$109-$495	635
39 / p. 624		Hampton Inn & Suites-Woodland Hills	◆◆◆	$92-$101	631
40 / p. 624		Staybridge Suites	◆◆◆	$109-$199	635
41 / p. 624		SpringHill Suites by Marriott	◆◆◆	$105-$130	635
42 / p. 624		Residence Inn by Marriott	◆◆◆	$120-$165	635
43 / p. 624		Candlewood Suites	◆◆◆	Failed to provide	628
44 / p. 624		Hilton Tulsa Southern Hills	◆◆◆	$89-$159	631
45 / p. 624		Hilton Garden Inn Tulsa South	◆◆◆	Failed to provide	631
		TULSA - Restaurants			
1 / p. 624		Caz's Chowhouse	◆◆	$6-$17	636
2 / p. 624		The Chalkboard	◆◆◆	$16-$27	636
3 / p. 624		Chimi's Mexican Food	◆◆	$6-$16	637
4 / p. 624		Camerellis Ristorante Italiano	◆◆◆	$9-$20	636
5 / p. 624		Te Kei's	◆◆◆	$9-$21	640
6 / p. 624		McGill's	◆◆◆	$10-$27	638
7 / p. 624		Fleming's Prime Steakhouse & Wine Bar	◆◆◆	$21-$36	637
8 / p. 624		Polo Grill	◆◆◆◆	$20-$35	639
9 / p. 624		Goldies Patio Grill	◆◆	$5-$8	638
10 / p. 624		Celebrity Restaurant	◆◆	$10-$28	636
11 / p. 624		Monte's Chop House	◆◆◆	$17-$33	639
12 / p. 624		Bodeans Seafood Restaurant	◆◆◆	$18-$38	636
13 / p. 624		Hideaway Pizza	◆◆	$5-$14	638
14 / p. 624		Royal Drason	◆◆	$8-$14	640
15 / p. 624		Rick's Cafe Americain	◆◆◆	$12-$19	639
16 / p. 624		The Green Onion	◆◆◆	$15-$25	638

Spotter/Map Page Number	OA	**TULSA - Restaurants (continued)**	Diamond Rating	Rate Range High Season	Listing Page
⑰ / p. 624		Ti Amo Restaurante	◆◆◆	$10-$24	640
⑱ / p. 624	◆◆◆	**La Roma Pizza**	◆	$5-$10	638
⑲ / p. 624		McGill's	◆◆◆	$10-$25	638
⑳ / p. 624		Goldies Patio Grill	◆◆	$5-$8	637
㉑ / p. 624		Atlantic Sea Grill	◆◆◆	$10-$26	636
㉒ / p. 624		Warren Duck Club	◆◆◆	$20-$43	640
㉓ / p. 624		Cyprus Grille	◆◆◆	$6-$25	637
㉔ / p. 624		Mahogany Prime Steakhouse	◆◆◆	$17-$40	638
㉕ / p. 624		Abuelo's Mexican Food Embassy	◆◆◆	$7-$19	635
㉖ / p. 624		Ron's Hamburgers & Chili	◆	$4-$6	640
㉗ / p. 624		The French Hen	◆◆◆	$14-$28	637
㉘ / p. 624		Mexicali Border Cafe	◆◆	$8-$14	638
㉙ / p. 624		Da' Boat	◆◆	$6-$10	637
㉚ / p. 624		Ron's Hamburgers & Chili	◆	$4-$6	639
㉛ / p. 624		Hideaway Pizza	◆◆	$5-$14	638
㉜ / p. 624		Chimi's Mexican Food	◆◆	$6-$15	637
㉝ / p. 624		Bourbon Street Cafe	◆◆	$9-$20	636
㉞ / p. 624		Pepper's Grill	◆◆	$6-$16	639
㉟ / p. 624		The Bistro At Seville	◆◆◆	$10-$28	636
㊱ / p. 624		Hideaway Pizza	◆◆	$5-$14	638
		BROKEN ARROW - Lodgings			
㊽ / p. 624		Clarion Hotel - see color ad p 629	◆◆◆	$69-$79	641
㊾ / p. 624		Hampton Inn-Tulsa/Broken Arrow	◆◆◆	$199-$299	641
㊿ / p. 624		Comfort Inn	◆◆	$63-$250	641
		BROKEN ARROW - Restaurants			
㊴ / p. 624		Stone Mill BBQ and Steakhouse	◆◆	$7-$21	642
㊵ / p. 624		El Lorito	◆◆	$6-$13	642
㊶ / p. 624		China Star	◆	$6-$11	642
㊷ / p. 624		Mexico Viejo	◆◆	$5-$13	642
㊸ / p. 624		Jake's Cafe	◆◆	$6-$9	642
㊹ / p. 624		Big Daddys All American BBQ	◆	$4-$8	641
㊺ / p. 624		Ron's Hamburgers & Chili	◆	$4-$6	642
㊻ / p. 624		Goldies Patio Grill	◆◆	$5-$8	642
㊼ / p. 624		Peppers Grill	◆◆	$6-$16	642
		JENKS - Restaurant			
㊿ / p. 624		Los Cabos Mexican Grill & Cantina	◆◆	$8-$20	644

TULSA pop. 393,049   (See map and index starting on p. 624)

─────── WHERE TO STAY ───────

AMBASSADOR HOTEL   *Book at AAA.com*   Phone: (918)587-8200

▼▼▼▼   All Year   1P: $157-$193   2P: $157-$193

Historic
Small-scale Hotel

Location: Jct 14th and Main sts. 1324 S Main St 74119. Fax: 918/587-8208. **Facility:** Dating back to 1929, th Mediterranean-style hotel has been restored to its early day elegance. Designated smoking area. 55 uni 47 one-bedroom standard units. 8 one-bedroom suites ($214-$269) with whirlpools. 9 stories, interi corridors. *Bath:* combo or shower only. **Parking:** on-site and valet. **Terms:** cancellation fee impose package plans, small pets only ($50 fee, $150 deposit). **Amenities:** video games (fee), dual phone lines, voice mail, safe irons, hair dryers. *Some:* CD players. **Dining:** The Chalkboard, see separate listing. **Leisure Activities:** exercise room. Gue Services: valet laundry, area transportation, wireless Internet. **Business Services:** meeting rooms, PC. **Cards:** AX, CB, D DS, JC, MC, VI.

[ASK] [S/D] [⊞] [🛏] [🍴] [⊤] [♿] [✕] [🎥] [🔌] [▯]   FEE

AMERISUITES (TULSA/HYDE PARK)   *Book at AAA.com*   Phone: 918/491-4010

▼▼▼   Property failed to provide current rates

Small-scale Hotel

Location: I-44, exit 229 (Yale Ave/SR 66), 3 mi s to 71st St, then just e. 7037 S Zurich Ave 7413 Fax: 918/497-2053. **Facility:** 128 one-bedroom standard units. 6 stories, interior corridors. *Bath:* combo shower only. **Parking:** on-site. **Amenities:** high-speed Internet, voice mail, irons, hair dryers. *Some:* du phone lines. **Pool(s):** outdoor. **Leisure Activities:** exercise room. **Guest Services:** valet and coin laundry, wireless Interne **Business Services:** meeting rooms, PC.

SOME UNI

[🛏] [🍴] [♿] [🌊] [🏊] [VCR] [🎥] [🔌] [▯] [📶] [▯] / [✕] /

BAYMONT INN & SUITES TULSA   *Book at AAA.com*   Phone: (918)488-8777

▼▼▼ ▼▼▼   5/1-9/4 [CP]   1P: $64-$94   2P: $70-$100   XP: $6   F
9/5-2/29 [CP]   1P: $62-$92   2P: $92-$98   XP: $6   F
3/1-4/30 [CP]   1P: $59-$89   2P: $65-$95   XP: $6   F

Small-scale Hotel

Location: I-44, exit 229 (Yale Ave/SR 66), just s, then w. 4530 E Skelly Dr 74135. Fax: 918/488-0220. **Facility:** 1 units. 98 one-bedroom standard units. 3 one-bedroom suites ($99-$140). 4 stories, interior corridors. *Bath:* combo or show only. **Parking:** on-site. **Terms:** small pets only. **Amenities:** video games (fee), voice mail, irons, hair dryers. **Pool(s):** sm outdoor. **Leisure Activities:** exercise room. **Guest Services:** valet and coin laundry, wireless Internet. **Business Service** meeting rooms. **Cards:** AX, CB, DC, DS, MC, VI.

SOME UNITS

[ASK] [🛏] [🍴] [♿] [🌊] [🔌] [▯] / [✕] [▯] [🖨]

BEST WESTERN AIRPORT   *Book great rates at AAA.com*   Phone: (918)438-0780

(AAA) [SAVE]   All Year   1P: $69-$89   2P: $69-$89   XP: $5   F

▼▼ ▼▼
Small-scale Hotel

Location: I-244, exit 14 (Garnett Rd), just s. 222 N Garnett Rd 74116. Fax: 918/438-9296. **Facility:** 108 units. 1 one-bedroom standard units. 1 one-bedroom suite ($120-$150) with whirlpool. 2 stories (no elevato exterior corridors. **Parking:** on-site. **Terms:** package plans. **Amenities:** irons, hair dryers. *Some:* hig speed Internet. **Pool(s):** outdoor. **Guest Services:** coin laundry. **Business Services:** meeting rooms, P **Cards:** AX, DS, MC, VI. **Free Special Amenities: expanded continental breakfast and high-spee Internet.**

SOME UNITS

[S/D] [⊞] [⊤] [🌊] [🏋] [🎥] [▯] / [✕] [▯] [🖨]

BEST WESTERN INN & SUITES   *Book great rates at AAA.com*   Phone: (918)858-2100

(AAA) [SAVE]   7/26-8/15   1P: $95-$150   2P: $95-$150   XP: $6
3/1-7/25 & 8/16-2/29   1P: $75-$119   2P: $75-$119   XP: $6

▼▼▼▼▼
Small-scale Hotel

Location: I-44, exit 231 eastbound; exit 232 westbound, just sw. 3212 S 79th E Ave 74145. Fax: 918/622-271 **Facility:** 62 one-bedroom standard units, some with whirlpools. 3 stories, interior corridors. *Bath:* combo shower only. **Parking:** on-site. **Terms:** [ECP] meal plan available. **Amenities:** high-speed Internet, du phone lines, voice mail, irons, hair dryers. **Pool(s):** small heated indoor. **Leisure Activities:** sauna, limite exercise equipment. **Guest Services:** valet and coin laundry, wireless Internet. **Business Services:** business cent **Cards:** AX, DS, MC, VI. **Free Special Amenities: room upgrade (subject to availability with advance reservations).**

SOME UNITS

[S/D] [🍴] [♿] [🌊] [🎥] [▯] / [✕] [▯] [🖨]

BEST WESTERN TRADE WINDS CENTRAL INN   *Book great rates at AAA.com*   Phone: (918)749-5561

(AAA) [SAVE]   All Year   1P: $55-$75   2P: $59-$79   XP: $5   F

▼▼ ▼▼
Small-scale Hotel

Location: I-44, exit 228 (Harvard Ave), on northwest frontage road. 3141 E Skelly Dr 74105. Fax: 918/749-631 **Facility:** 164 one-bedroom standard units, some with whirlpools. 2 stories (no elevator), interior/exteri corridors. **Parking:** on-site, winter plug-ins. **Terms:** pets ($10 fee). **Amenities:** video games (fee), voi mail, irons, hair dryers. **Dining:** 6 am-10 pm, Sun-9 pm, cocktails, nightclu entertainment. **Pool(s):** heated outdoor. **Leisure Activities:** exercise room. **Guest Services:** valet and c laundry. **Business Services:** meeting rooms, business center. **Cards:** AX, CB, DC, DS, MC, VI. **Free Special Amenitie room upgrade (subject to availability with advance reservations) and high-speed Internet.**

SOME UNITS

[S/D] [⊞] [🌊] [🎥] [▯] / [✕] [▯] [🖨]   FEE

CANDLEWOOD SUITES   *Book at AAA.com*   Phone: 918/294-9000

▼▼▼▼   Property failed to provide current rates

Small-scale Hotel

Location: Just sw of jct 71st and 101st E Ave. 10008 E 73rd St S 74133. Fax: 918/294-9997. **Facility:** 72 units. one-bedroom standard units with efficiencies. 21 one-bedroom suites with kitchens. 3 stories, inter corridors. *Bath:* combo or shower only. **Parking:** on-site. **Terms:** check-in 4 pm, pets ($25 fe **Amenities:** video library, DVD players, high-speed Internet, dual phone lines, voice mail, irons, hair dryers. **Leisu Activities:** exercise room. **Guest Services:** complimentary evening beverages: Tues, complimentary and valet laund **Business Services:** meeting rooms, business center.

SOME UNIT

      FEE

(See map and index starting on p. 624)

COMFORT SUITES — *Book great rates at AAA.com* — **Phone: (918)622-6300** ⑳
AAA SAVE — All Year — 1P: $89-$109 — 2P: $95-$115 — XP: $5 — F
▼▼▼▼ — **Location:** I-44, exit 231 eastbound; exit 232 (Memorial Dr) westbound. 8039 E 33rd St S 74145. Fax: 918/665-7322. **Facility:** 63 units. 60 one-bedroom standard units, some with whirlpools. 3 one-bedroom suites ($120-$150) with whirlpools. 3 stories, interior corridors. *Bath:* combo or shower only. **Parking:** on-site. **Terms:** [BP] meal Small-scale Hotel plan available, package plans. **Amenities:** high-speed Internet, dual phone lines, voice mail, irons, hair dryers. **Pool(s):** heated indoor. **Leisure Activities:** whirlpool, exercise room. **Guest Services:** valet and coin laundry, wireless Internet. **Business Services:** meeting rooms, business center. **Cards:** AX, CB, DC, DS, JC, MC, VI.
Free Special Amenities: full breakfast and high-speed Internet.

⬛⬛⬛⬛⬛⬛⬛⬛⬛⬛⬛⬛

COMFORT SUITES-TULSA AIRPORT — *Book great rates at AAA.com* — **Phone: (918)628-0900** ⑫
▼▼▼ — All Year — 1P: $79-$120 — 2P: $79-$120
Small-scale Hotel — **Location:** Just nw of jct US 169 and 21st St. 1737 S 101st E Ave 74128. Fax: 918/663-5224. **Facility:** 57 one-bedroom standard units, some with whirlpools. 2 stories (no elevator), interior corridors. *Bath:* combo or shower only. **Parking:** on-site. **Terms:** [BP] meal plan available, package plans. **Amenities:** safes (fee), irons, hair dryers. **Pool(s):** heated indoor. **Leisure Activities:** whirlpool, exercise room. **Guest Services:** valet laundry, wireless Internet. **Cards:** AX, CB, DC, DS, MC, VI.

SOME UNITS
⬛⬛⬛⬛⬛⬛⬛⬛⬛ / ⬛⬛ /

COUNTRY INN & SUITES BY CARLSON — *Book at AAA.com* — **Phone: (918)234-3535** ③
▼▼▼ — All Year [ECP] — 1P: $59-$70 — 2P: $65-$75 — XP: $6 — F18
Small-scale Hotel — **Location:** I-244, exit 14 (Garnett Rd), just n. 1034 N Garnett Rd 74116. Fax: 918/234-2600. **Facility:** 48 units. 36 one-bedroom standard units, some with whirlpools. 12 one-bedroom suites ($74-$125), some with whirlpools. 2 stories (no elevator), interior corridors. **Parking:** on-site. **Terms:** 7 day cancellation notice. Amenities: irons, hair dryers. **Pool(s):** small heated outdoor. **Guest Services:** valet and coin laundry, wireless Internet. Cards: AX, CB, DC, DS, MC, VI.

SOME UNITS
⬛⬛⬛⬛⬛⬛⬛⬛ / ⬛ ⬛⬛ ⬛⬛ /

CROWNE PLAZA TULSA — *Book great rates at AAA.com* — **Phone: (918)582-9000** ⑦
AAA SAVE — All Year — 1P: $89-$169 — 2P: $99-$169
▼▼▼ — **Location:** Jct 2nd St and Boston; downtown. 100 E 2nd St 74103. Fax: 918/560-2292. **Facility:** 462 units. 457 one-bedroom standard units. 5 one-bedroom suites ($300-$325), some with whirlpools. 15 stories, interior corridors. *Bath:* combo or shower only. **Parking:** on-site (fee) and valet. **Terms:** package plans, pets ($50 Large-scale Hotel fee). **Amenities:** CD players, voice mail, irons, hair dryers. **Pool(s):** heated indoor/outdoor. **Leisure Activities:** exercise room, spa. **Guest Services:** gift shop, valet and coin laundry, area transportation-downtown, wireless Internet. **Business Services:** conference facilities, business center. **Cards:** AX, DC, DS, MC, VI.

SOME UNITS
⬛⬛⬛⬛⬛⬛⬛⬛⬛⬛ / ⬛⬛ /
FEE

(See map and index starting on p. 624)

DAYS INN   *Book great rates at AAA.com*   Phone: (918)496-9300   2

AAA SAVE
7/29-8/31   1P: $75   2P: $75   XP: $6
3/1-7/28 & 9/1-2/29   1P: $62   2P: $62   XP: $6

Location: I-44, exit 229 (Yale Ave/SR 66), just s. 4724 S Yale Ave 74135. Fax: 918/495-1944. **Facility:** 63 units. 6 one-bedroom standard units. 1 one-bedroom suite ($95). 2 stories (no elevator), exterior corridors. **Parking:** Small-scale Hotel on-site. **Terms:** pets ($50 deposit). **Amenities:** high-speed Internet, voice mail, irons, hair dryers. **Pool(s):** small outdoor. **Leisure Activities:** limited exercise equipment. *Fee:* game room. **Guest Services:** co laundry. **Business Services:** business center. **Cards:** AX, CB, DC, DS, JC, MC, VI. **Free Special Amenities:** continental breakfast and high-speed Internet.

SOME UNITS

[icons] FEE

DOUBLETREE HOTEL AT WARREN PLACE   *Book great rates at AAA.com*   Phone: (918)495-1000   3

All Year   1P: $109-$185   2P: $109-$185   XP: $25   F1

Location: I-44, exit 229 (Yale Ave/SR 66), 1.3 mi s. 6110 S Yale Ave 74136. Fax: 918/491-5914. **Facility:** 370 units. Large-scale Hotel   364 one-bedroom standard units. 6 one-bedroom suites, some with whirlpools. 9 stories, interior corridors. *Bath:* combo or shower only. **Parking:** on-site and valet. **Terms:** pets ($25 fee). **Amenities:** dual phor lines, voice mail, irons, hair dryers. **Dining:** Warren Duck Club, see separate listing. **Pool(s):** heated indoor. **Leisure Activities:** saunas, whirlpool, jogging, exercise room. **Guest Services:** gift shop, valet laundry, wireless Internet. **Business Services:** conference facilities, business center. **Cards:** AX, CB, DC, DS, JC, MC, VI.

SOME UNITS

[icons] FEE

DOUBLETREE HOTEL DOWNTOWN TULSA   *Book great rates at AAA.com*   Phone: (918)587-8000   8

All Year   1P: $149-$400   2P: $159-$410   XP: $10   F1

Location: Jct 7th St and Houston. 616 W 7th St 74127. Fax: 918/587-3001. **Facility:** 417 one-bedroom standard units, some with whirlpools. 17 stories, interior corridors. **Parking:** on-site (fee) and valet Large-scale Hotel **Terms:** cancellation fee imposed, small pets only ($50 fee). **Amenities:** video games (fee), dual phor lines, voice mail, irons, hair dryers. **Pool(s):** heated indoor. **Leisure Activities:** whirlpool, exercise room. **Guest Services:** g shop, valet and coin laundry, area transportation, wireless Internet. **Business Services:** conference facilities. **Cards:** AX, C DC, DS, JC, MC, VI.

SOME UNITS

[icons] FEE

ECONO LODGE AIRPORT   *Book great rates at AAA.com*   Phone: (918)437-9200   9

AAA SAVE
All Year   1P: $42-$85   2P: $49-$99   XP: $5   F1

Location: I-44, exit 235 (11th St); on southeast corner. 11620 E Skelly Dr 74128. Fax: 918/437-2935. **Facility:** 12 one-bedroom standard units. 2 stories (no elevator), interior corridors. **Parking:** on-site. **Terms:** [CP] me plan available, package plans. **Amenities:** high-speed Internet. *Some:* irons. **Dining:** 11 am-10 pm, Sat Motel   Sun from 11:30 am; closed Tues. **Pool(s):** outdoor, heated indoor. **Leisure Activities:** whirlpool. **Guest Services:** coin laundry. **Business Services:** meeting rooms, PC. **Cards:** AX, CB, DC, DS, JC, MC, V **Free Special Amenities:** continental breakfast and high-speed Internet.

SOME UNITS

[icons]

EMBASSY SUITES HOTEL   *Book at AAA.com*   Phone: (918)622-4000   13

All Year [BP]   1P: $99-$299   2P: $99-$299   XP: $10   F1

Location: I-44, exit 231 eastbound; exit 232 (Memorial Dr) westbound, just sw. 3332 S 79th E Ave 74145. Fax: 918/665-2347. **Facility:** 244 units. 4 one-bedroom standard units. 232 one- and 8 two-bedroom suite Large-scale Hotel   some with whirlpools. 9 stories, interior corridors. **Parking:** on-site. **Terms:** cancellation fee imposed package plans, pets ($25 extra charge). **Amenities:** video games (fee), dual phone lines, voice mail, irons, hair dryers. **Pool(s):** small heated indoor. **Leisure Activities:** sauna, whirlpool, exercise room. **Guest Services:** gift shop, complimentary evenin beverages, valet and coin laundry, wireless Internet. **Business Services:** conference facilities. **Cards:** AX, CB, DC, DS, JC MC, VI.

SOME UNITS

[icons] FEE

(ee map and index starting on p. 624)

**AIRFIELD INN BY MARRIOTT-TULSA/WOODLAND
HILLS** *Book great rates at AAA.com*   Phone: (918)252-7754   **36**
All Year   1P: $77-$97   2P: $82-$102   XP: $5   F18
Small-scale Hotel   **Location:** US 169, exit E 71st St, 1 mi w. 9020 E 71st St 74133. Fax: 918/252-7754. **Facility:** Smoke free premises. 64 one-bedroom standard units. 3 stories, interior corridors. **Bath:** combo or shower only. **Parking:** on-site. **Amenities:** irons, hair dryers. **Pool(s):** small heated indoor. **Leisure Activities:** whirlpool. **Guest Services:** valet laundry, wireless Internet. **Cards:** AX, DC, DS, MC, VI.

SOME UNITS
(ASK) (SD) (TV+) (⟳) (≈) (↔) (X) (▣) (🖥) (▭) /

GUEST HOUSE SUITES PLUS *Book at AAA.com*   Phone: 918/664-7241   **23**
Property failed to provide current rates
Small-scale Hotel   **Location:** 1.7 mi w of jct US 169. 8181 E 41st St 74145. Fax: 918/622-0314. **Facility:** 95 units. 69 one-bedroom standard units with kitchens. 26 one-bedroom suites with kitchens. 2 stories (no elevator), exterior corridors. **Parking:** on-site, winter plug-ins. **Terms:** pets ($50 fee). **Amenities:** video library, CD players, dual phone lines, voice mail, irons, hair dryers. **Some:** high-speed Internet (fee). **Pool(s):** small outdoor. **Leisure Activities:** exercise room, sports court. **Guest Services:** valet and coin laundry. **Business Services:** meeting rooms.

SOME UNITS
(🛏) (TV+) (⟳) (≈) (↔) (VCR) (X) (▣) (🖥) (▭) / (X) /
FEE

HAMPTON INN *Book great rates at AAA.com*   Phone: 918/663-1000   **18**
Property failed to provide current rates
Small-scale Hotel   **Location:** I-44, exit 231 eastbound; exit 232 (Memorial Dr) westbound, just sw. 3209 S 79th Ave E 74145. Fax: 918/663-0587. **Facility:** 148 units. 136 one-bedroom standard units. 12 one-bedroom suites. 4 stories, interior corridors. **Bath:** combo or shower only. **Parking:** on-site. **Terms:** pets ($25 deposit). **Amenities:** video games (fee), high-speed Internet, voice mail, irons, hair dryers. **Pool(s):** heated outdoor. **Guest Services:** valet laundry, wireless Internet. **Business Services:** meeting rooms.

SOME UNITS
(🛏) (TV+) (⟳) (≈) (↔) (X) (🖥) / (X) (▣) (🖥) /
FEE

HAMPTON INN & SUITES-WOODLAND HILLS *Book great rates at AAA.com*   Phone: (918)294-3300   **39**
All Year   1P: $92-$101   XP: $10   F18
Small-scale Hotel   **Location:** 1.2 mi w of jct US 169, exit 71st St. 7141 S 85th Ave E 74133. Fax: 918/294-1300. **Facility:** 74 units. 47 one-bedroom standard units. 27 one-bedroom suites, some with efficiencies and/or whirlpools. 4 stories, interior corridors. **Bath:** combo or shower only. **Parking:** on-site. **Terms:** check-in 4 pm, package plans. **Amenities:** video library, high-speed Internet, dual phone lines, voice mail, irons, hair dryers. **Some:** DVD players. **Pool(s):** outdoor. **Leisure Activities:** whirlpool, exercise room. **Guest Services:** sundries, valet and coin laundry, wireless Internet. **Business Services:** meeting rooms, business center. **Cards:** AX, CB, DC, DS, MC, VI.

SOME UNITS
(ASK) (SD) (TV+) (⟳) (≈) (☎) (🖥) / (X) (VCR) (▣) (🖥) /

HILTON GARDEN INN *Book great rates at AAA.com*   Phone: 918/838-1444   **2**
All Year   1P: $134-$199   2P: $134-$199
Small-scale Hotel   **Location:** Off SR 11, exit airport terminal. 7728 E Virgin Ct 74115. Fax: 918/834-6910. **Facility:** 120 one-bedroom standard units. 3 stories, interior corridors. **Bath:** combo or shower only. **Parking:** on-site. **Terms:** package plans. **Amenities:** video games (fee), high-speed Internet, dual phone lines, voice mail, irons, hair dryers. **Pool(s):** heated indoor. **Leisure Activities:** whirlpool, exercise room. **Guest Services:** sundries, valet and coin laundry, wireless Internet. **Business Services:** meeting rooms, business center. **Cards:** AX, DC, DS, JC, MC, VI.

SOME UNITS
(ASK) (🚡) (TV) (⟳) (≈) (🖥) (▣) (🖥) (▭) / (X)

HILTON GARDEN INN TULSA SOUTH *Book great rates at AAA.com*   Phone: 918/392-2000   **45**
Property failed to provide current rates
Small-scale Hotel   **Location:** US 169 S, exit 81st St, just w. 8202 S 100th Ave E 74133. Fax: 918/392-2099. **Facility:** 104 units. 98 one-bedroom standard units. 6 one-bedroom suites. 4 stories, interior corridors. **Bath:** combo or shower only. **Parking:** on-site. **Amenities:** video games (fee), high-speed Internet, voice mail, irons, hair dryers. **Pool(s):** heated outdoor. **Leisure Activities:** whirlpool, exercise room. **Guest Services:** sundries, valet and coin laundry, wireless Internet. **Business Services:** meeting rooms, business center.

SOME UNITS
(TV) (⛴M) (⟳) (≈) (🖥) (▣) (🖥) (▭) / (X)

HILTON TULSA SOUTHERN HILLS *Book great rates at AAA.com*   Phone: (918)492-5000   **44**
All Year   1P: $89-$159   2P: $89-$159   XP: $10   F18
Large-scale Hotel   **Location:** I-44, exit 227, 3 mi s. Located opposite Oral Roberts University. 7902 S Lewis 74136. Fax: 918/492-7256. **Facility:** 293 one-bedroom standard units, some with whirlpools. 11 stories, interior corridors. **Bath:** combo or shower only. **Parking:** on-site. **Terms:** [AP] & [BP] meal plans available, package plans, pets ($75 extra large). **Amenities:** dual phone lines, voice mail, irons, hair dryers. **Some:** Fee: high-speed Internet. **Pool(s):** outdoor. **Leisure Activities:** exercise room. **Guest Services:** sundries, valet laundry, wireless Internet. **Business Services:** conference facilities, business center. **Cards:** AX, CB, DC, DS, JC, MC, VI.

SOME UNITS
(ASK) (SD) (🚡) (🛏) (TV) (Y) (⟳) (≈) (🖥) (▭) / (X) (▣) (🖥) /
FEE   FEE FEE

HOLIDAY INN EXPRESS *Book at AAA.com*   Phone: (918)459-5321   **37**
All Year   1P: $75-$100   2P: $80-$105   XP: $5   F18
Small-scale Hotel   **Location:** US 169, exit 71st St, 1 mi w. 9010 E 71st St 74133. Fax: 918/459-5321. **Facility:** 64 one-bedroom standard units. 3 stories, interior corridors. **Bath:** combo or shower only. **Parking:** on-site, winter plug-ins. **Amenities:** dual phone lines, voice mail, irons, hair dryers. **Pool(s):** small heated indoor. **Leisure Activities:** whirlpool. **Guest Services:** valet laundry, wireless Internet. **Cards:** AX, DC, DS, MC, VI.

SOME UNITS
(ASK) (SD) (TV+) (⟳) (≈) (↔) (🖥) / (X) (▣) (🖥) /

(See map and index starting on p. 624)

HOLIDAY INN EXPRESS-TULSA CENTRAL   *Book great rates at AAA.com*   Phone: (918)665-4242 ❶
(AAA) (SAVE)   All Year [ECP]   1P: $99-$139   2P: $99-$139   XP: $10   F▮
▼▼▼▼   **Location:** I-44, exit 231 eastbound; exit 232 (Memorial Dr) westbound, just sw. 3215 S 79th Ave E 7414▮
Fax: 918/665-4343. **Facility:** 62 one-bedroom standard units, some with whirlpools. 3 stories, interi▮
Small-scale Hotel   corridors. *Bath:* combo or shower only. **Parking:** on-site. **Amenities:** high-speed Internet, dual phone line▮
voice mail, irons, hair dryers. **Pool(s):** small heated outdoor. **Leisure Activities:** sauna, exercise roor▮
Guest Services: valet and coin laundry, wireless Internet. **Business Services:** business center. **Cards:** A▮
CB, DC, DS, JC, MC, VI. **Free Special Amenities:** expanded continental breakfast and local telephone calls.

SOME UNITS
🍴➔ 👶M 👤 📶 🏊 🎥 💻 ✕ 🔌 📠

HOLIDAY INN-INTERNATIONAL AIRPORT   *Book at AAA.com*   Phone: (918)437-7660 ❹
▼▼▼▼   All Year   1P: $84
Location: I-244, exit 14 (Garnett Rd), just n. 1010 N Garnett Rd 74116. Fax: 918/438-7538. **Facility:** 158 on▮
Small-scale Hotel   bedroom standard units. 2 stories (no elevator), interior corridors. *Bath:* combo or shower only. **Parking:** on-
site. **Terms:** [BP] meal plan available, package plans, pets ($25 fee). **Amenities:** high-speed Internet, du▮
phone lines, voice mail, irons, hair dryers. **Pool(s):** small heated indoor. **Leisure Activities:** playground, exercise room. *Fe*
game room. **Guest Services:** valet laundry, wireless Internet. **Business Services:** meeting rooms, business center. **Cards:** A▮
CB, DC, DS, MC, VI.

SOME UNITS
(ASK) ➔ 🛏 🍴 🍸 👶M 👤 📶 🏊 ✕ 🎥 💻 ✕ 🔌 📠
FEE

HOLIDAY INN SELECT   *Book at AAA.com*   Phone: (918)622-7000 ❷
▼▼▼▼   All Year   1P: $79-$99   2P: $79-$99
Location: I-44, exit 229 (Yale Ave/SR 66); on south frontage road. 5000 E Skelly Dr 74135. Fax: 918/664-935▮
Small-scale Hotel   **Facility:** 313 units. 305 one-bedroom standard units. 8 one-bedroom suites ($159-$289), some wi▮
whirlpools. 4 stories, interior/exterior corridors. **Parking:** on-site. **Terms:** package plans, small pets on
($25 fee, $25 deposit). **Amenities:** video games (fee), high-speed Internet, voice mail, irons, hair dryers. *Some:* dual phor▮
lines. **Pool(s):** heated outdoor. **Leisure Activities:** exercise room. **Guest Services:** valet and coin laundry, area transportatio▮
wireless Internet. **Business Services:** meeting rooms, business center. **Cards:** AX, DC, DS, MC, VI.

SOME UNITS
(ASK) (S🌀) ➔ 🛏 🍴 🍸 📶 🏊 ✕ 🎥 💻 ✕ 🔌 📠
FEE   FEE FEE

LA QUINTA INN & SUITES TULSA CENTRAL   *Book great rates at AAA.com*   Phone: (918)665-2630 ❷
▼▼▼▼   All Year   1P: $89-$109
Location: I-44, exit 230, just s. 6030 E Skelly Dr 74135. Fax: 918/858-9744. **Facility:** 105 units. 86 one-bedroo▮
Small-scale Hotel   standard units. 19 one-bedroom suites ($109-$179), some with whirlpools. 4 stories, interior corridor▮
Parking: on-site. **Terms:** small pets only. **Amenities:** high-speed Internet, dual phone lines, voice ma▮
irons, hair dryers. *Some:* DVD players. **Pool(s):** outdoor. **Leisure Activities:** exercise room. **Guest Services:** valet and co▮
laundry, wireless Internet. **Business Services:** meeting rooms, business center. **Cards:** AX, CB, DC, DS, JC, MC, VI.

SOME UNIT▮
(ASK) (S🌀) 🛏 🍴➔ 📶 🏊 🎥 🔌 📠 💻 / ✕ /

LA QUINTA INN TULSA (AIRPORT)   *Book great rates at AAA.com*   Phone: (918)836-3931 ❸
▼▼▼ ▼▼▼   6/1-9/30   1P: $82-$105   2P: $82-$105   XP: $6   F▮
4/1-5/31 & 10/1-2/29   1P: $58-$94   2P: $58-$94   XP: $6   F▮
3/1-3/31   1P: $58-$83   2P: $58-$83   XP: $6   F▮
Small-scale Hotel   **Location:** I-244, exit 11 (Sheridan Rd). 35 N Sheridan Rd 74115-8718. Fax: 918/836-5428. **Facility:** 101 units. 9▮
one- and 2 two-bedroom standard units. 2 one-bedroom suites ($99-$125). 2 stories (no elevator), exterior corridors. **Parking:**
on-site. **Terms:** weekly rates available, [ECP] meal plan available, package plans. **Amenities:** video games (fee), voice ma▮
irons, hair dryers. **Pool(s):** small outdoor. **Cards:** AX, DS, MC, VI. **Free Special Amenities:** continental breakfast and hig▮
speed Internet.

SOME UNITS
(S🌀) 🛏 🍴➔ 📶 🏊 🎥 💻 / ✕ 🔌 📠

  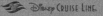

(See map and index starting on p. 624)

LA QUINTA INN TULSA (EAST)   *Book great rates at AAA.com*   Phone: (918)665-0220   **22**

5/18-8/18 [CP]	1P: $75-$105	2P: $81-$111	XP: $6	F18
8/19-2/29 [CP]	1P: $70-$100	2P: $76-$106	XP: $6	F18
3/1-5/17 [CP]	1P: $65-$95	2P: $71-$101	XP: $6	F18

Small-scale Hotel   **Location:** US 169, exit E 41st St. 10829 E 41st St 74146. **Fax:** 918/664-4810. **Facility:** 113 units. 112 one-bedroom standard units. 1 one-bedroom suite ($95-$141). 3 stories, exterior corridors. **Parking:** on-site, winter plug-ins. **Terms:** small pets only. **Amenities:** video games (fee), high-speed Internet, voice mail, irons, hair dryers. **Pool(s):** small outdoor. **Guest Services:** valet laundry. **Business Services:** meeting rooms. **Cards:** AX, CB, DC, DS, MC, VI.

SOME UNITS
(ASK) 🛏 🍴 🎱 🚲 🛜 🎬 💻 / ✕ 🔒 🖥 /

LA QUINTA INN TULSA (SOUTH)   *Book great rates at AAA.com*   Phone: (918)254-1626   **31**

4/14-7/27 [CP]	1P: $65-$99	2P: $75-$105	XP: $6	F18
7/28-2/29 [CP]	1P: $65-$95	2P: $71-$101	XP: $6	F18
3/1-4/13 [CP]	1P: $62-$92	2P: $68-$98	XP: $6	F18

Small-scale Hotel   **Location:** Broadway Arrow Expwy (SR 51), exit 129th and 51st sts, just s. 12525 E 52nd St S 74146-6207. **Fax:** 918/252-3408. **Facility:** 115 units. 104 one-bedroom standard units. 11 one-bedroom suites ($102-$145). 3 stories, exterior corridors. **Parking:** on-site, winter plug-ins. **Terms:** small pets only. **Amenities:** video games (fee), high-speed Internet, voice mail, irons, hair dryers. *Some:* dual phone lines. **Pool(s):** outdoor. **Guest Services:** coin laundry. **Business Services:** meeting rooms. **Cards:** AX, CB, DC, DS, MC, VI.

SOME UNITS
(ASK) 🛏 🍴 🎱 🚲 🛜 🎬 💻 / ✕ 🔒 🖥 /

MCBIRNEY MANSION BED & BREAKFAST   Phone: 918/585-3234   **11**

Property failed to provide current rates

Historic Bed & Breakfast   **Location:** US 64 and SR 51, exit Denver Ave, 0.5 mi sw. 1414 S Galveston 74127. **Fax:** 918/585-9377. **Facility:** The mansion sits on nicely landscaped grounds overlooking the Arkansas River. Smoke free premises. 8 units. 6 one-bedroom standard units, some with whirlpools. 2 one-bedroom suites, some with whirlpools. 4 stories (no elevator), interior/exterior corridors. *Bath:* combo or shower only. **Parking:** on-site. **Terms:** age restrictions may apply. **Amenities:** voice mail, irons, hair dryers. **Leisure Activities:** hiking trails. **Guest Services:** valet laundry. **Business Services:** meeting rooms.

SOME UNITS
✕ / (VCR) 🔒 💻 /

MICROTEL INN & SUITES   *Book at AAA.com*   Phone: (918)858-3775   **13**

All Year [CP]   1P: $55-$125   2P: $55-$125

Small-scale Hotel   **Location:** Just w of 21st St and Yale Ave. 4531 E 21st St 74114. **Fax:** 918/858-3776. **Facility:** 82 one-bedroom standard units. 3 stories, interior corridors. *Bath:* combo or shower only. **Parking:** on-site. **Terms:** pets ($25 fee). **Amenities:** video games (fee), voice mail. **Guest Services:** wireless Internet. **Business Services:** meeting rooms, PC. **Cards:** AX, CB, DC, DS, MC, VI.

SOME UNITS
(ASK) (S🔒) 🛏 ♿ 🎬 / ✕ 🔒 🖥 💻 /
FEE

MICROTEL INN & SUITES   *Book at AAA.com*   Phone: (918)234-9100

All Year   1P: $45-$65   2P: $45-$65

Small-scale Hotel   **Location:** I-44, exit 238 (161st Ave), just s. 16518 E Admiral Pl 74116. **Fax:** 918/234-3248. **Facility:** 46 one-bedroom standard units, some with whirlpools. 3 stories, interior corridors. *Bath:* combo or shower only. **Parking:** on-site. **Terms:** 2 night minimum stay - seasonal, [CP] meal plan available, small pets only ($10 extra charge). **Amenities:** irons, hair dryers. **Guest Services:** coin laundry, wireless Internet. **Cards:** AX, DC, DS, MC, VI.

SOME UNITS
(ASK) 🛏 ♿ 🎱 🎬 / ✕ 🔒 🖥 💻 /
FEE

POST OAK LODGE   Phone: (918)425-2112   **F16**

All Year   1P: $74-$99   2P: $84-$109   XP: $10

Small-scale Hotel   **Location:** 0.7 mi w of jct Apache/41st St. 5323 W 31st N 74127. **Fax:** 918/425-2288. **Facility:** Smoke free premises. 36 one-bedroom standard units. 2 stories (no elevator), interior corridors. **Parking:** on-site. **Terms:** cancellation fee imposed, [BP] & [CP] meal plans available, package plans, pets ($50 deposit). **Amenities:** video library, DVD players, voice mail, irons, hair dryers. **Pool(s):** heated outdoor. **Leisure Activities:** whirlpools, fishing, hiking trails, exercise room, basketball, horseshoes, volleyball. **Guest Services:** wireless Internet. **Business Services:** conference facilities, business center. **Cards:** AX, DS, MC, VI.

(ASK) (S🔒) 🛏 🍴 🚲 🎬 ✕ ✕
FEE

QUALITY SUITES   *Book great rates at AAA.com*   Phone: (918)858-9625   **15**

All Year [ECP]   1P: $75-$125   2P: $75-$125   XP: $7   F

Small-scale Hotel   **Location:** I-44, exit 232 (Memorial Dr), just sw. 3112 S 79th E Ave 74145. **Fax:** 918/665-7240. **Facility:** 69 one-bedroom standard units, some with whirlpools. 2 stories, interior/exterior corridors. *Bath:* combo or shower only. **Parking:** on-site. **Amenities:** high-speed Internet, voice mail, irons, hair dryers. **Pool(s):** small heated indoor. **Leisure Activities:** whirlpool, limited exercise equipment. **Guest Services:** valet and coin laundry, wireless Internet. **Business Services:** PC. **Cards:** AX, DS, MC, VI. **Free Special Amenities:** full breakfast and high-speed Internet.

SOME UNITS
(S🔒) 🍴 🚲 🎬 🔒 🖥 💻 / ✕ /

(See map and index starting on p. 624)

RADISSON TULSA   *Book great rates at AAA.com*   Phone: 918/627-5000   ②
▼▼▼   Property failed to provide current rates
Location: Just e of US 169. 10918 E 41st St 74146. Fax: 918/627-4003. **Facility:** 325 units. 323 one-bedroom
Large-scale Hotel   standard units. 2 one-bedroom suites with whirlpools. 11 stories, interior corridors. *Bath:* combo or shower
only. **Parking:** on-site. **Terms:** pets (with prior approval). **Amenities:** high-speed Internet, dual phone lines,
voice mail, irons, hair dryers. *Some:* fax. **Pool(s):** heated outdoor. **Leisure Activities:** sauna, whirlpool, exercise room. **Guest
Services:** gift shop, valet laundry, area transportation, wireless Internet. **Business Services:** conference facilities, PC.
(See color ad below)

SOME UNITS
⊞ 🐾 🍽 🍸 ⚿ 🕸 ⇄ ✕ 🎥 🖥 / ✕ 📼 /
FEE

RADISSON TULSA AIRPORT   *Book at AAA.com*   Phone: 918/835-9911   ①
▼▼▼   Property failed to provide current rates
Location: SR 11, exit airport terminal. 2201 N 77th East Ave 74115. Fax: 918/838-2452. **Facility:** 172 one-
Small-scale Hotel   bedroom standard units. 2 stories (no elevator), interior corridors. **Parking:** on-site. **Terms:** pets ($25 fee).
Amenities: video games (fee), dual phone lines, voice mail, irons, hair dryers. *Some:* high-speed Internet.
Pool(s): outdoor. **Leisure Activities:** exercise room. **Guest Services:** valet laundry, wireless Internet. **Business Services:**
conference facilities, PC.

SOME UNITS
⊞ 🐾 🍽 🍸 ⇄ 🎥 🖥 / ✕ 🔌 🖨 /
FEE

RED ROOF INN   *Book at AAA.com*   Phone: (918)622-6776   ㉗
▼▼   All Year [CP]   1P: $39-$300
Motel   **Location:** I-44, exit 229 (Yale Ave), just s. 4717 S Yale Ave 74135. Fax: 918/622-1809. **Facility:** 101 one-bedroom
standard units, some with whirlpools. 3 stories, exterior corridors. *Bath:* combo or shower only. **Parking:** on-
site. **Amenities:** high-speed Internet. **Pool(s):** small heated outdoor. **Guest Services:** coin laundry.
Business Services: PC. **Cards:** AX, DS, MC, VI.

SOME UNITS
(ASK) 🆂 🐾 🍽 ⇄ 🎥 / ✕ 🔌 🖨 /

**RENAISSANCE TULSA HOTEL & CONVENTION
CENTER**   *Book great rates at AAA.com*   Phone: (918)307-2600   ㉞
(AAA) (SAVE)   All Year   1P: $129-$229   2P: $129-$229   XP: $15
▼▼▼ ▼▼▼   **Location:** Just ne of jct US 169 and 71st St. 6808 S 107th E Ave 74133. Fax: 918/307-2907. **Facility:** Water
cascading over a rock wall and a stream winding through the lobby create a scenic and serene ambience at
Large-scale Hotel   this upscale hotel. Smoke free premises. 300 units. 265 one-bedroom standard units. 35 one-bedroom
suites ($189-$299), some with whirlpools. 9 stories, interior corridors. *Bath:* combo or shower only. **Parking:**
on-site. **Terms:** package plans. **Amenities:** high-speed Internet (fee), dual phone lines, voice mail, safes,
irons, hair dryers. *Some:* DVD players (fee). **Dining:** Cyprus Grille, see separate listing. **Pool(s):** heated indoor. **Leisure
Activities:** sauna, whirlpool, exercise room, spa. *Fee:* game room. **Guest Services:** valet and coin laundry, wireless Internet.
Business Services: conference facilities, business center. **Cards:** AX, CB, DC, DS, JC, MC, VI. **Free Special Amenities:**
newspaper.

SOME UNITS
🆂 🐾 🍽 🍸 ⚿ 🕸 ⇄ ✕ ✕ 🎥 🖥 / 🔌 🖨 /

(See map and index starting on p. 624)

RESIDENCE INN BY MARRIOTT · *Book great rates at AAA.com* · Phone: (918)250-4850 · 42
▼▼▼
All Year · 1P: $120-$160 · 2P: $125-$165 · XP: $5 · F18
Location: US 169, exit 71st St, just e. 11025 E 73rd St 74133. Fax: 918/250-4850. **Facility:** Smoke free premises.
Small-scale Hotel · 90 units. 37 one-bedroom standard units with efficiencies. 35 one- and 18 two-bedroom suites, some with efficiencies or kitchens. 3 stories, interior corridors. *Bath:* combo or shower only. **Parking:** on-site.
Terms: [BP] meal plan available, pets ($75 fee). **Amenities:** dual phone lines, voice mail, irons, hair dryers. **Pool(s):** heated door. **Leisure Activities:** whirlpool, exercise room, sports court. **Guest Services:** valet and coin laundry, wireless Internet. **Business Services:** meeting rooms, PC. **Cards:** AX, DC, DS, MC, VI.

SLEEP INN & SUITES TULSA CENTRAL · *Book great rates at AAA.com* · Phone: 918/663-2777 · 21
▼▼▼
Property failed to provide current rates
Location: I-44, exit 231 eastbound; exit 232 (Memorial Dr) westbound, just sw. 8021 E 33rd St S 74145.
Small-scale Hotel · Fax: 918/858-4445. **Facility:** 66 units. 63 one-bedroom standard units, some with whirlpools. 3 one-bedroom suites. 3 stories, interior corridors. *Bath:* combo or shower only. **Parking:** on-site, winter plug-ins.
Terms: pets ($10 extra charge). **Amenities:** voice mail, safes, irons, hair dryers. **Pool(s):** small heated indoor. **Leisure Activities:** sauna, whirlpool, limited exercise equipment. **Guest Services:** valet and coin laundry, wireless Internet. **Business Services:** business center.
SOME UNITS

SLEEP INN & SUITES TULSA SOUTH · *Book great rates at AAA.com* · Phone: (918)249-8100 · 33
AAA SAVE
All Year · 1P: $79-$129
▼▼▼ · **Location:** Just w of jct US 169 and 61st St. 10143 E 62nd St S 74133. Fax: 918/249-8101. **Facility:** Smoke free premises. 65 one-bedroom standard units, some with whirlpools. 3 stories, interior corridors. *Bath:* combo or
Small-scale Hotel · shower only. **Parking:** on-site. **Terms:** [ECP] meal plan available. **Amenities:** high-speed Internet, voice mail, irons, hair dryers. **Pool(s):** heated indoor. **Leisure Activities:** sauna, whirlpool, exercise room. **Guest Services:** valet and coin laundry. **Business Services:** PC. **Cards:** AX, DC, DS, MC, VI.
Free Special Amenities: high-speed Internet.

SPRINGHILL SUITES BY MARRIOTT · *Book great rates at AAA.com* · Phone: (918)254-1777 · 41
▼▼▼
All Year · 1P: $105-$125 · 2P: $110-$130 · XP: $5 · F18
Location: US 169, exit 71st St, just se. 11015 E 73rd St S 74133. Fax: 918/254-1777. **Facility:** Smoke free
Small-scale Hotel · premises. 76 one-bedroom standard units. 3 stories, interior corridors. *Bath:* combo or shower only.
Parking: on-site. **Amenities:** dual phone lines, voice mail, irons, hair dryers. **Pool(s):** heated indoor.
Leisure Activities: whirlpool, exercise room. **Guest Services:** valet and coin laundry, wireless Internet. **Business Services:** meeting rooms, business center. **Cards:** AX, DC, DS, MC, VI.

STAYBRIDGE SUITES · *Book at AAA.com* · Phone: (918)461-2100 · 40
▼▼▼
All Year [BP] · 1P: $109-$199
Location: Just se of jct US 169 and 71st St. 11111 E 73rd St S 74133. Fax: 918/461-2300. **Facility:** 85 units. 52 one-bedroom standard units with efficiencies. 26 one- and 7 two-bedroom suites with efficiencies. 4 stories,
Small-scale Hotel · interior corridors. **Parking:** on-site. **Terms:** weekly rates available, package plans, pets ($75 fee).
Amenities: high-speed Internet, voice mail, irons, hair dryers. **Pool(s):** heated outdoor. **Leisure Activities:** sauna, whirlpool, exercise room, basketball. **Guest Services:** sundries, complimentary evening beverages: Tues-Thurs, complimentary laundry. **Business Services:** meeting rooms, business center. **Cards:** AX, CB, DC, DS, JC, MC, VI.
SOME UNITS

STUDIOPLUS TULSA CENTRAL · *Book at AAA.com* · Phone: (918)660-2890 · 14
▼▼▼
6/1-9/30 · 1P: $59-$69 · 2P: $64-$74 · XP: $5
3/1-5/31 & 10/1-2/29 · 1P: $54-$64 · 2P: $59-$69 · XP: $5
Location: I-44, exit 231 eastbound; exit 232 (Memorial Dr) westbound, just sw. 7901 E 31st Ct 74145.
Small-scale Hotel · Fax: 918/660-4672. **Facility:** 73 units. 72 one-bedroom standard units with kitchens. 1 one-bedroom suite with kitchen. 3 stories, interior corridors. *Bath:* combo or shower only. **Parking:** on-site. **Terms:** pets ($25 extra charge).
Amenities: voice mail, irons. **Pool(s):** outdoor. **Leisure Activities:** exercise room. **Guest Services:** coin laundry, wireless Internet. **Cards:** AX, CB, DC, DS, MC, VI.
SOME UNITS

TULSA MARRIOTT SOUTHERN HILLS · *Book great rates at AAA.com* · Phone: (918)493-7000 · 38
▼▼▼
All Year · 1P: $109-$495 · 2P: $109-$495 · XP: $10 · F
Location: I-44, exit 227 (Lewis Ave), 2 mi s; jct 71st St and Lewis Ave. 1902 E 71st St 74136. Fax: 918/523-0950.
Facility: Smoke free premises. 383 units. 379 one-bedroom standard units, some with kitchens. 4 one-
Large-scale Hotel · bedroom suites. 11 stories, interior corridors. **Parking:** on-site, winter plug-ins. **Terms:** check-in 4 pm, [AP]
meal plan available, package plans. **Amenities:** video games (fee), voice mail, irons, hair dryers. *Some:* dual phone lines.
Pool(s): heated indoor. **Leisure Activities:** saunas, whirlpool, exercise room, spa. **Guest Services:** gift shop, valet laundry, wireless Internet. **Business Services:** conference facilities, business center. **Cards:** AX, DC, DS, MC, VI.
SOME UNITS

━━━━━━ **WHERE TO DINE** ━━━━━━

ABUELO'S MEXICAN FOOD EMBASSY · Lunch: $7-$13 · Dinner: $7-$19 · Phone: 918/249-1546 · 25
▼▼▼
Location: Just e of jct US 169. 10909 E 71st St S 74133. **Hours:** 11 am-10 pm, Fri & Sat-11 pm. Closed: 11/22,
12/24, 12/25. **Reservations:** not accepted. **Features:** The upscale and artistically decorated restaurant
Mexican · presents a menu of well-prepared and attractively presented dishes. Casual dress; cocktails. **Parking:** on-site. **Cards:** AX, DS, MC, VI.

(See map and index starting on p. 624)

ATLANTIC SEA GRILL **Lunch:** $7-$10 **Dinner:** $10-$26 **Phone:** 918/252-7966 ②
▼▼▼▼ Continental **Location:** 1.5 mi w of jct US 169 and 61st St; in Eton Square. 8321-A E 61st St 74133. **Hours:** 11:30 am-2:30 5:30-10 pm, Fri-11 pm, Sat 5:30 pm-11 pm, Sun 5:30 pm-10 pm. Closed major holiday **Reservations:** suggested. **Features:** Decorated in elegant, turn-of-the-20th-century San Francisco deco the restaurant nurtures a cozy, intimate atmosphere. Seafood specialties include lobster, Dover sole ar king crab legs, but selections of steak, veal, pasta and chicken also are prepared. Mouthwatering desserts are made in-hous Casual dress; cocktails. **Parking:** on-site. **Cards:** AX, CB, DC, DS, MC, VI.

THE BISTRO AT SEVILLE **Lunch:** $7-$28 **Dinner:** $10-$28 **Phone:** 918/296-3000 ③
▼▼▼▼ American **Location:** Jct 101st St. 10021 S Yale Ave 74145. **Hours:** 11 am-9 pm. Closed: 11/22, 12/2 **Reservations:** suggested. **Features:** Seafood, steak, pasta and chicken dishes are among the bistro varied menu offerings. Dressy casual; cocktails. **Parking:** on-site. **Cards:** AX, DS, MC, VI.

BODEANS SEAFOOD RESTAURANT **Lunch:** $8-$38 **Dinner:** $18-$38 **Phone:** 918/743-3861 ①
▼▼▼▼ Seafood **Location:** I-44, exit 228 (Harvard Ave), just se. 3323 E 51st St 74105. **Hours:** 11 am-2:30 & 5-10 pm, Sat & Su from 5 pm. Closed major holidays. **Reservations:** accepted. **Features:** On the menu are several fres seafood choices, as well as a nice selection of steaks. The attentive, knowledgeable staff provides servic in a comfortable yet formal manner. Casual dress; cocktails. **Parking:** on-site. **Cards:** AX, CB, DC, DS, JC MC, VI.

BOURBON STREET CAFE **Lunch:** $6-$9 **Dinner:** $9-$20 **Phone:** 918/298-0000 ③
▼▼▼ Cajun **Location:** I-44, exit 227 (Lewis Ave), 3.5 mi s. 8246 S Lewis Ave 74137. **Hours:** 11 am-9 pm, Fri-10 pm, Sat 3 pn 10 pm, Sun 11 am-9 pm. Closed major holidays. **Features:** Lively music sets the mood at the cafe, whic prepares blackened dishes and a nice assortment of seafood dishes to each diner's liking. Casual dres cocktails. **Parking:** on-site. **Cards:** AX, DS, MC, VI.

CAMERELLIS RISTORANTE ITALIANO **Lunch:** $6-$17 **Dinner:** $9-$20 **Phone:** 918/582-8900 ④
▼▼▼ Ethnic **Location:** 0.8 mi w of jct US 64. 1536 E 15th St 74120. **Hours:** 11 am-2 & 5-10:30 pm, Wed-Fri to 11:30 pm, S 5 pm-11:30 pm, Sun 5 pm-10:30 pm. Closed: 11/22, 12/25. **Reservations:** suggested. **Features:** Popul with couples and professionals who enjoy its lunch offerings, Camerellis offers authentic cuisine in a warr cozy and comfortable atmosphere. The seafood a la vodka and scampi primavera are excellent choice from their menu. Good service. Casual dress; cocktails. **Parking:** on-site. **Cards:** AX, CB, DC, DS, MC, VI.

CAZ'S CHOWHOUSE **Lunch:** $6-$17 **Dinner:** $6-$17 **Phone:** 918/588-2469 ①
▼▼▼ American **Location:** Just w of jct N Boston Ave. 18 E Brady St 74103. **Hours:** 11 am-9 pm, Fri-10 pm, Sat 5 pm-10 pn Closed: 11/22, 12/25; also Sun & Mon. **Features:** Creativity and attention to presentation are evident at th restaurant. Ingredients are fresh, and servers are conscientious. Casual dress; cocktails. **Parking:** on-sit **Cards:** AX, DC, DS, MC, VI.

CELEBRITY RESTAURANT **Lunch:** $6-$12 **Dinner:** $10-$28 **Phone:** 918/743-1800 ①
▼▼▼ Steak & Seafood **Location:** Jct 31st and Yale Ave; on southeast corner. 3109 S Yale Ave 74135. **Hours:** 11:30 am-2 & 5-9 pm, Fri Sat-10 pm. Closed major holidays; also Sun. **Reservations:** suggested, evenings. **Features:** An are institution for more than 30 years, the restaurant presents a concise selection of well-prepared items in semi-formal atmosphere that caters to couples and businesspeople. Caesar salad is a notable specialt Dressy casual; cocktails. **Parking:** on-site. **Cards:** AX, MC, VI.

THE CHALKBOARD **Lunch:** $9-$18 **Dinner:** $16-$27 **Phone:** 918/582-1964 ②
▼▼▼▼ Mediterranean **Location:** Jct 14th and Main sts; in Ambassador Hotel. 1324 S Main St 74105. **Hours:** 6:30-10 am, 11-2:30 & 5-1 pm, Fri & Sat-10:30 pm, Sun-9 pm. **Reservations:** accepted. **Features:** Equally well-suited for a busines lunch or romantic dinner with well-prepared and presented entree's and a nice selection of wines. Dres casual; cocktails. **Parking:** on-site. **Cards:** AX, DS, MC, VI.

CHARLESTON'S RESTAURANT **Lunch:** $8-$22 **Dinner:** $8-$22 **Phone:** 918/749-328
▼▼ ▼▼ Steak & Seafood **Location:** I-44, exit 226B, 1.6 mi n. 3726 S Peoria 74136. **Hours:** 11 am-9 pm, Fri & Sat-10 pm. Closed: 11/2 12/25. **Reservations:** accepted. **Features:** This casual dining spot boasts a friendly, club-like atmospher Fine steak and seafood, as well as hardwood-grilled dishes, are at the heart of the menu. The notewort baked potato soup is rich with onions and bacon bits. Casual dress; cocktails. **Parking:** on-site. **Cards:** A DS, MC, VI.

CHARLESTON'S RESTAURANT **Lunch:** $8-$22 **Dinner:** $8-$22 **Phone:** 918/495-351
▼▼ ▼▼ Steak & Seafood **Location:** I-44, exit 229 (Yale Ave), 3 mi s. 6839 S Yale Ave 74136. **Hours:** 11 am-10 pm, Fri & Sat-11 pm Closed: 11/22, 12/25. **Features:** This casual dining spot boasts a friendly, club-like atmosphere. Fine stea and seafood, as well as hardwood-grilled dishes, are at the heart of the menu. The noteworthy baked potat soup is rich with onions and bacon bits. Casual dress; cocktails. **Parking:** on-site. **Cards:** AX, DS, MC, VI

CHEDDAR'S **Lunch:** $6-$13 **Dinner:** $7-$14 **Phone:** 918/307-201
▼▼ ▼▼ American **Location:** Just e of jct US 169. 10708 E 71st St 74133. **Hours:** 11 am-11 pm, Fri & Sat-midnight. Closed majc holidays. **Features:** Enjoy the large, casual dining room and a large menu to choose from. Fresh soups an salads, sandwich board, seafood and burgers, steaks, pasta and desserts are all options at this fami friendly cafe. Casual dress; cocktails. **Parking:** on-site. **Cards:** AX, DS, MC, VI.

(See map and index starting on p. 624)

CHIMI'S MEXICAN FOOD Lunch: $5-$7 Dinner: $6-$15 Phone: 918/298-1570 [32]
Mexican
Location: I-44, exit 227 (Lewis Ave), 2 mi s at 81st St. 8144 S Lewis Ave 74137. **Hours:** 11 am-10 pm, Fri & Sat-11 pm. Closed: 11/22, 12/25. **Features:** The locally popular Chimi's features a good menu selection of traditional, well-prepared dishes. This large, busy restaurant has a casual atmosphere and a well-coordinated Mexican theme. The server staff is prompt and cordial. Casual dress; cocktails. **Parking:** on-site. **Cards:** AX, DS, MC, VI.

CHIMI'S MEXICAN FOOD Lunch: $6-$12 Dinner: $6-$16 Phone: 918/587-4411 [3]
Mexican
Location: At Peoria Ave; center. 1304 E 15th St 74120. **Hours:** 11 am-10:30 pm, Fri & Sat-11:30 pm. Closed: 11/22, 12/25. **Features:** A good menu selection is offered at Chimi's, which is quite popular with local residents. This large, busy, rustic restaurant features a casual atmosphere as the backdrop for its traditional, well-prepared dishes. Service is friendly and attentive. Casual dress; cocktails. **Parking:** on-site. **Cards:** AX, DS, MC, VI.

CYPRUS GRILLE Lunch: $6-$18 Dinner: $6-$25 Phone: 918/307-2600 [23]
Steak & Seafood
Location: Just ne of jct US 169 and 71st St; in Renaissance Tulsa Hotel & Convention Center. 6808 S 107th E Ave 74133. **Hours:** 6 am-2 & 5:30-10 pm, Sat & Sun from 7 am. **Features:** Entrees provide both visual and taste appeal. Everything from soups to desserts shows wonderful taste and presentation. Dressy casual; cocktails. **Parking:** on-site. **Cards:** AX, DS, MC, VI.

DA' BOAT Lunch: $6-$8 Dinner: $6-$10 Phone: 918/299-2900 [29]
Steak & Seafood
Location: I-44, exit 227 (Lewis Ave), 3.5 mi s. 8102-E S Lewis 74137. **Hours:** 11 am-9:30 pm, Fri & Sat-10:30 pm, Sun-9 pm. Closed: 11/22, 12/25. **Features:** The menu lists a nice selection of quality seafood dishes. A nice outdoor seating area complements the smallish indoor dining space. Casual dress; cocktails. **Parking:** on-site. **Cards:** AX, DC, DS, MC, VI.

ELEPHANT BAR RESTAURANT Lunch: $6-$16 Dinner: $8-$16 Phone: 918/254-4191
American
Location: Just n of jct 71st St. 7007 S Memorial Rd 74133. **Hours:** 11 am-10 pm. Closed: 11/22, 12/25. **Features:** Going on safari was never this much fun. Guests who unwind amid the bright jungle decor can sample fresh California cuisine prepared with Pacific Rim influences. Pizza cooked over a wood fire, sizzling cantina fajitas, wok-seared Shanghai cashew chicken and langoustines, and shrimp and chicken jambalaya are among dishes sure to wake up the taste buds. Service is great, too. Casual dress; cocktails. **Parking:** on-site. **Cards:** AX, DS, MC, VI.

FAMOUS DAVE'S Lunch: $6-$14 Dinner: $8-$14 Phone: 918/249-2140
Barbecue
Location: Just e of jct Memorial Rd; at Woodland Hills Mall. 8247 E 71st St 74133. **Hours:** 11 am-10 pm, Fri & Sat-11 pm. Closed: 11/22, 12/25. **Features:** Famous for its legendary pit barbecue, the fun and casual northwoods lodge-style eatery celebrates the many variations of barbecue styles, from Texas beef brisket and Georgian chopped pork to country roast chicken and pit barbecue ribs. Casual dress; cocktails. **Parking:** on-site. **Cards:** AX, CB, DC, DS, JC, MC, VI.

FLEMING'S PRIME STEAKHOUSE & WINE BAR Dinner: $21-$36 Phone: 918/712-7500 [7]
Steak House
Location: US 64, exit Utica Ave, s to 21st St, then just e. 1976 E 21st St 74114. **Hours:** 5 pm-10 pm, Fri & Sat-11 pm, Sun-9 pm. Closed: 11/22, 12/25. **Reservations:** accepted. **Features:** The warm, clubby atmosphere is the ideal setting for perfectly grilled steaks and seafood. Side dishes come in hearty portions, and salads are fresh and crisp. More than 100 wine selections are available. Dressy casual; cocktails. **Parking:** on-site. **Cards:** AX, DC, DS, MC, VI.

THE FRENCH HEN Lunch: $7-$13 Dinner: $14-$28 Phone: 918/492-2596 [27]
Continental
Location: I-44, exit 229 (Lewis Ave), 1.8 mi s. 7143 S Yale Ave 74136. **Hours:** 11 am-2 & 4-10 pm, Fri-11 pm, Sat 4 pm-11 pm. Closed major holidays; also Sun. **Reservations:** suggested. **Features:** A nice casual diner restaurant or casual business meeting place, serving a broad variety of American dishes. There are windows on three sides of the restaurant, which all face a courtyard, in which the restaurant is situated. The subdued lighting lends itself to the relaxing environment and the service is prompt and efficient. Dressy casual; cocktails. **Parking:** on-site. **Cards:** AX, CB, DC, DS, MC, VI.

GOLDIES PATIO GRILL Lunch: $5-$8 Dinner: $5-$8 Phone: 918/743-2188
American
Location: I-44, exit 227 (Lewis Ave), just s. 5200 S Lewis Ave 74136. **Hours:** 11 am-9 pm. Closed: 1/1, 11/22, 12/25. **Features:** The menu comprises grilled items, chicken, sandwiches and steak, but this place is bests known for its excellent charbroiled burgers. The decor incorporates 1950s and '60s memorabilia. Casual dress. **Parking:** on-site. **Cards:** AX, DS, MC, VI.

GOLDIES PATIO GRILL Lunch: $5-$8 Dinner: $5-$8 Phone: 918/438-6530
American
Location: Just s of jct 21st St. 2115 S Garnett 74146. **Hours:** 11 am-9 pm. Closed: 1/1, 11/22, 12/25. **Features:** The menu comprises grilled items, chicken, sandwiches and steak, but this place is bests known for its excellent charbroiled burgers. The decor incorporates 1950s and '60s memorabilia. Casual dress. **Parking:** on-site. **Cards:** AX, DS, MC, VI.

GOLDIES PATIO GRILL Lunch: $5-$8 Dinner: $5-$8 Phone: 918/747-2007
American
Location: Just w of jct US 64 and SR 51. 2005 E 21st St 74114. **Hours:** 11 am-9 pm. Closed: 1/1, 11/22, 12/25. **Features:** The menu comprises grilled items, chicken, sandwiches and steak, but this place is bests known for its excellent charbroiled burgers. The decor incorporates 1950s and '60s memorabilia. Casual dress. **Parking:** on-site. **Cards:** AX, DS, MC, VI.

GOLDIES PATIO GRILL Lunch: $5-$8 Dinner: $5-$8 Phone: 918/494-0330 [20]
American
Location: Just w of jct Sheridan Rd. 6121 E 61st St 74136. **Hours:** 11 am-9 pm. Closed: 1/1, 11/22, 12/25. **Features:** An area institution since the 1950s, the grill lines up a tempting selection of hamburgers, steak, chicken and entree salads. Casual dress; beer only. **Parking:** on-site. **Cards:** AX, DS, MC, VI.

(See map and index starting on p. 624)

GOLDIES PATIO GRILL
△▽△▽ △▽△▽
American

Lunch: $5-$8   **Dinner:** $5-$8   **Phone:** 918/747-4546
Location: Just w of jct Yale Ave. 4401 E 31st St 74135. **Hours:** 11 am-9 pm. Closed: 1/1, 11/22, 12/2
Features: An area institution since the 1950s, the grill lines up a tempting selection of hamburgers, stea
chicken and entree salads. Casual dress. **Parking:** on-site. **Cards:** AX, DS, MC, VI.

THE GREEN ONION
△▽△▽ △▽△▽
Continental

Lunch: $7-$10   **Dinner:** $15-$25   **Phone:** 918/481-3338
Location: I-44, exit 229, just s to 51st St, then just w. 4532 E 51st St 74135. **Hours:** 11 am-2 & 5-10 p
Fri & Sat-10:30 pm, Sun-2 pm. Closed major holidays. **Reservations:** suggested. **Features:** This nic
casual dining restaurant or casual business meeting place, serves a broad variety of American dishes ar
some Italian dishes. There is a small dance floor and entertainment is provided in the evenings. Th
subdued lighting lends itself to the relaxing environment and the service is prompt and efficient. Casual dress; cocktail
entertainment. **Parking:** on-site. **Cards:** AX, CB, DC, DS, MC, VI.

HIDEAWAY PIZZA
△▽△▽ △▽△▽
Pizza

Lunch: $5-$14   **Dinner:** $5-$14   **Phone:** 918/366-4777
Location: Just s of jct Memorial Rd. 8222 E 103rd St 74133. **Hours:** 11 am-10 pm, Fri & Sat-11 pm. Close
11/22, 12/25. **Features:** The restaurant is a favorite spot for pizza lovers who like a wide variety of toppi
choices. Casual dress; beer only. **Parking:** on-site. **Cards:** AX, DC, DS, MC, VI.

HIDEAWAY PIZZA
△▽△▽ △▽△▽
Pizza

Lunch: $5-$14   **Dinner:** $5-$14   **Phone:** 918/270-4777
Location: 1.2 mi w of jct US 169. 7877 E 51st St 74145. **Hours:** 11 am-10 pm, Fri & Sat-11 pm. Closed: 11/2
12/25. **Features:** Locals flock to this place for pizza, including a good selection of out-of-the-ordina
choices. Casual dress; beer only. **Parking:** on-site. **Cards:** AX, DC, DS, MC, VI.

HIDEAWAY PIZZA
△▽△▽ △▽△▽
Pizza

Lunch: $5-$14   **Dinner:** $5-$14   **Phone:** 918/492-4777
Location: Just s of jct 81st St. 8204 S Harvard Ave 74137. **Hours:** 11 am-10 pm, Fri & Sat-11 pm. Closed: 11/2
12/25. **Features:** Locals flock to this place for pizza, including a good selection of out-of-the-ordina
choices. Casual dress; beer only. **Parking:** on-site. **Cards:** AX, DC, DS, MC, VI.

LA ROMA PIZZA
🅰🅰🅰
△▽△▽
Ethnic

Lunch: $5-$10   **Dinner:** $5-$10   **Phone:** 918/491-6436
Location: I-44, exit 230, 2 mi s. 6027 S Sheridan Rd 74145. **Hours:** 11 am-3 & 5-9 pm, Fri & Sat-10 pm. Close
Sun. **Features:** La Roma's is a family-owned restaurant specializing in Mediterranean cuisine, homemac
pizza with fresh ingredients and authentic Lebanese dishes. They have a casual, serve-yourse
atmosphere. All desserts are made in-house and taste great. Casual dress; beer only. **Parking:** on-sit
Cards: AX, DC, DS, MC, VI.

MAHOGANY PRIME STEAKHOUSE
△▽△▽ △▽△▽ △▽△▽
Steak House

Dinner: $17-$40   **Phone:** 918/494-4043
Location: I-44, exit 229 (Yale Ave), 2.8 mi s. 6823 S Yale Ave 74136. **Hours:** 5:30 pm-10 pm, Fri & Sat-11 pr
Sun 5 pm-9 pm. Closed: 12/25. **Reservations:** suggested. **Features:** The house specialty is well-prepare
high-quality steak. Included in the selection of sides is fresh, flavorful corn. Dressy casual; cocktail
Parking: on-site. **Cards:** AX, DC, DS, MC, VI.

MCGILL'S
△▽△▽ △▽△▽
Steak & Seafood

Lunch: $8-$13   **Dinner:** $10-$27   **Phone:** 918/742-8080
Location: Just w of Utica Ave. 1560 E 21st St E 74114. **Hours:** 11 am-10 pm, Fri-11 pm, Sat 5 pm-11 pm, Sun
pm-9 pm. Closed: 11/22, 12/25. **Reservations:** suggested. **Features:** The restaurant is a good choice for
fine-dining experience centered on great-tasting steak, seafood and prime rib. Dressy casual; cocktail
Parking: on-site. **Cards:** AX, DC, DS, MC, VI.

MCGILL'S
△▽△▽ △▽△▽
Steak & Seafood

Lunch: $8-$12   **Dinner:** $10-$25   **Phone:** 918/388-8080
Location: I-44, exit 229 (Yale Ave), 1.3 mi s. 6058 S Yale Ave 74136. **Hours:** 11 am-10 pm, Sat 5 pm-10 pm, Su
4 pm-9 pm. Closed: 11/22, 12/25. **Reservations:** suggested. **Features:** Well-prepared entrees are mac
with enhanced flavors and presented attractively. The dining room has upscale appointments but is casu
enough to make everyone comfortable. Dressy casual; cocktails. **Parking:** on-site. **Cards:** AX, CB, DC, DS
JC, MC, VI.

MEXICALI BORDER CAFE
△▽△▽ △▽△▽
Mexican

Lunch: $6-$14   **Dinner:** $8-$14   **Phone:** 918/481-1114
Location: Just w of jct 71st St. 7104 S Sheridan Rd 74133. **Hours:** 11 am-10 pm. Closed major holiday
Features: A bar at the entry lends to the lively atmosphere that lures patrons to the Mexican cafe. Casu
dress; cocktails. **Parking:** on-site. **Cards:** MC, VI.

MIMI'S CAFE
△▽△▽ △▽△▽
American

Lunch: $6-$14   **Dinner:** $6-$17   **Phone:** 918/254-633
Location: 1.4 mi w of jct US 169 and 71st St. 8215 E 71st St 74133. **Hours:** 7 am-11 pm. Closed: 12/2
Reservations: accepted. **Features:** Breakfast, lunch and dinner are offered throughout the day at th
eclectic and popular eatery. With New Orleans inspired decor and a menu that features something f
everyone, finding a favorite dish should be no problem. Casual dress; beer & wine only. **Parking:** on-sit
Cards: AX, DS, MC, VI.

(See map and index starting on p. 624)

MONTE'S CHOP HOUSE
Steak House

Dinner: $17-$33   **Phone:** 918/744-9463   11

Location: I-44, exit 226B, 1.5 mi n. 3509 S Peoria St 74105. **Hours:** 5 pm-10 pm. Closed: Sun. **Reservations:** suggested, weekends. **Features:** You'll appreciate the fine dining at Monte's. Their signature steak, bone-in prime-rib chop and the roasted chicken with vegetables are excellent choices and served in large portions. Many top wines are offered by the glass. A cozy yet lively atmosphere. Dressy casual; cocktails. **Parking:** on-site. **Cards:** AX, MC, VI.

PEI WEI
Chinese

Lunch: $6-$9   **Dinner:** $6-$9   **Phone:** 918/497-1015

Location: I-44, exit 229 (Yale Ave), 1.3 mi s. 5954 S Yale Ave 74135. **Hours:** 10:30 am-9 pm, Fri & Sat-10 pm. Closed: 11/22, 12/25. **Features:** The small chain specializes in Asian cuisine. Guests can expect a combination of self-service and full service: Servers bring out orders and refills, but orders are placed at the counter upon entry. Noodle and rice bowls come with various combinations of vegetables and meats. Signature dishes borrow from Korean, Mongolian and Chinese cuisines. Casual dress. **Parking:** on-site. **Cards:** AX, CB, DC, DS, JC, MC, VI.

PEPPER'S GRILL
Tex-Mex

Lunch: $6-$16   **Dinner:** $6-$16   **Phone:** 918/296-0592   34

Location: Just e of jct Riverside Pkwy. 2809 E 9th St 74137. **Hours:** 11 am-10 pm, Fri & Sat-11 pm. Closed major holidays. **Features:** Guests don't come to the grill for anything fancy. Instead, they clamor for large portions of tasty Tex-Mex. Casual dress; cocktails. **Parking:** on-site. **Cards:** AX, DS, MC, VI.

POLO GRILL
Continental

Lunch: $6-$18   **Dinner:** $20-$35   **Phone:** 918/744-4280   8

Location: US 64, exit Utica Ave, s to 21st St, then just e. 2038 Utica Ave 74114. **Hours:** 11 am-10 pm, Fri & Sat-11 pm. Closed: Sun. **Reservations:** suggested. **Features:** This restaurant sports a stone front with a red English phone booth located just outside the entrance. A favorite spot for business working lunches and dinners, the menu is dominated by beef entrees. Wine and cocktail service is provided as well. Casual dress; cocktails; entertainment. **Parking:** on-site. **Cards:** AX, DC, DS, MC, VI.

RIB CRIB BARBECUE
Barbecue

Lunch: $6-$14   **Dinner:** $6-$14   **Phone:** 918/828-0010

Location: Just ne of jct 31st St. 3022 N Garnett 74129. **Hours:** 11 am-10 pm. Closed: 11/22, 12/25. **Features:** Most guests need extra napkins to tackle the ribs, brisket, ham, pork and chicken selections. The menu also lists sandwiches and wraps, along with tempting sides and large desserts. The decor is decidedly Western. Casual dress; beer only. **Parking:** on-site. **Cards:** AX, DC, DS, MC, VI.

RIB CRIB BARBECUE
Barbecue

Lunch: $6-$14   **Dinner:** $6-$14   **Phone:** 918/447-1400

Location: I-44, exit 223C, just se. 3232 W Skelly Dr 74104. **Hours:** 11 am-10 pm. Closed: 11/22, 12/25. **Features:** Most guests need extra napkins to tackle the ribs, brisket, ham, pork and chicken selections. The menu also lists sandwiches and wraps, along with tempting sides and large desserts. The decor is decidedly Western. Casual dress; beer only. **Parking:** on-site. **Cards:** AX, DC, DS, MC, VI.

RIB CRIB BARBECUE
Barbecue

Lunch: $6-$14   **Dinner:** $6-$14   **Phone:** 918/742-2742

Location: Just n of jct 21st St. 1601 S Harvard Ave 74112. **Hours:** 11 am-10 pm. Closed: 11/22, 12/25. **Features:** Most guests need extra napkins to tackle the ribs, brisket, ham, pork and chicken selections. The menu also lists sandwiches and wraps, along with tempting sides and large desserts. The decor is decidedly Western. Casual dress; beer only. **Parking:** on-site. **Cards:** AX, DC, DS, MC, VI.

RIB CRIB BARBECUE
Barbecue

Lunch: $6-$14   **Dinner:** $6-$14   **Phone:** 918/492-8627

Location: Just n of jct 81st St. 8040 S Yale Ave 74136. **Hours:** 11 am-10 pm. Closed: 11/22, 12/25. **Features:** Most guests need extra napkins to tackle the ribs, brisket, ham, pork and chicken selections. The menu also lists sandwiches and wraps, along with tempting sides and large desserts. The decor is decidedly Western. Casual dress; beer only. **Parking:** on-site. **Cards:** AX, DC, DS, MC, VI.

RIB CRIB BARBECUE
Barbecue

Lunch: $6-$14   **Dinner:** $6-$14   **Phone:** 918/663-4295

Location: Just n of jct 51st St. 5025 S Sheridan Rd 74145. **Hours:** 11 am-10 pm. Closed: 11/22, 12/25. **Features:** Most guests need extra napkins to tackle the ribs, brisket, ham, pork and chicken selections. The menu also lists sandwiches and wraps, along with tempting sides and large desserts. The decor is decidedly Western. Casual dress; beer only. **Parking:** on-site. **Cards:** AX, DC, DS, MC, VI.

RIB CRIB BARBECUE
Barbecue

Lunch: $6-$14   **Dinner:** $6-$14   **Phone:** 918/492-2440

Location: I-44, exit 227, 2 mi s. 6902 S Lewis Ave 74136. **Hours:** 11 am-10 pm. Closed: 11/22, 12/25. **Features:** Most guests need extra napkins to tackle the ribs, brisket, ham, pork and chicken selections. The menu also lists sandwiches and wraps, along with tempting sides and large desserts. The decor is decidedly Western. Casual dress; beer only. **Parking:** on-site. **Cards:** AX, DC, DS, MC, VI.

RICK'S CAFE AMERICAIN
American

Lunch: $8-$19   **Dinner:** $12-$19   **Phone:** 918/742-1076   15

Location: I-44, exit 228 (Harvard Ave), just se. 5107 S Harvard Ave 74135. **Hours:** 11 am-2:30 & 5:30-9:30 pm. Closed: 1/1, 11/22, 12/25; also Sun. **Features:** Desserts, dressing and breads, all made freshly on site, enhance skillfully prepared menu choices. The quaint dining room displays upscale enhancements. Casual dress; cocktails. **Parking:** on-site. **Cards:** AX, CB, DC, DS, JC, MC, VI.

RON'S HAMBURGERS & CHILI
American

Lunch: $4-$6   **Dinner:** $4-$6   **Phone:** 918/496-4328   30

Location: I-44, exit 228 (Harvard Ave), 3.5 mi s. 8201 S Harvard Ave 74105. **Hours:** 11 am-8:30 pm. Closed: 11/22, 12/25. **Features:** The restaurant's name gives a strong indication of the strengths—varied hamburgers and the popular chili—but a few surprises also lurk on the menu. Casual dress. **Parking:** on-site. **Cards:** AX, DS, MC, VI.

(See map and index starting on p. 624)

RON'S HAMBURGERS & CHILI
American
Lunch: $4-$6   **Dinner:** $4-$6   **Phone:** 918/250-7667   26
Location: 0.6 mi w of jct US 169. 7119 S Mingo 74133. **Hours:** 11 am-8:30 pm, Sun-3 pm. Closed: 11/22, 12/25.
Features: The restaurant's name gives a strong indication of the strengths—varied hamburgers and the popular chili—but a few surprises also lurk on the menu. Casual dress; cocktails. **Parking:** on-site.
Cards: MC, VI.

ROYAL DRASON
Chinese
Lunch: $7-$14   **Dinner:** $8-$14   **Phone:** 918/664-2245   14
Location: 1.2 mi w of jct US 169. 7837 E 51st St 74145. **Hours:** 11 am-10 pm. Closed: 11/22. **Features:** The well-stocked buffet bar is a favorite for the restaurant's regular patrons. Casual dress. **Parking:** on-site.
Cards: AX, CB, DC, DS, JC, MC, VI.

SMOKEY BONES BARBECUE & GRILL
Barbecue
Lunch: $6-$18   **Dinner:** $6-$18   **Phone:** 918/294-9395
Location: US 169, exit 71st St, 1 mi w. 9111 E 71st St 74133. **Hours:** 11 am-10 pm, Fri & Sat-11 pm. Closed: 11/22, 12/25. **Features:** Guests can feast on hand-pulled pork, St. Louis-style ribs, smoked turkey breast and other barbecue dishes in a casual, rustic setting that resembles a mountain lodge. Casual dress; cocktails. **Parking:** on-site. **Cards:** AX, DS, MC, VI.   ⛝

TE KEI'S
Asian
Lunch: $7-$13   **Dinner:** $9-$21   **Phone:** 918/382-7777   5
Location: 0.4 mi s of jct US 64/SR 51. 1616 S Utica Ave 74104. **Hours:** 11 am-10 pm, Fri & Sat-11 pm. Closed major holidays. **Reservations:** accepted. **Features:** Attractive, artistic and distinctive decor, along with diverse Asian dishes, are hallmarks of this place. Dressy casual; cocktails. **Parking:** on-site. **Cards:** AX, DS, MC, VI.   ⛝ ◥

TI AMO RESTAURANTE
Italian
Lunch: $7-$17   **Dinner:** $10-$24   **Phone:** 918/499-1919   17
Location: Just n of jct 61st St. 6024 S Sheridan Rd 74145. **Hours:** 11 am-2 & 5-9 pm, Fri & Sat-10 pm, Sun-9 pm. Closed: 11/22, 12/25. **Reservations:** suggested. **Features:** Attractive presentations and ample portions set the restaurant's traditional Italian food apart. Casual dress; cocktails. **Parking:** on-site. **Cards:** AX, DS, MC, VI.   ⛝

WARREN DUCK CLUB
Continental
Lunch: $10-$20   **Dinner:** $20-$43   **Phone:** 918/497-2158   22
Location: I-44, exit 229 (Yale Ave/SR 66), 1.3 mi s; in DoubleTree Hotel At Warren Place. 6110 S Yale Ave 74136. **Hours:** 6:30 am-2 & 5-10 pm. **Reservations:** suggested. **Features:** The intimate, sophisticated restaurant is ideally suitable for special occasions and business get-togethers. The menu features well-prepared American, Italian and European selections, including the signature duck. An excellent choice is blackened tenderloin prepared with Cajun spices. The dessert bar lays out an array of tantalizing selections. Dressy casual; cocktails. **Parking:** on-site. **Cards:** AX, CB, DC, DS, MC, VI.   ⛝

ZIO'S ITALIAN KITCHEN
Italian
Lunch: $4-$12   **Dinner:** $4-$12   **Phone:** 918/250-5999
Location: 0.6 mi w of jct US 169. 7111 S Mingo 74133. **Hours:** 11 am-10 pm, Fri & Sat-11 pm. Closed: 11/22, 12/25. **Reservations:** accepted. **Features:** The warm, comfortable atmosphere and Old World decor complement the menu. Meals are a good value, and so is the service. This small chain specializes in Italian cuisine, including oven-baked pizzas and pasta dishes. Guests are encouraged to get creative with their pizzas by mixing and matching from a list of 24 toppings. Particularly tempting dishes are Artichoke spinach pasta, chicken parmigiana, and Shrimp Limone. Casual dress; cocktails. **Parking:** on-site. **Cards:** AX, DC, MC, VI.   ⛝

The Tulsa Vicinity

BIXBY pop. 13,336

────── WHERE TO DINE ──────

EAST CHINA

Chinese

Lunch: $4-$8	**Dinner:** $6-$8	**Phone:** 918/369-6688

Location: Just s of jct 131st St. 13202 S Memorial Ave 74008. **Hours:** 11 am-10 pm, Fri & Sat-11 pm. Closed: 11/22, 12/25. **Features:** Offered for lunch and dinner, the restaurant's large buffet includes sushi and the popular Mongolian barbecue option. Casual dress. **Parking:** on-site. **Cards:** MC, VI.

RIB CRIB BARBECUE
Barbecue

Lunch: $6-$14	**Dinner:** $6-$14	**Phone:** 918/369-4799

Location: Just n of jct 131st St. 12850 S Memorial Ave 74008. **Hours:** 11 am-10 pm. Closed: 11/22, 12/25. **Features:** Most guests need extra napkins to tackle the ribs, brisket, ham, pork and chicken selections. The menu also lists sandwiches and wraps, along with tempting sides and large desserts. The decor is decidedly Western. Casual dress; beer only. **Parking:** on-site. **Cards:** AX, DC, DS, MC, VI.

BROKEN ARROW pop. 74,859   (See map and index starting on p. 624)

────── WHERE TO STAY ──────

CLARION HOTEL
Small-scale Hotel

Phone: (918)258-7085   **48**

All Year   1P: $69-$79

Location: Just s of jct SR 51. 2600 N Aspen Ave 74012. **Fax:** 918/251-6768. **Facility:** 196 units. 193 one-bedroom standard units. 3 one-bedroom suites ($99-$169). 4 stories, interior corridors. **Parking:** on-site. **Terms:** pets ($25 fee). **Amenities:** voice mail, irons, hair dryers. *Some:* high-speed Internet. **Pool(s):** small heated outdoor. **Leisure Activities:** exercise room. **Guest Services:** coin laundry, wireless Internet. **Business Services:** meeting rooms, PC. **Cards:** AX, DS, MC, VI. *(See color ad p 629)*

COMFORT INN   *Book great rates at AAA.com*
Small-scale Hotel

Phone: (918)258-8585   **50**

All Year	1P: $63-$150	2P: $63-$250	XP: $8	F18

Location: Just sw of jct SR 51 and Aspen Ave (145th St). 2301 W Concord 74012. **Fax:** 918/258-8586. **Facility:** 50 one-bedroom standard units, some with whirlpools. 2 stories (no elevator), interior/exterior corridors. *Bath:* combo or shower only. **Parking:** on-site, winter plug-ins. **Terms:** package plans. **Amenities:** high-speed Internet, voice mail, irons, hair dryers. **Pool(s):** small heated indoor. **Leisure Activities:** limited exercise equipment. **Guest Services:** valet and coin laundry, wireless Internet. **Business Services:** PC. **Cards:** AX, CB, DC, DS, JC, MC, VI.

HAMPTON INN-TULSA/BROKEN ARROW   *Book great rates at AAA.com*
Small-scale Hotel

Phone: (918)251-6060   **49**

7/6-8/15 [ECP]	1P: $199-$299	2P: $199-$299	XP: $25	F18
3/1-7/5 & 8/16-2/29 [ECP]	1P: $99-$199	2P: $99-$199	XP: $10	F18

Location: Just sw of jct SR 51 and Aspen Ave (145th St). 2300 W Albany 74012. **Fax:** 918/251-9090. **Facility:** 80 one-bedroom standard units, some with whirlpools. 4 stories, interior corridors. *Bath:* combo or shower only. **Parking:** on-site, winter plug-ins. **Terms:** cancellation fee imposed, package plans. **Amenities:** high-speed Internet, dual phone lines, voice mail, irons, hair dryers. **Pool(s):** small heated indoor. **Leisure Activities:** exercise room. **Guest Services:** valet and coin laundry, wireless Internet. **Business Services:** meeting rooms, business center. **Cards:** AX, CB, DC, DS, JC, MC, VI.

HOLIDAY INN EXPRESS HOTEL & SUITES   *Book at AAA.com*
Small-scale Hotel

Phone: (918)355-3200

All Year	1P: $99-$149	2P: $99-$149	XP: $10	F18

Location: I-64/51, exit Elm Pl, just ne of jct SR 51 and Elm Pl. 2201 N Stone Wood Cir 74012. **Fax:** 918/355-3443. **Facility:** 120 units. 114 one-bedroom standard units. 6 one-bedroom suites with whirlpools. 3 stories, interior corridors. *Bath:* combo or shower only. **Parking:** on-site. **Terms:** check-in 4 pm. **Amenities:** irons, hair dryers. *Some:* video games, dual phone lines. **Pool(s):** indoor. **Leisure Activities:** whirlpool, exercise room. *Fee:* miniature golf, game room. **Guest Services:** sundries, valet and coin laundry, wireless Internet. **Business Services:** meeting rooms, business center. **Cards:** AX, DC, DS, MC, VI.

────── WHERE TO DINE ──────

BAMBOO GARDEN
Chinese

Lunch: $3-$6	**Dinner:** $3-$6	**Phone:** 918/369-7863

Location: Just n of jct 131st St. 8210 S Elm Pl 74011. **Hours:** 11 am-9 pm. Closed: 11/22, 12/25; also Sun. **Features:** Large portions of a good variety of classic favorites line the menu in the modest restaurant. Casual dress. **Parking:** on-site. **Cards:** MC, VI.

BIG DADDYS ALL AMERICAN BBQ
Barbecue

Lunch: $4-$8	**Dinner:** $4-$8	**Phone:** 918/439-4460 **44**

Location: Just e of jct Aspen Ave (145th St). 201 W Houston 74012. **Hours:** 11 am-9 pm. Closed: 11/22, 12/25; also Sun. **Features:** Modest decor may hide the fact that locals lay claim to this place as a favorite for good barbecue. Casual dress. **Parking:** on-site. **Cards:** AX, DS, MC, VI.

(See map and index starting on p. 624)

CHINA STAR
~~~~ ~~~~
Chinese

Lunch: $4-$7   **Dinner:** $6-$11   **Phone:** 918/258-8899   41

Location: 1.4 mi s of SR 51. 803 N Aspen Ave 74012. **Hours:** 11 am-9 pm, Fri & Sat-9:30 pm. **Features:** Assorted seafood preparations are among offerings of varied Chinese favorites. Many locals enjoy the buffet choices. Casual dress. **Parking:** on-site. **Cards:** AX, DS, MC, VI.

DOOLEYS ANGUS INN
~~~~ ~~~~
American

Dinner: $8-$22   **Phone:** 918/258-2333

Location: Center. 201 S Main St 74012. **Hours:** 4:30 pm-9 pm, Fri & Sat-10 pm. Closed: 11/22, 12/25; also Sun. **Features:** Great tasting steaks, chops and chicken are served in the converted main-street drugstore. Portions are ample, and service is friendly. Casual dress; cocktails. **Parking:** on-site. **Cards:** AX, CB, DC, DS, JC, MC, VI.

EL LORITO
~~~~ ~~~~
Mexican

Lunch: $4-$13   **Dinner:** $6-$13   **Phone:** 918/251-5637   40

Location: Just s of jct SR 51. 941 N Elm Pl 74012. **Hours:** 11 am-9 pm. Closed: 11/22, 12/25. **Features:** The menu comprises traditional Mexican dishes. It's common for the dining room to fill during peak hours on Friday and Saturday. Casual dress; beer only. **Parking:** on-site. **Cards:** AX, DS, MC, VI.

GOLDIES PATIO GRILL
~~~~ ~~~~
American

Lunch: $5-$8   **Dinner:** $5-$8   **Phone:** 918/455-6128   46

Location: Just s of jct 91st St. 1912 S Elm Pl 74012. **Hours:** 11 am-9 pm. Closed: 11/22, 12/25. **Features:** An area institution since the 1950s, the grill lines up a tempting selection of hamburgers, steak, chicken and entree salads. Casual dress. **Parking:** on-site. **Cards:** AX, DS, MC, VI.

JAKE'S CAFE
~~~~ ~~~~
American

Lunch: $5-$9   **Dinner:** $6-$9   **Phone:** 918/258-7710   43

Location: 1.5 mi s of jct SR 51. 626 S Aspen Ave 74012. **Hours:** 6 am-8 pm, Sat & Sun 7 am-2 pm, Mon 6 am-2 pm. **Features:** The menu and decor are reminiscent of a 1950s diner. Freshness and hearty portions contribute to the popularity of the breakfast items. Casual dress. **Parking:** on-site. **Cards:** MC, VI.

MCALISTER'S DELI
~~~~
Deli/Subs
Sandwiches

**Lunch:** $4-$6    **Dinner:** $4-$6    **Phone:** 918/258-3354

**Location:** 1.1 mi s of jct SR 51. 720 N Aspen Ave 74012. **Hours:** 11:30 am-10 pm. Closed: 11/22, 12/25. **Features:** Patrons can choose from more than 30 sandwiches and 11 ways to have their extra-large baked potatoes served. Kentucky pie is a sinful favorite from the dessert menu. Casual dress. **Parking:** on-site. **Cards:** AX, DS, MC, VI.

**MEXICO VIEJO**
~~~~ ~~~~
Mexican

**Lunch:** $4-$6    **Dinner:** $5-$13    **Phone:** 918/259-3572    42

**Location:** Broken Arrow Expwy (SR 51), exit 145th E Ave, 1.5 mi s. 723 N Aspen Ave 74012. **Hours:** 11 am-10 pm, Fri & Sat-10:30 pm. Closed: 11/22, 12/25. **Features:** The quaint restaurant has traditional offerings, as well as other Mexican dishes with pork, shrimp and crab. Casual dress; cocktails. **Parking:** on-site. **Cards:** AX, DS, MC, VI.

**PEPPERS GRILL**
~~~~ ~~~~
Tex-Mex

**Lunch:** $6-$16    **Dinner:** $6-$16    **Phone:** 918/451-0593    47

**Location:** Just n of jct 101st St. 3226 S Elm Pl 74012. **Hours:** 11 am-10 pm, Fri & Sat-11 pm. Closed major holidays. **Features:** Guests don't come to the grill for anything fancy. Instead, they clamor for large portions of tasty Tex-Mex. Casual dress; cocktails. **Parking:** on-site. **Cards:** AX, DC, DS, MC, VI.

**RIB CRIB BBQ**
~~~~ ~~~~

**Phone:** 918/258-1559

**Location:** Just e of jct Elm St. 121 W Kenosha 74012. **Features:** Most guests need extra napkins to tackle the ribs, brisket, ham, pork and chicken selections. The menu also lists sandwiches and wraps, along with tempting sides and large desserts. The decor is decidedly Western.

**RON'S HAMBURGERS & CHILI**
~~~~
American

Lunch: $4-$6   **Dinner:** $4-$6   **Phone:** 918/451-7667   45

Location: Just s of jct 91st St. 1913 E Elm Pl 74012. **Hours:** 11 am-8 pm. Closed: 11/22, 12/25; also Sun. **Features:** The restaurant's name gives a strong indication of the strengths—varied hamburgers and the popular chili—but a few surprises also lurk on the menu. Casual dress. **Parking:** on-site. **Cards:** MC, VI.

STONE MILL BBQ AND STEAKHOUSE
~~~~ ~~~~
Barbecue

Lunch: $7-$21   **Dinner:** $7-$21   **Phone:** 918/258-4227   39

Location: 0.5 mi s of jct SR 51. 2000 W Reno 74012. **Hours:** 11 am-9 pm, Fri & Sat-10 pm. Closed: 11/22, 12/25. **Features:** Rustic decor sets the mood for freshly prepared steaks and barbecue. Hearty portions may make dessert a stretch. Casual dress. **Parking:** on-site. **Cards:** AX, DS, MC, VI.

CATOOSA pop. 5,449

——— WHERE TO STAY ———

CHEROKEE CASINO INN

▼▼▼

Motel

MC, VI.

All Year   1P: $49-$79   2P: $49-$79   XP: $10   F18

Phone: (918)266-7000

Location: I-44, exit 240A, just nw. 19250 Timbercrest Cir 74015. **Fax:** 918/266-3995. **Facility:** 113 one-bedroom standard units. 2 stories (no elevator), exterior corridors. **Parking:** on-site. **Terms:** check-in 4 pm, small pets only. **Dining:** McGill's, see separate listing. **Pool(s):** outdoor. **Guest Services:** coin laundry. **Cards:** AX, DS,

SOME UNITS

(ASK) (S🄳) 🐾 (🍽️➕) 🚥 (📷) / (✕) /

——— WHERE TO DINE ———

MCGILL'S

▼▼▼

Steak & Seafood

Lunch: $8-$20   **Dinner:** $12-$33   **Phone:** 918/384-7500

Location: I-44, exit 240A, just nw; in Cherokee Casino Inn. 777 W Cherokee St 74015. **Hours:** 11 am-2:30 & 5-10 pm, Fri & Sat-11 pm, Sun 4 pm-9 pm. **Reservations:** suggested. **Features:** Inside the Cherokee casino, the sophisticatedly decorated fine-dining restaurant is limited in size, making reservations a wise idea. Dressy casual; cocktails. **Parking:** on-site and valet. **Cards:** AX, DS, MC, VI.

MOLLY'S

(AAA)

▼▼▼

Steak & Seafood

Lunch: $5-$9   **Dinner:** $15-$35   **Phone:** 918/266-7853

Location: I-44, exit 241, 3.6 mi n. 3700 N Hwy 66 74015. **Hours:** 11 am-10 pm, Sat from noon. Closed: 1/1, 12/25; also Sun. **Features:** Nestled beside a river just off Historic Route 66, Molly's Landing is an unusual restaurant housed in a log cabin that features mounted wildlife and leather rawhide chairs in a casual and rustic atmosphere. Good menu selection and pleasant service. Casual dress; cocktails. **Parking:** on-site. **Cards:** AX, CB, DC, DS, MC, VI.

(🍸) (🔌)

CLAREMORE pop. 15,873

——— WHERE TO STAY ———

CLAREMORE MOTOR INN

(AAA) (SAVE)

▼

Motel

All Year   1P: $32-$42   2P: $39-$49   XP: $7   F

Phone: (918)342-4545

Location: 1.2 mi n on SR 66. 1709 N Lynn Riggs Blvd 74017. **Fax:** 918/342-4315. **Facility:** 29 one-bedroom standard units. 2 stories (no elevator), interior/exterior corridors. **Parking:** on-site. **Terms:** cancellation fee imposed, [CP] meal plan available, pets ($5 fee). **Amenities:** high-speed Internet. *Some:* DVD players (fee), hair dryers. **Guest Services:** wireless Internet. **Business Services:** meeting rooms, PC. **Cards:** AX, DS, MC, VI.

SOME UNITS

(S🄳) 🐾 (♿) (📷) 🖥️ 📠 / (✕) (VCR) /
    FEE   FEE

DAYS INN CLAREMORE   *Book great rates at AAA.com*

▼▼

Small-scale Hotel

Business Services: meeting rooms.

Property failed to provide current rates

Phone: 918/343-3297

Location: 1.6 mi s on SR 66. 1720 S Lynn Riggs Blvd 74017. **Fax:** 918/341-1971. **Facility:** 58 one-bedroom standard units. 2 stories (no elevator), interior corridors. **Parking:** on-site, winter plug-ins. **Terms:** small pets only ($10 extra charge). **Amenities:** hair dryers. **Pool(s):** small outdoor. **Guest Services:** wireless Internet.

SOME UNITS

🐾 (🛁) 🚥 (♿) (📷) / (✕) 🖥️ 📠 💻 /
       FEE

MICROTEL INN & SUITES   *Book great rates at AAA.com*

(AAA) (SAVE)

▼▼ ▼▼

Small-scale Hotel

Internet.

All Year   1P: $50-$95   2P: $50-$155

Phone: (918)343-2868

Location: 2.6 mi s on SR 66. 10600 E Mallard Lake Rd 74017. **Fax:** 918/343-2869. **Facility:** 57 one-bedroom standard units, some with whirlpools. 3 stories, interior corridors. *Bath:* combo or shower only. **Parking:** on-site. **Terms:** weekly rates available, package plans, pets ($10 extra charge). **Amenities:** safes. *Some:* irons, hair dryers. **Pool(s):** small outdoor. **Leisure Activities:** whirlpool. **Guest Services:** wireless Internet. **Cards:** AX, DS, MC, VI. **Free Special Amenities:** expanded continental breakfast and high-speed

SOME UNITS

(S🄳) 🐾 (📷) 🚥 (📷) / (✕) (VCR) 🖥️ 📠 💻 /
    FEE

SUPER 8 MOTEL   *Book great rates at AAA.com*

(AAA) (SAVE)

▼▼ ▼▼

Small-scale Hotel

All Year [ECP]   1P: $56-$66   2P: $64-$74   XP: $5   F12

Phone: (918)341-2323

Location: I-44, exit 255, just w. 1100 E Will Rogers Blvd 74017. **Fax:** 918/341-5342. **Facility:** 40 one-bedroom standard units, some with whirlpools. 2 stories, interior/exterior corridors. **Parking:** on-site. **Terms:** pets ($5 extra charge). **Amenities:** high-speed Internet, hair dryers. *Some:* DVD players. **Guest Services:** coin laundry, wireless Internet. **Business Services:** PC. **Cards:** AX, DC, DS, MC, VI. **Free Special Amenities:** continental breakfast and high-speed Internet.

SOME UNITS

(S🄳) 🐾 🚥 🖥️ 📠 / (✕) /
    FEE

——— WHERE TO DINE ———

GOLDIES PATIO GRILL
American

Lunch: $5-$8   **Dinner:** $5-$8   **Phone:** 918/342-3744
Location: Center. 967 W Will Rogers Blvd 74017. **Hours:** 11 am-9 pm. Closed: 11/22, 12/25. **Features:** The menu comprises grilled items, chicken, sandwiches and steak, but this place is bests known for its excellent charbroiled burgers. The decor incorporates 1950s and '60s memorabilia. Casual dress. **Parking:** on-site. **Cards:** AX, DS, MC, VI.

HAMMETT HOUSE RESTAURANT   *Menu on AAA.com*   **Lunch:** $6-$8   **Dinner:** $7-$23   **Phone:** 918/341-7333
American
Location: On SR 88; adjacent to Will Rogers Memorial Park. 1616 W Will Rogers Blvd 74017. **Hours:** 11 am-9 pm. Closed: 11/22, 12/25; also Mon. **Features:** Hammet House has a casual style and family atmosphere with daily specials and a great variety of home-style American dishes. They also serve homemade pie and freshly baked rolls. The server staff is attentive, friendly and efficient. A regionally known dining establishment for over 30 years. Casual dress; beer only. **Parking:** on-site. **Cards:** AX, CB, DC, DS, MC, VI.

RIB CRIB BARBECUE
Barbecue

Lunch: $6-$14   **Dinner:** $6-$14   **Phone:** 918/283-4600
Location: Center. 1736 S Lynn Riggs Blvd 74017. **Hours:** 11 am-10 pm. Closed: 11/22, 12/25. **Features:** Most guests need extra napkins to tackle the ribs, brisket, ham, pork and chicken selections. The menu also lists sandwiches and wraps, along with tempting sides and large desserts. The decor is decidedly Western. Casual dress; beer only. **Parking:** on-site. **Cards:** AX, DC, DS, MC, VI.

GLENPOOL pop. 8,123

——— WHERE TO STAY ———

BEST WESTERN GLENPOOL/TULSA   *Book great rates at AAA.com*   **Phone:** (918)322-5201
Small-scale Hotel
All Year   1P: $79-$99   2P: $89-$109   XP: $10   F18
Location: I-44, exit 224, 9.5 mi s on US 75. 14831 S Casper St 74033 (PO Box 520). **Fax:** 918/322-9604. **Facility:** 64 one-bedroom standard units, some with whirlpools. 2 stories (no elevator), exterior corridors. **Parking:** on-site, winter plug-ins. **Terms:** [CP] meal plan available, small pets only ($50 deposit). **Pool(s):** outdoor. **Guest Services:** coin laundry, wireless Internet. **Business Services:** PC. **Cards:** AX, CB, DC, DS, JC, MC, VI.
Free Special Amenities: continental breakfast and high-speed Internet.

SOME UNITS

JENKS pop. 9,557   (See map and index starting on p. 624)

——— WHERE TO STAY ———

——— *The following lodging was either not evaluated or did not meet AAA rating requirements but is listed for your information only.* ———

BEST WESTERN AQUARIUM INN & SUITES   **Phone:** 918/296-7300
[fyi]   Did not meet all AAA rating requirements for some property operations at time of last evaluation on 07/06/2006. **Location:** Just s of jct Main St and Riverfront Dr. 150 Aquarium Dr 74037. Facilities, services, and decor
Small-scale Hotel   characterize a mid-range property.

——— WHERE TO DINE ———

LOS CABOS MEXICAN GRILL & CANTINA   **Lunch:** $7-$20   **Dinner:** $8-$20   **Phone:** 918/298-2226   [50]
Mexican
Location: Just n of jct Main St. 300 Riverwalk Terr 74037. **Hours:** 11 am-10 pm, Fri & Sat-11 pm. Closed: 11/22, 12/25. **Features:** The popular grill and cantina turns out tasty, freshly prepared Mexican favorites. Casual dress; cocktails. **Parking:** on-site. **Cards:** AX, DS, MC, VI.

OWASSO pop. 18,502

──────── WHERE TO STAY ────────

BEST WESTERN OWASSO INN & SUITES   *Book great rates at AAA.com*   Phone: (918)272-2000

AAA SAVE

Small-scale Hotel

All Year   1P: $84-$89   2P: $84-$89   XP: $5   F12
Location: Just ne of jct US 169 and 76th St. 7653 N Owasso Expwy 74055. Fax: 918/272-6664. **Facility:** 62 units. 60 one-bedroom standard units, some with whirlpools. 2 one-bedroom suites ($129-$199). 2 stories, interior/exterior corridors. *Bath:* combo or shower only. **Parking:** on-site, winter plug-ins. **Terms:** cancellation fee imposed. **Amenities:** voice mail, irons, hair dryers. **Pool(s):** small outdoor. **Leisure Activities:** exercise room. **Guest Services:** valet and coin laundry, wireless Internet. **Business Services:** meeting rooms. **Cards:** AX, CB, DC, DS, MC, VI. **Free Special Amenities:** expanded continental breakfast and early check-in/late check-out.

SOME UNITS

HOLIDAY INN EXPRESS   *Book at AAA.com*   Phone: 918/274-4100

Small-scale Hotel

All Year   1P: $89-$160   2P: $89-$160
Location: Just se of jct US 169 and 76th St. 7551 N Owasso Expwy 74055. Fax: 918/274-9799. **Facility:** 60 one-bedroom standard units, some with whirlpools. 3 stories, interior corridors. *Bath:* combo or shower only. **Parking:** on-site. **Terms:** cancellation fee imposed, weekly rates available. **Amenities:** dual phone lines, voice mail, irons, hair dryers. *Some:* DVD players. **Pool(s):** heated indoor. **Leisure Activities:** sauna, whirlpool, exercise room. **Guest Services:** valet and coin laundry, wireless Internet. **Business Services:** meeting rooms, business center. **Cards:** AX, DC, DS, MC, VI.

SOME UNITS

──────── WHERE TO DINE ────────

GOLDIES PATIO GRILL   Lunch: $5-$8   Dinner: $5-$8   Phone: 918/272-8501

American

Location: Just e of jct US 169. 8591 N Owasso Expwy 74055. **Hours:** 11 am-9 pm. Closed: 1/1, 12/25. **Features:** The menu comprises grilled items, chicken, sandwiches and steak, but this place is bests known for its excellent charbroiled burgers. The decor incorporates 1950s and '60s memorabilia. Casual dress. **Parking:** on-site. **Cards:** AX, DS, MC, VI.

RIB CRIB BARBECUE   Lunch: $6-$14   Dinner: $6-$14   Phone: 918/376-2600

Barbecue

Location: Just s of jct E 86th St N. 8551 N 129th Ave 74055. **Hours:** 11 am-10 pm. Closed: 11/22, 12/25. **Features:** Most guests need extra napkins to tackle the ribs, brisket, ham, pork and chicken selections. The menu also lists sandwiches and wraps, along with tempting sides and large desserts. The decor is decidedly Western. Casual dress; beer only. **Parking:** on-site. **Cards:** AX, DC, DS, MC, VI.

RON'S HAMBURGERS & CHILI   Lunch: $4-$6   Dinner: $4-$6   Phone: 918/272-6996

American

Location: Just n of jct US 169 and 86th St. 9100 N Garnett 74055. **Hours:** 11 am-8 pm. Closed: 11/22, 12/25. **Features:** The restaurant's name gives a strong indication of the strengths—varied hamburgers and the popular chili—but a few surprises also lurk on the menu. Casual dress. **Parking:** on-site. **Cards:** MC, VI.

SAND SPRINGS pop. 17,451

──────── WHERE TO STAY ────────

BEST WESTERN SAND SPRINGS INN & SUITES   *Book great rates at AAA.com*   Phone: (918)245-4999

AAA SAVE

Small-scale Hotel

All Year [CP]   1P: $71-$75   2P: $71-$82
Location: US 64 and 412, exit 81st W Ave, just sw. 211 S Lake Dr 74063. Fax: 918/245-5862. **Facility:** 54 one-bedroom standard units, some with whirlpools. 2 stories (no elevator), interior/exterior corridors. *Bath:* combo or shower only. **Parking:** on-site, winter plug-ins. **Terms:** small pets only ($10 fee). **Amenities:** high-speed Internet, voice mail, safes, irons, hair dryers. **Pool(s):** outdoor. **Leisure Activities:** exercise room. **Guest Services:** coin laundry, wireless Internet. **Business Services:** meeting rooms. **Cards:** AX, DS, MC, VI. **Free Special Amenities:** expanded continental breakfast and high-speed Internet.

SOME UNITS

FEE

──────── *The following lodging was either not evaluated or did not* ────────
meet AAA rating requirements but is listed for your information only.

HAMPTON INN-TULSA/SAND SPRINGS   Phone: 918/245-8500

fyi

Small-scale Hotel

Did not meet all AAA rating requirements for some property operations at time of last evaluation on 12/06/2005. **Location:** Off US 64 and 412, exit 81st W Ave, just nw. 7852 W Parkway Blvd 74127. Facilities, services, and decor characterize a mid-range property.

──────── WHERE TO DINE ────────

RIB CRIB BARBECUE   Lunch: $6-$14   Dinner: $6-$14   Phone: 918/241-5200

Barbecue

Location: Just w of jct SR 97. 450 W Wekiwa 74063. **Hours:** 11 am-10 pm. Closed: 11/22, 12/25. **Features:** Most guests need extra napkins to tackle the ribs, brisket, ham, pork and chicken selections. The menu also lists sandwiches and wraps, along with tempting sides and large desserts. The decor is decidedly Western. Casual dress; beer only. **Parking:** on-site. **Cards:** AX, CB, DC, DS, JC, MC, VI.

RON'S HAMBURGERS & CHILI   Lunch: $4-$6   Dinner: $4-$6   Phone: 918/245-6010

American

Location: Just s of jct Charles Page Blvd. 233 S Adams Rd 74063. **Hours:** 11 am-8 pm. Closed: 11/22, 12/25; also Sun. **Features:** The restaurant's name gives a strong indication of the strengths—varied hamburgers and the popular chili—but a few surprises also lurk on the menu. Casual dress. **Parking:** on-site. **Cards:** MC, VI.

SAPULPA pop. 19,166

—— WHERE TO DINE ——

RIB CRIB BARBECUE

Lunch: $6-$14   **Dinner:** $6-$14   **Phone:** 918/248-6800

Barbecue

Location: Center. 705 S Mission 74066. **Hours:** 11 am-10 pm. Closed: 11/22, 12/25. **Features:** Most guests need extra napkins to tackle the ribs, brisket, ham, pork and chicken selections. The menu also lists sandwiches and wraps, along with tempting sides and large desserts. The decor is decidedly Western. Casual dress; beer only. **Parking:** on-site. **Cards:** AX, DC, DS, MC, VI.

Tulsa Garden Center / © Gibson Stock Photography

This ends listings for the Tulsa Vicinity.
The following page resumes the alphabetical listings of cities in Oklahoma.

VINITA pop. 6,472

------ WHERE TO STAY ------

HOLIDAY INN EXPRESS HOTEL & SUITES   *Book at AAA.com*   **Phone:** (918)256-4900
All Year   1P: $80-$129   2P: $80-$129   XP: $10
Small-scale Hotel **Location:** I-44, exit 289, 0.7 mi nw. 232 S 7th St 74301. Fax: 918/256-5100. **Facility:** 60 one-bedroom standard units, some with whirlpools. 3 stories, interior corridors. *Bath:* combo or shower only. **Parking:** on-site.
Terms: [ECP] meal plan available. **Amenities:** high-speed Internet, dual phone lines, voice mail, irons, hair dryers. **Pool(s):** heated indoor. **Leisure Activities:** whirlpool, exercise room. **Guest Services:** coin laundry, wireless Internet. **Business Services:** meeting rooms. **Cards:** AX, DC, DS, MC, VI.

SOME UNITS
(ASK) (SD) (&M) (🔲) (🏊) (📹) (🖥) / (✉) (🔲) (🍴) /

WEATHERFORD pop. 9,859

------ WHERE TO STAY ------

BEST WESTERN MARK MOTOR HOTEL   *Book great rates at AAA.com*   **Phone:** (580)772-3325
(AAA) (SAVE)   All Year [BP]   1P: $59-$149   2P: $69-$149   XP: $5   F17
Location: I-40, exit 82, 0.5 mi n. 525 E Main St 73096. Fax: 580/772-8950. **Facility:** 63 units. 61 one-bedroom standard units. 2 two-bedroom suites ($139-$169) with kitchens. 2 stories (no elevator), exterior corridors.
Small-scale Hotel   *Bath:* combo or shower only. **Parking:** on-site, winter plug-ins. **Amenities:** voice mail, irons, hair dryers. *Some:* high-speed Internet. **Pool(s):** outdoor. **Guest Services:** wireless Internet. **Business Services:** PC.
(See color ad below)   **Cards:** AX, CB, DC, DS, MC, VI. **Free Special Amenities:** full breakfast and high-speed Internet.

SOME UNITS
(SD) (🍴) (🛗) (&) (🔲) (🏊) (📹) (🍴) (🖥) (🔲) / (✉) (VCR) /

COMFORT INN & SUITES   *Book great rates at AAA.com*   **Phone:** (580)772-9100
(AAA) (SAVE)   All Year   1P: $75-$99   2P: $75-$99
Location: I-40, exit 82, on north side. 1311 E Main St 73096. Fax: 580/772-8100. **Facility:** 71 one-bedroom standard units, some with kitchens (no utensils) and/or whirlpools. 4 stories, interior corridors. *Bath:* combo or shower only. **Parking:** on-site. **Terms:** cancellation fee imposed, [ECP] meal plan available, package
Small-scale Hotel   plans. **Amenities:** high-speed Internet, irons, hair dryers. **Pool(s):** heated indoor. **Leisure Activities:** exercise room. **Guest Services:** coin laundry, wireless Internet. **Business Services:** meeting rooms, business center. **Cards:** AX, CB, DC, DS, MC, VI. **Free Special Amenities:** expanded continental breakfast and high-speed Internet.

SOME UNITS
(SD) (🍴) (🛗) (&M) (&) (🔲) (🏊) (📹) (🍴) (🔲) (🖥) / (✉) /

—————— *The following lodging was either not evaluated or did not* ——————
meet AAA rating requirements but is listed for your information only.

HOLIDAY INN EXPRESS HOTEL & SUITES   Phone: 580/774-0400
[fyi]   Did not meet all AAA rating requirements for some property operations at time of last evaluation on 03/30/2006. **Location:** I-40, exit 84, just nw. 3825 E Main St 73096. Facilities, services, and decor characterize a mid-range property.
Small-scale Hotel

—————— **WHERE TO DINE** ——————

ALFREDO'S MEXICAN CAFE   **Lunch:** $6-$12   **Dinner:** $6-$12   Phone: 580/772-3696
▽▽ ▽▽   **Location:** I-40, exit 82, just n. 1231 E Main St 73096. **Hours:** 11 am-9 pm, Fri & Sat-9:30 pm. Closed major holidays; also Sun. **Features:** Open and inviting dining room decor sets the mood for an enjoyable meal; hearty portions of Mexican favorites are available. Casual dress. **Parking:** on-site. **Cards:** AX, DS, MC, VI.
Mexican

K-BOB'S STEAKHOUSE   **Lunch:** $6-$18   **Dinner:** $6-$18   Phone: 580/772-0271
▽▽ ▽▽   **Location:** I-40, exit 82, just e. 1333 E Main St 73096. **Hours:** 11 am-9 pm. Closed major holidays. **Features:** The steakhouse prepares a great variety of plump, juicy fillets. A fireplace opens up into both dining rooms, and antique clocks decorate the walls. Rustic wagon-wheel chandeliers illuminate the room. Casual dress.
Steak House   **Parking:** on-site. **Cards:** AX, DC, DS, MC, VI.

NEW YOUNG CHINA   **Lunch:** $4-$7   **Dinner:** $6-$8   Phone: 580/774-2845
◆   **Location:** I-40, exit 82, 1 mi n. 205 W Main St 73096. **Hours:** 11 am-9:30 pm, Sun-9 pm. Closed: 11/22, 12/25.
Chinese   **Features:** Patrons can choose from the lunch or dinner buffet or select from the many choices on the menu. Orders also are available for carryout. Casual dress. **Parking:** on-site. **Cards:** AX, DS, MC, VI.

T-BONE STEAK HOUSE   **Dinner:** $6-$20   Phone: 580/772-6329
▽▽ ▽▽   **Location:** I-40, exit 82, 1 mi e on north frontage road. 1805 E Main St 73096. **Hours:** 5 pm-10 pm. Closed: 11/22, 12/25; also for dinner 12/24. **Features:** Slow-cooked, smoked prime rib, flavorful steaks and bacon-wrapped
Steak House   charbroiled shrimp are excellent choices here. A sports-bar motif is featured on one side; a beautiful brick fireplace dominates the other side of the warm, inviting atmosphere. Casual dress; cocktails. **Parking:** on-site. **Cards:** AX, CB, DC, DS, MC, VI.   ▯▯ ▯▯

WOODWARD pop. 11,853

—————— **WHERE TO STAY** ——————

NORTHWEST INN   Phone: 580/256-7600
(AAA) [SAVE]   All Year   1P: $69-$79   2P: $79-$89   XP: $10   F18
▽▽ ▽▽   **Location:** 1.4 mi s of jct US 183, 270, SR 3 and 34. Hwy 270 S & 1st St 73802 (PO Box 1006). **Fax:** 580/254-2274.
Facility: 124 one-bedroom standard units. 2 stories (no elevator), interior/exterior corridors. **Parking:** on-site. **Terms:** [BP] meal plan available, pets ($10 fee). **Amenities:** irons. *Some:* hair dryers. **Dining:** 6 am-10
Small-scale Hotel   & 5-9 pm, Sun 6 am-10 & 11-2 pm, cocktails. **Pool(s):** heated indoor. **Leisure Activities:** billiards, table tennis, limited exercise equipment. **Guest Services:** valet and coin laundry, wireless Internet. **Business Services:** meeting rooms, PC. **Cards:** AX, DC, DS, MC, VI. **Free Special Amenities:** newspaper and high-speed Internet.
(See color ad below)

SOME UNITS
🛏️ 🍽️ 🍸 🏊 📷 🖥️ / ✕ 📶 🖨️ /
FEE

—————— **WHERE TO DINE** ——————

K-BOB'S STEAKHOUSE   **Lunch:** $6-$18   **Dinner:** $6-$18   Phone: 580/256-9413
▽▽ ▽▽   **Location:** US 183/270 at Anderson Rd. 270 Northwest Highway St 73801. **Hours:** 11 am-9 pm. Closed major holidays. **Features:** The steakhouse prepares a great variety of plump, juicy fillets. A fireplace opens up into
Steak House   both dining rooms, and antique clocks decorate the walls. Rustic wagon-wheel chandeliers illuminate the room. Casual dress. **Parking:** on-site. **Cards:** AX, DC, DS, MC, VI.

YUKON — *See Oklahoma City p. 615.*

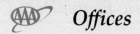 *Offices*

Cities with main offices are listed in **BOLD TYPE** and toll-free member service numbers in *ITALIC TYPE.*
All are closed Saturdays, Sundays and holidays unless otherwise indicated.
The type of service provided is designated below the name of the city where the office is located:

✛ Auto travel services, including books/maps, marked maps and on-demand TripTik® maps
● Auto travel services, including books/maps, marked maps, but no on-demand TripTik® maps
■ Provides books/maps only. No marked maps or on-demand TripTik® maps available
▲ Travel agency services

NATIONAL OFFICE: 1000 AAA DRIVE, HEATHROW, FLORIDA 32746-5063, (407) 444-7000

ARKANSAS

FAYETTEVILLE—AAA MISSOURI, 4262 FRONTAGE RD, 72703.
MON-FRI 8:30-5. (479) 444-9222. *(800) 822-5356.* ✛

LITTLE ROCK—AAA MISSOURI, 9116 RODNEY PARHAM RD,
72205. MON-FRI 8:30-5, SAT 9-1. (501) 223-9222.
(800) 632-6808. ✛▲

KANSAS

HUTCHINSON—AAA ALLIED GROUP INC, 4 E 12TH AVE,
67501. MON-FRI 9-6. (620) 663-2169. ✛

LAWRENCE—AAA ALLIED GROUP INC, 3514 CLINTON PKY #L,
66047. MON-FRI 9-6, SAT 9-3. (785) 843-1600.
(800) 234-1442. ✛▲

MANHATTAN—AAA ALLIED GROUP INC, 321 SOUTHWIND
RD, 66503. MON-FRI 8:30-5:30, SAT 9-3. (785) 776-3131.
(800) 579-9470. ✛▲

OVERLAND PARK—AAA ALLIED GROUP INC, 10600A METCALF, 66212.
MON-FRI 8:30-5, SAT 9-1. (913) 649-2280. *(800) 422-6375.* ✛▲

PITTSBURG—AAA ALLIED GROUP INC, 101 S BROADWAY,
66762. MON-FRI 8:30-5:30. (620) 231-7080.
(800) 288-6157. ✛▲

SHAWNEE—AAA MISSOURI, 15810 B SHAWNEE MSN PKY,
66217. MON-FRI 8:30-5, SAT 9-1. (913) 248-1627.
(866) 222-2288. ✛▲

TOPEKA—AAA ALLIED GROUP INC, 1223 SW WANAMAKER,
66604. MON-FRI 9-6, SAT 9-1. (785) 233-0222. ✛▲

WICHITA—AAA ALLIED GROUP INC, 2110 N MAIZE RD STE
400, 67212. MON-FRI 9-6, SAT 9-3. (316) 942-0008.
(800) 789-4222. ✛▲

WICHITA—AAA ALLIED GROUP INC, 4817 E DOUGLAS AVE,
67218. MON-FRI 9-6, SAT 9-3. (316) 685-5241.
(800) 759-7222. ✛▲

MISSOURI

CAPE GIRARDEAU—AAA MISSOURI, 1903 BROADWAY, 63701.
MON-FRI 9-5, SAT 9-1. (573) 334-3038. *(800) 922-0941.* ✛▲

CLAYTON—AAA MISSOURI, 8235 FORSYTH BLVD, 63105.
MON-FRI 9-5, SAT 9-1. (314) 862-8021. ✛▲

COLUMBIA—AAA MISSOURI, 2101 W BROADWAY #D, 65203.
MON-FRI 8:30-5, SAT 9-1. (573) 445-8426. *(800) 822-5567.* ✛▲

FLORISSANT—AAA MISSOURI, 2686 N HWY 67, 63033.
MON-FRI 9-5, SAT 9-1. (314) 838-9900. *(800) 477-2224.* ✛▲

INDEPENDENCE—AAA MISSOURI, 4201 S NOLAND RD #Y,
64055. MON-FRI 8:30-5, SAT 9-1. (816) 373-1717.
(800) 722-6978. ✛▲

JEFFERSON CITY—AAA MISSOURI, 757A W STADIUM BLVD,
65109. MON-FRI 8:30-5, SAT 9-1. (573) 634-3322.
(800) 438-5222. ✛

JOPLIN—AAA MISSOURI, 2639 E 32ND ST #D, 64804. MON-FRI
8:30-5, SAT 9-1. (417) 624-2000. *(800) 822-9132.* ✛

KANSAS CITY—AAA MISSOURI, 3245 BROADWAY, 64111.
MON-FRI 8:30-5, SAT 9-1. (816) 931-5252. *(800) 345-4283.* ✛▲

KANSAS CITY—AAA MISSOURI, 7679 NW PRAIRIE VIEW RD,
64151. MON-FRI 8:30-5, SAT 9-1. (816) 455-4900.
(866) 222-8800. ✛▲

O'FALLON—AAA MISSOURI, 2277 HWY K, 63368. MON-FRI
9-5, SAT 9-1. (636) 926-0426. ✛▲

SAINT JOSEPH—AAA MISSOURI, 1301 VILLAGE DR, 64506.
MON-FRI 8:30-5, SAT 9-1. (816) 233-1377. *(800) 221-2582.* ✛

SAINT LOUIS—AAA MISSOURI, 12901 N FORTY DR, 63141.
MON-FRI 8:30-5, SAT 9-1. (314) 523-7300. *(800) 222-7623.* ✛▲

SAINT LOUIS—AAA MISSOURI, 3917 LINDELL BLVD, 63108.
MON-FRI 9-5, SAT 9-1. (314) 531-0700. *(800) 315-3222.* ✛

SAINT LOUIS—AAA MISSOURI, 9005 WATSON, 63126.
MON-FRI 9-5, SAT 9-1. (314) 962-2282. *(800) 986-4222.* ✛▲

SAINT PETERS—AAA MISSOURI, 591 MID RIVERS MALL DR,
63376. MON-FRI 9-5, SAT 9-1. (636) 279-2299.
(800) 983-4222. ✛▲

SEDALIA—AAA MISSOURI, 1204 WINCHESTER, 65301.
MON-FRI 8:30-5, SAT 9-1. (660) 826-1800. *(800) 822-8692.* ✛▲

SPRINGFIELD—AAA MISSOURI, 2552 S CAMPBELL #B, 65807.
MON-FRI 8:30-5, SAT 9-1. (417) 882-8040. *(800) 922-7350.* ✛▲

WASHINGTON—AAA MISSOURI, 1053 WASHINGTON SQ,
63090. MON-FRI 9-5, TUE & THUR 9-12 (SUMMER HOURS SAT
9-1). (636) 239-6791. *(800) 922-2451.* ✛▲

OKLAHOMA

ARDMORE—AAA OKLAHOMA, 1505 N COMMERCE #103,
73401. MON-FRI 8:30-5. (580) 223-5170. *(800) 499-5170.* ✛▲

BARTLESVILLE—AAA OKLAHOMA, 112 SE FRANK PHILLIPS
BLVD, 74003. MON-FRI 8:30-5:30. (918) 335-1212.
(800) 688-2701. ✛▲

BROKEN ARROW—AAA OKLAHOMA, 3746 S ELM PL, 74011.
MON-FRI 8:30-6. (918) 455-4764. *(800) 380-6443.* ✛▲

DEL CITY—AAA OKLAHOMA, 4605 SE 29TH ST, 73115.
MON-FRI 8:30-6. (405) 670-1474. ✛▲

EDMOND—AAA OKLAHOMA, 3222 SOUTH BLVD, 73013.
MON-FRI 8:30-6. (888) 841-9127. ✛▲

MUSKOGEE—AAA OKLAHOMA, 1021 W OKMULGEE ST,
74401. MON-FRI 8:30-5:30. (918) 683-0341.
(800) 259-9299. ✛▲

NORMAN—AAA OKLAHOMA, 1021 24TH AVE NW, 73069.
MON-FRI 8:30-6. (405) 360-7771. *(877) 314-3489.* ✛▲

OKLAHOMA CITY—AAA OKLAHOMA, 3557 W MEMORIAL
RD, 73134. MON-FRI 8:30-6. (888) 434-2270. ✛▲

OKLAHOMA CITY—AAA OKLAHOMA, 3625 NW 39TH ST,
73112. MON-FRI 8:30-6, SAT 9-1. (405) 717-8200.
(800) 926-9922. ✛▲

TULSA—**AAA OKLAHOMA**, 2121 E 15TH ST, 74104. MON-FRI
8:30-6. (918) 748-1122. *(800) 222-2582.* ✛▲

TULSA—AAA OKLAHOMA, 10051 S YALE STE 106, 74137.
MON-FRI 8:30-6. (918) 296-9600. ✛▲

TULSA—AAA OKLAHOMA, 8013 S SHERIDAN RD, 74133.
MON-FRI 8:30-6, SAT 9-1. (918) 496-0496. *(800) 745-5222.* ✛▲

Metric Equivalents Chart

TEMPERATURE

To convert Fahrenheit to Celsius, subtract 32 from the Fahrenheit temperature, multiply by 5 and divide by 9.
To convert Celsius to Fahrenheit, multipy by 9, divide by 5 and add 32.

ACRES

1 acre = 0.4 hectare (ha)   1 hectare = 2.47 acres

MILES AND KILOMETRES

Note: A kilometre is approximately 5/8 or 0.6 of a mile.
To convert kilometres to miles multiply by 0.6.

Miles/Kilometres		Kilometres/Miles	
15	24.1	30	18.6
20	32.2	35	21.7
25	40.2	40	24.8
30	48.3	45	27.9
35	56.3	50	31.0
40	64.4	55	34.1
45	72.4	60	37.2
50	80.5	65	40.3
55	88.5	70	43.4
60	96.6	75	46.6
65	104.6	80	49.7
70	112.7	85	52.8
75	120.7	90	55.9
80	128.7	95	59.0
85	136.8	100	62.1
90	144.8	105	65.2
95	152.9	110	68.3
100	160.9	115	71.4

Celsius °	Fahrenheit °
100	BOILING	212
37		100
35		95
32		90
29		85
27		80
24		75
21		70
18		65
16		60
13		55
10		50
7		45
4		40
2		35
0	FREEZING	32
-4		25
-7		20
-9		15
-12		10
-15		5
-18		0
-21		-5
-24		-10
-27		-15

LINEAR MEASURE

Customary	Metric
1 inch = 2.54 centimetres	1 centimetre = 0.4 inches
1 foot = 30 centimetres	1 metre = 3.3 feet
1 yard = 0.91 metres	1 metre = 1.09 yards
1 mile = 1.6 kilometres	1 kilometre = .62 miles

LIQUID MEASURE

Customary	Metric
1 fluid ounce = 30 millilitres	1 millilitre = .03 fluid ounces
1 cup = .24 litres	1 litre = 2.1 pints
1 pint = .47 litres	1 litre = 1.06 quarts
1 quart = .95 litres	1 litre = .26 gallons
1 gallon = 3.8 litres	

WEIGHT

If You Know:	Multiply By:	To Find:
Ounces	28.000	Grams
Pounds	0.450	Kilograms
Grams	0.035	Ounces
Kilograms	2.200	Pounds

PRESSURE

Air pressure in automobile tires is expressed in kilopascals. Multiply pound-force per square inch (psi) by 6.89 to find kilopascals (kPa).

24 psi = 165 kPa   28 psi = 193 kPa
26 psi = 179 kPa   30 psi = 207 kPa

GALLON AND LITRES

Gallons/Litres				Litres/Gallons			
5	19.0	12	45.6	10	2.6	40	10.4
6	22.8	14	53.2	15	3.9	50	13.0
7	26.6	16	60.8	20	5.2	60	15.6
8	30.4	18	68.4	25	6.5	70	18.2
9	34.2	20	76.0	30	7.8	80	20.8
10	38.0	25	95.0	35	9.1	90	23.4

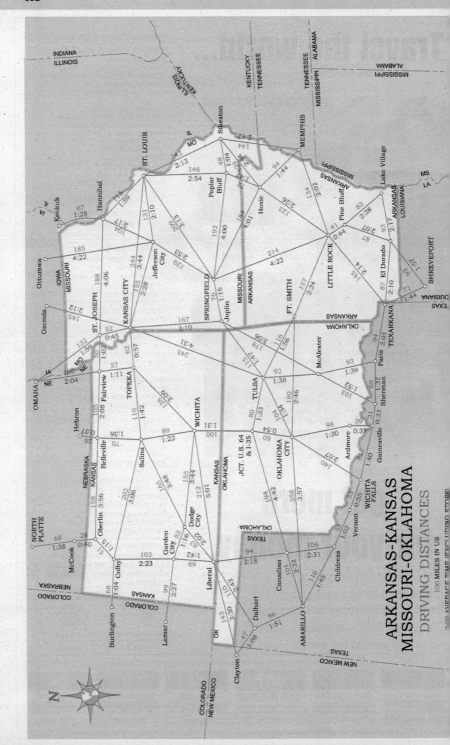

ARKANSAS-KANSAS
MISSOURI-OKLAHOMA
DRIVING DISTANCES

100 MILES IN US

Points of Interest Index

Index Legend

NB...................................national battlefield	NR.......................................national river
NBP.........................national battlefield park	NS.....................................national seashore
NC...................................national cemetery	NWR...........................national wildlife refuge
NF.......................................national forest	PHP......................provincial historic(al) park
NHM...................national historic(al) monument	PHS.......................provincial historic(al) site
NHP......................national historic(al) park	PP.......................................provincial park
NHS.......................national historic(al) site	SF...state forest
NL...................................national lakeshore	SHM........................state historic(al) monument
NME..................................national memorial	SHP.........................state historic(al) park
NMO..................................national monument	SHS.........................state historic(al) site
NMP.............................national military park	SME...................................state memorial
NP.......................................national park	SP...state park
NRA..........................national recreation area	SRA..........................state recreation area

▽ GEM: Points of Interest Offering a *Great Experience for Members*®

ARTS & CRAFTS

AUDITORIUMS

BATTLEFIELDS

BATTLE RE-ENACTMENTS

BIRTHPLACES & CHILDHOOD HOMES

EXHIBITS & COLLECTIONS-AVIATION

EXHIBITS & COLLECTIONS-CIVIL WAR

EXHIBITS & COLLECTIONS-CLOCKS

EXHIBITS & COLLECTIONS-COINS

EXHIBITS & COLLECTIONS-DOLLS & TOYS

EXHIBITS & COLLECTIONS-HISTORICAL

EXHIBITS & COLLECTIONS-INDIAN

HISTORIC BUILDINGS & HOUSES

HISTORIC DOCUMENTS, MANUSCRIPTS & RARE BOOKS

HISTORIC SITES

INDIAN MOUNDS, REMAINS & RUINS

INDIAN BURIAL GROUNDS

INDIAN PICTOGRAPHS & PETROGLYPHS

INDIAN RESERVATIONS & VILLAGES

INDUSTRIAL TOURS

JAILS

LAKES, PONDS & RESERVOIRS

LIBRARIES, ARCHIVES

LOCKS

MARKETS

MEMORIALS

MILLS

MUSIC HALLS & OPERA HOUSES

MYTHICAL PERSONS & ANIMALS

NATIONALITIES & ETHNIC AREAS

NATURAL BRIDGES

PARKS, NATIONAL

SIGHTSEEING-AIRCRAFT RIDES & TOURS

SIGHTSEEING-HOT AIR BALLOON RIDES & TOURS

SIGHTSEEING TOURS

WALKING TOURS

WATERFALLS

WATER PARKS

WAX MUSEUMS

WILDERNESS AREAS

SAVE *Attraction Admission Discount Index*

Bed & Breakfast Lodgings Index

Some bed and breakfasts listed below might have historical significance. Those properties are also referenced in the Historical index. The indication that continental [CP] or full breakfast [BP] is included in the room rate reflects whether a property is a Bed-and-Breakfast facility.

Country Inns Index

Some of the following country inns can also be considered as bed-and-breakfast operations. The indication that continental [CP] or full breakfast [BP] is included in the room rate reflects whether a property is a Bed-and-Breakfast facility.

Historical Lodgings & Restaurants Index

Some of the following historical lodgings can also be considered as bed-and-breakfast operations. The indication that continental [CP] or full breakfast [BP] is included in the room rate reflects whether a property is a Bed-and-Breakfast facility.

Historical Lodgings & Restaurants (cont'd)

Resorts Index

Many establishments are located in resort areas; however, the following places have extensive on-premises recreational facilities:

Comprehensive City Index

Here is an alphabetical list of all cities appearing in this TourBook® guide. Cities are presented by state/province. Page numbers under the POI column indicate where points of interest text begins. Page numbers under the L&R column indicate where lodging and restaurant listings begin.

Comprehensive City Index (cont'd)

Comprehensive City Index (cont'd)

Comprehensive City Index (cont'd)

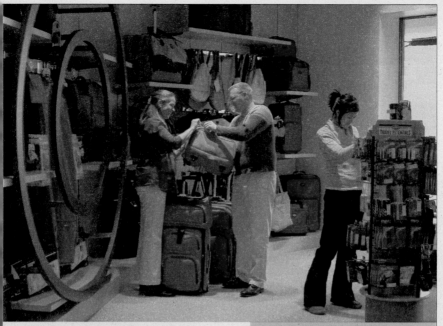

The Little Extras That Make Travel Better

AAA offers a wide variety of great travel books, top quality luggage, automotive and travel accessories, children's products, and much more. Visit your local AAA Travel Store to take advantage of significant AAA member discounts today.

AAA TRAVEL STORE

Travel with AAA

...the only travel agency with thousands of highly trained travel professionals at more than 1,000 offices in the United States and Canada and on aaa.com, AAA's complete travel planning Web site.

Trust AAA for complete travel planning with exclusive savings and benefits on cruises, drive vacations, packages, flights, car rentals and more. Plus, get:

- ◆ Low member prices at AAA Approved and Diamond rated hotels.
- ◆ Famous maps and TripTiks®.
- ◆ Worldwide destination information.
- ◆ Show Your Card & Save® member values at more than 150,000 locations.
- ◆ And, more!

VISIT
AAA offices

CLICK
aaa.com

CALL
your AAA office or
Hotel savings: (866) AAA-SAVE
Roadside help: (800) AAA-HELP

Products and services available through participating AAA clubs.

700

A Partnership You Can Book On!

Show Your Card & Save

BARNES&NOBLE.com

AAA and Barnes & Noble.com have teamed up to create a new online bookstore exclusively for AAA members.

AAA members receive 5% off Barnes & Noble.com's already low online prices!

Discount applies only to items purchased on www.aaa.com/barnesandnoble and cannot be combined with Barnes & Noble's Reader's Advantage or Student Advantage Programs. Not valid at Barnes & Noble retail locations or on www.barnes&noble.com. AAA Membership number required at checkout.

AAA Members Save 5%!

Travel Rule #1:
When kids smile,
you relax.

Holiday Inn®
LOOK AGAIN.™

At Holiday Inn®, we know it's easy to make kids happy when you travel: a sparkling pool, a comfy bed, and room to explore. That's why our hotels offer even more to please tiny travelers and grown-up adventurers.

www.holidayinn.com/aaa

- Kids Eat & Stay Free*
- Swimming pools
- Free high-speed Internet access
- Fresh, cooked to order breakfast available

PRIORITYCLUB REWARDS Earn points or miles. | **BOOK** WITH **CONFIDENCE**® 1-800-734-4275